OZ CLARKE'S
WINE
BUYING
GUIDE
2002

EIGHTEENTH EDITION

'WEBSTER'S'
THE COMPLETE WINE
BUYER'S HANDBOOK

WEBSTERS

LITTLE, BROWN AND COMPANY
BOSTON NEW YORK LONDON

The information and prices contained in the Guide were correct to the best of our knowledge when we went to press, and the impression of relative price and relative value is almost certainly still accurate, even if a particular price has changed.

Although every care has been taken in the preparation of the Guide, neither the publishers nor the editors can accept any liability for any consequences arising from the use of information contained herein.

Oz Clarke's Wine Buying Guide *is an annual publication. We welcome any suggestions you might have for the next edition.*

Editor Maggie Ramsay
Price Guides Editor Julie Ross
Wine Editor Margaret Rand
Editorial Assistants Sarah Cooke, Jo Turner, Andrew Walker, Athina Ypsilanti
Indexer Elizabeth Atkinson
Database Managing Editor Lorna Bateson
DTP Consultant Keith Bambury
Production Kâren Connell
Managing Editor Anne Lawrance
Art Director Nigel O'Gorman
Photography for Oz Clarke's Wine Style Guide Nigel James

Corporate Sales
Companies, institutions and other organizations wishing to make bulk purchases of this or any other Oz Clarke title published by Little, Brown should contact the Sales Department on +44(0)20-7911 8090

Advertising Sales
Logie Bradshaw Media Limited,
Strathallan House, Fernville Lane,
Midland Road, Hemel Hempstead,
Herts HP2 4LS
tel 0144 2233331, fax 0144 2231131

A LITTLE, BROWN/WEBSTERS BOOK

This edition first published in 2001 by
Little, Brown and Company (UK)
Brettenham House
Lancaster Place
LONDON WC2E 7EN

Created and designed by
Websters International Publishers Limited
Axe and Bottle Court
70 Newcomen Street
LONDON SE1 1YT
www.websters.co.uk
www.ozclarke.com

Oz Clarke's Wine Buying Guide 2002 Edition
Copyright © 2001 Websters International
Publishers

A CIP catalogue for this book is available from the British Library.

ISBN 0-316-85709-2

Printed and bound in the UK by
Clays Ltd, St Ives plc

CONTENTS

Oz Clarke's Wine Style Guide: centre pages

INTRODUCTION

Wow, things change fast. Since 1 January 2000 the world seems to have been in a whirligig of change that leaves me breathless and cross-eyed as I try to keep pace. The way wine is sold, the sort of wine that is sold, to whom it is sold, and where – all in a state of flux that has already raised up and then hurled down various places and players, and which promises to make a significant difference to the long-established producers, grape varieties and selling operations as well as the newcomers.

What remains unchanged is that in Britain we have the best organized and best supplied wine retailing business in the world. Our high street wine shops, supermarkets and specialist merchants give us the chance to travel the world of flavours, the chance to experiment with the wines of every continent, to taste different grape varieties, many of them hardly known in the countries where they grow. The proof is in the pages of this book. And if you want my personal take on some of the most exciting flavours in the world today, turn to my Ideal Cellar on page 35. A few of them are not available in the UK – yet – but I have every faith in the buyers who put the wine on our shelves; if there's a good wine out there, they'll bring it to us.

WELL RED

The simple fact is that we're all drinking more in the UK every year. Each year the total volume drunk goes up. Each year the per capita consumption goes up. And two things become immediately apparent if you wade through the figures. Firstly the New World is creaming it at the moment. Almost without exception the New World countries are increasing their share each year, in several cases quite dramatically. And secondly, we're becoming a nation of red wine drinkers.

Ten years ago, around two thirds of the wine we bought was white. Now the split is officially around 50:50, and when I talk to supermarketeers, wine retailers and restaurant people – and consumers – the kind of figure that emerges is a split of about 60 red to 40 white. And when I try to be clever with restaurateurs and say, 'but aren't people eating more fish nowadays?', they say, sure, and they're quite happy to drink red wine with their fish.

Suddenly the raison d'être of boring, basic white wine is out the window. And if you can disentangle the figures for boring old German hock, boring old Soave, boring old Muscadet and Bordeaux Blanc from the masses of statistics – you'll see just what it is we are *not* drinking more of.

So where does that leave Chardonnay? Has the great golden balloon of white wine drinking suddenly gone pop? Well, in parts, yes, and, in parts, absolutely not. Let's look at the positive side. The quality of top Chardonnay has never been better; it isn't cheap, but it still virtually sells itself. White Burgundy (the heartland of Chardonnay) is making superb wines right now; the major New World producers are producing fine Chardonnay every vintage; leading European countries like France, Italy and Spain offer us a vast selection of Chardonnays; and so do Greece, Hungary, Bulgaria, Moldova.

Now hang on. This sounds as though absolutely everyone worldwide can offer you a whole palette of Chardonnays. Correct. They can. So Chardonnay isn't that special then? No, everybody makes it. And, remarkably, most people make it to a reasonable standard. So has it become a bit predictable, a bit boring? Got it in one. Chardonnay, the great white grape, is becoming a victim of its own success. Because it is remarkably adept at making decent wine wherever you plant it, suddenly it's boring, passé, yesterday's wine.

We're not drinking less Chardonnay, and the world isn't *producing* less Chardonnay, but it is increasingly seen as simply 'a glass of white'. A generation of wine drinkers bought up on grape varieties' names – and Chardonnay was the leading variety – don't see Chardonnay as a real grape variety any more; it's in danger of becoming a generic term for decent white wine. Is that all the thanks Chardonnay gets for blazing the trail for all of us modern wine drinkers? Well, think for a moment. How many of you started on Liebfraumilch? How many of you give thanks to *that* brew? From dominating our wine shelves 15 years ago, Liebfraumilch is in freefall, and with it the whole health of German wine in the UK.

AUSTRALIA RULES

So which country is Chardonnay most associated with? I'd say Australia, wouldn't you? Is Australia under threat? Not quite! At the end of this year, Australia is likely to take over from France as the number one wine supplier, almost certainly in shops and supermarkets, though bars and restaurants will take a while to catch up. That's an astonishing thought. France has been our dominant supplier for hundreds of years. Only 15 years ago many shops didn't stock any Australian wine and most of the supermarkets weren't convinced the wines were any good or that anyone would drink them. Well, the wines *were* good, hordes of us drank them, and we drank them because for the first time, after centuries of being starved of ripeness in our wines, suddenly we could taste the joyous, fruity ripeness of 'sunshine in a bottle'. The whole pulsating New World success story followed in Australia's wake.

But there are seeds of concern in this success story. I'm beginning to hear people say that they don't buy Australian wines – not old fuddy duddies who *never* bought Australian wines, but young 20- and 30-somethings who used to buy Australian wine, but got bored by it. Shades of Germany and Liebfraumilch? Possibly.

One of the crucial strengths of Australian wines is in its brands – you know, names like Lindemans, Jacob's Creek, Banrock Station. Currently seven of the top ten brands in Britain are Australian. And on average the top ten brands are showing increases in sales of 30 per cent a year; some are doubling, year on year. If you add in the formidable own-label sales of the Safeways, Sainsburys and Tescos of this world, you can sort of see the danger of mould-breaking new Australia becoming predictable, reliable old Australia.

If these brands were all Australia had to offer, I'd be worried – although I'd also ask those of you who dare to cast your minds back to recall the flavours of Hirondelle, of Piat d'Or, Don Cortez, Black Tower, Mateus and the rest. Which would you rather drink? Those tired old things, or Jacob's Creek Cabernet Sauvignon, Banrock Station Shiraz or Lindemans Bin 65? I thought so. The modern brands. And why? Because they are so much better than the old brands.

Australia led the way in introducing the New World to us. The rest followed. Australia now leads the way in high-quality, entirely reliable branded wines. With the exception of California and its ubiquitous E & J Gallo, the rest of the New World has got a lot of catching up to do yet. And if you think Australia still sounds boring – check out our Best Buys top dozen, and then the 20 runners up. The quality of the top Aussies was simply stunning, and they took half the awards. If the brands provide consistency and the estates provide the thrills, Australia will prove a worthy leader in 2002 – and a worthy target for other countries to try to emulate.

HOW TO USE THIS BOOK

If you are looking for specific wines, turn straight to the **Price Guides.** These are the pages on which we have collated the current retail prices of the thousands of wines we hold on our computer database. **The letters in brackets are abbreviations for the names of the stockists for each of the wines listed.** The key to these abbreviations is on the facing page and full details of these and other wine retailers appear in the **Retailers Directory** on pages 40–78.

If you want to find local suppliers, retailers are listed by region on page 79; if you want to find a specialist in a particular country's wines, these are listed at the beginning of each country's Price Guides.

Please remember that the Price Guides are not meant to replace up-to-date retailers' lists. What they *do*, however, is give you a unique opportunity to compare prices; to develop a sense of what you can expect to pay for any given wine; to spot a bargain – *and to find it.*

Buying wine can feel like a lucky dip when you are faced with shelves or lists full of unfamiliar names: the chapters on the **wine-producing countries** of the world provide a quick introduction to the grapes, wine styles, regions and producer names. In most of these chapters you'll also find specific recommendations in the form of an **Instant Cellar:** a selection of wines to help you acquaint yourself with the region.

The **Producers Who's Who** sections feature our pick of the top producers from each country. In addition, a producer may be awarded one or more stars for the overall quality of wine being made, ranging from particularly good in its category ★ to excellent ★★ or world class ★★★.

We aim to improve this *Guide* every year. Please let us know what you think: that way we can produce an even better guide next year.

USING THE PRICE GUIDES

When using the **Price Guides** you should be aware of the following:

● All prices listed are *per bottle inclusive of VAT*, unless otherwise stated. The prices are those which applied in the early summer of 2001. When comparing prices remember that some retailers sell only by the case. In this instance, we have arrived at a bottle price by dividing by 12 the VAT-inclusive price of a single case. Where retailers who sell by the case will sell cases of mixed bottles, we have used the bottle price that would apply in a mixed case.

● When clubs have both member and non-member prices we have used the *non-member* prices.

● Wines are listed in price bands, and in alphabetical order within each band. If more than one vintage of the same wine appears within one price band, these run from the most recent to the oldest.

● All stockists for a particular wine are listed in ascending order of price. The wines are placed in bands according to the lowest price for which each is available. This means that the highest prices may overstep the upper limit of the price band in which the wine is featured. Variations in price are the result of a combination of factors: wine warehouses, for example, often come out much cheaper than individual merchants because they sell only by the case, they do not deliver, they do not have smart high street premises to maintain, and so on.

● The **Red Bordeaux Price Guides** are a special case. The châteaux are listed alphabetically, then in order of vintage. There are some dramatic price variations here; for a full explanation, see page 174.

● **NV** denotes non-vintage wines in the **Champagne Price Guides.**

● A ★ in the Price Guides indicates a wine recommended by Oz Clarke in the **Best Buys** section which begins on page 8.

RETAILER NAME CODES

These are the retailers whose prices are featured in the Price Guides. The abbreviations are shown in brackets after the price of each of the listed wines they stock.

AD	Adnams		MI	Millésima
AME	Amey's Wines		MON	Montrachet
ARM	John Armit		MOR	Moreno Wines
AS	Ashley Scott		MORR	Morrisons
ASD	Asda		MV	Morris & Verdin
AUS	Australian Wine Club		NEZ	Le Nez Rouge
BAC	Bacchus		NI	James Nicholson
BAL	Ballantynes of Cowbridge		NO	The Nobody Inn
BALL	Balls Brothers		NZW	New Zealand Wines Direct
BAN	H & H Bancroft		OD	Oddbins
BEN	Bennetts		PAU	Paulson Rare Wine
BER	Berry Bros. & Rudd		PEN	Penistone Court Wine Cellars
BIB	Bibendum		PIP	Christopher Piper Wines
BOT	Bottoms Up		PLA	Terry Platt
BO	Booths		PLAY	Playford Ros
BODX	Bordeaux Index		POR	Portland Wine Co
BU	Butlers Wine Cellar		RAE	Raeburn Fine Wines
BUD	Budgens		RES	La Réserve
BY	Anthony Byrne		RIC	Richardson
CAP	Cape Province Wines		RIP	Howard Ripley
CB	Corney & Barrow		RSJ	RSJ Wine Company
CO	CWS (Co-op)		SAF	Safeway
COC	Cockburns of Leith		SAI	Sainsbury's
CON	Connolly's		SAV	Savage Selection
CRO	Croque-en-Bouche		SO	Somerfield
DI	Direct Wine Shipments		SOM	Sommelier Wine Co
DOM	Domaine Direct		STA	Frank Stainton Wines
FA	Farr Vintners		STE	Stevens Garnier Wine Merchants
FLE	Le Fleming Wines		SUN	Sunday Times Wine Club
FORT	Fortnum & Mason		TAN	Tanners
FRI	Friarwood		TES	Tesco
GAU	Gauntleys		THR	Thresher
GN	Great Northern Wine Co		TUR	Turville Valley
GW	Great Western Wine		TW	T & W Wines
HAH	Haynes Hanson & Clark		UN	Unwins
HAW	Roger Harris Wines		VA	Valvona & Crolla
HED	Hedley Wright		VIC	Victoria Wine
HIC	Hicks & Don		VIL	Villeneuve
HIG	High Breck Vintners		VIN	Vintage Wines Ltd
JER	Jeroboams		VINV	Vin du Van
JON	S H Jones		WAI	Waitrose
JU	Justerini & Brooks		WAT	Waterloo Wine Co
LA	Laymont & Shaw		WHI	Whitesides of Clitheroe
LAI	Laithwaites		WIN	The Winery
LAY	Lay & Wheeler		WIW	Wines of Westthorpe
LEA	Lea & Sandeman		WR	Wine Rack
LIB	Liberty Wines		WRI	Wright Wine Co
LLO	Lloyd Taylor Wines		WS	Wine Society
MAJ	Majestic		WY	Peter Wylie Fine Wines
MAR	Marks & Spencer plc		YAP	Yapp Brothers
MAY	Mayfair Cellars		YOU	Noel Young Wines

BEST BUYS

There's an enormous amount of wine out there, and we've sipped and slurped our way through hundreds of bottles to bring you the cream of the crop, the individualistic and memorable characters that really impressed us

These are exciting times in the world of wine. But not all the excitement is good. High street stores are being closed down – in my area of London alone we've lost two Threshers and a Wine Rack this year. Famous names like Oddbins are up for sale. New and worrying diseases threaten the vineyards of Europe and California, and the depletion of water supplies in Australia could wreak havoc in an industry almost totally dependent on a regular supply of clean, non-saline water for irrigation. Does all this bad news make you feel you need a drink? Fear not. There is a vast global surplus of wine at the moment – almost 9 *billion* bottles at the last count! Not all of it good, I grant you, but the threat of vast oceans of unwanted wine clogging up the system should wonderfully concentrate the minds of the wine industry. And right now we've got a dazzling array of wines from every corner of the globe capable of ripening a grape, available to every one of us who wants to pop to the local shop or supermarket, pick up the phone, or tap out an e-mail.

Please bear in mind that wines are not made in infinite quantities – some of these may well sell out, but the following year's vintage should then become available
The retailers listed here submitted the winning wines; see Price Guides for other stockists

MY 2002 TOP DOZEN

A stunning bunch of wines from all kinds of grape varieties, and from merchants great and small. And convincing proof to any doubters that Australia can make world-class wine – and lots of it

① 1998 The Dead Arm Shiraz, d'Arenberg, McLaren Vale, £17.99, Bibendum (red, Australia)
The unbridled throaty roar of old vine Shiraz in full cry. I've seen these vines: wizened, ancient, sprouting tiny bunches of tiny black grapes from their tired old limbs. And what wine they make! The fruit is as thick as blood, dark and brooding; the richness is the aggressive richness of black chocolate and black treacle; the perfume is a spearing scent of minerals, dill, anise and thyme.

② 1998 Châteauneuf-du-Pape Cuvée Réservée, Domaine du Pegaü, £21.35, Gauntleys (red, Rhône)
Rich, high-octane red, hurling its flavours together in a maelstrom of sunbaked ripeness from the southern Rhône. The richness just builds and builds in your mouth with such unlikely partners as loganberries, dates, stewed cherries and Nesquik chocolate powder all battling it out with the warm hillside scents of rosemary and thyme. It's deep and exciting now and will improve for five to ten years yet.

③ 1998 Semillon, Tim Adams, Clare Valley, £7.99, Australian Wine Club (white, Australia)
Tim Adams may be most famous for his Herculean reds, but he also makes one of Australia's greatest Semillons: austere and assertive but marvellously rich if you let the wine open out in your mouth. Wax, confectioners' cream and butter all coat the lemon acidity in warmth and mellow the scents of leather and sage.

4 1998 Pinot Noir, Saintsbury, Carneros, £18.95, Adnams (red, USA)

If you want your Pinot to be sensuous, lush in the mouth and beautifully ripe on the tongue, don't automatically look to Burgundy: California often does it better – if differently. This is almost syrup smooth, and with about as much strawberry and red plum fruit as a wine can pack in without breaking the bottle.

5 1998 The Angelus Cabernet Sauvignon, Wirra Wirra Vineyards, Coonawarra, £14.55, Waitrose (red, Australia)

Am I glad to see this back on form. It used to be one of South Australia's best Cabernets before entering a long period when it never seemed quite as ripe and lush as before. Now it's back, bristling with superripe fruit, darkly scented oak and mint. But above all, it's black, black, black – the intense, impenetrable sweetness of black cherry and black plums submerged in a flood of black chocolate.

6 1999 Old Garden Mourvèdre, Hewitson, Barossa Valley, £12.95, Waterloo Wine (red, Australia)

Each year throws up more ancient Australian vines no-one ever knew existed, and luckily there are people like Dean Hewitson scouring every last plot of overgrown garden in South Australia to make sure none gets missed. These vines were planted in 1853 and produce wonderfully ripe fruit: juicy loganberry and strawberry nestled in syrup, with sprigs of thyme floating casually on the surface.

7 1998 Riesling Vorbourg Clos St Landelin, René Muré, £19.30, Gauntleys (white, Alsace)

Most wine lovers don't realize that Alsace Riesling is one of France's classic wine styles. Well, here's your chance to check it out. This wine, from a great vineyard site, has a heavenly mix of honey, ripe apple flesh and the sweet grapiness of sultanas, streaked with the perfumed purity of lime zest.

8 1999 Shiraz, Tim Adams, Clare Valley, £8.99, Australian Wine Club (red, Australia)

A real class act, rich and soft and beautifully balanced with deep plum and black cherry fruit wrapped in the sweetness of pastry dough and coconut.

9 1999 Sauvignon Blanc/Semillon, Cullen, Margaret River, £11.95, Adnams (white, Australia)

This is one of the classic Western Australia whites. It matches and resembles the great dry Bordeaux whites of Pessac-Léognan with lovely zingy acid and perhaps even more nectarine and custard depth than Bordeaux manages. It's lovely now but will happily age ten years.

10 2000 Semillon/Sauvignon Blanc, Cape Mentelle, Margaret River, £9.99, Waitrose (white, Australia)

This is still slightly severe, but attractively so, because it does quickly open up in the mouth, and as it ages it will become richer and more succulent. Even now you can see an enticing mix of tropical fruit, above all white peaches, gentle spice and the cuddly warmth of nuts and custard.

11 1999 Riesling, Waipara West, Waipara, £8.29, Waterloo Wine (white, New Zealand)

Riesling in all its naked glory. Dry, aggressive, with bone dry apple peel fruit and lemon zest attack – even the honey seems strangely gaunt and dry. Impressive, severe now, it will get richer and more honeyed over the next few years.

12 Caballo Loco No. 4, Valdivieso, Central Valley, £14.95, Waitrose (red, Chile)

A magnificent brute with a powerful kick of bitter black chocolate combined with a richness almost of fruit in brandy – and that fruit demonstrates the brilliant piercing quality of blackcurrant, black cherry and plum that only Chile can achieve.

THE RUNNERS UP

Another set of fantastic wines. Again, Australia dominates proceedings, with France weighing in with a very different bunch of flavours, but I hoped for more excitement from the other heavyweights, like South America, South Africa, California and Spain

1 2000 Sauvignon Blanc, Forrest Estate, Marlborough, £7.95, Adnams (white, New Zealand)
Balance is everything in this delicious tongue-tingler. It has tremendous blackcurrant leaf, nettle and gooseberry attack, it throws the flavour gauntlet down with grapefruit, passionfruit and coffee bean – and yet it somehow manages to be mild-mannered and gently persuasive rather than argumentative and abrupt.

2 1997 Pinot Gris Clos Windsbuhl, Domaine Zind-Humbrecht, £22.60, Anthony Byrne (white, Alsace)
Nothing aggressive, in-your-face or modern here, just the magical Pinot Gris ability to be rich with runny honey and fruit syrup, yet to suggest the savoury aroma of fresh sweat, and match this with an unmistakable sense of the clean cool soil of the vineyard.

3 2000 Gamekeeper's Reserve, St Hallett, Barossa, £6.99, Australian Wine Club (red, Australia)
I've always enjoyed this riproaring red party animal from St Hallett, but this vintage is more serious than usual; darker, burlier, indeed almost needing another few months for its splash of strawberry fruit and slash of herb scent to clamber out of the glass.

4 1999 Cabernet Sauvignon, Tatachilla, Padthaway, £8.99, Safeway (red, Australia)
Padthaway is always talked of as a white wine area, but the locals have been whispering for years that it's just as good for reds, if not better! Well, this marvellous ripe but serious red, bulging with chocolate and plums, orange blossom and mint, tells me not only is the quality good but the flavours are excitingly different.

5 1998 Shiraz/Cabernet, Stonyfell Metala, Saltram, Langhorne Creek, £6.99, Safeway (red, Australia)
A potent, utterly gluggable Aussie brew, with loads of blackcurrant, toffee and licorice and even a little pepper and mint – the mint cream in a chocolate bar.

6 1999 Côtes du Rhône-Villages Rasteau, Domaine Gourt de Mautens/Jerome Bressy, £17.99, Raeburn (red, Rhône)
This *is* expensive, and it *is* tannic – so much so that you wonder, will it ever soften? It will eventually, and when it does, the dark, brutal carapace will dissolve into a welter of perfumed cherry and mulberry fruit, toastily soft oak and a black-hearted richness of licorice, chocolate, pepper and kitchen spice.

7 2000 Verdelho, Chapel Hill, McLaren Vale, £6.99, Australian Wine Club (white, Australia)
Really original stuff that marries a ripeness of biscuit, butter and beeswax with the raw scent of herbs and the citrus sweetness of lemon and lime marmalade.

8 1998 Riesling Mount Barker, Plantagenet, Western Australia, £7.95, Vin du Van (white)
This manages to be rich and ripe, almost fat, but still pings with lime juice acidity and the wafting strains of an open petrol can.

9 2000 Sauvignon Blanc, Wither Hills, Marlborough, £7.99, Great Western Wine (white, New Zealand)
Bursting with lively fruit and acidity, this throws out showers of lime and lemon fruit, and blackcurrant leaf and coffee bean perfume, and yet manages to feel full and ripe – a classic Kiwi Sauvignon.

⑩ 1998 Shiraz, Steve Hoff Wines, Barossa, £9.99, Australian Wine Club (red, Australia)
Fiery, passionate Shiraz, brimful of old-time flavours of rich, ripe, dark cherry and black plum fruit soused in black treacle.

⑪ 1999 The Growers Semillon, Mitchell, Clare Valley, £6.95, Balls Brothers (white, Australia)
This probably needs another year or so to show its full personality. Right now it's on the dry side, but is already beginning to taste of fluffy apple flesh and dried apricot fruit, smoky leather perfume and a rather attractive waxy fatness.

⑫ 1999 Crozes-Hermitage Cuvée Albéric Bouvet, Gilles Robin, £9.99, Great Western Wine (red, Rhône)
Full of the sunshine of the south, this remarkably combines the perfume of lilies with the scorched smell of burnt cheese on toast. That plus powerful ripe red fruit makes for a pretty interesting mouthful.

⑬ 2000 Chardonnay, Allandale, Hunter Valley, £8.50, Australian Wine Club (white, Australia)
Fruitier and more scented than the 1998 vintage, which swept the board in our tasting a couple of years ago, the 2000 has more of the almost syrupy ripe character of Hunter Valley fruit.

⑭ 2000 Shiraz/Cabernet Sauvignon, The Wattles Wine Company, South Australia, £5.75, The Wine Society (red)
This is lovely stuff, really ripe and rich, but expertly, refreshingly balanced too. Spicy chocolate, black treacle, and plum and loganberry fruit make for a real hedonist's mouthful – at a *very* keen price.

⑮ 1994 Wehlener Sonnenuhr Spätlese, Joh. Jos. Prüm, Mosel-Saar-Ruwer, £13.99, Waitrose (white, Germany)
The epitome of elegance. This delightful Mosel mixes honey and lime with the scrape of slate and the juicy crackle of a Bramley cooking apple, and yet remains mild-mannered and perfect for a contemplative sip in the late summer sun.

⑯ 1999 Côtes du Rhône-Villages Séguret, Domaine la Montagne d'Or, Corinne et Alain Mahinc, £6.45, Tanners (red, Rhône)
This is ripe, bursting with raspberry and strawberry fruit, herb perfume and just a touch of tannin to keep it half serious.

⑰ 1997 Chianti Classico Riserva, Castello di Fonterutoli, £22.95, Waitrose (red, Italy)
The new exciting face of Chianti Classico. It's a serious wine, but that doesn't stop it being intensely enjoyable if you're in the right mood. You'll get deep cherry, strawberry and nut kernel fruit, the husks of nut splashed with tomato, a dry, haughty flavour but ripe and in no way rough.

⑱ 1995 Olmo's Reward, Frankland Estate, Great Southern, £12.50, Morris & Verdin (red, Australia)
This wine is fairly mature, deep and dark, showing some of the savoury excitement of well-aged Cheddar cheese to temper its ripe, sweet black cherry fruit.

⑲ 1998 Reserve Chardonnay – Barrique-Fermented, Delegat's, Hawkes Bay, £8.99, Safeway (white, New Zealand)
New Zealand Chardonnay is fleshier, more lush than the leaner French style, yet nothing like the broad, slightly sweet style of the Americas. This has a lovely ripe mix of grilled nuts and syrup and cream, but it is refreshingly balanced by piercing acidity.

⑳ 1998 St-Émilion Grand Cru, Château Plaisance, £12.95, The Wine Society (red, Bordeaux)
Classic St-Émilion, with gentle, cherryish fruit rounded with cream and a light but appetizing perfume of grilled nuts. Drink it now or keep it for at least five years.

BEST BUYS UNDER £5

I was very relieved to see how many good Chilean wines surfaced in this category. Last year South America threatened to sweep all before it. The threat didn't materialize – except here, in the under a fiver section

1 1993 Ürziger Würzgarten Riesling Spätlese, Weingut Prälat, Mosel, £4.99, Majestic (white, Germany)
Majestic always have some beautiful mature Mosels from top producers and top vineyard sites at giveaway prices. This little treasure is a classic marriage of high acidity, lime flower perfume scratched with the cool scent of slate, and licked with cream.

2 1999 Poema Garnacha Viñas Viejas, Bodegas y Viñedos del Jalon, Calatayud, £4.99, Moreno Wines (red, Spain)
Calatayud, in north-central Spain, is as yet barely known, but it soon will be if it keeps producing delightful juicy strawberry and herb flavoured reds like this.

3 2000 Cabernet Sauvignon Rosé Santa Digna, Miguel Torres, Curicó, £4.99, Direct Wine Shipments (red, Chile)
This rosé is a delight, with a lovely summery strawberry fruit and blackcurrant leaf scent to match its shimmering cherry-pink hue.

4 2000 Syrah, Inycon, Sicily, £4.99, Enotria Winecellars/Sainsbury's (red, Italy)
Inycon is a new project in Sicily and the 2000 vintage is a big leap forward in quality: really interesting Syrah with loads of plum fruit, a soft texture like caramel melted into fluffy egg white and a suggestion of violets.

5 2000 Carmenère, Cooperativa Agricola Vitivinicola de Curicó, Curicó Valley, £4.99, Co-op (red, Chile)
Smashing wine: deep and ripe, packed with toffee and black cherry fruit but daringly smeared with soy sauce and pepper.

6 1999 Dry English Table Wine, £4.99, The Nobody Inn (white, UK)
For those of you yet to try English wine: firstly, shame on you; secondly, this fragrant,

mouthwatering mix of grapefruit, passionfruit and green leafy acidity should persuade you.

7 1999 Zinfandel Peteroa, Vinicola Montealegre, Central Valley, £4.71, Wines of Westhorpe (red, Chile)
Zinfandel doesn't get quite as ripe in Chile as it does in California, but that's not a problem: it's still 13.5% alcohol by volume, and it keeps its rich date and raisin and plum depth, but in a slightly more restrained manner.

8 1997 Vin de Pays d'Ardèche Syrah, Ptomaine des Blagueurs, £4.99, Oddbins (red, Rhône)
I've watched with interest as this has developed into a really interesting, mature wine, with more than a suggestion of Crozes-Hermitage about its soft plum fruit, its smoky scent and its strange but attractive potato savouriness.

9 2000 Argento Malbec, Catena, Mendoza, £4.99, Sainsbury's (red, Argentina)
Argentina has, on the whole, failed to build on its bright start of a year or two ago; its wines have become both less fruity and less affordable. Argento, though, has held its price and improved its quality and is a good sturdy red, with ripe black fruit, a flicker of spice and a handful of herbs.

10 1999 The Society's Chilean Merlot, Concha y Toro, Rapel Valley, £4.95, The Wine Society (red, Chile)
Really nice juicy red – and very Chilean in style. Lovely black plum and blackcurrant fruit that is positively rich in the mouth, and then a savoury, soy sauce earthiness emerges to keep the whole thing on the right side of serious.

BEST BUYS UNDER £4

The £3.99 price point is an important one for many wine buyers. We've found some good wines, but not much from the New World. France rules here, and Hungary is making a decent stab at things too

1 2000 Vin de Pays d'Oc Viognier Cuvée Prestige, Les Chevalerets, £3.95, Anthony Byrne (white, southern France)
What a lovely wine to sneak in under the £4 barrier. This is a delightfully scented dry white, smelling of flowers and talc, and tasting of apricots stewed in syrup, but with their stalks imparting a touch of graininess to the end product.

2 1999 Vin de Pays de Côtes de Thongue Syrah, Domaine la Condamine l'Evêque, £3.95, The Wine Society (red, southern France)
Impressive Syrah, full of herbs and shrivelled plum fruit, but with a touch of the farmyard to keep you firmly on the ground.

3 1999 The Society's Ruppertsberg Trocken, Pfalz, £3.95, The Wine Society (white, Germany)
An excellent dry yet soft German wine, marvellously mild, scented with orange blossom and tasting of fluffy English eating apples drizzled with honey.

4 2000 Vin de Pays d'Oc Merlot Cuvée Prestige, Les Chevalerets, £3.95, Anthony Byrne (red, southern France)
Good, fresh, balanced young red. It's quite difficult to get Merlot right in the south of France: it's usually either raw or soupy, with not much in between. This is the in between: bright plum fruit, a touch of redcurrant and youthful yeast and some blackcurrant leaf to lift the palate.

5 2000 'The Unpronounceable Grape' Cserszegi Füszeres, Hilltop Neszmély, Duna Region, £3.49, First Quench (white, Hungary)
I'm not surprised these guys call it the Unpronounceable Grape: when you try to pronounce it it sounds as though you're

sneezing and choking at the same time – not at all the effect you want from a soft, fresh, gently floral dry white like this, just pleasantly streaked with lime zest.

6 2000 Pinot Gris, Nyakas Pince, Budai, £3.49, Wines of Westhorpe (white, Hungary)
New-wave Hungarian whites are some of our best bargains at the moment, and this Pinot Gris is classy: gentle in texture, delicately balanced with acidity, and blending honey with soft eating apples and peach.

7 1999 Quiltro Cabernet Sauvignon, Viñedos del Pacifico, Maipo Valley, £3.99, Oddbins (red, Chile)
Not one of Chile's real stars, but it is pleasant, a bit overripe but soft and full, and there *is* some of Chile's famed blackcurrant there if you look for it.

8 2000 Sauvignon Blanc, Nyakas Pince, Budai, £3.99, Wines of Westhorpe (white, Hungary)
It's difficult to find better Sauvignon than this at the price. Clouds of elderflower scent, aggressive nettles and lime leaf acidity and a quite appetizing cool earthiness to round it off.

9 2000 Vin de Pays des Coteaux de Peyriac, Domaine de Subremont, £3.49, Waterloo Wine (red, southern France)
A bit raw and young, but it's balanced and gutsy, and I can see it calming down and softening up by the time you read this.

10 2000 Malbec, La Riojana, Famatina Valley, £3.99, Co-op (red, Argentina)
I'd longed for much more good Argentinian wine at this level, but this is the only one – and it's a pleasant mix of mildly floral perfume and savoury middleweight fruit.

RHÔNE RAVERS

The most successful area of France for red wines at the moment is the Rhône Valley. Prices are reasonable; quality is excellent. Several have made the top selection, but here are half a dozen more

1 1998 Côtes du Rhône-Villages Rasteau, Domaine Saint Gayan, £7.50, Yapp Brothers
Rasteau is not a well-known village, but the wines are increasingly good and fairly priced. This is soft, rich and steeped in hillside herbs, bringing a mouthwatering attack to the gentle cherry, plum and sultana fruit.

2 1999 Côtes du Rhône-Villages Cairanne, Domaine de l'Ameillaud, £5.99, Unwins
This property is run by an Englishman and this dense, powerful vintage is his best yet, almost baked in its richness, almost bitter in its seriousness, but stuffed with deeply satisfying ripe black fruit.

3 1999 Côtes du Rhône, Domaine Cros de la Mûre, £5.95, The Wine Society
Deep, warm, plummy wine that gets better and better the longer you leave it in the glass – so make sure you employ a big glass and fill it well, otherwise you'll have a thirsty half hour wait for this to develop its full black plum and cherry fruit and its appetizing bay leaf scent.

4 1998 Côte-Rôtie, Patrick et Christophe Bonnefond, £14.99, Great Western Wine
Côte-Rôtie represents scent and succulence of texture, a beguiling beauty rather than the thrusting jaw of Hermitage. And that's what we have here: a gentle red with dry, ripe plum fruit, a hint of floral scent, and a coating of coffee and cream.

5 1998 Crozes-Hermitage Les Machonnières, Charles et François Tardy, £10.70, Christopher Piper Wines
At first taste this may seem a little surly and dark, but the flavour soon opens out with lilac perfume, a chocolate cream richness and an invigorating peppery finish. It'll be even better in a couple of years.

6 1997 St-Joseph, Domaine Rochevine, £8.99, Majestic
St-Joseph is less bedevilled by excessive use of new oak barrels than some of its neighbours, so the beauty of the fruit can shine through. This is still a little tough at the edge, but has full ripe plum fruit, and the delightful perfume of lily stems.

MAGNIFICENT MISFITS

We uncover such an array of different styles and flavours in our tastings each year that some real beauties fall between the cracks and just miss out on the top selections. Here's a dozen that are...not less good...just *different*

1 1999 Deheso Gago, Bodegas Toresanas, Toro, £6.50, Adnams (red, Spain)
Toro is a tremendous area, capable of producing intense black fruit, but short on good winemakers. Enter Spain's roving star Telmo Rodriguez. Here he's made a marvellous wine packed with dark sweet plum and cherry fruit, scented with flowers and sprinkled with peppercorns.

2 1999 Coteaux du Languedoc Les Garrigues, Domaine Clavel, £5.95, Tanners (red, southern France)
The far south is producing some of France's best red wines at the moment, and now's the time to try them, because vintages are good and prices are keen. This is powerful stuff, meaty, dry but stuffed with heavy black fruit, and a splash of Angostura bitters.

3 1999 Bourgogne Grand Ordinaire Pinot Noir Terres Dorées, Jean-Paul Brun, £8.04, Savage Selection (red, Burgundy)

Bourgogne Grand Ordinaire is a wine title so lowly we virtually never see it this side of the channel. But this inspired example boasts a cherry and plumskin core wrapped round with leather and soft oak and thrust through with a shaft of cold shiny metal. Really interesting – and it will age for two to three years.

4 1998 Minervois, Château de Beaufort, £7.59, Great Northern Wine Company (red, southern France)

Some Minervois is soft and scented but this one is sterner stuff: brawny, powerful, packed with bitter chocolate and black plums, strewn with bay leaves and a perfumed streak of Angostura.

5 1999 Cabernet Franc, Waipara West, Waipara, £7.99, Waterloo Wine (red, New Zealand)

Waipara is sunny but it's cool, and the Cabernet Franc grape from cool Bordeaux may find it an ideal spot to ripen. Certainly this gentle strawberry-flavoured red flecked with a hint of sage perfume bodes well.

6 2000 Pinot Gris, Mount Langi Ghiran, Victoria, £10.25, Vin du Van (white, Australia)

Mount Langi Ghiran is famous for its rich, sensuous red Shiraz. But clearly Pinot Gris works here too. This is full and soft, but with good ripe apple acidity and a mild warm perfume of honeysuckle and new leather.

7 1993 Chardonnay, Vicker's Vineyard, Idaho, £12.53, Savage Selection (white, USA)

An eight-year-old Chardonnay from Idaho? Sure, why not? This high-acid white has slowly evolved into a strange but delicious blend of Burgundian oatmeal and grilled cashew nuts now taking over from the sage leaves and lemon acidity of its youth.

8 1996 Graciano, Milawa Estate, Brown Brothers, King Valley, £8.50, Christopher Piper Wines (red, Australia)

Graciano is a rare grape from Rioja in Spain. You'd hardly expect to find it in Australia, but the Brown Brothers are inveterate experimenters, and this interesting mélange of squashy strawberry and blackberry fruit mingled with tobacco, menthol and sandalwood shows the experiment was worth it.

9 1998 Côtes de Provence, Château Vannières, £10.95, Gauntleys (red, southern France)

Most Côtes de Provence wine is drunk on the French Riviera – and is often pretty dull. But this is good, perhaps a bit tannic, but it has good dark red fruit, a little floral perfume and a brush of maquis herbs.

10 1999 Vin de Pays Catalan Carignan, Domaine Ferrer Ribere, £7.50, Yapp Brothers (red, southern France)

The Carignan is *not* a trendy grape, but these vines are not trying to be trendy: they're122 years old. At this age, they give dark, treacly, pruney wine, almost port-like in its richness but still vibrant and exciting.

11 1997 Foral Vinho Tinto, Aliança, Douro DOC, £4.99, Noble Rot Wine Warehouses (red, Portugal) Tel: (01527) 575606

The Douro Valley is where they make port – but they make impressive table wine too. This big, old-style bruiser, dry but ripe, packed with herbs, black fruit and chocolate, is a pretty good example.

12 2000 Soave Classico Superiore Monte Fiorentine, Ca' Rugate, £5.99, Unwins (white, Italy)

Cheap commercial brands have given Soave such a bad name we don't take it seriously. But those estates with good traditional vineyards who keep their yields low make delightful wine, overflowing with the fresh ripe fruit of eating apples and the scented acidity of lemon slices.

SWEETIES

High street retailer and restaurateur alike report declining interest in sweet wines, but here's a tasty half dozen for those of you who've kept the faith

1 1998 Torcolato, Maculan, Breganze, £12.99/half bottle, Oddbins (Italy)
This is one of the true originals in the sweet wine firmament: it manages to balance its rich, powerful fruit with a finely judged, and very refreshing, hint of sourness. The wine seems at first to be a splendid medley of pineapple, barley sugar and peach – and so it is – but when that delightful streak of sourness starts to make itself felt around the edges of your tongue then you know this isn't a run of the mill mouthful of goo in any shape or form.

2 1997 Pacherenc du Vic Bilh, Brumaire, Alain Brumont, £10.92/50cl, Anthony Byrne (southern France)
This is a very rare wine from France's deepest South-West, but stuff this good deserves to be better known, with its luscious cling peach in syrup, barley sugar and orange treacle pudding richness, its coconut perfume and its refreshing acidity.

3 1995 Monbazillac, Château les Charmes de Saint-Mayme, £7.99, Marks & Spencer (southern France)
What a surprise to find this carefully made, mature sweetie on the supermarket shelves.

It has very attractive pineapple chunks and barley sugar sweetness which just stops short of true lusciousness. A sort of 'semi-Sauternes', at a 'semi-Sauternes' price.

4 1996 Botrytis Semillon, Nine Pines Vineyards, Cranswick Estate, New South Wales, £4.98/half bottle, ASDA (Australia)
Big, thick, sweet stuff, simply oozing ripe pineapple and sticky barley sugar richness and yet keeping some nice acidity to stop it cloying. Subtle it ain't, but at £4.99 for a bottleful of blazing Aussie sunshine, who's asking for subtlety?

5 1999 Moscatel de Valencia, Bodessa, £3.99, Marks & Spencer (Spain)
I have to include one of these – the perfect bargain basement glass of grape juice and honey, lemon flower and orange blossom.

6 1998 Recioto di Soave La Perlara, Ca' Rugate, £12.99/50cl, Valvona & Crolla (Italy)
This is 'half-sweet': it's got the barley sugar and the peaches and the pineapple, but it doesn't have the syrup, so drink it by itself rather than with the tiramisu.

FORTIFIEDS

If it weren't for the tiny band of excellent winners each year, I fear we might give up having a fortified section altogether. There is so much good fortified wine being made, yet many British retailers are content to offer drab stuff. Oh dear. Still, try these and you won't be disappointed

1 1972 Vino Dulce de Postre Gran Reserva Pedro Ximenez, Toro Albalá, Montilla Moriles, £9.49/half bottle, Moreno Wines (Spain)
You can't comprehend just how sweet and powerful a wine can be until you've tasted a drop or two of this. It is the traditional

sweet wine of the sherry region, although it is made in nearby Montilla. It's so thick it hardly pours from the bottle, and then it stains the glass as it clings lasciviously to the sides. And all the while it's exuding an intense aroma of Christmas pudding, treacle, nutmeg, ginger and honey bread.

2 1986 Banyuls Grand Cru Cuvée Réservée, L'Etoile, £16.17, Anthony Byrne Fine Wines (southern France)
This is a rare but brilliant style of wine, from way, way down on the Mediterranean coast, where the sun bakes the grapes senseless as they perch over the cool blue sea. You can get young Banyuls, all purple and fiery, but this is a grand old man: beautifully mature, rich but not overpowering, just beginning to give up the tempestuous joys of youth for a mellow, nutty middle age.

3 The Society's Fino, Jerez, £4.25, The Wine Society (Spain)
A classic dry sherry – and for no more than the price of a mediocre Chardonnay. This is exactly how I hope a fino will be when offered a glass: bready, soft, apple fresh, distinctly dry and redolent of old wooden

stairs and the undisturbed dust on a spinster aunt's landing.

4 1996 Maury, Mas Amiel, £9.60, Nicolas (southern France), Tel: 020-8964 5469
Excellent example of the young, beautiful, fruit-drenched style of the fortifieds made in Roussillon down near the Spanish border. This one's blackberry and loganberry is so dark and sweet and soft, you forget that this is a fortified wine at all.

5 1996 Late Bottled Vintage Port, J W Burmester, £11.50, Fortnum & Mason (Portugal)
Burmester is an ancient port house, but has failed to impress me until recently. This is good, though, full of sweet, dark plum and blackberry fruit but shot through with peppercorn and the rasp of hillside herbs.

FIZZ

We were impressed by what the supermarkets had to offer (see page 26), but most other fizz was distinctly unfestive. Here's half a dozen that hit the spot

1 1996 Rory Brut, Kim Crawford, Auckland, £10.95, Liberty Wines (New Zealand)
This is what Champagne *should* taste like, but this comes from the other side of the world. It's soft, has a soothingly foaming bubble, and the gentle flavours of cream and nuts and porridge oats wash blithely over your palate.

2 Champagne NV Cuvée Selection Brut, Le Brun de Neuville, £13.25, Waterloo Wine
Nice stuff. I could drink this very happily through a reasonably long party. Gently foaming, with attractive hazelnut and oatmeal ripeness.

3 Premium Brut NV, Morton Estate, £8.99, Le Nez Rouge (New Zealand)
Lovely fizz – fairly dry, very fresh, but with a nice foam and a subtle undertow of nuts and soft fruit.

4 Champagne NV Henri Harlin Brut, P & C Heidsieck, £14.99, Oddbins
One of the high street's most reliable Champagne brands, always fairly full-bodied, always enjoyable. This release has a little honeyed richness to go with the soft fruit and the seductively foaming fizz.

5 Champagne NV Brut Réserve, Theophile Roederer, £18.95, Fortnum & Mason
This is *a* Roederer rather than *the* (Louis) Roederer, but it's nice wine: quite full and fat, foaming and ripe, the flavour like loft apples in syrup. A little oatmeal or brioche would improve the apple, but there you go.

6 Champagne NV Brut, Brossault, £12.49, Majestic
More loft apples, but this time there is something extra, rather like the breakfast aromas of puffed wheat and porridge.

SUPERMARKET SELECTION

The wine department shelves may be bulging with big brands – most of them Australian – but our supermarkets are also adept at talent-spotting and bringing us new and exciting tastes at very reasonable prices

It's rather fashionable at the moment to complain that the supermarkets are offering increasingly bland and homogeneous wines to the drinking public. Well, there is no doubt that the big, heavily advertised brands are more dominant in the supermarkets than they were. The supermarkets say they like them because they allow nervous shoppers the chance to feel confident amid the jungle of confusing wine names. They also say that they offer people a base from which to become more adventurous and start to try less familiar wines. I sort of agree. Although I'm sure there's all kinds of hard bargaining going on about which brand gets what kind of exposure on the shelves, I have to say that the majority of the big brands are surprisingly good nowadays and I for one wouldn't mind spending an evening drinking most of them. But the supermarkets are also right when they say well-known names offer a good springboard from which to leap into the unknown. We found more exciting, individualistic wines exclusive to supermarkets than ever before, at either end of the price scale. The geographical spread was also excellent, with France, in particular, making a real comeback. The biggest disappointment was how South America, and particularly Argentina, has not built on the success of last year.

Please bear in mind that wines are not made in infinite quantities – some of these may well sell out, but the following year's vintage should then become available.

SUPERMARKET SUPERSTARS

Any merchant would be more than happy to have these delights on their list – but these are all supermarket wines, available in hundreds of outlets throughout the country. And that's a resounding endorsement of the job our supermarkets are doing at the moment

1 1999 Chardonnay, Tatachilla, Adelaide Hills, £8.99, Safeway (white, Australia)
Burgundy, eat your heart out. What a beaut. This has all the lush dryness of toast and cashew nuts and oatmeal that makes great Burgundy and adds to it a silky, glyceriny patina that sensuously coats your palate with pleasure.

2 2000 Sauvignon Blanc, Neil Ellis, Groenekloof, £7.99, Safeway (white, South Africa)
I've always thought of New Zealand as the leader of the world's Sauvignon Blanc producers, but those guys in the Cape are turning it into one of their specialities too. Using grapes from the new area of Groenekloof on the Atlantic coast, Neil Ellis has made a brilliant Sauvignon, bristling with nettles, gooseberry and green pepper, perfumed with mint and blackcurrant leaves, yet with just enough honey to soften the tingling, mouthwatering fruit.

3 2000 Sauvignon Blanc, Old Renwick Vineyard, Craggy Range Winery, Marlborough, £8.99, Waitrose (white, New Zealand)
A cracking good wine, throbbing with nettle, gooseberry and capsicum aggression,

but also with lovely tropical passionfruit and lime aromas and a gentleness that belies its zingy taste.

4 **1999 Touriga Nacional/Tinta Roriz, Manta Preta, D F J Vinhos, Estremadura, £5.99, Waitrose (red, Portugal)**
New-wave Portuguese reds are some of Europe's most original wines – just look at this example. Using two of Portugal's best grape varieties, this is bursting with the richest of red fruit, wrapped in syrup, with crumbs of cherry cake thrown into the vat.

5 **1999 Crozes-Hermitage, Etienne Barret, £6.99, Safeway (red, Rhône)**
Surprisingly gentle but delicious red, with a perfume of lilies, a savoury warmth of grilling meat and a sweetness of red plums and cream. If you like northern Rhône reds, Crozes-Hermitage offers the best value at the moment.

6 **2000 Riesling, McLean's Farm, St Hallett Wines, Eden Valley, £7.99, Marks & Spencer (white, Australia)**
This ace dry Riesling is just the thing to get your appetite moving, with its cutting acidity of lime zest and grapefruit overlaid with lemon flower, apple blossom and the juice of a Cox's Orange Pippin.

7 **2000 Carmenère, Los Robles, Curicó Valley, £4.99, Sainsbury's (red, Chile)**
A real original, rippling with the ripeness of damsons and plums yet unable to shake off a marvellous earthy mixture of soya and beef stew fired up with spice after long hours on the hob.

8 **1998 Côtes du Roussillon, Domaine de l'Auris, £8.99, Safeway (red, southern France)**
Magnificent, haughty red from down near the Pyrenees, swathed in perfume, packed with fruit, encased in bittersweet tannins. You might even think this wine is a bit too fierce. Don't be a faintheart. Smell the heady aroma of violets and bay leaf. Drink

in the sweetness of morello cherries and damsons and then worry about the tannin as you prepare yourself a steak to go with the wine and reflect that it'll be even better if you stash a bottle or two away for a couple of years.

9 **1999 Vila Santa, João Portugal Ramos, Alentejo, £7.99, Waitrose (red, Portugal)**
This wine needs another couple of years to show at its best, but João Ramos is one of Portugal's top winemakers, and it will blossom in time. For now, it's rich, deep and tannic, but with a fabulous ripeness of mulberries and plums in syrup just waiting to clamber out into the light.

10 **1998 St-Joseph Cuvée Côte-Diane, Cave de Saint-Désirat, £9.99, Marks & Spencer (red, Rhône)**
St-Joseph is the most perfumed of all the Rhône reds, sometimes exhibiting a floral scent so marked it quite puts you off your stride. This one won't cause you to stumble, but it is a gentle dry red with an irresistible scent of lilies and black peppercorns and sandalwood to ginger up its soft red plum and cherry fruit.

11 **1998 Faugères, Domaine des Lauriers, £4.75, Safeway (red, southern France)**
Faugères wines are famously scented, and this one has a scent of violet and bay leaf and Imperial Leather soap and talc that fills the room. However, this one is more tannic than usual and would be better with a couple more years to round out.

12 **2000 Sancerre Les Bonnes Bouches, Henri Bourgeois, £8.99, Safeway (white, Loire)**
Hah! What a nice surprise. We have got so used to the powerful, assertive flavours of New World Sauvignon Blanc that it's easy to forget that Sancerre has been growing it in France for centuries. This is gentle and classy, mixing honey and lemon flower with blackcurrant leaf and a whiff of 'gunflint' for the traditionalists.

HIGH-STREET HEROES

An inspiring selection that really shows the strengths of our supermarkets, with 20 excellent wines from 10 different countries – and most are under £10

1 **1996 Classic Selection Rioja Reserva, La Rioja Alta, Rioja DOC, £7.99, Sainsbury's (red, Spain)**
Pure class. There's so little good Rioja around at the moment at a fair price that this brings back all the memories of the good times Rioja used to guarantee. The flavour of coconut, banana, strawberry and plum, a coating of cream smoothing away any acidity and tannin – that's how Rioja used to be. Luckily, Rioja Alta still make it that way.

2 **1997 Hattenheimer Schützenhaus Riesling Auslese, Hans Lang, Rheingau, £7.99, Waitrose (white, Germany)**
One day, people will start to drink fine German wine again, and this is just the thing to encourage them. This is slightly sweet, with an uplifting marriage of peach and pear, honey and even grapes, topped off with crème fraîche and knitted together with fine acidity.

3 **1998 Cabardès, Château Salitis, £5.49, Safeway (red, southern France)**
From a little-known area near Toulouse – half Bordeaux, half Mediterranean – this is almost overripe at first taste, then develops a ripe plum and honey fruit, yet never loses its powerful herb and pepper core.

4 **1998 Shiraz, Haselgrove, McLaren Vale, £7.99, Safeway (red, Australia)**
Big, ripe red with loads of licorice blackness as well as toffee, chocolate and plum. Not as brawny as some McLaren Vale Shirazes, but a lovely ripe red mouthful with respectable table manners.

5 **1999 Single Vineyard Zinfandel, MontGras, Colchagua Valley, £6.99, Sainsbury's (red, Chile)**
All the lush briary richness of a typical Zinfandel but with a cooler, calmer character than the typical California example. A little more acidity, a brighter, drier fruit, but no lack of ripe bramble and syrup, honeycomb and tobacco leaf.

6 **1999 Pinot Noir Kaituna Hills Reserve, Montana Wines, Marlborough, £9.99, Marks & Spencer (red, New Zealand)**
New Zealand is convinced it's going to become the New World's number one Pinot producer, and if this is anything to go by, it might well. It's a gentle, glyceriny, strawberry and cherry-flavoured wine, lightly brushed with cream and definitely touched with class.

7 **1997 Fronsac, Château la Vieille Cure, £10.99, Sainsbury's (red, Bordeaux)**
High street Bordeaux doesn't give me a lot of joy nowadays, but this year there are signs of improvement and this vintage of an old Sainsburys' regular is the best yet – not massively ripe but very attractive, with gentle plum fruit and a toasted nuts aroma from its time spent maturing in oak barrels.

8 **2000 Viognier, Fairview, Coastal Region, £8.99, Waitrose (white, South Africa)**
Viognier is the top white grape of France's Rhône Valley; in the hands of this South African producer it makes rich, succulent wine, with a core of apricot fruit and a slightly over the top blanket of sweet, toasty oak.

9 **1997 Wehlener Sonnenuhr Riesling Kabinett, S A Prüm, Mosel-Saar-Ruwer, £6.99, Safeway (white, Germany)**
One of Germany's greatest producers, one of Germany's greatest vineyard sites – in a supermarket? This is simply delightful, with its penetrating green apple acid, its austere

slatey coolness that quickly gives in to a pastry softness, and an orchard bouquet of honeysuckle, greengage and honeycomb.

10 Pinotage, Beyers Truter, Coastal Region, £4.99, Tesco (red, South Africa)
I love Pinotage – it is so different from the mainstream European grapes. This has loads of unashamed flavour – marshmallows toasting over the fire, coal smoke, mulberry, even banana, all squashy and ready to be made into sandwiches. Yum.

11 1994 Viña Mara Rioja Gran Reserva, Bodegas Berberana, £9.99, Tesco (red, Spain)
This is classy Rioja – it's quite mature and mellow, but is still holding on to a pleasant, wistful strawberry fruit wrapped in a coconut cream cocoon.

12 1998 'Bentwing' Shiraz, Haselgrove, Wrattonbully, £8.99, Safeway (red, Australia)
Wrattonbully is a new cool-climate area way south of Adelaide in South Australia, so this isn't your classic Aussie Shiraz, all blood and thunder. No, it's more demure, with a non-threatening plummy fruitiness, some toffee softness and a suggestion of sweetness like the smell of manila envelopes.

13 2000 Tannat Polo Sur, Pisano, Progreso, £9.99, Marks & Spencer (red, Uruguay)
Tannat is a wild, brutish grape from southern France that seems to have found its natural home in the warmer climes of Uruguay. This is dark, rumbling with gruff earth and mineral tastes, but there's loads of plum and damson fruit and a surprising but reasonably attractive smell of bakelite.

14 1999 Vacqueyras, Domaine la Bouscatière, £6.99, Safeway (red, Rhône)
Old-style, powerful Rhône, full of fruit baked by the sun to a deep, stewed cherry ripeness that battles with tannin and herbs and the gaunt dryness of pebbles for supremacy.

15 1998 Vin de Pays d'Oc Les Romains, Les Domaines Camplazens, £7.99, Marks & Spencer (red, southern France)
At the moment this is burly and brooding, but keep it for another couple of years and it will open out to a syrupy soft display of plum and blackberry.

16 2000 Bonarda, Finca El Retiro, Mendoza, £5.99, Sainsbury's (red, Argentina)
The Bonarda grape from the north of Italy looks set to assume a star role in Argentina, with fascinating flavours of eucalyptus and thyme, lime leaf and menthol all bouncing around on a bed of soft red fruit.

17 2000 Torrontés La Nature (organic), La Riojana, Famatina Valley, £4.47, Asda (white, Argentina)
You must give this a try at least once for its riot of rose-petal scent, ginger spice and grapefruit, peach, lemon zest fruit.

18 1999 Dão, Touriga Nacional/Jaen, Dom Ferraz, £4.95, Budgens (red, Portugal)
Deep, serious red that manages to balance dark black fruit with redcurrant freshness, heady kitchen spice with the scent of shiny new leather. A great food wine.

19 1999 Single Vineyard Syrah, MontGras, Colchagua Valley, £6.99, Sainsbury's (red, Chile)
Pour a glass and give it a good shake, because this wine has a rather meaty smell that needs dissipating. Once you've done that, though, you'll find a deep, satisfying red that mingles violet perfume with plum and black cherry fruit and a twist of pepper.

20 2000 Vin de Pays d'Oc Coeur de Vallée Chardonnay/Roussanne, Pierre de Passendale, £4.99, Marks & Spencer (white, southern France)
Roussanne brings exotic white peach and apricot flavours to titillate the banana, pear and coconut spice of the Chardonnay.

ECONOMY CLASS

Lots of really tasty stuff here, showing that the £3.99 price point is capable of truly mouthfilling flavours when the supermarkets make enough effort to locate them. And when I pull out a synthetic closure instead of a traditional cork I know that a fruity, drink-me-now wine will taste as fresh as its producer intended, with no risk of corky mustiness.

The biggest disappointment this year has been South America: hardly anything from Chile and nothing from Argentina, yet both countries have vast acreages of vineyards capable of lovely ripe flavours at a fair price

1 1999 Garnacha, Viña Fuerte, Calatayud, £3.99, Waitrose (red, Spain)
Spain's lesser-known areas make some fantastic reds, and this gorgeous brute leads the way: powerful, palate-smothering loganberry and blackberry fruit, pepped up by some celery-stick greenness and pepper and allspice scent. All this, and it's 14.5% alcohol by volume – don't drink this one standing up in a gale.

2 Laid Back Ruby – Ruby Cabernet, California, £3.99, Co-op (red, USA)
Laid back Ruby? In yer face Ruby, more like. Straight between the eyes Ruby. This is a gutsy red – full, sturdy, throbbing with plum and blackcurrant fruit and with a good, rough, earthy undertow. This is the kind of decent California red we're all crying out for. Bring on the rest of Ruby's family.

3 Shiraz/Cabernet Sauvignon, South Eastern Australia, £3.99, Tesco (red)
Those Aussies are making some good grog at the moment; no other country offers the richness of fruit yet keeps the wine balanced and invigorating. This bursts with prunes and toffee, loganberries and plum and finishes off with just a lick of tar. [Plastic cork]

4 2000 Karalta Shiraz/Cabernet, Thomas Hardy & Sons, South Australia, £3.49, Asda (red)
Another whopper, a bit younger than the Tesco one above, with great gobs of blackberry jam, plums in treacle and the appetizing smells of fresh grilled nuts. [Plastic cork]

5 2000 Oaked Viura, Alteza, Manchuela, £3.99, Sainsbury's (white, Spain)
Very nice, dry, well oaked white. The acidity is quite marked, but there's loads of ripe peach and Cox's apple fruit and a fragrant dusting of spicy new oak.

6 Shiraz, South Eastern Australia, £3.27, Tesco (red)
What a bargain! This has all the loganberry and plum syrup ripeness you could ask for with some rice pudding and toffee oak softness. Buy it now; it'll get deeper and richer over the next year or so. [Plastic cork]

7 2000 Vin de Pays d'Oc Sauvignon Blanc, Foncalieu, £3.98, Asda (white, southern France)
Bright, fresh Sauvignon, full of lemon zing, banana and Bramley apple fruit and a touch of coffee bean.

8 2000 Young Vatted Valpolicella, Sartori, Veneto, £3.49, Safeway (red, Italy)
Valpolicella as it ought to be: a happy-go-lucky, bright, breezy pale red, smelling of pears and banana split toffees and tasting much the same, with a ladleful of straw-berries and cream to round off the flavours.

9 2000 Shiraz/Ruby Cabernet, Thomas Hardy & Sons, South Australia, £3.99, Safeway (red)
Safeway have had good, lusty, own-label Aussie wines for years and this continues the successful line: big, toasty, rip-roaring red, rich and chewy as Harrogate toffee, sweet as plums stewed in syrup. [Plastic cork]

10 1999 Sémillon, Mountain Vines, Sodap, £3.99, Co-op (white, Cyprus)

What a surprise! A really classy Cypriot white. Things have changed dramatically in Cyprus in the last few years, and this is a good example of the modern style. Still young, it tastes of apples and nuts with a touch of vanilla custard, but promises to age to quince, honey and custard richness in two to four years.

11 2000 Spätlese, Langenbach, Rheinhessen, £3.99, Safeway (white, Germany)

This is exactly what the label says, 'full-flavoured and fruity', off-dry, with a gentle honey and grape richness and clean, unsulphurous character.

12 2000 Grecanico/Chardonnay, Il Padrino, Sicily, £3.99, Budgens (white, Italy)

Soft, easy, mild Sicilian white with melon and pear fruit, refreshing lemony acidity and a touch of cream. Very nice modern wine, showing imaginative use of local and international grape varieties. [Plastic cork]

13 Valencia Oak-aged Bobal/Monastrell/Tempranillo, £3.79, Sainsbury's (red, Spain)

Valencia has so much potential – big modern wineries, loads of investment and export know-how – yet so far all we've seen is Moscatel de Valencia. Well, things are changing at last: there are vast plantations of native red grape varieties crying out for star treatment, and this is a really good modern red, with a touch of spicy oak and toffee and a good, full, bright, plum fruit.

14 Jumilla Monastrell/Merlot, £3.99, Sainsbury's (red, Spain)

Jumilla is just inland from Valencia, and is bursting with superripe red grapes – as this deep, stewy plum and sultana red shows.

15 2000 Sauvignon Blanc, Lontue, £3.48, Asda (white, Chile)

The lone Chilean wine in this price range – and a white one at that – but at least this is a good, snappy dry white with aggressive grapefruit and apple flavours. [Plastic cork]

16 2000 Vin de Pays des Côtes de Gascogne, £3.49, Marks & Spencer (white, southern France)

Another good snappy white, packed with blackcurrant leaf and coffee bean savouriness and an unusual but attractive flavour a bit like really fresh sausagemeat. I'm not kidding! Try it! [Plastic cork]

17 Chardonnay, South Australia, £3.99, Sainsbury's (white)

The £3.99 own-label Aussie Chardonnays are better this year than last. This one has loads of peach skin and quince fruit and a touch of grilled cashewnut smokiness – but is not too oaky or fat. [Plastic cork]

18 2000 Gewürztraminer Bin 066, Hilltop Neszmély, Mór Region, £3.99, Sainsbury's (white, Hungary)

Hungary does these light tasty whites really well; this is a lovely wine with a scent of rose petals and talc, adding an exotic lift to the apple, grapefruit and lily stem flavour.

FOR MORE WINE RECOMMENDATIONS SEE:
OZ CLARKE'S WINE STYLE GUIDE
How to find the flavours you like

Red wines: young and juicy; silky, strawberryish; blackcurranty; spicy; sweet-sour, herby
White wines: crisp and neutral; tangy; intense and nutty; ripe and toasty; aromatic
on the centre pages

See also **Ideal Cellars** on pages 28–37 and the **Retailers Directory** on pages 40–78.
Look out for the **Instant Cellar** lists in the wine region chapters, too.

19 1999 Soave Classico, Vigneti di Costalta, £4.49, Tesco (white, Italy)
Nice bright Italian white, with a flavour like apple pie and cream – that's the fruit *and* the pastry. Soave has been discredited by bad wine for too long, but when properly made, especially in the Classico zone, it's a delightful north Italian thirstquencher.

20 Cabernet/Merlot, South Eastern Australia, £3.49, Tesco (red)
Well, guess what – *another* of Tesco's own-label Aussies! Tesco has a full-time wine buyer living in Australia and it's clearly having an effect: this is a very attractive mix of blackcurrant and red plum fruit with just a touch of welcome earthiness. [Plastic cork]

BARGAIN BASEMENT

It looks as though the surplus of wine that is building up around the world is starting to have a positive effect for us wine drinkers in search of a bargain. One of the most crisis-ridden areas is southern France: half our top tipples at around the £3 price point came from there. Indeed Europe completely dominates the basement, with 11 of my 12 choices.
But what does this mean? Does it mean the New World no longer wishes to play at the bottom end? Yes it does. And if they're not careful, some European producers, happy enough to take whatever price they're offered right now, will struggle to break out from the basement when and if the global surplus of wine diminishes

1 1999 Corbières, Georges Badriou, £5.95/150cl, Safeway (red, southern France)
Don't think I'm not on the consumers' side, but I almost start to fret when wine this good is so cheap. This is an excellent dry red, with a good dollop of raspberry and strawberry fruit, not too much tannin and a splash of Angostura bitters and bay leaf scent.

2 2000 Vin de Pays du Gers, £2.99, Marks & Spencer (white, southern France)
Wow! If you want a white wine that positively spits its aggressive green fruit at you, mixing green apples and lime leaves, kiwi fruit and a touch of mint all together into a tongue-tingling triumph – this is your wine. [Plastic cork]

3 1999 Minervois, Georges Badriou, £2.99, Safeway (red, southern France)
Safeway have clearly got some inspired contacts down in the south of France. This is another smasher. Fresh, juicy, jammy strawberry fruit, the scratch of a sprig of

thyme and a sprinkling of violet perfume – spot on.

4 2000 Irsai Oliver, Hilltop Neszmély, Duna Region, £2.99, Safeway (white, Hungary)
You've got to like your wine scented to like this: it's almost as though someone has sprinkled a bottle of rosewater into the vat, to marry up with the delightful fresh crunchy taste of muscatel grapes. And it's dry! Lovely.

5 Portuguese Red, J P Vinhos, Terras do Sado, £2.99, Somerfield (red, Portugal)
Really interesting basic red: it has lots of deep raspberry juice fruit and slightly sour cream that have to battle a wild savoury roughness that threatens to disrupt the wine, but never does.

6 1999 Vin de Pays du Gers La Loustère, £2.99, Safeway (white, southern France)
Excellent snappy white, bristling with the aggressive scents of lemon zest and sharp

green apples and soothed just a little by a suggestion of roasting coffee beans. Gers, in South-West France, is currently the best place in France for good, cheap, tingly whites. [Plastic cork]

7 Chardonnay, Danie de Wet, Robertson, £2.99, Tesco (white, South Africa)

This represents quite a coup for Tesco to get an own-label from Danie de Wet, because he's one of South Africa's top Chardonnay producers, and this is good stuff, with mild melon and apple fruit, a touch of chalk dust, and finished off with a lick of honey.

8 Merlot, Boyar International, Rousse, £2.99, Sainsbury's (red, Bulgaria)

Bulgaria lost its way a little during the 1990s, but now seems to be recovering its knack of making tasty cheap reds. This has a gentle cakey quality just like Merlot should, some red plum and cherry fruit and even a little cream to soften the tannin.

9 Sicilian White, Cantine Settesoli, Sicily, £2.99, Sainsbury's (white, Italy)

Bright, soft, simple, refreshing white, a bit of pear flesh fruit, some apple acidity and a flicker of spice. [Plastic cork]

10 Corbières, £2.99, Sainsbury's (red, southern France)

Quite full and tough, but lots of black plum skin fruit to counteract the toughness and a definite sprig or two of mountain herbs. [Plastic cork]

11 2000 Young Vatted Merlot, Domaine Boyar, Sliven Region, £3.49, Safeway (red, Bulgaria)

This is young all right! In fact it's only just beginning to soften up its tannins and acidity, but it's got nice strawberry, cherry and plum fruit, dusted with a little vineyard earth.

12 1999 Vin de Pays de Vaucluse, Du Peloux, £2.99, Safeway (red, Rhône)

Nice, soft, mild strawberryish red showing a little of the baking sun of the south of France. Superior plonk. [Plastic cork]

SUPERMARKET FORTIFIEDS

Not for the first time, we thought the standard of fortified wines was pretty ordinary. I can't understand why the big groups don't make more effort with their dry sherry: if this is a declining sector, it'll decline even faster unless the quality bucks up a bit. Even so, two supermarkets – Marks & Spencer and Waitrose – clearly take their ports and sherries fairly seriously

1 Solera Reserva Dry Oloroso Sherry, Diego Romero, Jerez, £5.59, Waitrose

We need more sherries like this if we're ever going to make sherry a popular drink again. This is *fantastic* stuff, sensuously deep and golden brown, purring with the richess of hazelnuts drenched in toffee, sultanas, dates and apricots. And it's totally dry. At this price, one of the bargains of the year.

2 1994 Late Bottled Vintage Port, CD Vintners, £8.49, Marks & Spencer

If you think port should give you a great big foursquare smack in the mouth,

bruising your gums and staining your tongue with black plum and cherry fruit, the sandpaper of pepper and spice and tannin – and a lovely warm glow in your tummy – look no further.

3 Fino Sherry, Luis Caballero, Jerez, £4.89, Waitrose

It doesn't really surprise me that people don't buy dry sherry if it's always stale and flat when they try it. This example, however, is how dry sherry should be: fresh, bready, with a nice acid tang – it's wonderfully refreshing.

4 10 Year Old Tawny Port, Skeffington Vinhos, Douro DOC, £7.99, Waitrose
The more serene and civilized face of port. Tawny in colour, it has soft date and raisin fruit and a certain nutty softness, but it still has a touch of aggression for those who want it.

5 Rich Cream Sherry (Extra Sweet), Williams & Humbert, Jerez, £4.99, Marks & Spencer
Big, sweet and grapy, with a rich pruny depth and a surprising and welcome floral scent. Very pleasant if unfashionable style of sherry – it'll be just the thing with your Christmas mince pies.

6 20 Year Old Port, CD Vintners, £16.99, Marks & Spencer
This is good port, but ideally a 20-year-old should be smoother and subtler than this. Never mind – it's big, full, relatively rich and gooey, with lots of date and plum fruit and dusty oak.

SUPERMARKET CHAMPAGNE

The quality of own-label Champagne is way up on last year. And the reason is we didn't drink enough last year and all the supermarket suppliers had an awful lot left over. So it's a year older, a year softer, a year classier. Whatever some experts say, own-label Champagne is *much* better with an extra year's age. These'll be *fab* this Christmas

1 Brut NV, Bonnet, £27.95/magnum, Waitrose
Wow! This is gorgeous. Beautiful soft stuff, quite mature in a seductive, hazelnut and oatmeal way, and so creamy and soft that the bubbles burst across your palate like velvet foam. And it's in magnums! Fantastic! Invite a friend round.

2 1990 Blanc de Blancs Brut – Cuvée Orpale, de Saint-Gall/Alain Coharde, £30, Marks & Spencer
Another smasher. It's a pretty stiff price, but lubbly bubbly – a beautiful honeycomb ripeness coating grilled hazelnuts and finishing the whole thing off with cream – classic Blanc de Blancs style. Sure you have to pay, but for once in Champagne-land, it's worth it.

3 Blanc de Noirs Brut, Bonnet, £11.95, Waitrose
Made from black grapes only, you expect Blanc de Noirs to be a bit weightier – and it is, but not in a clumsy way. This has a beautiful strawberries and cream ripeness – and I mean it – *real* strawberries and cream! You could almost swear it was candyfloss pink. Well in taste, it is.

4 Blanc de Blancs Brut NV, de Saint-Gall, £16.99, Marks & Spencer
Back to an all white grapes blend, so you lose the strawberries, but you don't lose the cream. This has oodles of soft gooey cream quality and something savoury too – like an ace cream of mushroom soup. In fact, a splash of this *in* a cream of mushroom soup *would* be ace.

5 1995 Albert Etienne Special Cuvée Brut, Lanson, £16.99, Safeway
1995 is a bit young for a vintage Champagne, but the fruit was soft and ripe in 95 and doesn't need as much age as usual, so this is pretty well ready to go: creamy and nutty, but with a bit of acidity underneath it all to show it will still age well. A couple of years under the stairs and it will be very nice indeed.

6 Champagne Premier Cru Extra Dry NV, Duval-Leroy, £14.99, Sainsbury's
Another fizz that has benefited from the build-up of stocks in Champagne. Full, nutty, yeasty and a nice round oatmeal smoothness. But don't buy too much all at once, or you'll use up all the mature stuff.

SUPERMARKET FIZZ

You don't need to spend Champagne money to get Champagne quality

1 Sparkling Shiraz, Banrock Station, South Australia, £7.99, Waitrose
A gorgeous, sexy, plum- and mulberry-saturated burst of colour and scented fruit splashing into the glass and foaming wickedly over the rim.

2 Chandon Australia Brut, Domaine Chandon Australia, £9.99, Safeway
This isn't Champagne – but it's made in the same way, with the same grapes. Soft, oatmealy, warm brioche flavours and gentle foam make for a smashing drink, wherever it's from.

3 English Sparkling Brut, £6.99, Co-op
Gloriously, unashamedly English, with a fabulous elderflower and hedgerow scent and soft, brimming foam that conjures up images of a perfect early summer's day.

4 Bluff Hill Brut NV, Auckland, £7.50, Marks & Spencer (New Zealand)
Full, toasty, slightly honeyed fizz that makes an excellent Champagne lookalike – they use the same grape varieties as Champagne – for a lot less money.

5 Chandon Argentina Brut Fresco, Bodegas Chandon Argentina, Mendoza, £7.99, Safeway
A very nice foaming wine with soft brioche and hazelnut flavours. Real easy-to-drink stuff.

6 Asti, Tosti, £5.99, Marks & Spencer
Good Asti is a delightful drink – I can't work out why it's so unfashionable. But it is. So fly in the face of fashion and enjoy this slightly sweet mouthful of muscatel grapes and elderflower scented with honeysuckle.

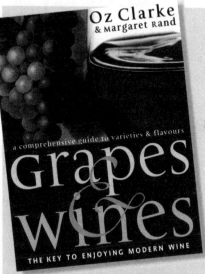

IDEAL CELLARS

If we gave you £100, £500 or £1000 to spend on wine, what would you buy? That's the question we asked our guest writers, and between them they've come up with a tempting mix of wines to drink right now and others that will emerge in their full glory in five or ten years' time. And if you're concerned about what sort of a world it will be in ten years' time, why not support the growing band of winemakers who really care about the future of the planet? Neil Palmer of Vintage Roots rose to our challenge to fill a cellar with a thrilling selection of organic wines from around the world. Meanwhile, I've gone on a money-no-object spending spree, packing my imaginary cellar with some of the fab wines I've tasted this year.

NEIL PALMER
VINTAGE ROOTS, ARBORFIELD, BERKSHIRE

Why choose organic wine? Well, like all organic produce, the grapes are grown without man-made fertilizers, fungicides or pesticides; traces of the 240 man-made compounds that have so far been found in non-organic wine could have worrying health implications. Other consumers choose organic products out of respect for the environment. All organic growers agree that naturally strong, healthy crops begin with healthy soil, and thrive within a naturally diverse ecosystem. As a practical illustration of the advantages of biodiversity, in California, growers for Fetzer's organic Bonterra wines are asked to plant plum trees around the edge of the vineyard to attract Anagrus wasps which eat the destructive vine leafhoppers.

And then there's biodynamism. Some people think of this as 'organic with frills' — the frills being the study of planetary and lunar cycles and the use of homeopathy to achieve balance in the vines. Tidal activity demonstrates the influence of the moon on Earth's great bodies of water, and when you consider that grapes (like us!) are over 90% water, perhaps it's not that far-fetched after all. Some of the world's top producers are wholeheartedly biodynamic — and the proof is in the quality of their wines.

All wines are available from Vintage Roots unless otherwise stated.

£100

Easy drinking with lots of organic fruitiness, and value for money in anyone's book!

2000 Vino da Tavola Bianco dell'Umbria, Di Filippo (white, Italy)
Intensely fresh with zingy mixed citrus fruits character and crisp acidity. **£25.50 for 6**

2000 Penedès Can Vendrell Blanco, Albet i Noya (white, Spain)
Chardonnay and Xarel-lo blend with fruit in the driving seat, backed up with tantalizing balancing acidity. **£25.20 for 6**

2000 Vin de Pays d'Oc Merlot Cuvée Gabriel, Domaine de Brau (red, southern France)
Easy, ripe, plummy Merlot with keen balancing tannins. An extremely well made wine from one of the top southern French organic estates.
£23.94 for 6

2000 Montalbano 'Organic Rosso', (red, Italy)
Sangiovese, Merlot and Montepulciano grapes combine superbly to deliver a broad, fruity style with a very appealing silky mouthfeel. **£25.50 for 6**

Total cost: £100.14

£500

These wines are all drinking well now and for the year ahead. The best way to invest in the future!

1999 Pinot Blanc, André Stentz (white, Alsace)
Superb musky richness in a slightly off-dry style. Wonderful, pleasing wine to enjoy with or without food.

£41.94 for 6

2000 Frascati Superiore, Casale Mattia (white, Italy)
Frascati is all too often light and characterless, but this Superiore version is definitely the real McCoy. Surprisingly weighty fruit with piercing zesty flavours and a creamy texture.

£65.40 for 12

2000 Sauvignon Blanc Kawarau, Central Otago (white, New Zealand)
Classic Kiwi Sauvignon from an up and coming area. Nettles, gooseberry and cats' pee in abundance! One to make you purr with delight.

£105.60 for 12

2000 Penedès Pinot Noir/Merlot D'Anyada, Albet i Noya (rosé, Spain)
Crimson cherry red in colour with gorgeous delicate ripe red fruit flavours. Drink chilled when hot!

£34.50 for 6

1999 Beaujolais, Domaine de Buis-Rond (red, Burgundy)
Beautiful Beaujolais: a superb expression of the Gamay grape, combining a light freshness with substance and texture, and lovely raspberry and cherry fruit.

£71.40 for 12

1999 Côtes du Luberon, Château la Canorgue (red, Rhône)
Concentrated red from southern France. Spicy, chewy, berried fruit; a great mix of Rhône and Provence styles. Drink or keep.

£83.40 for 12

1999 Penedès Cabernet Sauvignon Col.lecció, Albet i Noya (red, Spain)
One of Spain's best wines and organic too! Carefully crafted with sumptuous fruit, oaky structure and finely poised tannins. Spanish splendour indeed.

£90 for 8

Total cost: £492.24

£1000

Now for some outstanding, world-class wines made by some of the most forward-thinking producers around. Drink or keep.

1995 Champagne Brut, Fleury
Big, fruity, luscious Champagne – plenty of toasty richness and a long-lasting complex finish. 100% Pinot Noir, 100% biodynamic, 100% excellent!

£297 for 12

1999 Vouvray Sec – Le Mont, Huet (white, Loire)
This wine needs keeping; it will develop stunning richness and complexity in the years to come. Chenin Blanc at its best from the master, Huet. Biodynamic again.
£119.40 for 12

1998 Mâcon-Clessé Quintaine, Domaine Guillemot-Michel (white, Burgundy)
Sensational Chardonnay, rich and very complex on the palate. Great value Burgundy, could the quality be anything to do with the biodynamic methods used?
£65.70 for 6, T & W Wines

1998 St-Chinian Soulié des Joncs, Chateau de Soulié (red, southern France)
Hedgerow fruits, herbs and figs in a generously mouthfilling style. You can feel the terroir here.
£114 for 12

1998 Côtes de Provence Cuvée Columelle, Domaine Richeaume (red, southern France)
A spicy, potent wine with warm liquorice tones. Syrah, Cabernet Sauvignon and Merlot on top form together.
£65.94 for 6, Vinceremos

1999 Priorat FA206, Mas Igneus (red, Spain)
Organic wine from Spain is really progressing fast. This example from Priorat in Cataluña has piercing raspberry fruit and seductive tannins, coupled with the staggering 14% of alcohol this fashionable region is known for.
£114 for 12

1996 Barolo Bricco Viole, Viberti (red, Italy)
A wonderful traditional single-vineyard Barolo with earthy, gamy, truffle aromas giving way to an explosive palate of rich, well-ripened Nebbiolo fruit.
£117 for 6

1998 Saussignac Coup de Coeur, Château Richard (white, southern France)
Spellbinding dessert wine that has been likened to a hypothetical mix of two Sauternes superstars, Château Climens and Château d'Yquem.
£81 for 6/50cl bottles
Total cost: £974.04

Vintage Roots, freephone: 0800 980 4992
Vinceremos, tel: 0113 205 4545
T & W Wines, tel: 01842 765646

JEREMY PLATT
TERRY PLATT WINE MERCHANTS, LLANDUDNO

We pride ourselves on discovering well-made, highly individual wines from around the world; this often means we have wines that you will find nowhere else.

£100

A selection of wines that are ideal for barbecues and nick-pics!

2000 Chardonnay, Villa Rosa, Maule Valley (white, Chile)
This is a fresh and vibrant wine with hints of citrus fruit. Quite fat in style with notes of oak and vanilla.
£29.52 for 6

2000 Vin de Pays des Hautes de Badens Rosé, Domaine la Grave (rosé, southern France)
Produced by a good friend of ours at the family estate east of Carcassonne. This tastes of mixed fruit salad with cream! Dry with good acidity and a mouthfilling finish.
£27.84 for 6

2000 Cinsault-Pinotage, Rocheburg Selection, Western Cape (red, South Africa)
Excellent, easy-drinking red, with smoky, chocolaty, blackcurrant fruit. Ideal with

barbecued meats. Light in style yet full of flavour with good ripe tones.

£27.42 for 6

NV Champagne Brut Blanc de Blancs Grand Cru, Bonnaire

Ideal for a picnic for two, close to a stream! Produced by an excellent small grower based in Cramant, this is a yeasty, creamy fizz with good fruit and balanced acidity.

£15.22 for 1

Total cost: £100

£500

I reckon in this parcel of wines I have chosen enough for six good dinner parties!

2000 Sauvignon Blanc, Stonybrook, Franschhoek (white, South Africa)

Grassy gooseberry style with steely acidity and a lingering finish. £74.04 for 12

1998 Chardonnay, Broke's Promise, Hunter Valley (white, Australia)

Tropical fruit style with a hint of oak and a clean finish. The Broke's Promise vineyard is in the Broke region of the Hunter Valley.

£92.88 for 12

1999 Chablis Premier Cru Fourchaume, Pascal Bouchard (white, Burgundy)

Complex nose with good length and acidity. A striking wine, powerful and elegant.

£90.60 for 6

1997 Château Peuy Saincrit 'Montalon' (red, Bordeaux)

A well-balanced wine with plenty of smooth fruit flavours and good tannins. This particular château just gets better and better! £90.12 for 12

1999 Pinotage, Dellrust, Helderberg (red, South Africa)

Deep red in colour with a fruity character and delicate almond flavour. From Dellrust, a family-owned winery in the foothills of the Helderberg mountains near Stellenbosch.

£95.76 for 12

1994 Champagne Louis Roederer Cristal

An indulgence for a special night. I promise to pay the difference.

£91.06 for 1

Total cost: £534.46

£1000

As for the £500 selection, I have chosen these wines for a number of dinner parties. But how many and who do I invite?

1995 Champagne Brut Blanc de Blancs, Cramant Grand Cru, Bonnaire

Classic Blanc de Blancs champagne. An elegant wine with great depth of flavour.

£204.48 for 12

2001 Sauvignon Blanc, Whitehaven Winery, Marlborough (white, New Zealand)

A pungent and aromatic wine with tropical fruit on the nose. £88.68 for 12

1997 Chablis Grand Cru Les Clos, Pascal Bouchard (white, Burgundy)

A complex wine with rich mineral flavours. Nectar. £190.38 for 6

1997 Château Yon Figeac, St-Émilion Grand Cru Classé (red, Bordeaux)

This property is one of the great classed growths of St-Émilion. A distinguished wine with a brilliant colour and balanced tannins.

£281.28 for 12

1999 Stonybrook Reserve, Franschhoek (red, South Africa)

This exciting Cape blend, using Pinotage with Cabernet and Merlot, has rich aromas of blackberries and truffles with a hint of spice. This is heaven with cheese.

£108.48 for 12

1996 Bonnezeaux, Château de Fesles (white, Loire) –

A fantastic pudding wine with marmalade tones and a long finish.

£144.54 for 6/50cl bottles

Total cost: £1017.84

JONATHAN BUTT

FIRST QUENCH (BOTTOMS UP, THRESHER WINE SHOP, VICTORIA WINE, WINE RACK)

£100

These wines are easy to enjoy and inexpensive, to make wine an everyday occasion.

2000 Sauvignon Blanc Tohu, Marlborough (white, New Zealand)
This is what NZ Savvy is all about: pungent nettle and redcurrant, with the obligatory gooseberry. In your face and invigorating.
£47.94 for 6, Wine Rack, Bottoms Up

2000 Pinot Gris, Corazon, Mendoza (white, Argentina)
Deliciously crisp and fresh, with peach and nectarine scents and flavours.
£23.94 for 6, Wine Rack, Bottoms Up, Thresher Wine Shop

1999 Castelão Tinto, Pedras do Monte, Terras do Sado (red, Portugal)
A wonderful example of one of Portugal's finest indigenous grapes. Full and rich, with succulent berry fruit.
£29.94 for 6, Wine Rack, Bottoms Up, Thresher Wine Shop
Total cost: £101.82

£500

*This cellar should contain some **wow** wines with which to impress your friends, and also some easily approachable wines that are enjoyable to drink on their own while relaxing in front of the TV or in the garden.*

1995/6 Sparkling Shiraz, Seppelt (red, Australia)
Bright, red fizz with spicy plum and lots of character. Drink before, during and after your night out.
£56.94 for 6, Wine Rack, Bottoms Up, Thresher Wine Shop

1999 Tokay-Pinot Gris, Cave de Turckheim (white, Alsace)
Alsace is often overlooked, which is a pity as the standard of winemaking is exceptional. This is a honeyed pear and grapefruit beauty.
£35.94 for 6, Wine Rack, Bottoms Up, Thresher Wine Shop

2000 Sauvignon Blanc, Palliser Estate, Martinborough (white, New Zealand)
Consistently one of the best NZ Sauvignons on the market. Intense gooseberry and green capsicum, and some added weight on the finish of tropical fruit.
£59.95 for 5, Wine Rack, Bottoms Up

1997 Marsannay, Louis Jadot (white, Burgundy)
Serious stuff at affordable money. Butterscotch and smoke with a tangy lime and nutty edge. This will develop with time.
£77.94 for 6, Wine Rack, Bottoms Up

2000 Syrah Rosé Valley Oaks, Fetzer (rosé, California)
At last someone is taking rosé seriously. This has lots of weight and bags of raspberry and cranberry fruit.
£35.94 for 6, Wine Rack, Bottoms Up, Thresher Wine Shop

1998 Merlot, Delheim (red, South Africa)
A big, fleshy, earthy Merlot with bags of fruit, complexity and length.
£44.94 for 6, Wine Rack, Bottoms Up

1997 Côtes de Francs, Château de Francs (red, Bordeaux)
Nicely weighted, with expressive plum and blackberry fruit character. For drinking now.
£50.94 for 6, Wine Rack, Bottoms Up

1998 Grenache Bush Vine, Yalumba (red, Australia)
A big Aussie red; ripe, fleshy and packed full of juicy plum and berry fruit.
£47.94 for 6, Wine Rack, Bottoms Up

1997 Meursault Clos de Mazeray, Domaine Jacques Prieur (red, Burgundy)
Great weight and depth are the trademarks of this estate; this Pinot is rich and complex with amazing concentration of fruit.
£89.97 for 3, Wimbledon Wine Cellar Total cost: £500.50

£1000

Now for the serious stuff. This 'cellar' should contain wines that you are passionate about, and that you can share with friends around the dinner table.

2000 Sauvignon Blanc, Isabel Estate, Marlborough, (white, New Zealand)
I have fond memories of crushing the 97 vintage of this wine, but my choice is not based on unfounded loyalty. Superripe and rich with passionfruit, gooseberry and apricot – and I guarantee the 2001 will be just as good.   £71.94 for 6, La Reserve

1998 Viognier, Bonterra, California (white, USA)
Organically produced, with elegant apricot and peach fruit and a lime-edged finish.
£31.47 for 3, Wine Rack, Bottoms Up

1998 Pinot Gris Herrenweg, Zind-Humbrecht (white, Alsace)
This is immense, petrolly and vegetal on the nose with honeyed notes. The palate is loaded with mature lychee and ginger fruit and a grapefruit marmalade finish.
£83.94 for 6, Wine Rack, Bottoms Up

2000 Chardonnay, Te Mata, Hawkes Bay (white, New Zealand)
Magnificent Chardonnay to rival anything else, from anywhere else. Burgundian style with Kiwi attitude.
£107.88 for 12, Wine Rack, Bottoms Up

1999 Chardonnay, Kumeu River (white, New Zealand)
Another terrific New Zealand Chardonnay, with power and elegance.
£95.70 for 6, La Reserve

1999 Pinot Noir, Isabel Estate, Marlborough (red, New Zealand)
Fabulous Pinot with earthy blackberry and cherry notes, gamy and complex, with a beetrooty finish.
£95.94 for 6, Wimbledon Wine Cellar

1998 Pinot Noir, Fromm Vineyard, Marlborough (red, New Zealand)
This is a wild-flavoured, gamy, beetrooty masterpiece. A real gem for Pinot lovers.
£65.85 for 3, Lay & Wheeler

1997 Beaune Champs Pimont, Domaine Jacques Prieur (white, Burgundy)
Young and tight right now, but this will develop into an elegant beauty.
£179.94 for 6, Wimbledon Wine Cellar

1997 Ribera del Duero, Pesquera Tinto, (red, Spain)
A big opulent monster, always packed full of black fruit and character. Well worth cellaring but decent enough now.
£83.94 for 6, Wimbledon Wine Cellar

1997 Chianti Classico Riserva, Rocca Guicciarda, Barone Ricasoli (red, Italy)
A great vintage from a great Chianti producer. Classy morello cherry, warmth and bitter chocolate, very concentrated.
£59.94 for 6, Wine Rack, Bottoms Up

1998 Châteauneuf-du-Pape, Domaine Font de Michelle (red, Rhône)
Big, brooding and intense, packed with berry fruit and a big, sweet, hot finish. A powerhouse of a wine.
£63.96 for 4, Wine Rack, Bottoms Up

1990 Sauternes Château Filhot (white, Bordeaux)
Magnificent dessert wine with luscious honeysuckle and tangerine fruit and a super fresh lime zest finish.
£74.97 for 3, Wine Rack, Bottoms Up Total cost: £1015.47

Wimbledon Wine Cellar, 020 8540 9979

ZUBAIR MOHAMED
RAEBURN FINE WINES, EDINBURGH

£100

At this price level, I've chosen three wines that give value and pleasure – with personality.

Fino Sherry The Bottlers, Bodegas la Carrena (Spain)
For me, a crisp, freshly bottled fino, which has not had its alcohol boosted, is some of the best value in the world of wine.
£29.70 for 6

1996 Vin de Pays Comté Tolosan, Domaine de Callory (red, southern France)
An old favourite from near Toulouse. Complex, spicy, with a hint of liquorice and excellent balance.
£29.94 for 6

1999 Côtes du Rhône, Vieilles Vignes, Vinergie (white, Rhône)
A full-flavoured, peachy, mineral white Rhône from 65-year-old Clairette vines. Complex and moreish!
£41.94 for 6

Total cost: £101.58

£500

A step up – these wines will be delicious now, but will also keep well.

1998 Riesling, Vom Stein Federspiel, Nikolaihof, Wachau (white, Austria)
No point in having less than 12 bottles of this immensely drinkable wine. The Saahs family make stylish and intensely mineral dry Rieslings on their biodynamically run estate. Will improve with cellaring.
£162 for 12

1998 Malbec/Cabernet Sauvignon, Galah, Adelaide Hills (red, Australia)
From the legendary Wendouree estate in the Clare Valley, Stephen George, who is Wendouree's consultant, has an option on some of the wines, which he bottles under his Galah label. Stunning, complex and rich, yet with ripe, silky tannins and an opulent, baroque palate.
£144 for 12

NV Champagne Brut Cuvée Reserve, Henri Billiot (France)
My favourite Champagne. Mainly Pinot Noir, with a little Chardonnay, this is from 100% Grand Cru vineyards totally owned by the Billiot family. If only all Champagne could be so delicious!
£228 for 12

Total cost: £534

£1000

If you're looking to the future, these wines will bring pleasure in the years to come.

1998 Chablis 1er Cru Butteaux, François Raveneau (white, Burgundy)
This is Chablis at its best: flinty, mineral, complex and very elegant, with real concentration. Can be drunk now or kept for ten years or more.
£300 for 12

1999 Côtes du Rhône-Villages Rasteau, Domaine Gourt de Mautens (red, Rhône)
Fabulously concentrated red wine from absurdly low yields. Complex and classy; should be cellared until 2004, and will keep for much longer.
£222 for 12

1993 Pernand-Vergelesses 1er Cru Ile des Vergelesses, Domaine Rollin, (red, Burgundy)
From a great winemaker, this subtle and beautifully made wine is developing great complexity and finesse. Ideally, drink in 2005, though it will improve further after that.
£228 for 12

1996 Barolo Brunate, Poderi Marcarini (red, Italy)
From one of Piedmont's greatest recent vintages, this traditionally made Barolo will mature into a wine of great refinement and character. Start drinking this in 2006 or 2007 – but it will keep for at least 20 years!
£300 for 12

Total cost: £1050

OZ CLARKE

My editor has come up with the idea that I might like to put together my ideal cellar for a year's drinking. Good idea. It's a very particular delight fantasizing about spending an unlimited about of money – especially my publisher's money – on hundreds of cases of good grog. 'We thought perhaps 250 bottles.' Bottles? 250? Cases, yes, but...bottles? A whole year's drinking and only 250 bottles? Am I supposed to share these? Will I have to timidly advise my friends that they'll have to bring their own when they come round to watch the football? 'Well, see what you can do.' She stares disapprovingly and marches out of the room. 250 bottles a year, for a chap of my thirst and breadth of acquaintance. It's humiliating. Oh well, here goes....250 bottles! Whatever next?

[Ed: is anyone interested in hearing my side of the story? What I actually said was, 'Oz, you can't be trusted to stick to a budget, even an imaginary one, so just indulge your fantasies – but please try and keep it to two or three pages; how about 250 bottles?' Can I help it if he doesn't pay attention?]

Stockists for many of these wines can be found in the **Price Guides**.

Plonk

Not really plonk – but stuff that won't make much of a dent in the wallet – even if it is the publisher's money. Frankly, there's masses of good wine in the UK at the moment in the £3 to £4 class. I know that's with all the tax and profit margins and the rest, but I reckon penny for penny you can drink as well in the supermarkets of the UK as in those of France, Italy and Spain, because our wine buyers make so much more effort to locate decent stuff, and won't buy on reputation alone.

Hungary currently offers the best bargains in dry whites, either scented like **Irsai Oliver** and **Cserszegi Füszeres** (which Safeway sells as **Woodcutter's White**), or really snappy **Sauvignon Blanc** and soft **Chardonnay**. At £2.99 to £3.99 a bottle, they're a steal. I'll have a case or two of those.

I'll also have a case of **Soave**. What? Yes, Soave! Not any old Soave, but **Safeway** and **Sainsbury's** own labels are simple, clean, fresh gluggers for around £2.99. And if you find them too mild and bland, throw in a glass of Irsai Oliver and shake it up – that'll be the end of bland, for sure.

I also need red – and there are some stunning deep ripe Aussie reds at bargain basement prices: **Karalta** red is only £2.99 at **Asda**. Banrock Station Shiraz/Mataro costs a bit more (£3.99 at Morrisons and Unwins), but what a mouthful!

And for the brave, **Morocco** has leapt back into our drinking world. **Sainsbury's Moroccan Cabernet Sauvignon** and **Syrah** (£3.99) taste great and will shock the molars out of any wine snobs among your friends.

As for fizz, I'll have a case of whichever Spanish **Cava** is on offer. There's always something for £3.49 to £3.99, and as long as the fridge is working, that'll do me just fine.

Friends' grog

So, what shall I have for more important drinking – like when I actually recognize the people who turn up on my doorstep looking for a drink? For around £5 or £6, we can drink some of the most original flavours in the world of wine – and always afford a second bottle.

Argentina hasn't really kept up the progress of last year, but a few wineries have improved. The **Valle de Vistalba** wines from **Nieto Senetiner** are deep, rich and exciting. **Barbera** and **Bonarda** are my favourite reds; two old Italian workhorses made in a brilliantly different way in the lee of the Andes.

On the other side of the Andes, in **Chile**, the great lost red grape of Bordeaux, **Carmenère**, has made a reappearance full of throaty savoury scent and rich plum fruit. **Gracia Carmenère Reserva Especial** (£5.99, Co-op) and **Terra Noble Gran Reserva** (no retail outlet as yet) show the variety in all its glory.

And back to Europe. First stop as the crow flies is **Portugal**, a country which has revolutionized its winemaking in the past couple of years. The 1999 vintage was a revelation. Try the **Senda do Vale** (£5.99, Sainsbury's) and the equally exotic **Vale de Rosas** (£4.29, Asda) to catch a full frontal of the new Portugal.

The new **Greece** is equally remarkable, and **Oddbins** has been showing us the way. The Gaia Estate makes marvellous, serious yet scented reds: the Peloponnese **Nótios** (£5.99) and **Nemea** (£6.49) will do me. The islands are coming up with some fascinating whites. I can't decide between **Athini Villave** from Rhodes and **Boutari**'s sweet **Vi'Santo** from Santorini (£7.49 for 50cl); maybe I'll have both.

I could pick literally dozens of superb reds from the **Languedoc** in the south of France. Dark, ripe, perfumed with herbs and lightly cloaked with tannin; I'll just choose two scented bruisers for now: **Domaine de Blayac 1998 Minervois** (£5.99) and **Domaine de l'Auris 1998 Côtes du Roussillon** (£6.99). Oh, and perhaps a case of **Château de Villemourette 1998 Corbières** (£7.99). All from Safeway.

High days and holidays

Actually, with my kind of lifestyle there are no specific holidays or high days as such. Every dawn brings the potential of both, depending largely on whether or not I had a high day or holiday the day before, and am therefore too strung out to have another one. In which case I have to go to work.

But I'll have to have some fizz to set me straight. Champagne? In flavour, yes. In character and style, effervescence, beauty and effect, yes. But it'll come from **New Zealand**, where the talented winemakers of **Cloudy Bay** are producing stunning fizz called **Pelorus** (around £12 for non-vintage, £15 for vintage, various stockists, see page 411). And just for the pure, hedgerow-scented beauty of it, I'll have some **English** fizz: **Warden Brut** from Bedfordshire (£13.49, Hedley Wright).

Now I want some aromatic white wines, and **New Zealand** makes superb **Gewürztraminer**. Cloudy Bay, Stonecroft and Matawhero are all star Gewürz producers, but I'll go for a case of **Lawson's Dry Hills 2000** (£8.20, Lay & Wheeler) –

beautiful fragrant stuff – and just for the hell of it, I'll also have some of my most surprising aromatic discovery this year: **Enate**'s **Gewürztraminer 2000** (£8, Averys of Bristol) from the **Somontano** region in the Pyrenean foothills of northern **Spain**.

But back to **New Zealand**. The 1998 vintage produced stunning results for warm-climate grapes and I'm going to have me some. **Ata Rangi**'s rare but brilliant Syrah, **Unison**'s inspired Selection, **Stonecroft**'s Zinfandel and **Vidal**'s Cabernet Sauvignon/Merlot Reserve – all are great wines from great winemakers. New Zealand is not going to achieve these results with warm-climate grapes every year, but cool-climate grapes should triumph most years, so I'm going to choose some sublime Pinot Noir: **Quartz Reef Pinot Noir 1999** (£15.99, First Quench) and **Felton Road Block 5 Pinot Noir 2000** (p.o.a. Berry Bros. & Rudd), as well as some ace Riesling: **Felton Road Dry Riesling 2000** and **Gibbston Valley Riesling 2000**. I tasted all these in NZ and some are not yet available in the UK, but keep your eyes open for them.

But back to warmer climes. **Chile**'s got a lot of lovely juicy reds, though the prices are beginning to get a bit serious. Even so, I can't resist two fabulously dense, rich reds: **Cono Sur 20 Barrel Merlot 1999** (£11.99, Sainsbury's) and **Santa Rita Triple C 1997** (£12.50, Philglas & Swiggot).

And **South Africa**'s finally flexing her red wine muscles too, producing wines with the intensity and ripeness her climate has always promised but rarely delivered. I'll take some **Du Plessis Shiraz 1999** (not yet in UK) along with some **Neil Ellis Stellenbosch Shiraz 1999** (£9.99, Villeneuve Wines) and some **Verdun Cabernet Sauvignon 1997** (£11.99, Connolly's, Domaine Direct, Noel Young).

Over to **California**, where my old friend **Marimar Torres** is on form at the moment in her cool Sonoma vineyards. I'll have some of her classy, elegant Chardonnay 1998 and Pinot Noir 1998. **Viader**'s vineyards on Howell Mountain are warmer, and it shows in a superb 1998 Cabernet blend (£40,

Handford of Holland Park, tel: 020-7221
~~614~~). **Firesteed**, on the other hand, is
decidedly cool up in **Oregon**, which is probably
why their **1999 Pinot Gris** (£9.95, Mayfair
Cellars, Christopher Piper, Noel Young and
others) is such a delight.

Just a hop and skip in **Australia**, where I'll
pick up the ridiculously tasty but virtually
unheard of **Pencil Pine Chambourcin 1999**
(£5.97, Asda) from the Hunter Valley and the
unfashionable but unbeatably beautiful stickies
of South Australia: **Yalumba's Old Sweet
Wine** and **Antique Tawny** (about £8 a
bottle, but they're very rare here).

Now for Europe. **Portugal** first for a star
wine from the **Douro: Quinta do Fojo 1996**
(£32.70, Bibendum). It's a magnificent,
powerful, heady wine – you can see why they
choose such stuff as the base wine for port.

On to **France** and the **Rhône**, the French
area that is performing best at the moment
and which actually seems to take notice of
what we – the consumers – want. I've tasted
loads of good grog, in the south and the north,
but when I'm in the mood for great brooding
draughts of super-ripe Grenache I'll get them
from the south: **Domaine des Girasol
Vieilles Vignes 1998 Rasteau**; **Domaine
Gramenon Ceps Centenaires 1999
Montbrison** and **Domaine des Espiers 2000
Sablet** (£5.99, Noel Young). And for something
older but just as exciting I'll take **Domaine de
Mourchon 1996 Seguret.**

And to round off, **Italy**. But not just any old
Italy. I'm starting in the far north with a
brilliant, deep, exciting red: **Endrizzi Masetto
Nero 1998** (£9.95, Adnams). I'll follow that
with some **Amarone della Valpolicella**, dark
and bitter yet wonderfully scented and rich all
at once: **Brigaldara Classico 1997** and
Tedeschi 1996 are good (more on pages
386–7). And after that, with the great 1997
Chiantis coming on to the shelves, I can't resist
a couple from a vast array (pages 389–393):
I'll choose **Villa Cafaggio Riserva** and
Fattoria di Basciano Riserva.

So how many bottles is that? How do I
know? I stopped counting long ago.

BUYING WINE ON THE WEB

The early months of the New Millennium were boiling over with news of how wine e-tailing was going to change the wine trade for ever. Was it? Have you bought wine over the Net yet? If not, when are you proposing to start? Because the wine e-tailers that still survive are desperate to know. I remember, last year, surveying the rash of high-profile dot.com failures and thinking that most of them hadn't been providing anything that anybody needed, although some of them offered quite nice ideas. Well, 'quite nice' isn't good enough when you're trying to establish a stand-alone dot.com, regardless of what product you offer.

I'd always been told by marketing men that there was a single path to success in marketing. You had to make your product known, then wanted, and ultimately, triumphantly, you had to make your product needed. Firstly, most of the dot.coms weren't known at all when they arrived on the scene. It costs millions – don't ask me what all the money is spent on, but that's what it costs – to launch a successful major dot.com. That's just to get yourself known and attract customers.

So when you've found some customers, will they want either your wine or the way you plan to deliver it and charge for it? They might, to have a change. But the samples of wine I've seen from many of the dot.coms during the past 12 months have generally been poor and sometimes ranging on the cynical and disgraceful. Is that the way to get a repeat order? When the high streets are full of wine shops, when there is a glittering array of interesting independent merchants spread across the land – and when the supermarkets where you do your regular shopping are all busting a gut to get you to add a few bottles to your basket as you wander round the aisles. I haven't even mentioned the third stage: when the consumer 'needs' your product. Some people may decide they like the idea of dot.com wine. Few people in Britain actually need a dot.com to provide their wine.

It is interesting that the ones that are surviving, and possibly prospering in some small way, are those that have a powerful identity with which to trawl for customers – Virgin Wines, for instance – or that are bolted on to existing businesses like Laithwaites, the new name for Bordeaux Direct, or the operations of people like Waitrose for whom the Net provides a cost-efficient way of handling part of their business; many retailers are now geared up to take orders via the internet.

Destination Wine, a co-operation between Sainsbury's and Oddbins, offers cases of wine from the Taste Network website (www.taste.co.uk), an online 'magazine' channel, and should do well. Another online food and drink site (www.winetelegraph.co.uk) allows you to order from the huge range offered by everywine.co.uk. And there are plenty more where they came from: my own website (www.ozclarke.com) has links to other wine- and food-related sites.

If it's not chat you're after, but a bit of serious wine investment, don't part with your money until you've visited www.investdrinks.org. Jim Budd, the site's creator, has spent several years researching dodgy drinks deals, and the site is full of advice for potential wine investors.

Generally speaking, however, buying wine over the Net is not that different from the traditional mail-order scenario. Consider the following. Is this company offering the sort of wines you want? Will it deliver the wines swiftly and at your convenience? Are the prices (including delivery) competitive? What will happen if you are dissatisfied with the wine? And, ultimately, do you trust these people? Merchants with an established trading base are unlikely to let you down, and any serious online retailer will have invested in effective credit card security systems.

The internet can give us access to a greater range of wines than ever. Conventional wine retailing is not about to join the dinosaurs, but you know what? Buying online can be fun – and that's what wine is all about.

SAFE NET SHOPPING

- Find out who you are dealing with: well-known companies are more likely to have secure sites. UK-based companies are covered by UK laws.
- Look for the 'small print' telling you about the company, its guarantees, delivery systems and refund or returns policy. Beware of PO Box addresses, but look for a telephone number.
- Check that the company uses SSL (secure sockets layer) technology, which makes your details unavailable to other web users.
- Before you enter your credit card details a box should appear to tell you you are entering a secure connection, which scrambles the details in transit.
- Save all the information relating to your purchase, so you have proof if anything goes wrong.
- Check your credit card statement for unauthorized purchases.
- Look for a firm that abides by a code of practice; participating retailers will display the relevant logo. These include: Which? Web Trader Scheme (www.which.net/webtrader/index.html); Interactive Media in Retail Group (www.imrg.org); Consumer Assistance Bureau (www.isitsafe.com).

RETAILERS DIRECTORY

All these retailers have been chosen on the basis of the quality and interest of their lists. We feature wines from almost all of them in our Price Guides. The abbreviations used for these retailers in the Price Guides are shown in brackets after their names.

If you want to find local suppliers, merchants are listed by region in the Who's Where directory on page 79; if you're looking for a specialist in a particular country's wines, you'll find a list at the start of that country's Price Guides.

> The following services are available where indicated: **C** = cellarage, **G** = glass hire/loan, **M** = mail order, **T** = tastings and talks. There is a key to name abbreviations on page 7.

ADNAMS (AD)

Head office & mail order Sole Bay Brewery, Southwold, Suffolk IP18 6JW, (01502) 727220, fax (01502) 727223; mail order (01502) 727222
• The Cellar & Kitchen Store, Victoria Street, Southwold, Suffolk IP18 6JW • The Wine Shop, Pinkney's Lane, Southwold, Suffolk IP18 6EW
• The Grapevine, 109 Unthank Road, Norwich NR2 2PE, (01603) 613998
E-MAIL wines@adnams.co.uk
HOURS Mail order: Mon–Fri 9–6.30, Sat 9–12; Cellar & Kitchen Store and Wine Shop: Mon–Sat 10–6.30; The Grapevine: Mon–Sat 10–8 **CARDS** MasterCard, Switch, Visa **DISCOUNTS** 5% for 5 cases or more **DELIVERY** Free for complete cases, £5 part cases **MINIMUM ORDER** (mail order) 1 mixed case **EN PRIMEUR** Burgundy, California, Italy, Rhône. **C G M T**
A list that is gradually being reduced in breadth, though Adnams would no doubt say that it is losing nothing in depth. It is certainly very good. Alsace features such names as Domaines Blanck and Schoffit; the Rhône is interesting and Burgundy well-chosen. There are some super wines from Germany and some pretty irresistible stuff from Italy. The New World features producers other than the usual names.

1998 Châteauneuf-du-Pape, Vieux Mas des Papes, £11.95 This is the second wine of Domaine du Vieux Télégraphe, in an excellent year. Rich, broad and generous.
1998 Bourgogne Côte Chalonnaise, La Digoine, £11.95 The appellation may not sound thrilling, but this wine is from Aubert de Villaine, who co-owns the Domaine de la Romanée-Conti and is one of the most thoughtful, careful winemakers in Burgundy. This is all cherries and smoke, and remarkable value.
1998 Enkircher Batterieberg Riesling Spätlese Trocken, Immich-Batterieberg, £10.95 If you're going to drink Mosel trocken you should really choose a Spätlese. This has great concentration and depth.

AMEY'S WINES (AME)

83 Melford Road, Sudbury, Suffolk CO10 1JT, (01787) 377144
HOURS Tue–Sat 9–5.30 **CARDS** Amex, MasterCard, Switch, Visa **DISCOUNTS** 10% for a mixed dozen, 15% for 5 or more mixed cases **DELIVERY** Free within 20 miles of Sudbury for orders over £60. **G T**
France and the New World rule here, and the New World consists mostly of Australia and New Zealand, with lesser quantities from South Africa. There are a handful of wines from each of Germany, Austria (one wine here, and that a half bottle), Spain, Portugal and Italy. Australia, however, goes all out with an extremely well-chosen list of surprises. Australian Durif? Zinfandel from Margaret River? They're all here.
1997 Tannat, RPF Family Reserve, Pisano, £8.99 Well structured Uruguayan Tannat with intense but quite elegant fruit. Very much Old World in style.
1998 Fitou, Domaine de Roudène, £5.79 Wine that reminds you how good Fitou can be, with terrific concentration and minerally fruit.

JOHN ARMIT WINES (ARM)

5 Royalty Studios, 105 Lancaster Road, London W11 1QF, 020-7908 0600, fax 020-7908 0601

E-MAIL info@armit.co.uk
WEB SITE www.armit.co.uk
HOURS Mon–Fri 9–6 **CARDS** Amex, MasterCard,
Switch, Visa **DELIVERY** Free anywhere in UK
mainland **MINIMUM ORDER** 1 case **EN PRIMEUR**
Bordeaux, Burgundy, Italy. **C M T**
John Armit Wines has the reputation of selling
expensive wines to expensive people – and with
wines like Bodegas Roda in Rioja, Angelo Gaja in
Piedmont and Dominus from the Napa Valley, this
is exactly what the company does quite a lot of
the time. But expense is not its raison d'être. The
point of this company is that it seeks out the best,
most interesting wines – and sometimes those are
expensive and sometimes they're not. The new
own-label range, with labels based on colour-field
painting, features a wine called simply Italian Red,
which is Sangiovese from Castello di Argiano in
Chianti, and is £7.50 a bottle, and there is some
very good southern French stuff at around the
same level.
**1998 Chablis Domaine de la Genillotte,
Domaine Sourice-Depuydt, £9.33** Classically
minerally and steely, with hints of honey and
lemon.
**1997 Minervois Clos l'Angély, Domaine
Piccinini, £8.17** A complex palate of licorice, tar
and violets, chocolate and earth, with plenty of
concentration.
1999 Teroldego Rotaliano, Foradori, £10
Wonderfully tight, elegant stuff from a top
Trentino name.
1996 Rioja Reserva, Roda II, £17.50 This really
is good, from one of the best new-wave names
in Rioja. It's intense, tarry and leathery.

ASDA (ASD)

Head office Asda House, Southbank,
Great Wilson Street, Leeds LS11 5AD,
0113-241 9172, fax 0113-241 7766.
243 stores
WEB SITE www.asda.co.uk
HOURS Selected stores open 24 hours a
day – see local store for details **CARDS**
MasterCard, Switch, Visa **DISCOUNTS** £1
off any 4 bottles **DELIVERY** South London
only. **G T**
No thrills here, but then not a lot over a fiver
either. Asda is good at good-value basics –

though once you get away from the own-label
wines you have a better chance of finding something with some character. Choose carefully and
you'll find some sound everyday bottles; and funnily
enough there's a rather good (though quite short)
list of clarets.
1998 Le 'D' de Dassault, St-Emilion, £12.99
The second wine of the excellent Château
Dassault, in what was a terrific vintage in
St-Emilion.

ASHLEY SCOTT (AS)

PO Box 28, The Highway, Hawarden, Flintshire
CH5 3RY, tel & fax (01244) 520655
HOURS 24-hr answerphone **DISCOUNTS** 5%
unmixed case **DELIVERY** Free in North Wales,
Cheshire, Merseyside; elsewhere at cost
MINIMUM ORDER 1 mixed case **G M T**
A short list of attractive wines from around the
world. The emphasis is on straightforward, fruity,
soft flavours.
**1995 Crozes-Hermitage Rouge, Bernard
Chave, £8.95** Good smoky stuff, rich and ripe.

AUSTRALIAN WINE CLUB (AUS)

Kershaw House, Great Western Road,
Hounslow, Middx TW5 0BU, freephone order-
line (0800) 856 2004, freefax (0800) 856 2114,
enquiries tel 020-8538 0718
E-MAIL ukorders@austwine.co.uk
WEB SITE www.austwine.co.uk
HOURS Mon–Fri 8–7, Sat–Sun 9–4 **CARDS**
Amex, MasterCard, Visa **DELIVERY** £4.99 anywhere in UK mainland **MINIMUM ORDER**
1 mixed case **EN PRIMEUR** Australia. **M T**
Oddly enough, all the wines here are Australian.
Not every Australian wine is here, mind, but
there's enough variety to go round. The list reflects
fashions down under: it kicks off with Shiraz,
moves on to Rhône-style blends, and only then
gets round to Cabernet. There are not many Pinot
Noirs, but buckets of Chardonnay for those who
never, but never, get tired of tropical fruit salad
packed in oak.
**1999 Il Briccone (The Rogue), Primo Estate,
£10** A complex and rich but not overpowering
blend of Shiraz, Sangiovese, Barbera, Nebbiolo
and Cabernet, from the Adelaide Plains. Weird
and brilliant.

AVERYS OF BRISTOL

Orchard House, Southfield Road, Nailsea, Bristol
BS48 1JN, orderline (18457) 283797, enquiries
tel (01275) 811100, fax (01275) 811101
E-MAIL averywines@aol.com
HOURS Shop: 8 Park Street, Bristol: Mon–Sat
10–6; Wine Cellar: Culver Street, Bristol:
Mon–Sat 10–7 **CARDS** Amex, MasterCard,
Switch, Visa **DISCOUNTS** Monthly mail order
offers, Bin Club 10% off most list prices
DELIVERY Free 2 or more cases, otherwise
£5.50 per consignment (£2 in Bristol area) **EN
PRIMEUR** Bordeaux, Burgundy, Port. **C G M T**
*There's a decent list of lesser clarets here, and in
fact Bordeaux looks a lot better than Burgundy,
which relies on some slightly tired négociant names.
There are some good Rhônes, jazzed up this year
by the addition of three Condrieus from Georges
Vernay, and Germany has some decent stuff even
if, again, the producers are not the most exciting in
their areas. There is Tedeschi from Italy, which is a
step up, and there are some other good producers
from here as well. There are plenty of new additions
across the list, so perhaps it will gradually be
revamped. But on the other hand, if it ain't actually
broke, why fix it?*
**1999 Ripa della Mandorle, Castello
Vicchiomaggio, £10.20** This is Sangiovese plus
Cabernet, matured in French oak – a classic
Super-Tuscan recipe, in fact. It's forward and rich.

BACCHUS FINE WINES (BAC)

Warrington House Farm Barn, Warrington,
Olney, Bucks MK46 4HN, (01234) 711140,
fax (01234) 711199
E-MAIL wine@bacchus.co.uk
WEB SITE www.bacchus.co.uk
HOURS Mon–Fri 11–7, Sat 10–1.30 **CARDS**
Access, Amex, Diners, MasterCard, Switch, Visa
DISCOUNTS Loyalty account: 5% of purchase
price as credit for subsequent purchases
DELIVERY Free within 19 miles of Olney, £6 +
VAT per case elsewhere **MINIMUM ORDER**
1 mixed case. **G M T**
*There are lots of wines here that are miles away
from the standard ranges. There's Barbera from
Mexico and Santa Magdalena from the Alto Adige;*
*lots and lots from Austria, including wines from the
splendidly named Skoff; and some good Germans
as well. A well considered list that shows an interest
in subtle flavours.*
**1998 Zierfandler, Ried Badnerweg, Schellmann,
Gumpoldskirchen, £7.90** Zierfandler is the
grape, Ried Badnerweg the vineyard, Schellmann
the grower and Gumpoldskirchen the region of
Austria where spicy, rich, dry white Zierfandler is
a speciality.
1998 Langhe Nebbiolo, G D Vajra, £10.98
Barolo is so pricy now that even trading down
isn't cheap. But this is from an excellent
producer, and has plenty of class.
**1999 Fleurie Vieilles Vignes, Domaine de la
Grand Cour, £9.90** It's time to rediscover
Beaujolais: there are plenty of times when one
wants a red, but not a massive, overpowering
red. This has lovely depth and perfume.

BALLANTYNES OF COWBRIDGE (BAL)

3 Westgate, Cowbridge, Vale of Glamorgan CF71
7AQ, (01446) 774840, fax (01446) 775253
E-MAIL richard@ballantynes.co.uk
WEB SITE www.ballantynes.co.uk
HOURS Mon–Sat 9–5.30 **CARDS** MasterCard,
Switch, Visa **DISCOUNTS** 8% on mixed/unmixed
cases in shop **DELIVERY** £4.95 per case
EN PRIMEUR Bordeaux, Burgundy, Italy, Rhône.
C G M T
*Ballantynes is swimming firmly against the tide of
over-extracted, over-concentrated claret and looks
for elegance and finesse. Hooray. There are some
terrific Italian wines, too: I've picked all my
recommendations from among them, because
although Italy is brimming with original wines, you
wouldn't always think so to look at some lists. It's
worth looking at the Austrians here, as well: there
are a couple of traditional Gumpoldskirchners – the
full-bodied dry white wines made from Rotgipfler
and Zierfandler – and Gumpoldskirchner is a wine
you seldom see in Britain at the moment, more's
the pity.*
1999 Brachetto d'Acqui, Contero, £9.99 Weird
and wacky fizzy red from northern Italy. You
either love it or hate it. Me, I'm mad about it.

1999 Nero d'Avola, Villa Tonino, £4.99 This grape is one of the new darlings of southern Italy. It's dark, bittersweet and full of plums and earth.

BALLS BROTHERS (BALL)

313 Cambridge Heath Road, London E2 9LQ, 020-7739 6466, fax 0870 243 9775, direct sales 020-7739 1642
E-MAIL wine@ballsbrothers.co.uk
WEB SITE www.ballsbrothers.co.uk
HOURS Mon–Fri 9–5.30 **CARDS** Amex, Diners, MasterCard, Switch, Visa **DISCOUNTS** Negotiable for larger quantities **DELIVERY** Free 1 case or more locally; £6 1 case, free 2 cases or more, England, Wales and Scottish Lowlands; islands and Scottish Highlands phone for details. **T**

A helpful list that likes to point you round to different parts of it with suggestions of 'If you like this, try this'. So if you like a Sauvignon and Sémillon Bordeaux Blanc, you may well like an Australian Semillon. It's also terribly keen on recipes for snails, and indeed for seared kangaroo, which can be a little difficult to obtain round my way. But it makes up for such daftness by listing Alsace wines from Domaine Blanck, and Australia, New Zealand and California are also good. Much of the focus, however, is on Bordeaux and Burgundy, and these sections are excellent.

1998 Pouilly-Fumé, Château de Tracy, £9.95 Classic Sauvignon Blanc from one of the leading producers in the appellation. It's minerally and complex rather than fruit-driven.
1999 Tokay-Pinot Gris, Domaine Blanck, £8.50 Rich, smoky, dry Alsace wine of great finesse that will go a treat with many dishes.
1998 St-Chinian Comte Cathare, Château de Combebelle Prestige, £8.50 Wonderfully rich stuff, full of complexity. It's a blend of Syrah and Grenache, and influential wine writer Robert Parker loves it, so buy now while you can still afford it.

H + H BANCROFT (BAN)

Matrix House, Cambridge Business Park, 10 Cowley Park, Cambridge CB4 0WT, 0870 444 1700, fax 0870 444 1701
E-MAIL sales@handhbancroft.co.uk
HOURS Mon–Fri 9–6 **CARDS** MasterCard, Visa

DISCOUNTS Negotiable **DELIVERY** Free
MINIMUM ORDER 3 cases **EN PRIMEUR** Australia, Bordeaux, Burgundy, Rhône. **C M T**

Lots of unusual wines here, and lots to tempt money from one's wallet. There are plenty of great tastes from the south of France, genuinely interesting wines from appellations like Cahors, Madiran, La Clape and Pic St-Loup – all those names you wish you could use at Scrabble. There are no fewer than 13 wines from Banyuls and Maury alone; how many lists have even one? Bordeaux focuses on well-chosen lesser wines, and there's a good Beaujolais list – another rarity these days. Burgundy, too, has masses of wines one can both afford and would want to drink, as well as those one can't afford. Italy and Germany are both outstanding, Australia is good, and there's a healthy list of halves.

1998 Côtes du Rhône-Villages Cairanne Cuvée Tradition, Daniel & Denis Alary, £6.58 Classy stuff: peppery and herby, as you'd expect from the southern Rhône, but with some elegance too.
1997 Rioja Crianza, Domaine Ostatu, £9.70 Concentrated Tempranillo, Graciano and Mazuelo from old vines, made with great care.

BAT & BOTTLE

Knightly Grange Office, Grange Road, Knightley, Woodseaves, Staffordshire ST20 0JU, (01785) 284495, fax (01785) 284877
E-MAIL sales@batandbottle-wine.co.uk
HOURS Fri 2–7, Sat 11–4 **CARDS** MasterCard, Switch, Delta, Visa **DISCOUNTS** 5% on unmixed cases **DELIVERY** Free for orders of £150 or more, otherwise £4.99 per case. Timed and weekend deliveries available at extra charge. **MT**

This is a tremendous list. Bat & Bottle clearly make the effort to find wines for themselves rather than just buying from other shippers, and it shows. I'll bet the majority of the names on this list will be unfamiliar to you, but if I mention Charles Koehly and Domaine Ostertag in Alsace, Ascheri in Piedmont, Inama in Soave and Isabel Estate in Marlborough, it will give you an idea of the sort of level B&B operate at: these are characterful wines of subtlety and depth, yet prices don't look high. There's a pretty good sprinkling from everywhere, with the notable exception of Bordeaux. They also send out a gloriously loopy French card listing the wines (all French, naturally) that one should take for various maladies. So for obesity you should drink four glasses of Burgundy a day. For major obesity you need a bottle of Rosé de Provence. For abnormal thinness four glasses of Côtes de Beaune are required. And don't touch Anjou Blanc or Vouvray before a long journey: they are both, apparently, excellent cures for constipation.

1998 Chenin Blanc, Wildekrans, Bot River Valley, £5.75 Cool-climate wine full of concentrated honeyed fruit. Not a bit like most South African Chenin, but then this estate is one of the country's newest stars.

BENNETTS (BEN)

High Street, Chipping Campden, Glos GL55 6AG, (01386) 840392, fax (01386) 840974 **E-MAIL** enquiries@bennettsfinewines.com **WEB SITE** www.bennettsfinewines.com **HOURS** Mon–Fri 10–1 & 2–6, Sat 9–6 **CARDS** MasterCard, Switch, Visa **DISCOUNTS** On collected orders **DELIVERY** £6 per case, minimum charge £12 (£1 per case surcharge Scotland) **EN PRIMEUR** Burgundy, Italy, New Zealand, Rhône. **G M T**

Bennetts reckon that the south of France is currently producing better quality and value, and more interesting wines, than the New World. To prove it they have wines made with Grenache, Syrah, Carignan, Cinsaut, Gros Manseng, Colombard, Clairette, Chenin Blanc, Viognier, Marsanne and Rolle. From further north in France there are great Sauternes and Barsacs, including 1947 Château Gilette at £100. New World wines are pretty high up the quality scale, especially in Australia; Bennetts confess to not seeing the point of Chile, which is fair enough – one can't like everything – but they do see the point of Germany, even if their customers don't. ('Hard to move in any quantity', they say.) Everybody, presumably, sees the point of Italy, since there are yards of terrific wines from here. On the subject of South Africa, they say, 'We know people will criticize us for not having a comprehensive range, but try as we might we just can't find a bottle we would choose to drink with supper.' I say, far better that than a cynical attitude of buying anything you can sell, regardless of whether you believe in it.

1996 Vin de Glace, Domaine de Clovallon, £34 for 50cl Look, never mind that it's £34. This is the first ice wine ever made in the Languedoc, and that's about as unusual as you can get. It was picked on 28 December 1996, from grapes naturally frozen on the vines.

2000 Redoma Rosé, Quinta de Napoles, £8.99 Pink wine from the Douro; big, serious stuff.

2000 Pinot Gris, Mount Langi Ghiran, £10.90 Few Australians seem to understand this grape, but this succeeds brilliantly. It's spicy but not over the top.

BERRY BROS. & RUDD (BER)

3 St James's Street, London SW1A 1EG, 020-7396 9600, order number 0870 900 4300, fax 0870 900 4301 • Berry's Wine & Food Shop, Hamilton Close, Houndmills, Basingstoke, Hants RG21 6YB, (01256) 323566, fax (01256) 340144 • Terminal 3 departures, Heathrow Airport, TW6 1JH, 020-8564 8361/3, fax 020-8564 8379 • Terminal 4 departures, Heathrow, TW6 3XA 020-8754 1961/1970, fax 020-8754 1984 **E-MAIL** orders@bbr.com **WEB SITE** www.bbr.com **HOURS** Orders office Mon–Fri 9–6, Sat 10–4; St James's Street: Mon–Fri 9–5.30, Sat 10–4; Berry's Wine & Food Shop: Mon–Thur 10–6, Fri 10–8, Sat 10–4; Heathrow: Daily 6am–10pm **CARDS** Amex, Diners, MasterCard, Switch, Visa **DISCOUNTS** variable **DELIVERY** Free for orders of £100 or more, otherwise £7.50 **EN PRIMEUR** Bordeaux, Burgundy, Rhône. **C G M T**

Berry Bros pulls off the trick of having the world's most traditional image, while actually offering one of the most go-ahead ranges to be found in this country. It's a pretty classy list, as you'd expect, but not everything is expensive, and the everyday wines are characterful and well-chosen. Burgundy is at every price from under a tenner to nearly £40, and the Loire and Rhône are excellent too. All the fans of German wine in the country must come here, because BBR is one of the few companies to be able to sustain a top-class list of these wines, and you'll find plenty to tempt money from your pocket

---

C = cellarage   **G** = glass loan/hire   **M** = mail order   **T** = tastings and talks

in Italy, too. And if you want to pay over £50 for a bottle of Napa Valley Cabernet blend, now's your chance. Personally I'd rather pay less and have a top Burgundy, but that's just me. Chile, Argentina and South Africa don't fill as many pages as some of the classic regions, but the wines are considerably more interesting than in many lists. And Australia and New Zealand are tremendous.

1998 Sancerre Rouge, Les Cailleries, Domaine Vacheron, £11.50 Denis Vacheron makes superb red Sancerre that is ageworthy, complex and full of ripe cherry fruit.

1995 Vom Stein Federspiel, Nikolaihof, £14.75 Riesling of great purity and clarity – and complexity – from one of Austria's top names.

1996 Cordoba Crescendo, Stellenbosch, £15.45 A Cabernet Franc and Merlot blend from South Africa with considerably depth and finesse.

1999 Mount Difficulty Chardonnay, Central Otago, £16.50 Very serious Chardonnay from New Zealand, a country rapidly proving that it can make complex, top-class examples of the grape. This is minerally and citrus, with a creamy palate and a very long finish.

BIBENDUM (BIB)

113 Regents Park Road, London NW1 8UR, 020-7916 7706, fax 020-7916 7705
E-MAIL bibendum@bibendum-wine.co.uk
WEB SITE www.bibendum-wine.co.uk
HOURS Mon–Fri 9–6 **CARDS** Amex, MasterCard, Switch, Visa **DELIVERY** London and Home Counties £10; elsewhere on application; free for orders over £100 **MINIMUM ORDER** 1 case (minimum 6 bottles of any one wine)
EN PRIMEUR Bordeaux, Burgundy, New World, Rhône. **C G M T**

A consistently adventurous and wide-ranging list, always adding new wines to stay ahead of the game. And Bibendum does look for wines that nobody else is shipping, which makes for a very different sort of list. New this year are the wines of Michel Laroche in Chablis; two young growers from Burgundy, in the shape of Dominique Cornin at Domaine Lalande in Mâcon, and Jean Paul Mestre in Meursault; Solatione in Chianti; Bric Cencurio in Piedmont; Luigi Maffini in Campania; Mas d'en Gil in Priorat and Alexia of Nelson in New Zealand.

2000 Arneis, Bric Cencurio, £8.13 A lovely, spicy, concentrated example of this fascinating white grape, which is Italy's answer to Viognier.
1998 Priorat Coma Vella, Mas d'en Gil, £18 A Priorat new to Britain, from low-yielding vines. The wines are dense and concentrated.

BOOTHS (BO)
4 Fishergate, Preston PR1 3LJ, (01772) 251701, fax (01772) 204316. 25 stores
HOURS Office: Mon–Fri 9–5; shop hours vary
CARDS MasterCard, Switch, Visa **DISCOUNTS** 5% any 6 bottles. **G T**
A good list for a merchant, never mind a supermarket. There's a long list of Australians all the way up to Penfolds Grange at £105. It doesn't say how many stores this is available in, but I think we can assume it's not in many. If top Aussie Chardonnay is your preference, there's Petaluma Tiers at £34.99. Well, it's cheaper than Grange. Cheaper still are the wonderful Chablis from Defaix, good Faugères from Gilbert Alquier and Langhe Nebbiolo from Vajra. Admittedly, they also stock Piat d'Or, but we'll gloss over that little embarrassment.
2000 Vin Ruspo, Capezzana, £6.99 Beautifully structured rosé from Tuscany, classy and good value.

BORDEAUX DIRECT
See Laithwaites.

BORDEAUX INDEX (BODX)
1st Floor, 3–5 Spafield Street, London EC1R 4QB, 020-7278 9495, fax 020-7278 9707
E-MAIL dylan.paris@bordeauxindex.com
WEB SITE www.bordeauxindex.com
HOURS Mon–Fri 8.30–6 **CARDS** Access, Amex, MasterCard, Switch, Visa (transaction fees apply)
DELIVERY Free for orders over £2000 UK mainland **MINIMUM ORDER** £100 **EN PRIMEUR** Australia, Bordeaux, Burgundy, Piedmont, Rhône, Tuscany. **C**
This is a company for serious spenders only. There are classic wines from classic producers: if you want garage wines from Bordeaux from the hugely expensive 2000 vintage, this is one of the places to

start queuing – except that it's probably already too late. There are older vintages as well, back to 1961, and in spite of the company name, stacks of top Burgundies. There are some Rhônes, Italians and a handful of wines from elsewhere, like Penfolds Grange from Australia and the inevitable Cloudy Bay from New Zealand.
1961 Château Palmer, Margaux, £805 Yes, per bottle: it's a classic wine from a classic vintage.

BOTTOMS UP (BOT)
See First Quench.

BUDGENS (BUD)
Head office PO Box 9, Stonefield Way, Ruislip, Middx HA4 0JR, 020-8422 9511, fax 020-8864 2800, for nearest store call 0800 56002.
210 stores in South-East
WEB SITE www.budgens.com
HOURS Usually Mon–Sat 8–8, Sun 10–4 **CARDS** MasterCard, Switch, Visa **G T**
Well, I suppose you wouldn't make a special trip to Budgens for wine, any more than you would if you wanted balsamic vinegar or unpasteurized cheese. So it's no good expecting anything startling. The printed list doesn't even give vintages. Bland brands are the order of the day – mostly perfectly pleasant, if you're not interested in drinking anything better.
Valdepeñas Viña Albali Gran Reserva, £5.99 Soft, strawberryish Spanish red.

BUTLERS WINE CELLAR (BU)
247 Queens Park Road, Brighton BN2 2XJ, (01273) 698724, fax (01273) 622761
E-MAIL henry@butlers-winecellar.co.uk
WEBSITE www.butlers-winecellar.co.uk
HOURS Tue–Wed 10–6, Thur–Sat 10–7 **CARDS** Amex, MasterCard, Switch, Visa **DELIVERY** Free locally 1 case or more; free UK mainland 3 or more cases. **G M T**
You probably need to look at the website to get full value from this list, or at least be on the mailing list: it's the odds and ends that are the main point, and they change all the time. There are mature Australian reds like St Hallett Old Block 1994 and Wirra Wirra The Angelus 1990, and Late Harvest

---

C = cellarage   **G** = glass loan/hire   **M** = mail order   **T** = tastings and talks

Chardonnay from Romania, which has to be worth a try at £4.95.

1997 Shiraz McCrae Wood, Jim Barry, £17
Lovely tarry, damsony red from the Clare Valley in Australia; at its peak now.

ANTHONY BYRNE (BY)

Ramsey Business Park, Stocking Fen Road, Ramsey, Cambs PE26 2UR, (01487) 814555, fax (01487) 814962
E-MAIL anthony@abfw.co.uk or claude@abfw.co.uk
WEB SITE www.abfw.co.uk
HOURS Mon–Fri 9–5.30 **CARDS** None
DISCOUNTS available on cases **DELIVERY** Free 5 cases or more, or orders of £250 or more; otherwise £6 **MINIMUM ORDER** 1 case **EN PRIMEUR** Bordeaux, Burgundy, Rhône. **C M T**
Anthony Byrne has always been good at finding interesting wines from rural France, but there's some pretty smart stuff from well-known vineyards too. The sparkiest, liveliest Sancerre comes from flinty silex soil, and Anthony Byrne has examples from Serge Laloue and Domaine Gueneau. He also has Pouilly-Fumé from Dageneau. There is an extremely serious list of Burgundy, and from Alsace enough Zind-Humbrecht wines to sink a ship. There are good selections from elsewhere in the world, too, but France is the focus of the list.

1997 Madiran, Château Montus, £11.54 A serious wine at a fairly serious price. This is concentrated and spicy.

1998 Aligoté Bouzeron, Villaine, £8.17 Lovely structured white from Burgundy. Aubert de Villaine's Aligoté is about as good as the grape gets – he's also part-owner of the Domaine de la Romanée Conti.

D BYRNE & CO

Victoria Buildings, 12 King Street, Clitheroe, Lancs BB7 2EP (01200) 423152
HOURS Mon–Sat 8.30–6 **CARDS** MasterCard, Switch, Visa **DELIVERY** Free within 50 miles; nationally £10 1st case, £5 subsequent cases **EN PRIMEUR** Bordeaux, Burgundy, Rhône, Germany. **G M T**
D Byrne has been sadly absent from this guide for several years, but let's hope it is now back to stay. The list is as good as ever: Bordeaux, Burgundy, the

Loire, the Rhône, Beaujolais, Alsace and southern France are all excellent, as are Germany, California, South Africa, Spain, Chile, Argentina, Portugal, Austria... Bravo.

1992 Somontano Pinot Noir, Viñas del Vero, £6.35 Good value Pinot from northern Spain. The remarkable thing is that it really does taste like Pinot – and nice Pinot, too.

CAPE PROVINCE WINES (CAP)

77 Laleham Road, Staines, Middx TW18 2EA, (01784) 451860, fax (01784) 469267
E-MAIL capewines@msn.com
WEB SITE www.capewinestores.co.uk
HOURS Mon–Sat 9–5.30 **CARDS** Access, MasterCard, Switch, Visa **DELIVERY** £7.95 1 case UK mainland **MINIMUM ORDER** 6 bottles. **G M T**
The entire list is of Cape wines, though of course not every Cape wine is here. Quality is generally good, and the producers are well-established names rather than new discoveries.

1995 Marlbrook, Klein Constantia, £9.48 This is a mainly Merlot Bordeaux blend with good fruit and richness.

CAVE CRU CLASSÉ

Unit 13 The Leathermarket, Weston Street, London SE1 3ER, 020-7378 8579, fax 020-7378 8544 and 7403 0607
E-MAIL enquiries@ccc.co.uk
WEB SITE www.cave-cru-classe.com
HOURS Mon–Fri 9–5.30 **CARDS** Amex, MasterCard, Visa **DELIVERY** £15 per order in London and the South-East; price according to distance for other addresses **MINIMUM ORDER** 1 mixed case **EN PRIMEUR** Bordeaux. **M T**
How do you choose wine if you're very, very rich? Do you end up buying far more than you can possibly drink, and then one day flog the lot at auction for about 25 times what you paid for it? Well, this is one of the places you'd buy it. There are yards and yards of clarets and Burgundies, several feet of Rhônes and a couple of inches of other French stuff. You can buy standard non-vintage Champagne here, too, though with Roederer at £29.38 you might prefer to go elsewhere. From California there are such stars as Dalla Valle, and there are all sorts of smart Cognacs like 1800 Fine Champagne at

£1169. I think that must be per bottle, though I admit I find the list a little confusing on this point. If I drank more Cognac of that sort I'd probably know straight off.

1998 Château Smith-Haut-Lafitte Blanc, £22 Lovely nutty, complex white Graves from one of the region's top producers of white. The red is pretty decent stuff, too.

COCKBURNS OF LEITH INCORPORATING J E HOGG (COC)

The Wine Emporium, 7 Devon Place, Haymarket, Edinburgh EH12 5HJ, 0131-346 1113, fax 0131-313 2607
E-MAIL jhogg@winelist.co.uk
WEB SITE www.winelist.co.uk
HOURS Mon–Fri 9–6; Sat 10–5 **CARDS** MasterCard, Switch, Visa **DELIVERY** Free 12 or more bottles within Edinburgh; elsewhere £6 1–2 cases, free 3 cases or more **EN PRIMEUR** Bordeaux, Burgundy. **G T**

There are the greatly improved Burgundies of Bouchard Père here, and a nice list of Beaujolais. You'll find some interesting Italians, too, and some good South Africans, one of which is described as 'screaming fruit'. And people accuse me of writing bizarre tasting notes. A good all-round list, with no particular favourite countries or regions, but well-chosen wines across the board.

1999 Verdicchio dei Castelli di Jesi Classico Macrina, Antonio Garofoli, £6.70 Classy, substantial Italian white for when you want weight and depth but not powerful flavour.

CONNOLLY'S WINE MERCHANTS (CON)

Arch 13, 220 Livery Street, Birmingham B3 1EU, 0121-236 9269/3837, fax 0121-233 2339
E-MAIL connowine@aol.com
WEB SITE www.connollyswine.co.uk
HOURS Mon–Fri 9–5.30, Sat 10–4 **CARDS** Amex, MasterCard, Switch, Visa **DELIVERY** Surcharge outside Birmingham area **DISCOUNTS** 10% for cash & carry **EN PRIMEUR** Bordeaux, Burgundy, Port. **G M T**

Bordeaux, Burgundy and the Rhône all look very good, and there is an interesting German list, too.

Italy has names like Isole e Olena and Allegrini and from Spain there are Riojas from Faustino and Artadi. Top Aussies include Grant Burge and Shaw & Smith.

1996 Zinfandel, Lytton Springs, Ridge, £19.65 Expensive, yes – but it's one of the best examples of the grape you can get. Not the most massive or alcoholic, but big and complex, and it ages fantastically. So it's world-class stuff. And for California, this price is nothing. Ridge's Monte Bello Cabernet is £65. Yes, per bottle.

CORNEY & BARROW (CB)

Head office 12 Helmet Row, London EC1V 3TD, 020-7539 3200, fax 020-7608 1373/1142 • 194 Kensington Park Road, London W11 2ES, 020-7221 5122 • Belvoir House, High Street, Newmarket CB8 8DH, (01638) 600000 • 26 Rutland Square, Edinburgh EH1 2BW, 0131-228 2233 • Corney & Barrow (Scotland) with Whighams of Ayr, 8 Academy Street, Ayr KA7 1HT, (01292) 267000
E-MAIL wine@corbar.co.uk
WEB SITE www.corneyandbarrow.com
HOURS Mon–Fri 9–6 (24-hr answerphone); Kensington Mon–Sat 10.30–9; Newmarket Mon–Sat 9–6; Edinburgh Mon–Fri 9–6; Ayr Mon–Sat 9–6 **CARDS** Amex, MasterCard, Switch, Visa **DELIVERY** Free 2 or more cases within M25 boundary, elsewhere free 3 or more cases. Otherwise £9 plus VAT per delivery. For Scotland and East Anglia, please speak with the relevant office. **EN PRIMEUR** Bordeaux, Burgundy, Italy, Spain. **C G M T**

If you want certain Pomerols like Pétrus, Trotanoy, la Fleur-Pétrus and Latour à Pomerol, Corney & Barrow is where you have to come. At least, if you want them en primeur. They have other exclusivities in Bordeaux, too: Château Moulin Pey-Labrie in Canon-Fronsac, which is pretty serious stuff, and Château Roylland in St-Emilion among them. Burgundy kicks off with Domaine de la Romanée-Conti and proceeds via names like Domaine Trapet and Domaine Joseph Roty. The rest of France is equally impressive, and C&B are good at finding new and interesting producers. But Europe is their main focus, and while there is good stuff from Australia and South America, selections are, well, select.

Champagne Delamotte NV, £17.63 Invariably elegant and very good value.

1998 Morellino di Scansano, Moris Farms, £8.75 Peppery, cherryish Sangiovese from Tuscany. The curious name is that of the Moris family, who emigrated to Italy from Spain in 1700.

CROQUE-EN-BOUCHE (CRO)

221 Wells Road, Malvern Wells, Worcestershire WR14 4HF, (01684) 565612

E-MAIL mail@croque-en-bouche.co.uk
WEB SITE www.croque-en-bouche.co.uk
HOURS No fixed hours; open by appointment 7 days a week **CARDS** Access, MasterCard, Switch, Visa **DISCOUNTS** 4% on orders of £500 or more, if cash and collected; 2.5% if paid by credit card **DELIVERY** Free locally 2 or more cases; elsewhere for orders over £400; otherwise £9.50 **MINIMUM ORDER** 1 mixed case. **M**

A wonderful list with a curious habit of giving certain wines the accolade, in capital letters, of 'GREAT WINEMAKING'. What does that say about the wines that don't get it? Particularly if they're from the same company? Cape Mentelle's Zinfandel is GREAT WINEMAKING, but not, apparently, the same producer's Shiraz and Cabernet. But even if the winemaking is perfectly dreadful, at least there are mature Australian reds here from the early 1980s to the mid-1990s, and terrific stuff from the Rhône as well. The Rhône list is full of starry names – expect prices to match. There are lots of Alsace wines, with Zind-Humbrecht predominating, and a good sprinkling from every other French region. They stock two Vin Jaunes, a 1961 and a 1953, and say, 'every year or so we sell a bottle'.

1996 Cabernet Cuvée Alexandre, Casa Lapostolle, £11.50 Punchy, blackcurrant Chilean wine, super-ripe, with rich tannins. There's also a Merlot version, for £1 more.

1996 Bárbara Forés, Ferrer Escoda, £8.90 The list describes this Spanish red as 'squeeky clean', and very modern. Lots of fruit.

THE CO-OPERATIVE GROUP/CWS (CO)

Head office New Century House, Manchester M60 4ES, freephone 0800 0686 727 for stock

details, fax 0161-827 5117. 1872 licensed stores
WEB SITE www.co-op.co.uk
HOURS Variable **CARDS** Variable **M T**

A decent list of commercial flavours, with some gloriously bizarre restrictions on what gets sold where. Penfolds Grange 1995 (£89) is only available in the North-East, as is Cloudy Bay Pelorus (£13.99) and indeed Cloudy Bay Sauvignon Blanc (£10.99). And two English wines for which neither producer nor vintage is listed, England Dry and Penny Black, are sold only in the Midlands. These facts are, however, the most eccentric things in the list; otherwise it's a sound list of familiar names.

Cabernet Franc Reserve, Valdivieso, £8.99 No vintage is given for this quite elegant, structured, redcurrant-fruited Chilean red.

DIRECT WINE SHIPMENTS (DI)

5/7 Corporation Square, Belfast, Northern Ireland BT1 3AJ, 028-9050 8000, fax 028-9050 8004

E-MAIL enquiry@directwine.co.uk
WEB SITE www.directwine.co.uk
HOURS Mon–Fri 9–6.30 (Thur till 8), Sat 9.30–5.30 **CARDS** Access, MasterCard, Switch, Visa **DISCOUNTS** 10% in the form of complimentary wine with each case **DELIVERY** Free Northern Ireland 1 case or more; £10 per case UK mainland **EN PRIMEUR** Bordeaux, Rhône. **C G M T**

It's amazing the way Direct Wines have built up the company – and the list – from what was basically a corner grocer's shop. Now it can compete with any wine merchant in the United Kingdom. It's a first-class list with all the top names you can think of. Burgundy looks outstanding, as – happily – does Germany. And Italy is very good. There are some seriously expensive Spanish wines here – things like L'Ermita 1996 from Alvaro Palacios in Priorat at £145. Chile is more routine, but there's terrific stuff here from pretty well everywhere. Lucky Northern Ireland.

1999 Muscat Cuvée Tradition, Hugel, £8.99 Lovely dry Muscat from Alsace – crisp, aromatic and delicious.

1998 Chinon Terroir, Charles Joguet, £7.99 The Loire can provide some of France's best bargains at the moment – it's unfashionable, so prices haven't shot up, although winemaking is far better than it was. This is a lovely, minerally, juicy red.

DOMAINE DIRECT (DOM)

6–9 Cynthia Street, London N1 9JF, 020-7837 1142, fax 020-7837 8605
E-MAIL info@domainedirect.co.uk
WEB SITE www.domainedirect.co.uk
HOURS 8.30–5.30; or answering machine
CARDS Mastercard, Switch, Visa **DELIVERY** Free London; elsewhere in UK mainland 1 case £9.99, 2 cases £12.93, 3 or more free **MINIMUM ORDER** 1 mixed case **EN PRIMEUR** Burgundy.
M T
Domaine Direct has discovered the New World, which is very good news given that it has applied the same high standards as it does to its Burgundy list. So from Australia you'll find wines from the Leeuwin Estate; from California producers like Etude, Viader (expensive but beautifully structured) and Spottswoode. But Burgundy is still the main focus and it's still terrifically good, with a sensational selection.
1999 Savigny-lès-Beaune Blanc, Jean-Marc Pavelot, £14.69 Good value white from a mostly red village, and beautifully ripe and balanced.

BEN ELLIS WINES

Brockham Wine Cellars, Wheelers Lane, Brockham, Surrey RH3 7HJ, (01737) 842160, fax (01737) 843210
E-MAIL sales@benelliswines.com
WEB SITE www.benelliswines.com
HOURS Mon–Fri 9–6 **CARDS** MasterCard, Switch, Visa **DELIVERY** Free 1 case local area and Central London, elsewhere free 5 cases or orders over £400; other orders £10 **MINIMUM ORDER** 1 mixed case **EN PRIMEUR** Bordeaux, Burgundy, Rhône. **C G M T**
This is an extremely well thought out list of characterful, subtle wines – and wines that you won't find everywhere else. Exactly what independent wine merchants should be doing, in other words: challenging people to try new flavours and new producers. The list groups them by grape variety, so that Semillon and Semillon/Sauvignon blends range from a £5.50 Bordeaux Blanc (Château Haut-Rian) to a £39.50 Pessac-Léognan,

taking in the Hunter Valley, Margaret River and Napa Valley on the way. There is Pinot Gris from Italy, Argentina, Alsace and Australia, some interesting Italian and Spanish reds, and Portuguese beer. And could Austria's Schloss Gobelsburg Grüner Veltliner Grub be the ultimate food wine?
1999 Verdelho, Margan, Hunter Valley, £9.50 Lovely limes and toast white from Australia, for when you're sick of Chardonnay.
1998 Bush Vine Pinotage, Trafalgar, The Pinotage Co, £7.30 Rich and ripe, which sets it apart from a lot of South African Pinotage. Supple, too.

FARR VINTNERS (FA)

19 Sussex Street, London SW1V 4RR, 020-7821 2000, fax 020-7821 2020
E-MAIL sales@farr-vintners.com
WEB SITE www.farr-vintners.com
HOURS Mon–Fri 10–6 **CARDS** None **DELIVERY** London £1 per case (min £10); elsewhere £4 per case (min £12) **MINIMUM ORDER** £500 plus VAT **EN PRIMEUR** Bordeaux. **C M T**
A fantastic list of the world's finest wines, be they from Bordeaux, Burgundy or the Crimea. (You want Crimean 1948 Tokay South Coast at £125 per bottle plus VAT? No problem.) The Italian list looks particularly good, with names like Castello di Ama.
1983 Château Guiraud, Sauternes, £27.42 This is a remarkable price for a world-class wine. 'Sweet wine seems to be out of fashion', say Farr Vintners.

FIRST QUENCH GROUP: BOTTOMS UP (BOT), THRESHER (THR), VICTORIA WINE (VIC), WINE RACK (WR)

Head office Enjoyment Hall, Bessemer Road, Welwyn Garden City, Herts AL7 1BL, (01707) 387200, fax (01707) 387350; national delivery via Drinks Direct, 0800 232221.
95 Bottoms Up stores, 707 Thresher Wine Shops, 1016 Victoria Wine stores, 216 Wine Rack stores
HOURS Mon–Sat 9–10 (some 10.30), Sun 12–3, 7–10; Scotland 12.30–10.30 **CARDS** MasterCard, Switch, Visa **DISCOUNTS** Various offers **DELIVERY** Free locally, some branches.
G T

A major high street presence, First Quench is presumably a faithful reflection of everyday wine drinking in Britain. There is a huge variety of wines but rather less variety of flavours; Chile is here in force; there's a decent selection of cheap clarets and Rhônes and, more adventurously, a very respectable selection of Alsace; and people are clearly prepared to pay more for Burgundy than they are for Bordeaux. Germany is pretty much a write-off, and Italy seems to be limited by price. But New Zealand, Australia and South Africa are in demand.

1999 Verdelho David Traeger, Victoria, £8.49 Lovely limey-fresh stuff, rich and dry.

LE FLEMING WINES (FLE)
19 Spenser Road, Harpenden, Hertfordshire AL5 5NW, (01582) 760125
E-MAIL cherry@lefleming.swinternet.co.uk
HOURS 24-hour answering machine **DISCOUNTS** 5% on large orders **DELIVERY** Free locally
MINIMUM ORDER 1 case. **G M T**
Australia looks terrific here, with lots of serious and not so serious wines. South Africa, too, is good, with wines like Clos Malverne Pinotage Reserve and Hamilton Russell Chardonnay. The list is basically the New World and France, plus a few wines from Italy and Spain, but not many. They're more mixed, too, with Tuscany's Isole e Olena rubbing shoulders with Piedmont's Terre del Barolo.

1998 Quinta do Crasto, £6.85 Spicy damsons and lots of character. This is one of the Douro Valley's best red table wines.
1997 Riesling Green Hills, Henschke, £10.65 Classic Aussie Riesling, from a top producer.
1998 Cabernet Sauvignon/Malbec, Colome la Salta, £14.33 Hugely concentrated Argentinian red, with lots of alcohol: not a light lunchtime wine, this. But it's well balanced.

FORTNUM & MASON (FORT)
181 Piccadilly, London W1A 1ER, 020-7734 8040, fax 020-7437 3278
E-MAIL info@fortnumandmason.co.uk
WEB SITE www.fortnumandmason.co.uk
HOURS Mon–Sat 10–6.30 **CARDS** Amex, Diners, MasterCard, Switch, Visa **DISCOUNTS**

1 free bottle per dozen **DELIVERY** £6 per delivery address **EN PRIMEUR** Bordeaux. **M T**
As you'd expect, a fine list, and strongest in the classics. Bordeaux and Burgundy are very good, and there's a sprinkling of top names from other French regions, but Australia is much smaller – although, again, very good. There are some nice Germans and Austrians. Prices are on the high side, but presumably if you do your food shopping at Fortnums you don't mind that.

1999 Bardolino Classico Tacchetto, Guerrieri-Rizzardi, £7.75 Lovely fresh strawberryish summer red. Well, reddish.

FRIARWOOD (FRI)
26 New King's Road, London SW6 4ST, 020-7736 2628, fax 020-7731 0411
E-MAIL sales@friarwood.com
WEB SITE www.friarwood.com
HOURS Mon–Fri 10–7.30, Sat 10–7 **CARDS** Amex, Diners, MasterCard, Switch, Visa
DISCOUNTS 5% on mixed cases, 10% unmixed
DELIVERY Free locally; £5 1 or 2 cases in London; elsewhere at cost **EN PRIMEUR** Bordeaux, Burgundy. **C G M T**
There are new wines from the south of France here, but the focus is still Burgundy and Bordeaux. The former is mostly from Domaine Antonin Guyon, and the latter includes a good selection of petits châteaux as well as classed growths; vintages go back to 1982, or 1967 for Yquem. From the US there is Bonny Doon, Qupé and Ridge.

1997 Saussignac, Vendanges d'Autrefois, £7.95 for 50cl Saussignac is a lesser-known sweet wine region in the Bordeaux area: expect lighter weight than Sauternes, and good delicate flavours.

GAUNTLEYS (GAU)
4 High Street, Exchange Arcade, Nottingham NG1 2ET, 0115-911 0555, fax 0115-911 0557
E-MAIL rhone@gauntleywine.com
WEB SITE www.gauntleywine.com
HOURS Mon–Sat 9–5.30 **CARDS** Amex, MasterCard, Switch, Visa **DELIVERY** Free within Nottingham area, otherwise 1–2 cases £8 plus VAT, 3–5 cases £13 plus VAT **MINIMUM ORDER**

C = cellarage **G** = glass loan/hire **M** = mail order **T** = tastings and talks

1 case **EN PRIMEUR** Alsace, Burgundy, Italy, Loire, Rhône, Southern France, Spain. **M T**

Do you know, if this list didn't exist I think I'd have to invent it. It's full of wines that are not just unusual, but that are also from the sorts of places that offer both character and good value. There are just two wines from Bordeaux: isn't that extraordinary? Bravo for having the nerve to do it. In fact if you were a Cabernet Sauvignon fan I think you might have rather a thin time of it here. There's lots of lovely stuff from the south of France, but it tends to be Coteaux du Languedoc or Bandol or Jurançon or Minervois or Maury: flying winemaker reds are few and far between. Alsace features heavily, with star names like Schoffit, Trimbach and Josmeyer, and Champagne is from Vilmart, which makes wonderfully big, rich wines that need ages. There's a long list of Burgundy, and lots of Loire as well, and some good Spanish and Italians.

1995 Minervois Blanc La Dame Blanche, Château de Violet, £6.36 This southern French white is 100% Marsanne and is beautifully herby, almondy and fresh.

Champagne Vilmart Grande Reserve NV, £18.12 Astonishing Champagne aged in a proportion of new barrels. Yes, it does have the weight to stand it.

GOEDHUIS & CO

6 Rudolf Place, Miles Street, London SW8 1RP, 020-7793 7900, fax 020-7793 7170
E-MAIL goedhuis@btinternet.com
HOURS Mon–Fri 9–6.30 **CARDS** MasterCard, Visa **DELIVERY** Free 3 or more, otherwise £10 England, elsewhere at cost **MINIMUM ORDER** 1 unmixed case **EN PRIMEUR** Bordeaux, Burgundy. **C G M T**

Goedhuis is very much a fine wine specialist. That doesn't mean that everything on the list is tremendously expensive or rare, but it does mean that everything is good, and if you buy your everyday wines here you'll get very good quality. Here there are masses of Bordeaux and Burgundies, plus Rhône, Loire, a few French country wines, very good Italians, and shorter lists from Spain, Chile, California, South Africa, Australia and New Zealand. There are good ports and

Champagnes, too, but really the Bordeaux and Burgundies are the core of the list.

1997 Château Potensac, £14.20 A very useful château, this: it's making wine of far higher quality than its Cru Bourgeois classification would suggest, and 1997 is an attractively forward year.

THE GREAT NORTHERN WINE COMPANY (GN)

The Warehouse, Blossomgate, Ripon, N. Yorks HG4 2AJ, (01765) 606767, fax (01765) 609151, accounts (01765) 609177
E-MAIL info@greatnorthernwine.com
WEB SITE www.greatnorthernwine.com
HOURS Mon–Fri 9–6, Sat 9–5 **CARDS** Amex, MasterCard, Switch, Visa **DISCOUNTS** 5% for orders over £100 **DELIVERY** Free local area; elsewhere at cost, free 5 cases or more
MINIMUM ORDER (for deliveries) £25 plus VAT
EN PRIMEUR Bordeaux, Port. **G M T**

A sound list that mixes well-known and less familiar names and offers good drinking: there are wines like Tyrrell's and Devil's Lair, Campbells and Allanmere from Australia; Ca'vit and Tedeschi from Italy; Thelema and Clos Malverne from South Africa, among many many others.

Sancerre les Roches, Domaine Vacheron, £10.99 The list GNW sent us doesn't list vintages, but Vacheron is highly reliable, always producing characterful, minerally wines.

GREAT WESTERN WINE (GW)

The Wine Warehouse, Wells Road, Bath BA2 3AP, (01225) 322800, fax (01225) 442139
E-MAIL post@greatwesternwine.co.uk
WEB SITE www.greatwesternwine.co.uk
HOURS Mon–Fri 10–7, Sat 10–6 **CARDS** Amex, MasterCard, Switch, Visa **DISCOUNTS** Negotiable
DELIVERY Free 3 or more cases, otherwise £5
MINIMUM ORDER 1 mixed case **EN PRIMEUR** Bordeaux, Burgundy. **C G M T**

A highly individual list of highly individual wines. It would be fatal to turn up here knowing what you wanted: you'd feel obliged to by-pass all the other things that might be even more delicious. All sorts of lovely Loire wines, for example, or Viognier from Tuscany, or Yarra Yering's peerless Cabernet

---

C = cellarage   **G** = glass loan/hire   **M** = mail order   **T** = tastings and talks

Sauvignon from Australia's Yarra Valley. A list to browse through at leisure.

1998 Soave Classico, Pra, £7.40 Serious Soave made from low-yielding vines.

PETER GREEN & CO

37A/B Warrender Park Road, Edinburgh EH9 1HJ, tel & fax 0131-229 5925
HOURS Tues–Thur 9.30–6.30, Fri 9.30–7.30, Sat 9.30–7 **CARDS** MasterCard, Switch, Visa
DISCOUNTS 5% on a case or two unmixed half-dozens **DELIVERY** 1 case £6; extra cases £4 each.
G M T

There's a good list of Burgundies from interesting producers here, and the Loire boasts names like Baumard, Vacheron and Prince Poniatowski. The Rhône has a fair number of stars, too – names of the calibre of Chapoutier and Perrin – and Germany, Italy and Portugal are also very strong. Australia and New Zealand are equally well chosen, and there's plenty of stuff to tempt you from Chile. In fact, it's hard to see anywhere where you'd go wrong.

1998 Blaufränkisch Mörbisch Prestige, Lenz Moser, £6.95 Tasty, ripe red from Austria.

ROGER HARRIS WINES (HAW)

Loke Farm, Weston Longville, Norfolk NR9 5LG, (01603) 880171, fax (01603) 880291
E-MAIL sales@rogerharriswines.co.uk
WEB SITE www.Beaujolaisonline.co.uk
HOURS Mon–Fri 9–5 **CARDS** Amex, MasterCard, Visa **DELIVERY** next working day UK mainland, £3 for orders up to £100, £2 up to £150, free over £150 **MINIMUM ORDER** 1 mixed case. **M**

If you love good Beaujolais, look no further. Roger Harris specializes in the stuff, and his list has yards of advice on how to choose it, drink it and serve it. And no, it's not stuffy advice; more suggestions along the lines of which wines are good chilled and which are spoiled by chilling, and which can actually benefit from decanting. All very useful stuff. And the list is terrific, both in breadth and depth. It also ventures into the Mâconnais, and into the south of France, if you feel like a brief change of scene.

1998 Juliénas, Château de Juliénas, £8.55 Well structured and with a deft touch of oak. Lovely fresh fruit, but depth, too.

HAYNES HANSON & CLARK (HAH)

Sheep Street, Stow-on-the-Wold, Glos GL54 1AA, (01451) 870808, fax (01451) 870508
• 25 Eccleston Street, London SW1W 9NP, 020-7259 0102, fax 020-7259 0103
E-MAIL stow@hhandc.co.uk or london@hhandc.co.uk
HOURS Stow: Mon–Fri 9–6, Sat 9–5.30; London: Mon–Fri 9–7 **CARDS** Amex, MasterCard, Switch, Visa **DISCOUNTS** 10% unsplit case
DELIVERY Free central London and Glos; elsewhere 1 case £8, 2–3 cases £5.20 per case, 4 or more cases £4.50 per case, free orders over £500 **MINIMUM ORDER** 1 bottle (mail order)
EN PRIMEUR Bordeaux, Burgundy, Port, Rhône.
G M T

HH&C's preference is for wines of subtlety and elegance, so you won't find too many hefty blockbusters here. It's most famous for Burgundy – the Hanson in the name is Anthony Hanson MW, a leading authority on the subject – but there are also lovely Loires, Alsace and Rhônes, German wines and some good Australians and Californians. Their Bordeaux is also extremely well chosen, and biased towards the affordable end of things. Prices are rather good, too, and their Champagne, Pierre Vaudon, is invariably a winner.

1997 Gevrey-Chambertin Clos de Meixvelles, Domaine Pierre Gelin, £15.90 Smoky, earthy Pinot Noir with lots of spice and substance. The 1997s are drinking very well right now.

1996 Chinon, La Croix Boissée, Bernard Baudry, £12.95 Complex spice and redcurrant flavours mixed with minerals and earth. Very classy Loire red.

HEDLEY WRIGHT (HED)

11 Twyford Centre, London Road, Bishop's Stortford, Herts CM23 3YT, (01279) 465818, fax (01279) 465819
E-MAIL justin@j.waples.fsnet.co.uk
HOURS Mon–Wed 9–6, Thur–Fri 9–7, Sat 10–6
CARDS Access, Amex, MasterCard, Switch, Visa
DELIVERY £5 per delivery, free for orders of £200 or more **MINIMUM ORDER** 1 mixed case
EN PRIMEUR Bordeaux, Chile, Port. **C G M T**

A good all-round list that does justice to most French regions; it has Alsace wines from Charles Koehly, which is always a treat. Portugal and

Spain both look good, even if the wines from Quinta do Fojo have shot up in price to absurd heights. Italy, something of a speciality, has wines from the likes of Pieropan, Franz Haas and Pra. There is a good selection of German wines – from the wonderful Selbach-Oster and Dr Loosen, among others – Chile and Argentina are interesting, and from New Zealand there are the wines of Jackson Estate. Ports are from Churchill Graham: look out for the Traditional LBV.

1995 Château de Landiras Blanc, Graves, £12.95 Pure Sémillon from Bordeaux, very rich and creamy.

1999 Chinon Rosé, Château de la Grille, £10.95 A sort of Chinon for beginners, all raspberry flavours and summer freshness.

HICKS & DON (HIC)

Order office 4 Old Station Yard, Edington, Westbury, Wiltshire BA13 4NT (01380) 831234, fax (01380) 831010 • Park House, North Elmham, Dereham, Norfolk NR20 5JY (01362) 668571, fax (01362) 668573 **E-MAIL** mailbox@hicksanddon.co.uk **WEB SITE** www.hicksanddon.co.uk **HOURS** Mon–Fri 9–5 **CARDS** Access, MasterCard, Visa **DISCOUNTS** Negotiable **DELIVERY** Free 3 cases or more UK mainland, otherwise £4 per case, next day delivery in London extra £12 **MINIMUM ORDER** I case **EN PRIMEUR** Bordeaux, Burgundy, Chile, Italy, Port, Rhône. **C G M T**

Another company that has no truck with ultra-fashionable wines; it simply sells what it likes, and what it likes is subtle, well-made wines that go with food. The list is sensibly organized by grape variety, regardless of origin. It also follows Chardonnay, Sauvignon Blanc and Sémillon with 'White wines of individuality', though since this last section includes Vin de Pays des Côtes de Gascogne and Muscadet as well as Pieropan's Soave Classico, I don't think it's intended as a slur on the lack of character of the likes of Mountadam Chardonnay. Dessert wines include the intriguingly named Markgraflerland Bugginger Maltesgarten Spätburgunder Eiswein from Baden, and there's a good list of other German wines.

1998 Merlot, De Leuwen Jagt, Paarl, £8.29 Big, minty, blackcurranty South African red with plenty of flavour. It's well-focused, though, and has some elegance.

1997 Crozes-Hermitage Clairmonts Blanc, Silviane Borja, £8.89 Ripe, full and well-structured Marsanne. Drinking well now.

HIGH BRECK VINTNERS (HIG)

11 Nelson Road, London N8 9RX, 020-8340 1848, fax 020-8340 5162 **E-MAIL** hbv@richanl.freeserve.co.uk **WEB SITE** www.hbvwines.co.uk **HOURS** Mail order **DELIVERY** Free to the South-East, 3 or more cases; supplements payable for smaller orders or other locations **MINIMUM ORDER** I mixed case **EN PRIMEUR** Bordeaux. **C G M T**

A shortish list with the focus on France. Wines tend to come from lesser-known appellations, like St-Bris or Costières de Nîmes, which can provide good drinking at lower prices. Sancerre is from Gitton Père et Fils, who are reliably good, and the red Bordeaux list looks interesting. Outside France there is a sprinkling of wines from Italy and Spain, Australia and the Lebanon.

1998 Sauvignon de St-Bris, Domaine des Remparts, £6.50 You don't see Sauvignon de St-Bris that often in Britain, but it can be rather good. This is crisp and pungent, and good value.

JEROBOAMS (INCORPORATING LAYTONS) (JER)

Head office Jeroboams: 8–12 Brook Street, London W1S 1BH, 020-7629 7916, fax 020-7495 3314 **Mail order** Laytons: 7–9 Elliot's Place, London N1 8HX 020-7288 8888, fax 020-7359 2616 • 50–52 Elizabeth Street, London SW1W 9PB, 020-7730 8108, fax 020-7730 9284 • 51 Elizabeth Street, London SW1W 9PP, 020-7823 5623, fax 020-7823 5722 • 25 Elystan Street, London SW3 3NT, 020-7581 2660, fax 020-7581 1203 • 20 Davies Street, London W1Y 1LH, 020-7499 1015, fax 020-7491 3052 • 77–78 Chancery Lane, London WC2A 1AB, 020-7405 0552, fax 020-7405 0553 • 96 Holland Park Avenue,

---

C = cellarage   **G** = glass loan/hire   **M** = mail order   **T** = tastings and talks

London W11 3RB, 020-7727 9359, fax 020-7792 3672 • 6 Pont Street, London SW1X 9EL, 020-7235 1612, fax 020-7235 7246 • The Market Place, Cirencester, Glos GL7 2PE, (01285) 655842, fax (01285) 644101 **E-MAIL** sales@jeroboams.co.uk and sales@laytons.co.uk **WEB SITES** www.jeroboams.co.uk and www.laytons.co.uk **HOURS** Offices Mon–Fri 9–6, shops Mon–Sat 9–7 (may vary) **CARDS** Amex, MasterCard, Switch, Visa **DELIVERY** Shops: free for orders of £50 or over in central London; mail order: free for orders over £150, otherwise £10 **EN PRIMEUR** Bordeaux, Burgundy, Germany, Rhône. **C G M T**

There are some sensibly priced everyday clarets here – together with a realistic appraisal of the vintages of the 1990s. It's a little surprising to see Jura wines listed under Burgundy, but then it's surprising to see any Jura wines at all, and the Burgundies themselves look very interesting. Other regions of France are covered quite well though in less depth. Ditto Italy, Germany, Spain and Portugal. Outside Europe, Australia looks particularly good.

1998 Riesling, Alkoomi, Frankland River, Western Australia, £8.40 Intense lemon and lime fruit, weighty and full.

1997 Valpolicella Classico Superiore, Tomasso Bussola, £13.96 Yes, this is pricy for Valpol, but Tomasso Bussola is very, very good. He has a range called TB, for those given to conspicuous consumption.

S H JONES (JON)

27 High Street, Banbury, Oxfordshire OX16 5EW, (01295) 251179, fax (01295) 272352 • 9 Market Square, Bicester, Oxfordshire OX6 7AA (01869) 322448, fax (01869) 244588 • 121 Regent Street, Leamington Spa, Warwickshire CV32 4NU, (01926) 315609 **E-MAIL** sh.jones@btconnect.com **HOURS** Mon–Sat 8.30–6 **CARDS** Access, MasterCard, Switch, Visa **DELIVERY** Free within van delivery area for 1 case or more; 'small delivery charge' otherwise. Elsewhere £8.50; free for orders over £250 **EN PRIMEUR** Bordeaux, Port. **C G M T**

There are good Burgundies here, from the likes of Faiveley, Domaine Parent and Tollot-Beaut, and there's a very good list of clarets which tends towards the expensive end of the spectrum. In the Loire, à propos of Muscadet, the list comments obliquely that 'affordable oysters will aid recovery'. Sounds like one of those dialogues between spies: 'The cat has eaten its kittens.' 'The daffodils are wilting.' You know the sort of thing. Perhaps I'd be better off in Alsace (mostly Schlumberger with a dash of Trimbach) or Germany (Bassermann-Jordan, Friedrich-Wilhelm-Gymnasium and Dr Loosen). Spain is good, with Albariño from Martin Codax, and Australia, California, Argentina and Chile have good drinking.

1999 Coteaux d'Aix-en-Provence, Château de Fonscolombe, £4.89 Fonscolombe seems to get better and better. This is fresh, herby, and with a touch of melons.

1998 Botrytis Riesling, Lindemans, Coonawarra, £6.19 half bottle Rich and concentrated, with lots of acidity to balance the sweetness.

JUSTERINI & BROOKS (JU)

61 St James's Street, London SW1A 1LZ, 020-7484 6400, fax 020-7499 4699 • 45 George Street, Edinburgh EH2 2HT, 0131-226 4202, fax 0131-225 2351 **HOURS** London, Mon–Fri 9–5.30; Edinburgh, Mon–Sat 9.30–6 **CARDS** Amex, MasterCard, Switch, Visa **DELIVERY** £9 for 1–23 bottles; free 24 bottles and over in UK mainland **EN PRIMEUR** Bordeaux, Burgundy, Rhône. **C G M T**

The Bordeaux list is generally well chosen, although it does include the overhyped and overpriced vin de garage Le Dôme; the 1998 will cost you £120 a bottle. Burgundy, however, is tremendous, with lots of excellent domaines and plenty of wines under £20, too. The Rhône, Alsace (lovely Domaine Weinbach wines), the Loire, all look splendid, and J&B has one of the best German lists around. You may point out that the competition is not enormous, but really this list is spectacular. Italy is equally good: there are eight different Dolcettos from the 1999 vintage alone. And there is good New World stuff, though the focus of the list is Europe.

1994 Saarburger Rausch Riesling Kabinett, Zilliken, Mosel-Saar-Ruwer, £8.90 Zilliken's

wines are extraordinarily tense and refined. This
is just beginning to drink.
**1995 Marsannay, Les Longeroies, Domaine
Bruno Clair, £14** Lovely red Burgundy from a
rich, concentrated vintage, drinking now.

KWIKSAVE
See Somerfield.

LAITHWAITES (LAI)
New Aquitaine House, Exeter Way, Theale,
Reading, Berks RG7 4PL, orderline 0870-444
8383, fax 0870-444 8182, enquiries tel 0118-
903 0903, fax 0118-903 1073
E-MAIL orders@laithwaites.co.uk
WEB SITE www.laithwaites.co.uk
HOURS Mon–Fri 9–9, Sat–Sun 9–6 **CARDS**
DISCOUNTS Special offers **DELIVERY** £4.99 per
order **EN PRIMEUR** Australia, Bordeaux,
Burgundy, Rhône. **C M T**
*Bordeaux Direct say that they are now known as
Laithwaites because they don't want to be
associated only with Bordeaux wines. Fair enough.*

*The lists are essentially the same as those for the
Sunday Times Wine Club. I find the lists from both
establishments pretty baffling, with some wines
hyped to the skies, and others that don't mention the
growers. But there are good wines here, if you've got
the patience to trawl through endless bits of paper.*
1998 Château Rozier, St-Emilion, £10.65 This
was a very good year on the Right Bank, and this
Grand Cru has lots of concentrated spice and
plum fruit.

LAY & WHEELER (LAY)
The Wine Centre, Gosbecks Park, Colchester
CO2 9JT, (01206) 764446, fax (01206) 560002
E-MAIL sales@laywheeler.com
WEB SITE www.laywheeler.com
HOURS Mon–Sat 9–6; telephone orders Mon–Fri
8–6, Sat 8.30–4 **CARDS** Amex, MasterCard,
Switch, Visa **DISCOUNTS** 10% on 5 or more
mixed cases, £3 per case if collected **DELIVERY**
£7.95; free for orders over £150 **EN PRIMEUR**
Alsace, Australia, Bordeaux, Burgundy, California,
Germany, Italy, Rhône, Spain. **C G M T**

C = cellarage   **G** = glass loan/hire   **M** = mail order   **T** = tastings and talks

There's enough first-class Bordeaux and Burgundy to satisfy the most demanding drinker here; the Rhône, the Loire and Alsace are all excellent, and actually, so is everything else. Australia has some fascinating wines – Henschke, Veritas, Penley Estate, Vasse Felix – and there are great Californians, too. Germany is famously good here, and so is Italy: lots of interesting flavours from the south, among others. A must-have list.

1999 Bourgogne Blanc, Domaine Leflaive, c. £13.11 Marvellously pure, focused fruit with a mineral edge. Domaine Leflaive is run by Anne-Claude Leflaive, who is committed to biodynamic viticulture. The bottle price is an estimate because the wine is not yet shipped.

LAYMONT & SHAW (LA)

The Old Chapel, Millpool, Truro, Cornwall TR1 1EX, (01872) 270545, fax (01872) 223005 **E-MAIL** info@laymont-shaw.co.uk **WEB SITE** www.laymont-shaw.co.uk **HOURS** Mon–Fri 9–5 **CARDS** MasterCard, Visa **DISCOUNTS** £2.50 per case if wines collected, also £1 per case for 2 cases, £2 for 3–5, £3 for 6 or more **DELIVERY** UK mainland delivery included in wine price **MINIMUM ORDER** 1 mixed case. **G M T**

An excellent, knowledgeable list that specializes in Spain and Portugal. And when I say 'specializes', I mean that they seek out individual wines that you won't find in supermarkets because the quantities are too small. From Portugal come the wines of Montez Champalimaud, a maverick port producer who in fact concentrates on table wines of great concentration and style. There is also Luis Pato of Bairrada, who makes startlingly characterful wines unlike any other. From Spain there are lots of Riojas and wines from other well-known regions like Navarra and Penedès; there are some goodies from Ribera del Duero and Toro as well, and new-wave stuff from Priorat. The list makes the point that 'If independent wine merchants are to survive then they must offer better service than their huge rivals. We do not need to be obsessed with price-points at the expense of quality. We can offer advice, inform, even entertain.' Too right. Laymont & Shaw do all these things superbly.

1997 Ribera del Duero Teófilo Reyes, Bodegas Reyes, £17.50 All tar, mulberries and damsons,

very long and concentrated and ripe. First-class wine from an ultra-careful producer.
Manzanilla Pasada, Pastrana, Hidalgo y Cía £9.25 A superb dry sherry that combines depth with lightness, finesse and elegance.

LAYTONS

See Jeroboams.

LEA & SANDEMAN (LEA)

170 Fulham Road, London SW10 9PR, 020-7244 0522, fax 020-7244 0533 • 211 Kensington Church Street, London W8 7LX, 020-7221 1982 • 51 Barnes High Street, London SW13 9LN, 020-8878 8643 **E-MAIL** info@leaandsandeman.co.uk **HOURS** Mon–Sat 10–8 **CARDS** Amex, MasterCard, Switch, Visa **DISCOUNTS** 5–15% by case, other discounts, 10 cases or more **DELIVERY** £5 for less than 1 case; free 1 case or more London, and to UK mainland south of Perth on orders over £250 **EN PRIMEUR** Bordeaux, Burgundy, Cahors. **C G M T**

Lea & Sandeman is increasingly a Burgundy specialist, and there's a succession of excellent names, chosen with great care. But you'll also find fascinating wines from all corners of Europe here: L&S really do seek out unknown treasures, so it's worth taking the time to study the list carefully. This is also a remarkably honest list, pointing out when they think a wine is less fine than its stablemate, or when a grower reckons he picked a bit too late. Well, they can afford to be honest with wines like these. There are a few wines from the Rhône, Alsace and the Loire, and the south of France is well represented. Bordeaux is interesting, with wines at all price levels. Italy is good, as well, and there are short but fascinating ranges from other countries – the US, Spain, Australia, South Africa.
1999 Mâcon Pierreclos, Domaine Guffens-Heynen, £11.95 Round and balanced Mâcon from the region's most outstanding estate.
2000 Pinot Grigio La Casteletta, Boccadigabbia, £8.50 Minerally, spicy wine from the Italian Marches. Intense and full with a very long finish.
1995 Cabernet Sauvignon, Robert Keenan Winery, Spring Mountain, £23.95 Deep, rich, ripe Cabernet from California, very chocolaty and with fine tannins.

LIBERTY WINES (LIB)

Unit A53, New Covent Garden Food Market, London SW8 5EE, 020-7720 5350, fax 020-7720 6158
E-MAIL order@libertywine.co.uk
HOURS 7.30–5.30 **CARDS** Mastercard, Switch, Visa **DELIVERY** Free 1 mixed case or more **MINIMUM ORDER** 1 mixed case. **M**
The Californian side of this list is on the increase, with Seghesio and Testarossa leading the way. There are new producers too from Australia's Hunter Valley, from the Loire – Clos Baudoin in Vouvray – and from the Rhône. They join a list that majors in Italy, with superb wines and pretty well all the best producers from all over the country. If you want Aldo Conterno, Aldo Vajra, Allegrini, Pieropan, Castelnuovo Berardenga, Fontodi – I could go on – Liberty Wines should be your first port of call.
2000 Viognier, Lindsay Hill, £11.95 The problem with Viognier is getting the right amount of flavour into the grapes: this one, from the Hunter Valley, succeeds brilliantly.
1999 Chardonnay Sleepy Hollow, Testarossa, £27.95 Complex, nutty wine from a new small-scale producer. The vineyard is in the Santa Lucia Highlands, in Monterey County.

LLOYD TAYLOR WINES LTD (LLO)

Unit 6, Mercian Buildings, Shore Road, Perth PH2 8BZ, (01738) 444994, fax (01738) 447979
E-MAIL sales@lloyd-taylor-wines.com
HOURS Mon–Wed 9–5, Thur–Fri 9–5.30, Sat 12–3 **CARDS** Access, MasterCard, Switch, Visa **DELIVERY** Free UK mainland **MINIMUM ORDER** 1 mixed case **EN PRIMEUR** Bordeaux. **G M T**
A strange list, in some ways – there are lots of large-scale producers, and sometimes they're very good, like Australia's Capel Vale or Burgundy's Faiveley or Alsace's Schlumberger. But I can't see why anyone would want to stock Canard-Duchêne Champagne, though the draft list I have here passes over the wines with no comment. I advise you to do the same, and stick to producers like Barbadillo in Sanlúcar, or the well-selected red Bordeaux.
1999 Santenay, Faiveley, £14 Good village Burgundy from a lesser commune, but weighty and ripe for all that.

MAJESTIC (MAJ)

Head office Majestic House, Otterspool Way, Watford, Herts WD25 8WW, (01923) 298200, fax (01923) 819105. 95 stores nationwide
E-MAIL info@majestic.co.uk
WEB SITE www.majestic.co.uk
HOURS Mon–Sat 10–8, Sun 10–6 (may vary)
CARDS Amex, Diners, MasterCard, Switch, Visa **DELIVERY** Free UK mainland **MINIMUM ORDER** 1 mixed case **EN PRIMEUR** Bordeaux, Port. **G M T**
This has long been one of the best places to come for Champagne, with a good range and good discounts for buying in quantity. Elsewhere the range is a bit mixed, with real stars rubbing shoulders with some relatively undistinguished names. At the moment the stars seem to have more space than the others, which is good news. The Loire is good, as are Alsace, Germany, Italy, Chile and most of the New World.
1997 Amarone della Valpolicella, Tedeschi, £12.99 Wonderfully rich north Italian red, full of prunes and bitter cherries.

MARKS & SPENCER (MAR)

Head office Michael House, 47–67 Baker Street, London W1A 1DN, 020-7935 4422; 293 licensed stores nationwide
WEB SITE www.marksandspencer.com
HOURS Variable **DISCOUNTS** 12 bottles for the price of 11. **T**
Safe, fruity, well-made wines from large-scale producers. M&S wines are perfectly good examples of their type, but most of them won't startle you with character. They're crowd-pleasers rather than trailblazers.
1997 Trilogy, Warwick Estate, South Africa, £9.99 Warwick Estate has long been one of South Africa's most reliable top performers, and this Bordeaux blend is classically balanced and structured.

MAYFAIR CELLARS (MAY)

Miniver House, 19–20 Garlick Hill, London EC4V 2AL, 020-7329 8899, fax 020-7329 8880
E-MAIL sales@mayfaircellars.co.uk
HOURS Mon–Fri 8.30–6.00, **CARDS** Access,

C = cellarage   **G** = glass loan/hire   **M** = mail order   **T** = tastings and talks

MasterCard, Visa **DELIVERY** England & Wales free; Scotland ring for details
MINIMUM ORDER 1 mixed case
EN PRIMEUR Bordeaux, Burgundy. **C M T**
There are some excellent producers at this merchant: from Alsace, for example, there are Albert Mann and Bruno Sorg, and from the Saar there is Schloss Saarstein. The Pfalz has Rainer Lingenfelder and the Nahe, Paul Anheuser, though it has to be said that none of these names are represented in great depth. Italy looks promising as well, and there are good names from Burgundy. Mayfair Cellars has also just taken on Lalla Gully from Australia – now, I can't claim to know about these things, but wasn't that one of the Teletubbies?
1998 Rosso Conero, Alessandro Moroder, £7.95 *Spicy, strawberryish red from the Italian Marches.*

MILLÉSIMA (MI)

87 Quai de Paludate, BP 89, 33038 Bordeaux Cedex, France, 0033 557 808813, fax 0033 557 808819, Freephone 00800 267 33289 or 0800 917 0352

E-MAIL millesima@millesima.com
WEB SITE www.millesima.com
HOURS Mon–Fri 8–5.30 **CARDS** MasterCard, Switch, Visa **DELIVERY** Free for orders over £500. Otherwise £20 **EN PRIMEUR** Bordeaux.
C M
Millésima describes itself as 'Your négociant in Bordeaux', and indeed it is: as well as being a merchant, selling by the case (which can be mixed), it is a Bordeaux négociant, operating in Bordeaux's Byzantine internal marketplace. This could mean paying one mark-up less and so getting better prices, but the Bordeaux system is so complicated that it's always worth comparing prices with those of other merchants. The selection of Bordeaux is very good, and it's particularly good if you want big bottles like magnums, double magnums, jeroboams or imperiales. There are wines from outside Bordeaux, and they tend to be a sprinkling of top established names: Hugel, Zind-Humbrecht and Trimbach in Alsace, Guigal and Jaboulet in the Rhône. From further afield there is Quinta do Crasto from Portugal, Gaja and Sassicaia from Italy. If you know what you want,

this is a very good place to find it. But it's not a source of new discoveries.

1998 Sarget de Gruaud-Larose, St-Julien, £15.83 The second wine of the reliable Château Gruaud-Larose. If you want the Grand Vin of the same year, it costs £38.33.

1997 Le Petit-Cheval, St-Emilion, £26.66 The vintage wasn't a great one, but it's drinking very well now. This is the second wine of Cheval Blanc (£89.16 a bottle for the Grand Vin of the same year) and is very hard to find.

MILLE VIGNES

90 rue Carnot, 62930 Wimereux, 0033 3 21 32 60 13, fax 0033 3 21 32 56 37
E-MAIL nick@millevignes.com
WEB SITE www.millevignes.com
HOURS Tues–Sat 10–1.30 & 3–7, Sun 10–1, Closed Mon **CARDS** MasterCard, Maestro, Visa
DISCOUNTS 7.5% on 60–119 bottles, 10% on 120 bottles or more. **T**

Worth a visit next time you're in Calais, as they don't ship to the UK. Burgundy looks particularly good here, with Olivier Merlin, Tollot-Beaut and Bonneau du Martray (the last is Corton-Charlemagne 1994, FF399). Champagne is from Billecart-Salmon, among others, and the Rhône looks good – better than Bordeaux, actually, though Mille Vignes say the list changes constantly. The one they sent us also had the delicious Vouvrays of Domaine du Clos de Naudin.

1998 Mâcon la Roche-Vineuse Les Cras, Olivier Merlin, FF115 Merlin is a tremendously careful grower, and this white is made from low-yielding old vines for depth and character.

MONTRACHET (MON)

59 Kennington Road, London SE1 7PZ, 020-7928 1990, fax 020-7928 3415
E-MAIL admin@montrachetwine.com
WEB SITE www.montrachetwine.com
HOURS Office/mail order Mon–Fri 8.30–5.30,
CARDS MasterCard, Visa **DELIVERY** England and Wales £5 plus VAT 1 case, free 2 or more cases; Scotland ring for details **MINIMUM ORDER** 1 unmixed case **EN PRIMEUR** Bordeaux, Burgundy. **M T**

An impressive range, with Chablis featuring William Fèvre and Jean Brocard. In the Côte d'Or there are wines from Marquis d'Angerville, Lucien Boillot, Louis Carillon, Jacques Gagnard-Delagrange, Comte de Vogüé; the Rhône includes top names such as Bernard Gripa, Marc Sorrel. Bordeaux is also excellent at all price levels. So is Germany, which is very much a speciality. So you'll find a big range from the agency Lingenfelder in the Pfalz. Rainer Lingenfelder is a slightly batty character with, apparently, an obsession with the letter Y. He's named a Silvaner Ypsilon, and declassified it to table wine so as to be able to spell the grape the French way, Sylvaner, and he makes a Dornfelder called Onyx.

1999 Volnay 1er Cru Fremiets, £23.50 All ripe cherries on the palate, with good backbone.
1999 Meursault 1er Cru Charmes, £24.48 A beautifully honeyed and nutty Meursault with lots of cream and weight.

MORENO WINES (MOR)

11 Marylands Road, London W9 2DU, 020-7286 0678, fax 020-7286 0513
E-MAIL morenowi@dialstart.net
HOURS Mon–Wed 4–10, Thur–Fri 4–10.30, Sat 10–10.30, Sun 12–8 **CARDS** Amex, MasterCard, Switch, Visa **DISCOUNTS** 5% 1 or 2 cases, 10% 3 or more cases **DELIVERY** Free locally. **C G M T**

This Spanish specialist has a new range of wines called Poema from Aragon, which are cheap and very cheerful; it also has Getariako Txakolina from the Basque country, which at £11.25 can hardly be described as good value unless you want to pass a merry hour getting your friends to pronounce it. There's also Vega Sicilia and Pesquera and buckets of Priorat. And if what you crave is old vintages of classic wines like Marqués de Murrieta, they've got those as well. From outside Spain there are some Portuguese wines, plus some from Argentina, Bolivia, Chile and Oregon.

1999 Marqués de Alella Clásico, Parxet, £5.99 I have a weakness for the Pansa Blanca grape, which is what this is: it's true that it's only boring old Xarel-lo under a different name, but in Alella it really does take on some lovely lime cordial flavour.

C = cellarage   **G** = glass loan/hire   **M** = mail order   **T** = tastings and talks

1995 Priorat, Clos Mogador, £25 Cult wine that is as beefy as they come – but can be drunk early.

MORRIS & VERDIN (MV)

10 The Leathermarket, Weston Street, London SE1 3ER, 020-7357 8866, fax 020-7357 8877 **E-MAIL** info@m-v.co.uk
HOURS Mon–Fri 8–6 **DISCOUNTS** 10% unmixed cases; further discounts 10 or more cases **DELIVERY** Free central London and Oxford; elsewhere £10 up to 3 cases, free 4 or more **MINIMUM ORDER** 1 mixed case **EN PRIMEUR** Bordeaux, Burgundy. **C G M T**

M&V are, they say, 'moving by stealth into the kaleidoscopic vinous world of Italy, unable to resist the excitement of so many extraordinary native varieties and winemaking styles any longer.' So far there's only a Dolcetto from Servetti and a Greco di Tufo from Benito Ferrara, but more are promised. At the moment the list focuses on France – especially Burgundy – Germany, and California. From Spain there is Vega Sicilia, from Hungary the glorious Tokaji Oremus, from Portugal Quinta de la Rosa, and from Austria, Prager and Dr Unger. New Zealand has Isabel Estate, Gunn Estate and Clos de Ste Anne, the latter being the ultra-super range from biodynamic producer Millton Vineyards. A surprisingly high proportion of M&V's producers seem to have tried philosophy first, then given it up for wine. Curious, that.
1998 Pinot Noir Naboth's Vineyard, Clos de Ste Anne, £13.05 An unfiltered, wild-yeast-fermented number from New Zealand, aged in old Burgundy barrels.

WILLIAM MORRISON SUPERMARKETS (MORR)

Head office Wakefield 41 Industrial Estate, Wakefield, West Yorkshire WF2 0XF, (01924) 870000, fax (01924) 875250 100 licensed branches **HOURS** Variable, generally 8–8 **CARDS** MasterCard, Switch, Visa. **G T**
A good range of inexpensive, often tasty wines. The whole world is covered pretty effectively, though there's not much danger of dying of excitement.
1999 Brown Brothers Late-Picked Muscat, £5.99 Sweet dessert wine from Australia, and good value.

NADDER WINES LTD

See Stevens Garnier.

NEW ZEALAND WINES DIRECT (NZW)

PO Box 476, London NW5 2NZ, 020-7482 0093, fax 020-7267 8400 **E-MAIL** margaret.harvey@btinternet.com **WEB SITE** www.fwnz.co.uk
HOURS Mon–Sat 9–5 **CARDS** MasterCard, Visa **DISCOUNTS** 2 or more cases **DELIVERY** Free UK mainland, £15 per case N Ireland **MINIMUM ORDER** 1 mixed case. **M T**

Margaret Harvey was a pioneer of New Zealand wines in this country, and she has a small but good list from names like Ata Rangi, Te Motu (Waiheke Vineyards), Aotea, Kumeu River, Hunters, Waipara West and others. New this year are Quartz Reef in Central Otago and Pegasus Bay in Waipara.
1999 Pinot Noir, Quartz Reef, £16 Ripe and supple Pinot from Central Otago.

LE NEZ ROUGE (NEZ)

Berkmann Wine Cellars, 10/12 Brewery Road, London N7 9NH, 020-7609 4711, fax 020-7607 0018
• Pagendam Pratt, Unit 456, Thorpe Arch Trading Estate, Wetherby, Yorkshire LS23 7BJ, (01937) 844711, fax (01973) 541058
• T M Robertson, 10 Gilmore Place, Edinburgh EH3 9PA, 0131-229 4522
E-MAIL info@berkmann.co.uk
WEB SITE www.berkmann.co.uk
HOURS Mon–Fri 9–5.30 **CARDS** MasterCard, Switch, Visa **DISCOUNTS** £3.50 per unmixed case collected **DELIVERY** Free for 1 case or more to UK mainland (excluding the Highlands) **MINIMUM ORDER** 1 mixed case.
C G M

Lots more New World wines are joining the list here: Santa Rita from Chile, Bulletin Place from South Australia (Len Evans' new label) and lots of South Africans. But France hasn't been forgotten: there are Loire wines from Sauvion, Dagueneau and others, Chablis from Jean-Marc Brocard, good Burgundies from a stack of good growers, and Beaujolais from Duboeuf. Claret looks largely affordable. Italy has a range of wines from Antinori, including the beautiful whites from Castello della

Sala. The top wine, Cervaro della Sala, is around £22 so perhaps I'd better pick something else. Antinori also owns the house of Prunotto in Piedmont, so there are Barolos and Barbarescos here, too.

1998 Muscadet de Sèvre et Maine sur lie, Château du Cléray, £6.25 No, I haven't lost my senses; I'm just starting to rediscover Muscadet. For the last ten years I've been delighted to have forgotten it, and it's coming as a great surprise to see again how good it can be.

1998 Syrabec, Syrconnection, £9.95 This is a blend of Syrah and Malbec from the Coteaux du Languedoc; there's also Syrache, which is Syrah and Grenache, and Syraz, which is pure Syrah. The structure is lovely, and the fruit is distinctly classy.

JAMES NICHOLSON (NI)

27A Killyleagh Street, Crossgar, Co. Down, Northern Ireland BT30 9DG, 028-4483 0091, fax 028-4483 0028
E-MAIL info@jnwine.com
WEB SITE www.jnwine.com
HOURS Mon–Sat 10–7 **CARDS** Access, MasterCard, Switch, Visa **DISCOUNTS** 10% mixed case **DELIVERY** Free in Eire and Northern Ireland; UK mainland £6.95, 12 bottles or more **EN PRIMEUR** Bordeaux, Burgundy, California.
G M T
The south of France is a strength here – in fact most regions of France look rather appealing. There's a good selection of affordable Burgundy – as affordable as decent Burgundy ever is, anyway – and the Loire and Rhône are full of interest. Spain has some lovely new-wave wines from the likes of Telmo Rodriguez and Cellers de Capçanes, and there's some excellent drinking from Germany, with names like von Buhl, von Kesselstatt and Dr Loosen. You won't go far wrong in Italy either, with Anselmi, Castello di Fonterutoli and others. Australia is well chosen, and there are the Oregon Pinots of Domaine Drouhin. A list which shows just how much variety there is to be found at reasonable prices.

1999 Gamay, Domaine de la Charmoise, Touraine, £5.75 Good concentrated stuff with lots of juicy fruit and some elegance. Excellent summer red from the Loire.

1997 Finca la Sarda, Navarra £8.85 A Bordeaux blend that shows how good Navarra can be when somebody puts their mind to it.

THE NOBODY INN (NO)

Doddiscombsleigh, Nr Exeter, Devon EX6 7PS, (01647) 252394, fax (01647) 252978
E-MAIL inn.nobody@virgin.net
WEB SITE www.thenobodyinn.com
HOURS Mon–Sat 12–2.30 & 6–11 (summer), 6–11 (winter), Sun 12–3 & 7–10.30; or by appointment **CARDS** Amex, MasterCard, Switch, Visa **DISCOUNTS** 5% per case **DELIVERY** £7.20 for 1 case, 2 or more cases £3.20 per case. **G M T**
What I want to know is this: where do they keep all this wine? The selection is extraordinary. It's also extraordinary at all price levels: there are masses of interesting wines at affordable levels, and there's also some 1959 Yquem at £500 a bottle, which apparently is less than auction price. Everywhere is brilliant: France, Germany, California, Italy, you name it. The list is the same as the one used in the restaurant, and the mark-ups on the restaurant prices are not high. Other restaurants, take note.

1996 Colome Tinto Fino, Vinas de Davalos, £14.57 Licorice- charcoal-, bitter chocolate- and cherry-flavoured wine, with soft tannins. Masses of character – very good indeed.

ODDBINS (OD)

Head office 31–33 Weir Road, London SW19 8UG, 020-8944 4400, fax 020-8944 4411
Mail order Oddbins Delivers, 0870-601 0015, fax 0870-601 0069. 249 shops
WEB SITE www.oddbins.com
HOURS Generally Mon–Sat 10–10, Sun 10–8 in England & Wales, 12.30–8 Scotland **CARDS** Access, Amex, MasterCard, Switch, Visa **DISCOUNTS** 5% split case wine. 7 bottles of Champagne and sparkling wine for the price of 6 **DELIVERY** Free locally from most shops **EN PRIMEUR** Bordeaux. **G M T**
It's easy to think of Oddbins as a New World specialist, but actually it has a pretty serious list of classic Europeans as well. Your local branch may not have the full range, but isn't that what the Internet is for? Vintages are mostly the not-utterly-thrilling 1997 and the considerably better 1998.

There are some nice Beaujolais – a wine which doesn't look so expensive these days, and which makes a welcome change from the general run of over-concentrated, over-extracted reds. Burgundy, the Loire and the Rhône also look good, and there's a pretty extensive range from Greece, a country of which Oddbins was the pioneer. Italy looks decent, but Australia is where Oddbins really comes into its own: 42 Aussie Chardonnays to choose from at the last count.

2000 Falanghina, Feudi di San Gregorio, £6.79
This is the sort of thing I like: Falanghina is a rare white grape from the south of Italy, quite aromatic but well-built enough for food.

PAULSON RARE WINE

Postfach 1250, 94062 Waldkirchen, Germany, 0049 08581 910145, fax 0049 08581 910147
E-MAIL sales@rare-wine.com
WEB SITE www.rare-wine.com
CARDS Amex, Eurocard, MasterCard, Visa
DELIVERY Price on application.
A German merchant that operates principally via the Internet. It lives up to its name with Bordeaux and Burgundy back to the 1920s and, on the list they sent us, 1947 Moulin à Vent. They warn that they sell out quickly, but I suppose it's possible they may still have the Beaujolais by the time you read this. They may also still have the 1950 Luxembourg Vin de Moselle, unless some Luxembourgeois collector has pounced. They have old Riojas and Italian wines too, and of course modern vintages.

1943 Lalanne, Aragon, £71.43 I haven't the faintest idea what this is like, but I believe the Lalanne family discovered the Somontano region of northern Spain in the 1890s. Whatever this is, it should be mature by now.

PENISTONE COURT WINE CELLARS (PEN)

The Railway Station, Penistone, Sheffield, South Yorkshire S36 6HP, (01226) 766037, fax (01226) 767310
E-MAIL pcwc@dircon.co.uk
HOURS Mon–Fri 10–6, Sat 10–3 **DELIVERY** Free locally, rest of UK mainland charged at cost 1 case or more. **G M**

There are good wines but few surprises on this list: it's a list for those who want the same producers over and over again, and names they recognize. And why not? Spain has Torres, Martínez Bujanda, Vega Sicilia and a few others; Italy has Banfi, Castello Vicchiomaggio and others – quite a good list here, actually – and Australia has names like Brown Brothers, Penfolds, Lindemans, Wynns and Pipers Brook. California looks interesting, with Sonoma-Cutrer, Swanson, Simi and Far Niente, and there's Domaine Drouhin from Oregon. Loire is Mellot, Alsace Wunsch et Mann and Rhône mostly Chapoutier and Guigal. So you're in good hands.

1998 Blaufränkisch Goldberg, J. Heinrich, £6.99
Light redcurranty red from Austria, unusual and appealing.

PHILGLAS & SWIGGOT

21 Northcote Road, London SW11 1NG, 020-7924 4494, fax 020-7642 1308
E-MAIL karen@philglasandswiggot.co.uk
HOURS Mon–Sat 10–7.30, Sun 12–6 **CARDS** Amex, MasterCard, Switch, Visa **DISCOUNTS** 5% per case **DELIVERY** Free 1 case West End, Wandsworth and other South London boroughs, elsewhere £7. **G M T**
A very good list, although looking a bit pricy in places. P&S started off as Australian specialists and still have an excellent Aussie selection – and of subtle, interesting wines, not blockbuster brands. The same philosophy applies to the wines they buy from elsewhere, so you'll find serious Italians and lots of good French – Burgundy is particularly noteworthy. Austria fits the bill nicely and the Chilean and Argentinian sections are above average. This is a good place to come for dessert wines, too, and sherry.

1997 Santa Rita Triple C, £12.50 The grapes, in case you hadn't guessed, are Cabernet Sauvignon and Franc, plus Carmenère; a very modern, lush and structured Chilean red, with finesse as well.

1999 Riesling Mount Barker, Plantagenet, £8.99
Crisp, fresh and minerally, with perfect focus, from a relatively cool area in the Great Southern region of Western Australia.

C = cellarage   **G** = glass loan/hire   **M** = mail order   **T** = tastings and talks

CHRISTOPHER PIPER WINES (PIP)

I Silver Street, Ottery St Mary, Devon EX11
1DB, (01404) 814139, fax (01404) 812100
WEB SITE www.chrispiperwines.freeserve.co.uk
HOURS Mon–Fri 8.30–5.30, Sat 9–4.30 **CARDS**
Access, MasterCard, Switch, Visa **DISCOUNTS**
5% mixed case, 10% 3 or more cases **DELIVERY**
Free for 4 cases, otherwise £7.05 **MINIMUM**
ORDER I mixed case **EN PRIMEUR** Bordeaux,
Burgundy, Rhône. **C G M T**

*Oh, Oh, Oh what a lovely list. There's nothing
routine here – just pages and pages of interesting,
well chosen wines: lots of Sauternes, for example,
and some of them are not even hideously
expensive; Burgundies from domaines of the
standing of Chantal Lescure and Rossignol-Trapet;
Beaujolais, lovely Italians and Californians and
Australians and New Zealanders and South
Africans. I could go on, but my editor will be cross if I
miss my deadline.*

**1998 Vin de Pays de l'Hérault Cabernet Franc,
Domaine des Lenthérics, £5.85** Cabernet Franc
gets far riper here than it does in Bordeaux – in
fact it's positively plummy. But there's still a
touch of cut grass to give it freshness.

**1998 Dry Country Grenache, Rockford Wines,
Barossa Valley, £10.60** Tarry, fleshy wine of
great complexity which will age brilliantly. This is
very good value.

TERRY PLATT (PLA)

Council Street West, Llandudno LL30 1ED,
(01492) 874099, fax (01492) 874788
E-MAIL plattwines@clara.co.uk
WEB SITE www.terryplattwines.co.uk
HOURS Mon–Fri 8.30–5.30 **CARDS** Amex,
MasterCard, Switch, Visa **DELIVERY** Free locally
and UK mainland 5 cases or more **MINIMUM**
ORDER I mixed case. **G M T**

*A good list that effectively skims the surface of most
regions, with a sprinkling of good growers. Australia
is strong, with Cape Mentelle, Tyrrell's and others;
California has Rodney Strong; the Loire has Pascal
Jolivet. You need to choose carefully in Burgundy.*

1998 Muscat Reserve, Trimbach, £10.28
Marvellously crunchy and fresh wine. Drink it in
the summer, in the garden.

PLAYFORD ROS (PLAY)

Middle Park House, Sowerby, Thirsk, Yorkshire
YO7 3AH, (01845) 526777, fax (01845) 526888
E-MAIL sales@playfordros.com
WEB SITE www.playfordros.com
HOURS Mon–Fri 8–5 **CARDS** MasterCard, Visa
DISCOUNTS 2.5% on orders over 6 cases
DELIVERY Free Yorkshire, Derbyshire, Durham,
Newcastle; elsewhere on UK mainland (per
case), £8.50 I case, £5.50 2 cases, £4.50 3 cases,
£3.50 4 cases, free 5 cases **MINIMUM ORDER**
I mixed case **EN PRIMEUR** Bordeaux, Burgundy.
C G M T

*A carefully chosen list, with reassuringly
recognizable representatives from Bordeaux and
Burgundy, Alsace, the Rhône and the Loire.
Australia looks exceptional, with a range that
includes some top wines like Wynn's Mountadam
The Red at £19.25. Similar standards apply
elsewhere: New Zealand, North and South
America, Spain and Germany all look good, and
Italy is excellent. But if you don't fancy splashing out*

C = cellarage   **G** = glass loan/hire   **M** = mail order   **T** = tastings and talks

£82.50 on a bottle of 1994 Sassicaia, Playford Ros has thoughtfully pulled out a selection of 'everyday' wines at around the £5 to £6 mark, from every corner of the globe. A good all-round, serious range.
2000 Château de Sours Rosé, Bordeaux, £10.32 This is, admittedly, a pretty high price for rosé, but this is good, all toast and fresh fruit.

PORTLAND WINE CO (POR)

16 North Parade, off Norris Road, Sale, Cheshire M33 3JS, 0161-962 8752, fax 0161-905 1291
• 152a Ashley Road, Hale WA15 9SA, 0161-928 0357
• 82 Chester Road, Macclesfield SK11 8DL, (01625) 616147
E-MAIL portwineco@aol.com
WEB SITE www.portlandwine.co.uk
HOURS Mon–Sat 10–10, Sun 12–3 & 7–9.30
CARDS Amex, MasterCard, Switch, Visa
DISCOUNTS 10% off 1 mixed case **DELIVERY** Free locally 1 case or more **EN PRIMEUR** Bordeaux. **G M T**
There's a promising-looking list of lesser clarets here, with some around a tenner. The southern Rhône selection looks good, and Italy is interesting – classy wines from the Veneto like Tedeschi's Amarone Classico and Pra's Soave Classico Superiore Montegrande. Portugal looks good too – and Portugal is my current benchmark for good-value, interesting flavours. Spain has interesting stuff from Valdepeñas and Priorat. The New World looks equally well chosen.
1998 Pinot Noir Don Miguel Vineyard, Marimar Torres, £19.99 Rich, balanced and perfumed. Not cheap, but then nor is Burgundy, and this is a serious competitor from California.
1998 Chianti Rufina, Selvapiana, £9.95 Selvapiana always makes such elegant Chianti.

RAEBURN FINE WINES (RAE)

21/23 Comely Bank Road, Edinburgh EH4 1DS, 0131-343 1159, fax 0131-332 5166
E-MAIL raeburn@netcomuk.co.uk
WEB SITE www.raeburnfinewines.com
HOURS Mon–Sat 9.30–6, Sun 12.30–5 **CARDS** Amex, MasterCard, Switch, Visa **DISCOUNTS** 5% unsplit case, 2.5% mixed **DELIVERY** Free local area 1 or more cases (usually); elsewhere £7.50 1–3 cases, free 4 or more **EN PRIMEUR**

Bordeaux, Burgundy, Germany, Languedoc-Roussillon, Rhône. **G M T**
Lots of wonderful wines to keep the good people of Edinburgh happy. There are oodles of Vouvrays from Huet, in vintages going back to 1924, and interesting wines from the south of France. Everything is carefully chosen: if you want obvious wines you won't like this list. They've got some red and white table wines from the Douro from the 1950s and 1960s, too, which I'd be happy to bet no-one else has; and first-class current drinking from California and South Africa.
1995 Blaufränkisch Tradition, Weinbau Pretterebner, £14.73 Good ripe, juicy red that will keep a year or two, from a producer in the Neusiedlersee-Hugelland region of Burgenland in Austria.

REID WINES (1992) LTD

The Mill, Marsh Lane, Hallatrow, Nr Bristol BS39 6EB, (01761) 452645, fax (01761) 453642
HOURS Mon–Fri 9–5.30 **CARDS** MasterCard, Visa (3% charge) **DELIVERY** Free within 25 miles of Hallatrow (Bristol), and in central London **EN PRIMEUR** Burgundy, Italy, Rhône.
C G M T
I'm sure it's unfair on Reid wines to go on quoting the worst wines from their utterly wonderful and fascinating list, but I get a bit desperate for jokes when I'm doing this directory, and Reid's is the list I look forward to most. So: 1936 Château Lestage, Listrac, £55 'Almost certainly dreadful – poor château, poorer vintage = recipe for disaster.' 1938 Château Gilette, £145, 'Probably fake.' 1962 Anjou Moulin Touchais, £42.50, 'old stock so has a chance of being vaguely genuine.' As always, a mix of great old wines, old duds and splendid current stuff. Germany, Italy, USA, port, Madeira and Cognac look tremendous.
Shiraz/Cabernet Vixen Cuvée 6 NV, Fox Creek, McLaren Vale, £9.85 Sparkling red from Australia – yum yum.
1993 Chardonnay/Welschriesling Nouvelle Vague, Kracher, £22.75 half bottle Says the list 'Kracher is thought of as one of Austria's top winemakers...PLEASE somebody buy these – I am getting so bored of tripping over them in the cellar not to mention putting them in the list.' Go on. Help them out.

LA RÉSERVE (RES)

Knightsbridge: 56 Walton Street, London SW3
1RB, 020-7589 2020, fax 020-7581 0250
• Battersea: 7 Grant Road, London SW11 2NU,
020-7978 5601, fax 020-7978 4934
• Hampstead: 29 Heath Street, Hampstead,
London NW3 6TR, 020-7435 6845, fax 020-
7431 9301
• Marble Arch: 47 Kendal Street, London W2
2BU, 020-7402 6920, fax 020-7402 5066
• Fulham: 203 Munster Road, London SW6
6BX, 020-7381 6930, fax 020-7385 5513
E-MAIL realwine@la-reserve.co.uk
WEB SITE www.la-reserve.co.uk
HOURS Vary from shop to shop **CARDS** Amex,
MasterCard, Switch, Visa **DISCOUNTS** 5% per
case except accounts **DELIVERY** Free 1 case or
more central London and orders over £200 on
UK mainland. Otherwise £7.50 **EN PRIMEUR**
Bordeaux, Burgundy, Italy, Rhône. **C G T**
*My kind of list – varied, intelligent and without a
trace of pomposity. 'The Bordelais continue to be
the most irritating of people to deal with', it says,
and I couldn't agree more. Bordeaux, Burgundy, the
Loire, Spain, Italy, North America and Australia are
all excellent, with well-chosen wines (Jermann, Gaja,
Allegrini in Italy, for example). There's nothing run-
of-the-mill here, nothing boring. Well done, La
Réserve.*
**1998 Bourgogne Rouge, Anne-Françoise Gros,
£11.95** If I'm going to spend £12 on a bottle of
basic Burgundy I'd like it to be from Anne-
Françoise Gros, because I know then that it
won't be the least bit basic. She makes lovely
wines, with great depth and character.

RICHARDSON & SONS (RIC)

2A Marlborough Street, Whitehaven, Cumbria
CA28 7LL, (01946) 65334, fax (01946) 599549
HOURS Mon–Sat 10–5.30 **CARDS** Amex, Delta,
MasterCard, Switch, Visa **DELIVERY** Free locally;
UK mainland £10 first case and £2 each
additional case; orders over £150 free **G M T**
*A patchy list – patchy geographically, that is, not in
quality. And I'm all in favour of merchants favouring
the regions they love and ignoring everything else if
they want. Far better that than something routine
and predictable. This one covers Spain and South
America, Australia, South Africa (a bit) and New*

*Zealand (barely). France is Bordeaux, Burgundy,
the South and a dribble from the Loire; there's a bit
from Italy, a bit from the USA, and that's it. But
everything is well chosen.*
**1998 Sancerre, Jean Thomas, £4.70 per half
bottle** Good classic Sancerre, grassy and
minerally.

HOWARD RIPLEY LTD (RIP)

25 Dingwall Road, London SW18 3AD
020-8877 3065, fax 020-8877 0029
E-MAIL info@howardripley.com
WEB SITE www.howardripley.com
HOURS Mon–Fri 9–8, Sat 9–1 **DELIVERY**
Minimum charge £11 plus VAT, free UK
mainland on orders over £500 ex-VAT
MINIMUM ORDER 1 mixed case **EN PRIMEUR**
Burgundy, Germany. **M T**
*If you're serious about Burgundy, this is one of
perhaps half a dozen lists that you need. Forget the
general merchants with their arrays of big négociant
houses: if you're a Burgundy freak you'll want the
small domaines, notes on the finer points of
adjacent vineyards and stocks of several vintages:
Howard Ripley manages to list as many as four
vintages of many wines. Yes, the wines are
expensive – great Burgundy is expensive, and that's
all there is to it – but they're not excessive.*
**1999 Chassagne-Montrachet Rouge, Les
Chaumes, Guy Amiot, £12.93** Howard Ripley
reckons this is a bargain, and I reckon he's right.
Guy Amiot wines are usually both reasonably
priced and utterly delicious.

ROBERSON

348 Kensington High Street, London W14 8NS,
020-7371 2121, fax 020-7371 4010
E-MAIL wines@roberson.co.uk
WEB SITE www.roberson.co.uk
HOURS Mon–Sat 10–8 **CARDS** Amex, Diners,
MasterCard, Switch, Visa **DISCOUNTS** Mail
order 5% on unmixed cases; shop 10% unmixed
cases, 5% mixed **DELIVERY** Free locally 1 case or
more, free UK mainland for orders over £150,
otherwise £5 per case **EN PRIMEUR** Bordeaux,
Burgundy, Italy. **C G M T**
*A terrific list, with fine and rare stuff from all over the
world. There's not much under a fiver here, but then
if you want the likes of Castillo Ygay 1970 you're not*

going to worry about that: Roberson is not about simple, everyday wine. All of France is excellent; so is Italy, and there's some Port from 1935.

1998 Pinot Blanc Bergheim, Marcel Deiss, £10.50 Marcel Deiss regards this as one of his simplest wines, but everything he makes is refined and subtle.

THE RSJ WINE COMPANY (RSJ)

115 Wootton Street, London SE1 8LY, 020-7633 0881, fax 020-7401 2455
E-MAIL tom.king@rsj.uk.com
WEB SITE www.rsj.uk.com
HOURS Mon–Fri 9–5, answering machine at other times **CARDS** MasterCard, Visa **DELIVERY** Free central London, minimum 1 case; England and Wales (per case), £8.25 1 case, £5.50 2 cases, £4.60 3–5 cases. **G M T**
The restaurant attached to this wine list is where Loire growers come for dinner in London. 'You can't find a wine list like this in France,' they say; and nor can you. Here, for example, you can find Muscadet with bottle age: 1989, for example. I kid you not. If it's made to age, it will age, and get wonderfully honeyed. But then this list is a roll-call of great Loire names. From Savennières there is Domaine aux Moines, from Anjou Mark Angeli, Vouvray from Huet, to mention just a few. Quite a number of these producers farm biodynamically, and it really does seem to make a difference to the flavour. But now there are wines from outside the Loire as well: Bordeaux, Beaujolais, and even the odd wine from Australia and New Zealand. Whatever next?

1998 Bourgueil Clos Senechal, Catherine and Pierre Breton, £8.95 Lovely ripe Cabernet Franc from limestone soil, and given a year in oak. It needs a bit of time, even in this fairly early-maturing vintage.

1996 Anjou Rouge Les Fouchardes, Mark Angeli, £13.80 Another star. Mark Angeli is committed to biodynamism and his wines have great complexity.

SAFEWAY (SAF)

Head office 6 Millington Road, Hayes, Middlesex UB3 4AY, 020-8848 8744, fax 020-8573 1865. 480 stores nationwide

WEB SITE www.safeway.co.uk
HOURS Mon–Sat 8–10, Sun 10–4 (most stores)
CARDS Amex, MasterCard, Switch, Visa
DISCOUNTS 5% on six or more bottles (not fortified wines and Montilla). **G**
A list which swings weirdly between the cheap and routine and the expensive and fabulous – though one wonders just how many bottles of Château Guiraud 1990 are stocked at £39.99 each. Safeways fine wine stores also stock Château Haut-Bailly 1997 at £31.99, and Château Poujeaux 1995 at £25.99. You can buy both these wines more cheaply elsewhere – see the price guides for details. You will, however, be reasonably safe if you stick to less ambitious names and prices. There's a handful of good Burgundies, including Domaine Parent's Beaune Premier Cru Les Epenottes 1998, and the New World looks good: Cloudy Bay Sauvignon 2000 is £10.99, which is excellent value.

1999 Pinot Grigio Alto Adige, St Michael-Eppan/San Michele-Appiano, £5.99 Crisp, light white from north-eastern Italy. Hats off to Safeway for stocking an Alto Adige wine.

SAINSBURY'S (SAI)

Head office Stamford House, Stamford Street, London SE1 9LL, 020-7695 6000
435 stores nationwide (including Savacentres)
WEB SITE www.sainsburys.co.uk
HOURS Variable, many open late **CARDS** Amex, MasterCard, Switch, Visa. **G**
There's a good list of affordable clarets here, though most are only available in a relatively small number of stores. As with all supermarkets, if you want a

---

C = cellarage   **G** = glass loan/hire   **M** = mail order   **T** = tastings and talks

decent range of wines you've got to go to a big branch. Strangely, the more expensive clarets are less impressive: from Margaux, for example, there is the underperforming Rauzan-Gassies. If you're going to spend £35 on a bottle of red this Guide can point you in many better directions in which to spend it. In Burgundy you'd be better off going to a specialist, though there is the odd interesting grower, like Jacques Prieur. All through the list, in fact, good names are dotted in with the routine ones. There's Sancerre from Fouassier, for example, and Chianti from Castello di San Polo in Rosso. There's also supposed to be Royal Tokaji's Tokaji Aszú 5 Puttonyos at a price of £13.99 for 50cl. **2000 Merlot, Valdivieso, £4.99** Good value stuff from a producer that always gets a bit of extra character into the wine.

SAVAGE SELECTION (SAV)

The Ox House, Market Place, Northleach, Cheltenham, Glos GL54 3EG, (01451) 860896, fax (01451) 860996. The Ox House retail shop and wine bar at same address, tel (01451) 860680
E-MAIL savage.selection@virgin.net
WEB SITE www.savageselection.co.uk
HOURS Office: Mon–Fri 9–6; shop: Tue/Wed 10–7.30, Thur–Sat 10–10, Sun/Mon closed
CARDS Amex, MasterCard, Switch, Visa
DELIVERY Free locally 1 case, elsewhere on UK mainland free 3 cases, otherwise £10 per consignment **EN PRIMEUR** Bordeaux. **C G M T**
Really well-chosen wines from names that you may never have heard of – that's because Mark Savage takes the trouble to find wines himself rather than just buy them in from other people. Savage says, 'Any idiot can make powerful wine; it is much harder, and more worthwhile, to make wine that has subtlety, delicacy, elegance and balance... I like wine to be refreshing, not exhausting.' Hear hear. So there are some glorious wines from Austria, for example, particularly the dessert wines of Heidi Schröck and the remarkable Riesling from Nikolaihof; South Africans are the cream of that country's producers and Oregon wines are from The Eyrie Vineyard and Tyee Wine Cellars. There's a wine bar now at The Ox House, and they now

serve food as well, which sounds a very cheerful way of doing your shopping.
1999 Aba da Serra Tinto, £4.75 Good, spicy, plummy, juicy red from the south of Portugal, and notably good value.
1999 Beaujolais Cuvée à l'Ancienne, Terres Dorées, £6.76 Good value again: this is an old-vine cuvée, with excellent depth and fruit.

SECKFORD WINES

Dock Lane, Melton, Suffolk IP12 1PE, (01394) 446622, fax (01394) 446633
E-MAIL sales@seckfordwines.co.uk
WEB SITE www.seckfordwines.co.uk
CARDS MasterCard, Switch, Visa **DELIVERY** £10 per consignment, UK mainland; elsewhere at cost. **MINIMUM ORDER** 1 mixed case. **C**
Seckford sent us their Bordeaux 2000 offer, and I note that it is open about wines that are not, how shall we say, quite up to scratch. Lynch-Bages is noted as having some 'rusticity to it. The tannins seemed firm, the wine sold but it lacked generosity and real flair.' Go for the Durfort-Vivens instead: 'A very subtle and attractive wine.' I agree entirely. But of course, given the hysteria currently afflicting the Bordeaux 2000 market, you might prefer to go for older vintages, and Seckford have got plenty of these, of years back to 1964. Burgundy and the Rhône are packed with top growers, and there's serious stuff from Italy, Spain, Austria and Germany as well. There's a bit from Australia, and rather less from the US and New Zealand.
1999 Riesling Loibenberg Smaragd, Emmerich Knoll, £18.50 Austrian wine is not bargain basement stuff, but this is lovely, with beautiful balance.

SOMERFIELD (SO)

Head office Somerfield House, Hawkfield Business Park, Whitchurch Lane, Bristol BS14 0TJ, 0117-935 9359. 533 Somerfield stores and 793 Kwiksave stores nationwide
WEB SITE www.somerfield.co.uk
HOURS Mon–Sat 9–8, variable late opening Friday all stores **CARDS** MasterCard, Switch, Visa
DISCOUNTS 5% off 6 bottles **DELIVERY** Small selection available via Somerfield Direct. **M T**

C = cellarage **G** = glass loan/hire **M** = mail order **T** = tastings and talks

The Languedoc looks the most interesting region here. To judge from the list, Somerfield customers don't much care for New Zealand wines, but do quite like new-style Spanish ones. They prefer Bordeaux to Burgundy, and when it comes to Australia, they like what they know. What they particularly like is the safety of Somerfield own-labels. They're prepared to experiment with different grape varieties, though. In other words a list with some decent drinking, but no surprises.

1999 Gewurztraminer, Caves de Turckheim, £5 Few supermarkets these days dare to have something as esoteric as Alsace Gewurztraminer, and Turckheim is a good reliable, inexpensive source.

1997 Petite Sirah, LA Cetto, £4.99 Earthy, chunky Mexican red.

SOMMELIER WINE CO (SOM)

23 St George's Esplanade, St Peter Port, Guernsey, Channel Islands, GY1 2BG (01481) 721677, fax (01481) 716818 **HOURS** Mon–Thur 10–5.30, Fri 10–6, Sat 9.30–5.30; 24-hour answerphone **CARDS** MasterCard, Switch, Visa **DISCOUNTS** 5% 1 case or more **DELIVERY** Free locally 1 unmixed case. Customs legislation restricts the shipping of wine to the UK mainland. **G T**

An excellent selection, this: all well-thought-out, interesting, unusual wines. It's a big selection, too: there are yards of lovely subtle Italian whites, three Viogniers from Australia (Heggies, Heathcote and Yalumba The Virgilius), and lots and lots of lovely Loires. Burgundy looks excellent, and South Africa, Chile and Argentina all look good, though Australia outdoes them all – quite rightly, since the wines are so terrific. There's hardly a wine here that I don't crave to have in my racks.

Quadratura del Cerchio, Secondo Viaggio, Roberto Cipresso, £8.25 This means 'Squaring the circle', and it doesn't have a vintage. It's a Tuscan blend of Sangiovese and Primitivo. Some claim this is a traditional blend in Tuscany, but of course they can't be right.

SPRINGBOK WINES

Unit 4a, Yorkhill Quay, Glasgow G3 8QE, (0141) 400 6065, fax (0141) 400 6068 **E-MAIL** springbokwines@hotmail.com

HOURS Mon–Fri 9–6, Sat 10–3 **CARDS** MasterCard, Switch, Visa **DISCOUNTS** 10% on an unmixed case **DELIVERY** Free central Scotland; elsewhere varies depending on area and number of cases ordered. **M T**

A South African specialist with a shortish list of wines not widely available elsewhere. Producers include Agust Wines, Cabriere Estate, Cordoba Wines, Elephant Pass Vineyard, Furter Wines, Meerlust, Morgenhof, Muratie, Sylvanvale, Verdun and Whalehaven, and there are a few wines from Chile, France and Spain.

1997 Pinot Noir, Haute Cabrière, £10.99 One of the Cape's best Pinots.

FRANK STAINTON WINES (STA)

3 Berry's Yard, Finkle Street, Kendal, Cumbria LA9 4AB, (01539) 731886, fax (01539) 730396 **E-MAIL** admin@stainton-wines.co.uk **HOURS** Mon–Sat 9–5.30 **CARDS** Access, MasterCard, Switch, Visa **DISCOUNTS** 5% mixed case **DELIVERY** Free Cumbria and North Lancashire; elsewhere (per case) £9 1 case, £6 2–4 cases, £4 5–9 cases, 10 cases free.

C G M T

There are some interesting Burgundy growers here, but on the whole Bordeaux is better. Germany is largely from Kesselstatt, a company now making greatly improved wines, and Italy has a selection of leading names, all making wines of character: among others, you'll find Allegrini's Valpolicella, and Carmignano from Capezzana. New from Chile are the wines of Casa Silva, which have real character and subtlety. Prices overall look good value, and the wines are cleverly chosen. Lucky Kendal.

1998 Château Fourcas Hosten, £11.25 Excellent value claret. Fourcas Hosten is a good, reliable Cru Bourgeois, and 1998 a well-structured year. You'll need to put this aside for a few years, but you'll be glad you did.

1999 Jurançon Sec, Domaine Cauhapé, £8.95 Lovely, characterful, spice and apricot-flavoured dry white wine from South-West France.

1999 Old Vine Semillon, Eikehof Estate, £8.20 These Semillon vines are 97 years old, apparently, and this Stellenbosch wine has great depth as a result. Good waxy flavours and balancing acidity.

J. Straker, Chadwick & Sons

—— Established 1872 ——

conduct regular auctions of

FINE, RARE AND INTERESTING WINES

throughout the year.

We offer a personal, helpful and professional service to buyers and sellers alike of single bottles or complete cellars.

NO BUYERS PREMIUM

Further information from
The Wine Department,
Market Street Chambers,
Abergavenny, Mon. NP7 5SD

Tel: 01873 852624 / Fax: 01873 857311

STEVENS GARNIER WINE MERCHANTS (STE)

47 West Way, Botley, Oxford OX2 0JF, (01865) 263303, fax (01865) 791594
E-MAIL info@stevensgarnier.co.uk
WEB SITE www.stevensgarnier.co.uk
HOURS Mon–Wed 10–6, Thur–Fri 10–7, Sat 9.30–6 **CARDS** Amex, MasterCard, Switch, Visa
DISCOUNTS 10% on an unmixed case
DELIVERY Free locally 5 days a week; 'competitive rates' elsewhere. **G T**
The south of France is a strength here, and this is one of the few places you can buy wine from Savoie. Loires are from Vacheron, Basseville in Muscadet and others, and Rhônes are from Chapoutier and Max Aubert. Alsace is from Pierre Sparr, Portugal from Sogrape. The New World follows the same pattern of well-known, established names with no surprises. That being said, the wines are generally very good, and there's quite a lot under a fiver. A good, reliable list.
1999 Nobilis Dry Rosé, Sogrape, £4.75 Very good crisp rosé with plenty of fruit and a touch of spice. Reliable and delicious.

SUNDAY TIMES WINE CLUB (SUN)

New Aquitaine House, Exeter Way, Theale, Reading, Berks RG7 4PL, 0118-903 0903, fax 0118-903 1073; order line 0870 220 0010, fax 0870-220 0030
E-MAIL orders@wine-club.co.uk
WEB SITE www.sundaytimeswineclub.co.uk
HOURS Mail order, 24-hr answerphone **CARDS** Amex, Diners, MasterCard, Switch, Visa
DISCOUNTS On special offers **DELIVERY** £4.99 per order **EN PRIMEUR** Australia, Bordeaux, Burgundy, Rhône. **C M T**
The associate mail order company of Laithwaites, with essentially the same list. The membership fee is £10 per annum. The club also runs tours and tastings and an annual festival in London, and does monthly promotions to its members. See Laithwaites for more details.

T & W WINES (TW)

51 King Street, Thetford, Norfolk IP24 2AU, (01842) 765646, fax (01842) 766407
E-MAIL contact@tw-wines.co.uk
WEB SITE www.tw-wines.co.uk
HOURS Mon–Fri 9.30–5.30, Sat 9.30–1.00
CARDS Amex, Diners, MasterCard, Visa
DELIVERY (most areas) 7–47 bottles £10.95 plus VAT, 4 or more cases free **EN PRIMEUR** Burgundy. **C G M T**
There's another peculiar watercolour on the cover of this year's list – I feel I ought to warn you so that you don't leave it around to be seen by persons of a nervous disposition. It claims to be a plum pudding, but reminds me more of an illustration for the sort of thriller where a bleeding head is found in a sack. Anyway. Prices for wines are not low here, but the list is a good one, featuring Burgundies from Joseph Matrot, Daniel Defaix and Domaine Guillemot-Michel (sweet white Mâcon), and if you like sherry, as every civilized person does, you'll find single-vineyard wines here. Loire wines come from luminaries like Huet and Charles Joguet, and from Sauternes there are the wines of Château Gilette, which are aged for decades in cement vats before release; the youngest wine here is 1962.
1976 Riesling, Cuvée Frederic Emile, Trimbach, £42.30 per half bottle The ideal wine if you're both very rich and not at all greedy.

TANNERS (TAN)

26 Wyle Cop, Shrewsbury, Shropshire SY1
1XD, (01743) 234500, fax (01743) 234501
• 4 St Peter's Square, Hereford HR1 2PG,
(01432) 272044, fax (01432) 263316 • 36 High
Street, Bridgnorth WV16 4DB, (01746) 763148
•Severn Farm Enterprise Park, Welshpool SY21
7DF, (01938) 552542, fax (01938) 556565
E-MAIL sales@tanners-wines.co.uk
WEB SITE www.tanners-wines.co.uk
HOURS Shrewsbury Mon–Sat 9–6, branches
9–5.30 **CARDS** Amex, MasterCard, Switch, Visa
DISCOUNTS 5% I mixed case (cash &
collection); 2.5% for 3 mixed cases, 5% for 5,
7.5% for 10 (mail order) **DELIVERY** Free I
mixed case or more locally, or nationally over
£80, otherwise £5.95 **EN PRIMEUR** Bordeaux,
Burgundy, Rhône, Port. **G M T**

*The sort of list from which it's extremely difficult to
choose, because you simply want everything on it.
And since one of everything is never enough (if you
like it you'll want another bottle) drinking one's way
through Tanners' stock could be a real problem.
There are lots of lovely white Rhônes and even
more lovely red Rhônes, with some new growers
added this year: Leméncier, Montagne d'Or and
Colombier. Bordeaux and Burgundy are both
terrific; there's some very interesting Spanish stuff;
Italy looks very good; and Germany looks
wonderful: obviously somebody's buying enough of
the stuff to encourage Tanners to go on selling it.
Hooray. Australia, South Africa and California all
show what these places can do, with the biggest
selection coming from Australia. Now there's a
surprise.*

**Champagne, Tanners Brut Extra Réserve
Spécial, £14.20** Very good value non-vintage
Champagne: it's got fresh, biscuity fruit, good
length and plenty of elegance.
**1998 Château Doisy-Daëne Vin Blanc Sec,
£11.75** One of the best of all dry wines from
Sauternes châteaux. This is rich, with lots of fresh
flavour.

TESCO (TES)

Head office Delamare Road, Cheshunt, Herts
EN8 9SL, (01992) 632222, fax (01992) 630794,
Customer Service (0800) 505555.
566 licensed branches
WEB SITE www.tesco.co.uk
HOURS Variable (open Sunday) **CARDS**
MasterCard, Switch, Visa **DISCOUNT** 5% on 6
bottles or more **EN PRIMEUR** Bordeaux.
G M T

*This is looking increasingly like a place to do some
serious wine shopping – shopping like St Hallett
Old Block Shiraz from the Barossa at £14.99,
Saintsbury Carneros Pinot Noir at £13.99 and
Valdivieso Cabernet Franc Reserva at £8.99. Not
bargain basement wines, you'll agree. There are lots
of cheapies here for when your budget is strictly of
the baked-bean-and-scrambled-egg sort, but when
you're flush with cash do take a look at the better
wines. I'm not sure that I'd cross the road for the
Burgundies, I'd certainly cross the road to avoid the
Germans, and the thought of Mexican Chardonnay
does not make my eyes light up, but credit where
credit's due. Australia seems to inspire the good
buyers of Tesco most. Well, I'm not about to argue
with that. A thought, though: what is it about the
word 'finest' that makes one instantly distrustful?
Tesco has a Tesco Finest Coonawarra Cabernet
Sauvignon at £6.99 and a Tesco Finest Margaux at
£10.99 and a Tesco Finest Red Burgundy at £6.49,
and so on and so forth. Now, in my experience the
finest Coonawarra Cab costs a great deal more
than that. The same goes for the finest Margaux
and the finest red Burgundy. A pity they feel they
have to resort to this sort of fake poshness.*
**1996 Cabernet Sauvignon St George,
Lindemans, £16.99** Classic minty Aussie stuff
with great intensity and balance.

THRESHER (THR)

See First Quench.

TURVILLE VALLEY WINES (TUR)

The Firs, Potter Row, Great Missenden, Bucks
HP16 9LT (01494) 868818, fax (01494) 868832
E-MAIL info@turville-valley-wines.com
WEB SITE www.turville-valley-wines.com
HOURS Mon–Fri 9–5.30 **CARDS** None
DELIVERY By arrangement **MINIMUM ORDER**
£300, minimum 12 bottles. **C M**

| **C** = cellarage | **G** = glass loan/hire | **M** = mail order | **T** = tastings and talks |

Serious wines for serious spenders. The Bordeaux is all classic stuff – no lesser wines here – and there are buckets of DRC Burgundies. There are top names too from Spain, Italy, the Rhône, California (there are five bottles of Screaming Eagle on the current list, if you feel inspired to spend £1200) and odds and ends from all over.

1990 Romanée Conti, Domaine de la Romanée Conti, £3113.75 How about this for a serious wine?

UNWINS (UN)

Head office Birchwood House, Victoria Road, Dartford, Kent DA1 5AJ, (01322) 272711, fax (01322) 294469; 451 branches in South-East England
E-MAIL info@unwins.co.uk
WEB SITE www.unwins.co.uk
HOURS Variable, usually Mon–Sat 10–10, Sun 11–10 **CARDS** Amex, Diners, MasterCard, Switch, Visa **DISCOUNTS** 10% mixed case, 5% on six bottles **DELIVERY** Free locally
EN PRIMEUR Bordeaux. **C G M T**
Unwins' purchase of the Fullers shops has given it rather more presence on the High Street than it had before, and the list seems to have improved, too. Gone are the days when I could pass an Unwins shop with hardly a second glance: nowadays they actually have wines I want. There are good flavours from South America, and there's Opus One from North America if you happen to have £90 or so going spare; there are some serious clarets, too. Alsace is reliable, with Kuentz-Bas and the Turckheim co-op, and Australia looks good. Parts of Europe – Spain, for example – aren't bad but could do with a revamp to update them a little. Italy has just had that, it seems, and there are some interesting new wines, though it would be nice to see some of the old ones being chucked.

1997 Shiraz, Balbi, £5.49 Good juicy-spicy stuff from Argentina. It's got structure, too.
1996 Pyrus, Lindemans, £16.99 This old favourite Bordeaux blend looks decent value against many clarets of the same price.
2000 Fiano di Avellino Pietracaida, Feudi di San Gregorio, £8.99 A single-vineyard, late-harvested example of this lesser-known Italian white. It has lots of minerally fruit streaked with honey and figs.

VALVONA & CROLLA (VA)

19 Elm Row, Edinburgh EH7 4AA,
0131-556 6066, fax 0131-556 1668
E-MAIL wine@valvonacrolla.co.uk
WEB SITE www.valvonacrolla.com
HOURS Mon–Wed 8–6, Thur–Fri 8–7.30, Sat 8–6 **CARDS** Amex, MasterCard, Switch, Visa
DISCOUNTS 7% 1-3 cases, 10% 4 or more
DELIVERY Free on orders over £100, £5 otherwise for 8 day service, £8 for next day service. **G M T**
There's a nice list of Australian wines here (names like Mount Langi Ghiran and Cape Mentelle), some quirky Californians (Ridge for example), some good Spanish wines and the odd bottle from the south of France or Germany, but they are not what V&C is about. It's an Italian shop, run by Italians for, I suppose, Scots – plus anyone else who wants to avail themselves of mail order. And you know, if you're fond of Italian wines you should be shopping here. The list has three closely printed pages of wines from Piedmont, and three-and-a-half from Tuscany; that's not to mention the wines from Lombardy, Basilicata, the Marche, Sicily, the Veneto, and the page of dessert wines. It's a simply fabulous selection, and at all prices. V&C demonstrates very successfully that if you want interesting flavours on a budget Italy should be at the top of your list. Yes, the names are often unfamiliar, but that's what wine merchants are for, isn't it?

1994 Frascati Superiore Colle Gaio, Colli Catone, £19.95 Hang on – 1994 Frascati? Have I gone mad? I have not. This is serious Malvasia of concentration and depth, and it's terrific. Trust me. Or if that's out of the question, trust V&C.

VICTORIA WINE (VIC)

See First Quench.

LA VIGNERONNE

105 Old Brompton Road, London SW7 3LE,
020-7589 6113, fax 020-7581 2983
E-MAIL lavig@aol.com
WEB SITE www.lavigneronne.co.uk
HOURS Mon–Fri 10–8, Sat 10–6 **CARDS** Amex, Diners, MasterCard, Switch, Visa
DISCOUNTS 5% mixed case (collected)

DELIVERY Free locally, £10 mainland England and Wales for orders under £250; mainland Scotland at cost **EN PRIMEUR** Bordeaux, Burgundy, Rhône. **M T**

They do have classic wines here – in fact rather good ones, to judge from their offer of 1998 Burgundies. But one always associates the shop with the quirky and just-discovered, with unknown names and properties they've found for themselves. The south of France is a particular love, and there are classics like Mas Jullien, Daumas Gassac, Domaine Tempier and Domaine de Trévallon, plus hard-to-find wines like Château Simone's Palette. But there are lots of others, too.

1999 Marmandais Rosé, Chante Coucou, £12 *An unfiltered rosé which improves in bottle – how about that? The Côtes du Marmandais is just south of Bordeaux, and the grapes are Syrah, Merlot, Cabernet and Abouriou.*

VILLENEUVE WINES (VIL)

1 Venlaw Court, Peebles, Scotland EH45 8AE, (01721) 722500, fax (01721) 729922 • 82 High Street, Haddington EH41 3ET, (01620) 822224, fax (01620) 822279 • 49A Broughton Street, Edinburgh, EH1 3RJ (0131) 558 8441, fax (0131) 558 8442

E-MAIL wines@villeneuvewines.com
WEB SITE www.villeneuvewines.com
HOURS (Peebles) Mon–Thur 9–8, Fri–Sat 9–9, Sun 12.30–5.30; (Haddington) Mon–Thur 10–7, Fri 10–8, Sat 9–8; (Edinburgh) Mon–Sat 9–10, Sun 12.30–10 **CARDS** MasterCard, Switch, Visa **DISCOUNTS** 5% per case **DELIVERY** 48 hour service. Free locally, £7.50 per case elsewhere. **G M T**

A top-class list with (as befits a Scottish merchant) yards and yards of single malts. And while this is not meant to be a whisky guide, I do recommend Clynelish, and Glenmorangie Fino Finish. Anyway, back to the wines. It's full of names that inspire confidence, like Zind-Humbrecht in Alsace, Guy Saget in the Loire, Domaine Parent in Burgundy and Aldo Vajra in Barolo. From Spain there is supple Joan d'Anguera from Tarragona, plus unusual wines from Ribera del Duero, Cigales and Priorat: Spain is clearly an enthusiasm. There are

excellent estate wines from southern Portugal, too, and from Germany and Austria, plus old vintages of Chateau Musar in the Lebanon. From California there are wines from Phelps and Shafer, Stag's Leap and Sanford, and from South Africa there are Thelema Mountain Vineyards and De Wetshof. It seems to be impossible to fault this list.

1998 Quinta do Côtto Tinto, Champalimaud, £9.99 *Tremendously characterful stuff, with soft, leathery, almost animal-perfumed fruit, very long and silky.*

1997 Carneros Unfiltered Chardonnay, Saintsbury, £13.99 *Good complex, tight-grained Chardonnay; rich but subtle.*

VIN DU VAN (VINV)

Appledore, Kent TN26 2BX, (01233) 758727 **HOURS** Mon–Fri 9–5, Sat 9–1 (phone orders only) **CARDS** MasterCard, Visa **DISCOUNTS** 10% for 6 or more bottles collected; other discounts negotiable **DELIVERY** Free locally. Mail order £5.95 for first case, further cases free. Highlands & Islands ask for quote **MINIMUM ORDER** 1 case. **G M**

An almost entirely Australian list, with just a few New Zealand wines to leaven the blend. It won Wine magazine's International Challenge Wine List of the Year 2000/01 Award, so the wines are clearly well chosen. But this is no ordinary list. One of the shortest tasting notes, for a Barossa Shiraz, reads: 'As richly concentrated, full and spicy as a beaker of Vegemite.'

1998 Riesling Polish Hill, Logan, £9.50 *Lime and toast: classic stuff.*

VINCEREMOS

19 New Street, Leeds LS18 4BH, 0113 205 4545, fax 0113 205 4546
E-MAIL info@vinceremos.co.uk
WEB SITE www.vinceremos.co.uk **CARDS** Amex, Delta, MasterCard, Switch, Visa, **DISCOUNTS** 5% on 5 cases or over, 10% on 10 cases or over **DELIVERY** £5.95 per order, free 5 cases or more. Outside UK mainland, £10 per case postage. For 3 cases or more outside UK mainland, please ask for quote. **M**

C = cellarage	**G** = glass loan/hire	**M** = mail order	**T** = tastings and talks

An organic specialist which very properly prints its list on recycled paper. Now, my attitude to organic wines is that while they're a very good thing for the birds and the bees, I'm only going to drink them if they taste as good as any other wines. The idea that they're automatically going to taste better is, sadly, not true in practice. So, as always, you should go for a good producer – who just happens to be organic. You'll find some on this list – names like Château de Caraguilhes in Corbieres, or Huet or Bossard in the Loire, or Château le Barradis in Monbazillac, or Millton Vineyard in New Zealand. Fetzer's Bonterra wines from California are here as well; from Australia there are wines from Penfolds, Eden Ridge and Glenara. There are also spirits, beers and ciders.

1999 Muscadet de Sèvre et Maine sur lie, Guy Bossard, £5.29 Superb wine from a biodynamic producer. Bossard's Muscadets always have tremendous grace and focus.

VINTAGE WINES LTD (VIN)

116 Derby Road, Nottingham NG1 5FB, 0115-947 6565/941 9614, fax 0115-950 5276
E-MAIL michellewalker@btconnect.com
WEB SITE www.vintagewinesltd.co.uk
HOURS Mon–Fri 9–5.15, Sat 9–5 **CARDS** MasterCard, Switch, Visa **DISCOUNTS** 10% for 6 or more bottles collected, other discounts negotiable **DELIVERY** Free within 60 miles **EN PRIMEUR** Bordeaux. **C G M T**

This list gives an explanation for the curious fact that all the vineyards of Montagny are Premier Cru, when they clearly don't deserve to be so. Apparently during the Second World War the Germans were allowed to help themselves to any wines they wanted up to but not including those of Premier Cru standard. The local mayor got wind of the arrival of occupying forces 24 hours in advance and issued a proclamation putting all the vineyards of the commune out of their reach. Clever, no? Champagne is good here, and you can buy Vega Sicilia; most other countries and regions here look a little routine, though perfectly respectable, and there's some good drinking.

1997 Old Vine Grenache, McLaren Vale, Simon Hackett, £10.85 Good juicy rich stuff with lots of depth and complexity.

WAITROSE (WAI)

Head office Doncastle Road, Southern Industrial Area, Bracknell, Berks RG12 8YA (01344) 424680 **Mail order** freephone 0800 188881, freefax 0800 188888.
118 licensed stores
E-MAIL dee_blackstock@waitrose.co.uk
WEB SITE www.waitrose.co.uk
HOURS Mon–Tue 8.30–6, Wed–Thur 8.30–8, Fri 8.30–9, Sat 8.30–6 **CARDS** Amex, Delta, MasterCard, Switch, Visa **DISCOUNTS** 5% for 6 bottles or more **DELIVERY** (From Waitrose Direct/Findlater Mackie Todd) Free for orders of £75 or more throughout UK mainland or Isle of Wight, otherwise £3.95 **EN PRIMEUR** Bordeaux, Port. **G M T**

Still ahead of the other supermarkets in quality and value, and still proving that being a supermarket doesn't have to mean being terrified of offering anything unusual. There are some very good clarets, and some serious Burgundies, though the top wines tend to be available through Waitrose Direct rather than actually in the shops.

1997 Château Léoville-Barton, £22.50 This is excellent value for this invariably delicious St-Julien (take a look at the price guides for comparisons). It will keep, but you could drink it pretty soon if you wanted to.

1998 Saumur-Champigny, Château de Targé, £6.99 Lovely light, elegant summery red with good structure.

1998 Syrah Dominio de Valdepusa, Marqués de Griñon, £10.99 Wonderfully exotic stuff from Spain, all spices and leather and lovely concentration.

WATERLOO WINE CO (WAT)

6 Vine Yard, London SE1 1QL, 020-7403 7967, fax 020-7357 6976; shop at 59–61 Lant Street, London SE1 1QN
E-MAIL sales@waterloowine.co.uk
WEB SITE www.waterloowine.co.uk
HOURS Mon–Fri 10–6.30, Sat 10–5 **CARDS** Amex, MasterCard, Switch, Visa **DELIVERY** Free 5 cases in central London (otherwise £5); elsewhere (per case), 1 case £8.23, 2 cases £5.88, 3 cases £5.29, 4 cases £4.99, further reductions according to quantity. **G T**

A very quirky, personal list, of which the strengths

are the Loire and Germany. But there are finds in lots of regions, and the finds are the reason to come here: 1988 Sauternes from Château Lamothe-Guignard – a second growth – for £22.59;and 1988 Château Haut-Gardère Blanc from Pessac-Léognan for just £9.65; 1962 Vouvray Moelleux Clos de Bourg from Huet for £44; and the utterly delicious 1993 Bourgueil Cuvée Prestige from Lamé-Delisle-Boucard for £8.65. There's also something rather endearing about a company that stocks just one Argentinian wine – and it's a Riesling.

1993 Bourgueil Cuvée Prestige, Lamé-Delisle-Boucard, £8.65 This was a good year for Loire reds, and Lamé-Delisle-Boucard is a top-notch producer. This is rich, cherryish and complex, and drinking beautifully at the moment.

1985 Forster Mariengarten Riesling Kabinett, Bürklin-Wolf, £7.75 An astonishingly low price for such a mature wine. I'd guess that it wants drinking, but if you like old Riesling this is for you.

WHITESIDES OF CLITHEROE (WHI)

Shawbridge Street, Clitheroe, Lancs BB7 1NA, (01200) 422281, fax (01200) 427129
E-MAIL wine@whitesideswine.co.uk
HOURS Mon–Fri 9–6, Sat 9–5.30 **CARDS** MasterCard, Switch, Visa **DISCOUNTS** 5% per case. **G M T**

A safe list of familiar names and flavours. I can find a reasonable number of wines I'd choose to drink here, but it's not the place if you want to be surprised or challenged. Australian wines are mainly from McGuigan and Rosemount and there are a couple of Duca di Salaparuta wines from Sicily.

1997 Baga/Trincadeira, Casa do Lago £4.41 Rich, ripe, chocolaty red from Portugal.

WINEMARK

3 Duncrue Place, Belfast BT3 9BU, 028 90 746274, fax 028 90 751755. 71 branches
WEB SITE www.winemark.com
HOURS Branches vary, but in general Mon–Sat 10–10, Sun 12–8 **CARDS** Delta, MasterCard, Switch, Visa **DISCOUNTS** 5% on 6–11 bottles, 10% on 12 bottles or more. **G M T**

The recipes in this list include one for Barbeque

Aussie Platter, for which you need four pieces of crocodile fillet. I ate crocodile once – it was like trying to eat a handbag. Perhaps Belfast crocodiles are more delicate creatures. Reptiles aside, this is a decent list of mostly big company wines: from California there's Gallo and Mondavi; Chile has Errazuriz and Caliterra; Portugal has Sogrape, and there's a good list of Bordeaux. There's decent drinking here, even if not many surprises.

1996 Nebbiolo d'Alba, Fontanafredda, £10.99 Forward, early-drinking stuff from a reliable producer.

WINE RACK (WR)

See First Quench.

THE WINE SOCIETY (WS)

Gunnels Wood Road, Stevenage, Herts SG1 2BG, (01438) 741177, fax (01438) 761167; order line tel (01438) 740222
E-MAIL memberservices@thewinesociety.com
WEB SITE www.thewinesociety.com
HOURS Mon–Fri 8.30–9, Sat 9–2; showroom: Mon–Fri 9–5.30, Sat 9–4 **CARDS** MasterCard, Switch, Visa **DISCOUNTS** (per case) £1 for 5–9, £2 for 10 or more, £3 for collection **DELIVERY** Free 1 case or more UK mainland and Northern Ireland. Collection facility at Hesdin, France at French rates of duty and VAT **EN PRIMEUR** Bordeaux, Burgundy, Germany, Port, Rhône.
C G M T

This is an outstanding list – as good as any in the country, and a great deal better than nearly all.

C = cellarage   **G** = glass loan/hire   **M** = mail order   **T** = tastings and talks

Prices are competitive, and they include delivery. Bordeaux is excellent, with masses of well-chosen affordable wines as well as big names; Burgundy ditto; Rhône ditto; Loire, Italy, Spain, Portugal, all ditto. There's a single Bulgarian red for diehards, and lovely, classy New World wines for the rest of us. The recommendations that follow are picked entirely at random: if you close your eyes and choose wines from this list with a pin, you'll always get something wonderful.

1996 Meritage Reserve Paragon Vineyard, Edna Valley, Carmenet, £12.50 A white Graves-style blend from California. It's two-thirds Sauvignon and one-third Semillon, barrel-fermented and with lots of rich, dry depth.

1996 Altos de Temporada Gran Vino, £10.97 This Argentinian will improve in bottle, but it's delicious already, with good structure, depth and rich redcurrant fruit.

1998 Pin, Monferrato Rosso, La Spinetta, £18.50 Yes, I promise it really is called Pin. It's from Piedmont, and is made from half Nebbiolo and a quarter each from Barbera and Cabernet. It's weighty and complex.

WINE TREASURY

69–71 Bondway, London SW8 1SQ, 020-7793 9999, fax 020-7793 8080
E-MAIL quality@winetreasury.com
WEB SITE www.winetreasury.com
HOURS Mon–Fri 9.30–5.30 **CARDS** MasterCard, Visa **DISCOUNTS** 5% for unmixed cases; £60 per year Syndicate membership gives 25% discount **DELIVERY** £6 1 case, free 2 or more cases, England and Wales; Scotland phone for details **MINIMUM ORDER** 1 mixed case. **M T**

If you want to be able to serve a wine from a producer called Blockheadia Ringnosii, this is the place to go. You want to know more about it? There's a Zinfandel and Sauvignon Blanc, and very good they are too. There's also the sublime (and expensive) Kistler Chardonnay from California, but there's not much of it, and it's on allocation. Other California goodies include Stag's Leap Wine Cellars, Stonestreet, Shafer, Lokoya and Sanford: good Californians are, as you might gather, a speciality here. In fact the whole New World shows pretty well. Italy looks good, too, as does France.

1996 Shiraz/Cabernet Sauvignon, Penley Estate, £11.85 You don't see this erstwhile classic blend so much these days, but this is a terrific example: all spice and black fruit, pepper and mint.

THE WINERY (WIN)

4 Clifton Road, London W9 1SS, 020-7286 6475, fax 020-7286 2733
E-MAIL dmotion@globalnet.com
HOURS 11–9.30 **CARDS** MasterCard, Switch, Visa **DISCOUNTS** 5% on a case (can be mixed) **DELIVERY** £8.50 per case, free for 3 cases or more **MINIMUM ORDER** 1 case. **G M T**

Burgundy, Rhône and California are the specialities at this merchant, and Italy looks pretty good, too. From California there is Green & Red, Robert Sinskey, Bacio Divino and other seldom-seen names (they're agencies here, so perhaps we'll see more of them now) and from Burgundy a good long list of interesting-looking domaines. It's a company that takes the trouble to source and ship wines for itself, rather than just buying from other merchants, so it's a list to linger over (and a shop to linger in) rather than one from which you just pick something familiar. And beer-lovers might want to try the bottle-fermented beers from Brittany.

1998 Gigondas, Château Redortier, £12.50
Traditional winemaking and a wine of real depth and class. Truffly fruit, very fine tannins.

1999 Dão Tinto, Quinta do Pereiro, £4.50 A modern, rich blend of Touriga Nacional, Rufete and Aragones grapes.

1997 The Adventures of Commander Zinskey Zinfandel, Robert Sinskey, £13.99 Daft name, but rather good wine. It's Zin from Carneros, which is unusual – most Zin comes from hotter climates. This is all damsons and cherries, with good length.

WINES OF WESTHORPE LTD (WIW)

Marchington, Staffs ST14 8NX, (01283) 820285, fax (01283) 820631
E-MAIL wines@westhorpe.co.uk
WEB SITE www.westhorpe.co.uk
HOURS Mon–Sat 8.30–6 **CARDS** Access, MasterCard, Switch, Visa **DISCOUNTS** (per case) £2 for 6–13; £4.50 for 14–20; £5.20 for 21–27; £6 for 28–41; £6.50 for 42-55; £7 for 56 **DELIVERY** Free UK mainland (except Northern Scotland) **MINIMUM ORDER** 1 mixed case. **M**
An excellent list for devotees of Bulgarian and Hungarian wines. Wines of Westhorpe do a determined job of offering Eastern European wines when most other merchants have deserted everything except Tokaj. Wines of Westhorpe's Tokaji is in the 'traditional' (whatever that means) oxidized style – not new-wave, in other words. There are also some Australians and Chileans.
1998 Cabernet Sauvignon, Tibor Gál, £6.99
I haven't tasted this, to be honest, but Tibor Gál is one of Hungary's star winemakers, who made his name when he was hired to make Super-Tuscan red Ornellaia. So it's got to be worth a try.

WRIGHT WINE CO (WRI)

The Old Smithy, Raikes Road, Skipton, N. Yorks BD23 1NP, (01756) 700886, 24-hour answerphone (01756) 794175, fax (01756) 798580
E-MAIL Bob@wineandwhisky.co.uk
WEB SITE www.wineandwhisky.co.uk
HOURS Mon–Sat 9–6 **CARDS** MasterCard, Switch, Visa **DISCOUNTS** Wholesale price unsplit case, 5% mixed case **DELIVERY** Free within 30 miles, elsewhere at cost. **G**

Burgundy is good and well chosen here, without being hideously expensive – well, less so than some. Alsace, with names like Albert Mann, Schlumberger and Josmeyer, looks incredibly cheap in comparison. It's really far wiser to cultivate a taste for unfashionable wines than for the likes of Bordeaux and Burgundy. In the meantime you can have great fun with Australia, though I'm afraid the top Shirazes may be out of reach: Cabernet is looking better value at the moment. Wright Wine also stocks a lot of rums, including 1979 vintage from J Bally and New Orleans Premium Golden Rum, Small Batch Louisiana, which apparently is possibly the smallest rum distillery in the world.
1996 Cartuxa de Evora Reserva, Alentejo, £13.50 Rich, elegant, classy red from the south of Portugal. Think plums, earth and a touch of chocolate and coffee.
1990 Reflets de Cissac, Médoc, £9.25 This is the second wine of Château Cissac. It's not so very long ago that you could get the grand vin for this price, but there you are. At least 1990 is the sort of year in which it is worth buying second wines – and this is tasty.

PETER WYLIE FINE WINES (WY)

Plymtree Manor, Plymtree, Cullompton, Devon EX15 2LE, (01884) 277555, fax (01884) 277557
E-MAIL peter@wylie-fine-wines.demon.co.uk
WEB SITE www.wyliefinewines.co.uk
HOURS Mon–Fri 9–6 **CARDS** None
DISCOUNTS Unsplit cases **DELIVERY** (per case) 1 case £20, 2 cases £11, 3–4 £6, 5 or more £4.50 **EN PRIMEUR** Bordeaux. **C M**
There's something fascinating about browsing through a list of very old wines. There's a 'pre-1860' Château Belair Marquis d'Aligré here – I mean, 1860! And for a mere £80 you can have 1914 Château Pontet-Canet. There are umpteen 1961 clarets and a decent selection of serious wines from every vintage since, though the list alleges that 'the châteaux are reputed to set aside all their best casks to be bottled into grand formats' – magnums, double magnums and so on. I don't think that's true. Well, it may be reputed to be so, but I don't think they do. If they did you'd be getting a different blend. Serious Bordeaux, red, dry white and sweet white, is the top performer on this list, and as usual

NOEL YOUNG WINES

Award Winning Independent Wine Merchant
Small Independent Wine Merchant of the Year
International Wine Challenge *95/96, 97/98,
98/99, 99/00*

Which? Wine Guide Awards
*Independent Merchant of the Year 1996
East of England Wine Merchant of the Year 1998
New World Wine Specialist Award 2000*

Please call now for our latest regular news-
letters and our extensive fine and rare wine list.

56 HIGH STREET, TRUMPINGTON,
CAMBRIDGE, CB2 2LS
TELEPHONE: 01223 844744
FACSIMILE: 01223 844736
www.nywines.co.uk
email: admin@nywines.co.uk

the prices for Sauternes compare favourably with
those for reds of equivalent age and quality. There
are a few Rhônes and Burgundies, and ports going
back to 1912. The Madeiras, on the other hand, go
back to 1834.
**1992 Meursault les Perrières, Joseph Drouhin,
£14 per half bottle** This would be a perfect treat
to buy just for oneself. Gloriously mature wine
from a top vintage and a very good producer.

YAPP BROTHERS (YAP)

The Old Brewery, Mere, Wilts BA12 6DY,
(01747) 860423, fax (01747) 860929
E-MAIL sales@yapp.co.uk
WEB SITE www.yapp.co.uk
HOURS Mon–Sat 9–5 **CARDS** MasterCard,
Switch, Visa **DISCOUNTS** £3 per case on
collection, quantity discount on 6 or more cases
DELIVERY £3 single case, 2 or more cases free.
C G M T
*Anybody who loves Loire and Rhône wines must
already know Yapps, and if they don't they should,
because they're missing out. The Yapps pretty well
invented the Rhône in Britain – or at least were the*

*first to specialize in it – and every starry name is
here. But while everything is good, not everything is
famous. The Yapps have always headed off the
beaten track in search of lesser-known names and
wines, and so there's good stuff from the Ardèche
as well as from Hermitage; from St-Pourçain as well
as Sancerre. They also have the extremely hard-to-
find wines of Bellet and Cassis from Provence and,
in case you get sick of French wines, Jasper Hill
from Victoria.*
1998 Château des Tours, £12.50 This is pure
Grenache, and was accordingly refused the
Vacqueyras AC. It's rich, powerful and
wonderful.
1999 Saumur Rouge, Château Fouquet, £7.50
Cabernet Franc of great depth and richness.

NOEL YOUNG WINES (YOU)

56 High Street, Trumpington, Cambridge CB2
2LS, (01223) 844744, fax (01223) 844736
E-MAIL admin@nywines.co.uk
WEB SITE www.nywines.co.uk
HOURS Mon–Thur 10–8, Fri-Sat 10-9, Sun 12–2
CARDS Access, Amex, MasterCard, Switch, Visa
DISCOUNTS 5% for orders over £500 **DELIVERY**
£7 first case, £4 subsequent cases, larger orders
negotiable **MINIMUM ORDER** 1 mixed case
EN PRIMEUR Australia, Burgundy, Rhône.
G M T
*There are fantastic wines from just about
everywhere here. Think of a sexy region – Priorat
in Spain, Napa Valley, anywhere – and you'll find
the best wines on Noel Young's list. Okay, having
a good list of mostly pricy Bordeaux isn't difficult –
there's a lot of it about – but getting decent
Burgundy is an altogether trickier proposition.
The Rhône is excellent, too, with lots of Condrieu,
and Alsace is from Domaine Weinbach. Noel
Young has a famously good Austrian list, and lots
of terrific Germans, as well. In fact everywhere
is good: California, Italy, Australia. How does he
do it?*
**1999 Eschendorfer Lump Riesling Kabinett
Trocken, Horst Sauer, £8.99** The vineyard
sounds unappealing in English, but it's one of
Franken's finest; the wine is crisp and focused.
**1997 Riesling Select, Weingut Wieninger,
Austria, £10.99** Dry Riesling from Vienna. Great
power and body.

WHO'S WHERE

Name codes are shown
for retailers whose wines
appear in the Price Guides.
All merchants are listed in
the Retailers Directory.

LONDON

John Armit	ARM
Balls Brothers	BALL
Berry Bros. & Rudd	BER
Bibendum	BIB
Bordeaux Index	BODX
Cave Cru Classé	
Corney & Barrow	CB
Domaine Direct	DOM
Farr Vintners	FA
Fortnum & Mason	FORT
Friarwood	FRI
Goedhuis & Co	
Haynes Hanson & Clark	HAH
Jeroboams	JER
Justerini & Brooks	JU
Lea & Sandeman	LEA
Liberty Wines	LIB
Mayfair Cellars	MAY
Montrachet	MON
Moreno Wines	MOR
Morris & Verdin	MV
NZ Wines Direct	NZW
Le Nez Rouge	NEZ
Philglas & Swiggot	
La Réserve	RES
Howard Ripley	RIP
Roberson	
RSJ Wine Company	RSJ
Unwins	UN
La Vigneronne	
Waterloo Wine Co	WAT
Wine Treasury	
The Winery	WIN

SOUTH-EAST AND HOME COUNTIES

Australian Wine Club	AUS
Bacchus	BAC
Berry Bros. & Rudd	BER
Budgens	BUD
Butlers Wine Cellar	BU
Cape Province Wines	CAP
Ben Ellis Wines	
Le Fleming Wines	FLE
High Breck Vintners	HIG

Seckford Wines	
Turville Valley Wines	TUR
Unwins	UN
Vin du Van	VINV

WEST AND SOUTH-WEST

Averys of Bristol	
Bennetts	BEN
Croque-en-Bouche	CRO
Great Western Wine	GW
Haynes Hanson & Clark	HAH
Hicks & Don	HIC
Laymont & Shaw	LA
The Nobody Inn	NO
Christopher Piper Wines	PIP
Reid Wines (1992) Ltd	
Savage Selection	SAV
Peter Wylie Fine Wines	WY
Yapp Brothers	YAP

EAST ANGLIA

Adnams	AD
Amey's Wines	AME
H & H Bancroft	BAN
Anthony Byrne	BY
Corney & Barrow	CB
Roger Harris Wines	HAW
Hicks & Don	HIC
Lay & Wheeler	LAY
T & W Wines	TW
Noel Young Wines	YOU

MIDLANDS

Bat & Bottle	
Connolly's	CON
Gauntleys	GAU
Hedley Wright	HED
SH Jones	JON
William Morrison	MORR
Portland Wine Co	POR
Stevens Garnier	STE
Tanners	TAN
Vintage Wines Ltd	VIN
Wines of Westhorpe	WIW

NORTH

Booths	BO
D Byrne	
Great Northern Wine Co	GN
William Morrison	MORR
Le Nez Rouge	NEZ
Penistone Court	PEN

Playford Ros	PLAY
Richardson & Sons	RIC
Frank Stainton Wines	STA
Vinceremos	
Whitesides of Clitheroe	WHI
Wright Wine Co	WRI

WALES

Ashley Scott	AS
Ballantynes of Cowbridge	BAL
Terry Platt	PLA
Tanners	TAN

SCOTLAND

Cockburns of Leith	COC
Corney & Barrow	CB
Peter Green & Co	
Justerini & Brooks	JU
Lloyd Taylor Wines	LLO
Le Nez Rouge	NEZ
Raeburn Fine Wines	RAE
Springbok Wines	
Valvona & Crolla	VA
Villeneuve Wines	VIL

CHANNEL ISLANDS

Sommelier Wine Co	SOM

NORTHERN IRELAND

Direct Wine Shipments	DI
James Nicholson	NI
Winemark	

COUNTRYWIDE

Asda	ASD
Bottoms Up	BOT
CWS (Co-op)	CO
Laithwaites	LAI
Majestic	MAJ
Marks & Spencer	MAR
Millésima	MI
Oddbins	OD
Paulson	PAU
Safeway	SAF
Sainsbury's	SAI
Somerfield	SO
Sunday Times Wine Club	SUN
Tesco	TES
Thresher	THR
Victoria Wine	VIC
Waitrose	WAI
Wine Rack	WR
Wine Society	WS

ARGENTINA

Argentinian Malbec is fast becoming a staple of our drinking – so perhaps it's time to trade up to the better wines

Argentina is very much a red wine country. This is not to say that it doesn't make whites, nor that the whites aren't worth looking at: just that reds are so far what it does best, and most. This is of course very nice for Argentina, since reds of just this lush, sweet-fruited sort are the style that everybody wants at the moment.

And for 'Argentinian red', read 'Malbec'. There's actually more Bonarda planted in the vineyards, but Malbec is what producers are focusing on for exports. It ranges from simple, soft reds of pretty undemanding flavours to, at the top end, some sensationally complex, dense wines – but

these, you will be unsurprised to hear, do not come cheap.

What should we be looking for? Well, it's remarkably easy to buy Malbec that is perfectly attractive and drinkable. Nearly all of it is reasonably well made, but to an Identikit pattern of sweet damson fruit and perhaps a bit of new oak. (At its wackiest it can have a distinct taste of sugar mice, if you remember what they taste like, and a scent of violets.) But by paying a bit more – £6 or £7, maybe – you can get something much more stylish. And look out for blends of different grapes, too: some of the finest reds are blends.

GRAPE VARIETIES

BARBERA (red) Don't imagine that Argentina is busy reproducing the acidic, rasping style of Barbera beloved of Italophiles – or even the more modern oaky examples. Argentinian Barbera is a much sweeter proposition. But it can be attractive in its own right.

BONARDA (red) A middling quality grape that is planted in enormous quantities. It probably isn't the same as the Bonarda found in north-western Italy, but since the flavour can be good that's neither here nor there. Expect ripe wines with good concentration and sweet fruit. Most is blended with other varieties, however.

CABERNET SAUVIGNON (red) Of course Argentina makes Cabernet: who doesn't? It can be made as a varietal or blended, often with Merlot. Flavours are rich, ripe, and sometimes a bit jammy.

CHARDONNAY (white) Good but not great, but getting better: that's my verdict

on Argentinian Chardonnay. It remains to be seen how much plantings will increase now that the world is demanding more and more red wine.

MALBEC (red) Argentina's best-known red variety. Elsewhere (which mostly means France) Malbec produces rather plain, rustic wine; but in Mendoza the wines are concentrated, balanced and lush, and almost gamy in flavour: think of red Bordeaux crossed with Australian Shiraz, but softer than either. The best can age surprisingly well, too.

MERLOT (red) There's quite a lot of the world's most fashionable red grape in Argentina; a fair amount of it gets made as an easy-drinking varietal wine, and a lot is blended in with Cabernet Sauvignon; both grapes play second fiddle (both in quantity and in quality) to Malbec.

SANGIOVESE (red) Don't expect Argentinian Sangiovese to taste like Chianti:

it doesn't. Instead it's chunkier, with sweeter fruit and an altogether lusher style. It doesn't have that austere bite that Tuscan examples have, nor the elegance. Drink it on its own terms.

SYRAH (red) There's more and more of this planted every year, though overall quantities are still small. It seems thoroughly at home, but yields are still too high to give of its perfumed best.

TEMPRANILLO (red) Spain's best native red grape can make pretty good quality in Argentina so long as yields are kept down. Often they aren't, and the wines are then light and dilute. Sometimes called Tempranilla.

TORRONTÉS (white) A wildly aromatic grape with a slightly Muscatty smell of air freshener. It succeeds in having good crisp acidity as well, and it needs this to balance all that perfume. It's Argentina's best and most original white, although there are in fact several varieties using this name – some more perfumed than others.

OTHER VARIETIES These include Sauvignon Blanc, which has yet really to succeed here, Riesling and Semillon. Individual examples can be good. Chenin Blanc and Ugni Blanc are less likely to be exported. Red varieties that are sometimes seen include Nebbiolo and Pinot Noir; the former probably has more potential here, but neither is particularly easy to grow.

WINE REGIONS

Nearly all the vineyards are in the western part of the country, and can go up to astonishing altitudes as producers search for cooler climates. Most are semi-desert: if it wasn't for all that melted snow pouring from the mountains there would be no wine made here at all.

MENDOZA This is where the majority of the wine industry is situated, and where most of the wine we see over here comes from. Some three-quarters of Argentina's wine, in fact, comes from here, which includes cheap bulk wine for the domestic market. Malbec rules among the better grapes, though there's quite a bit of Tempranillo, too, and some Italian varieties. There are lots of sub-regions, of which the best are Luján de Cuyo (especially for Malbec), Agrelo, Maipú and Tupungato (some promising Chardonnay). Good producers include: *Altos de Temporada, Anubis, Balbi, Valentin Bianchi, Luigi Bosca, Catena, Etchart, Fabre Montmayou, Finca El Retiro, Finca Flichman, La Agrícola, La Rural, Bodegas J & F Lurton, Nieto Senetiner, Norton, Pascual Toso, Peñaflor, Santa Ana, Trapiche, Villa Atuel, Weinert.*

SAN JUAN It gets far hotter here than it does in Mendoza, and the idea of making high quality wine is relatively new. The Pedernal Valley looks promising.

SALTA This relatively small region in the north of the country is where some of the most exciting wines are being made. The sub-region of Cafayate is the home of Torrontés, and the wines are ripe, quite weighty, and with a wonderful, seductive Muscat perfume. Cabernet Sauvignon also does well here. The vineyards are at terrifically high altitude – the Calchaquíes Valley is at around 1500 metres – which gives elegance to the wines in spite of the hot, dry climate. Look for wines from *Etchart* and *Michel Torino*.

RíO NEGRO Well to the south, this cool-climate region in Patagonia is showing considerable promise for wines; Torrontés, Sauvignon Blanc, Semillon and Malbec look good so far. Good names to look for include *Infinitus* (Chardonnay/Semillon, Cabernet/Merlot and Malbec/Syrah) and *Humberto Canale*, which is even trying some Pinot Noir down here.

PRODUCERS WHO'S WHO

ANUBIS ★ Impressive wines – Malbec, Bonarda, Merlot and Cabernet Sauvignon – from an accomplished winemaking team. The same team makes Villa Atuel wines.

BODEGA ALTA VISTA ★ Bordeaux comes to Argentina: the winemaker of Ch. Clinet in Pomerol makes subtle Malbec and Cabernet Sauvignon. Red blend Alto is terrific.

HUMBERTO CANALE Getting better year by year. The Malbec and Merlot are better bets than the Pinot Noir.

NICOLAS CATENA ★★ The Catena Alta range is tops: rich, complex Chardonnay is beautifully made; Cabernet Sauvignon is dense, chocolaty and will age; Malbec is all blackberries and licorice. Alamos wines, especially the Cabernet Sauvignon, Malbec and Chardonnay, are also well worth a look.

> ## INSTANT CELLAR: ARGENTINIAN REDS
>
> • 1996 Colome Tinto Fino, Vinas de Davalos, £14.57, The Nobody Inn Licorice- charcoal-, bitter chocolate- and black cherry-flavoured wine, with soft tannins. Masses of character – very good indeed.
> • 1997 Shiraz, Balbi, £5.49, Unwins Good juicy-spicy stuff. It's got structure, too. A very good buy.
> • 1997 Altos de Temporada Gran Vino, £10.95, The Wine Society This will improve in bottle, but it's delicious already, with good structure, depth and rich redcurrant fruit.
> • 1998 Cabernet Sauvignon/Malbec, Colome la Salta, £14.33, Le Fleming Hugely concentrated, and with lots of alcohol: not a light lunchtime wine, this. But it's well balanced.
> • 1999 Malbec Reserva, Altos Las Hormigas, £14, Justerini & Brooks Concentrated herby, tobaccoey red with sweet, silky tannins. A beauty.

ETCHART ★★ Top wine Arnaldo B is a blend of Malbec and Cabernet Sauvignon. The Cafayate range includes wonderfully grapy Torrontés, real cassis Cabernet Sauvignon and good Malbec.

FINCA FLICHMAN ★ Spicy Syrah; leathery Reserva Malbec is also excellent.

LA AGRíCOLA ★ Labels include Santa Julia and Picajuan Peak. Reds are reliable. Look for the Bonarda/Sangiovese.

NIETO SENETINER ★★ Supple and complex Cadus Malbec, very good Reserva Syrah, and elegant Torrontés.

NORTON ★ Top wine Norton Privada is a Cabernet Sauvignon/Malbec/Merlot blend full of blackberry and cloves. Ever-improving range includes attractive Torrontés.

FELIPE RUTINI Look for the Apartado blended red. More basic wines are sold under the Libertad label.

TERRAZAS DE LOS ANDES ★ Well-structured Gran Malbec; Reserva and Gran Reserva wines are also very good.

TRAPICHE ★ Chardonnay is improving here, as are Merlot and Cabernet Sauvignon, especially the top Medalla range.

DOMAINE VISTALBA ★★ A French-owned group that includes Fabre Montmayou, Altos de Temporada and Infinitus. Look for Fabre Montmayou Grand Vin, a complex blend of Malbec and Cabernet Sauvignon. Altos de Temporada has promising Merlot, Malbec and Cabernet. Infinitus has some good blends.

WEINERT ★★ Very good peppery, fleshy Malbec, and good chocolaty Cabernet. Cavas de Weinert (Malbec/Cabernet/Merlot) is intense and complex.

ARGENTINA PRICES

RED

Under £4.00

Bonarda/Sangiovese La Agricola Santa Julia **1999** £3.99 (MORR)
★ Malbec La Riojana **2000** £3.99 (CO)
Malbec/Bonarda Rutini Libertad **1999** £3.70 (BAC)
Mission Peak Red **Non-vintage** £3.29 (BO)
Tempranillo/Malbec Etchart Rio de Plata **2000** £3.99 (BUD)
Tempranillo/Malbec Etchart Rio de Plata **1999** £3.99 (MORR)

£4.00 → £4.99

Barbera La Riojana La Nature Organic **2000** £4.49 (SAF) £4.49 (CO)
Barbera Vistalba **1999** £4.99 (CON)
Bonarda Alto Agrelo **1999** £4.99 (VIL)
Bonarda Bodegas Lurton **1999** £4.79 (UN)
Bonarda Medrano **1999** £4.86 (PEN)
Bonarda/Malbec Emperador **Non-vintage** £4.35 (AS)
Cabernet Sauvignon Etchart Rio de Plata **1997** £4.47 (ASD)
Cabernet Sauvignon Finca El Retiro **1999** £4.85 (SOM) £5.95 (POR) £5.99 (VA) £6.15 (BU) £7.65 (HIC)
Cabernet Sauvignon La Agricola Santa Julia **1999** £4.49 (MORR)
Cabernet Sauvignon Norton **1997** £4.99 (UN)
Cabernet Sauvignon Viniterra Omnium **1999** £4.95 (STE)
Cabernet Sauvignon/Malbec Artina Classic Collection **1999** £4.95 (AS)
Cabernet Sauvignon/Syrah Viniterra Terra **1996** £4.20 (STE)
Malbec Alto Agrelo **1999** £4.99 (VIL)
Malbec Balbi **2000** £4.49 (SAF)
Malbec Balbi **1999** £4.39 (MORR)
Malbec Balbi **1998** £4.49 (OD)

★ Malbec Nicolas Catena Argento **2000** £4.99 (BUD) £4.99 (TES) £4.99 (BO) £4.99 (VIC) £4.99 (THR) £4.99 (BOT) £4.99 (SAI)
Malbec Nicolas Catena Argento **1999** £4.99 (WR) £4.99 (CO)
Malbec Finca El Retiro **1999** £4.85 (SOM) £5.89 (BO) £5.95 (POR) £5.95 (BAC) £5.99 (WAI) £6.49 (VA) £6.98 (HIC)
Malbec Norton **1999** £4.99 (UN) £4.99 (TES) £5.99 (NEZ) £5.99 (OD)
Malbec Terrazas Alto **1999** £4.90 (CRO)
Malbec Viniterra Omnium **1997** £4.95 (STE) £5.95 (BALL)
Malbec/Bonarda Rutini Libertad **2000** £4.11 (BIB)
Malbec/Cabernet Sauvignon La Agricola Magdalena River **1997** £4.99 (UN)
Malbec/Cabernet Sauvignon La Agricola Santa Julia **1998** £4.49 (WAI)
Malbec/Sangiovese Trapiche Parral **2000** £4.45 (STE)
Merlot La Rural Libertad **2001** £4.61 (BIB)
Merlot Villa Atuel **2000** £4.99 (LIB)
Pinot Noir La Agricola Santa Julia **1999** £4.99 (WR)
Sangiovese Alto Agrelo **1999** £4.99 (VIL)
Sangiovese Finca El Retiro **2000** £4.99 (LIB) £4.99 (STA)
Sangiovese Norton **1999** £4.99 (NEZ)
Sangiovese/Bonarda La Agricola Magdalena River **1998** £4.99 (UN)
Shiraz Balbi **1999** £4.75 (MORR)
Shiraz Graffigna Reserve **1999** £4.99 (CO)
Syrah Goyenechea **1996** £4.64 (PEN)
Syrah Nieto Senetiner Valle de Vistalba **1998** £4.95 (SOM)
Syrah Villa Atuel **1999** £4.90 (BAC) £4.95 (WS) £4.99 (LIB) £4.99 (WR) £5.25 (BU) £5.99 (VA)
Tempranillo Finca El Retiro **1999** £4.50 (SOM) £5.49 (WAI) £5.75 (BU) £5.79 (BAL)
Tempranillo La Agricola Santa Julia Oak-Aged **1999** £4.49 (TES) £4.99 (SO)

RETAILERS SPECIALIZING IN ARGENTINA
see Retailers Directory (page 40) for details

No merchant actually specializes in Argentian wines, though some have better lists than others. Most only stock a few wines at best. Try Adnams (AD),Bennetts (BEN), D Byrne, Hedley Wright (HED), Lloyd Taylor (LLO), Moreno Wines (MOR), Sommelier Wine Co (SOM), The Wine Society (WS), Wine Treasury.

£5.00 → £5.99

Barbera Nieto Senetiner Valle de Vistalba
  2000 £5.05 (LLO)
Cabernet Sauvignon Nicolas Catena
  Alamos **1997** £5.95 (BAC)
Cabernet Sauvignon Finca El Retiro **2000**
  £5.99 (LIB)
Cabernet Sauvignon Goyenechea **1996**
  £5.39 (PEN)
Cabernet Sauvignon Navarro Correas
  Correas **1996** £5.49 (MOR)
Cabernet Sauvignon Norton **1999** £5.50
  (TAN) £5.99 (NEZ) £5.99 (OD)
Cabernet Sauvignon Terrazas Alto **2000**
  £5.93 (PLA)
Cabernet Sauvignon Terrazas Alto **1999**
  £5.99 (UN) £5.99 (JON) £5.99 (VIL)
Cabernet Sauvignon Trapiche **1997** £5.49
  (DI)
Cabernet Sauvignon Vistalba **1999** £5.99
  (CON)
Malbec Alta Vista **1997** £5.95 (JU)
Malbec Valentin Bianchi **1999** £5.50 (GW)
Malbec Nicolas Catena Alamos **1999**
  £5.99 (TES) £6.26 (BIB)
Malbec Nicolas Catena Alamos **1997**
  £5.95 (WS)
Malbec La Agricola Santa Julia Oak
  Reserve **1997** £5.99 (UN)
Malbec Bodegas Lurton **1999** £5.49 (POR)
  £5.75 (TAN) £5.95 (JER)
Malbec Bodegas Lurton **1998** £5.69 (JON)
Malbec Medrano **1999** £5.21 (PEN)
Malbec Navarro Correas Correas **1998**
  £5.49 (MOR) £5.73 (LLO)
Malbec Bodegas Orfila **2000** £5.99 (HED)
Malbec Terrazas Alto **2000** £5.93 (PLA)
Malbec Michel Torino Coleccion **1999**
  £5.99 (VIL) £6.40 (CRO)
Merlot Goyenechea **1997** £5.15 (PEN)
Merlot Norton **1999** £5.99 (NEZ) £5.99
  (OD)
Merlot Michel Torino Coleccion **1999**
  £5.99 (VIL)
Pedro del Castillo Weinert **1998** £5.45
  (STE)
Shiraz Balbi **1997** £5.49 (UN)
Syrah Finca El Retiro **2000** £5.99 (POR)
Syrah Medrano **1999** £5.33 (PEN)
Syrah Navarro Correas Correas **1998**
  £5.74 (LLO)
Syrah Navarro Correas Correas **1997**
  £5.49 (MOR)
Syrah Vistalba **1999** £5.99 (CON)

Tempranillo Anubis **2000** £5.99 (LIB)
Tempranillo Anubis **1999** £5.95 (WS)
Tempranillo Finca El Retiro **2000** £5.95
  (STA) £5.99 (LIB)
Tempranillo La Agricola Santa Julia Oak
  Reserve **1999** £5.99 (UN) £6.96 (ASD)

£6.00 → £6.99

Bonarda Nicolas Catena Alamos **1999**
  £6.26 (BIB)
Cabernet Sauvignon Domaine Vistalba
  Altos de Temporada **1996** £6.95 (WS)
Cabernet Sauvignon Domaine Vistalba
  Fabre Montmayou **1997** £6.99 (OD)
Cabernet Sauvignon Terrazas Reserva
  1997 £6.99 (VIL)
Cabernet Sauvignon Michel Torino Don
  David **1998** £6.99 (VIL)
Cabernet Sauvignon Trapiche Oak Cask
  1995 £6.99 (DI)
Cabernet Sauvignon/Merlot Domaine
  Vistalba Infinitus **1999** £6.95 (WS)
Carrascal Weinert **1997** £6.45 (STE) £6.99
  (BO) £7.79 (CON) £7.90 (TAN) £9.17 (ARM)
Malbec Humberto Canale **1997** £6.99
  (HED)
Malbec Domaine Vistalba Altos de
  Temporada **1996** £6.95 (WS)
Malbec Domaine Vistalba Fabre
  Montmayou **1997** £6.99 (OD)
Malbec Finca El Retiro **2000** £6.20 (STA)
Malbec Trapiche Oak Cask **1995** £6.99
  (DI)
Malbec/Syrah Domaine Vistalba Infinitus
  1997 £6.99 (BAL)
Malbec/Syrah Domaine Vistalba Infinitus
  1996 £6.79 (BO) £7.65 (RAE)
Merlot Humberto Canale **1999** £6.99
  (JON)
Merlot Humberto Canale **1996** £6.99
  (HED)
Merlot Domaine Vistalba Fabre
  Montmayou **1997** £6.99 (OD)
Pinot Noir Humberto Canale **1998** £6.99
  (HED)
Syrah Luigi Bosca **1996** £6.90 (CRO) £7.50
  (RIC)
Syrah Trapiche Oak Cask **1997** £6.99 (DI)
Syrah/Bonarda Anubis **2000** £6.99 (LIB)

> *Stars (★) indicate wines selected by
> Oz Clarke in the Best Buys section which
> begins on page 8.*

£7.00 → £8.99

Cabernet Sauvignon Luigi Bosca **1996** £7.50 (AD)

Cabernet Sauvignon Nicolas Catena Agrelo **1996** £8.40 (NO)

Cabernet Sauvignon Bodegas Lurton Gran Lurton **1997** £8.99 (UN) £10.99 (POR)

Cabernet Sauvignon Norton Reserve **1997** £8.99 (NEZ)

Cabernet Sauvignon Viña Amalia **1998** £7.49 (OD)

Cabernet Sauvignon Viniterra **1997** £7.95 (STE)

Cabernet Sauvignon Weinert **1991** £8.99 (MOR)

Cabernet Sauvignon/Merlot Domaine Vistalba Infinitus **1996** £7.65 (RAE)

Carrascal Weinert **1995** £7.49 (JON)

Malbec La Agricola Familia Zuccardi 'Q' **1998** £8.99 (WAI)

Malbec Bodegas Lurton Reserva **1999** £7.52 (CB)

Malbec Norton **2000** £7.25 (NI)

Malbec Terrazas Reserva **1997** £8.99 (GN)

Malbec Trapiche Oak Cask **1998** £7.79 (JON)

Malbec Viña Amalia **1999** £7.49 (OD)

Malbec Weinert **1995** £8.45 (STE) £9.99 (CON) £10.20 (TAN) £11.30 (MOR)

Malbec Weinert **1994** £8.25 (WS) £8.45 (STE) £9.62 (NO) £9.95 (BAL) £11.25 (ARM)

Malbec Weinert **1992** £8.45 (MOR)

Merlot Viniterra **1997** £7.95 (STE)

Merlot Weinert **1992** £8.45 (MOR)

Miscelánea Weinert **1997** £7.95 (STE)

Privada Norton **1998** £8.99 (WR)

Syrah Navarro Correas **1995** £8.99 (MOR)

Tempranillo La Agricola Familia Zuccardi 'Q' **1998** £7.99 (TES)

£9.00 → £9.99

Barbaro Balbi **1998** £9.99 (MORR)

Barbaro Balbi **1997** £9.99 (SAF)

Cabernet Sauvignon Anubis Reserva **1999** £9.95 (WS)

Cabernet Sauvignon Nicolas Catena **1996** £9.80 (BAC)

Cabernet Sauvignon Nicolas Catena Agrelo **1999** £9.31 (BIB)

Cabernet Sauvignon Nicolas Catena Agrelo **1997** £9.95 (WS)

Cabernet Sauvignon La Agricola Familia Zuccardi 'Q' **1998** £9.99 (TES)

Cabernet Sauvignon Weinert **1995** £9.75 (STE) £11.50 (BAL) £11.75 (CON) £12.93 (PLAY) £13.75 (ARM)

Cavas de Weinert Weinert **1996** £9.95 (STE) £12.25 (CON)

Cavas de Weinert Weinert **1994** £9.95 (STE) £10.95 (WS) £11.06 (NO)

Centenario Goyenechea **1990** £9.90 (RIC)

Malbec Nicolas Catena **1997** £9.95 (RES) £9.99 (OD)

Malbec Nicolas Catena Agrelo **1999** £9.79 (BIB)

Malbec Navarro Correas **1993** £9.40 (RIC)

Malbec Navarro Correas Privada Reserva **1997** £9.49 (MOR)

Malbec Norton Reserve **1998** £9.99 (NEZ)

Merlot Rutini Reserva **1997** £9.31 (BIB)

Syrah Navarro Correas **1994** £9.40 (RIC)

Over £10.00

Cabernet Sauvignon Nicolas Catena Alta **1997** £21.54 (BIB)

Cabernet Sauvignon Terrazas Gran Reserva **1997** £19.95 (GN) £19.99 (VIL) £20.95 (RES)

Cabernet Sauvignon Weinert **1994** £11.45 (JON)

Malbec Nicolas Catena **1996** £10.00 (BAC)

Malbec Terrazas Gran **1997** £16.90 (CRO) £19.95 (GN) £19.99 (VIL)

Merlot Weinert **1996** £10.95 (BALL) £11.40 (CB) £11.54 (PLAY) £11.67 (ARM)

Privada Norton **1999** £10.99 (NEZ) £12.75 (NI)

WHITE

Under £4.00

Semillon/Chardonnay Valentin Bianchi Elsa **2000** £3.99 (CO)

Torrontés/Chardonnay Etchart Rio de Plata **1999** £3.59 (MORR) £3.79 (SO)

Torrontés/Chardonnay Etchart Rio de Plata **1998** £3.59 (BUD)

Torrontés/Chardonnay Navarro Correas Correas **2000** £3.99 (VIC) £3.99 (THR) £3.99 (BOT) £3.99 (WR) £4.83 (LLO)

£4.00 → £4.99

Chardonnay Anubis **2000** £4.95 (WS)

Chardonnay Nicolas Catena Argento **2001** £4.99 (BUD)

Chardonnay Nicolas Catena Argento **2000** £4.99 (TES) £4.99 (ASD)

Chardonnay Etchart Rio de Plata 1999
£4.59 (MORR)
Chardonnay Finca El Retiro 2000 £4.99
(STA)
Chardonnay La Agricola Magdalena River
1999 £4.99 (UN)
Chardonnay Rutini Libertad 2001 £4.61
(BIB)
Chardonnay Viniterra Omnium 1999
£4.95 (STE) £5.33 (NO) £5.95 (BALL)
Chardonnay/Chenin Blanc Parral 2000
£4.45 (STE)
Chenin Blanc/Sauvignon Blanc Rutini
Libertad 2000 £4.11 (BIB)
Pinot Gris Bodegas Lurton 2000 £4.29
(WAI) £4.49 (UN) £4.99 (POR) £5.35
(TAN) £5.68 (CB)
Semillon/Chardonnay Norton 2000 £4.99
(WR) £5.99 (NEZ)
Torrontés Artina Classic Collection 1999
£4.95 (AS)
Torrontés La Riojana La Nature Organic
2000 £4.47 (ASD) £4.49 (BUD) £4.49 (CO)
Torrontés Norton 2000 £4.49 (VIC) £4.49
(THR) £4.49 (BOT) £4.49 (WR) £4.99 (NEZ)
£4.99 (OD) £5.75 (TAN) £5.90 (CRO)
£6.40 (NI)
Torrontés/Chardonnay Navarro Correas
Correas 1998 £4.99 (MOR)
Torrontés/Chenin Blanc Emperador
Non-vintage £4.35 (AS)
Viognier La Agricola Santa Julia 2000
£4.49 (TES)
Viognier La Agricola Santa Julia 1999
£4.99 (WR)

£5.00 → £5.99

Chardonnay Nicolas Catena Alamos
1997 £5.95 (WS) £5.95 (BAC) £5.99
(UN)
Chardonnay La Agricola Santa Julia Oak
Reserve 1999 £5.99 (UN)
Chardonnay Medrano 1999 £5.33 (PEN)
Chardonnay Terrazas Alto 2000 £5.99
(GN)
Chardonnay Terrazas Alto 1999 £5.99
(UN) £5.99 (VIL)
Chardonnay Vistalba 1999 £5.95 (CON)
Chardonnay/Riesling Humberto Canale
1999 £5.79 (JON)

*A key to name abbreviations
is available on page 7.*

Chenin Blanc Bodegas Lurton 2000 £5.95
(JER)
Pinot Gris Bodegas Lurton 1998 £5.09
(JON)
Sauvignon Blanc Norton 2000 £5.99
(NEZ) £7.45 (NI)

£6.00 → £6.99

Chardonnay Nicolas Catena Alamos
2000 £6.26 (BIB)
Chardonnay Nieto Senetiner Valle de
Vistalba 2000 £6.00 (LLO)
Chardonnay Terrazas Reserva 1997
£6.99 (VIL) £8.99 (GN) £10.95 (RES)
Chardonnay Michel Torino Don David
1999 £6.99 (VIL)
Chardonnay Viña Amalia 1999 £6.99 (OD)
Chardonnay/Semillon Domaine Vistalba
Infinitus 1997 £6.99 (BAL) £7.65 (RAE)

£7.00 → £9.99

Chardonnay Nicolas Catena 1999 £9.90
(BAC)
Chardonnay Nicolas Catena 1997 £8.99
(OD) £9.49 (UN)
Chardonnay Nicolas Catena Agrelo 1999
£8.99 (WAI)
Chardonnay Nicolas Catena Agrelo 1997
£8.95 (WS)
Chardonnay Bodegas Lurton 1995 £7.90
(CRO)
Chardonnay Trapiche Oak Cask 1997
£7.99 (JON)
Chardonnay Viniterra 1999 £7.95 (STE)
Riesling Luigi Bosca 1999 £7.50 (AD)

Over £12.00

Chardonnay Nicolas Catena Alta 1999
£19.59 (BIB)
Chardonnay Nicolas Catena Alta 1997
£21.95 (RES)

ROSÉ

c. £4.00

Malbec Santa Ana 1999 £3.99 (SAF)

SPARKLING

c. £8.00

Chandon Argentina Non-vintage £7.88
(BY) £7.99 (SAF) £8.03 (BIB) £8.75 (STE)
£8.99 (VIL)

AUSTRALIA

**Australia is restlessly moving forward into new grape
varieties and new flavours. Italian grape varieties are the latest
things to start looking for**

How much odder can Australian wine names get? When you've got Broken Fishplate and The Footbolt (Sauvignon Blanc and Shiraz respectively, both from d'Arenberg), then it's hard to see that things can get any more peculiar. I suppose calling a wine Log Jail (from Currabridge) is no weirder than calling a wine Hermitage, and Isolation Ridge (Frankland Estate) is wonderfully evocative of the exploration of Australia. So don't get me wrong. I love these names. Even Fetlers Rest (from Jindalee). What's a fetler? Someone who fettles, I suppose.

Not that any of this is much to the point. And the point is (yes, I am coming to it) that Australia is leading the way in introducing us to all sorts of other names we had never associated with the country: names like Sangiovese, Arneis, Nebbiolo and Barbera. Australia is taking a serious interest in Italian grape varieties, and there'll be lots more in years to come, including southern Italian grapes like Negro d'Avola, Primitivo and Aglianico.

Now, it's true that Californians are also experimenting with these grapes – but so far, with less success. Among consultant winemakers Australian producers have the reputation of thinking things through before planting new varieties – they don't just stick them in the ground anywhere and assume they'll grow. Instead they do very detailed research into soil and climatic conditions; and not just temperature, either. Humidity, hours of sunlight, amount of cloud cover and the times of the year at which these things occur are all just as important.

Even with all this research, it still takes time to learn about new varieties. The first really convincing examples of Italian varieties are just appearing, and the best ones taste recognizably of their variety but also recognizably Australian. It's a hard balance to find. And when you've found it, why not celebrate with a daft name?

GRAPE VARIETIES

CABERNET SAUVIGNON (red) This can be rich and chocolaty in the Barossa, austere and minty in Victoria's Pyrenees, full of moss, tobacco and cedar flavours in the Eden Valley, and dense, phenolic and black in the Hunter. Sometimes it can be all of these, sometimes it can taste of nothing more than simple blackcurrant jelly. It's an Aussie staple these days, and even cheaper ones generally have clear fruit, without the muddiness that can mar cheap claret. And when it's good, it's breathtaking. It's also often blended with other grapes, particularly Shiraz or the Bordeaux varieties Cabernet Franc and/or Merlot. Best: *Peter Lehmann, St Hallett Cabernet/Merlot, Seppelt's Dorrien,*

Yalumba The Menzies and *The Signature* (Barossa); *Grosset, Wendouree* (Clare); *Bowen Estate, Hollick's Ravenswood, Katnook Odyssey, Lindemans Pyrus, Lindemans Limestone Ridge* and *Lindemans St George, Parker, Penley Estate, Petaluma, Wynns Coonawarra* and *John Riddoch* (Coonawarra); *Heggies, Henschke Cyril Henschke, Mountadam The Red* (Eden Valley); *Tahbilk* (Goulburn Valley); *Mount Langi Ghiran* (Grampians); *Frankland Estate, Goundrey, Howard Park, Plantagenet* (Great Southern); *Brokenwood, Lake's Folly* (Hunter); *Cape Mentelle, Capel Vale, Xanadu, Cullen, Devil's Lair, Leeuwin Estate, Moss Wood, Sandstone, Vasse Felix The Heytesbury* (Margaret River);

Chapel Hill The Vicar, Reynella, Coriole, d'Arenberg Coppermine Road, Reynella Basket Press, Shottesbrooke, Wirra Wirra (McLaren Vale); Dromana Estate (Mornington Peninsula); Taltarni (Pyrenees); Freycinet (Tasmania); Mount Mary, Yarra Yering (Yarra); Geoff Merrill, Penfolds (various).

CHARDONNAY (white) Australia has done more than most to give this grape mass appeal with its rich, fruity wines. Most are now far more restrained than they were, but the fruit is still there. The best have kept their original appeal and gained complexity. Best: Ashton Hills, Penfolds, Petaluma, Shaw & Smith Reserve (Adelaide Hills); St Hallett, Peter Lehmann (Barossa); Giaconda (Beechworth); Grosset (Clare); Katnook (Coonawarra); Henschke, Seppelt's Partalunga (Eden Valley); Bannockburn (Geelong); Howard Park, Plantagenet, Wignalls (Great Southern); Allandale, Brokenwood, Rosemount (Hunter); Reynella, Wirra Wirra (McLaren Vale); Cape Mentelle, Cullen, Evans & Tate, Leeuwin Estate, Moss Wood, Pierro, Xanadu (Margaret River); Dromana Estate (Mornington Peninsula); Hardy Eileen Hardy (Padthaway); Pipers Brook (Tasmania); Coldstream Hills (Yarra).

FORTIFIEDS Shiraz and other Rhône-type grapes are often used to make port styles. Vintage is wonderful. Best: Reynella, Montara, Penfolds, Seppelt, Stanton & Killeen.

GEWÜRZTRAMINER (white) Decent, faintly spicy examples smelling of lychees and honeydew melon are made by Brown Brothers, Delatite and Lillydale (Victoria),

Pipers Brook (Tasmania) and Knappstein (Clare). Orlando Flaxman's (Eden Valley) and Tolleys (Barossa) are always good. Rymill's botrytis version (Coonawarra) is intense.

GRENACHE (red) The Southern Vales and the Barossa Valley, south and north of Adelaide, are the heartland of this Mediterranean variety, and the rediscovery of old vines sitting there squeezing out more and more concentrated grapes has resulted in a range of wonderful wines; the Turkey Flat vines have been in constant production since 1847. Best: Charles Cimicky's Daylight Chamber Grenache, Charles Melton, RBJ, Rockford, St Hallett Gamekeeper's Reserve, Turkey Flat, Yalumba Bush Vine Grenache (Barossa); Tim Adams The Fergus (Clare); Mitchelton III (Goulburn); d'Arenberg Ironstone Pressings, Tim Gramp (McLaren Vale).

MARSANNE (white) In Central Victoria, both Tahbilk and Mitchelton have made big, broad, ripe Marsanne.

MUSCAT (white) There are two types of Muscat in Australia: first, the bag-in-box Fruity Gordo or Muscat of Alexandria – fruity, sweetish, swigging wine, from a heavy-cropping lowish-quality grape grown along the Murray River; second, liqueur Muscat, made from the Brown Muscat, a strain of the top quality Muscat à Petits Grains, grown in Victoria. It is a sensation: dark, treacly even, with a perfume of strawberry and honeyed raisins. Best producers: All Saints, Baileys, Brown Brothers, Campbells, Chambers, McWilliam's, Morris.

LANGTON'S CLASSIFICATION OF AUSTRALIAN WINES

This is put together by Langton's, the Australian auction house, and ranks 89 Australian wines as Exceptional (7 wines), Outstanding (24 wines), Excellent (29 wines) and Distinguished (29 wines). The seven Exceptional wines are: Penfolds Grange; Henschke Hill of Grace Shiraz; Mount Mary Quintet Cabernets; Leeuwin Estate Art Series Chardonnay; Moss Wood Cabernet Sauvignon; Penfolds Bin 707 Cabernet Sauvignon; and Wendouree Shiraz.

PINOT NOIR (red) Better clones, viticulture and general understanding of the variety are producing some serious examples. Best: *Ashton Hills* (Adelaide Hills); *Giaconda* (Beechworth); *Mountadam* (Eden Valley); *Bannockburn* (Geelong); *Wignall's* (Great Southern); *Tyrrell Vat 6* (Hunter); *Ashton Hills, Lenswood Vineyards* (Lenswood); *Moss Wood* (Margaret River); *Stonier* (Mornington Peninsula); *Freycinet, Pipers Brook* (Tasmania); *Coldstream Hills, Mount Mary, St Huberts, Tarrawarra, Yarra Yering* (Yarra).

RIESLING (white) On a roll in Australia, and increasingly fashionable. The wines are highly individual, and all share a lime aroma: some are clean and crisp (*Ashton Hills, Pewsey Vale, Leeuwin Estate*), some softer and more rounded (*Heritage, Skillogalee*), and others beg to be aged (*Orlando Steingarten, Mount Langhi Ghiran*). It's a wonderful apéritif and the perfect partner for Thai and Pacific Rim cooking: not many white wines could stand up to those flavours, but Australian Riesling sails through them. Other good ones: *Rockford* (Barossa); *Tim Adams, Jim Barry, Grosset, Knappstein, Mitchell, Petaluma, Pikes* (Clare); *Heggies, Leo Buring, Orlando St Helga, St Hallett, Seppelt's Partalunga* (Eden Valley); *Frankland Estate, Howard Park* (Great Southern); *Henschke* (Lenswood or Eden Valley); *Tim Gramp* (McLaren Vale); *Pipers Brook* (Tasmania); *Delatite* (Victoria). Botrytis-affected wines: *Mount Horrocks, Petaluma.*

SAUVIGNON BLANC (white) A riper but still pungent style is emerging – less gooseberryish than New Zealand's, and more white peach and melon. Cool Adelaide Hills is proving its worth, with *Lenswood* and *Shaw & Smith*, while Margaret River's richer styles are like southern hemisphere Graves (*Cullen*). Best producers: *Pikes* (Clare); *Katnook* (Coonawarra); *Hill-Smith Estate* (Eden Valley); *Amberley Estate* (Margaret River); *Wirra Wirra* (McLaren Vale).

SEMILLON (white) Unoaked Aussie Semillon is rare and great; lean and grassy when young, and needing years for its flavours of toast and honey to emerge. That makes it hopelessly uncommercial: you can hardly blame the producers for opting for oak barrels and a quick sale. *Glenguin, McWilliams Elizabeth* and *Tyrrell's Vat 1* are the unoaked versions to look for. But oaked Semillon is delicious as well, waxy and toasty, and the best will age. Try: *Peter Lehmann, Grant Burge* (Barossa); *Mitchell* (Clare); *Henschke* (Eden Valley); *Brokenwood, Lindemans, Peterson, Rothbury* (Hunter); *Knappstein* (Lenswood); *Evans & Tate, Moss Wood* (Margaret River). Best blends with Sauvignon: *St Hallett* (Barossa); *Brokenwood* (Hunter); *Cape Mentelle, Cullen, Pierro, Xanadu Secession* (Margaret River); *Wirra Wirra* (McLaren Vale). *Geoff Merrill* blends with Chardonnay. Best sweet wines: *Peter Lehmann, Tim Adams, de Bortoli.*

SHIRAZ (red) The most widely planted red vine in Oz, but look for wine from old vines for greatest depth of flavour. There's the dense, black iron intensity of Clare, the chocolate, earth and moss of the Barossa, the black pepper of the cooler bits of Victoria and Western Australia, or the simple red berry sweetness of the hot Murray Valley. Try: *Basedow, Grant Burge Meshach, Greenock Creek, Peter Lehmann, Charles Melton, Rockford, St Hallett Old Block, Yalumba Octavius* (Barossa); *McWilliams* (Barwang); *Jasper Hill* (Bendigo); *Tim Adams, Jim Barry The Armagh, Mitchell, Pikes, Wendouree* (Clare); *Bowen, Majella, Wynns, Zema* (Coonawarra); *Henschke, David Wynn Patriarch* (Eden); *Bannockburn* (Geelong); *Tahbilk* (Goulburn); *Mount Langi*

Ghiran (Grampians); *Plantagenet* (Great Southern); *Allandale Matthew, Brokenwood, McWilliams Old Paddock* and *Old Hill, Tulloch Hector,* Tyrrell's *Vat 9* (Hunter); *Craiglee* (Macedon); *Cape Mentelle* (Margaret River); *Chapel Hill,* d'Arenberg *Old Vine* and *Dead Arm, Hardy, Reynella* (McLaren Vale); *Dalwhinnie, Taltarni* (Pyrenees); *Baileys 1920s Block* (Victoria); *Yarra Yering* (Yarra Valley); *Hardy, Penfolds* (various).

SPARKLING WINES In the lead for quality are *Croser, Green Point,* Pipers Brook *Pirie* and *Jansz.* Cheaper ones include: *Seaview Brut, Angas Brut.* Upmarket: Seppelt's *Blanc de Blancs* and *Pinot Noir/Chardonnay.* And try Yalumba's *Cabernet* and Seppelt's *Shiraz* (sparkling red).

VERDELHO (white) Rich, dry, lime-flavoured wines that are fast becoming Australian classics. Look for *Chapel Hill, Pendarves Estate, Rothbury Estate.*

OTHER GRAPES Viognier gets better and better, with *Yalumba* out there in the lead. Look too for Rhône grapes like Mourvèdre and Grenache, and blends of these from *Basedow, Grant Burge, d'Arenberg, Tim Gramp* and *St Hallet. Dromana Estate* is so far making the best Arneis, Sangiovese, Barbera and Nebbiolo; *Brown Brothers* are also interested in Italian varieties. There's a bit of Chenin Blanc, but it's rarely taken seriously, except in Western Australia, and is generally fuller, fruitier and blander in style than its steely Loire counterpart. Pinot Gris/Grigio can be better, but tends to lack excitement. *Mount Langi Ghiran* and *T'Gallant* are very good. There's an increasing amount of good Petit Verdot, often made as a varietal with rich tannins and chocolatey, violet-scented fruit. Good ones include *Yaldara Julians, Simeon Kingurra, McGuigan Lennard's Crossing.* Oh, and *Brown Brothers* has a rather attractive Graciano.

WINE REGIONS

The Australian Geographical Indication system aims to identify areas that produce wines with their own distinct character. But it also has to accommodate the widespread system of inter-regional blending: that is, trucking grapes from several different regions, possibly in different states, to a central winery for blending together. Some of Australia's most famous wines *(Grange,* for example) are blended like this.

The most general designation is Produce of Australia. The next most general is South-Eastern Australia, which is much seen; it covers most of the wine-producing area. Then there is the more specific State of Origin, and then there are zones, regions and sub-regions. In all there will be about 400 Geographical Indications by the time the process is complete.

ADELAIDE HILLS (South Australia) Cool area pioneered by *Petaluma,* now joined by *Shaw & Smith, Stafford Ridge,*

Henschke and *Lenswood,* making classically pure Sauvignon Blanc, Chardonnays with great length and classy Pinot Noir. *Penfolds* is making a bid for white wine fame here.

BAROSSA VALLEY (South Australia) This is the heart of the Australian wine industry, planted originally by immigrants from Silesia. Most of Australia's wine passes through the Barossa Valley, if only for bottling or aging. It's also a source of wonderful old-vine Grenache and Shiraz. Best: *Basedow, Beringer Blass, Grant Burge, Greenock Creek, Hewitson, Peter Lehmann, Charles Melton, Orlando, Penfolds, Rockford, St Hallett.*

BENDIGO (Victoria) Destroyed by phylloxera, this region has been replanted with excellent Cabernet, good Shiraz and Pinot Noir. *Balgownie* is the leader, with *Chateau Leamon, Harcourt Valley, Heathcote, Mount Ida* and *Passing Clouds* important.

CANBERRA DISTRICT (ACT) Some modest wineries are at last beginning to find some kind of wine style and identity.

CLARE VALLEY (South Australia) An upland complex of four valleys (Skillogalee, Clare, Watervale and Polish River), Clare is all things to many grapes: cool and dry for steely, limy Riesling (*Adams, Jim Barry, Leo Buring, Grosset, Knappstein, Pikes*) and soft, light Chardonnay (*Penfolds*), but warm enough for rounded Semillon (*Mitchell*) and long-living reds (*Adams, Knappstein, Leasingham, Skillogalee, Watervale, Wendouree*).

COONAWARRA (South Australia) A big, flat, wide open landscape with the famous cigar-shaped strip of *terra rossa* soil over limestone at its heart. It is Australia's most profitable red wine vineyard, and its incredibly expensive land is jam-packed with great names. Coonawarra is best at Cabernet and unirrigated Shiraz. Try: *Bowen, Brand's, BRL Hardy, Hollick, Katnook, Lindemans, Majella, Mildara, Orlando, Penfolds, Penley, Petaluma, Rouge Homme, Rosemount, Rymill, Wynns* and *Zema*. Other similar limestone ridges nearby are currently being planted, with promising results.

EDEN VALLEY (South Australia) Home to some of Australia's oldest vineyards, like *Henschke*'s 120-year-old Hill of Grace, and some of the newest and most high-tech (*Mountadam* and *Seppelt*'s *Partalunga*). Most of the major Barossa companies take fruit from these rolling uplands. *Yalumba* is here, with *Heggies* and *Hill-Smith Estate* vineyards.

GEELONG (Victoria) Best are intense Cabernets from vineyards like *Idyll* and *Bannockburn*, Pinot Noir from *Prince Albert* and *Bannockburn*, and whites from *Idyll*.

GOULBURN VALLEY (Victoria) This houses *Mitchelton*, a medium-sized modern winery, and *Tahbilk*, one of the nation's oldest, still making traditional intense reds and long-lived Marsanne.

INSTANT CELLAR:
NEW FLAVOURS

- **2000 Viognier, Lindsay Hill, £11.95, Liberty Wines** The problem with Viognier is getting the right amount of flavour into the grapes: this one, from the Hunter Valley, succeeds brilliantly.
- **2000 Pinot Gris, Mount Langi Ghiran, £10.90, Bennetts** Few Australians seem to understand this grape, but this succeeds brilliantly. It's spicy but not over the top.
- **1999 Gewürztraminer Dead Man's Hill, Delatite, £9.17, John Armit Wines** Firm, with a mineral edge and floral fruit.
- **1998 Petit Verdot, Pirramimma, £8.99, Majestic** One of Bordeaux's rarer red grapes, famed for its colour, perfume and late ripening, makes solid and undeniably ripe wines in Australia.
- **1991 Sangiovese 'i', Garry Crittenden, £9.34, The Nobody Inn** Australia's best Sangiovese so far. It's not Chianti, but it has style.
- **1999 Il Briccone (The Rogue), Primo Estate, £10, Australian Wine Club** A complex and rich but not overpowering blend of Shiraz, Sangiovese, Barbera, Nebbiolo and Cabernet, from the Adelaide Plains. Weird and brilliant.

GRAMPIANS (Victoria) The new name for Great Western; still the source of base wine for *Seppelt*'s *Great Western* fizz, but more exciting for its reds. Shiraz is full of chocolate, coconut and cream at *Cathcart Ridge*, or licorice and pepper at *Mount Langi Ghiran*. *Best's, Montara* and *Seppelt* are other top names for Shiraz. Excellent Chardonnay from *Best's* and *Seppelt*, Cabernet from *Mount Langi Ghiran* and *Best's*, fortified from *Montara*.

GRANITE BELT (Queensland) The vines are planted high up in what is otherwise a banana and mango belt. Most wines serve the local market and some (*Ballandean, Kominos Wines, Rumbalara, Robinsons Family* and *Stone Ridge*) are good. *Ironbark Ridge* is one to watch.

GREAT SOUTHERN (Western Australia) One of Australia's most promising wine areas, good for Riesling, limy Chardonnay, peppery Shiraz and magnificent Cabernet. Try *Alkoomi, Goundrey, Frankland Estate, Plantagenet* and *Howard Park*, home of *Madfish* blends.

HILLTOPS (New South Wales) Excellent-value Shiraz and Cabernet. Restraint and elegance are the watchwords.

HUNTER VALLEY (New South Wales) Old-established region, home to wonderful individual Semillons that last for decades, and great leathery Shiraz. Best producers include: *Allandale, Glenguin, McWilliam's Mount Pleasant, Reynolds, Rosemount* and its *Roxburgh* vineyard, *Rothbury* and *Tyrrell's*.

KING VALLEY (Victoria) Cool, high-altitude region with fine Riesling, Shiraz and fizz, plus exciting Italian varietals.

MACEDON RANGES (Victoria) Region dominated by small wineries, with good Pinot Noir, Chardonnay, Riesling and fizz. The cool climate can be just a bit *too* cool.

MARGARET RIVER (Western Australia) A source of increasingly beautiful wines that reek of a sense of place, combining richness of fruit with elegance of structure. *Cape Mentelle, Cullen, Leeuwin Estate, Moss Wood, Pierro* and *Vasse Felix*

are the names to watch, and while Semillon and Sauvignon, Cabernet and Chardonnay are the most common wines, there is a scattering of other grapes like Zinfandel, Malbec, Sangiovese and Nebbiolo.

McLAREN VALE (South Australia) Some wonderful old Shiraz vineyards are now under tarmac, thanks to the spread of Adelaide suburbia. Building has been slowed by a revival of interest in the quality of the area's fruit: the boldness of the black pepper Shiraz and the sweet concentration of Grenache and Chardonnay. Recommended are *Chapel Hill Chardonnay, Coriole Redstone Shiraz/Cabernet, d'Arenberg (Ironstone Pressings, Twenty Eight Road, Custodian* and *Coppermine Road), Four Sisters, Geoff Merrill, Mount Hurtle, Reynella Basket Pressed Shiraz*.

MORNINGTON PENINSULA (Victoria) One of the coolest Aussie wine zones, this is a weekend playground for the Melbourne rich. Good for light Chardonnay, sparkling wine, Merlot, sometimes Pinot Noir, and now Italian varieties. Among the best wineries are *Dromana, T'Gallant, Stonier* and *Moorooduc Estate*.

MUDGEE (New South Wales) Mudgee has grown high quality grapes for generations, but most of them ended up in nearby Hunter Valley. A few memorable wines have surfaced from the scattering of

MATURITY CHART

1998 Barossa Old Vines Shiraz

Often approachable early, yet these wines can last and last

Bottled	Ready	Best	Fading	Tired

| 0 | 1 | 2 | 3 | 4 | 5 | 6 | 7 | 8 | 9 | 10 | 11 | 12 | 13 | 14 | 15 | 16 | 17 | 18 | 19 | 20 | 21 | 22 | years |

local wineries, and the quality of full, ripe Cabernet and Shiraz and lovely, intense Chardonnay is starting to shine. Best: *Craigmoor, Huntington, Miramar, Montrose, Rosemount.*

ORANGE (New South Wales) A new cool-climate region already making intense Loire-style Sauvignon Blanc (*Highland Heritage*) and cashew nut Chardonnay *(Rosemount)*, while the reds, notably Shiraz Cabernet and Merlot (from *Bloodwood, Reynolds* and *Rosemount*) are outstanding.

OVENS VALLEY (Victoria) Former tobacco region now making steely Riesling and Chardonnay, but also intense Merlot, Cabernet and Shiraz.

PADTHAWAY (South Australia) Region initially lauded for high quality whites, notably Chardonnay, Riesling and Sauvignon Blanc. There is some excellent sweet Riesling, also, but lately a series of superb reds are showing Padthaway to be a fantastic all-round area. Best: *Hardy, Lindemans, Seppelt;* major names like *Orlando* and *Penfolds* also use the grapes.

PEMBERTON (Western Australia) Promising region for cool-climate Pinot Noir, Chardonnay and Sauvignon Blanc.

PYRENEES (Victoria) Very dry, dense Shiraz and Cabernet reds, and mostly Sauvignon whites. Tops: *Dalwhinnie, Mount Avoca, Redbank, Taltarni, Warrenmang,* and for fizz, *Chateau Remy* (also stylish Cabernet and Chardonnay) and *Taltarni.*

RIVERINA (New South Wales) The vast irrigated Riverina (which used to be called Murrumbidgee Irrigation Area) provides ten to 15 per cent of the total Australian crop. Most is bulk wine, but *McWilliam's* makes some attractive wines, as does *De Bortoli.*

RIVERLAND (South Australia) A vast irrigation project on the Murray River,

providing a large chunk of the national crop. Dominated by the huge *Angove's* winery, and the even bigger *Berri-Renmano-Loxton* group (part of BRL Hardy), it makes huge amounts of bag-in-box wines. But it also yields fresh, fruity Riesling, Chardonnay, Chenin, Sauvignon, Colombard, Cabernet and Shiraz. *Deakin Estate, Oxford Landing* and *Kingston Estate* stand out for good, fresh flavours.

RUTHERGLEN (Victoria) Here and Glenrowan to the south make up the centre of the fortified wine tradition. The white table wines are generally dull, except for the reliably fine *St Leonards.* The reds are rich and robust. The fortifieds, either as solera-method 'sherries', as 'vintage ports', or as intense, brown sugar-sweet Tokays, are all memorable. The true heights are achieved by sweet Muscats, unbearably rich but irresistible with it. Best: *Bullers, Campbells, Chambers, Morris, Stanton & Killeen* (Rutherglen); *Baileys* (Glenrowan).

SWAN DISTRICT (Western Australia) This hot region made its reputation on big, rich reds and whites, but even the famous Houghton HWB is now much lighter and fresher. Good names: *Evans & Tate, Houghton, Moondah Brook, Sandalford.*

TASMANIA Only tiny amounts, but rapidly making a reputation for sparkling wine. Tazzie grapes are increasingly used in top mainland sparklers. There are fine whites from *Pipers Brook* and *Moorilla Estate* and scented Pinot Noir from *Freycinet.*

YARRA VALLEY (Victoria) Victoria's superstar. It suits the Champagne grapes, Pinot Noir and Chardonnay, for fizz, plus Cabernet and Pinot for frequently excellent reds. Best producers include: *Coldstream Hills, de Bortoli, Diamond Valley, Lillydale, Mount Mary, St Huberts, Seville, Tarrawarra, Yarra Burn, Yarra Ridge, Yarra Yering* and *Yeringberg.* Lots of big names are moving in, so expect more Yarra wines on the shelves.

PRODUCERS WHO'S WHO

TIM ADAMS ★★ (South Australia) Spellbinding Semillon, wild Grenache and dense, full-flavoured Shiraz.

ALLANDALE ★★ (New South Wales) One of the best Hunter Semillons; also complex, slightly honeyed Chardonnay and the excellent Matthew Shiraz.

BAILEYS OF GLENROWAN ★★ (Victoria) Traditional winery famous for stunning sweet Muscats and Tokays. Has been through a rather lean spell, but burly dark red table wines are showing a return to form.

BANNOCKBURN ★★ (Victoria) Some of cool-climate Geelong's best-known wines: a rich Pinot Noir, full-bodied Chardonnay and Shiraz.

BAROSSA VALLEY ESTATE ★★ (South Australia) Jointly owned by local growers and *BRL Hardy*, this specializes in good quality, cheap wine, but also makes some mighty Shiraz.

JIM BARRY ★★ (South Australia) Clare Valley winery; unwooded Chardonnay, Watervale Riesling, delicious Cabernet Sauvignon and a pair of splendid Shiraz: McCrae Wood and The Armagh.

BASEDOW (South Australia) Barossa winery with big, toasty, oaky Chardonnay and Semillon, chocolaty Shiraz and Cabernet. Old-fashioned in the best way.

BERINGER BLASS (South Australia) Own labels include Cabernet-based Robertson's Well and red blend Jamiesons Run; also a Jamiesons Run Chardonnay. Owned by brewing giant Fosters, with umpteen subsidiaries, including Annie's Lane, Yarra Ridge and Yellowglen; see also *Baileys of Glenrowan, Wolf Blass, Rothbury* and *St Huberts*.

WOLF BLASS ★ (South Australia) The wines are decent at this Beringer Blass-owned winery – modern, well plumped out with fruit and oak – but rarely match the silky, come-hither brilliance of the old days. Voluptuous Chardonnay, good Riesling and five styles of red which have, in rising price order, red, yellow, grey, brown and black labels.

BOWEN ESTATE ★★ (South Australia) The best value in Coonawarra: elegant Cabernet/Merlot and razor-fine Shiraz renowned for consistency and quality. Very good Riesling and Chardonnay.

BRL HARDY ★ (South Australia) Huge company making both high-standard, cheap own-labels and Hardy's impressive range from Nottage Hill to Reynella and Eileen Hardy. Look out, too, for Hardy's rich, sweet Botrytized Riesling.

BROKENWOOD ★★ (New South Wales) Small, high-class Hunter Valley winery noted for eclectic blends such as Hunter/Coonawarra Cabernet and latterly Hunter/McLaren Vale Semillon/Sauvignon Blanc. Low-yielding Graveyard vineyard produces one of Australia's best Shirazes: concentrated, profound and long-living.

BROWN BROTHERS ★ (Victoria) A huge range of middling to good wine. The best vineyards are the cool Koombahla and even cooler Whitlands; there are lots of unusual grape varieties, but some can seem a little short on character.

CAPE MENTELLE ★★ (Western Australia) Excellent Cabernet and variations on the Semillon/Sauvignon theme as well as Shiraz – and Zinfandel.

CHAPEL HILL ★★ (South Australia) Impressive wines with restraint and style include toasty Eden Valley Riesling, unwooded Chardonnay and chocolaty, blackberry-flavoured The Vicar, a blend of Cabernet and Shiraz.

COLDSTREAM HILLS ★★ (Victoria) Top-class Pinot Noir, exciting Chardonnay and Cabernet-Merlot blend, Briarston. Now owned by giant Southcorp, which seems to want to maintain quality.

CULLEN ★★★ (Western Australia) Intense wines with great purity of fruit. Releases include a benchmark Chardonnay, a very refined Sauvignon Blanc-Semillon, a richly elegant Cabernet/Merlot and good Pinot Noir.

D'ARENBERG ★★ (South Australia) Firmly traditional winemaking produces powerfully rich Dead Arm Shiraz, concentrated, velvety Footbolt Shiraz and Twenty Eight Road Mourvèdre; all require long aging. Also sweetly fruity Custodian Grenache; The Other Side Chardonnay; and 12-year-old fortified Nostalgia.

DE BORTOLI ★ (New South Wales) Rich sweet Noble One Botrytis Semillon, plus a string of well-priced basics. Rare Dry Botrytis Semillon has bags of marmalade flavour but little subtlety. De Bortoli's Yarra Valley property makes good Chardonnay, Cabernet and Shiraz.

DELATITE ★★ (Victoria) Wines with individuality of style plus superb wine-making which puts them in the top class. Dry Riesling is delicious, the sweet version superb, while Pinot Noir, Gewürztraminer, Cabernet and Shiraz are brilliant.

DROMANA ESTATE ★ (Victoria) Excellent Chardonnay, promising Pinot Noir and first-class Cabernet/Merlot, as well as a fascinating new range of Italian varietals, especially very good Arneis.

EVANS & TATE ★★ (Western Australia) Beautifully crafted, stylish wines; in particular weighty Semillon (straight and blended with Sauvignon), Merlot and Shiraz.

GOUNDREY ★★ (Western Australia) Wines of real concentration, including Reserve Riesling and Cabernet Sauvignon, and Shiraz from Mount Barker.

GREEN POINT ★★ (Victoria) Moët & Chandon's Australian outpost, making possibly Australia's best sparklers from Champagne grape varieties. The standard fizz is now called Chandon Australia.

HENSCHKE ★★★ (South Australia) Old red vines, some of them 100 years old, that yield deep, dark top-class wines, such as Hill of Grace Shiraz. Mount Edelstone Shiraz comes a close second. Cyril Henschke Cabernet Sauvignon is terrifically rich. Whites are equally stunning – Riesling, Semillon and Chardonnay.

HERITAGE/STEVE HOFF (South Australia) Among Barossa's boisterous winemakers, Heritage is a hidden gem, quietly producing classic wines from a wide range of varieties: limy Riesling, softly honeyed Semillon and tasty Shiraz.

HOLLICK ★ (South Australia) Some of Coonawarra's suavest reds; rich Wilgha Shiraz and an outstanding Bordeaux blend, Ravenswood. There is also fine Chardonnay and the district's most successful Riesling.

HOWARD PARK ★★ (Western Australia) Expensive but superb, long-living wines. Intense Riesling, structured Chardonnay and rich Cabernet/Merlot. All need cellaring. Second label: Madfish.

KNAPPSTEIN ★ (South Australia) Ageworthy Riesling, spicy, restrained Gewürztraminer, and ripe Enterprise Cabernet Sauvignon.

LAKE'S FOLLY ★★★ (New South Wales) Tiny Hunter Valley winery making highly idiosyncratic Chardonnay and cedary, structured red blend Lake's Folly.

LEEUWIN ESTATE ★★ (Western Australia) Ultra-high profile, ultra-high prices for brilliant Chardonnay and Pinot Noir, blackcurrant-and-leather Cabernet Sauvignon, powerful Riesling and crisp Sauvignon Blanc. Look for Prelude Vineyards Chardonnay and Pinot Noir.

LINDEMANS ★★ (Victoria) Exceptionally good basic varietals, while Coonawarras, Padthaways and Hunters are among Australia's finest. Coonawarra reds Limestone Ridge and St George are tip-top, as is the Bordeaux blend, Pyrus. New is smoky, leafy Bin 70: Semillon, Verdelho, Sauvignon and Chardonnay. Bin 65 Chardonnay is consistently good value.

MCWILLIAM'S ★★ (New South Wales) Unoaked Mount Pleasant Elizabeth Semillon repays aging. Also some fine Shiraz.

CHARLES MELTON ★★ (South Australia) A small Barossa winery with Grenache-based Nine Popes and a Shiraz of exceptional concentration and character.

GEOFF MERRILL (South Australia) Wines here include worthy Cabernet, full Chardonnay, crisp Sauvignon/Semillon and thirst-quenching Grenache rosé under the Mount Hurtle label.

MITCHELTON ★ (Victoria) Wide range of styles, notably fine, full-flavoured Rieslings, ripe, spicy Shiraz, and the speciality of the house, oak-matured Marsanne. Chardonnay and Cabernet Sauvignon are increasingly good. The Preece label offers ripe, bright fruit and good value.

MOORILLA ESTATE ★★ (Tasmania) A polished range of crisp, cool-climate wines. Pinot Noir is a speciality; aromatic Riesling, Chardonnay and Gewürztraminer are also good.

MORRIS ★★ (Victoria) The leading producer of sweet liqueur Muscat and Tokay which give a new meaning to the words 'intense' and 'concentrated'.

MOSS WOOD ★ (Western Australia) Superbly original wines. Semillon, with and without wood-aging, is some of the best in Australia. Pinot Noir is daring and delicious, Chardonnay less daring but just as delicious, Cabernet rich and structured. All have lots of polished fruit.

MOUNTADAM ★ (South Australia) French-trained Adam Wynn makes complex, Burgundian Chardonnay, substantial Pinot Noir, idiosyncratic Riesling and lean Cabernet. David Wynn Patriarch is a rich, fruit-laden Shiraz. The Red is a Cabernet/Merlot blend, and there's good rosé fizz, too.

MOUNT LANGI GHIRAN ★★ (Victoria) Grampians winery making richly flavoured, dry, intense Shiraz, long-lived Cabernet Sauvignon, good lime cordial Riesling and properly spicy Pinot Gris.

MOUNT MARY ★★ (Victoria) Finely structured Cabernet-based Bordeaux blend Quintet and white Triolet; also a Pinot Noir improving with age. Tiny production, much sought-after.

ORLANDO ★★ (South Australia) Barossa winery with fine quality at every level. St Helga and Steingarten Riesling, Lawson's Padthaway Shiraz and St Hugo Cabernet are among the best. Excellent Jacaranda Ridge Cabernet from Coonawarra. Jacob's Creek basics are deservedly successful.

PENFOLDS ★★★ (South Australia) Great red wine producer, and now good in whites too, particularly Old Vine Barossa Valley Semillon. Its basics are clean and tasty, its varietals packed with flavour, and its special selection reds, culminating in the deservedly legendary Grange, are superlative wines of world class. Overpriced Yattarna Chardonnay from Adelaide Hills is supposed to be the 'white Grange'.

PENLEY ESTATE ★ (South Australia) There's rich, concentrated Shiraz/Cabernet from here as well as ageworthy Cabernet Sauvignon, supple Phoenix Cabernet and elegant Chardonnay.

PETALUMA ★★ (South Australia) Brian Croser's fizz is now softer and more enjoyable than before. Outstanding Tiers Chardonnay, though regular Chardonnay is now less exciting. Full, limy Riesling. Coonawarra red is good, sometimes excellent.

PIPERS BROOK ★★ (Tasmania) Steely aromatic Riesling, classically reserved Chardonnay, serious Gewürztraminer and Pinot Gris are joined by excellent traditional-method fizz, Pirie.

PLANTAGENET ★★ (Western Australia) Noted for peppery Shiraz, melony/nutty Chardonnay, fine limy Riesling and elegant Cabernet Sauvignon. Sparkling wine is good too, as is Pinot Noir.

REYNOLDS ★ (New South Wales) This small Upper Hunter estate has gained its reputation with its chocolaty Cabernet, powerful Shiraz and well-structured, fragrant unoaked Semillon.

ROCKFORD ★★ (South Australia) The individuality of Rocky O'Callaghan's wines, especially his Basket Press Shiraz, has made him a Barossa cult. Grenache and Riesling are marvellous, too, and all improve with aging. Sparkling Black Shiraz is a world-class wine, heady with spicy berried fruit.

ROSEMOUNT ★ (New South Wales) The company which did more than any to help Australia take Britain by storm with Chardonnay, Fumé Blanc and Cabernet. The last two are no longer so good, though Chardonnay is on the way back and the single-vineyard Roxburgh and Show Reserve Chardonnays are impressive. Exciting new Mountain Blue and Hill of Gold wines from Mudgee, surprising Pinot Noir and excellent Semillon and Shiraz. McLaren Vale reds are tops. Newly merged with Southcorp (which controls Lindemans and Penfolds).

ROTHBURY ESTATE ★ (New South Wales) Idiosyncratic but successful when it was under Len Evans' obsessive control; now owned by Beringer Blass. Can produce the Hunter's greatest Semillon and juicy, fat crowd-pleasing Chardonnays. Has produced Shiraz and Pinot Noir on occasion, too.

ST HALLETT ★★ (South Australia) Full, oaky Semillon and Chardonnay, good Riesling and a rich Shiraz, Old Block, from

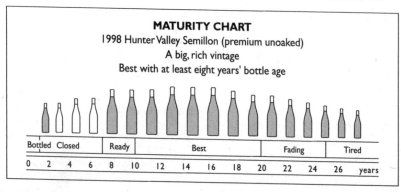

MATURITY CHART
1998 Hunter Valley Semillon (premium unoaked)
A big, rich vintage
Best with at least eight years' bottle age

Bottled	Closed		Ready		Best			Fading		Tired	

| 0 | 2 | 4 | 6 | 8 | 10 | 12 | 14 | 16 | 18 | 20 | 22 | 24 | 26 | years |

old vines. Gamekeeper's Reserve is Shiraz, Grenache, Mourvèdre and Touriga Nacional, brambly and spicy. One of the leading names in the Barossa revival.

ST HUBERTS (Victoria) At best produces superb Chardonnays, exciting Cabernets and Pinots plus the odd thrilling sweetie, but has never settled into a totally reliable groove and some vintages fail to convince. Now owned by Beringer Blass.

SEPPELT ★★ (Victoria) Leading makers of quality fizz from Champagne grapes, peaking with Salinger. Also fruity, easy-drinking styles, and blackberryish sparkling red Shiraz.

SHAW & SMITH ★ (South Australia) Fine Sauvignon Blanc and Chardonnay – including an unoaked version.

STONIER ★★ (Victoria) Good cool-climate Chardonnay, Pinot Noir and Cabernet from this Mornington Peninsula winery.

TAHBILK ★ (Victoria) Historic Goulburn Valley winery with great traditional Shiraz and Cabernet, and excellent Marsanne.

TALTARNI ★ (Victoria) Remarkable bone-dry, grassy-sharp Fumé Blanc; fine Cabernet and Shiraz which soften (after about a decade) into classy, if austere reds.

TYRRELL'S ★ (New South Wales) Eccentrically brilliant Hunter winery which sells 'port' and 'blackberry nip' to tourists through the front door while making some classic wines out the back. Vat 1 Semillon is excellent, as is the 'plonk' – Long Flat Red and White. Vat 9 is supple, leathery Shiraz.

VASSE FELIX ★★ (Western Australia) One of the original Margaret River wineries, producing a classic regional style of rich, leafy, curranty Cabernet and spicy, fleshy Shiraz. Chardonnay, Semillon and Sauvignon Blanc are equally good. Heytesbury Red, a Bordeaux blend, is tops.

GEOFF WEAVER/STAFFORD RIDGE ★★ (South Australia) Adelaide Hills winery with pure and intense Sauvignon Blanc, delicate but long Chardonnay and crisp Riesling.

WIRRA WIRRA ★★ (South Australia) Fine, concentrated reds, whites and sparkling wine, and exceptional Angelus Cabernet.

WYNNS ★★ (South Australia) Well-structured Cabernet, powerful Shiraz and big, oaky Chardonnay from this Coona-warra company. Top-line John Riddoch Cabernet is expensive but exceptional stuff.

YALUMBA/HILL-SMITH ★★ (South Australia) Good wines under the Yalumba and Hill-Smith labels, and exceptional ones under the Heggies and Pewsey Vale labels, where dry and sweet Rieslings are some of the finest in Australia. Yalumba Signature is an outstanding blend of Cabernet Sauvignon and Shiraz. Also look out for Yalumba's Octavius Shiraz and Antipodean Red – a blend of Shiraz and other Rhône grapes. Very fine Viognier and lovely classic old stickies. Some attractive quaffers in the Oxford Landing range.

YARRA YERING ★★ (Victoria) Wonderful Yarra Valley winery, where Bailey Carrodus labels his Cabernet-based wine Dry Red No.1 and his Shiraz-based wine Dry Red No. 2: exceptional, powerful and concentrated yet fragrant reds. Fine Pinot Noir and Chardonnay as well, in a very personal style.

YERINGBERG ★★ (Victoria) This small Yarra Valley winery, established in 1862 is one of Australia's oldest. Its Cabernet-based blend, Yeringberg, is a terrific wine with great aging potential; Pinot Noir is supple and silky, with cherry and strawberry fruit.

AUSTRALIA PRICES

RED

Under £4.00

Dry Red Dalwood **Non-vintage** £3.60 (SOM)

Dry Red Lindemans Cawarra 1999 £3.99 (WAI)

Dry Red Rolleston Vale **Non-vintage** £3.95 (CON) £3.99 (VIL) £3.99 (GN)

Malbec/Ruby Cabernet Angove's Nanya Estate 1999 £3.99 (WAI) £4.49 (THR)

Shiraz/Mataro Hardys Banrock Station 2000 £3.99 (MORR) £4.49 (BUD) £4.49 (VIL) £4.49 (SAF)

Shiraz/Mataro Hardys Banrock Station 1999 £3.99 (UN)

Shiraz/Merlot Barramundi **Non-vintage** £3.98 (TES) £3.98 (ASD)

Shiraz/Merlot Barramundi 1999 £3.99 (MORR)

£4.00 → £4.99

Cabernet Sauvignon/Shiraz/Merlot Hardys Crest 1998 £4.99 (MORR)

Dry Red Dalwood 2000 £4.50 (LLO)

Grenache Peter Lehmann Vine Vale 1998 £4.46 (ASD) £4.69 (UN)

Grenache/Mourvèdre/Cabernet Yaldara Stoney Vale 1998 £4.99 (RAE)

Grenache/Shiraz Orlando Jacob's Creek 1999 £4.99 (BUD) £4.99 (SO) £4.99 (WAI)

Red Ochre d'Arenberg 1998 £4.95 (WS)

Shiraz/Cabernet Sauvignon Canoe Tree 1999 £4.95 (STE)

Shiraz Hardys Banrock Station 1999 £4.99 (TES) £4.99 (VIL)

Shiraz Lindemans Bin 50 1999 £4.75 (WS) £4.99 (MORR) £5.49 (TES) £5.49 (MAJ)

Shiraz McGuigan Brothers Black Label 2000 £4.99 (WHI)

Shiraz Yaldara Berrigan Point 1998 £4.50 (BU)

Shiraz/Cabernet Dalwood 1999 £4.82 (BY)

Shiraz/Cabernet Sauvignon Aldridge Estate 1999 £4.99 (CON)

Shiraz/Cabernet Sauvignon De Bortoli Sacred Hill 1999 £4.95 (STE) £4.95 (LEA)

Shiraz/Cabernet Sauvignon Hardys Stamp 2000 £4.75 (TES) £5.29 (BUD) £5.29 (THR) £5.29 (WR) £5.29 (SAF) £5.29 (MORR)

Shiraz/Cabernet Sauvignon Hardys Stamp 1999 £4.99 (UN) £4.99 (WAI)

Shiraz/Cabernet Sauvignon Hardys Stamp 1998 £4.99 (SO)

Shiraz/Cabernet Sauvignon Lindemans Cawarra 2000 £4.98 (TES) £4.99 (BUD)

Shiraz/Cabernet Sauvignon Lindemans Cawarra 1999 £4.99 (UN) £4.99 (CO)

Shiraz/Cabernet Sauvignon Lindemans Cawarra 1998 £4.99 (SO)

Shiraz/Cabernet Sauvignon Lonsdale Ridge 2000 £4.79 (BIB)

Shiraz/Cabernet Sauvignon Lonsdale Ridge 1999 £4.60 (BAC)

Shiraz/Cabernet Sauvignon Orlando Jacob's Creek 2000 £4.77 (ASD) £5.49 (SAF)

Shiraz/Cabernet Sauvignon Orlando Jacob's Creek 1999 £4.59 (MORR) £4.77 (TES) £5.49 (THR) £5.49 (WR) £5.49 (WAI)

Shiraz/Cabernet Sauvignon Penfolds Rowlands Brook 2000 £4.99 (TAN)

Shiraz/Cabernet Sauvignon Penfolds Rowlands Brook 1999 £4.69 (JON)

Shiraz/Cabernet Sauvignon Rolleston Vale 1998 £4.70 (PEN)

Shiraz/Cabernet Sauvignon Tatachilla Wattle Park 1998 £4.95 (BAN)

RETAILERS SPECIALIZING IN AUSTRALIA
see Retailers Directory (page 40) for details

Virtually every retailer will be able to sell you some Australian wines. But for more than the usual, try: Adnams (AD), Australian Wine Club (AUS), Averys of Bristol, Ballantynes (BAL), Bennetts (BEN), Bibendum (BIB), Anthony Byrne (BY), Direct Wine Shipments (DI), Domaine Direct (DOM), First Quench Group (BOT, THR, VIC, WR), Lay & Wheeler (LAY), James Nicholson (NI), The Nobody Inn (NO), Oddbins (OD), Terry Platt (PLA), Philglas & Swiggot, Raeburn Fine Wines (RAE), Roberson, Sainsbury's (SAI), Safeway (SAF), Sommelier Wine Co (SOM), Tanners (TAN), Wine Society (WS), Vin du Van (VINV), Wine Treasury (WT), Noel Young (YOU).

£5.00 → £5.99

Black Label Red McGuigan Brothers **2000**
£5.39 (CON)

Black Label Red McGuigan Brothers **1999**
£5.63 (PLA)

Cabernet Sauvignon Deakin Estate **2000**
£5.49 (BIB) £5.99 (DI)

Cabernet Sauvignon Lindemans Bin 45
1999 £5.98 (PEN) £5.99 (MORR)

Cabernet Sauvignon Lindemans Bin 45
1998 £5.80 (BAC) £5.99 (MAJ) £6.61 (BY)

Cabernet Sauvignon McWilliams
Hanwood **1997** £5.95 (COC)

Cabernet Sauvignon Sunnycliff **1999**
£5.35 (HAH) £6.49 (POR)

Cabernet Sauvignon Sunnycliff **1998**
£5.45 (TAN) £5.49 (JON)

Cabernet Sauvignon Tatachilla Breakneck
Creek **2000** £5.49 (SAF)

Cabernet Sauvignon David Wynn **1999**
£5.70 (SOM) £6.95 (NI) £8.00 (MV)

Cabernet Sauvignon/Mourvèdre Grant
Burge Oakland **1997** £5.49 (UN)

Cabernet Sauvignon/Shiraz Hardys
Nottage Hill **2000** £5.99 (VIL) £5.99 (SAF)

Cabernet Sauvignon/Shiraz Hardys Nottage
Hill **1999** £5.28 (TES) £5.49 (SAI) £5.79
(WAI) £5.99 (BUD) £5.99 (VIC) £5.99 (THR)
£5.99 (BOT) £5.99 (WR) £5.99 (MORR)

Cabernet Sauvignon/Shiraz Hardys
Nottage Hill **1998** £5.79 (UN)

Cabernet Sauvignon/Shiraz Penfolds
Koonunga Hill **1999** £5.99 (SOM) £6.89
(POR) £6.99 (COC) £6.99 (OD)

Cabernet Sauvignon/Shiraz Yalumba Oxford
Landing **2000** £5.49 (THR) £5.49 (SAF)

Cabernet Sauvignon/Shiraz Yalumba Oxford
Landing **1999** £5.49 (UN) £5.49 (TES)
£5.49 (WAI) £5.69 (BUD)

Cabernet Sauvignon/Shiraz/Merlot
Woolshed **1999** £5.99 (SAF)

Grenache/Shiraz Rosemount **2000** £5.82
(WHI) £6.79 (TES) £6.99 (BUD) £6.99 (WAI)

Long Flat Red Tyrrell's **1999** £5.31 (COC)
£5.49 (VIL) £5.55 (GN)

Long Flat Red Tyrrell's **1997** £5.90 (RIC)

Merlot Casella Mallee Point **1999** £5.90
(BAC)

---

*Stars (★) indicate wines selected by
Oz Clarke in the Best Buys section which
begins on page 8.*

Merlot Deakin Estate **1999** £5.49 (WAI)
£5.50 (BAC) £5.99 (DI)

Rawson's Retreat Bin 35 Penfolds **2000**
£5.99 (BUD) £5.99 (POR) £5.99 (SAF)

Rawson's Retreat Bin 35 Penfolds **1999**
£5.49 (WAI) £5.50 (BAC) £5.97 (TES) £5.99
(UN) £5.99 (BO) £5.99 (THR) £5.99 (MORR)

Red Ochre d'Arenberg **1999** £5.38 (BIB)

Richardsons Red Block Rouge Homme
1995 £5.99 (AME) £8.95 (POR)

Shiraz Deakin Estate **2000** £5.49 (OD)

Shiraz Hardys Nottage Hill **1998** £5.99
(BUD)

Shiraz Peter Lehmann Vine Vale **1998**
£5.25 (BO) £6.29 (VIN)

Shiraz Lindemans Bin 50 **2000** £5.99 (BUD)

Shiraz Lindemans Bin 50 **1998** £5.99 (UN)

Shiraz McGuigan Brothers Bin 2000 **2000**
£5.86 (WHI)

Shiraz McGuigan Brothers Black Label
1998 £5.10 (RIC)

Shiraz Simon Gilbert Card Series Mudgee
1999 £5.99 (BAL)

Shiraz Tyrrell's Long Flat **1998** £5.99 (VIL)

Shiraz Willandra **1999** £5.90 (BAC) £6.49
(HED) £6.65 (LLO)

Shiraz/Cabernet Sauvignon Orlando Jacob's
Creek **1998** £5.49 (UN) £5.49 (BUD)

Shiraz/Cabernet Sauvignon Penfolds
Koonunga Hill **1999** £5.99 (SOM) £6.99
(TES) £6.99 (VIC) £6.99 (THR) £6.99 (BOT)
£6.99 (WR) £6.99 (SAF) £7.19 (JON)

★ Shiraz/Cabernet Sauvignon The Wattles
Wine Co **2000** £5.75 (WS)

Shiraz/Grenache Ironstone **1998** £5.99
(UN) £6.49 (BO) £6.99 (VIL) £7.70 (AD)

Shiraz/Mourvèdre Penfolds Bin 2 **1998**
£5.60 (SOM) £6.49 (TES) £6.98 (PEN)

Tarrango Brown Brothers **2000** £5.79
(JON) £5.95 (POR) £5.99 (TES)

Tarrango Brown Brothers **1999** £5.28
(WHI) £5.75 (CON) £5.95 (STE) £5.99
(BO) £5.99 (WAI) £5.99 (DI) £6.55 (AD)

£6.00 → £6.99

Barbera Brown Brothers **1997** £6.95 (WS)
£7.49 (CON) £7.70 (PEN) £7.99 (VIL)

Cabernet Sauvignon Best's Victoria **1994**
£6.50 (CRO)

Cabernet Sauvignon Wakefield **1999**
£6.79 (BO)

Cabernet Sauvignon Wakefield **1998** £6.99
(UN) £7.63 (PLA) £7.99 (GN) £8.29 (BAL)

Cabernet Sauvignon Wakefield **1997**
£6.99 (RAE)

Cabernet Sauvignon David Wynn **1998**
£6.74 (FLE) £7.25 (STE) £8.54 (HIC)
Cabernet Sauvignon/Merlot St Hallett
1997 £6.49 (TES) £8.21 (DOM)
Cabernet Sauvignon/Merlot Yaldara
Reserve **1998** £6.70 (FLE) £8.72 (VIN)
Cabernet Sauvignon/Shiraz Penfolds
Koonunga Hill **1998** £6.99 (UN)
Cabernet Sauvignon/Shiraz Riddoch **1997**
£6.95 (BALL)
Cabernet Sauvignon/Shiraz Rosemount
1999 £6.79 (UN)
Cabernet Sauvignon/Shiraz/Merlot De
Bortoli Windy Peak **1998** £6.99 (BAL)
Durif De Bortoli Vat 1 **1998** £6.79 (AME)
★ Gamekeeper's Reserve St Hallett **2000**
£6.99 (AUS)
Grenache Basedow Bush Vine **1998**
£6.85 (BIB)
Grenache Bethany **1999** £6.49 (MAJ)
Grenache Bethany **1998** £6.79 (UN)
Grenache Simon Hackett McLaren Vale
Old Vine **1998** £6.92 (FLE) £7.38 (GN)
Grenache/Shiraz Rosemount **1999** £6.99
(VIC) £6.99 (THR) £6.99 (BOT) £6.99 (WR)
Merlot Dromana Estate Schinus **1999**
£6.82 (FLE) £7.35 (AS)
Merlot McGuigan Brothers Bin 3000
1998 £6.20 (RIC)
Merlot Willandra **1999** £6.65 (LLO)
Pinot Noir De Bortoli Windy Peak **1997**
£6.99 (BAL)
Pinot Noir Fox River **1998** £6.87 (ASD)
Pinot Noir Tyrrell's Old Winery **1999**
£6.99 (UN) £6.99 (VIL) £6.99 (GN)
Pinot Noir Tyrrell's Old Winery **1998**
£6.64 (PEN) £6.72 (COC)
Pinot Noir David Wynn **1999** £6.95 (NI)
Pinot Noir/Shiraz Montara 'M' **1997**
£6.15 (SOM) £6.90 (CRO)
Shiraz Best's Victoria **1999** £6.99 (GW)
Shiraz Best's Victoria **1998** £6.99 (UN)
Shiraz Simon Hackett Anthony's Reserve
1997 £6.92 (FLE)
Shiraz Hardys Bankside **1999** £6.99 (VIL)
Shiraz Hardys Bankside **1998** £6.99 (UN)
Shiraz Haselgrove Sovereign **1999** £6.49
(VIL)
Shiraz Rosemount **1998** £6.90 (CRO)
£7.49 (SO)
Shiraz Rothbury Mudgee **1997** £6.90 (CRO)
Shiraz Tyrrell's Old Winery **1997** £6.80
(RIC)
Shiraz Wolf Blass **1999** £6.99 (TES)
Shiraz Wolf Blass **1998** £6.99 (UN)

Shiraz Wyndham Estate Bin 555 **1999**
£6.99 (SAF)
Shiraz Wyndham Estate Bin 555 **1998**
£6.99 (COC) £6.99 (MAJ)
Shiraz David Wynn **1998** £6.74 (FLE)
Shiraz Wynns Coonawarra Estate **1998**
£6.99 (BUD) £6.99 (MAJ) £7.95 (POR)
Shiraz Wynns Coonawarra Estate **1997**
£6.80 (BAC)
Shiraz Yaldara Reserve **1999** £6.99 (GW)
Shiraz/Cabernet Sauvignon Penfolds
Koonunga Hill **2000** £6.99 (BUD)
Shiraz/Cabernet Sauvignon Penfolds
Koonunga Hill **1998** £6.95 (WS) £6.98
(PEN) £6.99 (SO) £6.99 (TAN) £7.66 (BY)
Shiraz/Cabernet Sauvignon Penfolds
Koonunga Hill **1997** £6.99 (WAI)
Shiraz/Cabernet Sauvignon Rosemount
2000 £6.49 (SAI) £6.79 (SAF) £6.99 (MORR)
Shiraz/Cabernet Sauvignon Rouge Homme
1998 £6.49 (AME) £6.99 (BAL)
★ Shiraz/Cabernet Sauvignon Saltram
Stonyfell Metala **1998** £6.99 (SAF)
Shiraz/Cabernet Sauvignon Wolf Blass
Red Label **1999** £6.99 (VIL)
Shiraz/Grenache Ironstone **1997** £6.60 (RIC)

£7.00 → £7.99

Barbera Brown Brothers **1998** £7.75 (STA)
Barbera Dromana Estate Garry
Crittenden 'I' **1999** £7.88 (FLE) £8.95
(BU) £10.99 (WAI)
Cabernet Sauvignon Best's Victoria **1998**
£7.50 (FLE)
Cabernet Sauvignon Brown Brothers **1997**
£7.95 (STE) £8.25 (CON) £8.65 (PEN)
Cabernet Sauvignon Chateau Tahbilk
1998 £7.75 (WS)
Cabernet Sauvignon Heathfield Ridge
Endeavour **1999** £7.99 (SAF)
Cabernet Sauvignon/Merlot Brookland
Valley Verse 1 **1998** £7.99 (OD)
Cabernet Sauvignon Montara Estate **1997**
£7.75 (SOM) £8.95 (AD)
Cabernet Sauvignon Rosemount **1999**
£7.49 (SAI) £7.49 (TES) £7.49 (BO)
Cabernet Sauvignon Water Wheel **1999**
£7.99 (AUS)
Cabernet Sauvignon Wolf Blass Yellow
Label **2000** £7.49 (SAF)
Cabernet Sauvignon Wolf Blass Yellow
Label **1999** £7.48 (TES) £7.49 (SAI) £7.49
(MAJ) £7.49 (ASD) £8.78 (BY)
Cabernet Sauvignon Wolf Blass Yellow
Label **1998** £7.49 (BUD) £7.99 (VIL)

Cabernet Sauvignon/Franc Normans Signature Langhorne Creek **1996** £7.99 (SAF)

Cabernet Sauvignon/Merlot Knappstein **1998** £7.99 (SAF)

Cabernet Sauvignon/Merlot Neil Paulett **1997** £7.90 (JU)

Cabernet Sauvignon/Merlot St Hallett **1998** £7.99 (AUS)

Cabernet Sauvignon/Merlot Trentham **1998** £7.99 (JON)

Cabernet Sauvignon/Merlot Tyrrell's Old Winery **1998** £7.73 (PLAY)

Cabernet Sauvignon/Shiraz Yalumba **1998** £7.95 (WS)

Cabernet Sauvignon/Shiraz/Merlot Wynns Coonawarra Estate **1996** £7.99 (TES) £8.29 (JON)

Clancy's Red Peter Lehmann **1999** £7.99 (SAI) £7.99 (WAI)

Clancy's Red Peter Lehmann **1998** £7.99 (UN) £7.99 (OD)

Coonawarra Red Jamiesons Run **1998** £7.99 (MORR)

Grenache Simon Hackett McLaren Vale Old Vine **1999** £7.49 (CON)

Grenache Yalumba Barossa Growers Bush Vine **1998** £7.99 (VIC) £7.99 (THR) £7.99 (BOT) £7.99 (WR) £8.25 (FORT)

Merlot Brown Brothers **1997** £7.49 (CON) £7.70 (PEN) £7.99 (DI)

Merlot Kingston Estate **1999** £7.63 (PLA)

Merlot Kingston Estate **1997** £7.50 (RIC)

Merlot Miranda High Country **1997** £7.41 (COC)

Merlot/Cabernet Sauvignon Rymill **1997** £7.99 (ASD)

Pinot Noir De Bortoli Windy Peak **1999** £7.25 (STE)

Pinot Noir Ninth Island **2000** £7.95 (SOM)

Pinot Noir David Wynn **1998** £7.25 (STE)

Sangiovese Coriole **1998** £7.75 (WS)

Sharefarmer's Red Petaluma **1995** £7.95 (RIC) £8.50 (STE)

Shiraz Brown Brothers Victoria **1998** £7.63 (WHI) £7.99 (TES) £8.45 (STE) £8.70 (TAN)

Shiraz Grant Burge Barossa Vines **1999** £7.50 (HIG)

Shiraz Chateau Tahbilk **1997** £7.75 (WS)

Shiraz Lindemans Limestone Coast **1998** £7.50 (BAC)

Shiraz McGuigan Brothers Shareholders **1997** £7.86 (WHI)

Shiraz McWilliams JJ McWilliam **1998** £7.35 (COC)

Shiraz Penfolds Kalimna Bin 28 **1997** £7.80 (SOM) £8.95 (WS) £8.99 (PEN) £8.99 (VIL) £9.99 (COC) £9.99 (TES) £9.99 (BO) £9.99 (THR) £9.99 (BOT) £9.99 (WR) £9.99 (JON)

Shiraz Plantagenet Omrah **1999** £7.90 (BAC) £7.95 (BU) £7.99 (AME) £7.99 (VIL)

Shiraz Plantagenet Omrah **1998** £7.95 (POR) £7.99 (SO)

Shiraz Rosemount **1999** £7.49 (UN) £7.49 (TES) £7.49 (VIC) £7.49 (THR) £7.49 (SAF) £7.49 (ASD) £7.49 (CO) £7.49 (MORR)

Shiraz Rothbury Hunter Valley **1999** £7.99 (DI)

Shiraz Seaview Edwards & Chaffey **1998** £7.66 (BY)

Shiraz St Hallett Faith **1999** £7.99 (TES) £8.99 (AUS)

Shiraz Wakefield **1998** £7.65 (RAE) £8.29 (BAL)

Shiraz Water Wheel **1998** £7.93 (WHI) £8.80 (PLA)

Shiraz Yaldara Reserve **1998** £7.04 (PLA) £8.28 (PLAY)

Shiraz Yalumba Barossa Growers **1998** £7.99 (BAL) £8.75 (WS)

Shiraz/Cabernet Sauvignon Penfolds Clare Valley Organic **1998** £7.99 (VIL)

Shiraz/Cabernet Sauvignon Saltram Stonyfell Metala **1997** £7.49 (BO)

Shiraz/Grenache d'Arenberg d'Arry's Original **1999** £7.99 (OD) £8.23 (BIB)

Shiraz/Grenache d'Arenberg d'Arry's Original **1998** £7.49 (BO)

Shiraz/Grenache Ironstone **1999** £7.29 (LLO) £9.15 (NI)

Shiraz/Mourvèdre Penfolds Bin 2 **2000** £7.99 (POR)

£8.00 → £8.99

Billi Billi Creek Mount Langi Ghiran **1998** £8.99 (UN) £8.99 (VIL) £11.95 (FORT)

Cabernet Franc Chatsfield **1999** £8.50 (AS) £8.99 (DI)

Cabernet Franc Knappstein **1998** £8.49 (BO)

Cabernet Sauvignon Brown Brothers Milawa **1998** £8.39 (JON)

Cabernet Sauvignon Chateau Xanadu **1998** £8.99 (DI)

Cabernet Sauvignon d'Arenberg The High Trellis **1999** £8.23 (BIB)

Cabernet Sauvignon Mitchell **1999** £8.99 (JON)

Cabernet Sauvignon Mitchell **1996** £8.25 (TAN) £8.50 (BALL) £8.60 (HAH)

A CLUB WITH A FINE WINE CELLAR

The Royal Over-Seas League has a long history of welcoming diplomats, business people, writers and artists from around the world to its London and Edinburgh clubhouses and providing an international network of reciprocal clubs, branches or honorary representatives.

The London clubhouse, comprising two period houses, is in a prime location bordering Green Park and has a private garden, al fresco dining, restaurant, excellent wine list, buttery for light meals, bar, drawing room, 72 ensuite bedrooms and seven conference and private dining rooms. The Edinburgh clubhouse is centrally situated on Princes Street.

Benefits of membership include economical pricing due to the League's not-for-profit status, varied events programmes including champagne, wine and whisky tastings, quarterly journal, discounts on certain Swan Hellenic cruises and Cox & Kings tours, in-house concerts, evening speakers and short term access to over 50 other clubs around the world.

Annual subscription rates range from £78 - £198 and initial joining fees from £21.50 - £100. For further details please contact the Membership Department.

Royal Over-Seas League

Over-Seas House, Park Place, St James's Street, London SW1A 1LR
Tel: **020 7408 0214** (exts. 216 and 315). Enquiries: 9.30am-5.30pm Mon-Fri.
Fax: **020 7499 6738**

Website: www.rosl.org.uk
E-mail: info@rosl.org.uk

Cabernet Sauvignon Pewsey Vale 1996
£8.99 (TES)

Cabernet Sauvignon Rouge Homme 1996
£8.49 (AME) £10.63 (HIC)

Cabernet Sauvignon Tatachilla McLaren
Vale 1998 £8.99 (MAJ)

★ Cabernet Sauvignon Tatachilla Padthaway
1999 £8.99 (SAF)

Cabernet Sauvignon/Malbec Galah 1998
£8.99 (AUS)

Cabernet Sauvignon/Shiraz Ironstone
1995 £8.50 (CRO)

Cabernet Sauvignon/Shiraz Riddoch 1998
£8.99 (DI)

Cabernet Sauvignon/Shiraz Wirra Wirra
Church Block 1998 £8.99 (OD) £9.49
(WAI)

Dry Red Madfish 1999 £8.62 (SAV)

★ Graciano Brown Brothers Milawa 1996
£8.50 (PIP)

Grenache d'Arenberg The Custodian
1998 £8.95 (WS)

Grenache Yalumba Barossa Growers
Bush Vine 1997 £8.99 (BEN)

Merlot/Cabernet Sauvignon Brokenwood
Cricket Pitch 1998 £8.99 (OD) £9.50 (WS)

Nebbiolo Brown Brothers 1996 £8.99 (BO)

Pinot Noir Hollick Coonawarra 1999
£8.95 (NI)

Pinot Noir Hollick Coonawarra 1998
£8.99 (HED)

Pinot Noir Ninth Island 1998 £8.15 (PEN)
£8.95 (BALL)

Pinot Noir Yarra Valley Hills 1998 £8.99
(OD)

★ Shiraz Tim Adams 1999 £8.75 (WS) £8.99
(AUS) £8.99 (TES)

Shiraz Basedow 1997 £8.23 (BIB)

Shiraz Bridgewater Mill 1996 £8.68 (PEN)

Shiraz Bridgewater Mill 1995 £8.70 (RIC)

Shiraz Brown Brothers Victoria 1999
£8.75 (POR)

Shiraz Capel Vale CV 1999 £8.28 (LLO)

Shiraz Coriole 1997 £8.95 (TAN)

Shiraz Evans & Tate Margaret River 1999
£8.85 (AS) £8.99 (SAF)

Shiraz Madfish 1999 £8.99 (GW) £9.25
(BAN) £9.60 (SAV) £9.99 (YOU)

Shiraz Madfish 1998 £8.45 (SOM) £10.50
(NI) £10.95 (BAL)

Shiraz Mitchell Peppertree 1999 £8.70
(TAN) £8.95 (POR) £8.95 (AD) £8.99
(JON) £9.25 (HAH)

Shiraz Montara Estate 1997 £8.95 (AD)
£8.99 (FLE)

Shiraz Penfolds Coonawarra Bin 128 1997
£8.20 (SOM) £9.99 (COC) £9.99 (TES)
£9.99 (VIL) £9.99 (MORR) £10.73 (BY)

Shiraz Penfolds Kalimna Bin 28 1996 £8.99
(SO) £9.74 (BY) £9.99 (UN) £15.83 (MI)

Shiraz Plantagenet Omrah 2000 £8.20 (STA)

Shiraz Plantagenet Omrah 1997 £8.75 (STE)

Shiraz Riddoch 1999 £8.91 (BIB)

Shiraz St Hallett 1998 £8.99 (THR)

Shiraz Taltarni 1998 £8.95 (BER) £9.25
(CON) £9.50 (MAY)

Shiraz David Traeger 1998 £8.99 (AUS)

Shiraz Trentham 1997 £8.99 (AME)

Shiraz/Grenache Veritas Christa-Rolf
1999 £8.95 (LAY)

Shiraz/Grenache Veritas Christa-Rolf
1998 £8.50 (RIC)

Shiraz/Grenache/Mourvèdre Penfolds Old
Vine 1996 £8.65 (SOM) £11.84 (BY)

Tamar Cabernets Ninth Island 1998
£8.99 (VIL) £9.25 (CON)

£9.00 → £9.99

Cabernet Franc Knappstein 1994 £9.00
(CRO)

Cabernet Sauvignon Jim Barry 1998 £9.20
(TAN) £9.40 (BEN) £9.99 (DI)

Cabernet Sauvignon Best's Great
Western 1993 £9.50 (CRO)

Cabernet Sauvignon Bremerton 1996
£9.79 (LLO)

Cabernet Sauvignon Bremerton 1995
£9.50 (BAC)

Cabernet Sauvignon Grant Burge 1998
£9.95 (BALL) £9.99 (UN) £10.85 (AS)

Cabernet Sauvignon Grant Burge 1997
£9.95 (RES) £10.00 (RIC)

Cabernet Sauvignon Eden Ridge 1997
£9.50 (AD)

Cabernet Sauvignon/Merlot Vasse Felix
1999 £9.20 (TAN)

Cabernet Sauvignon Pikes Clare Valley
1998 £9.95 (LEA)

Cabernet Sauvignon Rouge Homme 1994
£9.90 (VIN)

Cabernet Sauvignon Saltram Mamre
Brook 1998 £9.99 (SAF)

Cabernet Sauvignon Wynns 1996 £9.99
(PEN)

Cabernet Sauvignon Wynns Coonawarra
Estate 1997 £9.99 (MAJ) £10.73 (BY)

Cabernet Sauvignon Wynns Coonawarra
Estate 1996 £9.99 (SUN) £9.99 (LAI)

Cabernet Sauvignon Wynns Coonawarra
Estate 1995 £9.99 (AME)

Cabernet Sauvignon/Malbec Leasingham Bin 56 **1997** £9.99 (THR) £9.99 (WR)

Cabernet Sauvignon/Merlot Bethany **1999** £9.99 (CO)

Cabernet Sauvignon/Merlot Cape Mentelle **1999** £9.98 (PLA) £10.79 (YOU)

Cabernet Sauvignon/Merlot Cape Mentelle **1998** £9.85 (CON) £9.99 (JON) £9.99 (VIL) £9.99 (BAL) £10.50 (STA) £10.85 (AD)

Cabernet Sauvignon/Merlot Hollick Coonawarra **1998** £9.95 (NI)

Cabernet Sauvignon/Merlot Hollick Coonawarra **1996** £9.49 (HED)

Durif Morris **1994** £9.65 (SOM)

The Fergus Tim Adams **1999** £9.99 (AUS)

The Fergus Tim Adams **1998** £9.99 (WR)

Fifth Leg Devil's Lair **1998** £9.69 (GW)

Grenache Charles Cimicky **1998** £9.50 (CRO)

Grenache Simon Hackett McLaren Vale Old Vine **1997** £9.76 (VIN)

Grenache Rockford Dry Country **1997** £9.30 (FLE) £10.75 (TAN) £10.99 (YOU)

Grenache Woodstock **1998** £9.39 (GN)

GSM Simon Gilbert McLaren Vale **1998** £9.99 (BAL)

Merlot Mitchelton Preece **1997** £9.60 (HIC)

Merlot Oakridge **1998** £9.90 (CRO)

Pinot Noir Dromana Estate **1999** £9.99 (FLE) £9.99 (YOU)

Pinot Noir Scotchman's Hill **1997** £9.90 (JU)

Pinot Noir Yering Station **1999** £9.99 (YOU)

Shiraz Alkoomi **1999** £9.85 (JER)

Shiraz Baileys 1920s Block **1996** £9.95 (AME)

Shiraz Chapel Hill McLaren Vale **1998** £9.99 (AUS)

Shiraz Fern Hill **1995** £9.95 (FRI)

Shiraz Simon Hackett Anthony's Reserve **1998** £9.99 (GN) £12.99 (CON)

★ Shiraz Steve Hoff Wines **1998** £9.99 (AUS)

Shiraz Leasingham **1997** £9.99 (ASD)

Shiraz Leasingham **1996** £9.99 (UN)

Shiraz Lindemans Padthaway **1996** £9.72 (BY)

Shiraz McWilliams Mount Pleasant **1994** £9.95 (COC)

Shiraz Mitchelton Goulburn Valley **1996** £9.60 (HIC)

Shiraz Penfolds Coonawarra Bin 128 **1998** £9.49 (POR) £9.99 (SO) £9.99 (SAF)

Shiraz Penfolds Coonawarra Bin 128 **1996** £9.99 (UN) £9.99 (BO)

Shiraz Penley Estate Hyland **1999** £9.95 (LAY)

Shiraz Penley Estate Hyland **1996** £9.99 (VIL)

Shiraz Pikes Clare Valley **1998** £9.95 (LEA)

Shiraz Rosemount Hill of Gold **1999** £9.99 (SAF)

Shiraz Rothbury Brokenback **1998** £9.99 (DI)

Shiraz Saltram Mamre Brook **1997** £9.99 (SUN) £9.99 (LAI)

Shiraz Taltarni **1996** £9.40 (PEN)

Shiraz The Willows Vineyard **1998** £9.99 (AUS)

£10.00 → £10.99

Cabernet Sauvignon Best's Great Western **1996** £10.99 (UN) £11.99 (GW)

Cabernet Sauvignon Richard Hamilton Hut Block **1996** £10.99 (SUN) £10.99 (LAI)

Cabernet Sauvignon Katnook **1998** £10.99 (YOU) £11.99 (DI) £12.24 (BIB)

Cabernet Sauvignon Seaview Edwards & Chaffey Section 353 **1997** £10.80 (BY)

Cabernet Sauvignon Taltarni **1996** £10.75 (STA)

Cabernet Sauvignon Taltarni **1995** £10.00 (CON)

Cabernet Sauvignon Vasse Felix **1999** £10.75 (SOM) £13.55 (BEN) £14.95 (LAY)

Cabernet Sauvignon Yalumba Menzies **1995** £10.85 (SOM)

Cabernet Sauvignon/Merlot Dromana Estate **1998** £10.99 (YOU)

Cabernet Sauvignon/Merlot Mount Helen **1997** £10.83 (LAI)

GSM Rosemount **1996** £10.56 (WHI)

Mourvèdre d'Arenberg The Twenty Eight Road **1998** £10.96 (BIB)

Pinot Noir Old Kent River **1998** £10.75 (JER)

Pinot Noir Stonier **1998** £10.99 (DI) £11.49 (YOU) £11.52 (BY)

Shiraz Balgownie **1997** £10.99 (AME)

Shiraz Best's Great Western **1997** £10.99 (GW)

Shiraz Cape Mentelle **1999** £10.40 (CRO)

Shiraz Delatite **1996** £10.42 (ARM)

Shiraz Frankland Estate Isolation Ridge **1998** £10.99 (YOU)

Shiraz Tim Gramp **1996** £10.75 (SOM)

Shiraz Woodstock **1998** £10.99 (GN)

- All prices for each wine are listed together in ascending order.
- Price bands refer to the lowest price for which the wine is available.

£11.00 → £11.99

Cabernet Sauvignon Alkoomi 1997
£11.00 (JER)
Cabernet Sauvignon Balgownie 1998
£11.99 (RAE) £12.95 (BEN) £12.95 (BAL)
Cabernet Sauvignon Best's Great
Western 1997 £11.45 (NI)
Cabernet Sauvignon Chain of Ponds
Amadeus 2000 £11.55 (BIB)
Cabernet Sauvignon Leconfield 1997
£11.95 (JU)
Cabernet Sauvignon Plantagenet Mount
Barker 1998 £11.95 (LIB)
Cabernet Sauvignon Plantagenet Mount
Barker 1997 £11.99 (VIL) £12.20 (HAH)
Cabernet Sauvignon Wolf Blass
President's Selection 1996 £11.46
(COC) £12.31 (BY) £12.59 (JON)
Cabernet Sauvignon/Malbec Leasingham
Bin 56 1995 £11.25 (BALL)
Cabernet Sauvignon/Merlot Hollick
Coonawarra 1995 £11.25 (FORT)
£11.69 (TW)
Cabernet Sauvignon/Merlot Leeuwin
Estate Prelude 1998 £11.52 (DOM)
Cabernet Sauvignon/Merlot Voyager
Estate 1995 £11.50 (JU)
Cabernet Sauvignon/Shiraz Penfolds Bin
389 1997 £11.40 (SOM) £12.99 (VIL)
£14.85 (TAN) £14.99 (TES) £14.99 (WR)
Coonawarra Petaluma 1998 £11.16 (FA)
Grenache/Shiraz Richard Hamilton
Marion Vineyard 1998 £11.20 (SOM)
Obliqua Ashton Hills 1998 £11.99 (AUS)
Pinot Noir Pipers Brook Pellion 2000
£11.25 (SOM)
Pinot Noir Plantagenet Mount Barker
Pemberton 1998 £11.99 (VIL) £13.99 (VA)
Shiraz Tim Adams 1998 £11.95 (FORT)
Shiraz Balgownie 1998 £11.99 (RAE)
£12.95 (BEN) £12.95 (BAL)
Shiraz Jim Barry McCrae Wood 1995
£11.75 (SOM) £21.00 (BU)
Shiraz Best's Great Western Bin 'O'
1997 £11.99 (NI)

- *Wines are listed in A–Z order within each price band.*
- *For each wine, vintages are listed in descending order.*
- *Each vintage of any wine appears only once.*

Shiraz Bowen Estate 1997 £11.49 (YOU)
Shiraz Grant Burge 60-year-old vines
1998 £11.50 (CON)
Shiraz Grant Burge Filsell Vineyard Old
Vine 1998 £11.50 (HIG) £11.95 (RES)
Shiraz Grant Burge Old Vine 1998 £11.45
(AS) £11.75 (BU) £12.99 (VIL)
Shiraz Chateau Reynella Basket Pressed
1998 £11.99 (WAI)
Shiraz De Bortoli Yarra Valley 1997
£11.95 (STE)
Shiraz Penfolds Magill Estate 1996 £11.75
(SOM)
Shiraz St Hallett Blackwell 1997 £11.99
(AUS) £12.49 (VIC) £12.99 (WR)
Shiraz Wolf Blass President's Selection
1997 £11.86 (BY) £11.99 (VIL)
Shiraz David Wynn Patriarch 1996
£11.95 (NI) £14.75 (WRI)
Shiraz/Grenache/Mourvèdre Penfolds Old
Vine 1997 £11.99 (PEN) £11.99 (VIL)

£12.00 → £12.99

Cabernet Sauvignon Maxwell Lime Cave
1999 £12.99 (YOU)
Cabernet Sauvignon McGuigan Brothers
Personal Reserve 1997 £12.16 (WHI)
Cabernet Sauvignon/Merlot Devil's Lair
1998 £12.15 (BAN)
Cabernet Sauvignon Vasse Felix 1998
£12.99 (YOU) £14.95 (RES)
Limestone Ridge Lindemans 1994 £12.05
(SOM) £14.98 (PEN)
Merlot Tatachilla Clarendon Vineyard
1997 £12.79 (YOU)
★ Mourèvdre Hewitson Old Garden 1999
£12.95 (WAT)
★ Olmo's Reward Frankland Estate 1995
£12.50 (MV)
Pinot Noir Cullen 1999 £12.99 (YOU)
Pinot Noir Cullen 1998 £12.50 (CRO)
Pinot Noir Nepenthe 1999 £12.79 (PLA)
£12.99 (YOU) £14.90 (CRO)
Pinot Noir Nepenthe 1998 £12.99 (GW)
Pinot Noir Pipers Brook Pellion 1998
£12.50 (POR) £12.71 (PEN) £13.75 (STA)
Shiraz Bremerton Old Adam 1998 £12.99
(YOU)
Shiraz Brokenwood 1997 £12.95 (RES)
Shiraz/Cabernet Sauvignon/Malbec
Henschke Keyneton Estate 1995
£12.20 (SOM) £15.00 (FLE) £24.68 (FA)
Shiraz Chateau Reynella 1997 £12.99 (VIL)
Shiraz De Bortoli Yarra Valley 1998
£12.95 (STA)

Shiraz Elderton **1997** £12.99 (OD)
Shiraz Hewitson Barossa Valley **1998**
£12.95 (WAT)
Shiraz Maxwell Ellen Street **1998** £12.90
(CRO) £12.99 (YOU)
Shiraz Miranda Family Reserve Old Vine
1998 £12.49 (YOU)
Shiraz Picardy **1997** £12.00 (JU)
Shiraz Vasse Felix **1997** £12.45 (SOM)
Shiraz David Wynn Patriarch **1997**
£12.35 (SOM) £13.58 (FLE) £13.90 (CRO)

£13.00 → £13.99

The Blend Balnaves **1998** £13.95 (LIB)
Cabernet Sauvignon Chain of Ponds
Amadeus **1994** £13.40 (SOM)
Cabernet Sauvignon Devil's Lair **1995**
£13.75 (SOM)
Cabernet Sauvignon Stonier Reserve
1995 £13.99 (DI)
Cabernet Sauvignon Taltarni **1998** £13.28
(TW)
Cabernet Sauvignon Vasse Felix **1996**
£13.50 (BAL)
Cabernet Sauvignon Yalumba Menzies
1996 £13.50 (FORT) £13.99 (LAI) £14.95
(RES) £14.95 (BAL)
Cabernet Sauvignon/Merlot Leeuwin
Estate Prelude **1996** £13.20 (SOM)
Cabernet Sauvignon/Merlot Nepenthe
Fugue **1997** £13.99 (GW) £14.79 (YOU)
'Mary Kathleen' Coriole **1997** £13.79
(YOU)
Pinot Noir Barratt **1997** £13.85 (FLE)
Pinot Noir Mountadam **1997** £13.29 (FLE)
Shiraz De Bortoli Yarra Valley **1996**
£13.50 (BAL)
Shiraz Hillstowe Mary's Hundred **1997**
£13.57 (NO) £14.50 (FLE)
Shiraz Hollick Wilgha **1997** £13.30 (NI)
Shiraz Kingston Estate Reserve **1997**
£13.99 (RIC)
Shiraz Charles Melton **1998** £13.60 (SOM)
£16.25 (NI) £19.99 (VIL)
Shiraz Mount Horrocks Clare Valley
1998 £13.12 (FA) £17.95 (STA)
Shiraz Plantagenet Mount Barker **1997**
£13.95 (BEN) £13.95 (LIB) £13.95 (BU)
£13.99 (VIL)
Shiraz St Hallett Old Block **1997** £13.99
(BOT) £13.99 (WR) £14.99 (TES) £15.86
(DOM) £15.99 (POR)
Shiraz Turkey Flat **1998** £13.12 (FA)
Shiraz Veritas Heysen Vineyard **1996**
£13.12 (FA)

£14.00 → £15.99

★ Angelus Wirra Wirra **1998** £14.49 (OD)
£14.50 (WS) £14.55 (WAI)
Cabernet Sauvignon Barossa Valley Estate
Ebenezer **1996** £15.99 (YOU)
Cabernet Sauvignon Devil's Lair **1997**
£14.85 (FLE) £15.76 (GW)
Cabernet Sauvignon Simon Hackett Foggo
Road **1998** £14.88 (NO) £15.50 (WRI)
Cabernet Sauvignon Simon Hackett Foggo
Road **1997** £15.50 (CON)
Cabernet Sauvignon/Merlot Devil's Lair
1997 £14.99 (YOU)
Cabernet Sauvignon Mountadam **1994**
£14.99 (YOU)
Cabernet Sauvignon Rosemount Orange
Vineyard **1993** £15.03 (WHI)
Cabernet Sauvignon Rosemount Show
Reserve **1997** £14.99 (MORR)
Cabernet Sauvignon Seppelt Drumborg
1994 £15.49 (AME)
Cabernet Sauvignon Yalumba Menzies
1997 £14.99 (YOU) £15.00 (WRI)
Cabernet Sauvignon/Merlot Nepenthe
Fugue **1998** £14.90 (CRO)
Cabernet Sauvignon/Shiraz Penfolds Bin
389 **1998** £14.99 (POR) £14.99 (OD)
£14.99 (SAF)
Cabernet Sauvignon/Shiraz Penfolds Bin
389 **1995** £14.00 (CRO) £14.99 (COC)
Cabernet Sauvignon/Shiraz Penfolds Bin
389 **1994** £14.95 (FORT)
Coonawarra Petaluma **1997** £14.75 (BEN)
Diva Coriole **1998** £14.95 (HED)
The Fergus Tim Adams **1996** £15.00 (BU)
Grenache/Mourvèdre/Shiraz Penfolds
Barossa Valley Old Vine **1996** £14.29
(JON)
GSM Rosemount **1997** £14.95 (WAI)
£14.99 (SUN) £14.99 (WR) £14.99 (LAI)
GSM Rosemount **1995** £15.90 (CRO)
Mentor Peter Lehmann **1996** £15.99
(UN)
Merlot Charles Cimicky **1997** £15.99
(GW)
Nine Popes Charles Melton **1998** £15.99
(SOM) £18.99 (YOU) £19.95 (BEN) £19.95
(BAL) £19.99 (VIL) £23.95 (RES)
Olmo's Reward Frankland Estate **1994**
£15.25 (FORT)
Opimian Pipers Brook **1998** £14.75 (CON)
Pinot Noir De Bortoli **1998** £15.50 (BAL)
Pinot Noir De Bortoli Yarra Valley **1997**
£15.45 (STE)

Pinot Noir Henschke Giles **1994** £14.26
(NO) £23.00 (CRO)
Pinot Noir Lenswood **1998** £14.55 (SOM)
£16.99 (NEZ)
Pinot Noir Mountadam **1998** £14.99 (OD)
Pinot Noir Mountadam **1996** £15.25
(FORT) £15.95 (AD)
Pyrus Lindemans **1996** £14.98 (PEN)
£15.39 (JON) £16.99 (UN)
St George Lindemans **1996** £14.95 (WS)
St George Lindemans **1995** £14.98 (PEN)
Shiraz Barossa Valley Estate Ebenezer
1997 £14.99 (UN) £14.99 (VIL)

Shiraz Jim Barry McCrae Wood **1997**
£14.95 (TAN) £15.50 (BEN) £15.99 (DI)
Shiraz Jim Barry McCrae Wood **1996**
£14.00 (NO) £14.99 (SUN) £14.99 (OD)
£14.99 (LAI) £14.99 (YOU) £15.49 (JON)
Shiraz Jim Barry The Armagh **1994**
£14.10 (FA)
Shiraz Bremerton Old Adam **1997** £14.49
(AME)
Shiraz Chapel Hill McLaren Vale **1994**
£14.50 (BU)
Shiraz Charles Cimicky **1996** £14.94 (GW)
Shiraz Coriole **1996** £14.00 (CRO)
Shiraz Tim Gramp **1997** £15.95 (AD)
Shiraz Hollick Wilgha **1998** £15.99 (AME)
Shiraz Leasingham Classic Clare **1997**
£14.99 (UN) £19.99 (VIL) £19.99 (YOU)
Shiraz Lengs & Cooter Clare Valley Old
Vine **1995** £15.15 (NO) £15.75 (CON)
Shiraz Mount Langi Ghiran Langi **1997**
£15.99 (SOM) £17.90 (FLE) £18.99 (BO)
£18.99 (YOU) £19.50 (STA) £19.75 (WRI)
£19.99 (BAL) £20.15 (HAH) £21.95 (RES)
Shiraz Plantagenet Mount Barker **1998**
£14.80 (HAH)
Shiraz St Hallett Old Block **1996** £14.95
(FLE) £16.99 (JON)
Shiraz St Hallett Old Block **1994** £15.50
(CRO) £22.50 (BU)
Shiraz Saltram No 1 **1997** £15.99 (YOU)
£16.99 (AME)

Shiraz Taltarni **1988** £14.00 (CRO)
Shiraz Tatachilla Foundation **1997** £14.50
(WS)
Shiraz Vasse Felix **1999** £14.99 (YOU)
Shiraz Wirra Wirra R.S.W. **1998** £14.50
(WS)
Shiraz Wolf Blass President's Selection
1993 £15.00 (CRO)
Traditional Rosemount **1998** £14.99 (UN)
The Vicar Chapel Hill **1998** £14.99 (YOU)

£16.00 → £19.99

The Aberfeldy Tim Adams **1998** £18.49
(YOU)
The Aberfeldy Tim Adams **1997** £18.95
(FORT)
Angelus Wirra Wirra **1990** £19.50 (BU)
Cabernet Sauvignon Balnaves **1998**
£17.99 (YOU) £18.95 (LIB)
Cabernet Sauvignon Brown Brothers
Family Reserve **1992** £16.92 (PEN)
Cabernet Sauvignon Cape Mentelle **1996**
£17.95 (BAL) £18.19 (NO) £18.75 (NI)
Cabernet Sauvignon Cape Mentelle **1995**
£16.20 (TAN) £16.99 (VIL) £18.42 (PLAY)
Cabernet Sauvignon Dalwhinnie **1997**
£17.00 (JU)
Cabernet Sauvignon d'Arenberg The
Coppermine Road **1998** £17.33 (BIB)
£17.50 (WS)
Cabernet Sauvignon Haselgrove H Series
1998 £18.99 (SAF) £23.99 (VIL)
Cabernet Sauvignon Hollick Ravenswood
1994 £18.99 (AME) £19.89 (JON) £22.95
(RES)
Cabernet Sauvignon Howard Park **1996**
£19.02 (GW)
Cabernet Sauvignon Leasingham Classic
Clare **1996** £19.99 (VIL) £19.99 (YOU)
Cabernet Sauvignon Leeuwin Estate Art
Series **1997** £17.63 (DOM)
Cabernet Sauvignon Leeuwin Estate Art
Series **1995** £19.35 (SOM)
Cabernet Sauvignon Penley Estate **1995**
£17.95 (LAY)
Cabernet Sauvignon Seppelt Black Label
1983 £18.00 (CRO)
Cabernet Sauvignon Turkey Flat **1998**
£16.95 (BAL) £16.99 (YOU)
Cabernet Sauvignon Yarra Yering Dry
Red No.1 **1997** £18.75 (SOM)
Cabernet Sauvignon/Merlot Cullen **1997**
£19.95 (AD) £19.95 (DI) £21.00 (CRO)
Cabernet Sauvignon/Merlot Henschke
Abbott's Prayer **1995** £19.95 (SOM)

Cabernet Sauvignon/Merlot Howard Park
1998 £19.50 (BAN) £21.79 (YOU)
Cabernet Sauvignon/Merlot Howard Park
1995 £17.10 (SOM) £23.95 (FORT)
Cabernet Sauvignon/Merlot Mount
Horrocks Clare Valley **1998** £16.95
(BEN)
Cabernet Sauvignon/Shiraz Yalumba The
Signature **1996** £18.95 (LAY)
Cabernet Sauvignon/Shiraz Yalumba The
Signature **1995** £18.95 (RES)
Cabernet Sauvignon/Shiraz/Merlot
Elderton **1995** £18.95 (BER)
Cabernets Pierro **1997** £19.95 (BER)
Gaia Grosset **1997** £16.06 (FA)
Grenache Clarendon Hills Blewitt Springs
Vineyard Old Vines **1999** £19.00 (JU)
Grenache Clarendon Hills Kangarilla
Vineyard Old Vines **1997** £17.04 (FA)
£19.00 (JU) £19.99 (YOU)
Grenache/Shiraz d'Arenberg Ironstone
Pressings **1998** £17.33 (BIB) £17.50 (WS)
£17.99 (YOU) £19.95 (FORT)
The Holy Trinity Grant Burge **1997**
£19.75 (BU) £19.90 (RIC)
The Holy Trinity Grant Burge **1996**
£19.50 (HIG) £21.50 (BALL) £21.95 (CON)
Limestone Ridge Lindemans **1997** £16.99
(UN)
Merlot/Cabernet Sauvignon Yaldara
Farms Barossa Valley **1996** £16.99
(SUN) £16.99 (LAI)
Merlot Mountadam **1996** £19.95 (AD)
£20.75 (NI)
Merlot Taltarni **1992** £18.00 (CRO)
Nine Popes Charles Melton **1999** £17.25
(NI) £21.95 (LIB) £21.95 (VA)
Nine Popes Charles Melton **1991** £19.00
(CRO)
Pinot Meunier Best's Great Western Old
Vine **1994** £17.00 (CRO)
Pinot Noir Bannockburn **1998** £18.00 (TAN)
Pinot Noir Bannockburn **1997** £19.95 (RES)
Pinot Noir Barratt **1999** £16.75 (BAN)
Pinot Noir Coldstream Hills Reserve
1998 £16.99 (OD)
Pinot Noir Dromana Estate Reserve
1999 £17.99 (YOU)
Pinot Noir Henschke Giles **1998** £18.79
(YOU)
Pinot Noir Lenswood **1997** £16.70 (HAH)
Pinot Noir Lenswood **1996** £16.00 (CRO)
Pinot Noir Moss Wood **1999** £16.50 (JER)
Pinot Noir Stonier Merricks Reserve
1997 £19.95 (RES)

Pinot Noir Stonier Reserve **1997** £16.99
(DI)
Pyrus Lindemans **1997** £16.01 (BY)
The Red Mountadam **1996** £18.99 (YOU)
£19.45 (NI) £19.95 (AD) £20.42 (HIC)
The Red Mountadam **1994** £18.50 (FLE)
Shiraz Bannockburn **1998** £16.99 (YOU)
Shiraz Bannockburn **1995** £17.95 (BAL)
Shiraz/Cabernet Sauvignon/Malbec
Henschke Keyneton Estate **1997**
£17.80 (RIC) £17.95 (LAY) £21.15 (JER)
Shiraz Capel Vale Reserve Kinnaird **1998**
£19.99 (LLO)
Shiraz Dalwhinnie **1997** £17.00 (JU)
£17.99 (YOU)
★ Shiraz d'Arenberg Dead Arm **1998**
£17.50 (WS) £17.99 (BIB) £17.99 (OD)
£17.99 (YOU) £19.25 (FORT)
Shiraz Henschke Mount Edelstone **1995**
£19.95 (SOM) £28.75 (NI) £42.00 (CRO)
Shiraz Maglieri Steve Maglieri **1993**
£19.00 (CRO)
Shiraz McWilliams Maurice O'Shea **1994**
£17.70 (COC)
Shiraz Charles Melton **1997** £18.50 (AD)
Shiraz Mount Langi Ghiran Langi **1998**
£16.06 (FA) £18.99 (YOU) £19.75 (CON)
£19.95 (BEN) £19.95 (LIB) £19.99 (VIL)
Shiraz Neil Paulett Andreas **1996** £16.50
(JU)
Shiraz Penfolds Kalimna Bin 28 **1991**
£16.00 (CRO)
Shiraz Rockford Basket Press **1997**
£16.95 (WRI)
Shiraz Saltram No 1 **1996** £16.66 (SUN)
Shiraz Turkey Flat **1997** £17.95 (BAL)
Shiraz Wakefield St Andrews **1996**
£18.99 (RAE)
Shiraz Woodstock 'The Stocks' **1998**
£18.95 (GN)
Shiraz Woodstock 'The Stocks' **1996**
£16.85 (WRI)
Shiraz/Cabernet Sauvignon Saltram
Stonyfell Metala **1996** £18.27 (NO)
Shiraz/Cabernet Sauvignon Yalumba The
Signature **1996** £16.95 (BAL) £16.99 (YOU)
Shiraz/Mourvèdre Leconfield **1997**
£18.00 (JU) £18.99 (YOU)

Oz Clarke's Wine Buying Guide
is an annual publication.
We welcome your suggestions for
next year's edition.

£20.00 → £29.99

The Aberfeldy Tim Adams 1996 £25.00 (BU)

Cabernet Sauvignon Chateau Reynella Basket Pressed 1985 £22.00 (CRO)

Cabernet Sauvignon Henschke Cyril Henschke 1997 £28.55 (JER)

Cabernet Sauvignon Hollick Ravenswood 1996 £22.95 (NI)

Cabernet Sauvignon Howard Park 1995 £22.95 (BAL)

Cabernet Sauvignon Lake's Folly 1987 £25.00 (CRO)

Cabernet Sauvignon Leeuwin Estate Art Series 1996 £27.50 (MAY)

Cabernet Sauvignon Moss Wood 1997 £25.00 (WS)

Cabernet Sauvignon Moss Wood 1989 £27.00 (CRO)

Cabernet Sauvignon Parker Coonawarra Estate Terra Rossa 1996 £25.85 (FA)

Cabernet Sauvignon Penfolds Bin 707 1997 £29.95 (SOM) £35.00 (WS) £36.99 (VIL) £36.99 (YOU) £40.00 (FORT) £47.50 (MI)

Cabernet Sauvignon Rosemount Show Reserve 1985 £23.00 (CRO)

Cabernet Sauvignon Taltarni 1982 £25.00 (BU)

Cabernet Sauvignon Wynns John Riddoch 1994 £28.45 (SOM) £36.62 (FA)

Cabernet Sauvignon Yarra Yering Dry Red No.1 1998 £22.99 (YOU) £25.50 (BEN)

Cabernet Sauvignon Yarra Yering Dry Red No.1 1996 £24.95 (NI)

Cabernet Sauvignon/Merlot Cullen 1998 £21.99 (VIL) £22.50 (WS) £24.99 (VA)

Cabernet Sauvignon/Merlot Cullen 1996 £20.00 (YOU)

Cabernet Sauvignon/Merlot Henschke Abbott's Prayer 1997 £28.99 (YOU)

Cabernet Sauvignon/Merlot Henschke Abbott's Prayer 1991 £29.38 (FA) £30.00 (CRO)

Cabernet Sauvignon/Merlot Howard Park 1996 £25.00 (WS)

Cabernet Sauvignon/Merlot/Shiraz Blue Pyrenees Estate 1982 £24.00 (CRO)

Cabernet Sauvignon/Shiraz Yalumba The Reserve 1992 £24.75 (SOM)

Cabernet Sauvignon/Shiraz/Merlot Houghton Jack Mann 1996 £28.99 (YOU)

E&E Black Pepper Shiraz 1997 £29.99 (UN) £35.00 (WRI) £39.99 (VIL) £46.00 (YOU)

E&E Black Pepper Shiraz 1993 £29.00 (CRO)

Grenache Clarendon Hills Clarendon Vineyard Old Vines 1998 £21.93 (BODX)

Limestone Ridge Lindemans 1988 £29.00 (CRO)

Merlot Clarendon Hills 1997 £23.40 (FA) £26.00 (JU) £26.99 (YOU)

Mountain Blue Rosemount 1995 £22.31 (WHI)

Nine Popes Charles Melton 1997 £20.50 (WRI)

Octavius Yalumba 1995 £26.12 (FLE)

Octavius Yalumba 1993 £24.95 (SOM)

Pinot Noir Yarra Yering 1998 £28.95 (BEN)

Pinot Noir Yarra Yering 1994 £24.17 (ARM)

St George Lindemans 1988 £28.00 (CRO)

Shadrach Grant Burge 1996 £28.50 (BU) £29.95 (LEA) £31.50 (BALL) £34.99 (VIL)

Shiraz Basedow Johannes Barossa 1996 £27.41 (BIB)

Shiraz Brokenwood Graveyard Vineyard 1998 £29.50 (BAN)

Shiraz Brokenwood Graveyard Vineyard 1996 £28.86 (NO)

Shiraz Brokenwood Rayners Vineyard 1998 £22.95 (RES)

Shiraz/Cabernet Sauvignon/Malbec Henschke Keyneton Estate 1996 £24.50 (FORT) £25.85 (FA) £29.00 (CRO)

Shiraz Clarendon Hills 1998 £22.91 (FA)

Shiraz Clarendon Hills 1996 £21.00 (JU)

Shiraz Dalwhinnie 1998 £23.99 (YOU)

Shiraz Elderton Command 1995 £29.95 (POR)

Shiraz Hardys Eileen Hardy 1997 £27.95 (WAI) £28.99 (YOU) £29.99 (UN)

Shiraz Henschke Mount Edelstone 1997 £28.85 (LAY) £32.80 (JER) £38.58 (FA)

Shiraz Jasper Hill Georgia's Paddock 1999 £29.75 (YAP)

Shiraz Charles Melton 1999 £21.95 (VA)

Shiraz Penfolds Magill Estate 1997 £24.86 (PEN) £29.99 (VIL) £29.99 (YOU)

Shiraz Penfolds St Henri 1996 £24.86 (PEN) £24.99 (VIL) £35.00 (MI)

Shiraz Rockford Basket Press 1995 £24.00 (CRO)

Shiraz Taltarni 1982 £26.00 (CRO)

Shiraz Tyrrell's Vat 9 Winemakers Selection 1990 £25.00 (CRO)

Shiraz Wynns Michael 1994 £28.45 (SOM) £36.99 (PEN) £39.56 (FA)

Shiraz Yarra Yering Underhill 1998 £22.99 (YOU) £26.00 (BAL) £27.95 (BER)

Shiraz Yarra Yering Underhill 1996 £24.95 (NI)

Shiraz/Cabernet Sauvignon Seppelt
  Moyston **1971** £25.00 (BU)
Syrah Rosemount Balmoral **1997** £22.31
  (WHI) £34.99 (SUN) £34.99 (LAI)
Terra Rossa First Growth Parker
  Coonawarra Estate **1998** £26.46 (CB)
Terra Rossa First Growth Parker
  Coonawarra Estate **1996** £29.99 (VIL)

£30.00 → £39.99

Cabernet Sauvignon Chateau Tahbilk
  1982 £32.00 (CRO)
Cabernet Sauvignon Moss Wood **1998**
  £35.00 (JER)
Cabernet Sauvignon Moss Wood **1987**
  £36.00 (CRO)
Cabernet Sauvignon Penfolds Bin 707
  1998 £39.99 (POR) £39.99 (YOU)
Cabernet Sauvignon Penfolds Bin 707 **1996**
  £36.94 (BY) £36.99 (UN) £50.33 (FA)
Cabernet Sauvignon Penfolds Bin 707
  1994 £32.90 (PEN) £39.99 (GN) £51.23
  (NO) £54.00 (CRO)
Cabernet Sauvignon Rouge Homme **1982**
  £35.00 (CRO)
Cabernet Sauvignon Taltarni **1980** £30.00
  (CRO)
Cabernet Sauvignon Wynns John Riddoch
  1996 £34.99 (YOU) £36.99 (UN) £36.99
  (PEN)
Cabernet Sauvignon/Shiraz Wolf Blass
  Black Label **1996** £39.99 (VIL)
Limestone Ridge Lindemans **1984** £35.00
  (CRO)
Meshach Grant Burge **1997** £37.50 (RIC)
Meshach Grant Burge **1996** £39.95 (CON)
Meshach Grant Burge **1995** £38.75 (STA)
  £39.95 (LEA) £39.99 (UN) £42.84 (PLAY)
Octavius Yalumba **1996** £32.99 (YOU)
  £35.00 (FORT) £35.75 (LAY) £38.00 (BAL)
Pinot Noir Giaconda **1998** £32.00 (YOU)
Shiraz Jim Barry The Armagh **1998**
  £34.99 (YOU)
Shiraz Jim Barry The Armagh **1997**
  £34.95 (BEN) £35.20 (TAN) £37.00 (BAL)
Shiraz Jim Barry The Armagh **1996**
  £31.94 (NO) £34.99 (OD) £36.40 (JER)
Shiraz d'Arenberg Dead Arm **1997**
  £35.64 (FA)
Shiraz Elderton Command **1993** £36.62
  (FA)
Shiraz Henschke Mount Edelstone **1996**
  £30.00 (FORT) £38.58 (FA) £39.00 (CRO)
Shiraz Jasper Hill Georgia's Paddock **1998**
  £39.50 (BAL)

Shiraz Peter Lehmann Stonewell **1994**
  £30.75 (BODX) £34.08 (TUR)
Shiraz Penfolds Kalimna Bin 28 **1978**
  £35.00 (CRO)
Shiraz Wynns Michael **1998** £39.99 (POR)
Shiraz Wynns Michael **1991** £49.00 (CRO)
Shiraz Yarra Yering Dry Red No.2 **1989**
  £30.00 (CRO)
Syrah Rosemount Balmoral **1996** £34.99
  (UN)

£40.00 → £59.99

Cabernet Sauvignon Henschke Cyril
  Henschke **1996** £43.95 (RES)
Cabernet Sauvignon Henschke Cyril
  Henschke **1994** £40.89 (NO) £46.41 (FA)
Cabernet Sauvignon Henschke Cyril
  Henschke **1988** £55.00 (CRO)
Cabernet Sauvignon Parker Coonawarra
  Estate Terra Rossa **1988** £40.00 (CRO)
Cabernet Sauvignon Penley Estate **1989**
  £45.00 (CRO)
Cabernet Sauvignon/Merlot Henschke
  Abbott's Prayer **1996** £40.89 (NO)
Cabernet Sauvignon/Shiraz Petaluma
  1985 £44.00 (CRO)
Octavius Yalumba **1994** £52.00 (CRO)
Pinot Noir Bass Phillip Premium **1998**
  £45.99 (BEN)
Shiraz Penfolds Magill Estate **1990** £48.37
  (FA)

£60.00 → £99.99

Cabernet Sauvignon Penfolds Bin 707
  1989 £68.00 (CRO)
Grange Penfolds **1995** £97.88 (BY) £99.99
  (UN) £110.00 (YOU) £120.00 (GN) £126.21
  (FA) £131.11 (BODX) £135.13 (TUR)
Grange Penfolds **1993** £80.72 (BY) £119.00
  (CRO) £129.25 (TUR) £140.25 (NO)
Pinot Noir Bass Phillip Reserve **1998**
  £78.55 (BEN) £97.00 (BAL)
Shiraz Lindemans Hunter Valley **1970**
  £88.00 (CRO)

£100.00 → £199.99

Grange Penfolds **1992** £102.00 (CRO)
  £130.00 (BEN) £134.83 (NO) £146.88 (TUR)
Grange Penfolds **1991** £143.35 (FA)
  £149.81 (NO) £164.50 (TUR)
Grange Penfolds **1988** £150.00 (BU)
Grange Penfolds **1986** £199.00 (BEN)
  £229.13 (TUR)
Grange Penfolds **1980** £160.00 (TUR)
Grange Penfolds **1972** £177.62 (FA)

Shiraz Clarendon Hills Astralis **1997**
£110.00 (JU)
Shiraz Clarendon Hills Astralis **1996**
£104.18 (FA) £105.75 (TUR) £109.08
(BODX)
Shiraz Henschke Hill of Grace **1991**
£152.00 (NO) £165.87 (FA)

Over £200.00

Grange Penfolds **1990** £209.74 (NO)
£226.58 (FA) £265.75 (TUR) £275.00 (BEN)
Grange Penfolds **1971** £412.62 (FA)

WHITE

Under £4.00

Chardonnay Hardys Banrock Station
2000 £3.99 (TES) £3.99 (MORR) £4.49
(BUD) £4.49 (VIL)
Chardonnay Hardys Banrock Station
1999 £3.99 (UN)
Chardonnay McGuigan Brothers Up a
Gum Tree **2000** £3.99 (CON)
Colombard/Chardonnay Hardys Banrock
Station **2001** £3.99 (SAF)
Colombard/Chardonnay Hardys Banrock
Station **2000** £3.49 (MORR) £3.79 (TES)
Colombard/Chardonnay Hardys Banrock
Station **1999** £3.99 (UN)
Colombard/Chardonnay Lindemans
Cawarra **2000** £3.60 (SOM) £4.45 (BY)
Dry White Dalwood **2000** £3.60 (SOM)
£4.37 (LLO)
Dry White Rolleston Vale **Non-vintage**
£3.79 (CON) £3.99 (VIL) £3.99 (GN)
£4.18 (PEN)
Rawson's Retreat Bin 202 Penfolds **2000**
£3.99 (SOM) £4.99 (BUD) £4.99 (VIC) £4.99
(THR) £4.99 (BOT) £4.99 (WAI) £5.04 (BY)
Rawson's Retreat Bin 21 Penfolds **2000**
£3.98 (SOM) £4.99 (BUD) £4.99 (BO)
£4.99 (VIC) £4.99 (THR) £4.99 (BOT)
Riesling Peter Lehmann Vine Vale **2001**
£3.99 (SAF)
Semillon Basedow ½ bottle **1998** £3.38
(BIB)
Semillon/Chardonnay Barramundi **Non-vintage** £3.98 (TES) £3.98 (ASD) £3.99
(MORR)
Semillon/Chardonnay Lindemans Cawarra
1999 £3.90 (BAC)
Semillon/Chardonnay Orlando Jacob's
Creek **2000** £3.69 (MORR) £3.83 (TES)
£3.99 (ASD) £4.59 (VIC) £4.59 (THR)

£4.00 → £4.99

Chardonnay Cockatoo Ridge **1999** £4.50
(SOM) £4.99 (BAL)
Chardonnay Dalwood **2000** £4.62 (LLO)
£4.79 (BY)
Chardonnay Deakin Estate **2000** £4.99
(OD) £4.99 (BIB) £5.49 (DI)
Chardonnay Hardys Nottage Hill **2000**
£4.68 (TES) £5.49 (BUD) £5.49 (VIL) £5.49
(MORR)
Chardonnay Hardys Nottage Hill **1999**
£4.99 (UN) £4.99 (SO) £4.99 (WAI)
Chardonnay Lindemans Bin 65 **2000**
£4.35 (SOM) £4.49 (TES) £4.50 (WS)
£4.99 (SAI) £4.99 (WAI) £4.99 (MORR)
£5.49 (MAJ) £5.50 (BY) £5.99 (BUD) £5.99
(POR) £5.99 (VIC) £5.99 (THR) 5.99 (OD)
Chardonnay Lindemans Bin 65 **1999** £4.90
(BAC) £4.99 (SO) £4.99 (PEN) £5.99 (UN)

Chardonnay Lindemans Cawarra
Unoaked **2001** £4.99 (SAF)
Chardonnay Lindemans Cawarra
Unoaked **2000** £4.49 (ASD) £4.98 (BY)
£4.99 (BUD) £4.99 (TES) £4.99 (MAJ)
£4.99 (VIC) £4.99 (THR) £4.99 (MORR)
Chardonnay McGuigan Brothers Black
Label **2000** £4.99 (WHI)
Chardonnay Orlando Jacob's Creek **2000**
£4.99 (TES) £4.99 (VIC) £4.99 (THR) £4.99
(BOT) £4.99 (WR)
Chardonnay Orlando Jacob's Creek **1999**
£4.99 (UN) £4.99 (BUD)
Chardonnay Penfolds Koonunga Hill
1999 £4.80 (SOM) £4.95 (WS) £5.49 (SO)
£5.49 (PEN) £5.99 (UN) £5.99 (VIC) £5.99
(THR) £5.99 (BOT) £5.99 (WR) £5.99
(JON) £5.99 (CO) £6.50 (FORT)
Chardonnay Penfolds Rowlands Brook
1998 £4.95 (BALL)
Chardonnay Rolleston Vale **1999** £4.95
(CON)
Chardonnay Tatachilla Breakneck Creek
2001 £4.49 (SAF)

Chardonnay Yalumba Oxford Landing
  2001 £4.99 (SAF)
Chardonnay Yalumba Oxford Landing
  2000 £4.98 (ASD) £5.75 (STE)
Chardonnay/Sauvignon Blanc Hardys
  Crest **1997** £4.99 (UN)
Chardonnay/Semillon Hardys Stamp **2001**
  £4.79 (SAF)
Chardonnay/Semillon Hardys Stamp **2000**
  £4.48 (ASD) £4.79 (VIC) £4.79 (THR)
Chardonnay/Semillon Wolf Blass **1999**
  £4.99 (VIL)
Chenin Blanc Brown Brothers **1999**
  £4.99 (MORR) £5.04 (WHI) £5.45 (STE)
  £5.75 (DI) £5.82 (PLA)
Chenin Blanc/Semillon/Sauvignon Blanc
  Tatachilla Growers **1998** £4.40 (BAN)
Colombard Deakin Estate **2000** £4.99 (BIB)
Colombard Deakin Estate **1998** £4.99 (DI)
Colombard/Chardonnay Lonsdale Ridge
  2000 £4.79 (BIB)
Colombard/Chardonnay Sunnycliff **1999**
  £4.49 (JON) £4.95 (POR)
Long Flat White Tyrrell's **1999** £4.99 (VIL)
  £5.55 (GN)
Medium Dry White Dalwood **2000** £4.37
  (LLO)
Muscat Grant Burge Dry Late-Picked
  1998 £4.99 (UN)
Rawson's Retreat Bin 202 Penfolds **2001**
  £4.99 (SAF)
Rawson's Retreat Bin 21 Penfolds **1999**
  £4.99 (UN) £4.99 (COC) £4.99 (MORR)
Riesling Orlando Jacob's Creek Dry **2000**
  £4.99 (TES) £5.49 (THR) £5.49 (WR)
Riesling/Gewürztraminer Hardys Stamp
  2000 £4.79 (VIC) £4.79 (THR)
Riesling/Gewürztraminer Hardys Stamp
  1999 £4.49 (UN)
Sauvignon Blanc Deakin Estate **2000**
  £4.99 (BO) £4.99 (BIB) £5.49 (DI)
Sauvignon Blanc Lindemans Bin 95 **1990**
  £4.81 (BY)
Sauvignon Blanc Sunnycliff **1999** £4.89
  (JON) £4.95 (BALL) £5.99 (POR)
Sauvignon Blanc Sunnycliff **1998** £4.65 (TAN)
Sauvignon Blanc Yalumba Oxford Landing
  2001 £4.99 (SAF)
Sauvignon Blanc Yalumba Oxford Landing
  2000 £4.95 (WS) £4.99 (SO) £4.99 (TES)
  £4.99 (VIC) £4.99 (THR) £4.99 (WR)
Sauvignon Blanc Yalumba Oxford Landing
  1999 £4.99 (UN)
Semillon/Chardonnay Aldridge Estate
  1999 £4.99 (CON)

Semillon/Chardonnay Casella Painters
  Cove **2000** £4.40 (BAC)
Semillon/Chardonnay Dalwood **2000**
  £4.54 (BY) £4.72 (LLO)
Semillon/Chardonnay De Bortoli Sacred
  Hill **2000** £4.95 (STE) £4.99 (BU)
Semillon/Chardonnay De Bortoli Sacred
  Hill **1999** £4.95 (STE) £4.95 (LEA)
Semillon/Chardonnay Hardys Stamp **2000**
  £4.45 (TES) £4.48 (ASD) £4.79 (BUD)
  £4.79 (MORR)
Semillon/Chardonnay Miranda Opal Ridge
  1999 £4.99 (CON)
Semillon/Chardonnay Orlando Jacob's
  Creek **2001** £4.59 (SAF)
Semillon/Chardonnay Orlando Jacob's
  Creek **1999** £4.59 (UN) £4.59 (WAI)
  £4.69 (BUD)
Semillon/Chardonnay Penfolds Rowlands
  Brook **1999** £4.50 (BALL) £4.69 (JON)
  £4.90 (HAH) £4.95 (POR)
Semillon/Chardonnay Tatachilla Wattle
  Park **1997** £4.95 (BAN)
Semillon/Chardonnay Yaldara Stoney Vale
  1999 £4.99 (RAE)

£5.00 → £5.99

Chardonnay Aldridge Estate **1999** £5.95
  (CON) £6.05 (NO)
Chardonnay Deakin Estate **1998** £5.00
  (BAC)
Chardonnay Hardys Nottage Hill **2001**
  £5.49 (SAF)
Chardonnay Katnook ½ bottle **1998**
  £5.97 (BIB)
Chardonnay Miranda **1999** £5.45 (CON)
Chardonnay Penfolds Koonunga Hill
  2000 £5.49 (WAI) £5.99 (BUD) £5.99
  (POR) £5.99 (COC) £5.99 (TES) £5.99
  (MORR) £6.54 (BY)
Chardonnay Penfolds Private Bin **2000**
  £5.82 (BY)
Chardonnay Penfolds The Valleys **1999**
  £5.95 (SOM) £6.95 (SO) £6.99 (SAI) £6.99
  (PEN) £7.49 (POR)
Chardonnay Rosemount **2000** £5.93 (TES)
  £6.95 (ASD) £6.99 (BUD) £6.99 (MORR)
Chardonnay Simon Gilbert Card Series
  Hunter **1999** £5.99 (BAL)
Chardonnay Sunnycliff **1999** £5.25 (BALL)
  £5.45 (HAH) £5.49 (JON) £5.70 (TAN)
  £5.99 (POR)
Chardonnay Tyrrell's Long Flat **1999**
  £5.99 (UN) £5.99 (VIL) £5.99 (GN)
Chardonnay Willandra **1999** £5.99 (HED)

Chardonnay Woolshed 1999 £5.99 (SAF)
Chardonnay David Wynn 1999 £5.70
(SOM) £6.35 (FLE) £7.98 (HIC)
Chardonnay Yaldara Berrigan Point 2000
£5.83 (LLO)
Chardonnay/Sauvignon Blanc Hardys
Crest 1999 £5.49 (MORR) £5.99 (VIL)
Chenin Blanc Brown Brothers 1998
£5.45 (STE) £5.49 (POR)
Chenin Blanc Brown Brothers 1997
£5.04 (WHI)
Colombard Deakin Estate 1999 £5.49 (DI)
GTR Rosemount 2000 £5.95 (ASD) £5.99
(BUD) £5.99 (CO) £5.99 (MORR)
GTR Rosemount 1999 £5.82 (WHI)
HWB Houghton 1999 £5.97 (ASD) £5.99
(WAI)
HWB Houghton 1998 £5.95 (WS)
Marsanne Chateau Tahbilk 1999 £5.95 (WS)
Marsanne Chateau Tahbilk 1997 £5.99 (BO)
£6.57 (COC)
Marsanne Mitchelton Thomas Mitchell
1999 £5.99 (VIC) £5.99 (THR)
Marsanne Mitchelton Unoaked 1998
£5.49 (OD)
Muscat Brown Brothers Dry 2000 £5.49
(POR) £5.99 (DI)
Muscat Brown Brothers Dry 1999 £5.41
(PEN) £5.49 (TES) £5.49 (JON) £5.50 (WRI)
£5.60 (TAN) £5.70 (STA) £5.82 (PLA)
£5.96 (COC) £6.99 (VIL)
Muscat Brown Brothers Dry 1998 £5.45
(STE) £5.49 (POR) £5.69 (GW)
Muscat Grant Burge Dry Late-Picked
1999 £5.95 (BU) £5.99 (CON)
Poachers Blend St Hallett 2001 £5.99 (AUS)
Poachers Blend St Hallett 1999 £5.40
(SOM) £5.79 (POR)
Riesling Best's Victoria 2000 £5.50 (CRO)
£6.50 (GW)
Riesling Bethany 2000 £5.49 (MAJ)
Riesling Orlando Jacob's Creek Dry 1999
£5.49 (BUD)
Riesling Peter Lehmann Eden Valley 1999
£5.49 (ASD)
Riesling Pewsey Vale 1999 £5.99 (TES)
£5.99 (VIC) £5.99 (THR) £5.99 (BOT)
£5.99 (WR) £6.30 (BEN)
Riesling Wakefield 1992 £5.99 (RAE)
£6.50 (WRI)
Riesling Wolf Blass 1999 £5.99 (VIL)
Riesling Wynns Coonawarra Estate 1998
£5.29 (JON)
Sauvignon Blanc Deakin Estate 1999
£5.49 (DI)

Sauvignon Blanc Rosemount 2000 £5.99
(WAI) £6.99 (TES)
Sauvignon Blanc Yaldara Reserve 2000
£5.86 (PLA)
Semillon Peter Lehmann 2000 £5.49 (SAF)
Semillon Peter Lehmann 1999 £5.49 (UN)
Semillon Rosemount 2000 £5.99 (MORR)
Semillon/Chardonnay Ironstone 1999
£5.49 (UN) £5.99 (BO) £5.99 (VIL) £6.49
(CON) £7.33 (PLAY)
Semillon/Chardonnay Penfolds Barossa
Valley 1999 £5.99 (VIC) £5.99 (THR)
£5.99 (BOT) £6.89 (POR)
Semillon/Chardonnay Penfolds Barossa
Valley 1998 £5.20 (SOM) £5.99 (WR)
£6.73 (BY)
Semillon/Chardonnay Rosemount 2001
£5.99 (SAF)
Semillon/Chardonnay Rosemount 2000
£5.95 (TES) £5.99 (BUD) £6.49 (VIC)
Semillon/Sauvignon Blanc Rosemount
2000 £5.99 (TES)
Viognier Yalumba Oxford Landing 2000
£5.95 (WS) £5.99 (BO) £5.99 (SAF) £6.95
(STE)
White Clare Wakefield 1998 £5.99 (UN)
White Ochre d'Arenberg 2000 £5.38 (BIB)

£6.00 → £6.99

Chardonnay Jim Barry Clare Valley 1999
£6.49 (JON)
Chardonnay Jim Barry Clare Valley Un-
wooded 2000 £6.20 (TAN)
Chardonnay Best's Victoria 1999 £6.60
(NI)
Chardonnay Bethany 1998 £6.49 (CO)
£8.90 (NO)
Chardonnay Grant Burge Barossa Vines
1999 £6.35 (CON) £6.95 (RES) £7.00
(HIG)
Chardonnay Chapel Hill Unwooded 1999
£6.99 (TES)
Chardonnay d'Arenberg Olive Grove
1999 £6.50 (WS)
Chardonnay De Bortoli Deen Vat 7 1999
£6.95 (STE)
Chardonnay De Bortoli Windy Peak
1998 £6.99 (BAL) £7.25 (STE)
Chardonnay Evans & Tate Gnangara 2000
£6.45 (AS)
Chardonnay Simon Hackett Barossa
Valley 1999 £6.99 (CON)
Chardonnay Haselgrove Sovereign 1999
£6.49 (VIL)
Chardonnay Leasingham 1998 £6.99 (WAI)

Chardonnay Peter Lehmann Vine Vale
1999 £6.29 (VIN)
Chardonnay Lindemans Limestone Coast
1998 £6.99 (UN)
Chardonnay Madfish Unwooded **2000**
£6.95 (SOM) £7.99 (GW) £8.25 (BAN)
£8.62 (SAV) £8.95 (NI)
Chardonnay Penfolds The Valleys **1998**
£6.99 (VIL)
Chardonnay Plantagenet Omrah Unoaked
2000 £6.99 (SO) £6.99 (LIB) £7.25 (STA)
Chardonnay Riddoch **1997** £6.95 (BALL)
Chardonnay Rosemount **1999** £6.99 (BO)
£6.99 (VIC) £6.99 (THR) £6.99 (BOT)
Chardonnay Saltram Mamre Brook **2000**
£6.99 (SAF)
Chardonnay Seaview Edwards & Chaffey
1999 £6.61 (BY)
Chardonnay Tatachilla Padthaway **2000**
£6.49 (SAF)
Chardonnay Tyrrell's Old Winery **1997**
£6.64 (PEN)
Chardonnay Wakefield **1998** £6.99 (UN)
Chardonnay Water Wheel **1999** £6.76
(WHI) £7.98 (PLA)
Chardonnay Wolf Blass **2000** £6.99 (WAI)
£6.99 (MORR)
Chardonnay David Wynn **1998** £6.95
(AD) £6.99 (UN) £7.25 (STE)
Chardonnay Wynns Coonawarra Estate
1999 £6.99 (PEN)
Chardonnay Yaldara Reserve **1999** £6.49
(GW)
Chardonnay Yalumba Antipodean Un-
wooded **1999** £6.29 (OD)
Colombard Primo Estate La Biondina
2000 £6.99 (AUS)
Marsanne Chateau Tahbilk **2000** £6.99
(WAI)
Riesling Jim Barry Watervale **1999** £6.30
(BEN) £6.50 (WRI) £6.99 (DI)
Riesling Knappstein **2000** £6.99 (OD)
Riesling Stanley Leasingham Rhine Bin 7
2000 £6.99 (SAF)
Riesling Mitchell Watervale **1999** £6.75
(TAN) £6.75 (BALL) £6.95 (POR) £6.95
(HAH)
Riesling Mitchelton Blackwood Park **1999**
£6.99 (WR) £7.25 (WS)
Riesling Wakefield **1998** £6.69 (GN)
Riesling David Wynn **1998** £6.35 (FLE))
Sauvignon Blanc Dromana Estate Schinus
2000 £6.82 (FLE)
Sauvignon Blanc Plantagenet Omrah **1999**
£6.95 (POR) £6.99 (VIL)

Sauvignon Blanc Riddoch **1997** £6.95
(BALL)
Sauvignon Blanc Rymill **1999** £6.99 (ASD)
Sauvignon Blanc David Wynn **1999** £6.35
(FLE) £6.95 (AD) £6.95 (NI) £8.00 (MV)
Semillon Basedow **1998** £6.62 (BIB)
Semillon Bethany **1997** £6.15 (NO)
Semillon Haselgrove Sovereign **1999**
£6.49 (VIL)
Semillon Penfolds Barossa Valley Old Vine
2000 £6.90 (SOM) £7.60 (BY)
Semillon Simon Hackett **1999** £6.99
(CON)
★ Semillon Mitchell The Growers **1999**
£6.95 (BALL)
Semillon Mitchell The Growers **1998**
£6.95 (POR)
Semillon/Chardonnay Ironstone **2000**
£6.77 (LLO) £8.65 (NI)
Semillon/Chardonnay Tatachilla Wattle
Park **2000** £6.99 (VIC) £6.99 (THR) £6.99
(BOT)
Verdelho Bleasdale Lady Ayres **2000**
£6.99 (SAF)
Verdelho McGuigan Brothers Bin 6000
2000 £6.45 (PLA)
Verdelho Rothbury Hunter Valley **1999**
£6.99 (DI)
Viognier Yalumba Oxford Landing **1998**
£6.49 (JON)

£7.00 → £7.99

Chardonnay Aldridge Estate **1998** £7.50
(BU)
Chardonnay Basedow **1998** £7.41 (BIB)
Chardonnay Bridgewater Mill **1999** £7.49
(SAI)
Chardonnay Brown Brothers **1999** £7.99
(DI) £8.70 (TAN)
Chardonnay Capel Vale CV Unwooded
1999 £7.99 (UN)
Chardonnay Chapel Hill Unwooded **2001**
£7.99 (AUS)
Chardonnay Diamond Valley Vineyards
1998 £7.45 (BU)
Chardonnay Simon Hackett Barossa
Valley **1998** £7.50 (FLE)

Please remember that
Oz Clarke's Wine Buying Guide
*is a price **guide** and not a price list. It is
not meant to replace up-to-date
merchants' lists.*

Chardonnay Heathfield Ridge Endeavour
Barrel-Fermented 1999 £7.99 (SAF)
Chardonnay Jamiesons Run 1999 £7.99
(MORR)
Chardonnay Leasingham 1997 £7.95 (BALL)
Chardonnay Leconfield 1999 £7.90 (JU)
Chardonnay Peter Lehmann 1999 £7.99
(GN)
Chardonnay Lindemans Padthaway 1998
£7.99 (UN) £8.49 (BOT) £8.65 (BY)
Chardonnay McWilliams JJ McWilliam
1998 £7.35 (COC)
Chardonnay Mitchelton Preece 1998
£7.93 (HIC) £8.44 (PLAY)
Chardonnay Nepenthe Unwooded 2000
£7.99 (OD)
Chardonnay Ninth Island 2000 £7.25 (SOM)
Chardonnay Ninth Island 1999 £7.99 (POR)
£7.99 (TES) £7.99 (BO) £8.65 (CON) £8.99
(VIL) £9.40 (MV)
Chardonnay Neil Paulett 1997 £7.90 (JU)
Chardonnay Riddoch 1999 £7.34 (BIB)
Chardonnay Riddoch 1998 £7.00 (BAC)
Chardonnay Rothbury Hunter Valley
1999 £7.99 (JON)
Chardonnay Trentham 1999 £7.75 (BALL)
Chardonnay Wakefield Unwooded 1999
£7.99 (BAL)
Chardonnay Wolf Blass 1998 £7.72 (BY)
£7.95 (JER)
Chardonnay Yering Station 1994 £7.45
(SOM)
Chardonnay/Verdelho Brokenwood
Harlequin 1999 £7.50 (BAN)
Chenin Blanc Richard Hamilton 1998
£7.10 (SOM)
Fifth Leg Devil's Lair 1998 £7.95 (SOM)
Gewürztraminer Knappstein 1999 £7.85
(WRI)
Muscat Brown Brothers Dry 1997 £7.05
(NO)
Riesling Tim Adams 2001 £7.99 (AUS)
Riesling Alkoomi 2000 £7.99 (SAF)
Riesling Chain of Ponds 2000 £7.93 (BIB)
Riesling Tim Gramp Watervale 1997
£7.99 (UN)
Riesling Howard Park 2000 £7.50 (BAN)
£9.75 (WS) £10.99 (YOU)
Riesling Leconfield 1997 £7.20 (JU)

Riesling Mount Langi Ghiran 1998 £7.99
(VA) £8.99 (CON)
Riesling Neil Paulett 1998 £7.50 (JU)
Riesling Pikes Clare Valley 2000 £7.95 (LEA)
★ Riesling Plantagenet Mount Barker 1998
£7.95 (VINV)
Sauvignon Blanc Alkoomi 2000 £7.99 (SAF)
Sauvignon Blanc Brown Brothers 2000
£7.45 (STE)
Sauvignon Blanc d'Arenberg The Broken
Fishplate 2000 £7.73 (BIB)
Sauvignon Blanc Neil Paulett 1998 £7.95
(JU)
Sauvignon Blanc Riddoch 2000 £7.34 (BIB)
Sauvignon Blanc Taltarni 1999 £7.85 (CON)
Sauvignon Blanc David Wynn 1998 £7.25
(STE)
Sauvignon Blanc/Chardonnay Capel Vale
CV 1998 £7.99 (UN)
Sauvignon Blanc/Chardonnay/Semillon
Vasse Felix 1999 £7.35 (SOM) £9.20
(TAN)
Sauvignon Blanc/Semillon Brokenwood
Cricket Pitch 1999 £7.95 (WS) £7.99 (OD)
Sauvignon Blanc/Semillon Chain of Ponds
2000 £7.93 (BIB)
Sauvignon Blanc/Semillon Hollick
Coonawarra 1998 £7.99 (HED)
Sauvignon Blanc/Semillon Madfish 2000
£7.95 (BAN)
★ Semillon Tim Adams 1998 £7.99 (AUS)
£7.99 (TES) £8.99 (BOT) £8.99 (WR)
£10.95 (FORT)
Semillon Brown Brothers 1996 £7.99 (DI)
Semillon Grant Burge Old Vine 1999
£7.95 (BU) £7.95 (CON) £8.00 (WRI)
£8.99 (VIL)
Semillon Grant Burge Old Vine 1997
£7.99 (UN)
Semillon Chain of Ponds 2000 £7.93 (BIB)
Semillon Maglieri 1995 £7.65 (RAE)
Semillon McWilliams Mount Pleasant
Elizabeth 1994 £7.99 (TES)
Semillon Penfolds Barossa Valley Old Vine
1997 £7.70 (NO)
Verdelho Bremerton 1999 £7.52 (FLE)
£7.99 (HED)
Verdelho Capel Vale 1999 £7.99 (BO)
£7.99 (MAJ) £8.65 (WRI)
★ Verdelho Chapel Hill 2000 £7.99 (AUS)
Verdelho Chapel Hill 1998 £7.49 (BOT)
£8.49 (WR)
Verdelho David Traeger 2000 £7.99 (AUS)
Viognier Yalumba Barossa Growers 1998
£7.99 (BAL) £9.75 (FORT)

Stars (★) indicate wines selected by
Oz Clarke in the Best Buys section which
begins on page 8.

£8.00 → £8.99

★ Chardonnay Allandale **2000** £8.50 (AUS)
Chardonnay Brown Brothers King Valley **1999** £8.39 (JON) £8.45 (STE) £8.95 (POR)
Chardonnay Brown Brothers King Valley **1998** £8.25 (CON) £11.28 (TW)
Chardonnay Brown Brothers King Valley **1997** £8.75 (STA)
Chardonnay Capel Vale CV Unwooded **2000** £8.28 (LLO)
Chardonnay Chatsfield **1998** £8.99 (DI)
Chardonnay Hollick Coonawarra **1996** £8.99 (HED) £9.49 (AME) £10.95 (FORT)
Chardonnay Lindemans Padthaway **1999** £8.49 (WR)
Chardonnay Madfish Unwooded **1999** £8.99 (BAL)
Chardonnay Nepenthe Unwooded **1998** £8.99 (GW) £9.50 (CRO)
Chardonnay Ninth Island **1998** £8.15 (PEN) £8.60 (STA)
Chardonnay Penfolds The Valleys **1997** £8.25 (BY)
Chardonnay Rymill **1995** £8.99 (RAE)
Chardonnay St Hallett **2000** £8.99 (AUS)
Chardonnay St Hallett **1999** £8.21 (DOM)
Chardonnay Stonier **1998** £8.99 (DI)
Chardonnay Tatachilla Adelaide Hills **1999** £8.99 (SAF)
Chardonnay Water Wheel **2000** £8.99 (AUS)
Chardonnay Yaldara Reserve **1998** £8.72 (VIN)
Chardonnay Yarra Valley Hills **1999** £8.99 (OD)
Chardonnay/Sauvignon Blanc Penfolds Clare Valley **1996** £8.24 (BY)
Gewürztraminer Pipers Brook **1999** £8.55 (SOM)
Marsanne Mitchelton **1997** £8.49 (AME)
Marsanne Mitchelton Victoria Reserve **1994** £8.90 (TAN)
Marsanne Mitchelton Wood-Matured **1994** £8.95 (WRI)
Pinot Gris Ninth Island **2000** £8.99 (VIL)
Pinot Gris Pipers Brook **1999** £8.55 (SOM) £10.75 (CON) £10.99 (VIL) £10.99 (YOU)
Riesling Alkoomi **1999** £8.95 (JER)
Riesling Best's Great Western **2000** £8.50 (NI)
Riesling Brown Brothers Family Reserve **1995** £8.99 (DI) £9.99 (PEN)

Riesling Capel Vale **2000** £8.74 (LLO)
Riesling Tim Gramp Watervale **1998** £8.40 (AD)
Riesling Heggies Vineyard **1987** £8.99 (BAL)
Riesling Henschke Julius Eden Valley **1997** £8.70 (SOM) £13.25 (NI)
Riesling Knappstein **1997** £8.48 (NO)
Riesling Leeuwin Estate Art Series **1999** £8.88 (DOM)
Riesling Mount Langi Ghiran **1999** £8.99 (BEN) £8.99 (LIB) £8.99 (VIL) £9.21 (FLE)
Riesling Pipers Brook **2000** £8.65 (SOM)
Riesling St Hallett Eden Valley **2000** £8.99 (AUS)
Riesling David Wynn **1999** £8.00 (MV)
Sauvignon Blanc Nepenthe **2000** £8.99 (OD) £8.99 (SAF) £9.99 (GW)
Sauvignon Blanc Ninth Island **1999** £8.95 (BALL) £8.99 (VIL)
Sauvignon Blanc Shaw & Smith **1999** £8.85 (BAC) £9.35 (CON)
Sauvignon Blanc Shaw & Smith **1998** £8.99 (BO)
Sauvignon Blanc Taltarni **1998** £8.21 (PEN)
Sauvignon Blanc/Chardonnay/Semillon Vasse Felix **1996** £8.99 (BEN)
Sauvignon Blanc/Semillon Henschke Eden Valley **1998** £8.55 (SOM) £12.70 (JER)
Sauvignon Blanc/Semillon Hollick Coonawarra **2000** £8.25 (NI)
Semillon Grant Burge Old Vine **1998** £8.95 (RES) £9.25 (PLAY)
Semillon Chateau Xanadu **1998** £8.99 (OD)
Semillon Coriole Lalla Rookh **1998** £8.40 (TAN) £9.95 (HED) £10.90 (CRO)
Semillon De Bortoli Rare Dry Botrytis **1996** £8.99 (AME)
Semillon Fern Hill **1997** £8.75 (FRI)
Semillon Henschke **1997** £8.20 (SOM)
Semillon St Hallett Select **1998** £8.99 (AUS)
Semillon Tyrrell's Lost Block **1997** £8.90 (CRO)
Semillon Voyager Estate **1997** £8.90 (JU)

> • Wines are listed in A–Z order within each price band.
> • For each wine, vintages are listed in descending order.
> • Each vintage of any wine appears only once.

Semillon Willows Vineyard 1998 £8.50 (AUS)

Semillon Willows Vineyard 1997 £8.49 (BOT) £8.49 (WR)

Semillon/Sauvignon Blanc Cape Mentelle 1999 £8.34 (NO) £8.99 (VIL) £9.25 (CON) £9.29 (JON) £9.50 (STA) £11.16 (PLAY) £11.34 (TW)

Semillon/Sauvignon Blanc Woodstock 1998 £8.45 (GN)

Verdelho Allanmere Hunter Valley 1999 £8.99 (GN) £10.50 (BALL)

Verdelho Capel Vale 2000 £8.74 (LLO)

Verdelho Pendarves Estate 1998 £8.75 (STA)

Verdelho David Traeger 1999 £8.49 (VIC)

£9.00 → £9.99

Chardonnay Jim Barry Clare Valley 1998 £9.20 (TAN)

Chardonnay Capel Vale 1999 £9.72 (LLO)

Chardonnay Chateau Reynella 1999 £9.99 (VIL)

Chardonnay Dromana Estate 1999 £9.99 (FLE) £10.99 (YOU) £12.50 (MAY)

Chardonnay Fern Hill 1997 £9.25 (FRI)

Chardonnay Haselgrove H Series 1999 £9.99 (SAF)

Chardonnay Heggies Vineyard 1998 £9.95 (WS) £10.95 (RES) £12.99 (YOU) £13.25 (FORT)

Chardonnay Hollick Coonawarra 1997 £9.19 (JON)

Chardonnay Lindemans Padthaway 1996 £9.27 (BY)

Chardonnay McWilliams Mount Pleasant 1996 £9.45 (COC)

Chardonnay Mount Helen 1997 £9.66 (SUN)

Chardonnay Oakridge 1998 £9.99 (GW)

Chardonnay Penley Estate 1996 £9.99 (VIL)

Chardonnay Pipers Brook 1996 £9.85 (SOM) £13.75 (STA) £15.50 (BALL)

Chardonnay Plantagenet Mount Barker 1999 £9.90 (BAC) £9.95 (LIB) £9.99 (VIL)

Chardonnay Rosemount Show Reserve 1999 £9.99 (WAI) £9.99 (SAF) £9.99 (MORR)

Chardonnay Rosemount Show Reserve 1998 £9.99 (UN) £9.99 (VIC) £9.99 (THR)

Chardonnay Scotchman's Hill 1997 £9.90 (JU)

Chardonnay Shaw & Smith Unoaked 2000 £9.95 (LIB)

Chardonnay Shaw & Smith Unoaked 1999 £9.99 (TES) £9.99 (VIL) £10.90 (TAN)

Chardonnay Wirra Wirra 1999 £9.99 (OD)

Chardonnay Wolf Blass President's Selection 1999 £9.60 (CRO) £10.40 (BY)

Chardonnay Wolf Blass President's Selection 1998 £9.99 (VIL)

Fifth Leg Devil's Lair 1999 £9.80 (BAN)

Gewürztraminer Delatite Dead Man's Hill 1999 £9.17 (ARM)

Marsanne Mitchelton 1998 £9.25 (BALL)

Pinot Gris Mount Langi Ghiran 1999 £9.95 (BEN) £10.95 (RES) £10.99 (VIL)

Pinot Gris Mount Langi Ghiran 1998 £9.65 (CON) £11.45 (FORT)

Riesling Geoff Weaver 1998 £9.49 (BAL)

Riesling Howard Park 1999 £9.06 (GW) £11.90 (CRO)

Riesling Leeuwin Estate Art Series 1998 £9.95 (SOM)

Riesling Nepenthe 2000 £9.49 (YOU)

Riesling Penfolds Eden Valley Reserve 2000 £9.99 (WAI)

Riesling Penfolds Eden Valley Reserve 1999 £9.99 (VIL)

Riesling Petaluma 1998 £9.80 (TAN) £10.50 (FORT)

Riesling Petaluma 1997 £9.95 (BEN)

Sauvignon Blanc Alkoomi 1999 £9.70 (JER)

Sauvignon Blanc Delatite 1999 £9.17 (ARM)

Sauvignon Blanc Eden Ridge 1998 £9.50 (AD)

Sauvignon Blanc Katnook 2000 £9.99 (BIB)

Sauvignon Blanc Lenswood 1999 £9.99 (NEZ)

Sauvignon Blanc Scotchman's Hill 1996 £9.90 (JU)

Sauvignon Blanc Shaw & Smith 2001 £9.95 (LIB)

Sauvignon Blanc Shaw & Smith 2000 £9.50 (BEN) £9.90 (FLE) £9.95 (WRI) £9.95 (STA) £9.98 (BY) £9.99 (POR) £9.99 (TES) £9.99 (VIL) £11.30 (TAN) £11.50 (RES) £11.95 (FORT)

Semillon Amberley Estate 1999 £9.99 (MAJ)

Semillon McWilliams Mount Pleasant Elizabeth 1995 £9.45 (COC)

Semillon/Chardonnay Henschke Tilly's Vineyard Eden Valley 1998 £9.95 (LAY)

Semillon/Chardonnay Henschke Tilly's Vineyard Eden Valley 1997 £9.95 (FORT) £10.10 (RIC)

★ Semillon/Sauvignon Blanc Cape Mentelle
2000 £9.34 (PLA) £9.49 (MAJ) £9.49 (OD)
£9.60 (HAH) £9.60 (TAN) £9.99 (WAI)
£10.50 (NI)
Semillon/Sauvignon Blanc Cape Mentelle
1998 £9.49 (AME)

£10.00 → £10.99

Chardonnay Alkoomi **1998** £10.75 (JER)
Chardonnay Allanmere Durham **1997**
£10.85 (GN)
Chardonnay Ashton Hills **1998** £10.99
(AUS)
Chardonnay Best's Great Western **1998**
£10.64 (FLE) £10.69 (GW)
Chardonnay Best's Victoria **1996** £10.69
(GW)
Chardonnay Blue Pyrenees Estate **1997**
£10.79 (TES)
Chardonnay Cape Mentelle **1998** £10.99
(VIL) £11.49 (AME) £12.50 (FORT) £13.09
(PLAY)
Chardonnay De Bortoli Yarra Valley
1998 £10.95 (WRI) £10.95 (BAL) £11.45
(STE) £11.99 (WAI)
Chardonnay Heggies Vineyard **1996**
£10.95 (BALL)
Chardonnay Howard Park **1997** £10.00
(GW) £12.25 (SOM) £14.99 (YOU)
Chardonnay Katnook **1997** £10.99 (BO)
Chardonnay Lenswood **1997** £10.40 (SOM)
Chardonnay Mountadam **1998** £10.75
(NI) £11.98 (FLE)
Chardonnay Old Kent River **1998** £10.35
(JER)
Chardonnay Penfolds Adelaide Hills **1996**
£10.35 (SOM) £12.89 (BY)
Chardonnay Rosemount Show Reserve
1997 £10.16 (WHI)
Chardonnay Voyager Estate **1999** £10.99
(WAI)
Chardonnay Wolf Blass President's
Selection **2000** £10.40 (BY)
Chardonnay Woodstock **1998** £10.49
(GN)
Gewürztraminer Pipers Brook **2000**
£10.99 (YOU)
★ Pinot Gris Mount Langi Ghiran **2000**
£10.25 (VINV)
Riesling Delatite **1988** £10.69 (BY)
Riesling Henschke Green's Hill **1997**
£10.65 (FLE)
Riesling Mount Horrocks Watervale
2000 £10.99 (POR) £11.50 (STA) £11.95
(BEN)

Riesling Pipers Brook **1999** £10.99 (VIL)
Sauvignon Blanc Geoff Weaver **1999**
£10.75 (BAN) £10.99 (BAL)
★ Sauvignon Blanc/Semillon Cullen **1999**
£10.99 (DI) £11.95 (AD) £11.95 (WS)
£11.99 (YOU) £12.50 (BAL)
Semillon Brokenwood **2000** £10.49 (YOU)
Semillon Nepenthe **1999** £10.33 (PLA)

£11.00 → £12.99

Chardonnay Barossa Valley Estate
Ebenezer **1998** £11.99 (VIL)
Chardonnay Best's Great Western **1997**
£11.45 (NI)
Chardonnay Cape Mentelle **1999** £12.65
(HAH) £12.79 (YOU) £12.99 (NI)
Chardonnay Chateau Xanadu **1996**
£12.95 (DI)
Chardonnay De Bortoli Yarra Valley
1997 £12.25 (STA)
Chardonnay Devil's Lair **1996** £11.70 (SOM)
Chardonnay Frankland Estate **1997**
£11.95 (FORT)
Chardonnay Geoff Weaver **1997** £12.95
(BAL)
Chardonnay Green Point **1993** £12.50
(CRO)
Chardonnay Heggies Vineyard **1999**
£12.95 (YOU)
Chardonnay Hollick Coonawarra **1998**
£11.69 (TW)
Chardonnay Leeuwin Estate Prelude
1999 £11.52 (DOM) £16.75 (MAY)
Chardonnay Miranda Family Reserve
1998 £11.99 (YOU)
Chardonnay Mount Horrocks Clare
Valley **1999** £12.50 (BEN)
Chardonnay Mountadam **1997** £11.25
(SOM) £12.50 (WRI) £12.95 (AD) £13.75
(STE) £14.25 (FORT) £14.72 (HIC)
Chardonnay Nepenthe **1997** £11.98 (GW)
Chardonnay Penfolds Adelaide Hills **1999**
£11.95 (POR)
Chardonnay Pipers Brook **1998** £12.50
(POR) £12.71 (PEN) £13.99 (TES) £13.99
(CON)
Chardonnay Pipers Brook **1993** £12.50
(CRO)

- *All prices for each wine are listed
together in ascending order.*
- *Price bands refer to the lowest price
for which the wine is available.*

Chardonnay Seville Estate 1998 £11.99
(YOU)

Chardonnay Shaw & Smith Reserve 1998
£12.99 (YOU) £13.35 (CON) £13.99 (VIL)

Chardonnay Vasse Felix 1999 £11.95 (LAY)

Chardonnay Wyndham Estate Bin 222
1991 £12.50 (BU)

Riesling Grosset Polish Hill 2000 £11.75
(WS) £13.99 (BEN)

Riesling Henschke Green's Hill 1999
£12.48 (NO)

Riesling Henschke Julius Eden Valley 1999
£12.99 (YOU)

Riesling Leeuwin Estate Art Series 1996
£12.75 (FORT)

Riesling Mount Horrocks Clare Valley
Cordon Cut 1999 £11.99 (BEN)

Riesling Mount Horrocks Watervale
1999 £11.50 (BU)

Riesling Pipers Brook 1997 £11.95 (BALL)

Sauvignon Blanc Leeuwin Estate Art
Series 1999 £11.16 (DOM)

Sauvignon Blanc/Semillon Chain of Ponds
1997 £11.95 (BAL)

Semillon Henschke Louis 1999 £12.80
(LAY)

Semillon Henschke Louis 1998 £12.19
(NO) £12.70 (JER) £13.50 (FORT)

Semillon Mount Horrocks Clare Valley
1999 £12.50 (BEN)

Viognier Heggies Vineyard 1998 £12.75
(WRI) £13.25 (FORT)

Viognier/Roussanne Mitchelton 1997
£12.99 (WR)

£13.00 → £15.99

Chardonnay Bannockburn 1998 £15.99
(YOU) £16.90 (TAN)

Chardonnay Barratt 1998 £15.49 (YOU)

Chardonnay Brokenwood 1998 £13.50
(RES)

Chardonnay Brookland Valley 1999
£13.99 (OD)

Chardonnay Capel Vale Reserve
Frederick 1997 £15.50 (WRI)

Chardonnay Chain of Ponds 1998 £15.49
(YOU)

Chardonnay Coldstream Hills Reserve
1997 £14.99 (YOU)

Chardonnay Dalwhinnie 1997 £14.00 (JU)

Chardonnay d'Arenberg The Other Side
1999 £13.04 (BIB)

Chardonnay Devil's Lair 1998 £14.99 (SUN)

Chardonnay Diamond Valley Vineyards
Estate 1998 £14.99 (YOU)

Chardonnay Grosset Piccadilly 1999
£14.95 (WS)

Chardonnay Hardys Eileen Hardy 1996
£14.99 (VIL)

Chardonnay Henschke Croft 1998
£13.35 (SOM) £19.95 (JER)

Chardonnay Henschke Eden Valley 1994
£15.00 (CRO)

Chardonnay Howard Park 1999 £14.20
(BAN) £14.90 (NI) £14.99 (YOU)

Chardonnay Kingston Estate Reserve
1997 £13.99 (RIC)

Chardonnay Moss Wood 1995 £13.50
(CRO)

Chardonnay Mountadam 1994 £14.00
(CRO)

Chardonnay Petaluma 1998 £13.99 (YOU)
£14.20 (TAN) £14.70 (BEN) £14.72 (BY)
£14.99 (SUN) £15.50 (FORT)

Chardonnay Petaluma 1996 £15.95 (BALL)

Chardonnay Pipers Brook 1999 £13.69
(AME)

Chardonnay Rosemount Orange Vineyard
1998 £14.99 (MORR)

Chardonnay Shaw & Smith Reserve 1999
£13.90 (FLE)

Chardonnay Tyrrell's Vat 47 1997 £15.90
(CRO) £17.10 (NO) £21.50 (WRI)

Chardonnay Vasse Felix Heytesbury 1999
£14.99 (YOU)

Riesling Grosset Polish Hill 1998 £14.75
(FORT)

Riesling Jasper Hill 1999 £13.95 (YAP)

Riesling Mount Horrocks Clare Valley
Cordon Cut 2000 £13.75 (BEN)

Semillon Moss Wood Wooded 1991
£13.50 (CRO)

Viognier Heggies Vineyard 1997 £13.25
(BALL)

The Virgilius Yalumba 1999 £13.75 (SOM)
£19.90 (CRO)

£16.00 → £19.99

Chardonnay Bannockburn 1997 £16.95
(BEN) £17.95 (RES)

Chardonnay Brokenwood Graveyard
1998 £17.50 (BAN) £21.95 (RES)

Chardonnay Capel Vale Reserve
Frederick 1998 £16.03 (LLO)

Chardonnay Chain of Ponds 1996 £16.99
(VA)

Chardonnay Cullen 1999 £16.95 (DI)
£17.95 (AD) £18.49 (YOU)

Chardonnay Dromana Estate Reserve
1999 £17.99 (YOU)

Chardonnay Henschke Croft **1999** £18.20 (NO)

Chardonnay Stonier Merricks Reserve **1997** £17.95 (RES)

Chardonnay Vasse Felix Heytesbury **1998** £16.25 (FORT)

Riesling Howard Park **1996** £16.00 (BU)

Semillon Clarendon Hills **1997** £19.00 (JU)

Semillon Henschke **1993** £16.00 (CRO)

Semillon Tyrrell's Vat 1 **1994** £19.99 (SUN) £20.95 (TAN)

Semillon Tyrrell's Vat 1 **1993** £19.95 (FORT)

The Virgilius Yalumba **1998** £17.50 (FORT)

£20.00 → £24.99

Chardonnay Clarendon Hills Kangarilla Vineyard **1997** £23.00 (JU)

Chardonnay Clarendon Hills Norton Summit Vineyard **1997** £22.00 (JU)

Chardonnay Oakridge Reserve **1998** £20.99 (GW)

Chardonnay Rosemount Roxburgh **1996** £22.31 (WHI)

Over £25.00

Chardonnay Giaconda **1999** £43.00 (BAN) £54.99 (YOU)

Chardonnay Lake's Folly **1986** £28.00 (CRO)

Chardonnay Leeuwin Estate Art Series **1998** £27.61 (DOM) £34.00 (RES)

Chardonnay Leeuwin Estate Art Series **1997** £35.00 (FORT)

Chardonnay Rosemount Roxburgh **1997** £34.99 (UN)

Chardonnay Rosemount Roxburgh **1992** £33.00 (CRO)

Chardonnay Yarra Yering **1997** £28.50 (FORT)

Yattarna Penfolds **1998** £37.00 (GN)

Yattarna Penfolds **1996** £29.95 (SOM) £40.00 (BU) £60.12 (FA)

ROSÉ

Under £9.50

Grenache/Shiraz Hardys Stamp **2000** £4.49 (TES) £4.99 (SAF)

Grenache/Shiraz Hardys Stamp **1999** £4.79 (WAI)

Rose of Virginia Charles Melton **2000** £9.25 (NI) £10.95 (LIB) £10.99 (VIL)

SPARKLING

Under £5.00

Angas Brut **Non-vintage** £4.75 (SOM) £5.99 (UN) £5.99 (TES) £5.99 (VIC) £5.99 (THR) £5.99 (BOT) £5.99 (WR) £5.99 (OD)

Angas Brut Rosé **Non-vintage** £4.75 (SOM) £5.99 (UN) £5.99 (TES) £6.49 (OD)

Killawarra Brut **Non-vintage** £4.50 (SOM) £5.90 (BY) £5.99 (JON) £6.25 (GN)

Killawarra Rosé **Non-vintage** £4.50 (SOM) £5.69 (GW) £5.95 (TAN) £5.99 (POR) £5.99 (JON) £6.06 (BY) £6.43 (LLO) £6.80 (GN)

Rolleston Vale Brut **Non-vintage** £4.99 (VIL) £4.99 (GN)

£5.00 → £5.99

Aldridge Estate Brut **Non-vintage** £5.99 (CON)

Barramundi Brut **Non-vintage** £5.29 (ASD)

Carrington Vintage Brut **1996** £5.99 (UN)

Deakin Estate Brut **1999** £5.80 (BAC) £6.37 (BIB) £6.99 (DI)

Hardys Stamp Sparkling Chardonnay/Pinot Noir **Non-vintage** £5.99 (TES) £6.49 (BUD)

Jacob's Creek Sparkling Chardonnay/Pinot Noir **Non-vintage** £5.99 (UN) £6.99 (SAI) £6.99 (TES) £6.99 (WAI) £6.99 (SAF)

Penfolds Rowlands Brook **Non-vintage** £5.99 (JON) £6.49 (POR)

Richmond Royal Brut **Non-vintage** £5.58 (WHI)

Seaview Brut **Non-vintage** £5.99 (TES) £6.49 (VIC) £6.49 (WAI) £6.50 (WS) £6.99 (UN) £6.99 (VIL) £6.99 (SAF) £7.73 (BY)

£6.00 → £7.99

Banrock Station Sparkling Shiraz NV **Non-vintage** £7.99 (SAI) £7.99 (WAI) £7.99 (VIL)

Nottage Hill Chardonnay Brut Hardys **Non-vintage** £6.99 (SAI)

Nottage Hill Chardonnay Brut Hardys **1999** £6.99 (SAF)

Oz Clarke's Wine Buying Guide
is an annual publication.
We welcome your suggestions for
next year's edition.

Rosemount 'V' **Non-vintage** £6.94 (ASD)
£6.99 (BUD)
Seaview **Non-vintage** £6.49 (BO) £6.49
(MAJ)
Seaview Brut Rosé **Non-vintage** £6.49
(WAI) £6.99 (UN) £6.99 (VIL) £6.99 (SAF)
Seppelt Great Western Brut **Non-vintage** £7.49 (VIC) £7.49 (THR)
Seppelt Great Western Brut Rosé **Non-vintage** £6.49 (BOT) £6.49 (WR)
Tatachilla Brut Non-Vintage **Non-vintage** £6.55 (BAN)
Yaldara Brut **Non-vintage** £6.40 (PLA)
Yalumba Pinot Noir/Chardonnay Cuvée
One Prestige **Non-vintage** £6.50
(SOM)

£8.00 → £9.99

Brown Brothers Sparkling Pinot
Noir/Chardonnay **Non-vintage** £8.99
(JON) £9.99 (DI) £10.33 (PLA) £10.45
(STE) £10.50 (PEN)
Chandon Australian **Non-vintage** £9.89
(BUD) £9.99 (UN) £9.99 (COC) £9.99
(JON) £9.99 (VIL) £9.99 (SAF) £9.99 (BIB)
£10.56 (PLA) £10.58 (BY) £11.75 (JER)
Jansz Pipers River Brut **1996** £9.45 (SOM)
Miranda Family Reserve Sparkling Shiraz
1994 £8.90 (CRO) £13.95 (POR)
Seaview Chardonnay Blanc de Blancs
1996 £8.99 (VIL) £8.99 (SAF)
Seaview Edwards & Chaffey **1995** £9.99
(VIL)
Seaview Pinot Noir/Chardonnay **1997**
£8.99 (UN)
Seppelt Salinger Brut **1994** £8.99 (OD)
Seppelt Sparkling Shiraz **1996** £8.99 (OD)
Seppelt Sparkling Shiraz **1995** £8.99 (UN)
£9.44 (BY) £9.49 (WR) £10.90 (CRO)
Taltarni Brut Taché **Non-vintage** £8.95
(STA) £8.99 (CON) £9.28 (PEN) £9.30
(COC) £11.69 (TW)
Wolf Blass Brut **Non-vintage** £9.33 (BY)
Yellowglen Brut **1998** £9.99 (OD)
Yellowglen Brut **1997** £9.99 (MAJ) £10.99
(VIL)
Yellowglen Pinot Noir/Chardonnay **Non-vintage** £8.99 (VIL)

£10.00 → £11.99

Fox Creek The Vixen Sparkling
Shiraz/Cabernet Franc **Non-vintage**
£10.99 (YOU)
Green Point Brut **Non-vintage** £11.99
(WAI) £12.50 (CRO)

Green Point Brut **1997** £11.49 (TES)
£11.99 (OD) £13.35 (HAH)
Green Point Brut **1996** £10.40 (SOM)
£11.49 (VIC) £11.49 (THR) £11.49 (BOT)
£11.49 (WR) £11.99 (UN) £11.99 (JON)
£11.99 (VIL) £13.34 (BY) £13.85 (PLA)
£13.95 (JU) £13.95 (FORT)
Green Point Brut **1995** £10.10 (RAE)
Green Point Brut **1994** £11.99 (COC)
Green Point Brut Rosé **1995** £11.25 (SOM)
Padthaway Estate Eliza Brut **1996** £10.99
(AME)

£12.00 → £15.99

Clover Hill **Non-vintage** £12.93 (PEN)
Clover Hill **1996** £13.50 (MAY) £14.50 (STA)
Clover Hill **1995** £12.99 (AME)
Croser **1995** £13.17 (BY) £14.25 (FORT)
Green Point Brut Rosé **Non-vintage**
£12.99 (JON)
Green Point Brut Rosé **1996** £12.99 (VIL)
£14.50 (FORT)
Jansz **1995** £12.99 (BEN)
Pipers Brook Pirie **1995** £15.20 (SOM)
£16.71 (NO) £18.99 (AME)

Over £16.00

Croser **1994** £18.00 (CRO)
Charles Melton Sparkling Red **Non-vintage** £18.99 (NI) £24.99 (YOU)
£25.70 (FLE) £28.49 (LIB) £28.99 (VIL)
Mountadam Chardonnay/Pinot Noir
Non-vintage £19.95 (FLE)
Pipers Brook Pirie **1996** £18.99 (VIL)

SWEET & FORTIFIED

Under £5.00

★ Cranswick Estate Botrytis Semillon Nine
Pines ½ bottle **1996** £4.99 (ASD)
Morris Liqueur Muscat **Non-vintage**
£4.99 (TES)
Penfolds Magill Tawny ½ bottle **Non-vintage** £4.99 (UN) £4.99 (JON) £4.99
(OD) £4.99 (VIL) £5.65 (SOM) £5.99 (BO)

£5.00 → £5.99

Best's Late-Harvest Muscat **1997** £5.95
(BU)
Brown Brothers Muscat Late-Harvest
1999 £5.88 (PEN) £5.99 (DI) £5.99 (MORR)
£6.19 (JON) £6.40 (TAN) £6.50 (STA)
Brown Brothers Orange Muscat & Flora
½ bottle **Non-vintage** £5.58 (WHI)

Brown Brothers Orange Muscat & Flora ½ bottle **1999** £5.88 (PEN) £5.95 (WRI) £5.99 (UN) £5.99 (JON) £5.99 (WAI) £5.99 (OD) £5.99 (DI) £6.20 (GW) £6.25 (STE) £6.25 (CON) £6.29 (VIN) £6.40 (TAN) £6.50 (STA) £7.73 (PLAY)

Brown Brothers Orange Muscat & Flora ½ bottle **1995** £5.99 (COC)

Brown Brothers Orange Muscat & Flora ½ bottle **1994** £5.90 (CRO)

Lindemans Coonawarra Botrytis Riesling ½ bottle **1997** £5.90 (SOM) £6.19 (JON)

Penfolds Botrytis Semillon **1998** £5.99 (VIL)

Seppelt Show Fino DP117 ½ bottle **Non-vintage** £5.99 (OD) £6.42 (NO)

£6.00 → £6.99

Best's Late-Harvest Muscat **Non-vintage** £6.95 (NI)

Campbells Rutherglen Liqueur Muscat **Non-vintage** £6.85 (GN) £13.40 (NO)

Cranswick Estate Botrytis Semillon ½ bottle **1996** £6.99 (CB) £9.99 (OD)

Rymill Botrytis Gewürztraminer **1998** £6.99 (RAE)

Stanton & Killeen Rutherglen Liqueur Muscat ½ bottle **Non-vintage** £6.25 (WS) £6.45 (WAT) £6.49 (UN) £6.49 (BAL) £6.69 (CON) £6.99 (AME) £7.19 (NO) £7.25 (FORT) £7.89 (HIC)

£7.00 → £9.99

Brown Brothers Muscat Late-Harvest ½ bottle **1999** £7.87 (VIN)

Brown Brothers Muscat Reserve **Non-vintage** £9.49 (JON)

Brown Brothers Noble Riesling ½ bottle **1998** £9.99 (VIL)

Brown Brothers Noble Riesling ½ bottle **1997** £9.45 (STE) £9.85 (VIN)

Brown Brothers Noble Riesling ½ bottle **1994** £9.35 (WRI)

Brown Brothers Noble Riesling Family Reserve ½ bottle **1997** £9.28 (PEN)

d'Arenberg Noble Riesling ½ bottle **1998** £8.93 (BIB) £9.99 (OD)

Miranda Golden Botrytis **1996** £7.95 (CON)

Primo Estate Joseph 'La Magia' Botrytis Riesling ½ bottle **1996** £9.99 (AUS)

Seppelt Show Reserve DP63 ½ bottle **Non-vintage** £7.49 (OD)

Vasse Felix Noble Riesling ½ bottle **1996** £7.25 (SOM) £8.95 (BEN) £10.69 (PLAY)

Yalumba Pewsey Vale Botrytis Late-Harvest Riesling ½ bottle **1991** £9.25 (NO)

£10.00 → £11.99

Grant Burge Fine Old Tawny **Non-vintage** £10.95 (BALL)

Cranswick Estate Botrytis Semillon ½ bottle **Non-vintage** £11.29 (BO)

Cranswick Estate Botrytis Semillon ½ bottle **1995** £11.85 (WRI) £12.75 (NO)

d'Arenberg Vintage Fortified Shiraz **1998** £11.90 (BIB)

De Bortoli Noble One Botrytis Semillon ½ bottle **1996** £10.85 (SOM) £12.99 (BAL) £13.25 (WRI) £13.99 (AME) £14.75 (MAY) £14.95 (LEA) £15.95 (JER)

Primo Estate Joseph 'The Fronti' V ½ bottle **Non-vintage** £11.99 (AUS)

£12.00 → £13.99

Brown Brothers Liqueur Muscat **Non-vintage** £12.75 (DI) £13.51 (PEN) £13.52 (GW) £13.99 (JON)

Chambers Special Liqueur Muscat **Non-vintage** £13.79 (NO) £15.99 (YOU)

De Bortoli Black Noble ½ bottle **Non-vintage** £12.99 (BAL) £13.50 (LEA) £13.99 (OD) £14.50 (WRI) £14.95 (STE) £15.95 (MAY)

De Bortoli Noble One Botrytis Semillon ½ bottle **1999** £13.20 (HIG)

De Bortoli Noble One Botrytis Semillon ½ bottle **1995** £13.75 (STE) £13.95 (STA)

Seppelt Old Trafford **Non-vintage** £12.85 (NO)

£14.00 → £19.99

Chambers Rutherglen Liqueur Muscat **Non-vintage** £14.00 (CRO)

Chambers Rutherglen Old Vine ½ bottle **Non-vintage** £15.99 (YOU)

Over £20.00

Brown Brothers Noble Riesling **1982** £20.00 (CRO)

Campbells Merchant Prince Liqueur Muscat **Non-vintage** £59.57 (NO)

Campbells Old Rutherglen Liqueur Muscat **Non-vintage** £39.64 (NO)

De Bortoli Noble One Botrytis Semillon **1993** £20.95 (FA)

Stars (★) indicate wines selected by Oz Clarke in the Best Buys section which begins on page 8.

CHILE

Chile is making some terrific reds at the top end – but don't assume that triple the price means triple the quality

First there was one; then two; then four. Now they're proliferating like dotcom companies, though I hope they'll last a bit longer. I'm referring, of course, to super-premium Chilean reds.

'Super-premium' is a pretty daft term, really. Apart from sounding like petrol, it's imprecise and can mean whatever the user chooses: a super-premium wine can be one that costs £15 or £40. And what worries me a little is that the £40 super-premium numbers from Chile are not necessarily two and a half times as good as the £15 ones.

Should they be? The hard truth is that by charging £40 for a wine you create demand among a certain class of consumer. Price, once you hit this level, becomes almost immaterial. The wine has to be very good (and mostly they are very good), but it does not have to prove that it is good value. A £15 wine does not have this luxury.

I'm not saying we should avoid the priciest Chilean reds. If somebody else is paying, I'm all for drinking them. What I am saying is: don't be misled into thinking that more expensive always means better. I'll always advocate trading up from the basic level, and paying a bit more in order to get something better, but there are limits. To my pocket, if not to Chilean ambition.

GRAPE VARIETIES

CABERNET SAUVIGNON (red) Characterized by relatively soft but piercing blackcurrant fruit; unusually, Chilean Cab often doesn't need Merlot to fill it out. Unoaked versions are best within two years of the vintage. Best premium (including blends): *Almaviva, Canepa Magnificum, Carmen Gold Reserve, Concha y Toro Don Melchor, Errázuriz Don Maximiano, Montes Alpha M, Santa Rita Casa Real, Seña.*

CARMENÈRE (red) Marvellously spicy wines, sometimes under its alias of Grande Vidure. This could well become Chile's classic style. Try *Bisquertt Casa La Joya, Carmen, Casa Silva, Gracia, Los Robles.*

CHARDONNAY (white) As with Cabernet, subtler oaking is increasingly the norm. Cool-climate Casablanca tends to produce a crisper, more citrus-fresh Chardonnay than its Central Valley counterparts. Best: *Caliterra, Casa Lapostolle, Concha y Toro, Errázuriz, La Palmería, San Pedro, Viña Casablanca Santa Isabel Estate.*

GEWÜRZTRAMINER (white) The lychee and rose petal packed *Viña Casablanca* version of this grape is still the best. Most others seem to lack heart.

MERLOT (red) Ever more fashionable, and bursting with colour, vibrant, plummy fruit and savoury depth. Try *Canepa, Carta Vieja, Castillo de Molina, La Fortuna, Santa Monica* (all for drinking young); *Carmen, Casa Lapostolle, Concha y Toro, Cono Sur 20 Barrels, Errázuriz, La Palmería, Montes Alpha, Mont Gras, Viña Porta* (all with aging potential).

PINOT NOIR (red) Chile is a prime source of inexpensive Pinot Noir, but there's still not that much. Try *Carmen, Cono Sur, Gracia, Valdivieso, Villard.*

SAUVIGNON BLANC (white) The Casablanca region leads and has a distinct style (ripe gooseberry and asparagus fruit, and firm acidity). *Caliterra, Viña Casablanca's Santa Isabel Estate, Concha y Toro* and *Villard* are the labels to watch. The Curicó Valley is also producing some goodies (*Viña Casablanca White Label, Montes, San Pedro*).

SEMILLON (white) Plantings are falling rapidly. Occasionally blended with Chardonnay or Sauvignon Blanc.

SYRAH (red) There is more and more Syrah being planted, and some lovely smoky, spicy wines being made. A lot is being blended, with excellent results. Best: *Carmen, Errázuriz, Montes Alpha, Mont Gras, Tarapacá*.

OTHER VARIETIES Some Riesling is planted – and occasionally late-harvested. Both Malbec and Zinfandel are making some good red wines.

WINE REGIONS

Although grapes are grown in the far north and pretty far south, quality wine is only produced in a 400km stretch of this long, narrow country. Frost and rain limit development further south, searing heat and desert are the problems to the north.

Recent appellation legislation splits the main wine-growing area into Aconcagua (incorporating the sub-region of Casablanca), the Central Valley (including the valleys of Maipo, Rapel, Curicó and Maule) and the Southern Region (including the valleys of Itata and Bío-Bío).

ACONCAGUA VALLEY Dominated by one producer (*Errázuriz*) in Panquehue. The main vine is Cabernet Sauvignon (*Errázuriz' Don Maximiano* is one of the top Cabernets in Chile) and new plantings of Sangiovese, Nebbiolo and Zinfandel add to the red bias.

CASABLANCA VALLEY Chile's premier white wine region, and the only one with an identifiable style. Chardonnay dominates, with Sauvignon Blanc and Gewürztraminer, and small amounts of Cabernet Sauvignon, Merlot and Pinot Noir. Chardonnay tends to be green and citrus-flavoured, often with figgy aromas, and Sauvignons are grassy and crisp with firm acidity. Best: *Caliterra, Concha y Toro, Veramonte, Villard, Viña Casablanca*.

CURICÓ Mainly known for its Chardonnay (*Valdivieso, Montes, San Pedro, Caliterra*). Valdivieso has emerged as the leading producer, also making beautiful Pinot Noir, Merlot and Cabernet. The Lontué Valley is a sub-region of Curicó.

MAIPO Birthplace of the Chilean wine industry and home to some of the biggest and most traditional players (*Santa Rita, Concha y Toro, Santa Carolina*). Cabernet Sauvignon made the valley's name and is still the main grape, although excellent Chardonnay is made here, too. The spread of Santiago's suburbs and smog is creating pressure on some producers, but most are beginning to push away from the valley floor with good results. Best: *Canepa, Carmen, Concha y Toro, Tarapacá*.

MAULE A handful of producers (*Carta Vieja, Domaine Oriental, TerraNoble*) are achieving variable results, with reds (particularly Merlot) so far beating whites hands down on quality.

RAPEL A seedbed of new winery activity with two zones: Cachapoal Valley and Colchagua Valley to the south, where *Mont Gras, Luis Felipe Edwards* and *Casa Lapostolle* are producing good Chardonnay and Cabernet. Top Pinot Noir comes from *Cono Sur*, and Merlot from *La Rosa* and *Concha y Toro. Viña Porta* and *Santa Monica* make top-class Cabernet and Merlot.

SOUTHERN REGION *Concha y Toro* has produced a top-class Gewürztraminer from Mulchen, and *Gracia*'s Chardonnay and Pinot Noir are sourced from Bío-Bío.

PRODUCERS WHO'S WHO

FRANCISCO DE AGUIRRE Clean, fresh Chardonnay and Cabernet under the Palo Alto label.

BISQUERTT ★ Top wines, sold under the Casa La Joya label, include Gran Reservas Chardonnay, Merlot and Carmenère.

CALITERRA ★ Citrus-edged Chardonnay, intense Sauvignon Blanc, and impressive Arboleda Carmenère and Merlot.

CANEPA ★ The company behind many of the best own-labels here. Carmenère, Zinfandel and Magnificum Cabernet are its top reds.

CARMEN ★★ State-of-the-art sister operation to Santa Rita. Reds are best; beautiful Merlot Reserve, Grande Vidure, Cabernet and Winemakers Red blend.

INSTANT CELLAR: CHILE'S FINEST

• **Caballo Loco No 4, Valdivieso, £14.99, Majestic** An enormously characterful non-vintage blend of Heaven knows what – Cabernet, Syrah, Merlot, Carmenère?
• **1999 Carmenère Reserva De Gras, Mont Gras, £7.34, The Nobody Inn** Supple and concentrated, with vanilla and redcurrant fruit.
• **1996 Cuvée Alexandre Cabernet, Casa Lapostolle, £11.50, Croque-en-Bouche** Punchy, blackcurranty wine, superripe, with rich tannins. There's also a Merlot version, for £1 more.
• **1999 Merlot Reserva De Gras, Mont Gras, £7.99, Noel Young** Much better than the 1998: deep cherries and plums fruit, with a touch of creamy oak. Very approachable, and drinking well now.
• **1997 Santa Rita Triple C, £12.50, Philglas & Swiggot** The grapes, in case you hadn't guessed, are both Cabernets plus Carmenère; very modern, lush and structured, with finesse as well.

CARTA VIEJA Old Maule Valley winery delivering good value, inexpensive wine. Reds are best. Very good Merlot.

CASA LAPOSTOLLE ★★ No-expense-spared winery making grassy Sauvignon, rich, buttery Chardonnay and spectacular Cuvée Alexandre Merlot.

CASA SILVA ★★ Colchagua Valley's new star, with excellent Carmenère, Merlot, Cabernet Sauvignon and Chardonnay.

CONCHA Y TORO ★★ Chile's biggest winery has resources to reach both good value and premium ends. Trio reds and whites are superb, as are Amelia Chardonnay and constantly improving Don Melchor Cabernet. Latest is a joint venture with Ch. Mouton-Rothschild in Bordeaux to produce super-pricy Almaviva.

CONO SUR ★★ Tasty Pinot Noir at every price level, and very good Merlot and Cabernet. Top label, 20 Barrel, can be excellent. Isla Negra reds are good value.

COUSIÑO MACUL Traditionalist making disappointing old-style reds under the Santiago smog. The move to new vineyards should help.

DOMAINE PAUL BRUNO Cabernet Sauvignon made by Bordelais duo Paul Pontallier of Ch. Margaux and Bruno Prats (formerly of Ch. Cos d'Estournel). Quality is puzzlingly unpredictable.

ECHEVERRÍA Leading boutique winery with vineyards in Curicó Valley. Good Reserva Chardonnay and Cabernet.

LUIS FELIPE EDWARDS ★ Large specialist in Chardonnay and Cabernet.

ERRÁZURIZ ★★ Excellent Merlot, Cabernet Sauvignon, Syrah and

Chardonnay; there is also a wild yeast Chardonnay. A joint venture with Robert Mondavi of California has produced Seña, an extremely expensive, lush Cabernet Sauvignon/Carmenère blend.

GRACIA ★ Good Merlot, Cabernet, and Pinot Noir Reserva Lo Mejor.

LA ROSA ★ Top unwooded Chardonnay and Merlot. Look out for La Palmería Cabernet and Merlot.

LOS ROBLES ★ Curicó co-operative making upfront, flying winemaker-style Cabernet, Carmenère and Merlot.

LOS VASCOS ★ Ch. Lafite-Rothschild of Bordeaux's venture in Chile. So far, the Cabernet has not lived up to its potential.

MONTES ★★ Slightly erratic, but currently on form with intense Malbec, good Merlot and premium Montes Alpha range Merlot, Syrah and Cabernet.

MONT GRAS ★ Go for the reds here: Cabernet, Merlot and Syrah are all good. Whites are less impressive so far.

PORTA ★ Consistently good oak-aged Chardonnay and Cabernet, and a good, concentrated Merlot.

SAN PEDRO★ Good-value 35 Sur Sauvignon Blanc and 35 Sur Chardonnay. The Castillo de Molina label includes a ripe, rich Merlot.

SANTA CAROLINA ★ Large, old winery, finally waking up to the modern world with fruity whites and substantial, if oaky Barrica Selection reds.

SANTA INÉS Small company, whose top label, De Martino, covers whites and reds.

SANTA RITA ★★ The 120 range is reliable, and the latest release of premium

> ### ON THE CASE
> Sauvignon Blanc from Chile can be good but often isn't thrilling: there's still too much dull Sauvignonasse in the vineyards

Casa Real shows welcome restraint with the new oak. Triple C is a fine Chilean response to the classic Bordeaux blend.

TARAPACÁ ★ Rapidly improving winery. Premium reds include Reserva Privada Syrah and Last Edition, an unusual red blend.

TERRANOBLE ★ Very good Sauvignon Blanc, Merlot and Gran Reserva Carmenère.

TORRÉON DE PAREDES ★ Good range, particularly an award-winning Merlot. Don Amado is the top red.

MIGUEL TORRES ★ Spanish investment has been slow to deliver the goods, but recent vintages are at last showing good form. Top wine is Manso de Velasco Cabernet, from old vines.

VALDIVIESO ★★ Traditional sparkling wine producer, now top of the premium still wine league. Excellent oaked Pinot Noir, Merlot, Malbec, and red blend (grapes vary from year to year) Caballo Loco.

VILLARD ★★ Good Sauvignon, Chardonnay and Pinot Noir from Casablanca, and fruity Merlot from Maipo.

VIÑA CASABLANCA ★★ White label wines come from outside the Casablanca area. From the valley itself, Santa Isabel Estate Sauvignon Blanc, Chardonnay and Gewürztraminer are all excellent, as are the Merlot and Cabernet Sauvignon.

VIU MANENT ★ The 19th-century San Carlos winery makes ripe Semillon, buttery Chardonnay Reserva and intense Malbec Reserva and Merlot Reserva.

CHILE PRICES

RED

Under £4.00

Arena Negra Red **1999** £2.99 (MORR)
★ Cabernet Sauvignon Viñedos del Pacifico Quiltro **1999** £3.99 (OD)
Cabernet Sauvignon Santiago **1999** £3.99 (MOR)
Merlot Las Colinas **2000** £3.99 (WR)
Merlot Las Colinas **1999** £3.99 (VIC) £3.99 (THR) £4.49 (BOT)
Merlot Santa Carolina Antares **2000** £3.95 (MORR)

£4.00 → £4.49

Cabernet Sauvignon Casa Leona **1999** £4.49 (MAR)
Cabernet Sauvignon Peteroa **1999** £4.49 (WIW)
Cabernet Sauvignon San Pedro Sur 35 **1999** £4.19 (MORR) £4.49 (ASD) £4.79 (SAF)
Cabernet Sauvignon Santa Carolina Antares **1999** £4.49 (VIL)
Cabernet Sauvignon Viña Gracia **1999** £4.49 (BUD) £4.49 (MORR)
Cabernet Sauvignon/Merlot La Rosa La Palmeria **1999** £4.49 (BOT)
Cabernet Sauvignon/Merlot Norte Chico **1999** £4.25 (CON)
Campero Chilean Red **Non-vintage** £4.25 (CON)
Merlot Concha y Toro **2000** £4.39 (WAI) £4.99 (POR) £4.99 (TAN) £4.99 (JON) £5.25 (HAH)
Merlot Cono Sur **1999** £4.49 (ASD)
Merlot Peteroa **1999** £4.49 (WIW)
Merlot Santa Carolina Antares **1999** £4.49 (VIL)
Merlot Santa Emiliana Acacias Estate **1998** £4.45 (SOM)
Merlot Viña Gracia **1999** £4.49 (MORR)

£4.50 → £4.99

Cabernet Sauvignon Caliterra **1999** £4.99 (VIC) £4.99 (THR) £4.99 (BOT) £4.99 (WR)
Cabernet Sauvignon Concha y Toro **1999** £4.75 (BALL) £4.99 (POR) £5.20 (TAN)
Cabernet Sauvignon Concha y Toro **1998** £4.99 (VIL) £5.39 (PLA)
Cabernet Sauvignon Concha y Toro Casillero del Diablo **2000** £4.99 (SAF)
Cabernet Sauvignon Concha y Toro Casillero del Diablo **1999** £4.99 (VIC)
Cabernet Sauvignon Concha y Toro Casillero del Diablo **1998** £4.99 (BOT) £4.99 (OD) £6.29 (CON)
Cabernet Sauvignon Cono Sur **1999** £4.95 (WS) £4.99 (BO) £4.99 (WAI) £4.99 (SAF)
Cabernet Sauvignon Cono Sur Isla Negra **1999** £4.99 (WAI) £5.49 (OD)
Cabernet Sauvignon Cono Sur Isla Negra **1998** £4.99 (TES) £4.99 (BOT)
Cabernet Sauvignon Luis Felipe Edwards Pupilla **1998** £4.99 (VIL)
Cabernet Sauvignon Francisco de Aguirre Tierra Arena **2000** £4.75 (GN)
Cabernet Sauvignon Linderos **1998** £4.99 (BO) £5.45 (STE)
Cabernet Sauvignon Santa Rita 120 **1998** £4.99 (WAI)
Cabernet Sauvignon Terra Andina **2000** £4.99 (BUD)
Cabernet Sauvignon TerraMater **2000** £4.79 (TES)
Cabernet Sauvignon Valdivieso **2000** £4.79 (SAI)
Cabernet Sauvignon Villa Montes **1999** £4.99 (MORR) £5.49 (SAI)
Cabernet Sauvignon Viña Porta **1999** £4.99 (UN)
Cabernet Sauvignon Vistamar Vistasur **1999** £4.79 (MAJ)
Cabernet Sauvignon/Merlot Concha y Toro **1999** £4.85 (STA)

RETAILERS SPECIALIZING IN CHILE
see Retailers Directory (page 40) for details

Not many retailers stock a long list, but the following have a good choice: D Byrne, First Quench Group (BOT, THR, VIC, WR), Hedley Wright (HED), Lay & Wheeler (LAY), Oddbins (OD) – few independent merchants have as much variety, Safeway (SAF), Sommelier Wine Co (SOM), Tanners (TAN), Noel Young (YOU).

★ Carmenère Cooperativa Agricole
  Vitivinicola de Curicó 2000 £4.99 (CO)
Malbec TerraMater 1999 £4.99 (CO)
Merlot Concha y Toro 1999 £4.75 (BALL)
  £4.99 (CON) £5.39 (PLA)
Merlot Concha y Toro 1998 £4.99 (VIL)
Merlot Cono Sur 2000 £4.95 (WS)
Merlot La Rosa La Palmeria 2000 £4.89
  (OD)
Merlot La Rosa La Palmeria 1999 £4.99
  (UN)
Merlot MontGras 1999 £4.79 (TES)
Merlot MontGras 1998 £4.95 (SOM)
Merlot San Pedro Sur 35 1999 £4.79 (SAF)
Merlot Santa Emiliana Andes Peaks 1999
  £4.85 (CON)
Merlot Santa Inés 1998 £4.99 (THR)
Merlot Undurraga 2000 £4.99 (MORR)
Merlot Valdivieso 2000 £4.99 (SAI)
Merlot Valdivieso 1999 £4.99 (UN) £4.99
  (BO) £4.99 (VIC) £4.99 (THR) £4.99 (BOT)
Merlot Villa Rosa 1999 £4.69 (WHI)
Merlot Viña Porta 1999 £4.99 (UN)
Pinot Noir Concha y Toro 1998 £4.99
  (VIL)
Pinot Noir Cono Sur 2000 £4.99 (ASD)
  £4.99 (SAI) £4.99 (TES)
Pinot Noir Cono Sur 1999 £4.98 (ASD)
Pinot Noir Undurraga 2000 £4.99 (TES)
Red Norte Chico 1998 £4.51 (PEN)
Zinfandel Canepa 2000 £4.99 (TES)
Zinfandel Canepa 1998 £4.99 (UN)
★ Zinfandel Peteroa 1999 £4.71 (WIW)

£5.00 → £5.99

Cabernet Sauvignon Aresti Montemar
  1999 £5.50 (RES)
Cabernet Sauvignon Carmen 1999 £5.02
  (FLE)
Cabernet Sauvignon Carmen 1996 £5.69
  (UN)
Cabernet Sauvignon Concha y Toro Trio
  1999 £5.99 (THR) £5.99 (BOT) £5.99
  (OD)
Cabernet Sauvignon Concha y Toro Trio
  1998 £5.99 (WR) £5.99 (VIL)
Cabernet Sauvignon Cono Sur Reserve
  1999 £5.99 (ASD)
Cabernet Sauvignon Errázuriz 1999 £5.49
  (VIC) £5.49 (THR) £5.49 (WR) £5.99 (UN)
  £6.49 (SO) £6.49 (SAF) £6.99 (BO)
Cabernet Sauvignon Los Vascos 1999
  £5.90 (CRO) £6.95 (LEA) £6.99 (BEN)
  £6.99 (POR) £6.99 (BAL) £7.25 (HAH)
  £7.83 (PLAY)

Cabernet Sauvignon Montes Oak-Aged
  Reserve 1997 £5.46 (WHI) £7.24 (PLAY)
Cabernet Sauvignon MontGras 1999
  £5.99 (SAI)
Cabernet Sauvignon Palomar Estate 1999
  £5.90 (JU)
Cabernet Sauvignon Portal del Alto 1998
  £5.50 (BALL)
Cabernet Sauvignon San Pedro Castillo de
  Molina Reserva 1999 £5.99 (MORR)
Cabernet Sauvignon Santa Emiliana
  Palmeras Estate 1999 £5.35 (CON)
Cabernet Sauvignon Santa Emiliana
  Palmeras Estate 1998 £5.29 (BO)
Cabernet Sauvignon Santa Rita 1999
  £5.49 (NEZ) £5.99 (VA)
Cabernet Sauvignon Santa Rita 120 1999
  £5.49 (DI)
Cabernet Sauvignon Santiago 2000 £5.10
  (LLO)
Cabernet Sauvignon Torres 1999 £5.95
  (POR)
Cabernet Sauvignon Torres Santa Digna
  1999 £5.99 (DI)
Cabernet Sauvignon Veramonte Central
  Valley 1999 £5.99 (SOM)
Cabernet Sauvignon Viña Casablanca
  Miraflores 1999 £5.88 (LLO)
Cabernet Sauvignon Viña Casablanca
  Miraflores 1998 £5.50 (WS)
Cabernet Sauvignon Viña Gracia Reserva
  Especial 1999 £5.99 (CO)
Cabernet Sauvignon/Merlot La Rosa La
  Palmeria Reserve 1999 £5.99 (UN)
Carmenère Viña Gracia Reserva Especial
  1999 £5.99 (CO)
Malbec TerraMater 1997 £5.99 (RAE)
Malbec Viña Casablanca White Label
  1999 £5.49 (MOR) £5.75 (BAC)
Merlot Aresti Montemar 1999 £5.50 (RES)
Merlot Bouchon Las Mercedes 1999
  £5.95 (BAN)
Merlot Carmen 1999 £5.49 (BO) £5.95
  (WS) £6.95 (JER)
Merlot Carmen 1998 £5.26 (FLE)
Merlot Casas del Bosque 2000 £5.97
  (ASD)
Merlot Château Los Boldos Tradition
  2000 £5.95 (STA)

*Stars (★) indicate wines selected by
Oz Clarke in the Best Buys section which
begins on page 8.*

Merlot Cono Sur Isla Negra **2000** £5.49 (SAF)

Merlot Cono Sur Isla Negra **1999** £5.79 (TES)

Merlot Errázuriz **1999** £5.99 (UN) £5.99 (TES) £6.95 (HAH)

Merlot La Rosa Cornellana **1999** £5.25 (AD)

Merlot La Rosa Cornellana **1998** £5.00 (AS)

Merlot M de Gras **1998** £5.80 (FLE) £6.99 (VA)

Merlot Morandé Terrarum **1999** £5.99 (SO)

Merlot Peteroa Oak-Aged **1997** £5.73 (WIW)

Merlot Santa Emiliana Andes Peaks **2000** £5.30 (MV)

Merlot Santa Rita **2000** £5.49 (NEZ)

Merlot Torreón de Paredes **2000** £5.85 (GN) £5.99 (AME)

Merlot Veramonte **1999** £5.99 (SOM) £6.99 (BOT)

Merlot Villa Rosa **2000** £5.16 (PLA)

Merlot Viña Casablanca White Label **1998** £5.49 (MOR) £5.75 (BAC) £6.99 (BAL)

Merlot/Syrah Morandé **1999** £5.99 (UN)

Pinot Noir Concha y Toro **1999** £5.99 (CON)

Pinot Noir Concha y Toro Explorer **1998** £5.49 (UN) £5.99 (VIL)

Syrah Concha y Toro Explorer **1998** £5.99 (JON) £5.99 (VIL)

£6.00 → £6.99

Cabernet Sauvignon Caliterra Reserve **1998** £6.99 (THR) £6.99 (BOT) £6.99 (WR)

Cabernet Sauvignon Carmen **1998** £6.26 (HIC)

Cabernet Sauvignon Carmen Reserve **1998** £6.89 (FLE) £6.95 (WS) £6.95 (STE)

Cabernet Sauvignon Casa Lapostolle **1999** £6.99 (VIC) £6.99 (THR) £6.99 (BOT)

Cabernet Sauvignon Casa Lapostolle **1998** £6.49 (MAJ)

Cabernet Sauvignon Concha y Toro Casillero del Diablo **1997** £6.99 (VIL)

Cabernet Sauvignon Cousiño Macul Antiguas Reservas **1997** £6.95 (POR) £6.95 (BALL) £7.25 (WRI) £7.49 (VIL) £7.50 (TAN)

Cabernet Sauvignon Domaine Oriental Clos Centenaire **1998** £6.30 (COC)

Cabernet Sauvignon Luis Felipe Edwards Reserva **1997** £6.99 (VIL)

Cabernet Sauvignon Los Vascos **1998** £6.51 (COC)

Cabernet Sauvignon Los Vascos **1996** £6.56 (PEN)

Cabernet Sauvignon M de Gras **1998** £6.99 (VA)

Cabernet Sauvignon Mapocho Reserva **1998** £6.99 (MORR)

Cabernet Sauvignon Montes **1999** £6.24 (PLAY)

Cabernet Sauvignon Montes **1998** £6.49 (POR) £7.75 (TW)

Cabernet Sauvignon Montes Oak-Aged Reserve **1998** £6.99 (AME)

Cabernet Sauvignon Montes Reserve **1998** £6.99 (HED)

Cabernet Sauvignon MontGras Reserva **1998** £6.25 (SOM)

Cabernet Sauvignon Santa Rita Reserva **1999** £6.99 (MAJ) £6.99 (NEZ) £6.99 (SAF)

Cabernet Sauvignon Torres Curico **1999** £6.49 (AME)

Cabernet Sauvignon Torres Santa Digna **1995** £6.44 (PEN)

Cabernet Sauvignon Valdivieso Barrel Selection **1999** £6.37 (BIB)

Cabernet Sauvignon Valdivieso Reserve **1998** £6.99 (TES) £6.99 (BOT) £6.99 (WR)

Cabernet Sauvignon Veramonte Central Valley **1998** £6.99 (OD)

Cabernet Sauvignon Villard **1998** £6.95 (TAN)

Cabernet Sauvignon Viña Alamosa Reserve **1999** £6.50 (GW)

Cabernet Sauvignon Viña Gracia Reserve **1997** £6.99 (WAI) £7.95 (POR)

Carmenère Luis Felipe Edwards **1997** £6.99 (VIL)

Carmenère William Fèvre La Misión **2000** £6.95 (STA)

Malbec Villa Montes **2000** £6.49 (POR)

Merlot Bouchon Las Mercedes **1997** £6.72 (SAV)

Merlot Casa Lapostolle **1999** £6.99 (BOT) £6.99 (WR) £7.86 (PLA) £7.99 (JON) £8.04 (LLO) £8.50 (WRI) £8.55 (HAH) £8.95 (FORT)

Merlot Concha y Toro Marques de Casa **1997** £6.99 (VIL) £7.96 (HIC)

Merlot Domaine Oriental Clos Centenaire **1997** £6.30 (COC)

Merlot Luis Felipe Edwards **1998** £6.99 (VIL)

Merlot Francisco de Aguirre Palo Alto Reservado **1999** £6.89 (COC)

Merlot M de Gras **2000** £6.60 (NI)

Merlot MontGras Reserva **1999** £6.25 (SOM) £7.37 (FLE)

Merlot Santa Rita Reserva **1999** £6.99 (DI)
Merlot Valdivieso Barrel Selection **1999** £6.37 (BIB)
Merlot Veramonte **1998** £6.99 (WR)
Merlot Viña Casa Silva **1999** £6.50 (STA)
Pinot Noir Concha y Toro Explorer **1997** £6.23 (PEN)
Pinot Noir Cono Sur Reserve **1999** £6.99 (UN) £6.99 (OD)
Pinot Noir Cono Sur Reserve **1998** £6.99 (TES)
Pinot Noir Peteroa Oak-Aged **1998** £6.66 (WIW)
Pinot Noir Undurraga **1997** £6.50 (BALL)
Pinot Noir Valdivieso Reserve **1997** £6.99 (WAI)

£7.00 → £7.99

Cabernet Sauvignon Casa Lapostolle **2000** £7.49 (POR)
Cabernet Sauvignon Concha y Toro Marques de Casa **1998** £7.70 (TAN)
Cabernet Sauvignon Cousiño Macul Antiguas Reservas **1998** £7.29 (JON) £7.75 (STA) £8.20 (MV)
Cabernet Sauvignon Cousiño Macul Antiguas Reservas **1996** £7.19 (PEN) £7.27 (PLA) £7.59 (CON)

Cabernet Sauvignon Echeverria Reserva **1998** £7.95 (MAY) £8.29 (COC)
Cabernet Sauvignon Valdivieso Reserve **1999** £7.34 (BIB)
Cabernet Sauvignon Viña Casablanca El Bosque **1998** £7.99 (POR) £7.99 (MOR)
Carmenère M de Gras Reserva **1999** £7.99 (VIL)
Carmenère M de Gras Reserva **1998** £7.99 (VA)
Chardonnay De Martino Prima Reserva **1999** £7.95 (BALL)
Grande Vidure/Cabernet Sauvignon Carmen **1998** £7.49 (BO) £8.25 (WRI)
Grande Vidure/Cabernet Sauvignon Carmen **1997** £7.50 (FLE) £8.29 (JON)

Malbec Villa Montes **1998** £7.75 (TW)
Merlot Carmen Reserve **1999** £7.45 (STE) £9.10 (JER)
Merlot Carmen Reserve **1998** £7.95 (WS)
Merlot Cousiño Macul **1998** £7.25 (WRI)
Merlot De Martino Prima Oaked **1999** £7.40 (AS)
Merlot M de Gras Reserva **1999** £7.99 (VIL)
Merlot Viña Casablanca White Label **1997** £7.95 (POR)
Merlot Viña Gracia Reserva **1998** £7.49 (UN)
Pinot Noir Valdivieso Reserve **1998** £7.99 (BOT) £7.99 (WR)
Quatro MontGras **1999** £7.99 (VIL)

£8.00 → £9.99

Cabernet Franc Valdivieso Single Vineyard Reserve **1999** £9.31 (BIB)
Cabernet Franc Valdivieso Single Vineyard Reserve **1998** £8.99 (SAF)
Cabernet Franc Valdivieso Single Vineyard Reserve **1997** £8.95 (WS) £9.99 (UN)
Cabernet Sauvignon Carmen Nativa Organic **1998** £8.95 (STE) £9.69 (OD)
Cabernet Sauvignon Cousiño Macul Antiguas Reservas **1999** £8.35 (NI)
Cabernet Sauvignon M de Gras Reserva **2000** £8.85 (NI)
Cabernet Sauvignon Montes Alpha **1998** £9.99 (POR) £9.99 (OD) £10.75 (WRI) £10.75 (PLA) £10.95 (HED)
Cabernet Sauvignon Montes Alpha **1997** £9.39 (WHI) £10.50 (CRO) £11.37 (PLAY)
Cabernet Sauvignon Santa Rita Medalla Real **1999** £8.99 (NEZ)
Cabernet Sauvignon Santa Rita Medalla Real **1998** £8.99 (DI)
Cabernet Sauvignon Viña Alamosa Prestige Reserve **1998** £8.70 (GW)
Cabernet Sauvignon Viña Casablanca El Bosque **1997** £8.95 (WS)
Carmenère/Cabernet Sauvignon Casa Donoso 1810 **1999** £9.99 (UN)
Merlot Echeverria Reserva **1998** £8.29 (COC)
Merlot M de Gras Reserva **2000** £8.85 (NI)
Merlot Montes Alpha **1998** £8.99 (MORR) £9.99 (POR)
Merlot Montes Alpha **1997** £9.39 (WHI) £10.80 (CRO) £10.95 (HED) £11.37 (PLAY)
Merlot Valdivieso Single Vineyard Reserve **1999** £9.31 (BIB)
Merlot Valdivieso Single Vineyard Reserve **1998** £8.99 (MAJ) £8.99 (ASD)

Merlot Viña Casablanca Santa Isabel **1998**
£8.99 (MOR) £10.99 (POR)

Merlot Viña Casablanca Santa Isabel **1997**
£8.95 (WS)

Ninquen MontGras **1997** £9.99 (FLE)
£14.99 (VIL)

Pinot Noir Carmen Reserve **1998** £8.45
(STE) £9.69 (NO)

Pinot Noir Villard **1998** £8.30 (SOM)
£8.49 (AME) £8.99 (OD)

Primus Veramonte **1998** £8.95 (SOM)

Syrah Errázuriz Reserva **1998** £9.99 (UN)
£9.99 (SAF) £10.95 (POR)

Syrah Santa Carolina Barrica Selection
1999 £8.99 (MORR)

£10.00 → £12.99

Cabernet Sauvignon Casa Lapostolle
Cuvée Alexandre **1998** £11.61 (LLO)

Cabernet Sauvignon Casa Lapostolle
Cuvée Alexandre **1997** £10.99 (VIL)
£11.99 (UN)

Cabernet Sauvignon Concha y Toro
Terrunyo **1998** £11.95 (WS)

Cabernet Sauvignon Montes Alpha **1996**
£10.99 (AME)

Cabernet Sauvignon Torres Manso de
Velasco **1995** £12.95 (DI) £14.69 (PEN)

Cordillera Torres **1999** £10.75 (DI)

Cordillera Torres **1998** £11.99 (AME)
£11.99 (YOU) £12.19 (GN)

Merlot Casa Lapostolle Cuvée Alexandre
1999 £12.99 (POR) £13.99 (BOT) £13.99
(WR) £13.99 (SAF) £14.16 (LLO)

Merlot Casa Lapostolle Cuvée Alexandre
1998 £12.95 (JER) £14.42 (HIC) £14.75
(FORT) £14.99 (OD) £15.49 (JON)

Merlot Casa Lapostolle Cuvée Alexandre
1997 £12.50 (CRO) £23.86 (MI)

Merlot Cono Sur 20 Barrels **1998** £10.95
(WS)

Pinot Noir Cono Sur 20 Barrels **1997**
£10.99 (WR)

Over £13.00

Alpha 'M' Montes **1997** £29.00 (CRO)
£30.00 (HED) £34.25 (PLAY) £36.95 (POR)

Alpha 'M' Montes **1996** £30.62 (NO)

★ Caballo Loco No 4 Valdivieso **Non-vintage** £14.95 (RES) £14.95 (WAI)
£14.99 (UN) £14.99 (MAJ) £14.99 (YOU)

Caballo Loco No 5 Valdivieso **Non-vintage** £15.66 (BIB)

Cabernet Sauvignon Carmen Gold
Reserve **1997** £18.95 (STE) £19.50 (WRI)

Cabernet Sauvignon Concha y Toro Don
Melchor **1997** £18.65 (TAN) £19.95 (STA)

Cabernet Sauvignon Concha y Toro Don
Melchor **1996** £16.99 (CON)

Cabernet Sauvignon Concha y Toro Don
Melchor **1994** £13.99 (VIL)

Cabernet Sauvignon De Martino Reserva
de Familia **1996** £19.95 (BALL)

Cabernet Sauvignon Echeverria Family
Reserve **1997** £13.99 (COC)

Cabernet Sauvignon Errázuriz Don
Maximiano Reserva **1998** £19.99 (UN)

Cabernet Sauvignon Errázuriz Don
Maximiano Founders Reserve **1998**
£17.95 (POR)

Cabernet Sauvignon Errázuriz Don
Maximiano Founders Reserve **1997**
£17.99 (WR)

Cabernet Sauvignon Torres Manso de
Velasco **1996** £13.95 (POR) £14.99 (AME)

Casa Real Santa Rita **1997** £18.50 (DI)
£18.99 (NEZ)

Clos Apalta Casa Lapostolle **1998** £26.00
(FORT)

Clos Apalta Casa Lapostolle **1997** £42.20
(MI)

Donoso Domaine Oriental **1997** £16.95
(COC)

Finis Terrae Cousiño Macul **1997** £15.85
(WRI) £15.95 (TAN) £15.99 (JON) £17.50
(STA) £17.99 (VIL)

Finis Terrae Cousiño Macul **1996** £16.50
(CON)

Seña Errázuriz **1997** £30.75 (FA) £36.00
(VIL)

WHITE

Under £4.00

Chardonnay Santa Carolina Antares **2000**
£3.95 (MORR)

Sauvignon Blanc Antu Mapu Reserva
2000 £3.99 (MORR)

Semillon Canepa **2000** £3.99 (WAI)

Semillon Canepa **1999** £3.99 (UN)

Semillon Peteroa **2000** £3.83 (WIW)

£4.00 → £4.99

Campero Chilean White **Non-vintage**
£4.25 (CON)

Chardonnay Caliterra **2000** £4.99 (VIC)
£4.99 (THR) £4.99 (BOT) £4.99 (WR)

Chardonnay Caliterra **1999** £4.75 (WAI)

Chardonnay Casa Donoso **1999** £4.49 (UN)

Chardonnay Concha y Toro **1999** £4.75
(BALL) £4.99 (POR) £4.99 (CON) £4.99
(VIL) £5.20 (TAN) £5.39 (PLA)

Chardonnay Concha y Toro Casillero del
Diablo **1999** £4.99 (UN) £4.99 (OD)

Chardonnay Concha y Toro Casillero del
Diablo **1998** £4.99 (BOT) £6.99 (VIL)

Chardonnay Cono Sur **2000** £4.49 (ASD)
£4.99 (SAF)

Chardonnay Cono Sur Isla Negra **1999**
£4.99 (BO) £5.49 (VIC) £5.49 (THR)

Chardonnay La Rosa La Palmeria **1999**
£4.49 (VIC) £4.49 (THR) £4.99 (UN)

Chardonnay MontGras **1999** £4.95 (SOM)

Chardonnay Peteroa **2000** £4.49 (WIW)

Chardonnay San Pedro Sur 35 **2000**
£4.69 (MORR) £4.79 (SAF)

Chardonnay Santa Carolina Antares **1999**
£4.49 (VIL)

Chardonnay Santa Carolina Reservado
1999 £4.99 (MORR)

Chardonnay Santa Emiliana Andes Peaks
1999 £4.85 (CON)

Chardonnay Terra Andina **1999** £4.99
(BUD)

Chardonnay TerraMater **2000** £4.79 (TES)

Chardonnay Valdivieso **1998** £4.99 (UN)

Chardonnay Viña Casablanca **2000** £4.99
(BO) £5.19 (BAL) £5.88 (LLO) £6.90 (NI)

Chardonnay Viña Casablanca **1999** £4.99
(POR)

Chardonnay Viña Casablanca White Label
1999 £4.95 (WS) £5.49 (MOR)

Chardonnay Vistamar Vistasur **2000**
£4.79 (MAJ)

Chardonnay/Sauvignon Blanc Norte
Chico **2000** £4.25 (CON)

Chardonnay/Semillon Santiago **2000**
£4.49 (BAL) £5.10 (LLO)

Chardonnay/Semillon Santiago **1999**
£4.25 (MOR)

Gewürztraminer Concha y Toro **2000**
£4.99 (VIL) £5.49 (JON) £5.50 (STA)

Gewürztraminer Concha y Toro **1999**
£4.49 (UN) £4.99 (CON)

Gewürztraminer Cono Sur **1999** £4.95
(WS) £4.99 (TES) £4.99 (BOT) £4.99 (WR)

Sauvignon Blanc Canepa **1999** £4.49 (UN)

Sauvignon Blanc Carmen **2000** £4.74 (FLE)
£6.35 (JER)

Sauvignon Blanc Concha y Toro **2000**
£4.49 (OD) £4.99 (POR) £4.99 (TAN)
£5.39 (PLA)

Sauvignon Blanc Concha y Toro **1999**
£4.75 (BALL) £4.99 (VIL)

Sauvignon Blanc Francisco de Aguirre
Tierra Arena **2000** £4.75 (GN) £5.20
(COC)

Sauvignon Blanc Francisco de Aguirre
Tierra Arena **1999** £4.85 (CON)

Sauvignon Blanc San Pedro Sur 35 **2000**
£4.49 (ASD) £4.69 (MORR) £4.79 (SAF)

Sauvignon Blanc San Pedro Sur 35 **1999**
£4.49 (WAI)

Sauvignon Blanc Santa Carolina Antares
1999 £4.49 (VIL)

Sauvignon Blanc Santa Emiliana Andes
Peaks **1999** £4.85 (CON)

Sauvignon Blanc Santiago **2000** £4.48
(LLO) £4.49 (BAL)

Sauvignon Blanc Santiago **1999** £4.25 (MOR)

Sauvignon Blanc Villa Montes **1999** £4.99
(MORR)

Sauvignon Blanc Villard **1999** £4.75 (SOM)

Sauvignon Blanc Viña Casablanca White
Label **2000** £4.99 (POR)

Semillon Las Casas del Toqui **1999** £4.99
(BO)

Semillon Peteroa Barrel-Fermented **1999**
£4.72 (WIW)

Semillon Viña Alamosa **2000** £4.80 (GW)

Viognier Cono Sur **2000** £4.99 (MAJ)

White Norte Chico **1998** £4.51 (PEN)

£5.00 → £5.99

Chardonnay Aresti Montemar **1999**
£5.50 (RES)

Chardonnay Carmen **2000** £5.95 (BER)
£6.35 (JER)

Chardonnay Carmen **1999** £5.99 (OD)

Chardonnay Casa Lapostolle **2000** £5.79
(NO) £8.04 (LLO)

Chardonnay Château Los Boldos
Tradition **1999** £5.95 (STA)

Chardonnay Concha y Toro Terrunyo
1999 £5.90 (HIC)

Chardonnay Concha y Toro Trio **2000**
£5.99 (OD)

Chardonnay Concha y Toro Trio **1999**
£5.99 (VIC) £5.99 (THR) £5.99 (VIL)

Chardonnay Cono Sur Isla Negra **1998**
£5.49 (BOT) £5.99 (UN)

Please remember that
Oz Clarke's Wine Buying Guide
is a price guide and not a price list. It is
not meant to replace up-to-date
merchants' lists.

Chardonnay Cono Sur Reserve **1999**
£5.99 (MAJ) £5.99 (ASD)
Chardonnay Cousiño Macul **1999** £5.79
(POR) £5.95 (TAN) £5.99 (VIL) £6.19 (JON)
£6.35 (STA)
Chardonnay Luis Felipe Edwards **1999**
£5.99 (VIL)
Chardonnay Errázuriz **2000** £5.49 (VIC)
£5.49 (THR) £5.49 (BOT) £5.79 (TES)
£5.99 (SO) £5.99 (OD)
Chardonnay Errázuriz **1999** £5.99 (SAF)
Chardonnay Francisco de Aguirre Palo
Alto **1999** £5.95 (BALL)
Chardonnay La Rosa Cornellana **1999**
£5.25 (AD)
Chardonnay MontGras Reserva **1999**
£5.99 (SAI)
Chardonnay Palomar Estate **1998** £5.90
(JU)
Chardonnay Peteroa Barrel-Fermented
1999 £5.73 (WIW)
Chardonnay San Pedro Casillo de Molina
Reserva **1999** £5.99 (MORR)
Chardonnay Santa Emiliana Palmeras
Estate **1998** £5.25 (BU)
Chardonnay Santa Rita 120 **2000** £5.39
(DI)
Chardonnay Santa Rita Reserva **1999**
£5.99 (NEZ) £6.49 (SAF) £6.99 (DI)
Chardonnay Veramonte **1999** £5.99
(SOM) £6.99 (BOT) £6.99 (WR)
Chardonnay Viña Casablanca White Label
1998 £5.49 (UN)
Chardonnay Vistamar Subsol **1997** £5.69
(BAC)
Riesling/Gewürztraminer Torres Don
Miguel **1999** £5.99 (GN)
Sauvignon Blanc Bouchon Las Mercedes
2000 £5.50 (BAN)
Sauvignon Blanc Caliterra **1999** £5.44
(PLA)
Sauvignon Blanc Casa Lapostolle **2000**
£5.49 (VIC) £5.49 (THR) £5.49 (BOT)
£5.95 (POR) £5.98 (PLA) £5.99 (WR)
Sauvignon Blanc Concha y Toro Casillero
del Diablo **1998** £5.99 (VIL)

- *Wines are listed in A–Z order within
  each price band.*
- *For each wine, vintages are listed in
  descending order.*
- *Each vintage of any wine appears
  only once.*

Sauvignon Blanc Concha y Toro Explorer
2000 £5.99 (JON)
Sauvignon Blanc Concha y Toro Explorer
1999 £5.99 (CON)
Sauvignon Blanc Concha y Toro Explorer
1998 £5.65 (WRI)
Sauvignon Blanc Echeverria **2000** £5.99
(COC) £6.35 (JER)
Sauvignon Blanc Errázuriz **2000** £5.99
(VIC) £5.99 (THR) £5.99 (BOT) £5.99 (WR)
Sauvignon Blanc Montes **2000** £5.50 (HED)
£5.62 (PLA) £6.24 (PLAY) £6.58 (TW)
Sauvignon Blanc Montes **1999** £5.75 (FORT)
Sauvignon Blanc Montes **1998** £5.50 (JU)
Sauvignon Blanc Montes Oak-Aged **2000**
£5.46 (WHI)
Sauvignon Blanc Santa Emiliana Andes
Peaks **2000** £5.30 (MV)
Sauvignon Blanc Torreón de Paredes
2000 £5.79 (GN)
Sauvignon Blanc Torres **2000** £5.45 (STA)
Sauvignon Blanc Torres **1999** £5.49 (POR)
Sauvignon Blanc Torres Santa Digna **2000**
£5.49 (GN) £5.58 (PEN) £5.69 (JON)
£5.99 (DI)
Sauvignon Blanc Villard Aconcagua **2000**
£5.75 (BU)
Sauvignon Blanc Viña Casablanca **2000**
£5.19 (BAL) £5.40 (LLO) £6.90 (NI)
Sauvignon Blanc Viña Casablanca Santa
Isabel **1999** £5.99 (TES)

£6.00 → £6.99

Chardonnay Caliterra Reserve **1998** £6.99
(VIC) £6.99 (THR) £6.99 (BOT) £6.99 (WR)
Chardonnay Carmen Reserve **1997** £6.25
(STE) £7.00 (WRI)
Chardonnay Casa Lapostolle **1999** £6.99
(UN) £7.49 (POR) £7.99 (JON)
Chardonnay Cousiño Macul Antiguas
Reservas **1997** £6.95 (POR) £6.95 (BALL)
Chardonnay Domaine Oriental Clos
Centenaire **1999** £6.21 (COC)
Chardonnay Echeverria Unwooded **1999**
£6.39 (COC)
Chardonnay La Rosa La Palmeria Gran
Reserva **1998** £6.99 (OD)
Chardonnay Los Vascos **1999** £6.56 (PEN)
£7.86 (PLAY)
Chardonnay Montes Barrel-Fermented
1999 £6.25 (HED) £7.75 (TW)
Chardonnay Montes Reserve **1999** £6.95
(BER)
Chardonnay Santa Rita Medalla Real **1997**
£6.99 (NEZ)

Chardonnay Torres Maquehua **1999**
£6.99 (DI) £6.99 (GN)
Chardonnay Torres Miguel **1999** £6.99
(POR)
Chardonnay Valdivieso Barrel Selection
2000 £6.37 (BIB)
Chardonnay Veramonte **1998** £6.99 (OD)
Chardonnay Villard **1997** £6.95 (WS)
Chardonnay Viña Alamosa Grand Reserve
1999 £6.99 (GW)
Chardonnay Viña Casa Silva **1999** £6.25
(STA)
Chardonnay Viña Casablanca Barrel-
Fermented **1999** £6.99 (OD)
Chardonnay Viña Casablanca Santa Isabel
1998 £6.90 (BAC)
Chardonnay Viña Gracia Reserve **1997**
£6.99 (WAI)
Gewürztraminer Viña Casablanca **1998**
£6.99 (BAL)
Gewürztraminer Viña Casablanca Santa
Isabel **2000** £6.99 (OD) £7.06 (LLO)
Gewürztraminer Viña Casablanca Santa
Isabel **1999** £6.99 (POR) £6.99 (MOR)
Sauvignon Blanc Casa Lapostolle **2001**
£6.26 (LLO)
Sauvignon Blanc Echeverria **1999** £6.50
(MAY)
Sauvignon Blanc Errázuriz **1999** £6.60 (HAH)
Sauvignon Blanc William Fèvre La Misión
1999 £6.35 (STA)
Sauvignon Blanc Santa Rita Reserva **2000**
£6.49 (MAJ) £6.49 (NEZ) £6.99 (DI)
Sauvignon Blanc Viña Casablanca Santa
Isabel **1997** £6.99 (MOR)

£7.00 → £8.99

Chardonnay Carmen Nativa Organic
1999 £7.95 (STE) £8.95 (WRI) £8.99 (BO)
Chardonnay Carmen Nativa Organic
1998 £8.18 (NO)
Chardonnay Carmen Reserve **1998** £8.75
(JER)
Chardonnay Casa Lapostolle **1998** £8.25
(WRI) £8.25 (FORT)
Chardonnay Cousiño Macul Antiguas
Reservas **1998** £7.25 (WRI)
Chardonnay Cousiño Macul Antiguas
Reservas **1996** £7.19 (PEN) £7.59 (CON)
Chardonnay Errázuriz Reserva **1995**
£7.90 (CRO)
Chardonnay Errázuriz Wild Ferment
1999 £8.99 (SAI) £9.95 (BER) £9.99 (OD)
Chardonnay M de Gras Reserva **1999**
£7.99 (VA)

Chardonnay Montes **1999** £7.26 (PLAY)
Chardonnay Montes Alpha **1999** £8.99
(MORR) £9.99 (POR) £10.95 (HED)
Chardonnay Santa Rita Medalla Real **1999**
£7.99 (DI)
Chardonnay Valdivieso Reserva **1999**
£7.34 (BIB)
Chardonnay Villard Reserve **1998** £8.20
(SOM) £9.95 (TAN)
Chardonnay Viña Casablanca Santa Isabel
Barrel-Fermented **1998** £7.99 (MOR)
Chardonnay Viña Gracia Reserve **1999**
£7.49 (UN)
Gewürztraminer Viña Casablanca **2000**
£7.90 (NI)
Sauvignon Blanc Casa Lapostolle **1998**
£7.46 (HIC)
Sauvignon Blanc Santa Rita Medalla Real
1998 £8.99 (NEZ)

Over £9.00

Chardonnay Carmen Winemakers
Reserve **1997** £10.45 (STE)
Chardonnay Casa Lapostolle Cuvée
Alexandre **1999** £9.99 (SAF) £10.99 (UN)
£10.99 (VIL) £11.49 (JON) £12.90 (JER)
Chardonnay Casa Lapostolle Cuvée
Alexandre **1997** £12.50 (WRI) £12.50
(FORT) £23.86 (MI)
Chardonnay Concha y Toro Amelia **1998**
£17.50 (STA) £17.99 (VIL)
Chardonnay Concha y Toro Terrunyo
1998 £9.99 (VIL)
Chardonnay Montes Alpha **1998** £9.39
(WHI)

ROSÉ

Under £5.00

★ Cabernet Sauvignon Torres Santa Digna
Rosado **2000** £4.99 (DI) £4.99 (WHI)
£5.39 (JON)
Cabernet Sauvignon Torres Santa Digna
Rosado **1999** £4.98 (NO) £4.99 (WHI)
Cabernet Sauvignon Torres Santa Digna
Rosado **1998** £4.99 (POR)

SPARKLING

Under £7.00

Santa Carolina Brut **1996** £5.69 (MORR)
Valdivieso Brut Reserve Methode
Traditionelle **1997** £6.26 (BIB) £6.90 (BAC)

EASTERN EUROPE

At last Eastern Europe is getting there, with fresh flavours and an understanding of what we want

Poor old Eastern Europe. It's ten years and more since the Iron Curtain came down, and it found itself having to start again from scratch just when other countries, like Chile, were forging ahead. It hasn't been easy. But it is, at last, happening. Hungary, with the aid of an army of outside winemakers and consultants, is producing some excellent flavours at good prices (though the Hungarian wines you taste in Hungary are, I can tell you, a different kettle of fish). Bulgaria is slowly finding its feet, with modern reds and a few fresh whites. Other countries, like Moldova, Romania, Slovenia, Georgia and the Ukraine have as yet unrealized poential.

GRAPE VARIETIES

CABERNET SAUVIGNON (red) Capable of producing ripe, long-lived wines.

CHARDONNAY (white) Sometimes barrel fermented, sometimes overoaked.

FURMINT (white) Top quality Tokaji grape; good acidity, concentration, and long life.

GAMZA (red) Soft, light, early maturing.

GEWÜRZTRAMINER (white) Usually known as Traminer, and typically spicy.

GRÜNER VELTLINER (white) Intense greengage fruit at best.

HÁRSLEVELÜ (white) Earthy, big, peachy, long-lived.

IRSAI OLIVÉR (white) Very perfumed.

KADARKA (red) Usually tough, green.

KÉKFRANKOS/FRANKOVKA/ BLAUFRÄNKISCH (red) Mostly vegetal young reds.

MAVRUD (red) Hefty dark reds; best examples have plummy fruit.

MELNIK (red) Firm, spicy reds.

MERLOT (red) Reasonably good and soft.

MUSCAT OTTONEL (white) Perfumed but short-lived.

PINOT BLANC/GRIS (white) At their best similar to dry Alsace.

PINOT NOIR (red) Often poorly handled.

PLAVAC MALI (red) Good, tannic red with potential to age.

RHINE RIESLING (white) Rarely as intense as good German versions.

ST LAURENT/BLAUER LIMBERGER (red) Soft reds with black cherry flavours.

SAPERAVI (red) Very good spicy wine; lots of potential.

SAUVIGNON BLANC (white) Can be good and pungent.

TĂMÎIOASĂ ROMÂNEASCĂ (white) Classic noble rot grape. Very sweet, raisiny flavours, long-lived.

WELSCHRIESLING/LASKI RIZLING/ OLASZ RIZLING (white) Earthy, lowish-acid, but can be good.

WINE REGIONS AND PRODUCERS

BULGARIA Soft, juicy modern reds and crisp whites. It's best to go for young wines and drink them fast – and don't be surprised if 'reserve' turns out to be a euphemism for more oak than is good for anyone. There's much less overoaking than there was, though, and an understanding too that older isn't necessarily better. Look for *Assenovgrad, Blueridge, Domaine Boyar, Iambol, Khan Krum, Preslav, Rousse, Shumen, Sliven, Suhindol, Stara Zagora, Vinogradi.*

CZECH REPUBLIC AND SLOVAKIA The latter got most of the former Czechoslovakia's vineyards. Both countries produce light, gently spicy whites of unremarkable quality.

GEORGIA Known for primitive, tannic whites; Western influence is now appearing, for example in plummy Matrassa reds.

HUNGARY Quality is erratic, but there are quite a few exceptions, and luckily it's the exceptions we see over here, often from top Hungarian winemakers such as Tibor Gál and Ákos Kamocsay. White wines are what Hungary does best: Sauvignon Blanc, Chardonnay and Pinot Gris can be seriously good, and renewed interest in native grape varieties such as Irsai Olivér, Cserszegi Füszeres and Leányka is resulting in some tasty and original wines. Look for *Chapel Hill, Hilltop (Riverview), Vylyan.*

The other big exception is the sweet white wine of Tokaj. This is the name of the region; Tokaji is the name of the wine (the English used to spell it Tokay). The style has also changed: from being oxidized and tasting like ancient sherry, it is now (as a result of Western investment) fresher and infinitely more delicious. The grapes are Furmint, Muscat Lunel and Hárslevelü. It's made from botrytized grapes (known as *aszú*) which are added to dry base wine in measures known as *puttonyos*. A three-puttonyos Tokaji will be sweet, a four-puttonyos one sweeter, and a five or six-puttonyos one very concentrated and rich. Aszú Eszencia is sweeter again, and Eszencia on its own means juice too sweet to ferment to more than a few per cent alcohol; it's used for blending in tiny quantities into lesser wines to pep them up or (according to legend) for reviving dying monarchs. Tokajis of three to six puttonyos are a more practical buy: they have a smokiness and acidity to their fruit which sets them apart from all other dessert wines, and they age superbly. Best: *Disznókö, Istvan Szepsy, Chateau Megyer, Oremus, Chateau Pazjos, Royal Tokaji Wine Company, Tokaji Kereskedöház.*

MOLDOVA Plenty of potential in both whites and reds. Look for *Crikova, Hincesti, Purkar.*

ROMANIA Patchy quality again. The sweet whites from the Tămîîoasă grape can be sensational. Not much else is.

SLOVENIA Quality is promising – the wines are well-structured, balanced and often quite aromatic – but prices are on the high side and we don't see many.

EASTERN EUROPEAN CLASSIFICATIONS

Quality wine, equivalent to France's Appellation Contrôlée, is Minöségi bor in Hungary, Controliran in Bulgaria, and in Slovenia Vrhunsko Vino or, below this, Kakovostno Vino. Romania's system is too complicated to give in full, but the best are VSOC, which can be late harvest up to nobly rotten; VSO from specific grapes and regions; VS for quality wine.

EASTERN EUROPE PRICES

BULGARIA RED

Under £3.00

Boyar International Merlot **NV** £2.99 (SAI)
Iambol Cabernet Sauvignon **1999** £2.99 (MORR)
Iambol Merlot **1999** £2.99 (MORR)
Lovico Suhindol Cabernet Sauvignon/Cinsault **1998** £2.98 (WIW)
Shumen Cabernet Sauvignon **1999** £2.99 (CO)
Stara Zagora Merlot/Cabernet **1999** £2.98 (WIW)

£3.00 → £3.99

Blueridge Merlot Barrique **1999** £3.99 (BUD) £3.99 (WAI)
Bulgarian Vintners Merlot Reserve **1997** £3.99 (SAI)
Domaine Boyar Cabernet Sauvignon Reserve **1997** £3.79 (MORR)
Domaine Boyar Merlot Young Vatted **2000** £3.49 (SAF)
Iambol Cabernet Sauvignon Reserve **1996** £3.99 (BOT)
Iambol Merlot **1998** £3.49 (UN)
Liubimetz Merlot Reserve **1997** £3.32 (WIW)
Lovico Suhindol Cabernet Sauvignon **1999** £3.95 (WS)
Oriachovitza Cabernet Sauvignon **2000** £3.10 (WIW)
Oriachovitza Cabernet Sauvignon Reserve **Non-vintage** £3.99 (UN)
Oriachovitza Cabernet Sauvignon Reserve **1997** £3.32 (WIW)
Oriachovitza Merlot **2000** £3.10 (WIW)
Oriachovitza Merlot/Cabernet Sauvignon **1999** £3.07 (WIW)
Oriachovitza Merlot/Cabernet Sauvignon Reserve **1997** £3.32 (WIW)

£4.00 → £4.99

Domaine Boyar Merlot Premium Oak **1999** £4.99 (TES)
Domaine Boyar Merlot Premium Oak **1998** £4.99 (SAI) £4.99 (MORR)
Shumen Cabernet Sauvignon Premium Oak **Non-vintage** £4.99 (UN)
Shumen Merlot Premium Cuvée **Non-vintage** £4.49 (UN)

BULGARIA WHITE

Under £4.00

Khan Krum Chardonnay **2000** £3.20 (WIW)
Khan Krum Chardonnay Reserve **1998** £3.60 (WIW)
Preslav Chardonnay Bin 63 **2000** £3.82 (WIW)
Shumen Chardonnay **1999** £3.29 (CO)

HUNGARY WHITE

Under £3.50

Chapel Hill Irsai Oliver **2000** £3.29 (WAI)
Chapel Hill Irsai Oliver **1999** £3.29 (TES) £3.79 (OD)
Chapel Hill Irsai Oliver **1998** £3.49 (UN)
Gyorgy Chardonnay Villa Etyeki **2000** £3.47 (WIW)
★ Hilltop Neszmély 'The Unpronouncable Grape' Cserszegi Füszeres **2000** £3.49 (THR) £3.49 (WR) £3.49 (BOT) £3.49 (VIC)
Hilltop Neszmély Irsai Oliver **2000** £2.99 (SAF)
Lellei Chardonnay **2000** £3.23 (WIW)
Lellei Pinot Gris **2000** £3.23 (WIW)
Lellei Tramini **2000** £3.23 (WIW)
★ Nyakas Pince Pinot Gris **2000** £3.65 (WIW)

RETAILERS SPECIALIZING IN EASTERN EUROPE

see Retailers Directory (page 40) for details

If you want to look beyond bargain Cabernet Sauvignon, try the following merchants: Butlers Wine Cellar (BU) – good for curiosities, First Quench Group (BOT, THR, VIC, WR), Morris & Verdin (MV), Sainsbury's (SAI), Safeway (SAF), T&W Wines (TW) – good for old Tokaji, Wines of Westhorpe (WIW).

£3.50 → £4.49

Badacsonyi Szürkebarát **1999** £4.49
(WIW)
Chapel Hill Chardonnay **1999** £3.69
(BO)
Chapel Hill Chardonnay Oaked **2000**
£4.49 (WAI)
Gyöngyös Estate Chardonnay **1999** £3.79
(CO)
Hilltop Neszmély Gewürztraminer Bin
066 2000 £3.99 (SAI)
Nagyréde Dry Muscat **1999** £3.79
(OD)
Nagyréde Pinot Gris Oaked Reserve
1999 £3.99 (OD)
★ Nyakas Pince Sauvignon Blanc **2000** £3.99
(WIW)

£4.50 → £9.99

Tibor Gal Chardonnay Barrique Eger
1999 £6.08 (WIW)
Tokaji Aszú 5 Putts ½ litre, Château
Messzelato **1988** £8.33 (WIW)
Tokaji Fordítás Dessewffy **1988** £7.50
(CRO)
Tokaji Furmint Disznókö **1993** £4.50
(CRO)
Tokaji Szamorodni Dry ½ litre, Oremus
1993 £5.99 (DI)
Tokaji Szamorodni Sweet ½ litre, Oremus
1989 £5.99 (DI)

£10.00 → £19.99

Tokaji Aszú 5 Putts ½ litre, Disznókö
1993 £18.99 (OD)
Tokaji Aszú 5 Putts ½ litre, Oremus **1994**
£19.49 (YOU) £19.95 (FORT)
Tokaji Aszú 5 Putts ½ litre, Oremus **1993**
£18.95 (HED)
Tokaji Aszú 5 Putts ½ litre, Tokaji
Kereskedöhóz **1993** £18.50 (STA)
Tokaji Aszú 6 Putts ½ litre, J Monyok
1993 £13.13 (WIW)

£20.00 → £39.99

Tokaji Aszú 5 Putts ½ litre Birsalmàs,
Royal Tokaji Wine Co. **1993** £25.50
(TAN)
Tokaji Aszú 5 Putts ½ litre Nyulaszo,
Royal Tokaji Wine Co. **1993** £36.30
(TAN)
Tokaji Aszú 5 Putts ½ litre, Royal Tokaji
Wine Co. **1995** £21.50 (HAH) £22.33
(CB) £23.21 (PLA)

Over £40.00

Tokaji Aszú Essencia ½ litre, J Monyok
1983 £46.65 (WIW)
Tokaji Aszú Essencia ½ litre, Oremus
1975 £250.00 (FORT)
Tokaji Aszú Essencia ½ litre, Royal Tokaji
Wine Co. **1993** £89.50 (LEA)

HUNGARY RED

Under £4.00

Bull's Blood Eger **1999** £3.49 (SAF)
Bull's Blood Eger **1998** £3.69 (MORR)
£3.79 (TES)
Bull's Blood Eger **1997** £3.99 (UN) £6.41
(WIW)
Chapel Hill Cabernet Sauvignon **1997**
£3.49 (MORR)

Lellei Cabernet Sauvignon **2000** £3.37
(WIW)
Lellei Merlot **1999** £3.32 (WIW)
Sopron Kékfrankos **2000** £3.13 (WIW)
Szekszardi Kadarka Sweet **1999** £3.47
(WIW)

Over £4.00

Tibor Gal Cabernet Sauvignon **1998**
£6.99 (WIW)
Tiffáns Cabernet Sauvignon **1998** £9.16
(WIW)
Tiffáns Cabernet Sauvignon/Kékfrankos
Cuvée **1998** £7.33 (WIW)
Tiffáns Kékoportó **2000** £5.38 (WIW)

ROMANIA

Under £5.00

Romanian Classic Pinot Noir **1998** £2.99
(MORR)
Romanian Merlot Special Reserve Barrel
Matured **1999** £4.95 (WRI)

FRANCE

There's not much to be said for France's Appellation Contrôlée system, but I'm still rather glad to have some things preserved in AC aspic

I'm going to do something extremely unfashionable. I'm going to stand up for the Appellation Contrôlée system.

Not wholeheartedly, you understand. It doesn't do the job it is supposed to do – which is maintain or improve quality – and it is, most of the time, a godsend to lazy producers who are happy to abide by the rules and milk the system as hard as they can. And since the rules were tailored to just this sort of producer in the first place, it is not surprising that too many ACs in France produce wines that are a disgrace to the system. Basic Bordeaux Rouge, for example, is being taken in hand now, but not by the Institut National des Appellations d'Origine (INAO). It is the Bordelais themselves who have got fed up with the poor quality of

much of their basic wine: it's a local rebellion against the idleness of the national authorities.

Doesn't sound as though I'm standing up for the system, does it? Well, this is what I have to say in its favour. It has preserved a great many obscure grape varieties from the inroads of Chardonnay and Cabernet – grapes like Tannat, which is the star of Uruguay of all places. I predict a renaissance of this grape in South-West France once the South American versions catch our imaginations. Or Gros and Petit Manseng – as luscious and aromatic as Viognier and again, found in the South-West. Winemakers these days are wild for 'new' grapes, and it is at least partly because of the jobsworths at INAO that they're still there to be rediscovered.

WINE CLASSIFICATIONS

The French have the most far-reaching system of wine control of any nation, even though its adequacy as a form of quality control is now in question. The key factors are the 'origin' of the wine, its historic method of production and the use of the correct grape types. The three defined levels are: AC, VDQS and vin de pays.

APPELLATION D'ORIGINE CONTRÔLÉE (AC, AOC) To qualify
for AC a wine must meet specific requirements on seven fronts:
Land: Suitable vineyard land is minutely defined. **Grape**: Only those grapes traditionally regarded as suitable can be used. **Degree of alcohol**: Wines must reach a minimum (or maximum) degree of natural alcohol. **Yield**: A basic permitted yield is set for each AC, but the figure may be increased or decreased (laugh!) year by year after consultation between the

growers of each AC region and the Institut National des Appellations d'Origine. **Vineyard practice**: AC wines must follow rules about pruning methods and density of planting. **Winemaking practice**: Each AC wine has its own regulations as to what is allowed. Typically, chaptalization – adding sugar during fermentation to increase alcoholic strength – is accepted in the North, but not in the South. **Tasting and analysis**: Since 1979 wines must pass a tasting panel.

VIN DÉLIMITÉ DE QUALITÉ SUPÉRIEURE (VDQS) This second
group is, in general, slightly less reliable in quality. It is in the process of being phased out. No more vins de pays are being upgraded to VDQS but there is still no news on when any of the existing ones will be upgraded to AC status (or downgraded to vin de pays).

VIN DE PAYS The third category gives a regional definition to France's basic blending wines. The rules are similar to AC, but allow a good deal more flexibility and some wonderful cheap wines can be found. Ambitious estates can use the regulations to make excellent, original reds and whites, although Vins de Pays d'Oc from leading grape varieties are frequently disappointing.

VIN DE TABLE 'Table wine' is the title for the rest. No quality control except as far as basic public health regulations demand. Vins de pays are always available for approximately the same price, and offer a far more interesting drink. Many vins de table here are dull and poorly made, and the branded, heavily advertised ones are seldom good value.

LOIRE	Main wine regions
CAHORS	Other regions

WINE-FINDER: FRANCE

France is packed with famous wine names, but if you don't know whereabouts in the country a wine comes from, life can get confusing. In the following 206 pages we have divided the huge number of appellations in France into eight clearly defined regions: Alsace, Bordeaux, Burgundy, Champagne, Jura & Savoie, Loire, Rhône and Southern France. In Burgundy, we have separated Basic Burgundy and the sub-regions Beaujolais, Chablis, Côte Chalonnaise, Côte d'Or and Mâconnais. So, if you know the name but are wondering which section to look in, this quick guide to some of the best-known wine names will help.

Aloxe-Corton – *Burgundy, Côte d'Or*
Auxey-Duresses – *Burgundy, Côte d'Or*
Bandol – *Southern France*
Barsac – *Bordeaux (sweet white)*
Beaune – *Burgundy, Côte d'Or*
Blagny – *Burgundy, Côte d'Or*
Bourgueil – *Loire (red)*
Brouilly – *Burgundy, Beaujolais*
Cadillac – *Bordeaux*
Cahors – *Southern France*
Cérons – *Bordeaux*
Chablis – *Burgundy, Chablis*
Chambolle-Musigny – *Burgundy, Côte d'Or*
Chassagne-Montrachet – *Burgundy, Côte d'Or*
Châteauneuf-du-Pape – *Rhône*
Chénas – *Burgundy, Beaujolais*
Chinon – *Loire (red)*
Chiroubles – *Burgundy, Beaujolais*
Chorey-lès-Beaune – *Burgundy, Côte d'Or*
Clairette de Die – *Rhône (sparkling)*
Condrieu – *Rhône (white)*
Corbières – *Southern France*
Cornas – *Rhône (red)*
Coteaux du Tricastin – *Rhône*
Côte-Rôtie – *Rhône (red)*
Côtes de Beaune – *Burgundy, Côte d'Or*
Côtes de Bourg – *Bordeaux*
Côtes de Nuits – *Burgundy, Côte d'Or*
Côtes du Ventoux – *Rhône*
Crozes-Hermitage – *Rhône*
Entre-deux-Mers – *Bordeaux*
Fitou – *Southern France*
Fixin – *Burgundy, Côte d'Or*
Fleurie – *Burgundy, Beaujolais*
Fronsac – *Bordeaux*
Gevrey-Chambertin – *Burgundy, Côte d'Or*
Gigondas – *Rhône (red)*
Givry – *Burgundy, Côte Chalonnaise*
Graves – *Bordeaux (dry white)*
Hautes-Côtes de Beaune – *Burgundy, Côte d'Or*
Hautes-Côtes de Nuit – *Burgundy, Côte d'Or*
Haut-Médoc – *Bordeaux*
Hermitage – *Rhône*
Juliénas – *Burgundy, Beaujolais*
Languedoc-Roussillon – *Southern France*
Listrac – *Bordeaux*

Loupiac – *Bordeaux*
Mâcon – *Burgundy, Mâconnais*
Margaux – *Bordeaux*
Marsannay – *Burgundy, Côte d'Or*
Médoc – *Bordeaux*
Mercurey – *Burgundy, Côte Chalonnaise*
Meursault – *Burgundy, Côte d'Or*
Minervois – *Southern France*
Montagny – *Burgundy, Côte Chalonnaise*
Monthelie – *Burgundy, Côte d'Or*
Morey-St-Denis – *Burgundy, Côte d'Or*
Morgon – *Burgundy, Beaujolais*
Moulin-à-Vent – *Burgundy, Beaujolais*
Moulis – *Bordeaux*
Muscadet – *Loire (dry white)*
Muscat de Beaumes-de-Venise –
    Rhône (fortified white)
Nuits-St-Georges – *Burgundy, Côte d'Or*
Pauillac – *Bordeaux*
Pernand-Vergelesses – *Burgundy, Côte d'Or*
Pessac-Léognan – *Bordeaux*
Pomerol – *Bordeaux*
Pommard – *Burgundy, Côte d'Or*
Pouilly-Fuissé – *Burgundy, Mâconnais*
Pouilly-Fumé – *Loire (dry white)*
Provence – *Southern France*
Puligny-Montrachet – *Burgundy, Côte d'Or*
Régnié – *Burgundy, Beaujolais*
Rully – *Burgundy, Côte Chalonnaise*
St-Amour – *Burgundy, Beaujolais*
Ste-Croix-du-Mont – *Bordeaux*
St-Émilion – *Bordeaux*
St-Estèphe – *Bordeaux*
St-Joseph – *Rhône (red)*
St-Julien – *Bordeaux*
St-Véran – *Burgundy, Mâconnais*
Sancerre – *Loire*
Saumur-Champigny – *Loire (red)*
Sauternes – *Bordeaux (sweet white)*
Sauvignon de St-Bris – *Burgundy, Basic*
Savigny-lès-Beaune – *Burgundy, Côte d'Or*
Tavel – *Rhône (rosé)*
Vins de pays – *various; mainly Southern France*
Volnay – *Burgundy, Côte d'Or*
Vosne-Romanée – *Burgundy, Côte d'Or*
Vougeot – *Burgundy, Côte d'Or*
Vouvray – *Loire*

ALSACE

Alsace has been quietly making benchmark wines for many years; they may be dragged reluctantly into the spotlight as producers in other parts of the world discover their subtle, scented charms

I'm beginning to think there may even be hope for Alsace wines. Relatively speaking, of course. No-one in their right minds would describe them as exactly hopeless, and the growers are neither on the breadline nor despairing of ever selling the stuff. The locals, and the more discerning sorts of foreigner, lap up all the Alsace wines they can get.

But the style is not fashionable in the wider world. So what? you might say. If the wines are good, and the producers are happy, what does it matter whether there are queues at the supermarkets? And I agree, it doesn't. But I am interested to see that little by little, millimetre by millimetre, growers of Alsace grapes in other parts of the world are creeping towards a more Alsace style of wine. By 'Alsace grapes' I mean mostly Pinot Gris, Pinot Blanc and Gewurztraminer; and it's New World sources of these grapes I'm thinking of. Growers in Oregon and New Zealand, though they seldom inject the same excitement into their versions, are just beginning to work towards a bit more concentration and focus. Which is a long-overdue acceptance that Alsace is one of the great benchmark wine styles of the world. Not oaky, not obvious, but benchmark nevertheless. So let's hear it for complexity, elegance and scent.

GRAPE VARIETIES

In Alsace, wines are generally labelled according to their grape variety. Cheap blends of two or more varieties are sold as Edelzwicker; go instead for upmarket ones.

AUXERROIS Fatter and more buttery than Pinot Blanc, with a touch of spice and musk. Generally inexpensive, and often blended with Pinot Blanc. Best: *Kientzler, Marc Kreydenweiss, Josmeyer, Albert Mann, Rolly Gassmann.*

CHASSELAS Rare now in Alsace, Chasselas has never been very demanding; the few true examples can be fruity enough but must be drunk young. Best: *Kientzler, Josmeyer, Pfaffenheim co-op, Schoffit.*

CLASSIC BLENDS Using varieties like Riesling, Gewurztraminer and Pinot Gris in blends with Pinot Blanc, Sylvaner, even Muscat, these can be superb. Generally best in riper years. Best: *Hugel Gentil, Marc Kreydenweiss Clos du Val d'Eléon, Ribeauvillé* co-op *Clos du Zahnacker, 'S' de Schlumberger, Jean Sipp Cuvée Cristal, Louis Sipp Gentil.*

EDELZWICKER This is the region's everyday blend, usually based on Sylvaner, Pinot Blanc, Auxerrois; seldom exciting, but *Rolly Gassmann* makes an aromatic version.

GEWURZTRAMINER The least dry of all Alsace, though *Léon Beyer Cuvée des Comtes d'Eguisheim* and *Trimbach Cuvée des Seigneurs de Ribeaupierre* are bone dry. Gewurztraminer is the most voluptuous, upfront and fleshy of all Alsace wines, overflowing with exotic aromas. In hot years it can lack acidity but still intrigue you. Best: *Léon Beyer, Blanck, Ernest Burn, Marcel Deiss, Dopff au Moulin, Eguisheim* co-op, *Hugel, Marc Kreydenweiss, Kuentz-Bas, Albert Mann, Meyer-Fonné, Mittnacht-Klack, René Muré, Ostertag, Rolly Gassmann, Martin Schaetzel, Schlumberger, Schoffit, Louis Sipp, Marc Tempé, Trimbach, Turckheim* co-op, *Weinbach, Zind-Humbrecht.*

MUSCAT Light, fragrant, wonderfully grapy. Imagine crushing a fistful of green grapes and gulping the juice. That's how fresh and grapy a good Muscat should be. Best in cooler years. Seldom made sweet in Alsace. Look for *Becker, Albert Boxler, Ernest Burn, Théo Cattin, Dirler, Marc Kreydenweiss, Kuentz-Bas, Albert Mann, René Muré, Rolly Gassmann, Pfaffenheim co-op, Schoffit, Bruno Sorg, Weinbach, Zind-Humbrecht.*

PINOT BLANC At its best, this is plump, rich and ripe, with apple or floral overtones and a long creamy finish. May also be called Klevner. Best: *J B Adam, Blanck, Albert Boxler, Cléebourg co-op, Marcel Deiss, Dopff au Moulin, Hugel, Josmeyer, Charles Koehly, Marc Kreydenweiss, Albert Mann, Meyer-Fonné, René Muré, Ostertag, Rolly Gassmann, Schlumberger, Schoffit, Turckheim co-op, Weinbach, Zind-Humbrecht.*

PINOT NOIR The Burgundy grape makes light reds, perfumed and strawberryish, but lacking in complexity. Most are overpriced for the quality. Best include *J B Adam, Barmès-Buecher, Jean Becker, Marcel Deiss, Hugel, Albert Mann, Pfaffenheim co-op, Turckheim co-op, Wolfberger.*

RIESLING Powerful, structured, steely wines that grow 'petrolly' with age. It's with Riesling that the subtleties of Grand Cru soils are most evident. Can be long-lived. Best producers: *Becker, Léon Beyer, Blanck, Albert Boxler, Marcel Deiss, Dirler, Dopff au Moulin, Hugel, Kientzler, Marc Kreydenweiss, Kuentz-Bas, René Muré, Ostertag, Rolly Gassmann, Charles Schleret, Schlumberger, Schoffit, Sick-Dreyer, Jean Sipp, Louis Sipp, Bruno Sorg, Trimbach, Weinbach, Zind-Humbrecht.*

SYLVANER Light, tart, slightly earthy. With age it tastes of tomatoes, for some reason. Best: *Seppi Landmann, Ostertag* (especially *Vieilles Vignes), Martin Schaetzel, Schoffit, Weinbach, Zind-Humbrecht.*

TOKAY-PINOT GRIS Rich, musky and honeyed, though it can run to flab if badly made. Even the lighter ones are luscious behind their dry fruit. The best can age well. Best: *J-B Adam, Lucien Albrecht, Barmès-Buecher, Léon Beyer, Blanck, Bott-Geyl, Ernest Burn, Dopff & Irion, Kientzler, Charles Koehly, Marc Kreydenweiss, Kuentz-Bas, Albert Mann, Ostertag, Schlumberger, Schoffit, Bruno Sorg, Turckheim co-op, Weinbach, Zind-Humbrecht.*

WINE CLASSIFICATIONS

ALSACE, AC The generic term 'Vin d'Alsace' is usually seen on the label in conjunction with Appellation Alsace Contrôlée. The appellation covers the whole Alsace region and is normally used with a grape name.

CRÉMANT D'ALSACE, AC White, Champagne-method fizz, made mainly from Pinot Blanc. Usually crisp and decent quality. Look for wines from *Blanck, Dopff & Irion, Dopff au Moulin, René Muré, Ostertag, Pfaffenheim co-op, P Sparr, Turckheim co-op.*

ALSACE GRAND CRU, AC A decree of 1992 brought the number of Grand Cru vineyards to 50; in theory these are the best sites within the Alsace AC. They can only be planted with Riesling, Tokay-Pinot Gris, Gewurztraminer or Muscat, and notably lower (but still high) yields apply. Grand Cru wines should reflect the great variety of soils to be found in Alsace – limestone, schist, granite, clay, sandstone – offering a superb palate of flavours and nuances. The best do – but only when yields are kept reasonable.

HIER

ON

Europe's most exclusive reds and whites

Quality you didn't know existed

Swiss Wine UK Tel: 020 7851 1731, Fax: 020 7851 1730, Web: www.swisswine.ch
Email UK: swisswine@stlondon.com, Email Switzerland: info@swisswine.ch

We trample the grapes not the growers

PRODUCE OF CHILE

Chilean
CARMENÈRE
Valle de Curicó

2000

FAIR TRADE

Bottled by Cooperativa Agricola
Vitivinicola de Curicó Ltda.
Imported for CWS Ltd.,
M60 4ES, UK

This fairly traded wine, made possible by Fairtrade, has
been produced using Carmenère grapes grown by a
co-operative in Chile and a through a partnership with a
A truly co-operative relationship

Fair Trade

There for **you**

Fairtrade

Guarantees
a better deal
for Third World
Producers

your

wine finder

With over 20,000 different wines already online we'll find the one you want.

www.everywine.co.uk

Your wish...is our command.

Click on **www.everywine.co.uk** or **Freephone 0800 072 0011** We'll help you find the wine you're looking for...even if we don't list it!

decanter.com
the route to all good wine

fine wine tracker®

news & views

wine finder

learning route

good living

from the publishers of Decanter magazine

VENDANGE TARDIVE The lesser of two 'super-ripe' categories, made from late-picked grapes, as opposed to the botrytized ones used for *sélection de grains nobles*. Only applies to Riesling, Tokay-Pinot Gris, Muscat (rare) and Gewurztraminer. They are very full, fairly alcoholic and vary in sweetness from richly dry to dessert-sweet. They can be aged, particularly if from Grand Cru vineyards. Up to ten years is a good rule of thumb.

SÉLECTION DE GRAINS NOBLES (SGN) The higher of the two 'super-ripe' categories, applying to very sweet wines made from botrytized grapes. It applies only to Riesling, Tokay-Pinot Gris, Muscat (very rare) and Gewurztraminer; the wines are not dissimilar to Sauternes in style, though the flavour is different. Acidity levels can be lower, especially from Pinot Gris or from Gewurztraminer. All benefit from aging for ten years or more. For some of Alsace's top tastes, try producers such as *Beyer, Blanck, Bott-Geyl, Hugel, Kuentz-Bas, Meyer, René Muré, Ostertag, Schlumberger, Schoffit, Trimbach, Weinbach, Zind-Humbrecht.*

> **ON THE CASE**
> *If you want a serious wine from Alsace, go for a Grand Cru. More basic wines won't have the same depth*

ALSACE VINTAGES

2000 A good, but not outstanding year. Most should be ripe and well-structured.

1999 There'll be a lot of dilute wines this year. Choose top names only.

1998 A very good year for sweet wines – but don't open them for a while.

1997 Potentially great: beautifully ripe wines of good body and weight.

1996 A mostly good, ripe vintage with nice acidity levels. Small quantities of *vendange tardive* and even *sélection de grains nobles* were made.

1995 Similar to 1994, but possibly with lower acidity. Stick to good names.

1994 Mixed: some wines are too light; but conversely other producers made phenomenally rich late-harvest wines.

1993 Good to average, but there is excellent Riesling.

1992 The wines are sound, and range from dilute to excellent. Choose wines from good producers, who have a reputation to maintain.

1991 Fresh, clean wines, but it is not a late-harvest year. Not one to keep, either.

1990 With healthy grapes and no noble rot, 1990 was a *vendange tardive* year. Rieslings are powerful and will age well.

1989 Very good but not top quality. The wines have lively fruit, though some are low in acidity. Abundant and superb late-harvest wines.

1988 Pleasant, but hardly inspiring wine. Tokay-Pinot Gris and Riesling are best.

1987 Not great, but better than first thought. Good single-vineyard wines.

1986 The best are at their peak. Good *vendange tardive* and even some SGN.

ALSACE PRICES

Under £5.00

Pinot Blanc Blanck Frères 1998 £4.95 (WAI)
Pinot Blanc Preiss-Zimmer 1999 £4.39 (MORR)
Pinot Blanc Tradition, Cave Vinicole de Turckheim 1999 £4.50 (WS)
Pinot Blanc Cave Vinicole de Turckheim 2000 £4.49 (BO) £6.20 (NI)
Sylvaner Hugel 1999 £4.95 (WS)

£5.00 → £5.99

Chevalier d'Alsace, Hügel et Fils 1995 £5.95 (JU)
Gentil Hugel 1999 £5.99 (DI)
Gewürztraminer Preiss-Zimmer 1999 £5.49 (MORR)
Gewürztraminer Cave Vinicole de Turckheim 1999 £5.95 (WS) £5.95 (SO) £6.49 (UN) £6.99 (AME)
Pinot Blanc Cuvée Reservée, Schaetzel 1999 £5.99 (GW)
Pinot Blanc Horstein, Cave Vinicole de Pfaffenheim 1999 £5.35 (HAH) £5.59 (JON)
Pinot Blanc Réserve, Seltz 1998 £5.39 (WAT)
Pinot Blanc Cave du Roi Dagobert 1998 £5.75 (FRI)
Pinot Blanc Cave Vinicole de Turckheim 1998 £5.29 (OD)
Riesling Horstein, Cave Vinicole de Pfaffenheim 1998 £5.99 (POR)
Riesling Cave Vinicole de Turckheim 1998 £5.99 (UN)
Tokay-Pinot Gris Cave de Beblenheim 1998 £5.75 (WAI)
Tokay-Pinot Gris Tradition, Vinicole de Turckheim 1999 £5.50 (WS)
Tokay-Pinot Gris Cave Vinicole de Turckheim 1999 £5.99 (UN) £6.29 (OD)

£6.00 → £6.99

Fleur d'Alsace, Hugel 1999 £6.45 (STA) £6.99 (PLA)
Fruits de Mer, Wiederhirn 1998 £6.00 (HIG)
Gewürztraminer Hornstein, Cave Vinicole de Pfaffenheim 1999 £6.40 (HAH) £6.59 (JON)
Muscat Réserve, Cave Vinicole de Turckheim 1999 £6.29 (OD)
Pinot Blanc Auxerrois Vieilles Vignes, Albert Mann 1999 £6.99 (OD)
Pinot Blanc Cattin 1999 £6.99 (CB)
Pinot Blanc Hugel 1998 £6.99 (DI) £7.25 (CON)
Pinot Blanc Muré 1998 £6.95 (NEZ)
Pinot Blanc A Willm 2000 £6.30 (BU)
Pinot d'Alsace Blanck 1999 £6.50 (BALL)
Sylvaner Deiss 1994 £6.99 (BAL)
Sylvaner Rolly Gassmann 1997 £6.64 (BIB)
Tokay-Pinot Gris Hornstein, Cave Vinicole de Pfaffenheim 1999 £6.79 (POR) £6.95 (TAN)

£7.00 → £7.99

Gewürztraminer Sipp 1998 £7.58 (WHI)
Gewürztraminer Wiederhirn 1997 £7.20 (HIG)
Pinot Blanc Hugel 1999 £7.50 (STA)
Pinot Blanc Rolly Gassmann 1996 £7.95 (RAE)
Pinot Blanc Schlumberger 1999 £7.83 (LLO) £7.95 (FORT) £7.99 (POR) £7.99 (JON) £8.17 (PLA)
Pinot Blanc Schlumberger 1998 £7.95 (WRI)
Pinot Blanc Tradition, Kuentz-Bas 1999 £7.13 (COC)
Pinot Blanc Vieilles Vignes, Meyer-Fonné 1999 £7.75 (LAY)
Riesling Cuvée Reservée, Schaetzel 1999 £7.48 (GW)

RETAILERS SPECIALIZING IN ALSACE

see Retailers Directory (page 40) for details

Adnams (AD), Ballantynes (BAL), Bennetts (BEN), Berry Bros (BER), Butlers (BU), A Byrne (BY), D Byrne, Croque-en-Bouche (CRO), Direct Wine (DI), Cockburns (COC),

First Quench (BOT, THR, VIC, WR), Lay & Wheeler (LAY), Mayfair (MAY), Morris & Verdin (MV), Oddbins (OD), Reid, T&W (TW), Wine Society (WS), Noel Young (YOU).

Riesling Kuentz-Bas 1999 £7.62 (COC)
Riesling Albert Mann 1998 £7.50 (MAY)
Riesling A Willm 1996 £7.50 (BU)
Sylvaner Schleret 1998 £7.25 (YAP)
Sylvaner Vieilles Vignes, Domaine
  Ostertag 1999 £7.75 (WRI) £8.00 (MV)
Tokay-Pinot Gris Hornstein, Cave Vinicole
  de Pfaffenheim 1998 £7.39 (JON)
Tokay-Pinot Gris Tradition, Kuentz-Bas
  1998 £7.99 (UN)
Tokay-Pinot Gris Wiederhirn 1997 £7.20
  (HIG)

£8.00 → £8.99

Chasselas Cuvée Caroline, Schoffit 1998
  £8.50 (GAU)
Edelzwicker Rolly Gassmann 1999 £8.23
  (BIB)
Gewürztraminer Beyer 1999 £8.95 (WS)
Gewürztraminer Blanck 1999 £8.50
  (BALL) £8.95 (AD)
Gewürztraminer Cuvée Reservée,
  Schaetzel 1999 £8.70 (GW)
Gewürztraminer Dopff au Moulin 1997
  £8.90 (CRO)
Gewürztraminer Hugel 1999 £8.95 (STA)
  £9.99 (DI)
Gewürztraminer Albert Mann 1998 £8.95
  (MAY) £9.25 (WRI)
Gewürztraminer Cave du Roi Dagobert
  1998 £8.50 (FRI)
Gewürztraminer A. Willm 1999 £8.95 (BU)
Muscat Koehly 1998 £8.70 (HAH)
Muscat Albert Mann 1999 £8.49 (OD)
Muscat Réserve, Trimbach 1998 £8.50
  (WS) £10.28 (PLA)
Muscat Tradition, Hugel 1998 £8.95 (STA)
  £8.99 (DI)
Pinot Blanc Blanck Frères 1999 £8.00
  (FLE)
Pinot Blanc Rolly Gassmann 1997 £8.18
  (BIB)
Pinot Blanc Schleret 1998 £8.35 (YAP)
Riesling Hugel 1999 £8.95 (STA)
Riesling Hugel 1998 £8.99 (OD) £8.99 (DI)
Riesling Hugel 1997 £8.65 (CON)
Riesling les Princes Abbés, Schlumberger
  1997 £8.93 (LLO)
Riesling Schleret 1998 £8.95 (YAP)
Riesling Trimbach 1997 £8.95 (WS) £8.99
  (COC) £9.60 (GN)
Sylvaner Reserve Fut 1, Domaine
  Weinbach 1996 £8.95 (JU)
Tokay-Pinot Gris Réserve Personnelle,
  Seltz 1997 £8.09 (WAT)

£9.00 → £10.49

Auxerrois Seefel, Rolly Gassmann 1993
  £9.30 (RAE)
Chasselas Vieilles Vignes, Schoffit 1999
  £9.24 (FLE)
Gewürztraminer Bollenberg, Cattin 1998
  £9.99 (CB) £12.99 (VIL)
Gewürztraminer Cuvée des Evêques,
  Hügel et Fils 1999 £9.90 (JU)
Gewürztraminer Hugel 1998 £9.49 (OD)
  £9.50 (CON)
Gewürztraminer Hugel 1996 £9.19 (SUN)
  £9.19 (LAI)
Gewürztraminer Kuentz-Bas 1998 £9.45
  (COC)
Gewürztraminer Réserve Personnelle,
  Wiederhirn 1998 £9.50 (HIG)
Gewürztraminer Schléret 1998 £10.25
  (YAP)
Gewürztraminer Trimbach 1998 £9.95
  (WS) £10.59 (COC) £12.37 (PLAY)
Gewürztraminer Zind-Humbrecht 1999
  £9.99 (WR) £10.72 (BY)
Gewürztraminer Zotzenberg, Seltz 1997
  £9.09 (WAT)
Muscat Deiss 1991 £9.49 (BAL)
Muscat Schleret 1996 £9.75 (YAP)
Pinot Blanc Burn 1997 £9.50 (BEN)
Pinot Blanc Réserve, Domaine Weinbach
  1996 £9.95 (JU)
Pinot d'Alsace Zind-Humbrecht 1998
  £9.99 (WAI)
Riesling Bennwihr, Deiss 1997 £9.95 (LEA)
Riesling Bennwihr, Deiss 1996 £9.49 (BAL)
Riesling Frédéric Émile, Trimbach 1998
  £9.00 (FLE) £9.95 (BER)
Riesling Meyer-Fonné 1997 £9.50 (FORT)
Riesling Patergarten, Blanck 1999 £9.95
  (BALL)
Riesling Rolly Gassmann 1998 £9.49 (BIB)
Riesling Wintzenheim, Zind-Humbrecht
  1996 £9.49 (BY) £24.95 (NI)
Sylvaner Réserve, Domaine Weinbach
  1995 £9.45 (JU)
Sylvaner Zind-Humbrecht 1999 £9.69
  (BY)

Please remember that
Oz Clarke's Wine Buying Guide
*is a price guide and not a price list. It is
not meant to replace up-to-date
merchants' lists.*

Tokay-Pinot Gris Barriques, Domaine Ostertag **1995** £10.35 (SOM)

Tokay-Pinot Gris Patergarten, Blanck **1999** £9.75 (BALL)

Tokay-Pinot Gris Réserve Personnelle, Wiederhirn **1998** £9.50 (HIG)

Tokay-Pinot Gris Tradition, Kuentz-Bas **1999** £9.05 (COC)

£10.50 → £12.99

Auxerrois 'H' Vieilles Vignes, Josmeyer **1997** £11.90 (GAU)

Auxerrois Rolly Gassmann **1993** £10.50 (GAU)

Gewürztraminer Clos Gaensbroennel, A Willm **1998** £12.95 (AS)

Gewürztraminer Cuvée Caroline Harth, Schoffit **1998** £11.50 (AD)

Gewürztraminer Kessler, Schlumberger 50cl **1997** £12.50 (TAN)

Gewürztraminer les Princes Abbés, Schlumberger **1999** £10.79 (JON) £10.82 (LLO)

Gewürztraminer les Princes Abbés, Schlumberger **1998** £11.20 (TAN) £12.70 (JER)

Gewürztraminer les Princes Abbés, Schlumberger **1997** £10.95 (FORT)

Gewürztraminer Rolly Gassmann **1995** £12.43 (BIB)

Gewürztraminer St-Hippolyte, Deiss **1995** £11.50 (BAL)

Gewürztraminer Steingrubler, Albert Mann **1999** £12.95 (LAY)

Gewürztraminer Tradition, Hugel **1997** £10.95 (WS) £10.99 (OD) £11.95 (STA)

Muscat Deiss **1999** £10.95 (LEA)

Muscat Herrenweg de Turckheim, Zind-Humbrecht **1999** £12.56 (BY)

Muscat Tradition, Hugel **1997** £12.95 (FORT)

Muscat Zind-Humbrecht **1990** £11.74 (BY)

Pinot Blanc Réserve, Domaine Weinbach **1995** £11.50 (JU)

Pinot Blanc Domaine Weinbach **1999** £11.40 (TAN)

Pinot Blanc Zind-Humbrecht **1998** £11.13 (BY)

Pinot Blanc Zind-Humbrecht **1995** £10.61 (FLE)

Riesling Altenberg de Bergheim, Koehly **1996** £11.55 (HAH)

Riesling Clos St-Imer, Burn **1997** £11.50 (BEN)

Riesling Cuvée Caroline Harth, Schoffit **1999** £11.75 (AD)

Riesling Ecaillers, Beyer **1996** £12.95 (WS)

Riesling les Pierrets, Josmeyer **1995** £12.85 (GAU)

Riesling Réserve, Trimbach **1997** £12.50 (MI)

Riesling Schlossberg, Albert Mann **1998** £11.75 (LAY)

Riesling Schoenenbourg, Wiederhirn **1997** £11.00 (HIG)

Riesling Tradition, Hugel **1996** £10.99 (OD) £15.00 (FORT)

Riesling Turckheim, Zind-Humbrecht **1998** £12.56 (BY)

Riesling Wineck-Schlossberg, Meyer-Fonné **1997** £11.95 (LAY)

Riesling Wintzenheim, Zind-Humbrecht **1998** £12.90 (CRO)

Tokay-Pinot Gris Beblenheim, Deiss **1995** £11.95 (BAL)

Tokay-Pinot Gris Cuvée Caroline, Schoffit **1998** £10.95 (BER) £11.90 (FLE)

Tokay-Pinot Gris Cuvée Caroline, Schoffit **1997** £10.50 (GAU)

Tokay-Pinot Gris Furstentum, Albert Mann **1999** £12.90 (LAY)

Tokay-Pinot Gris Grand Cru Brand, Cave Vinicole de Turckheim **1997** £10.69 (AME)

Tokay-Pinot Gris Hatschbourg, Cattin **1997** £11.41 (CB)

Tokay-Pinot Gris Hinterberg de Katzenthal, Meyer-Fonné **1999** £11.35 (LAY)

Tokay-Pinot Gris les Princes Abbés, Schlumberger **1997** £10.99 (POR)

Tokay-Pinot Gris Réserve, Trimbach **1998** £11.00 (WS)

Tokay-Pinot Gris Rolly Gassmann **1997** £10.67 (BIB)

Tokay-Pinot Gris Schleret **1998** £11.95 (YAP)

Tokay-Pinot Gris Tradition, Hugel **1998** £11.75 (STA)

£13.00 → £14.99

Gewürztraminer Herrenweg, Zind-Humbrecht **1998** £14.62 (BY) £16.99 (VIL)

Gewürztraminer Jubilee, Hugel **1988** £13.95 (CON)

Gewürztraminer Kappelweg, Rolly Gassmann **1993** £14.99 (RAE)

Gewürztraminer Kessler, Schlumberger **1997** £14.99 (POR)

Gewürztraminer Réserve, Trimbach **1990** £13.95 (WS)

Gewürztraminer St-Hippolyte, Deiss **1999** £13.95 (LEA)

Muscat Herrenweg de Turckheim, Zind-Humbrecht **1996** £14.00 (CRO)

Muscat Moenchreben, Rolly Gassmann **1994** £13.50 (RAE)

Muscat Réserve No 6, Domaine Weinbach **1996** £14.50 (JU)

Pinot Blanc Zind-Humbrecht **1997** £13.50 (CRO)

Pinot d'Alsace Zind-Humbrecht **1997** £14.20 (NI)

Riesling Brand, Zind-Humbrecht **1998** £14.25 (BY)

Riesling Clos Haüserer, Zind-Humbrecht **1997** £14.49 (BOT) £14.49 (WR) £16.06 (FA)

Riesling Heissenberg **1997** £13.00 (MV)

Riesling Herrenweg, Zind-Humbrecht **1998** £13.99 (BY) £16.99 (VIL)

Riesling Kappelweg, Rolly Gassmann **1993** £14.50 (JU)

Riesling Kitterlé, Schlumberger **1997** £14.99 (POR)

Riesling Réserve, Trimbach **1995** £13.00 (GAU)

Riesling Rosenberg Vendange Tardive, Albert Mann ½ litre **1995** £14.95 (LAY)

Riesling Schlossberg, Blanck **1998** £14.95 (BALL)

Riesling Schlossberg, Blanck **1996** £14.95 (AD)

Riesling Schlossberg, Albert Mann **1997** £13.79 (YOU)

Riesling Schoenenbourg, Dopff au Moulin **1997** £13.41 (COC)

Riesling Turckheim, Zind-Humbrecht **1999** £13.79 (BY) £16.20 (FLE)

Riesling Turckheim, Zind-Humbrecht **1996** £13.99 (VIL)

Riesling Wintzenheim, Zind-Humbrecht **1997** £13.12 (FA) £15.90 (CRO)

Tokay-Pinot Gris Beblenheim, Deiss **1999** £14.95 (LEA)

Tokay-Pinot Gris Furstentum, Albert Mann **1997** £13.99 (YOU)

Tokay-Pinot Gris Réserve Millésime, Rolly Gassman **1994** £14.95 (RAE) £18.90 (JU)

Tokay-Pinot Gris Tradition, Hugel **1996** £14.68 (TW)

£15.00 → £19.99

Gewürztraminer Cuvée Laurence, Domaine Weinbach **1995** £19.50 (JU)

Gewürztraminer Cuvée Théo, Domaine Weinbach **1995** £16.50 (JU)

Gewürztraminer Herrenweg, Zind-Humbrecht **1999** £16.05 (BY) £21.67 (MI)

Gewürztraminer Herrenweg, Zind-Humbrecht **1997** £19.21 (NI)

Gewürztraminer Jubilee, Hugel **1997** £15.50 (DI)

Gewürztraminer Jubilee, Hugel **1996** £15.15 (PLA)

Gewürztraminer Réserve, Trimbach **1994** £15.00 (MI)

Gewürztraminer Seigneurs de Ribeaupierre, Trimbach **1988** £17.50 (MI)

Gewürztraminer Seigneurs de Ribeaupierre, Trimbach **1986** £17.99 (YOU)

Gewürztraminer Wineck-Schlossberg, Meyer-Fonné **1999** £15.95 (LAY)

Muscat Goldert, Zind-Humbrecht **1998** £18.99 (VIL)

Muscat Goldert, Zind-Humbrecht **1996** £16.00 (CRO)

Muscat, Domaine Weinbach **1995** £17.95 (JU)

Pinot Blanc Zind-Humbrecht **1996** £15.50 (CRO)

Riesling Clos Haüserer, Zind-Humbrecht **1996** £17.85 (GAU)

Riesling Clos Haüserer, Zind-Humbrecht **1992** £19.00 (CRO)

Riesling Clos St-Imer Cuvée Chapelle, Burn **1998** £16.15 (GAU) £17.95 (BEN)

Riesling Clos St-Imer Cuvée Chapelle, Burn **1997** £16.95 (BAL) £17.95 (BEN)

★ Riesling Clos St-Landelin, Muré **1998** £16.99 (NEZ) £19.30 (GAU)

Riesling Cuvée Théo, Domaine Weinbach **1996** £16.00 (JU)

Riesling Frédéric Émile, Trimbach **1995** £19.17 (MI) £19.99 (SUN) £19.99 (LAI) £20.35 (GAU) £24.44 (TW)

Riesling Frédéric Émile, Trimbach **1993**
£19.95 (BAL) £19.96 (PLA) £21.03
(PLAY)

Riesling Herrenweg, Zind-Humbrecht
1999 £15.23 (BY)

Riesling Herrenweg, Zind-Humbrecht
1996 £18.80 (CRO) £21.67 (MI)

Riesling Jubilee, Hugel **1997** £15.95 (CON)

Riesling Jubilee, Hugel **1995** £16.90 (WS)

Riesling Jubilee, Hugel **1993** £18.95 (DI)

Riesling Jubilee Réserve Personnelle,
Hugel **1996** £17.50 (STA)

Riesling Kitterlé, Schlumberger **1995**
£17.45 (BER)

Riesling Muenchberg, Domaine Ostertag
1999 £18.75 (NI)

Riesling Muenchberg, Domaine Ostertag
1998 £17.50 (MV)

Riesling Muenchberg, Domaine Ostertag
1997 £17.50 (MV)

Riesling Muenchberg, Domaine Ostertag
1996 £17.99 (YOU) £18.50 (BEN)

Riesling Saering, Schlumberger **1986**
£15.08 (FA)

Riesling Saering, Schlumberger **1983**
£16.06 (FA)

Riesling Schlossberg II, Domaine
Weinbach **1996** £19.00 (JU)

Riesling Turckheim, Zind-Humbrecht
1997 £15.55 (NI) £16.06 (FA)

Tokay-Pinot Gris Bergheim, Deiss **1995**
£17.20 (GAU)

Tokay-Pinot Gris Clos St-Imer Cuvée
Chapelle, Burn **1999** £17.95 (BEN)

Tokay-Pinot Gris Clos St-Imer Cuvée
Chapelle, Burn **1997** £16.95 (BAL)

Tokay-Pinot Gris Heimbourg, Zind-
Humbrecht **1997** £18.60 (BY) £19.00
(FA) £25.83 (MI)

Tokay-Pinot Gris Jubilee, Hugel **1996**
£17.33 (PLA)

Tokay-Pinot Gris Réserve Personnelle,
Trimbach **1996** £15.57 (FA) £18.33 (MI)
£19.70 (GAU)

Tokay-Pinot Gris Réserve, Rolly
Gassmann **1989** £18.99 (RAE)

Tokay-Pinot Gris Vendange Tardive,
Deiss **1994** £18.95 (BAL)

Tokay-Pinot Gris Zind-Humbrecht **1996**
£17.00 (CRO)

---

*A key to name abbreviations
is available on page 7.*

£20.00 → £24.99

Gewürztraminer Altenbourg Cuvée
Laurence, Domaine Weinbach **1995**
£22.00 (JU)

Gewürztraminer Clos Windsbuhl, Zind-
Humbrecht **1998** £23.83 (BY)

Gewürztraminer Cuvée Laurence,
Domaine Weinbach **1996** £21.00 (JU)

Gewürztraminer Fronholz Vendange
Tardive, Domaine Ostertag **1998**
£22.90 (NI)

Gewürztraminer Goldert, Zind-
Humbrecht **1997** £23.42 (BY)

Gewürztraminer Kitterlé, Schlumberger
1997 £21.00 (WS) £22.95 (BER)

Gewürztraminer Seigneurs de
Ribeaupierre, Trimbach **1996** £20.99
(YOU)

Gewürztraminer Vendange Tardive,
Wiederhirn **1990** £22.50 (HIG)

★ Pinot Gris Clos Windsbuhl, Zind-
Humbrecht **1997** £22.60 (BY)

Riesling Brand, Zind-Humbrecht **1996**
£22.60 (BY) £26.99 (VIL)

Riesling Clos Haüserer, Zind-Humbrecht
1994 £23.00 (CRO)

Riesling Clos St-Théobald Rangen de
Thann, Schoffit **1997** £24.50 (GAU)

Riesling Cuvée Ste-Catherine II, Domaine
Weinbach **1997** £20.99 (YOU)

Riesling Cuvée Ste-Catherine, Domaine
Weinbach **1995** £22.50 (JU)

Riesling Frédéric Émile, Trimbach **1997**
£21.99 (YOU) £23.29 (JON)

Riesling Frédéric Émile, Trimbach **1996**
£22.00 (WS)

Riesling Furstentum, Blanck **1998** £20.30
(JER)

Riesling Réserve, Trimbach **1989** £20.86
(TW)

Riesling Schoenenbourg Vendange
Tardive, Dopff au Moulin **1981** £22.00
(CRO)

Tokay-Pinot Gris Cuvée Ste-Cathérine,
Domaine Weinbach **1996** £21.49 (YOU)

Tokay-Pinot Gris Heimbourg, Zind-
Humbrecht **1996** £20.95 (FA) £21.53
(BY) £25.83 (MI) £27.50 (FORT)

Tokay-Pinot Gris Réserve Personnelle,
Hugel **1983** £23.49 (YOU)

Tokay-Pinot Gris Réserve, Rolly
Gassmann **1983** £22.95 (RAE)

Tokay-Pinot Gris Vendange Tardive,
Deiss **1989** £24.50 (BAL)

£25.00 → £29.99

Gewürztraminer Altenbourg Cuvée Laurence, Domaine Weinbach 1997 £28.49 (YOU)

Gewürztraminer Altenbourg Cuvée Laurence, Domaine Weinbach 1996 £26.00 (JU)

Gewürztraminer Clos Windsbuhl, Zind-Humbrecht 1999 £25.46 (BY)

Gewürztraminer Clos Windsbuhl, Zind-Humbrecht 1996 £25.85 (FA) £28.99 (VIL)

Gewürztraminer Cuvée Christine, Schlumberger 1989 £29.88 (NO)

Gewürztraminer Furstentum Cuvée Laurence, Domaine Weinbach 1995 £29.00 (JU)

Gewürztraminer Hengst, Zind-Humbrecht 1999 £25.46 (BY)

Gewürztraminer Hengst, Zind-Humbrecht 1998 £25.05 (BY)

Gewürztraminer Hengst, Zind-Humbrecht 1997 £28.00 (CRO) £29.17 (MI)

Gewürztraminer Herrenweg Vendange Tardive, Zind-Humbrecht 1997 £29.38 (FA)

Gewürztraminer Seigneurs de Ribeaupierre, Trimbach 1983 £25.00 (MI) £35.00 (CRO)

Riesling Brand, Zind-Humbrecht 1991 £29.00 (CRO)

Riesling Clos St-Urbain, Zind-Humbrecht 1995 £28.39 (FA)

Riesling Frédéric Émile, Trimbach 1989 £25.00 (CRO)

Riesling Frédéric Émile, Trimbach 1986 £27.00 (CRO)

Riesling Réserve Personnelle, Hugel 1983 £29.00 (CRO)

Riesling Schlossberg Cuvée Ste-Catherine, Domaine Weinbach 1998 £28.50 (TAN)

Riesling Schlossberg Cuvée Ste-Catherine, Domaine Weinbach 1995 £28.00 (JU)

Riesling Schoenenbourg Vendange Tardive, Dopff au Moulin 1983 £29.00 (CRO)

Riesling Vendange Tardive, Hugel 1995 £29.00 (WS)

Tokay-Pinot Gris Clos St-Imer Vendange Tardive, Burn 1995 £29.95 (BEN)

Tokay-Pinot Gris Cuvée Ste-Catherine II, Domaine Weinbach 1996 £25.00 (JU)

Tokay-Pinot Gris Cuvée Ste-Catherine III, Domaine Weinbach 1995 £29.00 (JU)

£30.00 → £39.99

Gewürztraminer Altenbourg Cuvée Laurence, Domaine Weinbach 1998 £33.90 (TAN)

Gewürztraminer Clos Windsbuhl, Zind-Humbrecht 1991 £34.00 (CRO)

Gewürztraminer Cuvée Christine, Schlumberger 1991 £36.35 (TAN)

Gewürztraminer Furstentum Cuvée Laurence, Domaine Weinbach 1996 £30.00 (JU)

Gewürztraminer Herrenweg Vendange Tardive, Zind-Humbrecht 1995 £30.75 (FA) £32.00 (CRO)

Gewürztraminer Vendange Tardive, Hugel 1994 £34.17 (MI)

Gewürztraminer Vendange Tardive, Hugel 1989 £32.50 (DI) £40.13 (TW)

Gewürztraminer Vendange Tardive, Trimbach 1996 £33.33 (MI)

Riesling Altenberg Sélection des Grains Nobles, Deiss 1989 £37.50 (GAU)

Riesling Brand, Zind-Humbrecht 1997 £33.30 (NI)

Riesling Brand, Zind-Humbrecht 1990 £39.00 (CRO)

Riesling Clos St-Urbain, Zind-Humbrecht 1997 £37.50 (MI)

Riesling Clos Ste-Hune, Trimbach 1986 £33.00 (BAL) £38.00 (CRO) £61.69 (TW)

Riesling Frédéric Émile, Trimbach 1985 £38.00 (CRO)

Riesling Frédéric Émile, Trimbach 1983 £36.45 (GAU) £41.13 (FA)

Riesling Frédéric Émile, Trimbach 1981 £35.13 (TW)

Riesling Frédéric Émile Vendange Tardive, Trimbach 1990 £36.99 (YOU) £37.50 (MI) £37.60 (FA) £39.95 (RES)

Riesling Frédéric Émile Vendange Tardive, Trimbach 1983 £39.17 (MI) £52.29 (TW)

Riesling Herrenweg, Zind-Humbrecht 1989 £38.00 (CRO)

Riesling Vendange Tardive, Dopff & Irion 1976 £33.00 (CRO)

Riesling Vendange Tardive, Hugel 1989 £34.17 (MI)

Riesling Vendange Tardive, Hugel 1983 £39.95 (DI)

Riesling Vendange Tardive, Wiederhirn 1983 £31.00 (CRO)

Tokay-Pinot Gris Clos St-Landelin Sélection de Grains Nobles, Muré 1996 £36.99 (NEZ)

Tokay-Pinot Gris Clos St-Urbain, Zind-
Humbrecht **1997** £39.17 (MI)
Tokay-Pinot Gris Vendange Tardive,
Hugel **1990** £34.17 (MI)
Tokay-Pinot Gris Zind-Humbrecht **1990**
£37.00 (CRO)

£40.00 → £49.99

Gewürztraminer Cuvée Anne,
Schlumberger **1989** £40.05 (TUR)
£42.00 (BAL) £55.06 (NO) £57.80 (BEN)
Gewürztraminer Cuvée Christine,
Schlumberger **1990** £47.00 (CRO)
Gewürztraminer Cuvée Christine,
Schlumberger **1983** £47.00 (TUR)
Gewürztraminer Herrenweg, Zind-
Humbrecht **1990** £40.00 (CRO)
Gewürztraminer Vendange Tardive,
Trimbach **1989** £46.51 (PLAY)
Riesling Clos Ste-Hune, Trimbach **1993**
£49.35 (TW)
Riesling Frédéric Émile, Trimbach **1979**
£43.18 (TW)
Tokay-Pinot Gris Vendange Tardive,
Faller **1983** £46.00 (CRO)

£50.00 → £59.99

Gewürztraminer Cuvée Christine,
Schlumberger **1985** £56.00 (CRO)
Gewürztraminer Seigneurs de
Ribeaupierre, Trimbach **1976** £54.00
(CRO)
Gewürztraminer Sélection de Grains
Nobles, Hugel **1989** £59.17 (MI)
Gewürztraminer Sélection de Grains
Nobles, Hugel **1986** £57.00 (WS)
Gewürztraminer Sélection de Grains
Nobles, Fuchs **1989** £55.06 (NO)
Riesling Clos Ste-Hune, Trimbach **1996**
£50.00 (FORT)
Riesling Réserve Personnelle, Hugel **1976**
£54.00 (CRO)
Riesling Vendange Tardive, Hugel **1976**
£59.00 (CRO) £92.83 (TW)
Riesling Vendange Tardive, Domaine
Weinbach **1990** £54.00 (JU)
Tokay-Pinot Gris Clos St-Imer Sélection
de Grains Nobles, Burn **1994** £59.50
(BEN)
Tokay-Pinot Gris Cuvée Clarisse,
Schlumberger **1989** £52.29 (FA) £58.00
(CRO)
Tokay-Pinot Gris Furstentum Sélection de
Grains Nobles, Albert Mann ½ bottle
1994 £51.55 (LAY)

£60.00 → £74.99

Gewürztraminer Clos St-Imer Sélection
de Grains Nobles, Burn **1994** £66.00
(BEN)
Gewürztraminer Furstentum Sélection
des Grains Nobles, Domaine Weinbach
1994 £62.00 (JU)
Gewürztraminer Sélection de Grains
Nobles, Hugel **1983** £69.91 (FA)
Riesling Frédéric Émile, Trimbach **1976**
£65.00 (CRO)
Riesling Frédéric Émile Vendange Tardive,
Trimbach **1989** £61.69 (TW)

£75.00 → £99.99

Gewürztraminer Cuvée Anne,
Schlumberger **1976** £99.29 (FA)
£120.00 (CRO)
Gewürztraminer Cuvée Christine,
Schlumberger **1976** £92.00 (CRO)
Gewürztraminer Sélection de Grains
Nobles, Hugel **1976** £80.00 (CRO)
£92.82 (TW) £94.00 (TUR)
Tokay-Pinot Gris Sélection de Grains
Nobles, Hugel **1976** £92.00 (CRO)

Over £100.00

Gewürztraminer Cuvée d'Or
Quintessence Sélection des Grains
Nobles, Domaine Weinbach **1994**
£138.00 (JU)
Riesling Frédéric Émile, Trimbach **1992**
£224.09 (TW)
Riesling Sélection de Grains Nobles,
Hugel **1976** £105.75 (TUR)

RED

Under £10.00

Pinot Noir Hugel **1997** £8.95 (STA)
Pinot Noir Hugel **1993** £9.95 (DI)

£10.00 → £20.00

Pinot Noir Réserve, Rolly Gassmann
1990 £19.99 (RAE)
Pinot Noir Schleret **1998** £10.65 (YAP)

SPARKLING

c. £9.50

Crémant d'Alsace Cuvée Julien, Dopff au
Moulin **Non-vintage** £9.44 (COC)

BORDEAUX

It's true that the 2000 vintage is being hyped to the skies – but there'll be some good affordable wines there. Or you could just hang on and wait for the 1997s to come down in price

What should you be buying from Bordeaux at the moment? Should you rush to snap up the 2000 vintage? Or should you hang on and wait?

The 2000 wines are certainly worth a punt. It's a genuinely good year, although it's not quite as even as the Bordelais would have us believe. The Médoc, particularly Margaux, and Graves are very good, and Pomerol has made some wonderfully seductive wines. St-Émilion is less thrilling, with too many over-extracted, over-tannic monsters being made to please millionaire collectors.

Luckily there are hundreds of properties – great and small, in major communes and minor, but all joined by the common thread of not being over-hyped – that have made their best wines for a generation. Some have made their best wines ever, but can't charge the earth because, except for the handful of superstars, Bordeaux is not popular in general at the moment. So these you should buy: the price is fair for the quality. But you'll clearly possess more money than sense if you shell out for the superstars: the 50 or so châteaux who have been hyped to the skies and who can therefore sell their wines for silly money to well-heeled label snobs. Many of their prices have doubled since being offered. They started expensive, they'll stay expensive – and you can do without.

And if you want to drink Bordeaux, you don't *have* to get sucked into the 2000 vintage frenzy. Are you a label drinker or a 'nice flavour at a fair price' drinker? If it's the latter - well, remember 1997? The wines weren't massively ripe, the prices were silly; no-one bought. So there are warehouses full of 1997 just sitting there and now, at four years old, the wines are looking rather good. And the prices have, if anything, gone down. 1998 and 1999 also both started too expensive and have been eclipsed by 2000. But they're still there, taking up warehouse space, sucking up the merchants' resources in interest charges. They'll have to be sold sometime. Bide your time, keep your eyes and ears open and buy them in bottle. They'll be drinking better, and they'll be cheaper than 2000.

GRAPE VARIETIES

Fine claret has the most tantalizing and appetizing combination of flavours of any red wine. There's the blast of pure, fragrant blackcurrant fruit, and then the exotic, dry perfumes of lead pencil shavings, fresh-wrapped cigars and cedar to weave an endlessly fascinating balance of sweet and dry tastes with the buttery overlay of new oak barrels.

Bordeaux's vineyards are so poised on the knife-edge of ripening their grapes or failing to do so that every vintage is fascinatingly different. If the year gets too hot, the flavour can be rich, strong and burnt, more like the Californian or Italian versions of claret. If the summer rains and autumn gales roll in off the Bay of Biscay and the grapes can't ripen, then the taste may be thin and green, resembling the Cabernets of the Loire Valley. But in the years of balance, like 1990, '95, '96, '98 and 2000, those astonishing ripe but dry, fruity and tannic flavours mix to produce the glory that is claret.

As for the whites – well, for years the sweet, botrytized wines of Sauternes and Barsac were the only ones that could compete in quality with the reds, and not always successfully. But recent years have seen a revolution. The sweet whites have improved beyond measure, helped by massive investment and a run of excellent vintages in the 1980s, but so have the dry ones. Inexpensive Bordeaux Blanc, based on Sauvignon, is usually crisp and grassy these days, while fine oak-aged white Graves has taken its place among the greats.

CABERNET FRANC (red) The lesser of the two Cabernets, giving lighter-coloured, softer wines than Cabernet Sauvignon, often slightly earthy but with good, blackcurranty fruit. It's always blended in Bordeaux. In St-Émilion and Pomerol it can give fine flavours and is widely planted. Château Cheval-Blanc in St-Émilion is two-thirds Cabernet Franc.

CABERNET SAUVIGNON (red) This world-famous Bordeaux grape surprisingly covers only a fifth of the vineyard area. Crucially, a wine built to age needs tannin and acidity, and the fruit and extract to keep up with them. Cabernet Sauvignon has all these in abundance. It gives dark, tannic wine with a strong initial acid attack, and stark blackcurrant fruit. When aged in new oak, it can be stunning. It's the main grape of the Haut-Médoc, but other varieties soften it and add complexity.

MALBEC (red) A rather bloated, juicy grape, little seen nowadays in Bordeaux, though it appears in some blends, especially in Bourg and Blaye. In Bordeaux it tastes rather like a feeble version of Merlot, soft and low in acidity. Upriver in Cahors it has real style, which probably explains why there's lots of it there and little in Bordeaux.

MERLOT (red) Bordeaux has more Merlot than Cabernet Sauvignon. It covers almost a third of the vineyard, and is the main grape in St-Émilion and Pomerol, whereas in the Médoc and Graves it's used to soften and enrich the Cabernet. It ripens early and gives a gorgeous, succulent, minty,

blackcurranty or plummy wine, which explains why Pomerols and St-Émilions are easier to enjoy than Médocs. It also makes less long-lived wine than Cabernet, and tends to peak and fade sooner.

MUSCADELLE (white) A very little (up to five per cent) of this headily perfumed grape often goes into the Sauternes blend. In dry white blends a few per cent can add a very welcome honeyed softness. It is now being produced in small quantities as a varietal: dry, lean, but perfumed.

PETIT VERDOT (red) A dark, tough grape with a liquorice-and-plums taste, and a violet perfume, used for colour and complexity. It adds quality in a ripe year.

SAUVIGNON BLANC (white) There has been a rush to plant more of this fashionable grape in Bordeaux in recent years, and everybody's learnt how to handle it. *Couhins-Lurton, Malartic-Lagravière* and *Smith-Haut-Lafitte* make splendid versions, but most of the best are blended with Sémillon. Many of the cheaper dry white Bordeaux are entirely Sauvignon, and these are almost always fresh and pungent. *Benoit & Valerie Calvet, Coste, Dourthe, Ginestet* and *Mau* are among the names to look for. A little Sauvignon adds acidity to Sauternes and other sweet whites.

SÉMILLON (white) The most important grape of Sauternes, and vital to the best dry wines, too. With modern techniques one can hardly tell a good dry Sémillon from a Sauvignon, except that it's a little fuller. But ideally they should be blended, with Sémillon the main variety. It gives a big, round dry wine, slightly creamy but with an aroma of fresh apples and a lanolin smoothness in the mouth. The result is a wonderful, soft, nutty dry white, often going honeyed and smoky as it ages for seven to 15 years. Like this it produces one of France's great whites, and is an antidote to anyone getting just a little tired of varietals.

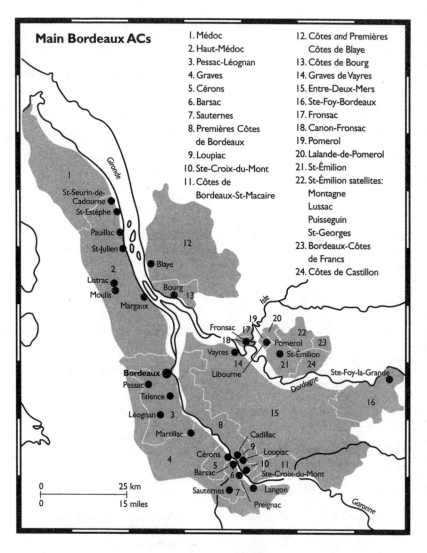

Main Bordeaux ACs

1. Médoc
2. Haut-Médoc
3. Pessac-Léognan
4. Graves
5. Cérons
6. Barsac
7. Sauternes
8. Premières Côtes de Bordeaux
9. Loupiac
10. Ste-Croix-du-Mont
11. Côtes de Bordeaux-St-Macaire
12. Côtes *and* Premières Côtes de Blaye
13. Côtes de Bourg
14. Graves de Vayres
15. Entre-Deux-Mers
16. Ste-Foy-Bordeaux
17. Fronsac
18. Canon-Fronsac
19. Pomerol
20. Lalande-de-Pomerol
21. St-Émilion
22. St-Émilion satellites:
    Montagne
    Lussac
    Puisseguin
    St-Georges
23. Bordeaux-Côtes de Francs
24. Côtes de Castillon

WINE REGIONS

BARSAC, AC (sweet white) The only one of the five Sauternes villages with the right to use its own name as an official appellation (it may also call itself Sauternes – or Sauternes-Barsac). The wines tend to be lighter, and the best combine marvellous richness with a certain delicacy of texture.

BORDEAUX BLANC, AC (dry white) This AC is the catch-all name for all white Bordeaux. Château wines are usually the best and should generally be drunk as young as possible. Recommended names include: *Birot, Grand-Mouëys, du Juge, Lamothe, Reynon*. Good blends are likely from the following merchants: *B & V Calvet, Coste, Dourthe, Dubroca, Ginestet, Joanne, Lurton, Mau, Sichel* and *Univitis*.

Some classy properties in red areas make good, dry white which is allowed only this AC. *Château Margaux*'s white, for instance, is a simple AC Bordeaux Blanc. Many great Sauternes châteaux make a dry wine from the grapes deemed unsuitable for Sauternes. These also take the Bordeaux Blanc AC and are often named after the initial letter of the château's name – as in 'G' of *Guiraud*, 'R' of *Rieussec* and 'Y' of *Yquem*. They're expensive but complex and unusual. 'Y' can really be spectacular.

BORDEAUX BLANC SUPÉRIEUR, AC (dry white) Rarely used, but requires higher basic strength and lower vineyard yield than Bordeaux Blanc AC.

BORDEAUX ROUGE, AC (red) Unless qualified by one of the other ACs below, this is the everyday red wine of Bordeaux, from co-ops, from properties in undistinguished localities, or wine disqualified from one of the better ACs. It is a delicious, appetizing meal-time red when good – and a palate-puckering disappointment when bad. Too many are muddy, coarse and lacking in style.

BORDEAUX SUPÉRIEUR, AC (red) Similar to Bordeaux Rouge but with more alcohol and produced from a slightly lower yield. The same comments on quality apply. Best results are often from properties producing white Entre-Deux-Mers and from the Premières Côtes. Best châteaux: *Brethous, Cayla, Domaine de Terrefort, Fayau, la Gabory, le Gay, Grand-Moüeys, Gromel Bel-Air, Jalousie-Beaulieu, Jonqueyres, du Juge, Lacombe, Méaume, Peyrat, Pierredon, Reynon, la Roche, Tanesse, Thieuley, de Toutigeac, de la Vieille Tour*.

CADILLAC, AC (sweet white) This small region can produce attractive sweet whites, but many properties produce more commercial dry whites and reds – which do *not* qualify for the AC Cadillac. The AC is so involved that few growers bother with it.

CÉRONS, AC (sweet white) Good, fairly sweet whites, but many growers now prefer to produce dry whites instead, which can be sold as Graves. *Château Archambeau* is typical, producing tiny amounts of very good Cérons and larger amounts of good, fresh dry Graves. *Château Cérons* makes splendidly complex sweet whites worthy of the AC of Barsac. Other good names to look out for: *Grand Enclos du Château Cérons, Haura*.

CÔTES DE BLAYE, AC (dry white) and **PREMIÈRES CÔTES DE BLAYE, AC** (red, dry white) The reds are sometimes a little 'cooked' in taste, but they're improving. The whites are getting better, too. Good names: *Bas Vallon, Bourdieu, Charron, Crusquet-Sabourin, l'Escadre, Fontblanche, Grand Barail, Haut-Bertinerie, Haut-Sociondo, Jonqueyres, Peybonhomme*.

CÔTES DE BOURG, AC (red) The rather full, savoury style of these reds is backed up by sweet Merlot fruit and occasionally a touch of new oak. As Médoc and St-Émilion prices spiral, Bourg wines are coming into their own. Best châteaux: *de Barbe, du Bousquet, Brûlésécaille, la Croix, Dupeyrat, Falfas, Grolet, Haut-Guiraud, Haut-Rousset, de Millorit, Roc de Cambes, Tayac* and wines from the co-op at *Tauriac*.

CÔTES DE CASTILLON, AC (red) and **BORDEAUX-CÔTES DE FRANCS, AC** (red) Two small regions which are turning out an increasing number of exciting wines. They can be a little too earthy, but at their best they combine a grassy Cabernet Franc freshness with a gorgeous, juicy, minty Merlot sweetness. Several leading Bordeaux proprietors have bought properties here. Best châteaux in the Côtes de Castillon: *Arthus, Beau-Séjour, Belcier, Brisson, Canon-Monségur, La Clarière-*

Laithwaite, Ferrasses, Fonds Rondes, Grand Taillac, les Hauts-de-Grange, Lessacques, Moulin-Rouge, Parenchère, Peyrou, Pitray, Poupille, Rocher-Bellevue, Vernon. The Côtes de Francs in particular produces fruity, light, delicious wines to drink early, using a lot of Cabernet Franc. Best châteaux here are la Claverie, de Francs, Lauriol, Marsau, du Moulin-la-Pitié, la Prade, Puygueraud.

ENTRE-DEUX-MERS, AC (dry white) Every vintage produces more good, fresh, grassy wines here. Many properties make red, which take the AC of Bordeaux or Bordeaux Supérieur. Best: Bonnet, Ducla, de Florin, Moulin-de-Launay, Tertre du Moulin, Thieuley, Union des Producteurs de Rauzan.

FRONSAC, AC (red) with the (in theory) superior **CANON-FRONSAC, AC** (red) St-Émilion lookalikes, sometimes a bit grassy and tannic, but often supple, balanced clarets of some elegance – even in light years like 1997. Best: Barrabaque, Canon-de-Brem, Canon-Moueix, Cassagne Haut-Canon, La Croix-Canon, Dalem, La Dauphine, Fontenil, Grand-Renouil, Mayne-Vieil, Mazeris, Moulin Haut-Laroque, Moulin Pey-Labrie, la Rivière, Toumalin, La Vieille Cure, Villars, Vrai Canon Bouché.

GRAVES, AC (red, dry white) Red Graves run the gamut of claret flavours, and are less easy to sum up than others. Though Cabernet Sauvignon is the dominant grape in the North, as in the Médoc, there's more stress on Merlot, so the wines are slightly softer. They tend to have some of the blackcurrant and cedar of the Médoc, but without the size of, say, Pauillac; they have some of the plummy richness of St-Émilion, yet it never dominates; and there is a slightly gravelly quality in many of them, too. The less well-known châteaux are good value.

Modern white Graves, even at the level of commercial blends, can be sharply fruity and full in style, although too many are overoaked. Best châteaux: Archambeau, Bouscaut, Cabannieux, Carbonnieux, Domaine de Chevalier, Couhins-Lurton, de Cruzeau, Domaine la Grave, de Fieuzal, la Garance, la Garde, Haut-Brion, Landiras, Latour-Martillac, Laville-Haut-Brion, la Louvière, Malartic-Lagravière, Montalivet, Rahoul, Respide, Rochemorin, Roquetaillade-la-Grange, Smith-Haut-Lafitte. (Note that in 1987 the top properties in the North were grouped into a separate AC, Pessac-Léognan.)

GRAVES SUPÉRIEURES, AC (sweet or dry white) Graves with a minimum natural alcohol of 12 degrees. Often made sweet. Best property: Clos St-Georges.

HAUT-MÉDOC, AC (red) Geographically, the prestigious southern part of the Médoc, nearest Bordeaux. The AC, however, covers the less exciting vineyards because the really juicy business gets done at Margaux, St-Julien, Pauillac, St-Estèphe, Listrac and Moulis, which have their own ACs. Even so, the AC Haut-Médoc has five Classed Growths including two superb ones – Cantemerle and la Lagune – and an increasing number of fine bourgeois properties like Beaumont, de Castillon, Cissac, Hanteillan, Lamarque, Lanessan, Liversan, Pichon, Sociando-Mallet and la Tour-du-Haut-Moulin – plus lots of lesser properties, such as châteaux Bernadotte, Cambon-la-Pelouse, Coufran, le Fournas, Grandis, du Junca, Larose-Trintaudon, Malescasse, Maucamps, Moulin de Labarde, Quimper, Sénéjac and Verdignan.

LALANDE-DE-POMEROL, AC (red) Pomerol's equally tiny northern neighbour is often accused of being overpriced, but since it can produce rich, plummy wines with a distinct resemblance to those of Pomerol at a distinctly less painful price, this criticism is not entirely justified. Best: Annereaux, Bel-Air, Belles-Graves, Bertineau-St-Vincent, Clos des Moines, Clos des Templiers, la Croix Bellevue, la Fleur St-Georges, Garraud, Grand Ormeau, Haut-Ballet, Haut-Chaigneau, les Hauts-Tuileries, Lavaud-la-Maréchaude, Siaurac, les Templiers, Tournefeuille, de Viaud.

LISTRAC, AC (red) One of the less prestigious communes of the Haut-Médoc. The wines contain a higher proportion of Merlot than elsewhere, but nevertheless are rather tough and charmless, only lightly perfumed wines. But some properties rise above this, such as *la Bécade, Cap-Léon-Veyrin, Clarke, Fonréaud* (since 1988), *Fourcas-Dupré, Fourcas-Hosten, Fourcaud, Lestage* and the *Grand Listrac* co-op.

LOUPIAC, AC (sweet white) These wines are not as sweet as Sauternes, and most are light, lemony, honeyed Barsac styles. The general improvement in Bordeaux's sweet wines has filtered down here, as well. Best: *Domaine du Noble, Loupiac-Gaudiet, Ricaud.*

MARGAUX, AC (red) Rather sludgy, solid wines at one extreme, and the most fragrant, perfumed red wines France has yet dreamed up at the other. The best include: *d'Angludet, la Gurgue, d'Issan, Labégorce-Zédé, Margaux, Monbrison, Palmer, Prieuré-Lichine, Rauzan-Ségla, du Tertre.* Among the next best are *Durfort-Vivens, Giscours, Lascombes, Marquis d'Alesme-Becker, Marquis de Terme, Siran* and *la Tour-de-Mons.*

MÉDOC, AC (red) This name covers the long tongue of land north of Bordeaux town, between the Gironde river and the sea, including the Haut-Médoc and all its famous communes. As an AC it refers to the less-regarded but important northern part of the area. Médoc reds, with a high proportion of Merlot grapes, are drinkable more quickly than Haut-Médocs and the best have a refreshing, grassy, juicy fruit, and just enough tannin and acidity. Easily the best property is *Potensac.* Other good wines are *Cardonne, David, d'Escot, la Gorce, Greysac, Haut-Canteloup, Lacombe-Noaillac, Loudenne, Noaillac, Ormes-Sorbet, Patache d'Aux, la Tour-de-By, la Tour-St-Bonnet, Vieux-Château-Landon.* Most of the co-ops — especially *Bégadan, Ordornac, St-Yzans* — make good fruity stuff in the best years.

MOULIS, AC (red) Another lesser commune of the Haut-Médoc next door to, and similar to, Listrac, but with more potentially outstanding properties and a softer, more perfumed style in the best which can equal Classed Growths. Best are *Bel-Air-Lagrave, Brillette, Chasse-Spleen, Duplessis-Fabre, Dutruch-Grand-Poujeaux, Grand-Poujeaux, Gressier-Grand-Poujeaux, Maucaillou, Moulin-à-Vent, Poujeaux.*

PAUILLAC, AC (red) The most famous of the Haut-Médoc communes, Pauillac has three of the world's greatest red wines sitting inside its boundaries: *Latour, Lafite* and *Mouton-Rothschild.* This is where the blackcurrant really comes into its own. The best wines are almost painfully intense, a celestial mixture of blackcurrant and lead pencil sharpenings that sends well-heeled cognoscenti leaping for their cheque books. Best: *d'Armailhac* (formerly known as *Mouton-Baronne-Philippe*), *Grand-Puy-Lacoste, Haut-Bages-Avérous, Haut-Bages-Libéral, Lafite-Rothschild, Latour, Lynch-Bages, Mouton-Rothschild, Pichon-Baron, Pichon-Lalande.* Next best: *Batailley, Clerc-Milon-Rothschild, Duhart-Milon, Grand-Puy-Ducasse, Haut-Bages-Monpelou.*

PESSAC-LÉOGNAN, AC (red, dry white) Traditionally the Graves' best area, containing all the *crus classés.* The whites at their best offer a depth surpassed only by the best Burgundies. They start out with a blast of apricot, peach and cream ripeness and slowly mature to a superb nutty richness with a dry savoury finish. The reds have a biscuity, bricky warmth. Best reds: *Carbonnieux, Carmes-Haut-Brion, Cruzeau, Domaine de Chevalier, Domaine de Gaillat, Domaine la Grave, Ferrande, de Fieuzal, Haut-Bailly, Haut-Brion, Haut-Portets, Latour-Martillac, la Louvière, Malartic-Lagravière, la Mission-Haut-Brion, Pape-Clément, Rahoul, Rochemorin, de St-Pierre, Smith-Haut-Lafitte, Roquetaillade-la-Grange, Tourteau-Chollet.* Best whites: *Bouscaut, Carbonnieux, Couhins-Lurton, Domaine de Chevalier, de Fieuzal,*

Haut-Brion, Latour-Martillac, la Louvière, Malartic-Lagravière, Rochemorin, Smith-Haut-Lafitte.

POMEROL, AC (red) The Merlot grape is even more dominant in Pomerol than in St-Émilion, and most Pomerols have a deeper, rounder flavour, the plummy fruit going as dark as prunes in great years, but with the mineral backbone of toughness preserving it for a very long time. Pomerol harbours the *Château Pétrus*, and what is often the world's most expensive red wine, *Le Pin*. Other top names: *Beauregard, le Bon Pasteur, Bourgneuf-Vayron, Certan-de-May, Certan-Giraud, Clinet, Clos René, Clos du Clocher, Clos l'Église, la Conseillante, la Croix-de-Gay, l'Église Clinet, l'Évangile, le Gay, la Grave-Trigant-de-Boisset, Lafleur, la Fleur-de-Gay, Lafleur-Gazin, la Fleur-Pétrus, Lagrange-à-Pomerol, Latour-à-Pomerol, Petit-Village, Le Pin, Trotanoy, Vieux-Château-Certan. Vray Croix de Gay.*

PREMIÈRES CÔTES DE BORDEAUX, AC (red, white) Some very attractive reds and excellent dry whites in the bang-up-to-date, fruit-all-the-way style, plus some reasonable sweetish wines. Best châteaux: *de Berbec, Brethous, Cayla, Fayau, Grands-Moüeys, du Juge, Lamothe, de Lucat, Peyrat, la Roche, Reynon, Tanesse.*

ST-ÉMILION, AC (red) Traditionally soft, round and rather generous wines, because the main grape is the Merlot, aided by Cabernet Franc and Malbec, and only slightly by Cabernet Sauvignon. St-Émilions don't always have Pomerol's minerally backbone, and the sweetness is usually less plummy and more buttery, toffeed or raisiny. Top wines add to this a blackcurranty, minty depth. However, the region is plagued by the fashion for massive, over-extracted wines: the 2000 vintage, in particular, should be chosen with care. Basic St-Émilions are seldom exciting, and quality is extremely

---

THE ST-ÉMILION CLASSIFICATION

St-Émilion Grand Cru is a superior appellation within St-Émilion AC, and of the several hundred Grand Cru wines a certain number are classified. The first classification was in 1954, and it was slightly modified in 1969, 1985 and 1996. The possibility of re-grading can help to maintain quality.

Premiers Grands Crus Classés (A)
Ausone, Cheval-Blanc

Premiers Grands Crus Classés (B)
Angélus, Beau-Séjour-Bécot, Beaséjour (Duffau-Lagarosse), Belair, Canon, Clos Fourtet, Figeac, La Gaffelière, Magdelaine, Pavie, Trottevieille

Grands Crus Classés
l'Arrosée, Balestard-la-Tonnelle, Bellevue, Bergat, Berliquet, Cadet-Bon, Cadet-Piola, Canon-la-Gaffelière, Cap de Mourlin, Chauvin, Clos des Jacobins, Clos de l'Oratoire, Clos St-Martin, la Clotte, la Clusière, Corbin, Corbin-Michotte, la Couspaude, Couvent des Jacobins, Curé-Bon, Dassault, la Dominique, Faurie de Souchard, Fonplégade, Fonroque, Franc Mayne, les Grandes Murailles, Grand-Mayne, Grand-Pontet, Guadet-St-Julien, Haut-Corbin, Haut-Sarpe, Lamarzelle, Laniote, Larcis Ducasse, Larmande, Laroque, Laroze, Matras, Moulin du Cadet, Pavie-Decesse, Pavie-Macquin, Petit-Faurie-de-Soutard, le Prieuré, Ripeau, St-Georges (Côte Pavie), la Serre, Soutard, Tertre-Daugay, la Tour Figeac, la Tour du Pin Figeac (Giraud-Bélivier), la Tour du Pin Figeac (J M Moueix), Troplong- Mondot, Villemaurine, Yon-Figeac.

variable. The top châteaux are *Cheval-Blanc* and *Ausone*. Some satellite areas also annex the name, like St-Georges-St-Émilion or Puisseguin-St-Émilion. These would be better value if they didn't trade greedily on the St-Émilion handle. Best in satellites: *Montaiguillon, St-Georges, Tour du Pas St-Georges* (St-Georges-St-Émilion); *Haut-Gillet, de Maison Neuve* (Montagne-St-Émilion); *Bel Air, la Croix-de-Berny* (Puisseguin-St-Émilion); *Lyonnat* (Lussac-St-Émilion). Best St-Émilion: *Angélus, l'Arrosée, Ausone, Balestard-la-Tonnelle, Beauséjour-Duffau-Lagarosse, Canon, Canon-la-Gaffelière, Cheval-Blanc, Clos des Jacobins, la Dominique, Figeac, Fonroque, Larmande, Magdelaine, Pavie, Pavie-Decesse, Soutard, Tertre-Rôteboeuf, Troplong-Mondot.* Next best: *Belair, Cadet-Piola, Berliquet, Cap-de-Mourlin, Cardinal Villemaurine, Carteau, Clos Fourtet, Corbin-Michotte, Côtes Daugay, Couvent des Jacobins, Destieux, de Ferrand, Fombrauge, Franc-Mayne, la Gaffelière, Grand-Mayne, Gravet, Magnan-la-Gaffelière, Mauvezin, Monbousquet, Pavie-Macquin, Rolland-Maillet, Tour-des-Combes, la-Tour-du-Pin-Figeac, Trappaud, Trottevieille, Villemaurine.* There's a trend towards producing *micro-vins*: take perhaps a single hectare of vines, make a wine of great concentration and oak, then charge a fortune for it. *Valandraud* and *La Mondotte* are leading players; also *Le Dôme*.

CRUS BOURGEOIS

The 419 Crus Bourgeois of the Médoc have just been given a shiny new classification, and about time too. There will be three levels: Crus Bourgeois, Crus Bourgeois Supérieurs and Crus Bourgeois Exceptionnels, and the rankings will be determined in 2002. And this classification, unlike that of the Crus Classés, will be revised every ten years, so that it really will be a genuine guide to quality. However, prices of the top wines are likely to rise as a result.

ST-ESTÈPHE, AC (red) The northernmost of the great Haut-Médoc communes is a more everyday performer. There are few famous names, and most are relatively cheap. Best: *Calon-Ségur, Chambert-Marbuzet, Cos d'Estournel, Haut-Marbuzet, Lafon-Rochet, Marbuzet, Meyney, Montrose, les Ormes-de-Pez, de Pez, Phélan-Ségur.* Next best: *Andron-Blanquet, Beausite, du Boscq, Cos Labory, le Crock, Lavillotte.*

ST-JULIEN, AC (red) There are two main styles here. One is almost honeyed: gentle, round, wonderfully easy-to-love. The other has glorious cedar-cigar-box fragrance and just enough fruit to make it satisfying as well as exciting. Best: *Beychevelle, Ducru-Beaucaillou, Gruaud-Larose, Lagrange, Lalande-Borie, Langoa-Barton, Léoville-Barton, Léoville-Las-Cases, Léoville-Poyferré, St-Pierre, Talbot.* Next: *Branaire-Ducru, Gloria, Hortevie* and *Terrey-Gros-Caillou.*

STE-CROIX-DU-MONT, AC (sweet white) Very attractive when properly made. *Château Loubens* is the best-known wine, but *la Grave, Lousteau-Vieil, la Rame, Domaine du Tich, des Tours* and the minuscule *de Tastes* are also good.

SAUTERNES, AC (sweet white) The overall appellation for a group of five villages: Sauternes, Bommes, Fargues, Preignac and Barsac. (Barsac wines may use their own village name.) Concentrated by noble rot, the Sémillon, along with Sauvignon and Muscadelle, produces at its best a brilliantly rich and glyceriny wine, combining honey and cream, pineapple and nuts when young; becoming oily and penetrating with age. In the finest wines the sweetness has an intensity of volatile flavours, like a peach, bruised and browned in the sun, then steeped in syrup. Best include: *Bastor-Lamontagne, Climens, Doisy-Daëne, Doisy-Védrines, de Fargues, Gilette, Guiraud, Lafaurie-Peyraguey, Lamothe-Guignard, Rabaud-Promis, Raymond-Lafon, Rayne-Vigneau, Rieussec, St-Amand, Suduiraut, la Tour Blanche, d'Yquem.*

THE 1855 CLASSIFICATION

This is the most famous and enduring wine classification in the world – but it was intended merely as an impromptu guide to the Bordeaux wines entered for the Great Paris Exhibition of 1855, based on the prices the wines had obtained over the previous century.

Since this classification applies only to the Médoc and one château, Haut-Brion, in the Graves, all the wines are red. The Graves has its own classification, for reds and whites, and Sauternes and St-Émilion are also classified. Pomerol steers clear of any official hierarchy. The only change so far has been the promotion of Mouton-Rothschild to First Growth in 1973.

In general, classified properties do deserve their status, but that's never yet stopped anyone from arguing about it.

CLARET CLASSIFICATIONS

First Growths (1ers crus)
Margaux – *Margaux*; Lafite-Rothschild, Latour, Mouton-Rothschild (promoted in 1973) – *Pauillac;* Haut-Brion – *Pessac-Léognan* (formerly *Graves*).

Second Growths (2èmes crus)
Brane-Cantenac – *Cantenac-Margaux*; Durfort-Vivens, Lascombes, Rauzan-Gassies, Rauzan-Ségla – *Margaux*; Pichon-Longueville, Pichon-Longueville-Lalande (formerly Pichon-Lalande) – *Pauillac;* Cos d'Estournel, Montrose – *St-Estèphe*; Ducru-Beaucaillou, Gruaud-Larose, Léoville-Barton, Léoville-Las-Cases, Léoville-Poyferré – *St-Julien.*

Third Growths (3èmes crus)
Boyd-Cantenac, Cantenac-Brown, d'Issan, Kirwan, Palmer – *Cantenac-Margaux*; Giscours – *Labarde-Margaux*; la Lagune – *Ludon-Haut-Médoc;* Desmirail, Ferrière, Malescot-St-Exupéry, Marquis d'Alesme-Becker – *Margaux*; Calon-Ségur – *St-Estèphe;* Lagrange, Langoa-Barton – *St-Julien.*

Fourth Growths (4èmes crus)
Pouget, Prieuré-Lichine – *Cantenac-Margaux*; Marquis-de-Terme – *Margaux*; Duhart-Milon-Rothschild – *Pauillac;* Lafon-Rochet – *St-Estèphe*; Beychevelle, Branaire (formerly Branaire-Ducru), St-Pierre, Talbot – *St-Julien;* la Tour-Carnet – *St-Laurent-Haut-Médoc.*

Fifth Growths (5èmes crus)
du Tertre – *Arsac-Margaux*; Dauzac – *Labarde-Margaux*; Cantemerle – *Macau-Haut-Médoc;* d'Armailhac (formerly Mouton-Baronne-Philippe), Batailley, Clerc-Milon-Rothschild, Croizet-Bages, Grand-Puy-Ducasse, Grand-Puy-Lacoste, Haut-Bages-Libéral, Haut-Batailley, Lynch-Bages, Lynch-Moussas, Pédesclaux, Pontet-Canet – *Pauillac;* Cos Labory – *St-Estèphe*; Belgrave, de Camensac – *St-Laurent-Haut-Médoc.*

SAUTERNES CLASSIFICATIONS

Grand 1er cru   d'Yquem – *Sauternes.*

1er crus   Climens, Coutet – *Barsac*; Haut-Peyraguey, Lafaurie-Peyraguey, Rabaud-Promis, Rayne-Vigneau, Sigalas-Rabaud, la Tour-Blanche – *Bommes;* Rieussec – *Fargues*; Suduiraut – *Preignac*; Guiraud – *Sauternes.*

2èmes crus   Broustet, Caillou, Doisy-Daëne, Doisy-Dubroca, Doisy-Védrines, Nairac, de Myrat, Suau – *Barsac*; Romer-du-Hayot – *Fargues*; de Malle – *Preignac*; d'Arche, Filhot, Lamothe, Lamothe-Guignard – *Sauternes.*

PRODUCERS WHO'S WHO

ANGÉLUS *1er grand cru classé St-Émilion* ★★★ Wonderful: gutsy, rich and soft, though sometimes verging on the over-extracted. It excelled even in the difficult years of the early 1990s. 1996 is superb, '95 even better, '97 and '98 excellent. 1999 is very good, and 2000 lush.

D'ANGLUDET *cru bourgeois Margaux* ★ **£** Tremendous value *bourgeois* red easily attaining Classed Growth standards. Much of the perfume of good Margaux without ever going through the traditional lean period. 1983 and '90 were beauties; '95 and '96 are worthy of their vintages. 2000 looks tremendous.

D'ARCHE *2ème cru Sauternes* ★ A little-known property now increasingly highly thought of.

D'ARMAILHAC *5ème cru classé Pauillac* ★ (formerly Mouton-Baronne-Philippe) A red of very good balance, with the cedar perfume particularly marked. 1996 is especially good, '95 even better. 1999 and 2000 are very good.

AUSONE *1er grand cru classé St-Émilion* ★★★ A new winemaker was appointed for the 1995, and the wines are altogether gutsier. The 1985, '86, '89 and above all the '90, are especially good, as are the '96 and '97; 1999 is spectacular; 2000 utterly seductive.

BASTOR-LAMONTAGNE *cru bourgeois Sauternes* ★ Marvellous, widely available sweet whites. Pricy, but as rich as many Classed Growths. 1983, '86, '88, '89

> **£** *This symbol denotes producers who offer particularly good value – that's not the same as saying that they're cheap.*

and '90 epitomize quality Sauternes. 1996 and '97 are good, too.

BATAILLEY *5ème cru classé Pauillac* ★ **£** The wines have been reliably good quality for a generation. Drinkable young, they age well too. 1990 is excellent, and relatively affordable. Look out for the 1995 and '96, too, but '97, '98 and '99 were less convincing. 2000 should be nice enough.

BEAU-SÉJOUR BÉCOT *1er grand cru classé St-Émilion* ★★ Improvements during the late 1980s and 1990s have brought this estate back to top form, producing ripe, richly textured wines. that need at least 8–10 years to develop.

BELAIR *1er grand cru classé St-Émilion* ★★ Biodynamic since 1994, Belair steadfastly ignores the fashion for ever more richness and focuses instead on seriousness and finesse. The 2000 is superb.

BEYCHEVELLE *4ème cru classé St-Julien* ★ The most expensive Fourth Growth; only the best vintages merit the high price. It takes time to mature to a beautifully balanced, scented, blackcurranty red. 1990 is sublime, but there is still sometimes a tendency to overproduce. '95 and '96 are both worthy of the property, and 2000 looks like a winner.

BRANAIRE *4ème cru classé St-Julien* ★ (formerly Branaire-Ducru) Soft, smooth red with plums and chocolate flavours, achieving a classic, cedary St-Julien perfume in maturity. The 1980s were erratic, but 1989 and '90 saw a return to form. Recent vintages are excellent.

BRANE-CANTENAC *2ème cru classé Margaux* ★ A famous property which was underachieving when most of the other Second Growths were shooting ahead. Late-'90s vintages look far more positive.

CALON-SÉGUR *3ème cru classé St-Estèphe* ★ Intensely traditional claret that needs time. 1995, '96 and '98 are all impressive.

CANON *1er grand cru classé St-Émilion* ★ Mature Canon reeks of the soft, buttery Merlot grape as only a top St-Émilion can. It's marvellously rich stuff, though 1998 was the first really good vintage of the '90s.

CANON-LA-GAFFELIÈRE *grand cru classé St-Émilion* ★★ German owners have invested a fortune here, and everything is of the most modern, including the wine: rich, seductive, luscious. Very good 1990, '93 and '97, glorious 1999 and 2000.

CANTEMERLE *5ème cru classé Haut-Médoc* ★ Often up to Second Growth standards. The 1999 is attractive, 2000 splendidly concentrated.

CARBONNIEUX *cru classé Pessac-Léognan* ★ Balanced reds and oaky whites. 2000 is creamy and rich.

CHASSE-SPLEEN *cru bourgeois Moulis* ★ A tremendously consistent wine, at the top of the *bourgeois* tree. It sells above the price of many Classed Growths, but it's worth it. Look for the superb 2000.

CHEVAL-BLANC *1er grand cru classé St-Émilion* ★★★ There's some sturdy richness here, but wonderful spice and fruit too, perhaps due to the very high proportion of Cabernet Franc. 1999 and 2000 are tops.

DOMAINE DE CHEVALIER *cru classé Pessac-Léognan* ★★★ (white) The white is simply one of France's greatest; the red has a good balance of fruit and oak. Look also for the sweetly oaky white and refined red second wines, Esprit de Chevalier.

CISSAC *cru grand bourgeois Haut-Médoc* ★ £ Well-structured wine made in

ON THE CASE
Don't think of basic Médoc or Haut-Médoc as being wine of remarkable quality. Apart from leading petits châteaux and crus bourgeois, most are simple, but not cheap, everyday wines

traditional, slow-maturing style. It is best in richly ripe years, such as 2000. Otherwise can be a bit tough.

CLIMENS *1er cru Barsac* ★★★ Undoubtedly the best property in Barsac, making some of the most consistently fine sweet wines in France. The delicious second wine, les Cyprès, is well worth seeking out in off-vintages.

CLOS DE L'ORATOIRE *grand cru classé St-Émilion* ★★ Muscular style, and top-class winemaking. Expect lush, dense fruit. Very good 1999 and 2000.

COS D'ESTOURNEL *2ème cru classé St-Estèphe* ★★★ The undoubted leader of St-Estèphe. The wines are dark, tannic and oaky: classically made for long aging.

COUHINS-LURTON *cru classé Pessac-Léognan* ★★ 100 per cent Sauvignon dry white fermented in new oak barrels, producing a blend of grassy fruit and oaky spice. Recent vintages have been excellent.

COUTET *1er cru Barsac* ★ A great sweet wine property but never a match for neighbouring Climens; also a dry white.

DOISY-DAËNE *2ème cru Sauternes* ★★ Very good, consistent, relatively light, but extremely attractive sweet wine, plus a particularly good dry white.

DOISY-VÉDRINES *2ème cru Barsac* ★★ £ A rich, concentrated sweet white which is usually good value. 1989 and '90 are very good, and '95 is good.

DUCRU-BEAUCAILLOU *2ème cru classé St-Julien* ★★★ Great depth and warmth, and lovely balance. Back on form again after a few problematic years in the late '80s: 1999 is full of finesse, 2000 tremendous: big, dense and expressive.

DURFORT VIVENS *Margaux* ★ The quality is rising fast here, and prices are lagging a bit behind: it's currently looking a very good buy. 2000 is beautifully balanced and elegant.

L'ÉGLISE CLINET *Pomerol* ★★★ Very old vines and an owner-winemaker who is completely dedicated to quality account for the depth and elegance of the wines; they are expensive but worth seeking out.

L'ÉVANGILE *Pomerol* ★★ Top-line Pomerol, lacking the sheer intensity of its neighbour Pétrus, but irresistibly perfumed and rich. In huge demand, so it's expensive. 1999 is terrific; 2000 is soft, rich and concentrated.

DE FARGUES *cru bourgeois Sauternes* ★★ Stunning, rich wines in the best years. Generally sells at exactly half the price of Yquem, so it ain't cheap.

FERRIERE *3ème cru classé Margaux* ★★ A change of ownership in 1992 has seen huge strides in quality here, and the ripe, rich and perfumed wines are now among the best in Margaux – with correspondingly high prices.

DE FIEUZAL *cru classé Pessac-Léognan* ★★ (white) One of the stars of Pessac-Léognan, the white only just behind Domaine de Chevalier. The red starts plum-rich and buttery, but develops earthiness and cedar scent allied to lovely fruit. The unclassified white is scented, complex, deep and exciting. Both are very good in 2000.

FIGEAC *1er grand cru classé St-Émilion* ★★ Figeac shares many of the qualities of Cheval Blanc but it's always ranked as the ever-reliable star of the second team. The reason is inconsistency, because a sublime, scented vintage can so often be followed by something below par. 1990s were erratic, but '96, '98 and '99 seem good. The 2000, however, seems to have a bit too much green tannin.

FILHOT *2ème cru Sauternes* ★ The wines are fairly light, and not particularly complex, although Crème de Tête, made in the best years, is a winner.

LA FLEUR-PÉTRUS *Pomerol* ★★ This red is in the top flight, having some of the mineral roughness of much Pomerol, but also tremendous perfume and length.

FOURCAS-DUPRÉ *cru bourgeois Listrac* A top performer in this generally underperforming AC: tough and closed when young, but opening up attractively into rich fruit and spice. 2000 looks promising.

FOURCAS-HOSTEN *cru bourgeois Listrac* Slightly fuller than its neighbour, Fourcas-Dupré, and making wines in a similarly long-lived, austere style. All the '90s vintages have been good, and 2000 just has the edge on its neighbour.

GAZIN *Pomerol* ★★ Lovely perfume and sweetness. 1998 and '99 were great, and 2000 is all buttery plumskins.

GILETTE *cru bourgeois Sauternes* ★★ This property ages its sweet whites in concrete tanks for 20 to 30 years before releasing them. Usually delicious, with a dry richness that is unique in Sauternes thanks to the long maturation and absence of wood.

GISCOURS *3ème cru classé Margaux* ★ Exceedingly nice wines in '91, '92 and '93, then a bit of a blip in the mid-90s. 1999 is seductive, and 2000 is tremendous.

GLORIA *cru bourgeois St-Julien* ★ The quality of this quick-maturing red has not always lived up to its hype. But 1995 is super, '96 is very good and '94 is good for the vintage. Gloria is never cheap, though.

GRAND-PUY-DUCASSE *5ème cru classé Pauillac* ★ £ Nice, but lagging behind Grand-Puy-Lacoste in quality. Excellent 2000.

GRAND-PUY-LACOSTE *5ème cru classé Pauillac* ★★ £ Perfume, power and consistency: Pauillac at its brilliant best. Blackcurrant and cigar-box perfumes are rarely in better harmony than here. Showing exceptional class in the 2000 vintage.

GRUAUD-LAROSE *2ème cru classé St-Julien* ★★ Often starts rich, chunky and sweetish but will achieve its full cedary glory in time, while still retaining a lovely sweet centre. 2000 is well on form.

GUIRAUD *1er cru Sauternes* ★★ The wines are difficult to taste when young but are very special, and outstanding in 1990, '96 and '97.

HAUT-BAILLY *cru classé Pessac-Léognan* ★ Haut-Bailly red (there is no white) tastes sweet, rich and perfumed from its youth. However, there is new ownership, and the last couple of vintages have been disappointing.

HAUT-BATAILLEY *5ème cru classé Pauillac* ★ Stylish, relatively light wine, although 2000 looks concentrated as well as supple and refined.

HAUT-BRION *1er cru classé Pessac-Léognan* ★★★ The wines are not big, but are almost creamy in their gorgeous ripe taste. 1996 is outstanding, '95 even better, 2000 stunning. Also makes a little fine, long-lived white (appealing when young, too). 1999 and 2000 are spectacular.

INSTANT CELLAR: 1998s TO WATCH

- **1998 Sarget de Gruaud-Larose, £15.83, Millésima** The second wine of the reliable Château Gruaud-Larose. If you want the Grand Vin of the same year, it costs £38.33.
- **1998 Château Fourcas-Hosten, £11.25, Frank Stainton** Excellent value claret. Fourcas-Hosten is a good, reliable Cru Bourgeois. You'll need to put this aside for a few years, but you'll be glad you did.
- **1998 Château d'Angludet, £13.40, Tanners** Lovely rich stuff with good structure.
- **1998 Château Plaisance, St-Émilion, £12.95, The Wine Society** Really creamy, silky stuff. Very seductive.
- **1998 Château Petit Clos Figeac, St-Émilion Grand Cru, £9.75, H&H Bancroft** St-Émilion did brilliantly in 1998, and this has good concentration and supple fruit.
- **1998 Le 'D' de Dassault, St-Émilion, £12.99, Asda** The second wine of the excellent Château Dassault.

D'ISSAN *3ème cru classé Margaux* Traditionally one of the truest Margaux wines, austere when young, but perfumed and deep after ten to 12 years. Fabulous in 1990, but underperformed in the '90s. 2000 is intense, perfumed and balanced.

KIRWAN *3ème cru classé Margaux* ★★ Hugely improved, thanks largely to the efforts of oenologist Michel Rolland. Riper, richer – you name it. 2000 looks good.

LAFAURIE-PEYRAGUEY *1er cru Sauternes* ★★★ Fine sweet wine property once more regarded as one of the best Sauternes of all. Good in difficult years, and stunning in '83, '86, '88 and '90; 1997 also looks very good.

LAFITE-ROTHSCHILD *1er cru classé Pauillac* ★★★ Most difficult of all the great Médocs to get to know. It doesn't stand for power like Latour, or perfume like Mouton, but for the elegant, restrained balance that is the perfection of great claret. It often

> **ON THE CASE**
> The crus bourgeois of the
> Médoc are in the process of being
> reclassified: see page 160
> for details

shows poorly young, and needs years to develop, but '99 and 2000 look spectacular.

LAFLEUR *Pomerol* ★★★ The only Pomerol with the potential to be as great as Pétrus. They couldn't be further apart in style, and Lafleur has an astonishing austere concentration of dark fruit and tobacco spice perfume. 1999 is glorious, and the second wine, Pensées de Lafleur, is also great.

LAFON-ROCHET *4ème cru classé St-Estèphe* ★ A perennial favourite of mine for its austere but beautifully focused blackcurrant fruit and cedar perfume. 2000 is spicy and substantial.

LAGRANGE *3ème cru classé St-Julien* ★★ Continually impressive since the mid-80s, in good years and bad. The vineyard is high quality though set a little back from the traditionally superior river bank. Look particularly for the 1995, '96 and 2000.

LA LAGUNE *3ème cru classé Haut-Médoc* ★★ Making Second Growth-standard red, with a rich, soft intensity. 1995 and '96 are very good, 2000 very promising.

LAMOTHE-GUIGNARD *2ème cru Sauternes* ★ Recent years have seen dramatic improvements here. Usually pretty good these days.

LANESSAN *cru bourgeois Haut-Médoc* ★ Ever correct, consistently attractive. 1990 is a wine of balance and depth. Very promising 1995 and 1996.

LANGOA-BARTON *3ème cru classé St-Julien* ★★ £ Very good, in the dry, cedary style, and sometimes regarded as a lesser version of Léoville-Barton. 1989 and '96 almost matched Léoville-Barton for elegance and '90 and '95 were its equal. 1997 looks good, as does 2000.

LARRIVET-HAUT-BRION *Pessac-Léognan* ★★ The red 1996 here is superb wine with lots of finesse, but '98 wasn't so hot. 2000 is on form again, with plenty of tannin and rich, honeyed plums fruit. Lovely white, especially in 2000.

LASCOMBES *2ème cru classé Margaux* One of Bordeaux's great underachievers, with a poor track record since the mid-80s. Regular rumours of improvements are not substantiated by the mediocre quality in the glass. 2000 is attractive, but not outstanding.

LATOUR *1er cru classé Pauillac* ★★★ The easiest of all the First Growths to comprehend. It's a huge, dark, hard brute when young, eventually spreading out to a superb, blackcurrant and cedar flavour. It used to take ages to come round, but some recent vintages have seemed a little softer and lighter, whilst retaining their tremendous core of fruit. The superb '96 is the best wine of its year. 2000 has marvellous poise and balance. The second wine, les Forts-de-Latour, is of upper Classed-Growth level: look for the 2000. A third wine, simply called Pauillac, is made in most years, and very good it is too.

LATOUR-MARTILLAC *cru classé Pessac-Léognan* ★ Some ancient vines in a strictly organic vineyard have been fulfilling their potential since the mid-1980s, and quality stepped up again in the 90s. Ageworthy reds and whites that represent real value for money.

LATOUR-A-POMEROL *Pomerol* ★★ Directed by Christian Moueix of Pétrus, this property makes luscious wines with loads of gorgeous fruit and enough tannin to age well. Super-expensive.

LAVILLE-HAUT-BRION *cru classé Pessac-Léognan* ★★ This should be one of the greatest of all white Pessac-Léognan, since it is owned by Haut-Brion, but despite some great successes, the general effect is patchy. But 2000 looks stunning, all unctuous limes and smoke.

LÉOVILLE-BARTON *2ème cru classé St-Julien* ★★★ £ Traditionalist's dream, making superlative, old-fashioned wine for long aging. 1995, '96, '97, '98, '99 and 2000 are tremendous. All the wines are fairly priced, though hardly cheap.

LÉOVILLE-LAS-CASES *2ème cru classé St-Julien* ★★★ The most renowned of the St-Juliens, combining all that sweet, honeyed ripeness with strong, dry, cedary perfume. Prices are startlingly high. Recent vintages seem to me to be somewhat too manipulated. I wish they'd let the simple brilliance of the vineyard sing out.

LÉOVILLE-POYFERRÉ *2ème cru classé St-Julien* ★★ Things have been looking up here for some while, and 1995 is wonderful. The 1994 is remarkably good and 1996, too, is extremely attractive. 1999 and 2000 are intense.

LOUDENNE *cru bourgeois Médoc* Both red and white are fruity and agreeable, and best drunk young. New ownership is putting in more investment; it could be one to watch. 2000 looks appealing.

LA LOUVIÈRE *cru bourgeois Pessac-Léognan* ★★ (white) Lovely, modern, oak-aged whites. Reds are also very good, and quite earthy. Quality seems to be on a roll. White looks better than red in 2000.

LYNCH-BAGES *5ème cru classé Pauillac* ★★ Astonishingly soft and drinkable when very young, yet it ages brilliantly, and has one of the most beautiful scents of minty blackcurrant in all Bordeaux. 2000 is deep and tannic.

MAGDELAINE *1er grand cru classé St-Émilion* ★★ Combines the soft richness of Merlot with the sturdiness needed to age. Expensive, but one of the best.

MALARTIC-LAGRAVIÈRE *cru classé Pessac-Léognan* ★ Improving under its new ownership, but still a tough, traditional style. 1997 and '98 continue the good work. The 2000 red is good and ripe, the white attractive and grassy.

MALESCOT-ST-EXUPÉRY *3ème cru classé Margaux* ★★ Rather light in the 1980s, but since the 1995 vintage has returned to a beautiful perfumed style of classic Margaux.

DE MALLE *2ème cru Sauternes* ★ Good, relatively light sweet white. It went through a bad patch in the 1980s, but since '88 the wines have been back on course.

MARGAUX *1er cru classé Margaux* ★★★ Refinement and sheer, ravishing perfume: weightier and more consistent than in the past, yet with all its beauty intact. In the difficult '91 and '92 vintages the wines were better than most First Growths, and the '95 is stunning. 2000 is as good as claret gets.

MEYNEY *cru bourgeois St-Estèphe* ★ £ This epitomizes St-Estèphe reliability, yet is better than that. It is big, meaty and strong, but never harsh. Recent wines are increasingly impressive, although 1996 seems a touch disappointing.

LA MISSION-HAUT-BRION *cru classé Pessac-Léognan* ★★★ La Mission likes to put itself in a class apart, between Haut-Brion and the rest. Yet one often feels this red relies more on weight and massive, dark fruit and oak flavours than on any great subtleties. Even so it has considerable richness, with great consistency and fragrance. Glorious 1999 and 2000.

MONTROSE *2ème cru classé St-Estèphe*
★★ Famous for its dark, tannic character,
and its slow, ponderous march to maturity.
Wines in the 1990s have been more
forthcoming: '95, '96 and '97 are excellent.

MOUTON-ROTHSCHILD *1er cru
classé Pauillac* ★★★ An astonishing flavour,
piling intense cigar-box and lead-pencil
perfume on to the rich blackcurrant fruit.
The 1982 is already a legend, '86 and '89
are likely to join it, but '88 and '90 are
below par. The 1990s saw a parade of good
to superb wines: '95 is fabulous, '96 very
fine, and 2000 massive and dense.

NENIN *Pomerol* ★ Old-fashioned red,
rather chunky and solid with quite a tough
core for a Pomerol, which doesn't always
attain mellow fruitfulness. Recent vintages

VINS DE GARAGE

Okay, the name was originally a joke,
but it has stuck. These are wines made
on a tiny scale – *Le Pin* and *Valandraud*
are typical – from a couple of hectares
or less. The ideal is that you carve out
the very best nugget of vines, which
will give you something superb. (This
ideal is somewhat tarnished by the fact
that not all are on the very best
terroir.) They're made on so small a
scale that you could make them in
your garage. Geddit? Most are in St-
Émilion – there's *La Mondotte* and *Le
Dôme*, but Margaux now boasts
Marogallia, Pessac-Léognan has *Branon*,
and Entre-Deux-Mers has *Presidial*. All
are Merlot-based, if not entirely
Merlot. What they also share is a
super-concentrated style that critics
say masks the terroir; their critics also
say they can lack balance, so that they
dry out in a few years and age poorly.
People who love cult wines simply
adore them, however, and prices are
astronomical.

have improved, though, with a much better
1995 and '96, a seductive '99 and very
promising 2000.

PALMER *3ème cru classé Margaux* ★★
Palmer can occasionally out-perform some
First Growths in tastings. The 1980s weren't
so good, and the '83 surprisingly lacks some
of its neighbours' class. But 1990 was better
than most of them and '91 a great success in
a poor year. 1996 is very good, '99 lovely, as
is 2000. Second wine Alter Ego is excellent
in 2000.

PAPE-CLÉMENT *cru classé Pessac-
Léognan* ★★ Capable of mixing
considerable sweetness from ripe fruit and
new oak with a good deal of tough
structure. Outstanding since 1985, with the
1990 and '95 both examples of Pessac-
Léognan at its best. 2000 is dense, leathery
and classic; the white is balanced and
concentrated.

PAVIE *1er grand cru St-Émilion* ★
Generally good but not wonderful, stylish
but not grand. But it has the gentle flavours
of true St-Émilion. The best recent releases
show a deeper, more passionate style
which puts it into the top flight. 1990, '95,
'96 and '99 are good examples.

PETIT-VILLAGE *Pomerol* ★★ Not
usually one of the softest, most plummy
Pomerols. The wine is worth laying down,
but the price is always high. 2000 is
beautifully buttery.

PÉTRUS *Pomerol* ★★★ One of the
world's most expensive reds, and often one
of the greatest, its fame has been acquired
since 1945. 1982, '89, '90, '95, '98 and 2000
were stupendous; 1985, '96 and '99 aren't
far off.

DE PEZ *cru bourgeois St-Estèphe* ★ Almost
always of Classed Growth standard: big,
rather plummy and not too harsh. 1995 and
'96 are both successful.

PHÉLAN-SÉGUR *cru bourgeois St-Estèphe* ★ £ Classed Growth quality at a *bourgeois* price. Good rich fruit, and it ages well. 1995 and '96 are well worth a punt, and 2000 looks extremely promising.

PICHON-LONGUEVILLE *2ème cru classé Pauillac* ★★ Often described as more masculine than its 'sister', Pichon-Longueville-Lalande, this very correct Pauillac (formerly Pichon-Longueville-Baron) turned out a tremendous 1995, a very good '96 and '97 and a good '94. The 1990 is one of the Médoc's greatest. 2000 is wonderfully rich and supple.

PICHON-LONGUEVILLE-LALANDE *2ème cru classé Pauillac* ★★★ Rich, concentrated red of great quality. Its price has risen inexorably and it wishes to be seen as equal to St-Julien's leading pair, Léoville-Las-Cases and Ducru-Beaucaillou. Well, in general, it is. 1989 and '90 are below par, and easily outclassed by its neighbour Pichon-Longueville. But since then Lalande has been right back on form, and seems to have the edge on Longueville since '95 and '96.

LE PIN *Pomerol* ★★★ Tiny property that makes one of the most expensive wines in the world. It's very, very good, and utterly seductive. It reached cult status in the late '80s – if you didn't buy it then you probably can't afford it now. 1997 is lovely, though.

PONTET-CANET *5ème cru classé Pauillac* ★★ Famous but unpredictable, and still trying to regain its traditionally reliable form. Throughout the 1990s, however, the deep, ripe blackcurrant fruit has been in evidence, and 1995, '97 and '99 are very good.

POTENSAC *cru bourgeois Médoc* ★★ £ Delicious blackcurrant fruit, greatly improved by a strong taste of oak. Not expensive for the level of quality. Beats many *crus classés* every year for sheer

---

> ## ON THE CASE
> *Simple Bordeaux Blanc, at around £4 a bottle, is one of today's bargains – nearly all are excellent value*

flavour. Both the 1995 and '96 look good buys, as does 2000.

POUJEAUX *cru bourgeois Moulis* ★★ Good, spicy, rich wine with plenty of concentration; made to last. 1990, '93, '94, '95 and '97 are all excellent, as is 2000.

PRIEURÉ-LICHINE *4ème cru classé Margaux* ★ £ Reliable, fairly priced and, though not that perfumed, good and sound. 1990 was the first real excitement for some time. Throughout the 1990s progress was erratic, but things really showed improvement with excellent 1996 and good '99 and 2000.

RABAUD-PROMIS *1er cru Sauternes* ★★ Not well known, but a quality producer of serious sweet wine.

RAHOUL *cru bourgeois Graves* ★ A leader of the modern oak-aged white style, and generally good red.

RAUZAN-GASSIES *2ème cru classé Margaux* ★ One of the poorest Margaux Classed Growths despite its supposedly exalted Second Growth status. 1996 was the first exciting wine for a generation, and '99 continued the improvement. 2000 isn't quite as good as neighbouring Rauzan-Ségla.

RAUZAN-SÉGLA *2ème cru classé Margaux* ★★ Massive investment is producing dividends in terms of quality here. 1995 and '96 were excellent and '98 on top form. 2000 is a wine of great clarity and refinement.

RAYMOND LAFON *cru bourgeois Sauternes* ★★ Owned by the former manager of neighbouring d'Yquem, this is fine wine but overpriced.

RIEUSSEC *1er cru Sauternes* ★★★ One of the richest, most exotic Sauternes; will age superbly for 20 years or more. 1996, '97 and '98 confirm Rieussec's status.

ST-PIERRE *4ème cru classé St-Julien* ★★ Small property producing superb, slow-maturing, old-fashioned red. Produced wonderful wines in the 1980s, and judging by 1995 and '96 is still well on form.

SÉNÉJAC *cru bourgeois Haut-Médoc* Finesse rather than concentration. It made an excellent 1995 and has in fact been good pretty well every year. The white, made entirely from Sémillon, will age.

SIRAN *cru bourgeois Margaux* ★ All vintages have been good lately. 1995 and '96 look worth buying, as does 2000.

SMITH-HAUT-LAFITTE *cru classé Pessac-Léognan* ★★ Wonderfully elegant, exotic reds and ripe, white peach whites. Whites have been superb right through the 1990s and reds are now equally good. Excellent 2000.

SOCIANDO-MALLET *cru bourgeois Haut-Médoc* ★★ One of Bordeaux's star *crus bourgeois*. The wine has every sign of great classic red Bordeaux flavours to come – if you can wait for 10 to 15 years. The 2000 is attractive.

SUDUIRAUT *1er cru Sauternes* ★★ At its best, rich, exciting Sauternes, but doesn't always live up to its reputation as being only a step or so behind d'Yquem.

TALBOT *4ème cru classé St-Julien* ★ Has seemed in recent years to be lagging behind in quality. The 1990 seems to lack concentration, and the early '90s are disappointing. 1996 looks better, and 2000 is intense and tannic.

DU TERTRE *5ème cru classé Margaux* ★ Slightly uneven of late. At best it has a lot of body for a Margaux, and the flavour is pure. 1995 was disappointing but '96 is better.

TERTRE RôTEBOEUF *grand cru St-Émilion* ★★ Exceptional quality from an unclassified estate. The wines are rich, unctuous and complex, and quality is consistently good; the 1998 is stunning.

LA TOUR-DE-BY *cru bourgeois Médoc* ★ Well-made: plenty of juicy fruit, good structure and a touch of rusticity. Reliable: look for 1995, '96, '97 and 2000.

TROPLONG MONDOT *grand cru classé St-Émilion* ★★ A property ripe for promotion. Lovely lush wines, even in difficult years.

TROTANOY *Pomerol* ★★ This used to be considered just below Pétrus, and usually performed up to expectation. The wine is still excellent, but has been surpassed by other Pomerols as it has lost some of its concentrated richness.

VALANDRAUD *St-Émilion* ★★ The idea at this micro-property is to do everything with extreme care – which should be the norm at top Bordeaux properties, but isn't. How the wines will age is unproven, since the first vintage was 1991. 2000 is super-ripe, super-extracted.

VIEUX CHÂTEAU CERTAN *Pomerol* ★★ Sometimes practically as good as Pétrus, but more austere. 1995 is terrific, '96 very good, '97 lovely, '99 complex.

D'YQUEM *grand 1er cru classé Sauternes* ★★★ Almost every vintage of d'Yquem is a masterpiece and its outlandish price is almost justified, since d'Yquem at its best is undoubtedly the greatest sweet wine in the world. And it lasts – well, forever, really. There's also a dry white made here, called Ygrec, which can be remarkable.

BORDEAUX VINTAGES

Generic wines like Bordeaux Rouge rarely need any aging. A *petit château* wine from a good vintage might need five years to be at its best, a good *bourgeois* might need ten, and a *premier cru* might need 20. Pomerols and St-Émilions come round faster than Médocs.

2000   Very good, but not uniformly so. The Médoc, especially Margaux, Graves and Pomerol look lovely; St Émilion has too many over-extracted wines in what is anyway a very tannic year. Lesser wines should be chosen with caution, again because of that tannin. Good dry whites; very little Sauternes.

1999   An erratic vintage, spoiled by last-minute rain. Dry whites should be good, reds supple and ripe. Sauternes suffered from rot of the wrong sort.

1998   A Merlot year rather than a Cabernet one; Pomerol and St-Émilion look very good. There'll be some good Sauternes, too.

1997   A mixed vintage of mostly soft, semi-ripe wines, attractive for relatively early drinking. The wines have a certain uniformity – not only in flavour, but in being offered for sale at a price not related to their middling quality.

1996   The 1994s were hyped, the 1995s were hyped, and the 1996s too. Increasingly they look good but not great, and they're certainly expensive. Sauternes are good in parts.

1995   Red wines of charm and structure, with a handful of really great wines at the top. Not much noble rot in Sauternes, though the dry whites of the Graves look good.

1994   Most successful in Pomerol, though most regions produced reds with good concentration, but usually a rather over-aggressive tannic punch.

1993   A dilute year, in which the good wines are drinking nicely now. St-Émilion and Pomerol are probably best. Decent dry whites but little of quality in Sauternes.

1992   An unripe vintage: stick to reliable names and drink early.

1991   Wildly variable for reds, and few thrills in Sauternes. Dry whites were good. Most should have been drunk by now.

1990   Excellent quality; the third of a great trio of vintages. Reds are immensely rich, as are Sauternes; lesser regions like Loupiac also came up trumps. It was a bit too hot for the dry whites, though.

1989   Famous as a superripe Pomerol and St-Émilion year, though there were also many excellent Médocs. Graves and Pessac-Léognan were uneven, as was Sauternes. Dry whites were rather overripe.

1988   Classically balanced reds and very fine Sauternes.

1987   These have proved to be soft, attractively drinkable reds – but drink them up.

1986   Superb Sauternes, dripping with noble rot, and drinking beautifully now. Reds are good, sometimes very good, dark, deep and ripe.

1985   Pretty well all the reds are delicious now. Sauternes are pleasant but light.

1983   Fine claret, especially in Margaux, and delicious now. Superb, rich, exciting Sauternes.

EARLIER BORDEAUX VINTAGES

1981   Good but not spectacular. Quite light wines, which need drinking. A slightly graceless year in Sauternes.

1980   Nice light, grassy claret, which should have been drunk by now. The best Sauternes are still drinking well.

1979   All but the very best should be drunk up. There was attractive, mid-weight Sauternes.

1978   All but the top wines are starting to dry out now. Graves and St-Émilion are lovely, and won't improve.

1976   Rather soft and sweet; not inspiring, drink up. Best Sauternes are still fat and rich.

1975   Very tannic wines; frequently they went stale and brown before they had time to soften. The best may yet bloom; I'm not sure when. Nice, well-balanced Sauternes.

1966   All the wines are ready, and some are tipping over the edge.

1961   One of the classic vintages of the century, but now beginning to fade a little. Well, they had an amazing innings.

Most other vintages of the 1960s will now be risky; '64s can still be good, rather solid wines and '62, one of the most gorgeous, fragrant vintages since the war, is showing its age. If your godfather's treating you, and offers '59, '55 or '53, accept with enthusiasm. If he offers you '49, '47 or '45, get it in writing before he can change his mind.

MATURITY CHARTS
1997 Sauternes Premier Cru Classé
Complex wines that are delicious young but will also age well

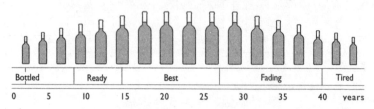

1999 Pessac-Léognan Cru Classé (white)

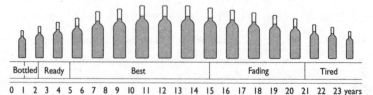

MATURITY CHARTS
1995 Cru Classé Médoc
A vintage for the medium to long term

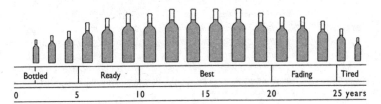

| Bottled | Ready | Best | Fading | Tired |

0   5   10   15   20   25 years

1995 Good Cru Bourgeois Médoc

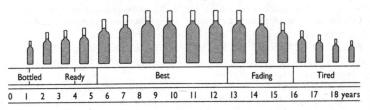

| Bottled | Ready | Best | Fading | Tired |

0 1 2 3 4 5 6 7 8 9 10 11 12 13 14 15 16 17 18 years

1996 Cru Classé Médoc
A good year, but less long-lived than 95

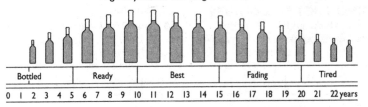

| Bottled | Ready | Best | Fading | Tired |

0 1 2 3 4 5 6 7 8 9 10 11 12 13 14 15 16 17 18 19 20 21 22 years

1996 Good Cru Bourgeois Médoc

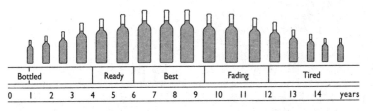

| Bottled | Ready | Best | Fading | Tired |

0 1 2 3 4 5 6 7 8 9 10 11 12 13 14 years

BUYING CLARET EN PRIMEUR

In the spring after the vintage the Bordeaux châteaux make their opening offers. This means that their capital is not tied up in very expensive stock for the next year or two, until the wines are bottled and ready to ship. In theory this also means that you can buy the wine at a preferential price – but do not forget that the cost of shipping, duties and other taxes will appear on your final bill. Traditionally merchants would buy for stock while offering their customers the chance to take advantage of the opening prices as well. In the heady days of the 1980s, however, the market really took off.

There is a lot to be said for buying en primeur. For one thing, you may be able to find the finest and rarest wines far more cheaply than they will ever appear again. This was especially true of the 1990 vintage.

But you should be aware of the risks: prices can go down as well as up. They may easily not increase significantly in the few years after the campaign (witness prices for 1985s and 1989s). The second risk is that a tasting assessment is difficult at an early date. However, consideration can be given to both the producer's reputation for consistency and to the general vintage assessment for the region.

Another risk is that the merchant you bought the wine from may not still be around to deliver it to you two years later. Buy from a merchant you can trust, one with a solid trading base in other wines.

Once the wines are shipped you may want your merchant to store the wine for you. If so, you should insist that (1) you receive a stock certificate; (2) your wines are stored separately from the merchant's own stocks; and (3) your cases are identifiable as your property and are labelled accordingly. All good merchants will offer these safeguards as a minimum service. Of course, in an ideal world your house is equipped with its own temperature-controlled cellar, because the best solution is certainly to take possession of your cases yourself.

USING THE PRICE GUIDES

In the Red Bordeaux Price Guides the châteaux are listed alphabetically regardless of appellation or class, with prices for each château given in order of vintage from the most recent to the oldest.

In the Médoc, there is a middle level of châteaux – cru bourgeois – below the crus classés. The bourgeois properties adhere to fairly strict rules governing winemaking, and are often excellent value.

There are some dramatic price variations here. Note that while most of the prices are per bottle, inclusive of all duty and VAT charges, others are per case, with extra to pay on top before you can have the wine delivered.

A wine quoted **EC** (ex-cellars) is offered on an en primeur basis (i.e. as a young wine) in Bordeaux or at the château in the summer following the vintage; one quoted **IB** (in bond) is offered in bond in the UK. All EC and IB prices are **per case**.

The EC price simply includes the price of the wine in the bottle and excludes shipping, duties and taxes such as VAT. The IB price includes shipping, but still excludes duties and taxes.

The EC price is usually payable when the wine is offered en primeur. Other costs (including VAT on both invoices) become payable when the wine is shipped. The crus classés and better bourgeois are shipped two years after the wine is offered, the petits châteaux and the lesser bourgeois after a year. You should check beforehand the exact terms of sale with your merchant who will give you a projection of the final 'duty paid delivered' price at current rates of shipping, duty and VAT.

RED BORDEAUX PRICES

d'Aiguilhe *Côtes de Castillon*
1998 IB £65.00 (BODX) £75.00 (FA)
1997 £7.99 (WAI)
1996 £8.72 (BIB)

Amiral-de-Beychevelle *St-Julien*
1995 £18.55 (GN)

Andron-Blanquet *cru grand bourgeois exceptionnel St-Estèphe*
1995 £13.10 (GN) £14.99 (AME)

Angélus *1er grand cru classé St-Émilion*
1999 £50.32 (MON)
1999 IB £470.00 (JU) £480.00 (RAE)
1998 £45.00 (FORT) £75.83 (MI)
1998 IB £540.00 (BAN) £595.00 (BODX) £710.00 (FRI) £880.00 (WY)
1997 £59.00 (BAL) £63.00 (JU) £66.95 (WAI) £70.00 (FORT)
1996 £52.88 (BAN) £62.08 (WY) £69.00 (JU) £84.00 (FRI)
1995 £77.26 (WY) £77.55 (BAN)
1995 IB £700.00 (FA) £750.00 (TUR)
1994 £32.00 (WS) £51.70 (BAN) £65.00 (BAL)
1993 £45.83 (FA)
1990 £141.98 (TUR) £164.50 (WY)
1990 IB £1,420.00 (FA)
1959 £164.50 (WY)

d'Angludet *cru bourgeois supérieur exceptionnel Margaux*
1999 £16.40 (NI)
1998 £14.95 (NI) £116.50 (TAN)
1997 £11.99 (BO) £16.49 (JON) £16.75 (NI) £18.50 (CON) £19.20 (TAN)
1996 £16.00 (FLE) £24.50 (CON)

1995 IB £140.00 (BODX)
1994 £18.49 (SUN) £18.49 (LAI) £18.99 (YOU) £22.03 (PLA)
1993 £16.00 (FLE)
1989 £24.68 (FA)
1988 £40.00 (FORT)
1987 £13.71 (TUR)
1986 £35.00 (CRO)
1983 £31.00 (HIG)
1982 £35.00 (BU)
1978 £48.00 (CRO)

des Annereaux *Lalande-de-Pomerol*
1997 £9.99 (POR) £11.49 (AME) £12.63 (PLAY)
1996 £8.95 (GN)
1995 £9.25 (CON)

Anthonic *cru bourgeois supérieur Moulis*
1999 IB £99.00 (CB)
1998 £12.16 (CB)
1997 £13.97 (PLA) £13.99 (VIL)
1989 £10.58 (BAN)

d'Ardennes *Graves*
1996 £10.52 (BAN)

d'Armailhac (was Mouton-Baronne-Philippe) *5ème cru classé Pauillac*
1999 IB £130.00 (HIG)
1997 £15.83 (MI) £17.00 (HIG)
1996 £18.50 (SOM) £18.99 (SUN) £18.99 (LAI) £19.50 (BU) £19.50 (HIG) £22.50 (UN) £24.17 (MI) £27.95 (STA) £29.65 (VIN)
1996 IB £155.00 (FA)
1995 £22.50 (UN) £23.89 (WY) £36.75 (TAN)

RETAILERS SPECIALIZING IN BORDEAUX
see Retailers Directory (page 40) for details

Adnams (AD), Averys, Ballantynes (BAL), Bennetts (BEN), Berry Bros. & Rudd (BER), Bibendum (BIB), Bordeaux Index (BODX), Butlers (BU), Anthony Byrne (BY), D Byrne, Cave Cru Classé, Corney & Barrow (CB), Croque-en-Bouche (CRO), Direct Wine (DI), Farr Vintners (FA), First Quench Group (BOT, THR, VIC, WR), Fortnum & Mason (FORT), Friarwood (FRI), Goedhuis & Co,

Great Western (GW), High Breck (HIG), Justerini & Brooks (JU), Lay & Wheeler (LAY), Millésima (MI), Montrachet (MON), Oddbins (OD), Paulson Rare Wines (PAU), Christopher Piper (PIP), Raeburn Fine Wines (RAE), Reid, T&W Wines (TW), Tanners (TAN), Turville Valley (TUR), Wine Society (WS), Peter Wylie (WY), Noel Young (YOU).

1994 £28.65 (TAN) £32.82 (PLAY)
1990 £27.00 (FLE)
1989 IB £350.00 (FA)
1986 IB £340.00 (FA)
1961 £282.00 (WY)
1945 £340.75 (WY)
1914 £334.88 (WY)

Arnauld *Haut-Médoc*
1997 £8.50 (WS)
1996 £11.09 (WAT)

d'Arricaud *Graves*
1988 £14.10 (BAN)

l'Arrosée *grand cru classé St-Émilion*
1998 £35.00 (MI)
1997 £26.67 (MI)
1996 £28.33 (MI) £35.00 (WS) £38.00 (JU)
1996 IB £240.00 (FA)
1994 £21.67 (MI)
1990 IB £500.00 (FA)
1988 £39.00 (CRO)
1986 IB £450.00 (FA)
1985 £55.23 (FA)
1982 IB £900.00 (FA)
1981 IB £265.00 (FA)
1981 magnum IB £695.00 (BODX)
1980 £14.10 (FA)

Ausone *1er grand cru classé St-Émilion*
1999 IB £1,150.00 (JU)
1998 £215.00 (MI)
1998 IB £1,250.00 (FA) £1,470.00 (FRI)
1997 £100.00 (WS) £120.00 (JU)
1996 £180.00 (JU) £215.00 (MI)
1995 IB £1,300.00 (FA)
1994 £133.33 (MI)
1994 IB £700.00 (FA)
1993 £90.28 (BY)
1990 £231.67 (MI)
1990 IB £1,350.00 (FA)
1989 £105.75 (BODX) £264.17 (MI)
1988 £94.90 (BY) £95.00 (CON)
1985 £88.13 (FA) £110.00 (FRI) £153.11
(PLAY)
1983 £111.63 (BODX)

---

*EC (ex-cellar) price per dozen,
excluding shipping, duty and VAT.
IB (in bond) price per dozen,
excluding duty and VAT.
All other prices, per bottle incl VAT.*

1982 £176.25 (BODX) £217.38 (TUR)
1982 IB £2,200.00 (FA)
1978 £84.13 (PAU)
1976 £108.10 (FA)
1936 £252.63 (WY)
1934 £230.00 (JU)

Bahans-Haut-Brion *Graves*
1999 IB £180.00 (JU)
1997 £24.95 (BAL) £26.00 (JU)
1995 £32.90 (WY)
1995 IB £245.00 (BODX) £260.00 (FA)
1995 ½ bottle £16.45 (WY)
1953 £87.30 (PAU)

Balestard-la-Tonnelle *grand cru classé
St-Émilion*
1995 £36.00 (STA)
1990 £23.50 (FA)

Baret *Pessac-Léognan*
1996 £11.75 (HIG)

Barreyres *cru bourgeois Haut-Médoc*
1998 £7.99 (SAI)
1995 £7.58 (CB)

Batailley *5ème cru classé Pauillac*
1999 IB £118.00 (HIG)
1998 £20.60 (NI)
1997 £17.50 (HIG) £19.95 (DI) £22.42 (BY)
1996 £19.58 (HIG) £19.99 (VIL)
1994 £19.99 (YOU)
1990 £35.00 (WS)
1986 £24.68 (FA) £34.99 (SUN)
1985 £27.03 (FA) £37.50 (BAL)
1983 IB £300.00 (TUR)
1982 IB £380.00 (FA)
1976 IB £240.00 (BODX)
1970 £31.00 (CRO)
1970 IB £240.00 (FA)
1966 £47.62 (PAU) £52.00 (YOU)

Beau-Séjour-Bécot *1er grand cru classé
St-Émilion*
1998 £26.60 (TAN)
1997 £33.19 (CB) £35.70 (TAN)
1996 £32.99 (OD)
1986 £44.99 (BO)

Beau-Site *cru grand bourgeois
exceptionnel St-Estèphe*
1996 £10.99 (OD) £14.75 (HAH)
1995 £13.75 (WS)
1982 £15.28 (FA)

Beaumont *cru grand bourgeois Haut-Médoc*
1997 £12.50 (MAY)
1996 £9.75 (WS) £11.75 (BAN) £12.35 (HIC) £12.95 (CON) £13.95 (RIC)
1995 £11.16 (BIB) £12.95 (WS) £15.25 (BALL)

Beausejour *Côtes de Castillon*
1998 £7.05 (CB)
1997 £6.40 (HAH)

Beauséjour *cru bourgeois St-Estèphe*
1966 £25.00 (BU)

Beauséjour-Duffau-Lagarrosse *1er grand cru classé St-Émilion*
1999 IB £298.00 (JU)
1996 £50.00 (JU)
1992 IB £190.00 (BODX)
1990 IB £3,050.00 (FA)
1970 £29.50 (BU)
1959 £45.00 (BU)

Bel-Air *Pomerol*
1997 £18.86 (CB)
1989 IB £140.00 (FA)

Bel-Air *Puisseguin-St-Émilion*
1985 £43.50 (STE)

Bel-Air-Marquis d'Aligre *cru bourgeois supérieur exceptionnel Margaux*
1986 £25.00 (MI)

Belair *1er grand cru classé St-Émilion*
1996 £27.92 (ARM)
1995 £25.00 (BU)

de Belcier *Côtes de Castillon*
1996 £7.99 (CON)
1994 £7.29 (GN) £8.99 (AME)

Belgrave *5ème cru classé Haut-Médoc*
1999 £10.57 (MON)
1998 £18.33 (MI)
1996 £14.99 (YOU) £19.17 (MI)
1995 £15.99 (SAI) £20.00 (PEN)
1970 £52.87 (TW)

Belles-Graves *Lalande-de-Pomerol*
2000 EC £74.00 (MON)

Bellevue *grand cru classé St-Émilion*
1996 IB £90.00 (FA)
1966 £22.50 (BU)

Bertin *Montagne-St-Émilion*
1999 IB £70.00 (CB)
1998 £8.70 (CB)

Beychevelle *4ème cru classé St-Julien*
1999 IB £150.00 (JU)
1998 £25.75 (NI) £25.83 (MI)
1997 £21.67 (MI)
1996 £19.98 (FA) £24.68 (BAN) £30.53 (PLAY) £31.50 (FRI) £31.67 (MI) £39.45 (STE)
1996 double magnum £91.65 (WY)
1995 £29.00 (HIG) £29.38 (WY) £29.95 (CON) £30.83 (MI)
1994 £22.33 (BAN) £24.50 (UN) £26.67 (MI) £35.50 (STA)
1994 IB £185.00 (FA)
1993 £25.83 (MI) £26.83 (WY)
1993 IB £230.00 (TUR)
1990 IB £460.00 (FA)
1990 magnum IB £460.00 (FA)
1989 £86.22 (PLAY)
1989 IB £520.00 (FA)
1988 £47.50 (FRI) £58.28 (BY)
1988 IB £420.00 (FA)
1988 magnum IB £420.00 (FA)
1987 IB £270.00 (BODX)

1986 £59.00 (FRI)
1986 IB £490.00 (FA)
1985 £29.38 (BAN)
1985 IB £475.00 (BODX)
1984 £26.95 (FRI)
1983 £47.00 (BODX)
1983 magnum £115.00 (FRI)
1982 £89.00 (FRI) £92.00 (BAL)
1982 IB £720.00 (FA)
1981 £47.00 (WY)
1978 £45.00 (BAL)
1975 double magnum £146.88 (FA)
1970 £43.00 (YOU)
1970 IB £420.00 (BODX)
1967 IB £330.00 (BODX)
1961 £246.75 (WY)
1961 IB £1,750.00 (TUR)
1959 £173.90 (WY)
1959 IB £1,200.00 (FA)
1955 £55.55 (PAU)
1949 £206.35 (PAU)
1945 £440.63 (WY)
1937 £58.75 (WY)
1934 £93.65 (PAU)
1928 £352.50 (FA)

le Bon-Pasteur *Pomerol*
1999 IB £340.00 (FRI)
1998 £79.00 (POR)
1998 IB £420.00 (FA)
1998 magnum IB £430.00 (FA)
1997 £26.67 (MI)
1996 £27.77 (CB)
1995 £49.75 (STA)
1990 £47.00 (FA) £61.90 (PAU)
1959 £49.20 (PAU)

la Bonnelle *St-Émilion*
1998 £10.24 (GN)

Bonnet *Bordeaux Supérieur*
1998 £7.49 (BOT) £7.49 (VIC) £7.49 (WR)
1997 £7.49 (THR)

le Boscq *cru bourgeois supérieur St-Estèphe*
1998 £16.67 (MI)
1997 £13.00 (JU) £14.17 (MI) £14.50 (TAN)
1996 £14.00 (JU) £17.50 (MI)

Bouscaut *cru classé Pessac-Léognan*
1996 £16.50 (UN)
1989 £16.99 (RAE)
1967 £38.99 (RAE)
1962 £30.15 (PAU)

Boyd-Cantenac *3ème cru classé Margaux*
1992 IB £115.00 (FA)
1986 IB £250.00 (FA)
1982 IB £320.00 (FA)
1980 £14.50 (BU)

Branaire *4ème cru classé St-Julien*
1998 £25.83 (MI)
1997 £21.67 (MI) £23.56 (CB) £26.50 (FORT) £26.90 (TAN)
1996 £26.50 (FORT) £27.90 (TAN) £28.50 (NI) £31.67 (MI)
1996 IB £185.00 (FA)
1995 £25.00 (FLE) £29.38 (WY)
1995 IB £230.00 (FA)
1995 double magnum £152.75 (WY)
1994 £26.95 (LEA)
1992 IB £150.00 (BODX)
1990 £48.00 (AME)
1989 IB £400.00 (FA)
1986 £35.25 (BODX)
1982 IB £450.00 (FA)
1979 IB £240.00 (FA)
1979 double magnum £94.00 (FA)
1978 £29.38 (WY)
1975 IB £290.00 (BODX)
1970 £48.00 (CRO)
1959 £129.25 (WY)
1929 £250.00 (CRO)

Brane-Cantenac *2ème cru classé Margaux*
1999 IB £171.00 (RAE) £175.00 (FRI)
1997 £21.67 (MI)
1997 IB £150.00 (BAN)
1995 £18.80 (BAN) £35.00 (UN)
1988 IB £310.00 (BODX)
1987 magnum £55.00 (BALL)
1986 IB £360.00 (FA)
1983 IB £380.00 (FA)
1978 £25.85 (FA) £32.31 (BAN)
1975 magnum £47.00 (BODX) £50.92 (TUR)
1970 IB £220.00 (FA) £340.00 (BODX)
1967 £22.50 (BU)
1962 £47.62 (PAU)
1961 £141.00 (WY)
1928 £320.00 (JU)
1928 IB £3,000.00 (FA)
1920 £200.00 (CRO)

du Breuil *cru bourgeois supérieur Haut-Médoc*
1996 £9.99 (UN)
1995 £12.30 (TAN)

Brillette *cru bourgeois supérieur exceptionnel Haut-Médoc*
1989 £12.95 (BU)

Cabannieux *Graves*
1995 £7.75 (CON)
1959 £55.55 (PAU)
1953 £47.62 (PAU)

Cadet-Piola *grand cru classé St-Émilion*
1995 £39.99 (VIL)
1989 IB £250.00 (FA)
1985 IB £220.00 (FA)
1983 IB £240.00 (FA)
1936 £111.11 (PAU)

Calon *Montagne-St-Émilion*
1961 £99.88 (WY)

Calon-Ségur *3ème cru classé St-Estèphe*
1999 IB £155.00 (JU) £204.00 (CB)
1998 £20.00 (JU)
1997 £17.53 (WY) £18.50 (JU) £20.40 (TAN)
1997 IB £210.00 (BAN)
1996 £29.38 (BAN) £30.00 (UN) £31.95 (DI) £35.00 (JU) £35.25 (WY) £36.00 (FRI) £36.67 (MI) £39.99 (CON)
1996 IB £265.00 (FA) £340.00 (TUR)
1995 £41.13 (WY) £47.80 (TAN) £50.00 (VIL) £51.00 (FRI) £70.93 (BY)
1995 IB £360.00 (FA) £380.00 (TUR)
1994 £23.50 (UN) £23.50 (BAN) £34.00 (TAN)
1993 £25.50 (UN)
1990 IB £520.00 (FA) £560.00 (TUR)
1989 £58.75 (WY)
1989 IB £420.00 (FA)
1988 £43.50 (WRI)
1986 £41.13 (BODX) £44.00 (CRO) £49.50 (BU)
1986 IB £420.00 (FA)
1985 £37.60 (TUR)
1983 £41.13 (WY)
1981 £28.20 (WY)
1966 £45.00 (BU)
1959 £164.50 (WY)
1955 £61.90 (PAU)
1945 £105.75 (WY) £206.35 (PAU)
1943 £111.11 (PAU)
1936 £142.85 (PAU)

Cambon-la-Pelouse *cru bourgeois supérieur Haut-Médoc*
1998 £10.95 (LEA)

de Camensac *5ème cru classé Haut-Médoc*
1996 £22.50 (UN)
1996 IB £110.00 (BODX)
1995 £14.50 (BU)
1993 £25.85 (WRI)
1989 £18.50 (BU)
1988 IB £180.00 (FA)
1985 £20.00 (BU)

Cana *Côtes de Bourg*
1996 £6.50 (FRI)
1995 £6.50 (FRI)

Canon *1er grand cru classé St-Émilion*
1999 IB £113.00 (CB)
1997 £9.58 (ARM) £26.67 (MI) £32.67 (CB)
1996 IB £250.00 (TUR)
1995 £15.83 (ARM) £25.00 (CON) £33.50 (FRI) £37.50 (UN)
1994 £12.08 (ARM) £27.50 (MI) £35.89 (JON)
1990 £64.63 (WY)
1990 IB £440.00 (FA)
1989 £75.00 (FORT)
1989 IB £495.00 (BODX)
1988 £35.25 (FA) £47.50 (FRI) £53.26 (BY)
1986 £44.65 (FA) £59.00 (FRI) £75.22 (PLAY)
1985 £49.35 (FA) £60.00 (JU)
1982 £88.13 (TUR) £112.50 (BEN)
1982 IB £900.00 (FA)
1979 £31.73 (FA)
1978 £35.25 (BODX)
1971 £47.62 (PAU)
1966 IB £650.00 (FA)
1962 £47.62 (PAU)

Canon-de-Brem *Canon-Fronsac*
1997 £12.57 (CB)
1996 £14.04 (CB)
1993 £11.75 (WS)

Canon-la-Gaffelière *grand cru classé St-Émilion*
1997 £39.90 (TAN)
1996 £32.31 (BAN) £35.00 (CON) £37.50 (MI) £44.59 (CB)
1996 IB £245.00 (FA) £270.00 (TUR)
1995 £29.95 (CON)

All châteaux are listed alphabetically regardless of class.

1993 £17.63 (BODX)
1990 IB £500.00 (FA)
1989 £235.00 (WY)
1989 IB £450.00 (FA)
1985 £29.38 (FA)
1983 £29.38 (WY)
1966 £35.00 (BU)

Canon-Moueix *Canon-Fronsac*
1999 IB £108.00 (CB)
1996 £14.28 (CB)
1995 £15.00 (ARM)

Canteloup *1ères Côtes de Blaye*
1998 £7.50 (WIN)

Cantemerle *5ème cru classé Haut-Médoc*
1999 IB £105.00 (HIG)
1998 £20.00 (MI) £22.00 (POR)
1997 £15.00 (MI)
1996 £15.86 (BAN) £18.35 (SOM) £19.75
  (NI) £19.99 (SAI) £22.00 (WRI) £22.50
  (MI) £22.50 (UN) £24.50 (CON)
1996 IB £160.00 (BODX) £160.00 (FA)
  £185.00 (TUR)
1995 £19.98 (BAN) £20.00 (MI) £20.00
  (ARM) £22.25 (STE) £22.50 (UN) £22.99
  (VIL)
1995 IB £185.00 (TUR)
1994 £21.15 (BAN)
1990 £29.75 (WRI) £30.00 (HIG) £33.78
  (BAN)
1990 IB £375.00 (BODX)
1989 £53.60 (TAN)
1989 IB £420.00 (BODX) £420.00 (FA)
1986 £30.55 (BAN)
1981 £23.50 (BODX)
1979 £27.50 (BU) £28.20 (FA)
1957 £39.68 (PAU)

Cantenac-Brown *3ème cru classé Margaux*
1998 £22.50 (MI)
1997 £18.33 (MI)
1996 £17.04 (BAN) £30.00 (UN)
1995 £24.50 (AME) £24.99 (VIL) £29.50
  (UN)
1990 £21.15 (FA)
1966 IB £345.00 (BODX)
1955 £39.68 (PAU)

Cap-de-Faugères *Côtes de Castillon*
1997 £7.80 (BAC) £7.95 (HAH)
1996 £7.98 (BIB)
1995 £7.64 (BAN)

Cap-de-Mourlin *grand cru classé St-Émilion*
1978 IB £155.00 (FA)
1959 £34.92 (PAU)

Carbonnieux *cru classé Pessac-Léognan*
1998 £20.00 (MI)
1996 £20.83 (MI)
1994 £17.50 (MI)
1988 IB £165.00 (BODX)

de Cardaillan *Graves*
1996 £9.95 (COC)

la Cardonne *cru grand bourgeois Médoc*
1997 £9.99 (POR)
1996 £9.99 (OD)
1995 £10.00 (PEN) £14.50 (CRO)

les Carmes-Haut-Brion *Pessac-Léognan*
1995 £17.63 (WY)
1959 £117.50 (FA)

Caronne-Ste-Gemme *cru grand bourgeois exceptionnel Haut-Médoc*
1997 £9.99 (MORR) £11.99 (BUD)
1996 IB £86.00 (FA)
1995 £11.95 (SOM) £14.20 (JER)
1994 £11.99 (BUD) £13.40 (TAN) £14.99
  (POR)
1993 £14.95 (BALL)
1990 IB £155.00 (FA)
1983 IB £145.00 (FA)
1970 £20.00 (BU)

Carruades de Lafite (Moulin des Carruades until 1987) *Pauillac*
1999 IB £155.00 (JU) £160.00 (FA) £165.00
  (HIG)
1998 £17.63 (BODX) £21.00 (JU) £25.00
  (MI)
1998 IB £170.00 (HIG) £185.00 (TUR)
1997 £17.50 (WS) £21.00 (JU)
1997 IB £165.00 (TUR)
1996 £23.44 (BAN) £24.00 (CRO) £25.00
  (UN) £25.50 (NI) £25.85 (WY) £27.00 (JU)
  £30.00 (MI) £35.00 (VIL)
1996 IB £210.00 (FA) £225.00 (BODX)
1995 £29.17 (MI) £29.38 (WY)
1995 IB £250.00 (FA)
1993 £22.50 (BU)
1990 £42.30 (TUR)
1989 IB £360.00 (FA)
1983 IB £330.00 (FA) £350.00 (BODX)
1934 £152.75 (WY)

Carsin *lères Côtes de Bordeaux*
1998 £6.99 (SAI)
1997 £9.25 (WAI)

Cazebonne *Graves*
1997 £8.85 (JER)

Certan-Giraud *Pomerol*
1997 £31.02 (CB)
1995 £29.50 (WS) £38.87 (CB)
1982 IB £400.00 (FA)

Certan-de-May *Pomerol*
1999 IB £440.00 (JU) £585.00 (CB)
1998 £72.00 (JU)
1998 IB £595.00 (FA)
1997 £46.00 (JU) £55.28 (CB)
1996 £44.50 (LAY) £60.34 (CB) £70.00 (JU)
1995 IB £420.00 (FA)
1993 IB £250.00 (FA)
1990 £61.90 (PAU) £140.00 (JU)
1990 IB £695.00 (BODX) £720.00 (FA)
1988 £29.38 (TUR) £80.00 (FORT)
1988 IB £620.00 (BODX)
1986 IB £550.00 (FA)
1982 £196.23 (FA)
1982 IB £2,500.00 (TUR)
1979 £52.88 (FA)
1975 £79.36 (PAU)
1975 IB £680.00 (FA)
1950 £301.59 (PAU)

la Chapelle de la Mission *Pessac-Léognan*
1999 IB £135.00 (FA) £140.00 (JU)
1998 £21.00 (JU)
1996 IB £180.00 (FA)

Charmail *cru bourgeois Haut-Médoc*
1999 £9.20 (MON)
1998 £13.95 (LEA)
1996 £10.00 (UN)
1995 £11.16 (BAN)

Charron *lères Côtes de Blaye*
1997 £7.50 (TAN)
1992 £10.52 (TW)

Chasse-Spleen *cru grand bourgeois exceptionnel Moulis*
1999 IB £115.00 (JU)
1998 £16.99 (OD) £17.50 (FORT) £20.83 (MI)
1998 IB £180.00 (BAN)
1997 £18.60 (TAN) £18.95 (FORT)

1996 £19.99 (UN) £20.00 (JU) £21.67 (MI) £22.91 (PLA) £24.95 (FRI) £25.50 (STA) £28.50 (LAY) £30.32 (BY)
1995 £17.95 (CON) £22.99 (VIL) £26.95 (FRI)
1994 £19.17 (MI) £30.00 (FORT)
1992 IB £135.00 (FA)
1990 IB £350.00 (FA)
1989 £34.35 (NO) £46.60 (TAN)
1986 £39.00 (CRO)
1986 IB £350.00 (FA)
1986 magnum £164.97 (NO)
1985 £42.00 (CRO)
1985 IB £350.00 (FA)
1983 £31.00 (CRO)
1982 IB £380.00 (FA) £395.00 (BODX)
1971 £22.50 (BU)

Chauvin *grand cru classé St-Émilion*
1998 £18.99 (SUN) £18.99 (LAI)
1995 £25.00 (JU)

Cheval-Blanc *1er grand cru classé St-Émilion*
1999 IB £1,200.00 (TUR) £1,200.00 (FA) £1,250.00 (JU)
1998 £198.33 (MI)
1998 IB £1,950.00 (FA)
1997 £89.17 (MI) £98.85 (TAN) £99.00 (JU)
1997 IB £790.00 (FA) £852.00 (BAN)
1996 £105.00 (TAN) £108.69 (BAN) £110.00 (UN) £119.50 (LAY) £135.00 (FRI) £148.00 (JU) £165.83 (MI)
1995 £122.20 (BAN) £125.00 (WS) £169.00 (FRI) £180.00 (STA) £206.67 (MI)
1995 IB £1,225.00 (FA) £1,250.00 (BODX)
1994 £70.50 (BAN) £70.50 (FA) £125.00 (PEN) £133.33 (MI)
1994 IB £750.00 (BODX) £770.00 (TUR)
1994 ½ bottle IB £720.00 (FA)
1993 £48.00 (FLE)
1993 IB £680.00 (FA)
1992 £93.50 (BAL)
1992 IB £720.00 (FA) £725.00 (BODX)
1990 £284.13 (PAU) £293.75 (TUR) £350.00 (JU)
1990 magnum £596.90 (FA)
1989 £117.50 (TUR) £129.25 (BODX) £140.00 (BEN) £239.17 (MI)
1989 IB £1,350.00 (FA)
1988 £110.00 (BEN) £123.38 (WY) £173.90 (TW)
1988 IB £1,150.00 (BODX) £1,150.00 (FA)
1988 ½ bottle £56.40 (FA)
1988 magnum £215.03 (FA)

1986 £210.56 (BY)
1986 IB £1,320.00 (FA)
1986 magnum £276.13 (WY)
1986 magnum IB £1,320.00 (FA)
1985 £195.00 (DI)
1983 IB £1,900.00 (FA)
1982 £350.00 (JU) £411.25 (BODX)
£525.00 (FORT) £4,200.00 (FA)
1982 IB £4,400.00 (TUR)
1981 £111.63 (WY)
1981 IB £950.00 (FA)
1979 £88.13 (FA)
1978 £130.00 (JU)
1978 IB £950.00 (FA)
1975 £135.13 (BODX) £166.67 (PAU)
1975 IB £1,400.00 (FA)
1974 IB £500.00 (BODX)
1974 magnum IB £575.00 (BODX)
1970 £164.50 (WY) £174.60 (PAU)
1970 IB £1,280.00 (FA)
1970 ½ bottle £70.50 (WY)
1966 £205.63 (WY)
1964 £311.38 (TUR) £352.50 (FA)
1959 £164.50 (WY)
1953 £323.13 (WY)
1953 ½ bottle £111.63 (WY)
1952 £174.60 (PAU)
1950 £446.50 (FA)
1949 ½ bottle £235.00 (WY)
1945 £933.38 (WY)
1934 £300.00 (JU)

Chicane *Graves*
1997 £9.60 (TAN)

Cissac *cru grand bourgeois exceptionnel Haut-Médoc*
1999 IB £85.00 (JU)
1998 IB £96.00 (BAN)
1998 EC £98.00 (TAN)
1997 £12.50 (TAN) £13.95 (DI)
1997 IB £144.00 (BAN)
1996 £11.75 (BAN) £14.75 (BU) £14.95 (DI)
£14.99 (UN) £15.95 (POR) £17.95 (CON)
£19.75 (VIN)
1996 magnum £38.99 (UN)
1995 £13.95 (CON) £14.10 (BAN) £15.75
(BU) £15.99 (JON)
1995 magnum £37.99 (UN)
1994 £14.10 (BAN)
1994 magnum £34.99 (UN)
1993 £16.25 (BALL)
1990 £26.95 (TAN)
1989 £22.91 (BAN) £26.20 (TAN)
1988 £21.74 (BAN) £27.60 (TAN)

Citran *cru grand bourgeois exceptionnel Haut-Médoc*
1998 £14.17 (MI) £14.50 (FORT)
1997 £13.50 (HIG) £14.50 (FORT)
1996 £15.00 (MI) £16.49 (SUN) £16.49 (LAI)
1995 £19.39 (DOM)
1988 IB £170.00 (BODX)

la Clare *cru bourgeois Médoc*
1997 £8.99 (VIL)
1996 £8.87 (PLA)

Clarke *cru bourgeois Listrac*
1983 IB £200.00 (FA)
1982 IB £240.00 (FA)

Clerc-Milon *5ème cru classé Pauillac*
1998 £26.67 (MI)
1997 £20.00 (MI) £27.95 (DI)
1996 £22.33 (BAN) £24.95 (DI) £32.50 (MI)
£35.00 (UN)
1995 £21.50 (DI) £29.50 (UN) £41.13 (WY)
1994 £24.50 (UN)
1993 £17.50 (WS)
1992 £14.69 (TUR)
1989 £70.50 (FA)
1986 IB £380.00 (FA)
1985 £54.05 (WY)

Clinet *Pomerol*
1999 IB £455.00 (JU)
1998 £62.00 (JU)
1998 IB £576.00 (BAN) £580.00 (FA)
£750.00 (WY)
1997 £32.70 (WY) £48.00 (JU)
1996 £64.63 (BAN) £85.00 (JU)
1996 IB £520.00 (FA) £540.00 (BODX)
£550.00 (TUR)
1995 £82.25 (BAN)
1995 IB £720.00 (TUR) £780.00 (FA)
1994 £37.60 (BAN) £49.35 (WY)
1993 IB £350.00 (FA)
1990 £141.00 (WY)
1989 £200.00 (JU)
1989 IB £1,975.00 (BODX)

Clos Beauregard *Pomerol*
1999 £10.18 (MON)
1995 £20.00 (FLE)

Clos du Clocher *Pomerol*
1999 IB £130.00 (FA) £140.00 (JU)
1998 IB £160.00 (FA)
1995 £23.50 (BALL)
1989 £50.00 (JU)

Clos de l'Eglise *Lalande-de-Pomerol*
1999 IB £60.00 (JU)
1998 £10.50 (JU)
1998 IB £750.00 (FA) £760.00 (BODX)
 £780.00 (FRI)
1992 IB £140.00 (BODX)
1990 £27.03 (FA)
1982 £52.95 (NI)

Clos Fourtet *1er grand cru classé St-Émilion*
1998 £37.50 (MI)
1998 IB £330.00 (FRI)
1996 £30.83 (MI) £39.00 (JU) £48.00 (STA)
1996 IB £240.00 (FA)
1995 £33.50 (FRI)
1994 £25.00 (MI) £25.00 (MAY) £25.99 (VIL)
1986 £23.50 (FA)
1982 £39.68 (PAU)
1950 £125.40 (PAU)
1949 £170.38 (WY)

Clos des Jacobins *grand cru classé St-Émilion*
1996 £27.03 (BAN)
1995 £18.80 (BAN)
1989 IB £250.00 (FA)
1985 £23.50 (FA)
1936 £111.11 (PAU)

Clos du Marquis *St-Julien*
1999 IB £130.00 (JU) £169.00 (CB)
1998 £24.32 (CB)
1998 IB £180.00 (WY)
1997 £16.00 (WS) £23.50 (BAL) £25.00 (JU)
 £25.50 (CB)
1996 £25.99 (OD) £27.35 (SOM) £31.49
 (CB) £32.00 (JU)
1996 IB £175.00 (BODX) £180.00 (FA)
 £195.00 (TUR)
1995 £30.00 (JU) £33.50 (NI)
1995 IB £195.00 (FA)
1994 £20.42 (ARM)
1994 IB £195.00 (TUR)
1990 IB £360.00 (FA)
1986 £29.38 (BODX)
1986 IB £365.00 (FA)

Clos René *Pomerol*
1998 £19.50 (JU)
1998 IB £180.00 (BAN) £180.00 (FRI)
 £180.00 (FA)
1996 £17.50 (MI) £17.50 (WS)
1995 £17.49 (SUN) £17.49 (LAI) £21.00
 (BAC) £30.80 (BY)
1994 £18.33 (MI) £22.99 (TES)
1989 £24.68 (FA)
1988 IB £250.00 (FA)
1961 £246.75 (WY)

du Clos Renon *Bordeaux*
1995 £7.50 (FRI)

Connétable de Talbot *St-Julien*
1997 £14.10 (JER)
1996 £16.67 (MI)
1996 IB £105.00 (FA)
1995 £16.67 (MI) £17.90 (RIC)

la Conseillante *Pomerol*
1998 £72.00 (JU) £84.17 (MI) £94.00 (CB)
1998 IB £680.00 (FRI)
1996 £49.50 (LAY) £50.00 (MI) £60.00 (JU)
 £70.89 (CB)
1996 IB £360.00 (FA)
1995 £56.00 (FRI) £62.00 (FLE) £70.00 (JU)
1994 £40.83 (MI) £42.00 (WS) £50.00 (PEN)
1994 magnum £85.00 (BU)
1990 £123.38 (BODX)
1990 IB £1,400.00 (FA)
1989 £135.13 (TUR) £172.72 (WY)
1989 IB £1,320.00 (FA)
1986 magnum IB £480.00 (FA)
1982 £122.20 (FA) £193.88 (WY)
1982 IB £1,320.00 (BODX) £1,350.00 (TUR)
1975 magnum £117.50 (BODX)
1962 £47.62 (PAU)
1945 £258.50 (WY)

Corbin *grand cru classé St-Émilion*
1996 £19.99 (UN)

Cos d'Estournel *2ème cru classé St-Estèphe*
1999 IB £320.00 (FRI)
1998 £40.00 (JU) £47.50 (MI)
1998 IB £345.00 (WY) £380.00 (FRI)
1997 £47.50 (MI) £49.95 (BAL) £51.00 (JU)
 £53.30 (TAN) £55.58 (CB)
1996 £64.63 (WY) £67.50 (FRI) £71.67 (MI)
 £79.50 (BU)
1996 magnum £180.00 (FORT)
1996 imperial £493.50 (WY)

1995 £50.00 (FORT) £66.00 (FRI)
1995 IB £520.00 (FA)
1995 imperial £470.00 (WY)
1994 £42.99 (VIL)
1990 £86.07 (WY)
1990 IB £850.00 (FA)
1989 £69.00 (FRI) £77.70 (LAY) £79.90 (TAN) £94.56 (PLAY)
1989 IB £645.00 (BODX) £650.00 (TUR) £650.00 (FA)
1989 magnum IB £650.00 (FA)
1988 £47.50 (CON)
1986 £70.50 (TUR) £72.50 (CON)
1986 IB £750.00 (BODX) £760.00 (FA)
1985 £70.00 (BU) £81.03 (PLA) £86.07 (WY) £97.50 (BEN)
1985 IB £750.00 (FA)
1985 double magnum £311.38 (FA)
1983 £45.00 (BU) £47.00 (WY) £49.35 (TUR)
1983 IB £450.00 (FA)
1983 magnum £135.00 (CON)
1982 £117.50 (TUR) £130.00 (BEN)
1982 IB £1,250.00 (BODX) £1,280.00 (FA)
1981 £35.00 (YOU) £45.00 (BAC)
1978 IB £520.00 (FA)
1977 £20.00 (YOU)
1977 imperial £164.50 (FA)
1975 £70.00 (PEN)
1970 £55.00 (BU) £82.25 (WY)
1970 IB £500.00 (FA)
1970 magnum £158.63 (WY)
1970 magnum IB £500.00 (FA)
1966 £47.00 (FA) £61.90 (PAU)
1961 £323.13 (WY)
1947 £174.60 (PAU)

Cos Labory *5ème cru classé St-Estèphe*
1996 £22.75 (NI)
1995 £22.50 (STA)
1994 £17.50 (RIC)
1986 £22.50 (BU)

Coufran *cru bourgeois Haut-Médoc*
1996 £12.99 (SAI)
1995 £14.95 (BER) £15.99 (VIL)
1994 £12.70 (STE)

---

*EC (ex-cellar) price per dozen,
excluding shipping, duty and VAT.
IB (in bond) price per dozen,
excluding duty and VAT.
All other prices, per bottle incl VAT.*

---

la Couspaude *grand cru St-Émilion*
1998 £36.67 (MI) £38.60 (NI)
1998 IB £320.00 (FA)
1996 £33.95 (DI)
1995 £23.75 (NEZ) £26.67 (MI)

Couvent-des-Jacobins *grand cru classé St-Émilion*
1996 £26.00 (WS)

le Crock *cru grand bourgeois exceptionnel St-Estèphe*
1998 £13.22 (BIB)
1993 £13.95 (BALL) £15.98 (LLO)
1990 £24.68 (COC)
1949 £79.36 (PAU)

la Croix *Pomerol*
1993 £22.43 (NO)

la Croix-du-Casse *Pomerol*
1998 £26.00 (JU)
1998 IB £264.00 (BAN)
1997 £19.95 (BAL) £22.00 (JU) £24.25 (BER)
1996 £21.50 (BAL) £22.99 (YOU) £23.00 (JU) £32.90 (BAN)
1995 £30.00 (JU) £31.73 (BAN)
1995 IB £180.00 (FA)
1994 £16.45 (BAN)
1989 IB £300.00 (FA)

la Croix-de-Gay *Pomerol*
1999 £15.56 (MON)
1998 IB £210.00 (FRI) £216.00 (BAN) £240.00 (FA)
1995 £31.50 (FRI)
1995 IB £185.00 (TUR)
1990 IB £265.00 (FA)
1955 £79.36 (PAU)

la Croix-des-Moines *Lalande-de-Pomerol*
1997 £10.87 (BIB)
1996 £10.87 (BIB) £10.99 (RAE)
1990 £19.50 (BAL)

Croizet-Bages *5ème cru classé Pauillac*
1996 £22.50 (UN)
1995 £22.50 (UN)

Croque-Michotte *grand cru classé St-Émilion*
1998 IB £108.00 (BAN)
1995 £18.50 (FRI)
1990 IB £220.00 (FA)
1983 £24.50 (BU)

1982 £30.79 (PAU)
1982 IB £240.00 (FA)
1979 £22.50 (BU)
1979 IB £165.00 (FA)
1959 £49.20 (PAU)
1947 £111.11 (PAU)

Curé-Bon-la-Madeleine *grand cru*
classé St-Émilion
1997 £21.95 (DI)
1992 £28.79 (TW)
1986 IB £200.00 (FA)
1978 £22.50 (BU)
1953 £47.62 (PAU)

Dalem *Fronsac*
1997 £13.99 (DI)

la Dame de Montrose *St-Estèphe*
1997 £13.99 (GW) £16.75 (WRI) £17.50
 (MI)
1996 £22.50 (MI) £27.24 (LLO)
1996 IB £145.00 (FA)
1995 £20.00 (MI) £25.00 (FORT)
1994 £18.33 (MI)
1989 £44.00 (FORT)

Dassault *grand cru classé St-Émilion*
1997 £20.00 (FORT)
1994 £23.95 (LEA)

de la Dauphine *Fronsac*
1999 IB £90.00 (CB)
1997 £7.67 (ARM) £12.69 (CB)

Dauzac *5ème cru classé Margaux*
1996 £28.50 (FRI)
1995 £29.50 (FRI)
1989 IB £225.00 (FA)
1988 £18.80 (FA)

Deyrem-Valentin *cru bourgeois Margaux*
1998 £16.75 (STA)
1997 £12.00 (SOM)

Domaine de Chevalier *cru classé*
Pessac-Léognan
1999 IB £195.00 (JU) £330.00 (RAE)
1999 EC £208.00 (HAH)
1998 £30.00 (MI)
1998 IB £230.00 (HIG) £270.00 (FRI)
1997 £25.83 (MI)
1996 £18.80 (BAN) £25.99 (RAE) £29.50
 (FRI) £30.00 (FORT) £33.33 (MI)
1996 ½ bottle IB £195.00 (BODX)

1995 £21.85 (WAT) £25.99 (RAE) £27.95
 (AD) £31.45 (NI) £32.50 (FORT) £35.00
 (JU)
1995 IB £200.00 (FA)
1994 £23.33 (MI) £24.99 (RAE)
1994 IB £170.00 (FA)
1993 £18.95 (RAE) £21.67 (MI)
1993 ½ bottle £9.99 (RAE)
1992 £20.00 (MI)
1990 £45.99 (RAE) £63.33 (MI)
1989 £41.13 (TUR) £51.49 (RAE) £63.33
 (MI) £70.50 (WY)
1989 IB £480.00 (FA)
1988 ½ bottle £22.50 (CRO)
1986 IB £400.00 (FA)
1983 £54.00 (CRO)
1983 IB £480.00 (FA)
1981 £32.90 (FA) £65.00 (BALL)
1978 ½ bottle £29.50 (CRO)
1975 £42.00 (BAL)
1975 IB £260.00 (FA)
1970 £50.00 (FLE)
1966 £72.00 (CRO)
1964 IB £720.00 (FA)

Domaine de l'Eglise *Pomerol*
1999 IB £130.00 (HIG)
1998 IB £155.00 (HIG)
1996 £18.95 (DI) £19.50 (HIG)
1990 IB £270.00 (FA)
1985 IB £220.00 (FA)

Domaine de la Solitude *Pessac-Léognan*
1998 £11.67 (MI)
1997 £9.17 (MI)
1996 £12.50 (MI) £12.50 (BALL)
1995 £9.99 (WAT) £11.67 (MI)

la Dominique *grand cru classé St-Émilion*
1999 IB £325.00 (CB)
1998 £35.00 (MI) £41.13 (CB)
1998 IB £325.00 (YOU)
1997 £28.33 (MI) £29.95 (BAL) £33.61 (CB)
1996 £34.50 (BAL) £35.00 (CON) £38.00
 (JU) £43.00 (FRI) £43.89 (CB)
1995 £29.95 (CON) £35.25 (WY) £36.00
 (FRI) £40.00 (JU)
1994 £34.00 (JON)
1994 IB £200.00 (FA) £215.00 (BODX)
1990 IB £475.00 (BODX)
1989 IB £450.00 (FA)

Ducluzeau *cru bourgeois Listrac*
1996 £11.85 (HIC) £15.00 (ARM)
1994 £9.95 (BALL)

Ducru-Beaucaillou *2ème cru classé St-Julien*
1999 £32.70 (MON) £47.75 (NI)
1999 IB £300.00 (JU) £315.00 (HIG)
£315.00 (RAE) £360.00 (FRI)
1998 £45.00 (FORT) £46.00 (JU) £47.50 (MI)
£51.50 (NI)
1998 IB £345.00 (BODX) £350.00 (TUR)
£380.00 (FRI) £450.00 (BAN)
1998 EC £460.00 (TAN)
1998 ½ bottle IB £345.00 (BODX)
1997 £37.78 (PAU) £39.50 (LAY) £41.67
(MI) £47.00 (BAL) £49.00 (JU) £49.88 (CB)
£50.90 (TAN) £60.00 (JER)
1997 magnum £100.00 (FORT)
1996 £56.40 (BAN) £60.00 (FLE) £71.67 (MI)
£72.50 (FRI) £75.00 (FORT) £82.25 (GW)
1996 IB £580.00 (BODX) £600.00 (FA)
1996 imperial £470.00 (FA) £581.63 (WY)
1995 £78.33 (MI) £82.25 (WY) £89.00 (FRI)
1995 IB £720.00 (BODX) £750.00 (FA)
1995 imperial £746.13 (WY)
1994 £55.00 (BAL)
1994 IB £320.00 (FA)
1994 jeroboam £258.50 (WY)
1993 £35.00 (MI)
1993 magnum IB £320.00 (FA)
1990 £65.83 (MI) £76.38 (WY)
1990 IB £485.00 (BODX)
1989 £63.33 (MI) £64.63 (WY)
1989 IB £475.00 (BODX) £480.00 (FA)
1989 double magnum £276.13 (WY)
1988 £37.50 (BU)
1988 IB £450.00 (FA) £485.00 (BODX)
1986 £47.50 (CON) £69.25 (BY) £76.38
(WY) £80.00 (FORT)
1985 IB £645.00 (BODX) £650.00 (FA)
1983 £52.88 (WY) £59.27 (BY)
1982 £100.82 (NO) £105.00 (YOU)
£111.63 (TUR) £117.50 (WY)
1982 IB £1,000.00 (FA) £1,040.00 (BODX)
1981 £41.13 (FA) £47.62 (PAU)
1979 £47.50 (BAL)
1979 IB £380.00 (FA)
1979 double magnum £170.38 (FA)
1978 £52.88 (FA)
1978 IB £570.00 (BODX)
1975 jeroboam £315.00 (DI)
1970 £90.00 (CRO) £99.50 (BEN) £125.40
(PAU)
1970 IB £880.00 (FA)
1969 £29.38 (BODX)
1966 £70.50 (FA) £93.65 (PAU)
1961 £340.75 (WY)
1952 £79.36 (PAU)

Duhart-Milon *4ème cru classé Pauillac*
2000 EC £140.00 (MON)
1999 IB £130.00 (JU)
1998 £22.50 (MI)
1998 IB £145.00 (BODX) £180.00 (FRI)
1997 £18.33 (MI) £25.95 (DI)

1996 £24.50 (HIG) £27.50 (UN) £28.50 (NI)
£217.38 (TUR)
1996 IB £175.00 (FA)
1995 £25.00 (UN) £25.83 (MI)
1995 IB £230.00 (TUR)
1990 £35.25 (BODX)
1989 IB £320.00 (FA)
1985 £46.00 (FRI)
1985 IB £300.00 (FA)
1964 £42.85 (PAU)

Durand-Laplagne *Puisseguin-St-Émilion*
1997 £7.55 (AD)
1996 £7.95 (BALL)

Durfort-Vivens *2ème cru classé Margaux*
1997 £18.75 (BER)
1995 £22.00 (YOU) £29.50 (FRI)
1978 £35.00 (BALL)
1970 £27.50 (BU)
1950 £79.36 (PAU)

Dutruch-Grand-Poujeaux *cru grand bourgeois exceptionnel Moulis*
1999 IB £99.00 (CB)
1997 £7.95 (WS)
1996 £19.59 (YOU)

l'Église-Clinet *Pomerol*
1999 IB £830.00 (JU) £840.00 (RAE)
1998 IB £1,800.00 (FA)
1997 £72.00 (BAL)
1996 IB £720.00 (FA) £720.00 (TUR)
1995 £123.38 (TUR) £160.00 (JU)
1995 IB £1,200.00 (BODX)
1994 IB £480.00 (FA) £550.00 (TUR)
1990 £140.00 (JU)
1990 IB £1,100.00 (FA)

1989 £90.48 (FA) £95.00 (WS) £120.00 (JU)
1988 £55.00 (JU)
1986 IB £840.00 (FA)
1985 £135.00 (BEN)
1982 £70.50 (FA) £200.00 (JU)
1981 IB £420.00 (FA)
1979 £71.43 (PAU)
1979 IB £480.00 (FA)
1975 £93.65 (PAU)
1975 IB £1,300.00 (FA)

l'Enclos *Pomerol*
1998 IB £135.00 (BODX) £216.00 (BAN)
1997 £16.50 (HED) £23.50 (POR)
1995 £19.98 (WY) £21.50 (STE) £21.99 (VIL)
1990 £23.00 (CRO)
1945 £166.67 (PAU)

l'Éperon *Bordeaux*
1999 £6.99 (VIL)
1998 £6.99 (VIL)

l'Ermitage de Chasse-Spleen *Haut-Médoc*
1998 £10.83 (MI) £11.66 (BIB)
1997 £10.00 (MI)
1996 £13.95 (CON)
1994 £10.95 (WRI)
1993 £16.40 (BY)

l'Etoile *Graves*
1996 £6.50 (BALL)
1995 £6.95 (BALL)

l'Évangile *Pomerol*
1999 IB £795.00 (JU) £910.00 (FRI)
1998 £108.33 (MI)
1998 IB £1,050.00 (FA) £1,600.00 (WY)
1997 £65.00 (MI) £69.95 (WAI) £72.00 (BAL)
  £72.00 (JU) £81.47 (CB) £85.00 (RES)
1996 £75.83 (MI) £85.00 (JU) £90.87 (CB)
1995 £99.88 (TUR) £130.00 (JU) £157.50
  (MI)
1995 IB £780.00 (FA)
1994 IB £440.00 (BODX) £440.00 (FA)
1993 £35.25 (BODX) £47.40 (TAN)
1990 £21.15 (WY) £117.50 (TUR)
1990 IB £1,450.00 (FA)
1989 £131.11 (WY)
1985 £193.88 (WY)
1975 IB £2,300.00 (TUR)
1971 IB £720.00 (FA)
1970 £96.35 (WY)
1955 £182.54 (PAU)
1937 £188.89 (PAU)

Falfas *Côtes de Bourg*
1998 £7.99 (WAI) £8.99 (GW)
1997 £9.25 (AD)
1996 £12.95 (GW)

Fayau *1ères Côtes de Bordeaux*
1998 £6.60 (MV)

Ferrière *3ème cru classé Margaux*
1998 £18.00 (JU)
1994 £44.00 (FORT)

Feytit-Clinet *Pomerol*
1999 IB £174.00 (CB)
1995 £26.95 (BALL)

les Fiefs-de-Lagrange *St-Julien*
1998 £14.99 (ASD) £15.00 (MI)
1998 IB £110.00 (WY)
1997 £12.50 (MI) £14.50 (WS)
1996 £16.67 (MI) £20.95 (BALL)
1996 IB £125.00 (FA) £140.00 (TUR)
1994 IB £100.00 (FA)

de Fieuzal *cru classé Pessac-Léognan*
1996 £18.80 (BAN) £25.00 (MI)
1995 £18.21 (BAN) £22.85 (SOM) £27.50
  (HED) £34.50 (NI)
1995 IB £195.00 (FA)
1994 £14.10 (BAN) £14.75 (BU) £22.50
  (BER)
1989 £29.38 (BODX) £32.99 (NO)
1988 £55.00 (BALL)
1988 IB £240.00 (FA) £280.00 (BODX)
1986 £40.00 (PEN)
1982 IB £300.00 (FA)

Figeac *1er grand cru classé St-Émilion*
2000 EC £395.00 (MON)
1998 £55.00 (JU) £59.17 (MI)
1998 IB £460.00 (FRI) £480.00 (FA)
1996 £40.50 (FLE) £47.50 (MI)
1995 £40.00 (FLE) £47.50 (FRI) £52.50
  (POR)
1990 IB £780.00 (FA)
1989 £52.88 (FA) £68.00 (WS) £76.38 (WY)
1988 IB £530.00 (TUR)
1988 magnum £116.75 (BEN)
1986 £58.75 (FA)
1985 IB £600.00 (FA) £620.00 (BODX)
1983 IB £600.00 (FA)
1982 £94.00 (TUR)
1981 £79.99 (POR)
1979 IB £420.00 (FA) £495.00 (TUR)
1975 £88.13 (WY)

la Fleur-Pétrus *Pomerol*
1999 IB £315.00 (JU) £350.00 (FA) £456.00 (CB)
1998 IB £685.00 (FA)
1995 £55.00 (JU)
1988 £53.00 (CRO)
1982 IB £1,150.00 (FA)

Fombrauge *grand cru St-Émilion*
1998 £17.50 (MI)
1994 £129.25 (BAN)
1966 £23.80 (PAU)

Fonpiqueyre *cru bourgeois Haut-Médoc*
1978 £19.00 (CRO)

Fonplégade *grand cru classé St-Émilion*
1988 IB £150.00 (FA)
1979 IB £130.00 (FA)

Fonréaud *cru bourgeois Listrac*
1996 £9.95 (TAN) £11.67 (MI)
1995 £10.83 (MI)
1979 £12.75 (BU)

Fonroque *grand cru classé St-Émilion*
1998 £15.99 (JON)
1997 £10.17 (ARM) £14.92 (CB)
1994 £13.75 (ARM) £15.50 (WS)

les Forts-de-Latour *Pauillac*
1999 IB £230.00 (JU)
1998 £30.00 (FORT) £31.67 (MI)
1997 £19.50 (WS) £27.95 (BAL) £28.50 (LAY) £30.00 (JU) £31.26 (CB)
1996 £45.00 (JU)
1996 IB £330.00 (FA) £365.00 (TUR)
1995 £33.00 (FLE) £37.50 (YOU) £37.60 (WY)
1995 IB £350.00 (FA)
1990 £55.00 (WS) £79.00 (CRO)
1990 IB £720.00 (FA)
1982 £70.50 (FA)
1979 £44.00 (PEN)
1970 £71.43 (PAU)

Fourcas-Dupré *cru grand bourgeois exceptionnnel Listrac*
2000 EC £56.00 (MON)
1955 £23.80 (PAU)

All châteaux are listed alphabetically regardless of class.

Fourcas-Hosten *cru grand bourgeois exceptionnnel Listrac*
1999 IB £65.00 (HIG)
1998 £10.00 (MI) £11.25 (STA)
1997 £10.50 (HIG)
1996 £9.99 (HIG) £10.95 (STA) £12.99 (POR) £13.80 (TAN) £14.04 (LLO) £14.95 (BALL)
1995 £9.99 (HIG) £14.04 (LLO)
1989 £19.50 (BAL)

Franc-Mayne *grand cru classé St-Émilion*
1997 £15.83 (MI)
1996 £16.67 (MI)
1995 £29.99 (UN)

de Francs *Côtes de Francs*
1997 £7.99 (BOT) £7.99 (THR) £7.99 (VIC) £7.99 (WR)

la Gaffelière *1er grand cru classé St-Émilion*
1998 £36.67 (MI)
1998 IB £252.00 (BAN) £280.00 (FRI)
1996 £30.83 (MI)
1995 £33.50 (FRI) £34.17 (MI)
1994 £29.50 (UN) £30.83 (MI)
1990 IB £370.00 (FA)
1948 £119.05 (PAU)

de Gaillat *Graves*
1996 £8.70 (HAH) £9.99 (JON) £10.00 (ARM)
1995 £8.95 (BALL)
1994 £8.20 (NEZ)

la Garde *Pessac-Léognan*
1996 £9.21 (PAU)

le Gay *Pomerol*
1998 IB £210.00 (FA)
1996 £19.17 (ARM)
1995 IB £240.00 (FA)
1994 £16.67 (ARM)
1990 IB £450.00 (FA)
1959 £111.11 (PAU)

Gazin *Pomerol*
1999 IB £513.00 (CB)
1999 EC £397.65 (HAH)
1998 magnum IB £420.00 (FA)
1997 £38.00 (JU) £45.00 (TAN) £45.47 (CB)
1995 £38.09 (WY) £50.00 (JU)
1995 IB £320.00 (FA)
1989 £63.33 (MI)

1988 £31.73 (FA) £52.00 (BALL)
1988 magnum IB £340.00 (BODX)
1983 £28.20 (FA)
1982 £52.30 (TAN)
1982 IB £385.00 (FA) £390.00 (BODX)
1982 magnum IB £385.00 (FA)
1955 £79.36 (PAU)

Giscours *3ème cru classé Margaux*
1999 IB £135.00 (HIG)
1998 £22.50 (MI)
1997 £18.33 (MI) £24.95 (DI)
1996 £25.00 (MI) £26.95 (FRI) £30.00 (UN)
  £33.75 (WRI)
1995 £27.02 (PLA) £27.50 (UN) £29.50 (FRI)
  £31.00 (YOU)
1990 £47.50 (MI) £49.35 (WY)
1990 IB £350.00 (FA)
1989 £47.50 (MI)
1988 IB £360.00 (BODX)
1982 £68.15 (WY)
1982 IB £440.00 (FA)
1975 £49.50 (BAL)
1973 £23.50 (BODX)
1971 £27.50 (BU)
1966 £76.38 (WY)
1966 IB £360.00 (FA)
1961 £55.55 (PAU) £211.50 (WY)
1959 £141.00 (WY)

du Glana *cru grand bourgeois exceptionnel St-Julien*
1997 £14.81 (BAN)
1975 £18.75 (BU)

Gloria *cru bourgeois St-Julien*
1998 £20.00 (MI) £21.00 (NI)
1997 £18.33 (MI)
1996 £20.83 (MI) £22.50 (UN) £25.95 (FRI)
1995 £23.99 (SUN) £23.99 (LAI) £28.00
  (FRI)
1994 £18.33 (MI)
1993 magnum £34.99 (VIL)
1990 £29.38 (COC)
1989 IB £320.00 (FA)
1986 IB £285.00 (FA)
1983 £23.50 (FA)
1978 £38.50 (BAL)

Grand-Barrail-Lamarzelle-Figeac
  grand cru classé St-Émilion
1983 £26.24 (BY)
1982 IB £200.00 (FA)
1981 IB £135.00 (BODX)
1953 £47.62 (PAU)

Grand-Corbin *grand cru classé St-Émilion*
1998 IB £168.00 (BAN)
1996 £14.20 (NI) £25.22 (PLAY)
1994 £129.25 (BAN)
1985 IB £250.00 (FA)
1959 £47.62 (PAU)

Grand-Lartigue *St-Émilion*
1995 £9.99 (RAE)
1993 £11.75 (BAN)

Grand-Mayne *grand cru classé St-Émilion*
1998 £34.99 (OD)
1998 IB £255.00 (FA)
1995 £30.21 (BY) £37.00 (JU)
1994 £21.50 (BAL)
1990 £39.95 (TUR)

du Grand-Moueys *1ères Côtes de Bordeaux*
1994 £7.55 (NEZ)

Grand Ormeau *Lalande-de-Pomerol*
1997 £14.49 (SAV)

Grand-Pey-Lescours *St-Émilion*
2000 EC £73.00 (MON)

Grand-Pontet *grand cru classé St-Émilion*
1996 £19.17 (ARM) £25.00 (JU)
1995 £19.99 (SUN) £19.99 (LAI) £30.00 (JU)

Grand-Puy-Ducasse *5ème cru classé Pauillac*
1998 £20.83 (MI)
1998 IB £160.00 (FRI) £300.00 (BAN)
1997 £15.83 (MI) £19.95 (DI)
1996 £18.21 (BAN) £20.50 (NI)
1995 £25.00 (BU)
1990 IB £250.00 (FA) £310.00 (BODX)
1989 £39.00 (COC)
1989 IB £280.00 (FA) £360.00 (BODX)
1986 £29.38 (FA)
1983 IB £240.00 (BODX)
1961 £150.00 (CRO) £170.38 (WY)

Grand-Puy-Lacoste *5ème cru classé Pauillac*
1999 £20.46 (MON)
1999 IB £185.00 (JU) £225.00 (FRI) £256.00
  (CB)
1998 £27.00 (JU) £32.84 (CB)
1998 IB £215.00 (BODX) £235.00 (TUR)
  £270.00 (FRI)
1998 magnum IB £290.00 (FRI)

1997 £23.80 (PAU) £27.75 (WAI) £28.00
(JU) £30.61 (CB) £30.80 (TAN) £37.14
(BY)
1997 IB £230.00 (BODX) £235.00 (TUR)
1996 £35.25 (BAN) £51.00 (FRI)
1996 IB £380.00 (BODX) £380.00 (FA)
1996 magnum £84.99 (WY)
1995 £52.50 (FRI)
1995 IB £365.00 (BODX)
1994 £21.50 (WS) £31.20 (LAY) £38.50
(POR)
1994 IB £220.00 (FA)
1989 £48.00 (WS)
1986 IB £480.00 (FA)
1983 £37.50 (BAL)
1982 £72.00 (FLE)
1982 IB £860.00 (FA) £905.00 (BODX)
1979 £28.20 (FA) £39.00 (CRO)
1975 £29.38 (BODX) £66.00 (PEN)
1970 £48.35 (BY)
1961 £180.00 (CRO)
1947 £157.14 (PAU)

Grandes-Murailles *grand cru classé St-Émilion*
1998 £29.26 (CB)
1998 IB £200.00 (BODX)
1997 £26.50 (CB)
1971 £23.80 (PAU)
1964 £25.40 (PAU)

Grangeneuve de Figeac *grand cru St-Émilion*
1995 £20.00 (MI)
1995 IB £120.00 (BODX)
1994 £15.83 (MI)

de la Grave *Côtes de Bourg*
1998 £5.50 (WS)

la Grave-Trigant-de-Boisset *Pomerol*
1999 IB £145.00 (FA)
1996 IB £155.00 (FA)
1995 £27.03 (WY)
1994 IB £150.00 (FA)
1992 IB £120.00 (FA)
1990 £41.13 (WY)
1989 £76.38 (WY)
1988 IB £220.00 (FA)
1986 IB £200.00 (FA)
1985 IB £260.00 (FA)
1983 £38.78 (WY)
1982 IB £375.00 (FA)
1978 IB £250.00 (FA)
1975 IB £310.00 (BODX)

Gressier-Grand-Poujeaux *cru bourgeois supérieur Moulis*
1996 £16.50 (WS)

Gruaud-Larose *2ème cru classé St-Julien*
2000 EC £250.00 (MON)
1999 IB £225.00 (HIG) £230.00 (JU)
1998 £38.33 (MI)
1998 IB £300.00 (FRI)
1997 £35.83 (MI) £45.00 (FORT)
1997 IB £276.00 (BAN)
1996 £28.20 (BAN) £28.50 (FLE) £40.00
(FORT) £40.00 (FRI) £41.67 (MI) £43.50
(TAN) £45.00 (JU) £50.00 (UN)
1996 IB £265.00 (FA)
1996 magnum £80.00 (FORT)
1995 £39.17 (MI) £40.00 (UN) £47.50 (FRI)
1995 IB £290.00 (FA)
1994 £24.68 (BAN) £28.50 (UN) £30.83 (MI)
1994 IB £230.00 (FA)
1993 IB £240.00 (FA) £250.00 (TUR)
1992 £25.83 (MI)
1992 magnum £70.00 (BALL)
1990 £49.99 (OD) £55.81 (BAN) £59.17
(MI)
1990 IB £575.00 (FA)
1990 ½ bottle £40.00 (FORT)
1989 £44.06 (BAN) £62.08 (WY) £78.00
(WS)
1989 IB £495.00 (FA)

1988 £95.00 (BALL)
1986 £70.50 (TUR) £77.55 (WY)
1986 IB £680.00 (FA)
1986 double magnum £270.25 (FA)
1985 £52.88 (FA) £59.00 (CRO) £70.50
(WY) £75.00 (FORT)
1985 ½ bottle £32.00 (CRO) £32.90 (WY)
1983 £58.75 (WY)
1983 IB £520.00 (BODX) £520.00 (FA)
1983 ½ bottle £32.90 (WY)
1982 £111.63 (TUR) £125.00 (FORT)
£129.25 (WY)
1982 IB £1,095.00 (BODX) £1,100.00 (FA)
1982 magnum £215.03 (FA)
1981 £35.25 (FA) £42.50 (BAL)

1979 £34.08 (FA)
1978 IB £420.00 (FA)
1978 double magnum £211.50 (WY)
1975 £27.03 (FA) £54.99 (YOU)
1971 £82.25 (WY)
1970 £58.75 (WY) £89.50 (POR)
1970 IB £450.00 (FA)
1970 magnum £129.25 (WY)
1966 £94.00 (WY)
1966 IB £540.00 (FA)
1962 £125.40 (PAU)
1961 £317.25 (WY)
1961 IB £2,900.00 (FA)
1955 £164.50 (WY)
1952 £47.62 (PAU)
1950 £125.39 (PAU)
1936 £287.88 (WY)
1934 £111.11 (PAU) £129.25 (WY)
1924 £301.59 (PAU)
1920 £246.75 (WY)

Guillot *Pomerol*
1998 £21.00 (JU) £21.67 (MI)
1997 £15.83 (MI)
1996 £16.99 (SUN) £16.99 (LAI) £20.00 (MI)
1995 £21.67 (MI) £26.00 (JU)

Guionne *Côtes de Bourg*
1998 £6.59 (COC)
1996 £6.67 (ARM)

la Gurgue *cru bourgeois supérieur Margaux*
1998 £14.50 (FORT)
1997 £14.50 (TAN)
1990 IB £220.00 (FA)
1989 £24.00 (CRO)
1989 IB £220.00 (FA)

Hanteillan *cru grand bourgeois Haut-Médoc*
1996 £9.50 (WS)

Haut-Badon *grand cru St-Émilion*
1999 £9.41 (LLO)
1998 £9.41 (LLO)

Haut-Bages-Avérous *cru bourgeois Pauillac*
1998 £16.67 (MI)
1996 £18.33 (MI)
1995 £29.00 (STA) £31.00 (BY)
1993 £17.25 (WRI)
1990 IB £280.00 (BODX)
1988 IB £250.00 (FA)

Haut-Bages-Libéral *5ème cru classé Pauillac*
1998 £16.50 (FORT) £17.50 (MI)
1998 EC £154.00 (TAN)
1997 £15.83 (MI) £18.80 (TAN)
1997 magnum £42.50 (FORT)
1996 £21.67 (MI) £21.99 (VIL)
1995 £20.83 (MI) £21.50 (STE)
1994 £17.90 (RIC)
1990 £27.03 (MI)
1989 IB £265.00 (FA)
1986 IB £340.00 (FA)
1985 £52.17 (BY)
1978 £23.50 (BODX)

Haut-Bages-Monpelou *cru bourgeois Pauillac*
1997 £18.51 (BY)
1996 £11.30 (BER)
1970 £25.00 (BU)
1970 ½ bottle £19.95 (BAL)

Haut-Bailly *cru classé Pessac-Léognan*
1999 IB £199.00 (JU)
1998 £30.83 (MI)
1997 £23.33 (MI)
1996 £24.00 (WS) £29.49 (YOU) £30.95 (BALL) £33.33 (MI)
1995 £37.50 (FORT)
1995 IB £250.00 (FA)
1994 £16.45 (FA) £24.50 (STA)
1993 IB £165.00 (FA)
1990 IB £450.00 (FA)
1988 £35.25 (BODX)
1988 IB £320.00 (FA)
1986 £29.38 (BODX)
1986 IB £320.00 (FA)
1985 £35.25 (FA)
1984 IB £140.00 (BODX)
1983 IB £300.00 (FA)
1970 £35.25 (FA)
1966 £61.90 (PAU)

Haut-Batailley *5ème cru classé Pauillac*
1999 £14.58 (MON)
1999 IB £130.00 (JU)
1998 £20.83 (MI)
1998 IB £135.00 (WY)
1997 £14.95 (WS) £17.95 (LAY) £19.00 (JU) £19.68 (CB) £20.00 (MI) £22.90 (TAN)
1996 £23.33 (MI) £23.89 (WY) £24.68 (BAN) £29.00 (JU) £30.00 (UN)
1996 IB £200.00 (FA)
1995 £21.99 (SUN) £21.99 (LAI) £25.00 (BAC) £26.50 (WRI) £27.03 (WY)

1994 £20.00 (MI)
1994 IB £160.00 (FA)
1993 £18.51 (WY)
1990 £34.92 (PAU)
1989 IB £280.00 (FA) £340.00 (BODX)
1986 IB £340.00 (FA)
1983 magnum IB £290.00 (FA)
1982 IB £420.00 (FA)
1978 £35.25 (BY)
1973 £18.73 (PAU)

Haut-Bergey *Pessac-Léognan*
1996 £13.50 (GN) £16.50 (NO)

Haut-Brion *1er cru classé Pessac-Léognan*
1999 IB £900.00 (FA) £900.00 (JU)
1998 £120.00 (JU) £198.33 (MI)
1997 £89.17 (MI) £89.95 (LAY) £98.90
   (TAN) £99.00 (JU) £109.57 (CB) £129.95
   (DI)
1997 IB £820.00 (TUR)
1996 £105.75 (BAN) £119.50 (LAY)
   £130.00 (JU) £135.00 (UN) £135.00 (FRI)
   £206.67 (MI)
1996 IB £1,050.00 (TUR) £1,150.00 (FA)
1996 imperial £822.50 (FA) £940.00 (WY)
1995 £105.75 (BAN) £155.00 (FRI) £160.00
   (JU) £165.83 (MI) £230.69 (BY)
1995 IB £1,150.00 (FA)
1995 imperial £846.00 (FA)
1994 £67.50 (UN) £70.00 (PEN) £70.50
   (TUR) £70.50 (BAN) £72.00 (BAL) £95.00
   (WAI) £99.00 (POR) £116.67 (MI)
1994 IB £725.00 (FA)
1994 magnum £145.00 (UN)
1993 £84.17 (MI) £117.22 (BY)
1993 IB £700.00 (FA)
1991 £124.06 (BY)
1990 £206.35 (PAU)
1990 IB £1,950.00 (FA) £2,050.00 (TUR)
1990 magnum £381.88 (FA)
1989 £293.75 (TUR) £311.38 (WY) £495.00
   (CON)
1989 IB £3,000.00 (FA) £3,095.00 (BODX)
1988 £125.00 (FORT)
1988 IB £1,180.00 (FA)
1987 £99.82 (BY)

1986 £85.00 (CON) £119.99 (OD) £141.00
   (WY) £160.00 (FORT)
1986 IB £1,300.00 (FA)
1985 £123.38 (FA) £137.62 (BY)
1985 magnum £301.59 (PAU)
1983 £98.70 (WY) £125.00 (MI) £125.00
   (FORT)
1983 IB £950.00 (FA)
1982 £214.29 (PAU) £220.00 (BEN)
   £262.50 (NI)
1982 IB £2,100.00 (FA) £2,200.00 (TUR)
   £2,200.00 (BODX)
1981 IB £780.00 (FA)
1979 £94.00 (FA) £142.85 (PAU)
1975 £100.00 (BU)
1971 £76.38 (FA) £85.00 (BU)
1970 £114.73 (BY) £117.50 (WY)
1970 magnum £258.50 (WY)
1966 IB £1,400.00 (FA)
1964 £129.25 (FA) £174.60 (PAU)
1959 £728.50 (WY)
1952 £152.75 (WY) £182.54 (PAU)
1949 £687.38 (WY)
1944 £238.09 (PAU)
1929 £575.75 (WY)
1918 double magnum £3,149.00 (WY)

Haut-Canteloup *cru bourgeois Médoc*
1995 £9.50 (BAC)

Haut-Gardère *Pessac-Léognan*
1993 £8.79 (WAT)

Haut-Guiraud *Côtes de Bourg*
1998 £7.60 (JER)

Haut-Marbuzet *cru grand bourgeois
exceptionnel St-Estèphe*
1998 £25.83 (MI)
1997 £23.00 (JU) £23.33 (MI)
1996 £24.31 (NO) £26.67 (MI)
1995 IB £220.00 (FA)
1983 £29.50 (BAL)

Haut-Mazeris *Canon-Fronsac*
1996 £6.90 (PEN)

Haut-Milon *Pauillac*
1996 £13.50 (MAY)

Haut-Pontet *grand cru St-Émilion*
1996 IB £110.00 (BODX)

de Haut-Sociondo *1ères Côtes de Blaye*
1998 £5.50 (WS)

l'Hermitage *grand cru St-Émilion*
1998 IB £395.00 (BODX)
1997 £52.50 (MI)

Hortevie *cru bourgeois St-Julien*
1997 £9.95 (HED)
1996 £13.15 (GN) £15.25 (BER) £16.99
   (AME)
1995 £16.49 (JON)
1994 £18.50 (BAL)

d'Issan *3ème cru classé Margaux*
1999 IB £130.00 (HIG)
1998 £20.00 (MI)
1996 £21.00 (HIG) £23.33 (MI)
1995 £22.50 (MI) £25.00 (FLE) £29.50 (FRI)
   £38.16 (BY)
1994 £19.17 (MI)
1990 £35.00 (WS)
1986 £28.00 (CRO)
1986 IB £275.00 (FA)

Jonqueyres *Bordeaux Supérieur*
1998 £5.90 (JU)
1998 IB £108.00 (BAN)
1997 £8.00 (JU)
1996 £8.50 (JU) £9.99 (BU)

Kirwan *3ème cru classé Margaux*
1999 IB £188.00 (CB)
1998 £18.00 (JU)
1997 £21.00 (JU) £24.95 (DI)
1996 £30.00 (UN)
1996 magnum £54.64 (WY)
1995 £24.50 (LAY) £24.50 (UN) £28.20
   (WY) £35.00 (WRI)
1990 IB £265.00 (BODX)
1989 £49.50 (BALL)
1982 £29.95 (WAT)

Labégorce *cru bourgeois supérieur*
   Margaux
1996 £14.10 (BAN) £17.95 (NEZ) £18.15
   (HAH) £20.03 (CB)
1989 £29.38 (COC)

Labégorce-Zédé *cru bourgeois supérieur*
   Margaux
1999 IB £110.00 (JU)
1997 IB £115.00 (BODX)
1996 £17.63 (BAN) £18.50 (JU)
1995 £17.63 (WY) £21.45 (NI)
1992 £12.93 (BAN)
1982 IB £345.00 (BODX)
1945 £93.65 (PAU)

Lacombe-Noaillac *Médoc*
1997 £7.20 (HIG)

Lacoste-Borie *Pauillac*
1996 £15.50 (WS) £18.33 (MI)
1995 £16.67 (MI) £18.00 (CRO) £20.00 (JU)
   £20.45 (HIC) £27.50 (RES)
1994 £13.33 (MI) £20.76 (BY)
1988 £29.50 (BAL)

Lafite-Rothschild *1er cru classé Pauillac*
1999 £79.90 (MON)
1999 IB £800.00 (FA) £850.00 (JU) £950.00
   (FRI)
1998 £90.00 (JU) £108.33 (MI) £116.09
   (CB) £135.00 (VIL)
1998 IB £825.00 (WY) £888.00 (LAY)
   £1,100.00 (FRI) £1,200.00 (BAN)
1998 EC £895.00 (TAN)
1997 £89.17 (MI) £95.00 (BAL) £95.90
   (TAN) £99.00 (JU) £135.00 (POR)
1997 IB £840.00 (BAN)
1996 £140.00 (UN) £206.67 (MI) £220.00
   (JU) £225.00 (VIL) £245.00 (FRI)
1996 ½ bottle IB £1,900.00 (FA)
1996 magnum £425.00 (BU)
1995 £129.25 (TUR) £180.00 (FRI) £182.50
   (MI) £258.34 (BY)
1995 IB £1,300.00 (FA) £1,320.00 (BODX)
1995 double magnum £612.57 (WY)
1994 £76.38 (BAN) £78.73 (TUR) £89.00
   (PEN) £100.00 (JU) £104.05 (BY)
1994 IB £780.00 (FA) £800.00 (BODX)
1994 magnum IB £720.00 (FA)
1993 £76.38 (TUR) £84.17 (MI) £86.45
   (LAY) £117.22 (BY)
1993 IB £750.00 (FA)
1993 double magnum £305.50 (FA)
1993 imperial £611.00 (FA)
1992 £76.38 (BODX) £101.97 (BY)
1991 £70.50 (TUR)
1991 IB £780.00 (FA)
1991 magnum IB £690.00 (BODX) £780.00
   (FA)
1991 imperial £440.63 (BODX)
1990 £206.35 (PAU) £235.00 (FRI) £239.17
   (MI)
1990 IB £1,800.00 (FA) £1,850.00 (BODX)
   £1,975.00 (TUR)
1990 magnum IB £1,800.00 (FA)
1989 £140.00 (SUN) £152.75 (BODX)
   £173.00 (PAU) £223.33 (MI)
1989 IB £1,550.00 (FA)
1989 magnum £370.13 (WY)
1989 double magnum £622.75 (FA)

1988 £141.00 (TUR) £141.00 (WY) £169.00 (FRI)
1988 IB £1,440.00 (BODX) £1,450.00 (FA)
1988 ½ bottle £68.15 (FA)
1988 double magnum £799.00 (FRI)
1987 £70.50 (BODX) £74.03 (TUR) £75.00 (BAL) £110.00 (FRI)
1986 £200.00 (WY) £220.63 (PAU) £235.00 (WY) £247.50 (MI) £250.00 (FORT)
1986 IB £2,050.00 (FA

1985 IB £1,480.00 (FA)
1985 magnum £290.23 (FA) £301.59 (PAU)
1984 £58.75 (TUR) £58.75 (FA)
1984 magnum IB £600.00 (FA)
1983 £123.38 (TUR) £129.25 (BODX) £150.00 (FORT) £152.87 (BY)
1983 IB £1,250.00 (FA)
1983 magnum £350.00 (FORT)
1983 magnum IB £1,250.00 (FA)
1982 £350.00 (BU) £370.00 (CRO) £381.88 (WY) £390.00 (FRI) £495.00 (FORT)
1982 IB £3,500.00 (BODX) £3,500.00 (FA)
1982 double magnum £1,715.50 (WY)
1981 £90.00 (BEN) £94.00 (TUR)
1981 IB £900.00 (FA)
1979 £88.13 (FA) £139.00 (BAL)
1979 magnum £176.25 (TUR)
1978 £105.75 (FA) £123.38 (WY) £161.95 (VIN)
1976 IB £1,350.00 (FA)
1976 magnum £264.38 (FA)
1975 £166.67 (PAU)
1975 IB £1,320.00 (FA)
1974 £58.75 (WY)
1973 £69.00 (BAL)
1973 ½ bottle £37.50 (BU)
1971 £67.50 (BU) £117.50 (WY)
1971 double magnum £605.13 (WY)
1970 double magnum £540.50 (WY)
1966 £135.13 (WY)
1966 imperial £940.00 (FA) £1,468.75 (WY)
1961 £334.88 (FA) £804.88 (WY)
1961 ½ bottle £217.38 (WY)
1961 magnum £1,762.50 (WY)
1961 imperial £3,525.00 (FA) £4,230.00 (WY)

1956 magnum £188.00 (WY)
1955 £287.88 (WY)
1953 magnum £505.25 (WY)
1949 £555.55 (PAU) £699.13 (WY)
1949 magnum £2,526.25 (WY)
1948 £399.50 (WY) £495.00 (CRO)
1948 ½ bottle £135.13 (WY)
1945 £1,128.00 (WY)
1934 £305.50 (WY)
1931 £206.35 (PAU) £552.25 (WY)
1929 £1,039.88 (WY)
1929 magnum £2,526.25 (WY)
1928 £390.00 (JU) £752.00 (WY)
1923 £423.00 (WY)
1920 £3,348.75 (WY)
1918 £387.75 (WY)

Lafleur *Pomerol*
1999 IB £1,250.00 (JU) £1,500.00 (FA)
1998 £150.00 (JU) £182.13 (BODX)
1998 IB £1,775.00 (WY)
1997 £120.00 (JU)
1997 IB £900.00 (FA)
1996 £135.13 (BODX) £210.00 (JU)
1996 IB £1,250.00 (TUR) £1,350.00 (FA)
1995 £217.38 (TUR)
1995 IB £1,795.00 (BODX) £2,000.00 (FA)
1994 £76.38 (FA) £88.13 (BODX)
1993 £70.50 (BODX)
1993 IB £750.00 (FA)
1992 £60.00 (JU) £105.75 (WY)
1992 IB £760.00 (BODX)
1990 £423.00 (TUR)
1989 IB £2,900.00 (FA)
1988 £156.28 (WY)
1988 IB £1,850.00 (TUR)
1985 £293.75 (TUR)
1982 £822.50 (FA)

Lafleur-Gazin *Pomerol*
1999 IB £110.00 (JU)
1998 £35.00 (JU)
1997 £13.50 (JU) £16.49 (YOU)
1945 £166.67 (PAU)

Lafon-Rochet *4ème cru classé St-Estèphe*
1999 IB £120.00 (HIG)
1998 £20.00 (MI)
1998 IB £155.00 (HIG)
1997 £16.67 (MI) £19.68 (CB) £19.95 (BAL) £20.50 (JER) £20.70 (TAN)
1996 £24.95 (FRI) £27.50 (LAY)
1996 IB £180.00 (FA)
1995 £31.50 (FRI) £38.50 (WRI)
1995 IB £190.00 (BODX) £190.00 (FA)

1993 £30.34 (BY)
1988 IB £250.00 (FA)
1982 £41.13 (WY)
1982 IB £380.00 (WY)
1978 IB £210.00 (BODX)
1960 £82.25 (WY)

Lagrange *Pomerol*
1999 IB £188.00 (CB)
1998 £25.83 (MI)
1997 £21.55 (LAY) £21.67 (MI)
1995 £27.50 (WS)
1995 IB £225.00 (FA)
1994 £26.67 (MI)
1970 £35.00 (BU)

Lagrange *3ème cru classé St-Julien*
1998 IB £165.00 (WY)
1997 £24.32 (CB)
1996 £28.95 (DI) £31.00 (CON) £31.50
 (FRI) £35.00 (FORT) £49.50 (VIN)
1996 IB £200.00 (FA)
1995 £25.00 (CON) £29.38 (WY)
1993 £25.85 (WY) £33.53 (BY)
1990 £70.50 (WY)
1989 £68.15 (WY)
1988 IB £340.00 (FA) £345.00 (BODX)
1985 IB £380.00 (FA)
1983 IB £330.00 (FA)
1982 £47.00 (BAL)
1979 £22.50 (BU) £24.68 (WY)

la Lagune *3ème cru classé Haut-Médoc*
1998 £23.33 (MI)
1998 IB £140.00 (TUR) £180.00 (FRI)
1997 £18.33 (MI)
1997 magnum £40.00 (FORT)
1996 £20.50 (HIG) £24.99 (VIL) £26.75
 (POR) £26.95 (CON) £26.95 (FRI) £27.50
 (UN) £29.17 (MI)
1996 IB £205.00 (TUR)
1996 imperial £182.13 (WY)
1995 £25.85 (WY) £27.50 (MI) £29.50 (UN)
 £29.50 (FRI)
1995 IB £195.00 (FA)
1995 ½ bottle £15.75 (FRI)
1995 magnum £62.50 (FRI)
1995 double magnum £107.32 (WY)
1995 imperial £199.75 (WY)
1994 £21.50 (UN) £25.00 (MI)
1994 IB £200.00 (TUR)
1993 £24.17 (MI)
1993 IB £165.00 (FA)
1990 £48.00 (CRO)
1990 IB £420.00 (FA)

1989 £39.99 (SUN) £45.00 (YOU) £52.88
 (WY) £55.25 (BEN)
1989 magnum IB £420.00 (FA)
1988 IB £350.00 (FA)
1986 £45.00 (CON) £48.37 (WY)
1986 IB £400.00 (FA)
1985 £47.39 (WY)
1985 IB £400.00 (FA)
1983 £42.00 (CRO)
1983 IB £385.00 (FA) £395.00 (BODX)
1982 £72.00 (CRO) £75.00 (YOU)
1982 IB £650.00 (FA)
1982 double magnum £390.49 (WY)
1981 double magnum £99.88 (FA)
1980 imperial £146.88 (FA)
1979 £30.15 (PAU)
1978 £44.00 (CRO)
1978 IB £365.00 (BODX)
1975 IB £220.00 (FA)
1970 £56.00 (CRO)
1966 IB £440.00 (BODX)

Lalande d'Auvion *Médoc*
1995 £7.95 (BALL)

Lalande-Borie *cru bourgeois supérieur St-Julien*
1996 £18.33 (MI)
1996 IB £115.00 (FA)
1995 £17.50 (WS) £18.33 (MI)
1995 IB £120.00 (FA)
1994 £15.00 (MI) £17.95 (BALL)
1990 £26.67 (MI)
1989 IB £210.00 (FA)
1983 £19.36 (BY)
1983 IB £180.00 (FA)

de Lamarque *cru grand bourgeois Haut-Médoc*
1999 IB £100.00 (CB)
1998 £11.57 (CB)
1996 £15.45 (CB)

Lamothe-Bergeron *cru bourgeois Haut-Médoc*
1996 £11.80 (NEZ) £13.40 (MAY)
1995 £13.99 (COC)
1993 £10.50 (BALL)

Oz Clarke's Wine Buying Guide
is an annual publication.
We welcome your suggestions for
next year's edition.

Lamothe-Cissac *Haut-Médoc*
1998 £7.99 (DI)

Lanessan *cru bourgeois supérieur Haut-Médoc*
1998 £12.50 (MI)
1997 £10.83 (MI) £13.95 (DI)
1996 £13.99 (AME) £14.17 (MI)
1995 £19.75 (NI) £21.50 (FORT)
1994 IB £125.00 (FA)
1990 IB £260.00 (BODX)
1989 IB £220.00 (FA)
1986 £34.50 (BAL)

Langoa-Barton *3ème cru classé St-Julien*
1999 IB £160.00 (JU) £238.00 (CB)
1998 EC £240.00 (TAN)
1997 £19.95 (LAY) £21.95 (BER) £22.00 (JU)
£25.40 (TAN) £25.75 (AD)
1997 IB £150.00 (FA)
1996 £29.95 (DI) £30.60 (TAN) £55.58 (BY)
1995 £29.95 (DI) £29.99 (POR) £31.73
(WY) £44.31 (BY)
1994 £32.99 (JON) £35.91 (BY)
1993 £27.75 (BO)
1989 £38.00 (WS) £45.00 (CRO) £47.00
(WY)
1986 £30.88 (BY)
1986 IB £330.00 (FA)
1983 IB £325.00 (FA)
1981 magnum £53.00 (WY)
1978 IB £290.00 (BODX)

Larcis-Ducasse *grand cru classé St-Émilion*
1996 £20.50 (MAY)
1990 IB £250.00 (FA)
1975 IB £160.00 (BODX)

Larmande *grand cru classé St-Émilion*
1998 £25.00 (MI) £26.75 (NI)
1997 £20.00 (MI) £25.40 (TAN)
1996 £20.83 (MI) £25.95 (DI) £28.33 (ARM)
1995 £11.95 (LEA)
1995 IB £180.00 (FA)
1994 £19.99 (LAI) £25.26 (BAN)
1990 IB £300.00 (FA)
1983 £35.00 (WS)
1982 £27.03 (FA) £47.62 (PAU)

Laroque *grand cru St-Émilion*
1997 £13.45 (BER)
1996 £19.09 (BAN)
1995 £14.25 (WAI) £18.80 (BAN)
1993 £14.10 (BAN)

Larose-Trintaudon *cru grand bourgeois Haut-Médoc*
1996 £13.50 (FRI)

Laroze *grand cru classé St-Émilion*
1998 IB £168.00 (BAN)
1972 £23.80 (PAU)

Larrivet-Haut-Brion *Pessac-Léognan*
1998 £23.25 (NI)
1997 £18.90 (TAN)
1996 £14.10 (BAN) £18.00 (JU) £29.95 (NI)
1995 £26.95 (NI)
1982 £27.03 (FA)
1978 £18.73 (PAU)

Lascombes *2ème cru classé Margaux*
1997 £20.83 (MI)
1996 £21.15 (BAN) £28.50 (FRI) £45.00
(UN)
1995 £23.95 (NI) £25.99 (SUN) £25.99 (LAI)
£31.50 (FRI) £40.00 (UN)
1994 £25.85 (BAN) £28.50 (UN)
1993 IB £150.00 (FA)
1985 IB £350.00 (FA)
1982 IB £420.00 (FA)
1975 £65.00 (PEN)
1961 £146.88 (WY)
1953 £71.43 (PAU)

Latour *1er cru classé Pauillac*
1999 IB £840.00 (RAE) £900.00 (JU)
£950.00 (FRI)
1998 £85.00 (JU) £99.75 (NI) £108.33 (MI)
1998 IB £820.00 (FA) £1,100.00 (FRI)
£1,200.00 (BAN)
1997 £89.17 (MI) £98.90 (TAN) £99.00 (JU)
£100.00 (FORT) £109.57 (CB) £109.95
(BU) £123.00 (NI)
1997 IB £720.00 (FA) £792.00 (BAN)
£795.00 (TUR)
1996 £140.00 (UN) £152.75 (BAN) £185.00
(FRI) £206.67 (MI)
1996 IB £1,640.00 (BODX) £1,700.00 (FA)
£1,725.00 (TUR)
1996 double magnum £734.38 (WY)
1995 £141.00 (TUR) £142.18 (FA) £180.00
(FRI) £410.79 (BY)
1995 IB £1,550.00 (BODX)
1995 imperial £1,198.50 (FA)
1994 £82.25 (BAN) £119.26 (BY) £133.33
(MI)
1994 IB £855.00 (BODX) £900.00 (FA)
1994 magnum IB £900.00 (TUR)
1994 double magnum £352.50 (FA)

1993 £84.17 (MI) £85.00 (WS) £90.29 (BY)
1993 IB £795.00 (BODX) £800.00 (FA)
1993 magnum IB £745.00 (BODX)
1992 £76.38 (TUR) £124.49 (BY) £141.00
(BAN)
1992 magnum £141.00 (TUR)
1991 £74.03 (FA) £136.50 (BY)
1991 IB £785.00 (BODX)
1990 £295.00 (BU) £301.59 (PAU) £400.00
(FORT)
1990 IB £3,000.00 (BODX) £3,000.00 (FA)
£3,450.00 (TUR)
1990 magnum IB £3,000.00 (FA)
1989 £137.99 (SUN) £141.00 (TUR)
£154.70 (LAY) £169.00 (FRI) £173.00
(PAU) £183.17 (PLAY) £198.00 (NI)
1989 IB £1,440.00 (BODX) £1,450.00 (FA)
1989 magnum IB £1,450.00 (FA)
1989 double magnum £587.50 (FA)
1988 £105.75 (TUR) £138.34 (BY) £150.00
(FORT)
1988 magnum £249.20 (PAU) £300.00
(FORT)
1988 magnum IB £1,250.00 (FA)
1987 IB £720.00 (FA)
1986 £141.39 (WY) £157.14 (PAU) £182.50
(MI) £190.00 (NI)
1986 IB £1,340.00 (BODX) £1,350.00 (FA)
1986 magnum £315.87 (PAU)
1986 magnum IB £1,350.00 (FA)
1985 £129.25 (TUR) £190.00 (NI) £195.00
(FORT)
1985 magnum IB £1,400.00 (FA)
1985 imperial £1,116.25 (FA)
1983 £117.50 (WY) £125.00 (MI) £134.92
(PAU) £145.00 (FORT)
1983 IB £1,080.00 (FA) £1,100.00 (TUR)
£1,175.00 (BODX)
1983 magnum £277.78 (PAU)
1982 £352.50 (TUR) £393.63 (WY) £525.00
(FORT)
1982 IB £3,650.00 (BODX) £3,650.00 (FA)
1982 double magnum £1,686.13 (WY)
1982 imperial £3,818.75 (WY)
1981 £78.40 (BY) £99.88 (TUR) £111.63
(WY)
1980 £88.13 (BODX)
1979 £140.00 (FORT)
1979 double magnum £393.63 (FA)
1978 £117.50 (FA) £135.13 (WY) £158.50
(BY) £165.00 (BAL) £185.00 (FORT)
1977 IB £520.00 (FA)
1976 £88.13 (TUR)
1976 IB £750.00 (FA)
1976 double magnum £581.63 (WY)

1975 £166.67 (PAU)
1975 IB £1,300.00 (FA)
1971 £158.63 (WY)
1970 £287.88 (TUR) £305.50 (WY) £425.00
(FORT)
1970 IB £2,850.00 (FA)
1966 £270.00 (CRO) £279.65 (FA) £370.13
(WY) £395.00 (TAN) £400.00 (FORT)
1964 £315.00 (FORT)
1960 £264.38 (WY)
1959 IB £7,800.00 (FA)
1958 magnum £340.75 (WY)
1957 £142.85 (PAU) £170.38 (TUR)
1955 £525.00 (CRO)
1951 £575.75 (WY)
1949 £646.25 (WY)
1949 magnum £176.25 (WY)
1945 £1,233.75 (WY)
1940 £323.13 (WY)
1937 £301.59 (PAU)
1936 £505.25 (WY)
1934 £349.20 (PAU) £381.88 (WY)
1929 £387.75 (WY)
1916 £505.25 (WY)
1909 £752.00 (WY)

Latour-à-Pomerol *Pomerol*
1999 IB £250.00 (FA) £394.00 (CB)
1998 £47.00 (BODX)
1998 IB £420.00 (FA)
1997 £34.90 (CB)
1996 £36.84 (CB)
1995 £31.73 (FA)
1994 IB £245.00 (BODX)
1993 IB £240.00 (FA)
1990 £41.13 (TUR) £49.35 (FA)
1989 IB £450.00 (FA)
1988 £43.48 (WY)
1988 IB £420.00 (BODX)
1982 £123.38 (BODX) £132.78 (FA)
£135.13 (TUR) £170.38 (WY)
1981 £52.88 (WY)
1975 IB £400.00 (FA)
1970 £76.38 (FA)

Lavillotte *cru bourgeois Médoc*
1997 £12.50 (FORT)

---

*EC (ex-cellar) price per dozen,
excluding shipping, duty and VAT.
IB (in bond) price per dozen,
excluding duty and VAT.
All other prices, per bottle incl VAT.*

Léoville-Barton *2ème cru classé St-Julien*
1999 IB £249.00 (RAE) £280.00 (FRI)
    £325.00 (CB)
1998 £39.17 (MI) £40.60 (NI)
1998 IB £290.00 (FRI) £312.00 (BAN)
1998 EC £305.00 (TAN)
1997 £22.50 (WAI) £29.95 (BAL) £30.83
    (MI) £31.00 (JU) £31.80 (TAN) £33.50
    (HED) £35.00 (FORT) £35.19 (CB) £39.95
    (DI) £44.95 (BU)
1996 £32.90 (BAN) £44.50 (FRI) £47.00
    (GW) £49.95 (DI) £64.99 (BY)
1996 IB £320.00 (FA)
1995 £36.43 (BAN) £41.13 (WY) £41.99
    (VIL) £44.50 (LAY) £45.00 (FRI) £78.30
    (BY)
1995 double magnum £193.88 (WY)

1994 £26.44 (BAN) £28.79 (WY) £30.99
    (YOU) £31.00 (HIG) £31.41 (PLAY) £33.49
    (SUN) £33.49 (LAI) £36.99 (JON)
1994 IB £240.00 (BODX) £255.00 (FA)
1994 magnum £70.68 (WY)
1993 £29.95 (BU) £36.34 (BY)
1990 £65.00 (TAN) £80.00 (FORT) £96.00
    (BAL)
1990 IB £635.00 (BODX) £650.00 (FA)
1989 £52.88 (BODX) £62.90 (LAY) £64.43
    (BY) £64.60 (TAN) £65.80 (WY)
1988 £51.17 (BY) £58.70 (LAY)
1986 £45.00 (CON) £49.50 (BEN) £64.90
    (TAN) £70.00 (FORT)
1986 IB £550.00 (FA) £590.00 (BODX)
1986 magnum £129.25 (WY)
1985 £51.10 (NO) £75.00 (FORT)
1985 magnum £158.63 (WY)
1984 IB £170.00 (BODX)
1983 IB £425.00 (BODX) £440.00 (FA)
1983 magnum IB £425.00 (BODX)
1982 £84.75 (BEN)
1982 double magnum £381.88 (WY)
1981 IB £345.00 (BODX)
1975 £39.50 (BAL)
1970 magnum £176.25 (WY)
1966 £47.62 (PAU)
1961 £195.00 (CRO)

Léoville-Las-Cases *2ème cru classé St-Julien*
1999 £50.81 (MON)
1999 IB £490.00 (JU) £580.00 (FRI) £663.00
    (CB)
1998 £70.00 (JU) £88.13 (CB)
1998 IB £630.00 (FRI)
1997 £79.00 (JU) £79.50 (BAL) £89.95 (CB)
    £98.90 (TAN) £99.50 (CON)
1996 £105.75 (BAN) £125.00 (FRI) £150.00
    (JU)
1996 IB £1,050.00 (TUR) £1,050.00 (FA)
1996 double magnum £423.00 (FA)
1996 imperial £951.75 (WY)
1995 £77.55 (BAN) £85.00 (YOU) £89.00
    (FRI)
1995 IB £720.00 (FA)
1995 magnum IB £720.00 (FA)
1994 £47.00 (BAN) £59.50 (BAL) £59.95
    (WAI)
1994 IB £390.00 (BODX) £425.00 (FA)
    £520.00 (TUR)
1994 ½ bottle IB £425.00 (FA)
1994 double magnum £193.88 (FA)
1993 £38.78 (FA)
1990 £126.00 (TAN) £145.00 (POR)
1990 magnum IB £1,100.00 (FA)
1989 £76.38 (BODX) £88.13 (WY) £99.50
    (BAL)
1989 IB £750.00 (TUR) £750.00 (FA)
1989 magnum £193.88 (WY)
1988 £69.91 (WY) £77.60 (BY)
1988 IB £625.00 (BODX) £625.00 (FA)
1988 magnum IB £625.00 (FA)
1986 IB £1,095.00 (BODX)
1986 imperial £910.63 (FA)
1985 £89.50 (BEN)
1985 IB £780.00 (FA)
1983 £58.75 (WY) £90.00 (JU)
1982 £175.00 (POR) £180.00 (JU) £188.00
    (TUR) £191.53 (FA) £191.92 (TUR)
    £195.00 (BEN) £223.25 (WY) £250.00
    (FORT)
1982 IB £1,950.00 (BODX)
1981 IB £450.00 (FA) £455.00 (BODX)
1980 IB £280.00 (FA)
1980 imperial £193.88 (FA)
1979 £49.35 (FA) £53.50 (BEN)
1979 magnum IB £500.00 (FA)
1979 double magnum £217.38 (FA)
1978 £78.50 (BEN) £82.91 (BY)
1978 IB £640.00 (FA) £650.00 (BODX)
1978 magnum IB £640.00 (FA)
1978 imperial £564.00 (FA)
1975 £54.05 (FA)

1973 £23.50 (BODX)
1970 £41.13 (FA) £52.00 (HIG) £88.13 (WY)
1970 magnum £200.93 (WY)
1970 double magnum £411.25 (WY)
1961 £264.38 (WY)
1959 £188.00 (FA)
1955 £95.00 (CRO)
1945 £458.25 (WY)

Léoville-Poyferré 2ème cru classé St-Julien
1999 IB £190.00 (JU) £199.20 (RAE)
1998 £29.17 (MI)
1998 IB £195.00 (BODX) £240.00 (FRI)
1997 £26.67 (MI) £30.61 (CB) £31.00 (BER) £35.70 (TAN)
1996 £30.00 (FLE) £31.18 (BAN) £31.49 (RAE) £32.90 (LAY) £40.00 (FRI)
1996 IB £290.00 (FA) £320.00 (TUR)
1995 £35.25 (WY) £36.00 (FRI)
1995 IB £275.00 (FA) £315.00 (TUR)
1994 £22.91 (BAN) £25.50 (UN)
1994 IB £190.00 (FA) £220.00 (TUR) £230.00 (BODX)
1992 £20.56 (BAN)
1990 £68.15 (FA)
1989 £41.13 (FA)
1986 £34.95 (NI)
1986 IB £420.00 (FA)
1985 £50.00 (FLE)
1983 £56.90 (TAN)
1983 IB £385.00 (BODX) £420.00 (FA)
1983 imperial £387.75 (FA)
1982 £65.00 (FLE) £99.99 (VIL)
1982 IB £750.00 (FA)
1970 £31.73 (WY)
1966 £47.62 (PAU)
1961 £146.88 (WY)
1959 £64.63 (WY)
1953 £71.43 (PAU)
1924 £58.75 (WY)

Lestage cru bourgeois supérieur Listrac
1995 £11.70 (RIC)
1993 £7.99 (WAT)

Liversan cru grand bourgeois Haut-Médoc
2000 EC £45.00 (MON)
1999 £6.55 (MON)
1998 £9.99 (SAF)
1997 £9.99 (DI)
1996 £10.99 (UN)
1985 £28.00 (CRO)
1982 £14.50 (BU) £24.00 (CRO)
1966 £34.92 (PAU)

Loudenne cru grand bourgeois Médoc
1998 £12.50 (MI)
1996 £14.17 (MI)
1995 £12.50 (MI) £13.00 (JU)

la Louvière Pessac-Léognan
1995 £23.45 (NI)
1990 IB £265.00 (FA)
1970 IB £180.00 (FA)

Lynch-Bages 5ème cru classé Pauillac
1999 £23.40 (MON)
1999 IB £240.00 (FA) £260.00 (FRI)
1998 £32.50 (FORT) £35.75 (NI) £38.33 (MI)
1998 IB £265.00 (WY) £280.00 (FRI) £360.00 (BAN)
1998 magnum IB £300.00 (FRI)
1997 £35.83 (MI) £39.66 (CB) £40.60 (TAN)
1996 £35.25 (BAN) £40.00 (FRI) £42.50 (TAN) £43.33 (MI) £43.50 (CON) £55.00 (UN)
1996 IB £360.00 (TUR) £360.00 (FA)
1995 £35.25 (BAN) £39.17 (MI) £41.13 (WY) £46.00 (FRI) £74.41 (BY)
1995 IB £360.00 (TUR)
1995 magnum £96.00 (FRI)
1995 jeroboam £317.25 (WY)
1994 £29.38 (BAN) £29.99 (SUN) £29.99 (LAI) £31.67 (MI) £32.99 (YOU)
1994 IB £280.00 (FA)
1994 jeroboam £246.75 (WY)
1993 £30.83 (MI)
1993 IB £280.00 (FA)
1990 £90.00 (NO)
1990 IB £925.00 (BODX) £950.00 (FA)
1990 magnum £225.00 (FRI)
1990 magnum IB £950.00 (FA)
1989 £100.00 (WAI) £102.75 (LAY) £112.50 (BEN) £135.13 (WY)
1989 IB £1,050.00 (FA)
1989 magnum IB £1,050.00 (FA)
1988 £70.50 (WY)
1988 IB £720.00 (FA)
1988 jeroboam £493.50 (FA)
1986 £85.00 (FORT)
1986 IB £780.00 (FA)
1986 magnum IB £780.00 (FA)

1985 £94.00 (TUR) £99.88 (WY) £120.00
   (FORT)
1985 IB £935.00 (BODX) £940.00 (FA)
1985 magnum £235.00 (BEN)
1983 £76.38 (WY)
1983 magnum IB £680.00 (FA)
1983 jeroboam £481.75 (FA)
1982 £141.00 (WY)
1982 IB £1,250.00 (FA)
1982 jeroboam £1,350.00 (FRI)
1978 £58.75 (WY)
1978 IB £400.00 (FA) £435.00 (BODX)
1976 IB £270.00 (FA)
1975 £385.00 (FA)
1975 IB £425.00 (BODX)
1970 £105.75 (TUR) £112.80 (FA) £117.50
   (BODX) £125.50 (BEN) £129.25 (WY)
1969 £29.38 (BODX)
1966 magnum £229.13 (WY)
1961 £276.13 (WY)
1949 £238.09 (PAU)
1945 £505.25 (WY)

Lynch-Moussas *5ème cru classé Pauillac*
1998 £17.50 (MI)
1997 £15.00 (MI)
1996 £14.69 (TUR) £14.99 (OD) £18.33 (MI)
1981 IB £165.00 (FA)
1978 £26.50 (BU)

du Lyonnat *Lussac-St-Émilion*
1998 £10.99 (JON) £11.44 (PLAY)
1997 £9.99 (POR)

Macquin-St-Georges *St-Georges-St-Émilion*
1998 £7.95 (TAN) £7.99 (POR) £8.25 (HAH)
   £9.11 (CB)
1997 £7.50 (BALL)
1996 £8.25 (BALL)

Magdelaine *1er grand cru classé St-Émilion*
1999 IB £319.00 (CB)
1998 £35.25 (CB) £35.25 (BODX)
1997 IB £160.00 (BODX)
1992 £25.50 (BO) £29.38 (BODX)
1988 IB £365.00 (BODX)
1985 £29.38 (FA)
1983 £29.38 (FA)
1982 £74.03 (FA) £87.30 (PAU)
1982 IB £710.00 (BODX)
1981 IB £340.00 (BODX)
1978 IB £390.00 (BODX)
1959 £79.36 (PAU)

Malartic-Lagravière *cru classé Pessac-Léognan*
1998 £20.83 (MI)
1997 £16.67 (MI)
1952 £47.62 (PAU)

Malescasse *cru bourgeois Haut-Médoc*
1999 IB £78.00 (HIG)
1996 £12.99 (UN) £14.95 (CON)
1995 £13.25 (HIG) £15.99 (AME)
1994 £12.15 (NEZ)
1988 £18.50 (FLE)
1985 £21.00 (CRO)

Malescot-St-Exupéry *3ème cru classé Margaux*
1997 £22.50 (BAL) £29.99 (POR)
1996 £24.00 (JU)
1995 £32.50 (AME)
1990 IB £330.00 (FA)
1988 £29.99 (BAL)
1988 magnum IB £250.00 (FA)
1986 IB £250.00 (FA)
1983 magnum IB £250.00 (FA)
1981 IB £225.00 (BODX)
1978 IB £200.00 (FA)
1975 £22.50 (BU)
1972 £220.63 (PAU)
1961 £105.75 (WY)

de Malleret *cru grand bourgeois Haut-Médoc*
1997 £10.40 (HAH)
1985 IB £80.00 (FA)

de Marbuzet *cru grand bourgeois exceptionnel St-Estèphe*
1996 £21.00 (JU)
1989 IB £225.00 (FA)
1988 IB £245.00 (BODX)

la Maréchaude *Lalande-de-Pomerol*
1997 £7.05 (BAN)

Margaux *1er cru classé Margaux*
1999 £79.90 (MON)
1999 IB £850.00 (JU)
1998 £11.99 (BOT) £11.99 (THR) £11.99
   (VIC) £90.00 (JU) £99.75 (NI) £108.33 (MI)
1998 IB £880.00 (FA) £888.00 (LAY)
   £1,100.00 (FRI) £1,200.00 (BAN)
1998 EC £895.00 (TAN)
1997 £89.17 (MI) £98.90 (TAN) £99.00 (JU)
   £110.69 (CB)
1997 IB £850.00 (FA) £960.00 (BAN)

1996 £140.00 (UN) £160.00 (DI) £170.38 (BAN) £188.00 (FA) £205.00 (FRI) £205.63 (WY) £206.67 (MI) £245.00 (CON) £259.00 (POR)
1995 £158.63 (BAN) £170.38 (TUR) £245.00 (FRI)
1994 £109.00 (PEN) £119.26 (BY)
1994 IB £1,000.00 (FA)
1993 £85.00 (PEN) £150.00 (FLE)
1993 IB £980.00 (TUR) £990.00 (BODX) £1,000.00 (FA)
1993 magnum IB £1,000.00 (FA)
1992 IB £930.00 (TUR)
1991 £83.43 (FA)
1991 magnum IB £895.00 (TUR)
1990 £275.00 (YOU)
1990 IB £3,100.00 (FA)
1990 magnum IB £3,100.00 (FA)
1989 £158.63 (TUR) £206.35 (PAU) £220.00 (FORT)
1989 IB £1,750.00 (FA)
1989 magnum IB £1,750.00 (FA)
1988 £141.00 (WY) £145.00 (BEN) £146.88 (BODX) £1,500.00 (FA)
1988 magnum IB £1,430.00 (BODX) £1,500.00 (FA)
1986 £188.00 (TUR) £214.29 (PAU) £250.00 (FORT) £275.00 (BAL)
1986 IB £2,000.00 (FA)
1985 £180.00 (BAL)
1985 IB £1,950.00 (TUR) £2,000.00 (BODX) £2,000.00 (FA)
1983 £175.00 (WS) £193.88 (BODX) £200.00 (BEN) £200.00 (JU) £245.00 (FORT) £305.50 (TW)
1983 IB £2,000.00 (FA)
1982 £329.00 (BODX) £475.00 (FORT)
1982 IB £3,500.00 (FA)
1982 magnum £685.03 (FA)
1981 IB £1,200.00 (FA)
1979 IB £1,325.00 (BODX) £1,380.00 (FA)
1978 £132.78 (FA)
1967 £71.43 (PAU)
1961 magnum IB £8,000.00 (FA)
1959 £229.13 (WY) £325.50 (FA)
1949 £540.50 (WY)
1945 £293.75 (FA) £922.38 (WY) £1,000.00 (DI)
1944 £238.09 (PAU)
1926 £740.25 (WY)
1921 £628.63 (WY)

Marquis d'Alesme-Becker 3ème cru classé Margaux
1982 £47.00 (WY)

Marquis-de-Terme 4ème cru classé Margaux
1996 £19.00 (JU) £21.50 (WS) £25.95 (CON)
1996 IB £135.00 (FA)
1994 IB £150.00 (FA)
1992 IB £120.00 (FA)
1990 IB £300.00 (FA)
1988 IB £250.00 (FA)
1986 IB £300.00 (FA)
1983 IB £250.00 (FA)
1982 IB £250.00 (FA)
1981 £14.10 (FA)
1924 £129.25 (WY)
1920 £58.75 (WY)

Marsau Côtes de Francs
2000 EC £59.00 (MON)
1999 £7.24 (MON)
1998 IB £65.00 (FA)
1996 £9.90 (MV)

de Martouret Bordeaux
1998 £5.70 (BAC) £5.79 (AME)

Maucaillou cru bourgeois Moulis
1997 £15.95 (DI)
1996 £14.60 (HIG) £14.99 (JON) £19.99 (TES)
1995 £17.95 (STE) £18.99 (VIL)
1990 £29.50 (TAN)
1989 IB £210.00 (FA)

Mayne-Vieil Fronsac
1998 £6.85 (BO)
1996 £6.56 (NO)

Mazeris Canon-Fronsac
1999 IB £99.00 (CB)
1998 £11.87 (CB) £11.99 (JON)
1997 £7.92 (ARM)
1996 £11.00 (JU) £11.67 (ARM) £12.81 (CB)
1995 £12.98 (CB) £13.75 (ARM)
1994 £10.00 (ARM) £10.75 (BALL)
1994 IB £85.00 (FA)

Méaume Bordeaux Supérieur
1998 £5.90 (JU)
1997 £5.99 (MAJ)
1996 £6.90 (JU)

> *All châteaux are listed alphabetically regardless of class.*

Meyney *cru grand bourgeois exceptionnel*
St-Estèphe
1996 £16.45 (BAN) £17.99 (UN) £18.00 (JU)
£22.03 (PLA)
1996 IB £120.00 (FA)
1995 £14.69 (BAN) £20.99 (JON)
1995 IB £165.00 (FA)
1994 £18.80 (BAN)
1993 £15.95 (COC)
1991 £11.75 (BAN)
1990 IB £300.00 (FA)
1989 IB £330.00 (FA)
1988 £22.33 (FA)
1986 £47.62 (PAU)
1983 £44.00 (FORT)
1970 IB £300.00 (FA)

Millet *Graves*
1996 £10.95 (FRI)
1995 £10.95 (FRI) £15.04 (PLAY)

la Mission-Haut-Brion *cru classé Pessac-*
Léognan
1999 IB £495.00 (FA) £495.00 (JU) £540.00
(RAE)
1998 £72.00 (JU)
1998 IB £720.00 (FA) £790.00 (WY)
1997 £56.67 (MI) £65.00 (BAL) £65.00 (JU)
£68.21 (CB)
1996 £67.50 (MI) £75.00 (CON) £79.00 (JU)
1996 IB £495.00 (FA) £500.00 (TUR)
£540.00 (BODX)
1995 £49.35 (TUR) £50.00 (FLE) £70.50
(CON) £90.00 (JU)
1995 IB £580.00 (BODX)
1995 double magnum £269.86 (WY)
1994 £47.00 (TUR) £49.50 (BAL) £55.00
(POR) £70.00 (JU)
1994 IB £395.00 (FA)
1993 £47.62 (FLE)
1991 £37.60 (WY)
1991 IB £320.00 (FA)
1990 £112.80 (FA) £125.00 (MI)
1990 IB £94.00 (TUR)
1989 £246.75 (TUR)
1989 IB £2,450.00 (FA)
1989 magnum IB £2,450.00 (FA)
1988 £47.50 (CON) £66.00 (CRO)
1988 IB £575.00 (FA) £645.00 (BODX)
1986 £72.50 (CON) £82.00 (CRO) £82.25
(WY)
1986 IB £750.00 (FA)
1985 IB £820.00 (FA)
1983 IB £680.00 (FA) £685.00 (BODX)
1983 double magnum £346.63 (WY)

1982 £189.00 (NI) £217.00 (WY) £225.00
(FORT)
1982 IB £2,300.00 (FA)
1976 magnum £152.75 (WY)
1975 £346.63 (BODX)
1972 £45.00 (BU)
1971 £105.75 (WY)
1970 IB £920.00 (FA)
1967 £120.00 (JU)
1966 £223.25 (TUR)
1962 IB £1,250.00 (FA)
1920 £493.50 (WY)

Monbousquet *grand cru St-Émilion*
1999 IB £420.00 (FA)
1998 £39.00 (JU)
1997 IB £230.00 (FA)
1996 £26.44 (BAN) £30.99 (YOU) £33.40
(TAN)
1996 IB £235.00 (BODX) £240.00 (FA)
£250.00 (TUR)
1994 IB £200.00 (BODX) £220.00 (FA)
1990 IB £220.00 (FA)
1982 £36.92 (BY)

Monbrison *cru bourgeois Margaux*
1999 IB £138.00 (RAE)
1998 EC £152.60 (HAH)
1997 IB £168.00 (BAN)
1996 £17.04 (BAN) £21.00 (JU)
1994 IB £110.00 (BODX)
1990 IB £265.00 (FA)
1986 IB £270.00 (BODX)

Monlot-Capet *St-Émilion*
1997 £12.99 (CON)
1996 £13.65 (NEZ)

Montaiguillon *Montagne-St-Émilion*
1997 £9.80 (NEZ) £10.57 (VIN)
1959 £30.15 (PAU)

Montbrun *cru bourgeois Margaux*
1945 £88.13 (WY)

Montrose *2ème cru classé St-Estèphe*
1999 IB £260.00 (FRI) £306.00 (CB)
1998 £36.00 (JU) £41.67 (MI)
1998 IB £340.00 (FA)
1997 £13.95 (LEA) £37.50 (MI) £39.95 (BAL)
£42.00 (JU) £48.90 (TAN) £48.94 (CB)
£49.95 (JER)
1996 £47.50 (MI) £56.00 (FRI) £59.90 (TAN)
1996 IB £370.00 (TUR) £375.00 (FA)
£400.00 (BODX)

1995 £40.00 (YOU) £41.99 (VIL) £51.00 (FRI)
1995 IB £345.00 (BODX) £375.00 (FA)
1995 ½ bottle £26.00 (FRI)
1994 IB £285.00 (FA) £290.00 (BODX)
1993 £30.83 (MI) £48.75 (BY)
1990 £164.50 (WY) £182.54 (PAU)

1990 IB £1,600.00 (FA)
1989 £77.00 (FRI) £85.00 (JU)
1989 ½ bottle £39.00 (FRI)
1986 £58.75 (TUR) £59.00 (FRI) £60.83 (MI) £75.20 (WY)
1986 IB £580.00 (FA)
1985 £54.00 (FRI) £78.54 (PLAY)
1985 IB £420.00 (BODX) £440.00 (FA)
1982 £94.00 (WY)
1982 IB £700.00 (FA)
1982 jeroboam £810.00 (FRI)
1982 imperial £1,080.00 (FRI)
1981 £46.03 (PAU) £67.45 (VIN)
1978 £52.88 (WY)
1970 £93.50 (BU) £117.50 (WY) £117.50 (TAN) £140.00 (FORT)
1970 IB £920.00 (FA)
1966 £47.62 (PAU) £59.50 (BEN) £90.00 (BU)
1961 £200.00 (CRO)
1945 £464.13 (WY)
1934 £174.60 (PAU)

Moulin-du-Cadet *grand cru classé St-Émilion*
1996 £15.70 (HAH) £17.27 (CB)
1990 IB £185.00 (FA)
1955 £34.92 (PAU)

Moulin Haut-Villars *Fronsac*
1999 IB £55.00 (JU)
1998 £9.45 (JU)
1997 £8.95 (JU) £10.15 (JER)

Moulin Pey-Labrie *Canon-Fronsac*
1999 IB £119.00 (CB)

Moulin Rouge *Bordeaux Supérieur Côtes de Castillon*
1996 £8.70 (HIG)

Moulinet *Pomerol*
1997 £16.49 (BOT)
1978 £25.00 (BU)

Mouton-Rothschild *1er cru classé Pauillac*
1999 £79.90 (MON)
1999 IB £780.00 (FA) £850.00 (JU) £950.00 (FRI) £1,031.00 (CB)
1998 £108.33 (MI) £112.00 (NI)
1998 IB £1,100.00 (FRI) £1,200.00 (BAN)
1997 £89.95 (LAY) £98.90 (TAN) £99.00 (JU) £109.57 (CB) £129.95 (DI) £139.00 (POR)
1997 IB £750.00 (BODX) £780.00 (TUR) £792.00 (BAN)
1996 £120.00 (HIG) £135.00 (UN) £165.00 (FRI) £206.67 (MI)
1996 IB £1,200.00 (FA) £1,250.00 (TUR)
1996 magnum £265.00 (BU)
1996 imperial £963.50 (FA) £998.75 (WY)
1995 £133.95 (BAN) £145.00 (SUN) £205.00 (VIN) £282.90 (BY)
1995 IB £1,280.00 (FA) £1,325.00 (BODX) £1,500.00 (TUR)
1995 imperial £1,010.50 (FA)
1994 £76.38 (TUR) £78.14 (BAN) £80.00 (VIL) £91.00 (PEN) £95.00 (WAI) £96.35 (WY) £133.33 (MI)
1994 IB £780.00 (FA) £800.00 (BODX)
1994 imperial £611.00 (FA) £746.13 (WY)
1993 £77.55 (TUR) £84.17 (MI) £87.30 (PAU) £90.00 (UN) £94.00 (WY) £138.11 (BY)
1993 ½ bottle £42.50 (BU)
1993 double magnum £293.75 (FA)
1992 £71.43 (PAU) £88.13 (WY) £111.63 (PLA) £141.48 (BY)
1992 IB £750.00 (FA) £760.00 (TUR) £780.00 (BODX)
1992 imperial £564.00 (FA)
1991 £71.43 (PAU) £76.38 (TUR) £76.38 (BODX) £88.13 (WY) £135.64 (BY)
1991 IB £780.00 (FA)
1991 magnum £152.75 (FA)
1991 double magnum £270.25 (BODX)
1990 £129.25 (TUR) £129.25 (BODX) £135.13 (WY) £150.00 (JU) £154.00 (PEN) £159.00 (FRI) £182.50 (MI)
1990 IB £1,295.00 (FA)
1990 jeroboam £881.25 (FA)

1989 £152.75 (WY) £155.00 (BEN) £179.00 (FRI) £182.54 (PAU) £1,495.00 (BODX)
1989 IB £1,500.00 (FA) £1,600.00 (TUR)
1989 ½ bottle IB £1,500.00 (FA)
1989 magnum £340.75 (WY)
1989 magnum IB £1,500.00 (FA)
1989 double magnum £705.00 (WY)
1989 imperial £1,104.50 (FA)
1989 imperial IB £980.00 (TUR)
1989 jeroboam £940.00 (FA) £1,351.25 (WY)
1988 £120.00 (JU) £129.25 (TUR) £135.00 (BEN) £141.00 (WY) £150.79 (PAU) £175.00 (FORT)
1988 IB £1,280.00 (FA) £1,320.00 (BODX) £1,350.00 (TUR)
1988 ½ bottle IB £1,280.00 (FA)
1988 magnum IB £1,280.00 (FA)
1988 imperial £940.00 (FA)
1988 jeroboam £736.18 (FA)
1987 £97.50 (BEN) £99.88 (WY)
1987 IB £780.00 (FA)
1986 £25.85 (WY) £180.00 (BU) £277.78 (PAU) £350.00 (FORT)
1986 IB £2,500.00 (TUR) £2,500.00 (FA) £2,550.00 (BODX)
1985 £146.88 (TUR) £150.79 (PAU) £158.00 (BEN) £200.00 (FORT) £215.78 (VIN) £222.11 (PLAY)
1985 IB £1,450.00 (BODX) £1,480.00 (FA)
1984 £99.88 (WY)
1984 IB £720.00 (TUR)
1984 magnum IB £620.00 (FA)
1983 £129.25 (WY)
1983 IB £1,150.00 (FA) £1,200.00 (BODX)
1983 magnum £220.00 (BEN) £225.60 (FA) £246.75 (WY) £277.78 (PAU)
1983 double magnum £599.25 (WY)
1983 jeroboam £936.00 (PAU)
1982 £387.75 (WY) £395.00 (TAN) £550.00 (FORT)
1982 IB £3,900.00 (TUR) £3,950.00 (BODX) £3,950.00 (FA)
1982 magnum £793.13 (FA)
1982 jeroboam £3,760.00 (WY)
1981 £84.60 (BAN) £88.13 (WY)
1981 IB £850.00 (FA)
1981 double magnum £499.38 (WY)

Oz Clarke's Wine Buying Guide
is an annual publication.
We welcome your suggestions for
next year's edition.

1979 £88.13 (BODX) £93.65 (PAU) £99.88 (WY)
1979 IB £900.00 (FA)
1979 double magnum £323.13 (FA)
1979 jeroboam £493.50 (FA) £658.00 (BODX)
1978 £111.63 (WY)
1978 magnum £185.65 (FA)
1978 double magnum £540.50 (WY)
1978 jeroboam IB £460.00 (TUR)
1977 £64.63 (WY)
1976 £85.00 (YOU) £129.25 (WY)
1976 magnum £235.00 (WY)
1975 £88.13 (TUR) £111.63 (WY) £115.00 (BEN)
1975 IB £890.00 (FA)
1975 double magnum £616.88 (WY)
1975 imperial IB £690.00 (TUR)
1973 £229.13 (WY)
1973 magnum £305.50 (WY)
1971 £193.88 (WY) £207.85 (VIN)
1970 £150.00 (BEN) £193.88 (WY)
1970 IB £1,450.00 (FA)
1970 magnum £340.75 (WY)
1968 £411.25 (WY)
1966 £323.13 (WY) £355.50 (VIN)
1965 £311.38 (WY)
1962 £235.00 (FA) £411.25 (WY)
1961 £881.25 (FA) £1,527.50 (WY)
1957 £428.88 (WY)
1955 £225.00 (BEN)
1951 £969.38 (WY)
1947 £1,351.25 (WY)
1944 £511.13 (WY)
1943 £564.00 (WY)
1934 £364.25 (WY)
1929 £1,586.25 (WY)
1926 £1,363.00 (WY)
1921 £340.75 (WY)
1920 £440.63 (WY)
1914 £411.25 (WY)
1909 ½ bottle £158.63 (WY)

Nenin *Pomerol*
1998 £54.00 (JU)
1998 IB £400.00 (FA) £470.00 (FRI)
1997 £42.00 (BAL)
1996 IB £165.00 (FA)
1995 £32.50 (FRI)
1990 £41.23 (WY)
1983 £23.50 (BODX)
1982 IB £360.00 (FA)
1975 £61.90 (PAU)
1961 £85.00 (BAL)
1945 £206.35 (PAU)

Olivier *cru classé Pessac-Léognan*
1992 £11.95 (BY)
1959 £47.62 (PAU)

les Ormes-de-Pez *cru grand bourgeois
St-Estèphe*
1998 £19.17 (MI) £21.37 (BY)
1998 EC £144.50 (HAH)
1997 £15.00 (MI)
1996 £21.00 (STA) £22.50 (MI) £24.95 (FRI)
1995 £20.00 (MI) £22.69 (JON) £26.95 (FRI)
   £31.00 (BY)
1994 £18.99 (VIL) £19.17 (MI) £26.90 (BY)
1990 IB £265.00 (FA)
1989 £33.33 (PAU) £42.50 (FORT)
1986 IB £230.00 (BODX) £250.00 (FA)
1985 £37.00 (STE) £45.00 (FORT)

Les Ormes-Sorbet *cru grand bourgeois
Médoc*
1991 £14.00 (NEZ)
1990 IB £220.00 (FA)

Palmer *3ème cru classé Margaux*
1999 £70.50 (NI)
1999 IB £455.00 (JU)
1998 £55.00 (MI) £60.00 (JU) £62.25 (NI)
1998 IB £480.00 (FRI)
1997 £32.50 (BU) £49.90 (TAN) £52.50 (MI)
1996 £50.00 (FLE) £64.17 (MI) £65.00
   (CON) £65.95 (BALL)
1996 IB £420.00 (FA)
1995 £48.00 (FLE) £49.50 (CON) £57.00
   (NEZ) £58.75 (WY) £63.33 (MI) £69.00
   (BALL)
1994 £41.13 (BAN) £42.50 (MI)
1990 £70.50 (TUR) £75.00 (CON) £82.25
   (WY)
1990 IB £740.00 (FA)
1989 £80.00 (BU) £95.00 (CON) £107.00
   (FRI) £125.00 (MI) £150.24 (PLAY)
1989 IB £1,000.00 (FA) £1,020.00 (BODX)
1988 £75.00 (CON)
1988 IB £600.00 (BODX) £600.00 (FA)
1986 £64.63 (TUR) £64.63 (BODX) £75.00
   (CON) £75.00 (YOU) £76.00 (NI)
1985 £75.00 (CON) £82.25 (WY) £90.00
   (FORT) £110.00 (FRI)
1985 IB £650.00 (FA) £680.00 (BODX)
1983 £125.00 (WS) £135.00 (BEN) £142.00
   (STA) £145.00 (CRO) £146.88 (WY)
   £146.90 (TAN) £147.62 (PAU) £175.00
   (FORT)
1983 IB £1,350.00 (FA)
1983 magnum £330.00 (FORT)

1982 £75.00 (SOM)
1982 IB £850.00 (FA)
1982 magnum £223.25 (WY)
1982 magnum IB £850.00 (FA)
1981 £47.00 (TUR)
1981 IB £350.00 (FA)
1979 £48.18 (FA)
1978 IB £620.00 (FA)
1976 £31.73 (FA)
1975 £64.63 (FA) £88.13 (WY)
1975 IB £730.00 (BODX)
1970 £120.00 (BAL)
1970 magnum IB £1,400.00 (FA)
1966 £182.54 (PAU) £325.00 (FORT)
1961 £411.25 (WY)
1950 £58.75 (WY)

Pape-Clément *cru classé Pessac-Léognan*
1999 IB £235.00 (JU)
1998 £37.50 (MI)
1998 EC £340.00 (TAN)
1997 £29.95 (BAL) £31.00 (JU) £31.67 (MI)
1996 £37.00 (JU)
1996 IB £280.00 (FA)
1995 £47.50 (MI)
1994 IB £255.00 (BODX)
1993 IB £180.00 (FA) £225.00 (BODX)
1990 IB £480.00 (FA)
1989 £41.13 (FA) £44.95 (BEN) £47.62
   (PAU)
1988 IB £450.00 (FA)
1987 IB £340.00 (BODX)
1986 £59.50 (TAN) £61.90 (PAU)
1986 IB £480.00 (FA)
1985 IB £420.00 (FA)
1978 IB £280.00 (FA)
1975 £29.38 (BODX)
1962 £39.68 (PAU)

Patache d'Aux *cru grand bourgeois
Médoc*
2000 EC £45.00 (MON)
1999 £6.55 (MON)
1996 £9.75 (BU) £10.99 (POR) £10.99 (JON)
   £13.95 (COC)
1995 £8.35 (GN) £10.75 (BU)
1993 £10.90 (CRO)

---

*EC (ex-cellar) price per dozen,
excluding shipping, duty and VAT.
IB (in bond) price per dozen,
excluding duty and VAT.
All other prices, per bottle incl VAT.*

Pavie *1er grand cru classé St-Émilion*
1999 IB £695.00 (JU)
1998 £54.20 (JU) £71.67 (MI)
1998 IB £620.00 (FA)
1996 £36.00 (FRI)
1996 IB £305.00 (TUR)
1995 £33.50 (FRI)
1995 IB £240.00 (BODX)
1994 £32.50 (UN)
1990 £58.75 (FA)
1989 IB £450.00 (FA) £470.00 (BODX)
1988 £50.00 (JU) £53.26 (BY) £54.00 (FRI)
1988 IB £380.00 (FA) £425.00 (BODX)
    £465.00 (TUR)
1987 £33.50 (FRI)
1986 £59.00 (FRI) £75.22 (PLAY)
1985 IB £380.00 (FA) £465.00 (BODX)
    £490.00 (TUR)
1983 £51.00 (BY)
1983 IB £420.00 (FA)
1983 magnum IB £420.00 (FA)
1982 £88.13 (WY)
1982 IB £600.00 (FA)
1981 £21.15 (FA)
1981 magnum IB £340.00 (BODX)
1978 IB £355.00 (BODX)
1978 magnum IB £320.00 (FA)
1970 £50.00 (BU)
1970 magnum IB £495.00 (FA)
1947 £206.35 (PAU)
1924 £111.63 (WY)

Pavie-Decesse *grand cru classé St-Émilion*
1999 IB £380.00 (JU)
1998 IB £380.00 (FA)
1997 £44.17 (MI)
1995 £25.00 (UN) £29.50 (FRI)
1993 £17.63 (BAN)
1990 IB £330.00 (FA)
1989 IB £395.00 (BODX)
1985 IB £350.00 (FA)
1971 £87.30 (PAU)

Pavie-Macquin *grand cru classé St-Émilion*
1999 £52.60 (NI)
1999 IB £375.00 (JU) £380.00 (FA)
1998 £53.25 (JU) £63.33 (MI)
1998 IB £440.00 (BODX)
1997 £35.00 (JU) £45.00 (MI)
1996 £22.33 (FA) £30.00 (JU) £35.00 (WAI)
    £36.67 (MI)
1995 £37.00 (JU) £47.50 (MI)
1994 £18.80 (FA)
1970 £25.00 (BU)
1959 £55.55 (PAU)

Pavillon Rouge du Château Margaux
    Margaux
1999 IB £180.00 (JU)
1998 £23.50 (FORT) £25.00 (JU)
1998 IB £220.00 (WY)
1997 £25.00 (JU) £34.95 (DI)
1997 IB £240.00 (BAN)
1996 £25.95 (TUR) £31.85 (LAY) £34.17
    (MI) £36.00 (JU) £36.31 (CB)
1995 £37.60 (WY) £42.50 (BU)
1994 IB £200.00 (FA)
1989 IB £420.00 (FA)
1986 IB £450.00 (FA)
1985 £41.13 (FA) £58.75 (WY)
1983 £35.00 (WS) £68.15 (WY)
1982 IB £540.00 (FA)

Pédesclaux *5ème cru classé Pauillac*
1996 £20.00 (MI)
1995 £17.50 (MI)

Petit-Village *Pomerol*
1998 IB £350.00 (FRI)
1997 £26.67 (MI)
1996 £36.00 (FRI) £40.00 (FORT)
1995 £38.50 (FRI) £41.99 (VIL) £49.43 (BY)
    £49.50 (CON) £280.00 (FA)
1990 £52.38 (PAU)
1989 IB £540.00 (TUR)
1988 £50.00 (JU)
1985 £35.25 (FA)
1981 IB £320.00 (FA)
1979 £29.38 (BODX)
1970 £79.50 (POR)
1936 £111.11 (PAU)
1934 £220.00 (CRO)

la Petite Eglise *Pomerol*
1999 IB £99.00 (FA) £99.00 (JU)
1998 £17.00 (JU)
1997 IB £135.00 (FA)
1996 £15.86 (BAN) £19.00 (JU)
1996 IB £190.00 (FA) £195.00 (TUR)

Pétrus *Pomerol*
1999 IB £4,950.00 (FA) £5,600.00 (TUR)
1999 magnum £1,116.25 (TUR)
1998 £734.38 (FA)
1997 IB £3,200.00 (FA) £3,240.00 (BODX)
1996 IB £4,200.00 (FA) £5,200.00 (TUR)
1995 £567.53 (FA) £581.63 (WY) £587.50
    (TUR)
1995 IB £5,600.00 (BODX)
1994 £305.50 (WY)
1994 magnum £567.53 (FA)

1993 IB £2,850.00 (FA)
1990 £910.63 (WY) £940.00 (TUR)
1989 magnum £1,880.00 (TUR)
1988 £352.50 (TUR) £352.50 (BODX)
£500.00 (FORT)
1988 magnum IB £3,600.00 (BODX)
£3,600.00 (FA)
1986 £310.00 (JU) £352.50 (BODX)
1986 magnum £626.28 (FA)
1985 £550.00 (JU)
1982 £1,251.38 (BODX) £1,500.00 (FORT)
£2,500.00 (JU)
1982 IB £12,800.00 (FA)
1979 £289.05 (FA)
1978 IB £3,000.00 (FA)
1976 £364.25 (WY)
1971 £587.50 (FA)
1970 £1,000.00 (FORT)
1966 £500.00 (PAU)
1928 £2,500.00 (JU)

Peybonhomme-les-Tours *1ères Côtes de Blaye*
1998 £7.45 (NI) £7.95 (STE)

Peyrabon *cru grand bourgeois Haut-Médoc*
1998 £12.50 (MI)
1996 £13.33 (MI)

du Peyrat *1ères Côtes de Bordeaux*
1997 £7.46 (CB)

de Pez *cru bourgeois supérieur St-Estèphe*
1996 £17.50 (PEN) £17.99 (UN)
1995 £19.00 (PEN)
1994 £13.00 (UN)
1989 £25.00 (YOU)
1983 £24.50 (BU)

Phélan-Ségur *cru grand bourgeois exceptionnel St-Estèphe*
1998 £20.00 (MI) £27.85 (NI)
1997 £18.80 (TAN) £19.74 (CB)
1997 IB £180.00 (BAN)
1996 £19.95 (DI) £23.00 (JU) £23.50 (BAN)
£38.85 (NI)
1995 £22.69 (JON) £25.85 (BAN) £40.75
(NI)
1994 £21.15 (BAN)
1994 IB £130.00 (FA)
1990 £29.38 (BAN)
1988 £28.00 (BAL)
1982 £49.20 (PAU)
1955 £70.50 (FA)

Pibran *cru bourgeois Pauillac*
1998 £16.67 (MI)
1997 £14.17 (MI)
1996 £18.33 (MI) £18.50 (FORT)
1995 £17.50 (MI) £31.00 (BY)
1979 £19.50 (RIC)

Picard *cru bourgeois St-Estèphe*
1998 £4.95 (WS)
1996 £13.95 (WS)

Pichon-Longueville (called Pichon-Baron until 1988) *2ème cru classé Pauillac*
1999 IB £238.00 (JU) £270.00 (FRI) £313.00
(CB)
1998 £33.00 (FORT) £38.33 (MI) £39.75 (NI)
1998 IB £250.00 (FA) £310.00 (FRI)
1998 magnum IB £330.00 (FRI)
1997 £35.50 (LEA) £35.83 (MI) £38.00 (JU)
£40.19 (CB) £44.30 (HAH) £45.00 (RES)
£49.95 (DI) £51.25 (NI)
1996 £40.00 (FRI) £40.00 (JU) £41.67 (MI)
£43.50 (CON)
1996 IB £265.00 (FA) £345.00 (TUR)
1996 magnum £67.37 (WY)
1995 £29.95 (CON) £32.90 (WY) £42.50
(FRI) £58.64 (BY)
1995 IB £270.00 (BODX)
1994 £29.80 (AME) £30.83 (MI)
1994 IB £240.00 (FA) £265.00 (TUR)
1990 £85.00 (FRI) £85.50 (FLE) £98.41
(PAU)
1990 IB £925.00 (FA)
1989 £80.00 (JU) £89.00 (CRO) £94.00
(TUR) £146.88 (WY)
1988 £72.00 (BAL)
1986 £63.33 (MI) £70.00 (WS)
1985 IB £450.00 (BODX)
1983 £41.13 (BODX) £92.00 (CRO)
1983 IB £420.00 (FA)
1982 £103.17 (PAU) £170.00 (WS)
1982 IB £780.00 (FA)
1975 £98.90 (TAN)
1967 £42.85 (PAU)
1961 £223.25 (WY)
1928 £330.00 (JU)

Please remember that
Oz Clarke's Wine Buying Guide
*is a price **guide** and not a price **list**. It is not meant to replace up-to-date merchants' lists.*

Pichon-Longueville-Lalande (called Pichon-Lalande until 1993) *2ème cru classé Pauillac*
1999 £29.27 (MON)
1999 IB £280.00 (JU) £294.00 (RAE) £295.00 (HIG) £315.00 (FRI) £374.00 (CB)
1998 £49.00 (JU) £50.00 (FORT) £55.50 (NI)
1998 IB £440.00 (FRI)
1998 EC £498.00 (TAN)
1997 £39.50 (LAY) £45.00 (BAL) £48.90 (TAN) £49.00 (JU) £50.35 (CB)
1997 IB £300.00 (FA)
1997 magnum £100.00 (FORT)
1996 £62.86 (BAN) £63.65 (TUR) £76.50 (FRI) £90.00 (FORT) £95.00 (HED)
1996 imperial £493.50 (FA) £611.00 (WY)
1995 £70.50 (BAN) £85.00 (FRI) £86.45 (LAY)
1995 IB £695.00 (FA)
1995 jeroboam £622.75 (WY)
1994 £37.50 (NI) £41.13 (BAN) £41.13 (BODX) £45.00 (WS) £47.00 (BAL) £55.00 (WAI)
1994 IB £400.00 (FA)
1990 £69.50 (BEN) £74.03 (WY)
1990 IB £750.00 (TUR)
1990 magnum £175.00 (FRI)
1989 £75.00 (CON) £80.29 (TUR) £85.00 (FRI) £90.00 (JU) £94.00 (WY)
1989 IB £825.00 (FA)
1989 magnum £162.15 (FA)
1989 imperial £928.25 (WY)
1988 £73.00 (FRI) £79.90 (WY) £85.00 (FORT)
1988 IB £650.00 (BODX) £680.00 (FA)
1988 magnum IB £680.00 (FA)
1987 magnum IB £320.00 (FA)
1986 £110.00 (FRI) £125.00 (BAL)
1986 IB £900.00 (FA) £920.00 (BODX)
1986 magnum £176.25 (FA)
1985 £89.50 (BEN) £90.00 (WS) £99.88 (WY) £100.00 (FORT) £101.00 (STE)
1985 IB £850.00 (FA)
1983 £55.00 (FLE) £85.00 (JU) £97.53 (WY) £115.00 (FORT)
1983 IB £815.00 (BODX) £820.00 (FA)
1982 £170.00 (WS) £199.50 (BEN) £199.75 (TUR) £225.00 (FRI) £246.75 (WY) £290.00 (FORT)
1982 IB £2,200.00 (FA)
1982 magnum £431.23 (FA)
1982 jeroboam £1,890.00 (FRI)
1982 imperial £2,690.00 (FRI)
1981 IB £550.00 (FA)
1979 IB £600.00 (FA)

1978 £61.10 (FA) £79.00 (CRO)
1978 IB £830.00 (BODX)
1970 £89.00 (CRO) £105.75 (WY)
1959 £305.50 (WY)
1940 £176.25 (WY)
1914 £158.63 (WY)

le Pin *Pomerol*
1999 IB £2,975.00 (JU) £3,750.00 (FA)
1998 £300.00 (JU) £698.33 (MI)
1997 £188.00 (BODX) £250.00 (JU) £321.67 (MI)
1996 IB £3,200.00 (FA)
1995 £446.50 (TUR) £475.00 (BU)
1995 IB £4,200.00 (BODX)
1993 £264.38 (BODX)
1993 IB £2,700.00 (FA)
1993 magnum £528.75 (BODX)
1992 £215.42 (TUR)
1992 magnum IB £2,250.00 (FA)
1991 IB £2,400.00 (FA)
1990 £800.00 (JU)
1990 IB £8,000.00 (FA)
1989 £600.00 (JU) £646.25 (TUR)
1986 £538.54 (TUR) £600.00 (FORT)
1986 IB £5,000.00 (FA)

Pipeau *grand cru St-Émilion*
1996 £11.00 (TAN)

Pique-Caillou *Pessac-Léognan*
1998 £13.33 (MI)
1996 £13.49 (GW) £14.17 (MI)
1995 £13.33 (MI)
1993 £11.67 (MI)

Pitray *Bordeaux Supérieur Côtes de Castillon*
1997 £6.99 (HED)
1996 £7.50 (JU)
1995 £8.00 (JU)

Plagnac *cru bourgeois Médoc*
1996 £9.99 (UN)

Plaisance *Montagne-St-Émilion*
1998 £12.95 (WS)
1997 £7.49 (SO) £10.15 (JER)
1996 £8.90 (JU)

Plince *Pomerol*
1996 £14.17 (ARM)
1995 £17.95 (BALL)
1989 £25.99 (YOU)
1964 £30.15 (PAU)

la Pointe *Pomerol*
1999 IB £175.00 (CB)
1998 £19.00 (JU)
1998 IB £129.00 (BAN) £150.00 (FA)
£195.00 (WY) £210.00 (FRI)
1996 £21.17 (CB)
1995 £25.00 (MI) £27.50 (WRI)
1994 £21.67 (MI) £22.67 (JON) £28.20 (WY)
1993 IB £120.00 (FA)
1992 IB £95.00 (BODX)
1990 £39.50 (BEN)
1989 £26.00 (CRO)
1983 IB £165.00 (FA)
1978 £176.25 (FA)
1959 £61.90 (PAU)
1945 £206.35 (PAU)

Pontet-Canet *5ème cru classé Pauillac*
1999 IB £160.00 (HIG) £185.00 (FRI)
1998 £25.83 (MI)
1998 EC £188.85 (HAH)
1997 £22.00 (JU) £22.50 (MI) £24.95 (BAL)
£26.09 (CB) £26.40 (TAN) £29.95 (DI)
1997 IB £215.00 (TUR)
1996 £28.95 (DI) £31.00 (JU) £34.17 (MI)
1996 IB £245.00 (FA) £305.00 (TUR)
1995 £25.85 (FA) £32.50 (MI)
1994 £26.67 (MI) £29.99 (POR)
1994 IB £240.00 (FA)
1994 magnum £59.50 (POR)
1990 IB £330.00 (FA)
1989 £45.49 (SUN) £47.50 (MI)
1983 IB £285.00 (FA)
1970 £41.73 (WY)
1951 £111.11 (PAU)
1936 £111.11 (PAU)
1914 £135.13 (WY)

Potensac *cru grand bourgeois Médoc*
1999 IB £128.00 (CB)
1998 £16.67 (MI) £18.21 (CB)
1997 £12.38 (PAU) £15.83 (MI) £18.15 (CB)
1997 IB £105.00 (TUR)
1996 £14.58 (ARM) £15.99 (RAE) £16.25
(SOM) £17.00 (JU) £18.33 (MI) £22.50
(CON) £22.50 (FRI) £26.30 (GW)
1996 IB £115.00 (BODX) £125.00 (FA)
1995 £17.50 (MI) £18.40 (TAN) £26.30
(GW)
1994 £15.83 (MI) £19.99 (POR) £21.00
(BAL) £33.00 (FORT)
1994 IB £100.00 (FA)
1993 £15.00 (MI)
1990 £26.98 (PAU) £28.00 (CRO)
1990 IB £220.00 (FA)

1989 £19.58 (TUR) £22.99 (YOU)
1985 IB £240.00 (FA)
1983 IB £220.00 (BODX)
1982 IB £285.00 (FA)

Poujeaux *cru grand bourgeois exceptionnel Moulis*
1998 £18.99 (BAL) £20.00 (MI) £21.25 (NI)
1997 £15.83 (MI) £15.95 (WAI) £17.04 (CB)
£19.40 (TAN) £19.95 (DI) £22.50 (CON)
1996 £17.49 (OD) £18.80 (BAN) £20.00
(JU) £22.50 (CON)
1995 £17.95 (CON) £19.50 (WS) £19.99
(SUN) £19.99 (LAI) £20.00 (ARM) £27.41
(BY)
1995 IB £185.00 (FA)
1994 £18.33 (MI)
1994 IB £140.00 (FA)
1992 IB £120.00 (FA)
1990 £29.50 (BU)
1989 IB £255.00 (FA)
1988 £30.00 (BU)
1982 IB £320.00 (FA)
1953 £109.52 (PAU)

la Prade *Côtes de Francs*
1996 £7.50 (WS)

Prieur de Meyney *St-Estèphe*
1991 £8.23 (BAN)

Prieuré-Lichine *4ème cru classé Margaux*
1997 £22.44 (CB)
1996 £28.36 (CB)
1996 IB £160.00 (FA)
1995 £21.50 (HIG)
1990 IB £280.00 (FA)
1985 £39.00 (COC)
1982 £32.90 (FA)

Puy-Blanquet *grand cru St-Émilion*
1998 £11.50 (JU)
1994 £13.25 (BALL)

Puy-Castéra *cru bourgeois Haut-Médoc*
1998 £10.78 (SAV)
1997 £8.61 (SAV)
1995 £23.50 (SAV)
1993 £7.75 (CON)

Puygueraud *Côtes de Francs*
1998 £11.85 (NI)
1996 £12.90 (NI)
1995 £11.28 (BAN)

Ramage-la-Bâtisse *cru bourgeois Haut-Médoc*
1996 £11.49 (BOT) £11.49 (THR) £11.49 (VIC) £11.49 (WR)
1995 £11.45 (CON)
1994 £10.99 (BO) £12.99 (AME)
1987 £9.21 (PAU)

Rauzan-Gassies *2ème cru classé Margaux*
1996 £34.99 (SAI) £35.00 (UN)
1996 IB £165.00 (BODX)
1995 £35.00 (UN)
1983 IB £290.00 (BODX)
1961 £135.13 (WY)
1940 £111.63 (WY)
1928 £176.25 (WY)

Rauzan-Ségla *2ème cru classé Margaux*
1999 IB £281.00 (CB)
1998 £33.33 (MI)
1997 £27.50 (MI) £29.50 (WAI) £29.95 (BAL) £30.00 (JU) £32.25 (CB)
1996 £30.00 (FLE) £39.17 (MI) £40.11 (CB) £42.50 (FRI)
1996 IB £285.00 (FA)
1995 £34.66 (FLE) £42.99 (VIL)
1995 IB £280.00 (BODX) £330.00 (FA) £385.00 (TUR)
1993 £29.17 (MI)
1993 IB £130.00 (FA)
1992 IB £165.00 (BODX)
1990 £50.00 (FLE) £60.00 (PEN) £66.70 (TAN)
1990 IB £520.00 (BODX) £540.00 (FA)
1989 IB £425.00 (FA)
1986 £70.50 (FA)
1985 IB £420.00 (FA)
1983 magnum £77.55 (FA)
1982 IB £480.00 (FA)
1966 £38.09 (PAU)
1961 £100.00 (BU)
1937 £119.05 (PAU)

Réserve de la Comtesse *Pauillac*
1997 £19.50 (LAY)
1997 IB £120.00 (FA)
1996 £12.50 (WS) £19.00 (ARM) £23.50 (WY) £25.50 (STA)
1995 £26.00 (WS) £27.99 (RAE) £37.00 (JU)
1995 IB £205.00 (BODX)
1994 £16.50 (WS) £19.09 (TUR) £27.50 (TAN)
1993 £24.95 (BALL)
1988 IB £265.00 (FA)

Réserve du Château de la Tour *Bordeaux Supérieur*
1998 £7.95 (JU)
1996 £8.00 (JU)

la Réserve du Général *Margaux*
1997 £18.99 (MORR)
1995 IB £195.00 (BODX)
1989 £21.15 (FA)

Respide-Médeville *Graves*
1995 £19.39 (TW)

du Retout *cru bourgeois Haut-Médoc*
1995 £13.95 (WIN)

Reynier *Bordeaux Supérieur*
1996 £6.45 (STE)

la Rivière *Fronsac*
1994 £19.45 (TW)

Roc-de-Cambes *Côtes de Bourg*
1999 £23.50 (SAV)
1999 IB £220.00 (FA)
1998 £14.35 (NI)
1998 EC £220.00 (SAV)
1997 £15.83 (NI) £21.54 (SAV) £22.00 (FORT)
1997 IB £185.00 (BODX)
1996 £21.54 (SAV)
1995 IB £180.00 (FA)
1994 £15.97 (SAV)
1992 £18.95 (BU)
1991 £22.50 (BU)
1989 IB £260.00 (FA)

du Rocher *grand cru St-Émilion*
1994 £5.66 (NEZ)

Roquevieille *Côtes de Castillon*
1996 £6.95 (STA)

Rouet *Fronsac*
1994 £9.00 (BER)

Rouget *Pomerol*
1998 £28.00 (JU)
1949 £206.35 (PAU)

Rousset *Côtes de Bourg*
1995 £6.95 (WS)

Rozier *grand cru St-Émilion*
1998 £11.99 (SAF) £13.00 (MV)

Ruat-Petit-Poujeaux *cru bourgeois Moulis*
1994 £8.75 (CON)

St-Georges *St-Georges-St-Émilion*
1996 £16.25 (FRI)
1995 £16.25 (FRI)

St-Pierre *4ème cru classé St-Julien*
1998 £25.83 (MI)
1996 £23.95 (LEA) £31.67 (MI)
1995 £25.83 (MI) £27.99 (VIL)
1994 £26.67 (MI)
1974 £23.80 (PAU)

de Sales *Pomerol*
1998 £20.00 (MI)
1997 £14.17 (MI)
1996 £17.50 (MI) £19.99 (MAJ)
1995 £20.83 (MI) £31.00 (STA)
1993 IB £115.00 (BODX)
1990 IB £285.00 (FA)
1988 £17.63 (FA)
1985 £29.50 (BU)
1983 IB £225.00 (FA)
1982 £25.85 (FA)
1966 £23.80 (PAU)

Sarget de Gruaud-Larose *St-Julien*
1998 £15.83 (MI)
1994 £23.50 (STA)
1993 £22.49 (BO)

Segonzac *1ères Côtes de Blaye*
1998 £5.95 (WAI) £7.99 (SAI)

Sénéjac *cru bourgeois supérieur Haut-Médoc*
1996 £13.05 (BER)
1988 IB £110.00 (FA)
1945 £111.11 (PAU)

la Serre *grand cru classé St-Émilion*
1995 £25.99 (JON)
1955 £39.68 (PAU)

Siaurac *Lalande-de-Pomerol*
1998 £73.00 (TAN)
1995 £14.00 (JU)

Siran *cru bourgeois supérieur Margaux*
1996 £17.99 (UN) £19.55 (GN) £28.50 (STA)
1995 £29.95 (STA)
1993 £14.15 (COC)

Sirius *Bordeaux*
1998 £6.99 (BOT) £6.99 (THR) £6.99 (VIC) £6.99 (WR)
1997 £5.99 (SO)
1996 £7.25 (CON)

Smith-Haut-Lafitte *cru classé Pessac-Léognan*
1999 IB £275.00 (CB)
1998 £30.00 (MI)
1997 £29.02 (CB) £41.23 (BY)
1996 £33.00 (CON) £38.42 (CB) £47.17 (BY)
1996 IB £210.00 (BODX) £220.00 (FA)
1995 £49.43 (BY)
1995 IB £220.00 (BODX) £240.00 (FA)
1953 £55.55 (PAU)
1924 £82.25 (WY)

Sociando-Mallet *cru grand bourgeois Haut-Médoc*
1999 IB £165.00 (JU) £174.00 (RAE) £190.00 (FRI)
1998 £20.00 (JU) £25.83 (MI)
1998 IB £170.00 (BODX)

1997 £22.00 (JU) £22.50 (MI) £24.95 (BAL) £24.99 (ASD) £29.95 (DI)
1997 IB £185.00 (BODX)
1996 £24.00 (JU) £25.26 (BAN) £33.00 (CON) £39.99 (JON)
1995 £27.95 (CON)
1994 £25.00 (MI)
1993 £23.33 (MI)
1993 IB £165.00 (FA)
1990 £61.90 (PAU)
1990 IB £550.00 (FA)
1989 £41.13 (BODX)
1988 IB £320.00 (FA)
1986 £35.25 (TUR)
1986 IB £380.00 (FA)
1985 £37.60 (FA) £44.70 (TAN)

de Sours *Bordeaux Supérieur*
1999 IB £68.00 (CB)
1998 £8.52 (CB)

Soutard *grand cru classé St-Émilion*
1998 £21.50 (BAL)
1998 IB £240.00 (BAN)
1996 £18.33 (MI)
1994 £17.50 (MI)
1988 £23.50 (FA)
1972 £23.80 (PAU)

de Tabuteau *Lussac-St-Émilion*
1997 £8.99 (VIN) £9.24 (NO)

du Tailhas *Pomerol*
1995 £21.00 (RES)
1955 £39.68 (PAU)

Talbot *4ème cru classé St-Julien*
1999 IB £150.00 (HIG) £155.00 (FA)
   £155.00 (JU)
1998 £25.60 (NI) £25.83 (MI)
1998 IB £200.00 (FRI)
1997 £21.67 (MI) £24.68 (CB) £26.50
   (FORT) £27.50 (CON)
1997 IB £165.00 (TUR) £198.00 (BAN)
1996 £22.33 (BAN) £24.99 (LAI) £28.95
   (CON) £31.50 (FRI) £35.00 (UN)
1996 IB £230.00 (FA)
1996 double mgnum £119.07 (WY)
1995 £29.38 (WY) £29.95 (FRI) £30.33 (MI)
   £35.95 (LEA) £38.20 (JER) £38.95 (STA)
   £38.99 (PLAY)
1995 ½ bottle £16.45 (WY)
1994 £17.63 (WY) £20.00 (PEN) £26.67 (MI)
1994 IB £200.00 (FA)
1992 £37.99 (VIL)
1990 £39.50 (BU) £47.50 (MI) £47.62 (PAU)
   £58.75 (WY)
1989 £46.94 (PLA) £47.50 (MI) £54.99 (NO)
   £56.40 (WY)
1989 IB £440.00 (FA)
1988 double magnum £164.50 (FA)
1986 £70.50 (TUR) £77.55 (WY)
1986 IB £725.00 (FA) £730.00 (WY)
1986 magnum £142.18 (FA)
1985 IB £500.00 (FA)
1983 £54.05 (WY) £56.00 (CRO) £75.00
   (CON)
1983 magnum IB £495.00 (FA)

EC (ex-cellar) price per dozen,
excluding shipping, duty and VAT.
IB (in bond) price per dozen,
excluding duty and VAT.
All other prices, per bottle incl VAT.

1982 IB £800.00 (FA)
1982 ½ bottle £38.78 (FA)
1982 magnum £121.03 (FA)
1981 £31.73 (FA)
1981 magnum £62.28 (FA)
1970 IB £320.00 (FA)
1966 £44.65 (FA)
1955 £152.75 (WY)

Tanesse *1ères Côtes de Bordeaux*
1996 £5.82 (PEN)
1995 £7.50 (WS)

Terre Rouge *Médoc*
1997 £8.29 (HIC)
1996 £9.25 (MAY)
1995 £6.50 (BALL) £8.59 (JON)

Terrey-Gros-Cailloux *cru bourgeois St-Julien*
1997 £12.90 (BAC)
1993 £16.45 (BY)

du Tertre *5ème cru classé Margaux*
1998 £20.00 (MI)
1996 £19.39 (BAN)
1996 IB £140.00 (FA)
1989 £31.99 (SUN)

Tertre-Daugay *grand cru classé St-Émilion*
1999 IB £200.00 (CB)
1993 £22.50 (MI)
1990 £30.83 (MI)
1924 £105.75 (WY)

Tertre Rôteboeuf *St-Émilion*
1999 £58.75 (SAV) £65.50 (NI)
1999 IB £467.00 (CB) £550.00 (FA)
1998 £62.75 (CB)
1998 IB £780.00 (FA)
1998 EC £660.00 (SAV)
1997 £49.50 (NI) £55.00 (FORT) £55.81
   (SAV) £64.68 (CB)
1996 £64.63 (SAV) £83.07 (CB) £99.88
   (BODX)
1996 IB £550.00 (TUR)
1995 IB £780.00 (FA) £820.00 (BODX)
1993 IB £380.00 (FA) £410.00 (BODX)
1989 IB £1,550.00 (FA)
1988 £105.00 (CRO)
1988 IB £900.00 (FA)
1986 £99.00 (CRO) £99.88 (WY)
1985 £88.13 (FA) £95.50 (BEN)
1982 £129.25 (WY)

Teyssier *grand cru St-Émilion*
2000 EC £53.00 (MON)
1999 IB £85.00 (JU)
1998 £8.99 (SAF) £10.50 (JU) £14.95 (POR)
1997 £9.50 (JU) £9.52 (BAN) £11.99 (YOU)
   £12.02 (NO) £12.95 (AD) £12.99 (VIL)
   £13.99 (JON) £13.99 (DI)

Thieuley *Bordeaux Supérieur*
1999 £5.08 (MON)

la Tour-de-By *cru grand bourgeois Médoc*
1999 £11.90 (COC)
1998 EC £79.00 (TAN)
1997 £10.99 (POR)
1996 £10.49 (HED) £11.25 (NI) £11.99
   (JON) £11.99 (UN)
1995 £13.45 (STE)
1994 £11.50 (RIC)
1993 £15.60 (TAN)
1990 £19.99 (SUN)

la Tour-Carnet *4ème cru classé Haut-
   Médoc*
1996 £20.00 (UN)
1993 £15.12 (BY)
1990 £29.50 (BU)

la Tour-Figeac *grand cru classé St-Émilion*
1998 IB £165.00 (FA)
1997 £25.91 (CB)
1995 £26.50 (BALL)

la Tour-Haut-Brion *cru classé Pessac-
   Léognan*
1999 IB £210.00 (JU)
1998 £31.00 (JU) £34.17 (MI)
1997 £25.83 (MI) £29.95 (BAL)
1995 IB £220.00 (FA)
1990 £100.00 (FORT)
1989 £76.38 (WY)
1982 £206.35 (PAU)
1981 IB £280.00 (BODX)
1964 £103.17 (PAU)

Tour-Haut-Caussan *cru bourgeois
   Médoc*
1997 £11.50 (BAL) £12.93 (BIB)
1996 £12.95 (BAL)
1995 £13.50 (BALL)
1994 £11.50 (MV)

Tour-du-Haut-Moulin *cru grand
   bourgeois Haut-Médoc*
1999 £7.92 (MON)

la Tour-Martillac *cru classé Pessac-
   Léognan*
1998 £18.95 (LAY)
1994 IB £120.00 (FA)

Tour-du-Mirail *cru bourgeois Haut-
   Médoc*
1997 magnum £15.99 (UN)
1996 £8.99 (UN)

la Tour-de-Mons *cru bourgeois supérieur
   Margaux*
1998 £15.00 (MI)
1996 £15.83 (MI) £17.00 (JU) £18.99 (TES)
1995 £17.50 (BALL)
1989 £23.50 (BAN) £26.67 (MI)
1924 £84.13 (PAU) £135.00 (CRO)
1920 £160.00 (CRO)

Tour-du-Pas-St-Georges *St-Georges-St-
   Émilion*
1998 £7.75 (WS) £8.42 (BIB) £10.00 (MV)
1997 £8.42 (BIB)

la Tour-du-Pin-Figeac *grand cru classé
   St-Émilion*
2000 EC £124.00 (MON)
1998 IB £180.00 (FRI)
1959 £55.55 (PAU)

la Tour-St-Bonnet *cru bourgeois Médoc*
1998 £8.50 (JU)
1996 £8.72 (BIB) £9.95 (BU) £10.00 (JU)
   £11.75 (BER) £11.75 (BODX) £12.45 (JER)
1995 £10.99 (JON) £11.99 (SUN) £11.99
   (LAI)

les Tourelles de Longueville *Pauillac*
1998 £16.67 (MI)
1997 £14.59 (BIB) £15.83 (MI) £20.00
   (FORT)
1996 £18.49 (RAE) £20.00 (MI)
1995 £29.99 (WIN)
1988 IB £215.00 (BODX) £240.00 (FA)

Tournefeuille *Lalande-de-Pomerol*
1998 £15.09 (JON)
1996 £13.80 (RIC)

Tronquoy-Lalande *cru grand bourgeois
   St-Estèphe*
1998 £15.00 (MI)
1997 £12.63 (BAN) £13.33 (MI)
1996 £12.50 (WS) £16.67 (MI)
1995 £15.83 (MI)

Troplong-Mondot *grand cru classé St-Émilion*
1998 £40.00 (FORT) £43.33 (MI)
1998 IB £340.00 (FA)
1997 £35.83 (MI) £37.37 (CB) £40.00 (FORT)
1996 £29.95 (LAY) £37.50 (MI) £40.00 (JU) £44.18 (CB)
1996 IB £245.00 (FA) £250.00 (BODX) £255.00 (TUR)
1995 £34.00 (FLE) £60.00 (JU)
1994 £29.38 (BODX) £34.50 (MAY)
1994 IB £280.00 (FA)
1990 £141.00 (TUR)
1990 IB £1,250.00 (FA)
1989 £99.50 (TAN) £117.50 (TUR)
1989 IB £900.00 (FA)
1986 £27.03 (FA)
1986 IB £350.00 (BODX)
1981 IB £220.00 (BODX)
1959 £55.55 (PAU)

Trotanoy *Pomerol*
1999 IB £480.00 (FA)
1998 IB £1,850.00 (FA)
1997 £56.17 (CB)
1996 IB £350.00 (FA)
1993 £29.38 (FA)
1990 IB £1,080.00 (FA)
1989 £68.00 (CRO)
1987 £26.98 (PAU) £29.38 (FA)
1985 jeroboam £411.25 (FA)
1983 IB £520.00 (FA)
1982 £252.63 (WY)
1979 IB £500.00 (FA)
1975 £166.67 (PAU) £176.25 (BODX)
1970 £235.00 (TUR) £252.63 (WY)
1966 £61.90 (PAU)

Trottevieille *1er grand cru classé St-Émilion*
1996 £24.00 (HIG)
1994 £22.00 (HIG)
1983 £21.15 (FA)

de Valandraud *grand cru St-Émilion*
1999 IB £1,600.00 (FA) £1,680.00 (JU)
1998 £150.00 (JU) £534.17 (MI)
1998 IB £2,000.00 (FA)
1997 £200.00 (JU)
1996 £485.00 (MI)
1996 IB £2,100.00 (TUR) £2,100.00 (FA)
1995 £215.03 (FA)
1994 £176.25 (WY)
1994 IB £1,900.00 (FA)

Verdignan *cru grand bourgeois Haut-Médoc*
1996 £12.99 (SO)
1994 £11.80 (NEZ)
1969 £18.73 (PAU)

Vieux-Château-Certan *Pomerol*
1999 £79.35 (NI)
1999 IB £500.00 (FA) £510.00 (RAE) £550.00 (JU)
1998 IB £1,280.00 (FA)
1997 £41.67 (MI) £42.00 (BAL) £42.50 (LAY) £45.00 (JU) £52.29 (CB) £53.80 (TAN)
1996 £53.99 (RAE) £59.00 (FRI) £60.00 (JU) £60.87 (CB)
1995 £41.13 (FA) £55.99 (VIL) £58.75 (BAN) £70.00 (JU)
1995 IB £420.00 (BODX)
1994 £36.95 (RAE) £55.00 (JU)
1994 IB £315.00 (BODX)
1993 £30.00 (FLE) £36.67 (MI) £43.48 (BAN)
1993 IB £290.00 (BODX)
1992 £25.85 (BAN)
1989 £88.13 (WY)
1988 £80.00 (FORT)
1986 £70.00 (JU)
1982 IB £840.00 (FA)
1982 jeroboam £810.00 (FRI)
1981 £55.00 (FORT)
1981 double magnum £182.13 (FA)
1975 IB £680.00 (FA)
1975 magnum £132.78 (FA)
1970 £61.90 (PAU)
1958 £55.55 (PAU)
1953 £142.85 (PAU)

Villars *Fronsac*
1999 IB £91.00 (JU)
1998 £13.90 (JU)

Villegeorge *cru bourgeois supérieur exceptionnel Médoc*
1997 £14.20 (HAH)
1996 £12.83 (BIB)

Vray-Croix-de-Gay *Pomerol*
1996 £22.50 (ARM)
1962 £34.92 (PAU)

Yon Figeac *grand cru classé St-Émilion*
1997 £16.99 (BOT) £21.03 (NO)
1996 £16.99 (WR) £21.03 (NO) £23.44 (PLA)
1994 £19.99 (DI)
1985 IB £220.00 (FA)

WHITE BORDEAUX PRICES

DRY

Under £5.00

Bel Air **1999** £4.95 (WS) £5.70 (TAN)
Ducla **1999** £4.99 (UN)
Moulin de Launay **1999** £4.95 (TAN) £4.95
(BALL) £4.99 (POR) £4.99 (JON)
Thieuley **2000** £4.95 (SOM)
Trois Mouline Sauvignon **1999** £4.95 (JU)

£5.00 → £6.99

Antonins **1996** £5.99 (RAE)
Bonnet **2000** £5.99 (BOT) £5.99 (WR)
le Chec **1998** £6.95 (AD)
Civrac Lagrange **1995** £6.42 (BY)
Coucheroy **1999** £6.99 (VIC) £6.99 (THR)
£6.99 (BOT) £6.99 (WR)
l'Étoile **1999** £5.25 (WS) £5.95 (TAN)
£6.49 (JON)
l'Étoile **1998** £5.95 (BALL)
Haut-Rian **1999** £5.00 (BAC) £5.50 (COC)
£6.25 (FORT)
Lacroix **1999** £6.50 (JU)
Lacroix **1998** £5.20 (NO) £6.55 (AD) £6.99
(DI)
Montalivet **1998** £6.45 (SOM) £9.49 (BY)
Mouton-Cadet **1999** £5.99 (SAI) £5.99
(VIC) £5.99 (THR) £5.99 (BOT) £5.99 (WR)
Mouton-Cadet **1998** £5.99 (UN) £5.99
(BUD)
Reynon **1999** £6.83 (BY)
Reynon Vieilles Vignes **1999** £6.95 (WS)
Roquefort **1998** £5.75 (BAC)
Thieuley **1999** £5.95 (WS) £6.69 (JON)
Thieuley **1998** £6.49 (GW)

£7.00 → £8.99

Baret **1998** £7.50 (HIG)
Cabannieux **1995** £7.70 (CB)
Clos Floridène **1999** £8.95 (SOM)
Loudenne **1998** £8.50 (JU)
Reynon Vieilles Vignes **1998** £8.47 (BY)
de Sours **1999** £8.23 (CB)

£9.00 → £11.99

de Castelneau **1996** £9.99 (RAE)
Doisy-Daëne Grand Vin Sec **1998** £11.75
(TAN)
Domaine de la Solitude **1997** £10.83 (MI)
de Seuil **1998** £9.50 (JU)
de Seuil **1997** £9.50 (JU) £10.99 (DI)

Thieuley Cuvée Francis Courselle **1999**
£10.99 (CB)
Thieuley Cuvée Francis Courselle **1998**
£9.50 (BALL)
Thieuley Cuvée Francis Courselle **1997**
£9.99 (GW)

£12.00 → £14.99

Clos Floridène **1998** £12.97 (BY)
Clos Floridène **1996** £14.99 (JON)
Couhins-Lurton **1994** £14.50 (RAE)
Domaine de la Solitude **1998** £13.33 (MI)
Domaine de la Solitude **1994** £13.33 (MI)
Domaine de la Solitude **1993** £12.50 (MI)
de Landiras **1995** £12.95 (HED)

£15.00 → £19.99

Bouscaut **1996** £17.50 (UN)
Carbonnieux **1999** £19.50 (JU)
Carbonnieux **1998** £18.33 (MI)
Carbonnieux **1997** £17.50 (MI)
Carbonnieux **1996** £18.33 (MI)
Carbonnieux **1995** £18.33 (MI)
Domaine de la Solitude **1996** £15.00 (MI)
l'Esprit de Chevalier **1994** £19.17 (MI)
Latour-Martillac **1998** £17.50 (MI)
Latour-Martillac **1996** £19.17 (MI)
Latour-Martillac **1995** £17.50 (MI)
Latour-Martillac **1994** £17.50 (MI)
Latour-Martillac **1993** £16.67 (MI)
Malartic-Lagravière **1997** £18.33 (MI)
Smith-Haut-Lafitte **1995** £19.53 (BY)
£23.33 (MI)
Talbot Caillou Blanc **1998** £16.67 (MI)
Talbot Caillou Blanc **1997** £15.83 (MI)
Talbot Caillou Blanc **1996** £16.67 (MI)

£20.00 → £29.99

l'Esprit de Chevalier **1996** £21.67 (MI)
£22.00 (FORT)
l'Esprit de Chevalier **1995** £20.00 (MI)
de Fieuzal **1998** £26.33 (ARM)
de Fieuzal **1996** £26.67 (MI) £33.00 (JU)

- *Wines are listed in A–Z order within
  each price band.*
- *For each wine, vintages are listed in
  descending order.*
- *Each vintage of any wine appears
  only once.*

Latour-Martillac **1990** £25.83 (MI)
Malartic-Lagravière **1998** £20.83 (MI)
Pavillon Blanc du Château Margaux **1998**
  £23.40 (FA) £28.33 (MI) £28.33 (ARM)
  £31.33 (CB)
Pavillon Blanc du Château Margaux **1996**
  £29.17 (MI)
Smith-Haut-Lafitte **1998** £25.83 (MI)
  £27.83 (ARM) £30.00 (FORT) £31.10
  (HAH) £33.78 (CB)
Smith-Haut-Lafitte **1996** £25.83 (MI)
Smith-Haut-Lafitte **1994** £25.83 (MI)
Smith-Haut-Lafitte **1993** £24.17 (MI)

£30.00 → £39.99

Domaine de Chevalier **1998** £32.70 (FA)
Domaine de Chevalier **1997** £36.67 (MI)
Domaine de Chevalier **1993** £39.17 (MI)
Domaine de Chevalier **1992** £38.33 (MI)
de Fieuzal **1993** £37.90 (TAN)
de Fieuzal **1990** £39.50 (BEN)
Laville-Haut-Brion **1994** £35.64 (FA)
Smith-Haut-Lafitte **1997** £30.00 (FORT)

£40.00 → £49.99

Domaine de Chevalier **1996** £42.75 (BEN)
  £43.33 (MI)
Domaine de Chevalier **1995** £42.50 (MI)
  £45.00 (JU)
Domaine de Chevalier **1994** £45.00
  (FORT) £48.33 (MI)
Domaine de Chevalier **1989** £46.41
  (FA)
Laville-Haut-Brion **1997** £46.67 (MI)
Laville-Haut-Brion **1996** £47.50 (MI)
Laville-Haut-Brion **1992** £40.05 (FA)
Laville-Haut-Brion **1990** £48.33 (MI)
'Y' d'Yquem **1988** £47.00 (FA)

£50.00 → £69.99

Domaine de Chevalier **1990** £52.50 (MI)
  £52.88 (TUR) £58.16 (FA)
Domaine de Chevalier **1988** £58.75
  (WY)
Haut-Brion Blanc **1992** £58.75 (FA)
Laville-Haut-Brion **1998** £60.12 (FA)
Roumieu **1976** £52.88 (WY)

£70.00 → £99.99

Haut-Brion Blanc **1995** £95.00 (JU)
Haut-Brion Blanc **1994** £98.00 (JU)
Haut-Brion Blanc **1981** £76.38 (WY)
Laville-Haut-Brion **1967** £70.50 (WY)
Pavillon Blanc du Château Margaux **1924**
  £82.25 (WY)

Over £100.00

Haut-Brion Blanc **1997** £120.00 (JU)
Haut-Brion Blanc **1996** £115.00 (JU)
Haut-Brion Blanc **1988** £125.00 (FORT)
  £143.37 (BY)
Haut-Brion Blanc **1985** £118.87 (FA)
Olivier **1947** £129.25 (WY)
Pavillon Blanc du Château Margaux **1926**
  £141.00 (WY)
Roumieu **1950** £111.63 (WY)

SWEET

Under £7.00

Domaine du Noble ½ bottle **1996** £6.25
  (BALL)
Marquis de Beausoleil Ste-Croix-du-Mont
  1994 £5.99 (UN)
Tour Balot **1996** £6.70 (AS)

£7.00 → £8.99

des Arroucats **1998** £7.99 (CON)
des Arroucats **1997** £8.58 (CB) £9.44
  (HIC)
Bastor-Lamontagne ½ bottle **1915** £7.29
  (BODX)
la Caussade **1997** £7.75 (WAI)
Filhot ½ bottle **1996** £8.57 (FA) £9.99 (UN)
  £9.99 (MAJ) £10.96 (ARM)
Rabaud-Promis ½ bottle **1995** £8.99 (RAE)
  £12.50 (BU)
des Tours **1996** £8.95 (AD) £9.49 (JON)

£9.00 → £11.99

Broustet ½ bottle **1996** £11.50 (FRI)
  £13.95 (HED)
la Chartreuse ½ bottle **1996** £9.66 (HIC)
  £9.99 (SAI) £13.49 (CON)
Coutet ½ bottle **1996** £10.53 (WY) £16.95
  (WAI)
Doisy-Daëne **1996** £11.54 (BY) £19.75
  (WS) £23.26 (HIC) £24.40 (HAH) £25.00
  (JU) £25.20 (TAN) £25.25 (HIG) £25.95
  (DI) £27.03 (CB)
Doisy-Daëne ½ bottle **1996** £11.75 (HIC)
  £12.95 (RES) £14.95 (DI) £15.50 (STA)
Doisy-Védrines ½ bottle **1996** £9.75
  (ARM) £12.95 (LEA)
Fayau **1996** £9.00 (MV)
Filhot ½ bottle **1997** £9.49 (UN)
Liot ½ bottle **1997** £9.75 (WAI)
Liot ½ bottle **1996** £9.96 (HIC)
Lousteau-Vieil **1995** £9.40 (COC)

la Rame **1998** £11.75 (NI)
la Rame Reserve du Château **1995** £9.99 (OD)
Rayne-Vigneau ½ bottle **1997** £10.48 (BODX) £13.95 (LEA) £14.50 (RES)
Rayne-Vigneau ½ bottle **1996** £10.75 (BU) £12.95 (LEA)
Rayne-Vigneau ½ bottle **1995** £10.95 (TAN)
Rieussec ½ bottle **1998** £10.97 (BODX) £14.88 (FRI)
Peter A Sichel **1997** £11.99 (WR)
des Tours **1995** £9.90 (LAY)

£12.00 → £14.99

Bastor-Lamontagne **1997** £13.61 (BODX) £15.00 (MAY) £18.21 (CB)
Broustet **1999** £13.12 (FRI)
Climens ½ bottle **1995** £14.95 (LEA)
Clos d'Yvigne **1994** £13.50 (JU)
Doisy-Daëne ½ bottle **1997** £13.95 (LEA)
Filhot ½ bottle **1995** £12.85 (NI)
Guiraud ½ bottle **1990** £13.71 (FA)

£15.00 → £19.99

Accabailles de Barréjats **1995** £18.00 (JU)
Bastor-Lamontagne **1994** £17.90 (JU)
Broustet **1995** £18.95 (FRI)
Broustet ½ bottle **1997** £18.95 (HED)
la Chartreuse **1996** £17.64 (HIC) £18.95 (AD)
la Chartreuse **1988** £16.50 (BU)
Climens ½ bottle **1996** £19.95 (LEA) £19.99 (WAI)
Coutet **1995** £17.63 (FA) £28.00 (JU) £29.25 (HAH) £41.31 (PLAY)
Coutet ½ bottle **1997** £16.95 (RES) £19.50 (STA)
Coutet ½ bottle **1994** £16.97 (PLAY)
Cyprès de Climens **1997** £18.10 (HAH)
Doisy-Védrines **1998** £19.99 (OD) £22.50 (MI)
Doisy-Védrines **1996** £19.50 (ARM) £22.95 (LAY) £24.17 (MI)
Filhot **1998** £18.75 (HIG)
Filhot **1996** £15.18 (FA) £19.99 (UN) £21.91 (CB)
Filhot **1990** £19.97 (BODX) £21.92 (ARM) £22.99 (OD) £25.00 (WAI) £25.95 (VIC) £25.95 (THR) £25.95 (WR) £26.95 (BOT) £28.00 (JU) £31.35 (NI) £32.00 (RES) £40.00 (GN)
Filhot ½ bottle **1989** £17.50 (BU)
Guiraud **1999** £19.97 (HIG)
Guiraud **1995** £19.95 (TAN)

Guiraud ½ bottle **1996** £16.95 (WAI)
Guiraud ½ bottle **1989** £19.95 (BEN) £19.95 (STA)
Lafaurie-Peyraguey **1984** £16.45 (WY)
Lafaurie-Peyraguey ½ bottle **1997** £16.95 (RES)
Lafaurie-Peyraguey ½ bottle **1985** £18.00 (COC)
Liot **1998** £15.83 (MI)
Liot **1997** £17.50 (SUN) £17.50 (LAI) £18.83 (MI)
Liot **1996** £15.49 (SUN) £15.49 (LAI) £18.34 (HIC)
Liot **1995** £15.99 (JON)
Liot **1989** £18.33 (MI)
Loubens **1995** £16.70 (LAY)
Myrat **1998** £17.50 (MI)
Myrat **1996** £18.00 (JU) £18.33 (MI) £18.95 (DI)
Nairac ½ bottle **1997** £15.95 (LEA)
Nairac ½ bottle **1990** £15.95 (LEA)
Nairac ½ bottle **1983** £15.00 (CRO)
Rabaud-Promis **1997** £15.57 (BODX) £21.99 (RAE) £25.83 (MI)
Rabaud-Promis **1996** £18.99 (RAE) £23.00 (JU)
Rabaud-Promis **1995** £18.40 (BAC)
la Rame Reserve du Château **1990** £18.57 (NO)
Rayne-Vigneau **1997** £19.49 (BODX) £25.95 (LAY) £30.00 (MI)
Rayne-Vigneau ½ bottle **1988** £18.80 (WY)
Rieussec **1999** £19.58 (FA) £21.93 (HIG) £23.40 (FRI)
Rieussec ½ bottle **1997** £19.75 (TAN) £22.95 (STA)
Rieussec ½ bottle **1996** £16.95 (WAI) £18.95 (FRI)
Rieussec ½ bottle **1995** £17.95 (FRI)
Rieussec ½ bottle **1989** £19.34 (FA) £32.00 (STA)
Suduiraut ½ bottle **1998** £15.80 (HAH)
Suduiraut ½ bottle **1997** £15.95 (LEA) £16.50 (WS)
Suduiraut ½ bottle **1989** £17.29 (BO) £17.87 (TUR) £27.03 (WY)
Suduiraut ½ bottle **1983** £16.16 (TUR)

£20.00 → £29.99

d'Arche **1989** £29.32 (PLA)
Broustet **1997** £21.67 (MI)
Broustet **1988** £21.50 (FRI)
Caillou **1995** £20.00 (BU)
la Chartreuse **1989** £22.95 (BALL)
la Chartreuse **1983** £22.50 (BU)

Climens **1998** £28.89 (FA) £34.17 (MI)
Climens **1995** £29.00 (JU)
Climens **1991** £28.79 (PLA) £32.99 (RAE)
Climens **1985** £29.50 (FORT)
Climens **1974** £27.95 (RAE)
Climens ½ bottle **1988** £24.72 (FA)
Climens ½ bottle **1983** £27.50 (BEN)
Coutet **1998** £25.83 (MI)
Coutet **1997** £26.33 (ARM) £26.44 (FA)
£32.00 (JU) £32.49 (CB) £32.50 (MI)
£35.00 (HED) £35.95 (TAN) £35.95 (DI)
Coutet **1996** £21.54 (FA) £25.83 (MI)
£28.50 (LAY) £30.00 (JU) £31.50 (TAN)
£33.55 (CB) £40.00 (UN)
Coutet ½ bottle **1988** £22.95 (BEN)
Doisy-Daëne **1997** £25.73 (CB) £25.95
(LAY) £28.00 (JU)
Doisy-Daëne **1978** £23.50 (WY)
Doisy-Dubroca **1996** £29.50 (JER)
Doisy-Védrines **1997** £22.00 (MAY)
£25.56 (CB) £30.00 (MI)
Filhot **1997** £23.91 (CB) £25.00 (HED)
Filhot **1983** £27.00 (YOU)
Guiraud **1998** £28.33 (MI)
Guiraud **1996** £25.83 (MI) £29.00 (JU)
£32.43 (CB) £38.00 (UN)
Guiraud **1990** £26.44 (FA) £35.00 (CRO)
£38.95 (RES)
Guiraud **1988** £23.50 (FA)
Guiraud **1983** £27.42 (FA) £30.83 (MI)
Guiraud ½ bottle **1988** £21.95 (BEN)
£26.40 (NO)
les Justices ½ bottle **1996** £20.33 (TW)
Lafaurie-Peyraguey **1996** £29.50 (UN)
£30.00 (JU) £33.55 (CB)
Lafaurie-Peyraguey **1995** £22.50 (BU)
£29.50 (BER)
Lafaurie-Peyraguey **1989** £25.46 (FA)
£35.00 (HIG)
Lafaurie-Peyraguey **1985** £22.50 (BU)
Lafaurie-Peyraguey **1970** £25.00 (BU)
Lafaurie-Peyraguey **1969** £23.50 (WY)
de Malle **1998** £21.67 (MI)
de Malle **1997** £25.83 (MI) £27.00 (JU)
de Malle **1996** £22.45 (BER) £22.50 (MI)
£27.99 (JON)
de Malle **1995** £28.55 (CB)
Myrat **1997** £21.67 (MI)

- *All prices for each wine are listed
  together in ascending order.*
- *Price bands refer to the lowest price
  for which the wine is available.*

Nairac **1998** £29.50 (JER)
Nairac **1997** £28.50 (FORT) £32.80 (TAN)
Nairac **1996** £28.00 (HIG)
Nairac **1995** £20.56 (HIG) £31.31 (CB)
Nairac **1964** £23.50 (WY)
Nairac ½ bottle **1975** £24.00 (CRO)
Rabaud-Promis **1990** £21.00 (JU)
Rabaud-Promis **1989** £22.52 (FA)
Rayne-Vigneau **1998** £22.50 (MI)
Rayne-Vigneau **1996** £23.33 (MI) £27.03
(CB)
Rayne-Vigneau **1995** £21.67 (MI)
Rayne-Vigneau **1988** £21.05 (FA)
Rayne-Vigneau **1986** £20.07 (FA) £25.80
(TAN) £43.00 (CRO)
Rayne-Vigneau **1972** £25.00 (BU)
Rayne-Vigneau ½ bottle **1986** £24.00 (CRO)
Rieussec **1998** £20.56 (WY) £25.50 (HIG)
£27.81 (FRI) £30.83 (MI) £60.00 (VIL)
Rieussec **1996** £25.46 (FA) £32.00 (JU)
£32.31 (CB) £36.00 (FRI)
Rieussec **1995** £23.99 (FA) £32.50 (FRI)
Rieussec ½ bottle **1990** £23.99 (CON)
Rieussec ½ bottle **1988** £27.03 (WY)
£33.32 (NO)
Romer du Hayot **1982** £20.00 (BU)
Romer du Hayot **1976** £23.50 (FA)
Romer du Hayot **1971** £27.42 (FA)
Sigalas-Rabaud **1981** £27.95 (BU)
Sigalas-Rabaud **1975** £27.42 (FA)
Suduiraut **1998** £25.83 (MI)
Suduiraut **1997** £25.85 (BODX) £25.99 (OD)
£26.33 (ARM) £30.00 (WS) £30.00 (FORT)
£31.95 (TAN) £32.50 (MI) £32.72 (CB)
Suduiraut **1996** £25.83 (MI) £27.50 (FORT)
£32.50 (FRI) £33.19 (CB)
Suduiraut **1988** £26.44 (FA) £33.33 (MI)
£37.95 (TAN) £49.00 (BER)
Suduiraut **1986** £28.40 (TUR) £38.80 (TAN)
Suduiraut **1978** £27.50 (BU)
Suduiraut **1975** £29.38 (FA) £41.75 (BEN)
Suduiraut ½ bottle **1990** £26.00 (CRO)
la Tour Blanche **1996** £29.00 (JU)
la Tour Blanche **1995** £29.95 (FRI)
la Tour Blanche **1989** £25.46 (FA) £32.50
(FRI) £33.00 (JU)
la Tour Blanche **1985** £25.00 (BU)
la Tour Blanche **1983** £27.99 (JON)
la Tour Blanche ½ bottle **1996** £25.00 (NO)

£30.00 → £39.99

Climens **1996** £36.95 (RAE) £45.00 (JU)
Climens **1989** £35.25 (FA) £48.95 (BEN)
Climens **1979** £35.00 (BU)
Climens **1969** £35.00 (BAC)

Coutet **1990** £31.00 (COC) £31.14 (PLA)
 £47.99 (VIL)
Coutet **1989** £31.99 (YOU) £32.00 (CRO)
Coutet **1983** £31.70 (TAN)
Coutet **1975** £33.29 (FA)
Cru Barréjats **1992** £38.00 (JU)
Cru Barréjats **1991** £38.00 (JU)
Doisy-Daëne ½ bottle **1976** £30.55 (WY)
Doisy-Védrines **1990** £30.00 (MI)

de Fargues **1984** £30.83 (MI)
Filhot **1989** £32.90 (WY)
Filhot **1986** £37.60 (WY)
Guiraud **1997** £32.50 (MI) £32.72 (CB)
 £34.00 (JU)
Guiraud **1989** £32.50 (BU)
Guiraud **1986** £37.50 (CON)
Lafaurie-Peyraguey **1997** £32.72 (CB)
 £32.90 (HAH) £36.00 (JU)
Lafaurie-Peyraguey **1988** £39.17 (FA)
Lafaurie-Peyraguey **1938** £35.25 (WY)
de Malle **1989** £36.99 (JON)
de Malle **1988** £34.99 (NO)
de Malle **1986** £37.99 (JON) £39.98 (COC)
Rabaud-Promis **1971** £39.50 (BU)
Rayne-Vigneau **1971** £37.50 (BU)
Rieussec **1997** £30.00 (FORT) £36.00 (JU)
 £42.50 (HED)
Rieussec **1989** £35.15 (BODX) £37.00
 (TAN) £37.70 (FA) £48.01 (NO)
Rieussec **1983** £36.62 (BODX) £39.50 (BU)
 £48.96 (FA) £62.00 (RES) £65.99 (JON)
Sigalas-Rabaud **1997** £30.00 (JU)
Sigalas-Rabaud **1989** £32.50 (BEN) £46.50
 (BER)
Suduiraut **1995** £30.50 (FRI) £37.50 (BU)
Suduiraut **1990** £32.50 (MI) £33.29 (TUR)
 £49.50 (BU)
Suduiraut **1989** £32.32 (TUR) £34.59 (BO)
 £35.95 (BEN) £35.95 (DI) £49.99 (POR)
Suduiraut **1985** £35.00 (BU)
Suduiraut **1983** £30.84 (TUR) £35.25 (WY)
Suduiraut **1982** £34.00 (FRI)
Suduiraut ½ bottle **1988** £34.99 (NO)
la Tour Blanche **1997** £31.25 (ARM)
 £36.00 (JU)
la Tour Blanche **1934** £35.25 (WY)

£40.00 → £59.99

Climens **1997** £40.00 (FORT) £40.95 (RAE)
 £48.00 (JU) £55.00 (MI)
Climens **1990** £50.83 (MI)
Climens **1986** £47.00 (FA) £47.50 (MI)
Climens **1983** £45.04 (FA) £70.50 (WY)
Climens **1982** £45.00 (FORT)
de Fargues **1995** £50.00 (MI)
de Fargues **1990** £48.96 (FA) £50.83 (MI)
 £55.00 (JU) £80.00 (FORT)
de Fargues **1989** £50.83 (MI)
de Fargues **1988** £43.08 (FA)
de Fargues **1986** £45.00 (MI)
de Fargues **1985** £47.00 (WY)
Gilette **1956** £58.00 (CRO)
Guiraud ½ bottle **1924** £51.70 (WY)
les Justices **1985** £47.00 (TW)
les Justices **1983** £52.87 (TW)
Lafaurie-Peyraguey **1990** £45.00 (NO)
Lafaurie-Peyraguey **1980** £41.13 (WY)
Raymond-Lafon **1988** £47.00 (JU)
Rieussec **1990** £45.04 (TUR) £46.50 (TAN)
 £48.01 (NO)
Rieussec **1988** £49.99 (POR) £55.00 (FORT)
 £55.47 (NO) £61.00 (STA)
Rieussec **1986** £55.00 (FORT) £80.00 (RES)
Rieussec **1975** £54.00 (CRO)
la Tour Blanche **1923** £52.88 (WY)
d'Yquem ½ bottle **1994** £52.58 (BODX)

£60.00 → £99.99

Climens **1988** £60.00 (FORT)
Climens **1976** £99.88 (WY)
Climens **1975** £77.55 (WY)
Coutet **1971** £70.00 (CRO)
Coutet **1934** £88.13 (WY)
Coutet **1924** £94.00 (WY)
Doisy-Daëne **1953** £78.33 (FA)
Filhot **1975** £72.85 (WY)
Filhot **1934** £99.88 (FA) £146.88 (WY)
Lafaurie-Peyraguey **1926** £88.13 (WY)
Rieussec **1976** £90.00 (RES)
la Tour Blanche **1962** £66.00 (CRO)
 £99.88 (WY)
la Tour Blanche **1935** £88.13 (WY)
d'Yquem ½ bottle **1995** £71.68 (BODX)
d'Yquem ½ bottle **1993** £68.15 (WY)
d'Yquem ½ bottle **1990** £79.99 (OD)
 £81.76 (FA) £90.00 (WS) £90.48 (WY)
 £97.92 (TUR) £135.00 (RES)
d'Yquem ½ bottle **1989** £74.99 (OD)
 £87.39 (FA) £90.48 (WY) £95.00 (FRI)
 £96.45 (TUR) £120.00 (FORT)
d'Yquem ½ bottle **1981** £88.13 (WY)

£100.00 → £149.99

Climens **1967** £105.75 (WY)
Climens **1966** £129.25 (WY)
Climens **1962** £116.50 (BEN)
Coutet **1961** £129.25 (WY)
Doisy-Daëne **1961** £146.88 (WY)
Filhot **1930** £119.46 (FA)
Gilette **1962** £136.30 (TW)
Gilette Crème de Tête **1971** £105.75 (WY)
Rabaud-Promis **1918** £117.50 (WY)
Rayne-Vigneau **1948** £111.63 (WY)
Rayne-Vigneau **1947** £129.25 (WY) £160.00 (BU)
Rayne-Vigneau **1939** £135.13 (WY)
Rayne-Vigneau **1926** £117.50 (WY)
Rayne-Vigneau **1918** £141.00 (WY)
Suduiraut **1971** £111.63 (WY)
Suduiraut **1962** £146.88 (WY)
d'Yquem **1995** £143.35 (BODX) £157.50 (MI) £191.00 (HAH)
d'Yquem **1994** £105.16 (BODX) £115.55 (LAY) £125.00 (MI) £127.00 (TAN)
d'Yquem **1991** £116.67 (MI)
d'Yquem **1990** £143.35 (BODX) £143.94 (FA) £149.99 (OD) £155.00 (TAN) £158.63 (WY) £161.67 (MI) £170.00 (WS) £170.86 (TUR) £180.00 (JU)
d'Yquem **1989** £139.04 (FA) £144.99 (OD) £157.50 (MI) £158.63 (WY) £160.00 (JU) £163.52 (TUR) £195.00 (BEN) £215.00 (FORT)
d'Yquem **1988** £146.88 (BODX) £148.83 (FA) £150.00 (DI) £165.83 (MI) £165.97 (TUR) £176.25 (WY) £210.00 (FRI) £225.00 (FORT)
d'Yquem **1987** £129.25 (WY)
d'Yquem **1986** £141.00 (TUR) £148.85 (FA) £174.17 (MI) £176.25 (WY) £200.00 (FORT) £230.00 (RES)
d'Yquem **1985** £134.15 (TUR)
d'Yquem **1980** £123.38 (FA)
d'Yquem **1968** £111.63 (WY)
d'Yquem ½ bottle **1960** £135.13 (WY)

£150.00 → £199.99

Caillou **1943** £160.00 (CRO)
Climens **1953** £180.00 (BEN)
Filhot **1929** £199.00 (YOU) £223.25 (WY)
Gilette **1952** £190.35 (TW)
Gilette **1950** £164.50 (WY)
Rayne-Vigneau **1945** £176.25 (WY)
Rieussec **1961** £182.13 (WY)

Sigalas-Rabaud **1919** £152.75 (WY)
d'Yquem **1983** £188.00 (FA) £193.88 (WY) £235.00 (VA) £235.00 (FORT)
d'Yquem **1981** £170.38 (WY) £225.00 (RES)

£200.00 → £299.99

Climens **1928** £229.13 (WY)
Climens **1927** £229.13 (WY)
Suduiraut **1949** £250.00 (BEN)
d'Yquem **1976** £217.38 (TUR) £264.38 (FA) £345.00 (FORT)
d'Yquem **1960** £264.38 (WY)

£300.00 → £399.99

Coutet **1921** £330.00 (CRO)
Gilette **1934** £311.37 (TW)
Rayne-Vigneau **1941** £305.50 (WY)
d'Yquem **1971** £387.75 (WY)
d'Yquem **1967** £350.00 (DI) £675.00 (FRI) £750.00 (FORT)
d'Yquem **1963** £395.00 (VA)
d'Yquem **1957** £393.63 (WY)
d'Yquem **1918** £364.25 (WY)

£400.00 → £499.99

d'Yquem **1961** £434.75 (WY)
d'Yquem **1956** £435.00 (VA)
d'Yquem **1955** £495.00 (BEN) £495.00 (YOU)
d'Yquem **1953** £425.00 (BEN) £458.25 (FA) £540.50 (WY) £700.00 (VA)
d'Yquem **1925** £499.38 (WY) £900.00 (VA)
d'Yquem **1919** £423.00 (WY)

Over £500.00

d'Yquem **1959** £500.00 (NO)
d'Yquem **1950** £528.75 (TW)
d'Yquem **1948** £564.00 (WY)
d'Yquem **1947** £910.63 (WY)
d'Yquem **1934** £940.00 (VA)
d'Yquem **1933** £622.75 (WY)
d'Yquem **1931** £810.75 (WY)
d'Yquem **1926** £975.00 (VA)
d'Yquem **1900** £2,937.50 (WY)

ROSÉ

Under £7.00

Bel Air **2000** £5.50 (WS)
Lacroix **1999** £6.99 (DI)
Lacroix **1998** £5.83 (NO)
de Sours Rosé **2000** £6.99 (MAJ) £7.93 (CB) £9.85 (PLAY)
Thieuley Clairet **1998** £4.95 (SOM)

BURGUNDY

Experimenting with Burgundy is expensive, and yes, there are pitfalls. So how do you get to know this most fascinating of all red wines? Ask somebody who knows, that's how

How do you get to know Burgundy if you're not a millionaire and can't afford to experiment much?

Well, to be honest you've got to be able to afford to experiment a bit. If your normal price limit is £5 a bottle, you're better off in other regions and with other grapes. Sorry and all that, but it's a fact. Burgundy doesn't come cheap, and the silky seductiveness that makes people love Pinot Noir especially doesn't come cheap.

But if you're prepared to go to £15 or £20 a bottle, then we're in business. (And even that isn't expensive for Burgundy: take a look at the price guides and see what the rarest wines cost.) And what I would suggest is: adopt a merchant. We list lots here who have a great knowledge of Burgundy: you could start off by ringing them and asking for a list. Study the lists and see which companies you like the feel of best. You might have one near you, in which case, go in and have a chat.

Get to know the people, either face to face or over the telephone, and get them to guide you through the wines. Try a bottle of this, then a bottle of that. And never be afraid to ask questions. I know it's easier and quicker to grab a bottle off the supermarket shelf, but at these prices you'll make fewer mistakes if you get advice.

I'm not saying you'll never have a disappontment. Great Burgundy is elusive stuff – but good Burgundy these days is relatively easy to come by. Just don't blame me if you come to believe that it's the most gloriously elegantly fascinating wine in the world. Many people think it is.

GRAPE VARIETIES

ALIGOTÉ (white) Not planted in the best sites – though there are a few vines in Corton-Charlemagne. Aligoté from old vines can produce a lovely, refreshing wine, scented like buttermilk soap yet as sharp and palate-cleansing as a squeeze of lemon juice. *Jayer-Gilles*, *Denis Mortet* and a few others use new oak with surprising success. A & P de *Villaine*'s Aligoté de Bouzeron is tops.

CHARDONNAY (white) Burgundy makes the most famous Chardonnay of all. Even in the decidedly dicky Burgundian climate, it produces good to excellent wine almost every year. Chardonnays made without the use of oak barrels for aging will taste very different from barrel-aged wines. A Mâcon produced in stainless steel will have appley fruit; Côte Chalonnaise Chardonnay is generally rather taut and chalky-dry, but given some oak, it can

become delicately nutty. In the north of the Beaujolais region Chardonnay has a stony dryness; in the south it is nearer to the fatter, softer, wines of southern Burgundy. Chablis generally produces lean wine, but in riper years and with some oak aging it can get much rounder. The Côte d'Or is the peak of achievement and top wines from the Côte de Beaune are luscious, creamy and honeyed yet totally dry, the rich, ripe fruit entwined with the scents of oak in a surprisingly powerful wine – from the right producer, the world's greatest dry white.

GAMAY (red) The Gamay has no pretensions: in Beaujolais it can simply make one of the juiciest, most gulpable, gurgling wines the world has to offer. *Can*, I stress: not all Beaujolais is like this. Ideally it is simple, cherry-sharp, with candy-like fruit, sometimes with hints of raspberry or strawberry. The wines from the *crus* go further, but in the main their similarity from the grape is greater than the differences in the places they come from. All but the wines of the top villages should be drunk as young as you can find them.

PINOT BEUROT (white) Known elsewhere as Pinot Gris. Very rare in Burgundy, but it produces rich, buttery wine usually used to soften Chardonnay. There is a little blended Pinot Beurot in the Hautes-Côtes and Aloxe-Corton.

PINOT BLANC (white) There is a little of this in the Côte d'Or – in Aloxe-Corton, for instance, where it makes a soft, quick-maturing wine. Rully in the Côte Chalonnaise has some and it ripens well in the Hautes-Côtes. There is also an odd white mutation of Pinot Noir – found in Nuits-St-Georges where the *premier cru* vineyard la Perrière makes a savoury white, and in the Monts Luisants vineyard in Morey-St-Denis.

PINOT NOIR (red) The sulkiest, trickiest fine-wine grape in the world is the exclusive grape in almost all red Burgundies. It needs a more delicate balance of spring, summer and autumn climate than any other variety to achieve greatness. In the past, no other part of the world could produce a Pinot Noir to match those of Burgundy, but isolated growers in Oregon, California, New Zealand, Australia and South Africa are now making very fine examples. Even so, Burgundy is still the only place on earth where fine Pinot Noirs are made in any great quantity. There are some awful ones, too – heavy, chewy and sweet-fruited or thin and pallid – but quality is far higher than it used to be. It should be light, elegant, intense, and perfumed with raspberry or strawberry fruit and a hint of violets. Oak will add spicier, complex notes, and old vines will produce deeper, darker fruit. Except for wine from the very top vineyards, Burgundy can be drunk young with pleasure. But a great *cru* from a great vintage really benefits from a decade or more in bottle.

WINE REGIONS

ALOXE-CORTON, AC (Côte de Beaune; red, white) Overwhelmingly a red-wine village, and it has the only red *grand cru* in the Côte de Beaune, le Corton, also sold under various subdivisions like Corton-Bressandes and Corton Clos du Roi and more widely available than the other *grands crus* of Burgundy. Corton is broad, rich and savoury. Village wines normally keep the broad texture though they lose a little savouriness in favour of a mellow soft fruit. Go for *Chandon de Briailles, Chapuis, Delarche, Dubreuil-Fontaine, Faiveley, Follin-Arvelet, Jadot, Jaffelin, Leroy, Comte Senard, Tollot-Beaut* and *Michel Voarick*.

The village also has one of the Côte's most famous white *grands crus*, Corton-Charlemagne. This can be a magnificent, blasting wall of flavour, not big on nuance, but strong, buttery and ripe, traditionally supposed to require long aging to show its full potential. See Corton-Charlemagne for producers, if you think you can afford it.

AUXEY-DURESSES, AC (Côte de Beaune; red, white) A village with a deservedly high reputation for full, but fairly gentle, nicely fruity reds. Look for *Comte Armand, Diconne, Duc de Magenta, Alain Gras, Leroy, Pascal Prunier, Roy, Thévenin*.

The best whites here can be excellent, from producers like *Ampeau, Diconne, Duc de Magenta, Jadot, Leroy* and *Pascal Prunier*. Leroy's are probably the best of all, but prices at that domaine are astronomical.

BÂTARD-MONTRACHET, AC (Côte de Beaune; white) *Grand cru* of Chassagne and Puligny lying just below le Montrachet and, from a good producer, displaying a good deal of its dramatic flavour, almost thick in the mouth, all roast nuts, butter,

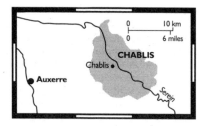

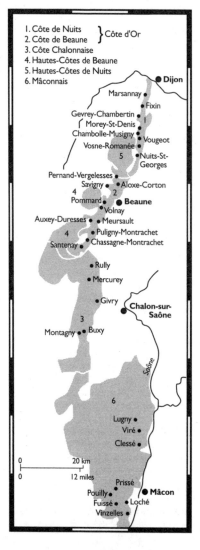

1. Côte de Nuits ⎫
2. Côte de Beaune ⎬ Côte d'Or
3. Côte Chalonnaise
4. Hautes-Côtes de Beaune
5. Hautes-Côtes de Nuits
6. Mâconnais

CLASSIFICATIONS

Burgundy has five different levels of classification:

Non-specific regional appellations with no geographical definition, e.g. Bourgogne, which may come from inferior land or young vines.

Specific regional appellations, e.g. Côte de Beaune-Villages, generally a blend from one or more villages. Côte de Nuits-Villages is usually better.

Village commune wines Each village has its vineyards legally defined. Vineyards with no special reputation are usually blended together under the village name. But there is a growing move towards even relatively unknown vineyards appearing on the label. These unclassified vineyards are called *lieux-dits* or 'stated places'. They can only appear on the label in letters half the size of the village name.

Premier cru It's typical of Burgundy that *premier cru* or 'First Growth' actually means 'Second Growth', because these are the second-best vineyard sites. Even so, they contain some of Burgundy's finest wines. They are classified by both village and vineyard names, e.g. Gevrey-Chambertin, Combe-aux-Moines. The vineyard name must follow the village name on the label, and it may be in the same size print. Confusingly, some growers use smaller print, but the appellation should make it clear whether it is a *premier cru* or a *lieu-dit*.

Grand cru These are the real top growths. Not every village has one. The reds are mostly in the Côte de Nuits, the whites in the Côte de Beaune. A *grand cru* vineyard name can stand alone on the label without the village – for example, Chambertin from the village of Gevrey-Chambertin. (Note that by tradition, a Burgundy village is allowed to tack on the name of its *grand cru* vineyard, and use the compound name for wines that have nothing to do with the *grand cru*, for instance Puligny-Montrachet.)

toast and honey. Should be wonderfully exciting, if expensive. Good names: *Blain-Gagnard, Carillon, Jean-Noël Gagnard, Leflaive, Bernard Morey, Pierre Morey, Michel Niellon, Paul Pernot, Poirier, Ramonet* and *Sauzet*.

BEAUJOLAIS, AC (red) This covers all the basic wines, the produce of the flatter, southern part of Beaujolais. Much of the best is now sold as Nouveau. Run-of-the-mill Beaujolais, apart from Nouveau, can be good, fruity stuff but generally costs too much for the quality. Best: *Blaise, Carron, Charmet, Ch. de la Plume*, the co-op at *Bully, Duboeuf Bouteille Cristal, Garlon, Labruyère, Loron, Paul Sapin, Domaine des Vissoux*.

BEAUJOLAIS BLANC, AC (white) Usually quite expensive, and seldom has much character. At best it should be light and minerally.

BEAUJOLAIS NOUVEAU (or PRIMEUR) (red) The new vintage wine of Beaujolais, released in the November after the harvest. It will normally improve for several months in bottle, and even longer in good Nouveau vintages – a couple of years, maybe. There's seldom much difference in quality between Beaujolais-Villages Nouveau and simple Beaujolais Nouveau.

BEAUJOLAIS ROSÉ, AC (rosé) Usually an apology for a wine, although a good one can be very good indeed. But it's usually too expensive.

BEAUJOLAIS SUPÉRIEUR, AC (red) *Supérieur* means that the basic alcoholic content is higher. It doesn't ensure a better wine, and is rarely seen on the label.

BEAUJOLAIS-VILLAGES, AC (red) Thirty-eight villages can use this title. The wines are certainly better than basic Beaujolais, a little fuller and deeper, and the cherry-sharp fruit of the Gamay is usually more marked. However, always look for a wine bottled in the region, and preferably

one from a single domaine. *Noël Aucoeur, Château Gaillard, Château des Loges, Château des Vergers, Jacques Dépagneux, Domaine de la Brasse, Domaine de la Chapelle de Vatre (Sarrau), de Flammerécourt, Gutty Père et Fils, André Large, Jean-Charles Pivot, Jean-Luc Tissier* and *Trichard* are good and local, but most domaines are bottled by one of the region's merchants. Labelling by domaine is on the increase.

BEAUNE, AC (Côte de Beaune; red, white) One of the few reliable commune wines, usually quite light, with a soft, 'red fruits' sweetness and a flicker of something minerally to smarten it up nicely. The wines are nearly all red. Beaune has the largest acreage of vines of any Côte d'Or commune, and they are mostly owned by merchants. It has no *grands crus* but many excellent *premiers crus*, for example Grèves, Marconnets, Teurons, Boucherottes, Vignes Franches and Cent Vignes. Prices tend to be reasonable, as Beaune is less fashionable than many. The best producers here are *Morot, Drouhin, Jadot, Lafarge* and *Tollot-Beaut*, but reliable wines are also made by *Besancenot-Mathouillet, Bouley, Germain, Jaffelin* and *Morey*. Drouhin's Clos des Mouches is a cut above the rest.

BIENVENUES-BÂTARD-MONTRACHET, AC (Côte de Beaune; white) A tiny *grand cru* situated in Puligny below le Montrachet, and within the larger Bâtard-Montrachet AC, whose wines are similar. The Bienvenues wines are often lighter and more elegant, although they may lack a tiny bit of Bâtard's drive. Best: *Carillon, Clerc, J-N Gagnard, Leflaive, Pernot, Ramonet*.

BLAGNY, AC (Côte de Beaune; red) The red wines are usually a bit fierce, but then this is the white wine heartland of Burgundy, so I'm a bit surprised they grow any red at all. Best: *Leflaive, Matrot*.

BONNES-MARES, AC (Côte de Nuits; red) Usually one of the most – or should I say one of the relatively few – reliable *grands crus*, which ages extremely well over ten to 20 years to a lovely smoky, chocolate-and-prunes richness. Best names: *Domaine des Varoilles, Drouhin, Dujac, Groffier, Jadot, Roumier, de Vogüé*.

BOURGOGNE ALIGOTÉ, AC

(white) Usually rather sharp and green except where old vines make exciting wine, but the locals add crème de cassis to it to make kir – which tells you quite a lot about it. Best: *Coche-Dury, Confuron, Devevey, Diconne, Jobard, Rion, Rollin*.

BOURGOGNE ALIGOTÉ DE BOUZERON, AC (Côte Chalonnaise;

white) The white wine pride of the Côte Chalonnaise. The vines are frequently old – this seems to be more crucial for Aligoté than for most other wines – and the buttermilk-soap nose is followed by a very dry, slightly lemony, pepper-sharp wine, too good to mix with cassis. The best Aligoté of all, rich and oaky, comes from *de Villaine*. *Chanzy* and *Bouchard Père et Fils* are also good. Top ones can age for five years or so.

BOURGOGNE BLANC, AC (white)

Anything from a basic Burgundy grown in the less good spots anywhere between Chablis and the Mâconnais to a carefully matured wine from a serious producer, either from young vines or from vineyards that just miss a superior AC, especially on the borders of Meursault. Best: *Boisson-Vadot, Michel Bouzereau, Boyer-Martenot, Boisson-Morey, Coche-Dury, J Deverey, Dussort, Jadot, Javillier, Jobard, Labouré-Roi, Lafon, René Manuel, Millot-Battault* and the *Buxy* co-op (look for *Clos de Chenoves*).

BOURGOGNE GRAND ORDINAIRE, AC (red) Très ordinaire.

Pas très grand. Usually denotes the bottom of the Burgundy barrel, and rarely seen outside Burgundy, but the occasional exception can be a pleasant surprise. It may be made from Pinot Noir and Gamay.

BOURGOGNE PASSE-TOUT-GRAINS, AC (red) Often decent, lightish

wine made usually in the Côte d'Or or the Côte Chalonnaise from Gamay blended with a minimum of one-third Pinot Noir. In some years it may be mostly Pinot. *Chanson* and *Rodet* make it well; *Chaley, Cornu, Léni-Volpato, Rion* and *Thomas* are also good. But even at its absolute best, true Burgundy it ain't.

BOURGOGNE ROUGE, AC (red) The

basic red AC, stretching from Chablis in the north to the Beaujolais *crus* in the south. Unknown Bourgogne Rouge is best avoided – much of it is very basic indeed. Domaine-bottled Bourgogne Rouge from good growers – and a handful of merchants – can be excellent value. The best wines come from vineyards just outside the village appellations. Look for *Bourgeon, Coche-Dury, Germain, d'Heuilly-Huberdeau, Juillot, Lafarge, Mortet, Parent, Pousse d'Or, Rion* and *Rossignol*. Good merchants include *Drouhin, Faiveley, Jadot, Jaffelin, Labouré-Roi, Latour, Olivier Leflaive, Leroy, Rodet, Vallet*. The co-ops at *Buxy* and *Igé* are also good as is the *Caves des Hautes-Côtes*. Most wines should be drunk quite young.

BROUILLY, AC (Beaujolais; red) Brouilly

usually makes one of the lightest *cru* wines, and in general rarely improves much with keeping. In fact, it makes a very good Nouveau. A few properties make a bigger wine to age – but even then, nine months to a year is quite enough. Good names include *Château de la Chaize, Château de Fouilloux, Château de Nevers, Château de Pierreux, Domaine Crêt des Garanches, Domaine de Combillaty (Duboeuf), Domaine de Garanches, Hospices de Belleville* and *André Large. Château des Tours*, although lovely young, can age longer.

CHABLIS, AC (white) Simple Chablis,

mostly soft, sometimes acidic, covers the widest area of the appellation. So it covers a multitude of sins, with a lot of wine going

CHABLIS VINEYARDS

GRand Crus

Blanchots, Bougros, les Clos, Grenouilles, Preuses, Valmur, Vaudésir. La Moutonne, considered a *grand cru*, is from a parcel in Preuses and Vaudésir.

Premiers Crus

Fourchaume (including Fourchaume, Vaupulent, Côte de Fontenay, Vaulorent, l'Homme Mort); Montée de Tonnerre (including Montée de Tonnerre, Chapelot, Pied d'Aloup); Monts de Milieu; Vaucoupin; les Fourneaux (including les Fourneaux, Morein, Côte des Prés-Girots); Beauroy (including Beauroy, Troesmes); Côte de Léchet; Vaillons (including Vaillons, Châtains, Séché, Beugnons, les Lys); Mélinots (including Mélinots, Roncières, les Epinottes); Montmains (including Montmains, Forêts, Butteaux); Vosgros (including Vosgros and Vaugiraut); Vaudevey.

under négociants' labels, and a lot being sold by the local co-op, *la Chablisienne* – they make most of the négociants' stuff too. Some of the co-op's best *cuvées* are outstandingly good, but many are too bland and soft. New oak, which is lavishly used by growers such as Droin, often smothers the steely and minerally qualities that make top Chablis so exciting. Best: *Pascal Bouchard, Jean-Marc Brocard, la Chablisienne co-op, Jean Collet, René Dauvissat, Defaix, Jean-Paul Droin, Joseph Drouhin, William Fèvre, Alain Geoffroy, Jean-Pierre Grossot, Michel Laroche, Bernard Légland, Long Depaquit, Louis Michel, Dom. des Milandes, Moreau, Guy Mothe, Raveneau, Regnard, Savary, Simmonet-Fèbvre, Vocoret.*

CHABLIS GRAND CRU, AC (white) The seven *grands crus* (Blanchots, Preuses, Bougros, Grenouilles, Valmur, Vaudésir and les Clos) can be outstanding, though they seldom rival the *grands crus* of the Côte de Beaune. To get the best out of them, you need to age them, preferably after oaking, although *Louis Michel's* oak-free wines age superbly. Some wines are marred by clumsy or excessive use of new oak. *William Fèvre* used to be a prime exponent of new oak, but has changed its ways, and the wines are now tremendous.

CHABLIS PREMIER CRU, AC (white) There are some 30 vineyard names in this category, but they have been rationalized into 12 main plots. Expansion mania has meant that many hardly suitable pieces of vineyard are now accorded *premier cru* status, so the difference in quality between basic Chablis and *premier cru* isn't always all that it should be. However, in recent years there has been a definite move towards quality by the better growers and *la Chablisienne* co-op.

CHAMBERTIN, AC (Côte de Nuits; red) Most famous of the eight *grands crus* of Gevrey-Chambertin, this vineyard should and can make wines that are big, strong and intense in their youth, mellowing to a complex, perfumed, plummy richness with age – good ones need ten to 15 years. Best: *Drouhin, Faiveley, Leroy, Denis Mortet, Ponsot, Rebourseau, Rousseau, Tortochot.*

CHAMBERTIN CLOS-DE-BÈZE, AC (Côte de Nuits; red) *Grand cru* in the village of Gevrey-Chambertin next to Chambertin both geographically and in quality. It needs seven to ten years in bottle. May be sold as Chambertin. Best: *Drouhin, Bruno Clair, Faiveley, Gelin, Mugneret-Gibourg, Rousseau, Thomas-Moillard* and *Damoy* since 1992.

CHAMBOLLE-MUSIGNY, AC (Côte de Nuits; red) This village can make light, cherry-sweet, intensely perfumed Burgundy. Best is *Georges Roumier,* with wonderful wines in every vintage from 1985. The best *premier cru* is les Amoureuses: it deserves to be *grand cru* and is priced accordingly. Top producers: *Barthod-Noëllat, Château de*

Chambolle-Musigny, Drouhin, Dujac, Groffier, Hudelot-Noëllat, Rion, Serveau, de Vogüé.

CHAPELLE-CHAMBERTIN, AC

(Côte de Nuits; red) The wines of this grand cru are typically lighter and more delicate than the other grands crus. But over-lightness – resulting from over-production – is their curse. The best producers are Damoy (since 1993), Louis Jadot and Rossignol-Trapet.

CHARMES-CHAMBERTIN, AC

(Côte de Nuits; red) This is the biggest of the grands crus of Gevrey-Chambertin. It can be fine, strong, sensuous wine, but as with all of them, it can also be disgracefully light. Best producers: Bachelet, Charlopin-Parisot, Drouhin, Dugat, Dugat-Py, Dujac, Rebourseau, Roty, Rousseau, Tortochot.

CHASSAGNE-MONTRACHET, AC

(Côte de Beaune; red, white) Its fame lies in its large share of the white grand cru vineyard of le Montrachet. The reds are a puzzle. At their best they're good value, if a bit heavy, plummy and earthy. The best names for red are Amiot, Carillon, Colin, Duc de Magenta, Jean-Noël Gagnard, Gagnard-Delagrange, René Lamy, Albert Morey, Moreau, Jean Pillot, Ramonet. Of the whites, the grands crus are excellent, but the premiers crus rarely dazzle quite like those of nearby Puligny-Montrachet. Best: Blain-Gagnard, Carillon, Colin, Duc de Magenta, Fontaine-Gagnard, Jean-Noël Gagnard, Gagnard-Delagrange, Lamy-Pillot, Laguiche, Château de la Maltroye, Moreau, Albert Morey, Bernard Morey, Niellon, Fernand Pillot and Ramonet. Jaffelin is the top merchant.

CHÉNAS, AC

(Beaujolais; red) This is the second-smallest Beaujolais cru, making strong, dark wines, sometimes a bit tough, that can be drunk a year after the harvest, or aged to take on a Pinot Noir-like flavour. Look out for Louis Champagnon, Charvet, Château de Chénas, Domaines des Brureaux, Domaine Chassignon, Domaine de la Combe

Remont (Duboeuf), Pierre Perrachon and Émile Robin.

CHEVALIER-MONTRACHET, AC

(Côte de Beaune; white) A grand cru vineyard of the village of Puligny, giving a leaner wine than le Montrachet itself, but one with a deep flavour as rich and satisfying as a dry white wine can get. Good ones will last 20 years. Best: Bouchard Père et Fils, Clerc, Jadot, Latour, Leflaive, Niellon.

CHIROUBLES, AC

(Beaujolais; red) A cru for early drinking: naturally light, similar to Beaujolais-Villages in weight, but with a cherry scent that makes it France's favourite Beaujolais cru. Look for Georges Boulon, René Brouillard, Cheysson, Château Javernand, Château de Raousset, Jean-Pierre Desvignes, Duboeuf, Méziat and Georges Passot.

CHOREY-LÈS-BEAUNE, AC

(Côte de Beaune; red) Good value, soft, fruity reds. The village isn't overhyped, so makes some of the few affordable Burgundies. Drouhin, Germain and Tollot-Beaut are best.

CLOS DES LAMBRAYS, AC

(Côte de Nuits; red) This single-owner grand cru in Morey-St-Denis changed hands recently. The estate had become run down. Let's hope things change now.

CLOS DE LA ROCHE, AC

(Côte de Nuits; red) Largest and finest grand cru of Morey-St-Denis. If not too light, it can be splendid, redcurrant-and-strawberry rich when young, like pretty good Chambertin after ten years. Best: Amiot, Dujac, Leroy, Hubert and Georges Lignier, Ponsot, Rousseau.

CLOS ST-DENIS, AC

(Côte de Nuits; red) Has rarely achieved great heights and is probably least famous of all the grands crus. Best known is Dujac's; look for Charlopin-Parisot, Georges or Hubert Lignier, Ponsot.

CLOS DE TART, AC

(Côte de Nuits; red) Grand cru of Morey-St-Denis owned

by Beaujolais merchants *Mommessin*. At best it is light but intense wine which lasts.

CLOS DE VOUGEOT, AC (Côte de Nuits; red) Over 80 growers share this *grand cru* and, while the land at the top of the slope is very fine, the land by the road is not. That rare thing, a good bottle of Clos de Vougeot, is fat, rich, strong and thick with the sweetness of perfumed plums and honey, unsubtle but exciting. It is only found in top vintages, and then only from the best producers. Best: *Arnoux, Ch. de la Tour, Jacky Confuron, Drouhin-Laroze, Engel, Grivot, Gros, Hudelot-Noëllat, Jadot, Lamarche, Leroy, Meo-Camuzet, Mugneret, Raphet.*

CORTON, AC (Côte de Beaune; red, white) The only red *grand cru* vineyard in the Côte de Beaune. Ideally, red Corton should have something of the richness and strength of Clos de Vougeot, but it tends to be four-square and unrewarding until it is mature, and then only the top wines are good. Best producers include: *Chandon de Briailles, Dubreuil-Fontaine, Faiveley, Gaunoux, Laleur-Piot, Maldant, Prince de Mérode, Rapet, Daniel Senard, Tollot-Beaut.* The finest white is the *Hospices de Beaune's* Corton-Vergennes, and *Chandon de Briailles* makes Corton-Bressandes that is half Pinot Blanc.

CORTON-CHARLEMAGNE, AC (Côte de Beaune; white) *Grand cru* of Aloxe-Corton and Pernand-Vergelesses that occupies the upper half of the hill of Corton. It is planted almost entirely with Chardonnay, but a little Pinot Blanc or Pinot Beurot can add intriguing fatness to the wine. Look for: *Bitouzet, Bonneau du Martray, Chandon de Briailles, Chapuis, Coche-Dury, Dubreuil-Fontaine, M Juillot, Hospices de Beaune, Jadot, Laleure-Piot, Latour, Rapet, Rollin.*

CÔTE CHALONNAISE, AC (red, white) Light, usually clean-tasting Chardonnay predominates among the whites – although at long last the idea of oak-aging is catching on. But the Côte

Chalonnaise has one star that cannot be overshadowed by the famous Côte d'Or: the village of Bouzeron makes the finest and the most famous Aligoté in all France. The top three villages of Rully, Mercurey and Givry all produce good reds, too, with a lovely, simple strawberry-and-cherry fruit.

CÔTE DE BEAUNE, AC (red, white) Wine from a small plot of land on the terraces to the west of the town of Beaune. Not much found.

CÔTE DE BEAUNE-VILLAGES, AC (red) Catch-all red wine appellation for 16 villages on the Côte de Beaune. Only Aloxe-Corton, Beaune, Volnay and Pommard cannot use the appellation. Rarely seen nowadays, and rarely exciting. Still, it *is* worth checking out the wines of *Bachelet, Jaffelin* and *Lequin-Roussot.*

CÔTE DE BROUILLY, AC (Beaujolais; red) The Mont de Brouilly, a pyramid-shaped hill in the middle of the *cru* of Brouilly, makes quite different wine to Brouilly itself. The soil is of volcanic origin, and the slopes lap up the sun. Best: *Château Thivin, Conroy, Domaine de la Pierre Bleue, Jean Sanvers, Lucien Verger, Chanrion.*

CÔTE DE NUITS (red, white) The northern part of the Côte d'Or, in theory producing the biggest wines. It is almost entirely devoted to Pinot Noir. Standards have risen in recent years. This doesn't mean you won't ever be disappointed, because unpredictability is built into red Burgundy. But your chances are an awful lot better than they used to be.

CÔTE DE NUITS-VILLAGES, AC (red) Covers the three southernmost villages of Prissey, Comblanchien and Corgoloin, plus Fixin and Brochon in the north. Usually fairly light and dry, it can have good cherry fruit and the delicious vegetal decay taste of good Côte de Nuits red. Often good value. Best producers: *Durand,*

Rion, Rossignol and *Tollot-Voarick*, especially *Chopin-Groffier* and *Domaine de l'Arlot.*

CÔTE D'OR

(red, white) The source of Burgundy's fame – a thin sliver of land worth its weight in gold. It has two halves, the Côte de Nuits in the north and the Côte de Beaune in the south, with a fine crop of illustrious wines.

CRÉMANT DE BOURGOGNE, AC

(white, rosé) Good, eminently affordable sparkling wine, made by the Champagne method, from Chardonnay and Pinot Noir. Try *Caves de Lugny* for white and *Caves de Bailly* for lovely fresh, strawberryish pink.

CRIOTS-BÂTARD-MONTRACHET, AC

(Côte de Beaune; white) Tiny *grand cru* in Chassagne-Montrachet nuzzled up against Bâtard-Montrachet. The wines resemble Bâtard's power and concentration but are leaner, more minerally – and rarely seen. Best: *Blain-Gagnard, Fontaine-Gagnard.*

CRU

The ten Beaujolais *crus* or growths (Fleurie, Moulin-à-Vent, Brouilly, Chénas, Côte de Brouilly, Chiroubles, Juliénas, St-Amour, Morgon, Régnié) are the top villages in the steeply hilly, northern part of Beaujolais. All *should* have definable characteristics, but the produce of different vineyards and growers is all too often blended to a mean by merchants elsewhere. There's also a distressing tendency now to age the wines in new oak, which destroys their point. Any old red can taste of new oak; only good Beaujolais has the juiciness of Gamay. Always buy either a single-estate wine, or one from a good local merchant like *Chanut Frères, la Chevalière, Duboeuf, Dépagneux, Ferraud, Loron, Sarrau, Louis Tête,* and *Trenel.* Elsewhere in Burgundy the best vineyards are labelled *grand cru,* and the second-best *premier cru.*

ÉCHÉZEAUX, AC

(Côte de Nuits; red) Large, slightly second-line *grand cru* vineyard in Vosne-Romanée. Best: *Domaine de la*

INSTANT CELLAR: CLASSIC WHITES

- 1999 Meursault 1er Cru Charmes, Domaine Yves Boyer-Martinot, £24.48, Montrachet A beautifully honeyed and nutty Meursault with lots of cream and weight.
- 1992 Meursault les Perrières, Joseph Drouhin, £14 a half bottle, Peter Wylie Fine Wines This would be a perfect treat to buy just for oneself and it's really not extravagantly priced, either. Gloriously mature wine from a top vintage and a very good producer.
- 1998 Chablis Domaine de la Genillotte, Domaine Sourice-Depuydt, £9.33, John Armit Wines Classically minerally and steely, with hints of honey and lemon.
- 1999 Savigny-lès-Beaune Blanc, Jean-Marc Pavelot, £14.69, Domaine Direct Good value white from a mostly red village, and beautifully ripe and balanced.
- 1998 Mercurey Blanc Les Mauvarennes, Maison J Faiveley, £12.25, Haynes Hanson & Clark Rich, spicy, supple wine, and nicely balanced oak.
- 1999 Bourgogne Blanc, Domaine Leflaive, c. £13.11, Lay & Wheeler Marvellously pure, focused fruit with a mineral edge. The bottle price is an estimate because the wine is not yet shipped.

Romanée-Conti, Engel, Faiveley, Forey, Louis Gouroux, Grivot, Mongeard-Mugneret, Mugneret-Gibourg, Rouget.

EPINEUIL, AC

(red) Tiny region in the north of Burgundy, producing light but fragrant styles of Pinot Noir.

FIXIN, AC

(Côte de Nuits; red) A suburb of Dijon, Fixin can make some of Burgundy's sturdiest reds: deep, strong, tough but plummy when young; capable of mellowing with age. Such wines are slowly reappearing. If you want to feel you're drinking Gevrey-Chambertin without shouldering the cost, Fixin from the following producers could fit the bill: *Bordet,*

> **ON THE CASE**
> *Don't despise Beaujolais just because it's fallen out of fashion. A good cru wine is an ideal summer red: never heavy, always refreshing*

Charlopin-Parizot, Bruno Clair, Fougeray, Roger Fournier, Gelin, Guyard, Joliet, Jadot, Moillard, Philippe Rossignol.

FLAGEY-ÉCHÉZEAUX (Côte de Nuits; red) A commune that sells its basic wines as Vosne-Romanée but has two *grands crus*: Échézeaux and Grands-Échézeaux.

FLEURIE, AC (Beaujolais; red) Often the most delicious of the *crus*, gentle and round, its sweet cherry-and-chocolate fruit just held firm by a touch of tannin and acid. Its deserved popularity in Britain and the US has led to high prices. Look out for: *Château de Fleurie (Loron), Chauvet, Chignard, Colonge, Domaine de la Grand, Grand Pré (Sarrau), Domaine de la Presle, Domaine des Quatre Vents, Duboeuf*'s *la Madone, Bernard Paul, Verpoix,* the *Fleurie* co-op's *cuvées, Cuvée Présidente Marguerite* and *Cuvée Cardinale.*

GEVREY-CHAMBERTIN, AC (Côte de Nuits; red) This village has eight *grands crus*, and two of them, Chambertin and Chambertin Clos-de-Bèze can be some of the world's greatest wines. They should have rough, plumskins and damson strength, fierce when young, but assuming a wafting perfume and intense, plummy richness when mature. Look out for *Bachelet, Boillot, Burguet, Dugat, Michel Esmonin, Philippe Leclerc, Mortet, Naddef* and *Rossignol-Trapet* among younger producers. Of the old estates, *Rousseau* is best but *Domaine des Varoilles* is also good. Also look for *Frédéric Esmonin, René Leclerc, Maume* and *Roty*, and for the merchants' bottlings from *Drouhin, Faiveley, Jadot* and *Jaffelin.* Look out for overpriced horrors with the sacred name.

GIVRY, AC (Côte Chalonnaise; red) Small but important red wine village. At their best, the wines are deliciously warm and cherry-chewy with a slightly smoky fragrance to them, but too many are mediocre, especially from négociants. *Baron Thénard* is best, but *Chofflet, Clos Salomon, Joblot, Laborbe, Lespinasse, Mouton* and *Ragot* are also worth investigating.

LA GRANDE RUE, AC (Côte de Nuits; red) This vineyard is wholly owned by the Lamarche family. Elevated to *grand cru* status in 1990, more because of its potential than because of recent wines.

GRANDS-ÉCHÉZEAUX, AC (Côte de Nuits; red) A *grand cru* capable of delicately scented, plum-and-woodsmoke wine which goes rich and chocolaty with age. Best names: *Domaine de la Romanée-Conti, Drouhin, Engel, Mongeard-Mugneret.*

GRIOTTE-CHAMBERTIN, AC (Côte de Nuits; red) One of the smallest *grands crus* of Gevrey-Chambertin. Best: *Drouhin, Claude Dugat, Frédéric Esmonin, Ponsot, Roty.*

HAUTES-CÔTES DE BEAUNE and HAUTES-CÔTES DE NUITS (red, white) A hilly backwater consisting of 28 villages which make fairly good, light, strawberry-like Pinot and reasonably good, light, dry Chardonnay at a decent price. The red grapes do not always ripen fully every year. Look out for the red Hautes-Côtes de Nuits wines of *Cornu, Domaine des Mouchottes, Jayer-Gilles, Thévenet* and *Verdet* and the red Hautes-Côtes de Beaunes of *Bouley, Capron Manieux, Chalet, Guillemard, Joliot, Mazilly* and *Plait.* The *Caves des Hautes-Côtes* is beginning to produce some of the best-value wines in the whole of Burgundy. Good whites come from *Chaley, Cornu, Devevey, Goubard, Jayer-Gilles, Thévenot-le-Brun, Alain Verdet* (organic).

IRANCY, AC (red) Mostly Pinot Noir from vineyards just to the south-west of

Chablis, sometimes with a little of the darker, tougher local grape, César. Rarely deep in colour, but always perfumed, slightly plummy and attractive. Cool years can unfortunately provide disappointingly thin wines. Best drunk while young and fresh. Good producers: *Léon & Serge Bienvenu, Bernard Cantin, Anita & Jean-Pierre Colinot, André & Roger Delaloge, Gabriel Delaloge, Patrice Fort, Jean Renaud, Simmonet-Fèbvre.*

JULIÉNAS, AC (Beaujolais; red) This *can* be big, with tannin and acidity, but many of the best more closely resemble the mixture of fresh red fruit and soft, chocolaty warmth that makes for good Fleurie. Good: *Château du Bois de la Salle, Château des Capitans, Château de Juliénas, Domaine des Bucherats, Domaine de la Dîme, Domaine de la Vieille Église, Duboeuf, René Monnet, Pelletier.*

LADOIX-SERRIGNY, AC (Côte de Beaune; red) Overshadowed by the more famous Aloxe-Corton next door. But it's worth a look: *Capitain-Gagnerot, Chevalier, Cornu, Prince de Mérode* and *Ravaut* all make decent, crisp wines at fair prices.

LATRICIÈRES-CHAMBERTIN, AC (Côte de Nuits; red) Small *grand cru* vineyard in Gevrey-Chambertin and very similar in style to Chambertin though without all the power. Best producers: *Leroy, Ponsot, Rossignol-Trapet.*

MÂCON BLANC, AC (Mâconnais; white) This should be good-value, light Chardonnay, but too often it's not. Most Mâcon simply cannot compete with the best-value New World wines.

MÂCON ROUGE, AC (Mâconnais; red) There's a lot of red wine made in the Mâconnais but it's usually fairly lean, earthy Gamay without the spark of Beaujolais' fruit. If it appeals, try wines from Igé and Mancey, or *Lafarge*'s wine from Bray. *Lassarat* is improving things by using new oak.

MÂCON-VILLAGES, AC (Mâconnais; white) One step up from basic Mâcon Blanc, this must come from the 43 Mâcon communes with the best land. The rare good ones show the signs of honey and fresh apples and some of the nutty, yeasty depth associated with fine Chardonnay. These come from those villages that add their own village names (Mâcon-Chaintry, etc). Wines from four of the best villages have now been renamed Viré-Clessé. There is a handful of growers making serious, oak-aged wine from low-yielding vines. *Guffens-Heynen, Merlin, Rijckaert* and *Jean Thévenet* are names to look for. Others include: *Bicheron, Bonhomme, Danauchet, Goyard, Guillemot-Michel, Josserand, Lassarat, Manciat-Poncet, Signoret, Talmard* and *Thévenet-Wicart.*

MARANGES, AC (Côte de Beaune; red) The sturdy, rustic reds from this AC created in 1989 are now beginning to come into their own. *Drouhin*'s is good and so are *Bachelet, Charlot, Girardin* and *Rijckaert.*

MARSANNAY, AC (Côte de Nuits; red, rosé) Used to produce mostly rosé under the name Bourgogne Rosé de Marsannay, but the introduction of an appellation for reds in 1987 has encouraged growers to switch. The results of this new seriousness are most encouraging and some lovely wines are now emerging, usually quite dry and cherry-perfumed, sometimes more full-blown and exciting. One to watch. Best: *Bouvier, Charlopin-Parizot, Bruno Clair, Collotte, Fougeray, Fournier, Geantet-Pansiot, Huguenot, Jadot, Naddef, Roty.*

MAZIS-CHAMBERTIN, AC (Côte de Nuits; red) This *grand cru* in Gevrey-Chambertin can have a superb deep blackberry-pip, damson-skin and black-currant fruit which gets more exciting after around six to 12 years. Best producers include: *Faiveley, Gelin, Hospices de Beaune, Maume, Rebourseau, Roty, Rousseau, Tortochot.*

MAZOYÈRES-CHAMBERTIN, AC

(Côte de Nuits; red) *Grand cru* of Gevrey-Chambertin, rarely seen since producers generally take up the option of using the *grand cru* Charmes-Chambertin instead. *Perrot-Minot* produces a fine example.

MERCUREY, AC (Côte Chalonnaise;

red, white) The biggest Chalonnais village, producing half the region's wines. Indeed many call the Côte Chalonnaise the 'Région de Mercurey'. It's mostly red wine, often fairly full, with attractive strawberry fruit and a little smoky fragrance. *Faiveley* and *Juillot* make a fine range of red Mercureys, but look out also for *Chandesais, Chanzy, Ch. de Chamirey, Domaine la Marche, Dufouleur, Jacqueson, de Launay, Meix-Foulot, Monette, Saier* and *de Suremain*. Whites have been improving, as rising prices have spurred producers to greater efforts. Good examples come from *Château de Chamirey, Faiveley, M Juillot, Protheau, Rodet*.

MEURSAULT, AC (Côte de Beaune;

white) It has by far the largest white production of any commune in the Côte d'Or, and this is one of several reasons why its traditionally high overall standard is gradually being eroded. The wines should be big and nutty and have a delicious, vegetal lusciousness, and sometimes even peachy, honeyed flavours. Try *Ampeau, Pierre Boillot, Boisson-Vadot, Boyer-Martenot, Michel Bouzereau, Buisson-Battault, Coche-Debord, Coche-Dury, Comtes Lafon, Fichet, Gauffroy, Henry Germain, Jean Germain, Grivault, Patrick Javillier, François Jobard, René Manuel, Matrot, Michelot-Buisson, Millot-Battault, Pierre Morey, Prieur, Roulot*.

MONTAGNY, AC (Côte Chalonnaise;

white) Quite nice round, ripe wines. Best: *Arnoux*, the co-op at *Buxy, Latour, Olivier Leflaive, B Michel, de Montorge, Rodet, Alain Roy* and *Vache*.

MONTHELIE, AC (Côte de Beaune;

red) These wines deserve recognition: they're full, dry, rather herby or piney, but with a satisfying rough fruit. Often a good buy but stick to growers, not négociants. Best: *Boussey, Caves des Hautes-Côtes, Château de Monthelie, Deschamps, Doreau, Garaudet, Monthelie-Douhairet, Potinet-Ampeau, de Suremain, Thévenin-Monthelie*.

LE MONTRACHET, AC (Côte de

Beaune; white) This is white Burgundy at its absolute greatest, the finest of fine white *grands crus* in the villages of Puligny and Chassagne. Does it mean most enjoyable, most happy-making? Not really. In fact the flavours can be so intense it's difficult sometimes to know if you're having fun drinking it or merely giving your wine vocabulary an end-of-term examination. So be brave if someone opens a bottle and let the incredible blend of spice and smoke, honey and ripeness flow over you. Best: *Amiot, Comtes Lafon, Domaine de la Romanée-Conti, Drouhin's Laguiche, Jadot, Pierre Morey, Prieur, Thénard* and, since 1991, *Leflaive*.

MOREY-ST-DENIS, AC (Côte de

Nuits; red) Expensive, and can suffer from overproduction. At their best they blend the perfume of Chambolle-Musigny with the body of Gevrey-Chambertin, and exhibit a slight savouriness that mellows into a rich chocolaty mouthful. You'll find exciting bottles from *Pierre Amiot, Charlopin, Bruno Clair, Dujac, Heresztyn, Dominique Laurent, Georges Lignier, Hubert Lignier, Marchand, Perrot-Minot, Ponsot, Serveau* and *Vadey-Castagnier*.

MORGON, AC (Beaujolais; red) The

wines of this *cru* can be glorious. They can start thick and dark, and age to a chocolaty, plummy depth with an amazing cherries smell. Look also for *Aucoeur, Georges Brun, Calot, Dom de la Chanaise, Charvet, Collonge, Descombes, Desvignes, Jean Foillard, Lapierre, Plateau de Bel-Air, Savoye, Georges Vincent*.

MOULIN-À-VENT, AC (Beaujolais;

red) Enter the heavy brigade. These *cru*

wines should be solid, and should age for three to five years and more from good years. The best of them have a big, plummy, Burgundian style, and their toughness doesn't give you much option but to wait for them to mellow. This is one of the few Beaujolais *crus* that can respond well to discreet oak aging. *Louis Champagnon*'s is good, as is *Brugne, Charvet, Château des Jacques, Château du Moulin-à-Vent, Château Portier, Domaine de la Tour de Bief, Duboeuf, Jacky Janodet, Raymond Siffert* and *Héritiers Maillard* (formerly *Héritiers Tagent*).

MUSIGNY, AC (Côte de Nuits; red, white) Extremely fine *grand cru* which gave its name to Chambolle-Musigny. All but a third of a hectare is planted with Pinot Noir, capable of producing Burgundy's most heavenly scented wine. Look for *Château de Chambolle-Musigny, Jadot, Leroy, Jacques Prieur, Georges Roumier, de Vogüé* (white, too).

NUITS-ST-GEORGES, AC (Côte de Nuits; red) When it's good, this has an enthralling decayed – rotting even – brown richness of chocolate and prunes rising out of a fairly light, plum-sweet fruit – gorgeous, whatever it sounds like. It is expensive but increasingly reliable. *Labouré-Roi* is the most consistent merchant for Nuits, although *Jadot, Jaffelin* and *Moillard* are increasingly good particularly at *premier cru* level. The most famous growers are *Robert Chevillon, Gouges, Michelot* and *Daniel Rion*, but excellent wines are also made by *Ambroise, Jean Chauvenet, Chicotot, Jean-Jacques Confuron, Domaine de l'Arlot*, and then there's the amazingly deep (and amazingly expensive) *Leroy*.

PERNAND-VERGELESSES, AC (Côte de Beaune; red, white) The village whites are generally fairly lean and need time to soften, but can be gently nutty and very enjoyable from a good producer. They can also be quite good value. Best names in white: *Dubreuil-Fontaine, Germain, Laleure-Piot, Pavelot, Rapet, Rollin*. Some quite

attractive, softly earthy reds are made. Look for the *premier cru* Île de Vergelesses. Best reds: *Besancenot-Mathouillet, Caves des Hautes-Côtes, Chandon de Briaillès, Delarche, Dubreuil-Fontaine, Laleure-Piot, Pavelot, Rapet* and *Rollin*.

PETIT CHABLIS, AC (Chablis; white) There used to be lots of this grown on the least-good slopes. But the growers objected that it made their wine sound like a lesser form of Chablis. Nowadays pretty well the whole lot is called 'Chablis' – so we can't tell what's what, the growers are all richer, they're happy, we're not… I give up.

POMMARD, AC (Côte de Beaune; red) From good producers, Pommard can have a strong, meaty sturdiness, backed by slightly jammy but attractively plummy fruit. Not subtle, but many people's idea of what red Burgundy should be. They need ten years to show their class. The most consistently fine wines are made by *Comte Armand, de Courcel* and *de Montille*, but also look out for the wines of *Boillot, Château de Pommard, Girardin, Lahaye, Lejeune, Jean Monnier, Parent, Pothier* and *Pousse d'Or*.

POUILLY-FUISSÉ, AC (Mâconnais; white) Prices here yo-yo according to supply and demand. It is sometimes best in years which are not too rich. Best: *Barraud, Béranger, Cordier, Corsin, Duboeuf*'s top selections, *Ferret, M Forest, Guffens-Heynen, Leger-Plumet, Loron*'s les Vieux Murs, *Manciat-Poncet, Noblet, Roger Saumaize, Valette, Vincent* at *Château Fuissé*. Adjoining villages Pouilly-Loché, AC and Pouilly-Vinzelles, AC are similar at half the price.

PULIGNY-MONTRACHET, AC (Côte de Beaune; white) The peak of great white pleasure is to be found in the various Montrachet *grands crus*. Le Montrachet is peerless, showing how humble words like honey, nuts, cream, smoke, perfume and all the rest do no honest service to a wine that seems to combine every memory of ripe fruit and scent with a dry, penetrating savouriness. Several other *grands crus* are less intense, but offer the same unrivalled mix. There are *premiers crus* as well. Standards here have risen. Look for *Amiot-Bonfils, Jean-Marc Boillot, Boyer-Devèze, Carillon, Gérard Chavy, Drouhin, Jadot, Labouré-Roi, Laguiche*, both *Domaine Leflaive* and *Olivier Leflaive, Pernot, Ramonet-Prudhon, Antonin Rodet, Sauzet, Thénard.*

RÉGNIÉ, AC (Beaujolais; red) Beaujolais' tenth *cru*. Quite similar to Brouilly in ripe years but a bit weedy when the sun doesn't shine. *Duboeuf Bouteille Cristal* is best.

RICHEBOURG, AC (Côte de Nuits; red) Exceptional *grand cru* of Vosne-Romanée. At its best, it manages to be fleshy yet filled with spice and perfume and the clinging richness of chocolate and figs. Best producers: *Domaine de la Romanée-Conti, Grivot, Anne Gros, A-F Gros, Leroy, Méo-Camuzet.*

ROMANÉE, AC (Côte de Nuits; red) The smallest of Burgundy's *grands crus*, solely owned by the Liger-Belair family and sold by *Bouchard Père et Fils*. There's not much of it but it's exciting stuff, steadily improving under the new ownership at Bouchard.

LA ROMANÉE-CONTI, AC (Côte de Nuits; red) This tiny *grand cru* is capable of a more startling brilliance than any other Burgundy. The 7000 or so bottles it produces per year are instantly seized on by the super-rich before we mortals can even get our tasting sheets out. Wholly owned by the *Domaine de la Romanée-Conti.*

ROMANÉE-ST-VIVANT, AC (Côte de Nuits; red) *Grand cru* in the village of Vosne-Romanée. It is far less easy to taste young than its neighbouring *grands crus* and needs a good 12 years to show what can be a delicious, savoury yet sweet personality. Best names: *Arnoux, Domaine de la Romanée-Conti, Latour, Leroy.*

RUCHOTTES-CHAMBERTIN, AC (Côte de Nuits; red) This is the smallest Gevrey-Chambertin *grand cru*, with wines of deeper colour and longer-lasting perfumed richness than most of the village's other *grands crus*. Best producers: *F Esmonin, Georges Mugneret, Roumier, Rousseau.*

RULLY, AC (Côte Chalonnaise; red white) This village gets my vote for the most improved white AC in Burgundy. The use of new oak to ferment and age the wine is producing wonderfully soft, spicy Burgundies of good quality – and still at relatively low prices. Relative to the rest of Burgundy, that is. Best whites: *Bêtes, Chanzy, Cogny, Delorme, Domaine de la Folie, Drouhin, Dury, Duvernay, Jacqueson, Jaffelin, Olivier Leflaive, Rodet.* Best for red: *Chanzy,*

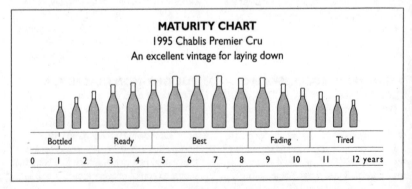

MATURITY CHART
1995 Chablis Premier Cru
An excellent vintage for laying down

Bottled	Ready	Best	Fading	Tired

0   1   2   3   4   5   6   7   8   9   10   11   12 years

Ch. de Rully, Delorme, Domaine de la Folie, Duvernay, Faiveley, Jacqueson, Jaffelin.

ST-AMOUR, AC (Beaujolais; red) This pink-red wine usually has freshness and peachy perfume and good, ripe fruit all at once. It isn't that common here and yet it is frequently the most reliable and enjoyable *cru*. Look for *Buis, Château de St-Amour, Domaine des Billards (Loron), Domaine des Ducs, Domaine du Paradis, Patissier, André Poitevin, Francis Saillant, Paul Spay.*

ST-AUBIN, AC (Côte de Beaune; red, white) Some of Burgundy's best-value wines, though the reds are a touch earthy. They are reliable, and can give real pleasure after a few years of aging. Best: *Bachelet, Clergy, Lamy, Prudhon, Gérard Thomas* and *Roux,* but wines from négociants *Jadot* and *Olivier Leflaive* are their equal. Good whites come from *Bachelet, Clerget, Lamy, Olivier Leflaive, Prudhon, Thomas* and *Roux.*

ST-ROMAIN, AC (Côte de Beaune; red, white) Full, rather broad-flavoured, cherry-stone dry reds, that perform best in very warm years. Often sold cheaper than they deserve. Look for *Bazenet, Buisson, Gras, Thévenin* and *Thévenin-Monthelie.* The flinty, dry whites are often of decent quality and pretty good value. Beware cooler vintages, when the grapes sometimes don't ripen properly. Best are: *Bazenet, Buisson, Germain, Gras, Thévenin, Thévenin-Monthelie.*

ST-VÉRAN, AC (Mâconnais; white) Pouilly-Fuissé's understudy, capable of simple, soft, quick-maturing but attractive, rather honeyed white Burgundy. Best: *Corsin, Dépardon, Dom. des Deux Roches, Duboeuf, Grégoire, Lassarat, de Montferrand, Saumaize, Thibert, Vincent* – and, above all, *Drouhin.*

SANTENAY, AC (Côte de Beaune; red) Rough and ready red. At its best it has a strong, savoury flavour and good strawberry fruit, though nowadays is frequently rather lean and earthy. Best: *Belland, Drouhin, Girardin, Lequin-Roussot, Morey, Pousse d'Or, Prieur-Bonnet, Roux.* Even these are variable.

SAVIGNY-LÈS-BEAUNE, AC (Côte de Beaune; red) Gaining in reputation at the expense of Aloxe-Corton. Light, attractive earthiness and strawberry fruit, but prone to leanness. Try *Bize, Camus-Bruchon, Capron-Manieux, Chandon de Briailles, Écard-Guyot, Girard-Vollot, Guillemot, Pavelot, Tollot-Beaut.*

SAUVIGNON DE ST-BRIS, VDQS (white) Wine of AC quality grown south-west of Chablis that languishes as a VDQS because Sauvignon Blanc is not an AC grape in the area. Can be one of the most nettly, most greeny-gooseberryish of all French Sauvignons, but it has not really faced up to the competition from Bordeaux – and New Zealand. Best: *Louis Bersan, Jean-Marc Brocard, Robert & Philippe Defrance, Michel Esclavy, Goisot, André Sorin.*

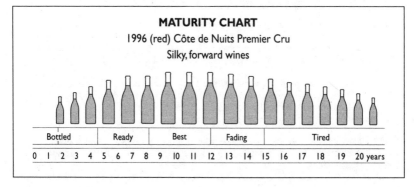

MATURITY CHART
1996 (red) Côte de Nuits Premier Cru
Silky, forward wines

Bottled	Ready	Best	Fading	Tired

0 1 2 3 4 5 6 7 8 9 10 11 12 13 14 15 16 17 18 19 20 years

LA TÂCHE, AC (Côte de Nuits; red)
Another *grand cru* monopoly of the
Domaine de la Romanée-Conti. The wine is
heavenly, so rich and heady that the
perfumes are sometimes closer to age-old
brandy than table wine and the flavour
loaded with spice, dark fruits and the acrid
richness of really good black chocolate.

VOLNAY, AC (Côte de Beaune; red)
One of the most perfumed red Burgundies,
with a memorable cherry-and-strawberry
spice, but also, in its *premiers crus*, able to
turn on a big, meaty style without losing the
perfume. The best are *Lafon, Lafarge,
Marquis d'Angerville, de Montille* and *Pousse
d'Or*. Other good names to look out for
include: *Ampeau, Blain-Gagnard, Boillot,
Bouley, Clerget, Delagrange, Vaudoisey-Mutin,
Voillot*.

VOSNE-ROMANÉE, AC (Côte de
Nuits; red) The greatest Côte de Nuits
village. Its *grands crus* cost more than any
red on earth, and, remarkably for Burgundy,
they are dominated by a single estate,
Domaine de la Romanée Conti. These
vineyards make wines capable of more
startling brilliance than any other, with
flavours as disparate yet as intense as the
overpowering, creamy savouriness of fresh
foie gras and the deep, sweet scent of ripe
plums and prunes in brandy. There are also
fine *premiers crus*, and the village wines can
reflect their leaders. The Domaine de la
Romanée Conti is by far the most famous
estate here, but *Leroy*, owned by a former
director of the DRC, is making wines that
rival it in both quality and price. Others
making terrific wine: *Arnoux, Sylvain Cathiard,
Confuron-Cotétidot, Engel, Grivot, Jean Gros,
Hudelot-Noëllat, Georges Jayer, Henri
Lamarche, Méo-Camuzet, Mongeard-
Mugneret, Georges Mugneret, Pernin-Rossin,
Rouget, Daniel Rion* and *Jean Tardy*.

VOUGEOT, AC (Côte de Nuits; red) A
village famous only because of its *grand cru*,
Clos de Vougeot, which at its best is
plummy and broad. However, there are
some decent wines made outside the Clos
– most notably from *Bertagna* and *Clerget*.

BURGUNDY AND BEAUJOLAIS VINTAGES

Red Burgundy is more subject to vintage fluctuation than white; with the latter, most
years can produce a fair amount of pretty good wine. The rule for Beaujolais: drink as
young as possible. Only top wines from the best villages will benefit much from aging,
although Nouveau may improve with a month or two's rest.

2000 Whites look very promising indeed, with good structure and plenty of flavour.
Reds had a more difficult year, and acidity looks low. Colour is quite pale, too, and there
was some rot. A year for careful winemaking and committed vineyard management.

1999 Quite good to very good, in spite of tricky weather. Whites may lack some
acidity, and some reds and whites will be a bit insubstantial. The best reds have good
colour and structure, but there was rain at the end of September, which affected the
Côte de Nuits more than the Côte de Beaune – the former was largely picked by then.

1998 A mixed year. Reds are often big, substantial and tannic with lots of acidity – and
all that is fine if they have the fruit to go with it. Some do, some don't. A lot of the reds
lack silkiness, which is surely the main reason for spending all that money on them.
Whites can be superb, but at the lower end lack acidity. Taste before you buy.

1997 Soft, approachable reds and whites of middling to good quality which should be
ready before the 1996s. Not a vintage to buy without tasting first, but there are some
very attractive wines.

1996   Excellent, concentrated, classic Chablis; the Côte d'Or whites and reds are also ripe, with good acidity, and should age well, with the reds having particularly succulent fruit. Whites are not as concentrated as in 1995.

1995   A year of low yields, ripe tannins and good concentration in the reds, and good quality but not greatness in the whites. For once, there is little to choose in quality between the Côte de Beaune and the Côte de Nuits. In Chablis quality is first-rate.

1994   Light wines with attractive, reasonable colours and lowish acidity. The best whites show a raciness and vigour. Now a vintage to drink up rather than keep.

1993   The reds from the best producers have good depth of colour, power of fruit and well-constructed tannins. Most are drinking very nicely now, but the best will still improve. The whites turned out far better than at first seemed likely. They plumped up nicely and had plenty of fruit, but it's time to drink them up now.

1992   Acidity is low among the reds, but it's a good year to choose in restaurants, as the wines are fast developers. The whites were far better, with masses of exuberant fruit and seemingly better acidity than their 1991 counterparts. All are drinking now.

1991   There were some very good concentrated reds made, but it's a very patchy vintage. Don't keep them any longer. The whites also should be drunk.

1990   The 1990 reds are brilliantly fruity, naturally high in sugars. Most producers now consider this the best of the great trio of 1988, 1989 and 1990. Almost all are drinking beautifully now; the best are sumptuously rich. The whites are proving to be less exciting than the reds. A good rather than a great vintage for white Burgundy but, that said, there is some excellent Premier Cru and Grand Cru in the Côte de Beaune and Chablis. At their peak now.

1989   A lot of good reds, but only a few exceptional ones. They are softer than the 1988s, though some are superbly concentrated, particularly in the Côte de Beaune. It was an outstanding year for white Burgundy. Almost all the best growers' wines are beautifully balanced, despite their richness, but you should be drinking them now.

1988   Many growers produced firm, concentrated reds, now at their best. Some superb wines, but quite a few dour ones, too. Whites have matured slowly but are mostly at their peak. Beaujolais was good and long-lived for once.

1987   The best 1987 reds are very good indeed, Côte de Beaune having the edge over Côte de Nuits. The lesser wines aren't as good as those of 1985, but are better than those of 1986. Drink now, especially the whites.

1986   The reds are showing good perfume but need drinking soon, as do most whites. Chablis *grands crus* are drinking well.

1985   The reds turned out unevenly, and only the very best are still good. Chablis started out with a lesser reputation, but top Grand Cru wines from good producers can still be good, as can top Côte de Beaunes.

1983   Some impressive reds from well-managed vineyards, but the majority of wines were spoilt by rot. Whites were mostly rather heavy and leaden, though tasty. None should be kept further.

BASIC BURGUNDY PRICES

RED

Under £7.00

Bourgogne Clos de Chenôves, Cave de Buxy 1998 £6.99 (WAI)

Bourgogne Rouge, Jean-Claude Boisset 1999 £6.50 (MAR)

Bourgogne Rouge, Jean-Claude Boisset 1998 £5.99 (WAI)

Bourgogne Rouge, Vallet 1997 £6.99 (MORR) £9.99 (GN)

£7.00 → £7.99

Bourgogne Lucien Denizot 1996 £7.50 (JU)

Bourgogne Passe-Tout-Grains, Lafarge 1998 £7.99 (CON) £8.75 (GAU) £10.99 (WIN)

Bourgogne Rouge, Cave de Buxy 1998 £7.99 (MAR)

Bourgogne Rouge, Prudhon 1997 £7.50 (JU)

Bourgogne Rouge, Roger et Joël Remy 1998 £7.50 (LEA)

£8.00 → £9.99

Bourgogne Côtes d'Auxerre, Goisot 1999 £8.17 (DOM)

★ Bourgogne Grand Ordinaire Pinot Noir Terres Dorées J-P Brun 1999 £8.04 (SAV)

Bourgogne Passe-Tout-Grains, Lafarge 1999 £8.13 (RAE)

Bourgogne Rouge, Jean-Marc Boillot 1997 £8.32 (MON)

Bourgogne Rouge, Chevillon 1998 £9.50 (FORT)

Bourgogne Rouge, Chevillon 1997 £9.90 (JU)

Bourgogne Rouge, Faiveley 1998 £8.99 (DI)

Bourgogne Rouge, Jadot 1999 £8.49 (THR)

Bourgogne Rouge, Machard de Gramont 1997 £8.81 (CB)

Bourgogne Rouge, Merlin 1998 £9.90 (MV)

Bourgogne Rouge, Thierry Mortet 1996 £9.95 (LEA)

Bourgogne Rouge, Parent 1997 £8.65 (NEZ)

Bourgogne Rouge, Nicholas Potel 1997 £8.50 (WS) £9.95 (CON)

£10.00 → £12.99

Bourgogne la Digoine, Villaine 1995 £11.67 (ARM)

Bourgogne de Montille 1997 £11.95 (BER)

Bourgogne Rouge, Burguet 1996 £10.90 (JU)

Bourgogne Rouge, Leroy 1997 £10.18 (TUR) £10.83 (ARM) £14.00 (JU)

Bourgogne Rouge, Méo-Camuzet 1999 £12.14 (BODX)

Bourgogne Rouge, Denis Mortet 1999 £12.14 (BODX)

Bourgogne Rouge, Denis Mortet 1997 £11.16 (DOM)

Bourgogne Rouge, Mugneret-Gibourg 1999 £11.95 (LEA)

Bourgogne Rouge, Georges Roumier 1998 £10.67 (BODX) £11.80 (TAN)

Over £13.00

Bourgogne de Montille 1996 £14.17 (ARM)

Bourgogne Perrières, Bize 1997 £13.33 (ARM)

Bourgogne Rouge, Dugat-Py 1997 £15.20 (NI)

Bourgogne Rouge, Méo-Camuzet 1997 £14.00 (JU) £14.50 (RAE)

Bourgogne Rouge, Georges Roumier 1996 £13.12 (BODX)

RETAILERS SPECIALIZING IN BURGUNDY
see Retailers Directory (page 40) for details

Adnams (AD), Averys, Ballantynes (BAL), Bancroft (BAN), Bennetts (BEN), Berry Bros (BER), Bibendum (BIB), Bordeaux Index (BODX), Butlers (BU), A Byrne (BY), D Byrne, Cave Cru Classé, Corney & Barrow (CB), Direct Wine (DI), Domaine Direct (DOM), Farr Vintners (FA), Fortnums (FORT), Goedhuis, Roger Harris (HAW) – for Beaujolais, Haynes Hanson (HAH), Justerini & Brooks (JU), Lay & Wheeler (LAY), Lea & Sandeman (LEA), Montrachet (MON), Morris & Verdin (MV), Le Nez Rouge (NEZ), J Nicholson (NI), Oddbins (OD), Paulson (PAU), Christopher Piper (PIP), Raeburn (RAE), Reid, La Reserve (RES), Howard Ripley (RIP), T&W (TW), Tanners (TAN), Turville Valley (TUR), Wine Soc (WS), Wine Treasury (WT), Peter Wylie (WY), Noel Young (YOU).

WHITE

Under £6.00

Bourgogne Aligoté, Brocard **1999** £5.99 (POR)
Bourgogne Blanc, Jean-Claude Boisset **1998** £5.99 (WAI)

£6.00 → £7.99

Bourgogne Aligoté, Brocard **1998** £6.99 (JON)
Bourgogne Aligoté, Goisot **1999** £6.76 (DOM)
Bourgogne Aligoté, Lafarge **1998** £7.99 (CON) £8.75 (GAU) £10.99 (WIN)
Bourgogne Aligoté, Olivier Leflaive **1998** £6.29 (PLAY)
Bourgogne Aligoté, Mouton **1998** £6.55 (TAN) £7.33 (ARM)
Bourgogne Aligoté, Rollin **1997** £7.90 (BAC)
Bourgogne Aligoté, Rollin **1996** £7.50 (JU)
Bourgogne Blanc, Guy Amiot **1998** £7.74 (BODX) £8.95 (BAN) £8.99 (DI)
Bourgogne Blanc Anniversaire, Latour **1997** £6.84 (PEN)
Bourgogne Blanc, Clos de Chenôves **1998** £6.49 (WAI)
Bourgogne Blanc, Cuvée Icarus **1997** £6.50 (BU)
Bourgogne Blanc, Matrot **1998** £6.99 (BO) £8.95 (CON)
Bourgogne Blanc les Setilles, Olivier Leflaive **1999** £7.95 (LAY) £8.34 (CB)
Bourgogne Blanc, J-P Sorin **1997** £7.35 (GN)

£8.00 → £9.99

Bourgogne Aligoté de Bouzeron, Villaine **1999** £8.95 (AD) £9.75 (CB)
Bourgogne Aligoté, Jayer-Gilles **1997** £9.00 (JU)
Bourgogne Blanc, Guy Amiot **1997** £8.71 (BODX) £10.25 (SOM)
Bourgogne Blanc, Faiveley **1997** £8.99 (DI)
Bourgogne Blanc, Matrot **1997** £8.45 (CON)
Bourgogne Blanc, Domaine Michelot **1999** £9.31 (BIB)
Bourgogne Blanc, Sauzet **1999** £9.80 (TAN)
Bourgogne Blanc, Verget **1998** £8.95 (LEA) £9.95 (LAY)
Bourgogne Blanc, Verget **1997** £8.99 (SUN) £8.99 (LAI)
Bourgogne Côtes d'Auxerre, Goisot **1998** £8.22 (DOM)

£10.00 → £14.99

Bourgogne Blanc, Boyer-Martenot **1997** £10.28 (MON)
Bourgogne Blanc Clos du Château, Château de Puligny-Montrachet **1999** £10.58 (BIB)
Bourgogne Blanc Cuvée des Forgets, Patrick Javillier **1998** £12.10 (BAN)
Bourgogne Blanc Cuvée des Forgets, Patrick Javillier **1997** £11.70 (LAY)
Bourgogne Blanc, Charles et Remi Jobard **1998** £10.95 (LEA)
Bourgogne Blanc, François Jobard **1996** £14.00 (JU)
Bourgogne Blanc, François Jobard **1992** £13.99 (RAE)
Bourgogne Blanc, Leroy **1996** £10.83 (ARM) £11.95 (JU)
Bourgogne Blanc, Matrot **1994** £12.34 (TW)
Bourgogne Blanc, Domaine Michelot **1997** £12.95 (RES)
Bourgogne Blanc Oligocène, Javillier **1997** £11.75 (BAN) £13.95 (LAY)
Bourgogne Blanc, Sauzet **1998** £11.95 (RES) £13.51 (DOM)
Bourgogne Blanc, Sauzet **1997** £10.67 (BODX) £12.50 (JU)
Bourgogne Blanc, Sauzet **1996** £14.90 (JU)

Over £15.00

Bourgogne Blanc, Clos du Château de Meursault **1995** £18.95 (GN)
Bourgogne Blanc, Clos du Château de Meursault **1994** £17.99 (VIN)
Bourgogne Blanc, Domaine Leflaive **1998** £17.50 (ARM) £18.90 (JU)
Bourgogne Blanc, Domaine Leflaive **1997** £17.99 (RAE)

ROSÉ

c. £7.00

Bourgogne Rosé de Marsannay, Bruno Clair **1999** £6.75 (SOM)

SPARKLING

Under £7.50

Crémant de Bourgogne Cave de Lugny **Non-vintage** £5.70 (SOM) £8.70 (HAH)
Crémant de Bourgogne Rosé Cave de Lugny **Non-vintage** £7.49 (WAI)

BEAUJOLAIS PRICES

RED

Under £6.00

Beaujolais Cuvée Tradition, Brun 1997
£5.75 (JU)
Beaujolais Loron 1999 £5.40 (TAN) £5.99
(DI)
Beaujolais Château de Pizay 1999 £5.75
(CON)
Beaujolais Ravier 2000 £4.99 (OD)
Beaujolais Cave de Sain Bel 2000 £5.90
(HAW)
Beaujolais Paul Sapin 2000 £5.50 (MAR)
Beaujolais-Villages Château du Basty
2000 £5.69 (OD)
Beaujolais-Villages les Champs Bouthier,
Sapin 1999 £5.95 (STA)
Beaujolais-Villages Colonge 1999 £5.80
(BAC) £6.29 (AME) £6.75 (STA)
Beaujolais-Villages Duboeuf 2000 £5.49
(VIC) £5.49 (THR) £5.49 (BOT) £6.75 (NI)
Beaujolais-Villages Duboeuf 1999 £4.99
(MAJ) £5.49 (UN)
Beaujolais-Villages Jadot 1999 £5.88 (ASD)
£5.99 (TES) £5.99 (WAI)
Beaujolais-Villages Château de Lacarelle
1999 £5.50 (WS)
Beaujolais-Villages Pivot 1999 £5.86 (DOM)
Coteaux du Lyonnais, Cave de Sain Bel
1999 £5.75 (HAW)
Régnié Paul Sapin 1999 £5.49 (MAJ)

£6.00 → £6.99

Beaujolais Aucoeur 1999 £6.30 (HIC)
Beaujolais Blaise Carron 2000 £6.45 (HAW)
Beaujolais Cave du Bois d'Oingt 2000
£6.10 (HAW)
Beaujolais Charmet 2000 £6.95 (HAW)
Beaujolais Pierre Jomard 2000 £6.25 (HAW)
Beaujolais-Lancié Geny de Flammerécourt
1999 £6.90 (HAW)
Beaujolais Lantignié, Domaine Joubert
1999 £6.60 (AD)
Beaujolais Domaine de Milhomme 2000
£6.40 (HAW)
Beaujolais Cave de St-Verand 2000 £6.10
(HAW)
Beaujolais Vieilles Vignes, Garlon 2000
£6.50 (HAW)
Beaujolais Vieilles Vignes, Cave de St-
Vérand 2000 £6.40 (HAW)

Beaujolais-Villages Domaine Dalicieux
2000 £6.26 (BIB)
Beaujolais-Villages Dumas 1998 £6.95 (LEA)
Beaujolais-Villages Domaine de la Pavé
2000 £6.80 (HAW)
Beaujolais-Villages le Perréon, Bererd
2000 £6.60 (HAW)
Beaujolais-Villages Pivot 2000 £6.65 (HAW)
Beaujolais-Villages Roux 1999 £6.65 (HAW)
Beaujolais-Villages Domaine St Cyr 1999
£6.10 (HAW)
Brouilly Duboeuf 1999 £6.99 (VIC)
Chénas Domaine des Vieilles Caves,
Charvet 1999 £6.75 (WS)
Chiroubles Loron 1999 £6.85 (SOM)
£7.25 (TAN) £7.30 (BAC)
Côte de Brouilly Domaine de la Pierre
Bleue, Ravier 2000 £6.99 (OD)
Fleurie les Garans, Latour 1988 £6.99 (PEN)
Fleurie Domaine des Raclets 2000 £6.99
(SAF)
Juliénas Duboeuf 1999 £6.99 (TES)
Juliénas Domaine Joubert 1999 £6.75
(BALL) £6.95 (WS) £6.95 (TAN) £7.60 (AD)
Morgon Côte de Py, Gaget 1999 £6.95
(WS)
Morgon Côte de Py, Gaget 1998 £6.95
(BER)
Morgon Jambon 1999 £6.49 (ASD)
Morgon Château de Pizay 1998 £6.99
(CON)
Régnié Château Chassantour, Perroud
1998 £6.95 (TAN)

£7.00 → £7.99

Beaujolais-Villages les Larmoises Vieilles
Vignes, Lacondemine 1998 £7.90 (JU)
Brouilly Domaine de Combillaty, Duboeuf
2000 £7.55 (NEZ)
Chénas Benon 1999 £7.70 (HAW)
Chénas Château de Chénas 1998 £7.59
(JON)
Chénas Léspinasse 1999 £7.50 (HAW)
Chiroubles Domaine de la Grosse Pierre
1999 £7.39 (CON)
Côte de Brouilly Domaine de la Glaciere,
Loron 1995 £7.64 (PEN)
Côte de Brouilly Domaine du Griffon
1999 £7.85 (HAW)
Côte de Brouilly Loron 1999 £7.20 (TAN)
Côte de Brouilly Château Thivin 1999
£7.49 (GW) £8.40 (HAW) £8.99 (DI)

OZ CLARKE'S
WINE STYLE GUIDE

You probably know whether you fancy red or white, but then what? A fruit-packed, vanilla-spiced white or an appetizing, tangy style? A mouthwatering, food-friendly red or a party quaffer? Use my guide to the wine styles of the world to help you find the flavour you want

Buying wine in the UK has never been more fun than it is today. You can dash into a supermarket on your way home from work, log on to the internet or linger over a list of fine wines from a specialist merchant – and from the thousands of bottles you will find, the chances are that the wine you choose will be well made, clean and fresh. But what will it taste like? Well, despite the hundreds of grape varieties, from dozens of countries, all those thousands of wines fall into the 14 broad styles I describe on the following pages. So, even if you don't know a thing about grape varieties and wine-producing regions, just choose a style that appeals and I'll point you in the right direction.

RED WINES
Cheap and cheerful reds
At budget prices, you're looking for a wine that's light on its feet, with clean, fresh fruity flavours, and maybe a deep breath of vanilla oak – but often better without. There are plenty of good examples around, mostly in supermarkets, proving that simple doesn't have to mean characterless. It really doesn't matter whether it's a happy-go-lucky blend from southern France, or a simple glugger from Italy, Portugal, Eastern Europe, South Africa, Australia or South America.
● Minervois, Georges Badriou, £2.99, Safeway (southern France)
● Portuguese Red, J P Vinhos, Terras do Sado, £2.99, Somerfield
● Merlot, Boyar International, Rousse, £2.99, Sainsbury's (Bulgaria)

Juicy, fruity reds
The definitive modern style for easygoing reds. Tasty, refreshing and delicious with or without food, they pack in loads of crunchy fruit while minimizing the tough, gum-drying tannins that characterize most traditional

red wine styles. Beaujolais is the prototype, but now hi-tech producers all over the world are working the magic with a whole host of grape varieties. I'm going to crack ahead with a Chilean Carmenère, bursting

---

THE CORKSCREW
The first step in tasting any wine is to extract the cork. Look for a corkscrew with an open spiral, a comfortable handle and a mechanism that you like using. Corkscrews with a solid core that looks like a giant woodscrew tend to mash up delicate corks or get stuck in tough ones. With a simple non-levered screw the heroic effort required to pull the cork can turn into a circus-strongman act. The Screwpull brand is still far and away the best, with a high-quality open spiral. 'Waiter's friend' corkscrews – the type you see used in restaurants, funnily enough – are good too, once you get the knack. Those awful 'butterfly' corkscrews with the twin lever arms and a bottle opener on the end are incapable of removing a cork in a single smooth action and tend to leave cork crumbs floating in the wine; avoid them if possible.

with blackberry, blackcurrant and plum fruit. Carmenère and Merlot are always good bets, and Grenache (Garnacha) and Tempranillo usually come up with the goods. Italian grapes like Bonarda, Barbera and Sangiovese seem to double in succulence under Argentina's blazing sun. And at around £5 even Cabernet Sauvignon – if it's from somewhere warm like Australia, South America, South Africa or Spain – or a vin de pays Syrah from southern France, will emphasize the fruit and hold back on the tannin.

● 2000 Carmenère, Los Robles, Curicó Valley, £4.99, Sainsbury's (Chile)
● 2000 Malbec, La Riojana, Famatina Valley, £3.99, Co-op (Argentina)
● 1999 Garnacha Viña Fuerte, Calatayud, £3.99, Waitrose (Spain)

Silky, strawberryish reds

Here we're looking for some special qualities, specifically a gorgeously smooth texture and a heavenly fragrance of strawberries, raspberries or cherries. We're looking for soft, decadent, seductive wines. One grape – Pinot Noir – and one region – Burgundy – stand out and prices are high to astronomical. Good red Burgundy is addictively hedonistic and all sorts of strange decaying aromas start to hover around the strawberries as the wine ages. Pinot Noirs from New Zealand, California and Oregon come close, but they're expensive, too. Don't despair, because Chile can do the business for around £6 a bottle and you can get that strawberry perfume (though not the silky texture) from other grapes in Navarra or Rioja in Spain or from the blends of the southern Rhône: look for fairly light examples of Côtes du Rhône-Villages or Vacqueyras.

● 1999 Pinot Noir Reserve, Montana, Marlborough, £9.99, Oddbins, Safeway, Tesco, Waitrose, Wine Rack (New Zealand)
● 2000 Pinot Noir, Cono Sur, £4.99, Asda, Sainsbury's, Tesco (Chile)
● 1998 Pinot Noir Reserve, Valdivieso, £7.99, Bottoms Up, Wine Rack (Chile)

Intense, blackcurranty reds

These are firm, intense wines which only reveal their softer side with a bit of age, and Cabernet Sauvignon is the grape, on its own or blended with other varieties. Bordeaux is the classic region but I could show you 100 overpriced underachievers for every decent, good-value wine here. And Cabernet's image has changed. You can still choose the austere and tannic style, in theory aging to a heavenly cassis and cedar maturity, but most of the world is taking a fruitier blackcurrant-and-mint approach. Chile can't grab all the glory, but it does the fruity style *par excellence*. To back her up I'll pick New Zealand, which can deliver Bordeaux-like flavours, but in a faster-maturing wine, laden with fruit and a delicious hint of blackcurrant leaf. Or Australia, which can add a medicinal eucalyptus twist or a dollop of blackcurrant jam. You can find some very serious kit from about £7 in Oz; you'll have to pay a little more for Kiwi wines.

● 1998 Cabernet Sauvignon Nativa (organic), Carmen, £8.95, Stevens Garnier/£9.69, Oddbins (Chile)

THE WINE GLASS

When you're tasting wine you need a glass that will showcase the wine rather than the creative talents of the glass designer. So forget blue glasses, green glasses, flared glasses, thick, heavy glasses and rustic tumblers. The ideal wine glass is a fairly large tulip shape, made of fine, clear glass, with a slender stem. This shape helps to concentrate the aromas of the wine and enhances your enjoyment of its colours and texture. For sparkling wine choose a tall, slender glass, as it helps the bubbles to last longer.

Look after your glasses carefully. Detergent residues or grease can affect the flavour of any wine and reduce the bubbliness of sparkling wine. Always rinse glasses thoroughly after washing and allow them to air-dry. Ideally, wash them in very hot water and don't use detergent at all. Store your wine glasses upright to avoid trapping stale odours.

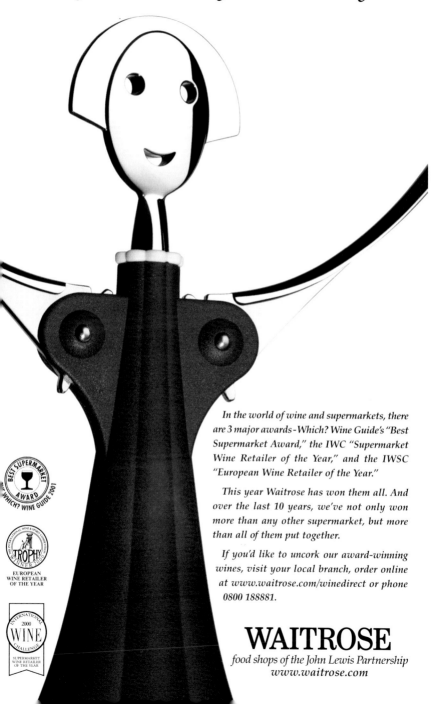

- 1998 Cabernet Sauvignon/Merlot Reserve, Villa Maria, £13.99, Safeway (New Zealand)
- 1998 Cabernet Sauvignon, The Willows Vineyard, Barossa, £9.99, Australian Wine Club (Australia)

Spicy, warm-hearted reds

Australian Shiraz is the epitome of this rumbustious, riproaring style: dense, rich, chocolaty, sometimes with a twist of pepper, a whiff of smoke, or a slap of leather. But it's not alone any more. There are southern Italy's Primitivo and Nero d'Avola, Argentina's Malbec, South Africa's Pinotage, California's Zinfandel, Mexico's Petite Sirah, Toro from Spain and some magnificent Greek reds. In southern France the wines of the Languedoc are increasingly showing this kind of warmth, roughed up with hillside herbs. And if you want your spice more serious, more smoky, and minerally, go for the classic wines of the northern Rhône Valley. You can find all the spice and richness you need for a mere £5, but the wines just get more potent and more individual from there on up.

- 1999 Organic Zinfandel, California Old Vines Estate, £5.99, Aldi (USA)
- 1999 Santa Cecilia, Planeta, Sicily, £20.95, La Reserve (Italy)
- 1999 Chambourcin, Pencil Pine, £5.97, Asda (Australia)

THE WINE COOLER

The temperature of wine has a bearing on its flavour. Heavy reds are happy at room temperature, but the lighter the wine the cooler it should be. For quick chilling you have a number of options. The traditional method is the ice bucket. Fill it with ice and cold water, plus a few spoonfuls of salt if you're in a real hurry. This is much more effective than a fridge or ice on its own. You can buy gel 'sleeves' to keep in the freezer for emergencies or a domestic version of the chiller machines offered in some off-licences. If the wine is already cool a vacuum-walled cooler is ideal for maintaining the temperature.

Mouthwatering, sweet-sour reds

Sounds weird? This style is the preserve of Italy, and it's all about food: the rasp of sourness cuts through rich, meaty food, with a lip-smacking tingle that works equally well with pizza or tomato-based pasta dishes. But there's fruit in there too – cherries and plums – plus raisiny sweetness and a herby bite. Italy does move with the times but it sticks to its guns, too, so the wines are better made than ever, with more seductive fruit, but holding on to those fascinating flavours. You'll have to shell out £7 or so for a decent Chianti; more for Piedmont wines (especially Barolo and Barbaresco, so try the Langhe DOC instead). Valpolicella can be very good at £5 up but you need to choose with care. Portugal can deliver something of the same character with its sour-cherries reds from the Douro and down south.

- 1996 Amarone della Valpolicella Classico, Allegrini, £19.99, Valvona & Crolla (Italy)
- 1997 Chianti Classico Riserva, Villa Cafaggio, £12.99, Villeneuve/£13.99, Sunday Times Wine Club, Laithwaites (Italy)
- 1999 Trincadeira/Cabernet Sauvignon, Senda do Vale, Ribatejano, £5.99, Sainsbury's (Portugal)

Delicate (and not-so-delicate) rosé

Rosé can be wonderful as long as it's made dry, with flavours of strawberries and maybe herbs. Look for wines made from sturdy grapes like Cabernet or Merlot, or go for Grenache, the classic rosé grape of Spain and the Rhône Valley. South America is a good, flavoursome bet. You don't need to pay much because most rosé is ridiculously unfashionable.

- 2000 Santa Julia Syrah Rosé, La Agricola, Mendoza, £4.99, Sainsbury's, Somerfield (Argentina)
- 2000 Cabernet Sauvignon Rosé Santa Digna, Miguel Torres, £4.99, Direct Wine Shipments (Chile)
- 2000 Goats do Roam Rosé, Fairview, £4.99, Tesco (South Africa)

Château Kirwan

Schröder & Schÿler S.A. propriétaires.
BP 113 - 33027 Bordeaux Cedex - France
Tél. 33 5 57 87 64 55 . Fax. 33 5 57 87 57 20

mail@schroder-schyler.com

HOW TO TASTE WINE

If you just knock your wine back like a cold beer, you'll be missing most of whatever flavour it has to offer. Take a bit of time to pay attention to what you're tasting and I guarantee you'll enjoy the wine more.

1 Read the label

There's no law that says you have to make life hard for yourself when tasting wine. So have a look at what you're drinking and read the notes on the back label if there is one. The label will tell you the vintage, the region and/or the grape variety, the producer and the alcohol level.

2 Look at the wine

Pour the wine into a glass so it is a third full and tilt it against a white background so you can enjoy the range of colours in the wine. Is it dark or light? Is it viscous or watery? As you gain experience the look of the wine will tell you one or two things about the age and the likely flavour and weight of the wine. As a wine ages, whites lose their springtime greenness and gather deeper, golden hues, whereas red wines trade the purple of youth for a paler brick red.

3 Swirl and sniff

Give the glass a vigorous swirl to wake up the aromas in the wine, stick your nose in and inhale gently. This is where you'll be hit by the amazing range of smells a wine can produce. Interpret them in any way that means something to you personally: it's only by reacting honestly to the taste and smell of a wine that you can build up a memory bank of flavours against which to judge future wines.

4 Take a sip

At last! It's time to drink the wine. So take a decent-sized slurp – enough to fill your mouth about a third full. The tongue can detect only very basic flavour elements: sweetness at the tip, acidity at the sides (saltiness too, but you won't find that in many wines) and bitterness at the back. The real business of tasting goes on in a cavity at the back of the mouth which is really part of the nose. The idea is to get the fumes from the wine to rise up into this nasal cavity. Note the toughness, acidity and sweetness of the wine then suck some air through the wine to help the flavours on their way. Gently 'chew' the wine and let it coat your tongue, teeth, cheeks and gums. Jot down a few notes as you form your opinion and then make the final decision… Do you like it or don't you?

Swallow or spit it out

If you are tasting a lot of wines, you will have to spit as you go if you want to remain upright and retain your judgement. Otherwise, go ahead and swallow and enjoy the lovely aftertaste of the wine.

SupremeCorq®. The closure that keeps wine as the winemaker *intended.*

The difference between a wine being "magnificent" and "musty" is often the length of the cork. Which is why hundreds of wineries have chosen to bottle their wines with SupremeCorq. SupremeCorq is a revolutionary cork that virtually eliminates the leakage and off-flavours associated with traditional closures. It opens with a regular corkscrew, won't break, and is recyclable. In short, it is perhaps the wine world's most perfect seal. Look for them topping off bottles in pubs, fine restaurants and wine shops worldwide. Visit us at: www.supremecorq.com.

SUPREME**CORQ**®

Designed to keep fine wine fine.

specialist gifts for lovers of wine and food

www.w-f-e.com

 Vin Pulla Opens a bottle of wine in just seconds. So easy to use. Place on your bottle of wine, pull down the lever, lift up and the cork is out! From £59.95

 Slica A perfect slice every time. This retro looking electric food slicer is safe and simple to use, fully adjustable for thickness from bread to Parma ham. Retails at £69.95

 Vin Chilla Chills to perfection in a matter of minutes. This stylish electric ice bucket will chill a bottle of wine or champagne from room temperature to perfection in as little as 4 minutes. From £69.95

Now available in rechargeable version to use anywhere, anytime.

 Vin Sava The only way to keep a wine fresh is by using nitrogen. VIN SAVA fits neatly on top of your bottle of wine or port, the wine is dispensed by pressing the lever. It then replaces the air with nitrogen, keeping the wine as fresh as the day of opening for up to three weeks. Retails £69.95

The wine & food
enthusiast

For a catalogue of all our products visit www.w-f-e.com

or call **020 8891 6464**

Rare Species from Banrock Station, Australia.

Banrock Station Sparkling Shiraz is now available in the UK. For every bottle sold, a donation is made to the Wildfowl and Wetlands Trust charity to preserve endangered wetland habitats and their wildlife.

BRL Hardy Wine Company
140 High Street, Esher, Surrey, KT10 9QJ.
Tel: 01372 473000. Fax: 01372 473100.

Discover our wines...
And uncover the soul
of a terroir

The Cave de Tain l'Hermitage vinifies
five famous appellations which typify the
character of the northern Rhône valley.
Bathed in soft sunshine, the steep,
granite terraces breathe
their soul into our wines.

ave de Tain l'Hermitage
RHONE VALLEY

WHITE WINES

Budget whites

There are budget versions of most of the styles of white I talk about below. The most successful, if they're cleanly made, are tangy Sauvignon Blancs – or vin de pays blends made to be tongue-tingling rather than toasty – which can send a shiver of acidity down your spine, and aromatic styles like Hungarian Irsai Oliver or Argentinian Torrontés, which can deliver a lovely rush of floral fragrance. You can still pick up ripe, peachy, none-too-subtle Aussie Chardonnay for £3.99, too.

● Soave, Sartori, £2.59, Sainsbury's (Italy)
● 2000 Cape White, Culemborg, £2.99, Waitrose (South Africa)
● 2000 Irsai Oliver, Hilltop Neszmély, Duna, £2.99, Safeway (Hungary)

Bone-dry, neutral whites

Neutral wines exist for the sake of seafood or to avoid interrupting you while you're eating. It's a question of balance, rather than aromas and flavours, but there will be a bit of lemon, yeast and a mineral thrill in a good Muscadet sur lie or a proper Chablis. Loads of Italian whites do the same thing, but Italy is increasingly picking up on the global shift towards fruit flavours and maybe some oak. Cheaper

French wines are often too raw whereas low-priced Italian whites tend to be insipid, but you don't need to spend much to get a result here.

● Sicilian White, Cantine Settesoli, Sicily, £2.99, Sainsburys (Italy)
● 2000 Soave Superiore Terra Viva (organic), £4.99, Tesco (Italy)
● 1999 Pinot Blanc Cuveé Réserve, Turckheim, £4.99, Oddbins (Alsace)

Green, tangy whites

For nerve-tingling refreshment, Sauvignon Blanc is the classic grape, full of fresh grass, gooseberry and nettle flavours. I always used to head straight for New Zealand versions, but I'm now more inclined to reach for an inexpensive bottle from South Africa or Hungary. Or even a simple white Bordeaux, because suddenly Bordeaux Sauvignon is buzzing with life. Most Sancerre and the other Loire Sauvignons are overpriced.

Alternatively, look at Riesling. Australia serves it up with bountiful lime and toast flavours while classic German versions are steelier and green-apple fresh, with intriguing peach and smoke flavours in their youth. Expect to pay £7 upwards.

● 2000 Kiwi Cuvée Vin de Pays du Jardin de la France, £3.99, Oddbins, Somerfield, Tesco (Loire)
● 2000 Sauvignon Blanc, Neetlingshof, £5.99, Oddbins (South Africa)
● 2000 Riesling, Tim Adams, £7.49, Tesco (Australia)

Intense, nutty whites

The best white Burgundy from the Côte d'Or cannot be bettered for its combination of soft nut and oatmeal flavours, subtle, buttery oak and firm, dry structure. Prices are, as you might expect, hair-raising and sadly the cheaper wines rarely offer much Burgundy style. For £6 or £7 your best bet is oaked Chardonnay from an innovative Spanish region such as Somontano or Navarra. You'll get a nutty, creamy taste and nectarine fruit with good

Unique & Innovative Wine Accessories

WINESERVER

Vacuum Wine Savers

WINEMASTER Corkscrew & Foilcutters

BOTTLE COASTER

Rapid Ice PRESTIGE COOLER

RAPID ICE 'Ultra Fast' drinks chillers

oak-aged white Bordeaux from around £10 or you could search out traditional white Rioja. The very best Chardonnays from New World countries – and Italy for that matter – can emulate Burgundy, but once again we're looking at serious prices.

● 1999 Vin de Pays d'Oc Chardonnay Reserve, Domaine Bégude, £8.99, Oddbins (southern France)
● 2000 Oaked Viura Alteza, Manchuela, £3.99, Sainsbury's (Spain)
● 2000 Sigalas Vareli, Santorini, £7.99, Oddbins, (Greece)

Ripe, toasty whites

Aussie Chardonnay conquered the world with its upfront flavours of peaches, apricots and tropical fruits, spiced up by the vanilla, toast and butterscotch richness of new oak. This winning style has now become a standard-issue flavour produced by all sorts of countries, though I still love the traditional Aussie stuff. You don't need to spend more than a fiver for a great big friendly golden labrador of a wine, though a well-spent £8 or so will give you more to relish beyond the second glass. However, many Australian winemakers are becoming increasingly restrained, and if you see the words 'unoaked' or 'cool-climate' on the bottle, expect an altogether leaner drink.

● 1999 Barrel-fermented Chardonnay, Sacred Hill, Hawkes Bay, £8.99, Unwins (New Zealand)
● 1999 Chardonnay, Bonterra, Fetzer, £8.49, Morrisons, Sainsbury's, Waitrose, Wine Rack (USA)
● 1998 Chardonnay, Montes Alpha, Curicó, £8.99, Morrisons/£9.99, Majestic, Portland Wine (Chile)

Aromatic whites

Every wine has an aroma, of course, but only with a few of them is it the aroma that we pay for. Alsace has always been a plentiful source. There's Gewürztraminer with its rose and lychee scent or Muscat with its floral, hothouse grape perfume,

and both are reliably good from £6 upwards. The world is currently discovering the joys of Viognier, traditionally the grape of Condrieu in the northern Rhône, but now appearing in vins de pays from all over southern France and also from California and Australia. Viognier should have a floral, apricotty aroma but lots of bottles fail to live up to the hype. Condrieu is expensive (£18 will get you entry-level stuff and no guarantee that it will be fragrant); vin de pays wines start at around £5 and are just as patchy. Albariño from Rías Baixas in Spain is another apricotty charmer. It's more reliable but it's in short supply, so prices start at about £7. For aroma on a budget grab some Hungarian Irsai Oliver or Argentinian Torrontés.

● 2000 Gewürztraminer, Paul Cluver, Elgin, £7.15, Christopher Piper (South Africa)
● 1999 Rías Baixas Albariño, Fillaboa, £8.80, Savage Selection (Spain)
● 2000 Torrontés La Nature (organic), Famatina Valley, £4.47, Asda/£4.49, Budgen (Argentina)

SPARKLING WINES

Champagne can be the finest sparkling wine on the planet and the very best is sublime, but fizz made by the traditional Champagne method in Australia, New Zealand or California is often just as good and cheaper. It might be a little more fruity, where Champagne concentrates on bready, yeasty or nutty aromas, but a few are dead ringers for the classic style. Fizz is also made in other parts of France: Crémant de Bourgogne is one of the best. England's cool climate – not that far removed from that of Champagne – is beginning to show its potential for sparkling wines.

● Pelorus NV, Cloudy Bay, £11.99, Villeneuve, Wine Rack (New Zealand)
● Limoux Les Etoiles Organic Sparkling, B Delmas, £6.99, Tesco (southern France)
● 1994 Classic Cuvée, Nyetimber (01798 813989 for stockists), £17 (England)

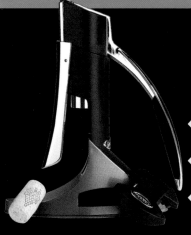

CHAMPAGNE
TAITTINGER
Reims

Stockists :
Asda, Bottoms Up,
Madaboutwine.com,
Majestic Wine Warehouse,
Oddbins, Safeway, Tesco,
Threshers, Victoria Wine,
Wine Cellar, Unwins.

Côte de Brouilly Domaine de la Voûte des Crozes, Chanrion **1999** £7.30 (RSJ)
Fleurie Denojean **1999** £7.86 (WHI)
Fleurie Loron **1999** £7.60 (TAN)
Fleurie Sapin **2000** £7.99 (MAR)
Juliénas Domaine de Beauvernay **1998** £7.80 (COC)
Juliénas Domaine Joubert **1998** £7.69 (JON) £7.99 (POR)
Juliénas Château de Juliénas **1997** £7.64 (PEN)
Juliénas Domaine de la Seigneurie, Duboeuf **2000** £7.49 (NEZ)
Juliénas Domaine de la Seigneurie, Duboeuf **1999** £7.99 (VIL)
Juliénas Domaine de la Vieille Église, Loron **1999** £7.99 (DI)
Morgon Aucoeur **2000** £7.30 (RSJ)
Morgon Domaine de la Chanaise **1998** £7.95 (FORT)
Morgon Domaine Jean Descombes, Duboeuf **2000** £7.49 (NEZ) £8.60 (NI)
Morgon Domaine Jean Descombes, Duboeuf **1999** £7.99 (VIL)
Morgon Château Gaillard **1998** £7.95 (COC)
Morgon Domaine des Vieux Cèdres, Loron **1998** £7.04 (PEN)
Moulin-à-Vent Cave du Château de Chénas **1999** £7.75 (HAW)
Moulin-à-Vent Duboeuf **1998** £7.99 (UN)
Moulin-à-Vent Fessy **1999** £7.99 (OD)
Moulin-à-Vent Domaine les Fine Graves, Janodet **1997** £7.25 (SOM)
Moulin-à-Vent Domaine Gay-Coperet **1998** £7.95 (LEA)
Moulin-à-Vent Domaine Janin **1999** £7.99 (RAE) £8.81 (DOM)
Régnié Desplace **1999** £7.30 (HAW)
Régnié Roux **1999** £7.50 (HAW) £7.61 (FLE)
St-Amour Domaine des Duc **1999** £7.49 (MAJ) £9.00 (HAW)
St-Amour Domaine des Pins, Echallier **1998** £7.99 (AME)

£8.00 → £8.99

Brouilly Drouhin **1998** £8.53 (PEN)
Brouilly Michaud **2000** £8.60 (MV)
Brouilly Michaud **1999** £8.60 (WRI)
Brouilly Château Thivin **2000** £8.20 (HAW)
Brouilly Château Thivin **1999** £8.25 (AD)
Brouilly Château des Tours **1999** £8.70 (BAC) £8.91 (NO) £8.95 (STA)

Chénas Oak-Aged, Benon **1998** £8.80 (HAW)
Chénas Domaine de Mongrin, Gaec des Ducs **1998** £8.81 (BIB)
Chénas Domaine de Mongrin, Gaec des Ducs **1995** £8.50 (RAE)
Chénas Trenel **1999** £8.99 (BEN)
Chiroubles Méziat **1999** £8.10 (HAW)
Chiroubles Passot **1999** £8.40 (HAW)
Chiroubles Château de Raousset **1998** £8.45 (JU)
Chiroubles la Maison des Vignerons **2000** £8.20 (HAW)
Côte de Brouilly Château Thivin **1998** £8.99 (DI)
Fleurie Domaine Paul Bernard **1999** £8.99 (OD)
Fleurie Duboeuf **1999** £8.49 (THR)
Fleurie Cuveé Bienfaiteur, Cave Co-op de Fleurie **1999** £8.50 (HAW)
Fleurie Château de Fleurie, Loron **1999** £8.37 (PEN) £8.75 (WRI)
Fleurie Domaine de la Grand Cour **1999** £8.85 (BAC) £8.99 (AME)
Fleurie Grille Midi **1999** £8.61 (BIB)
Fleurie Château de Labourons **1998** £8.65 (HAW)

Fleurie la Madone, Duboeuf **2000** £8.49 (NEZ)

Fleurie la Madone, Duboeuf **1999** £8.99 (VIL)

Fleurie Domaine des Quatre Vents, Duboeuf **2000** £8.49 (NEZ) £9.70 (NI)

Fleurie Château de Raousset **2000** £8.95 (JU)

Fleurie la Roilette, Coudert **1999** £8.97 (SAV)

Juliénas Condemine **1998** £8.55 (HAW)

Juliénas Drouhin **1998** £8.17 (PEN)

Morgon Aucoeur **1999** £8.25 (HAW)

Morgon Charmes Domaine des Pillets **2000** £8.61 (BIB)

Morgon Château de Raousset **1999** £8.45 (JU)

Moulin-à-Vent Domaine Charvet **1999** £8.90 (BAC)

Moulin-à-Vent Domaine les Fine Graves, Janodet **1999** £8.50 (BER) £8.75 (STA)

Moulin-à-Vent Grille Midi **1999** £8.85 (CON)

Moulin-à-Vent Janin **1998** £8.81 (DOM)

Moulin-à-Vent Domaine Lemonon, Loron **1997** £8.11 (PEN)

Moulin-à-Vent Loron **1996** £8.50 (BALL)

Moulin-à-Vent Le Vieux Domaine **1999** £8.35 (HAW)

Moulin-à-Vent Le Vieux Domaine **1998** £8.99 (GW)

Régnié Domaine des Pillets **2000** £8.13 (BIB)

St-Amour Poitevin **1999** £8.90 (HAW)

£9.00 → £10.99

Beaujolais Château de Fleurie, Loron **1999** £9.99 (DI)

Fleurie Berrod **1999** £9.95 (AD)

Fleurie Colonge **1999** £9.20 (TAN)

Fleurie Drouhin **1999** £10.46 (PEN)

Fleurie Dumas **1999** £9.50 (LEA)

Fleurie Cave Co-op de Fleurie **1998** £9.25 (FRI)

Fleurie les Garans, Latour **1999** £9.40 (WY)

Fleurie les Garans, Latour **1998** £9.76 (COC)

Fleurie la Madone, Louis Tête **1998** £9.56 (COC)

Oz Clarke's Wine Buying Guide
is an annual publication.
We welcome your suggestions for
next year's edition.

Fleurie la Roilette, André Metrat **1999** £10.38 (BIB)

Fleurie la Roilette, André Metrat **1998** £9.95 (RAE)

Morgon Domaine de la Chanaise **1999** £9.28 (PLAY)

Morgon Charmes Château Fuissé, Vincent **1998** £9.60 (AD)

Morgon Côte de Py, Lieven **1996** £10.50 (JER)

Morgon Marcel Lapierre **2000** £10.28 (BIB)

Moulin-à-Vent Domaine Berrod **1998** £9.95 (AD)

Moulin-à-Vent Cuvée Exceptionnelle, Château du Moulin-à-Vent **1998** £10.45 (HAW)

Moulin-à-Vent Drouhin **1998** £9.64 (PEN)

Moulin-à-Vent Château du Moulin-à-Vent **1998** £9.10 (HAW)

c. £15.00

Moulin-à-Vent Lafond **1988** £15.00 (CRO)

WHITE

Under £7.00

Beaujolais Blanc Château de Chanzé **1999** £6.60 (HAW)

Beaujolais Blanc Château de Pizay **1998** £6.69 (CON)

Beaujolais Blanc Domaine des Terres Dorées **1999** £6.76 (SAV)

Coteaux du Lyonnais, Cave de Sain Bel **1999** £5.90 (HAW)

£7.00 → £8.99

Beaujolais Blanc Pierre Carron **1999** £7.30 (HAW)

Beaujolais Blanc Charmet **1997** £8.10 (HAW)

Beaujolais Blanc Jean-Jacques Martin **1999** £8.55 (HAW)

Beaujolais Blanc Domaine des Terres Dorées **1998** £7.95 (AD)

Beaujolais Blanc Domaine des Terres Dorées **1997** £7.50 (JU)

ROSÉ

c. £7.00

Beaujolais Rosé Cave Beaujolais du Bois d'Oingt **1999** £6.55 (HAW)

CHABLIS PRICES

WHITE

Under £7.00

Chablis Servin 1999 £6.99 (MAJ)
Petit Chablis Brocard 1998 £6.99 (POR)
Sauvignon de St-Bris, Brocard 1998 £4.99 (WAI)
Sauvignon de St-Bris, Goisot 1999 £4.95 (SOM) £6.75 (DOM) £7.35 (RAE)
Sauvignon de St-Bris, Domaine des Remparts 1998 £6.50 (HIG)

£7.00 → £7.99

Chablis Alain Geoffroy 1999 £7.99 (OD)
Chablis la Chablisienne 1997 £7.25 (SOM) £7.95 (WS) £7.99 (MAR)
Chablis Durup 1999 £7.99 (BO) £8.52 (DOM)
Chablis Hamelin 1999 £7.95 (AS)
Chablis Domaine des Manants, Brocard 1998 £7.95 (BALL) £7.99 (POR) £8.59 (JON)
Chablis J Moreau 1999 £7.39 (WHI)
Chablis Tremblay 1998 £7.50 (BAC)
Chablis Domaine des Valéry, Durup 1998 £7.99 (TAN)
Petit Chablis Château de Maligny 1999 £7.49 (VIC) £7.49 (THR) £7.69 (BOT)
Sauvignon de St-Bris, Defrance 1998 £7.99 (WIN)
Sauvignon de St-Bris, Sorin-Defrance 1999 £7.00 (WRI)

£8.00 → £9.99

Chablis 1er Cru Grand Cuvée, la Chablisienne 1997 £9.75 (GN)
Chablis Beauroy, Hamelin 1998 £9.97 (HIC)
Chablis Domaine de Biéville, J Moreau 1999 £8.99 (VIC) £8.99 (THR) £8.99 (BOT)
Chablis Pascal Bouchard 1999 £9.15 (PLA)
Chablis Brocard 1999 £8.29 (OD)
Chablis la Chablisienne 1998 £8.57 (FLE)
Chablis Droin 1998 £9.99 (DOM)
Chablis Drouhin 1998 £9.87 (PEN)
Chablis Domaine de l'Églantière 1999 £8.79 (AME)
Chablis Domaine de l'Églantière 1998 £8.90 (BAC)
Chablis Grand Cru, Château de Grenouille 1995 £9.65 (GN) £23.00 (JU)
Chablis Domaine des Iles, Tremblay 1999 £8.59 (COC)

Chablis Laroche 1999 £8.99 (DI)
Chablis Latour 1998 £8.55 (PEN)
Chablis Latour 1997 £9.80 (RIC)
Chablis Légland 1999 £8.72 (BIB)
Chablis Long-Depaquit 1998 £8.95 (BAL)
Chablis Château de Maligny 1998 £8.99 (THR) £8.99 (BOT) £8.99 (WR) £9.19 (BY)
Chablis Pautré 1998 £9.00 (HIG)
Chablis Cuvée Reserve, Pautré 1998 £9.80 (HIG)
Chablis Picq 1999 £9.40 (MV)
Chablis Domaine Ste-Claire, Brocard 1998 £8.32 (HIC)
Chablis Servin 1994 £9.99 (WIN)
Chablis Tribut 1999 £9.95 (JU) £10.95 (LEA)
Chablis Tribut 1998 £9.99 (DOM)
Chablis Vieilles Vignes, Brocard 1996 £9.99 (NEZ) £12.50 (JU)
Chablis Vieilles Vignes, Château de Maligny 1998 £9.59 (BY)
Chablis Vocoret 1999 £8.99 (MAJ)
Petit Chablis Pautré 1998 £8.00 (HIG)

£10.00 → £11.99

Chablis 1er Cru, Drouhin 2000 £11.65 (NI)
Chablis Adhémar Boudin, Domaine de Chantemerle 1998 £10.95 (LEA)
Chablis Chevallier 1996 £10.25 (BEN)
Chablis Domaine de la Conciergerie, Adine 2000 £10.50 (JER)
Chablis Daniel Defaix 1998 £10.99 (VIC) £10.99 (THR) £10.99 (BOT) £10.99 (WR)
Chablis Fèvre 1999 £10.25 (FORT)
Chablis Fourchaume, Durup 1999 £11.52 (DOM)
Chablis Fourchaume, Durup 1998 £10.90 (BAC) £13.19 (JON)
Chablis Fourchaume, Domaine des Valéry 1998 £10.90 (TAN)
Chablis Montée de Tonnerre, Durup 1999 £11.52 (DOM)
Chablis Montmains, Brocard 1998 £11.95 (POR) £12.95 (AD) £12.99 (JON)
Chablis Montmains, Brocard 1996 £11.95 (BALL) £14.00 (JU)
Chablis Montmains, Légland 1999 £11.75 (BIB)
Chablis Montmains, Race 1999 £11.50 (MV) £11.75 (WRI)
Chablis Tremblay 1996 £10.35 (VIN)
Chablis Vau de vey Domaine des Valéry, Durup 1998 £10.90 (TAN) £15.74 (TW)

Chablis Vau-Ligneau, Alain Geoffroy **1999**
£10.99 (OD)

Chablis Vau-Ligneau, Hamelin **1998**
£11.49 (NEZ)

Chablis Vieilles Vignes, Daniel Defaix
1998 £10.99 (BO) £12.50 (LAY)

Chablis Vieilles Vignes, Daniel Defaix
1997 £10.25 (GN) £10.95 (CON)

Chablis Vieilles Vignes, Daniel Defaix
1996 £11.50 (BALL) £15.57 (TW)

Petit Chablis Dauvissat-Camus **1997**
£10.90 (JU)

£12.00 → £13.99

Chablis 1er Cru Grand Cuvée, la
Chablisienne **1996** £12.99 (MAR)

Chablis 1er Cru, Domaine Vocoret **1997**
£13.49 (VIN)

Chablis Beauroy, la Chablisienne **1997**
£12.95 (STE)

Chablis Côte de Léchet, Tribut **1998**
£12.50 (JU) £13.95 (LEA) £14.10 (DOM)

Chablis Cuvée Reserve, Pautré **1999**
£12.59 (VIN)

Chablis la Forêt, Domaine Dauvissat-
Camus **1998** £13.40 (TAN) £16.00 (JU)

Chablis la Forêt, Pinson **1997** £13.95 (NO)

Chablis Fourchaume, la Chablisienne
1998 £13.99 (VIL)

Chablis Fourchaume, Domaine des
Malandes **1995** £13.95 (WS)

Chablis Fourchaume, Château de Maligny
1997 £12.56 (BY) £13.99 (BOT)

Chablis Mont de Milieu, Pascal Bouchard
1999 £13.99 (SUN) £13.99 (LAI)

Chablis Mont de Milieu, Moreau **1997**
£12.62 (COC)

Chablis Montée de Tonnerre, Brocard
1998 £12.25 (HIC)

Chablis Montée de Tonnerre, Louis
Michel **1998** £13.55 (HAH)

Chablis Montée de Tonnerre, Servin
1996 £13.16 (CB)

Chablis Montée de Tonnerre, Domaine
de Vauroux **1999** £12.45 (LAY)

Chablis Montmains, Domaine Adine **2000**
£12.70 (JER)

Chablis Montmains, Laroche **2000** £13.90
(BIB)

Chablis Montmains, J Moreau **1997**
£13.60 (RIC)

Chablis Montmains, Domaine de Vauroux
1998 £12.49 (CON)

Chablis Vaillons, Daniel Defaix **1995**
£13.45 (GN) £15.95 (BALL) £22.56 (TW)

Chablis Vaillons, Laroche **1998** £13.28
(WHI)

Chablis Vau-Ligneau, Chevallier **1999**
£12.99 (BEN)

Chablis Vau-Ligneau, Hamelin **1999**
£12.99 (BEN)

Chablis Vaucoupin, Grossot **1998** £13.95
(LAY)

Chablis Vaudevey, Laroche **1998** £12.90
(CRO) £15.99 (DI)

Chablis Vaudevey, Château de Maligny
1998 £12.56 (BY)

£14.00 → £16.99

Chablis 1er Cru, Drouhin **1997** £16.33
(PEN)

Chablis Côte de Léchet, Etienne et Daniel
Defaix **1996** £15.60 (TAN)

Chablis Côte de Léchet, Etienne et Daniel
Defaix **1995** £15.95 (CON) £16.50
(BALL) £17.99 (BOT)

Chablis la Forest, René et Vincent
Dauvissat **1999** £14.69 (DOM)

Chablis Fourchaume Vieilles Vignes,
Laroche **2000** £15.66 (BIB)

Chablis Fourchaume Vieilles Vignes,
Laroche **1999** £16.99 (YOU)

Chablis les Lys, Daniel Defaix **1995**
£15.95 (CON)

Chablis Montée de Tonnerre, Droin
1999 £15.45 (BER)

Chablis Montée de Tonnerre, Louis
Michel **1999** £15.00 (FORT)

Chablis Montmains, Droin **1999** £14.69
(DOM)

Chablis Séchet, Domaine Dauvissat-
Camus **1998** £14.95 (JU)

Chablis Vaillons, Collet **1998** £14.15 (JER)

Chablis Vaillons, Domaine Dauvissat-
Camus **1998** £14.95 (JU)

Chablis Vaillons, René et Vincent
Dauvissat **1999** £14.69 (DOM)

Chablis Vaillons, Daniel Defaix **1996**
£16.95 (BER) £17.89 (JON)

Chablis Vaillons, Droin **1999** £14.10 (DOM)

£17.00 → £19.99

Chablis les Clos, Pinson **1999** £19.19 (BIB)
Chablis les Clos, Servin **1999** £19.69 (SUN) £19.69 (LAI) £26.99 (WIN)
Chablis Côte de Léchet, Etienne et Daniel Defaix **1997** £17.99 (WR)
Chablis la Forest, René et Vincent Dauvissat **1996** £19.97 (BODX)
Chablis Fourchaume, Laroche **1997** £18.99 (DI)
Chablis Grand Cru, Château de Grenouille **1998** £19.99 (MAR) £33.50 (FRI)
Chablis Grand Cru, Château de Grenouille **1997** £19.99 (SAF) £29.50 (STE)
Chablis Séchet, René et Vincent Dauvissat **1997** £17.53 (FA) £19.49 (BODX) £21.25 (FORT)
Chablis Vaillons, Drouhin **1997** £17.00 (JU)

£20.00 → £24.99

Chablis Blanchots, Laroche **1999** £23.99 (BIB) £25.99 (YOU)
Chablis Bougerots, Laroche **1999** £22.52 (BIB)
Chablis Bougros, Domaine de Vauroux **1997** £20.95 (CON)
Chablis les Clos, Pascal Bouchard **1998** £22.25 (WAT)
Chablis les Clos, Brocard **1996** £23.00 (JU)
Chablis les Clos, Brocard **1994** £22.87 (FLE)
Chablis les Clos, Droin **1998** £23.50 (DOM)
Chablis les Clos, Droin **1997** £23.75 (JON)
Chablis les Clos, Louis Michel **1998** £21.60 (HAH)
Chablis les Clos, J Moreau **1996** £21.20 (COC)
Chablis Côte de Léchet, Etienne et Daniel Defaix **1993** £22.09 (TW)
Chablis la Forest, René et Vincent Dauvissat **1998** £22.00 (FORT)
Chablis Grenouilles, Louis Michel **1998** £21.60 (HAH)
Chablis Montée de Tonnerre, Verget **1999** £20.07 (FA)
Chablis la Moutonne, Long-Depaquit **1997** £23.50 (UN)
Chablis les Preuses, la Chablisienne **1998** £24.25 (STE)
Chablis les Preuses, la Chablisienne **1995** £21.00 (JU)
Chablis les Preuses, Domaine Dauvissat-Camus **1998** £22.60 (TAN)

Chablis Séchet, René et Vincent Dauvissat **1998** £21.50 (FORT)
Chablis Valmur, Droin **1998** £23.50 (DOM)
Chablis Vaudésir, Droin **1997** £23.75 (JON)
Chablis Vaudésir, J Moreau **1996** £20.95 (COC)

£25.00 → £29.99

Chablis les Blanchots, Servin **1999** £26.99 (WIN)
Chablis Butteaux, Raveneau **1997** £29.38 (BODX) £30.26 (TUR) £32.70 (FA)
Chablis les Clos, Domaine Dauvissat-Camus **1998** £25.00 (JU)
Chablis les Clos, René et Vincent Dauvissat **1998** £26.44 (DOM) £29.28 (FA) £29.50 (LEA) £40.00 (FORT)
Chablis les Clos, Drouhin **1998** £29.95 (BEN)
Chablis Grenouilles, Droin **1998** £25.26 (DOM)
Chablis Grenouilles, La Chablisienne **1998** £27.95 (FRI)
Chablis la Moutonne, Long-Depaquit **1998** £26.95 (BER) £29.50 (BAL)
Chablis les Preuses, René et Vincent Dauvissat **1999** £26.44 (DOM)
Chablis les Preuses, René et Vincent Dauvissat **1998** £29.28 (FA) £37.50 (FORT)
Chablis les Preuses, René et Vincent Dauvissat **1997** £29.38 (BODX)
Chablis Vaillons, Raveneau **1998** £29.77 (FA)
Chablis Vaudésir, Drouhin **1997** £26.00 (JU) £26.95 (BEN)

Over £30.00

Chablis les Clos, René et Vincent Dauvissat **1997** £38.78 (TUR)
Chablis les Clos, Laroche **1999** £31.82 (BIB) £33.99 (YOU)
Chablis Montée de Tonnerre, Raveneau **1997** £32.70 (FA) £35.25 (BODX) £41.17 (ARM)
Chablis Valmur, Raveneau **1998** £38.58 (FA)
Chablis Valmur, Raveneau **1992** £52.88 (BODX)
Chablis Vaudésir, Drouhin **1999** £31.50 (NI)
Chablis Vaudésir, Drouhin **1998** £31.26 (PEN)
Chablis Vaudésir, Louis Michel **1988** £37.00 (CRO)
Chablis Vaulorent, Fèvre **1983** £31.00 (CRO)

CÔTE CHALONNAISE PRICES

RED

Under £9.00

Givry Latour **1997** £7.99 (PEN)
Rully Varot Domaine de la Renarde,
Delorme **1997** £8.69 (WAT)

£9.00 → £10.99

Givry Boischevaux, Thenard **1998** £10.95
(JER)
Givry le Pied de Clou, Lumpp **1999**
£10.95 (LEA)
Givry le Pied de Clou, Lumpp **1998**
£10.95 (LEA)
Givry le Pied de Clou, Lumpp **1997**
£10.95 (LEA)
Mercurey Latour **1997** £10.34 (PEN)
Rully Dureuil-Janthial **1999** £9.65 (RAE)
Rully Dureuil-Janthial **1998** £10.50 (RAE)

£11.00 → £14.99

Givry Clos Jus, Lumpp **1999** £12.95
(LEA)
Givry Clos Jus, Lumpp **1998** £12.95
(LEA)
Givry Clos Jus, Lumpp **1997** £12.95
(LEA)
Givry Clos Jus, Mouton **1999** £11.30
(TAN)
Givry Clos Jus, Mouton **1998** £11.75 (BU)
£12.08 (ARM)
Givry Clos Jus, Mouton **1997** £13.95
(POR)
Givry la Grande Berge, Ragot **1996**
£13.95 (BEN)
Givry Gérard Mouton **1996** £12.60 (STA)
Mercurey Carillon **1997** £11.75 (MON)
Mercurey Carillon **1996** £12.75 (STE)
Mercurey Château de Chamilly **1993**
£12.99 (JON)
Mercurey Château de Chamirey, Rodet
1998 £14.95 (STE)

Mercurey Château de Chamirey, Rodet
1997 £13.38 (WHI) £13.50 (WS)
Mercurey Château de Chamirey, Rodet
1996 £13.38 (WHI)
Mercurey les Combins, Juillot **1998**
£12.50 (LEA)
Mercurey les Combins, Juillot **1997**
£12.95 (LEA) £12.95 (BALL)
Mercurey Domaine de la Croix Jacquelet,
Faiveley **1998** £12.34 (PLA) £12.35
(CON)
Mercurey Domaine de la Croix Jacquelet,
Faiveley **1997** £11.95 (WRI) £12.50
(ARM)
Mercurey la Framboisière, Faiveley **1999**
£12.75 (LLO)
Mercurey la Framboisière, Faiveley **1998**
£13.99 (VIL) £14.50 (BEN)
Mercurey Juillot **1997** £11.69 (DOM)
Mercurey Juillot **1995** £12.87 (DOM)
Mercurey Maréchal **1996** £11.48 (NO)
Mercurey les Mauvarennes, Faiveley **1998**
£11.99 (DI) £12.25 (HAH)
Rully 1er Cru les Cloux, Jacqueson **1998**
£11.95 (LEA) £14.20 (NI)
Rully 1er Cru les Cloux, Jacqueson **1996**
£12.95 (NEZ)
Rully les Chaponnières, Jacqueson **1996**
£14.99 (POR)
Rully Faiveley **1999** £11.50 (BEN)
Rully les Préaux, Jean-Claude Brelière
1998 £11.95 (BALL)
Rully Préaux, Eric de Suremain **1997**
£13.90 (JU)
Rully Château de Rully, Rodet **1998**
£12.99 (UN)

£15.00 → £17.99

Givry Clos de la Servoisine, Jean-Marc
Joblot **1998** £17.95 (RES)
Givry Clos de la Servoisine, Jean-Marc
Joblot **1997** £16.00 (JU)
Givry Clos de la Servoisine, Jean-Marc
Joblot **1996** £16.50 (JU)
Mercurey Clos des Barraults, Juillot **1996**
£17.04 (DOM)
Mercurey Clos des Barraults, Juillot **1995**
£17.04 (DOM)
Rully Préaux, Eric de Suremain **1996**
£16.00 (JU)
Rully Préaux, Eric de Suremain **1995**
£16.00 (JU)

- *Wines are listed in A–Z order within
  each price band.*
- *For each wine, vintages are listed in
  descending order.*
- *Each vintage of any wine appears
  only once.*

Over £18.00

Mercurey les Combins, Juillot **1992** £26.62 (TW)
Mercurey Juillot **1996** £18.95 (FORT)

WHITE

Under £9.00

Montagny 1er Cru les Loges, Cave de Buxy **1999** £8.95 (TAN)
Montagny 1er Cru les Loges, Cave de Buxy **1998** £8.95 (BALL) £8.95 (AD)
Montagny Latour **1999** £8.99 (POR)
Montagny les Vignes de la Croix, Cave de Buxy **1998** £6.60 (STE)
Rully 1er Cru Margoté, Dury **1998** £8.50 (BALL)
Rully Jaffelin **1996** £8.99 (MAJ)

£9.00 → £10.99

Bourgogne Blanc les Clous, Villaine **1996** £9.50 (WS)
Givry Clos des Vignes Rondes, Lumpp **1999** £10.95 (LEA)
Givry Clos des Vignes Rondes, Lumpp **1998** £10.95 (LEA)
Mercurey Juillot **1998** £10.95 (LEA)

Mercurey Domaine du Meix-Foulot **1998** £9.95 (SOM)
Montagny 1er Cru, Cave de Buxy **1998** £9.50 (FRI) £9.90 (NI)
Montagny 1er Cru, Olivier Leflaive **1999** £10.22 (CB) £10.35 (LAY)
Montagny Coères, Bertrand et Juillot **1998** £9.58 (ARM)
Montagny Coères, Bertrand et Juillot **1997** £10.42 (ARM)
Montagny Latour **1997** £9.95 (STA)
Montagny Roy **1999** £10.85 (WRI)
Rully 1er Cru Meix Cadot, Dury **1997** £9.95 (RAE)
Rully la Chaume, Chartron et Trébuchet **1998** £10.99 (VIL)

Rully la Chaume, Dury **1998** £9.99 (JON)
Rully Faiveley **1997** £10.99 (DI)
Rully Grésigny, Jacqueson **1998** £10.90 (BAC) £11.75 (BAN) £14.95 (POR)
Rully Domaine de l'Hermitage, Chanzy **1997** £9.76 (HIC)
Rully Château de Rully, Rodet **1998** £10.99 (SAI)

£11.00 → £12.99

Mercurey Juillot **1997** £12.87 (DOM)
Montagny Latour **1998** £11.07 (PLAY)
Rully Bouchard Père **1997** £11.90 (COC)
Rully les Clous, Olivier Leflaive **1997** £11.95 (LAY)
Rully Olivier Leflaive **1999** £11.15 (HAH)
Rully Marissou, Dury **1990** £11.95 (RAE)
Rully la Pucelle, Jacqueson **1999** £11.95 (LEA)
Rully la Pucelle, Jacqueson **1998** £11.95 (LEA) £13.80 (NI)
Rully les St-Jacques, Villaine **1999** £12.81 (CB)

£13.00 → £14.99

Mercurey Château de Chamirey, Rodet **1998** £14.95 (BER)
Mercurey Château de Chamirey, Rodet **1997** £13.99 (YOU)
Mercurey Clos Rochette, Faiveley **1996** £14.75 (WRI)
Rully 1er Cru, de Suremain **1997** £13.90 (JU)
Rully 1er Cru, de Suremain **1996** £14.50 (JU)
Rully la Chaume, Chartron et Trébuchet **1999** £13.20 (JER)
Rully Grésigny, Jacqueson **1999** £13.80 (NI)

Over £15.00

Mercurey Clos Rochette, Faiveley **1999** £15.22 (PLA)
Mercurey Juillot **1996** £18.95 (FORT)
Montagny Latour **1990** £23.50 (WY)

- *All prices for each wine are listed together in ascending order.*
- *Price bands refer to the lowest price for which the wine is available.*

CÔTE D'OR PRICES

RED

Under £7.00

Hautes-Côtes de Beaune, Caves des
  Hautes-Côtes 1998 £6.99 (TES)
Hautes-Côtes de Beaune, Caves des
  Hautes-Côtes 1997 £6.75 (AS)

£7.00 → £7.99

Chorey-lès-Beaune Roger et Joël Remy
  1997 £7.95 (LEA)
Hautes-Côtes de Beaune Tête de Cuvée,
  Caves des Hautes-Côtes 1997 £7.49
  (WAI)
Hautes-Côtes de Nuits Tête de Cuvée,
  Caves des Hautes-Côtes 1997 £7.60
  (AS)
St-Aubin le Paradis, Hubert Lamy 1996
  £7.95 (LEA)

£8.00 → £9.99

Auxey-Duresses Bouchard Père 1994
  £9.08 (BY)
Chorey-lès-Beaune Roger et Joël Remy
  1998 £9.95 (LEA)
Côte de Beaune-Villages Bouchard Père
  1996 £9.28 (BY)
Côte de Beaune-Villages Chanson 1996
  £8.95 (POR) £9.95 (BALL)
Côte de Nuits-Villages Lucien Boillot
  1998 £9.99 (MON)
Fixin Gelin 1996 £8.95 (SOM)
Hautes-Côtes de Beaune Rollin 1997
  £8.90 (JU)
Hautes-Côtes de Nuits, Michel Gros
  1998 £9.70 (TAN)
Hautes-Côtes de Nuits, Michel Gros
  1996 £9.50 (TAN)
Monthélie Paul Garaudet 1993 £9.05
  (NEZ)
St-Aubin Prudhon 1998 £9.25 (WS)
St-Aubin Prudhon 1997 £8.95 (BALL)
  £9.90 (JU)
St-Aubin Prudhon 1993 £9.50 (BALL)
Santenay Clos des Hâtes, Hubert Lamy
  1997 £9.95 (LEA)
Santenay Clos des Hâtes, Hubert Lamy
  1996 £8.95 (LEA)
Santenay les Gravières, Roger Belland
  1995 £9.99 (WAT)
Santenay Latour 1996 £9.48 (PEN)

£10.00 → £11.99

Auxey-Duresses Michel Prunier 1997
  £11.55 (TAN)
Chambolle-Musigny Faiveley 1974 £11.75
  (FA)
Chassagne-Montrachet Blain-Gagnard
  1998 £10.95 (HAH)
Chassagne-Montrachet Carillon 1998
  £11.75 (MON)
Chassagne-Montrachet les Chaumes, Guy
  Amiot 1994 £10.95 (BAL)
Chassagne-Montrachet Henri Germain
  1997 £10.95 (LEA) £12.95 (TAN) £13.75
  (AD)
Chorey-lès-Beaune Tollot-Beaut 1998
  £11.50 (TAN) £12.34 (DOM) £12.50 (AD)
  £12.99 (DI)
Chorey-lès-Beaune Château de Chorey-
  lès-Beaune, Jacques Germain 1997
  £11.46 (WHI) £14.50 (AS)
Clos de Vougeot Méo-Camuzet 1989
  £11.75 (BODX)
Corton Viénot 1988 £11.16 (FA)
Côte de Beaune-Villages Chanson 1997
  £10.29 (LLO)
Fixin Gelin 1997 £11.85 (HAH)
Hautes-Côtes de Beaune Rollin 1995
  £11.50 (JU)
Marsannay les Longeroies, Bruno Clair
  1996 £11.95 (SOM) £14.00 (JU)
Marsannay les Vaudenelles, Bruno Clair
  1997 £10.75 (SOM) £12.00 (JU) £13.30
  (TAN)
Marsannay les Vaudenelles, Bruno Clair
  1996 £10.50 (SOM) £13.00 (JU)
Monthélie Château de Monthélie,
  Suremain 1995 £10.45 (SOM) £19.00 (JU)
Pernand-Vergelesses Rollin 1999 £11.55
  (BIB)
Pernand-Vergelesses Rollin 1997 £11.60
  (TAN)
Pommard Bouchard Père 1988 £11.16 (FA)
St-Aubin les Frionnes, Prudhon 1999
  £10.48 (RAE)
St-Aubin les Frionnes, Prudhon 1998
  £10.70 (TAN) £11.50 (RAE) £12.39 (JON)
St-Aubin les Frionnes, Prudhon 1997
  £11.50 (JU)
St-Aubin les Frionnes, Prudhon 1994
  £11.95 (BALL) £14.00 (JU)
St-Aubin Prudhon 1995 £10.90 (JU)

St-Aubin Sentier du Clou, Prudhon **1999** £11.84 (BIB)
St-Aubin Sentier du Clou, Prudhon **1995** £11.95 (WS)
St-Romain Buisson **1997** £11.46 (DOM)
St-Romain Gras **1997** £10.90 (TAN)
Santenay Drouhin **1996** £11.75 (WY)

Savigny-lès-Beaune Girard-Vollot **1996** £11.95 (BALL)
Savigny-lès-Beaune Latour **1998** £10.85 (TAN) £11.46 (PLA) £11.50 (WHI) £15.04 (PLAY)
Savigny-lès-Beaune Latour **1997** £11.67 (PEN)
Volnay Jean-Marc Boillot ½ bottle **1999** £10.95 (LEA)

£12.00 → £13.99

Aloxe-Corton Roger et Joël Remy **1998** £13.95 (LEA)
Auxey-Duresses Roulot **1996** £13.22 (DOM) £16.67 (ARM)
Chassagne-Montrachet Blain-Gagnard **1999** £12.50 (JER)
Chassagne-Montrachet Carillon **1997** £12.24 (MON)
Chassagne-Montrachet les Chaumes, Guy Amiot **1998** £13.95 (LEA) £13.99 (DI)
Chassagne-Montrachet Henri Germain **1998** £13.95 (TAN)
Chassagne-Montrachet la Goujonne, Hubert Lamy **1998** £13.50 (LEA) £18.50 (WIN)
Chassagne-Montrachet Latour **1997** £12.40 (PLA)
Chassagne-Montrachet Morgeot, J-M Pillot **1997** £13.95 (LEA) £22.50 (NI)
Chorey-lès-Beaune Maillard **1995** £13.00 (CRO)
Chorey-lès-Beaune Tollot-Beaut **1997** £13.09 (JON)
Chorey-lès-Beaune Tollot-Beaut **1996** £12.50 (BALL)
Chorey-lès-Beaune Château de Chorey-lès-Beaune, Jacques Germain **1998** £12.93 (DOM)

Côte de Beaune Drouhin **1998** £13.70 (NI)
Côte de Beaune-Villages Carillon **1995** £12.75 (STE)
Côte de Beaune-Villages Drouhin **1998** £12.70 (NI)
Côte de Nuits-Villages Faiveley **1997** £13.25 (CON)
Côte de Nuits-Villages Vallet **1997** £12.95 (GN)
Maranges Clos des Loyères, Girardin **1998** £12.80 (TAN) £15.95 (NI)
Marsannay Clos du Roy, Regis Bouvier **1998** £13.81 (DOM)
Marsannay Grasse-Tête, Bruno Clair **1997** £12.00 (JU)
Marsannay Grasse-Tête, Bruno Clair **1996** £13.95 (WS)
Marsannay les Longeroies, Bruno Clair **1997** £13.50 (JU)
Monthélie Darviot-Perrin **1998** £13.75 (JER)
Nuits-St-Georges Gouges **1997** £13.25 (SOM) £20.59 (YOU)
Pernand-Vergelesses Bouchard Père **1998** £12.83 (BY)
Pernand-Vergelesses Rollin **1996** £13.95 (BALL)
Pernand-Vergelesses Rollin **1993** £12.50 (RAE)
Pernand-Vergelesses Sous le Bois de Noël et Belles Filles, Rollin **1997** £12.50 (JU)
Pommard les Cras, Belland **1995** £13.95 (WAT)
St-Aubin les Castets, Hubert Lamy **1998** £12.34 (DOM) £12.60 (LAY) £13.50 (LEA)
St-Aubin les Frionnes, Prudhon **1991** £12.50 (BALL)
St-Aubin le Paradis, Hubert Lamy **1997** £13.99 (WIN)
St-Aubin Pitangerets, Carillon **1997** £12.73 (MON)
Santenay Clos des Hâtes, Hubert Lamy **1998** £13.50 (LEA)
Savigny-lès-Beaune aux Grands Liards, Bize **1996** £12.45 (SOM) £24.09 (TW)
Savigny-lès-Beaune Latour **1993** £12.93 (WY)
Savigny-lès-Beaune les Lavières, Camus-Bruchon **1997** £13.95 (BALL) £14.50 (RAE)
Savigny-lès-Beaune Pavelot **1997** £12.34 (DOM) £17.50 (FORT)
Savigny-lès-Beaune Nicolas Potel **1997** £12.95 (BALL)

£14.00 → £15.99

Aloxe-Corton Rollin **1999** £14.06 (RAE)
£16.65 (BIB)

Auxey-Duresses Roulot **1995** £14.17 (ARM)

Beaune Bressandes, Henri Germain **1997**
£15.75 (TAN) £18.95 (LEA)

Beaune Cent Vignes, Roger et Joël Remy
1998 £14.95 (LEA)

Beaune Cent Vignes, Roger et Joël Remy
1995 £15.95 (LEA)

Beaune Épenottes, Parent **1998** £14.99
(SAF)

Beaune Teurons, Jadot **1999** £15.08 (FA)

Beaune Vignes Franches, Latour **1997**
£15.95 (WRI) £15.97 (PLA)

Chassagne-Montrachet Clos St-Jean, J-N
Gagnard **1997** £15.00 (JU)

Chassagne-Montrachet Latour **1993**
£14.10 (WY)

Chassagne-Montrachet Vieilles Vignes,
Bernard Morey **1998** £14.10 (DOM)

Chassagne-Montrachet Vieilles Vignes,
Bernard Morey **1997** £15.50 (BALL)

Côte de Beaune-Villages Drouhin **1997**
£14.52 (HIC)

Côte de Nuits-Villages Clos du Chapeau,
Domaine de l'Arlot **1998** £15.42 (ARM)

Côte de Nuits-Villages Clos du Chapeau,
Domaine de l'Arlot **1997** £15.00 (ARM)
£15.02 (BY)

Côte de Nuits-Villages Clos du Chapeau,
Domaine de l'Arlot **1996** £14.17 (ARM)
£14.41 (BY) £17.86 (TW)

Fixin Berthaut **1996** £15.36 (NO)

Fixin la Croix Blanche, André Geoffroy
1997 £14.00 (JU)

Fixin la Croix Blanche, André Geoffroy
1994 £14.00 (JU)

Gevrey-Chambertin Rossignol-Trapet
1998 £15.99 (SAF)

Marsannay Clos du Roy, Regis Bouvier
1997 £14.04 (DOM)

Marsannay les Longeroies, Bruno Clair
1995 £14.00 (JU)

Marsannay Monchenevoy, Charlopin-
Parizot **1994** £14.00 (MV)

Please remember that
Oz Clarke's Wine Buying Guide
*is a price **guide** and not a price **list**. It is
not meant to replace up-to-date
merchants' lists.*

Meursault Pierre Morey **1999** £14.99 (GW)

Monthélie Clos Gauthey, Parent **1998**
£14.75 (HAH) £21.99 (WIN)

Monthélie Pierre Morey **1997** £15.23 (BY)

Monthélie Parent **1997** £15.49 (JON)

Morey-St-Denis en la Rue de Vergy, Bruno
Clair **1996** £15.75 (SOM) £20.00 (JU)

Nuits-St-Georges Jean Chauvenet **1999**
£14.94 (RAE) £19.50 (POR)

Nuits-St-Georges Labouré-Roi **1998**
£14.99 (SAF)

Pernand-Vergelesses Île de Vergelesses,
Chandon de Briailles **1999** £14.69
(MON) £16.95 (LEA)

Pernand-Vergelesses Sous le Bois de Noël
et Belles Filles, Rollin **1996** £14.00 (JU)

Pernand-Vergelesses les Vergelesses,
Pavelot **1997** £14.69 (DOM)

Pommard Bouchard Père **1995** £15.49
(COC)

Pommard Coste-Caumartin **1992** £14.50
(BU)

St-Aubin les Frionnes, Prudhon **1996**
£15.00 (JU)

Santenay Clos Tavannes, Domaine de la
Pousse d'Or **1994** £15.95 (DI)

Santenay les Gravières, Colin-Deléger
1998 £14.99 (RAE)

Santeney les Gravières, Girardin **1998**
£14.68 (MON) £16.50 (AD)

Savigny-lès-Beaune les Bourgeots, Bize
1997 £14.59 (JON) £17.50 (ARM)

Savigny-lès-Beaune les Bourgeots, Bize
1996 £14.95 (BALL) £15.83 (ARM)

Savigny-lès-Beaune Champs-Chevrey,
Tollot-Beaut **1999** £14.00 (RAE)

Savigny-lès-Beaune les Fourneaux, Bize
1997 £14.25 (SOM)

Savigny-lès-Beaune aux Grands Liards,
Javillier **1998** £14.75 (LAY)

Savigny-lès-Beaune les Guettes, Pavelot
1998 £14.69 (DOM)

Savigny-lès-Beaune Domaine Guyon **1996**
£15.75 (FRI)

Savigny-lès-Beaune les Lavières, Camus-
Bruchon **1999** £14.06 (RAE)

Savigny-lès-Beaune les Lavières, Chandon
de Briailles **1998** £15.45 (HAH) £15.95
(LEA)

Savigny-lès-Beaune Narbantons, Camus-
Bruchon **1995** £14.99 (JON)

Savigny-lès-Beaune Pavelot **1999** £14.69
(DOM)

Savigny-lès-Beaune Nicolas Potel **1999**
£14.40 (NI)

£16.00 → £17.99

Aloxe-Corton Chandon de Briailles **1997** £17.49 (YOU)

Aloxe-Corton Latour **1998** £17.49 (POR)

Aloxe-Corton Latour **1996** £17.04 (PEN)

Aloxe-Corton Rollin **1997** £16.99 (RAE) £17.00 (JU)

Aloxe-Corton Rollin **1995** £16.99 (RAE) £19.50 (BALL)

Beaune Cent Vignes, Lois Dufouleur **1998** £17.25 (JER)

Beaune Clos des Avaux, Guillemard-Pothiers **1992** £16.95 (CON)

Beaune Clos du Dessus des Marconnets, Pernot **1997** £17.50 (WIN)

Beaune Clos du Dessus des Marconnets, Pernot **1996** £16.25 (NEZ)

Beaune Clos du Roi, Camus-Bruchon **1996** £17.50 (RAE)

Beaune Clos du Roi, Camus-Bruchon **1995** £17.95 (BALL)

Beaune Vignes Franches, Latour **1996** £16.45 (PEN) £17.50 (STA) £18.01 (PLAY)

Chambolle-Musigny Ghislaine Barthod **1996** £17.50 (RAE)

Chambolle-Musigny Georges Roumier **1999** £17.99 (GW) £23.40 (BODX)

Chambolle-Musigny Georges Roumier **1998** £17.99 (GW) £25.95 (RES) £26.49 (YOU)

Chassagne-Montrachet Clos St-Jean, J-N Gagnard **1996** £17.00 (JU)

Chassagne-Montrachet la Maltroie, Guy Amiot **1997** £16.95 (LEA)

Chassagne-Montrachet Vieilles Vignes, Bernard Morey **1999** £17.63 (MON)

Gevrey-Chambertin Lucien Boillot **1999** £16.65 (MON)

Gevrey-Chambertin Chanson **1996** £16.99 (JON)

Gevrey-Chambertin Chanson **1995** £17.99 (POR)

Gevrey-Chambertin Fourrier **1999** £17.23 (BAL)

Gevrey-Chambertin Thierry Mortet **1998** £17.95 (LEA)

Gevrey-Chambertin Perrot-Minot **1999** £16.06 (BODX) £17.04 (BAL)

Gevrey-Chambertin Perrot-Minot **1996** £16.99 (SUN) £16.99 (LAI)

Gevrey-Chambertin Rebourseau **1997** £17.85 (SOM)

Gevrey-Chambertin Rodet **1995** £16.40 (RIC)

Gevrey-Chambertin Rossignol-Trapet **1997** £17.63 (CB)

Gevrey-Chambertin Rossignol-Trapet **1996** £16.09 (BY) £16.95 (CON) £22.27 (TW)

Gevrey-Chambertin Armand Rousseau **1992** £17.63 (FA)

Gevry-Chambertin les Jeunes Rois, Geantet-Pansiot **1997** £17.04 (BODX)

Hautes-Côtes de Nuits, Jayer-Gilles **1997** £16.00 (JU)

Hautes-Côtes de Nuits, Jayer-Gilles **1996** £17.00 (JU)

Monthélie Château de Monthélie, Suremain **1997** £16.00 (JU)

Monthélie Parent **1996** £16.99 (VIL)

Morey-St-Denis en la Rue de Vergy, Perrot-Minot **1999** £16.55 (BODX) £19.19 (BAL)

Nuits-St-Georges Domaine de l'Arlot **1997** £16.96 (BY) £19.17 (ARM)

Nuits-St-Georges Jean Chauvenet **1998** £16.05 (BIB) £16.50 (RAE)

Nuits-St-Georges Jean Chauvenet **1997** £16.99 (RAE)

Nuits-St-Georges Jean Chauvenet **1996** £16.99 (RAE)

Nuits-St-Georges Robert Chevillon **1997** £16.90 (JU)

Nuits-St-Georges les Fleurières, J-J Confuron **1999** £17.23 (BAL)

Nuits-St-Georges Gouges **1999** £17.14 (MON)

Nuits-St-Georges les Roncières, Robert Chevillon **1992** £16.45 (FA)

Pernand-Vergelesses Île de Vergelesses, Chandon de Briailles **1998** £16.50 (LEA)

Pernand-Vergelesses Île de Vergelesses, Chandon de Briailles **1997** £17.50 (LEA)

Pernand-Vergelesses Île de Vergelesses, Rollin **1999** £16.06 (RAE)

Pernand-Vergelesses Île de Vergelesses, Rollin **1997** £17.99 (RAE) £18.50 (JU)

Pernand-Vergelesses Île de Vergelesses, Rollin **1995** £17.95 (RAE) £24.00 (JU)

Pernand-Vergelesses Île de Vergelesses, Rollin **1994** £16.95 (BALL) £17.95 (RAE)

Pommard Clos Blanc, Albert Grivault **1993** £17.00 (JU)

Pommard Coste-Caumartin **1997** £16.00 (JU)

Pommard les Poutures, Lejeune **1988** £17.95 (RAE)

Pommard les Vignots, Coste-Caumartin **1997** £16.99 (GW) £17.00 (JU)

Santenay Clos Tavannes, J-N Gagnard
   1997 £16.00 (JU)
Santenay Grand Clos Rousseau, Bernard
   Morey **1997** £17.63 (DOM)
Santenay la Maladière, Girardin **1997**
   £16.85 (NEZ) £17.00 (WS) £18.75 (MAY)
Santeney les Gravières, Girardin **1997**
   £16.90 (JU) £17.70 (TAN)
Savigny-lès-Beaune la Dominode, Bruno
   Clair **1997** £17.60 (SOM) £22.00 (JU)
Savigny-lès-Beaune la Dominode, Pavelot
   1997 £17.63 (DOM) £25.50 (FORT)
Savigny-lès-Beaune aux Grands Liards,
   Bize **1997** £16.95 (BALL) £19.58 (ARM)
Savigny-lès-Beaune aux Guettes, Bize
   1998 £16.85 (LAY) £20.00 (ARM)
Savigny-lès-Beaune Domaine Guyon **1998**
   £16.25 (FRI)
Savigny-lès-Beaune les Lavières, Chandon
   de Briailles **1995** £16.60 (SAV)
Savigny-lès-Beaune les Lavières, Tollot-
   Beaut **1998** £16.99 (DI)
Savigny-lès-Beaune les Lavières, Tollot-
   Beaut **1997** £16.45 (DOM)
Savigny-lès-Beaune les Peuillets, Pavelot
   1998 £16.45 (DOM)
Volnay Lucien Boillot **1997** £17.45 (BER)
Volnay Champans, Monthélie-Douhairet
   1995 £16.90 (SOM)
Volnay Lafarge **1994** £17.95 (BALL)
Volnay Domaine de la Pousse d'Or **1997**
   £17.35 (CON)
Volnay Santenots Latour **1995** £17.05 (STA)
Vosne-Romanée Cacheux **1999** £16.16
   (MON)
Vosne-Romanée Engel **1998** £16.55
   (BODX) £20.50 (TAN) £21.95 (CON)
   £22.00 (MV)
Vosne-Romanée Engel **1997** £16.15 (GAU)
   £21.50 (CON) £22.95 (BALL) £25.00
   (FORT) £25.49 (YOU)
Vosne-Romanée Engel **1996** £17.95
   (CON) £17.95 (GN) £18.65 (SOM) £22.95
   (BALL) £25.00 (FORT)
Vosne-Romanée Engel **1995** £16.95 (GN)
   £17.25 (CON)
Vosne-Romanée les Hautes Maizieres,
   Clavelier **1999** £17.43 (SAV)

Oz Clarke's Wine Buying Guide
is an annual publication.
We welcome your suggestions for
next year's edition.

£18.00 → £19.99

Aloxe-Corton les Chaillots, Latour **1996**
   £18.95 (STA) £20.10 (PLAY)
Aloxe-Corton Tollot-Beaut **1997** £18.00
   (JU) £19.89 (JON)
Beaune Bressandes, Henri Germain **1996**
   £19.95 (LEA)
Beaune Clos du Roi, Camus-Bruchon
   1999 £18.41 (RAE)
Beaune Clos du Roi, Camus-Bruchon
   1998 £18.50 (RAE)
Beaune Clos du Roi, Camus-Bruchon
   1997 £18.50 (RAE) £19.50 (STA)
Beaune Clos des Ursules, Jadot **1999**
   £19.49 (FA)
Beaune Grèves, Tollot-Beaut **1999**
   £18.41 (RAE)
Beaune Marconnets, Chanson **1997**
   £19.95 (MAY)
Beaune les Montrevenots, Jean-Marc
   Boillot **1999** £19.95 (LEA)
Beaune les Montrevenots, Jean-Marc
   Boillot **1996** £19.68 (DOM) £20.95 (LEA)
Beaune Teurons, Bouchard Père **1997**
   £19.99 (COC)
Beaune Teurons, Bouchard Père **1995**
   £19.99 (COC)
Chambolle-Musigny Ghislaine Barthod
   1998 £19.50 (RAE)
Chambolle-Musigny Ghislaine Barthod
   1997 £18.50 (RAE) £20.00 (JU)
Chambolle-Musigny Ghislaine Barthod
   1995 £18.50 (RAE) £25.00 (JU)
Chambolle-Musigny les Véroilles, Bruno
   Clair **1997** £18.00 (JU)
Chassagne-Montrachet Gagnard-
   Delagrange **1998** £18.55 (BY)
Corton les Renardes, Delarche **1997**
   £19.25 (SOM)
Côte de Nuits-Villages Jayer-Gilles **1997**
   £19.50 (JU)
Gevrey-Chambertin Bouchard Père **1996**
   £19.62 (COC)
Gevrey-Chambertin Chanson **1997**
   £18.62 (LLO)
Gevrey-Chambertin Clos de la Justice,
   Vallet **1997** £18.95 (GN)
Gevrey-Chambertin Cuvée de l'Abeille,
   Ponsot **1998** £18.70 (BAL) £25.49 (YOU)
Gevrey-Chambertin Cuvée de l'Abeille,
   Ponsot **1997** £19.00 (BAL) £21.93
   (BODX)
Gevrey-Chambertin Cuvée de l'Abeille,
   Ponsot **1996** £19.50 (BAL) £20.83 (ARM)

Gevrey-Chambertin Latour **1997** £18.68 (PEN)

Gevrey-Chambertin Latour **1996** £19.50 (STA)

Gevrey-Chambertin Hubert Lignier **1998** £19.97 (BODX)

Gevrey-Chambertin Thierry Mortet **1999** £18.95 (LEA)

Gevrey-Chambertin Thierry Mortet **1997** £19.95 (LEA)

Gevrey-Chambertin Perrot-Minot **1998** £18.00 (WAT) £21.50 (CON) £21.50 (BAL)

Gevrey-Chambertin Vieilles Vignes, Marchand-Grillot **1997** £19.90 (LAY)

Gevry-Chambertin les Jeunes Rois, Geantet-Pansiot **1998** £19.39 (DOM)

Gevry-Chambertin Vieilles Vignes, Geantet-Pansiot **1997** £19.00 (BODX)

Meursault Coche-Debord **1998** £18.99 (RAE)

Meursault Coche-Debord **1996** £18.99 (RAE)

Monthélie Château de Monthélie, Suremain **1996** £18.00 (JU)

Monthélie sur la Velle, Château de Monthélie **1997** £18.50 (JU)

Morey-St-Denis Georges Lignier **1993** £19.95 (BALL)

Morey-St-Denis Hubert Lignier **1998** £19.97 (BODX)

Morey-St-Denis en la Rue de Vergy, Bruno Clair **1997** £19.00 (JU)

Morey-St-Denis en la Rue de Vergy, Perrot-Minot **1996** £19.50 (CON) £19.95 (BAL)

Nuits-St-Georges Domaine de l'Arlot **1996** £18.33 (ARM)

Nuits-St-Georges Robert Chevillon **1994** £18.00 (JU)

Nuits-St-Georges Clos des Argillières, Rion **1992** £18.13 (BY)

Nuits-St-Georges les Fleurières, J-J Confuron **1997** £18.95 (BAL)

Nuits-St-Georges les Fleurières, J-J Confuron **1996** £19.49 (BODX)

Nuits-St-Georges les Pruliers, Gouges **1997** £18.40 (SOM) £22.91 (BODX) £23.40 (FA) £26.99 (YOU)

Nuits-St-Georges les Pruliers, Gouges **1996** £18.95 (SOM) £27.99 (YOU)

Pernand-Vergelesses Île de Vergelesses, Rollin **1991** £19.95 (BALL)

Pommard Ampeau **1992** £19.95 (LEA)

Pommard les Argillières, Lejeune **1991** £18.79 (FLE)

Pommard Jean-Marc Boillot **1999** £18.41 (RAE)

Pommard Jean-Marc Boillot **1996** £18.95 (RAE)

Pommard Clos Blanc, Albert Grivault **1997** £18.00 (JU) £31.50 (WIN)

Pommard Clos Blanc, Albert Grivault **1995** £19.00 (JU)

Pommard Coste-Caumartin **1993** £19.00 (JU)

Pommard les Fremiers, Coste-Caumartin **1997** £18.50 (JU)

Pommard Parent **1992** £19.00 (CRO)

Pommard les Vignots, Coste-Caumartin **1996** £19.00 (JU)

Santenay Clos Tavannes, J-N Gagnard **1996** £18.00 (JU)

Santenay Clos Tavannes, J-N Gagnard **1995** £19.00 (JU)

Santenay les Passetemps, Faiveley **1988** £19.50 (JU)

Santeney les Gravières, Girardin **1999** £18.99 (POR) £19.65 (NI)

Savigny-lès-Beaune les Lavières, Bouchard Père **1996** £18.90 (COC)

Savigny-lès-Beaune les Lavières, Tollot-Beaut **1994** £18.00 (JU)

Savigny-lès-Beaune les Serpentières, Drouhin **1998** £19.35 (NI)

Volnay Jean-Marc Boillot **1997** £19.39 (DOM) £21.50 (LEA)

Volnay Clos d'Audignac, Domaine de la Pousse d'Or **1996** £19.88 (FA)

Volnay Pitures, Nicolas Potel **1999** £19.97 (BODX)

Volnay Santenots Roger Belland **1997** £18.00 (WAT)

Vosne-Romanée Champs Perdrix, Bruno Clair **1993** £19.90 (JU)

Vosne-Romanée Michel Gros **1998** £19.95 (TAN)

Vosne-Romanée les Hautes Maizieres, Clavelier **1997** £18.41 (SAV)

Vosne-Romanée les Hautes Maizieres, Clavelier **1996** £19.75 (BU)

Vosne-Romanée la Montagne, Clavelier **1999** £18.41 (SAV)

Vosne-Romanée la Montagne, Clavelier **1997** £19.00 (SAV)

Vosne-Romanée, Mugneret-Gibourg **1999** £19.95 (LEA)

Vosne-Romanée, Mugneret-Gibourg **1996** £18.80 (SAV) £19.95 (HAH) £19.95 (LEA)

Vosne-Romanée Rion **1996** £19.75 (SOM)

£20.00 → £22.49

Beaune Bressandes, Henri Germain 1995
£21.95 (LEA)

Beaune Clos du Roi, Tollot-Beaut 1998
£22.27 (DOM)

Beaune les Mariages, Rossignol-Trapet
1995 £21.74 (TW)

Beaune les Montrevenots, Jean-Marc
Boillot 1998 £20.50 (LEA) £20.56 (DOM)

Beaune les Sizies, Michel Prunier 1999
£21.00 (JU)

Beaune les Sizies, Michel Prunier 1996
£21.00 (JU)

Beaune Teurons, Jacques Germain 1997
£22.27 (DOM)

Beaune Teurons, Rossignol-Trapet 1996
£21.50 (TW)

Chambolle-Musigny Christian Clerget
1998 £20.75 (BY)

Chambolle-Musigny Confuron 1997
£20.95 (BAL)

Chambolle-Musigny Hudelot-Noëllat
1998 £20.00 (ARM)

Chambolle-Musigny Hudelot-Noëllat
1997 £20.00 (ARM)

Chambolle-Musigny Georges Roumier
1997 £21.20 (TAN) £28.50 (FORT)

Chambolle-Musigny Georges Roumier
1996 £21.15 (SOM)

Chambolle-Musigny les Véroilles, Bruno
Clair 1996 £20.00 (JU)

Chambolle-Musigny de Vogüé 1983
£21.15 (WY)

Chassagne-Montrachet les Vergers, Guy
Amiot 1999 £20.95 (BODX)

Côte de Nuits-Villages Jayer-Gilles 1996
£22.00 (JU)

Gevrey-Chambertin les Corbeaux, Lucien
Boillot 1997 £21.54 (MON)

Gevrey-Chambertin Drouhin-Laroze
1996 £21.20 (HAH)

Gevrey-Chambertin Fourrier 1998
£21.50 (BAL)

Gevrey-Chambertin Fourrier 1997
£20.95 (BAL)

Gevrey-Chambertin Denis Mortet 1998
£21.15 (DOM) £23.25 (RAE) £24.70 (TAN)

Gevrey-Chambertin Perrot-Minot 1997
£21.50 (CON) £21.50 (BAL)

Gevrey-Chambertin Armand Rousseau
1997 £22.40 (BY) £22.42 (BODX) £27.50
(FORT) £27.99 (YOU)

Gevrey-Chambertin Vieilles Vignes, Alain
Burguet 1996 £22.00 (JU)

Hautes-Côtes de Nuits, Jayer-Gilles 1995
£20.00 (JU)

Monthélie sur la Velle, Château de
Monthélie 1994 £21.00 (JU)

Monthélie sur la Velle, Château de
Monthélie 1993 £22.00 (JU)

Morey-St-Denis Hubert Lignier 1997
£20.95 (FA)

Morey-St-Denis en la Rue de Vergy,
Bruno Clair 1995 £22.00 (JU)

Nuits-St-Georges 1er Cru, Domaine de
l'Arlot 1993 £20.83 (ARM)

Nuits-St-Georges Domaine de l'Arlot
1998 £20.00 (ARM)

Nuits-St-Georges Domaine de l'Arlot
1995 £21.00 (FLE)

Nuits-St-Georges les Chaignots, Robert
Chevillon 1997 £22.00 (JU)

Nuits-St-Georges Robert Chevillon 1995
£21.00 (JU)

Nuits-St-Georges Clos des Porets,
Gouges 1993 £21.93 (FA)

Nuits-St-Georges Clos des Porets St-
Georges, Gouges 1999 £22.03 (MON)

Nuits-St-Georges Faiveley 1998 £21.75
(TAN)

Nuits-St-Georges Gouges 1998 £20.95
(RES)

Nuits-St-Georges A Michelot 1997
£20.35 (NEZ)

Nuits-St-Georges les Pruliers, Lucien
Boillot 1996 £22.03 (FA)

Nuits-St-Georges les Pruliers, Domaine
Jean Grivot 1996 £21.50 (SOM) £27.50
(BAL)

Nuits-St-Georges Richemone, Pernin-
Rossin 1996 £21.50 (BAN)

Nuits-St-Georges les Roncières, Robert
Chevillon 1997 £22.00 (JU)

Nuits-St-Georges les St-Georges, Gouges
1997 £22.35 (SOM)

Nuits-St-Georges les Vaucrains, Gouges
1997 £22.35 (SOM) £27.81 (BODX)

Nuits-St-Georges les Vaucrains, Gouges
1996 £21.75 (SOM) £30.99 (YOU)

Pernand-Vergelesses Île de Vergelesses,
Chandon de Briailles 1992 £20.00
(CRO) £26.44 (TW)

Pommard Jean-Marc Boillot 1998 £20.50
(RAE)

Pommard Jean-Marc Boillot 1997 £20.50
(RAE)

Pommard Clos des Boucherottes, Coste-
Caumartin 1997 £20.50 (GW) £21.00
(JU)

Pommard Clos des Épeneaux, Comte Armand **1994** £21.93 (BODX) £25.95 (LEA) £29.00 (MV) £37.01 (TW)

Pommard Clos des Épeneaux, Comte Armand ½ bottle **1995** £20.39 (TW)

Pommard Coste-Caumartin **1995** £20.00 (JU)

Pommard les Fremiers, Coste-Caumartin **1996** £21.00 (JU)

Santenay Clos Tavannes, Domaine de la Pousse d'Or **1992** £22.21 (TW)

Savigny-lès-Beaune les Marconnets, Bize **1996** £20.83 (ARM)

Savigny-lès-Beaune les Marconnets, Bize **1995** £21.67 (ARM)

Savigny-lès-Beaune Narbantons, Maurice Écard **1997** £21.99 (WIN)

Savigny-lès-Beaune Tollot-Beaut **1993** £20.00 (YOU)

Savigny-lès-Beaune aux Vergelesses, Bize **1998** £20.83 (ARM)

Volnay Marquis d'Angerville **1997** £20.00 (JU) £25.00 (ARM)

Volnay Marquis d'Angerville **1996** £21.00 (JU)

Volnay Jean-Marc Boillot **1999** £20.50 (LEA)

Volnay Jean-Marc Boillot **1996** £20.95 (LEA)

Volnay les Caillerets, Michel Prunier **1997** £22.00 (JU)

Volnay Drouhin **1995** £20.56 (PEN)

Volnay Lafarge **1998** £20.50 (GAU) £26.50 (WIN)

Volnay Lafarge **1997** £20.50 (GAU)

Volnay Santenots Matrot **1997** £22.40 (GAU)

Volnay Taillepieds, Marquis d'Angerville **1994** £21.67 (ARM) £21.93 (FA)

Volnay Taillepieds, Bouchard Père **1993** £20.99 (COC)

Volnay Vendange Selectionée, Lafarge **1998** £21.95 (CON) £28.99 (WIN)

Vosne-Romanée Cacheux **1996** £21.50 (BALL)

Vosne-Romanée Champs Perdrix, Bruno Clair **1997** £22.00 (JU)

Vosne-Romanée Hudelot-Noëllat **1998** £20.00 (ARM)

Vosne-Romanée, Mugneret-Gibourg **1998** £20.95 (LEA)

Vosne-Romanée les Suchots, Hudelot-Noëllat **1997** £20.65 (SOM)

Vosne-Romanée les Violettes, Georges Clerget **1998** £21.78 (BY)

Vosne-Romanée les Violettes, Georges Clerget **1996** £22.03 (PLA)

£22.50 → £24.99

Aloxe-Corton les Fournières, Tollot-Beaut **1997** £23.00 (JU)

Aloxe-Corton les Vercots, Tollot-Beaut **1998** £22.95 (DI)

Beaune Clos du Roi, Ampeau **1984** £22.50 (LEA)

Beaune Clos du Roi, Tollot-Beaut **1997** £23.49 (JON)

Beaune Clos des Ursules, Jadot **1998** £22.99 (YOU)

Beaune Clos des Ursules, Jadot **1997** £24.49 (YOU)

Beaune Épenottes, Jean Boillot **1998** £23.25 (LEA)

Beaune Grèves, Tollot-Beaut **1998** £22.95 (DI)

Beaune Teurons, Jacques Germain **1998** £23.50 (DOM)

Beaune Vignes Franches, François Germain **1996** £24.68 (DOM)

Blagny la Pièce sous le Bois, Matrot **1993** £24.95 (BALL)

Chambolle-Musigny Beaux Bruns, Ghislaine Barthod **1996** £23.50 (RAE)

Chambolle-Musigny Beaux Bruns, Ghislaine Barthod **1995** £23.99 (RAE)

Chambolle-Musigny Clos du Village, Domaine Guyon **1993** £23.50 (FRI)

Chambolle-Musigny les Cras, Ghislaine Barthod **1995** £23.99 (RAE)

Charmes-Chambertin Camus **1996** £23.95 (FLE)

Corton Bonneau du Martray **1996** £24.87 (FA) £41.35 (HAH)

Corton Bonneau du Martray **1993** £23.50 (FA)

Corton Clos des Meix, Comte Senard **1988** £24.87 (FA)

Corton Clos de la Vigne au Saint, Latour **1992** £24.68 (PEN)

Corton Maréchaudes, Chandon de Briailles **1999** £22.52 (MON)

Côte de Nuits-Villages Jayer-Gilles **1995** £23.00 (JU)

Gevrey-Chambertin Clos Prieur, Thierry Mortet **1999** £24.50 (LEA)

Gevrey-Chambertin Clos Prieur, Thierry Mortet **1997** £23.95 (LEA)

*A key to name abbreviations
is available on page 7.*

Gevrey-Chambertin Clos St-Jacques,
Fourrier **1993** £24.17 (ARM)

Gevrey-Chambertin les Corbeaux,
Bachelet **1993** £23.50 (FA)

Gevrey-Chambertin Drouhin **1997**
£23.65 (NI)

Gevrey Chambertin Estournelles-St-
Jacques, Frédéric Esmonin **1998** £23.00
(BAN)

Gevrey-Chambertin Lavaux-St-Jacques,
Maume **1996** £24.99 (RAE) £39.56 (FA)

Gevrey-Chambertin Hubert Lignier **1996**
£23.50 (BODX)

Gevrey-Chambertin Denis Mortet **1999**
£24.38 (BODX)

Gevrey-Chambertin Armand Rousseau
1996 £24.00 (JU)

Gevrey-Chambertin Armand Rousseau
1995 £24.87 (FA)

Monthélie sur la Velle, Château de
Monthélie **1995** £24.00 (JU)

Morey-St-Denis Clos de la Bussière,
Georges Roumier **1998** £23.89 (BODX)
£26.00 (WS)

Morey-St-Denis Clos des Ormes,
Georges Lignier **1992** £23.25 (PLA)

Morey-St-Denis Cuvée des Grives,
Ponsot **1997** £22.91 (BODX)

Morey-St-Denis Hubert Lignier **1996**
£22.91 (FA)

Morey-St-Denis en la Rue de Vergy,
Perrot-Minot **1998** £22.65 (CON)
£23.00 (BAL)

Nuits-St-Georges Domaine de l'Arlot
1993 £22.50 (CRO)

Nuits-St-Georges les Boudots, Domaine
Jean Grivot **1996** £23.25 (SOM)

Nuits-St-Georges les Boudots, Domaine
Jean Grivot **1994** £24.17 (ARM)

Nuits-St-Georges aux Chaignots, Faiveley
1994 £23.33 (ARM)

Nuits-St-Georges les Chaignots, A
Michelot **1997** £23.50 (DOM)

Nuits-St-Georges les Chaignots, Georges
Mugneret **1996** £24.48 (SAV)

Nuits-St-Georges Clos de l'Arlot,
Domaine de l'Arlot **1997** £24.17 (ARM)

Nuits-St-Georges Clos des Forêts St-
Georges, Domaine de l'Arlot **1992**
£23.83 (BY) £24.17 (ARM)

Nuits-St-Georges Clos de la Maréchale,
Faiveley **1998** £23.95 (HAH)

Nuits-St-Georges Clos de la Maréchale,
Faiveley **1997** £24.50 (CON) £26.32
(LLO)

Nuits-St-Georges les Damodes, Jean
Chauvenet **1998** £24.99 (RAE)

Nuits-St-Georges les Damodes, Jean
Chauvenet **1996** £24.50 (RAE)

Nuits-St-Georges Drouhin **1996** £24.68
(PEN)

Nuits-St-Georges Jadot **1992** £22.99 (YOU)

Nuits-St-Georges Méo-Camuzet **1995**
£23.50 (FA)

Nuits-St-Georges les Perrières, Jean
Chauvenet **1995** £24.50 (RAE)

Nuits-St-Georges les Perrières, Robert
Chevillon **1997** £23.00 (JU) £28.99 (YOU)

Nuits-St-Georges les Porets, A Michelot
1997 £22.91 (DOM)

Nuits-St-Georges les Pruliers, Lucien
Boillot **1999** £22.52 (MON)

Nuits-St-Georges les Pruliers, Gouges
1998 £24.95 (TAN)

Nuits-St-Georges les Pruliers, Domaine
Jean Grivot **1997** £24.50 (SOM) £29.95
(BAL)

Nuits-St-Georges les Roncières, Robert
Chevillon **1998** £23.50 (FORT)

Nuits-St-Georges les St-Georges, Gouges
1996 £22.85 (SOM)

Nuits-St-Georges les St-Georges, Gouges
1994 £23.95 (BALL)

Nuits-St-Georges les Vaucrains, A
Michelot **1997** £24.68 (DOM)

Pommard Boigelot **1997** £22.50 (BAC)

Pommard Clos des Boucherottes, Coste-
Caumartin **1996** £24.00 (JU)

Pommard Clos-du-Cîteaux, J Monnier
1997 £22.81 (BY)

Pommard les Cras, Belland **1998** £22.50
(FRI)

Pommard les Épenots, Latour **1996**
£22.91 (PEN)

Pommard les Vignots, Coste-Caumartin
1995 £23.00 (JU)

Savigny-lès-Beaune la Dominode, Bruno
Clair **1994** £23.00 (JU) £29.00 (CRO)

Savigny-lès-Beaune aux Guettes, Bize
1997 £22.50 (ARM)

Savigny-lès-Beaune les Marconnets, Bize
1993 £22.50 (ARM)

Savigny-lès-Beaune Narbantons, Leroy
1972 £23.50 (CRO)

Savigny-lès-Beaune aux Vergelesses, Bize
1997 £24.17 (ARM)

Savigny-lès-Beaune aux Vergelesses, Bize
1995 £22.50 (ARM) £30.27 (TW)

Savigny-lès-Beaune aux Vergelesses, Bize
1994 £23.38 (TW)

Volnay les Caillerets, Domaine de la Pousse d'Or **1993** £23.93 (CON) £28.95 (BALL)

Volnay les Caillerets, Domaine de la Pousse d'Or **1992** £22.95 (DI)

Volnay Carelle sous la Chapelle, Jean-Marc Boillot **1999** £22.52 (RAE)

Volnay Carelle sous la Chapelle, Jean-Marc Boillot **1996** £23.50 (RAE)

Volnay Carelles, Pernot **1997** £23.50 (WIN)

Volnay Champans, Marquis d'Angerville **1997** £24.87 (FA) £27.00 (JU)

Volnay Champans, Gagnard-Delagrange **1998** £24.88 (BY)

Volnay Clos des Chênes, Domaine Guyon **1993** £24.95 (FRI)

Volnay Frémiets, Marquis d'Angerville **1999** £23.50 (MON) £25.00 (JU)

Volnay Frémiets, Marquis d'Angerville **1998** £22.50 (ARM)

Volnay Frémiets, Marquis d'Angerville **1996** £23.68 (CB) £24.87 (FA)

Volnay la Gigotte, Darviot-Perrin **1998** £23.75 (MAY)

Volnay Santenots Pierre Boillot **1997** £23.01 (SAV)

Volnay Santenots Matrot **1996** £22.74 (CB)

Volnay Vendange Selectionée, Lafarge **1997** £22.50 (CON)

Volnay Vendange Selectionée, Lafarge **1996** £22.50 (CON) £23.95 (HAH)

Volnay Vendange Selectionée, Lafarge **1993** £23.50 (BALL)

Vosne-Romanée les Brûlées, Engel **1998** £22.91 (BODX) £24.95 (CON)

Vosne-Romanée les Brûlées, Engel **1997** £24.95 (CON) £27.49 (YOU)

Vosne-Romanée Champs Perdrix, Bruno Clair **1996** £24.00 (JU)

Vosne-Romanée Confuron-Cotétidot **1999** £22.50 (LEA)

Vosne-Romanée Confuron-Cotétidot **1997** £22.50 (LEA)

£25.00 → £27.49

Beaune Épenottes, Jean Boillot **1997** £25.50 (LEA)

Beaune Toussaints, Albert Morot **1989** £25.99 (YOU)

Blagny la Pièce sous le Bois, Matrot **1996** £25.85 (CB) £27.95 (BALL)

Chambolle-Musigny Beaux Bruns, Ghislaine Barthod **1998** £26.99 (RAE)

Chambolle-Musigny les Charmes, Ghislaine Barthod **1994** £27.00 (RAE)

Chambolle-Musigny Clos du Village, Domaine Guyon **1998** £25.95 (FRI)

Chambolle-Musigny la Combe d'Orveaux, Clavelier **1997** £25.95 (SAV)

Chambolle-Musigny les Cras, Ghislaine Barthod **1997** £25.99 (RAE)

Chambolle-Musigny les Feusselottes, Georges Mugneret **1998** £26.00 (HAH) £28.95 (LEA)

Chambolle-Musigny les Feusselottes, Georges Mugneret **1996** £26.93 (SAV)

Chambolle-Musigny les Veroilles, Ghislaine Barthod **1997** £27.00 (JU) £33.99 (YOU)

Clos de la Roche Armand Rousseau **1992** £27.03 (FA)

Corton-Bressandes Chandon de Briailles **1999** £26.44 (MON) £29.95 (LEA)

Corton-Bressandes Dubreuil-Fontaine **1992** £25.89 (BY)

Corton Clos de la Vigne au Saint, Latour **1996** £27.03 (PEN)

Corton Clos de la Vigne au Saint, Latour **1976** £25.00 (BU)

Corton Grancey, Latour **1995** £26.91 (PEN) £26.99 (MAJ) £32.00 (JON) £33.57 (PLAY) £34.50 (STA) £35.00 (FORT)

Corton Latour **1996** £27.03 (PEN)

Corton Latour **1992** £26.50 (POR)

Corton Maréchaudes, Chandon de Briailles **1997** £25.49 (YOU) £35.95 (RES)

Corton Maréchaudes, Chandon de Briailles **1996** £26.40 (HAH) £28.99 (YOU)

Corton Maréchaudes, Chandon de Briailles **1995** £26.50 (HAH) £33.19 (FA)

Fixin la Croix Blanche, André Geoffroy **1996** £25.00 (JU)

Gevrey-Chambertin Cazetiers, Bruno Clair **1997** £27.03 (FA) £37.00 (JU) £38.80 (TAN)

Gevrey-Chambertin Champeaux, Denis Mortet **1992** £25.50 (RAE)

Gevrey-Chambertin Clos du Fonteny, Bruno Clair **1997** £27.32 (FA) £30.00 (JU)

Please remember that
Oz Clarke's Wine Buying Guide
is a price guide and not a price list. It is not meant to replace up-to-date merchants' lists.

Gevrey-Chambertin Lavaux-St-Jacques,
Maume **1999** £27.22 (RAE) £28.40 (BAL)
Gevrey-Chambertin Denis Mortet **1995**
£26.00 (JU)
Gevrey-Chambertin au Vellé, Denis
Mortet **1998** £27.03 (DOM) £29.00 (WS)
£29.50 (TAN) £30.95 (RES)
Gevrey-Chambertin au Vellé, Denis
Mortet **1997** £25.00 (JU)

Gevrey-Chambertin Vieilles Vignes,
Charlopin-Parizot **1996** £25.50 (LEA)
Mazis-Chambertin Frédéric Esmonin
1997 £25.99 (SOM)
Meursault les Cras, Brunet **1988** £25.95
(BALL)
Morey-St-Denis Clos de la Bussière,
Georges Roumier **1999** £26.34 (BODX)
Morey-St-Denis Cuvée des Grives,
Ponsot **1998** £25.49 (YOU)
Morey-St-Denis Dujac **1997** £27.32 (FA)
Morey-St-Denis Dujac **1996** £25.36
(BODX)
Morey-St-Denis Dujac **1995** £25.00
(FORT) £29.75 (STA)
Nuits-St-Georges les Argillières, Dubois
1996 £25.06 (VIN)
Nuits-St-Georges les Cailles, Robert
Chevillon **1994** £27.00 (JU)
Nuits-St-Georges les Chaignots, Robert
Chevillon **1996** £25.00 (JU)
Nuits-St-Georges les Chaignots, Robert
Chevillon **1995** £27.32 (FA)
Nuits-St-Georges aux Chaignots, Faiveley
1997 £27.33 (ARM)
Nuits-St-Georges les Chaignots, Georges
Mugneret **1999** £26.95 (LEA)
Nuits-St-Georges Clos de l'Arlot,
Domaine de l'Arlot **1998** £26.67 (ARM)
£27.95 (LAY)
Nuits-St-Georges Clos des Forêts St-
Georges, Domaine de l'Arlot **1998**
£26.59 (RIP) £29.58 (ARM) £30.55 (LAY)
£30.58 (BY)
Nuits-St-Georges Clos des Forêts St-
Georges, Domaine de l'Arlot **1995**
£25.00 (FLE)

Nuits-St-Georges Clos de la Maréchale,
Faiveley **1994** £25.90 (WRI)
Nuits-St-Georges Clos de la Maréchale,
Faiveley **1989** £25.00 (FLE)
Nuits-St-Georges Clos des Porets,
Gouges **1997** £26.99 (YOU)
Nuits-St-Georges Clos des Porets St-
Georges, Gouges **1997** £26.00 (WS)
Nuits-St-Georges aux Cras, Clavelier
1997 £27.22 (SAV)
Nuits-St-Georges les Murgers, Hudelot-
Noëllat **1996** £26.67 (ARM)
Nuits-St-Georges les Perrières, Jean
Chauvenet **1997** £25.99 (RAE)
Nuits-St-Georges les Perrières, Robert
Chevillon **1996** £26.00 (JU)
Nuits-St-Georges les Porets St-Georges,
Faiveley **1993** £26.83 (FA)
Nuits-St-Georges les Pruliers, Domaine
Jean Grivot **1995** £26.00 (BAL)
Nuits-St-Georges les Roncières, Robert
Chevillon **1995** £27.00 (JU) £29.38 (FA)
Pommard les Fremiers, Coste-Caumartin
1993 £25.00 (JU)
Pommard les Jarollières, Jean-Marc Boillot
1996 £26.83 (FA)
Pommard les Jarollières, Domaine de la
Pousse d'Or **1994** £26.95 (DI)
Pommard Pezerolles, Domaine de
Montille **1994** £25.20 (HAH)
Pommard Pezerolles, Domaine de
Montille **1991** £26.00 (WS)
Volnay les Caillerets, Clos des 60
Ouvrées, Domaine de la Pousse d'Or
1996 £26.83 (FA) £28.95 (CON) £32.00
(WAI) £38.89 (TW)
Volnay les Caillerets Cuvée Carnot,
Bouchard Père **1999** £26.44 (BAL)
Volnay les Caillerets, Domaine de la
Pousse d'Or **1995** £25.50 (CON) £26.83
(FA)
Volnay Carelle sous la Chapelle, Jean-
Marc Boillot **1997** £25.50 (RAE)
Volnay Champans, Marquis d'Angerville
1999 £25.95 (MON)
Volnay Clos des Chênes, Domaine Guyon
1998 £26.95 (FRI)
Volnay Clos des Ducs, Marquis
d'Angerville **1994** £25.85 (FA) £27.00
(JU)
Volnay Frémiets, Comte Armand **1996**
£25.95 (LEA)
Volnay la Gigotte, Darviot-Perrin **1996**
£26.44 (TW)
Volnay Santenots Lafon **1994** £27.03 (FLE)

Vosne-Romanée les Beaux Monts, Clavelier **1997** £27.22 (SAV)

Vosne-Romanée les Beaux Monts, Domaine Jean Grivot **1997** £26.35 (SOM)

Vosne-Romanée les Brûlées, Clavelier **1999** £26.93 (SAV)

Vosne-Romanée les Brûlées, Engel **1999** £25.85 (BODX)

Vosne-Romanée Champs Perdrix, Bruno Clair **1995** £27.00 (JU)

Vosne-Romanée Jean Gros **1988** £27.03 (FA)

Vosne-Romanée Michel Gros **1993** £25.00 (JU)

Vougeot Clos de la Perrière, Bertagna **1997** £26.99 (OD)

£27.50 → £29.99

Beaune Clos des Fèves, Chanson **1990** £29.95 (DI)

Beaune Clos des Mouches, Drouhin **1998** £27.85 (NI)

Beaune Teurons, Bouchard Père **1964** £27.50 (BU)

Chambolle-Musigny la Combe d'Orveaux, Clavelier **1999** £27.91 (SAV)

Chambolle-Musigny les Cras, Ghislaine Barthod **1998** £27.99 (RAE)

Chambolle-Musigny Georges Lignier **1983** £28.00 (CRO)

Chassagne-Montrachet Clos St-Jean, Guy Amiot **1998** £29.95 (DI)

Chassagne-Montrachet les Vergers, Guy Amiot **1998** £29.95 (DI) £32.50 (BAL)

Clos de Vougeot Musigni, Gros Frère et Soeur **1995** £28.79 (FA)

Corton-Bressandes Chandon de Briailles **1998** £29.95 (LEA) £30.50 (TAN)

Corton Clos du Roi, Dubreuil-Fontaine **1993** £27.92 (BY)

Corton Grancey, Latour **1996** £27.91 (WY) £29.96 (PEN)

Corton Pougets, Jadot **1999** £28.79 (FA)

Corton Renardes, Prince Florent de Mérode **1995** £27.50 (WRI)

Corton le Rognet, Chevalier **1996** £27.85 (GW)

Corton Tollot-Beaut **1996** £28.50 (RAE)

Échézeaux Engel **1997** £29.49 (YOU) £31.50 (CON)

Échézeaux Engel **1996** £29.50 (CON) £29.95 (SOM)

Échézeaux Lamarche **1997** £27.75 (SOM) £34.50 (RAE)

Échézeaux Mongeard-Mugneret **1991** £29.38 (FA)

Gevrey-Chambertin Champeaux, Denis Mortet **1994** £27.95 (RAE)

Gevrey-Chambertin Champeaux, Denis Mortet **1993** £29.77 (FA)

Gevrey-Chambertin Clos St-Jacques, Fourrier **1995** £29.50 (BAL)

Gevrey-Chambertin la Combe aux Moines, Fourrier **1999** £27.71 (BAL)

Gevrey-Chambertin Lavaux-St-Jacques, Maume **1998** £27.99 (RAE) £31.50 (BAL)

Gevrey-Chambertin au Vellé, Denis Mortet **1999** £29.77 (BODX)

Morey-St-Denis Clos de la Bussière, Georges Roumier **1993** £29.38 (FA)

Nuits-St-Georges aux Chaignots, Faiveley **1996** £27.95 (DI)

Nuits-St-Georges aux Chaignots, Faiveley **1993** £28.40 (HAH)

Nuits-St-Georges Clos des Forêts St-Georges, Domaine de l'Arlot **1993** £29.17 (ARM)

Nuits-St-Georges Clos de la Maréchale, Faiveley **1993** £28.75 (TAN)

Nuits-St-Georges Clos des Porets, Gouges **1996** £27.99 (YOU)

Nuits-St-Georges les Murgers, Hudelot-Noëllat **1998** £27.50 (ARM)

Nuits-St-Georges les Porets St-Georges, Faiveley **1998** £27.95 (POR)

Nuits-St-Georges les Porets St-Georges, Faiveley **1996** £29.10 (HAH)

Nuits-St-Georges les Pruliers, Domaine Jean Grivot **1998** £28.75 (RAE) £33.00 (BAL)

Nuits-St-Georges les St-Georges, Robert Chevillon **1998** £28.50 (FORT)

Nuits-St-Georges les Vaucrains, Robert Chevillon **1998** £27.50 (FORT)

Nuits-St-Georges les Vaucrains, Robert Chevillon **1996** £28.79 (FA)

Nuits-St-Georges les Vaucrains, Robert Chevillon **1994** £28.00 (JU)

Nuits-St-Georges les Vaucrains, Gouges **1999** £28.89 (MON)

Pommard Clos des Boucherottes, Coste-Caumartin **1995** £28.00 (JU)

• *All prices for each wine are listed together in ascending order.*
• *Price bands refer to the lowest price for which the wine is available.*

Pommard Clos des Épeneaux, Comte Armand **1997** £28.79 (BODX)

Pommard Clos des Épeneaux, Comte Armand **1995** £29.95 (LEA) £30.00 (CON) £39.01 (TW) £41.13 (TUR)

Pommard les Épenots, Jean Luc Joillot **1998** £29.25 (NI)

Pommard Grand Clos des Épenots, Domaine de Courcel **1998** £29.95 (LEA)

Pommard Grand Clos des Épenots, Domaine de Courcel **1997** £28.95 (LEA)

Pommard les Jarollières, Jean-Marc Boillot **1999** £28.40 (RAE)

Pommard les Saucilles, Jean-Marc Boillot **1996** £28.79 (DOM)

Ruchottes-Chambertin Frédéric Esmonin **1997** £29.75 (BAN)

Volnay les Caillerets, Marquis d'Angerville **1995** £28.00 (JU)

Volnay les Caillerets, Clos des 60 Ouvrées, Domaine de la Pousse d'Or **1993** £29.77 (FA) £35.00 (WS)

Volnay Champans, Marquis d'Angerville **1996** £27.50 (CB) £30.75 (FA)

Volnay Frémiets, Comte Armand **1998** £27.50 (LEA)

Volnay Frémiets, Comte Armand **1997** £29.50 (LEA)

Vosne-Romanée les Brûlées, Engel **1996** £28.50 (YOU) £31.49 (TW)

Vosne-Romanée les Chaumes, Rion **1995** £28.30 (FA)

Vosne-Romanée Clos de la Fontaine, Michel Gros **1993** £28.00 (JU)

Vosne-Romanée les Malconsorts, Lamarche **1999** £27.81 (RAE)

Vosne-Romanée les Malconsorts, Lamarche **1997** £29.00 (RAE)

Vosne-Romanée Emmanuel Rouget **1996** £28.79 (FA)

Vosne-Romanée les Suchots, Domaine de l'Arlot **1998** £29.17 (ARM) £30.58 (BY)

£30.00 → £34.99

Beaune Clos des Mouches, Drouhin **1996** £32.90 (PEN) £44.50 (BAL)

Beaune Cuvée Maurice Drouhin, Hospices de Beaune **1996** £31.50 (BEN)

Beaune Grèves, Lafarge **1999** £33.68 (RAE)

Beaune Grèves, Lafarge **1998** £34.50 (CON)

Beaune Grèves Vigne de l'Enfant Jesus, Bouchard Père **1996** £34.00 (BAL)

Beaune Teurons, Leroy **1980** £32.00 (JU)

Chambolle-Musigny les Baudes, Hubert Lignier **1998** £32.70 (BODX)

Chambolle-Musigny les Fuées, Ghislaine Barthod **1997** £30.00 (JU)

Chambolle-Musigny les Fuées, Ghislaine Barthod **1994** £32.00 (JU)

Chambolle-Musigny de Vogüé **1998** £30.75 (FA)

Chambolle-Musigny les Charmes, Christian Clerget **1998** £33.04 (BY)

Chapelle-Chambertin Trapet **1997** £34.06 (BY)

Charmes-Chambertin Perrot-Minot **1996** £33.50 (CON)

Charmes-Chambertin Domaine Henri Rebourseau **1997** £32.75 (SOM)

Chassagne-Montrachet les Vergers, Guy Amiot **1997** £31.50 (BAL)

Clos de la Roche Armand Rousseau **1995** £33.04 (BY)

Clos de Vougeot J-J Confuron **1994** £30.75 (FA) £44.50 (BAL)

Clos de Vougeot Domaine Jean Grivot **1997** £31.40 (SOM) £35.00 (RAE) £36.62 (BODX) £40.58 (ARM) £42.00 (BAL)

Clos de Vougeot Domaine Jean Grivot **1996** £30.75 (SOM)

Clos de Vougeot Hudelot-Noëllat **1997** £33.45 (SOM) £42.50 (ARM)

Clos de Vougeot Hudelot-Noëllat **1996** £34.50 (SOM)

Clos de Vougeot Georges Roumier **1997** £33.50 (GW)

Corton Bouchard Père **1995** £33.00 (COC)

Corton-Bressandes Chandon de Briailles **1997** £32.20 (HAH) £32.50 (LEA)

Corton-Bressandes Chandon de Briailles **1996** £32.50 (YOU)

Corton-Bressandes Tollot-Beaut **1998** £32.21 (BODX) £36.00 (JU)

Corton-Bressandes Tollot-Beaut **1996** £30.75 (FA) £35.99 (JON)

Corton Clos des Cortons, Faiveley **1991** £30.70 (FLE)

Corton Clos du Roi, Chandon de Briailles **1999** £31.33 (MON)

Corton Clos du Roi, Chandon de Briailles **1998** £33.95 (LEA)

Corton Clos du Roi, Chandon de Briailles **1997** £30.99 (YOU)

Corton Clos de la Vigne au Saint, Latour **1989** £32.25 (WY)

Corton Pougets, Jadot **1996** £32.00 (YOU)

Corton Pougets, Jadot **1986** £32.90 (WY)

Corton Tollot-Beaut **1998** £32.21 (BODX)

Échézeaux Engel 1998 £31.50 (CON)
£35.15 (BODX) £37.49 (YOU)

Échézeaux Lamarche 1999 £33.09 (RAE)

Gevrey-Chambertin Cazetiers, Armand
Rousseau 1998 £31.00 (WS)

Gevrey-Chambertin Cazetiers, Armand
Rousseau 1997 £30.00 (YOU) £40.00
(FORT)

Gevrey-Chambertin Clos St-Jacques,
Fourrier 1999 £30.65 (BAL)

Gevrey-Chambertin la Combe aux
Moines, Faiveley 1993 £32.67 (ARM)

Gevrey-Chambertin les Fonteny, Joseph
Roty 1996 £33.68 (FA) £35.25 (TUR)

Gevrey-Chambertin au Vellé, Denis
Mortet 1995 £31.00 (JU)

Gevrey-Chambertin Vieilles Vignes, Alain
Burguet 1997 £33.99 (WIN)

Gevrey-Chambertin Vieilles Vignes, Alain
Burguet 1992 £33.49 (TW)

Gevry-Chambertin Domaine Taupenot-
Merme 1995 £31.36 (VIN)

Latricières-Chambertin Trapet 1997
£34.06 (BY) £45.43 (FA)

Nuits-St-Georges les Boudots, Domaine
Jean Grivot 1999 £32.80 (RAE)

Nuits-St-Georges les Chaignots, A
Michelot 1993 £34.00 (CRO)

Nuits-St-Georges Clos de l'Arlot,
Domaine de l'Arlot 1991 £34.90 (TW)

Nuits-St-Georges Clos des Forêts St-
Georges, Domaine de l'Arlot 1996
£32.01 (BY)

Nuits-St-Georges les Pruliers, Domaine
Jean Grivot 1999 £32.21 (RAE) £32.31
(BAL)

Nuits-St-Georges les Pruliers, Domaine
Jean Grivot 1992 £30.95 (BALL)

Nuits-St-Georges les Roncières, Robert
Chevillon 1994 £31.14 (TW)

Nuits-St-Georges les St-Georges, Robert
Chevillon 1995 £31.73 (TW)

Nuits-St-Georges les St-Georges, Robert
Chevillon 1994 £30.00 (JU)

Nuits-St-Georges les St-Georges, Gouges
1999 £33.78 (MON)

Nuits-St-Georges les Vaucrains, A
Michelot 1988 £34.00 (YOU)

Nuits-St-Georges Georges & Henri Jayer
1997 £33.00 (JU)

Pommard Clos des Épeneaux, Comte
Armand 1998 £32.95 (LEA)

Pommard Clos des Épeneaux, Comte
Armand 1996 £32.50 (CON) £33.50
(WRI) £41.83 (TW)

Pommard Clos des Épeneaux, Comte
Armand 1993 £30.26 (BODX)

Pommard Grand Clos des Épenots,
Domaine de Courcel 1996 £32.00 (LEA)

Pommard Grands Épenots, Pierre Morey
1997 £32.20 (LAY)

Pommard les Jarollières, Jean-Marc Boillot
1998 £32.65 (RAE) £33.50 (BALL)

Pommard les Jarollières, Jean-Marc Boillot
1997 £30.50 (RAE) £32.31 (DOM)

Pommard les Jarollières, Domaine de la
Pousse d'Or 1996 £30.50 (BALL) £42.95
(TW)

Pommard les Jarollières, Domaine de la
Pousse d'Or 1995 £30.00 (WS)

Pommard les Noizons, Jean Garaudet
1990 £30.93 (BY)

Pommard Rugiens, Domaine de Courcel
1999 £33.50 (LEA)

Pommard Rugiens, Domaine de Courcel
1997 £30.95 (LEA)

Pommard les Vignots, Leroy 1987 £30.00
(BU)

Savigny-lès-Beaune les Guettes, Machard
de Gramont 1985 £30.99 (YOU)

Savigny-lès-Beaune les Lavières, Ampeau
1976 £33.50 (LEA)

Savigny-lès-Beaune les Marconnets, Bize
1992 £33.49 (TW)

Volnay 1er Cru, Michel Lafarge 1998
£30.00 (CON)

Volnay 1er Cru, Michel Lafarge 1996
£30.00 (CON)

Volnay 1er Cru, Michel Lafarge 1995
£30.50 (RAE) £40.18 (TW)

Volnay les Caillerets, Marquis d'Angerville
1997 £31.00 (JU)

Volnay Champans, Marquis d'Angerville
1988 £31.73 (FA)

Volnay Clos de la Bousse d'Or, Domaine
de la Pousse d'Or 1996 £32.70 (FA)
£44.06 (TW)

Volnay Clos de la Bousse d'Or, Domaine
de la Pousse d'Or 1995 £32.70 (FA)

Volnay Clos des Ducs, Marquis
d'Angerville 1999 £33.78 (MON)

- *Wines are listed in A–Z order within
  each price band.*
- *For each wine, vintages are listed in
  descending order.*
- *Each vintage of any wine appears
  only once.*

Volnay Clos des Santenots, Prieur **1997**
£34.99 (YOU)

Volnay Santenots-du-Milieu, Lafon **1991**
£30.55 (FA)

Volnay Taillepieds, Marquis d'Angerville
1999 £30.35 (MON)

Volnay Taillepieds, Marquis d'Angerville
1997 £31.73 (FA)

Volnay Vendange Selectionée, Lafarge
1994 £31.49 (TW)

Vosne-Romanée les Beaux Monts,
Domaine Rion **1995** £31.28 (FLE)

Vosne-Romanée Cacheux **1990** £31.00
(CRO)

Vosne-Romanée les Chaumes, Arnoux
1999 £30.35 (MON)

Vosne-Romanée les Chaumes, Arnoux
1998 £32.00 (GW)

Vosne-Romanée les Malconsorts,
Lamarche **1998** £30.25 (RAE)

Vosne-Romanée Méo-Camuzet **1998**
£31.00 (WS) £31.95 (TAN)

£35.00 → £39.99

Beaune Clos des Mouches, Drouhin **1995**
£38.00 (CRO)

Beaune Grèves, Lafarge **1995** £36.50 (RAE)

Beaune Grèves Vigne de l'Enfant Jesus,
Bouchard Père **1999** £36.23 (BAL)

Chambolle-Musigny les Cras, Georges
Roumier **1999** £37.60 (BODX)

Chambolle-Musigny Jadot **1997** £35.00
(YOU)

Chambolle-Musigny Jadot **1986** £35.25
(WY)

Chambolle-Musigny les Veroilles,
Ghislaine Barthod **1995** £35.00 (JU)

Chambolle-Musigny de Vogüé **1997**
£35.00 (DI)

Chambolle-Musigny de Vogüé **1996**
£36.62 (FA)

Chambolle-Musigny de Vogüé **1994**
£35.00 (BAL) £35.95 (BALL)

Chambolle-Musigny les Charmes,
Christian Clerget **1997** £38.26 (PLAY)

Charmes-Chambertin Perrot-Minot **1997**
£37.85 (WAT) £41.65 (CON)

Please remember that
Oz Clarke's Wine Buying Guide
*is a price **guide** and not a price **list**. It is
not meant to replace up-to-date
merchants' lists.*

Charmes-Chambertin Armand Rousseau
1998 £38.95 (TAN)

Charmes-Chambertin Armand Rousseau
1997 £38.49 (YOU)

Charmes-Chambertin Armand Rousseau
1993 £38.58 (FA)

Clos de la Roche Armand Rousseau **1994**
£39.22 (BY)

Clos de Tart Mommessin **1993** £39.75
(WAI)

Clos de Vougeot Labouré-Roi **1998**
£39.17 (MI)

Clos de Vougeot Denis Mortet **1994**
£39.95 (RAE)

Corton Bonneau du Martray **1999** £38.09
(BAL)

Corton Bonneau du Martray **1997** £39.00
(JU)

Corton Bouchard Père **1999** £39.07 (BAL)

Corton Bouchard Père **1996** £39.50 (BAL)

Corton-Bressandes Chandon de Briailles
1995 £35.25 (SAV)

Corton Pougets, Jadot **1997** £38.49 (YOU)

Corton les Renardes, M Gaunoux **1997**
£39.99 (WIN)

Corton Viénot **1967** £39.00 (CRO)

Échézeaux Christian Clerget **1998** £38.16
(BY)

Échézeaux Domaine du Clos Frantin
1999 £37.11 (BAL)

Échézeaux Engel **1999** £35.64 (BODX)

Gevrey-Chambertin Cazetiers, Faiveley
1988 £38.68 (TUR)

Gevrey-Chambertin Champeaux, Denis
Mortet **1998** £36.75 (RAE) £39.00 (WS)

Gevrey-Chambertin Clos du Fonteny,
Bruno Clair **1995** £35.00 (JU)

Gevrey-Chambertin Clos Prieur,
Rossignol-Trapet **1993** £35.25 (TW)

Gevrey-Chambertin Clos St-Jacques,
Armand Rousseau **1992** £35.25 (FA)

Gevrey-Chambertin Coeur du Roy,
Dugat-Py **1997** £39.25 (NI)

Gevrey-Chambertin la Combe aux
Moines, Faiveley **1998** £35.00 (POR)

Gevrey-Chambertin Vieilles Vignes,
Dugat-Py **1998** £36.62 (FA)

Gevrey-Chambertin Vieilles Vignes,
Dugat-Py **1997** £35.25 (FA)

Latricières-Chambertin Faiveley **1992**
£39.00 (WRI)

Mazis-Chambertin Maume **1999** £38.09
(RAE) £40.44 (BAL)

Mazis-Chambertin Maume **1996** £36.00
(RAE) £43.00 (BAL) £58.16 (FA)

Mazis-Chambertin Armand Rousseau
1998 £38.95 (TAN)

Morey-St-Denis Clos de la Bussière,
Georges Roumier **1996** £36.58 (ARM)

Morey-St-Denis Clos des Lambrays,
Domaine des Lambrays **1998** £39.95
(LEA)

Morey-St-Denis Clos des Lambrays,
Domaine des Lambrays **1997** £35.30
(HAH) £36.75 (LEA)

Nuits-St-Georges Clos des Porets,
Gouges **1998** £36.50 (WIN)

Nuits-St-Georges Clos des Porets,
Gouges **1986** £35.00 (YOU)

Nuits-St-Georges Clos des Porets St-
Georges, Gouges **1996** £38.99 (YOU)

Nuits-St-Georges Hauts-Poiret, Jayer-
Gilles **1999** £39.56 (BODX)

Nuits-St-Georges Hauts-Poiret, Jayer-
Gilles **1997** £35.00 (JU) £35.64 (BODX)

Nuits-St-Georges Henri Jayer **1999**
£39.07 (BODX)

Pommard les Épenots, Comte Armand
1998 £36.50 (GAU)

Pommard les Épenots, Comte Armand
1997 £38.00 (GAU)

Volnay 1er Cru, Michel Lafarge **1992**
£38.19 (TW)

Volnay les Caillerets, Clos des 60
Ouvrées, Domaine de la Pousse d'Or
1990 £38.78 (FA)

Volnay les Caillerets, Domaine de la
Pousse d'Or **1991** £37.60 (TW)

Volnay les Caillerets, Domaine de la
Pousse d'Or **1990** £36.62 (FA)

Volnay Clos du Château des Ducs,
Lafarge **1998** £36.95 (CON) £46.99
(WIN)

Volnay Clos du Château des Ducs,
Lafarge **1997** £37.50 (RAE) £38.95
(CON)

Volnay Clos des Chênes, Lafarge **1998**
£36.95 (CON) £51.95 (WIN)

Volnay Clos des Chênes, Lafarge **1997**
£36.95 (CON)

Volnay Clos des Chênes, Lafarge **1992**
£38.95 (BALL)

Volnay Clos des Ducs, Marquis
d'Angerville **1997** £35.00 (JU) £38.58 (FA)

Volnay Frémiets, Marquis d'Angerville
1995 £35.67 (ARM)

Volnay Santenots Lafon **1997** £35.25
(BODX)

Volnay Santenots-du-Milieu, Lafon **1997**
£35.00 (JU)

Vosne-Romanée les Beaux Monts,
Domaine Jean Grivot **1998** £38.58 (FA)

Vosne-Romanée les Chaumes, Jean Tardy
1997 £39.95 (RES)

Vosne-Romanée Méo-Camuzet **1999**
£38.09 (BODX)

Vosne-Romanée Méo-Camuzet **1988**
£35.25 (FA)

Vosne-Romanée aux Reignots, Arnoux
1999 £38.19 (MON)

Vosne-Romanée aux Reignots, Arnoux
1996 £36.70 (GAU)

Vosne-Romanée Rion **1990** £37.00 (CRO)

Vosne-Romanée Emmanuel Rouget **1999**
£37.60 (BODX)

Vosne-Romanée Emmanuel Rouget **1998**
£35.99 (RAE)

£40.00 → £49.99

Beaune Cuvée Brunet, Latour **1990**
£47.00 (PEN)

Beaune Grèves, Lafarge **1994** £40.54 (TW)

Beaune Grèves, Lafarge **1992** £41.12 (TW)

Beaune Teurons, Jadot **1985** £41.13 (WY)

Bonnes-Mares Drouhin **1996** £44.45 (FA)

Bonnes-Mares Jadot **1999** £48.37 (FA)

Bonnes-Mares de Vogüé **1994** £42.50 (FA)
£49.00 (DI) £70.00 (FORT)

Bonnes-Mares de Vogüé **1987** £48.37 (FA)

Chambertin Clos-de-Bèze, Bruno Clair
1994 £48.00 (JU)

Chambertin Trapet **1997** £41.64 (BY)
£74.81 (FA)

Chambolle-Musigny les Amoureuses, de
Vogüé **1994** £49.00 (DI)

Chambolle-Musigny les Cras, Georges
Roumier **1996** £41.25 (HAH)

Chambolle-Musigny les Gruenchers,
Dujac **1994** £46.88 (TW)

Chambolle-Musigny de Vogüé **1993**
£47.00 (YOU) £49.50 (BAL)

Chapelle-Chambertin Ponsot **1992**
£47.50 (ARM)

Chapelle-Chambertin Trapet **1996**
£40.54 (FA)

Charmes-Chambertin Faiveley **1993**
£49.33 (ARM)

Charmes-Chambertin Faiveley **1988**
£43.87 (NO)

Charmes-Chambertin Perrot-Minot **1999**
£40.44 (BAL)

Charmes-Chambertin Perrot-Minot **1998**
£41.65 (CON)

Charmes-Chambertin Jean Raphet **1997**
£49.50 (BEN)

Chassagne-Montrachet Clos de la Boudriotte, Ramonet 1995 £47.50 (FORT)

Clos de la Roche Jean Raphet 1997 £49.50 (BEN)

Clos de la Roche Armand Rousseau 1998 £41.95 (TAN)

Clos de la Roche Armand Rousseau 1997 £41.23 (BY) £42.99 (YOU) £45.00 (BALL) £60.00 (FORT)

Clos de la Roche Armand Rousseau 1996 £45.50 (BALL) £48.99 (YOU) £49.75 (WAI) £55.50 (BEN)

Clos de Tart Mommessin 1994 £40.00 (WS)

Clos de Vougeot Arnoux 1999 £48.47 (MON)

Clos de Vougeot J-J Confuron 1999 £43.87 (BAL)

Clos de Vougeot J-J Confuron 1997 £47.00 (BAL) £50.33 (BODX)

Clos de Vougeot J-J Confuron 1990 £47.00 (FA)

Clos de Vougeot Confuron-Cotétidot 1998 £40.95 (LEA)

Clos de Vougeot Confuron-Cotétidot 1997 £40.95. (LEA)

Clos de Vougeot Engel 1999 £46.41 (BODX)

Clos de Vougeot Engel 1998 £45.43 (BODX) £46.50 (CON)

Clos de Vougeot Engel 1997 £41.52 (BODX) £46.50 (CON) £47.50 (FORT)

Clos de Vougeot Engel 1996 £45.00 (CON) £47.00 (BODX)

Clos de Vougeot Grand Cru, Prieur 1996 £43.99 (YOU)

Clos de Vougeot Domaine Jean Grivot 1999 £42.40 (BAL) £45.92 (BODX)

Clos de Vougeot Domaine Jean Grivot 1998 £40.05 (BODX) £40.50 (ARM) £44.00 (BAL)

Clos de Vougeot Georges Mugneret 1998 £49.50 (LEA)

Clos de Vougeot Rebourseau 1997 £44.20 (SOM)

Corton Clos des Cortons, Faiveley 1995 £49.95 (DI)

Corton les Renardes, Leroy 1994 £47.00 (FA)

Échézeaux Arnoux 1997 £49.90 (GW)

Échézeaux Drouhin 1995 £49.50 (BEN)

Échézeaux Jacqueline Jayer 1984 £41.95 (BALL)

Gevrey-Chambertin Champeaux, Denis Mortet 1999 £42.50 (BODX)

Gevrey-Chambertin Clos St-Jacques, Bruno Clair 1998 £40.00 (JU)

Gevrey-Chambertin Clos St-Jacques, Armand Rousseau 1997 £48.37 (FA) £52.99 (YOU) £58.75 (BODX)

Gevrey-Chambertin Clos St-Jacques, Armand Rousseau 1996 £49.43 (BY) £56.99 (YOU) £64.04 (FA) £66.00 (FORT)

Gevrey-Chambertin Coeur du Roy, Dugat-Py 1998 £48.37 (FA)

Gevrey-Chambertin Combettes, Dujac 1994 £46.41 (TW)

Gevrey-Chambertin Dugat 1998 £48.37 (FA)

Gevrey-Chambertin Faiveley 1996 £41.13 (PEN)

Gevrey-Chambertin Lavaux-St-Jacques, Dugat-Py 1997 £46.75 (NI)

La Grande Rue François Lamarche 1997 £48.45 (SOM) £61.00 (RAE) £69.95 (JER)

Grands-Échézeaux Engel 1997 £47.00 (BODX) £48.99 (YOU) £49.50 (CON)

Grands-Échézeaux Gros Frère et Soeur 1991 £44.94 (BODX)

Griotte-Chambertin Domaine des Chézeaux, Ponsot 1997 £40.50 (ARM)

Griotte-Chambertin Domaine des Chézeaux, Ponsot 1996 £45.43 (FA)

Griotte-Chambertin Fourrier 1999 £40.24 (BAL)

Griotte-Chambertin Fourrier 1998 £46.50 (BEN)

Griotte-Chambertin Ponsot 1994 £45.00 (BAL)

Latricières-Chambertin Leroy 1996 £42.30 (TUR)

Mazis-Chambertin Armand Rousseau 1996 £45.49 (YOU)

Mazis-Chambertin Armand Rousseau 1993 £44.45 (FA) £49.35 (BODX)

Mazis-Chambertin Armand Rousseau 1989 £42.00 (CRO)

Morey-St-Denis Clos des Ormes, Faiveley 1976 £49.94 (TW)

Nuits-St-Georges les Damodes, Jayer-Gilles 1999 £47.39 (BODX)

Nuits-St-Georges les Damodes, Jayer-Gilles 1997 £42.00 (JU)

Nuits-St-Georges Hauts-Poiret, Jayer-Gilles 1995 £45.00 (JU)

Pommard les Épenots, Comte Armand 1993 £40.00 (FORT)

Ruchottes-Chambertin Clos des Ruchottes, Armand Rousseau 1998 £45.95 (TAN)

Ruchottes-Chambertin Georges Roumier
1994 £45.43 (BODX)
Ruchottes-Chambertin Armand Rousseau
1997 £41.49 (YOU)
Ruchottes-Chambertin Armand Rousseau
1996 £46.41 (FA) £49.99 (YOU)
Ruchottes-Chambertin Armand Rousseau
1995 £48.37 (FA)
Ruchottes-Chambertin Armand Rousseau
1991 £47.00 (FA)
Volnay Clos du Château des Ducs,
Lafarge **1994** £42.00 (BALL) £44.53 (TW)
Volnay Clos des Chênes, Lafarge **1994**
£44.53 (TW)
Volnay Santenots Lafon **1993** £45.00
(CRO)
Vosne-Romanée les Brûlées, Engel **1990**
£40.54 (FA)
Vosne-Romanée les Chaumes, Méo-
Camuzet **1998** £40.05 (BODX)
Vosne-Romanée les Chaumes, Méo-
Camuzet **1997** £40.05 (BODX) £40.05
(FA)
Vosne-Romanée Cros Parantoux
Emmanuel Rouget **1992** £48.37 (FA)
Vosne-Romanée aux Reignots, Arnoux
1997 £45.95 (GAU)

£50.00 → £59.99

Bonnes-Mares Jadot **1998** £56.99 (YOU)
Bonnes-Mares de Vogüé **1992** £59.00 (DI)
Chambertin Clos-de-Bèze, Bruno Clair
1997 £55.00 (JU) £57.67 (FA)
Chambertin Clos-de-Bèze, Damoy **1997**
£54.10 (LAY)
Chambertin Clos-de-Bèze, Jadot **1986**
£58.75 (WY)
Chambolle-Musigny les Amoureuses,
Georges Roumier **1998** £52.00 (WS)
Chambolle-Musigny les Charmes, Leroy
1994 £58.75 (FA)
Chambolle-Musigny Latour **1969** £50.00
(YOU)
Charmes-Chambertin Faiveley **1995**
£55.25 (ARM)
Clos des Cortons Faiveley **1997** £54.00
(WS) £55.25 (ARM)
Clos de la Roche Dujac **1998** £57.18
(BODX)
Clos de Tart Mommessin **1998** £55.00
(HAH)
Clos de Tart Mommessin **1996** £54.00
(WS) £55.00 (JU)
Clos de Vougeot Drouhin **1995** £52.00
(BALL)

Clos de Vougeot Engel **1995** £58.75 (TW)
Clos de Vougeot Engel **1991** £57.50
(BALL)
Clos de Vougeot Faiveley **1997** £54.75
(ARM)
Clos de Vougeot Faiveley **1996** £58.17
(ARM)
Clos de Vougeot Domaine Jean Grivot
1993 £56.00 (CRO)
Clos de Vougeot Latour **1988** £51.70
(PEN)
Corton Clos des Cortons, Faiveley **1996**
£50.80 (HAH)
Corton Clos des Cortons, Faiveley **1993**
£52.90 (HAH)
Corton Tollot-Beaut **1990** £54.25 (FA)
Échézeaux Arnoux **1999** £51.41 (MON)
Échézeaux Arnoux **1998** £54.00 (GW)
Échézeaux Engel **1988** £56.00 (CRO)
Échézeaux Faiveley **1988** £50.33 (FA)
Échézeaux Domaine Jean Grivot **1999**
£55.22 (BODX)
Échézeaux Emmanuel Rouget **1994**
£54.00 (JU)
Gevrey-Chambertin Clos St-Jacques,
Armand Rousseau **1993** £56.40 (FA)
Gevrey-Chambertin Clos St-Jacques,
Armand Rousseau **1988** £58.75 (FA)
Gevrey-Chambertin Combettes, Dujac
1995 £56.99 (TW)
Gevrey-Chambertin Jadot **1985** £52.88
(WY)
La Grande Rue François Lamarche **1999**
£57.18 (RAE)
Grands-Échézeaux Engel **1999** £52.78
(BODX)
Grands-Échézeaux Engel **1998** £52.29
(BODX)
Grands-Échézeaux Gros Frère et Soeur
1996 £50.33 (FA)
Griotte-Chambertin Domaine des
Chézeaux, Ponsot **1995** £50.33 (FA)
Griotte-Chambertin Ponsot **1998** £58.75
(BODX) £64.92 (BAL) £73.99 (YOU)
Latricières-Chambertin Faiveley **1997**
£54.75 (ARM)
Mazis-Chambertin Faiveley **1997** £58.12
(ARM)

- *All prices for each wine are listed together in ascending order.*
- *Price bands refer to the lowest price for which the wine is available.*

Nuits-St-Georges aux Boudots, Leroy **1994** £52.88 (FA)

Nuits-St-Georges les Boudots, Méo-Camuzet **1999** £56.20 (BODX)

Nuits-St-Georges les Boudots, Méo-Camuzet **1997** £54.50 (TAN)

Nuits-St-Georges les Murgers, Méo-Camuzet **1999** £55.22 (BODX)

Nuits-St-Georges les Murgers, Méo-Camuzet **1997** £56.00 (TAN) £58.16 (FA)

Pommard Bouchard Père **1961** £50.00 (YOU)

Romanée-St-Vivant Domaine de la Romanée-Conti **1984** £58.75 (FA)

Ruchottes-Chambertin Georges Roumier **1997** £52.88 (DOM)

Ruchottes-Chambertin Armand Rousseau **1988** £54.25 (FA)

Santenay Remoissenet **1971** £54.99 (YOU)

Volnay Domaine de la Pousse d'Or **1990** £55.00 (BEN)

Vosne-Romanée les Brûlées, Méo-Camuzet **1993** £59.00 (CRO)

Vosne-Romanée Cros Parantoux Emmanuel Rouget **1994** £58.00 (JU)

£60.00 → £79.99

Bonnes-Mares Groffier **1998** £77.75 (BODX)

Bonnes-Mares Jadot **1997** £65.02 (FA)

Bonnes-Mares Georges Roumier **1998** £65.00 (WS)

Bonnes-Mares Georges Roumier **1997** £71.87 (FA)

Bonnes-Mares Georges Roumier **1991** £74.81 (FA)

Bonnes-Mares de Vogüé **1996** £72.00 (DI) £111.63 (TUR) £124.75 (FA)

Bonnes-Mares de Vogüé **1989** £74.81 (FA)

Chambertin Clos-de-Bèze, Damoy **1996** £75.31 (TW)

Chambertin Clos-de-Bèze, Drouhin **1995** £65.50 (BEN)

Chambertin Clos-de-Bèze, Faiveley **1993** £77.60 (HAH)

Chambertin Clos-de-Bèze, Jadot **1999** £64.04 (FA)

Chambertin Clos-de-Bèze, Jadot **1998** £76.99 (YOU)

Chambertin Clos-de-Bèze, Armand Rousseau **1994** £60.00 (JU)

Chambertin Armand Rousseau **1992** £60.12 (FA)

Chambertin Trapet **1996** £64.63 (BODX)

Chambolle-Musigny les Amoureuses, de Vogüé **1996** £72.00 (DI)

Chambolle-Musigny les Gruenchers, Dujac **1995** £61.69 (TW)

Chambolle-Musigny Latour **1971** £64.63 (WY)

Chapelle-Chambertin Ponsot **1998** £71.00 (YOU)

Chapelle-Chambertin Ponsot **1997** £69.42 (BODX)

Chapelle-Chambertin Ponsot **1996** £77.70 (LAY)

Chapelle-Chambertin Ponsot **1995** £67.95 (FA)

Chapelle-Chambertin Ponsot **1993** £76.38 (BODX)

Charmes-Chambertin Dujac **1996** £70.50 (BODX) £74.81 (FA)

Charmes-Chambertin Dujac **1995** £77.75 (BODX)

Clos de la Roche Ponsot **1998** £66.49 (BODX) £69.81 (BAL)

Clos de la Roche Ponsot **1997** £72.36 (BODX) £75.30 (BAL) £99.99 (YOU)

Clos de la Roche Vieilles Vignes, Ponsot **1997** £79.21 (FA)

Clos St-Denis Dujac **1996** £74.81 (FA)

Clos St-Denis Georges Lignier **1985** £60.00 (CRO)

Clos de Vougeot Latour **1990** £68.15 (PEN)

Clos de Vougeot Méo-Camuzet **1999** £78.72 (BODX)

Clos de Vougeot Méo-Camuzet **1998** £66.50 (TAN)

Clos de Vougeot Méo-Camuzet **1997** £60.00 (JU) £60.12 (FA) £64.63 (BODX) £67.50 (TAN)

Clos de Vougeot Denis Mortet **1999** £65.02 (BODX)

Clos de Vougeot le Prieuré, Ponnelle **1993** £76.37 (TW)

Clos de Vougeot Georges Roumier **1996** £74.81 (FA)

Corton Clos des Cortons, Faiveley **1998** £75.00 (POR)

Corton Méo-Camuzet **1999** £79.21 (BODX)

Corton Méo-Camuzet **1997** £63.00 (RAE) £64.63 (BODX)

Corton Méo-Camuzet **1993** £76.38 (BODX)

Échézeaux Georges Jayer **1994** £60.12 (FA)

Gevrey-Chambertin Latour **1971** £76.38 (WY)

La Grande Rue François Lamarche **1998**
£61.50 (RAE)
La Grande Rue François Lamarche **1996**
£65.02 (FA)
Griotte-Chambertin Ponsot **1996** £71.87
(FA)
Musigny Prieur **1997** £77.75 (FA) £82.99
(YOU)

Musigny Vieilles Vignes, de Vogüé **1994**
£65.02 (FA)
Musigny Vieilles Vignes, de Vogüé **1992**
£60.12 (FA)
Musigny Vieilles Vignes, de Vogüé **1976**
£70.50 (FA)
Nuits-St-Georges Richemone, Pernin-
Rossin **1985** £65.00 (CRO)
Nuits-St-Georges aux Vignerondes, Leroy
1997 £76.38 (FA)
Pommard Clos Micault, Parent **1978**
£75.00 (CRO)
Richebourg Gros Frère et Soeur **1993**
£69.91 (FA)
Richebourg Hudelot-Noëllat **1997** £77.50
(SOM)
Richebourg Mongeard-Mugneret **1991**
£60.12 (FA)
Romanée-St-Vivant Domaine de l'Arlot
1998 £74.42 (BY)
Romanée-St-Vivant Domaine de l'Arlot
1997 £66.83 (BY)
Romanée-St-Vivant Drouhin **1996** £60.12
(FA)
Romanée-St-Vivant Hudelot-Noëllat
1997 £77.50 (SOM) £93.33 (ARM)
Romanée-St-Vivant les Quatres Journaux,
Latour **1995** £68.15 (WY)
Romanée-St-Vivant les Quatres Journaux,
Latour **1989** £72.85 (WY) £77.55 (PEN)
Volnay Santenots Lafon **1983** £60.00
(CRO)
Vosne-Romanée les Brûlées, Méo-
Camuzet **1994** £62.00 (JU)
Vosne-Romanée Cros Parantoux, Méo-
Camuzet **1998** £77.75 (BODX)
Vougeot Clos de la Perrière, Bertagna
1978 £65.00 (CRO)

£80.00 → £99.99

Bonnes-Mares Dujac **1997** £85.95 (LAY)
Bonnes-Mares Groffier **1993** £80.00 (JER)
£99.88 (BODX)
Bonnes-Mares de Vogüé **1998** £97.33 (FA)
£99.88 (TUR)
Bonnes-Mares de Vogüé **1993** £88.13 (FA)
Chambertin Clos-de-Bèze, Drouhin **1976**
£99.88 (WY)
Chambertin Clos-de-Bèze, Faiveley **1997**
£80.17 (ARM)
Chambertin Clos-de-Bèze, Armand
Rousseau **1997** £90.00 (FORT)
Chambertin Armand Rousseau **1996**
£95.00 (FORT)
Chambolle-Musigny Ponnelle **1959**
£85.00 (YOU)
Clos de la Roche Vieilles Vignes, Ponsot
1998 £82.50 (YOU)
Clos de Vougeot Drouhin **1990** £91.65
(PEN)
Clos de Vougeot Faiveley **1978** £82.00
(CRO)
Clos de Vougeot Méo-Camuzet **1990**
£89.50 (FA)
Corton Bouchard Père **1966** £85.00 (YOU)
Corton Clos des Cortons, Faiveley **1978**
£88.00 (CRO)
Échézeaux Jayer-Gilles **1999** £89.01 (BODX)
Échézeaux Domaine de la Romanée-Conti
1997 £90.00 (FORT) £97.25 (LAY)
£111.63 (TUR) £185.00 (FRI)
Gevrey-Chambertin les Combottes,
Leroy **1997** £89.50 (FA)
Griotte-Chambertin Ponsot **1999** £98.31
(FA)
Latricières-Chambertin Leroy **1994**
£94.00 (FA)
Latricières-Chambertin Ponsot **1988**
£99.29 (FA)
Musigny Drouhin **1978** £95.00 (YOU)
Musigny Jadot **1999** £87.54 (FA)
Musigny Vieilles Vignes, de Vogüé **1989**
£99.29 (FA)
Nuits-St-Georges aux Boudots, Leroy
1997 £88.13 (FA)
Pommard les Épenots, Latour **1964**
£85.00 (YOU)
Pommard les Vignots, Leroy **1993** £89.50
(FA)
Richebourg Domaine Jean Grivot **1988**
£89.50 (FA)
Ruchottes-Chambertin Georges Roumier
1989 £95.37 (FA)

£100.00 → £149.99

Bonnes-Mares de Vogüé **1995** £118.87 (FA)

Chambertin Ponsot **1995** £129.25 (FA)

Chambertin Armand Rousseau **1993** £122.20 (FA)

Chambertin Armand Rousseau **1988** £145.00 (CRO)

Chambolle-Musigny les Amoureuses, de Vogüé **1995** £105.75 (FA)

Chambolle-Musigny les Amoureuses, de Vogüé **1989** £109.08 (FA)

Chambolle-Musigny les Charmes, Leroy **1996** £117.50 (FA)

Chambolle-Musigny les Charmes, Leroy **1995** £117.50 (FA)

Clos de la Roche Vieilles Vignes, Ponsot **1999** £116.91 (FA)

Clos de la Roche Vieilles Vignes, Ponsot **1995** £136.50 (FA)

Clos de Vougeot Leroy **1997** £143.35 (FA) £169.40 (LAY) £176.00 (JU)

Clos de Vougeot Leroy **1992** £138.45 (FA)

Clos de Vougeot Leroy **1989** £111.50 (ARM) £150.00 (JU) £232.65 (TW)

Clos de Vougeot Leroy **1988** £138.45 (FA) £140.00 (JU) £211.50 (TW)

Échézeaux Jayer-Gilles **1989** £146.88 (BODX)

Échézeaux Henri Jayer **1999** £131.11 (BODX)

Échézeaux Domaine de la Romanée-Conti **1996** £146.88 (WY) £152.75 (TUR)

Échézeaux Domaine de la Romanée-Conti **1995** £123.38 (BODX) £164.50 (TUR)

Échézeaux Domaine de la Romanée-Conti **1993** £111.63 (FA)

Échézeaux Domaine de la Romanée-Conti **1988** £146.88 (BODX)

Échézeaux Domaine de la Romanée-Conti **1982** £141.00 (TUR)

Échézeaux Domaine de la Romanée-Conti **1979** £146.88 (TUR)

Échézeaux Domaine de la Romanée-Conti **1976** £146.88 (TUR)

Échézeaux Domaine de la Romanée-Conti **1970** £129.25 (BODX)

Échézeaux Emmanuel Rouget **1999** £123.77 (BODX)

Échézeaux Emmanuel Rouget **1997** £117.89 (BODX)

Gevrey-Chambertin les Combottes, Leroy **1998** £107.08 (ARM)

Grands-Échézeaux Domaine de la Romanée-Conti **1995** £145.00 (FORT)

Musigny Vieilles Vignes, de Vogüé **1998** £126.70 (FA)

Musigny Vieilles Vignes, de Vogüé **1997** £133.56 (FA)

Musigny Vieilles Vignes, de Vogüé **1993** £148.25 (FA)

Richebourg Domaine Jean Grivot **1999** £133.56 (BODX)

Richebourg A-F Gros **1997** £110.00 (RES)

Romanée-St-Vivant Domaine de la Romanée-Conti **1994** £135.00 (FORT) £170.38 (TUR)

Romanée-St-Vivant Domaine de la Romanée-Conti **1986** £105.75 (FA) £217.38 (TUR)

Vosne-Romanée les Beaux Monts, Leroy **1996** £148.25 (FA)

Vosne-Romanée les Beaux Monts, Leroy **1989** £111.50 (ARM)

Vosne-Romanée les Brûlées, Méo-Camuzet **1999** £118.87 (BODX)

Vosne-Romanée les Brûlées, Méo-Camuzet **1995** £129.25 (FA)

Vosne-Romanée Cros Parantoux, Méo-Camuzet **1999** £142.37 (BODX)

Vosne-Romanée Cros Parantoux Emmanuel Rouget **1997** £146.88 (BODX)

£150.00 → £199.99

Clos de Vougeot Leroy **1996** £196.23 (FA) £207.00 (TUR) £220.50 (LAY)

Clos de Vougeot Leroy **1995** £191.53 (FA)

Échézeaux Domaine de la Romanée-Conti **1992** £164.50 (TUR)

Échézeaux Domaine de la Romanée-Conti **1972** £158.63 (TUR)

Grands-Échézeaux Domaine de la Romanée-Conti **1997** £159.02 (BODX) £160.49 (FA) £164.50 (TUR) £260.00 (FRI)

Grands-Échézeaux Domaine de la Romanée-Conti **1994** £188.00 (TUR)

Grands-Échézeaux Domaine de la Romanée-Conti **1993** £158.63 (FA) £176.25 (TUR)

Grands-Échézeaux Domaine de la Romanée-Conti **1992** £188.00 (TUR)

Grands-Échézeaux Domaine de la Romanée-Conti **1988** £176.25 (BODX) £185.00 (CRO)

Grands-Échézeaux Domaine de la Romanée-Conti **1982** £164.50 (TUR)

Musigny Vieilles Vignes, de Vogüé **1996** £166.20 (TW)

Musigny Vieilles Vignes, de Vogüé **1995** £177.62 (FA)

Nuits-St-Georges aux Boudots, Leroy **1995** £151.58 (FA)

Richebourg Méo-Camuzet **1997** £165.00 (TAN) £182.52 (FA)

Richebourg Méo-Camuzet **1994** £150.00 (FORT)

Richebourg Domaine de la Romanée-Conti **1994** £185.00 (FORT)

Richebourg Domaine de la Romanée-Conti **1993** £186.43 (BODX) £195.00 (BEN) £225.00 (FORT)

Richebourg Domaine de la Romanée-Conti **1982** £199.75 (TUR)

La Romanée Domaines du Château de Vosne-Romanée, Bouchard Père **1989** £170.00 (COC)

Romanée-St-Vivant Domaine de la Romanée-Conti **1997** £162.93 (BODX) £162.93 (FA) £188.00 (TUR) £215.00 (FORT)

Romanée-St-Vivant Domaine de la Romanée-Conti **1995** £153.14 (BODX) £171.55 (FA) £182.13 (TUR)

Romanée-St-Vivant Domaine de la Romanée-Conti **1993** £150.00 (BEN) £170.38 (TUR) £172.73 (FA)

Romanée-St-Vivant Domaine de la Romanée-Conti **1992** £176.25 (TUR)

Romanée-St-Vivant Domaine de la Romanée-Conti **1989** £182.13 (FA) £235.00 (TUR)

Romanée-St-Vivant Domaine de la Romanée-Conti **1988** £182.13 (FA) £188.00 (BODX)

Romanée-St-Vivant Domaine de la Romanée-Conti **1982** £176.25 (TUR)

Romanée-St-Vivant Domaine de la Romanée-Conti **1979** £176.25 (TUR)

£200.00 → £299.99

Bonnes-Mares d' Auvenay Leroy **1995** £264.38 (FA)

Chambertin Ponsot **1993** £259.68 (FA)

Chambertin Ponsot **1990** £246.16 (FA)

Clos de la Roche Vieilles Vignes, Ponsot **1993** £260.85 (FA)

Clos de la Roche Vieilles Vignes, Ponsot **1988** £216.79 (FA)

Échézeaux Henri Jayer **1993** £212.87 (FA)

Échézeaux Henri Jayer **1991** £211.50 (FA)

Échézeaux Henri Jayer **1986** £211.50 (FA)

Échézeaux Domaine de la Romanée-Conti **1980** £211.50 (TUR)

Grands-Échézeaux Domaine de la Romanée-Conti **1996** £205.63 (TUR)

Grands-Échézeaux Domaine de la Romanée-Conti **1989** £235.00 (TUR)

Grands-Échézeaux Domaine de la Romanée-Conti **1986** £217.38 (TUR)

Grands-Échézeaux Domaine de la Romanée-Conti **1983** £229.13 (TUR)

Grands-Échézeaux Domaine de la Romanée-Conti **1980** £293.75 (TUR)

Grands-Échézeaux Domaine de la Romanée-Conti **1979** £211.50 (TUR)

Grands-Échézeaux Domaine de la Romanée-Conti **1972** £217.38 (TUR)

Grands-Échézeaux Domaine de la Romanée-Conti **1964** £246.76 (TUR)

Grands-Échézeaux Domaine de la Romanée-Conti **1961** £229.13 (TUR)

Richebourg Méo-Camuzet **1999** £207.00 (BODX)

Richebourg Méo-Camuzet **1996** £235.00 (FA)

Richebourg Domaine de la Romanée-Conti **1997** £205.63 (TUR) £206.02 (BODX) £207.00 (FA) £225.00 (FORT) £425.00 (FRI)

Richebourg Domaine de la Romanée-
Conti **1996** £246.75 (TUR)
Richebourg Domaine de la Romanée-
Conti **1992** £211.50 (TUR)
Richebourg Domaine de la Romanée-
Conti **1991** £226.78 (TUR)
Richebourg Domaine de la Romanée-
Conti **1986** £235.00 (TUR)
Richebourg Domaine de la Romanée-
Conti **1983** £205.63 (FA)
Richebourg Domaine de la Romanée-
Conti **1979** £235.00 (TUR)
Richebourg Domaine de la Romanée-
Conti **1972** £235.00 (TUR)
La Romanée Domaines du Château de
Vosne-Romanée, Bouchard Père **1999**
£233.83 (BAL)
Romanée-St-Vivant Leroy **1997** £295.12
(FA)
Romanée-St-Vivant Domaine de la
Romanée-Conti **1996** £205.63 (TUR)
Romanée-St-Vivant Domaine de la
Romanée-Conti **1980** £293.75 (TUR)
Romanée-St-Vivant Domaine de la
Romanée-Conti **1972** £211.50 (TUR)
La Tâche Domaine de la Romanée-Conti
1997 £243.71 (BODX) £246.16 (FA)
£246.75 (TUR) £285.00 (FORT) £485.00
(FRI)
La Tâche Domaine de la Romanée-Conti
1995 £270.25 (BODX)
La Tâche Domaine de la Romanée-Conti
1994 £211.50 (TUR) £245.00 (FORT)
La Tâche Domaine de la Romanée-Conti
1993 £299.63 (TUR) £325.00 (FORT)
£375.95 (BEN)
La Tâche Domaine de la Romanée-Conti
1992 £202.50 (VIN) £258.50 (TUR)
La Tâche Domaine de la Romanée-Conti
1983 £247.50 (VIN) £299.63 (TUR)
La Tâche Domaine de la Romanée-Conti
1976 £293.75 (TUR)
La Tâche Domaine de la Romanée-Conti
1975 £217.38 (TUR)
La Tâche Domaine de la Romanée-Conti
1973 £211.50 (TUR)
La Tâche Domaine de la Romanée-Conti
1967 £235.00 (TUR)
Vosne-Romanée les Brûlées, Henri Jayer
1986 £211.50 (FA)

A key to name abbreviations
is available on page 7.

£300.00 → £499.99

Clos de la Roche Vieilles Vignes, Ponsot
1990 £314.70 (FA)
Clos de Vougeot Leroy **1993** £352.50 (FA)
Échézeaux Domaine de la Romanée-
Conti **1990** £329.00 (TUR)
Échézeaux Domaine de la Romanée-
Conti **1985** £334.88 (TUR)
Richebourg Leroy **1997** £314.70 (FA)
Richebourg Domaine de la Romanée-
Conti **1988** £305.50 (TUR)
Romanée-St-Vivant Leroy **1995** £493.50
(TUR) £530.12 (FA)
Romanée-St-Vivant Domaine de la
Romanée-Conti **1990** £412.62 (TUR)
La Tâche Domaine de la Romanée-Conti
1996 £314.70 (BODX) £317.25 (TUR)
La Tâche Domaine de la Romanée-Conti
1989 £346.63 (BODX) £411.25 (TUR)
La Tâche Domaine de la Romanée-Conti
1988 £411.25 (TUR)
La Tâche Domaine de la Romanée-Conti
1985 £450.00 (SOM) £763.75 (TUR)
Volnay Taillepieds, Marquis d'Angerville
1995 £364.10 (BODX)

Over £500.00

Clos de la Roche Ponsot **1996** £1,128.00
(TUR)
Clos de la Roche Ponsot **1995** £1,292.50
(TUR)
Richebourg Leroy **1995** £517.00 (TUR)
Richebourg Domaine de la Romanée-
Conti **1990** £646.25 (TUR)
Richebourg Domaine de la Romanée-
Conti **1978** £881.25 (TUR)
Romanée-Conti Domaine de la Romanée-
Conti **1997** £1,615.63 (TUR)
Romanée-Conti Domaine de la Romanée-
Conti **1996** £1,874.13 (TUR)
Romanée-Conti Domaine de la Romanée-
Conti **1994** £1,292.50 (BODX)
Romanée-Conti Domaine de la Romanée-
Conti **1992** £1,850.63 (TUR)
Romanée-Conti Domaine de la Romanée-
Conti **1990** £2,937.50 (TUR)
Romanée-Conti Domaine de la Romanée-
Conti **1985** £2,937.50 (TUR)
Romanée-Conti Domaine de la Romanée-
Conti **1980** £1,762.50 (TUR)
Romanée-Conti Domaine de la Romanée-
Conti **1978** £3,760.00 (TUR)
La Tâche Domaine de la Romanée-Conti
1990 £705.00 (TUR)

WHITE

Under £11.00

Hautes-Côtes de Nuits Clos du Vignon, Domaine Thévenot-le-Brun 1996 £10.95 (RES)

St-Aubin Prudhon 1998 £10.95 (JU)

St-Aubin la Pucelle, Roux 1998 £10.95 (WS)

St-Aubin Gerard Thomas 1997 £10.95 (CON)

St-Romain Gras 1997 £10.40 (TAN)

Santenay Clos des Champs des Carafe, Olivier Père et Fils 1996 £10.50 (HIG)

£11.00 → £11.99

Marsannay Bruno Clair 1996 £11.50 (JU)

St-Aubin Prudhon 1994 £11.95 (BALL)

St-Aubin Gerard Thomas 1996 £11.99 (BO)

St-Romain Buisson 1998 £11.16 (DOM)

£12.00 → £13.99

Auxey-Duresses Chartron et Trebuchet 1995 £12.95 (DI)

Auxey-Duresses Olivier Leflaive 1998 £13.95 (LAY)

Auxey-Duresses Michel Prunier 1998 £13.50 (TAN)

Chassagne-Montrachet Morey-Coffinet 1998 £13.65 (RAE)

Hautes-Côtes de Beaune Jayer-Gilles 1994 £12.50 (JU)

Marsannay Bruno Clair 1998 £13.25 (TAN)

Marsannay Bruno Clair 1997 £12.00 (JU)

Marsannay Jadot 1998 £12.49 (UN)

Marsannay Jadot 1997 £12.99 (VIC) £12.99 (THR) £12.99 (BOT) £12.99 (WR)

Pernand-Vergelesses Dubreuil-Fontaine 1997 £13.79 (BY)

Pernand-Vergelesses Jacques Germain 1995 £12.44 (WHI)

Pernand-Vergelesses Pavelot 1998 £13.95 (RES)

Pernand-Vergelesses Rollin 1999 £12.53 (RAE) £14.59 (BIB)

Pernand-Vergelesses Rollin 1991 £13.99 (RAE) £16.25 (BALL)

St-Aubin la Chatenière, Gerard Thomas 1999 £12.24 (MON)

St-Aubin Drouhin 1997 £12.95 (LEA) £16.00 (JU)

St-Aubin Frionnes, Hubert Lamy 1998 £12.87 (DOM) £14.95 (LEA)

St-Aubin les Murgers des Dents de Chien, Henri Prudhon 1997 £13.90 (JU)

St-Aubin la Pucelle, Lamy-Pillot 1998 £13.99 (BY) £14.99 (WR)

St-Romain Chartron et Trebuchet 1999 £13.75 (JER)

St-Romain Chartron et Trebuchet 1998 £12.99 (VIL)

St-Romain sous le Château, Coste-Caumartin 1998 £13.00 (GW)

St-Romain sous le Château, Coste-Caumartin 1995 £13.00 (JU)

Santenay le Biévaux, Olivier Père et Fils 1996 £12.50 (HIG)

Savigny-lès-Beaune Camus-Bruchon 1996 £13.99 (RAE)

Savigny-lès-Beaune Camus-Bruchon 1995 £13.65 (RAE)

Savigny-lès-Beaune Camus-Bruchon 1994 £13.99 (RAE)

Savigny-lès-Beaune Camus-Bruchon 1993 £13.75 (RAE)

£14.00 → £15.99

Auxey-Duresses Olivier Leflaive 1995 £14.00 (CRO)

Chassagne-Montrachet Guy Amiot 1999 £15.57 (BODX) £18.41 (BAL)

Chassagne-Montrachet Guy Amiot 1997 £15.08 (BODX)

Chassagne-Montrachet Jadot 1996 £15.99 (UN)

Hautes-Côtes de Beaune Jayer-Gilles 1996 £15.00 (JU)

Hautes-Côtes de Beaune Jayer-Gilles 1995 £15.00 (JU)

Pernand-Vergelesses Dubreuil-Fontaine 1998 £14.41 (BY)

Pernand-Vergelesses Jacques Germain 1998 £14.50 (AS)

Pernand-Vergelesses Rollin 1998 £15.35 (TAN)

Pernand-Vergelesses Rollin 1997 £14.95 (JU) £14.99 (RAE)

Pernand-Vergelesses Rollin 1996 £14.50 (RAE) £14.90 (JU)

Pernand-Vergelesses Rollin 1994 £15.50 (RAE)

Pernand-Vergelesses Rollin 1993 £14.95 (BALL)

Puligny-Montrachet Carillon 1998 £15.75 (SOM) £19.97 (BODX) £20.99 (YOU) £21.50 (BAN)

Puligny-Montrachet Chavy **1999** £15.66 (MON)

St-Aubin la Chatenière, Roux Père et Fils **1999** £14.59 (SAV)

St-Aubin Clos de la Chatenière, Hubert Lamy **1998** £15.22 (DOM) £16.95 (LEA)

St-Aubin Jadot **1997** £15.95 (VA)

St-Aubin les Murgers des Dents de Chien, Henri Prudhon **1996** £14.50 (JU)

St-Aubin en Remilly, Guy Amiot **1999** £15.57 (BODX)

St-Aubin en Remilly, Hubert Lamy **1998** £14.55 (LAY)

St-Aubin en Remilly, Château de Puligny-Montrachet **1999** £14.19 (BIB)

Santenay Blanc le St-Jean, Girardin **1999** £14.99 (POR) £16.65 (NI)

Santenay Blanc le St-Jean, Girardin **1998** £14.50 (TAN) £15.99 (UN)

Savigny-lès-Beaune Camus-Bruchon **1997** £14.50 (RAE)

Savigny-lès-Beaune les Vermots Dessus, Girardin **1999** £15.99 (POR)

£16.00 → £17.99

Chassagne-Montrachet F & L Pillot **1998** £16.95 (LEA)

Chassagne-Montrachet F & L Pillot **1997** £16.95 (LEA) £18.00 (BAC)

Hautes-Côtes de Beaune Jayer-Gilles **1997** £16.00 (JU)

Hautes-Côtes de Nuits Jayer-Gilles **1997** £16.00 (JU)

Hautes-Côtes de Nuits Jayer-Gilles **1996** £16.00 (JU)

Marsannay Bruno Clair **1993** £17.00 (CRO)

Meursault Clos du Cromin, Monnier **1997** £17.88 (BY)

Meursault Clos du Cromin, Monnier **1995** £17.75 (SUN)

Meursault Cuvée Charles Maxime, Latour-Giraud **1999** £16.84 (BIB)

Meursault Henri Germain **1998** £16.50 (TAN)

Meursault Henri Germain **1997** £17.95 (LEA)

Meursault Jadot **1996** £16.55 (FA)

Meursault Jadot **1995** £17.00 (CRO)

Nuits St-Georges Robert Chevillon **1995** £17.99 (YOU)

Pernand-Vergelesses les Caradeux, Chanson **1999** £16.99 (LLO)

Pernand-Vergelesses Île de Vergelesses, Domaine Chandon de Briailles **1999** £16.65 (MON)

Puligny-Montrachet les Charmes, Chavy **1999** £17.63 (MON) £19.00 (MV) £19.50 (BU)

Puligny-Montrachet les Charmes, Chavy **1997** £16.99 (SAF)

Puligny-Montrachet Clerc **1997** £16.95 (BAN)

St-Aubin la Chatenière, Chartron et Trébuchet **1998** £16.99 (VIL) £20.95 (DI)

St-Aubin Combe, Pierre Morey **1996** £17.00 (JU)

Savigny-lès-Beaune Montchenevoy, Javillier **1996** £16.95 (LAY)

Savigny-lès-Beaune Montchenevoy, Javillier **1993** £16.45 (BY)

£18.00 → £19.99

Chassagne-Montrachet Guy Amiot **1998** £19.00 (BODX) £22.50 (BAL) £24.50 (LEA)

Chassagne-Montrachet Bachelet **1995** £18.95 (BALL)

Chassagne-Montrachet Marc Colin **1997** £18.02 (BODX)

Chassagne-Montrachet les Macherelles, Guy Amiot **1997** £18.02 (BODX) £23.45 (SOM) £24.50 (LEA) £25.95 (DI)

Chassagne-Montrachet les Masures, J-N Gagnard **1998** £19.00 (FA)

Chassagne-Montrachet Morgeot, Gagnard-Delagrange **1999** £19.09 (MON)

Chassagne-Montrachet Niellon **1998** £19.97 (BODX) £20.95 (FA)

Chassagne-Montrachet J-M Pillot **1999** £18.11 (MON)

Marsannay Bruno Clair **1995** £19.50 (CRO)

Meursault Charmes, Brunet **1996** £18.00 (RIC)

Meursault Clos de la Barre, Monnier **1997** £18.29 (BY)

Meursault Clos du Cromin, Domaine Michelot **1996** £19.95 (BALL)

Meursault Clos du Cromin, Monnier **1998** £18.29 (BY)

Meursault Clos des Perrières, Albert Grivault **1993** £19.00 (FA)

- Wines are listed in A–Z order within each price band.
- For each wine, vintages are listed in descending order.
- Each vintage of any wine appears only once.

Meursault les Grands Charrons, Domaine Michelot **1995** £18.80 (FLE)

Meursault les Grands Charrons, Domaine Michelot **1993** £19.75 (BALL)

Meursault Lafarge **1998** £18.95 (CON) £20.65 (GAU) £22.99 (WIN)

Meursault les Meix Chavaux, Comte Armand **1996** £19.95 (LEA)

Meursault Monatine, Rougeot **1998** £18.75 (BAN)

Meursault les Narvaux, Girardin **1998** £19.99 (SUN) £25.95 (RES)

Meursault sous la Velle, Charles et Remi Jobard **1997** £19.95 (LEA)

Nuits St-Georges Robert Chevillon **1997** £19.00 (JU)

Pernand-Vergelesses les Caradeux, Chanson **1996** £19.95 (DI)

Puligny-Montrachet les Charmes, Chavy **1998** £19.50 (BAC)

Puligny-Montrachet Chavy **1998** £18.95 (MAY)

Puligny-Montrachet les Enseignères, Prudhon **1999** £18.44 (BIB)

St-Aubin Clos de la Chatenière, Hubert Lamy **1997** £19.99 (WIN)

St-Aubin Combe, Pierre Morey **1997** £18.90 (JU)

St-Aubin en Remilly, Hubert Lamy **1997** £19.99 (WIN)

Savigny-lès-Beaune les Vermots Dessus, Girardin **1998** £19.30 (NI)

£20.00 → £24.99

Chassagne-Montrachet la Boudriotte, Blain-Gagnard **1998** £24.25 (HAH)

Chassagne-Montrachet la Boudriotte, Gagnard-Delagrange **1999** £23.50 (MON)

Chassagne-Montrachet la Boudriotte, Gagnard-Delagrange **1998** £24.95 (HAH) £25.00 (ARM) £28.95 (BY)

Chassagne-Montrachet les Caillerets, Guy Amiot **1999** £24.38 (BODX) £27.42 (BAL)

Chassagne-Montrachet les Caillerets, Guy Amiot **1998** £23.40 (BODX) £29.75 (BAN) £31.00 (LEA)

Chassagne-Montrachet les Caillerets, J-N Gagnard **1998** £21.00 (JU) £30.75 (FA)

Chassagne-Montrachet les Caillerets, Morey-Coffinet **1999** £23.40 (RAE)

Chassagne-Montrachet les Champs Gains, Guy Amiot **1999** £20.46 (BODX) £24.09 (BAL)

Chassagne-Montrachet les Chenevottes, Colin-Deléger **1997** £23.89 (BODX)

Chassagne-Montrachet Clos St-Jean, Guy Amiot **1997** £22.91 (BODX) £27.00 (SOM)

Chassagne-Montrachet Clos St-Jean, Guy Amiot **1996** £24.38 (BODX)

Chassagne-Montrachet en Remilly, Colin-Deléger **1999** £24.87 (RAE)

Chassagne-Montrachet en Remilly, Colin-Deléger **1997** £24.38 (BODX)

Chassagne-Montrachet Fontaine-Gagnard **1997** £20.65 (SOM)

Chassagne-Montrachet les Houillères, Olivier Leflaive **1996** £24.90 (LAY)

Chassagne-Montrachet Latour **1997** £21.00 (PLAY)

Chassagne-Montrachet les Macherelles, Guy Amiot **1998** £24.50 (BAN) £28.50 (BAL)

Chassagne-Montrachet Morgeot, Gagnard-Delagrange **1997** £24.00 (BAN) £25.00 (ARM) £26.90 (BY)

Chassagne-Montrachet Morgeot, Gagnard-Delagrange **1996** £24.10 (HAH) £27.92 (BY)

Chassagne-Montrachet Morgeot, J-N Gagnard **1994** £22.91 (FA)

Chassagne-Montrachet J-M Pillot **1998** £21.95 (BER)

Chassagne-Montrachet en Pimont, Château de Chassagne-Montrachet **1998** £21.95 (FRI)

Chassagne-Montrachet Ramonet **1996** £23.89 (FA) £30.00 (FORT)

Chassagne-Montrachet Sauzet **1997** £21.93 (FA)

Chassagne-Montrachet Sauzet **1993** £20.95 (BALL)

Chassagne-Montrachet les Vergers, Colin-Deléger **1999** £24.87 (RAE)

Chassagne-Montrachet les Vergers, Colin-Deléger **1997** £24.38 (BODX) £30.89 (JON)

Chassagne-Montrachet Verget **1997** £23.49 (YOU) £27.50 (LEA)

Chassagne-Montrachet Vide-Bourse, F & L Pillot **1999** £23.49 (YOU)

Chassagne-Montrachet Vide-Bourse, F & L Pillot **1998** £24.50 (LEA)

Meursault en la Barre, François Jobard **1997** £23.00 (JU)

Meursault-Blagny, Latour **1997** £23.14 (WHI) £26.50 (STA)

Meursault-Blagny, Latour **1996** £24.50 (FORT)

Meursault-Blagny, Matrot **1992** £22.91 (BODX) £25.95 (CON)

Meursault-Blagny Thomas **1997** £21.95
(CON)
Meursault Chanson **1997** £21.10 (LLO)
Meursault Charmes, Henri Germain **1997**
£24.15 (TAN) £27.95 (LEA)
Meursault Charmes, Monnier **1996**
£20.25 (SOM)
Meursault Charmes, Pierre Boillot **1998**
£23.01 (SAV)
Meursault Chevalières, Charles et Remi
Jobard **1998** £24.50 (LEA)
Meursault Clos du Cromin, Domaine
Michelot **1997** £22.50 (BALL)
Meursault Darviot-Perrin **1998** £20.83
(ARM) £22.50 (MAY)
Meursault les Grands Charrons, Domaine
Michelot **1997** £22.95 (BALL)
Meursault Albert Grivault **1997** £24.00
(JU) £27.99 (WIN)
Meursault François Jobard **1995** £22.95
(RAE) £24.50 (BALL)
Meursault Latour **1997** £22.91 (PEN)
Meursault Limozin, Henri Germain **1997**
£22.95 (LEA)
Meursault les Luchets, Roulot **1998**
£22.08 (ARM) £23.50 (DOM)
Meursault Matrot **1998** £21.50 (CON)
£22.40 (GAU)
Meursault Matrot **1996** £22.95 (BALL)
Meursault les Meix Chavaux, Comte
Armand **1998** £20.95 (LEA)
Meursault les Meix Chavaux, Comte
Armand **1997** £21.95 (LEA)
Meursault les Meix Chavaux, Roulot
1998 £23.50 (DOM)
Meursault Domaine Michelot **1997**
£21.95 (STE)
Meursault les Narvaux, Girardin **1999**
£24.50 (NI)
Meursault les Narvaux, Girardin **1997**
£21.00 (JU)
Meursault Perrières, J-M Gaunoux **1997**
£22.45 (SOM) £32.00 (MAY)
Meursault Poruzots, François Jobard
1997 £24.87 (FA) £26.93 (SAV) £33.95
(RAE) £34.00 (JU)
Meursault Rougeots, Verget **1997** £22.91
(FA) £28.49 (YOU)

- All prices for each wine are listed
  together in ascending order.
- Price bands refer to the lowest price
  for which the wine is available.

Meursault Santenots, Marquis d'Angerville
1999 £23.50 (MON)
Meursault Santenots, Marquis d'Angerville
1998 £24.17 (ARM)
Meursault sous la Velle, Charles et Remi
Jobard **1998** £22.50 (LEA)
Meursault les Tillets, Javillier **1998** £21.00
(BAN)
Meursault Verget **1997** £23.49 (YOU)
Meursault les Vireuils, Dupont-Fahn **1998**
£24.75 (NI)
Meursault les Vireuils, Roulot **1998**
£22.08 (ARM)
Morey St-Denis Bruno Clair **1997** £23.00
(JU)
Morey-St-Denis Clos de Monts Luisants,
Ponsot **1996** £23.50 (TUR)
Puligny-Montrachet Jean-Marc Boillot **1999**
£20.95 (FA) £21.93 (BODX) £23.87 (RAE)
Puligny-Montrachet Carillon **1997** £20.07
(MON) £27.45 (STE)
Puligny-Montrachet Carillon **1996** £21.25
(FLE)
Puligny-Montrachet Champ Canet,
Carillon **1997** £22.45 (SOM) £40.55 (STE)
Puligny-Montrachet les Clavoillons, Chavy
1999 £20.56 (MON)
Puligny-Montrachet les Clavoillons, Chavy
1997 £22.50 (MAY)
Puligny-Montrachet Clos de la Mouchère,
Jean Boillot **1999** £24.97 (MON) £29.95
(LEA)
Puligny-Montrachet les Enseignères,
Prudhon **1996** £21.99 (JON)
Puligny-Montrachet les Folatières, Chavy
1999 £21.54 (MON) £24.00 (MV)
Puligny-Montrachet la Garenne, Thomas
1997 £21.95 (CON)
Puligny-Montrachet Latour **1995** £20.28
(COC)
Puligny-Montrachet Domaine Leflaive
1999 £24.87 (BODX)
Puligny-Montrachet Monnier **1997** £20.35
(BY)
Puligny-Montrachet Château de Puligny-
Montrachet **1999** £21.06 (BIB)
Puligny-Montrachet Sauzet **1998** £20.95
(BODX) £24.68 (DOM) £27.92 (BY) £28.75
(AD) £31.95 (RES)
Puligny-Montrachet sous le Puits, Verget
1998 £23.40 (FA) £33.50 (LEA)
Puligny-Montrachet sous le Puits, Bachelet
1997 £23.50 (RAE) £29.50 (BAL)
St-Aubin en Remilly, Guy Amiot **1998**
£22.95 (DI)

£25.00 → £29.99

Chassagne-Montrachet les Baudines, Bernard Morey 1998 £25.00 (BAN) £26.44 (DOM)

Chassagne-Montrachet les Caillerets, Guy Amiot 1997 £28.75 (SOM) £31.00 (LEA)

Chassagne-Montrachet les Caillerets, Morey-Coffinet 1998 £25.30 (RAE)

Chassagne-Montrachet les Caillerets, Morey-Coffinet 1997 £26.50 (RAE)

Chassagne-Montrachet les Champs Gains, Guy Amiot 1998 £27.95 (LEA)

Chassagne-Montrachet les Champs Gains, Guy Amiot 1996 £29.50 (LEA)

Chassagne-Montrachet Drouhin 1998 £28.75 (NI)

Chassagne-Montrachet Drouhin 1997 £26.00 (JU)

Chassagne-Montrachet les Embrazées, Bernard Morey 1998 £27.61 (DOM)

Chassagne-Montrachet en Remilly, Colin-Deléger 1998 £27.30 (LAY)

Chassagne-Montrachet Grandes, F & L Pillot 1998 £27.95 (LEA)

Chassagne-Montrachet Jadot 1997 £29.99 (BOT)

Chassagne-Montrachet Morgeot, Gagnard-Delagrange 1998 £25.00 (ARM) £27.92 (BY) £29.00 (JER)

Chassagne-Montrachet Morgeot, J-N Gagnard 1999 £29.77 (FA)

Chassagne-Montrachet Morgeot, Henri Germain 1998 £26.20 (TAN)

Chassagne-Montrachet Morgeot, Henri Germain 1997 £29.95 (LEA)

Chassagne-Montrachet Morgeot, Jadot 1999 £28.79 (FA)

Chassagne-Montrachet Morgeot Vieilles Vignes, Verget 1997 £29.38 (FA)

Chassagne-Montrachet Sauzet 1998 £25.87 (BY)

Chassagne-Montrachet Sauzet 1994 £26.50 (CRO)

Chassagne-Montrachet les Vergers, Colin-Deléger 1998 £27.99 (RAE)

Chassagne-Montrachet Verget 1998 £28.50 (LEA)

Chevalier-Montrachet Sauzet 1994 £26.40 (CRO)

Meursault en la Barre, François Jobard 1996 £25.00 (JU)

Meursault-Blagny, Jadot 1999 £27.81 (FA) £28.95 (POR)

Meursault-Blagny, Latour 1999 £26.25 (JER)

Meursault-Blagny, Matrot 1998 £27.50 (CON)

Meursault-Blagny, Matrot 1996 £28.50 (GAU) £29.50 (BALL)

Meursault-Blagny, Matrot 1994 £25.95 (CON) £30.00 (FORT)

Meursault-Blagny, Matrot 1993 £25.95 (CON)

Meursault Bouchard Père 1996 £26.99 (COC)

Meursault Charmes, Ampeau 1990 £29.00 (BAC)

Meursault Charmes, Darviot-Perrin 1998 £27.41 (RIP) £27.50 (ARM) £30.00 (MAY) £38.65 (TW)

Meursault Charmes, Henri Germain 1996 £29.95 (LEA)

Meursault Charmes, Jadot 1999 £28.79 (FA)

Meursault Charmes, Matrot 1998 £29.95 (CON) £31.45 (GAU)

Meursault Charmes, Monnier 1998 £27.92 (BY) £30.99 (WR)

Meursault les Clous, Javillier 1997 £25.65 (LAY)

Meursault Drouhin 1996 £28.50 (FORT)

Meursault Goutte d'Or, Latour 1999 £29.95 (POR)

Meursault Goutte d'Or, Latour 1996 £28.99 (JON)

Meursault François Jobard 1997 £27.95 (BER)

Meursault Limozin, Henri Germain 1996 £25.95 (LEA)

Meursault Pierre Morey 1998 £29.95 (RES) £31.00 (BY)

Meursault Pierre Morey 1997 £27.00 (JU)

Meursault les Narvaux, Pierre Morey 1993 £28.00 (CRO)

Meursault le Poruzot Dessus, Charles et Remi Jobard 1997 £29.95 (LEA)

Meursault Poruzots, Roux Père et Fils 1997 £27.50 (BEN)

Meursault Rougeots, Verget 1996 £29.? (FA)

Meursault Santenots, Marquis d'Anger 1997 £29.17 (ARM)

Meursault les Tessons Clos de Mon Plaisir, Roulot **1998** £26.67 (ARM) £29.38 (DOM)

Morey-St-Denis Clos de Monts Luisants, Ponsot **1998** £27.32 (BAL)

Nuits-St-Georges Clos de l'Arlot, Domaine de l'Arlot **1994** £29.71 (FLE)

Puligny-Montrachet Jean-Marc Boillot **1998** £27.50 (BALL) £27.50 (RAE)

Puligny-Montrachet Jean-Marc Boillot **1997** £26.50 (LEA) £29.50 (BALL)

Puligny-Montrachet Bouchard Père **1996** £29.89 (COC)

Puligny-Montrachet les Chalumeaux, Matrot **1995** £28.95 (BALL)

Puligny-Montrachet les Champs Gains, Michel Bouzereau **1999** £25.46 (MON)

Puligny-Montrachet les Champs Gains, Michel Bouzereau **1994** £28.20 (FLE)

Puligny-Montrachet Chartron et Trébuchet **1999** £27.50 (JER)

Puligny-Montrachet les Clavoillons, Chavy **1998** £25.00 (MAY)

Puligny-Montrachet Clerc **1998** £25.48 (FLE)

Puligny-Montrachet Clerc **1996** £29.50 (FRI)

Puligny-Montrachet Clos de la Mouchère, Jean Boillot **1996** £28.30 (BODX)

Puligny-Montrachet Drouhin **1998** £29.75 (NI)

Puligny-Montrachet Drouhin **1997** £27.00 (JU)

Puligny-Montrachet la Garenne, Sauzet **1998** £28.79 (BODX) £39.97 (BY)

Puligny-Montrachet Latour **1997** £25.26 (PEN)

Puligny-Montrachet Domaine Leflaive **1998** £26.25 (ARM) £34.00 (BAL)

Puligny-Montrachet Domaine Leflaive **1996** £29.99 (RAE)

Puligny-Montrachet Domaine Leflaive **1995** £26.74 (FLE)

Puligny-Montrachet les Levrons, Javillier **1998** £25.95 (LAY)

Puligny-Montrachet Sauzet **1997** £27.89 (JON) £27.92 (BY)

Puligny-Montrachet sous le Puits, Verget **1997** £26.83 (FA) £36.59 (YOU)

> ### Clarke's Wine Buying Guide
> is an annual publication.
> …come your suggestions for
> …xt year's edition.

£30.00 → £39.99

Beaune Clos des Mouches, Drouhin **1997** £34.00 (JU) £35.64 (FA) £45.00 (LEA)

Chassagne-Montrachet Blanchots Dessus, Darviot-Perrin **1998** £35.00 (ARM)

Chassagne-Montrachet la Boudriotte, Blain-Gagnard **1990** £38.00 (CRO)

Chassagne-Montrachet la Boudriotte, Ramonet **1996** £33.29 (TUR)

Chassagne-Montrachet les Caillerets, Guy Amiot **1996** £33.50 (LEA)

Chassagne-Montrachet les Caillerets, J-N Gagnard **1999** £30.75 (FA) £37.60 (BODX)

Chassagne-Montrachet les Caillerets, J-N Gagnard **1997** £38.00 (WS)

Chassagne-Montrachet les Caillerets, Jean-Marc Morey **1998** £32.56 (NO)

Chassagne-Montrachet les Caillerets, Ramonet **1996** £38.58 (FA)

Chassagne-Montrachet les Embrazées, Bernard Morey **1997** £32.89 (JON)

Chassagne-Montrachet Marquis de Laguiche, Drouhin **1997** £38.00 (WS) £38.00 (JU) £42.00 (LEA)

Chassagne-Montrachet Marquis de Laguiche, Drouhin **1996** £36.50 (BEN) £42.00 (LEA)

Chassagne-Montrachet Morgeot, Blain-Gagnard **1996** £36.23 (BY)

Chassagne-Montrachet Morgeot, J-N Gagnard **1997** £32.00 (JU)

Chassagne-Montrachet Morgeot, Jadot **1998** £38.08 (ARM)

Chassagne-Montrachet Morgeot, Ramonet **1996** £30.75 (FA)

Chassagne-Montrachet Morgeot Vieilles Vignes, Verget **1996** £33.68 (FA)

Chassagne-Montrachet Remilly, Verget **1997** £30.75 (FA) £45.00 (LEA)

Chassagne-Montrachet Sauzet **1995** £33.00 (CRO)

Chassagne-Montrachet les Vergers, J-M Pillot **1998** £34.95 (RES)

Chassagne-Montrachet les Vergers, Ramonet **1996** £30.75 (FA)

Chevalier-Montrachet Sauzet **1995** £33.00 (CRO)

Corton Domaine Chandon de Briailles **1999** £31.33 (MON)

Corton Domaine Chandon de Briailles **1998** £37.95 (LEA)

Corton Domaine Chandon de Briailles **1997** £39.60 (TAN) £45.00 (LEA)

Corton-Charlemagne Bonneau du
Martray 1993 £32.90 (FA) £64.63 (WY)

Corton-Charlemagne Domaine Chandon
de Briailles 1999 £36.72 (MON)

Corton-Charlemagne Dubreuil-Fontaine
1997 £37.14 (BY)

Corton-Charlemagne Labouré-Roi 1997
£36.67 (MI)

Corton-Charlemagne Latour 1999
£37.11 (TUR)

Corton-Charlemagne Latour 1998
£30.26 (FA) £35.25 (WY)

Corton-Charlemagne Latour 1997
£38.58 (FA) £38.78 (WY) £39.95 (PEN)
£39.99 (MAJ) £45.99 (JON) £49.20 (HIC)

Corton-Charlemagne Rollin 1999 £35.45
(RAE) £42.10 (BIB)

Corton-Charlemagne Rollin 1996 £39.00
(RAE) £60.00 (JU)

Meursault-Blagny, Jadot 1995 £34.99 (VIC)
£34.99 (THR) £34.99 (BOT)

Meursault Blagny, François Jobard 1998
£34.99 (RAE)

Meursault Blagny, François Jobard 1997
£33.95 (RAE)

Meursault Charmes, Charles et Remi
Jobard 1999 £32.21 (RAE)

Meursault Charmes, Charles et Remi
Jobard 1998 £35.00 (LEA)

Meursault Charmes, Matrot 1997 £31.45
(GAU) £33.95 (BALL)

Meursault Charmes, Domaine Michelot
1999 £30.50 (JER)

Meursault Charmes, Rougeot 1998
£31.50 (BAN)

Meursault Genevrières, Charles et Remi
Jobard 1998 £33.50 (LEA)

Meursault Genevrières, François Jobard
1999 £32.21 (RAE)

Meursault Genevrières, François Jobard
1998 £34.99 (RAE)

Meursault Genevrières, François Jobard
1997 £34.00 (JU)

Meursault Genevrières, Domaine
Michelot 1999 £33.29 (BIB)

Meursault Genevrières, Domaine
Michelot 1997 £35.95 (BALL)

Meursault Limozin, Henri Germain 1992
£35.00 (CRO)

Meursault Perrières, Chanson 1998
£32.49 (LLO)

Meursault Perrières, Darviot-Perrin 1998
£30.83 (ARM) £33.50 (MAY)

Meursault Perrières, J-M Gaunoux 1998
£31.50 (MAY)

Meursault Perrières, Albert Grivault
1997 £35.00 (JU)

Meursault Perrières, Albert Grivault
1988 £39.00 (YOU)

Meursault Perrières, Domaine Michelot
1997 £39.95 (RES)

Meursault le Poruzot Dessus, Charles et
Remi Jobard 1998 £31.00 (LEA)

Meursault Poruzots, François Jobard
1999 £32.21 (RAE)

Meursault Poruzots, François Jobard
1996 £35.00 (JU)

Meursault Rougeots, Verget 1995 £30.75
(FA)

Meursault les Tessons, Pierre Morey
1997 £33.00 (JU) £34.06 (BY) £38.95
(RES)

Puligny-Montrachet Jean-Marc Boillot
1994 £30.95 (BALL)

Puligny-Montrachet les Chalumeaux,
Matrot 1996 £31.50 (CON)

Puligny-Montrachet Champ Canet, Carillon
1998 £30.26 (BODX) £33.29 (MON)

Puligny-Montrachet Champ Canet, Sauzet
1998 £34.17 (BODX) £41.13 (DOM)

Puligny-Montrachet Champ Canet, Sauzet
1997 £33.19 (BODX) £36.62 (FA)

Puligny-Montrachet Clavoillons, Domaine Leflaive **1999** £37.60 (BODX)

Puligny-Montrachet Clavoillons, Domaine Leflaive **1998** £34.58 (ARM) £34.66 (TUR) £39.50 (TAN) £42.99 (JON) £43.59 (CB)

Puligny-Montrachet Clavoillons, Domaine Leflaive **1997** £36.62 (FA) £41.50 (RAE)

Puligny-Montrachet Clavoillons, Domaine Leflaive **1996** £38.58 (FA)

Puligny-Montrachet Clos de la Mouchère, Jean Boillot **1997** £35.95 (LEA)

Puligny-Montrachet les Combettes, Clerc **1999** £37.50 (FRI)

Puligny-Montrachet les Combettes, Sauzet **1997** £36.62 (BODX) £37.11 (FA) £54.40 (HAH)

Puligny-Montrachet les Demoiselles, Guy Amiot **1999** £36.13 (BODX)

Puligny-Montrachet les Demoiselles, Guy Amiot **1998** £38.58 (BODX)

Puligny-Montrachet les Folatières, Chartron **1997** £35.00 (BAN)

Puligny-Montrachet les Folatières, Clerc **1999** £38.00 (FRI)

Puligny-Montrachet les Folatières, Drouhin **1997** £36.00 (WS) £38.00 (JU) £39.95 (LEA)

Puligny-Montrachet les Folatières, Drouhin **1988** £38.78 (WY)

Puligny-Montrachet les Folatières, Jadot **1999** £31.73 (FA)

Puligny-Montrachet les Folatières, Latour **1995** £35.25 (WY)

Puligny-Montrachet les Folatières, Sauzet **1998** £35.25 (BODX)

Puligny-Montrachet Clos de la Garenne, Drouhin **1992** £35.25 (WY)

Puligny-Montrachet Clos de la Garenne, Drouhin **1988** £38.78 (WY)

Puligny-Montrachet la Garenne, Sauzet **1997** £30.75 (FA) £41.13 (DOM)

Puligny-Montrachet Domaine Leflaive **1997** £30.50 (RAE)

Puligny-Montrachet Domaine Leflaive **1994** £33.06 (PLAY)

Puligny-Montrachet Olivier Leflaive **1998** £34.66 (TW)

Puligny-Montrachet les Perrières, Carillon **1998** £30.26 (BODX)

Puligny-Montrachet les Perrières, Sauzet **1998** £30.26 (BODX) £39.97 (BY)

Puligny-Montrachet les Perrières, Sauzet **1997** £36.62 (FA) £39.00 (JU) £39.97 (BY)

Puligny-Montrachet les Perrières, Sauzet **1993** £39.50 (BALL)

Puligny-Montrachet les Referts, Carillon **1998** £33.80 (LAY) £44.00 (FORT)

Puligny-Montrachet les Referts, Sauzet **1998** £30.26 (BODX) £39.97 (BY)

Puligny-Montrachet les Referts, Sauzet **1997** £30.75 (FA) £43.20 (TAN)

Puligny-Montrachet les Referts, Sauzet **1995** £39.00 (FRI)

Puligny-Montrachet sous le Puits, Verget **1996** £30.75 (FA)

Puligny-Montrachet la Truffière, Colin-Deléger **1997** £36.13 (BODX)

£40.00 → £49.99

Bâtard-Montrachet Blain-Gagnard **1998** £48.75 (HAH)

Bâtard-Montrachet Blain-Gagnard **1997** £45.42 (ARM)

Bâtard-Montrachet Fontaine-Gagnard **1996** £46.50 (SOM)

Beaune Clos des Mouches, Drouhin **1998** £41.50 (NI) £60.00 (FORT)

Beaune Clos des Mouches, Drouhin **1993** £43.50 (BEN)

Bienvenues-Bâtard-Montrachet Bachelet **1997** £48.50 (RAE) £57.00 (BAL)

Chassagne-Montrachet les Caillerets, J-N Gagnard **1990** £42.50 (FA)

Corton Domaine Chandon de Briailles **1996** £49.00 (LEA)

Corton-Charlemagne Bonneau du Martray **1999** £46.41 (BAL)

Corton-Charlemagne Bonneau du Martray **1998** £42.99 (RAE) £44.94 (BODX) £49.50 (LEA)

Corton-Charlemagne Bonneau du Martray **1995** £48.38 (FA) £50.00 (WS)

Corton-Charlemagne Domaine Chandon de Briailles **1998** £45.00 (LEA)

Corton-Charlemagne Bruno Clair **1997** £46.00 (JU)

Corton-Charlemagne Dubreuil-Fontaine **1998** £40.21 (BY)

Corton-Charlemagne Jadot **1999** £46.41 (FA)

Corton-Charlemagne Juillot **1998** £45.83 (DOM)

Corton-Charlemagne Latour **1995** £44.86 (COC) £69.33 (WY)

Corton-Charlemagne Olivier Leflaive **1997** £43.12 (CB)

Corton-Charlemagne Rollin **1997** £41.50 (RAE) £47.25 (TAN) £48.00 (JU)

Corton-Charlemagne Rollin **1989** £45.00 (BALL)

Meursault Charmes, Pierre Morey **1997**
£42.00 (JU) £45.95 (RES)

Meursault Clos des Perrières, Albert
Grivault **1997** £45.00 (JU) £66.95 (WIN)

Meursault Clos des Perrières, Albert
Grivault **1990** £45.43 (FA)

Meursault Genevrières, Pierre Morey
1998 £41.85 (BY)

Meursault Genevrières, Pierre Morey
1997 £42.00 (JU)

Meursault Lafon **1998** £47.50 (BEN)

Meursault Lafon **1997** £48.95 (BEN)
£58.16 (FA)

Meursault Perrières, Chanson **1995**
£42.95 (DI)

Meursault les Perrières, Pierre Morey
1996 £48.00 (WS)

Puligny-Montrachet Champ Canet, Sauzet
1994 £46.00 (CRO)

Puligny-Montrachet les Combettes,
Domaine Leflaive **1998** £47.00 (TUR)

Puligny-Montrachet les Combettes,
Sauzet **1998** £40.05 (BODX) £47.00
(DOM)

Puligny-Montrachet les Combettes,
Sauzet **1996** £48.38 (FA)

Puligny-Montrachet les Demoiselles, Guy
Amiot **1997** £42.00 (LEA)

Puligny-Montrachet les Folatières,
Drouhin **1993** £42.30 (WY)

Puligny-Montrachet les Folatières, Jadot
1996 £43.08 (WY)

Puligny-Montrachet les Folatières,
Domaine Leflaive **1998** £44.45 (FA)
£47.00 (TUR) £51.50 (BALL)

Puligny-Montrachet les Folatières,
Domaine Leflaive **1994** £44.45 (FA)
£49.50 (FRI)

Puligny-Montrachet les Folatières, Sauzet
1996 £41.13 (FA)

Puligny-Montrachet Domaine Leflaive
1993 £42.50 (FRI)

Puligny-Montrachet les Perrières, Carillon
1997 £40.95 (STE)

Puligny-Montrachet la Truffière, Jean-
Marc Boillot **1999** £42.99 (BODX)

£50.00 → £69.99

Bâtard-Montrachet Gagnard-Delagrange
1999 £51.41 (MON)

Bâtard-Montrachet Gagnard-Delagrange
1998 £54.00 (BAN) £57.50 (HAH) £69.91
(BY)

Bâtard-Montrachet J-N Gagnard **1998**
£69.91 (FA)

Bâtard-Montrachet Latour **1996** £68.05
(WY)

Chassagne-Montrachet Marquis de
Laguiche, Drouhin **1989** £58.75 (WY)

Chassagne-Montrachet Marquis de
Laguiche, Drouhin **1988** £68.15 (WY)

Chassagne-Montrachet les Ruchottes,
Ramonet **1996** £54.05 (TUR)

Corton-Charlemagne Bonneau du
Martray **1996** £65.99 (YOU) £68.50
(BEN) £70.00 (JU)

Corton-Charlemagne Bonneau du
Martray **1985** £56.40 (WY)

Corton-Charlemagne Bouchard Père
1999 £56.60 (BAL)

Corton-Charlemagne Bouchard Père
1996 £60.00 (COC)

Corton-Charlemagne Jadot **1998** £58.17
(ARM)

Corton-Charlemagne Latour **1996**
£51.00 (STA) £51.08 (PLAY) £55.23 (FA)
£58.75 (WY)

Corton-Charlemagne Latour **1991**
£68.15 (WY)

Corton-Charlemagne Michel Voarick
1992 £58.75 (WY)

Criots-Bâtard-Montrachet Olivier Leflaive
1997 £67.80 (CB)

Meursault Clos de la Barre, Lafon **1998**
£55.00 (BEN)

Meursault Lafon **1996** £59.50 (BEN)

le Montrachet Thénard **1997** £67.95 (FA)

Puligny-Montrachet les Combettes, Clerc
1995 £58.75 (FA)

Puligny-Montrachet les Combettes,
Domaine Leflaive **1996** £63.65 (CB)
£66.00 (FA)

Puligny-Montrachet les Folatières,
Domaine Leflaive **1999** £55.22 (BODX)

Puligny-Montrachet les Folatières,
Domaine Leflaive **1996** £52.50 (BALL)
£63.06 (FA) £64.63 (TUR)

Puligny-Montrachet les Folatières,
Domaine Leflaive **1995** £54.05 (FA)

Puligny-Montrachet les Folatières, Sauzet
1999 £52.50 (JER)

Puligny-Montrachet les Pucelles, Domaine
Leflaive **1999** £62.57 (BODX)

Puligny-Montrachet les Pucelles, Domaine
Leflaive **1998** £52.29 (TUR) £56.25
(ARM) £63.45 (CB)

Puligny-Montrachet les Pucelles, Domaine
Leflaive **1997** £66.50 (LAY)

Puligny-Montrachet les Referts, Carillon
1996 £55.00 (FORT)

£70.00 → £99.99

Bâtard-Montrachet Jean-Marc Boillot
1999 £87.54 (BODX)

Bâtard-Montrachet Jean-Marc Boillot
1997 £88.13 (BODX)

Bâtard-Montrachet Jean-Marc Boillot
1996 £91.94 (BODX)

Bâtard-Montrachet Clerc **1998** £89.00
(FRI)

Bâtard-Montrachet J-N Gagnard **1999**
£74.81 (FA) £86.07 (BODX)

Bâtard-Montrachet J-N Gagnard **1997**
£79.00 (JU)

Bâtard-Montrachet J-N Gagnard **1992**
£99.29 (FA)

Bâtard-Montrachet Latour **1995** £78.00
(STA) £78.73 (PEN)

Bâtard-Montrachet Latour **1988** £85.50
(VIN)

Bâtard-Montrachet Latour **1981** £82.25
(WY)

Bâtard-Montrachet Domaine Leflaive
1998 £87.54 (FA) £89.58 (ARM) £103.81
(CB)

Bâtard-Montrachet Domaine Leflaive
1997 £90.47 (BODX) £99.00 (JU)
£103.80 (LAY)

Bâtard-Montrachet Domaine Leflaive
1993 £71.87 (FA)

Bâtard-Montrachet Pierre Morey **1997**
£94.50 (TAN)

Bâtard-Montrachet Ramonet **1997**
£89.50 (FA)

Bâtard-Montrachet Sauzet **1998** £77.75
(BODX) £92.83 (DOM)

Bâtard-Montrachet Sauzet **1997** £79.70
(FA)

Bienvenues-Bâtard-Montrachet Carillon
1998 £80.19 (BODX)

Bienvenues-Bâtard-Montrachet Carillon
1997 £76.38 (BODX)

Bienvenues-Bâtard-Montrachet Clerc
1999 £95.00 (FRI)

Bienvenues-Bâtard-Montrachet Domaine
Leflaive **1998** £84.58 (ARM) £90.00 (JU)

Bienvenues-Bâtard-Montrachet Domaine
Leflaive **1997** £91.45 (FA) £92.30 (TAN)
£95.00 (JU)

Chevalier-Montrachet Bouchard Père
1995 £79.00 (COC)

Chevalier-Montrachet Bouchard Père
1990 £79.90 (COC)

Chevalier-Montrachet Colin-Deléger
1999 £92.43 (FA)

Chevalier-Montrachet les Desmoiselles,
Latour **1997** £74.81 (FA)

Chevalier-Montrachet les Desmoiselles,
Latour **1996** £94.39 (FA) £100.00 (FORT)

Chevalier-Montrachet les Desmoiselles,
Latour **1995** £99.88 (WY)

Chevalier-Montrachet les Desmoiselles,
Latour **1994** £84.60 (PEN)

Chevalier-Montrachet Domaine Leflaive
1993 £89.50 (FA) £100.00 (FORT)

Chevalier-Montrachet Olivier Leflaive
1995 £82.26 (WY)

Chevalier-Montrachet Sauzet **1998**
£88.13 (BODX)

Chevalier-Montrachet Sauzet **1997**
£94.00 (BODX) £104.18 (FA) £120.00 (JU)

Corton-Charlemagne Drouhin **1985**
£99.88 (WY)

Corton-Charlemagne Jadot **1996** £80.00
(FORT)

Corton-Charlemagne, Verget **1997**
£77.20 (LAY) £77.75 (FA)

Corton-Charlemagne, Verget **1996**
£95.37 (FA)

Criots-Bâtard-Montrachet Olivier Leflaive
1995 £70.50 (WY)

Meursault Charmes, Lafon **1998** £78.00
(BEN)

Meursault Charmes, Lafon **1994** £88.13
(FA)

Meursault Clos de la Barre, Lafon **1997**
£77.55 (TUR) £77.75 (FA)

Meursault Clos de la Barre, Lafon **1996**
£94.00 (FA)

Meursault Clos de la Barre, Lafon **1995**
£89.50 (FA)

Meursault Perrières, Lafon **1998** £88.00
(BEN)

Meursault Rougeots, Coche-Dury **1998**
£88.13 (FA)

le Montrachet Bouchard Père **1997**
£89.50 (FA) £218.00 (COC)

le Montrachet Marquis de Laguiche,
Drouhin **1991** £98.00 (NI)

le Montrachet Latour **1998** £99.88 (PEN)

Puligny-Montrachet Domaine Leflaive **1989** £76.38 (WY)

Puligny-Montrachet les Pucelles, Domaine Leflaive **1994** £70.00 (FORT)

Puligny-Montrachet les Pucelles, Domaine Leflaive **1993** £76.38 (WY) £80.00 (BAL)

Puligny-Montrachet les Pucelles, Domaine Leflaive **1989** £90.00 (BAL)

Puligny-Montrachet les Pucelles, Domaine Leflaive **1988** £95.00 (BAL)

Puligny-Montrachet les Pucelles, Domaine Leflaive **1986** £95.00 (BAL)

£100.00 → £199.99

Bâtard-Montrachet Bouchard Père **1997** £110.00 (COC)

Bâtard-Montrachet Clerc **1999** £105.00 (FRI)

Bâtard-Montrachet Drouhin **1997** £129.00 (LEA)

Bâtard-Montrachet Latour **1986** £111.63 (WY)

Bâtard-Montrachet Domaine Leflaive **1999** £109.08 (BODX)

Bienvenues-Bâtard-Montrachet Domaine Leflaive **1999** £106.14 (BODX)

Chevalier-Montrachet Bouchard Père **1997** £118.00 (COC)

Chevalier-Montrachet Domaine Henri Clerc **1999** £110.00 (FRI)

Chevalier-Montrachet les Desmoiselles, Latour **1990** £135.13 (WY)

Chevalier-Montrachet Domaine Leflaive **1999** £148.25 (BODX)

Chevalier-Montrachet Domaine Leflaive **1998** £111.04 (FA)

Chevalier-Montrachet Domaine Leflaive **1997** £117.50 (FA) £135.18 (CB)

Chevalier-Montrachet Domaine Leflaive **1986** £176.25 (FA)

Corton-Charlemagne Drouhin **1989** £111.63 (WY)

Corton-Charlemagne Latour **1990** £129.25 (WY)

Corton-Charlemagne Latour **1978** £129.25 (WY)

Meursault Charmes, Lafon **1996** £148.25 (FA)

Meursault Charmes, Lafon **1995** £146.88 (FA)

Meursault Charmes, Lafon **1989** £146.88 (FA)

Meursault Clos de la Barre, Lafon **1990** £107.12 (FA)

Meursault Perrières, Lafon **1996** £177.62 (FA)

Meursault Perrières, Lafon **1995** £176.25 (FA)

le Montrachet Guy Amiot **1999** £158.63 (BAL)

le Montrachet Bouchard Père **1993** £110.00 (CRO)

le Montrachet Gagnard-Delagrange **1999** £112.60 (MON)

le Montrachet Marquis de Laguiche, Drouhin **1997** £113.98 (FA) £185.00 (FORT)

le Montrachet Marquis de Laguiche, Drouhin **1996** £170.00 (BEN)

le Montrachet Marquis de Laguiche, Drouhin **1987** £197.40 (TW)

le Montrachet Latour **1999** £126.21 (TUR)

le Montrachet Latour **1991** £117.50 (WY) £124.55 (PEN)

le Montrachet Sauzet **1999** £182.52 (FA)

le Montrachet Sauzet **1998** £146.88 (BODX) £229.13 (DOM)

le Montrachet Sauzet **1997** £160.00 (FA)

le Montrachet Sauzet **1994** £105.75 (FA) £110.00 (JU)

Musigny Comte de Vogüé **1987** £129.25 (TW)

£200.00 → £499.99

Corton-Charlemagne Coche-Dury **1998** £470.00 (FA)

le Montrachet Bouchard Père **1999** £201.51 (BAL)

le Montrachet Bouchard Père **1995** £218.00 (COC)

le Montrachet Lafon **1994** £375.00 (FORT)

le Montrachet Lafon **1993** £293.75 (TUR)

le Montrachet Domaine Leflaive **1998** £381.88 (FA)

le Montrachet Prieur **1997** £210.00 (YOU)

Over £500.00

le Montrachet Domaine Leflaive **1996** £616.88 (FA)

le Montrachet Domaine de la Romanée-Conti **1997** £646.25 (BODX)

le Montrachet Domaine de la Romanée-Conti **1996** £843.45 (TUR)

le Montrachet Domaine de la Romanée-Conti **1995** £843.45 (TUR)

le Montrachet Domaine de la Romanée-Conti **1986** £940.00 (TW)

le Montrachet Domaine de la Romanée-Conti **1972** £528.75 (TUR)

MÂCONNAIS PRICES

RED

Under £9.00

Mâcon la Roche Vineuse, Merlin 1999
£8.00 (MV)
Mâcon Rouge Bussières, Domaine de la
Sarazinière 1999 £6.99 (DOM)

WHITE

Under £6.00

Mâcon-Lugny Eugène Blanc, Cave de
Lugny 1997 £4.75 (SOM)
Mâcon-Lugny les Charmes, Cave de Lugny
1997 £5.99 (UN)
Mâcon-Villages Rodet 2000 £5.50 (MAR)

£6.00 → £6.99

Mâcon-Azé Domaine de Rochebin 2000
£6.07 (BIB)
Mâcon Chardonnay Talmard 2000 £6.55
(TAN) £6.75 (HAH) £6.99 (JON)
Mâcon Chardonnay Talmard 1999 £6.99
(POR)
Mâcon Chardonnay Talmard 1998 £6.50
(BALL)
Mâcon-Lugny les Charmes, Cave de Lugny
2000 £6.84 (LLO)
Mâcon-Lugny les Genièvres, Latour 1999
£6.49 (POR) £6.90 (TAN) £7.04 (PLA)
£7.15 (BEN) £7.35 (STA) £8.70 (COC)
Mâcon-Lugny les Genièvres, Latour 1998
£6.18 (PEN) £6.69 (WHI) £7.76 (HIC)
£7.87 (VIN) £7.95 (FORT) £8.99 (GN)
Mâcon-Lugny les Genièvres, Latour 1997
£6.69 (WHI) £7.50 (HIG) £7.50 (BALL)
Mâcon-Prissé Cave Co-op de Prissé 1999
£6.35 (HAH) £7.05 (HAW)
Mâcon-Uchizy Talmard 1999 £6.90 (JU)
£6.99 (BAL) £8.53 (PLAY)
Mâcon-Villages Cave de Lugny 1998
£6.25 (FRI) £6.50 (BU)
Mâcon-Villages Domaine des Teppes de
Chatennay 1998 £6.95 (CON)
Mâcon-Vinzelles Cave des Grands Crus
Blancs 1999 £6.95 (LEA) £7.15 (HAW)
St-Véran Domaine des Deux Roches
1999 £6.99 (BO) £7.70 (HAH) £7.99 (UN)
St-Véran Domaine St-Martin, Duboeuf
1998 £6.99 (NEZ)

£7.00 → £7.99

Mâcon-Clessé Michel 1997 £7.95 (RAE)
Mâcon-Lugny les Charmes, Cave de Lugny
1998 £7.25 (FRI)
Mâcon-Uchizy Talmard 2000 £7.45 (STE)
St-Véran en Creches, Jacques Saumaize
1999 £7.50 (WS) £8.07 (RAE)
St-Véran Caves des Grands Crus 1999
£7.39 (PLA) £7.55 (HAW)
St-Véran Domaine des Valanges, Paquet
2000 £7.99 (GW) £8.32 (BIB)
St-Véran Domaine des Valanges, Paquet
1998 £7.50 (BALL)

£8.00 → £9.99

Mâcon-Davaye Domaine des Maillettes,
Saumaize 1999 £8.60 (JER)
Mâcon Montbellet, Goyard 1998 £9.99
(BO) £11.26 (BIB) £11.99 (JON)
Mâcon la Roche Vineuse, Merlin 1998
£8.40 (MV)
Mâcon-Villages Tête de Cuvée, Verget
1998 £8.95 (LEA)
Mâcon-Viré Cuvée Spéciale, Bonhomme
1998 £8.81 (DOM)
Pouilly-Loché Domaine des Duc 1998
£9.10 (HAW)
Pouilly-Loché Cave des Grands Crus
Blancs 1998 £8.55 (HAW)
Pouilly-Vinzelles Blanc Cave des Grands
Crus 1999 £8.21 (PLA)
Pouilly-Vinzelles Jean-Jacques Martin
1999 £9.45 (HAW)
Pouilly-Vinzelles Château de Pouilly-
Vinzelles, Loron 1996 £8.92 (PEN)
St-Véran Domaine de la Collonge, Noblet
1999 £8.35 (LAY)
St-Véran Corsin 1999 £9.55 (GN)
St-Véran en Crèches, Daniel Barraud
1999 £8.95 (LEA)
St-Véran Domaine des Deux Roches 1998
£9.49 (VIC) £9.49 (THR) £9.49 (BOT)
St-Véran Drouhin 1998 £8.23 (PEN)
St-Véran Château Fuissé, Vincent 1998
£8.52 (DOM) £9.50 (RES)
St-Véran Jadot 1999 £9.75 (VA)
St-Véran Domaine des Valanges, Paquet
1999 £9.20 (NI)
St-Véran Verget 1999 £8.95 (LEA)
Viré-Clessé Chaland 1999 £8.55 (HAW)
Viré-Clessé Signoret 1999 £8.40 (HAW)

£10.00 → £12.49

Mâcon-Solutré Clos des Bertillonnes,
   Denogent 1998 £10.35 (GAU)
Mâcon-Viré Domaine Emilian Gillet,
   Thévenet 1998 £11.95 (SAV) £13.95 (LEA)
Mâcon-Viré Goyard 1997 £11.50 (JU)
Pouilly-Fuissé Domaine Béranger,
   Duboeuf 1998 £11.49 (NEZ)
Pouilly-Fuissé les Brûlés, Château Fuissé
   1997 £12.00 (CRO)
Pouilly-Fuissé Domaine de la Collonge
   1998 £11.75 (LAY)
Pouilly-Fuissé Corsin 1999 £12.45 (STE)
Pouilly-Fuissé Latour 1998 £11.46 (COC)
   £14.62 (PLAY)
Pouilly-Fuissé Manciat-Poncet 1998
   £11.90 (HAW)
Pouilly-Fuissé Pascal Renaud 1999 £10.95
   (CON)
Pouilly-Fuissé la Roche, Manciat-Poncet
   1997 £10.95 (JU)
Pouilly-Fuissé les Vieux Murs, Loron
   1999 £10.99 (POR)
Pouilly-Fuissé les Vieux Murs, Loron
   1997 £10.56 (PEN) £10.95 (BALL)
Pouilly-Vinzelles Bouchard Père et Fils
   1998 £11.99 (COC)
St-Véran en Crèches, Daniel Barraud
   1998 £11.99 (YOU)
St-Véran Cuvée Prestige Lassarat 1998
   £10.25 (STA)
St-Véran Château Fuissé, Vincent 1997
   £10.50 (BAN)
St-Véran Vieilles Vignes Domaine des
   Deux Roches 1996 £10.99 (POR)

£12.50 → £15.99

Mâcon-Clessé Domaine de la Bongran,
   Thévenet 1999 £15.85 (NI)
Mâcon-Clessé Domaine de la Bongran,
   Thévenet 1998 £12.50 (TAN) £14.88
   (SAV) £19.68 (TW)
Mâcon-Clessé Domaine de la Bongran,
   Thévenet 1997 £13.45 (AD) £15.00 (JU)
Mâcon-Viré Domaine Emilian Gillet,
   Thévenet 1999 £14.35 (NI)
Pouilly-Fuissé Clos du Bourg, Luquet
   1998 £12.95 (FORT)
Pouilly-Fuissé la Croix, Denogent 1999
   £13.71 (BIB)
Pouilly-Fuissé la Croix, Denogent 1998
   £14.00 (GAU)
Pouilly-Fuissé Château Fuissé, Vincent
   1999 £13.95 (TAN)

Pouilly-Fuissé Latour 1999 £13.99 (POR)
Pouilly-Fuissé Leger-Plumet 1997 £14.99
   (WIN)
Pouilly-Fuissé la Roche, Daniel Barraud
   1998 £12.99 (YOU) £13.95 (LEA)
Pouilly-Fuissé la Verchère, Daniel Barraud
   1998 £13.50 (LEA)
Pouilly-Fuissé Verget 1997 £14.95 (LEA)
Pouilly-Fuissé Vieilles Vignes, Manciat-
   Poncet 1997 £13.00 (JU)
St-Véran Cuvée Prestige Lassarat 1999
   £12.99 (POR)

£16.00 → £19.99

Mâcon-Clessé Domaine Emilian Gillet,
   Thévenet 1989 £18.57 (TW)
Pouilly-Fuissé le Clos, Château Fuissé
   1999 £17.04 (DOM)
Pouilly-Fuissé les Crays, Forest 1999
   £17.95 (BER)
Pouilly-Fuissé les Crays, Forest 1998
   £16.99 (YOU) £24.35 (BAN)
Pouilly-Fuissé les Crays, Forest 1997
   £18.75 (FORT)
Pouilly-Fuissé Cuvée Claude Vieilles
   Vignes, Denogent 1998 £18.25 (GAU)
Pouilly-Fuissé Château Fuissé Vieilles
   Vignes, Vincent 1999 £19.00 (SOM)
   £26.71 (PLAY)
Pouilly-Fuissé Château Fuissé Vieilles
   Vignes, Vincent 1998 £19.39 (DOM)
   £23.95 (RES)
Pouilly-Fuissé Château Fuissé Vieilles
   Vignes, Vincent 1997 £19.90 (RIC)
   £19.90 (JU)
Pouilly-Fuissé Tête du Cru, Ferret 1997
   £18.99 (BAL)
Pouilly-Fuissé Tête de Cuvée, Verget
   1998 £17.95 (LEA)

Over £20.00

Mâcon-Clessé Quintaine Sélection de
   Grains Cendrés, Guillemot-Michel
   1992 £24.00 (CRO)
Mâcon-Viré Domaine Emilian Gillet,
   Thévenet 1995 £20.56 (TW)
Pouilly-Fuissé les Carrons Vieilles Vignes,
   Denogent 1998 £20.35 (GAU)
Pouilly-Fuissé le Clos, Château Fuissé
   1998 £20.95 (RES)
Pouilly-Fuissé Clos des Petits Croux,
   Domaine Guffens-Heynen 1994 £22.91
   (FA)
Pouilly-Fuissé Hors Classe, Ferret 1997
   £23.50 (BAL)

CHAMPAGNE

**The big build-up of Champagne for the Millennium has *still* not been
exhausted, stocks are becoming softer and classier with age, and we, the
consumers, are reaping the benefits**

Well, there wasn't a shortage, was there? Come the end of last year, if you wanted Champagne there it was: lots of it, just for the taking. And this year there's been just as much around as ever. We didn't drink Champagne dry at the Millennium, although some of us did our level best.

As always, though, the wines on offer are sometimes just a wee bit young for comfort. The most common vintages on sale now are 1993 – decent but lean – and 1995 – potentially very good but still too young. The better wines need three or four years more.

Non-vintage wines, as ever, will benefit from being tucked away for another six months. The simplest way of buying Champagne is to wait until you see a good money-saving offer, then buy enough to see you through to the next lot of money-saving offers. Since they normally come in summer and winter it's quite easy to plan one's budget.

Why shops should cut the price of Champagne just when in theory everyone wants it is beyond me. I, in my innocence, would expect it to be the other way round: you cut the price when it's not selling. But what do I know?

GRAPE VARIETIES

CHARDONNAY Imparts elegance and freshness to the blend, not to mention acidity and structure. Good Chardonnay from here ages superbly, so just because Blanc de Blancs (which is entirely Chardonnay) has whiplash elegance, don't think you've got to drink it young.

PINOT NOIR Adds weight to the blend, even though it's vinified as a white wine, without the skins: a Champagne relying on Pinot Noir is certain to be heavier than those made from other grapes. It can also

go with food better. And yes, Champagne does make a very little still red wine from Pinot Noir, but it takes a hot year to make it attractive. Most Pinot made as red wine is used to colour rosé.

PINOT MEUNIER Champagne's second black grape, making a softer, fruitier style of wine, important for producing simple wines for drinking young, and useful for lightening the assertive weight of Pinot Noir. Soft, commercial blends are usually heavy on the Pinot Meunier, and none the worse for it.

WINE STYLES AND LABELLING

BLANC DE BLANCS Champagne made only from Chardonnay; it has become more fashionable as drinkers look for a lighter style. Should not only be fresh but creamy and bright as well, and should get deeper and richer as it ages. But with no easy-going Pinot Meunier to fatten out the wine, any fault is glaringly obvious, so stick to good producers. Excellent NV (non-

vintage) Blanc de Blancs is made by *Duval-Leroy, Gimonnet, Henriot, Mumm* and *Bruno Paillard*; the *Union* co-operatives at Avize and le Mesnil make the most of their positions at the heart of the Côte des Blancs. Among the best vintage Blanc de Blancs are *Billecart-Salmon, Delamotte, Deutz, Gardet, Jacquesson, Lanson, Pol Roger, Roederer, Jacques Selosse*. There are also de luxe cuvées: *Charles Heidsieck Blanc des Millénaires*, *Krug Clos de Mesnil*, *Dom Ruinart*, *Salon* and *Taittinger Comtes de Champagne* are the benchmarks.

BLANC DE NOIRS This white style is made from black grapes only. Few have the quality and longevity of *Bollinger*'s *Vieilles Vignes*, but none is even half as expensive. Most are rather solid. *Mailly* and *Pierre Vaudon* are elegant exceptions, and the *Sainsbury's* and *Waitrose* versions are good value, and benefit from bottle age.

BRUT Very dry – more so than either 'Sec' or 'Extra Dry'. Most non-vintage Champagne sold in Britain is Brut.

BUYER'S OWN BRAND (BOB) A wine blended to a buyer's specification or, more probably, to a price limit. The grapes are of lesser quality, the wines usually younger, and cheaper. However, *Safeway*, *Sainsbury's*, *Somerfield* and *Waitrose* Champagnes are consistent and good value.

CM Means *co-opérative-manipulant* and shows that the wine comes from a co-op, whatever the brand name implies.

COTEAUX CHAMPENOIS, AC Still wines, red, rosé or white and generally rather acid. A village name, such as Cramant (white) or Bouzy (red) may appear. *E Barnaut*'s *Bouzy*, *Egly-Ouriet*, *René Geoffroy*'s *Cumières* and *Jean Vesselle*'s *Bouzy* reds can be good, but all producers' still wines are as variable as the climate.

DE LUXE/CUVÉE DE PRESTIGE/ CUVÉE DE LUXE All these terms signify a highly prized blend, mostly vintage. Some are undeniably great wines and some gaudy coat-tailers. At these prices one is looking for immense complexity and refinement. In general these wines are drunk *far* too young. Most need a good ten years to shine. Some of the best: *Billecart-Salmon Cuvée NF Billecart*, *Bollinger RD*, *Cattier Clos du Moulin*,

---

> ## ON THE CASE
> If you buy Champagne to lay down, be sure to keep it somewhere cool and dark. Champagne is particularly susceptible to light

Deutz William Deutz, *Gosset Celebris*, *Alfred Gratien Cuvée Paradis*, *Charles Heidsieck Blanc des Millénaires*, *Dom Pérignon*, *Dom Ruinart*, *Krug Clos du Mesnil*, *Laurent-Perrier Grand Siècle*, *Perrier-Jouët Belle Époque*, *Philipponnat Clos des Goisses*, *Pol Roger Cuvée Sir Winston Churchill*, *Pommery Louise*, *Roederer Cristal*, *Taittinger Comtes de Champagne*, *Veuve Clicquot la Grande Dame*.

DEMI-SEC Medium-sweet. Rarely very nice, but *Louis Roederer* can be outstanding, and *Veuve Clicquot* is the most consistent.

DOUX Sweet. *Louis Roederer*'s is an excellent example.

EXTRA DRY Confusingly, this is less dry than 'Brut', but drier than 'Sec'.

GRAND CRU In Champagne it is communes that are classified, not individual vineyards, and the 17 Grand Cru communes in the region are the best. The next best are the Premiers Crus.

GRANDE MARQUE Ambiguous term meaning 'great brand', and now officially defunct, since the Syndicat is disbanded. It may re-form under a new name, eventually.

NM This means *négociant-manipulant* (merchant-handler) and shows that the producer is one of the 265 Champagne houses operating in the region.

NON-DOSAGE Most Champagne has a little sweetness – a 'dosage' – added just before the final cork is put in. A few have minimal dosage and will have names like Brut Zero. Best are *Laurent-Perrier*'s *Ultra*

Brut and *Gimonnet's Maxi Brut*. They're designed to show that it's the wine, not the dosage that provides the quality. Do they prove their point? Well, they need to be very ripe to be able to balance the austerity.

NON-VINTAGE (NV) The flagship of most houses, and the one by which a producer should be judged. The wines are generally based on one vintage and usually aged for three years. But many of the best provide greater depth and age, and ensure consistency by using up to 40 per cent of *vins de réserve* (wines from previous years) thus giving more depth and maturity to the blend. Quality is generally pretty good, and of the major names only *Canard-Duchêne, Heidsieck-Monopole, Mercier, Mumm* and *Perrier-Jouet* are disappointing. Rather more (like *Moët, Piper-Heidsieck*) have reached a level of good, reliable quality, but lack great personality. For real character try *Ayala, Besserat de Bellefon, Billecart-Salmon, Bollinger, Deutz, Gosset, Alfred Gratien, Charles Heidsieck* (excellent), *Henriot, Jacquart, Jacquesson, Krug, Mailly Grand Cru, Bruno Paillard, Joseph Perrier, Pol Roger, Pommery, Roederer, Ruinart, Taittinger, Pierre Vaudon, Veuve Clicquot* and *Vilmart*. All will improve if you keep them for a year or so. A new trend, led by *Charles Heidsieck*, is to feature the year of bottling on the label, so you can tell how long the wine has had to mature. It's a good idea but don't mistake these wines for vintage Champagne.

PREMIER CRU The 41 *premier cru* communes are those just below Grand Cru in quality. All the others are unclassified.

RC *Récoltant-co-opérateur* – a grower selling wine made at a co-op. It's supposed to stop growers from pretending they've made it themselves, when all they did was deliver the grapes. Should do, but somehow it doesn't seem to appear on labels that often.

RECENTLY DISGORGED A term for Champagnes that have been left in the cellars, drawing flavour from their yeast deposits, for much longer than usual before disgorging. The wines can rest for 20 or perhaps even 30 years on the lees but are usually released after seven to ten years. *Bollinger RD* is still the best; also good are *Deutz, Alfred Gratien* and *Laurent-Perrier*. The idea is that you should drink them as soon as you buy them, at which point they have freshness balanced by maturity.

RICH The sweetest Champagne. *Roederer* can be superbly balanced. *Veuve Clicquot* has a great vintage version.

RM *Récoltant-manipulant* means that the grower made it himself, rather than taking it to the co-op. Try: *Paul Bara, E Barnaut, Henri Billiot, J Charpentier, René Geoffroy, Gimonnet, Michel Gonet, André Jacquart, Larmandier-Bernier, Margaine, Serge Mathieu, Alain Robert, Vesselle, Vilmart*.

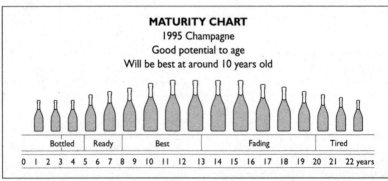

MATURITY CHART
1995 Champagne
Good potential to age
Will be best at around 10 years old

Bottled	Ready	Best	Fading	Tired

0 1 2 3 4 5 6 7 8 9 10 11 12 13 14 15 16 17 18 19 20 21 22 years

ROSÉ Usually made by adding a little still red to white wine before bottling. Only a few companies (like *Laurent-Perrier*) still make it by macerating red grapes on the skins until the right shade of pink is achieved. Ideally rosés are aromatic, fruity wines, with a delicious strawberry or cherry flavour. Sadly, many are indistinguishable from white. Most should be drunk young. Best: *Billecart-Salmon, Bollinger, Charbaut, Egly-Ouriet, Gosset, Charles Heidsieck, Jacquart Mosaïque, Jacquesson, Laurent-Perrier, Pol Roger, Louise Pommery, Roederer* and *Ruinart. Krug rosé* is way ahead in a class of its own, and at that price so it should be.

SEC Literally 'dry', but any Champagne so labelled will actually be medium dry. 'Extra Dry' and 'Brut' are drier.

SR *Société de Récoltants*. Label code for a family company of growers.

VINTAGE The wine produced from the grapes of a single, good year. Vintage Champagne should be fuller and deeper than non-vintage, but is almost always released too young, so you need to age it yourself. An awful lot of lesser producers make a vintage when they (and we) would be better off if they concentrated on improving their non-vintage. Best names to look for: *Beaumont des Crayères, Billecart-Salmon, Bollinger, Delamotte, Gosset, Alfred Gratien, Charles Heidsieck, Henriot, Jacquesson, Krug, Bruno Paillard, Joseph Perrier, Laurent-Perrier, Pol Roger, Pommery, Louis Roederer, Ruinart, Salon, Jacques Selosse, Taittinger* and *Veuve Clicquot*.

CHAMPAGNE HOUSES WHO'S WHO

BESSERAT DE BELLEFON ★ Makes, elegant, restrained Champagnes of good depth.

BILLECART-SALMON ★★★ Terrifically elegant Champagne from a family-owned house. Very refined, mature wines and a delicate rosé. Its vintage, Cuvée NF Billecart, is outstanding.

BOLLINGER ★★★ Like Krug, Bollinger makes 'English-style' Champagnes: rich, oaky, but more steely and almost half the price. The NV is excellent. RD is kept on its lees until just before sale.

F BONNET ★★ Inexpensive offshoot of Piper-Heidsieck and Charles Heidsieck, with mature and biscuity non-vintage.

DEUTZ ★★★ This house is back on form again with creamy-rich, biscuity non-vintage and an excellent quality prestige cuvée called William Deutz.

DRAPPIER ★★ Consistent quality, although the style bounces between ultra-

fruity and rich and biscuity according to how much bottle age the wine has.

DUVAL-LEROY ★★ Fresh, fragrant Chardonnay-dominated Champagne. Good value and consistent decent quality.

ALFRED GRATIEN ★★★ Serious, oak-fermented wine at a much lower price than Krug. Very long-lived vintage. Even the non-vintage needs extra bottle age.

CHARLES HEIDSIECK ★★★ Good value and reliable; rich, full style and good vanilla finesse. Excellent bottle-aged NV.

HENRIOT ★★★ Good bottle age and unrelenting high quality. Very rich and deep.

JACQUESSON ★★★ Good quality and finesse in both the elegant, flowery non-vintage and the rich, well-extracted vintage.

KRUG ★★★ Classic, mellow, rich. Oak-fermented Grande Cuvée is outstanding. The expensive rosé has incomparable Pinot Noir cherry fruit. Even more expensive

Clos de Mesnil is a rich, single-vineyard Blanc de Blancs.

LANSON ★★★ Classic, long-maturing vintage. Give the NV extra bottle age, too.

LAURENT-PERRIER ★★ One of the more reliable of NVs, with good rosé. Grand Siècle is a blend of several vintages; there's an expensive vintage version too.

MOËT & CHANDON ★★★ Brut Impérial is reliably good. The vintage wine is stylish. De luxe Dom Pérignon can be one of the greatest Champagnes of all.

MUMM ★★ A new winemaker has reversed Mumm's long-term quality slide, and Cordon Rouge is now fresh and clean. Elegant Blanc de Blancs Mumm de Cramant.

BRUNO PAILLARD ★★★ Fresh, elegant and satisfying Champagne from one of the most consistent producers.

JOSEPH PERRIER ★★★ The NV is extremely rich and well aged, with biscuity complexity and high but integrated acidity.

PERRIER-JOUËT ★ Famous but disappointing NV. De luxe cuvée Belle Époque is all flowery elegance.

POL ROGER ★★★ Delicious, delicate Blanc de Blancs. Top class across the board, including prestige cuvée Sir Winston Churchill and vintage Chardonnay.

POMMERY ★★★ Currently on good form, with wines of light, flowery elegance. Prestige cuvée Louise Pommery is superb.

LOUIS ROEDERER ★★★ Superb quality, lovely depth and finesse. The subtle, ripe NV is hard to beat, and prestige cuvée Cristal is wonderful. Good Demi-sec, too.

RUINART ★★★ The non-vintage ' R' de Ruinart has lots of bottle age and a style closer to the traditional 'English style' than many. Not for fans of light, young and delicate Champagne. The vintage is rich.

TAITTINGER ★★★ Traditionally a soft, foaming NV, but recently not as refreshing as usual. De luxe cuvée Blanc de Blancs Comtes de Champagne becomes sumptuously rich with age.

VEUVE CLICQUOT ★★★ The NV has a rich, warm style when on form, and prestige cuvée la Grande Dame is almost chocolate-rich.

VILMART ★★ Rich, full, traditionally made Champagnes. Good vintage Coeur de Cuvée and Grand Cellier d'Or.

CHAMPAGNE VINTAGES

In theory Champagne firms only make single-vintage wines in especially fine years. But only a few firms, like Bollinger and Krug, follow the theory. Most either opt too readily for vintage wines in marginal years or, increasingly, release wines after only five years in bottle, which may be okay for French tastes but leaves the average Brit with an acid stomach. Nevertheless, most firms come up with decent vintage.

2000 A warm, dry period just before harvest saved the vintage. Quality is likely to be variable but there's the possibility of some vintage wines.

1999 A highly promising year that will give some very good vintage wines. They'll be released long before they're ready to drink, as usual, and will need to be kept further. But they're ripe, fruity wines with good structure.

1998 Ripe wines that promise well. Expect plenty of vintage declarations.

1997 A ripe vintage with plentiful yields.

1996 Splendidly ripe, balanced wines that are likely to be widely declared. The non-vintage wines should be good, as well, when they start coming on stream. This and 1995 are the vintages to go for after 1990 – skip the intervening ones.

1995 The wines are significantly superior to those of the previous four years, and this will be the first widely declared vintage since the outstanding 1990.

1994 Of the few reputable producers likely to declare this a vintage, Vilmart's Grand Cellier d'Or will probably be the best.

1993 Roederer managed to produce a vintage Champagne after rejecting no less than half its own crop. Not a bad vintage, but there are better ones coming up behind.

1992 The 1992s are appearing on the shelves, and so far they're not impressive. Too many are green and coarse, though Perrier-Jouët might turn out okay.

1991 In the shops now, and looking surprisingly good. Elegance and structure seem to be the keys to this vintage, and it needs time. Try Billecart-Salmon, Philipponnat's Clos des Goisses, Pommery, Taittinger, and Vilmart's Coeur de Cuvée. Roederer declared a rosé.

1990 Many of the wines are superb, though few are still available. Try Jacquart, Lanson, Laurent-Perrier, Perrier-Jouët, Pommery, Roederer, Ruinart, Taittinger, Pierre Vaudon. They'll still improve.

1989 Most need a few years yet, though they're coming on beautifully. Look for Besserat de Bellefon, Gosset, Alfred Gratien, Bruno Paillard.

1988 The wines have bite, backbone and fruit, but most are already sold out.

1987 A lot of wine, but even the Champenois are not enthusiastic about its quality. Only Pommery declared a vintage, and any remaining bottles should really be drunk.

1986 Would have made a decent, if slightly hard vintage, but got sold far too young. One or two minor houses have wines available, and they're attractive.

1985 Fine wines, without any of the hardness of some vintages. There's very little still available, but if you've got any it should be delicious now.

CHAMPAGNE PRICES

SPARKLING WHITE

Under £10.00

Beerens Brut Reserve ½ bottle NV £9.60 (BIB)

Billecart-Salmon Brut Reserve ½ bottle NV £9.83 (SAV) £10.95 (LEA) £11.20 (AD)

Gardet Brut Special ½ bottle NV £8.65 (CON) £9.89 (VIN)

Gardet Cuvée St Flavy NV £9.95 (SOM) £13.95 (BAL) £13.99 (CON) £14.30 (HIC) £14.95 (STE) £14.99 (JON) £17.05 (VIN)

Duc de Marre Special Cuvée ½ bottle NV £7.99 (WAI)

Joseph Perrier Cuvée Royale NV £9.77 (HIC) £16.95 (STE) £17.50 (GN) £17.95 (BALL) £17.99 (GW) £19.75 (AS)

£10.00 → £11.99

Laurent-Perrier Brut LP ½ bottle NV £11.90 (GW) £12.53 (PLAY)

Moët & Chandon Brut Impérial ½ bottle NV £11.20 (TAN) £11.46 (PLA) £11.73 (BIB) £11.99 (BO) £12.49 (UN) £12.49 (BUD) £12.49 (TES) £12.49 (BOT) £12.49 (WR) £12.75 (OD) £12.99 (POR) £12.99 (VIL) £13.25 (FORT) £14.25 (JER)

£12.00 → £13.99

Benedick NV £12.95 (LEA)

★ **Brossault NV** £12.49 (MAJ)

★ **Le Brun de Neuville Cuvée Sélection NV** £13.25 (WAT)

Canard-Duchêne NV £13.90 (CRO) £15.57 (WHI) £15.99 (COC) £16.49 (BO) £16.99 (UN) £16.99 (WAI) £16.99 (SAF) £16.99 (MORR) £17.57 (LLO) £17.99 (MAJ) £18.41 (PLAY) £19.95 (JER)

Charles Ellner Brut NV £13.95 (BALL) £16.50 (LAY)

Duc de Marre Special Cuvée Extra Dry NV £13.99 (WAI)

Veuve Clicquot ½ bottle NV £12.95 (FRI) £12.95 (CON) £12.95 (BALL) £13.49 (BO) £13.51 (BIB) £13.99 (VIL) £14.50 (FORT) £14.69 (UN)

£14.00 → £15.99

Bauget-Jouette Carte Blanche NV £15.00 (HIG) £15.99 (AME)

Bollinger Special Cuvée ½ bottle NV £14.30 (TAN) £14.75 (CON) £15.30 (BEN) £15.30 (VIN) £15.51 (TW) £15.75 (STA) £15.95 (FORT) £15.99 (VIL) £15.99 (DI)

F Bonnet Brut Hermitage NV £15.99 (OD)

Le Brun de Neuville Blanc de Blancs Cuvée Chardonnay NV £14.15 (WAT)

Drappier Carte d'Or NV £15.43 (BY) £15.99 (VIC) £15.99 (THR) £15.99 (BOT) £15.99 (WR) £16.48 (FLE) £16.99 (POR) £17.50 (CRO)

Gardet Blanc de Blancs 1995 £14.95 (SOM)

Gardet Brut Special NV £15.45 (HIC) £15.99 (CON) £17.99 (VIN) £17.99 (JON)

Gimonnet Cuis Premier Cru Blanc de Blancs NV £14.99 (OD)

★ **Henri Harlin NV** £14.99 (OD)

Henri Harlin 1989 £15.99 (OD)

Heidsieck Dry Monopole NV £15.66 (BY) £15.99 (BUD) £15.99 (BO) £16.49 (OD) £16.49 (MORR) £16.99 (POR) £16.99 (JON)

Jacquart Tradition NV £15.99 (BO)

Lamiable Grand Cru NV £14.50 (HIG)

Mercier Demi-Sec NV £15.99 (MORR) £17.49 (TES) £17.49 (VIC) £17.49 (THR) £17.49 (BOT) £17.49 (WR) £17.99 (VIL)

RETAILERS SPECIALIZING IN CHAMPAGNE
see Retailers Directory (page 40) for details

Most good retailers have a fair variety of Champagnes, and generally list the most popular of the Grandes Marques, plus one or two cheaper ones. Most, too, have a pretty varied list of sparkling wines from other countries, and it is quite hard to single out merchants with exceptionally good lists of Champagne.

Nevertheless, for a wider than average choice, try especially: Adnams (AD), Averys of Bristol, Bennetts (BEN), Bibendum (BIB), Farr Vintners (FA), Justerini & Brooks (JU), Lea & Sandeman (LEA), Majestic (MAJ), Oddbins (OD), Roberson, T&W Wines (TW), Tanners (TAN), Peter Wylie (WY) – a few old vintages.

Le Mesnil Blanc de Blancs Brut **NV**
£15.99 (WAI)
Pol Roger ½ bottle **NV** £14.39 (VIN)
Pol Roger White Foil **NV** £14.20 (FA)
£15.95 (SOM) £20.74 (PLAY) £22.03 (BIB)
£22.50 (HIC) £22.90 (COC) £22.99 (VIC)
£22.99 (THR) £22.99 (BOT) £22.99 (WR)
£22.99 (JON) £23.45 (TAN) £23.50 (WS)
£23.50 (PEN) £23.54 (LLO) £23.95 (HAH)
£23.95 (VA) £23.95 (BER) £23.99 (BEN)
£23.99 (UN) £23.99 (HED) £23.99 (POR)
£23.99 (MAJ) £23.99 (CON) £23.99 (OD)
£23.99 (RIC) £24.00 (JU) £24.00 (MV)
£24.25 (WRI) £24.25 (VIN) £24.50 (RES)
£24.90 (JER) £24.95 (AS) £24.95 (STA)
£24.95 (BALL) £26.95 (LAY) £26.95
(FORT)

Ruelle-Pertois **NV** £15.20 (HAW)
de Telmont **NV** £14.65 (MAJ)
Thienot **NV** £15.99 (UN) £19.40 (HIC)
Pierre Vaudon 1er Cru **NV** £15.70 (HAH)

£16.00 → £17.99

Ayala Brut **NV** £16.49 (MAJ)
Bauget-Jouette Grande Réserve **NV**
£17.00 (HIG)
Beerens Brut Reserve **NV** £16.65 (BIB)
De Castelnau 1er Cru, Blanc de Blancs
NV £16.00 (JU)
Drappier Carte d'Or **1995** £16.90 (BY)
£18.50 (BAC) £22.00 (CRO)
Duchâtel **1994** £16.99 (UN)
Gardet Blanc de Blancs **1990** £17.95
(CON)
Gimonnet Gastonome Premier Cru Blanc
de Blancs **1995** £16.99 (OD)
Alfred Gratien ½ bottle **1990** £16.00 (WS)
Jacquesson Perfection **NV** £17.99 (DI)
£22.95 (MAY) £22.99 (BEN) £22.99 (VIL)
Legras Blanc de Blancs **NV** £16.95 (LEA)
Mercier **NV** £16.99 (COC) £17.49 (UN)
£17.49 (TES) £17.49 (VIC) £17.49 (THR)
£17.49 (BOT) £17.49 (WR) £17.49 (SAF)
£17.69 (BUD) £17.99 (VIL) £17.99 (ASD)
£18.44 (BY)

Moët & Chandon Brut Impérial **NV**
£17.04 (BODX) £19.49 (TES) £19.49
(WHI) £19.49 (ASD) £19.49 (MORR)
£19.90 (BAC) £20.50 (PLA) £20.56 (BIB)
£20.75 (WRI) £20.99 (UN) £20.99 (BUD)
£20.99 (POR) £20.99 (COC) £20.99 (BO)
£20.99 (VIC) £20.99 (THR) £20.99 (BOT)
£20.99 (VIN) £20.99 (WAI) £20.99 (VIL)
£20.99 (SAF) £21.30 (TAN) £21.50 (BALL)
£21.99 (CON) £22.05 (BY) £22.15 (JER)
£22.76 (PLAY) £22.80 (WAT) £22.95 (FRI)
£22.95 (VA) £23.95 (LAY) £23.97 (CB)
£24.25 (FORT) £25.00 (JU)
Pannier Sélection **NV** £16.99 (DI)
Louis Roederer Brut Premier **NV** £16.16
(FA) £19.96 (PLA) £23.95 (HIC) £23.95
(LEA) £24.00 (JU) £24.50 (WS) £24.50
(BALL) £24.68 (PEN) £24.80 (WRI) £24.95
(FRI) £24.95 (TAN) £24.95 (VA) £24.95
(CON) £24.95 (LAY) £24.99 (UN) £24.99
(COC) £24.99 (GW) £24.99 (TES) £24.99
(BO) £24.99 (MAJ) £24.99 (VIC) £24.99
(THR) £24.99 (BOT) £24.99 (WR) £24.99
(WAI) £24.99 (OD) £24.99 (SAF) £24.99
(LAI) £25.00 (ARM) £25.00 (FORT) £25.20
(VIN) £25.50 (HAH) £25.50 (RES) £25.95
(BEN) £26.44 (TW) £26.95 (POR) £26.95
(STA) £26.98 (CB) £26.99 (VIL) £27.45
(BER) £27.68 (PLAY) £29.00 (MV) £32.25
(NI)
Ruelle-Pertois **1996** £16.55 (HAW)
de Telmont **1993** £16.99 (MAJ)
Pierre Vaudon 1er Cru **1995** £17.90
(HAH)

£18.00 → £19.99

Billecart-Salmon Brut Reserve **NV** £18.49
(SAV) £19.95 (GAU) £19.95 (NI) £20.25
(JER) £20.95 (VA) £20.95 (LEA) £20.99
(CB) £21.50 (AD) £21.50 (FORT) £21.95
(BER) £21.99 (OD) £22.36 (HIC) £23.06
(BY) £24.00 (JU)
Henri Billiot Cuvée Réserve Brut **NV**
£18.99 (RAE)
H Blin **1995** £18.99 (OD)
Le Brun de Neuville Cuvée du Rois Clovis
NV £19.45 (WAT)
Le Brun de Neuville Millésime **1991**
£18.85 (WAT)

> *Stars (★) indicate wines selected by
> Oz Clarke in the Best Buys section which
> begins on page 8.*

Deutz Brut Classic NV £19.50 (JER)
£19.90 (CRO) £21.99 (NEZ)
**Duval-Leroy Fleur de Champagne Blanc
de Chardonnay 1993** £19.95 (PEN)
Nicolas Feuillatte Blanc de Blancs NV
£18.99 (SAF)
Gardet 1995 £19.92 (HIC) £24.99 (CON)
Henriot Blanc de Blancs NV £19.95 (COC)
Henriot Souverain NV £18.40 (COC)
Lamiable Le Club 1993 £19.00 (HIG)
Lanson NV £18.51 (PLA) £18.99 (UN)
£18.99 (SO) £18.99 (TES) £18.99 (WAI)
£18.99 (ASD) £18.99 (MORR) £19.50
(STA) £19.59 (CON) £19.99 (BUD) £19.99
(SAF) £20.40 (BY) £20.90 (WRI) £21.50
(VIN) £21.99 (VIC) £21.99 (THR) £21.99
(BOT) £21.99 (WR)
Laurent-Perrier Brut LP NV £19.59 (BIB)
£19.96 (PLA) £20.99 (GW) £21.67 (ARM)
£21.70 (BY) £21.95 (LEA) £21.99 (CON)
£22.33 (PEN) £22.50 (WS) £22.95 (HED)
£22.98 (CB) £22.99 (UN) £22.99 (MAJ)
£22.99 (VIC) £22.99 (THR) £22.99 (BOT)
£22.99 (WR) £22.99 (OD) £23.00 (JU)
£23.36 (PLAY) £23.95 (POR) £23.95 (LAY)
£24.00 (MV) £25.50 (JER)
Mumm Cordon Rouge NV £19.49 (TES)
£19.49 (ASD) £19.68 (BY) £19.99 (UN)
£19.99 (VIC) £19.99 (THR) £19.99 (BOT)
£19.99 (WR) £19.99 (OD) £19.99 (SAF)
£19.99 (MORR)
Bruno Paillard Première Cuvée NV
£19.59 (BIB) £19.99 (BO)
Pannier 1995 £19.95 (DI)
Perrier-Jouët Grand Brut NV £19.99 (VIC)
£19.99 (THR) £19.99 (SUN) £19.99 (LAI)
£20.99 (BO) £20.99 (MAJ) £20.99 (BOT)
£20.99 (WR) £20.99 (OD)
Piper-Heidsieck NV £18.98 (ASD) £18.99
(TES) £18.99 (WAI) £19.99 (UN) £19.99
(BO) £19.99 (VIC) £19.99 (THR) £19.99
(BOT) £19.99 (WR) £19.99 (SAF) £21.22
(PLAY)
Pol Roger 1993 £19.25 (SOM) £34.50
(CON) £34.99 (BEN) £35.00 (BALL) £36.99
(MAJ) £36.99 (OD) £40.00 (FORT)

- *Wines are listed in A–Z order within
  each price band.*
- *For each wine, vintages are listed in
  descending order.*
- *Each vintage of any wine appears
  only once.*

Pommery Royale NV £19.51 (BY) £20.99
(TES) £20.99 (SAF) £20.99 (ASD) £21.00
(FORT) £23.00 (JU)
★ **Theophile Roederer Réserve NV** £18.95
(FORT)
Taittinger Brut Réserve NV £18.45 (SOM)
£21.09 (PLA) £23.09 (PLAY) £23.95 (LEA)
£23.99 (POR) £23.99 (TES) £23.99 (WR)
£23.99 (JON) £24.45 (FORT) £24.95 (VA)
£24.99 (UN) £24.99 (MAJ) £24.99 (OD)
£24.99 (SAF) £24.99 (ASD) £25.07 (BY)
£25.50 (GW) £25.75 (STE)
Veuve Clicquot NV £18.95 (SOM) £22.74
(PLA) £22.90 (FLE) £22.90 (BAC) £22.95
(BAL) £23.00 (BIB) £23.49 (ASD) £23.50
(WY) £23.50 (PEN) £23.54 (LLO) £23.90
(TAN) £23.91 (WHI) £23.95 (VA) £23.95
(CON) £23.95 (BALL) £23.99 (BO) £23.99
(MORR) £24.17 (ARM) £24.25 (VIN)
£24.35 (JER) £24.49 (UN) £24.49 (VIC)
£24.49 (THR) £24.49 (SUN) £24.49 (BOT)
£24.49 (WW) £24.49 (WAI) £24.49 (VIL)
£24.49 (SAF) £24.49 (LAI) £24.50 (LEA)
£24.75 (WRI) £24.95 (FRI) £24.95 (STA)
£24.95 (GN) £24.99 (POR) £25.49 (COC)
£25.49 (TES) £25.49 (OD) £25.50 (HAH)
£25.52 (PLAY) £25.99 (MAJ) £26.00 (MV)
£26.39 (BY) £26.75 (FORT) £26.95 (LAY)
£27.03 (CB) £28.00 (JU)
Vilmart Grand Cellier NV £19.99 (DI)
£21.50 (GAU)

£20.00 → £21.99

Bauget-Jouette Grande Réserve 1993
£20.00 (HIG)
Canard-Duchêne 1991 £21.60 (WHI)
Drappier Grand Sendrée 1995 £21.33 (BY)
Henriot 1990 £21.49 (SUN) £21.49 (LAI)
Joseph Perrier Cuvée Royale 1995
£21.98 (GW) £22.20 (HIC) £22.50 (STE)
£24.95 (BALL)
'R' de Ruinart NV £21.99 (WR) £22.99
(BOT) £24.50 (FORT) £25.75 (LAY)
Veuve Clicquot Demi-Sec NV £21.95
(BALL) £23.90 (TAN) £23.91 (WHI) £24.49
(UN) £24.49 (THR) £24.49 (BOT) £24.49
(VIL) £24.95 (STA) £25.49 (OD) £26.40 (BY)

£22.00 → £23.99

Billecart-Salmon Blanc de Blancs 1983
£23.33 (MI)
Bollinger Special Cuvée NV £22.90 (CRO)
£23.90 (BAC) £25.26 (PLA) £25.31 (LLO)
£25.90 (TAN) £25.95 (VA) £25.95 (CON)
£25.95 (BALL) £25.95 (BAL) £25.99 (SO)

£25.99 (TES) £25.99 (ASD) £25.99 (MORR) £26.05 (BIB) £26.32 (WHI) £26.75 (WRI) £26.91 (PEN) £26.95 (FRI) £26.99 (VIN) £26.99 (BO) £27.00 (WS) £27.03 (WY) £27.50 (LEA) £27.60 (BEN) £27.77 (BY) £27.95 (BER) £27.95 (DI) £27.96 (TW) £27.98 (COC) £27.99 (UN) £27.99 (BUD) £27.99 (POR) £27.99 (MAJ) £27.99 (VIC) £27.99 (THR) £27.99 (BOT) £27.99 (WR) £27.99 (WAI) £27.99 (OD) £27.99 (VIL) £27.99 (SAF) £28.50 (STA) £28.76 (PLAY) £28.98 (CB) £29.00 (JU) £29.00 (MV) £29.10 (HAH) £29.50 (GW) £29.50 (LAY) £29.50 (FORT) £29.95 (YAP) £30.50 (JER)

Gosset Grande Réserve NV £23.45 (SOM) £27.80 (CRO) £27.95 (LEA) £28.00 (WRI) £28.50 (RES) £29.30 (GN) £29.99 (BOT) £29.99 (WR) £29.99 (BAL) £30.95 (BALL) £35.00 (FORT) £41.30 (NO)

Charles Heidsieck Brut Réserve Mis en Cave NV £23.49 (UN) £23.49 (WAI) £23.49 (SAF) £24.50 (POR) £30.00 (FORT)

Lanson 1995 £22.99 (ASD)

Laurent-Perrier Brut 1990 £22.52 (FA) £32.00 (WS) £33.99 (TES) £34.06 (WHI) £34.49 (LAI)

Legras St Vincent 1990 £23.95 (LEA)

Mercier 1995 £22.99 (VIL)

Mercier 1993 £22.99 (BOT)

Mercier Vendange 1993 £22.99 (VIC) £22.99 (THR) £22.99 (WR)

Piper-Heidsieck 1990 £23.99 (BOT) £23.99 (WR) £25.99 (SAF)

Pol Roger Chardonnay 1993 £22.35 (SOM) £44.00 (BEN) £45.00 (RES) £47.50 (FORT)

£24.00 → £25.99

Drappier Grand Sendrée 1988 £24.26 (BY)

Gardet 1990 £24.99 (CON) £31.36 (VIN)

Henriot Cuvée des Enchanteleurs 1985 £25.90 (BY)

Le Mesnil Réserve Sélection Blanc de Blancs Brut 1995 £24.49 (JON)

Mumm Cordon Rouge 1990 £25.99 (VIC) £25.99 (THR) £25.99 (BOT) £25.99 (WR)

Bruno Paillard Chardonnay Réserve Privée NV £25.49 (BO) £26.44 (BIB)

Joseph Perrier Cuvée Royale 1993 £24.95 (GN)

Louis Roederer Rich NV £25.75 (CON) £26.00 (WRI) £27.03 (PEN) £27.25 (BEN) £27.75 (STA) £28.86 (CB) £29.75 (HAH) £30.00 (FORT)

Veuve Clicquot Vintage Reserve 1995 £24.33 (ARM) £32.31 (PLA) £32.41 (BIB) £32.88 (LLO) £32.95 (CON) £33.70 (TAN) £34.36 (TW) £34.99 (VIL) £35.00 (WS) £35.25 (PLAY) £35.80 (WRI) £35.99 (WAI) £36.95 (HAH) £36.95 (LEA) £36.97 (CB) £36.99 (OD) £36.99 (ASD) £41.95 (JER)

Veuve Clicquot Vintage Reserve 1982 £25.00 (MI)

£26.00 → £29.99

Billecart-Salmon Cuvée N.F. Billecart 1995 £28.40 (SAV) £30.00 (FORT) £33.99 (OD) £34.95 (AD) £35.75 (NI) £37.95 (BER)

Billecart-Salmon Cuvée N.F. Billecart 1991 £29.95 (LEA) £33.30 (JER)

Deutz Brut 1995 £28.99 (NEZ)

Drappier Grand Sendrée 1990 £27.22 (NO) £28.02 (BY) £38.00 (GN) £49.00 (POR)

Lanson 1990 £27.99 (OD)

Laurent-Perrier Brut 1993 £28.50 (GN) £30.99 (HED) £34.38 (BY) £34.50 (ARM) £37.99 (CB) £41.80 (JER)

Laurent-Perrier Ultra Brut NV £28.95 (LEA) £29.99 (BOT) £29.99 (WR) £30.00 (FORT) £33.85 (BY)

Billecart-Salmon ★★★★ (★)

Terrifically elegant Champagne from a family-owned house. Very refined, mature wines and a delicate rosé. Its vintage, Cuvée NF Billecart, is also excellent.

(Oz Clarke's Wine Buying Guide 2000)

For further information on stockists please contact:

Billecart-Salmon (UK) Ltd

Tel: 020 8405 6345 Fax: 020 8405 6346
info@billecart-salmon.co.uk

Moët & Chandon Brut Impérial **1995**
£27.02 (PLA) £27.99 (BUD) £27.99 (ASD)
£28.49 (JON) £28.65 (TAN) £28.67 (BY)
£28.99 (TES) £28.99 (BO) £28.99 (OD)
£29.99 (VIL) £30.00 (FORT) £31.95 (LAY)

Moët & Chandon Brut Impérial **1993**
£26.73 (WHI) £26.95 (BIB) £27.50 (CON)
£27.50 (CON) £27.95 (VA) £27.99 (POR)
£27.99 (VIC) £27.99 (THR) £27.99 (BOT)
£27.99 (WR) £28.45 (WAT) £28.50 (FRI)
£28.99 (UN) £28.99 (BO) £29.45 (CB)
£29.50 (WRI) £29.50 (HAH) £29.95 (PLAY)
£29.99 (VIL) £31.50 (BALL) £32.80 (JER)

Moët & Chandon Brut Impérial **1992**
£26.79 (COC) £27.99 (VIC) £27.99 (THR)
£27.99 (BOT) £27.99 (WR) £30.94 (BIB)
£32.99 (WAI)

Mumm de Cramant Blanc de Blancs **NV**
£26.72 (BY)

Bruno Paillard **1995** £27.03 (BIB)

Joseph Perrier Cuvée Royale **1990**
£27.50 (BALL)

Perrier-Jouët Brut Millésimé **1995** £27.99
(OD)

Perrier-Jouët Brut Millésimé **1992** £27.99
(MAJ) £27.99 (VIC) £27.99 (THR) £27.99
(BOT) £27.99 (WR)

Pol Roger Chardonnay **1988** £27.91 (FA)
£47.00 (PEN)

Pommery **1992** £27.99 (TES) £28.11 (BY)
£31.50 (FORT)

'R' de Ruinart **1992** £26.99 (WR) £27.99
(BOT)

'R' de Ruinart **1990** £29.95 (LEA)

Taittinger **1996** £28.99 (POR)

Veuve Clicquot Vintage Reserve **1989**
£29.80 (CRO)

Vilmart Grand Cellier D'Or **1995** £28.95
(WRI) £29.50 (GAU)

£30.00 → £39.99

Beerens Brut Reserve magnum **NV**
£36.62 (BIB)

Billecart-Salmon Grande Cuvée **1991**
£34.95 (VA) £35.75 (NI)

Bollinger Grande Année **1989** £30.35 (FA)
£36.00 (CRO)

Deutz Blanc de Blancs **1995** £38.99 (NEZ)

• All prices for each wine are listed
together in ascending order.
• Price bands refer to the lowest price
for which the wine is available.

Drappier Carte d'Or **1983** £37.50 (POR)

Drappier Carte d'Or **1979** £39.00 (CRO)
£45.00 (POR)

Duval-Leroy Fleur de Champagne
magnum **NV** £32.90 (PEN)

Gardet Brut Special magnum **NV** £35.00
(CON) £41.35 (VIN)

Gosset Grande Millésime **1993** £36.00
(WRI) £36.99 (YOU) £39.95 (BOT) £39.95
(WR)

Gosset Grande Millésime **1989** £33.65
(SOM) £37.50 (BALL) £39.50 (LEA) £41.50
(RES) £44.00 (BAL) £47.50 (POR)

Charles Heidsieck Brut Reserve **1990**
£32.00 (JU)

Heidsieck Diamant Bleu **1989** £39.99 (OD)

Jacquesson Blanc de Blancs **1995** £39.95
(MAY)

Krug Grande Cuvée ½ bottle **NV** £35.64
(BIB) £36.50 (UN) £36.50 (VIC) £36.50
(THR) £36.50 (BOT) £36.50 (WR) £37.50
(STA) £38.00 (CRO) £39.36 (TW) £40.00
(FORT) £42.50 (FRI) £43.90 (JER)

Moët & Chandon Brut Impérial **1990**
£34.50 (FRI)

Moët & Chandon Brut Impérial magnum
NV £34.95 (MORR) £37.95 (WR) £38.95
(TES) £39.50 (BAC) £40.99 (BO) £41.20
(TAN) £41.95 (BOT) £41.99 (UN) £42.75
(WRI) £43.09 (BIB) £43.99 (JON) £45.00
(CON) £45.99 (VIL) £47.90 (LAY) £49.00
(FORT) £57.15 (JER)

Cuvée Orpale Blanc de Blancs **1995**
£30.00 (MAR)

Cuvée Orpale Blanc de Blancs **1990**
£30.00 (MAR) £31.95 (HAH)

Pol Roger **1990** £34.27 (BIB) £34.90 (COC)
£34.95 (RES) £34.99 (HED) £34.99 (VIC)
£34.99 (THR) £34.99 (SUN) £34.99 (BOT)
£34.99 (WR) £34.99 (LAI) £35.80 (HIC)
£36.00 (WS) £36.35 (TAN) £36.43 (PEN)
£36.45 (HAH) £36.95 (STA) £37.00 (MV)
£37.75 (VIN) £44.90 (GAU)

Pol Roger **1988** £36.99 (YOU)

Louis Roederer **1993** £38.67 (ARM)
£43.20 (TAN) £44.95 (VA) £45.00 (FORT)
£45.25 (STE) £47.00 (PEN)

Taittinger **1995** £35.99 (OD)

Taittinger **1991** £35.00 (JU)

Taittinger **1990** £34.99 (BOT) £34.99 (WR)

Veuve Clicquot Rich **1996** £35.99 (UN)

Veuve Clicquot Rich **1995** £34.99 (VIL)
£36.95 (HAH) £36.95 (LEA)

Veuve Clicquot Rich **1992** £36.95 (FORT)

Veuve Clicquot Rich **1988** £35.99 (WR)

Veuve Clicquot Vintage Reserve **1993**
£32.41 (BIB) £32.88 (LLO) £32.95 (CON)
£34.99 (VIL) £35.99 (SAF) £36.95 (FORT)
£36.99 (COC) £36.99 (MAJ) £36.99 (OD)
Veuve Clicquot Vintage Reserve **1991**
£35.95 (VA) £35.99 (VIC) £35.99 (THR)
£35.99 (AME) £35.99 (BOT) £35.99 (WR)
Veuve Clicquot Vintage Reserve **1990**
£31.00 (FLE) £32.95 (BALL) £35.99 (UN)
Veuve Clicquot Vintage Reserve **1988**
£37.99 (YOU) £38.99 (VIL)
Vilmart Coeur de Cuvée **1991** £36.95 (DI)

£40.00 → £49.99

Billecart-Salmon Cuvée N.F. Billecart
1990 £40.90 (GAU) £41.67 (MI)
Billecart-Salmon Cuvée N.F. Billecart
1989 £43.33 (MI)
Billecart-Salmon Grande Cuvée **1989**
£47.00 (SAV) £49.50 (LEA) £54.75 (NI)
£55.45 (GAU) £68.80 (JER)
Bollinger Grande Année **1993** £41.99
(VIC) £41.99 (THR) £42.95 (BALL) £45.85
(HAH) £45.95 (POR) £45.99 (ASD)
Bollinger Grande Année **1992** £40.00
(BAC) £41.50 (WS) £42.50 (LEA) £43.50
(BY) £43.95 (BEN) £43.95 (DI) £44.02
(CB) £44.99 (VIL) £45.00 (FRI) £45.95 (VA)
£45.99 (MAJ) £46.45 (STE) £46.50 (FORT)
£48.95 (RES) £49.95 (LAY) £56.60 (JER)
Bollinger Grande Année **1990** £41.51
(BIB) £41.99 (TES) £42.00 (WRI) £42.44
(PEN) £42.50 (CON) £42.90 (TAN) £43.19
(VIN) £44.78 (COC) £44.90 (GAU) £44.99
(VIL) £45.00 (FRI) £45.99 (UN) £48.00
(ARM) £48.25 (PLAY) £56.40 (TW)
Bollinger RD **1985** £49.95 (DI) £57.95 (VIC)
£57.95 (THR) £57.95 (BOT) £57.95 (WR)
£75.00 (VIL) £75.00 (FORT) £76.37 (TW)
Bollinger RD **1982** £49.50 (WRI) £50.43
(FA) £70.50 (PEN) £75.00 (LEA) £80.00
(FORT) £84.42 (TW) £85.00 (VIL)
Dom Ruinart Blanc de Blancs **1990**
£42.99 (BOT) £54.00 (LEA) £54.99 (WR)
Alfred Gratien **1985** £40.00 (FORT)
Charles Heidsieck Blanc des Millénaires
1988 £45.00 (FORT)
Lanson magnum **NV** £43.95 (VIC) £43.95
(THR) £43.95 (BOT) £43.95 (WR) £45.69
(UN)
Laurent-Perrier 'La Cuvée' Grande Siècle
NV £49.95 (BOT) £49.95 (WR) £50.51
(BY) £52.00 (WS) £52.88 (PEN)
Laurent-Perrier Brut LP magnum **NV**
£45.99 (MAJ)

Mumm René Lalou **1985** £47.00 (CRO)
Joseph Perrier Cuvée Joséphine **1989**
£42.75 (GW)
Joseph Perrier Cuvée Joséphine **1985**
£40.95 (GN) £45.50 (STE)
Pol Roger Chardonnay **1990** £44.50 (WRI)
£49.50 (VIN) £49.95 (GAU)
Pol Roger Cuvée Sir Winston Churchill
1990 £41.95 (SOM) £55.22 (BODX)
£57.28 (FA) £69.84 (PAU) £71.68 (PEN)
£72.50 (WRI) £75.00 (WS) £75.00 (WAI)
£75.00 (OD) £75.75 (HAH) £76.50 (BEN)
£79.00 (RES) £80.00 (FORT)
Pol Roger White Foil magnum **NV** £49.00
(RES) £49.35 (PEN) £50.00 (WRI) £55.00
(BALL) £55.00 (FORT)
Louis Roederer **1995** £44.40 (HAH)
Louis Roederer **1994** £43.99 (VIL)
Louis Roederer **1990** £44.00 (CRO)
£44.50 (STA) £44.95 (UN) £45.00 (WAI)
£48.70 (LAY) £52.88 (PEN)
Louis Roederer Blanc de Blancs **1995**
£49.95 (LAY)
Louis Roederer Blanc de Blancs **1994**
£44.99 (VIL)
Louis Roederer Blanc de Blancs **1993**
£42.10 (PEN) £43.00 (BEN) £46.50 (FORT)
Louis Roederer Blanc de Blancs **1991**
£44.50 (STA)
Veuve Clicquot la Grande Dame **1990**
£47.88 (BODX) £62.50 (CON) £64.34
(PLAY) £64.73 (BY) £65.00 (FORT) £67.95
(VA) £69.99 (MAJ) £69.99 (OD) £80.00 (MI)
Veuve Clicquot magnum **NV** £47.90
(CON) £48.95 (BALL) £48.99 (UN) £49.55
(BIB) £49.99 (VIC) £49.99 (THR) £49.99
(BOT) £49.99 (WR) £49.99 (VIL) £52.50
(LEA) £54.95 (VA) £55.00 (FORT)
Veuve Clicquot Vintage Reserve **1985**
£44.99 (VIL)

Vilmart Coeur de Cuvée **1993** £43.50 (GAU)

Vilmart Coeur de Cuvée **1992** £42.00 (YOU)

Vilmart Grand Cellier D'Or **1985** £45.00 (GAU)

£50.00 → £59.99

Bollinger RD **1988** £58.00 (LEA) £59.00 (VA) £65.00 (BALL) £69.00 (CRO) £78.75 (GAU)

Bollinger Special Cuvée magnum **NV** £54.95 (BALL) £55.00 (TAN) £56.00 (WS) £56.50 (CON) £58.75 (BEN) £58.95 (LAY) £59.00 (DI) £59.99 (VIL) £62.00 (YAP) £62.00 (FORT)

Deutz Cuvée de William Deutz **1995** £57.75 (JER)

Deutz Cuvée de William Deutz **1990** £59.99 (NEZ)

Dom Pérignon **1993** £57.77 (FA) £62.33 (BY) £62.50 (TAN) £63.15 (PLA) £63.30 (JER) £63.65 (BIB) £65.15 (HAH) £65.75 (WRI) £66.95 (LEA) £67.50 (FORT) £69.72 (CB) £69.95 (STA) £69.99 (UN) £71.99 (VIL) £74.99 (MAJ) £74.99 (OD)

Dom Pérignon **1992** £58.69 (WHI) £59.00 (WAT) £62.50 (CON) £63.65 (BIB) £64.99 (BOT) £64.99 (WR) £65.00 (BALL) £67.35 (PLAY) £69.99 (TES) £69.99 (BO) £71.99 (VIL) £74.99 (OD) £79.00 (FRI) £80.00 (MI)

Dom Pérignon **1990** £58.69 (COC) £65.60 (FA) £68.93 (BODX) £69.95 (VA) £70.50 (TUR) £74.17 (ARM) £76.38 (WY) £89.00 (POR) £89.99 (VIN) £90.00 (MI)

Gosset Célébris **1990** £59.50 (CRO) £64.99 (YOU)

Alfred Gratien **1983** £55.00 (WS) £61.00 (CRO)

Jacquesson Blanc de Blancs **1990** £55.00 (MAY)

Krug Grande Cuvée **NV** £54.83 (FA) £62.95 (SOM) £63.65 (BIB) £64.00 (WAT) £65.40 (RIC) £66.39 (PLA) £68.35 (VIN) £69.00 (FRI) £69.00 (BAL) £69.95 (TAN) £69.95 (CON) £69.95 (BER) £69.95 (GN) £69.99 (TES) £70.00 (BO) £70.50 (PEN) £71.28 (BY) £72.00 (CRO) £72.95 (CB) £72.99 (JON) £72.99 (VIL) £73.00 (UN) £73.00 (BOT) £73.33 (ARM) £73.95 (VA) £74.17 (PLAY) £74.50 (LEA) £74.99 (COC) £74.99 (OD) £75.00 (POR) £75.00 (VIC) £75.00 (THR) £75.00 (WR) £75.00 (BALL) £75.00 (JU) £76.55 (HAH) £77.25 (TW) £79.50 (LAY) £79.95 (RES) £80.00 (FORT) £86.75 (JER) £100.00 (MI)

Lanson Noble Cuvée **1988** £55.99 (WAI)

Lilbert-Fils Brut Blanc de Blancs **1976** £56.40 (TW)

Moët & Chandon Brut Impérial magnum **1995** £59.99 (VIL) £62.50 (FORT)

Moët & Chandon Brut Impérial magnum **1992** £55.95 (VIC) £55.95 (THR) £55.95 (BOT) £55.95 (WR) £56.50 (UN) £59.99 (VIL)

Perrier-Jouët Belle Époque **1995** £54.17 (BY) £54.99 (OD) £60.00 (FORT) £69.99 (VIL)

Perrier-Jouët Belle Époque **1990** £54.99 (VIC) £54.99 (THR) £54.99 (BOT) £54.99 (WR) £62.50 (FRI)

Philipponnat Clos des Goisses **1989** £58.50 (SOM)

Pol Roger Cuvée Sir Winston Churchill **1986** £50.92 (FA) £73.00 (COC)

Pommery Cuvée Louise **1990** £55.32 (BY)

Taittinger Comtes de Champagne Blanc de Blancs **1989** £58.66 (PLAY) £74.99 (GW)

Taittinger Comtes de Champagne Blanc de Blancs **1988** £59.00 (JU) £75.00 (BOT) £75.00 (WR)

Taittinger Vintage Collection **1992** £50.92 (FA) £75.00 (UN)

Taittinger Vintage Collection **1990** £55.81 (FA) £79.00 (UN)

Taittinger Vintage Collection **1988** £55.81 (FA) £79.00 (UN)

Veuve Clicquot la Grande Dame **1993** £52.75 (SOM) £57.77 (BIB) £61.98 (BY) £62.50 (CON) £62.99 (VIL) £69.50 (UN) £69.95 (HAH) £70.00 (MI) £73.55 (JER)

£60.00 → £74.99

Billecart-Salmon Blanc de Blancs **1988** £63.33 (MI)

Bollinger Grande Année magnum **1990** £74.42 (FA) £88.36 (PEN) £88.50 (CON) £90.00 (WS) £90.40 (TAN) £90.75 (BEN) £95.00 (VIL)

Dom Pérignon **1995** £64.99 (VIC) £64.99 (THR) £68.99 (JON)

Dom Pérignon **1985** £70.50 (FA) £79.17 (ARM) £88.13 (WY)

Dom Ruinart Blanc de Blancs **1993** £60.00 (FORT)

Alfred Gratien magnum **1990** £60.00 (WS)

Jacquesson Signature **1990** £60.00 (MAY)

Krug **1989** £70.00 (ARM) £85.00 (WS) £85.00 (LEA) £85.00 (OD) £87.50 (CON) £87.83 (BY) £89.09 (VIN) £92.30 (HAH) £93.75 (TAN) £95.00 (VIL) £95.76 (TW) £99.00 (VIC) £99.00 (THR) £99.00 (BOT) £99.00 (RES) £99.00 (WR) £99.30 (PLAY) £99.95 (UN) £140.00 (MI)

Lanson Noble Cuvée **1989** £61.99 (UN)

Laurent-Perrier Grande Siècle **1990** £70.00 (OD) £78.40 (PLAY) £90.00 (FORT)

Moët & Chandon Brut Impérial magnum **1990** £60.71 (FA)

Perrier-Jouët Belle Époque **1992** £71.09 (VIN)

Pol Roger Cuvée Sir Winston Churchill **1988** £71.68 (PEN) £80.00 (FORT)

Louis Roederer Cristal **1995** £65.60 (FA) £95.90 (HAH) £99.00 (POR)

Louis Roederer Cristal **1993** £72.46 (WY) £72.46 (FA) £88.50 (TAN) £89.95 (STA) £93.35 (PLAY) £94.00 (PEN) £94.50 (BEN) £95.00 (BALL) £98.80 (BODX) £99.99 (GW) £99.99 (OD) £99.99 (VIL) £109.86 (NO) £109.95 (VA) £111.63 (TUR) £115.00 (FRI)

Salon **1983** £61.10 (FA) £90.00 (FORT)

Taittinger Comtes de Champagne Blanc de Blancs **1990** £60.71 (FA) £75.00 (WAI) £79.99 (OD)

Taittinger Comtes de Champagne Blanc de Blancs **1986** £70.00 (YOU)

Taittinger Comtes de Champagne Blanc de Blancs **1961** £70.50 (WY)

Veuve Clicquot la Grande Dame **1995** £67.50 (BALL) £67.99 (JON)

Veuve Clicquot la Grande Dame **1988** £68.00 (BOT) £68.00 (WR)

£75.00 → £99.99

Bollinger Grande Année magnum **1992** £95.00 (VIL) £95.00 (FORT)

Bollinger RD **1981** £75.00 (LEA)

Bollinger RD **1979** £95.00 (LEA) £105.00 (GAU) £112.80 (TW) £130.50 (VIN)

Deutz Blanc de Blancs Amour de Deutz **1993** £80.00 (JER)

Jacquesson Dégorgement Tardif **1985** £95.00 (MAY)

Krug **1999** £93.99 (JON)

Krug **1988** £88.12 (PLA) £89.00 (BER) £94.98 (BIB) £95.00 (FORT) £99.00 (VIL) £104.99 (OD) £105.00 (STA)

Krug **1985** £90.00 (FA)

Lanson **1921** £82.25 (WY)

Perrier-Jouët Belle Époque **1989** £79.99 (VIL)

Pol Roger magnum **1993** £77.00 (FORT)

Pol Roger magnum **1988** £82.25 (PEN)

Louis Roederer Cristal **1994** £85.70 (WRI) £86.67 (ARM) £87.50 (CON) £91.06 (PLA) £93.14 (NO) £94.48 (CB) £99.00 (RES) £99.50 (UN) £99.99 (MAJ) £99.99 (OD) £99.99 (VIL) £105.00 (FORT) £115.00 (FRI) £127.00 (JER)

Louis Roederer Cristal **1989** £85.19 (FA) £115.00 (NO) £117.50 (TUR)

Salon **1988** £76.00 (GAU) £90.48 (CB)

Taittinger Comtes de Champagne Blanc de Blancs **1994** £75.00 (POR) £75.00 (FORT)

Taittinger Comtes de Champagne Blanc de Blancs **1993** £79.99 (MAJ)

Taittinger Vintage Collection **1983** £85.00 (YOU)

Veuve Clicquot la Grande Dame **1989** £80.00 (MI) £95.00 (MI)

Veuve Clicquot Vintage Reserve **1970** £76.67 (MI)

£100.00 → £129.99

Bollinger Grande Année magnum **1989** £117.50 (TW)

Bollinger RD **1975** £125.50 (BEN) £152.75 (TW)

Bollinger Special Cuvée jeroboam **NV** £119.00 (DI) £125.00 (TAN) £125.00 (CON) £125.73 (PEN) £134.10 (VIN) £136.00 (VIL) £140.00 (FORT)

Dom Pérignon **1975** £127.29 (FA)

Krug **1998** £101.99 (JON)

Krug **1982** £115.00 (ARM) £115.05 (FA)

Moët & Chandon Brut Impérial jeroboam **NV** £115.00 (UN) £115.00 (CON) £122.40 (COC) £130.00 (VIL) £135.00 (BOT) £135.00 (WR) £146.88 (BIB)

Please remember that
Oz Clarke's Wine Buying Guide
*is a price **guide** and not a price **list**. It is
not meant to replace up-to-date
merchants' lists.*

Pol Roger Cuvée Sir Winston Churchill magnum **1990** £114.56 (FA) £160.00 (FORT)

Louis Roederer Cristal **1990** £117.50 (TUR) £117.50 (FA) £121.91 (WY) £135.00 (YOU) £141.00 (TW) £150.00 (JU)

Salon **1985** £125.00 (GAU)

Veuve Clicquot jeroboam **NV** £120.00 (UN) £129.00 (BOT) £129.00 (WR)

£130.00 → £199.99

Bollinger Vieilles Vignes Françaises, Blanc de Noirs **1992** £159.00 (BAL)

Bollinger Vieilles Vignes Françaises, Blanc de Noirs **1989** £145.96 (NO)

Dom Pérignon **1983** £141.00 (TW)

Dom Pérignon magnum **1993** £145.00 (FORT)

Dom Pérignon magnum **1992** £145.00 (VIL)

Dom Pérignon magnum **1990** £131.21 (FA) £145.00 (VIL)

Dom Pérignon magnum **1988** £198.00 (VIN)

Dom Pérignon magnum **1985** £150.79 (FA)

Krug Clos du Mesnil Blanc de Blancs **1989** £164.81 (BY) £167.75 (HAH) £195.00 (FORT) £210.00 (MI)

Krug Clos du Mesnil Blanc de Blancs **1988** £158.63 (FA)

Krug Clos du Mesnil Blanc de Blancs **1986** £195.00 (VIL) £195.00 (YOU) £210.00 (MI)

Krug Grande Cuvée magnum **NV** £146.99 (VIL) £160.00 (RES) £160.00 (FORT)

Perrier-Jouët Belle Époque magnum **1995** £130.00 (FORT)

Perrier-Jouët Belle Époque magnum **1990** £135.99 (VIL)

Perrier-Jouët Belle Époque magnum **1989** £159.99 (VIL)

Pol Roger Cuvée Sir Winston Churchill magnum **1988** £160.00 (FORT)

Pol Roger Cuvée Sir Winston Churchill magnum **1986** £164.50 (PEN) £170.95 (VIN)

Pol Roger White Foil jeroboam **NV** £130.00 (WRI) £139.83 (PEN) £145.00 (FORT)

Louis Roederer Cristal **1988** £158.63 (FA)

Louis Roederer Cristal **1983** £140.00 (NO)

Louis Roederer Cristal magnum **1993** £144.92 (FA)

Salon magnum **1983** £141.76 (CB) £190.00 (FORT)

Veuve Clicquot la Grande Dame **1985** £130.00 (MI)

£200.00 → £299.99

Krug Collection **1979** £215.00 (YOU) £220.00 (VIL)

Moët & Chandon Brut Impérial methuselah **NV** £225.00 (UN) £239.00 (COC) £250.00 (VIL) £259.00 (WR)

Pol Roger White Foil methuselah **NV** £247.00 (WRI) £277.30 (PEN)

Louis Roederer Cristal magnum **1994** £200.00 (FORT)

Salon **1976** £225.00 (GAU)

Veuve Clicquot methuselah **NV** £280.00 (UN)

Over £300.00

Bollinger Grande Année jeroboam **1979** £470.00 (TW)

Moët & Chandon Brut Impérial salmanazar **NV** £330.00 (UN) £359.00 (BOT) £359.00 (WR) £370.00 (VIL)

Pol Roger White Foil salmanazar **NV** £367.00 (WRI) £425.00 (FORT)

SPARKLING ROSÉ

Under £20.00

Bauget-Jouette **NV** £17.99 (AME)

Beerens **NV** £18.60 (BIB)

Henri Billiot Cuvée Réserve **NV** £18.99 (RAE)

F Bonnet **NV** £16.99 (OD)

Alexandre Bonnet Prestige **NV** £15.99 (WAI)

Le Brun de Neuville Cuvée Rosé **NV** £17.35 (WAT)

Canard-Duchêne **NV** £16.50 (CRO) £19.49 (JON) £36.31 (LLO)

Charbaut **NV** £18.44 (PEN)

Gardet **NV** £17.95 (CON) £17.99 (JON) £24.25 (VIN)

Lamiable Grand Cru **NV** £15.50 (HIG)

Mercier **NV** £16.69 (COC) £17.49 (THR) £17.49 (BOT) £17.49 (WR) £17.99 (VIL)

Piper-Heidsieck **NV** £18.99 (TES) £18.99 (MORR)

Pol Roger **1993** £19.95 (SOM) £39.00 (WS) £39.75 (WRI) £39.95 (RES)

£20.00 → £29.99

Billecart-Salmon Brut NV £24.48 (SAV)
£25.90 (GAU) £26.99 (VIN) £27.50 (JER)
£27.50 (FORT) £27.95 (LEA) £29.50 (BER)
£29.50 (AD) £29.75 (NI) £29.95 (VA)
£30.60 (BY) £32.99 (OD) £36.42 (TW)
Gosset Grande Réserve NV £27.95 (BALL)
£29.50 (RES) £32.50 (FORT)
Lanson NV £23.58 (BY) £25.49 (UN)
£25.49 (VIC) £25.49 (THR) £25.49 (BOT)
£25.49 (WR)
Laurent-Perrier NV £27.50 (HIC) £27.90
(JER) £28.40 (BIB) £28.95 (GN) £28.99
(GW) £28.99 (SUN) £28.99 (LAI) £29.37
(PLA) £29.50 (WS) £29.50 (HED) £29.95
(BALL) £29.99 (POR) £29.99 (TES) £29.99
(VIL) £30.00 (JU) £30.00 (MV) £30.55
(PEN) £30.95 (FRI) £30.95 (VA) £30.96
(WHI) £30.99 (UN) £30.99 (MAJ) £30.99
(VIC) £30.99 (THR) £30.99 (BOT) £30.99
(WR) £30.99 (JON) £30.99 (OD) £31.22
(BY) £31.25 (WRJ) £31.50 (CON) £31.92
(CB) £32.03 (PLAY) £32.50 (FORT) £32.55
(TW) £33.00 (STA) £33.20 (TAN) £34.50
(HAH)
Moët & Chandon Brut Impérial NV
£24.92 (BY) £24.95 (CON) £24.99 (SAF)
£26.10 (VIN) £26.24 (BIB) £28.05 (PLAY)
£28.95 (JER) £29.99 (VIL)
Bruno Paillard NV £23.99 (SUN) £23.99
(LAI)
Bruno Paillard Première Cuvée NV
£22.71 (BIB)
Joseph Perrier Cuvée Royale NV £20.56
(GW) £22.95 (STE) £26.19 (GN)
Pommery NV £22.99 (TES) £23.17 (BY)
£23.50 (FORT)
'R' de Ruinart NV £25.99 (BO) £27.99
(BOT) £30.00 (FORT)
Taittinger NV £26.28 (PLAY) £27.95 (POR)
£28.47 (BY) £30.00 (FORT) £34.00 (JU)
Vilmart Cuvée Rubis NV £21.90 (GAU)
£23.75 (WRJ)

£30.00 → £39.99

Deutz 1990 £31.99 (NEZ)
Moët & Chandon Brut Impérial 1995
£33.50 (UN) £34.99 (VIL) £35.00
(FORT)
Moët & Chandon Brut Impérial 1993
£31.57 (BY) £32.50 (FRI) £34.99 (VIL)
£35.00 (FORT) £42.30 (JER)
Pol Roger 1990 £30.35 (FA) £37.50 (CON)
£42.50 (FORT) £44.65 (PEN)

Veuve Clicquot 1995 £34.50 (CON)
£34.99 (YOU) £36.27 (BY) £36.99 (VIL)
£39.50 (FORT)
Veuve Clicquot 1993 £38.50 (UN)
Veuve Clicquot 1991 £37.99 (VIC) £37.99
(THR)

£40.00 → £99.99

Bollinger Grande Année 1990 £41.99 (VIL)
£44.54 (PEN) £49.50 (FORT) £54.00 (TAN)
£54.40 (LAY)
Bollinger Grande Année 1985 £64.63 (WY)
Dom Ruinart 1986 £59.99 (WR) £87.90
(LAY)
Jacquesson Signature 1990 £68.00 (MAY)
Laurent-Perrier magnum NV £55.95
(BALL) £56.00 (CON) £64.82 (PLAY)
£67.50 (FORT) £67.70 (JER)
Perrier-Jouët Belle Époque 1990 £54.99
(VIC) £54.99 (THR) £54.99 (BOT) £54.99
(WR)
Perrier-Jouët Belle Époque 1989 £54.01
(BY) £65.00 (FORT)
Pol Roger 1988 £42.25 (VIN)
Louis Roederer 1995 £49.90 (HAH)
Louis Roederer 1994 £44.99 (VIL)
Louis Roederer 1993 £44.50 (STA) £48.95
(VA)
Louis Roederer 1986 £47.00 (PEN)
Taittinger Comtes de Champagne 1995
£68.54 (FA) £85.00 (FORT)
Taittinger Comtes de Champagne 1993
£64.17 (PLAY)
Taittinger Comtes de Champagne 1988
£69.95 (BAL)
Veuve Clicquot 1989 £52.88 (WY)
Veuve Clicquot 1985 £60.00 (MI)

Over £100.00

Dom Pérignon 1990 £153.65 (BY)
£153.73 (FA) £165.00 (VIL) £165.00
(FORT) £210.00 (MI)
Dom Pérignon 1988 £155.78 (PLAY)
Dom Pérignon 1986 £117.50 (WY)
£170.00 (UN) £200.00 (MI)
Dom Pérignon 1982 £176.25 (TUR)
£229.12 (TW) £260.00 (VA)
Krug NV £132.77 (PLA) £139.00 (POR)
£142.41 (TW) £145.00 (VIL) £160.00 (RES)
Louis Roederer Cristal 1993 £195.00
(FORT) £199.00 (OD)
Louis Roederer Cristal 1990 £166.46 (FA)
£190.00 (STA) £190.00 (VIL) £235.00 (TW)
Louis Roederer Cristal 1989 £146.88 (FA)
£165.00 (RES)

JURA & SAVOIE

By all means try these wines when you're on holiday in this part of France. But don't fall in love with them; they're very hard to find in the UK

These wines get more and more esoteric. To be honest, I sometimes wonder why I continue to write about them: if you want to find a bottle of any of them here in Britain you have to look very hard. The merchants at the bottom of this page stock some, but I can't believe the demand is enormous. They're included for the sake of completeness; and because if you go skiing in the French Alps you might come across one or two of them. And actually, they're rather interesting.

WINES & WINE REGIONS

ARBOIS, AC (red, white, rosé) The reds are thuddingly full of flavour. The Savagnin grape weaves its demonic spell on the whites, though Chardonnay sometimes softens it. There are some attractive light reds and rosés made from Pinot Noir or Poulsard. Best: *Henri Maire, Pupillin co-op*.

BUGEY, VDQS (red, white) Look for the deliciously crisp Chardonnays; they're among the most refreshing (and yes, fruity) in France.

CÔTES DU JURA, AC (red, white, rosé) Virtually indistinguishable in style and flavour (and grape varieties) from Arbois wines, though sometimes a little less weird.

CRÉPY, AC (white) The Chasselas grape here produces an even flimsier version of the already delicate Swiss Fendant, if that's possible. Drink young and fast, or not at all.

L'ÉTOILE, AC (white) Whites from Savagnin and Chardonnay. Also *vins jaunes*.

ROUSSETTE DE SAVOIE, AC (white) Fullest and softest of the Savoie whites.

SEYSSEL, AC AND SEYSSEL MOUSSEUX, AC (white) The Roussette (blended with a little Molette) makes quite full, flower-scented but sharp-edged whites. The fizz is light but pepper-pungent. Best: *Varichon et Clerc*.

VIN JAUNE (white) This grows the same yeasty *flor* as dry sherry, and its startlingly, painfully intense flavours from the Savagnin grape just get more and more evident as it matures. In fact it seems virtually indestructible. Château-Chalon AC is the most prized – and most pricy – and is difficult to find even in the region.

VIN DE SAVOIE, AC (red, white) These Alpine vineyards are some of the most beautiful in France and produce fresh, snappy wines. The white, from the Jacquère, Chardonnay or Chasselas, can be excellent, dry, biting, but with lots of tasty fruit. Drink young. The reds from Pinot Noir or Gamay are subtly delicious, while the Mondeuse produces some beefy beauties in hot years. A *cru* name may be on the best. Look for the villages of Abymes, Chignin, Apremont, Cruet, Montmélian, Chautagne and Arbin.

RETAILERS SPECIALIZING IN JURA AND SAVOIE
see Retailers Directory (page 40) for details

Very few of these wines are available in the UK. Nobody exactly specializes in them, but the following merchants have some:

Anthony Byrne (BY), Jeroboams (JER) S H Jones (JON), Terry Platt (PLA), Roberson, Tanners (TAN), Wine Society (WS).

LOIRE

**If you want wines that will match food but are
a joy to drink on their own, and yet aren't in the least showy and flashy,
this is your region**

Things are changing in the Loire. For the better? Yes, generally speaking. I hesitate very slightly because each of the three main white grapes – Muscadet, Chenin Blanc and Sauvignon – is evolving in a different way. Muscadet is getting less dilute, providing you pick a good producer, and Sauvignon Blanc is getting riper. The latter has looked at New Zealand examples and decided not to try and copy them: instead Sancerre and Pouilly Fumé are going for more minerally and less green gooseberry flavours; more white peach and less crushed nettles. Fair enough: why should all wines taste the same?

Chenin Blanc, too, is softening its act, and despite being fond of the austere, minerally style of Savennières or Vouvray, I have to applaud that. It needs years to mature, though, and who has time for that these days? So Savennières, and perhaps Vouvray too, is getting more user-friendly, and yes, that's a good thing. As long as it doesn't become wine for wimps.

GRAPE VARIETIES

CABERNET FRANC (red) The great quality grape of Anjou and Touraine. All the best reds are based on Cabernet Franc, and the styles span the spectrum from the palest, most fleeting of reds to deep, strong and sometimes austerely tannic wines of character and longevity. Often added to (white) sparkling wines, too.

CABERNET SAUVIGNON (red) This doesn't always ripen very well in the Loire, but even so it adds some backbone to the wines. It is really only at its best in the warmest, ripest years.

CHARDONNAY (white) Increasingly widespread in the Loire and producing lean, light but tangy results in Haut-Poitou, in Anjou as Vin de Pays du Jardin de la France and in Orléans as Vin de l'Orléanais (where it's called Auvernat) – *Clos St-Fiacre* is terrific. It also occurs in Muscadet (*le Chouan* and *Domaine Couillaud* are good) and adds character and softness to Anjou Blanc.

CHASSELAS (white) Makes adequate but dull wine at Pouilly-sur-Loire; it's actually best as a table grape, in a fruit salad.

CHENIN BLANC (white) A grape that cries out for sun and ripens long after the other varieties. It also performs superbly in the Loire in a few warm and misty mesoclimates (especially in Quarts de Chaume and Bonnezeaux), where noble rot strikes the Chenin with enough frequency to make it worthwhile going through all the pain and passion of producing great sweet wine, with steely acidity and the flavour of honeyed, ripe-apple fruit and quince jelly richness.

These wines can seem curiously disappointing when young, but fine sweet Chenin manages to put on weight and become sweeter for perhaps 20 years before bursting out into a richness as exciting as all but the very best from Germany or Bordeaux. And then it lasts and lasts… Because Chenin Blanc is unfashionable, these wines can be remarkably undervalued; but you have to be prepared to tuck them away in the cellar for a long time.

GAMAY (red) In the Loire this rarely achieves the lovely, juicy glugginess of Beaujolais, but when made by a careful modern winemaker it can have a fair amount of fruit, though it always seems to have a tough edge.

MELON DE BOURGOGNE (white) The grape of Muscadet, light and neutral. It's good at producing fresh white, usually quite biting, and with a creamy but minerally tang. It's usually for drinking young, though the odd good domaine-bottled *sur lie* can mature surprisingly well.

PINOT NOIR (red) In and around Sancerre this can, in warm years like the Loire has had lately, produce a lovely, light, cherry-fragrant wine that will be either a rosé or a light red. It's not Burgundy, but it's very attractive.

SAUVIGNON BLANC (white) The grape of Sancerre and Pouilly-Fumé, with a whole range of fresh, green, tangy flavours – anything from gooseberries to nettles and fresh-cut grass, and there's sometimes even a whiff of newly roasted coffee. The wines are usually quite tart – but thirst-quenching rather than gum-searing – and have loads of fruit. Sauvignon can age interestingly in bottle, but the odds are against it, except for the high-priced oak-aged cuvées.

WINE REGIONS

ANJOU BLANC SEC, AC (white) France's cheapest AC dry white made mostly from the hard-to-ripen Chenin Blanc. It *can* be good, steely and honeyed, from names such as *Domaine Richou* which mixes Chardonnay with the Chenin, for extra flavour and fruit. Other good names: *Mark Angeli (Cuvée Christine), Baranger, Château de Valliennes, Domaine de la Haute Perche, Jaudeau.*

ANJOU ROUGE CABERNET, AC (red) This ranges from mostly quite light when from the co-ops, to spicy, strong and capable of aging from the best estates. It can rival Bourgueil. Best producers include: *Mark Angeli (Cuvée Martial), Ch. d'Avrille, Ch. de Chamboureau (Soulez), Ch. d'Épiré, Clos de Coulaine, Dom. de la Petite Croix, Dom. du Petit Val, Dom. de Rochambeau, Dom. des Rochettes (Chauvin), Logis de la Giraudière (Baumard), Vincent Ogereau, Dom. Richou, Roussier.*

ANJOU ROUGE GAMAY, AC (red) Rarely more than adequate, but in the hands of a producer like *Richou*, the 'rooty' character is replaced by a fresh, creamy fruit that is sharp and soft at once, and *very* good. Look out for *Dom des Quarres* which is also worth a try.

ANJOU-VILLAGES, AC (red) Cabernets Franc and Sauvignon from the 46 best villages in Anjou. Some are labelled Anjou-Villages Val-de-Loire. Can be delicious, and even quite substantial. *Domaine de Montgilet, Domaine Ogereau, Jean-Yves Lebreton* and *Domaine Richou* are good.

BONNEZEAUX, AC (white) One of the most unfairly forgotten great sweet wines of France. Prices for the lovely noble rot-affected wines have risen, but are still low compared to Sauternes – which itself is cheap at the price. Look out for the outstanding wines of *Mark Angeli* (from old vines), *Château de Fesles, Denéchèr, Jean Godineau, Goizil* and *Renou.*

BOURGUEIL, AC (red) Some of the best reds of the Loire Valley. When they are young they can taste a bit harsh and edgy, but give them a few years and they will have a piercing blackcurrant fruit, sharp and thirst-quenching. They can age well too, developing complex leathery, meaty flavours. Best producers: *Audebert* (estate wines), *Pierre Breton, Paul Buisse, Caslot-Galbrun, J-F Demont, Domaine des Forges, Domaine des Ouches, Pierre-Jacques Druet, Lamé-Delisle-Boucard.*

CABERNET D'ANJOU, AC (rosé)

There is a reasonable chance of a pleasant drink here, because the Cabernets – mostly Franc, but often with Cabernet Sauvignon too – do give pretty tasty wine, usually less sweet than simple Rosé d'Anjou. Best: *Château de Valliennes, Domaine Baranger, Domaine de Hardières, Domaine Richou.*

CHEVERNY, AC (red, white) This

Touraine region is improving fast. Its claim to fame is the teeth-grittingly dry white Romorantin grape, but there is also Chardonnay, Sauvignon Blanc and Chenin. *Dom. des Huards* is delicate and fine, and the *Confrérie* at *Oisly-et-Thésée* is reliable. Others: *Cazin, Gendrier, Gueritte* and *Tessier.* Red Cheverny tends to be light and crisp, with a healthy dollop of Gamay perhaps beefed up with Cabernet Franc. *Oisly-et-Thésée's* is strawberryish with a fair bit of Pinot Noir in it.

CHINON, AC (red) In a ripe year (1995,

'96 or '97), Chinon can be delicious, exhibiting a great gush of blackcurrant and raspberry flavours. Winemaking standards have risen, and the wines are generally good to very good these days. Domaine wines are *far* better than négociant wines, which can be thin. Best: *Bernard Baudry, Jean Baudry, Couly-Dutheil, Domaine du Colombier, Domaine du Roncée, Domaine de la Tour, Druet, Gatien Ferrand, René Gouron, Charles Joguet, Alain Lorieux, Pierre Manzagol, Jean-François Olek, Jean-Maurice Raffault, Julien Raffault, Olga Raffault.*

COTEAUX DE L'AUBANCE, AC

(white) Quite cheap, pleasant semi-sweet whites. Best: *Domaine des Rochettes, Domaine Richou* and *Jean-Yves Lebreton.*

COTEAUX DU LAYON, AC (white)

A large AC producing varying qualities of sweet white wine, at its best rich and tasty with a taut acidity that allows the wine to age for a long time. *Mark Angeli, Château du Breuil* (from very old vines), *Château de la Guimonière, Château de la Roulerie, Clos Ste-Catherine, Domaine Ambinois, Domaine des Baumard, Domaine du Petit Val, Domaine de la Pierre St-Maurille, Domaine des Quarres, Domaine de la Soucherie* and *Ogereau* are worth trying. There are also six Coteaux du Layon-Villages ACs that usually offer higher quality. Some Anjou growers are now making *sélection de grains nobles*, very sweet, concentrated wines made only from botrytized grapes, and therefore in only the best years.

CRÉMANT DE LOIRE, AC (white)

Sparkling wine AC intended to denote higher quality than basic sparkling Saumur. Can be made partly or entirely from Chardonnay; Chenin-based ones are in fact indistinguishable from Saumur. Best include *Ackerman, Bouvet-Ladubay, Caves de Grenelle, Cave des Liards, Gratien & Meyer, Langlois-Château, St-Cyr-en-Bourg* co-op.

GROS PLANT, VDQS (white) Gros

Plant rejoices in being one of the rawest wines in France, and the prosperity of dentists in Nantes is thanks in no small measure to the locals' predilection for the stuff. That said, it *does* go amazingly well with seafood and seems to suit oysters. *Bossard's* is soft and honeyed. *Métaireau* and *Sauvion* have also tamed its fury. *Clos de la Sénaigerie* and *Clos de la Fine* from *Dom. d'Herbauges* are good.

HAUT-POITOU, VDQS (red, white)

Chardonnay and Sauvignon from the *Cave Co-opérative du Haut-Poitou* are good but tend to leanness, for the whites; the reds are fairly 'green' but reasonably enjoyable, and are usually made from Gamay.

JASNIERES, AC (white) A tiny

appellation producing long-lived bone-dry whites from the Chenin Blanc.

MENETOU-SALON, AC (red, white,

rosé) The Sauvignon is as good as that of Sancerre, and there are some fair reds and

ON THE CASE
A run of good to very good red vintages means that Loire reds are looking increasingly good buys. Better winemaking helps, too

rosés. *Henry Pellé* makes the best in Menetou, followed by *Domaine de Chatenoy, Chavet, Jean-Paul Gilbert, Alphonse Mellot, Jean-Max Roger* and *Jean Teiller.*

MONTLOUIS, AC (white) Chenin-based wines similar to Vouvray, but often more robust – which, when it comes to the Chenin grape, isn't always a good idea. *Domaine des Liards, Dominique Moye, Domaine de la Taille aux Loups* and *Jean-Pierre Trouvé* are good.

MUSCADET, AC (white) Simple, light, neutral wine from near the coast. Straight Muscadet, without any further regional title, is usually flat and boring. But at least it's light – the Muscadet ACs are the only ones in France to impose a *maximum* alcohol level (12.3 per cent).

MUSCADET DES COTEAUX DE LA LOIRE, AC (white) Quality in this sub-region isn't bad. *Pierre Luneau* is good.

MUSCADET CÔTES DE GRAND-LIEU, AC (white) Demarcated in 1994, this latest sub-region accounts for nearly half of the area that was basic Muscadet, and quality varies. At least most is *sur lie.*

MUSCADET DE SÈVRE-ET-MAINE, AC (white) The best Muscadet. A good one may taste slightly nutty, peppery or salty, even honeyed, sometimes with creaminess from being left on the lees and sometimes with a slight prickle. It should always have a lemony acidity, and should feel light. Buy domaine-bottled wine only, and check the address, looking out for St-Fiacre and le Pallet, two of the best villages.

MUSCADET SUR LIE (white) This is the most important thing to look for on a Muscadet label. The French apparently believe it means a wine that comes from the banks of the river Lie; in fact it indicates that the wine has been bottled straight off the lees (the yeast sediment from fermentation), thus having more depth than usual and a slight prickle. Best: *Sauvion's Ch. du Cléray* and *Découvertes* range, *Guy Bossard, Dom. de Coursay-Villages, Dom. du Grand Mouton, Pierre Luneau, Dom. de la Montaine, Ch. de Chasseloir, Clos de la Sénaigerie, Jean-Louis Hervouet, Dom. du 'Perdson-pain', Louis Métaireau, Huissier,* both *Michel* and *Donatien Bahuaud's* single-domaine wines, *Bonhomme* and *Guilbaud.*

POUILLY-FUMÉ, AC (white) These can be fuller than Sancerre, and the best have a mineral complexity, but there are too many under-achievers. Best: *Ch. Favray, J C Châtelain, Didier Dagueneau* (Pouilly's most brilliant winemaker), *Serge Dagueneau, André Figeat, Ch. du Nozet, Ch. de Tracy.*

POUILLY-SUR-LOIRE, AC (white) Made from the dull Chasselas grape which makes good eating but not memorable drinking. *Serge Dagueneau* is good.

QUARTS DE CHAUME, AC (white) Rare and expensive nobly-rotten sweet wines, with high acid stalking the rich apricot-and-honey fruit. Try *Jean Baumard, Ch. Bellerive, Ch. de l'Echarderie.*

QUINCY, AC (white) Crisp Sauvignon Blanc, usually more intense than Sancerre. *D Jaumier, Pierre Mardon, Jacques Rouzé* and *Jacques Coeur* co-op are good.

REUILLY, AC (white) Light, fragrant Sauvignon Blanc. *Gérard Cordier* and *Claude Lafond* are the main growers here. There is also some tasty red and rosé.

ROSÉ D'ANJOU, AC (rosé) The omnipresent and frequently omnihorrid

French rosé. It suffers in the main from lack of fruit and excess of sulphur. A few, like the co-op at *Brissac*, can make it fresh.

ROSÉ DE LOIRE, AC (rosé) A little-made dry rosé from Anjou or Touraine, generally much better than Rosé d'Anjou.

ST-NICOLAS-DE-BOURGUEIL, AC (red) These Cabernet reds tend to be lighter and more forward than the reds of nearby Bourgueil. They can be very good, but stick to warm years. Best: *Claude Ammeux, Caslot-Jamet, Couly-Dutheil, Jean-Paul Mabileau* and *Joël Taluau*.

SANCERRE, AC (white, red, rosé) Green, smoky, tangy white from the Sauvignon Blanc grape. At its best young, it should be super-fresh and fruity, tasting and smelling of gooseberries or cut grass. Look for single-domaine wines – especially from *Archambault, F & J Bailly, Bailly-Reverdy, Balland-Chapuis, Henri Bourgeois, R Champault, Francis & Paul Cotat, Lucien Crochet, Pierre & Alain Dézat, Gitton, Dom. Laporte, Alphonse Mellot, Paul Millérioux, Henri Natter, Reverdy, Jean-Max Roger, Pierre Riffault, Vacheron* and *André Vatan*.

The rosés can be very refreshing. The reds are, in general, overrated, but the best, in good years, have a lovely cherry fragrance and sweetness of strawberries that can survive a year or two in bottle. Silly prices, though. *Henri Bourgeois, Pierre & Alain Dézat* and *Domaine Vacheron* are all well worth trying.

SAUMUR, AC (red, white, rosé) White Saumur is usually ultra-dry Chenin Blanc, though it can be sweet, similar to Anjou Blanc. The reds, from Cabernet Franc, are usually light but the fruit can be attractively blackcurranty. The co-op at *St-Cyr-en-Bourg* is good, as is *Château Fouquet*.

SAUMUR-CHAMPIGNY, AC (red) Cabernet from the best villages in Saumur. It is way above other Loire reds thanks to a

---

INSTANT CELLAR:
CABERNET FRANC

• 1998 Bourgueil, Clos Senechal, Catherine and Pierre Breton, £8.95, RSJ Lovely ripe Cabernet Franc from limestone soil, and given a year in oak. It needs a bit of time.
• 1996 Anjou Rouge Les Fouchardes, Mark Angeli, £13.80, RSJ Another star from this specialist shipper. Mark Angeli is committed to biodynamism, and his wines have great complexity.
• 1997 Saumur Rouge, Réserve de la Paleine, Domaine de la Paleine, £5.70, Tanners Lovely raspberry-fruited light summer red, best slightly chilled.
• 1993 Bourgueil Cuvée Prestige, Lamé-Delisle-Boucard, £8.65, Waterloo Wine This is rich, cherryish and complex.
• 1998 Saumur-Champigny, Château de Targé, £6.99, Waitrose Lovely light, elegant summery red with good structure.
• 1996 Chinon, La Croix Boissée, Bernard Baudry, £12.95, Haynes Hanson & Clark Complex spice and redcurrant flavours mixed with minerals and earth.
• 1999 Château Fouquet, Saumur Rouge, £7.50, Yapp Cabernet Franc of great depth and richness.

---

firm structure and velvety softness, fruit that is slightly raw and rasping, yet succulent and rich at the same time. Although the term 'vieilles vignes' is open to interpretation it is always the best bet for quality. *Domaine Filliatreau* makes an outstanding one. Also good: *Château de Chaintres, Château du Hureau, Château de Targé, Domaine Dubois, Domaine Lavigne, Domaine Sauzay-Legrand, Domaine de Nerleux, Domaine des Roches Neuves, Domaine du Val Brun, Denis Duveau*.

SAUMUR MOUSSEUX, AC (white) Champagne-method fizz from Chenin Blanc, perhaps with the welcome addition of Chardonnay or Cabernet Franc to round out the acid Chenin. Quality is better than it's been for years, thanks to warm summers and better winemaking. Best: *Ackerman, Bouvet-Ladubay, Gratien & Meyer, Langlois-*

Château, Jacky Clée, Caves de Grenelle, Dom. Hauts de Sanziers.

SAVENNIÈRES, AC (white) Some of the world's steeliest, longest-living, diamond-dry white wines come from this tiny Anjou AC where the Chenin grape comes into its own. One vineyard, Coulée-de-Serrant, has its own AC within Savennières, and *Nicolas Joly*'s *Clos de la Coulée-de-Serrant* is excellent. Wine styles generally in Savennières are edging towards more softness, however, and that extreme steeliness could become a thing of the past. Also: *Yves Soulez* from the *Château de Chamboreau, Château d'Épiré, Clos du Papillon, Jean Baumard (Clos Ste-Catherine), Dom. de la Bizolière, Dom. aux Moines, Dom. du Closel, Mme Laroche.*

TOURAINE, AC (red, white) Everybody sees Touraine Sauvignon, with some justification, as a Sancerre substitute. The *Confrérie des Vignerons d'Oisly-et-Thésée* is good, as are *Paul Buisse, Ch. de l'Aulée, Dom. de la Charmoise (Marionnet), Ch. de Chenonceau, Dom. des Corbillières, Dom. Joël Delaunay* and *Dom. Octavie*. The reds have benefited from a run of warm years, though even at their ripest are seldom terrifically weighty. The *Domaine de la Charmoise (Marionnet)*, and the co-op of *Oisly-et-Thésée* produce fair Gamays. *Château de Chenonceau*'s is also good.

VIN DE PAYS DU JARDIN DE LA FRANCE (white, red, rosé) The general vin de pays of the Loire. Those based on Sauvignon Blanc and Chardonnay are the ones to go for, especially from *Ackerman-Laurence, Ch. de la Botinière, Ch. du Breuil* and *Domaine des Forges*.

VOUVRAY, AC (white) Sparkling and still whites from tangily dry to richly sweet, though often at its best in the off-dry demi-sec style. From a good producer this Chenin wine, initially all searing acidity, rasping dryness and green angelica fruit, over many years develops a deep honey-and-quince flavour. Best: *Daniel Allias, Bourillon-Dorléans, Brédif, Paul Buisse, Champalou, Ch. Gaudrelle, Ch. Moncontour, Dom. des Aubuisières, Dom. du Margelleau, Dom. de Vaugoudy, Foreau, Benoît Gautier, Huet, Pierre Mabille, Prince Poniatowski.*

LOIRE VINTAGES

Loire vintages are very variable, and can be radically different along the river length. In poor vintages, Muscadet is most likely to be okay, while in hot vintages Sauvignon goes dull, but the Chenin finally ripens. The red grapes need the warm years.

2000 A decent to good year, a bit too cool to be really good.

1999 A difficult vintage. The best will be good, and there'll be some great sweet Chenin.

1998 Less good and more mixed than '96 or '97. Sauvignon and Cabernet Franc look best.

1997 A splendid year for reds and for Chenin. Good fruity Sauvignon.

1996 The reds and the Chenin had a bumper year and should age well.

1995 Some luscious dessert wines as well as fine reds, but quality is not even.

1994 Fair dry whites, but Coteaux du Layon should be best of all. Reds are lightweight.

1993 Good, flinty whites. The best Coteaux du Layon is botrytized and concentrated.

LOIRE PRICES

DRY WHITE

Under £4.00

Sauvignon de Touraine Bougrier 1999
£3.95 (WS)
Sauvignon de Touraine Confrérie d'Oisly
et Thésée 2000 £3.99 (MAJ)

£4.00 → £4.99

VdP du Jardin de la France Chardonnay,
Cave du Haut-Poitou 1999 £4.15 (CON)
Muscadet de Sèvre-et-Maine des Ducs,
Chereau Carré 2000 £4.56 (BIB)
Muscadet de Sèvre-et-Maine Fief de la
Brie, Bonhomme 2000 £4.99 (TAN)
Muscadet de Sèvre-et-Maine Fief de la
Brie, Bonhomme 1998 £4.99 (POR)
Muscadet de Sèvre-et-Maine sur lie Carte
d'Or, Sauvion 1999 £4.95 (NEZ)
Muscadet de Sèvre-et-Maine sur lie Cuvée
Prestige, Saupin 1999 £4.95 (AD)
Muscadet de Sèvre-et-Maine sur lie Fief de
la Brie, Bonhomme 1999 £4.99 (JON)
Muscadet de Sèvre-et-Maine sur lie Fief de
la Brie, Bonhomme 1998 £4.95 (BALL)
Muscadet de Sèvre-et-Maine sur lie
Domaine des Ratelles 1999 £4.75 (WS)
Muscadet sur lie Côtes de Grand Lieu,
Clos de la Senaigerie 1998 £4.95 (JU)
Sauvignon de Touraine Domaine de
Bellevue, Tijou et Fils 2000 £4.95 (BER)
£5.75 (MAY)
Sauvignon de Touraine Domaine de la
Bergerie 2000 £4.95 (AD) £4.99 (GW)
Sauvignon de Touraine Caves de Coteaux
Romanais 1995 £4.95 (JU)
Sauvignon de Touraine Domaine de la
Renaudie 2000 £4.99 (OD)
Vouvray Speciale, Saget 1999 £4.99 (VIL)
£6.30 (VIN)

£5.00 → £5.99

Cheverny Domaine Salvard 1999 £5.75
(AD)
VdP du Jardin de la France Sauvignon
Blanc Petit Bourgeois, Henri Bourgeois
1999 £5.95 (CON)
Menetou-Salon Morogues, Pellé 1999
£5.75 (SOM) £6.95 (WS)
Muscadet de Sèvre-et-Maine Chon 2000
£5.58 (LLO)
Muscadet de Sèvre-et-Maine sur lie
Domaine du Bois Bruley 1999 £5.99 (BAL)
Muscadet de Sèvre-et-Maine sur lie
Domaine de Bois Joly 1999 £5.59 (CON)
Muscadet de Sèvre-et-Maine sur lie
Château de l'Oiselinière de la Ramée
1999 £5.50 (WS) £6.99 (BAL)
Muscadet de Sèvre-et-Maine sur lie
Domaine Saupin 2000 £5.95 (NI)
Muscadet sur lie Domaine de Basseville,
Bossard 1999 £5.45 (STE)
Muscadet sur lie Château de la
Galissonière 1999 £5.99 (DI)
St-Pourçain Cuvée Printanière, Union des
Vignerons 2000 £5.95 (YAP)
Saumur Blanc Domaine Langlois-Château
2000 £5.53 (GN)
Saumur Blanc Château de Villeneuve
1998 £5.95 (BAC)
Saumur Domaine des Hauts de Sanziers
1997 £5.00 (RSJ)
Saumur Cave des Vignerons de Saumur
2000 £5.45 (YAP)
Sauvignon de Touraine Domaine de la
Charmoise, Marionnet 1999 £5.25
(BALL) £6.70 (NI)
Sauvignon de Touraine Domaine de la
Preslé 1999 £5.50 (BAC) £5.95 (COC)
Touraine Azay-le-Rideau Pascal Pibaleau
1998 £5.35 (WAT)

RETAILERS SPECIALIZING IN THE LOIRE
see Retailers Directory (page 40) for details

Unusually imaginative lists can be found
at: Adnams (AD), Averys of Bristol,
Ballantynes (BAL), Bennetts (BEN),
Anthony Byrne (BY), D Byrne, Justerini &
Brooks (JU), Lay & Wheeler (LAY), The
Nobody Inn (NO), Terry Platt (PLA),
Raeburn Fine Wines (RAE), The RSJ Wine
Co (RSJ), T&W Wines (TW), Tanners
(TAN), Waterloo Wine (WAT), The Wine
Society (WS), Noel Young (YOU).

£6.00 → £6.99

Anjou Blanc le Haut de la Garde, Château de Pierre Bise 1998 £6.85 (RSJ)

Cheverny Domaine Salvard 2000 £6.55 (NI)

Coteaux du Giennois Gitton 1997 £6.50 (HIG)

Menetou-Salon Clos des Blanchais, Pellé 2000 £6.75 (SOM) £10.50 (MV)

Muscadet de Sèvre-et-Maine sur lie Château de Cléray 1999 £6.25 (NEZ) £7.10 (GAU)

Muscadet sur lie Domaine Grand Mouton, Métaireau 1998 £6.95 (RIC)

Pouilly-Fumé Bailly 1999 £6.99 (MORR)

Pouilly-Fumé Chatelain 1999 £6.50 (SOM) £8.99 (WAI)

Reuilly Beurdin 2000 £6.49 (MAJ)

Sancerre Cuvée Flores, Vincent Pinard 1999 £6.75 (SOM)

Sauvignon de Touraine Domaine de Bellevue, Tijou et Fils 1998 £6.50 (HIG)

Savennières Clos de la Coulaine, Château de Pierre Bise 1998 £6.95 (LEA) £7.95 (RSJ)

Vin de Thouarsais, Gigon 1999 £6.60 (YAP)

£7.00 → £7.99

Anjou Blanc le Haut de la Garde, Château de Pierre Bise 1997 £7.75 (LEA)

Menetou-Salon la Charnivolle, Fournier 2000 £7.99 (MAJ)

Menetou-Salon Roger 1999 £7.60 (TAN)

Montlouis les Batisses, Deletang 1995 £7.95 (WS)

Muscadet de Sèvre-et-Maine sur lie Château de la Ragotière 1998 £7.01 (VIN)

Pouilly Fumé Fine Caillottes, Pabiot 1998 £7.95 (AD)

Pouilly-Fumé les Bascoins, Masson-Blondelet 2000 £7.50 (BAN)

Pouilly-Fumé les Logères, Saget 1999 £7.95 (BALL) £8.99 (VIL) £10.30 (VIN) £11.99 (VA)

Quincy Jaumier 2000 £7.95 (YAP)

Reuilly Beurdin 1998 £7.80 (BAN)

- *Wines are listed in A–Z order within each price band.*
- *For each wine, vintages are listed in descending order.*
- *Each vintage of any wine appears only once.*

Sancerre Daulny 1999 £7.04 (WHI)

Sancerre Domaine du P'tit Roy 1999 £7.99 (BO)

Sancerre Domaine des Trois Piessons 2000 £7.99 (WR)

Savennières Clos du Papillon, Baumard 1997 £7.95 (SOM) £11.99 (VIL) £16.98 (TW)

Touraine Azay-le-Rideau la Basse Chevrière, Pavy 1997 £7.95 (YAP)

Vouvray Château Gaudrelle 1999 £7.50 (JER) £7.50 (JU) £8.45 (NI)

£8.00 → £9.99

Menetou-Salon Domaine de Chatenoy 1999 £8.99 (DI)

Menetou-Salon Clos des Blanchais, Pellé 1999 £8.40 (AD) £11.69 (TW)

Menetou-Salon la Charnivolle, Fournier 1999 £8.40 (STA)

Menetou-Salon Morogues, Pellé 2000 £9.20 (MV)

Menetou-Salon Pellé 1999 £8.00 (BAN)

Menetou-Salon Domaine du Prieuré 1999 £8.25 (CON)

Menetou-Salon Teiller 2000 £8.75 (YAP)

Pouilly-Fumé André Dezat 1999 £9.00 (BAC)

Pouilly-Fumé Chatelain 2000 £8.99 (MAR)

Pouilly-Fumé Serge Dagueneau 1999 £9.15 (HAH) £9.50 (JU)

Pouilly Fumé Fine Caillottes, Pabiot 1999 £8.65 (LAY) £8.79 (JON) £8.95 (BU)

Pouilly-Fumé les Berthiers, Claude Michot 2000 £8.72 (BIB)

Pouilly-Fumé les Chantes des Vignes, Mellot 1998 £9.04 (PEN)

Pouilly-Fumé Masson-Blondelet 2000 £8.49 (WAI)

Pouilly-Fumé Domaine des Rabichattes 1998 £8.99 (RAE)

Pouilly-Fumé Seguin 2000 £8.49 (VIC) £8.49 (THR) £8.49 (WR) £8.95 (LEA)

Pouilly-Fumé Domaine Thibault 1999 £8.75 (TAN) £9.36 (HIC) £9.99 (JON)

Pouilly-Fumé Château de Tracy 1998 £9.95 (BALL) £10.25 (HAH) £10.50 (WS)

Quincy Jean-Michel Sorbe 2000 £8.25 (NI)

Sancerre André Dézat 1999 £8.50 (TAN) £8.99 (JON) £9.11 (HIC)

Sancerre Clos du Chêne Marchand, Roger 2000 £9.95 (FORT)

Sancerre Clos du Roy, Millérioux 1998 £9.96 (COC)

Sancerre Daulny 2000 £8.19 (JON) £8.75 (HAH)

Sancerre Jean Thomas 2000 £8.42 (BIB)

Sancerre la Bourgeoise, Henri Bourgeois 1999 £9.95 (SOM)

Sancerre la Graveliere, Mellot 1999 £8.11 (PEN)

Sancerre le Chêne, Crochet 1999 £9.90 (JU)

Sancerre les Belles Dames, Gitton 1998 £9.20 (HIG)

Sancerre les Monts Damnés, Henri Bourgeois 1999 £9.50 (SOM) £10.99 (OD)

Sancerre les Perriers, Fournier 1998 £9.95 (STA)

Sancerre les Perriers, Vatan 2000 £9.95 (YAP)

Sancerre les Roches, Vacheron 1999 £9.95 (STE)

Sancerre Domaine de Montigny, Natter 1999 £9.85 (LAY) £9.99 (RAE)

Sancerre Domaine du Nozay, de Benoist 2000 £9.75 (CB)

Sancerre Paul Prieur 1999 £9.49 (BAL)

Sancerre Domaine du P'tit Roy 1998 £9.32 (COC)

Sancerre Roger 1999 £9.99 (BEN)

Saumur Blanc Château du Hureau 1996 £9.60 (MV) £11.69 (TW)

Savennières Clos des Maurières, Domaine des Forges 1997 £8.25 (HAH)

Savennières Domaine du Closel, Mme de Jessey 1997 £9.25 (YAP) £11.75 (FORT)

Savennières Château d'Epiré 1998 £8.75 (YAP)

Savennières Roche-aux-Moines, Domaine Aux Moines 1996 £8.95 (HAH) £9.85 (RSJ)

Vouvray Brédif 1998 £9.75 (CON) £9.99 (VIL) £10.96 (PLAY)

Vouvray Château Gaudrelle 2000 £8.50 (LEA)

Vouvray le Haut Lieu, Huet 1997 £8.99 (RAE)

Vouvray le Haut Lieu, Huet 1993 £9.31 (BIB)

Vouvray le Mont, Huet 1998 £9.90 (JU)

£10.00 → £14.99

Pouilly-Fumé André Dezat 2000 £10.25 (NI)

Pouilly-Fumé Domaine des Berthiers, Jean-Claude Dagueneau 1999 £10.75 (WRI)

Pouilly-Fumé Clos Joanne d'Orion, Gitton 1997 £10.50 (HIG)

Pouilly-Fumé les Pechignolles 1998 £10.00 (HIG)

Pouilly-Fumé Château du Nozet, de Ladoucette 1998 £14.99 (COC) £15.49 (MAJ) £16.00 (WS) £17.75 (JER)

Pouilly-Fumé Château de Tracy 1999 £10.95 (LEA) £10.99 (POR) £10.99 (JON) £11.35 (LAY) £11.99 (CB) £12.95 (JER)

Pouilly-Fumé Villa Paulus, Masson-Blondelet 1999 £11.06 (NO)

Sancerre André Dézat 2000 £10.25 (NI)

Sancerre Chavignol le Manoir, André Neveu 2000 £10.21 (BIB)

Sancerre Chavignol les Monts Damnés, Cotat 1998 £14.95 (BAL)

Sancerre Clos du Chaudenay Vieilles Vignes, Daulny 1999 £12.95 (POR)

Sancerre Comte Lafond, Château du Nozet 1999 £14.99 (MAJ)

Sancerre Culs de Beaujeu, Cotat 1998 £13.95 (RAE) £14.40 (GAU) £14.95 (BAL)

Sancerre Cuvée François de la Grange, Natter 1998 £12.24 (BIB)

Sancerre Cuvée Harmonie, Pinard 1997 £14.99 (UN)

Sancerre la Bourgeoise, Henri Bourgeois 1998 £13.49 (CON)

Sancerre la Grande Côte, Cotat 1998 £14.95 (RAE) £15.50 (GAU)

Sancerre la Croix au Garde, Pellé 2000 £10.00 (MV)

Sancerre les Baronnes, Henri Bourgeois 1998 £10.78 (NO)

Sancerre les Perriers, Reverdy Ducroux 1998 £10.99 (VA)

Sancerre les Roches, Vacheron 1998 £10.99 (UN) £10.99 (GN)

Sancerre Domaine de la Mercy Dieu, Bailly-Reverdy 1999 £11.95 (FORT)

Savennières Domaine de la Bizolière 1998 £11.25 (YAP)

Savennières Château de Chamboureau, Soulez 1996 £11.45 (YAP)

Savennières Clos du Papillon, Domaine du Closel 1997 £11.25 (YAP)

Savennières Clos St-Yves, Baumard 1996 £14.27 (TW)

Savennières Roche-aux-Moines, Château de Chamboureau 1996 £11.35 (NO)

Savennières Roche-aux-Moines Clos de la Coulée-de-Serrant, Joly 1992 £12.99 (DI)

Vouvray Aigle Blanc, Poniatowski 1996 £10.95 (BEN)

Vouvray Château Gaudrelle 1998 £12.60 (LAY)

£15.00 → £19.99

Pouilly-Fumé du Buisson Renard, Didier Dagueneau **1999** £15.20 (BAN)
Pouilly-Fumé en Chailloux, Didier Dagueneau **1999** £15.25 (TAN) £15.75 (BAN) £16.50 (JU) £17.95 (LAY)
Pouilly-Fumé Château du Nozet, de Ladoucette **1999** £15.95 (STA) £17.25 (FORT) £17.75 (BER)
Pouilly-Fumé Pur Sang, Didier Dagueneau **1999** £15.20 (BAN) £21.00 (JU)
Sancerre Chavignol la Grande Côte, Cotat **1998** £15.95 (BAL)
Sancerre Cuvée Harmonie, Pinard **1995** £18.00 (JU)
Vouvray le Haut Lieu, Huet **1989** £15.00 (WS)

£20.00 → £29.99

Pouilly-Fumé en Chailloux, Didier Dagueneau **1997** £21.09 (TW)
Pouilly-Fumé Pur Sang, Didier Dagueneau **1998** £27.90 (TW)
Pouilly-Fumé Silex, Didier Dagueneau **1999** £28.00 (BAN)
Savennières Coulée-de-Serrant Clos de la Coulée-de-Serrant, Joly **1996** £24.99 (RAE) £28.50 (BAL) £37.50 (MI)
Savennières Roche-aux-Moines Clos de la Coulée-de-Serrant, Joly **1981** £29.00 (CRO)

Vouvray le Haut Lieu, Huet **1969** £28.25 (WAT)

£30.00 → £39.99

Pouilly-Fumé Baron de L Château du Nozet **1997** £34.50 (WRI) £36.00 (FORT) £40.20 (JER)
Pouilly-Fumé Baron de L Château du Nozet **1996** £37.79 (PLAY)
Pouilly-Fumé Silex, Didier Dagueneau **1998** £38.48 (TW)
Pouilly-Fumé Silex, Didier Dagueneau **1995** £33.19 (FA)

Savennières Coulée-de-Serrant Clos de la Coulée-de-Serrant, Joly **1997** £31.00 (STA) £32.50 (MI)
Savennières Coulée-de-Serrant Clos de la Coulée-de-Serrant, Joly **1994** £38.33 (MI)
Savennières Roche-aux-Moines Clos de la Coulée-de-Serrant, Joly **1979** £39.00 (CRO)
Vouvray le Haut Lieu, Huet **1978** £31.00 (CRO)

Over £40.00

Savennières Coulée-de-Serrant Clos de la Coulée-de-Serrant, Joly **1976** £80.00 (MI)
Savennières Roche-aux-Moines Clos de la Coulée-de-Serrant, Joly **1998** £40.00 (YAP)
Savennières Roche-aux-Moines Clos de la Coulée-de-Serrant, Joly **1969** £62.00 (CRO)

SPARKLING

Under £8.00

Saumur Brut Bouvet-Ladubay **Non-vintage** £7.99 (MAJ) £8.50 (JU) £8.97 (BY)
Saumur Brut La Grande Marque **Non-vintage** £6.50 (BALL)
Saumur Brut La Grande Marque **1998** £6.95 (POR)
Saumur Brut La Grande Marque **1993** £6.99 (JON)

£8.00 → £9.99

Crémant de Loire Domaine Langlois-Château **Non-vintage** £8.25 (GN)
Montlouis Brut Domaine des Liards, Berger Frères **Non-vintage** £8.75 (YAP) £9.80 (JU)
Montlouis Demi-sec Domaine des Liards, Berger Frères **Non-vintage** £8.75 (YAP)
Saphir Bouvet-Ladubay **1998** £8.00 (HIG)
Saphir Bouvet-Ladubay **1997** £9.45 (NI)
Saumur Demi-Sec, Bouvet-Ladubay **Non-vintage** £8.50 (JU)
Saumur Domaine Langlois-Château **Non-vintage** £8.99 (DI)
Saumur Rosé Brut, Bouvet-Ladubay **Non-vintage** £8.00 (HIG) £9.00 (JU)
Saumur Rosé Excellence, Bouvet-Ladubay **Non-vintage** £9.95 (FORT)
Saumur Rosé Domaine Langlois-Château **Non-vintage** £9.99 (DI)

Vouvray Brut Brédif **Non-vintage** £9.99
(VIL) £10.99 (JON)
Vouvray Brut Jarry **Non-vintage** £8.95
(YAP)
Vouvray Pétillant Brut, Huet **1997** £8.95
(WS) £10.85 (RAE)

Over £10.00

Saumur Cuvée Flamme, Gratien & Meyer
Non-vintage £12.50 (CRO)
Vouvray Mousseux Méthode
Traditionelle, Huet **Non-vintage**
£10.77 (BIB) £10.85 (RAE)
Vouvray Pétillant Brut, Huet **Non-vintage** £10.50 (JU) £10.85 (RAE)

MEDIUM & SWEET WHITE

Under £7.00

Coteaux du Layon Château de Bellevue,
Tijou et Fils **1998** £6.50 (HIG)
Coteaux du Layon Château de Bellevue,
Tijou et Fils **1993** £6.99 (HIG)
Coteaux du Layon Chaume Château de
Bellevue, Tijou **1994** £6.75 (HIG)
Coteaux du Layon Domaine des Forges,
Branchereau **1999** £6.95 (AD)
Vouvray Demi-Sec Château Moncontour
1999 £5.95 (STE)
Vouvray Demi-Sec Château Moncontour
1998 £5.75 (BALL) £5.95 (STE) £6.99
(GN)
Vouvray Château Gaudrelle **1999** £6.95
(TAN)
Vouvray Philippe de Sivray **1999** £4.99
(JON) £6.49 (POR)
Vouvray Domaine de la Robinière **1999**
£5.49 (WAI)

£7.00 → £8.99

Coteaux de l'Aubance Domaine Richou
1997 £7.50 (WAT)
Coteaux du Layon Beaulieu, Chéné **1989**
£8.90 (JU)
Coteaux du Layon Chaume, Domaine des
Forges **1998** £8.99 (UN) £9.95 (NI)
Coteaux du Layon Chaume Château
Soucherie, Tijou **1993** £8.85 (WAT)
Coteaux du Layon Domaine du Petit Val
1998 £7.30 (TAN)
Coteaux du Layon St-Aubin de Luigné,
Domaine des Forges **1999** £8.00 (MV)
Coteaux du Layon St-Aubin de Luigné,
Domaine des Forges **1997** £8.60 (WRI)

Montlouis Domaine des Liards Vieilles
Vignes, Berger Frères **1999** £7.50 (YAP)
Montlouis Domaine des Liards Vieilles
Vignes, Berger Frères **1990** £7.95 (JU)
Touraine Azay-le-Rideau Moelleux,
Pibaleau **1995** £7.99 (WAT)
Vouvray Moelleux Jarry **1996** £8.95 (YAP)

£9.00 → £12.99

Bonnezeaux la Montagne Domaine du
Petit Val, Goizil **1989** £12.50 (JU)
Coteaux du Layon Chaume, Branchereau
1994 £12.45 (NO)
Coteaux du Layon Chaume, Domaine des
Forges **1995** £10.50 (JU)
Coteaux du Layon Chaume les Onnis,
Domaine des Forges **1999** £11.95 (TAN)
Coteaux du Layon Clos de Ste-Catherine,
Baumard **1998** £11.75 (SOM)
Coteaux du Layon Clos de Ste-Catherine,
Baumard **1995** £11.75 (COC)
Coteaux du Layon Rablay, Château la
Tomaze **1999** £9.25 (YAP)
Montlouis Domaine des Liards Vendange
Tardive, Berger Frères **1997** £11.25
(YAP)
Montlouis Domaine des Liards Vendange
Tardive, Berger Frères **1990** £12.90 (JU)
Quarts-de-Chaume Lalanne Bellerive
1992 £9.95 (WS)
Vouvray Clos du Bourg Demi-Sec, Huet
1994 £12.99 (RAE)
Vouvray Clos du Bourg Demi-Sec, Huet
1993 £11.99 (JON)
Vouvray Clos Naudin Demi-Sec, Foreau
1996 £11.90 (GAU)
Vouvray le Haut Lieu Demi-Sec, Huet
1989 £11.90 (JU) £12.30 (RAE)
Vouvray le Mont Demi-Sec, Huet **1998**
£11.66 (BIB)
Vouvray Moelleux Gilles Champion **1995**
£10.70 (LAY)

£13.00 → £15.99

Bonnezeaux la Montagne Domaine du
Petit Val, Goizil **1997** £14.50 (MV)
£15.00 (FORT)
Coteaux du l'Aubance les Trois
Demoiselles, Domaine Richou **1997**
£13.20 (HAH)
Coteaux du Layon Chaume les Onnis,
Domaine des Forges **1997** £14.00 (MV)
Coteaux du Layon Chaume les Onnis,
Domaine des Forges **1995** £13.50 (JU)
£19.90 (CRO)

Coteaux du Layon Chaume, Château de
la Roulérie **1995** £13.95 (DI)

Coteaux du Layon Rablay Cuvée des Lys,
Château la Tomaze **1995** £14.95 (YAP)

Montlouis Moelleux, Dominique Moyer
1995 £13.60 (LAY)

Quarts-de-Chaume Baumard **1993**
£13.45 (SOM)

Vouvray Clos du Bourg Demi-Sec, Huet
2000 £13.71 (BIB)

Vouvray Clos du Bourg Demi-Sec, Huet
1996 £15.51 (TW)

Vouvray Clos du Bourg Moelleux , Huet
1988 £14.50 (JU)

Vouvray le Haut Lieu Moelleux, Huet
1997 £14.50 (RAE) £21.37 (NO)

Vouvray le Mont Moelleux, Huet **1995**
£13.45 (WAT) £13.99 (RAE)

Vouvray Réserve Spéciale, Château
Gaudrelle **1997** £14.50 (LEA)

£16.00 → £19.99

Anjou Moulin, Touchais **1962** £19.50 (BU)

Coteaux du Layon Chaume les Aunis,
Château de la Roulerie **1997** £16.47 (NO)

Coteaux du Layon Chaume Cuvée
Corentine, Château de la Roulérie **1989**
£19.14 (NO)

Coteaux du Layon Chaume Cuvée Louis,
Château de la Roulérie **1990** £17.64 (NO)

Coteaux du Layon les Coteaux, Château
de la Roulérie **1990** £17.64 (NO)

Coteaux du Layon Rablay Cuvée des Lys,
Château la Tomaze **1990** £18.75 (YAP)

Coteaux du Layon Château de la Roulerie
1997 £19.99 (DI)

Jasnières les Truffieres, Pinon **1989**
£17.95 (YAP)

Montlouis Domaine des Liards Grains
Nobles de Pineau, Berger Frères **1990**
£18.00 (JU) £25.00 (YAP)

Montlouis Domaine des Liards Vendange
Tardive, Berger Frères **1989** £17.50
(YAP)

Quarts-de-Chaume Baumard **1996**
£18.60 (SOM) £32.97 (NO)

Quarts-de-Chaume Château de Bellerive
1989 £19.90 (JU)

• *All prices for each wine are listed
together in ascending order.*
• *Price bands refer to the lowest price
for which the wine is available.*

Quarts-de-Chaume Lalanne Bellerive
1986 £16.50 (WS)

Quarts-de-Chaume Domaine du Petit
Metris, Renou **1995** £19.90 (JU)

Sancerre Vendange du 27 Octobre 1995,
Crochet **1995** £19.50 (JU)

Vouvray Aigle Blanc Réserve, Poniatowski
1976 £17.00 (CRO)

Vouvray Clos du Bourg Demi-Sec, Huet
1997 £17.95 (FORT)

Vouvray le Mont Moelleux, Huet **1996**
£18.95 (AD)

Vouvray le Mont Moelleux, Huet **1990**
£17.32 (NO)

£20.00 → £29.99

Anjou Moulin, Touchais **1970** £29.50 (BU)

Bonnezeaux Château de Fesles **1996**
£24.09 (PLA)

Bonnezeaux Château de Fesles 50cl
bottle **1998** £23.99 (OD)

Bonnezeaux Château de Fesles 50cl
bottle **1997** £22.42 (NO) £23.95 (BER)

Coteaux du Layon Chaume les Aunis,
Château de la Roulerie **1994** £29.00
(NO)

Coteaux du Layon Clos de Ste-Catherine,
Baumard **1989** £29.50 (CRO) £36.00 (NO)

Coteaux de Saumur Moelleux, Château
du Hureau **1996** £20.74 (TW)

Montlouis les Batisses, Deletang **1990**
£22.00 (WS)

Quarts-de-Chaume Baumard **1997**
£26.50 (SOM) £44.38 (NO) £55.64 (TW)

Quarts-de-Chaume Château de Bellerive
1995 £22.50 (BAL)

Quarts-de-Chaume Château de Bellerive
1990 £20.00 (JU) £24.58 (NO)

Quarts-de-Chaume Château de Bellerive
1985 £22.00 (CRO)

Quarts-de-Chaume Bise **1999** £22.40 (RSJ)

Quarts-de-Chaume Lalanne Bellerive
1989 £22.93 (NO)

Vouvray Clos Baudoin Moelleux,
Poniatowski **1996** £26.95 (LIB)

Vouvray Clos du Bourg Moelleux , Huet
1989 £24.00 (JU) £25.00 (WS)

Vouvray Clos Naudin Demi-Sec, Foreau
1973 £21.00 (CRO)

Vouvray Cuvée Constance, Huet **1995**
£29.95 (RAE)

Vouvray Demi-Sec Domaine Peu de la
Moriette **1989** £21.00 (CRO)

Vouvray le Haut Lieu Demi-Sec, Huet
1976 £23.00 (CRO)

Vouvray le Haut Lieu Moelleux, Huet
1996 £20.74 (TW)
Vouvray le Mont Moelleux, Huet **1997**
£24.87 (FA)
Vouvray Moelleux Domaine Peu de la
Moriette **1989** £28.00 (CRO)
Vouvray Réserve Spéciale, Château
Gaudrelle **1989** £22.00 (JU)

£30.00 → £39.99

Bonnezeaux la Chapelle, Château de
Fesles **1990** £38.42 (NO)
Quarts-de-Chaume Baumard **1990**
£30.14 (NO) £56.98 (TW)
Savennières Liquoreux, Coulée de
Serrant **1995** £34.00 (JU)
Vouvray Brédif **1964** £32.00 (CRO)
Vouvray Clos Baudoin Moelleux,
Poniatowski **1989** £32.95 (LIB)
Vouvray Clos du Bourg Demi-Sec, Huet
1989 £39.00 (CRO)
Vouvray le Haut Lieu Demi-Sec, Huet
1949 £39.50 (RAE)
Vouvray le Haut Lieu Moelleux, Huet
1989 £35.00 (JU)

£40.00 → £49.99

Anjou Moulin, Touchais **1959** £49.50 (BU)
Bonnezeaux Château de Fesles **1997**
£45.76 (TW)
Vouvray Clos du Bourg Moelleux , Huet
1969 £47.00 (YOU)
Vouvray Clos du Bourg Moelleux , Huet
1962 £45.43 (FA) £48.50 (RAE)
Vouvray Doux Brédif **1964** £44.00 (CRO)
Vouvray le Mont Moelleux, Huet **1957**
£48.37 (FA) £69.80 (RAE)

£50.00 → £99.99

Anjou Moulin, Touchais **1949** £85.00 (BU)
Anjou Moulin, Touchais **1945** £95.00 (BU)
Anjou Rablay, Maison Prunier **1928**
£88.00 (CRO)
Bonnezeaux Château des Gauliers, Mme
Fourlinnie **1959** £68.00 (CRO)
Quarts-de-Chaume Baumard **1971**
£63.17 (NO)
Vouvray Brédif **1955** £50.00 (CRO) £75.00
(VIL)
Vouvray Cuvée Constance, Huet **1998**
£50.00 (YOU)
Vouvray le Haut Lieu Moelleux, Huet
1959 £50.00 (CRO)
Vouvray le Haut Lieu Moelleux, Huet
1949 £71.87 (FA)

Over £100.00

Bonnezeaux Château des Gauliers, Mme
Fourlinnie **1953** £105.00 (CRO)
Quarts-de-Chaume Baumard **1976**
£110.02 (NO)
Vouvray le Haut Lieu Moelleux, Huet
1924 £133.00 (RAE) £223.25 (TW)

ROSÉ

Under £8.50

Reuilly Pinot Gris, Cordier **1997** £7.75
(YAP)
Sancerre Rosé le Rabault, Mellot **1998**
£8.11 (PEN)

£8.50 → £9.49

Sancerre Rosé les Baronnes, Henri
Bourgeois **1998** £9.45 (CON)
Sancerre Rosé Domaine de la Mercy
Dieu, Bailly-Reverdy **1999** £8.95 (LAY)

Over £9.50

Sancerre Pinot-Rosé, Crochet **2000**
£9.60 (JU)
Sancerre Rosé André Dezat **1999** £9.59
(JON) £9.92 (HIC) £10.20 (LAY) £10.50
(FORT)
Sancerre Rosé Chavignol Domaine
Delaporte **2000** £9.95 (LEA)
Sancerre Rosé Cotat **1999** £9.95 (WS)
Sancerre Rosé les Romains, Vacheron
1999 £9.75 (STE)
Sancerre Rosé Domaine de Montigny,
Natter **1999** £10.20 (LAY)

RED

Under £5.00

VdP du Jardin de la France Gamay, Cave
du Haut-Poitou **1999** £4.15 (CON)
Saumur Cave des Vignerons de Saumur
1999 £4.95 (AD) £5.95 (YAP)

£5.00 → £6.99

Anjou Rouge Tijou **1998** £5.25 (HIG)
Bourgueil Cuvée Prestige, Lamé-Delille-
Boucard **1995** £6.05 (WAT)
Bourgueil Lamé-Delille-Boucard **1996**
£6.15 (WAT)
Chinon les Morillères, Caves Rabelais
1997 £5.45 (JU)

Côte Roannaise Vieilles Vignes, Serol
1999 £6.49 (BAL)

Gamay de Touraine Domaine de la
Charmoise, Marionnet **1999** £6.70 (NI)

St-Nicolas-de-Bourgueil Taluau **1998**
£6.95 (WS)

Saumur-Champigny Château des
Chaintres **1999** £6.75 (WS)

Saumur-Champigny Domaine de Nerleux
1999 £6.75 (RSJ) £7.10 (HAH)

Saumur-Champigny Domaine des Roches
Neuves **1996** £6.61 (NO)

Saumur-Champigny Château Villeneuve
1999 £6.95 (RSJ)

Saumur Domaine Langlois-Château **1999**
£5.70 (GN)

£7.00 → £8.99

Anjou-Villages Domaine des Rochelles,
Lebreton **1999** £7.35 (RSJ) £7.40 (TAN)

Bourgueil Domaine les Galichets **1999**
£8.35 (RSJ)

Chinon l'Arpenty, Desbourdes **2000**
£8.25 (YAP)

Reuilly Pinot Noir, Beurdin **1998** £7.80
(BAN)

St-Nicolas-de-Bourgueil la Source,
Domaine Amirault **1998** £8.95 (NI)

Sancerre André Dezat **1999** £8.50 (TAN)
£9.99 (JON)

Sancerre Reverdy **1999** £8.70 (GW) £9.50
(HAH)

Saumur-Champigny Domaine Dubois
1995 £8.50 (GAU)

Saumur-Champigny Domaine Filliatreau
2000 £7.75 (YAP)

Saumur-Champigny Grande Cuvée
Château du Hureau, Vatan **1997** £8.99
(GW) £9.00 (JU)

Saumur-Champigny Château du Hureau,
Vatan **1997** £8.50 (WS)

Saumur-Champigny Château Villeneuve
1998 £7.99 (JON) £8.25 (FORT)

Saumur Château Fouquet, Domaine
Filliatreau **1999** £7.50 (YAP)

£9.00 → £10.99

Bourgueil les Cent Boisselées, Druet
1996 £9.95 (YAP)

Bourgueil les Cent Boisselées, Druet
1995 £9.80 (JU)

Chinon Clos de Danzay, Druet **1996**
£9.90 (GAU) £10.75 (YAP)

Chinon Clos de la Cure, Joguet **1999**
£9.90 (BAC) £10.00 (MV)

Chinon les Grezeaux, Bernard Baudry
1999 £10.95 (LEA)

Sancerre la Croix du Roi, Crochet **1998**
£10.90 (JU)

Sancerre les Baronnes, Henri Bourgeois
1998 £10.99 (CON)

Sancerre les Cailleries, Vacheron **1998**
£9.50 (WS) £10.99 (UN) £11.50 (BER)

Sancerre Domaine de Montigny, Natter
1995 £10.95 (RAE)

Saumur-Champigny Grande Cuvée
Château du Hureau, Vatan **1999** £9.55
(NI)

Saumur-Champigny Château du Hureau,
Vatan **1998** £9.40 (MV)

Saumur-Champigny Terres Chauds,
Domaine des Roches Neuves **1999**
£9.95 (RSJ)

Saumur-Champigny Vieilles Vignes,
Filliatreau **1999** £10.50 (YAP)

£11.00 → £12.99

Anjou Rouge Château de la Roche, Nicolas
Joly **1990** £11.99 (BAL) £11.99 (RAE)

Chinon Clos de la Cure, Joguet **1996**
£12.34 (TW)

Chinon Clos de la Dioterie, Joguet **1997**
£12.90 (GAU) £16.99 (DI)

Chinon Clos du Chêne Vert, Joguet **1996**
£12.95 (GAU)

Chinon Cuvée des Varennes du Grand
Clos, Joguet **1997** £11.90 (GAU)

Saumur-Champigny Grande Cuvée Château
du Hureau, Vatan **1995** £11.04 (TW)

£13.00 → £14.99

Bourgueil Beauvais, Druet **1993** £13.00 (JU)

Chinon Domaine de la Chapellerie, Olek
1985 £14.50 (CRO)

Chinon Clos du Chêne Vert, Joguet **1998**
£14.00 (JU)

Chinon Cuvée des Varennes du Grand
Clos, Joguet **1995** £13.00 (JU)

Over £15.00

Bourgeuil Cuvée Vaumoreau, Druet **1995**
£25.00 (YAP)

Bourgueil Beauvais, Druet **1990** £17.00
(CRO)

Chinon Clos de la Dioterie, Joguet **1998**
£16.00 (MV) £16.50 (JU)

Chinon Clos de la Dioterie, Joguet **1996**
£20.38 (TW)

Saumur-Champigny Domaine des Roches
Neuves **1994** £15.57 (PLA)

RHÔNE

If you think you understand red wine, take a look at the 1998 Châteauneuf-du-Papes. They may come as a shock

The southern Rhône is the complete opposite of the northern Rhône. In fact it beats me that anyone ever thought of lumping them together in the same region. And it seems to me that the South is the bit that's the most difficult to understand.

For a start, it's much larger, and each appellation is more diverse. The cocktail of grapes complicates the picture still more: growers who put more Syrah and Mourvèdre in their wines make very different styles to those who concentrate on the broader, softer Grenache. And some vintages are Grenache vintages, while others are Syrah or Mourvèdre years.

If you want to see what a typically Grenache year is like, take a look at the 1998 vintage in Châteauneuf-du-Pape. It was a superripe year of plump, lush wines; not very dark in colour because Grenache isn't very dark in colour, but none the worse for that. Colour is not an automatic sign of quality, and don't ever dismiss the wine in your glass just because it's not jet-black and opaque.

And these wines will last. The secret of Grenache is alcohol and glycerine. All that fatness keeps it going, and the best wines from 1998 will easily last 15 or 20 years. And for all that they seem light now, they will improve, I promise.

Other years in Châteauneuf are darker and more tannic: years like 1990. These are years where the Syrah and Mourvèdre – grapes that were introduced to give a more classic structure to the warm, open reds of the appellation – are more dominant. Fans of the southern Rhône love this sort of difference, and I must say, I rather agree with them.

GRAPE VARIETIES

CARIGNAN (red) This grape is much maligned because in the far South it used to, and often still does, produce raw, fruitless wines that are the mainstay of the cheapest bulk wines. But old Carignan vines can produce strong, tasty, flavoursome wines that age well.

CINSAUT (red) Once widely planted for its high yields, this grape is now out of favour because of its inability to age. But if yields are kept low it can add pepperiness and acidity to the blend, and often makes a successful contribution to rosé blends.

CLAIRETTE (white) Makes sparkling Crémant de Die, but is a bit dull unless livened up with the aromatic Muscat. In the South it makes big, strong whites that can be creamy, but more often dull and nutty. Needs careful handling and early drinking.

COUNOISE (red) Rich, spicy, floral flavours, and highly regarded at *Ch. de Beaucastel* in Châteauneuf-du-Pape. Could be promising.

GRENACHE (red) One of the mainstays of the southern Rhône, giving loads of alcohol and a gentle, juicy, spicy fruit perked up by a whiff of pepper. It achieves its greatest power at Châteauneuf-du-Pape.

GRENACHE BLANC (white) Widely planted in the southern Rhône, producing rich, appley wines with a strong scent of aniseed. Good, but soft, so drink young.

MARSANNE (white) The dominant of the two grapes that go to make white Hermitage and Crozes-Hermitage, as well as white St-Joseph and St-Péray. Marsanne is weighty and can be flabby, but at its best it

ON THE CASE
Southern Rhône wines can be difficult to buy because quality is a bit uneven. Single-domaine wines are almost always superior

is rich and honeysuckle-scented. Further south it makes burly, lanoliny wine, but is capable of rich, exotic peach and toffee flavours, too. Increasingly fashionable.

MOURVÈDRE (red) This vine relishes ample warmth and sunshine. It contributes backbone and tannin to the blends of the South, and develops wonderful smoky, leathery, meaty flavours as it ages.

MUSCAT (white) Used to great effect blended with Clairette to make the sparkling Clairette de Die, but more famous for sweet Muscat de Beaumes-de-Venise.

ROUSSANNE (white) Altogether more delicate and fragrant than the Marsanne. Found chiefly in Hermitage and St-Péray in the North, though it also makes light, fragrant wines further south in Châteauneuf.

Look out for *Ch. de Beaucastel*'s Roussanne *Vieilles Vignes* – pricy but superb. Very fashionable at the moment.

SYRAH (red) The northern Rhône is dominated by Syrah – and it makes some of the blackest, most startling, pungent red wine in France. From Hermitage and Cornas, it rasps with tannin and tar and woodsmoke, backed by the deep, ungainly sweetness of black treacle. But give it five or ten years, and those raw fumes will have become sweet and pungent, full of raspberries, brambles and cassis.

VIOGNIER (white) The grape of Condrieu and Château-Grillet. It has one of the most memorable flavours of any white grape, blending the rich, musky scent of overripe apricots with that of spring flowers. The wine is made dry, but it is so rich you would hardly believe it. Sweet versions are making a comeback now. Viognier is enjoying a cult, with plantings increasing in the southern Rhône, southern France, California and Australia. As winemakers learn to handle it (and it's not an easy grape) flavours are improving.

WINE REGIONS

CHÂTEAU-GRILLET, AC (white; north) This single property is one of the smallest ACs in France. Wildly expensive, it's 100 per cent Viognier and is often surpassed in freshness and quality by top Condrieus. But unlike Condrieu, it can age interestingly.

CHÂTEAUNEUF-DU-PAPE, AC (red, white; south) This can be delicious, deep, dusty red, almost sweet and fat, low in acidity, but kept appetizing by back-room tannin. *Can* be. It can also be fruit-pastilly and pointless, or dark, tough and stringy. Thirteen different red and white grapes are permitted, and the resulting flavour is usually slightly indistinct, varying from one property to another. Around one-third of

the growers make good wine – and as much as two-thirds of the wine sold probably exceeds the permitted yields. So it makes sense always to go for a domaine wine and certainly not one bottled away from the region. Best: *Pierre André, Lucien Gabriel Barrot, Henri Bonneau, Bosquet des Papes, les Cailloux, Chante-Cigale, Chante-Perdrix, Chapoutier's la Bernadine, Château de Beaucastel, Château Fortia, Château de la Gardine, Château Rayas, Château St-André, les Clefs d'Or, Clos du Mont Olivet, Clos des Papes, Paul Coulon, Domaine du Grand Tinel, Domaine de Mont Redon, Domaine St-Benoît, Domaine du Vieux Télégraphe, Font du Loup, Font Michelle, la Gardine, la Janasse, Gabriel Meffre, Monpertuis, la Nerthe, Quiot, le Vieux Donjon.*

Few whites are made, but they can be outstandingly perfumed with a delicious nip of acidity, leaving you wondering how on earth such aromatic wines could come from such a hot, arid region. In its youth, the wine has a perfumed rush of springtime madness. Then it closes up for a few years, emerging at seven years as a rich, succulent, nutty mouthful. Best: *Château de Beaucastel* (its pure Roussanne *Vieilles Vignes* – and the Viognier white), *Clefs d'Or*, *Clos des Papes*, *Font de Michelle*, *Grand Tinel*, *Mont Redon*, *Nalys*, *Rayas*, *Vieux Télégraphe*.

CLAIRETTE DE DIE, AC (sparkling; south) Made from Clairette with a high proportion of Muscat, by the local *méthode dioise*, this is delicious, orchard-fresh and off-dry. The much duller Champagne-method sparkler, from 100 per cent Clairette grapes, is called Crémant de Die. The still wine is Coteaux de Die.

CONDRIEU, AC (white; north) An appellation on a roll, with new plantings, better quality and lots of chic. The apricot scent leaps out of the glass, and there's an exciting balance of succulent fruit and gentle acidity. Viognier is the only grape, and is difficult to cultivate; increased demand for the wine means that Condrieu is inevitably expensive. Always best young. Top names: *G Barge*, *P & C Bonnefond*, *Chapoutier*, *Clusel-Roch*, *Colombo*, *Cuilleron*, *Delas*, *Dumazet*, *Pierre Gaillard*, *Guigal's La Doriane*, *Dom. du Monteillet*, *Niero-Pinchon*, *Alain Paret*, *André*

Perret, *Jean Pinchon*, *Rostaing*, *Château du Rozay* and *Georges Vernay*.

CORNAS, AC (red; north) Black and tarry tooth-staining wine, often with much juicier fruit than of yore. They should be good for ten years in the cellar. Excellent blockbusters are made by *Auguste Clape*, *Robert Michel* and *Noël Verset*. It's also worth looking for *Allemand*, *René Balthazar*, *Guy de Barjac*, *Chapoutier*, *Colombo*, *Courbis*, *Delas*, *Jaboulet*, *Juge*, *Lemenicier*, *Jean Lionnet* (especially *Domaine de Rochepertuis*), *Tardieu-Laurent* (Vieilles Vignes), *Alain Voge*.

COTEAUX DU TRICASTIN, AC (red, rosé, white; south) Fast-improving, good-value, spicy, fruity reds, and quite full-flavoured, nutty whites. Best producers (reds): *les Domaines Bernard*, *Dom. de Grangeneuve*, *Dom. de St-Luc*, *Tour d'Elyssas* (100 per cent Syrah), *Dom. du Vieux Micocoulier*.

CÔTE-RÔTIE, AC (red; north) Together with Hermitage, the greatest wine of the northern Rhône. It can have exceptional finesse and a fragrance unexpected in a red wine thanks to the occasional addition of a dash of Viognier. The top wines, like *Guigal's La Landonne*, are now international blue chips. The top growers are *Barge*, *Domaine de Bonserine*, *Burgaud*, *Champet*, *Chapoutier*, *Clusel-Roch* (*Les Grandes Places*), *Delas*, *Gangloff*, *Gaillard*, *Gasse*, *Gerin*, *Guigal*, *Jaboulet*, *Jamet*,

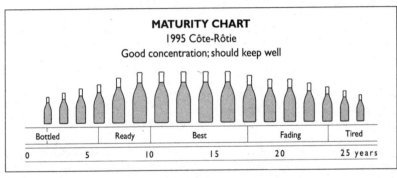

MATURITY CHART
1995 Côte-Rôtie
Good concentration; should keep well

Bottled	Ready	Best	Fading	Tired

| 0 | 5 | 10 | 15 | 20 | 25 years |

Jasmin, Ogier, Rostaing, Tardieu-Laurent, de Vallouit, Vidal-Fleury, F Villard.

CÔTES DU LUBÉRON, AC (red,
white; south) Lubéron makes decent reds, usually rather light, but capable of stronger personality. The *Val Joanis* rosé is one of the best in the South. Try also *Château la Canorgue, Château de l'Isolette, Mas du Peyroulet, Val Joanis* (also to be seen under the names of *Domaines Chancel* or *Domaine de la Panisse*), *la Vieille Ferme*. The whites are usually pleasant and light but little more, though much more fragrant, interesting styles come from *Château de l'Isolette, Mas du Peyroulet, Val Joanis* and *la Vieille Ferme*.

CÔTES DU RHÔNE, AC (red, white)
Well-made basic Côtes du Rhône reds are delicious when young, wonderfully fresh and fruity, like a soft Beaujolais. Or they can be fierce, black, grapeskins-and-alcohol monsters. Many of the weightiest are made by Châteauneuf growers (*Coudoulet de Beaucastel, Château de Fonsalette* from *Rayas*) or northern Rhône producers like *Guigal* and *Clape. Château du Grand Moulas* is spicy and attractive, with plenty of body. Also good: *Château de Goudray, Château de Ruth, Clos du Père Clément, Domaine des Aussellons, Domaine de Bel Air, Domaine de la Cantharide, Domaine de St-Estève, Jean Lionnet* and *Chapoutier's* rosé. Whites are generally fresh and fruity.

CÔTES DU RHÔNE-VILLAGES, AC
(red, white; south) Good, full reds that can also age, combining earthy, dusty southern heat with spicy, raspberry fruit. They come from a number of villages defined in the appellation contrôlée laws; 17 villages can add their names on the label, including Cairanne, Chusclan, Valréas, Beaumes-de-Venise and Rasteau. These wines often offer excellent value. Best: *Dom. Pélaquié* (Laudun); *Dom. de Grangeneuve, Dom. la Soumade* (Rasteau); *Jean-Pierre Cartier, Château de Trignon, Dom. de Boisson, Dom. Gourt de Mautens, Dom. St-Antoine, Dom. de*

Verquière (Sablet); *Dom. de l'Ameillaud, Dom. Brusset, Dom. l'Oratoire St-Martin, Dom. de la Présidente, Dom. Rabasse-Charavin, Marcel Richaud* (Cairanne); *Dom. Ste-Anne* (St-Gervais); *Dom. de Cabasse, Dom. Couronçonne* (Séguret); *Roger Combe, Dom. des Grands Devers, le Val des Rois* (Valréas). The whites are usually fresh, fruity and gulpable, especially from the villages of Laudun and Chusclan. *Dom. Pélaquié* is tops, and *Dom. Ste-Anne* is good.

CÔTES DU VENTOUX, AC (red,
white, rosé; south) Good area producing lots of fresh, juicy wine; the red is the best. Can even be quite special. Best: *Domaine des Anges, Dom. de Cascavel, Jaboulet, Pascal, la Vieille Ferme, Vieux Lazaret.*

CROZES-HERMITAGE, AC (red,
white; north) Red that varies from the light and juicy to well-structured smoky wine recognizable as a lesser cousin of the great Hermitage. *Etienne Pochon (Château Curson), Chapoutier's les Meysonniers* and *Varonniers, Graillot's Guiraude, Jaboulet's Thalabert* are tops. Also good are *Albert Belle, Cave des Clairmonts, Bernard Chave, Laurent Combier, Stéphane Cornu, Dom. des Entrefaux, Fayolle, Pradelle, Cave de Tain l'Hermitage* and *Vidal-Fleury.* The white is generally rather dull and strong, but there are good ones from *Château Curson, Combier, Entrefaux, Fayolle, Graillot, Jaboulet, Pradelle* and *Cave de Tain l'Hermitage.*

GIGONDAS, AC (red; south) Big,
chunky, plummy wines that can be short on finesse. This is Grenache country, and proud of it. Best: *Clos des Cazaux, Dom. de Cayron, Dom. les Gouberts, Dom. de Longue-Toque, Dom. l'Oustau Fauquet, Dom. les Pallières, Dom. Raspail-Ay, Dom. de Santa Duc, Dom. de St-Gayan.*

HERMITAGE, AC (red, white; north)
Grand, burly red; strong and fierily tough when young, it matures to a rich, brooding magnificence. There is always a medicinal or

smoky edge, and an unmatchable depth of raspberry and blackcurrant fruit. Although many people produce Hermitage of sorts, the stars are *Chave*, *Delas*, *Jaboulet* and *Chapoutier*'s *le Pavillon*. Also good: *Belle, Dom. du Colombier, Faurie, Fayolle, Grippat, Guigal, Sorrel, Cave de Tain l'Hermitage, Tardieu-Laurent*. The white can be heavy and dull, but it ages to a soft, rich nuttiness. *Chave* makes magnificent white Hermitage even in modest vintages. Other good producers include *Chapoutier, Ferraton, Grippat, Guigal, Marc Sorrel, Cave de Tain l'Hermitage*.

LIRAC, AC (red, white, rosé; south) A good, often underrated area making light, attractive wines. Reds are packed with fruit, often tinged with a mineral edge. The rosés are fresh. Whites are best young. Best: *Ch. d'Aquéria, Dom. des Causses et St-Eymes, Dom. de Ch. St-Roch, Dom. la Fermade, Dom. les Garrigues, Dom. de la Tour, Maby*.

INSTANT CELLAR:
SOUTHERN FLAVOURS

• 1999 Vacqueyras, Domaine Perrin, £9.05, Bibendum Tremendous depth and style from this serious producer.
• 1998 Châteauneuf-du-Pape, Domaine Font de Michelle, £14.95, Tanners Top-class stuff from a classic vintage. This is just starting to drink, but there's no hurry.
• 1998 Gigondas, Château Redortier, £12.50, The Winery Traditional winemaking and a wine of real depth and class.
v1998 Châteauneuf-du-Pape, Vieux Mas des Papes, £11.95, Adnams The second wine of Vieux Télégraphe. Rich, broad and generous.
• 1998 Côtes du Rhône-Villages Cairanne Cuvée Tradition, Daniel & Denis Alary, £6.58, H&H Bancroft Classy stuff: peppery and herby, but with some elegance too.
• 1997 Côtes du Rhône Coudoulet de Beaucastel, £9.90, Croque-en-Bouche Lovely stuff, made by Ch. de Beaucastel.
• 1998 Château des Tours, £12.50, Yapp This is pure Grenache, and was accordingly refused the Vacqueyras AC. It's rich, powerful and wonderful.

MUSCAT DE BEAUMES-DE-VENISE, AC (fortified white; south) The only Rhône village growing Muscat. This golden sweet wine – a *vin doux naturel* – is supremely delicious. Grapy, fresh, rich but not cloying. Best: *Dom. de Coyeux, Dom. Durban, Jaboulet, Beaumes-de-Venise co-op*.

RASTEAU, AC (fortified red, fortified white; south) Rasteau makes a few big, port-like fortified wines – *vins doux naturels* – but if you want that sort of thing you're probably better off with port itself. Young reds can have a delightful raspberry scent from the Grenache Noir. The whites are made from Grenache Blanc and are rarely exciting. Production is small. Try *Dom. de la Soumade, Rasteau co-op*.

ST-JOSEPH, AC (red; north) Almost smooth and sweet compared to their tougher neighbours, these reds can be fairly big, fine wines, stacked with blackcurrant in good years and sometimes scented with violets. *Chapoutier, Chave, Dom. du Chêne, Colombo, Courbis, Coursodon, Cuilleron, Delas, Gaillard, Graillot, Gripa, Grippat, Jaboulet, Monteillet, Paret* and *Tardieu-Laurent* are leading names. The white is decent and nutty. *Grippat* is good, but *Florentin*, an old-style oxidative, headbanging white, is more controversial. White Crozes is usually better value.

ST-PÉRAY, AC (white; north) Usually rather stolid and short on freshness. Quality is improving from the likes of *Chaboud, Domaine de Fauterie, Grippat* and Cornas estates such as *Clape, Lionnet* and *Voge*.

TAVEL, AC (rosé; south) Quite expensive, certainly tasty, rosés, but mostly they're too big and alcoholic to be very refreshing. Any of the Rhône grapes will do, but generally it's Grenache-dominated, with the addition of a little Cinsaut. Best producers: *Château d'Aquéria, Château de Trinquevedel, Domaine de la Forcadière, Domaine de la Genestière*.

VACQUEYRAS, AC (red, white, rosé; south) Reds and rosés of character and structure. Some white wine is also produced, but it tends to be on the heavy side. Cinsaut fanatic *Ch. de Montmirail* is good, as are *Clos des Cazaux, Dom. de la Fourmone, Dom. la Garrigue, le Sang des Cailloux, Ch. des Tours.*

VIN DE PAYS DES COLLINES RHODANIENNES (red; north) A usually impressive and expanding northern Rhône area, particularly for inexpensive, tasty Syrah-based reds, though the lighter, softer Gamays can also be good.

VIN DE PAYS DES COTEAUX DE L'ARDÈCHE (red, white; south) A source of delicious Nouveau-style Gamay, first-class Syrah, good Cabernet, plus Sauvignon, Pinot Noir – and Chardonnay, both for *Louis Latour*'s decent *Chardonnay de l'Ardèche* and the local co-ops (which give higher quality for far lower prices). This was one of the first vin de pays regions to smarten up its act; as happens to pioneers, it's been rather overtaken in the fashion stakes by others, notably those in the Languedoc. But it's still making good stuff, and it's worth looking out for. Most should be drunk young.

RHÔNE VINTAGES

2000 Looks good but not great. The South looks slightly better than the North, with rich, concentrated wines. Expect silky tannins and good ripeness in the North.

1999 A rain-affected vintage, but the wines look good to excellent all round, with the North just pipping the South.

1998 Tremendously hot year – so much so that some of the Northern wines appear a bit baked. The Southern reds are sumptuous and exciting.

1997 A year that looks like turning out as well as or better than 1996, at least in the South. Reds look set to age well.

1996 Superb for the northern reds, and for the whites from the whole region. Quality is less even in the South and the reds lack the intensity of those in the North.

1995 Top growers made very good wines, and there will be great wines in the North from those who, like Chapoutier and Chave, picked late.

1994 Succulent reds and lively, flowery whites this year. A very good year but not great.

1993 Châteauneuf-du-Pape and Côtes du Rhône did best. In the North attractive whites but raw and rather dilute reds from Hermitage, Crozes and Cornas.

1992 A poor year; buy only from top growers and drink up quickly.

1991 Côte-Rôtie is generally better than in 1990. The South was only moderately good.

1990 The North was more successful than the South. Choose 1990 for the North (though Côte-Rôtie is dodgy); 1989 for the South.

1989 Some undistinguished Hermitage and Cornas. Concentrated Châteauneuf-du-Pape.

1988 Best in Côte-Rôtie, Hermitage and Châteauneuf-du-Pape. Some is too tannic.

1987 The few good wines should have been drunk by now, though Côte-Rôtie and Hermitage provided some very good bottles, now drinking well.

1985 Brilliant Côte-Rôtie, St-Joseph and Cornas. Châteauneuf is delicious and juicy.

RHÔNE PRICES

RED

Under £4.00

VdP des Collines Rhodaniennes Syrah, Cave de Tain l'Hermitage 1999 £3.95 (WS)

VdP des Coteaux de l'Ardèche Duboeuf 1999 £3.95 (WS)

Côtes du Ventoux les Cailloux 1999 £3.99 (OD)

£4.00 → £4.99

★ VdP d'Ardèche Syrah, Ptomaine des Blagueurs 1997 £4.99 (OD)

Coteaux du Tricastin Domaine de Grangeneuve 1999 £4.99 (OD) £6.75 (YAP)

Côtes du Rhône André Brusset 1999 £4.50 (SOM)

Côtes du Rhône Jaume 1998 £4.95 (WS)

Côtes du Rhône-Villages Château la Courançonne 1999 £4.99 (SAI)

Côtes du Ventoux Jaboulet 1999 £4.95 (WS) £5.29 (OD) £6.20 (NI)

Côtes du Ventoux la Vieille Ferme 1999 £4.99 (MAJ) £5.76 (CB)

£5.00 → £5.99

VdP des Coteaux de l'Ardèche Gamay, Cave de St-Désirat 2000 £5.50 (YAP)

VdP des Coteaux de la Cèze, Domaine Maby 1998 £5.75 (YAP)

★ Côtes du Rhône Domaine Cros de la Mûre 1999 £5.95 (WS) £6.95 (AD)

Côtes du Rhône Cuvée des Capucines, Domaine du Vieux Chêne 1997 £5.45 (JU)

Côtes du Rhône Château du Grand Moulas 1999 £5.49 (POR) £5.60 (HAH) £5.85 (AD) £5.89 (JON)

Côtes du Rhône Guigal 1997 £5.29 (BODX) £5.88 (TUR) £6.90 (CRO) £7.95 (HIC)

Côtes du Rhône la Haie aux Grives, Domaine du Vieux Chêne 1997 £5.95 (JU)

Côtes du Rhône Jaume 1999 £5.48 (SAV)

Côtes du Rhône Domaine des Moulins 2000 £5.95 (NI)

Côtes du Rhône Caves des Vignerons de Vacqueyras 1999 £5.35 (TAN)

★ Côtes du Rhône-Villages Cairanne, Domaine de l'Ameillaud 1999 £5.99 (UN) £7.00 (ARM)

★ Côtes du Rhône-Villages Rasteau, Domaine St-Gayan 1998 £5.75 (YAP)

Côtes du Lubéron Château Val Joanis 1998 £5.53 (BY) £6.50 (CRO)

Côtes du Ventoux Jaboulet 1998 £5.49 (CON)

Côtes du Ventoux le Mont, la Vieille Ferme 1999 £5.29 (BIB)

Côtes du Ventoux la Vieille Ferme 1997 £5.99 (RAE)

Crozes-Hermitage Louis Mousset 1999 £5.99 (UN)

Crozes-Hermitage Cave de Tain l'Hermitage 1999 £5.65 (SOM) £5.99 (SAI) £5.99 (MORR) £7.37 (LLO) £7.49 (AME)

Lirac Domaine de la Mordorée 1997 £5.95 (SOM) £7.25 (SAV) £7.95 (LEA) £7.95 (BAL)

VdP de la Principauté d'Orange Cuvée des Templiers, Rieu Herail 2000 £5.35 (JER)

£6.00 → £6.99

Coteaux du Tricastin Domaine de Vieux Micocoulier 1995 £6.99 (GN)

Côtes du Rhône Domaine de l'Ameillaud 1998 £6.25 (ARM)

Côtes du Rhône Belleruche, Chapoutier 1999 £6.59 (DI) £6.69 (CON)

RETAILERS SPECIALIZING IN THE RHÔNE
see Retailers Directory (page 40) for details

Adnams (AD), Bennetts (BEN), Berry Bros & Rudd (BER), Bibendum (BIB), Anthony Byrne (BY), D Byrne, Direct Wine Shipments (DI), Ben Ellis, Farr Vintners (FA), Justerini & Brooks (JU), Lay & Wheeler (LAY), Oddbins (OD), James Nicholson (NI), The Nobody Inn (NO), Raeburn Fine Wines (RAE), Reid Wines, Savage Selection (SAV), T&W Wines (TW), Tanners (TAN), The Wine Society (WS), Yapp Brothers (YAP), Noel Young (YOU).

Côtes du Rhône André Brusset **1998**
£6.99 (VA)

Côtes du Rhône Cuvée Personnelle,
Pascal 1995 £6.95 (YAP)

Côtes du Rhône Guigal **1998** £6.99 (POR)
£6.99 (MAJ) £7.15 (FLE) £7.49 (UN) £7.49
(BO) £7.49 (OD) £7.73 (BY) £8.35 (JER)
£8.46 (CB)

Côtes du Rhône Guigal **1996** £6.99 (SOM)

Côtes du Rhône Jaboulet **1998** £6.95 (BER)

Côtes du Rhône Parallèle 45, Jaboulet
1999 £6.29 (OD) £7.60 (NI)

Côtes du Rhône Parallèle 45, Jaboulet
1998 £6.45 (CON) £7.04 (PLA)

Côtes du Rhône Parallèle 45, Jaboulet
1997 £6.95 (GAU)

Côtes du Rhône Rascasses, Berard **1995**
£6.99 (WAT)

Côtes du Rhône Domaine St-Gayan,
Meffre **1999** £6.25 (YAP)

Côtes du Rhône-Villages Château du
Grand Moulas **1999** £6.75 (TAN)

Côtes du Rhône-Villages Château du
Grand Moulas **1998** £6.95 (AD)

Côtes du Rhône-Villages Château du
Grand Moulas **1997** £6.99 (POR)

Côtes du Rhône-Villages Sablet, Château
du Trignon **1999** £6.99 (MAJ) £7.99 (VIL)

★ Côtes du Rhône-Villages Séguret,
Domaine la Montagne d'Or **1999** £6.45
(TAN)

Crozes-Hermitage Cave des Clairmonts
1999 £6.99 (WAI) £8.40 (MV)

Crozes-Hermitage Cave des Clairmonts
1998 £6.99 (JON) £8.89 (HIC)

Crozes-Hermitage Cave de Tain
l'Hermitage **1997** £6.45 (GN)

Lirac les Queyrades, Mejan **1998** £6.99
(JON)

Lirac les Queyrades, Mejan **1997** £6.95 (AD)

£7.00 → £7.99

Côtes du Rhône Coudoulet de Beaucastel
1997 £7.44 (FA) £8.95 (WS) £9.99 (RAE)

Côtes du Rhône Coudoulet de Beaucastel
1996 £7.25 (FA) £9.90 (CRO) £10.50
(FORT)

Côtes du Rhône Domaine Font de
Michelle **1994** £7.25 (JU)

---

*Stars (★) indicate wines selected by
Oz Clarke in the Best Buys section which
begins on page 8.*

Côtes du Rhône Château des Tours **1997**
£7.99 (RAE)

Côtes du Rhône-Villages Cairanne,
Domaine de l'Ameillaud **1998** £7.25
(ARM)

Côtes du Rhône-Villages Cairanne,
Domaine Brusset **1997** £7.00 (BAC)

Côtes du Rhône-Villages Cairanne,
Rabasse-Charavin **1999** £7.99 (AME)

Côtes du Rhône-Villages Jaboulet **1998**
£7.75 (STA)

Côtes du Rhône-Villages Rasteau,
Chapoutier **1998** £7.49 (DI) £7.75 (TAN)
£7.99 (CON)

Côtes du Rhône-Villages Sablet, Château
du Trignon **1998** £7.49 (UN) £8.75 (ARM)

Côtes du Rhône-Villages Domaine St-
Anne Notre Dame des Cellettes,
Steinmaier **1998** £7.95 (TAN)

Côtes du Rhône-Villages Domaine Ste-
Anne **1999** £7.15 (HAH)

Côtes du Rhône-Villages Domaine du
Vieux Chêne **1997** £7.00 (JU)

Crozes-Hermitage Domaine du
Colombier **1997** £7.25 (WAT)

Crozes-Hermitage Jaboulet **1998** £7.95
(WS) £8.60 (HAH)

Crôzes-Hermitage La Petite Ruche,
Chapoutier **1997** £7.48 (PEN) £7.99
(UN) £9.99 (POR) £10.75 (STE)

Crozes-Hermitage les Jalets, Jaboulet **1996**
£7.70 (WHI)

Crozes-Hermitage Pochon **1999** £7.95 (AD)

Hermitage Cuvée Louis Belle, Belle **1997**
£7.99 (OD)

Lirac la Fermade, Domaine Maby **1998**
£7.25 (YAP) £8.95 (RES)

Lirac Domaine de la Mordorée **1998**
£7.95 (LEA) £7.95 (BAL) £8.95 (BEN)

Vacqueyras Domaine le Clos des Cazaux
1998 £7.35 (AD)

Vacqueyras Cuvée Reservée, Domaine le
Clos des Cazaux **1995** £7.00 (JU)

£8.00 → £8.99

Côtes du Rhône Domaine Font de
Michelle **1999** £8.00 (ARM)

Côtes du Rhône Château des Tours **1999**
£8.20 (BIB)

Côtes du Rhône-Villages Cuvée de l'Ecu,
Château du Grand Moulas **1998** £8.95
(TAN) £9.40 (AD)

Côtes du Rhône-Villages Rasteau,
Domaine la Soumade **1998** £8.25 (STA)
£8.29 (AME) £8.45 (BER)

Côtes du Rhône-Villages Rasteau, Château du Trignon **1997** £8.50 (JU)

Côtes du Lubéron Château de Canorgue **2000** £8.25 (YAP)

Crozes-Hermitage Domaine du Colombier **1999** £8.32 (BIB)

Crozes-Hermitage Desmeure **1996** £8.99 (RAE)

Crozes-Hermitage Domaine des Entrefaux **1999** £8.26 (BY)

Crôzes-Hermitage La Petite Ruche, Chapoutier **1999** £8.50 (TAN) £10.75 (STE)

Crozes-Hermitage les Jalets, Jaboulet **1998** £8.99 (POR)

Crozes-Hermitage les Launes, Delas **1997** £8.49 (NEZ)

Crozes-Hermitage les Meysonniers, Chapoutier **1998** £8.99 (DI) £9.99 (CON) £9.99 (OD)

Gigondas Cuvée de la Tour Sarrazine, Domaine le Clos des Cazaux **1997** £8.90 (JU)

Lirac Sabon **1998** £8.95 (STA)

St-Joseph Domaine du Chêne **1998** £8.95 (WS)

★ St-Joseph Domaine Rochevine **1997** £8.99 (MAJ)

Vacqueyras Cuvée des Templiers, Domaine le Clos des Cazaux **1997** £8.50 (JU)

Vacqueyras Jaboulet **1997** £8.85 (CON)

£9.00 → £9.99

Châteauneuf-du-Pape Clos du Caillou **1998** £9.25 (SOM) £15.99 (YOU)

Châteauneuf-du-Pape Domaine du Grand Tinel **1997** £9.95 (WS) £10.90 (JU)

Châteauneuf-du-Pape Domaine de la Solitude **1998** £9.49 (SO)

Côtes du Rhône-Villages Rasteau, Chapoutier **1997** £9.45 (STE)

★ Crozes-Hermitage Cuvée Albéric Bouvet, Gilles Robin **1999** £9.99 (GW)

Crozes-Hermitage Château Curson, Pochon **1997** £9.90 (JU)

Crozes-Hermitage Delas **1999** £9.70 (JER)

Crozes-Hermitage Desmeure **1997** £9.99 (RAE)

Crozes-Hermitage Graillot **1999** £9.69 (BY) £11.95 (YAP)

Crozes-Hermitage les Jalets, Jaboulet **1999** £9.40 (NI)

Crozes-Hermitage les Launes, Delas **1996** £9.90 (CRO)

Gigondas Cuvée de la Tour Sarrazine, Domaine le Clos des Cazaux **1998** £9.95 (MAY)

Gigondas Domaine de Font-Sane **1999** £9.45 (BIB)

Gigondas Domaine de Gour de Chaulé **1997** £9.50 (JU)

Gigondas Domaine Santa Duc **1998** £9.75 (FORT) £11.85 (BAN) £11.99 (DI) £17.50 (CRO)

Gigondas Château du Trignon **1999** £9.49 (MAJ) £9.99 (VIL)

St-Joseph Clos de la Cuminaille, Gaillard **1997** £9.95 (WS) £10.95 (BER) £11.00 (JU) £11.21 (FLE)

St-Joseph le Grand Pompée, Jaboulet **1997** £9.60 (SAV) £9.75 (FORT) £9.99 (VIL) £11.20 (NI) £13.26 (PLA) £14.17 (MI)

Vacqueyras Jaboulet **1998** £9.85 (CON)

£10.00 → £11.99

Châteauneuf-du-Pape Château de Beaucastel **1991** £11.75 (FA)

Châteauneuf-du-Pape Domaine de Beaurenard **1997** £11.55 (NEZ)

Châteauneuf-du-Pape les Cailloux, Brunel **1997** £11.16 (BODX) £11.16 (FA) £13.99 (POR)

Châteauneuf-du-Pape Château des Fines Roches **1998** £10.99 (BO)

Châteauneuf-du-Pape Domaine Font de Michelle **1997** £11.95 (BALL) £12.80 (TAN) £12.95 (POR) £13.15 (HAH) £14.00 (JU) £14.29 (JON) £15.00 (ARM)

Châteauneuf-du-Pape Domaine Font de Michelle **1995** £11.95 (WS)

Châteauneuf-du-Pape Mont-Redon **1995** £11.75 (FA)

Châteauneuf-du-Pape Domaine de Nalys **1997** £11.71 (SAV)

Châteauneuf-du-Pape Domaine de Panisse **1997** £11.49 (CON)

Châteauneuf-du-Pape Domaine du Père Caboche **2000** £10.99 (OD)

Châteauneuf-du-Pape Domaine de la Roquette **1997** £11.95 (WS) £13.75 (LAY)

Châteauneuf-du-Pape Domaine du Vieux Lazaret **1998** £11.95 (BU)

Châteauneuf-du-Pape Vieux Mas des Papes **1998** £11.40 (TAN) £11.95 (AD) £12.90 (LAY) £12.99 (POR) £12.99 (JON)

Côtes du Rhône Coudoulet de Beaucastel **1998** £10.99 (OD) £11.50 (MV)

Crozes-Hermitage Graillot **1998** £10.94 (FLE)

★ Crozes-Hermitage les Machonnières,
   Charles et François Tardy **1998** £10.70
   (PIP)

Crozes-Hermitage Domaine de
   Thalabert, Jaboulet **1998** £11.99 (WAI)
   £12.49 (OD) £13.25 (CON) £14.25 (STA)

Crozes-Hermitage Domaine de
   Thalabert, Jaboulet **1997** £10.67 (BODX)
   £10.67 (FA) £11.65 (TUR) £12.39 (COC)
   £12.50 (FORT) £12.93 (SAV) £12.99 (VIL)
   £14.25 (STA) £14.30 (NI) £14.75 (LAY)
   £17.50 (MI)

Crozes-Hermitage Tour d'Albon, Delas
   1997 £10.95 (RAE)

Gigondas Domaine du Cayron **1998**
   £11.95 (AD) £13.33 (ARM)

Gigondas Cuvée de la Tour Sarrazine,
   Domaine le Clos des Cazaux **1999**
   £10.35 (JER)

Gigondas Domaine du Grand Montmirail
   1997 £10.35 (YAP)

Gigondas Domaine les Pallières **1998**
   £11.33 (COC) £11.60 (TAN)

Gigondas Perrin **1998** £10.18 (FA) £12.50
   (WS) £15.42 (ARM)

Gigondas Domaine St-Gayan, Meffre
   1998 £10.95 (YAP)

Gigondas Domaine les Tourelles,
   Cuillerat **1998** £10.00 (HIG)

Gigondas Château du Trignon **1998**
   £10.83 (ARM) £11.65 (FA)

Lirac Cuvée de la Reine des Bois,
   Domaine de la Mordorée **1999** £10.60
   (BAN)

St-Joseph Chapoutier **1998** £10.99 (OD)

St-Joseph Clos de la Cuminaille, Gaillard
   1998 £11.50 (JU)

St-Joseph Coursodon **1997** £11.99 (WIN)

St-Joseph Deschants, Chapoutier **1996**
   £11.50 (GAU) £12.59 (JON) £12.95 (STE)

St-Joseph Faurie **1997** £11.50 (JU)

St-Joseph Graillot **1999** £11.34 (BY)

St-Joseph Larmes du Père, Paret **1998**
   £11.99 (AME)

£12.00 → £13.99

Châteauneuf-du-Pape Lucien Barrot **1998**
   £12.95 (BAL) £15.00 (MV)

Châteauneuf-du-Pape Domaine de
   Beaurenard **1998** £13.12 (FA)

Châteauneuf-du-Pape Domaine Bosquet
   des Papes **1996** £13.65 (BAN)

Châteauneuf-du-Pape Chante-Cigale
   1998 £12.99 (POR) £12.99 (AME) £13.95
   (YAP)

Châteauneuf-du-Pape Chante-Cigale
   1996 £12.25 (CON) £13.35 (YAP)

Châteauneuf-du-Pape Chaupin, Domaine
   de la Janasse **1997** £13.12 (BODX)

Châteauneuf-du-Pape Clos du Caillou
   1999 £12.75 (BAN)

Châteauneuf-du-Pape Clos du Mont
   Olivet **1998** £13.99 (YOU) £14.19 (TUR)
   £14.59 (FA) £15.50 (CRO)

Châteauneuf-du-Pape Domaine du Grand
   Tinel **1998** £12.90 (CRO) £12.95 (CON)
   £12.99 (YOU)

Châteauneuf-du-Pape Domaine Grand
   Veneur **1997** £13.95 (GN)

Châteauneuf-du-Pape Domaine du Père
   Caboche **1999** £13.75 (YAP)

Châteauneuf-du-Pape Domaine de la
   Roquette **1996** £13.04 (NO) £14.50
   (FORT) £14.70 (TAN)

Châteauneuf-du-Pape Domaine Versino
   1997 £13.00 (JU)

Châteauneuf-du-Pape Domaine du Vieux
   Lazaret **1999** £12.09 (PLA)

Cornas le Reynard, Allemand **1992**
   £13.95 (RAE)

Cornas Rochepertuis, Jean Lionnet **1996**
   £13.50 (WS)

Crozes-Hermitage Cuvée Louis Belle,
   Belle **1998** £12.50 (CRO)

Crozes-Hermitage Graillot **1997** £12.50
   (FORT)

Crozes-Hermitage la Guiraude, Graillot
   1999 £12.77 (BY)

Crozes-Hermitage Pascal **1996** £12.19
   (VIN)

Gigondas Domaine du Cayron **1997**
   £12.50 (JU) £13.75 (ARM)

Gigondas Cuvée Pierre Aiguille, Jaboulet
   1998 £12.95 (CON)

Gigondas Domaine de Font-Sane **1998**
   £12.14 (FA)

Gigondas Guigal **1998** £13.49 (FLE)

Gigondas Guigal **1997** £12.99 (MAJ)
   £13.16 (BY) £13.95 (JER) £13.99 (POR)

Gigondas Hautes Garrigues, Domaine
Santa Duc 1998 £12.75 (FORT) £18.50
(GAU) £20.95 (FA) £20.99 (YOU) £28.50
(CRO)

Gigondas Perrin 1999 £13.71 (BIB)

Gigondas Domaine Raspail 1998 £13.12
(FA)

Gigondas Domaine St-Gayan, Meffre
1997 £12.59 (JON)

Gigondas Domaine Santa Duc 1997
£12.79 (YOU)

St-Joseph Clos de l'Arbalestrier, Florentin
1995 £12.99 (RAE)

St-Joseph Deschants, Chapoutier 1995
£12.95 (STE)

St-Joseph le Grand Pompée, Jaboulet
1996 £13.33 (MI)

St-Joseph Pascal 1997 £12.20 (VIN)

St-Joseph les Pierres, Pierre Gaillard
1995 £13.00 (JU)

Vacqueyras Grenat Noble, Domaine le
Clos des Cazaux 1995 £13.90 (GAU)

Vacqueyras Château des Tours 1999
£12.73 (BIB)

Vacqueyras Château des Tours 1998
£12.50 (YAP)

Vacqueyras Château des Tours 1994
£12.50 (RAE)

£14.00 → £15.99

Châteauneuf-du-Pape la Bernardine,
Chapoutier 1998 £14.95 (WAI) £16.99
(DI) £17.95 (CON) £17.99 (OD)

Châteauneuf-du-Pape Clos du Mont
Olivet 1997 £14.99 (POR)

Châteauneuf-du-Pape Clos des Papes,
Avril 1998 £15.28 (FA)

Châteauneuf-du-Pape Clos des Papes,
Avril 1997 £15.95 (BAL)

Châteauneuf-du-Pape Cuvée Etienne
Gonnet, Domaine Font de Michelle
1996 £15.00 (ARM) £17.95 (MAY)

Châteauneuf-du-Pape Château des Fines
Roches 1997 £14.50 (COC)

Châteauneuf-du-Pape Domaine Font de
Michelle 1998 £14.59 (FA) £14.95 (TAN)
£15.42 (ARM) £15.99 (WR) £16.99 (AME)

Châteauneuf-du-Pape Château Fortia
1998 £14.99 (YOU)

Châteauneuf-du-Pape Château Fortia
1997 £14.99 (POR)

Châteauneuf-du-Pape Mont-Redon 1997
£14.99 (POR)

Châteauneuf-du-Pape Domaine de Nalys
1998 £14.37 (NO)

Châteauneuf-du-Pape Château la Nerthe
1998 £14.59 (FA) £17.25 (SUN) £17.25
(LAI) £17.40 (NI)

Châteauneuf-du-Pape Domaine Terre
Ferme, Bérard 1994 £15.89 (WAT)

Châteauneuf-du-Pape Vieux Donjon,
Michel 1995 £15.50 (CRO)

Châteauneuf-du-Pape Domaine du Vieux
Télégraphe 1998 £15.95 (SOM) £17.50
(TAN) £19.99 (POR) £20.90 (CRO) £32.90
(TUR) £33.68 (FA) £34.17 (BODX)

Cornas Cuvée des Coteaux, Robert
Michel 1995 £15.00 (BAC)

Cornas Jean Lionnet 1997 £14.70 (COC)

Cornas Juge 1997 £14.75 (MAY)

Cornas la Chaillot, Allemand 1996 £14.95
(RAE)

Cornas Robert Michel 1984 £15.90 (GAU)

Cornas Rochepertuis, Jean Lionnet 1998
£14.50 (MAY) £15.20 (JER)

Cornas Rochepertuis, Jean Lionnet 1997
£14.95 (BER)

Cornas Noël Verset 1996 £14.50 (RAE)
£15.95 (GAU)

★ Côte-Rôtie Patrick et Christophe
Bonnefond 1998 £14.99 (GW)

Côte-Rôtie Brune et Blonde, Guigal 1996
£15.08 (FA) £15.57 (BODX) £22.23 (BY)
£23.95 (POR) £24.12 (HIC) £24.68 (PEN)
£25.83 (MI)

Crozes-Hermitage Domaine de
Thalabert, Jaboulet 1995 £15.68 (FLE)
£16.00 (CRO) £17.25 (FORT)

Gigondas Chapoutier 1997 £15.57 (PEN)

Gigondas Jaboulet 1996 £15.50 (STA)

Gigondas Domaine Santa Duc 1995
£15.00 (CRO)

Hermitage Desmeure 1995 £15.99 (RAE)
£21.90 (GAU)

St-Joseph Clos de la Cuminaille, Gaillard
1995 £15.60 (CRO)

St-Joseph le Grand Pompée, Jaboulet
1998 £15.00 (MI)

St-Joseph Grippat 1986 £15.00 (CRO)

St-Joseph les Pierres, Pierre Gaillard
1997 £14.00 (JU)

• Wines are listed in A–Z order within
  each price band.
• For each wine, vintages are listed in
  descending order.
• Each vintage of any wine appears
  only once.

£16.00 → £19.99

Châteauneuf-du-Pape Château de Beaucastel 1997 £16.06 (TUR) £16.06 (FA) £16.50 (RAE) £17.40 (TAN) £18.41 (SAV) £18.90 (CRO) £18.95 (BAL) £19.00 (JU) £20.50 (RAE) £20.60 (LAY) £20.99 (SUN) £20.99 (LAI) £21.49 (JON) £21.50 (NI)

Châteauneuf-du-Pape Château de Beaucastel 1996 £16.06 (TUR) £16.06 (FA) £19.99 (SUN) £19.99 (LAI) £20.50 (RAE) £21.50 (BAL) £24.75 (NI) £25.00 (FLE) £25.00 (TAN)

Châteauneuf-du-Pape Château de Beaucastel 1994 £18.99 (RAE) £21.44 (LLO) £22.91 (FA) £25.00 (FLE) £25.00 (CRO) £30.00 (FORT)

Châteauneuf-du-Pape Château de Beaucastel 1992 £17.04 (FA)

Châteauneuf-du-Pape la Bernardine, Chapoutier 1996 £18.21 (PEN)

Châteauneuf-du-Pape les Cailloux, Brunel 1998 £16.53 (BODX) £16.55 (FA) £16.95 (RES)

Châteauneuf-du-Pape les Cailloux, Brunel 1994 £16.00 (CRO)

Châteauneuf-du-Pape les Cèdres, Jaboulet 1997 £17.50 (STA) £20.95 (CON) £20.97 (PLA)

Châteauneuf-du-Pape Cuvée Etienne Gonnet, Domaine Font de Michelle 1998 £18.50 (MAY) £19.58 (ARM)

Châteauneuf-du-Pape Cuvée Etienne Gonnet, Domaine Font de Michelle 1997 £16.00 (JU) £17.95 (MAY) £18.33 (ARM)

Châteauneuf-du-Pape Cuvée Etienne Gonnet, Domaine Font de Michelle 1994 £18.99 (YOU)

Châteauneuf-du-Pape Cuvée Etienne Gonnet, Domaine Font de Michelle 1993 £16.00 (JU)

Châteauneuf-du-Pape Château la Nerthe 1995 £16.00 (WS)

Châteauneuf-du-Pape Réserve, Sabon 1998 £16.95 (STA)

Châteauneuf-du-Pape Domaine du Vieux Télégraphe 1994 £19.00 (CRO)

Châteauneuf-du-Pape Domaine du Vieux Télégraphe 1993 £16.00 (CRO)

Cornas Chapoutier 1998 £18.21 (PEN)

Cornas Chapoutier 1997 £16.99 (WAI)

Cornas Jaboulet 1997 £16.06 (TUR) £20.97 (PLA)

Cornas la Chaillot, Allemand 1997 £16.99 (RAE) £17.50 (GAU)

Cornas La Geynale, Robert Michel 1995 £18.80 (CRO)

Cornas le Reynard, Allemand 1998 £19.70 (GAU)

Cornas le Reynard, Allemand 1997 £19.50 (RAE)

Cornas les Ruchets, Colombo 1994 £19.70 (SOM) £33.95 (TW)

Cornas Noël Verset 1997 £16.20 (GAU)

Côte-Rôtie Brune et Blonde, Gaillard 1997 £19.34 (FLE) £20.00 (JU)

Côte-Rôtie Brune et Blonde, Gaillard 1995 £19.00 (JU)

Côte-Rôtie Brune et Blonde, Guigal 1995 £17.53 (FA) £23.33 (MI) £25.00 (FORT)

Côte-Rôtie Brune et Blonde, Guigal 1994 £18.50 (CRO) £22.50 (MI)

Côte-Rôtie Burgaud 1997 £19.00 (JU) £20.00 (YAP) £21.50 (WIN)

Côte-Rôtie Clusel-Roch 1997 £17.50 (LEA) £19.00 (JU)

Côte-Rôtie Cuvée du Plessy, Gilles Barge 1997 £17.99 (RAE)

Côte-Rôtie Cuvée du Plessy, Gilles Barge 1996 £16.99 (RAE) £19.20 (TAN)

Côte-Rôtie Guigal 1996 £19.99 (SUN) £19.99 (LAI) £22.99 (UN)

Côte-Rôtie Guigal 1992 £19.14 (WHI)

Côte-Rôtie René Rostaing 1996 £19.20 (GAU) £21.20 (HAH) £22.95 (NI)

Côte-Rôtie René Rostaing 1994 £19.00 (ARM) £21.00 (JU) £32.50 (FORT)

Côte-Rôtie René Rostaing 1992 £19.50 (CRO)

Côte-Rôtie de Vallouit 1997 £16.99 (VIL)

Côte-Rôtie la Viaillère, Champet 1997 £18.00 (JU) £18.95 (YAP)

Côtes du Rhône Château de Fonsalette 1997 £17.53 (FA)

★ **Côtes du Rhône-Villages Rasteau, Domaine Gourt de Mautens/Bressy 1999** £17.99 (RAE)

Crozes-Hermitage Domaine de Thalabert, Jaboulet **1982** £16.00 (CRO)

Gigondas Domaine les Gouberts **1985** £18.50 (CRO)

Gigondas Domaine Santa Duc **1996** £18.50 (CRO)

Hermitage Domaine du Colombier **1997** £18.65 (WAT) £21.00 (JU) £24.50 (BAL) £29.50 (JER)

Hermitage Cuvée des Miaux, Ferraton **1995** £19.00 (FA)

Hermitage Desmeure **1997** £19.50 (RAE)

Hermitage Desmeure **1994** £17.95 (RAE)

Hermitage Faurie **1993** £19.80 (BAC)

Hermitage la Sizeranne, Chapoutier **1994** £19.95 (BER) £25.99 (POR) £29.95 (BALL)

Hermitage Marquise de la Tourette, Delas **1994** £19.39 (PEN)

Hermitage Sorrel **1989** £17.63 (FA)

£20.00 → £24.99

Châteauneuf-du-Pape Château de Beaucastel **1995** £24.87 (FA) £27.50 (CRO) £35.00 (FORT)

Châteauneuf-du-Pape les Cèdres, Jaboulet **1996** £22.75 (NI)

Châteauneuf-du-Pape Chaupin, Domaine de la Janasse **1998** £22.99 (YOU) £24.87 (FA)

Châteauneuf-du-Pape Mont-Redon **1989** £24.87 (FA)

Châteauneuf-du-Pape Pignan **1997** £20.95 (FA)

★ Châteauneuf-du-Pape Cuvée Réservée, Domaine du Pegaü **1998** £21.35 (GAU)

Châteauneuf-du-Pape Domaine du Vieux Télégraphe **1996** £21.15 (WY)

Cornas Jaboulet **1983** £23.50 (WY) £26.44 (TUR)

Cornas le Reynard, Allemand **1996** £20.00 (WS)

Cornas les Ruchets, Colombo **1996** £22.91 (FA) £34.66 (TW) £36.00 (FORT)

Côte-Rôtie Brune et Blonde, Guigal **1997** £23.95 (JER) £25.99 (CON) £27.50 (MI)

Côte-Rôtie Burgaud **1998** £24.75 (YAP)

Côte-Rôtie Burgaud **1994** £22.00 (JU)

Côte-Rôtie Burgaud **1989** £24.87 (FA)

Côte-Rôtie Chapoutier **1997** £24.40 (TAN)

Côte-Rôtie Chapoutier **1995** £24.95 (DI)

Côte-Rôtie Côte Brune, Gentaz-Dervieux **1993** £23.95 (RAE)

Côte-Rôtie Guigal **1995** £23.50 (AME)

Côte-Rôtie Jasmin **1997** £22.75 (YAP)

Côte-Rôtie Jasmin **1996** £23.50 (YAP)

Côte-Rôtie la Landonne, René Rostaing **1996** £24.87 (FA) £29.40 (HAH) £35.25 (NI)

Côte-Rôtie la Mordorée, Chapoutier **1997** £22.95 (DI) £65.02 (FA) £69.00 (BAL) £70.50 (BODX) £77.75 (RAE)

Côte-Rôtie la Mordorée, Chapoutier **1992** £23.50 (FA) £47.00 (BODX)

Côte-Rôtie la Viaillère, Champet **1998** £20.00 (YAP)

Côte-Rôtie la Viaillère, René Rostaing **1996** £20.83 (ARM) £22.91 (FA) £30.55 (NI)

Côte-Rôtie la Viaillère, René Rostaing **1994** £24.00 (JU)

Côte-Rôtie les Jumelles, Jaboulet **1997** £20.95 (TUR) £25.00 (FORT) £26.99 (VIL) £32.31 (PLA) £32.70 (NI) £35.83 (MI)

Côte-Rôtie les Jumelles, Jaboulet **1992** £24.17 (MI)

Côte-Rôtie René Rostaing **1998** £21.67 (ARM) £23.89 (BODX)

Côte-Rôtie René Rostaing **1997** £20.83 (ARM) £23.50 (AD) £28.00 (JU)

Côte-Rôtie René Rostaing **1995** £22.00 (JU) £35.00 (CRO)

Côte-Rôtie Seigneur de Maugiron, Delas **1996** £29.00 (CRO)

Côte-Rôtie de Vallouit **1983** £20.00 (CRO)

Côtes du Rhône Château de Fonsalette **1998** £24.87 (BODX)

Côtes du Rhône Château de Fonsalette **1996** £20.95 (FA)

Côtes du Rhône Château de Fonsalette **1995** £23.50 (FA)

Côtes du Rhône Château de Fonsalette **1994** £21.15 (FA)

Côtes du Rhône Château de Fonsalette **1986** £23.00 (CRO)

Crozes-Hermitage Domaine de Thalabert, Jaboulet **1983** £22.00 (CRO)

Gigondas Jaboulet **1979** £21.00 (CRO)

Hermitage Albert Belle **1996** £24.95 (BEN)

Hermitage B Chave **1995** £23.00 (AME)

Hermitage Domaine du Colombier **1998** £23.30 (TAN) £24.50 (BAL)

Hermitage Domaine du Colombier **1994** £22.00 (JU) £30.25 (TW)

Hermitage Faurie **1997** £20.00 (JU)

Hermitage Faurie **1996** £20.40 (HAH)

Hermitage Faurie **1992** £24.00 (JU)

Hermitage Guigal **1994** £22.50 (MI) £25.99 (PLAY)

Hermitage la Chapelle, Jaboulet **1992**
£24.90 (COC) £29.17 (MI)
Hermitage la Chapelle, Jaboulet **1984**
£21.15 (WY)
Hermitage la Sizeranne, Chapoutier **1996**
£20.95 (FA) £24.95 (DI) £25.90 (GAU)
£27.99 (SUN) £27.99 (LAI) £28.00 (CRO)
£29.96 (PEN) £39.99 (UN)
Hermitage la Sizeranne, Chapoutier **1995**
£21.15 (FA)
Hermitage la Sizeranne, Chapoutier **1983**
£23.00 (CRO)
Hermitage Domaine des Remizières **1997**
£22.50 (WIN)
St-Joseph Graillot **1996** £23.50 (CRO)

£25.00 → £29.99

Châteauneuf-du-Pape Château de
Beaucastel **1998** £25.46 (MV) £37.60
(TUR) £39.90 (CRO)
Cornas Clape **1996** £29.50 (CRO)
Cornas Clape **1985** £25.85 (FA)
Cornas Jaboulet **1976** £29.00 (CRO)
Cornas les Ruchets, Colombo **1993**
£26.75 (NI)
Côte-Rôtie Brune et Blonde, Guigal **1983**
£29.28 (FA) £30.55 (WY)
Côte-Rôtie Chapoutier **1996** £25.00 (WS)
£28.95 (BEN) £29.38 (PEN)
Côte-Rôtie Côte Blonde, René Rostaing
1993 £28.00 (JU)
Côte-Rôtie Côte Brune, Dervieux-Thaize
1983 £26.34 (BODX)
Côte-Rôtie Gentaz-Dervieux **1986**
£28.00 (WY)
Côte-Rôtie Gentaz-Dervieux **1980**
£29.00 (CRO)
Côte-Rôtie Jasmin **1998** £25.75 (WAI)
£27.75 (YAP)
Côte-Rôtie la Landonne, René Rostaing
1994 £26.83 (FA)
Côte-Rôtie la Landonne, René Rostaing
1993 £28.00 (JU)
Côte-Rôtie les Grandes Places, Clusel-
Roch **1997** £27.50 (LEA)
Côte-Rôtie les Grandes Places, Clusel-
Roch **1994** £29.00 (JU)
Côte-Rôtie les Jumelles, Jaboulet **1995**
£25.00 (FLE)
Côte-Rôtie Rose Pourpe, Gaillard **1997**
£29.00 (JU)
Côte-Rôtie de Vallouit **1988** £27.00
(CRO)
Crozes-Hermitage Jaboulet **1983** £27.03
(WY)

Crozes-Hermitage Domaine de
Thalabert, Jaboulet **1990** £28.30 (FA)
£32.00 (CRO)
Hermitage J-L Chave **1984** £29.00 (CRO)
Hermitage Desmeure **1983** £27.00 (CRO)
Hermitage Faurie **1989** £25.85 (FA)
Hermitage Guigal **1997** £29.99 (POR)
£33.33 (MI) £34.00 (BY)
Hermitage Guigal **1996** £28.33 (MI)
Hermitage la Sizeranne, Chapoutier **1998**
£26.10 (GAU) £27.90 (TAN) £29.77 (FA)
£32.95 (DI)
Hermitage la Sizeranne, Chapoutier **1989**
£29.38 (FA) £47.90 (TAN)
Hermitage le Gréal, Sorrel **1996** £27.60
(GAU)
St-Joseph Jaboulet **1978** £27.00 (CRO)

£30.00 → £49.99

Châteauneuf-du-Pape Barbe Rac,
Chapoutier **1997** £35.00 (BAL) £35.20
(GAU) £37.80 (RAE) £57.95 (CON)
Châteauneuf-du-Pape Barbe Rac,
Chapoutier **1996** £40.05 (FA) £41.13
(TUR) £43.00 (DI)
Châteauneuf-du-Pape Barbe Rac,
Chapoutier **1993** £36.62 (FA)
Châteauneuf-du-Pape Château de
Beaucastel **1988** £36.62 (FA) £40.00
(CRO)
Châteauneuf-du-Pape Château de
Beaucastel **1986** £35.25 (FA) £39.00 (CRO)
Châteauneuf-du-Pape Château de
Beaucastel **1983** £45.43 (FA) £49.00
(TAN) £52.00 (CRO) £58.75 (WY)
Châteauneuf-du-Pape Château de
Beaucastel **1980** £36.62 (FA)
Châteauneuf-du-Pape Domaine Bosquet
des Papes **1985** £34.00 (CRO)
Châteauneuf-du-Pape les Cailloux, Brunel
1990 £36.00 (CRO)
Châteauneuf-du-Pape Pignan **1998** £41.13
(BODX)
Châteauneuf-du-Pape Pignan **1986** £32.00
(CRO)
Châteauneuf-du-Pape Château Rayas
1997 £39.95 (DI) £52.29 (FA)
Châteauneuf-du-Pape Château Rayas
1994 £36.50 (DI) £70.50 (TUR)
Châteauneuf-du-Pape Château Rayas
1992 £47.00 (FA) £52.88 (TUR)
Châteauneuf-du-Pape Vidal-Fleury **1985**
£32.25 (WY)
Châteauneuf-du-Pape Domaine du Vieux
Télégraphe **1989** £44.65 (WY)

Cornas Clape 1997 £34.00 (FORT)
Cornas Clape 1983 £49.00 (CRO)
Cornas les Ruchets, Colombo 1997
£35.20 (LAY)
Côte-Rôtie Brune et Blonde, Guigal 1990
£47.00 (CRO)
Côte-Rôtie Brune et Blonde, Guigal 1985
£33.68 (FA) £49.00 (CRO)
Côte-Rôtie Chapoutier 1978 £45.00 (CRO)
Côte-Rôtie Côte Blonde, René Rostaing
1996 £30.75 (FA)
Côte-Rôtie Côte Blonde, René Rostaing
1994 £47.00 (CRO)
Côte-Rôtie Côte Brune, Gentaz-
Dervieux 1983 £48.37 (FA)
Côte-Rôtie Jasmin 1990 £49.00 (CRO)
Côte-Rôtie Jasmin 1983 £45.00 (CRO)
Côte-Rôtie Jasmin 1979 £38.00 (CRO)
Côte-Rôtie la Mordorée, Chapoutier
1994 £45.43 (FA) £59.00 (YOU)
Côte-Rôtie la Mordorée, Chapoutier
1993 £35.64 (TUR) £35.64 (FA)
Côte-Rôtie les Grandes Places, Clusel-
Roch 1993 £32.00 (JU)
Côte-Rôtie les Jumelles, Jaboulet 1998
£34.17 (MI)
Côte-Rôtie les Jumelles, Jaboulet 1985
£35.25 (WY)
Côte-Rôtie les Jumelles, Jaboulet 1983
£38.78 (WY)
Côte-Rôtie René Rostaing 1991 £38.00
(CRO)
Côte-Rôtie René Rostaing 1990 £30.75
(FA)
Côtes du Rhône Château de Fonsalette
1993 £33.49 (TW)
Côtes du Rhône Château de Fonsalette
1990 £41.13 (FA)
Crozes-Hermitage Domaine de
Thalabert, Jaboulet 1989 £30.00 (CRO)
Ermitage le Pavillon, Chapoutier 1992
£41.13 (FA) £58.75 (BODX) £79.50 (BEN)
Gigondas Domaine les Gouberts 1981
£34.00 (CRO)
Gigondas Jaboulet 1978 £33.00 (CRO)
Hermitage J-L Chave 1997 £48.86 (BODX)
£50.00 (FORT) £50.33 (FA) £59.50 (BAL)
£64.63 (TUR)
Hermitage J-L Chave 1996 £48.37 (FA)
Hermitage J-L Chave 1991 £35.25 (FA)
Hermitage Faurie 1995 £35.00 (JU)
Hermitage Guigal 1986 £38.78 (WY)
Hermitage Guigal 1983 £41.13 (WY)
Hermitage Guigal 1982 £39.00 (CRO)
Hermitage Guigal 1978 £42.00 (CRO)

Hermitage la Chapelle, Jaboulet 1998
£39.99 (OD) £44.45 (FA) £46.75 (NI)
£46.90 (BODX) £48.50 (CON) £59.17 (MI)
Hermitage la Chapelle, Jaboulet 1997
£45.00 (VIL) £45.40 (HAH) £65.02 (TUR)
Hermitage la Chapelle, Jaboulet 1996
£35.00 (FORT) £36.62 (FA) £37.50 (CON)
£39.99 (VIL) £42.30 (NI) £45.53 (PLA)
Hermitage la Chapelle, Jaboulet 1995
£46.42 (TUR)
Hermitage la Chapelle, Jaboulet 1994
£30.00 (YOU)
Hermitage la Chapelle, Jaboulet 1991
£40.00 (WS)
Hermitage la Chapelle, Jaboulet 1987
£32.00 (CRO)
Hermitage la Sizeranne, Chapoutier 1991
£31.00 (CRO)
Hermitage Marquise de la Tourette, Delas
1990 £40.00 (WS)
Hermitage Marquise de la Tourette, Delas
1983 £49.00 (CRO)

£50.00 → £99.99

Châteauneuf-du-Pape Barbe Rac,
Chapoutier 1990 £91.00 (CRO) £99.29
(FA)
Châteauneuf-du-Pape Barbe Rac,
Chapoutier 1989 £72.00 (CRO)
Châteauneuf-du-Pape Château de
Beaucastel 1990 £58.50 (BEN) £64.63
(TUR) £65.01 (FA) £69.00 (CRO) £75.00
(FORT)
Châteauneuf-du-Pape Château de
Beaucastel 1989 £70.50 (TUR) £76.00
(CRO)
Châteauneuf-du-Pape Château de
Beaucastel 1981 £85.00 (CRO)
Châteauneuf-du-Pape Château de
Beaucastel 1978 £98.00 (CRO)
Châteauneuf-du-Pape Clos du Mont
Olivet 1978 £54.00 (CRO)
Châteauneuf-du-Pape Château Fortia
1978 £67.00 (CRO)
Châteauneuf-du-Pape Pignan 1989 £98.31
(FA)
Châteauneuf-du-Pape Pignan 1985 £80.00
(CRO)

- All prices for each wine are listed
  together in ascending order.
- Price bands refer to the lowest price
  for which the wine is available.

Châteauneuf-du-Pape Château Rayas
1996 £76.38 (TUR)
Châteauneuf-du-Pape Château Rayas
1993 £52.88 (TUR) £58.75 (TW)
Châteauneuf-du-Pape Château Rayas
1974 £66.00 (CRO)
Cornas Clape **1990** £55.00 (CRO)
Côte-Rôtie Brune et Blonde, Guigal **1978**
£84.00 (CRO)
Côte-Rôtie Côte Blonde, René Rostaing
1995 £55.00 (CRO)
Côte-Rôtie Côte Blonde, René Rostaing
1985 £69.42 (BODX)
Côte-Rôtie Gentaz-Dervieux **1985**
£59.00 (CRO)
Côte-Rôtie Gentaz-Dervieux **1982**
£66.00 (CRO)
Côte-Rôtie la Landonne, Guigal **1993**
£66.00 (FA) £164.50 (TW)
Côte-Rôtie la Landonne, Guigal **1981**
£99.29 (FA) £99.88 (BODX) £105.00
(CRO)
Côte-Rôtie la Landonne, René Rostaing
1991 £59.00 (CRO)
Côte-Rôtie la Landonne, René Rostaing
1990 £52.88 (FA)
Côte-Rôtie la Landonne, René Rostaing
1988 £61.00 (CRO)
Côte-Rôtie la Mordorée, Chapoutier
1996 £73.83 (ARM) £74.81 (FA) £85.00
(BEN)
Côte-Rôtie la Mordorée, Chapoutier
1995 £81.66 (FA)
Côte-Rôtie la Mordorée, Chapoutier
1990 £75.00 (CRO)
Côte-Rôtie la Mouline, Guigal **1997**
£63.07 (BY) £137.08 (TUR)
Côte-Rôtie la Mouline, Guigal **1993**
£64.63 (FA)
Côte-Rôtie la Mouline, Guigal **1981**
£89.00 (CRO) £89.01 (BODX)
Côte-Rôtie la Turque, Guigal **1997**
£63.07 (BY) £138.65 (TUR)
Côte-Rôtie la Turque, Guigal **1993**
£66.00 (BODX)
Côte-Rôtie la Turque, Guigal **1992**
£77.75 (FA)
Ermitage le Pavillon, Chapoutier **1997**
£71.50 (DI) £85.78 (FA) £96.55 (RAE)
£107.12 (BODX)
Ermitage le Pavillon, Chapoutier **1996**
£88.13 (BODX) £98.80 (FA) £101.33
(ARM) £105.75 (TUR)
Ermitage le Pavillon, Chapoutier **1994**
£55.23 (FA)

Hermitage J-L Chave **1999** £55.00 (YAP)
Hermitage J-L Chave **1988** £55.02 (NO)
£71.87 (FA)
Hermitage J-L Chave **1986** £74.03 (WY)
Hermitage J-L Chave **1985** £69.00 (CRO)
£70.50 (FA) £94.00 (WY) £108.12 (NO)
Hermitage J-L Chave **1983** £71.00 (CRO)
£98.31 (FA)
Hermitage la Chapelle, Jaboulet **1989**
£77.75 (FA)
Hermitage la Chapelle, Jaboulet **1988**
£52.50 (BEN)
Hermitage la Chapelle, Jaboulet **1985**
£59.00 (CRO) £64.67 (NO) £66.98 (WY)
£85.00 (FORT)
Hermitage la Chapelle, Jaboulet **1983**
£64.63 (TUR) £65.02 (BODX) £65.02 (FA)
£70.49 (NO) £70.50 (WY)
Hermitage la Chapelle, Jaboulet **1982**
£56.40 (TUR) £65.00 (CRO)
Hermitage la Chapelle, Jaboulet **1979**
£65.99 (FA) £69.00 (CRO) £70.50 (TUR)
Hermitage les Bessards, Delas **1997**
£50.13 (RAE)
Hermitage Marquise de la Tourette, Delas
1978 £75.00 (CRO)

£100.00 → £149.99

Châteauneuf-du-Pape Hommage à Jacques
Perrin, Château de Beaucastel **1994**
£120.00 (FORT) £141.00 (TUR) £152.75
(FA)
Châteauneuf-du-Pape Château Rayas
1976 £148.25 (FA)
Côte-Rôtie la Landonne, Guigal **1997**
£138.45 (TUR)
Côte-Rôtie la Landonne, Guigal **1996**
£108.59 (BODX) £118.87 (FA)
Côte-Rôtie la Landonne, Guigal **1994**
£121.32 (BODX) £123.77 (FA)
Côte-Rôtie la Landonne, Guigal **1987**
£113.98 (FA) £120.00 (CRO)
Côte-Rôtie la Landonne, Guigal **1986**
£105.75 (FA) £115.00 (CRO) £135.00
(FORT) £176.25 (TW)
Côte-Rôtie la Landonne, Guigal **1980**
£138.45 (TUR) £138.45 (FA)

Please remember that
Oz Clarke's Wine Buying Guide
*is a price **guide** and not a price **list**. It is
not meant to replace up-to-date
merchants' lists.*

Côte-Rôtie la Mouline, Guigal **1996**
£111.63 (BODX) £118.87 (FA) £137.08
(TUR)
Côte-Rôtie la Mouline, Guigal **1994**
£106.63 (BODX) £109.08 (FA) £117.50
(TUR)
Côte-Rôtie la Mouline, Guigal **1987**
£112.80 (FA) £125.00 (CRO)
Côte-Rôtie la Mouline, Guigal **1986**
£105.75 (FA) £115.00 (CRO) £176.25
(TW)
Côte-Rôtie la Mouline, Guigal **1979**
£117.50 (FA)
Côte-Rôtie la Turque, Guigal **1996**
£105.75 (BODX) £118.87 (FA) £141.00
(TUR)
Côte-Rôtie la Turque, Guigal **1994**
£109.08 (FA) £123.38 (TUR)
Côte-Rôtie la Turque, Guigal **1987**
£112.80 (FA)
Côte-Rôtie les Jumelles, Jaboulet **1962**
£123.37 (TW)
Ermitage le Pavillon, Chapoutier **1995**
£125.00 (CRO) £133.56 (FA)
Ermitage le Pavillon, Chapoutier **1989**
£145.00 (CRO)
Hermitage J-L Chave **1966** £135.00 (CRO)
Hermitage la Chapelle, Jaboulet **1976**
£103.40 (WY)

£150.00 → £249.99

Châteauneuf-du-Pape Hommage à Jacques
Perrin, Château de Beaucastel **1995**
£197.20 (FA) £200.00 (FORT)
Châteauneuf-du-Pape Hommage à Jacques
Perrin, Château de Beaucastel **1990**
£220.00 (CRO) £293.75 (TUR)
Châteauneuf-du-Pape Hommage à Jacques
Perrin, Château de Beaucastel **1989**
£210.00 (CRO) £248.12 (FA) £293.75
(TUR)
Châteauneuf-du-Pape Château Rayas
1998 £205.63 (TUR) £216.79 (BODX)
Châteauneuf-du-Pape Château Rayas
1995 £226.58 (BODX) £250.00 (YOU)
Châteauneuf-du-Pape Château Rayas
1988 £177.62 (FA) £211.50 (TUR)
Châteauneuf-du-Pape Château Rayas
1985 £176.25 (FA)
Côte-Rôtie la Landonne, Guigal **1995**
£152.75 (BODX) £160.00 (TUR)
Côte-Rôtie la Landonne, Guigal **1991**
£207.00 (FA) £270.25 (TUR)
Côte-Rôtie la Landonne, Guigal **1990**
£226.58 (FA) £293.75 (TUR)

Côte-Rôtie la Landonne, Guigal **1989**
£215.03 (FA) £258.50 (TUR)
Côte-Rôtie la Landonne, Guigal **1988**
£236.38 (FA)
Côte-Rôtie la Landonne, Guigal **1983**
£240.00 (JU) £265.00 (CRO) £270.25
(TUR)
Côte-Rôtie la Mouline, Guigal **1995**
£156.28 (FA)
Côte-Rôtie la Mouline, Guigal **1990**
£226.58 (FA)
Côte-Rôtie la Mouline, Guigal **1989**
£215.03 (FA) £258.50 (TUR)
Côte-Rôtie la Mouline, Guigal **1988**
£236.38 (FA)
Côte-Rôtie la Mouline, Guigal **1983**
£236.37 (BODX) £250.00 (CRO)
Côte-Rôtie la Turque, Guigal **1995**
£156.28 (FA)
Côte-Rôtie la Turque, Guigal **1991**
£207.00 (FA) £270.25 (TUR)
Côte-Rôtie la Turque, Guigal **1988**
£236.38 (FA)
Côte-Rôtie la Turque, Guigal **1986**
£188.00 (TW)
Côte-Rôtie les Jumelles, Jaboulet **1955**
£209.15 (TW)
Hermitage J-L Chave **1990** £182.13 (TUR)
Hermitage J-L Chave **1978** £182.13 (FA)
Hermitage la Chapelle, Jaboulet **1990**
£156.28 (FA) £188.00 (TUR)
Hermitage la Chapelle, Jaboulet **1978**
£220.00 (WS)
Hermitage la Chapelle, Jaboulet **1971**
£175.00 (CRO)
Hermitage la Chapelle, Jaboulet **1969**
£152.75 (FA) £195.00 (CRO)

Over £250.00

Châteauneuf-du-Pape Château Rayas
1990 £411.25 (TUR)
Châteauneuf-du-Pape Château Rayas
1989 £260.85 (FA)
Côte-Rôtie la Landonne, Guigal **1985**
£293.00 (CRO) £317.25 (TUR)
Côte-Rôtie la Landonne, Guigal **1978**
£324.50 (FA)
Côte-Rôtie la Mouline, Guigal **1985**
£260.00 (CRO)
Côte-Rôtie la Mouline, Guigal **1978**
£353.87 (FA)
Côte-Rôtie la Turque, Guigal **1989**
£258.50 (TUR)
Côte-Rôtie la Turque, Guigal **1985**
£317.25 (BODX) £353.87 (FA)

WHITE

Under £6.00

VdP des Coteaux de l'Ardèche
Chardonnay, Latour **2000** £4.99 (POR)
VdP des Coteaux de l'Ardèche
Chardonnay, Latour **1999** £5.41 (COC)
£5.49 (PEN) £5.49 (JON) £7.15 (TAN)
VdP des Coteaux de l'Ardèche
Chardonnay, Latour **1998** £5.95 (FORT)
VdP des Coteaux de l'Ardèche Viognier,
Duboeuf **1999** £5.99 (NEZ)
Côtes du Lubéron le Mont, la Vieille
Ferme **1999** £5.29 (BIB)
Côtes du Lubéron Château Val Joanis
1999 £5.53 (BY)
Côtes du Lubéron la Vieille Ferme **1998**
£5.70 (CB) £5.99 (RAE)
Lirac la Fermade, Domaine Maby **1998**
£5.95 (WS)

£6.00 → £7.99

Côtes du Rhône Belleruche, Chapoutier
1998 £6.58 (PEN) £6.69 (CON)
Côtes du Rhône Guigal **1999** £7.59 (JON)
£8.35 (JER) £10.69 (TW)
Côtes du Rhône Guigal **1998** £7.49 (UN)
Côtes du Rhône Parallèle 45, Jaboulet
1999 £7.04 (PLA)
Côtes du Rhône Domaine St-Gayan,
Meffre **1999** £6.95 (YAP)
Côtes du Rhône-Villages Blanc de Blancs,
Château du Grand Moulas **1998** £6.95
(AD)
Crozes-Hermitage Cave des Clairmonts
1999 £7.59 (JON) £8.50 (YAP)
Crozes-Hermitage Pochon **1997** £6.95
(JU)
Crozes-Hermitage Pradelle **1999** £7.50
(BALL)
Lirac la Fermade, Domaine Maby **1999**
£7.25 (YAP)

£8.00 → £9.99

Côtes du Rhône Coudoulet de Beaucastel
1999 £9.89 (RAE) £11.95 (AD)
Crozes-Hermitage Cave des Clairmonts
1997 £8.89 (HIC)
Crozes-Hermitage Domaine du
Colombier **2000** £8.72 (BIB)
Crozes-Hermitage Domaine du
Colombier **1999** £9.50 (JU)
Crozes-Hermitage Château Curson,
Pochon **1997** £9.90 (JU)

Crozes-Hermitage Delas **1999** £8.85 (JER)
Crozes-Hermitage Domaine des
Entrefaux **1999** £8.26 (BY)
Crozes-Hermitage la Mule Blanche,
Jaboulet **1999** £9.95 (WS)
Crozes-Hermitage Pochon **2000** £8.50
(MAY)
Crozes-Hermitage Pochon **1995** £8.50
(JU)
Hermitage Graillot **1999** £9.08 (BY)
St-Joseph Gaillard **1998** £9.85 (BAN)
St-Joseph le Grand Pompée, Jaboulet
1997 £9.30 (SAV)
St-Péray Thières **1998** £9.50 (YAP)

£10.00 → £14.99

Châteauneuf-du-Pape Domaine Font de
Michelle **1999** £13.95 (BALL)
Châteauneuf-du-Pape Domaine Font de
Michelle **1997** £13.50 (JU)
Châteauneuf-du-Pape Château Fortia
1999 £13.79 (YOU)
Châteauneuf-du-Pape Domaine Grand
Veneur **1996** £10.65 (GN)
Châteauneuf-du-Pape Domaine Grand
Veneur **1995** £10.65 (GN)
Châteauneuf-du-Pape Domaine de Nalys
1999 £11.82 (BY)
Châteauneuf-du-Pape Domaine de Nalys
1998 £11.08 (BY)
Châteauneuf-du-Pape Domaine du Père
Caboche **2000** £13.25 (YAP)
Châteauneuf-du-Pape Domaine de la
Roquette **1997** £11.70 (TAN)
Châteauneuf-du-Pape Domaine du Vieux
Télégraphe **1999** £14.95 (TAN)
Châteauneuf-du-Pape Domaine du Vieux
Télégraphe **1998** £14.95 (AD)
Côtes du Rhône Coudoulet de Beaucastel
1998 £10.99 (JON) £12.50 (MV)
Côtes du Rhône Coudoulet de Beaucastel
1997 £11.00 (WS)
Côtes du Rhône Coudoulet de Beaucastel
1996 £10.50 (CRO)
Côtes du Rhône Château de Fonsalette
1998 £13.12 (BODX)
Côtes du Rhône Château de Fonsalette
1995 £13.61 (FA)
Côtes du Rhône Viognier Clos de la
Cuminaille, Pierre Gaillard **1999** £13.95
(LEA)
Côtes du Rhône Viognier Domaine
Gramenon **1994** £10.00 (BAC)
Crozes-Hermitage la Mule Blanche,
Jaboulet **1998** £10.95 (TAN) £11.95 (STA)

Lirac Cuvée de la Reine des Bois,
Domaine de la Mordorée **1999** £10.25
(BAN) £10.95 (LEA) £11.99 (BEN)
Lirac Cuvée de la Reine des Bois,
Domaine de la Mordorée **1996** £10.58
(SAV)
St-Joseph Perret **1998** £11.00 (MV)
St-Joseph Perret **1996** £11.00 (JU)

£15.00 → £19.99

Châteauneuf-du-Pape Château de
Beaucastel **1999** £19.00 (FA) £21.35
(RAE) £22.95 (TAN) £25.00 (FORT)
Châteauneuf-du-Pape Château de
Beaucastel **1995** £15.28 (FA) £21.00
(CRO) £24.75 (NI)
Châteauneuf-du-Pape la Bernadine,
Chapoutier **1999** £17.95 (CON)
Châteauneuf-du-Pape la Bernadine,
Chapoutier **1997** £18.21 (PEN)
Châteauneuf-du-Pape les Cèdres, Jaboulet
1998 £16.75 (STA)
Châteauneuf-du-Pape Clos des Papes,
Avril **1999** £15.76 (RAE)
Châteauneuf-du-Pape Clos des Papes,
Avril **1998** £18.65 (GAU)
Châteauneuf-du-Pape Domaine Font de
Michelle **1998** £15.25 (MAY)
Châteauneuf-du-Pape Domaine du Vieux
Télégraphe **1997** £15.99 (JON)
Châteauneuf-du-Pape Domaine du Vieux
Télégraphe **1996** £16.90 (JU)
Condrieu Chapoutier **1999** £19.99 (DI)
Condrieu Coteau de Chéry, Perret **1999**
£19.95 (AD) £22.99 (YOU) £23.20 (GAU)
£26.95 (BEN)
Condrieu Delas **1994** £18.57 (PEN)
Condrieu Guigal **1998** £17.00 (CRO)
£19.95 (POR) £20.28 (BY) £22.49 (UN)
£23.33 (MI)
Condrieu Guigal **1997** £19.40 (BY) £22.50
(MI)
Condrieu Perret **2000** £19.35 (NI)
Condrieu Perret **1998** £18.90 (JU) £30.00
(FORT)
Côtes du Rhône Viognier, Gaillard **1996**
£16.00 (JU)
Côtes du Rhône Viognier, Gaillard **1994**
£16.95 (JU)
Hermitage Chante-Alouette, Chapoutier
1994 £17.63 (BODX) £25.00 (YOU)
Hermitage Faurie **1996** £18.40 (HAH)
£22.00 (JU)
St-Joseph Bernard Gripa **1995** £15.86
(TW)

£20.00 → £29.99

Châteauneuf-du-Pape Château de
Beaucastel **1997** £23.50 (GAU) £24.75
(NI)
Châteauneuf-du-Pape Château de
Beaucastel **1996** £21.00 (MV)
Châteauneuf-du-Pape Château de
Beaucastel **1993** £22.49 (YOU)
Châteauneuf-du-Pape Guigal **1990** £25.00
(CRO)
Châteauneuf-du-Pape Château Rayas
1998 £28.30 (BODX)
Condrieu Barge **1998** £21.40 (TAN)
Condrieu Chapoutier **1998** £23.75 (CON)
Condrieu Clos Chanson, Perret **1999**
£21.49 (YOU)
Condrieu Côte Fournet, Dumazet **1999**
£25.94 (BIB)
Condrieu Coteau de Chéry, Perret **2000**
£22.95 (NI)
Condrieu Coteau du Chéry, Clusel-Roch
1999 £21.95 (LEA)
Condrieu Dumazet **1999** £20.56 (BIB)
Condrieu Gaillard **1999** £20.60 (BAN)
Condrieu Gaillard **1997** £21.00 (GN)
Condrieu Guigal **1996** £22.50 (MI) £23.00
(CRO)
Condrieu la Bonnette, Rostaing **1999**
£24.99 (YOU) £28.99 (RAE)
Condrieu la Bonnette, Rostaing **1997**
£25.00 (JU)
Condrieu Perret **1996** £20.00 (JU)
Condrieu Château du Rozay **1999** £25.50
(YAP)
Condrieu Vernay **1997** £24.75 (YAP)
£28.50 (FORT)
Hermitage Chante-Alouette, Chapoutier
1995 £22.75 (DI) £25.00 (YOU)
Hermitage Chevalier de Stérimberg,
Jaboulet **1997** £22.91 (TUR) £32.20 (PLA)
£32.50 (CON)
Hermitage Faurie **1997** £23.00 (JU)
Hermitage Faurie **1994** £20.30 (HAH)
Hermitage Guigal **1996** £20.02 (BY)
Hermitage les Rocoules, Sorrel **1996**
£22.50 (GAU)

£30.00 → £39.99

Château-Grillet **1999** £36.00 (YAP)
Château-Grillet **1998** £35.00 (YAP)
Châteauneuf-du-Pape Château Rayas
1997 £33.95 (DI)
Châteauneuf-du-Pape Château Rayas
1994 £34.95 (DI) £64.62 (TW)

Châteauneuf-du-Pape Vieilles Vignes,
Château de Beaucastel **1997** £35.99
(RAE) £40.00 (YOU) £42.00 (MV)
Châteauneuf-du-Pape Vieilles Vignes,
Château de Beaucastel **1996** £30.50
(RAE) £51.98 (PLAY) £52.88 (TUR)
Châteauneuf-du-Pape Vieilles Vignes,
Château de Beaucastel **1995** £37.12
(NO)
Condrieu Coteau de Vernon, Vernay
1999 £39.00 (YOU)
Hermitage Chante-Alouette, Chapoutier
1997 £30.00 (WS)
Hermitage J-L Chave **1993** £37.50 (FORT)
Hermitage les Rocoules, Sorrel **1998**
£35.64 (FA)

Over £40.00

Châteauneuf-du-Pape Château Rayas
1978 £176.25 (FA)
Châteauneuf-du-Pape Vieilles Vignes,
Château de Beaucastel **1998** £41.40
(TAN)
Hermitage J-L Chave **1998** £52.75 (YAP)
Hermitage J-L Chave **1997** £45.00 (YAP)
Hermitage J-L Chave **1979** £99.88 (WY)
Hermitage de l'Orée, Chapoutier **1997**
£82.45 (RAE)
Hermitage de l'Orée, Chapoutier **1996**
£71.87 (FA) £89.50 (ARM)
Hermitage de l'Orée, Chapoutier **1995**
£64.63 (FA) £85.50 (BEN)
Hermitage de l'Orée, Chapoutier **1994**
£41.13 (FA)
Hermitage de l'Orée, Chapoutier **1992**
£41.13 (FA)

ROSÉ

Under £6.00

Côtes du Rhône Domaine de la
Mordorée à Tavel **1999** £4.95 (LEA)
Côtes du Lubéron Château Val Joanis
1999 £5.53 (BY)
Tavel la Forcadière, Domaine Maby **1999**
£5.95 (WS) £7.95 (YAP)

Over £6.00

Lirac Rosé la Fermade, Domaine Maby
1999 £7.25 (YAP)
Tavel Domaine André Méjan **1999** £6.99
(UN)
Tavel Domaine de la Mordorée **2000**
£8.95 (LEA)

SPARKLING

Under £10.00

Clairette de Die Brut Archard-Vincent
Non-vintage £9.50 (YAP)
Clairette de Die Tradition Demi-sec
Archard-Vincent **Non-vintage** £9.25
(YAP)
Côtes du Rhône Château St-Maurice
1999 £4.49 (WAI)

FORTIFIED

Under £7.00

Muscat de Beaumes-de-Venise Domaine
de Coyeux ½ bottle **1998** £6.31 (CB)
Muscat de Beaumes-de-Venise Domaine
de Durban ½ bottle **1997** £5.97 (SAV)

£7.00 → £9.99

Muscat de Beaumes-de-Venise Cave Co-
op de Beaumes-de-Venise **1999** £8.49
(OD)
Muscat de Beaumes-de-Venise
Chapoutier ½ bottle **1997** £8.12
(PEN)
Muscat de Beaumes-de-Venise Domaine
de Durban **1997** £9.60 (SAV)
Muscat de Beaumes-de-Venise Fenouillet
2000 £7.51 (BIB)
Muscat de Beaumes-de-Venise Jaboulet ½
bottle **Non-vintage** £8.95 (NI)
Muscat de Beaumes-de-Venise Cave des
Vignerons à Vacqueyras **Non-vintage**
£9.62 (PLAY) £9.95 (POR) £10.49 (JON)

£10.00 → £13.99

Muscat de Beaumes-de-Venise Domaine
de Coyeux **1996** £10.95 (JU)
Muscat de Beaumes-de-Venise Domaine
de Durban **2000** £12.35 (YAP)
Muscat de Beaumes-de-Venise Domaine
de Durban **1999** £11.50 (SOM)
Muscat de Beaumes-de-Venise Vidal-
Fleury **1998** £12.95 (SOM)
Muscat de Beaumes-de-Venise la Vieille
Ferme **Non-vintage** £11.99 (RAE)

Over £14.00

Muscat de Beaumes-de-Venise Jaboulet
1999 £16.04 (PLA)
Rasteau Domaine la Soumade **1998**
£18.74 (TW)

SOUTHERN FRANCE

Winemakers in the south of France are really working hard right now, experimenting with new grapes and vineyard sites and rediscovering old ones. And many of the wines are at bargain prices – what are you waiting for?

A few years ago, if you wanted exciting, modern wines from the South, you had a choice between a few private estates whose wines could be difficult to find, and a handful of huge companies whose wines were everywhere – and when I say everywhere I mean in every supermarket. The brand name might vary, but the wine didn't. It was perfectly nice wine – it still is perfectly nice wine. But what we're seeing now is a raft of smaller estates making wonderful, individual wines. Some are vins de pays, some are appellation contrôlée: it doesn't really seem to matter any more. Whether your wine is VdP or AC is increasingly a question of style and of region

– whether your property happens to fall within AC boundaries – but not of quality. There are fantastic sites here without an appellation to their name. All they need is somebody willing to discover them.

You see, the bits that were made Appellation Contrôlée were the bits that were making better wine at the time – which was decades ago. The rest of the land was producing bulk wine, and all anyone wanted to do was forget about it. But a new generation of ambitious owners is tramping the hills and cherry-picking the choicest spots. The estates are not large, so the wines are still not all over the place. But the winemakers went exploring; so can you.

WINE REGIONS

BANDOL, AC (Provence; red, rosé, white) Herby, tobaccoey, long-lived wines of top class, based on Mourvèdre. Some, like *Tempier,* are being made in a more supple style. The serious spicy rosés can also be excellent. Best estates: *Ch. la Rouvière (Bunan), Ch. de Pibarnon, Ch. Pradeaux, Dom. la Bastide Blanche, Dom. du Cagueloup, Dom. le Galantin, Dom. Ray-Jane, Dom. Tempier, Dom. Terrebrune, Dom. de la Tour de Bon, Ch. Ste-Anne, Ch. Vannières.* The whites can be delicious, with an aniseed-and-apple bite to them. Best whites: *Ch. de Pibarnon* and *Dom. Lafran-Veyrolles.*

BANYULS, AC (Languedoc-Roussillon; vin doux naturel, red) Grenache-based wine that can assume many guises: red or tawny, sweet or dryish, and can come, too, in an oxidized *rancio* style with burnt caramel flavours. *Cellier des Templiers, Clos des Paulilles, Dom. du Mas Blanc* and *Dom. de la Rectorie* are good. Wines aged for two-and-a-half years in wood may be labelled Grand Cru.

LES BAUX-DE-PROVENCE , AC (Provence; red, rosé) More characterful than their neighbours in Coteaux d'Aix-en-Provence, though limits on the use of Cabernet mean that top-notch *Domaine de Trévallon* has been demoted to vin de pays. *Mas de la Dame, Mas de Gourgonnier, Mas Ste-Berthe, Ch. Romanin* and *Terres Blanches* are also good.

BÉARN, AC (South-West; red, rosé, white) The reds are mainly from the Tannat grape, with other local varieties and both Cabernets thrown in. In spite of this they are basically undistinguished but you could try the wines of the *Vignerons de Bellocq co-op,* the *Crouseilles co-op, Domaine Cauhapé, Domaine Guilhemas (Lapeyre)* or *Nigri.*

BELLET, AC (Provence; red, white) An unusual nutty Rolle and Chardonnay white with a good local reputation. *Château de Crémat* and *Château de Bellet* are worth seeking out, though like everything else near

Nice, they're expensive. The same producers make a few reds and rosés, again from unusual local grapes such as Braquet and Folle Noire.

BERGERAC, AC (South-West; red, rosé) Bergerac is a kind of Bordeaux understudy: the rosés are often extremely good, deep in colour, dry and full of fruit; a good red can be a better bet than basic Bordeaux, and often cheaper. Bergerac Rouge is usually at its best at between one and four years old, depending on vintage and style. *Château la Jaubertie* led the way. *Château le Barradis*, *Château Belingard* and *Château Tour des Gendres* are also good, and *Château Court-les-Mûts* makes a delicious rosé and a good red.

BERGERAC SEC, AC (South-West; white) Bordeaux lookalikes. *Château Belingard*, *Château Court-les-Mûts*, *Château Fayolle*, *Château les Miaudoux* and *Château de Panisseau* are good but the star is *Château la Jaubertie* where tremendous flavour and panache are extracted from a Sauvignon, Sémillon and Muscadelle blend, and from a straight Sauvignon as well.

BUZET, AC (South-West; red, rosé, white) Claret lookalikes that can combine a rich blackcurrant sweetness with an arresting grassy greenness. They are for drinking at between one and five years old, depending on the vintage and the style. Look out for the wines of the co-op, which dominates the area: its *Baron d'Ardeuil*, *Château de Gueyze* and *Château Padère* are all pretty good.

CABARDÈS, AC (Languedoc-Roussillon; red) The aromatic originality and liveliness of these wines derives from the marriage of southern and south-western grape varieties, such as Grenache, Syrah, Merlot, Cabernet, Fer and Cot (Malbec). Best producers include *de Brau*, *Cabrol*, *Château de la Bastide*, *Château de Rayssac*, *Dom. Jouclary*, *Pennautier*, *Château Salitis* and *Ventenac*.

CAHORS, AC (South-West; red) Increasingly supple these days: the 'black wine' of yore has pretty well vanished, and that's no bad thing. Modern Cahors is likely to combine raisiny, plummy fruit with flavours of spices, tobacco and prunes, soft tannins and the potential for longevity. The grapes are largely Auxerrois (Bordeaux's Malbec), plus Merlot and Tannat. Good names: *Ch. des Bouysses* from the *Côtes d'Olt* co-op, *la Caminade*, *Ch. de Cayrou*, *Ch. du Cèdre*, *Ch. de Chambert*, *Ch. de Haute-Serre*, *Ch. de Poujol*, *Ch. St-Didier*, *Ch. de Treilles*, *Clos la Coutale*, *Clos de Gamot*, *Clos Triguedina*, *Domaine de Gaudou* and *Domaine de Quattre*, *Lagrezette*, *Lamartine*.

CASSIS, AC (Provence; red, white, rosé) The white dominates the AC – they say locally you should be able to taste the sea salt. Rosés are good, but red is increasingly rare. Look out for *Dom. du Bagnol*, *Dom. de la Ferme Blanche*, *Dom. du Paternel* and *Clos Ste-Magdelaine*.

CLAIRETTE DU LANGUEDOC, AC (Languedoc-Roussillon; white) The Clairette can be a difficult grape to vinify, but the quality of wines like *Dom. de la Condamine Bertrand*, the co-op at *Cabrières* and *Domaine St-André* show what can be done.

COLLIOURE, AC (Languedoc-Roussillon; red) Startling, intense reds dominated by Grenache, with increasing contributions from Mourvèdre. Best: *Casa Blanca*, *Cellier des Templiers*, *Clos des Paulilles*, *Dom. de Baillaury*, *Dom. du Mas Blanc*, *Dom. de la Rectorie*, *la Tour Vieille*.

CORBIÈRES, AC (Languedoc-Roussillon; red, white, rosé) Reds range from juicy upfront wines produced using carbonic maceration to powerful, serious, traditionally made bottles like *la Voulte-Gasparets*. Others: *R Balthazar*, *Bel Eveque*, *Caraguilhes*, *Ch. Cascadais*, *Courbis*, *E & J Durand*, *Étang des Colombes*, *Fontsainte*, *Grand Moulin*, *Ch. Hélène*, *Ch. de Lastours*,

Mansenoble, les Palais, St-Auriol, Dom. du Tunnel and the Mont Tauch co-op. There is less white, but it's increasingly good.

COSTIÈRES DE NÎMES, AC

(Languedoc; red, rosé, white) There are good rosés and meaty, smoky reds here, at prices that are still reasonable. Try Dom. de l'Amarine, Mas des Bressades, Mas Carlot (especially the Ch. Paul Blanc label), Ch. Mourgues du Grès, Ch. de la Tuilerie.

COTEAUX D'AIX-EN-PROVENCE, AC

(Provence; red, white, rosé) An increasing use of Cabernet and Syrah and subtle use of new oak are combining to make interesting reds and rosés in a semi-Bordelais style – such as Château Vignelaure. Also good: Ch. Bas, Ch. Crémade, Ch. de Calissanne, Ch. de Fonscolombe, Ch. du Seuil, Dom. de la Courtade, Dom. des Beatis, Dom. des Glauges, Revelette. There is little white, and frankly it's not that thrilling.

COTEAUX DU LANGUEDOC, AC

(Languedoc-Roussillon; red, white) This sprawling appellation incorporates 12 demarcated terroirs that may state their names on the labels. Among the better ones for reds are St-Saturnin, Pic St-Loup and La Clape. The classic southern grapes are used, and the growing presence of Syrah and Mourvèdre can be discerned in the complexity and breed of many wines. Best: Dom. l'Aiguelière, Dom. d'Aupilhac, Dom. de Brunet, Calage, Capion, Dom. de Cazeneuve, Clavel, Dom. de la Coste, Dom. de l'Hortus, Dom. des Jougla, Lascaux, Mas Bruguière, Mas des Chimères, Mas Jullien, Mas de Mortiès, Mas de la Seranne, Pech-Céleyran, Pech-Redon, Dom. Peyre-Rose, Prieuré de St-Jean de Bébian, de Terre-Mégère and the co-ops at Cabrières, Gabian (la Carignano), Montpeyrous, Neffiès and St-Saturnin. White winemaking is also being taken more seriously. Best: Boscary, Chamayrac, Ch. de Granoupiac, Claude Gaujal, Mas Jullien, Terre Mégère and the co-ops at Pine, Pomérols and St-Saturnin (le Lucian).

COTEAUX VAROIS, AC

(Provence; red, rosé, white) Quality is improving here. Try Château de Miraval for white, or Ch. la Calisse, Ch. Routas, Ch. St-Estève, Ch. St-Jean de Villecroze, Deffends, Dom. des Alysses, Dom. du Loou and Dom. de Triennes.

CÔTES DE BERGERAC, AC

(South-West; red, rosé) This is to Bergerac what Bordeaux Supérieur is to Bordeaux: from the same region, but with slightly higher minimum alcohol. Many are sold as basic Bergerac, although the excellent Château Court-les-Mûts now uses this AC.

CÔTES DE DURAS, AC

(South-West; red, white) Light, grassy claret lookalikes. Château de Pilar and le Seigneuret from the co-op are quite good and cheap. Also fairly good Sauvignon-based white that can be as fresh as good Bordeaux Blanc, but just a little chubbier. Château de Conti is good, as is Le Seigneuret from the co-op.

CÔTES DU FRONTONNAIS, AC

(South-West; red, rosé) At their best these are silky and plummy, sometimes with a touch of raspberry and licorice, but always with a twist of fresh black pepper. The Négrette grape dominates, and is wonderfully tasty. Best producers: *Baudare, Ch. Bellevue-la-Forêt, Ch. Flotis, Ch. Montauriol, Ch. la Palme, Le Roc.*

CÔTES DE LA MALEPÈRE, VDQS

(Languedoc-Roussillon; red) Similar grape varieties to those of Cabardès, with the addition of Cabernet Franc. Best: *Ch. de Festes, Dom. de Matibat, Cave du Razès.*

CÔTES DU MARMANDAIS, AC

(South-West; red) Simple, soft, fruity wines for drinking young, made from Cabernet Sauvignon, Cabernet Franc, Merlot, Fer and Abouriou. A few are designed for more serious aging, but it doesn't suit them.

CÔTES DE PROVENCE, AC

(Provence; red, white, rosé) Among the overpriced rosés made for the tourists there are many top-grade red and pink wines made by growers who take their calling seriously. They include *Dom. de la Bernarde, Commanderie de Bargemore, Commanderie de Peyrassol, la Courtade, Coussin Ste-Victoire, Dom. du Dragon, d'Esclans, Féraud, Maravenne, Dom. Ott, Presqu'île de St-Tropez, Dom. Rabiega, Richeaume, Rimauresq, St-Baillon, Ch. de Selle, Sorin.* For whites, *Castel Roubine, Château Ferry-Lacombe, Clos Bernarde, Gavoty, Dom. Richeaume, de Rasque, Réal Martin* and *St-André de la Figuière* are the leading lights.

CÔTES DU ROUSSILLON AND CÔTES DU ROUSSILLON VILLAGES, AC

(South-West; red, white) Up-and-coming for reds, although whites lag behind. Carignan still dominates the vineyards, though the tastier Syrah is increasing. The Villages AC covers 32 villages in the North. Try *Ch, de Casenove, Dom. Cazes, Dom. Gauby, Dom. Laporte,*

Dom. Piquemal, Dom. Sarda-Malet, Ferrer-Ribière, Les Hauts de Força Réal, Lafage, Mas Becha, Mas Crémat, Mas de la Garrigue.

CÔTES DE ST-MONT, VDQS

(South-West; red, white) These reds are increasingly made in a fresh, blackcurranty, modern style. By far the best examples come from the *Plaimont co-op.*

FAUGÈRES, AC (Languedoc-Roussillon;

red) The grapes here are Grenache, Syrah, Mourvèdre and Carignan. The wines have depth, class and character, in which cassis, black cherries and licorice predominate. In mature Faugères wines, complex game and leather aromas can often emerge. Best producers: *Alquier, Ch. Chenaie, Estanilles, Louison, Lubac, Ollier-Taillefer, Vidal* and the co-op at *Laurens.*

FITOU, AC (Languedoc-Roussillon; red)

A highly variable, old-style red in which Carignan has traditionally been dominant, but Grenache and, increasingly, Syrah and Mourvèdre are being used to add interest. *Paul Colomer, Robert Daurat-Fort* and *les Fenals* are the leading lights, along with co-ops at *Villeneuve* and at *Tuchan,* where the *Caves de Mont Tauch* is producing some of the most serious Fitou of all.

GAILLAC, AC (South-West; red, white)

The white, based on the bracing Mauzac grape, can be *moelleux* (medium-sweet), *perlé* (very faintly bubbly) or dry; the dry is usually a little neutral, though a few have a quite big apple-and-licorice fruit. The sparkling wines can be superb: peppery, honeyed, apricotty and appley all at the same time. From *Boissel-Rhodes, Canto Perlic Causses Marines, Cros* or *Plageoles,* they are very good value. There are two styles of red, Duras plus Fer Servadou and Syrah, or Duras plus Merlot and Cabernet. *Domaine Jean Cros* is delicious. Other producers worth a look are: *Dom. du Bosc-Long, Dom. de Labarthe, Ch. Larroze, Mas Pignou* and the co-ops at *Labastide-de-Lévis* and *Técou.*

IROULÉGUY, AC (South-West; red)
This comes from the foothills of the
Pyrénées, and it's mostly quite rough and
rustic, Tannat-based red, supplemented by
both Cabernets. Try *Domaine Brana* and
Domaine Ilarria.

JURANÇON, AC (South-West; white)
This can be sweet, medium or dry. The dry
wines are light and can be ravishingly
perfumed, while the sweet wines are
honeyed, raisiny and peachy, yet with a lick
of acidity. The pace-setter is *Henri
Ramonteu* of *Dom. Cauhapé*; others are *Clos
Lapeyre, Clos Thou* (dry), *Clos Uroulat*
(sweet), *Clos de la Vierge* (dry), *Cancaillaü*
(sweet), *Cru Lamouroux* (sweet), *Dom. Bru-
Baché* (dry), *Bellegarde, Dom. Castera, Dom.
Larrédya, Dom. de Souch.*

LIMOUX, AC (South-West; white)
Sparkling Blanquette de Limoux is mostly
from the Mauzac grape; Crémant de
Limoux has more Chardonnay, and is less
rustic. The still wines are based on barrel-
fermented Chardonnay, and tend to be
expensive. Best producers include: *Antech,
Dom. de l'Aigle, Caves du Sieur d'Arques,
Philippe Collin, Delmas, Sev Dervin, Robert.*

MADIRAN, AC (South-West; red)
Attractive, generally rather rustic reds based
on the Tannat grape, along with the
Cabernets and occasionally Fer. Good ones
include *Ch. d'Arricau-Bordes, Ch. d'Aydie* (alias
*Domaine Laplace), Ch. Bouscassé, Ch. de
Crouseilles, Ch. Montus, Ch. Peyros, Domaine
Berthoumieu, Domaine du Crampilh, Domaine
Damiens, Domaine Meinjarre, Domaine
Mouréou, Chapelle Lenclos, Laffitte-Teston*
and the *Plaimont co-op.*

MAURY, AC (Languedoc-Roussillon; *vin
doux naturel*, red) Grenache without the
finesse of Banyuls, but more explosive in its
nutty, toffee, prunes-in-brandy intensity. It
can also be made in the oxidized *rancio*
style. Try *la Coume du Roy, Mas Amiel,
Maurydoré, la Pleiade* and the *Maury* co-op.

MINERVOIS, AC (Languedoc-
Roussillon; red, white, rosé) Interesting reds
with good peppery berry fruit and violet
scent. A handful of crus – wines from areas
a cut above the rest – is planned; first will
be La Livinière, with wines based on Syrah.
Best include the co-op at *la Livinière*, plus
*Aires Hautes, Clos Centeilles, Château Fabas,
Château de Gourgazaud, Château d'Oupia,
Domaine Maris, Piccinini, Ste-Eulalie, la Tour
Boisée, Villerambert-Julien, Violet* and the co-
ops at *Peyriac* and *Azillanet*. White
Minervois is increasingly good and aromatic.

MONBAZILLAC, AC (South-West;
white) These sweet wines are never as rich
or weighty as a top Sauternes, but the
massive improvements in quality in
Sauternes have spurred the producers here
to sharpen up their act, too. The best are
very good indeed, and include *l'Ancienne
Cure, Belingard Blanche de Bosredon, Ch.
Haut-Bernasse, Ch. Hébras, Ch. Theulet, Ch.
du Treuil-de-Nailhac* and *Tirecul La Gravière.*

MONTRAVEL, AC (South-West; white)
Dry white from the Dordogne. Côtes de
Montravel is medium-sweet *moelleux* from
the same area; Haut-Montravel is a separate
area and sweeter. All are mostly sold as
Bergerac or Côtes de Bergerac.

MUSCAT (*vin doux naturel;* white) Not a
region but a grape. Wines range from the
syrupy *Tradition* made by the *Frontignan co-
op* to the elegant *Château de la Peyrade*
(Frontignan), *Domaine de la Capelle*
(Mireval), *Grés St-Paul* (Lunel), *Domaine de
Barroubie* and the co-op in *St-Jean-de-
Minervois.* All of these are made from the
Muscat à Petits Grains which gives more
finesse than the Muscat d'Alexandrie, used
in Muscat de Rivesaltes (*Cazes* and *Brial* are
the names to go for there).

PACHERENC DU VIC-BILH, AC
(South-West; white) One of France's most
esoteric whites, a blend of Gros and Petit
Manseng and Arrufiac – a grape peculiar to

the AC. At its best when dry and pear-skin-perfumed – and sometimes when rich and sweet. Best: *Château d'Aydie, Château Bouscassé, Domaine Berthoumieu, Domaine du Crampilh* and *Domaine Damiens*.

PALETTE, AC (Provence; red, white, rosé) A tiny AC dominated by *Château Simone*. The rosé beats the others.

PÉCHARMANT, AC (South-West; red) The best red wine of Bergerac, this must be aged for a minimum of a year before sale to distinguish it from Bergerac, which can be sold after only six months. It is deliciously blackcurranty when young, and at its best is a good claret lookalike. *Château de Tiregand* is very good indeed, but *Domaine du Haut-Pécharmant* is even better.

ST-CHINIAN, AC (Languedoc-Roussillon; red, rosé) Improving and often very attractive wines. Among the top are *Borie la Vitarèle, Canet Valette, Ch. Cazal-Viel, Ch. Coujan, Dom. des Jougla, la Dournie* (especially for its brilliant rosé), *Mas Chapart, Maurel Fonsalade*, and outstanding co-ops at *Berlou, Roquebrun, Roueire* and *St-Chinian*.

SAUSSIGNAC, AC (South-West; white) These sweet wines are generally less unctuous than their neighbours from Monbazillac. Notable exceptions are the concentrated *Château les Miaudoux* and *Château Richard*'s intense *Coup de Coeur*.

VIN DE CORSE, AC (Corsica; red, white, rosé) Things are slowly improving as Corsican producers begin to make the most of their local grape varieties. *Dom. de Torraccia* makes a tasty red redolent of spices and rosemary. Also good: *Clos Canarelli, Clos Landry, Dom. Culombu, Dom. Comte Peraldi* and *Bernard Renucci*. Good wines are just as likely to bear the all-island designation Vin de Pays de l'Île de Beauté.

VINS DE PAYS (red, white, rosé) This should be where it's all happening. The most innovative winemakers love the vin de pays classification for the freedom it gives them. There's plenty of Cabernet Sauvignon being used here, but some of the most exciting flavours come from Syrah and the other good grapes of the South, like Grenache or Mourvèdre. Australian influence in the winemaking is producing clear flavours and some creamy new oak. In the Pays d'Oc look for *de l'Aigle, du Bosc, Chais Baumière, Cousserges, Domaine de l'Arjolle, Domaine de la Colombette, Domaine la Condamine-l'Evêque, Domaine de la Jonction, Domaine de Limbardie, Domaine Virginie, L'Enclos Domeque, Fortant de France, la Grange des Quatre Sous, Peyrat, Raissac, Richemont, Rives de l'Argent Double* and *Top Forty Barrel-Fermented Chardonnay* (from Waitrose).

In the Gard, seek out *Domaine de Gournier, Domaine de Monpertuis, Listel* and *Mas Montel*; and, in the Roussillon, *Chichet, Laporte* and *Vaquer*. In the Vaucluse, look for *Domaine de l'Ameillaud*.

In the Hérault, look for *Domaine de Limbardie, Domaine de Poujol* and *Mas de Daumas Gassac* – in particular a Viognier-based white. From the Comté Tolosan, *Ribeton* makes good white; from the Comtés Rhodaniens, *les Vignerons Ardéchois* have a tasty Viognier. Look also for *Teisserenc* in the Côtes de Thongue; *Domaine d'Aupilhac* from Mont Baudille, and *Domaine de la Jasse Grande Olivette* from the Cevennes.

On the western side of France the Charente produces some good, grassy-fresh whites with fairly sharp acidity – which sometimes gets the better of the fruit. The region here is Vin de Pays Charentais. The equivalent from Armagnac country is Vin de Pays des Côtes de Gascogne. The Ugni Blanc is the major grape, and the Colombard adds a touch of class. Look for the co-op at *Plaimont*, though quality is variable. The *Grassa* family estates – notably *Domaines de Plantérieu* and *du Tariquet* – are worth seeking out. Also good are *Dom. le Puts, Dom. St-Lannes* and *San Guilhem*.

SOUTHERN FRANCE PRICES

RED

Under £4.00

Corbières Château de Caraguilhes 1999
£3.99 (WAI)

VdP des Coteaux de Murviel, Domaine de
Limbardié 1999 £3.95 (WS) £4.80 (TAN)
£4.95 (HAH) £5.40 (MV)

VdP des Coteaux de Murviel, Domaine de
Limbardié 1998 £3.50 (SOM)

★ VdP des Coteaux de Peyriac, Domaine de
Subremont 2000 £3.49 (WAT)

Côtes de St-Mont Producteurs Plaimont
1999 £3.25 (SOM) £3.99 (JON) £4.20 (HAH)

Côtes de St-Mont Producteurs Plaimont
1997 £3.95 (WS)

★ VdP des Côtes de Thongue Syrah, la
Condamine l'Évêque 1999 £3.95 (WS)
£4.35 (TAN)

VdP de l'Hérault Domaine Ste-Madeleine
1999 £2.99 (WAI)

VdP de l'Hérault Terrasses de Guilhem
2000 £3.95 (SOM)

VdP de l'Hérault les Trois Couronnes
1999 £2.89 (WAI)

Minervois Domaine du Moulin Rigaud
1999 £3.95 (WS)

Minervois Château d'Oupia 1998 £3.95
(SOM)

★ VdP d'Oc Merlot Cuvée Prestige, les
Chevalerets 2000 £3.95 (BY)

£4.00 → £4.99

Bergerac Château Tour des Gendres
2000 £4.99 (GW)

Bergerac Château Tour des Gendres
1995 £4.95 (JU)

Cahors Clos la Coutale 1998 £4.95 (WS)

Corbières Domaine Baillat 1998 £4.95 (WS)

Corbières Château de Montrabech 1999
£4.39 (JON)

Corbières Château de Montrabech 1998
£4.99 (POR)

Corbières Château de Montrabech 1996
£4.25 (BALL)

Corbières Domaine du Trillol, Sichel
1998 £4.95 (WS)

Costières de Nîmes Château de
Campuget 1998 £4.99 (POR)

Coteaux d'Aix-en-Provence Château de
Fonscolombe 1999 £4.95 (POR)

Coteaux d'Aix-en-Provence Château de
Fonscolombe 1998 £4.89 (JON)

VdP des Coteaux de Bessilles Cuvée
Traditionelle, Domaine St-Martin de la
Garrigue 1998 £4.95 (JU)

Coteaux du Languedoc La Clape, Château
Pech-Céleyran 1998 £4.50 (WS) £4.95
(POR) £5.29 (JON)

Coteaux du Languedoc La Clape, Château
Pech-Céleyran 1996 £4.95 (BALL)

Coteaux du Languedoc Pic St Loup, Mas
Bruguière 1999 £4.95 (SOM)

Côtes du Frontonnais Château Baudare
1998 £4.69 (GW)

VdP des Côtes de Gascogne Cabernet
Sauvignon, Brumont 1999 £4.31 (BY)

VdP des Côtes de Gascogne Merlot,
Brumont 1999 £4.31 (BY)

Côtes de la Malepère Château Malvies
1999 £4.75 (STE)

Côtes du Roussillon-Villages les Milleres,
Gardiès 1998 £4.99 (OD) £6.99 (BAL)

VdP des Côtes de Thongue, Clos
Ferdinand 1998 £4.49 (BO)

VdP des Côtes de Thongue Cuvée de
l'Arjolle, Teisserenc 1999 £4.95 (WS)

RETAILERS SPECIALIZING IN SOUTHERN FRANCE
see Retailers Directory (page 40) for details

Most good retailers have some. For
particularly good lists try the following
merchants: Adnams (AD), Averys of Bristol,
Ballantynes of Cowbridge (BAL), Bibendum
(BIB), Anthony Byrne (BY) – always
enterprising, D Byrne, Cockburns of Leith
(COC), Direct Wine (DI), Ben Ellis (ELL),
First Quench Group (BOT, THR, VIC, WR),

Gauntleys (GAU), Lay & Wheeler (LAY),
Majestic (MAJ), Oddbins (OD), The
Nobody Inn (NO), James Nicholson (NI),
Terry Platt (PLA), Raeburn Fine Wines (RAE),
Reid Wines, Sainsbury's (SAI), Savage
Selection (SAV), Somerfield (SO), Tanners
(TAN), The Wine Society (WS), Yapp
Brothers (YAP).

VdP des Côtes de Thongue Cuvée Harmonie, la Condamine l'Évêque **1999** £4.45 (TAN)

VdP des Côtes de Thongue Syrah, la Condamine l'Évêque **1998** £4.49 (JON) £4.50 (LEA)

Fitou Caves du Mont Tauch **1997** £4.49 (UN)

Gaillac Domaine de Labarthe **1999** £4.25 (SOM)

VdP de l'Hérault Cabernet Sauvignon, Domaine de Capion **1997** £4.35 (SOM)

VdP de l'Hérault Cabernet/Syrah, Domaine Montrose **1999** £4.95 (JU)

VdP de l'Hérault Domaine de Chapître **1999** £4.40 (MV)

VdP de l'Hérault Terrasses de Guilhem **1999** £4.22 (FLE)

Marcillac Domaine du Cros, Teulier **1998** £4.95 (WS)

Minervois Domaine de Ste-Eulalie **1999** £4.95 (HAH) £5.20 (TAN)

Minervois Domaine la Tour Boisée **1999** £4.39 (WAT)

VdP d'Oc Cabernet Sauvignon, Bellefontaine **1998** £4.29 (CON)

VdP d'Oc Cabernet Sauvignon, la Serre **2000** £4.41 (BIB)

VdP d'Oc Merlot, la Serre **2000** £4.41 (BIB)

VdP d'Oc Merlot, Domaine de Terre Megère **1999** £4.95 (LEA)

VdP d'Oc Merlot, Domaine Virginie **2000** £4.49 (MAR)

VdP d'Oc Syrah, Domaine de la Jonction **1999** £4.47 (CB)

VdP d'Oc Syrah, la Serre **2000** £4.41 (BIB)

VdP du Var les Trois Chenes, Domaine de l'Hermitage **1998** £4.39 (CON)

VdP de Vaucluse, Domaine de l'Ameillaud **1999** £4.60 (HAH)

VdP du Vaucluse Domaine Michel **1999** £4.95 (AD)

VdP du Vaucluse Domaine du Vieux Chêne **1999** £4.50 (JU)

- *Wines are listed in A–Z order within each price band.*
- *For each wine, vintages are listed in descending order.*
- *Each vintage of any wine appears only once.*

£5.00 → £5.99

Bergerac Château Tour des Gendres **1999** £5.99 (GN)

Cabardès Château de Pennautier **1997** £5.50 (RIC)

Cahors Clos la Coutale **1999** £5.97 (SAV)

Cahors Château St-Didier-Parnac, Rigal **1999** £5.49 (OD)

★ VdP Catalan Carignan, Domaine Ferrer Ribere **1999** £5.55 (YAP)

Corbières Château la Baronne **1998** £5.67 (JON) £7.93 (TW)

Corbières Château Cascadais **1995** £5.75 (BAL)

Corbières Cuvée Ullysses, Château Helene **1995** £5.70 (WAT)

Corbières Grande Réserve, Domaine Madelon **1997** £5.40 (HIC)

Costières de Nîmes Château de Belle-Coste **1999** £5.48 (HIG)

Costières de Nîmes Château de Nages **1998** £5.99 (POR)

Coteaux du Languedoc La Clape, Château Pech-Céleyran **1999** £5.20 (TAN)

★ Coteaux du Languedoc Les Garrigues, Domaine Clavel **1999** £5.95 (TAN)

Coteaux du Languedoc Pic St Loup, Château de Lascaux **1999** £5.49 (OD) £6.85 (NI)

Coteaux du Languedoc Pic St Loup, Château de Lascaux **1998** £5.95 (LEA) £6.76 (DOM)

Côtes du Marmandais Château de Beaulieu **1996** £5.95 (WS)

Côtes du Roussillon Domaine Sarda-Malet **1999** £5.50 (FORT)

VdP des Côtes de Thongue Champs de Coq, Domaine Boyer **1998** £5.95 (JU)

VdP des Côtes de Thongue Cuvée de l'Arjolle, Teisserenc **1998** £5.95 (JU)

Fitou Domaine d'Estradelle **1996** £5.29 (CON)

Fitou Château de Ségure **1996** £5.49 (UN)

VdP de l'Hérault Domaine du Poujol **1999** £5.40 (TAN)

Madiran Château Pichard **1996** £5.95 (WS)

Minervois Cuvée Opera, Château Villerambert-Julien **1999** £5.60 (TAN)

Minervois Domaine de Ste-Eulalie **1998** £5.19 (JON)

Minervois Domaine de Ste-Eulalie **1997** £5.25 (BALL)

VdP d'Oc Cabernet Sauvignon, Domaine de Terre Megère **1997** £5.45 (LEA)
VdP de Vaucluse Château des Tours **1997** £5.99 (RAE)
VdP de Vaucluse Domaine des Tours, Reynaud **1998** £5.95 (LEA)

£6.00 → £7.99

les Baux-de-Provence Mas de Gourgonnier **1998** £6.85 (FLE) £6.95 (AD)
Bergerac Cuvée Prestige, Château des Eyssards **1998** £6.99 (VA)
Cahors Château du Cèdre **1998** £6.95 (LEA) £6.99 (GW) £6.99 (BAL)
Cahors Clos la Coutale **1997** £6.67 (ARM)
Cahors Cuvée Classique, Domaine Eugenie **1996** £6.21 (HIC)
Cahors Domaine de Paillas **1994** £7.99 (RAE)
Cahors Domaine de la Pineraie **1998** £6.30 (SOM)
Costières de Nîmes Cuvée St Marc, Château de Belle-Coste **1999** £6.75 (HIG)
VdP des Coteaux de Bessilles Cuvée Bronzinelle, Domaine St-Martin de la Garrigue **1998** £6.95 (JU)
Coteaux du Languedoc Cuvée Prestige, Domaine de la Coste **1996** £6.46 (SAV)
Coteaux du Languedoc Montpeyroux, Domaine d'Aupilhac **1997** £7.95 (WS)
Coteaux du Languedoc Pic St Loup Terres Rouge, Château de Cazeneuve **1999** £6.29 (BAL)
Coteaux du Languedoc Pic St Loup Terres Rouge, Château de Cazeneuve **1998** £6.49 (UN)
Coteaux du Languedoc Pic St Loup Cuvée Classique, Domaine de l'Hortus **1997** £6.50 (BALL)
Coteaux du Languedoc Pic St Loup Cuvée Classique, Domaine de l'Hortus **1996** £6.99 (RAE)
Côtes de Bergerac Château la Borderie **1995** £7.58 (TW)
Côtes du Frontonnais Cuvée Reservée, Château le Roc **1998** £7.50 (LEA)
Côtes du Frontonnais Cuvée Reservée, Château le Roc **1997** £6.95 (LEA)
Côtes du Roussillon Domaine Cazes **1997** £6.95 (CON)
Côtes du Roussillon Élevé en Fûts, Domaine Gauby **1995** £7.50 (RAE)
Côtes du Roussillon Domaine Piquemal **1998** £6.29 (BAL)

Faugères Gilbert Alquier **1998** £7.79 (BO)
Faugères Gilbert Alquier **1997** £6.95 (WS) £6.95 (BALL) £7.95 (TAN) £8.39 (JON)
Faugères Gilbert Alquier **1994** £7.90 (GAU)
Faugères Reserve la Maison Jaune, Gilbert Alquier **1995** £7.99 (RAE) £8.95 (WS)
VdP de la Haute Vallée de l'Orb Cuvée Special, Domaine de la Croix Ronde **1997** £6.52 (CB)
Madiran Château d'Aydie **1997** £7.95 (WS)
Madiran Château d'Aydie **1996** £7.90 (CRO)
Madiran Château Bouscassé, Brumont **1994** £6.20 (SOM) £8.06 (BY)
Madiran Cuvée du Couvent, Domaine Capmartin **1998** £7.99 (GW)
Madiran Vieilles Vignes, Domaine Capmartin **1998** £6.99 (GW)
★ Minervois Château de Beaufort, **1998** £7.59 (GN)
VdP d'Oc La Cuvée Mythique, les Vignerons du Val d'Orbieu **1999** £6.49 (WAI)
VdP d'Oc La Cuvée Mythique, les Vignerons du Val d'Orbieu **1998** £6.49 (SAF)
VdP d'Oc Cuvée Pierre Elie, Les Chemins de Bassac **1994** £6.99 (BAL)
Pécharmant Château de Tiregand **1998** £6.95 (TAN)
VdP des Sables du Golfe du Lion Domaine du Bosquet **1998** £6.95 (NEZ)
VdP de Vaucluse Château des Tours **1999** £6.05 (BIB)

£8.00 → £9.99

Bandol Domaine de l'Hermitage **1996** £8.95 (CON)
les Baux-de-Provence Réserve, Mas de Gourgonnier **1997** £9.95 (FORT)
Bergerac Cuvée la Gloire de Mon Père, Château Tour des Gendres **1995** £8.95 (LEA)
Cahors Château du Cayrou **1988** £8.75 (WAT)
Cahors Château de Chambert **1996** £8.99 (DI)
Cahors Clos de Gamot **1992** £8.25 (WAT)
VdP des Cévennes Domaine de Baruel **1997** £8.30 (RAE)

A key to name abbreviations is available on page 7.

VdP des Cévennes Domaine de Baruel
1996 £8.99 (RAE)
VdP des Cévennes Cuvée Fontanilles,
Domaine de Baruel **1996** £9.95 (RAE)
Corbières Cuvée Helene de Troie,
Château Helene **1997** £8.45 (WAT)
Coteaux d'Aix-en-Provence Château
Vignelaure **1998** £9.95 (NI)
Coteaux du Languedoc Pic St Loup les
Nobles Pierres, Château de Lascaux
1998 £8.95 (LEA)
Coteaux du Languedoc Pic St Loup les
Nobles Pierres, Château de Lascaux
1997 £9.95 (NI)
Coteaux du Languedoc Terroir de la
Méjanelle la Copa Santa, Domaine
Clavel **1998** £8.99 (YOU) £9.30 (TAN)
£10.83 (ARM)
Coteaux du Languedoc Terroir de la
Méjanelle la Copa Santa, Domaine
Clavel **1997** £9.50 (MAY)
Côtes du Roussillon-Villages Tautavel,
Gardiès **1998** £8.99 (BAL)
Côtes de St-Mont Château de Sabazan
1997 £9.99 (POR)
VdP des Côtes de Thongue Cabernet de
l'Arjolle, Domaine Teisserenc **1998**
£8.90 (JU)
Faugères Cuvée Prestige, Château des
Estanilles **1998** £8.75 (BAC) £9.81 (HIC)
Faugères le Moulin Couderc, V Fonteneau
1997 £9.50 (BEN)
Faugères le Moulin Couderc, V Fonteneau
1995 £9.29 (BAL)
Faugères Reserve la Maison Jaune, Gilbert
Alquier **1996** £8.95 (BAC)
Fitou Terroir de Tuchan, Caves du Mont
Tauch **1998** £8.99 (WR)
Madiran Château Bouscassé, Brumont
1997 £8.47 (BY)
Madiran Château Bouscassé, Brumont
1995 £8.50 (HIG) £9.49 (BY)
Madiran Château Montus, Brumont **1994**
£9.25 (SOM) £11.54 (BY)
Minervois Château Villerambert-Julien
1999 £8.60 (TAN)
VdP d'Oc Syrah, Clovallon **1995** £9.29 (BAL)

£10.00 → £14.99

Bandol Cuvée Classique, Domaine
Tempier **1998** £12.00 (WS) £13.75 (LEA)
Bandol Cuvée Migoua, Domaine Tempier
1998 £14.69 (SAV)
Bandol Cuvée Migoua, Domaine Tempier
1995 £14.50 (GAU)

Bandol Cuvée Spéciale, Domaine Tempier
1998 £13.71 (SAV) £15.75 (LEA)
Bandol Cuvée Spéciale, Domaine Tempier
1997 £13.95 (LEA)
Bandol Cuvée Tourtine, Domaine
Tempier **1998** £14.69 (SAV)
Bandol Mas de la Rouvière, Bunan **1998**
£10.75 (YAP)
Bandol Château de Pibarnon **1997** £14.50
(GAU) £14.75 (NI) £15.95 (BAL) £17.07
(BY)
Bandol Château de la Rouvière, Bunan
1999 £14.75 (YAP)
Bandol Domaine Tempier **1998** £11.75
(SAV) £14.10 (GAU)
Bandol Domaine Tempier **1996** £12.99
(DI)
Bellet Château de Crémat, Jean Bagnis
1986 £13.50 (CRO)
Cahors Château du Cayrou **1983** £14.00
(CRO)
Collioure la Coume Pascole, Domaine de
la Rectorie **1997** £11.95 (BAL)
Collioure la Coume Pascole, Domaine de
la Rectorie **1996** £11.99 (RAE)
Coteaux d'Aix-en-Provence Domaine les
Bastides **1995** £10.58 (SAV)
Coteaux du Languedoc Pic St Loup,
Château la Roque **1998** £10.99 (NI)
Coteaux du Languedoc Prieuré de St-Jean
de Bébian **1997** £13.50 (RAE) £14.10
(GAU) £16.67 (MI)
Coteaux du Languedoc Prieuré de St-Jean
de Bébian **1996** £11.99 (RAE) £12.00
(WS) £14.10 (GAU)
Coteaux du Languedoc Prieuré de St-Jean
de Bébian **1995** £13.65 (RAE)
Coteaux du Languedoc Prieuré de St-Jean
de Bébian **1994** £12.95 (BAL) £14.90
(GAU) £19.17 (MI)
VdP des Côtes Catalanes
Cabernet/Merlot Le Credo, Domaine
Cazes **1996** £12.49 (CON)
Côtes de Provence Tradition Domaine
Richeaume, Hoesch **1999** £12.25 (YAP)
★ Côtes de Provence Château Vannières
1998 £10.95 (GAU)
Côtes du Roussillon-Villages la Torre,
Gardiès **1998** £10.95 (BAL)
Madiran Château Montus, Brumont **1997**
£11.54 (BY)
Madiran Château Montus, Brumont **1996**
£11.54 (BY)
Madiran Château Montus, Brumont **1995**
£11.00 (HIG) £12.56 (BY)

Madiran Château de Peyros **1982** £12.50 (CRO)

Minervois Clos de l'Escandil, Aires Hautes **1997** £10.90 (GAU)

Pécharmant Château de Tiregand **1985** £11.50 (CRO)

£15.00 → £19.99

Bandol Cuvée Migoua, Domaine Tempier **1997** £15.95 (LEA)

Bandol Cuvée Tourtine, Domaine Tempier **1997** £15.00 (WS)

Bandol Château de Pibarnon **1998** £15.95 (BAL) £16.45 (BY) £18.41 (FLE)

Bandol Château de Pibarnon **1996** £17.68 (BY) £18.41 (FLE)

Bandol Château Vannières **1997** £15.00 (MI)

Bandol Château Vannières **1988** £15.90 (GAU)

VdP des Bouches-du-Rhône Domaine de Trévallon **1997** £17.04 (FA) £23.75 (YAP)

VdP des Bouches-du-Rhône Domaine de Trévallon **1996** £19.00 (FA) £27.75 (YAP)

VdP des Bouches-du-Rhône Domaine de Trévallon **1995** £19.99 (DI) £26.00 (CRO)

Cahors Prince Probus, Clos Triguedina **1995** £15.18 (NO)

Coteaux du Languedoc Aurel, Domaine des Aurelles **1998** £16.50 (BAL)

Coteaux du Languedoc Prieuré de St-Jean de Bébian **1998** £17.50 (MI)

Côtes de Provence Columelle Domaine Richeaume, Hoesch **1998** £16.95 (YAP)

VdP de l'Hérault Mas de Daumas Gassac **1999** £16.80 (CRO)

VdP de l'Hérault Mas de Daumas Gassac **1998** £17.80 (CRO) £19.25 (NI)

VdP de l'Hérault Mas de Daumas Gassac **1997** £15.20 (FLE)

VdP de l'Hérault Mas de Daumas Gassac **1996** £16.95 (AD)

VdP de l'Hérault Mas de Daumas Gassac **1995** £18.00 (JU)

Madiran Cuvée Prestige Château Montus, Brumont **1998** £18.50 (HIG) £20.23 (BY)

Madiran Vieilles Vignes Château Bouscassé, Brumont **1998** £15.73 (BY)

Madiran Vieilles Vignes Château Bouscassé, Brumont **1997** £16.25 (BY)

Madiran Vieilles Vignes Château Bouscassé, Brumont **1992** £15.84 (BY)

Palette Château Simone **1998** £18.75 (YAP)

£20.00 → £29.99

VdP des Bouches-du-Rhône Domaine de Trévallon **1998** £27.25 (YAP)

VdP de l'Hérault Mas de Daumas Gassac **1983** £20.00 (CRO)

Madiran Cuvée Prestige Château Montus, Brumont **1995** £28.30 (FA) £41.30 (NO)

Palette Château Simone **1996** £25.00 (FORT)

Over £30.00

les Baux-de-Provence Domaine de Trévallon **1994** £32.00 (FORT)

les Baux-de-Provence Domaine de Trévallon **1990** £44.00 (CRO)

les Baux-de-Provence Domaine de Trévallon **1988** £42.00 (CRO) £50.00 (VIL)

les Baux-de-Provence Domaine de Trévallon **1985** £50.00 (CRO)

VdP des Bouches-du-Rhône Domaine de Trévallon **1989** £36.62 (FA)

VdP de l'Hérault Mas de Daumas Gassac **1990** £33.00 (CRO)

VdP de l'Hérault Mas de Daumas Gassac **1985** £35.00 (CRO)

Madiran Vieilles Vignes Château Bouscassé, Brumont **1995** £41.57 (NO)

DRY WHITE

Under £4.00

Bergerac Marquis de Beausoleil **2000** £2.99 (WAI)

VdP des Côtes de Gascogne Colombard, Plaimont **2000** £3.75 (TAN) £3.95 (AD)

VdP des Côtes de Gascogne Producteurs Plaimont **1999** £3.89 (JON)

VdP des Côtes de Gascogne Domaine de Planterieu **2000** £3.99 (WAI)

Côtes de St-Mont, les Hauts de Bergelle **1999** £3.70 (SOM)

Côtes de St-Mont, Producteurs Plaimont **1999** £3.99 (JON) £4.20 (HAH)

VdP de l'Hérault Grenache, Bésinet **1999** £3.75 (WS)

- All prices for each wine are listed together in ascending order.
- Price bands refer to the lowest price for which the wine is available.

VdP d'Oc Chardonnay, la Serre ½ bottle **2000** £2.71 (BIB)

VdP d'Oc Sauvignon Blanc, Domaine Virginie **2000** £3.99 (MAR)

VdP d'Oc Sauvignon Blanc, Domaine des Fontanelles **2000** £3.99 (MAJ)

★ VdP d'Oc Viognier Cuvée Prestige, les Chevalerets **2000** £3.95 (BY)

£4.00 → £4.99

Coteaux d'Aix-en-Provence Château de Fonscolombe **1999** £4.89 (JON) £4.95 (POR)

VdP des Coteaux des Baronnies Chardonnay, Bellefontaine **1998** £4.89 (CON)

Coteaux du Languedoc Picpoul de Pinet, Domaine St Peyre **2000** £4.95 (RES)

VdP des Côtes de Gascogne Chardonnay, Brumont **1999** £4.27 (BY)

VdP des Côtes de Gascogne Gros Manseng, Brumont **2000** £4.27 (BY)

VdP des Côtes de Gascogne Gros Manseng/Sauvignon, Brumont **1999** £4.27 (BY)

VdP des Côtes de Gascogne Domaine de Maubet **1999** £4.29 (CON)

VdP des Côtes de Gascogne Domaine de Rieux **2000** £4.35 (TAN)

VdP des Côtes de Gascogne Domaine de Rieux **1999** £4.25 (HAH) £4.25 (BALL) £4.39 (JON) £4.49 (POR)

VdP des Côtes de Gascogne Domaine San de Guilhem **2000** £4.99 (MV)

VdP des Côtes de Gascogne Sauvignon Blanc, Brumont **1998** £4.31 (BY)

VdP des Côtes de Gascogne Domaine de Tariquet **2000** £4.49 (VIC) £4.49 (THR) £4.49 (BOT) £4.49 (WR)

VdP des Côtes de Thau Sauvignon Blanc, Hugues de Beauvignac **2000** £4.95 (RES)

VdP des Côtes de Thongue Sauvignon de l'Arjolle, Teisserenc **1999** £4.95 (WS)

VdP de l'Hérault Chardonnay, Domaine Montrose **2000** £4.75 (JU)

VdP de l'Hérault Muscat Sec, Bésinet **1999** £4.50 (WS)

VdP d'Oc Chardonnay, James Herrick **2000** £4.99 (TES) £4.99 (SAF)

VdP d'Oc Chardonnay, James Herrick **1999** £4.99 (SAI) £4.99 (UN) £4.99 (BUD) £4.99 (BO) £4.99 (VIC) £4.99 (THR) £4.99 (BOT) £4.99 (WR) £4.99 (WAI)

VdP d'Oc Chardonnay, la Serre **2000** £4.79 (BIB)

VdP d'Oc Chardonnay, Domaine Virginie **2000** £4.49 (MAR)

VdP d'Oc Marsanne, Domaine Virginie **1999** £4.90 (TAN)

VdP d'Oc Roussane, Domaine du Bosc **1999** £4.99 (BAL)

VdP d'Oc Sauvignon Blanc, Domaine de Coussergues **2000** £4.56 (LLO)

VdP d'Oc Sauvignon Blanc Domaine des Salices, Lurton **1999** £4.75 (BALL) £5.65 (NI)

VdP d'Oc Sauvignon Blanc, la Serre **2000** £4.65 (BIB)

VdP du Vaucluse Domaine du Vieux Chêne **2000** £4.95 (JU)

£5.00 → £6.99

Bergerac Château de la Colline, Martin **1999** £5.88 (HIG)

Bergerac Cuvée des Conti, Château Tours des Gendres **1999** £5.99 (GW)

Bergerac Cuvée des Conti, Château Tours des Gendres **1998** £6.50 (LEA)

Bergerac Château Tours des Gendres **1999** £6.45 (JU)

Bergerac Château Tours des Gendres **1998** £5.99 (GN)

Coteaux du Languedoc Pic St Loup Cuvée Classique, Château de Lascaux **2000** £6.99 (BEN)

VdP des Côtes de Thongue Viognier, la Condamine l'Évêque **2000** £6.20 (TAN) £6.95 (LEA)

VdP des Côtes de Thongue Viognier, la Condamine l'Évêque **1999** £6.39 (JON)

VdP de l'Hérault Viognier, Domaine du Bosc **1999** £5.95 (WS) £5.99 (BAL)

Jurançon Sec, Domaine Castera **1999** £6.99 (GW)

Jurançon Sec, Clos Guirouilh **1999** £6.99 (VIL)

VdP d'Oc Chardonnay, Domaine de Gourgazaud **1999** £5.25 (WS)

VdP d'Oc Chardonnay, Domaine Virginie **1998** £5.50 (BALL)

VdP d'Oc Roussanne, Domaine Virginie **1999** £5.70 (LAY)

VdP d'Oc Roussanne, Domaine Virginie **1997** £5.30 (MV)

VdP d'Oc Sauvignon Blanc Domaine des Salices, Lurton **2000** £5.65 (NI)

VdP d'Oc Viognier, Domaine St-Hilaire **1999** £6.99 (GW)

VdP du Vaucluse Roussanne, Domaine du Vieux Chêne **1999** £5.45 (JU)

£7.00 → £9.99

Bandol Domaine de l'Hermitage **1998**
£8.95 (CON)

Bandol Mas de la Rouvière, Bunan **1998**
£9.45 (YAP)

Costières de Nîmes Cuvée Joseph
Torres, Château de Nages **1998** £7.49
(OD)

VdP des Côtes de Thongue Equinoxe,
Domaine de l'Arjolle **1999** £7.85
(JU)

VdP des Côtes de Thongue Equinoxe,
Domaine de l'Arjolle **1997** £8.49
(UN)

Jurançon Sec, Domaine Cauhapé **2000**
£9.40 (MV)

Jurançon Sec, Domaine Cauhapé **1997**
£8.99 (POR)

Jurançon Sec Chant des Vignes, Domaine
Cauhapé **2000** £7.95 (STE)

Jurançon Sec Chant des Vignes, Domaine
Cauhapé **1998** £7.95 (STE)

VdP d'Oc Chardonnay, Clovallon **1999**
£9.95 (BEN)

£10.00 → £19.99

Bandol Château de Pibarnon **1999** £12.40
(GAU) £12.97 (BY)

Bandol Château de Pibarnon **1997** £11.95
(BY)

Bandol Château de la Rouvière, Bunan
1996 £10.95 (YAP)

les Baux-de-Provence Coin Caché, Mas
de la Dame **1998** £16.40 (LAY)

Cassis Clos Ste-Magdeleine, Sack **1999**
£10.75 (YAP)

Coteaux du Languedoc Domaine
d'Aupilhac **1999** £10.95 (LEA)

VdP de l'Hérault, Mas de Daumas Gassac
1999 £15.95 (AD)

VdP de l'Hérault, Mas de Daumas Gassac
1996 £19.95 (NI)

VdP d'Oc Viognier, Clovallon **1999**
£11.99 (BEN)

Palette Château Simone **1999** £18.95 (YAP)

Over £20.00

VdP des Bouches-du-Rhône Domaine de
Trévallon **1999** £33.00 (YAP)

VdP des Bouches-du-Rhône Domaine de
Trévallon **1997** £40.00 (FORT)

Côtes de Provence Clos Mireille Blanc de
Blancs, Domaines Ott **1998** £20.00
(FORT)

SWEET WHITE

Under £8.00

Jurançon Domaine Castera ½ bottle **1997**
£7.81 (BIB)

Jurançon Vendange Tardive, Domaine
Cauhapé ½ bottle **1991** £6.95 (STE)

Jurançon Vendange Tardive du 2
Novembre, Domaine Cauhape ½ bottle
1996 £7.50 (POR)

★ Monbazillac Château les Charmes de Saint-
Mayme **1995** £7.99 (MAR)

Monbazillac Château Septy **1997** £7.58 (CB)

Monbazillac Château Septy **1996** £7.49
(JON)

£8.00 → £10.99

Jurançon Domaine Bellegarde, Labasse
1999 £9.95 (YAP)

Jurançon Domaine Cauhapé **2000** £9.70
(NI)

Jurançon Clos Guirouilh **1996** £8.99 (VIL)

Jurançon Vendange Tardive du 2
Novembre, Domaine Cauhape ½ bottle
1995 £9.50 (BEN)

Monbazillac Château Theulet **1997** £8.50
(WS) £8.95 (STE)

Monbazillac Château Theulet **1995**
£10.95 (GN)

★ Pacherenc du Vic-Bilh Brumaire, Brumont
50cl bottle **1997** £10.52 (BY)

£11.00 → £29.99

Monbazillac Château Tirecul la Gravière
1994 £27.00 (CRO)

Monbazillac Château Tirecul la Gravière
50cl bottle **1998** £18.95 (LEA)

Monbazillac Château Tirecul la Gravière
50cl bottle **1997** £19.95 (LEA)

Monbazillac Château Tirecul la Gravière
50cl bottle **1996** £19.95 (LEA) £23.50
(WY)

Monbazillac Château Tirecul la Gravière
50cl bottle **1994** £14.50 (JU) £18.50
(CRO)

Pacherenc du Vic-Bilh Vendange
Décembre Château Bouscassé,
Brumont ½ bottle **1989** £23.90 (NO)

---

*Stars (★) indicate wines selected by
Oz Clarke in the Best Buys section which
begins on page 8.*

Over £30.00

Monbazillac Château Tirecul la Gravière
Cuvée Madame 50cl bottle **1997**
£65.00 (LEA)
Monbazillac Château Tirecul la Gravière
Cuvée Madame 50cl bottle **1996**
£68.15 (WY)
Monbazillac Château Tirecul la Gravière
Cuvée Madame 50cl bottle **1992**
£40.00 (JU)

ROSÉ

Under £5.00

Coteaux d'Aix-en-Provence Cuvée
Spéciale, Château de Fonscolombe
1999 £4.75 (BALL)
Coteaux d'Aix-en-Provence Château de
Fonscolombe **1999** £4.95 (POR)
Coteaux d'Aix-en-Provence Château de
Fonscolombe **1998** £4.89 (JON)
VdP des Coteaux de Murviel, Domaine de
Limbardié **1999** £3.50 (SOM)
Côtes du Frontonnais Château le Roc
2000 £4.95 (LEA)
Côtes de St-Mont, Producteurs Plaimont
1999 £3.15 (SOM)
VdP de l'Hérault, Domaine Montrose
2000 £4.50 (JU)
VdP du Var les Trois Chenes, Domaine de
l'Hermitage **1998** £4.39 (CON)
VdP du Vaucluse Domaine du Vieux
Chêne **1999** £4.95 (JU)

£5.00 → £9.99

Bandol Domaine de l'Hermitage **1998**
£8.49 (CON)
Bandol Mas de la Rouvière **1999** £9.35
(YAP)
Bergerac Château Pique-Segue **1995**
£6.65 (HIC)
Côteaux du Languedoc Pic St Loup,
Château de Lascaux **2000** £5.99 (BEN)
VdP des Coteaux de Murviel, Domaine de
Limbardié **2000** £5.70 (MV)

Please remember that
Oz Clarke's Wine Buying Guide
*is a price guide and not a price list. It is
not meant to replace up-to-date
merchants' lists.*

Côtes de Provence Carte Noire,
Vignerons de St-Tropez **1999** £5.99
(NEZ)
Côtes de Provence Château la Moutete
1998 £5.59 (CON)
VdP des Côtes de Thongue Meridiene,
Domaine de l'Arjolle **1998** £8.50 (JU)

Over £10.00

Côtes de Provence Château de Selle,
Domaines Ott **1999** £25.40 (JER)
Côtes de Provence Château de Selle,
Domaines Ott **1998** £18.75 (FORT)
Palette Château Simone **1999** £17.60 (YAP)

SPARKLING

Under £9.00

Blanquette de Limoux Domaine des
Martinolles **1996** £8.99 (VIL)
Crémant de Limoux Cuvée St-Laurent,
Antech **1998** £6.95 (WS)
Crémant de Limoux Domaine des
Martinolles **1997** £7.95 (STE)

VINS DOUX NATURELS

Under £7.00

Muscat de Mireval Domaine du Moulinas
½ bottle **Non-vintage** £6.36 (NO)
Muscat de St-Jean-de-Minervois Les
Vignerons de Septimanie **Non-vintage**
£6.90 (LLO)

£7.00 → £9.99

Maury Vintage Mas Amiel ½ bottle **1997**
£7.95 (LEA)
Muscat de Frontignan Château de la
Peyrade **Non-vintage** £7.90 (CRO)
Muscat de Rivesaltes Domaine Cazes
1998 £9.65 (CON)
Muscat de Rivesaltes Domaine Cazes ½
bottle **1999** £7.25 (FORT)
Muscat de Rivesaltes Domaine Piquemal
1997 £8.95 (LEA)

Over £10.00

★ Banyuls Grand Cru Cuvée Réservée,
l'Etoile **1986** £16.17 (BY)
Muscat de Rivesaltes Sarda-Malet **1998**
£10.95 (FORT)
Banyuls Vieilles Vignes, Domaine du Mas
Blanc **1978** £40.00 (CRO)

GERMANY

What I can't understand is why German wines are still so cheap, when they're so extraordinarily good. Is it because you're still not drinking them? After all I've said?

Are you a wine buff? I'd say the answer is probably yes, since you're taking the trouble to read this page. If you are, you'll be pleased to learn that you and people like you make up just ten per cent of wine drinkers. But you get through 44% of the wine drunk in Britain. Congratulations: that's quite an achievement.

I know these figures because the Germans told them to me. And the Germans know them because you – yes, you – are their target market.

Actually, what surprises me most is that you're not drinking German wines already. We're not talking Liebfraumilch here, for goodness sake. We're talking about dry or off-dry Rieslings with balance and poise and acidity taut as piano wire; with smoky, peachy, ripe fruit that matures with age into petrolly maturity. Just your sort of wines, in other words. Particularly since they're still hugely undervalued. If I were you I'd take advantage of a run of good vintages and fill my cellar. Remember: Germany needs you.

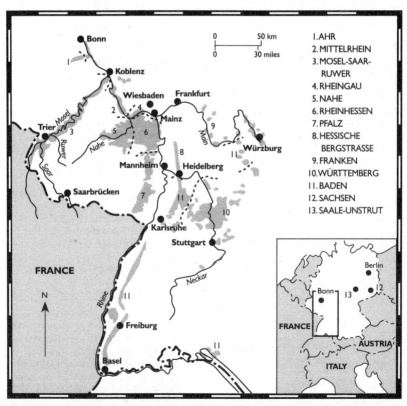

0 ——— 50 km
0 ——— 30 miles

1. AHR
2. MITTELRHEIN
3. MOSEL-SAAR-RUWER
4. RHEINGAU
5. NAHE
6. RHEINHESSEN
7. PFALZ
8. HESSISCHE BERGSTRASSE
9. FRANKEN
10. WÜRTTEMBERG
11. BADEN
12. SACHSEN
13. SAALE-UNSTRUT

QUALITY CONTROL

You'll see one of these terms on every German wine label: they are simply a way of classifying wine according to the ripeness of the grapes when they are picked.

DEUTSCHER TAFELWEIN Basic German table wine of supposedly tolerable quality; low natural alcohol, sugared at fermentation to increase it, no specific vineyard origin stated. Usually little more than sugar-water. However, at the other end of the price spectrum are expensive 'designer table wines' from adventurous producers who may age them in oak.

LANDWEIN Rarely seen German version of vin de pays; table wine from one of 20 designated areas. It can be Trocken (dry) or Halbtrocken (half-dry).

QbA (Qualitätswein bestimmter Anbaugebiete) Literally 'quality wine from designated regions' – Ahr, Hessische Bergstrasse, Mittelrhein, Nahe, Rheingau, Rheinhessen, Pfalz, Franken, Württemberg, Baden, Mosel-Saar-Ruwer, Saale-Unstrut and Sachsen. Quality varies from poor to very good, depending on the producer. Anything labelled Liebfraumilch, Niersteiner Gutes Domtal or Piesporter Michelsberg is unlikely to be worth a second glance. Go for top estates only, but 1997 yielded some splendidly concentrated QbAs.

QmP (Qualitätswein mit Prädikat) Literally, quality wine with special attributes. There are six categories, in order of increasing ripeness of the grapes: Kabinett, Spätlese, Auslese, Beerenauslese, Trockenbeeren-auslese and Eiswein. Drier wines (usually Kabinett or Spätlese) may be either Trocken (dry) or Halbtrocken (half-dry). Not all styles are made every year.

KABINETT Made from ripe grapes. Usually lighter in alcohol than ordinary QbA, and often delicious.

SPÄTLESE From late-picked (therefore riper) grapes. Often moderately sweet, though there are now dry (Trocken) versions.

AUSLESE From selected bunches of very ripe grapes. Usually sweet and sometimes touched by 'noble rot', a fungus that concentrates the sugar and acidity in the grapes. In many southern regions, such as Baden, they are fermented dry, making rich and powerful wines.

BEERENAUSLESE (BA) Wines made from selected single grapes almost always affected by the noble rot fungus. Beerenauslese from new, non-Riesling grapes can be dull. But Riesling Beerenauslese, and many a Scheurebe or Silvaner, will be astonishing.

EISWEIN Just that – 'ice wine' – often picked before a winter dawn when the grapes are frozen. They are dashed to the winery by the frost-bitten pickers; once there, quick and careful pressing removes just the slimy-sweet concentrate; the water, in its icy state, stays separate. Eiswein always has a high acidity that needs to be tamed by bottle age, though you do lose the lovely frosty, green apple flavours of youth.

TROCKENBEERENAUSLESE (TBA) 'Shrivelled selected berries' – that's a pedestrian translation of one of the world's great tastes. Individually picked grapes, shrivelled by noble rot, produce small amounts of intensely sweet juice, making TBAs among the sweetest wines in the world. The risks and the costs are both enormous. The vines are making a glass of wine each instead of a bottle, and the weather can easily ruin it all anyway. That's why TBAs are expensive – usually starting at £20 a half bottle ex-cellars. But, even then, a grower won't make money; it's his pride that makes him do it. And the wines can age for as long as you or I.

GRAPE VARIETIES

DORNFELDER (red) At its best this produces deep-coloured reds with great fruit concentration and firm structure. Made in two styles: reminiscent of Beaujolais and for early drinking or aged in barriques for longer keeping. Best: *Knipser, Lergenmüller, Lingenfelder Onyx, Messmer, Siegrist, Heinrich Vollmer* (Pfalz).

MÜLLER-THURGAU (white) The most widely planted German grape, propagated in 1883 to get Riesling style plus big yields. Well, you can't do it. It produces soft, pot-pourri-scented wines of no distinction, but it produces plenty of them. Occasionally it's made dry and aged in oak; this style is particularly successful in Baden when yields are severely reduced. For the oaked style try *Gunderloch, Karl H Johner, Dr Loosen*. *Juliusspital* in Franken makes a deceptively fragile unoaked version.

RIESLANER (white) A sensational crossing of Riesling and Silvaner, but not widely planted. Ripe, it tastes of apricots; unripe it tastes, less appealingly, of grass and gooseberries. Best as dessert wine from the Pfalz (especially *Müller-Catoir*) and Franken. Best producers: *Juliusspital, Rudolf Fürst, Robert Schmitt, Schmitt's Kinder* (Franken).

RIESLING (white) Most of Germany's best wines (except in Baden-Württemberg, where the soils are usually unsuitable) are made from this grape. When yields are controlled it produces wonderful flavours: from steely, slaty and dry as sun-bleached bones, through apples, peaches, apricots – more or less sweet according to the ripeness of the grapes and the intentions of the winemaker – and finally arriving at the great sweet wines. These can be blinding in their rich, honeyed concentration of peaches, pineapples, mangoes and even raisins, with acidity like a streak of fresh lime that makes them the most appetizing of sweet wines.

RULÄNDER (white) The French Pinot Gris. It can be strong, sweetish, broad-shouldered, with a whiff of spice and a splash of honey. When made dry it is often aged in small oak barriques and can make exciting drinking. Best: *Schlossgut Diel* (Nahe); *Koehler-Ruprecht, Müller-Catoir, Münzberg* (Pfalz); *Bercher, Dr Heger, Karl H Johner, Salwey, Stigler* (Baden); *Johann Ruck* (Franken).

SCHEUREBE (white) A tricky grape. When it's unripe, it can pucker your mouth with its rawness. But properly ripe, there's honey, and a crackling, peppery fire and pink grapefruit core which, in the Pfalz, Baden and Franken, produces dry wines as well as sweeter, sometimes outstanding

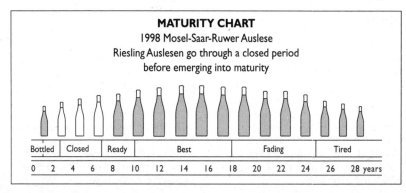

MATURITY CHART
1998 Mosel-Saar-Ruwer Auslese
Riesling Auslesen go through a closed period
before emerging into maturity

Bottled	Closed	Ready	Best	Fading	Tired

| 0 | 2 | 4 | 6 | 8 | 10 | 12 | 14 | 16 | 18 | 20 | 22 | 24 | 26 | 28 years |

Auslese and Beerenauslese. Best producers: *Darting, Lingenfelder, Messmer, Müller-Catoir* (Pfalz); *Andreas Laible, Wolff-Metternich* (Baden); *Rudolf Fürst, Wirsching* (Franken).

SILVANER (white) A workhorse grape, often dull, fat and vegetal, but can be impressive in Franken, where it develops honeyed weight with age. It suits the local pork cookery; good with asparagus, too. *Juliusspital* and *Lingenfelder Ypsilon* are good.

SPÄTBURGUNDER (red) There is a new, deeply coloured, rich and powerful style of this, the Pinot Noir of Burgundy.

Top producers: *Meyer-Näkel* (Ahr); *August Kesseler* (Rheingau); *Knipser, Koehler-Ruprecht, Lingenfelder, Müller-Catoir* (Pfalz); *Bercher, Dr Heger, Bernhard Huber, Karl H Johner* (Baden); *Rudolf Fürst* (Franken); *Dautel* (Württemberg).

WEISSBURGUNDER or **WEISSER BURGUNDER** (white) Can produce soft, creamy wines with a peach, melted butter, caramel and nuts flavour. Best: *Dönnhoff* (Nahe); *Heyl zu Herrnsheim, Schales* (Rheinhessen); *Bergdolt, Müller-Catoir, Rebholz, Wehrheim* (Pfalz); *Bercher, Dr Heger, Karl H Johner, Franz Keller, Salwey* (Baden).

WINE REGIONS AND STYLES

AHR This small area contrives to be famous for red wines, though their flavour and colour are pretty light, and the Rieslings are in fact more interesting. Top producers: *Deutzerhof, Meyer-Näkel.*

BADEN Dry Ruländer and Weisser Burgunder can be really special here in the balmy South. The Pinot family generally – even Spätburgunder – is on top, although the Ortenau area also has some fine dry Riesling. The area is dominated by the vast *Badische Winzerkeller* co-operative. Top names: *Bercher, Dr Heger, Bernhard Huber, Karl H Johner, Franz Keller, Andreas Laible, Schloss Neuweier, Salwey, Seeger, Wolff-Metternich.*

BEREICH A collection of villages, usually trading on the name of the most famous of them. Bereich wine is usually dull, dull, dull.

DEUTSCHER SEKT Often a sure route to intestinal distress and sulphur-led hangover, although *Dr Richter*'s and *Georg Breuer*'s are outstanding, but expensive. Interesting but rare smaller brands are *Graeger, Menger-Krug, Schloss Vaux.* Avoid at all costs the stuff made from imported wines, labelled Sekt (not Deutscher Sekt), or worse, Schaumwein.

FRANKEN (Franconia) Dry wine country. The slightly earthy, slightly vegetal, big and beefy Franken wines in their flagon-shaped 'Bocksbeutel' bottles are usually based on Silvaner or Müller-Thurgau. Quality is mixed, with only a few wines worth the high prices. Top names: *Rudolf Fürst, Juliusspital, Horst Sauer, Johann Ruck, Robert Schmitt, Schmitt's Kinder, Wirsching.*

GROSSLAGE An area smaller than a Bereich, but bigger than a single vineyard. The names sound like those of single vineyards (Piesporter Michelsberg is a Grosslage). Gross deceit is more like it.

HALBTROCKEN Half-dry. The wines need to have more body to balance the acidity, so the best Halbtrockens are from the Rheingau or Pfalz – not the Mosel.

HESSISCHE BERGSTRASSE A tiny side valley of the Rhine from which hardly anything is exported. Generally good Rieslings. Best: *Staatsweingut Bergstrasse.*

LIEBFRAUMILCH Liebfraumilch was a brilliant invention, innocuous and grapy and the perfect beginner's wine. Now mostly cheap sugar-water. *Blue Nun,* always one of the better ones, is no longer labelled Lieb.

MITTELRHEIN The Rhine at its most beautiful; tourists flock there and drink most of its wine, but *Toni Jost's* racy Rieslings still get away. Also good: *Fritz Bastian, Dr Randolph Kauer, Helmut Madess.*

MOSEL-SAAR-RUWER When they are made from Riesling and come from one of the many steep, slaty, south-facing sites in the folds of the river, these northerly wines are unlike any others. Think of a thrilling spring flowers flavour, allied to an alcohol level so low that it leaves your head clear. The lightest yet most intense Rieslings in the world, with a minerally character from the slate soil. The Saar and the Ruwer both need the warmest years to show at their best, and both can be longer-maturing, with even more steel. Best: *Joh. Jos. Christoffel, Fritz Haag, Reinhold Haart, von Hövel, Karthäuserhof, von Kesselstatt, Dr Loosen, Joh. Jos. Prüm, Max Ferd. Richter, Schloss Saarstein, Willi Schaefer, von Schubert, Selbach-Oster, Dr Wagner, Dr Weins-Prüm, Zilliken.*

NAHE At their best the Rieslings have quite high acidity and a mineral edge, but quality is not uniformly good. *Paul Anheuser, Dönnhoff, Crusius, Schlossgut Diel, Emrich-Schönleber, Kruger-Rumpf* and *Mathern* are all tops. The *Staatliche Weinbaudomäne* is back on good form.

PFALZ (formerly the Rheinpfalz) The northern half includes extremely good villages like Forst, Wachenheim, Deidesheim and Ruppertsberg. There's lots of fiery Riesling, and Scheurebe is excellent. The South is Germany's most dynamic region, with fewer big names to fly its flag but an astonishing overall improvement in quality. Look for *Bassermann Jordan, Bergdolt, Josef Biffar, von Buhl, Dr Bürklin-Wolf, Kurt Darting, Koehler-Ruprecht, Lingenfelder, Messmer, Georg Mosbacher, Müller-Catoir, Pfaffingen-Fuhrmann-Eymael, Rebholz, Karl Schaefer.*

RHEINGAU Some of Germany's most famous vineyards and renowned aristocratic

wine estates are here, and its supremely elegant Rieslings once defined top-quality German wines. However, many of the big estates here have been resting on their laurels for years. The best sign recently has been the classification of top vineyards. Look for these producers: *J B Becker, Georg Breuer, Domdechant Werner, August Eser, Johannishof, August Kesseler, Franz Künstler, Josef Leitz, Schloss Reinhartshausen, Balthasar Ress, J Wegeler-Erben (Deinhard), Robert Weil.* All are worth their high prices.

RHEINHESSEN The contrast between Rheinhessen's regular products and its top wines could not be more extreme. It is one of the main sources of Liebfraumilch, yet Nierstein's top Rieslings can match anything from the Rheingau. Top producers:

Gunderloch, Heyl zu Herrnsheim, Keller, St Antony, Schales, Georg Albrecht Schneider.

SAALE-UNSTRUT The largest wine region in what used to be East Germany. The climate is similar to Franken, the grapes mainly Müller-Thurgau and Silvaner. *Lützkendorf* has good Riesling and Traminer.

SACHSEN Müller-Thurgau dominates, but the best dry wines come from Weissburgunder, Kerner, Grauburgunder, Traminer and Riesling. *Klaus Zimmerling* is the best bet, but *Schloss Proschwitz* and *Schloss Wackerbarth* are also good.

SEKT bA (Sekt bestimmter Anbaugebiete) Germany's best sparkling wine comes from private estates. If the wine comes from one specific region it can be labelled accordingly – for instance, Rheinhessen Sekt. Riesling Sekt bA is especially worth looking out for. Best: *Bergdolt, Schloss Reinhartshausen.*

TROCKEN Dry: the driest German wines, austere and acidic in unripe vintages. The richer, more alcoholic wines of the Pfalz, Baden and Franken suit dryness best.

WÜRTTEMBERG More than half the wine is red, and most is drunk on the spot. The best grape is Lemberger, dark, spicy and suited to oak aging. Best: *Graf Adelmann, Hohenlohe-Öhringen, Graf von Neipperg.*

PRODUCERS WHO'S WHO

GEORG BREUER ★★ (Rheingau) Convincing promoter of dry Rheingau Riesling. Rüdesheimer Berg Schlossberg and Rauenthaler Nonnenberg are best.

H DÖNNHOFF ★★★ (Nahe) Classic Rieslings of great aromatic subtlety and racy intensity. Sensational Auslese and Eiswein.

GUNDERLOCH ★★★ (Rheinhessen) Explosively fruity, rich, seductive Rieslings from the great Nackenheimer Rothenberg. Jean-Baptiste Kabinett is good value; also Beerenauslese and Trockenbeerenauslese of other-worldly concentration and density.

FRITZ HAAG ★★ (Mosel-Saar-Ruwer) Wines of crystalline clarity and racy refinement from Brauneberger Juffer-Sonnenuhr.

VON HÖVEL ★★ (Mosel-Saar-Ruwer) Refined, elegant wines. Best are the succulent, beautifully balanced wines from Oberemmeler Hütte.

TONI JOST ★★ (Mittelrhein) Delicious racy Rieslings from the Bacharacher Hahn; exceptional Beerenauslese and Trockenbeerenauslese are also occasionally produced.

KARTHÄUSERHOF ★★★ (Mosel-Saar-Ruwer) Large Ruwer property making wines of tremendous concentration and character.

VON KESSELSTATT ★★ (Mosel-Saar-Ruwer) Huge estate showing big improvements. Look for Rieslings from Graach, Piesport and Wiltingen.

KOEHLER-RUPRECHT ★★★ (Pfalz) Powerful dry Rieslings plus excellent oak-aged whites and Germany's best Pinot Noir reds, sold under the Philippi label.

FRANZ KÜNSTLER ★★★ (Rheingau) Powerful and long-lived Rieslings. Best are the majestic dry and dessert wines from the Hochheimer Hölle.

DR LOOSEN ★★★ (Mosel-Saar-Ruwer) Rieslings, Spätlesen and Auslesen from Urziger Würzgarten, Erdener Prälat and Treppchen are tops. For value, try wines without vineyard names.

EGON MÜLLER ★★★ (Mosel-Saar-Ruwer) The ultimate in Riesling Auslese, Beerenauslese, Trockenbeerenauslese and Eiswein. No honey tastes this good. World-class prices.

MÜLLER-CATOIR ★★★ (Pfalz) Highly expressive, rich, dry and naturally sweet wines. Superb Scheurebe and Rieslaner as well as Rieslings. Also produce good red wine from Spätburgunder.

JOH. JOS. PRÜM ★★ (Mosel-Saar-Ruwer) Wines that need time to show their best; after a few years of aging they are supremely elegant. Wehlener Sonnenuhr can age for decades without losing vigour.

WILLI SCHAEFER ★★★ (Mosel-Saar-Ruwer) Small production; wines of great depth and elegance from Graach. They can easily age for ten years or more.

VON SCHUBERT ★★★ (Mosel-Saar-Ruwer) The Maximin Grünhaus estate makes exquisitely delicate, fragrant Rieslings that gain enormously with long aging.

SELBACH-OSTER ★★★ (Mosel-Saar-Ruwer) Superbly poised, concentrated Rieslings from Zeltingen.

WEINGUT ROBERT WEIL ★★ (Rheingau) Classic Rieslings which combine opulent fruit with clarity and crisp acidity. Best are the Kiedricher Gräfenbergs.

ZILLIKEN ★★ (Mosel-Saar-Ruwer) Estate specializing in Rieslings with minerally intensity from the Saarburger Rausch vineyard. Fashionable Eiswein.

GERMAN VINTAGES

2000 A good year for Kabinett and Spätlese, with lower quantities at higher ripeness levels.

1999 High quality, with some Beerenauslesen and Trockenbeerenauslesen wines that need long keeping.

1998 'Surprisingly good', according to the growers – it rained, in other words. But quality does look impressive, especially in the Mosel.

1997 Rich, concentrated wines: lots of Spätlesen and Auslesen. Some top estates had to declassify Spätlesen to QbA in order to have enough. Not an Eiswein year: too warm.

1996 Higher acidity than the 1997s; Kabinetts are drinking now.

1995 The best vintage since 1990. Lots of excellent Spätlesen and Auslesen.

1994 Strongest in the Mosel-Saar-Ruwer, but quite good generally. Outstanding at BA and TBA level.

1993 Rich, even opulent wines that have developed quite quickly. Best in the Rheingau, Pfalz and Mosel. Very good for dry Riesling. Drink now.

1992 Good, but a bit low on acidity. Drink up.

1991 The best are showing well now. Drink up.

1990 Fantastic wines that will age, though Kabinetts should have been drunk.

GERMANY PRICES

Kab.	=	Kabinett
Spät.	=	Spätlese
Aus.	=	Auslese
BA	=	Beerenauslese
TBA	=	Trockenbeerenauslese

RHINE WHITE

Under £3.50

Liebfraumilch Rudolf Müller 1998 £2.99 (UN)

Niersteiner Gutes Domtal, Rudolf Müller 1998 £3.29 (UN)

Rüdesheimer Rosengarten, Rudolf Müller 1999 £3.49 (TAN)

£3.50 → £4.49

Devil's Rock Riesling, St Ursula **Non-vintage** £3.99 (BUD) £3.99 (ASD)

Devil's Rock Riesling, St Ursula 1999 £3.99 (TES) £3.99 (VIC) £3.99 (THR) £4.99 (WAI)

Devil's Rock Riesling, St Ursula 1998 £3.99 (SAF)

Liebfraumilch Black Tower **Non-vintage** £3.99 (SO) £3.99 (VIC) £3.99 (THR) £3.99 (BOT) £3.99 (WR)

Liebfraumilch Black Tower 1998 £4.05 (SAF) £4.49 (BUD)

Liebfraumilch Blue Nun **Non-vintage** £3.99 (VIC) £3.99 (THR) £3.99 (BOT) £3.99 (WR) £3.99 (WAI)

Liebfraumilch Blue Nun 1999 £3.99 (MORR)

Liebfraumilch Blue Nun 1998 £3.99 (SAF)

Oppenheimer Krotenbrunnen Spät., Rudolf Müller 1997 £4.49 (JON)

★ Ruppertsberg Trocken, The Society's 1999 £3.95 (WS)

£4.50 → £5.99

Johannisberger Erntebringer Riesling Kab., Rudolf Müller 1998 £5.49 (JON)

Niersteiner Auflangen Riesling Spät., Rudolf Müller 1997 £4.95 (POR) £4.95 (BALL) £4.95 (AD)

Niersteiner Gutes Domtal, Langenbach 1998 £4.95 (PLAY)

Niersteiner Spiegelberg Riesling Spät., Rudolf Müller 1997 £5.49 (UN)

£6.00 → £6.99

Johannisberger Vogelsang Riesling Kab., Eser 1999 £6.95 (WS)

Niederhäuser Pfingstweide Riesling, Paul Anheuser 1998 £6.52 (HIC)

Niersteiner Hölle Riesling Kab., Senfter 1995 £6.86 (COC)

Riesling QbA, Dönnhoff 1995 £6.95 (JU)

Riesling Kab., Gunderloch 1995 £6.50 (JU)

Scheurebe Kab. Louis Philipp, Guntrum 1997 £6.75 (CON)

£7.00 → £7.99

Deidesheimer Leinhöhle Riesling Kab., Bassermann-Jordan 1989 £7.95 (JU)

Forster Mariengarten Riesling Kab., Bürklin-Wolf 1985 £7.75 (WAT)

Forster Pechstein Riesling Kab., von Buhl 1998 £7.95 (WS) £9.75 (NI)

Forster Pechstein Riesling Kab., von Buhl 1996 £7.90 (JU)

Forster Riesling, Bürklin-Wolf 1996 £7.75 (WRI) £7.99 (CON)

Niersteiner Bergkirche Riesling Kab., Guntrum 1997 £7.49 (CON)

Rauenthaler Rothenberg Riesling Kab., Eser 1994 £7.00 (BAC) £9.90 (JU)

Riesling QbA, Dönnhoff 1999 £7.35 (TAN)

Riesling QbA, Dönnhoff 1996 £7.90 (JU)

RETAILERS SPECIALIZING IN GERMANY
see Retailers Directory (page 40) for details

Adnams (AD), Averys of Bristol, Bennetts (BEN), Berry Bros & Rudd (BER), Bibendum (BIB), Butlers (BU) – particularly old vintages, D Byrne, Cockburns of Leith (COC), Direct Wine Shipments (DI), S H Jones (JON), Justerini & Brooks (JU), Lay & Wheeler (LAY), Montrachet (MON), Oddbins (OD), Majestic (MAJ), James Nicholson (NI), The Nobody Inn (NO), Reid Wines, Tanners (TAN), Waitrose (WAI), Waterloo Wine Company (WAT), The Wine Society (WS).

£8.00 → £8.99

Deidesheimer Leinhöhle Riesling Kab.,
Bassermann-Jordan **1994** £8.95 (JU)
Eltviller Sonnenberg Riesling Kab., von
Simmern **1985** £8.49 (WAT)
Forster Kirchenstück Riesling Kab.,
Bassermann-Jordan **1989** £8.50 (JU)
Forster Kirchenstück Riesling Spät.,
Bassermann-Jordan **1993** £8.00 (BAC)
Forster Pechstein Riesling Kab., von Buhl
1994 £8.95 (JU)
Hattenheimer Nussbrunnen Riesling Kab.,
von Simmern **1993** £8.85 (JU)
Hattenheimer Schützenhaus Riesling Kab.,
Ress **1996** £8.42 (MON)
Hochheimer Hölle Riesling Kab.,
Domdechant Werner **1994** £8.95 (JU)
Kreuznacher Kahlenberg Riesling Spät.,
Paul Anheuser **1998** £8.12 (HIC)
Nackenheimer Rothenberg Riesling Kab.
Jean Baptiste, Gunderloch **1993** £8.95
(JU)
Niersteiner Pettenthal Riesling Kab.,
Balbach **1996** £8.90 (JU) £8.95 (TAN)
Riesling Spät. Trocken, Lingenfelder **1997**
£8.66 (HIC) £9.30 (MON)

£9.00 → £9.99

Armand Kab., von Buhl **1998** £9.35 (NI)
Deidesheimer Hohenmorgen Riesling Kab.,
Bassermann-Jordan **1993** £9.95 (JU)
Deidesheimer Leinhöhle Riesling Spät.,
Bassermann-Jordan **1989** £9.90 (JU)
Erbacher Marcobrunnen Riesling Kab.,
von Simmern **1993** £9.45 (JU)
Freinsheimer Goldberg Riesling Aus.,
Lingenfelder **1994** £9.95 (FORT)
Geisenheimer Schlossgarten Riesling
Spät., Schönborn **1989** £9.50 (JU)
Hochheimer Reichestal Riesling Kab.,
Franz Kunstler **1998** £9.99 (DI)
Hochheimer Reichestal Riesling Kab.,
Franz Kunstler **1996** £9.00 (JU)
Hochheimer Riesling Aus., Domdechant
Werner **1994** £9.95 (AD) £25.00 (JU)
Nackenheimer Rothenberg Riesling Kab.,
Gunderloch **1996** £9.90 (JU)
Nackenheimer Rothenberg Riesling Kab.
Jean Baptiste, Gunderloch **1994** £9.90
(JU)
Oberhäuser Leistenberg Riesling Kab.,
Dönnhoff **1998** £9.46 (NO)
Oberhäuser Leistenberg Riesling Kab.,
Dönnhoff **1995** £9.50 (JU)

£10.00 → £11.99

Forster Jesuitengarten Riesling Spät.,
Bassermann-Jordan **1990** £11.50 (BAC)
Forster Jesuitengarten Riesling Spät., von
Buhl **1998** £10.95 (WS)
Forster Jesuitengarten Riesling Spät., von
Buhl **1997** £11.80 (NI) £14.69 (TW)
Forster Jesuitengarten Riesling Spät., von
Buhl **1995** £11.50 (JU)
Forster Kirchenstück Riesling Spät., von
Buhl **1994** £10.90 (JU)
Hattenheimer Pfaffenberg Riesling Spät.,
Schönborn **1996** £10.81 (CB)
Hattenheimer Pfaffenberg Riesling Spät.,
Schönborn **1989** £11.90 (JU)
Hochheimer Kirchenstück Riesling Spät.,
Geheimrat Aschrott'sche **1994** £10.50
(JU)
Johannisberger Klaus Riesling Spät.,
Schönborn **1990** £11.90 (JU)
Nackenheimer Rothenberg Riesling Spät.,
Gunderloch **1992** £10.50 (JU)
Nackenheimer Rothenberg Riesling Kab.
Jean Baptiste, Gunderloch **1995** £10.90
(JU)
Niederhauser Hermannshöhle Riesling
Spät., Dönnhoff **1993** £11.95 (JU)
Niersteiner Hipping Riesling Aus., Balbach
1989 £10.50 (JU)
Niersteiner Pettenthal Riesling Spät.,
Balbach **1999** £11.20 (TAN)
Oberhäuser Leistenberg Riesling Kab.,
Dönnhoff **1996** £10.20 (JU)
Schloss Vollrads Riesling Kab., Schloss
Vollrads **1999** £10.95 (LIB) £10.95 (STA)
£10.99 (VIL)
Wachenheimer Rechbächel Riesling Spät.
Trocken, Bürklin-Wolf **1999** £11.65
(TAN)

£12.00 → £14.99

Armand Kab., von Buhl **1995** £12.34 (TW)
Forster Jesuitengarten Riesling Aus.,
Bassermann-Jordan **1996** £12.45 (JU)
Forster Ungeheuer Riesling Aus., von
Buhl **1996** £13.50 (JU)
Hochheimer Kirchenstück Riesling Spät.,
Franz Kunstler **1998** £13.99 (DI)
Hochheimer Kirchenstück Riesling Spät.,
Franz Kunstler **1996** £13.90 (JU)
Hochheimer Kirchenstück Riesling Spät.,
Domdechant Werner **1994** £13.95 (JU)
Nackenheimer Rothenberg Riesling Spät.,
Gunderloch **1994** £13.90 (JU)

Niederhäuser Hermannshöhle Riesling
Spät., Staatliche Weinbaudomäne **1985**
£13.75 (WAT)
Niederhauser Hermannshöhle Riesling
Spät., Dönnhoff **1998** £14.76 (NO)
£16.00 (WS)
Niederhauser Hermannshöhle Riesling
Spät., Dönnhoff **1995** £14.95 (JU)
Oberhäuser Brücke Riesling Aus.,
Dönnhoff ½ bottle **1996** £14.00 (JU)
Riesling Montosa, Breuer **1998** £12.79
(YOU)
Schlossbockelheimer Kupfergrube
Riesling Spät., Dönnhoff **1999** £14.99
(YOU)
Wachenheimer Gerümpel Riesling Spät.,
J.L. Wolf **1996** £12.20 (NO)

£15.00 → £19.99

Deidesheimer Hohenmorgen Riesling
Aus., Bassermann-Jordan **1989** £18.90
(JU)
Erbacher Siegelsberg Riesling Spät.,
Auguste Eser **1994** £15.50 (JU)
Forster Kirchenstück Riesling Aus., von
Buhl **1995** £15.95 (JU)
Forster Kirchenstück Riesling Spät.,
Bassermann-Jordan **1994** £15.98 (TW)
Forster Ungeheuer Riesling Aus., von
Buhl **1994** £15.00 (JU)
Geisenheimer Rothenberg Riesling Aus.,
Deinhard **1989** £17.90 (JU)
Nackenheimer Rothenberg Riesling Spät.,
Gunderloch **1996** £15.00 (JU)
Nackenheimer Rothenberg Riesling Spät.,
Gunderloch **1995** £15.95 (JU)
Niederhauser Hermannshöhle Riesling
Spät., Dönnhoff **1999** £15.85 (TAN)
Niederhauser Hermannshöhle Riesling
Spät., Dönnhoff **1996** £15.50 (JU)
Niersteiner Hipping Riesling Aus., Balbach
1996 £15.00 (JU)
Oberhäuser Brücke Riesling Aus.,
Dönnhoff ½ bottle **1998** £16.88 (NO)
Oberhäuser Brücke Riesling Aus.,
Dönnhoff **1993** £19.00 (JU)
Schlossbockelheimer Felsenberg Riesling
Spät., Dönnhoff **1995** £15.95 (JU)

• *All prices for each wine are listed
together in ascending order.*
• *Price bands refer to the lowest price
for which the wine is available.*

Schlossbockelheimer Kupfergrube Riesling
Spät., Dönnhoff **1996** £16.00 (JU)
Wachenheimer Böhlig Riesling Aus.,
Bürklin-Wolf **1990** £15.95 (DI)
Wallufer Oberberg Riesling Aus., J B
Becker **1995** £17.00 (JU)

£20.00 → £24.99

Eltviller Sonnenberg Riesling Aus., J B
Becker **1995** £23.50 (JU)
Erbacher Marcobrunn Riesling Aus.,
Schönborn **1995** £20.62 (CB)
Kiedricher Gräfenberg Riesling Spät.,
Weil **1997** £21.50 (DI)
Nackenheimer Rothenberg Riesling Aus.
Fuder 20, Gunderloch **1996** £21.00 (JU)
Nackenheimer Rothenberg Riesling Aus.,
Gunderloch **1995** £22.00 (JU)
Niederhauser Hermannshöhle Riesling
Aus., Dönnhoff **1995** £21.00 (JU)

£25.00 → £49.99

Erbacher Marcobrunn Riesling Aus.,
Schönborn **1990** £49.00 (JU)
Forster Ungeheuer Riesling Eiswein,
Bassermann-Jordan ½ bottle **1996**
£35.00 (JU)
Nackenheimer Rothenberg Riesling Aus.
Goldkapsul, Gunderloch **1995** £43.00
(JU)
Nackenheimer Rothenberg Riesling BA,
Gunderloch ½ bottle **1996** £34.00 (JU)
Niederhäuser Hermannshöhle Riesling
Aus., Staatliche Weinbaudomäne **1997**
£25.95 (POR)
Oberhäuser Felsenberg Riesling BA,
Dönnhoff ½ bottle **1994** £40.00 (JU)
£48.75 (NI)

£50.00 → £99.99

Forster Jesuitengarten Riesling BA, von
Buhl **1994** £90.00 (JU)
Forster Jesuitengarten Riesling Eiswein,
von Buhl **1996** £69.00 (JU)
Forster Kirchenstück Riesling BA, von
Buhl **1996** £68.00 (JU)
Forster Ungeheuer Riesling Eiswein, von
Buhl ½ bottle **1995** £54.00 (JU)
Forster Ungeheuer Riesling TBA, von
Buhl ½ bottle **1996** £74.95 (NI)
Forster Ungeheuer Riesling TBA, von
Buhl ½ bottle **1994** £74.95 (NI)
Grosskarlbacher Burgweg Scheurebe
TBA ½ bottle, Lingenfelder **1985**
£50.00 (FORT)

Hochheimer Reichestal Riesling Eiswein,
Franz Kunstler ½ bottle 1998 £54.00
(DI)
Hochheimer Reichestal Riesling Eiswein,
Franz Kunstler ½ bottle 1996 £53.00
(JU)
Oberhäuser Brücke Riesling BA,
Dönnhoff ½ bottle 1995 £50.00 (JU)
Oberhäuser Brücke Riesling Eiswein,
Dönnhoff ½ bottle 1998 £65.20 (TAN)
Oberhäuser Brücke Riesling Eiswein,
Dönnhoff 1998 £71.14 (NO)
Oberhäuser Brücke Riesling Eiswein,
Dönnhoff ½ bottle 1995 £78.00 (JU)
Oberhäuser Brücke Riesling Eiswein,
Dönnhoff ½ bottle 1994 £72.00 (JU)
Oberhäuser Felsenberg Riesling Eiswein,
Dönnhoff ½ bottle 1993 £60.00 (JU)
Wachenheimer Böhlig Riesling BA,
Bürklin-Wolf 1989 £54.00 (JU)
Wachenheimer Luginsland Riesling TBA,
Bürklin-Wolf 1989 £92.00 (JU)

Over £100.00

Deidesheimer Hohenmorgen Riesling BA,
Bassermann-Jordan 1994 £110.00 (JU)
Forster Jesuitengarten Riesling TBA,
Basserman-Jordan 1989 £175.00 (JU)
Wallufer Walkenberg Riesling TBA, J B
Becker 1994 £136.00 (JU)

RHINE RED

£9.00 → £18.00

Spätburgunder QbA, Lingenfelder 1998
£9.95 (WS)
Spätburgunder QbA, Lingenfelder 1996
£11.95 (MON)
Wallufer Walkenberg Spätburgunder
Spät. Trocken, J B Becker 1994 £17.90
(JU)

MOSEL WHITE

Under £4.00

Piesporter Michelsberg Reh 2000 £3.99
(MAR)
Piesporter Michelsberg Rudolf Müller
1999 £3.99 (TAN)
Piesporter Michelsberg Rudolf Müller
1998 £3.99 (UN)
Reiler vom Heissen Stein Spät., Rudolf
Müller 1998 £3.95 (TAN)

£4.00 → £5.99

Deinhard Green Label 1998 £4.99 (GN)
Ockfener Bockstein Riesling, Dr Wagner
1999 £5.55 (WAI)
Reiler vom Heissen Stein Kab., Rudolf
Müller 1999 £4.59 (JON) £4.95 (POR)
Reiler vom Heissen Stein Kab., Rudolf
Müller 1997 £4.25 (BALL)
Riesling Dr 'L', Dr Loosen 1999 £5.99
(WAI) £6.25 (CON)
Riesling Trocken Dr 'L', Dr Loosen 1999
£5.95 (AD)
★ Urziger Wurzgarten Riesling Spät.,
Weingut Prälat 1993 £4.99 (MAJ)

£6.00 → £7.99

Brauneberger Juffer Sonnenuhr Riesling
Spät., Fritz Haag 1998 £6.95 (WS)
Erdener Treppchen Riesling Kab.,
Mönchhof 1997 £6.99 (RAE)
Graacher Himmelreich Riesling Kab., F-
W-Gymnasium 1996 £7.95 (POR)
Oberemmeler Hütte Riesling Kab., von
Hövel 1999 £7.50 (SAV) £8.50 (WS)
Ockfener Bockstein Riesling Kab., Dr
Wagner 1999 £7.85 (TAN)
Ockfener Bockstein Riesling Spät.,
Rheinart 1996 £7.63 (PLA)
Piesporter Goldtröpfchen Riesling,
Deinhard 1998 £6.99 (PEN)
Riesling, Fritz Haag 1996 £7.95 (JU)
Riesling Kab. Dr 'L', Dr Loosen 2000
£7.65 (NI)
Riesling Kab. Dr 'L', Dr Loosen 1997
£7.09 (CON)
Riesling QbA, Dr Loosen 1998 £6.25
(JON) £6.75 (STE) £7.23 (PLAY)
Scharzhofberger Riesling, Egon Müller-
Scharzhof 1995 £7.90 (JU)
Serriger Schloss Saarsteiner Riesling Kab.,
Schloss Saarstein 1998 £7.95 (MAY)

£8.00 → £9.99

Bernkasteler Lay Riesling Kab., Dr
Loosen 1999 £9.00 (WRI)
Brauneberger Juffer Riesling Kab., Richter
1997 £8.62 (MON)
Brauneberger Juffer Sonnenuhr Riesling
Kab., Fritz Haag 1996 £9.95 (RAE)
£10.90 (JU)
Eitelsbacher Karthäuserhofberg Riesling
Kab., Karthäuserhof 1999 £9.75 (TAN)
Erdener Treppchen Riesling Kab.,
Mönchhof 1995 £8.90 (JU)

Erdener Treppchen Riesling Spät.,
Mönchhof 1990 £9.95 (JU)
Erdener Treppchen Riesling Spät.,
Mönchhof 1985 £9.99 (RAE)
Erdener Treppchen Riesling Spät.,
Heinrich Schmitiges 1999 £9.39 (PLA)
Erdener Treppchen Riesling Spät.,
Heinrich Schmitiges 1995 £8.95 (JU)
Graacher Himmelreich Riesling Kab., J J
Prüm 1993 £9.75 (JU)
Graacher Himmelreich Riesling Kab., J J
Prüm 1992 £9.95 (JU) £13.92 (TW)
Graacher Himmelreich Riesling Spät.,
Richter 1996 £8.95 (FORT)
Graacher Himmelreich Riesling Spät.,
Richter 1995 £8.95 (FORT)
Josephshofer Riesling Spät., Kesselstatt
1999 £8.95 (WRI)
Josephshofer Riesling Spät., Kesselstatt
1996 £9.95 (STA)
Maximin-Grünhäuser Bruderberg Riesling,
Schubert 1996 £8.90 (JU)
Oberemmeler Hütte Riesling Spät., von
Hövel 1999 £8.80 (SAV)
Ockfener Bockstein Riesling Spät., Dr
Fischer 1989 £9.00 (JU)
Piesporter Goldtröpfchen Riesling Spät.,
Bischöfliches Priesterseminar 1989
£8.95 (JU)
Piesporter Goldtröpfchen Riesling Kab.,
Haart 1998 £9.99 (JON) £9.99 (BIB)
Piesporter Goldtröpfchen Riesling Kab.,
Haart 1996 £8.90 (JU)
Piesporter Goldtröpfchen Riesling Kab.,
Haart 1992 £9.50 (JU)
Piesporter Goldtröpfchen Riesling Kab.,
Kesselstatt 1998 £9.55 (NI)
Piesporter Goldtröpfchen Spät.,
Kesselstatt 1999 £9.95 (STA)
Riesling Kab., J J Prüm 1995 £9.45 (JU)
Riesling Kab., J J Prüm 1994 £8.95 (JU)
Riesling Spät. Dr 'L', Dr Loosen 1997
£8.95 (CON)
Saarburger Rausch Riesling Kab., Zilliken
1994 £8.90 (JU)
Scharzhofberger Riesling Spät., von Hövel
1997 £8.95 (WS)
Serriger Schloss Saarsteiner Riesling Kab.,
Schloss Saarstein 1999 £8.30 (HIC)
Urziger Würzgarten Riesling Kab.,
Mönchhof 1994 £8.95 (JU)
Urziger Wurzgarten Riesling Spät.,
Mönchhof 1990 £9.95 (JU)
Wehlener Sonnenuhr Riesling Aus., Dr
Loosen 1997 £9.33 (NO)

Wehlener Sonnenuhr Riesling Kab., Dr
Loosen 1998 £9.79 (CON)
Wehlener Sonnenuhr Riesling Kab., Dr
Loosen 1997 £9.95 (WRI)
Wehlener Sonnenuhr Riesling Kab., J J
Prüm 1996 £9.80 (WRI) £15.92 (TW)

£10.00 → £11.99

Brauneberger Juffer Riesling Aus., Richter
1996 £11.50 (FORT)
Brauneberger Juffer Sonnenuhr Riesling
Kab., Fritz Haag 1995 £11.50 (JU)
Brauneberger Juffer Sonnenuhr Riesling
Spät., Fritz Haag 1996 £11.99 (RAE)
£13.50 (JU)
Eitelsbacher Karthäuserhofberg Riesling
Kab., Karthäuserhof 1998 £11.55 (MON)
Eitelsbacher Karthäuserhofberg Riesling
Kab., Karthäuserhof 1995 £10.80 (JU)
Erdener Treppchen Riesling Kab., Dr
Loosen 1998 £10.99 (JON)
Erdener Treppchen Riesling Spät.,
Mönchhof 1994 £10.40 (JU)
Graacher Himmelreich Riesling Kab., J J
Prüm 1995 £10.90 (JU)
Graacher Himmelreich Riesling Kab., J J
Prüm 1994 £10.95 (JU)
Graacher Himmelreich Riesling Spät., F-
W-Gymnasium 1996 £10.95 (POR)
Graacher Himmelreich Riesling Spät., F-
W-Gymnasium 1995 £10.99 (JON)
Maximin-Grünhäuser Abtsberg Riesling
Kab., Schubert 1999 £11.95 (AD)
Maximin-Grünhäuser Abtsberg Riesling
Kab., Schubert 1996 £11.90 (JU)
Maximin-Grünhäuser Abtsberg Riesling,
Schubert 1995 £10.90 (JU)
Piesporter Goldtröpfchen Riesling Kab.,
Haart 1994 £10.50 (JU)
Piesporter Goldtröpfchen Riesling Spät.,
Haart 1996 £11.50 (JU)
Saarburger Rausch Riesling Spät., Zilliken
1996 £10.90 (JU)
Scharzhofberger Riesling Spät., Kesselstatt
1994 £11.25 (NI)
Schieferterrassen Riesling, Heymann-
Löwenstein 1999 £10.60 (MV)
Serriger Schloss Saarsteiner Riesling Spät.,
Schloss Saarstein 1996 £11.95 (MON)
Urziger Würzgarten Riesling Aus., Dr
Loosen 1999 £11.95 (NI)
Urziger Würzgarten Riesling Spät., Dr
Loosen 1995 £10.00 (BAC)
Urziger Wurzgarten Riesling Spät.,
Mönchhof 1995 £11.50 (JU)

Wehlener Sonnenuhr Riesling Kab., Dr
Loosen **2000** £11.50 (NI)
Wehlener Sonnenuhr Riesling Kab., Dr
Loosen **1996** £11.52 (PLAY)
Wehlener Sonnenuhr Riesling Kab., Dr
Loosen **1995** £10.25 (NO)
Wehlener Sonnenuhr Riesling Kab., J J
Prüm **1992** £10.95 (JU)
Wehlener Sonnenuhr Riesling Spät., S A
Prüm **1998** £10.50 (CON)

£12.00 → £14.99

Brauneberger Juffer Sonnenuhr Riesling
Aus., Fritz Haag **1992** £13.99 (RAE)
Brauneberger Juffer Sonnenuhr Riesling
Kab., Fritz Haag **1998** £12.60 (LAY)
Brauneberger Juffer Sonnenuhr Riesling
Spät., Fritz Haag **1999** £12.75 (HAH)
Brauneberger Juffer Sonnenuhr Riesling
Spät., Fritz Haag **1994** £14.95 (JU)
Enkircher Steffenberg Riesling Spät.
Halbtrocken, Immich-Batterieberg
1999 £13.95 (AD)
Erdener Treppchen Riesling Aus.,
Mönchhof **1990** £14.99 (RAE)
Erdener Treppchen Riesling Kab., Dr
Loosen **1995** £12.30 (NO)
Erdener Treppchen Riesling Spät., Dr
Loosen **1997** £14.65 (CON)
Graacher Himmelreich Riesling Kab., J J
Prüm **1996** £14.75 (TW)
Kaseler Kehrnagel Riesling Aus., Simon
1983 £13.75 (WAT)
Maximin-Grünhäuser Abtsberg Riesling
Kab., Schubert **1995** £13.50 (JU)
Maximin-Grünhäuser Abtsberg Riesling
Kab., Schubert **1994** £13.95 (JU)
Maximin-Grünhäuser Abtsberg Riesling
Kab., Schubert **1993** £13.00 (JU)
Maximin-Grünhäuser Abtsberg Riesling
Kab., Schubert **1992** £12.45 (JU)
Oberemmeler Hütte Riesling Aus., von
Hövel **1999** £12.60 (SAV)
Piesporter Goldtröpfchen Riesling Spät.,
Haart **1995** £13.90 (JU)
Scharzhofberger Riesling Kab. Fuder 21,
Egon Müller-Scharzhof **1994** £13.90 (JU)
Scharzhofberger Riesling Kab., Egon
Müller-Scharzhof **1999** £14.30 (TAN)
£14.95 (WAI)
Scharzhofberger Riesling Kab., Egon
Müller-Scharzhof **1998** £12.20 (TAN)
£14.49 (YOU)
Scharzhofberger Riesling Kab., Egon
Müller-Scharzhof **1992** £12.45 (JU)

Scharzhofberger Riesling Spät., Egon
Müller-Scharzhof **1997** £14.50 (FORT)
Scharzhofberger Riesling Spät., Egon
Müller-Scharzhof **1996** £14.50 (FORT)
£17.00 (JU)
Trittenheimer Apotheke Riesling Spät., F-
W-Gymnasium **1996** £12.95 (POR)
Urziger Würzgarten Riesling Spät., Dr
Loosen **1999** £14.50 (TAN)
Wehlener Sonnenuhr Riesling Spät., Dr
Loosen **1998** £13.99 (JON)
Wehlener Sonnenuhr Riesling Spät., Dr
Loosen **1995** £12.75 (WAI)
Wehlener Sonnenuhr Riesling Spät., J J
Prüm **1996** £14.50 (JU)
★ Wehlener Sonnenuhr Riesling Spät., J J
Prüm **1994** £13.99 (WAI)
Wintricher Ohligsberg Riesling Spät.,
Haart **1996** £13.22 (BIB)
Zeltinger Sonnenuhr Riesling Aus.,
Selbach-Oster **1996** £14.50 (RAE)
Zeltinger Sonnenuhr Riesling Aus.,
Selbach-Oster **1989** £13.99 (RAE)
Zeltinger Sonnenuhr Riesling Spät.,
Selbach-Oster **1998** £12.50 (MV)

£15.00 → £19.99

Bernkasteler Badstube Riesling Spät., J J
Prüm **1990** £19.15 (TW)
Bernkasteler Badstube Riesling Spät., J J
Prüm **1988** £19.45 (TW)
Bernkasteler Doctor Riesling Kab., H
Thanisch **1989** £18.00 (JU)
Brauneberger Juffer Sonnenuhr Riesling
Aus., Fritz Haag **2000** £16.13 (RIP)
Brauneberger Juffer Sonnenuhr Riesling
Aus., Fritz Haag **1996** £17.50 (JU)
Brauneberger Juffer Sonnenuhr Riesling
Aus., Fritz Haag **1995** £15.99 (RAE)
Brauneberger Juffer Sonnenuhr Riesling
Aus., Fritz Haag **1994** £19.50 (JU)
Brauneberger Juffer Sonnenuhr Riesling
Spät., Fritz Haag **1995** £15.00 (JU)
Eitelsbacher Karthäuserhofberg Riesling
Aus., Karthäuserhof **1999** £16.60 (HAH)
Eitelsbacher Karthäuserhofberg Riesling
Aus., Karthäuserhof **1995** £19.50 (JU)

Please remember that
Oz Clarke's Wine Buying Guide
*is a price **guide** and not a price **list**. It is
not meant to replace up-to-date
merchants' lists.*

Erdener Prälat Riesling Aus., Mönchhof
1997 £19.75 (RAE)
Erdener Prälat Riesling Aus., Mönchhof
1994 £15.00 (JU)
Erdener Treppchen Riesling Spät., Dr
Loosen **1981** £16.75 (NI)
Graacher Domprobst Riesling Aus.,
Richter **1997** £15.28 (MON)
Graacher Himmelreich Riesling Spät., J J
Prüm **1997** £15.20 (LAY)
Graacher Himmelreich Riesling Spät., J J
Prüm **1995** £19.62 (TW)
Graacher Himmelreich Riesling Spät., J J
Prüm **1985** £17.50 (FORT)
Josephshofer Riesling Aus., Kesselstatt
1983 £16.00 (WS)
Maximin-Grünhäuser Abtsberg Riesling
Spät., Schubert **1998** £16.95 (LAY)
Maximin-Grünhäuser Abtsberg Riesling
Spät., Schubert **1995** £15.75 (JU)
Maximin-Grünhäuser Abtsberg Riesling
Spät., Schubert **1994** £15.50 (JU)
Maximin-Grünhäuser Abtsberg Riesling
Aus., Schubert **1999** £19.95 (AD)
Maximin-Grünhäuser Herrenberg Riesling
Aus., Schubert **1995** £18.00 (RAE)
Piesporter Goldtröpfchen Riesling Aus.,
Haart **1996** £19.80 (JU)
Scharzhofberger Riesling Aus., Kesselstatt
1997 £16.63 (CB)
Scharzhofberger Riesling Kab., Egon
Müller-Scharzhof **1995** £15.50 (JU)
Scharzhofberger Riesling Spät. Fuder 17,
Egon Müller-Scharzhof **1993** £17.50 (JU)
Urziger Würzgarten Riesling Aus., Dr
Loosen **1998** £17.99 (YOU)
Urziger Würzgarten Riesling Aus.,
Mönchhof **1997** £15.99 (RAE)
Urziger Würzgarten Riesling Spät., Dr
Loosen **1998** £15.79 (YOU)
Wehlener Sonnenuhr Riesling Aus., Dr
Loosen **1995** £18.68 (NO)
Wehlener Sonnenuhr Riesling Aus., Dr
Loosen **1990** £16.99 (WAI)
Wehlener Sonnenuhr Riesling Aus., J J
Prüm **1997** £18.00 (WS)
Wehlener Sonnenuhr Riesling Aus., J J
Prüm **1995** £19.50 (JU) £26.55 (TW)

Wehlener Sonnenuhr Riesling Spät., J J
Prüm **1995** £16.50 (JU) £21.62 (TW)
Zeltinger Sonnenuhr Riesling Aus.,
Selbach-Oster **1998** £17.00 (MV)
Zeltinger Sonnenuhr Riesling Aus.,
Selbach-Oster **1995** £17.99 (RAE)

£20.00 → £29.99

Bernkasteler Doctor Riesling Spät., H
Thanisch **1993** £29.99 (VIL)
Bernkasteler Doctor Riesling Spät., H
Thanisch **1989** £26.00 (JU)
Brauneberger Juffer Sonnenuhr Riesling
Aus. Fuder 10, Fritz Haag **1996** £21.00
(JU)
Brauneberger Juffer Sonnenuhr Riesling
Aus. Fuder 12, Fritz Haag **1995** £22.80
(JU)
Brauneberger Juffer Sonnenuhr Riesling
Aus. Fuder 11, Fritz Haag **1994** £23.00
(JU)
Brauneberger Juffer Sonnenuhr Riesling
Aus. Goldkapsul, Fritz Haag **1996**
£24.99 (RAE) £49.00 (JU)
Brauneberger Juffer Sonnenuhr Riesling
Aus., Fritz Haag **1998** £21.35 (LAY)
Eitelsbacher Karthäuserhofberg Riesling
Aus. Fuder 30, Karthäuserhof **1995**
£23.00 (JU)
Erdener Prälat Riesling Aus., Dr Loosen
1998 £22.49 (YOU)
Erdener Prälat Riesling Aus., Dr Loosen
1997 £23.90 (TAN)

Erdener Treppchen Riesling Aus., Dr
Loosen **1995** £27.49 (NO)
Graacher Himmelreich Riesling Aus., J J
Prüm **1995** £22.91 (TW)
Maximin-Grünhäuser Abtsberg Riesling
Aus., Schubert **1996** £21.00 (JU)
Maximin-Grünhäuser Abtsberg Riesling
Aus., Schubert **1994** £24.00 (JU)
Maximin-Grünhäuser Herrenberg Riesling
Aus., Schubert **1994** £28.50 (FORT)
Mulheimer Helenenkloster Riesling Eiswein,
Richter ½ bottle **1998** £28.87 (HIC)

Mulheimer Helenenkloster Riesling
Eiswein, Richter ½ bottle **1995** £25.00
(FORT)
Ockfener Bockstein Riesling Aus., Dr
Fischer **1995** £24.48 (SAV)
Piesporter Goldtröpfchen Riesling Aus.
Fuder 10, Haart **1993** £24.00 (JU)
Piesporter Goldtröpfchen Riesling Aus.,
Haart **1994** £24.50 (JU)
Saarburger Rausch Riesling Aus., Zilliken
1995 £21.00 (JU)
Scharzhofberger Riesling Spät., Egon
Müller-Scharzhof **1999** £22.65 (HAH)
Scharzhofberger Riesling Spät., Egon
Müller-Scharzhof **1995** £21.00 (JU)
Urziger Würzgarten Riesling Aus., Dr
Loosen **1995** £22.91 (NO)
Wehlener Sonnenuhr Riesling Aus., J J
Prüm **1994** £22.50 (JU)
Wehlener Sonnenuhr Riesling Spät., J J
Prüm **1990** £25.00 (WS)
Zeltinger Sonnenuhr Riesling Aus.,
Selbach-Oster **1997** £21.00 (MV)

£30.00 → £59.99

Bernkasteler Doctor Riesling Aus., H
Thanisch **1993** £44.99 (VIL)
Brauneberger Juffer Sonnenuhr Riesling
Aus. Goldkapsul, Fritz Haag **1994**
£34.00 (JU)
Brauneberger Juffer Sonnenuhr Riesling
Aus. Goldkapsul, Fritz Haag **1989**
£30.00 (JU)
Erdener Prälat Riesling Aus., Dr Loosen
1989 £33.42 (NO)
Erdener Prälat Riesling Aus. Goldkapsul,
Dr Loosen **1998** £35.00 (YOU)
Erdener Prälat Riesling Aus. Goldkapsul,
Dr Loosen **1995** £34.83 (NO)
Erdener Prälat Riesling Aus. Goldkapsul,
Dr Loosen **1994** £31.33 (NO)
Erdener Treppchen Riesling Aus.
Goldkapsul, Dr Loosen **1994** £50.71
(NO)
Maximin-Grünhäuser Abtsberg Riesling
Eiswein, Schubert ½ bottle **1995** £49.00
(JU)
Maximin-Grünhäuser Abtsberg Riesling
Aus. Fuder 47, Schubert **1994** £40.00
(JU)
Maximin-Grünhäuser Abtsberg Riesling
Aus. Fuder 96, Schubert **1989** £47.00
(JU)
Maximin-Grünhäuser Herrenberg Riesling
Aus., Schubert **1976** £40.00 (CRO)

Piesporter Goldtröpfchen Riesling Aus.
Goldkapsul, Haart **1995** £37.00 (JU)
Wehlener Sonnenuhr Riesling Aus.
Goldkapsul, J J Prüm **1995** £43.00 (JU)
£60.51 (TW)

Over £60.00

Bernkasteler Doctor Riesling Aus., H
Thanisch **1989** £98.00 (JU)
Brauneberger Juffer Sonnenuhr Riesling
BA, Fritz Haag **1995** £120.00 (JU)
Eitelsbacher Marienholz Riesling Eiswein,
Bischöfliches Konvikt **1989** £85.00 (JU)
Maximin-Grünhäuser Abtsberg Riesling
Eiswein, Schubert **1993** £180.00 (JU)
Maximin-Grünhäuser Abtsberg Riesling
Eiswein, Schubert **1989** £160.00 (JU)
Maximin-Grünhäuser Abtsberg Riesling
BA, Schubert **1989** £220.00 (JU)
Maximin-Grünhäuser Abtsberg TBA,
Schubert ½ bottle **1995** £130.00 (JU)
Maximin-Grünhäuser Herrenberg Riesling
BA, Schubert **1995** £71.00 (RAE)
Maximin-Grünhäuser Herrenberg Riesling
BA, Schubert **1994** £125.00 (JU)
Maximin-Grünhäuser Herrenberg Riesling
BA, Schubert **1989** £127.00 (JU)
Ockfener Bockstein Riesling BA, Fischer
1989 £70.00 (JU)
Ockfener Bockstein Riesling Eiswein,
Fischer **1989** £85.00 (JU)
Scharzhofberger Aus. Fuder 29, Egon
Müller-Scharzhof **1990** £65.00 (JU)
Scharzhofberger Riesling Aus. Fuder 20,
Egon Müller-Scharzhof **1993** £65.00 (JU)
Scharzhofberger Riesling Aus. Goldkapsul
Fuder 23, Egon Müller-Scharzhof **1993**
£140.00 (JU)
Urziger Würzgarten Riesling TBA,
Mönchhof ½ bottle **1994** £165.00 (JU)

OTHER GERMAN WHITE

c. £8.50

Schloss Castell Silvaner Trocken, Fürstlich
Castell'sches Domänenamt **1998** £8.20
(TAN)

GERMAN SPARKLING

c. £7.00

Deinhard Lila Imperial Riesling **Non-
vintage** £6.99 (COC)

ITALY

Chianti's hard work is paying off: it's a wine to take seriously these days, with class and concentration to compete with any

Good grief, the price of Chianti these days. Anything halfway decent is at least £8 and quite possibly nearer £10. It's enough to drive anyone back to Bordeaux.

But don't let it drive you back. Yes, Chianti is no longer a cheap option – it's no longer the wine you first think of when you're skint and you want a bottle of red. And why should it be? The producers don't see it like that. They don't grow it like that, and they don't make it like that. Not any more.

Chianti these days is a very serious and grown-up wine region indeed. For some years now the producers have been studying their vineyards and their vines, and working out how they can do better. Once

growers start doing that, it's not long before quality starts shooting upwards – and that's just what it's been doing in Chiantiland. Chianti is now rich, supple and concentrated, but hasn't lost an iota of that characteristically Italian tea-like twist of flavour. And you don't even have to buy a Riserva to get good quality: pick a good estate and its regular wines will be excellent.

And the Super-Tuscans? Some have been eclipsed by the rise of Chianti. Some have been absorbed into the DOC system. They're no longer the force they were. Things move on. And so far, always in an upwards direction.

GRAPE VARIETIES

AGLIANICO (red) A southern grape at its most impressive in Aglianico del Vulture (Basilicata) and Taurasi (Campania).

BARBERA (red) The most prolific grape of the North-West, with high acidity and a sweet-sour, raisiny taste or even a brown-sugar sweetness. Some are lighter but intensely fruity. The grape does best in the Langhe hills around Alba in the hands of *Altare, Aldo Conterno, Conterno-Fantino, Gaja*.

BONARDA (red) Low acid, rich, plummy reds, often with a liquoricy, chocolaty streak. It's found most often in Emilia-Romagna where it is blended with Barbera as Gutturnio; also found in the Oltrepò Pavese.

CABERNET FRANC (red) Fairly widely grown in the North-East of Italy, especially in Alto Adige, Trentino, Veneto and Friuli. It can make gorgeous, grassy, yet juicy-fruited reds – wines that are easy to drink young but also capable of aging.

CABERNET SAUVIGNON (red) Very successful in the North-East and Tuscany. Check out *Gaja's Darmagi, Poliziano's Le Stanze* and Bordeaux-inspired *Tassinaia* and *Lupicaia* from *Tenuta del Terriccio*.

CANNONAU (red) Sardinian name for Grenache. Makes warm, full-blooded wine, sometimes DOC, usually inexpensive. Look for *Argiolas, Cantina Sociale di Dorgali, Gigi Picciau, Meloni, Sella & Mosca, Tonino Arcadu*.

CHARDONNAY (white) The typical Italian style is unoaked: lean, floral and sharply balanced from the Alto Adige, or try *Zeni* (Trentino) and *Gradnik* (Friuli). Oak-aged styles can be spicy and exciting, or just overoaked. Try *Gaja, Marchesi di Gresy* and *Pio Cesare* in Piedmont, *Zanella* in Lombardy, *Maculan* in the Veneto, *Caparzo* (*Le Grance*) and *Avignonesi* (*Il Marzocco*) in Tuscany, *Planeta* in Sicily. Many vary from year to year, and producers don't all have their winemaking sorted out.

Major Italian DOCs

RED AND WHITE
Oltrepò Pavese
RED
Bonarda
Valtellina
WHITE
Lugana
Franciacorta

RED
Kalterersee (Lago di Caldaro)
St-Magdalener (Santa Maddalena)

Cabernet
Lagrein
Rosenmuskateller
Schiava/Vernatsch

WHITE
Chardonnay
Gewürztraminer
Goldmuskateller
Müller-Thurgau
Pinot Bianco
Pinot Grigio
Sylvaner

RED
Cabernet Franc
Merlot
Refosco
WHITE
Chardonnay
Pinot Bianco
Pinot Grigio
Rhineriesling
Sauvignon
Tocai
Verduzzo

RED
Bardolino
Breganze
Colli Euganei
Merlot
Valpolicella

WHITE
Bianco di Custoza
Breganze
Colli Euganei
Prosecco
Soave

RED
Sangiovese di Romagna
Gutturnio
Lambrusco

WHITE
Albana di Romagna
Lambrusco Bianco
Pagadebit

RED
Rosso Conero

WHITE
Verdicchio

WHITE
Orvieto

RED AND WHITE
Torgiano

RED
Montepulciano d'Abruzzo
WHITE
Trebbiano d'Abruzzo

RED AND WHITE
Langhe
RED
Barbaresco
Barbera
Barolo
Carema
Dolcetto
Gattinara
Nebbiolo
WHITE
Arneis
Asti
Cortese di Gavi

RED AND WHITE
Bolgheri
Pomino
RED
Brunello di
  Montalcino
Carmignano
Chianti
Morellino di
  Scansano
Vino Nobile
  di Montepulciano
WHITE
Galestro
Vernaccia di
  San Gimignano
Vin Santo

WHITE
Est! Est!! Est!!!
di Montefiascone
Frascati

RED
Lacryma Christi
Taurasi
WHITE
Fiano di Avellino
Greco di Tufo

RED
Aglianico del Vulture

RED
Salice Salentino
Copertino
Castel del Monte
WHITE
Locorotondo

RED
Cannonau
Carignano del Sulcis
Monica di Sardegna
WHITE
Vermentino

FORTIFIED WINES
Marsala
Moscato di Pantelleria

VALLE
D'AOSTA

PIEDMONT   LOMBARDY
Po

TRENTINO-
ALTO
ADIGE
(SÜDTIROL)   FRIULI-
VENEZIA
GIULIA

VENETO

LIGURIA   EMILIA-ROMAGNA

Arno

TUSCANY   MARCHE

Tiber

UMBRIA

Rome

SARDINIA

LAZIO   MOLISE

ABRUZZO

CAMPANIA

PUGLIA

BASILICATA

CALABRIA

SICILY

N

0   100 km
0   50 miles

DOLCETTO (red) Usually light and refreshing with a bitter-cherry twist, though some producers in Alba, notably *Mascarello*, make it with attitude. Only the best will improve with age.

GARGANEGA (white) The principal grape of Soave, soft yet green-apple fresh when well made. Too much characterless Trebbiano Toscano spoils cheaper blends.

GEWÜRZTRAMINER (white) This seems to be getting more perfumed, though still light and fresh. Look out for examples from the North-East.

GRECO/GRECHETTO (white) Greco makes crisp, pale and refreshing wines with lightly spicy overtones in the South. Grechetto is part of the same family and its delicious, nutty, aniseed character adds dramatically to Trebbiano-dominated blends such as Orvieto in central Italy.

LAGREIN (red) Local grape of the Alto Adige and Trentino, making delicious, dark reds, strongly plum-sweet when young, aging slowly to a smoky, creamy softness. It also makes a good rosé, Lagrein Kretzer.

MALVASIA (white) This name and Malvoisie apply to a range of grape varieties, some not related. Malvasia is found mostly in Tuscany, Umbria and Lazio, giving a full, creamy nuttiness to dry whites like Frascati. It also produces brilliant, rich dessert wines with the density of thick brown-sugar syrup and the sweetness of raisins in Sardinia and the islands of Lipari north of Sicily.

MERLOT (red) Widely planted in the North-East. Often good in Friuli; provides lots of jug wine in the Veneto but when blended with Cabernet Sauvignon by *Loredan Gasparini* (Venegazzù) or *Fausto Maculan* (Trentino) achieves greater stature. Other Cabernet/Merlot blends are produced by *Mecvini* in the Marches and Trentino's *Bossi Fedrigotti* (Foianeghe). *Avignonesi* and *Castello di Ama* in Tuscany are promising, while *Ornellaia*'s *Masseto* (also Tuscany) is outstanding. It is becoming extremely fashionable.

MONTEPULCIANO (red) A source of much inexpensive, juicily plummy wine, usually with a decent tannic structure tucked into the finished product. A good, reliable buy.

ITALIAN CLASSIFICATIONS

Little more than 13 per cent of the massive Italian wine harvest comes under the heading of DOC or DOCG, and the regulations are treated in a fairly cavalier manner by many growers. Some producers choose to operate outside the regulations and classify their – frequently exceptional – wine simply as vino da tavola, the lowest grade. A new law means that more of these will come under the DOC umbrella.

Vino da Tavola   This currently applies to absolutely basic stuff but also to some maverick wines of the highest class, although many of these are now classified as IGT.

Indicazione Geografiche Tipici (IGT)   This applies to wines which are typical of their regions, but which do not qualify for DOC. It is equivalent to the French vin de pays.

Denominazione di Origine Controllata (DOC)   This applies to wines from specified grape varieties, grown in delimited zones and aged by prescribed methods. Most of Italy's traditionally well-known wines are DOC, but more are added every year.

Denominazione di Origine Controllata e Garantita (DOCG)   The top tier – a tighter form of DOC with more stringent restrictions on grape types, yields and a tasting panel. The new law is supposed to give recognition to particularly good vineyard sites.

MOSCATO (white) The Alto Adige has various Muscats, including Rosenmuskateller and Goldmuskateller, making dry wines to equal the Muscats of Alsace and sweet ones of unrivalled fragrance. But it is at its best in Piedmont with the delicious, grapy, sweetish fizz, Asti, and Moscato Naturale, a heartily perfumed sweet wine; generally best drunk young. It also makes fine dessert wines on the island of Pantelleria, near Sicily.

NEBBIOLO (red) The big, tough grape of the North-West, making – unblended – the famous Barolos and Barbarescos as well as Gattinara, Ghemme, Carema, Spanna and plain Nebbiolo. This is a fierce grape, producing wines that are stubborn and chewy with a shield of ripe tannin and acidity for the first few years; but which finally blossom out into a remarkable richness full of chocolate, raisins, prunes, and an austere perfume of tobacco, pine and herbs. The newer style still has a fairly hefty whack of tannin, but clever wine-making sheaths this in sleek and velvety fruit. These are ready much sooner. A few growers (*Altare, Clerico, Conterno-Fantino* and *Voerzio*) are producing some superb wines using barriques, or blending it with Barbera, or both. Most are sold under the Langhe DOC.

PINOT BIANCO (white) Produces some of its purest, honeyed flavours in the Alto Adige, and can do very well in Friuli, where the best are buttery and full.

PINOT GRIGIO (white) Popular in Friuli, where it makes fresh, lightly spicy wines. Good examples from *Livio Felluga, Alois Lageder, Schiopetto, Vie di Romans.*

PRIMITIVO (red) Genetically identical to California's Zinfandel, this is an increasingly popular variety in the South, combining outstanding ripeness and concentration with knockout alcoholic power. Don't expect elegance, though: these are chunky, often rustic wines.

> ### ON THE CASE
> *Brush up on your Italian grape names: they'll be appearing on labels much more now that Australia is planning to plant them, too*

RHEINRIESLING/RIESLING RENANO (white) The true German Riesling is grown in the Alto Adige for sharp, green, refreshing, steely dry wines. It can be OK, and slightly fatter, in Friuli and Lombardy. Riesling Italico, nothing to do with real Riesling, is the lesser Olasz/Laski/Welsch Rizling, still good if it's fresh.

SANGIOVESE (red) The mainstay of Chianti and all the other major Tuscan DOCGs. The wines have in common an austere, tea-like edge balanced by rich fruit. But the grape changes character when planted in the cool hills of Chianti, the warm clay soil of the coastal strip or the arid slopes of Montalcino. Quality has shot ahead in recent years.

SAUVIGNON BLANC (white) Spicy, grassy and refreshing from the Alto Adige and Friuli, though the style is usually more subtle than New World Sauvignon. Try *Avignonesi, Banfi, Castellare* and *Volpaia*.

SCHIAVA (red) Light reds with a unique taste that veers between smoked ham and strawberries. It's found in the Alto Adige, where the locals call it Vernatsch.

SYLVANER (white) Grown very high in the northern valleys of the Alto Adige, at its best this is dry, lemon-crisp and delicious.

TREBBIANO (white) Trebbiano Toscano is all too easy to grow, yielding mountains of grapes which make fruitless, sulphured wine. Trebbiano di Soave, the Veneto clone, is much better. Lombardy's Lugana can show character (*Zenato* is good), and Abruzzo's strain *can* be tasty from *Pepe, Tenuta del Priore* and *Valentini*.

VERNACCIA (white) We mostly just see two types of Vernaccia. In Sardinia Vernaccia di Oristano is a sort of Italian sherry, best dry – when it has a marvellous mix of floral scents, nutty weight and taunting sourness – but also medium and sweet. Vernaccia di San Gimignano *can* be Tuscany's best traditional white – full, golden, peppery but with a softness of hazelnuts and angelica. *Fagiuoli* and *Teruzzi & Puthod* show what can be done.

OTHER VARIETIES Arneis is producing some wonderfully peach-perfumed whites in Piedmont; Verdicchio and Vermentino make good leafy-fresh wines with some substance in Central Italy; Sicily's native Inzolia and Catarratto can produce fresh modern whites. But the really hot varieties are all red: Nero d'Avola, Negroamaro and Gaglioppo from the far South, if you want beefy, herby, bitter plums flavours; Teroldego and Refosco from the North-East for more elegance. Morellino, from Umbria, is Sangiovese under a different name, and often quite gutsy. Sagrantino, also from Umbria, is tannic with good cherry and smoke flavours.

WINE REGIONS

AGLIANICO DEL VULTURE, DOC (Basilicata; red) Superb, thick-flavoured red from gaunt Monte Vulture, in the wilds of Italy's 'instep'. The colour isn't particularly deep, but the tremendous almond paste and chocolate fruit is matched by a tough, dusty feel and quite high acidity. *Fratelli d'Angelo* (especially barriqued *Canneto d'Angelo*) and *Paternoster* are both good.

ALBANA DI ROMAGNA, DOCG (Emilia-Romagna; white) Can be dry or sweet, still or slightly fizzy, or very fizzy. At its best, the dry version can be delicately scented with an almondy finish; better are the sweet (*passito*) versions. Best producers: *Leone Conti, Fattoria Paradiso, Zerbina*.

ALTO ADIGE various **DOCs** (red, white, rosé) The reds here are attractive, light and made from the Vernatsch/Schiava grape, especially Kalterersee and St Magdalener. Cabernet, Pinot Nero, Lagrein and the tea-rose-scented Rosenmuskateller all make reds – and rosés – with stuffing and personality. Whites are light, dry and intensely fresh wines with spice and plenty of fruit, providing the producers haven't been too greedy about yields, which some of them are. Best: *Haas, Hofstätter, Lageder, Castello Schwanburg, Tiefenbrunner, Walch*, and *San Michele-Appiano* and *Terlano* co-ops.

ARNEIS (Piedmont; white) Potentially stunning, apples-pears-and-liquorice-flavoured wines from an ancient white grape of the same name, with high prices to match. Best producers: *Arneis di Montebertotto* by *Castello di Neive, Deltetto, Bruno Giacosa, Malvirà, Negro, Vietti, Voerzio*.

ASTI, DOCG (Piedmont; white) At its best it's wonderfully frothy, fruit-bursting young wine. Go for *Canelli, Cantina Duca d'Asti, Martini, Elio Perrone, Santo Stefano*, and don't even think of aging it.

BARBARESCO, DOCG (Piedmont; red) Nebbiolo reds with delicious soft, strawberryish fruit, edged with smoke, herbs and pine. Expect more softness and finesse than in Barolo. Best: *Castello di Neive, Cigliuti, Giuseppe Cortese, Gaja, Bruno Giacosa, Marchesi di Gresy, Moresco, Pasquero, Pelissero, Pertinace, Pio Cesare, Produttori del Barbaresco, Scarpa, La Spinona* and *Vietti*.

BARBERA, DOC (Piedmont and others; red) Italy's second most widely planted red vine after Sangiovese makes a good, gutsy wine, usually with a resiny, herby bite, insistent acidity and forthright, dry raisin sort of fruit. It is best in Piedmont as Barbera d'Alba or d'Asti, and also in Lombardy under the Oltrepò Pavese DOC.

Subscribe to **Wine Magazine** today and receive three **FREE** issues
Call 01795 414879 Ref: 210ZSUB

Vallformosa

Penedés Wines & Cavas
Spain

Vinexpo
France

London

Bruxelles

D.O.Pened

You are welcome to visit our web-page at:
www.vallformosa.es

sparkling wine of the year

Exclusively at Safeway

iWC 2001

- Over 100 exclusive wines from a range of 650 from around the globe

- Buy this and selected wines on line at www.safewaywinesdirect.co.uk

- Delivered direct to your door in 5 working days

VINOPOLIS

LONDON'S WINE TASTING VISITOR ATTRACTION

Immerse yourself in the Vinopolis world of wine, enjoyin
history. Five wine tastings included in the price. Tantalis
your taste buds at Cantina Vinopolis or Wine Wharf and t
complete your unique Vinopolis experience visit Majesti
Wine Store and Vinopolis Shop.

Call 0870 4444 777 for information and advance booking

No. 1 Bank End   Opening Times:
London   Mon 11:00 - 21:00 hrs Tues - Fri 11:00 -18:00 hr
SE1 9BU   Sat 11:00 - 20:00 hrs Sun 11:00 - 18:00 hrs
                  (last entrance is 2 hours prior to closure)

www.vinopolis.co.uk   Nearest Tube: London Bridg

DISCOVER

From the Western Cape growing region, sheltered by the spectacular Langeberg (Long Mountain in Africaans) range, come these sensational wines...

LONG MOUNTAIN

BORN IN SOUTH AFRICA

CHATEAU BLOSSOM HILL.

BLOSSOM HILL. CALIFORNIAN FOR GREAT WINE.

TWO OCEANS.
A WINE THAT'S MAKING A BIG SPLASH.

Available nationally from Londis, Southern Co-op
and all good convenience stores.

'A fresh breeze from the Cape'.

KUMA - AA - AA - AA - LA!

SOUTH AFRICA'S LEADING WINE RANGE

BARDOLINO, DOC (Veneto; red, rosé)
Pale-pinky reds with a frail, wispy cherry
fruit and a slight bitter snap to the finish.
There are also a few fuller, rounder wines
like *Boscaini's Le Canne* which can take
some aging. Also *Arvedi d'Emilei, Cavalchina,
Gardoni, Guerrieri-Rizzardi, Lenotti, Masi
(Fresco* and *La Vegrona), Portalupi, Le Vigne di
San Pietro, Zeni.*

BAROLO, DOCG (Piedmont; red) The
remarkable flavours of Nebbiolo – plums
and cherries, tobacco and chocolate,
liquorice and violets – whirl like a maelstrom
in the best wines. Modern winemaking
accentuates these flavours, and makes wines
that are drinkable in five years rather than 20.
　Producers are fighting for official
classification of the top sites: single-vineyard
wines can be the absolute best (and
absolute most expensive) but because
anyone's free to put any old vineyard name
on the label, standards are not consistent.
Best producers: *Altare, Azelia, Borgogno,
Bovio, Brovia, Cavallotto, Ceretto, Clerico, Aldo*
and *Giacomo Conterno, Conterno-Fantino,
Cordero di Montezemolo, Fontanafredda*
(only its *cru* wines), *Bruno Giacosa, Marcarini,
Bartolo* and *Giuseppe Mascarello, Pio Cesare,
Pira, Prunotto, Ratti, Rocche dei Manzoni,
Sandrone, Scarpa, Scavino, Sebaste, Vajra,
Vietti* and *Voerzio (Roberto* and *Gianni).*

BIANCO DI CUSTOZA, DOC
(Veneto; white) A Soave lookalike, though
generally better. *Gorgo, Tedeschi, Le Tende,
Le Vigne di San Pietro, Zenato* are good.

BOLGHERI, DOC (Tuscany; red, white,
rosé) A DOC for all colours, including reds
based on Cabernet, Merlot or Sangiovese in
various combinations, and even a special
category for *Sassicaia,* previously a vino da
tavola. It has intense Cabernet character but
higher acidity and slightly leaner profile than
most New World Cabernets. It needs eight
to ten years to approach its best. 1994, '96,
'97 and '99 are all excellent. Pre-1994
vintages are labelled as vino da tavola.

BREGANZE, DOC (Veneto; red, white)
Little-known but quite good wines from
near Vicenza. *Maculan* is best, and makes a
stunning dessert wine, *Torcolato.*

**BRUNELLO DI MONTALCINO,
DOCG** (Tuscany; red) A big, strong
neighbour of Chianti. In the right hands it
can achieve an amazing combination of
flavours: blackberries, raisins, pepper, acidity,
tannin and a haunting sandalwood perfume,
all bound together by the austere richness
of liquorice and fierce black chocolate.
Tops: *Altesino, Argiano, Banfi, Biondi Santi,
Campogiovanni, Caparzo, Casanova, Case
Basse, Il Casello, Castelgiocondo, Col d'Orcia,
Colombini, Costanti, Il Greppone Mazzi,
Pertimali, Poggio Antico, Il Poggione, Sassetti,
Talenti, Val di Suga.* Barbaresco star *Angelo
Gaja* has been here since 1994.

CAREMA, DOC (Piedmont; red)
Nebbiolo with some refinement. *Luigi
Ferrando* is the best producer; the wines
need five to six years to be at their best.

CARMIGNANO, DOCG (Tuscany;
red) A small enclave inside the Chianti zone
where the soft, clear blackcurranty fruit of
Cabernet Sauvignon makes a delicious
blend with the somewhat stark flavours of
the Sangiovese. There is also some good
toasty, creamy rosé and some sweet *vin
santo. Capezzana* is the original estate and
the only one which is regularly seen here.

**CHIANTI, DOCG and CHIANTI
CLASSICO, DOCG** (Tuscany; red)
There are two basic styles of Chianti. The
first is the sharp young red with a rather
attractive taste: almost a tiny bit sour, but
backed up by good, raisiny-sweet fruit, a
rather stark, peppery bite and tobacco-like
spice. The second type has usually been
matured for several years. Expect a range of
concentrated raspberry and blackcurrant
flavours backed up by a herby, tobaccoey
spice that is demanding but exciting. Best:
Badia a Coltibuono, Castellare, Castell'in Villa,

Castello di Ama, Castello dei Rampolla, Castello di San Polo in Rosso, Castello di Volpaia, Felsina Berardenga, Fontodi, Monsanto, Montesodi and *Nipozzano* (Frescobaldi), *Isole e Olena, Riserva Tenute del Marchese* and *Peppoli* (both *Antinori*), *Riecine, San Felice, Selvapiana, Vecchie Terre di Montefili, Vicchiomaggio, Villa di Vetrice*.

The Chianti territory is divided into seven sub-zones: Classico, Colli Aretini, Colli Fiorentini, Colli Senesi, Colline Pisane, Montalbano and Rufina. Most wines, however, are simply labelled 'Chianti'.

COLLI EUGANEI, DOC (Veneto; red, white) *Vignalta* produces a Cabernet Riserva and Merlot-based *Gemola* of good concentration.

COPERTINO, DOC (Puglia; red) The blend of Negroamaro and Malvasia Nera produces robust reds that can be elegant, and great bargains. Try the *Copertino co-op*.

DOLCETTO, some **DOC** (Piedmont; red) At its best, delicious. It's a full but soft, fresh, and dramatically fruity red, usually for gulping down fast and young, though some will age. The sub-regions of Asti and Acqui tend to produce the lightest. *Altare, Castello di Neive, Clerico, Aldo Conterno, Giacomo Conterno, Marcarini, Mascarello, Oddero, Pasquero, Prunotto, Ratti, Sandrone, Scavino, Vajra, Vietti* and *Voerzio* are wonderful.

ERBALUCE DI CALUSO, DOC (Piedmont; white) Half the price of Gavi, with a soft, creamy flavour. *Boratto, Ferrando* and *Marbelli* are good; *Boratto* also makes a rich but refreshing Caluso Passito.

FIANO DI AVELLINO, DOC (Campania; white) Suddenly very fashionable. *Mastroberardino*'s single-vineyard *Vignadora* has a brilliant spring flowers scent and honey, peaches and pearskins taste.

FRANCIACORTA, DOCG (Lombardy; red, white) Champagne method fizz made from Pinots Bianco and Nero and Chardonnay grapes. Best are *Bellavista* and *Ca' del Bosco*, though *Cavalleri, Monte Rosa, Ricci Curbastro* and *Uberti* are also recommended. The DOC of Terre di Franciacorta makes fine still white from Pinot and Chardonnay, and tasty red.

FRASCATI, DOC (Lazio; white) The best has a lovely, fresh, nutty feel with an attractive tang of slightly sour cream. *Casale Marchese, Colli di Catone* and *Villa Simone* are reliable. Or try *Fontana Candida*'s limited releases or *San Marco's Racemo*. Best of all is *Castel de Paolis*, with outstanding *Vigna Adriana*.

FRIULI, some **DOC** (red, white) Six different zones, of which Friuli Grave DOC produces the most. The reds are marked by vibrant fruit. Refosco has a memorable taste in the tar-and-plums mould – sharpened up with a fresh grassy acidity. Best: *Borgo Conventi, Ca' Ronesca, Collavini, La Fattoria, Pintar, Russiz Superiore*. Very good fruity and fresh varietal whites come from *Abbazia di Rosazzo, Attems, Borgo Conventi, Collavini, Dri, Eno Friulia, Gravner, Jermann, Livio Felluga* (especially *Molamatta*), *Puiatti, Ronchi di Cialla, Schiopetto, Villa Russiz, Volpe Pasini*. The almost mythical Picolit sweet wine is beautifully made by *Al Rusignul*.

GALESTRO (Tuscany; white) A name created to mop up the Trebbiano and Malvasia no longer used in red Chianti. Low alcohol, simple, lemony, greengage taste, high-tech style, best on its home territory.

GATTINARA, DOCG (Piedmont; red) Nebbiolo-based red that can be good. *Antoniolo, Brugo, Dessilani* and *Travaglini* are reliable.

GAVI, DOC (Piedmont; white) Cortese is the grape, its wine dry and sharp, like Sauvignon minus the tang, and fairly full, like Chardonnay without the class. Best: *Arione, Ca' Bianca, Chiarlo (Fior di Rovere), Deltetto*.

KALTERERSEE/LAGO DI CALDARO, DOC (Alto Adige; red)

Good, light, soft red with an unbelievable flavour of home-made strawberry jam and woodsmoke, made from the Schiava (alias Vernatsch) grape. It is best as a young gulper. Best producers: *Gries co-op*, *Lageder*, *Muri-Gries*, *Hans Rottensteiner*, *San Michele-Appiano co-op*, *Tiefenbrunner* and *Walch*.

LACRYMA CHRISTI DEL VESUVIO, DOC (Campania; red, white)

The most famous wine of Campania and Naples. It can be red, white, dry or sweet: *Mastroberardino*'s is the best.

LAGREIN DUNKEL, some DOC (Alto Adige; red)

Dark, chewy red with a tarry roughness jostling with chocolate-smooth ripe fruit. Look for the *Gries co-op*, *Lageder*, *Muri-Gries*, *Niedermayr* and *Tiefenbrunner* (also very good pink Lagrein Kretzer).

LAMBRUSCO, some DOC (Emilia-Romagna; red, white)

Good Lambrusco – lightly fizzy, low in alcohol, dry to vaguely sweet – should *always* have a sharp, almost rasping acid bite to it. Look for a DOC, from Sorbara, Santa Croce or Castelvetro. Most here is not DOC and softened for the UK market, but *Cavicchioli* is proper stuff.

LANGHE, DOC (Piedmont; red, white)

This recent DOC covers wines previously sold as vino da tavola. Look for tasty young Langhe Nebbiolo from good Barolo and Barbaresco producers at attractive prices.

LUGANA, DOC (Lombardy; white)

The Trebbiano di Lugana grape makes whites of solid structure and some fruity flavours from *Ca' dei Frati*, *Premiovini*, *Provenza*, *Visconti* and *Zenato*.

MARSALA (Sicily; fortified)

This has, at its best, a delicious, deep brown-sugar sweetness allied to a cutting, lip-tingling acidity that makes it surprisingly refreshing for a fortified dessert wine. The rare dry

---

ON THE CASE
If you want a good red in the middle price bracket vacated by Chianti, try Morellino di Scansano

---

Marsala Vergine is also good. But a once-great name is now in decline. A few good producers keep the flag flying: *De Bartoli* outclasses all the rest, and even makes an intense, beautifully aged, but *unfortified* non-DOC range called *Vecchio Samperi*. His *Josephine Dore* is in the style of *fino* sherry.

MONTEFALCO, DOC and SAGRANTINO DI MONTEFALCO, DOCG (Umbria; red)

Montefalco Rosso is tasty and often stylish. Sagrantino is a red of great size and strength, that comes in a dry version or as sweet Passito, using semi-dried grapes. Both can age impressively from *Adanti*, *Antonelli* and *Caprai*.

MONTEPULCIANO D'ABRUZZO, DOC (Abruzzo; red)

Good ones are citrus-fresh and plummily rich, juicy yet tannic, ripe yet with a tantalizing sour bite. Best: *Casal Thaulero co-op*, *Colle Secco*, *Illuminati*, *Mezzanotte*, *Pepe* and *Valentini*.

MORELLINO DI SCANSANO, DOC (Tuscany, red)

A similar grape-mix to that of Chianti gives austere wines with earthy tannins, deep, ripe fruit, and tarry spice. Best: *Le Pupille*, *Mantellassi*, *Moris Farms*.

MOSCATO D'ASTI, DOCG (Piedmont; white)

Sweet, slightly fizzy wine that captures all the crunchy green freshness of a fistful of ripe table grapes. Heavenly ones come from the following: *Ascheri*, *Michele Chiarlo*, *Bruno Giacosa*, *Rivetti*, *La Spinetta*, *I Vignaioli di Santo Stefano*.

MOSCATO PASSITO DI PANTELLERIA (Pantelleria; white)

Big, heavy wine with a great wodge of rich

Muscat fruit and a good slap of alcoholic strength. Best: *Marco De Bartoli's Bukkuram, Donnafugata's Ben Ryè*.

OLTREPÒ PAVESE, some **DOC** (Lombardy; red, white, rosé) This covers just about anything, including dry whites, sweet whites and fizz. Almost the only wine we see is non-DOC Champagne-method fizz based on Pinot Grigio/Nero/Bianco, and some red, which is good, substantial stuff.

ORVIETO, DOC (Umbria; white) Generally modern, pale and dry, sometimes peach-perfumed and honeyed. Best: *Antinori (Cervaro della Sala vino da tavola), Barberani, Bigi (Cru Torricella Secco* and medium-sweet *Cru Orzalume Amabile), Decugnano dei Barbi, Palazzone, Scambia.* Sweet, unctuous, noble rot-affected wines (*Antinori's Muffato della Sala* and *Barberani's Calcaia*) are rarely seen but delicious.

PIEMONTE, DOC (Piedmont; red, white) Applies to quality wines not covered by the other DOCs of Piedmont. The reds include Barbera, Bonarda, Brachetto and Grignolino. Whites, which may be sparkling, come from Chardonnay, Cortese, Moscato, Pinot Bianco, Pinto Grigio and Pinot Nero.

POMINO, DOC (Tuscany; red, white) The DOC also includes some sweet *vin santo*. The red, based on Sangiovese with Canaiolo, Cabernet and Merlot, becomes rich, soft, velvety and spicy with age. The only producers are *Frescobaldi* and *Giuntini*.

PROSECCO, some **DOC** (Veneto; white) Still or sparkling, it's a lovely fresh, bouncy, light white, often off-dry. The best is labelled Cartizze. Try *Canevel, Carpenè Malvolti, Le Case Bianche, Collavini, Zonin*.

ROSSO CONERO, DOC (Marche; red) Very good, sturdy red full of herb and fruit flavours, sometimes with some oak for richness. Best: *Bianchi, Garofoli, Marchetti, Mecvini* and *San Lorenzo (Umani Ronchi)*.

ROSSO DI MONTALCINO, DOC (Tuscany; red) DOC for producers of Brunello who want a second wine, perhaps for declassifying part of their crop. Softer, more approachable and cheaper than Brunello di Montalcino.

ROSSO DI MONTEPULCIANO, DOC (Tuscany; red) This is the DOC for 'lesser' Montepulciano, aged for less time in the cellar. Much the same style as big brother, but lighter, more approachable and drinkable younger.

SALICE SALENTINO, DOC (Puglia; red) Impressive wines, deep in colour, ripe and chocolaty, acquiring hints of roast chestnuts and prunes with age. Look out for wines from *Candido, Leone De Castris, Taurino, Vallone*.

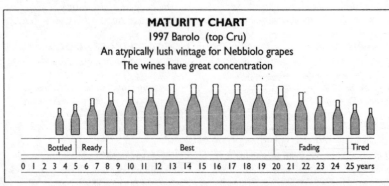

MATURITY CHART
1997 Barolo (top Cru)
An atypically lush vintage for Nebbiolo grapes
The wines have great concentration

Bottled	Ready	Best	Fading	Tired

0 1 2 3 4 5 6 7 8 9 10 11 12 13 14 15 16 17 18 19 20 21 22 23 24 25 years

SOAVE, DOC (Veneto; white) Usually attractive, soft, fair-priced white; slightly nutty, even creamy. Drink it as young as possible. *Bertani, Pasqua* and *Zenato* make a lot of decent basic stuff. On a higher level are *Anselmi* (try *Capitel Foscarino*) and *Pieropan,* especially single-vineyard wines *Calvarino* and *La Rocca.* Other good ones are *Bolla's Castellaro, Boscaini, Costalunga, Inama, Lenotti, Santi's Monte Carbonare, Tedeschi's Monte Tenda, Zenato* and the local co-operative's *Costalta. Anselmi* also makes a *Recioto di Soave I Capitelli* which is shockingly good in its pungent sweet-sour way, and *Pieropan's* unoaked *Recioto di Soave* is gorgeously redolent of apricots. Quality is better than it used to be, though it still pays to look for a top producer.

SPANNA (Piedmont; red) A Nebbiolo-based wine with a lovely raisin and chocolate flavour in the old style. Even cheap Spannas are a pretty good bet.

TAURASI, DOCG (Campania; red) Remarkable, plummy yet bitingly austere red, sometimes short on fruit or long on tannin, but worth trying. Tops: *Caggiano, Feudi di San Gregorio, Mastroberardino.*

TOCAI, DOC (Friuli, Veneto; white) Full, aromatic, softly nutty, honeyed wines. Best producers include: *Abbazia di Rosazzo, Borgo Conventi, Cà Bolani, Caccese, Collavini, Livio Felluga, Lazzarini, Maculan, Schiopetto, Villa Russiz, Volpe Pasini.*

TORGIANO, DOC and **DOCG** (Umbria; red, white) The region's fame rests on *Lungarotti.* The reds are strong, plummy, sometimes overbearing, usually carrying the trade name *Rubesco.* Quality is not as tip-top as it once was. Single-vineyard *Monticchio* and *San Giorgio* Cabernet Sauvignon are exciting. Torgiano Rosso Riserva is DOCG. White wines are clean and good. Lungarotti also makes good *flor*-affected sherry-type wine called *Solleone.*

TRENTINO, DOC (red, white) Some of Italy's best Pinot Bianco and Chardonnay comes from here, as well as some interesting whites from Riesling, Müller-Thurgau and excellent dry Muscat. Trento Classico DOC applies to Champagne-method sparkling wines. Look out especially for *Conti Martini, Gaierhof, Istituto di San Michele, Mandelli, Pojer e Sandri, Spagnolli* and *Zeni.* Fair *vin santo* comes from *Pisoni* and *Simoncelli.* Reds are made either from local grape varieties such as Lagrein, Teroldego and Marzemino, or the likes of Cabernet, Merlot and Pinot Noir. Go for *Conti Martini, Foradori, Guerrieri-Gonzaga, Istituto di San Michele, Pojer e Sandri, de Tarczal* and *Zeni.*

VALPOLICELLA, DOC (Veneto; red) This *should* have delicious, light, cherry fruit and a bitter almond twist to the finish – a bit fuller and deeper than Bardolino with a hint more sourness. Superiore has been aged for a year before release. Most of the commercial stuff is compared locally to twice-skimmed milk – i.e. insipid. Producers with good flavours: *Allegrini, Boscaini, Corte Sant'Alda, Guerrieri-Rizzardi, Masi, Quintarelli, Le Ragose, Santi, Tedeschi, Zenato.*

There are a few single-vineyard wines, like *Masi's Serègo Alighieri,* which are way ahead. They cost more, of course, but *Allegrini's La Grola* or *Tedeschi's Ca' Nicalo* show what Valpolicella should be about. You might also look for wine made by the traditional *ripasso* method, in which new wine is pumped over the skins and lees of Recioto or Amarone, starting a re-fermentation and adding an exciting sweet-sour dimension. Try *Masi, Quintarelli* and *Tedeschi.*

Best of all is the weird and wonderful Amarone della Valpolicella. It's made from half-shrivelled grapes and has a brilliant array of flavours – sweet grapeskins, chocolate, plums and woodsmoke – and a shocking, penetrating sourness. The good stuff is about three times the price of simple Valpolicella, but it's still good value. Wine labelled as Recioto della Valpolicella will be sweet and may be excellent – but a little less strangely special. Best producers include: *Allegrini, Bertani, Masi, Quintarelli, Le Ragose* and *Tedeschi*.

VALTELLINA, DOC (Lombardy; red) Slightly stringy Nebbiolo, not much seen over here.

VERDICCHIO, DOC (Marche; white) Reliable rather than exciting – usually extremely dry, lean, clean, nutty with a streak of dry honey, sharpened by slightly green acidity. *Fazi-Battaglia's* single-vineyard vino da tavola *Le Moie* shows the potential. There is also some fizz. The two leading areas are Verdicchio dei Castelli di Jesi and Verdicchio di Matelica. The rarer Matelica wines often have more flavour. *Bucci, Garafoli* and *Umani Ronchi* use new oak for their best wines. Also: *Brunori, Fabrini, Fazi-Battaglia, Mecvini, Monte Schiavo, Zaccagnini*.

VERDUZZO, DOC (Friuli and Veneto) This is usually a soft, nutty, low-acid yet refreshing light white. The DOC also includes a lovely, gentle fizz, and some of Italy's best sweet wines, in particular *Abbazia di Rosazzo's Amabile* and *Dri's Verduzzo di Ramandolo*.

VERNACCIA DI SAN GIMIGNANO DOCG (Tuscany) Can be attractively nutty, but the cheapest ones can be dull. Good: *Fagiuoli, Falchini, Frigeni, San Quirico, Teruzzi & Puthod* and *La Torre*.

VINO NOBILE DI MONTEPULCIANO, DOCG (Tuscany) Like Chianti only more so: more pepper, acid and tannin, and a higher price, but the best has a marvellous dry fragrance reminiscent almost of sandalwood, backed up by good Sangiovese spice, and a strong plumskins-and-cherries fruit. Look out for the following producers: *Avignonesi, Bindella, Boscarelli, La Casalte, Fassati, Fattoria di Casale, Fattoria del Cerro, Fognano, Poliziano* and *Trerose*.

VIN SANTO Can be one of the great sweet wines, but too often vaguely raisiny and very dull. It *should* have all kinds of splendid, rich fruit flavours – apricots, apples, the chewiness of toffee, smoke and liquorice. Try *Avignonesi, La Calonica* or *Isole e Olena* in Tuscany or *Adanti* in Umbria.

PRODUCERS WHO'S WHO

ABBAZIA DELL'ANNUNZIATA ★★ (Piedmont) One of the great producers of Barolo. All the wines are full of excitement and strongly perfumed, and they develop wonderfully in the bottle.

ALLEGRINI ★★ (Veneto) Splendid single-vineyard Valpolicellas, especially La Grola, Fieramonte and Palazzo della Torre. Top Amarone and Recioto. Also excellent vino da tavola, La Poja.

ELIO ALTARE ★★★ (Piedmont) New-wave producer – wines of firm structure and tannin behind perfumed fruit. Highly successful Barolo Vigneto Arborina, good Dolcetto and barrique-aged Langhe Larigi.

ALTESINO ★ (Tuscany) Excellent Brunello and some good vini da tavola, notably under the names of Alte d'Altesi and Palazzo Altesi.

CASTELLO DI AMA ★★ (Tuscany) Excellent single-vineyard Chianti Classico: San Lorenzo, La Casuccia, Bellavista; also a Merlot, Vigna L'Apparita.

ANSELMI ★★ (Veneto) Soave with character. Cru Capitel Foscarino is as good as it gets – as is his Recioto I Capitelli.

ANTINORI ★★★ (Tuscany) One of the great names of Chianti. Excellent Chianti Classico from estates Pèppoli and Badia a

Passignano; also Tignanello, the archetypal barrique-aged Sangiovese/Cabernet blend. Solaia has more Cabernet. Orvieto estate, Castello della Sala, makes wonderful IGT white, Cervaro della Sala. Brother Ludovico Antinori makes Ornellaia, a Cabernet-based superstar, and outstanding Masseto Merlot.

AVIGNONESI ★★★ (Tuscany) Serious Vino Nobile, and two excellent Chardonnays: Terre di Cortona, without oak, and Il Marzocco, an oak-fermented and aged wine of some considerable depth. I Grifi is barrel-aged Prugnolo and Cabernet Franc.

BADIA A COLTIBUONO ★★ (Tuscany) Produces good Chianti and even better 'Sangioveto', an IGT Toscana made from old vines.

BANFI ★★ (Tuscany) US-owned Montalcino winery making an excellent Brunello Poggio all'Oro, superb red blends, Summus and Excelsus, plus Tavernelle Cabernet and Mandrielle Merlot, amid a lot of other duller stuff.

FATTORIA DEI BARBI ★★ (Tuscany) Traditional methods produce serious Brunello and Rosso di Montalcino, as well as Brusco dei Barbi, and a single-vineyard wine, Vigna Fiore.

BIONDI-SANTI ★★ (Tuscany) Fabulously priced, but not always fabulous Brunello di Montalcino; old vintages are wonderful, new ones seem to be on the up after a long dip.

BOLLA (Veneto) Large scale producer of Soave and Valpolicella. Skip the basic wines and go for Valpolicella Jago.

BRAIDA-GIACOMO BOLOGNA ★★ (Piedmont) Saw early the potential of Barbera in barrique: deep, balanced and rich *cru* Bricco dell' Uccellone impresses. Equally good Bricco della Bigotta. Unoaked,

---

INSTANT CELLAR:
ONLY THE NORTH

- **1999 Gavi di Gavi Vigneti Montessora, La Giustiniana, £13.95, Liberty Wines** Wonderful intense apple fruit, all sappiness and freshness, from a grape which is always expensive and hardly ever as good as this.
- **1998 Dolcetto d'Alba, Aldo Conterno, £10.95, Liberty Wines** Classy Dolcetto that will benefit from some extra aging, from one of the country's top producers.
- **1997 Amarone della Valpolicella, Tedeschi, £12.99, Majestic** Wonderfully rich red full of prunes and bitter cherries.
- **1998 Pin, Monferrato Rosso, La Spinetta, £18.50, The Wine Society** Yes, I promise it really is called Pin. It's from Piedmont, and is made from half Nebbiolo and a quarter each from Barbera and Cabernet. It's weighty and complex.
- **1999 Teroldego Rotaliano, Foradori, £10, John Armit Wines** Wonderfully tight, elegant stuff from a Trentino name.
- **1998 Langhe Nenniolo, G D Vajra, £10.98, Bacchus** Barolo is so pricy now that even trading down isn't cheap. But this is from an excellent producer, and has plenty of class.

---

youthful Barbera, La Monella. Good Moscato d'Asti and Brachetto d'Acqui.

CA'DEL BOSCO ★★ (Lombardy) Good fizz from Franciacorta. Also vino da tavola called Maurizio Zanella, blended from both Cabernets and Merlot, which is expensive but terrific.

CAPARZO ★★ (Tuscany) High quality producer of Brunello di Montalcino and Rosso di Montalcino; also an oak-fermented Chardonnay called Le Grance, and Ca' del Pazzo, a barrique-aged blend of Cabernet Sauvignon and Sangiovese.

TENUTA DI CAPEZZANA ★★ (Tuscany) The leader in Carmignano, plus good Bordeaux blend, Ghiaie della Furba; Sangiovese-based Barco Reale; complex *vin santo* and delicious pink *vin ruspo*.

CASTELLARE ★★ (Tuscany) Nice Chianti, splendid vino da tavola I Sodi di San Niccolò, with a little Malvasia Nera adding perfume to the Sangiovese.

CERETTO ★★ (Piedmont) Barolo Bricco Rocche Bricco Rocche (yes!) and Barbaresco Bricco Asili are legendary with prices to match. Light Barbera and Dolcetto. Arneis is disappointing.

FATTORIA DEL CERRO ★ (Tuscany) Traditional producer of Vino Nobile, now working with barriques. Its best wine remains the DOCG Vino Nobile.

CLERICO ★★★ (Piedmont) Top modern producer; fine Nebbiolo-Barbera blend Arte, Barolo from two *crus* (Bricotto Bussia, Ciabot Mentin Ginestra).

ALDO CONTERNO ★★ (Piedmont) Great Barolo, traditionally made, slow to mature but worth the wait. Barbera d'Alba, Langhe Nebbiolo and Chardonnay, and Dolcetto also good.

GIACOMO CONTERNO ★★★ (Piedmont) Aldo's brother, making excellent traditional Barolo, plus top Dolcetto, Barbera and Friesa.

CONTERNO-FANTINO ★★ (Barolo, Monforte) Guido Fantino and Diego Conterno have earned a reputation for fine Barolo from the Ginestra hillside. Rich but forward, perfumed wines.

PAOLO CORDERO DI MONTEZEMOLO ★★ (Piedmont) The accent is on fruit. Standard-bearer is *cru* Monfalletto from La Morra. *Cru* Enrico VI is from Castiglione Falletto, refined, elegant, scented. Also Barbera and Dolcetto.

CARLO DELTETTO ★ (Roero, Canale) Good understated, intriguing whites from Arneis and Favorita. Reliable Roero and Gavi.

FELSINA BERARDENGA ★★ (Tuscany) Winery very much on the up. Vigneto Rancia single-vineyard Chianti, I Sistri barrique-aged Chardonnay. Fontalloro Sangiovese aged in barrique for a year.

FORADORI ★★★ (Trentino) The star of Trentino, making compact, powerful wines. Look for the Teroldegos.

FONTODI ★★ (Tuscany) Sleek Sangiovese, in the form of single-estate Chianto Classico or IGT red Flaccianello (plus white Meriggio, Pinot Bianco, Sauvignon and Traminer).

FRESCOBALDI ★★ (Tuscany) The best Frescobaldi estate is Castello di Nipozzano. Also excellent Pomino, including an oak-aged white, Il Benefizio. Excellent Brunello from the Castelgiocondo estate, plus good white under the Capitolato label and fine Cabernet Mormoreto red. A joint venture with Mondavi of California has produced a high-priced red, Luce.

ANGELO GAJA ★★★ (Piedmont) Innovative winemaker whose latest coup has been to renounce the Barbaresco and Barolo DOCGs for his best wines. His single-vineyard Barbarescos Costa Russi, Sorì San Lorenzo and Sorì Tildìn are now sold under the Langhe DOC. Barolo's Sperss and Conteisa are outstanding too.

BRUNO GIACOSA ★★★ (Piedmont) Traditional wines of, at their best, mind-blowing quality, especially Barbaresco *cru* Santo Stefano and, best of all, Vigna Rionda Barolo. Rich, concentrated but not overbearing, elegant. Also white Arneis and good fizz.

MARCHESI DI GRESY ★★ (Piedmont) The leading site, Martinenga, produces Barbaresco, two *crus* – Camp Gros and Gaiun – and a non-wood-aged Nebbiolo called Martinenga; all are elegant. Notable Sauvignon and Chardonnay, too.

ISOLE E OLENA ★★★ (Tuscany) Fine Chianti Classico. Also Cepparello, a rich pure Sangiovese wine, made from the oldest vines of the estate; outstanding sweet *vin santo* and a superb Syrah.

JERMANN (Friuli-Venezia Giulia) **★★★** Characterful, subtle vini da tavola: oak-aged Vintage Tunina and Chardonnay 'Were Dreams, Now it is just Wine'. Plain Pinot Grigio and Riesling are also very good.

LUNGAROTTI ★★ (Umbria) The main name in Torgiano. Also Chardonnays, Miralduolo and Vigna I Palazzi. San Giorgio is Cabernet plus Sangiovese.

GIUSEPPE MASCARELLO ★★★ (Piedmont) Superb *cru* Barolo Monprivato. Also Villero and other *crus*. Barbera d'Alba Ginestra is notable. Excellent inky Dolcetto.

MASI ★★★ (Veneto) Very good Soave and Valpolicella, especially Valpolicella Campo Fiorin. Brilliant Amarone and Recioto. Toar is oaky, cherryish new red vino da tavola.

MASTROBERARDINO ★★★ (Campania) Leading southern producer. Noteworthy Taurasi, and whites including Fiano di Avellino and Greco di Tufo.

MONTEVERTINE ★★★ (Tuscany) Outstanding Le Pergole Torte, a barrique-aged Sangiovese IGT Toscana, needs at least five years to open up. Il Sodaccio Sangiovese/Canaiolo can be drunk young.

CASTELLO DI NEIVE ★★ (Piedmont) Impeccable, finely crafted, austerely elegant Barbaresco from Santo Stefano. Barrique-aged Barbera from single *cru* Mattarello, firm, classic Dolcetto and revelatory Arneis.

FRATELLI ODDERO ★★ (Piedmont) Barolo, Barbera and Dolcetto from vineyards in prime sites in the area, plus Barbaresco from bought-in grapes. Good roundness, balance, style and value.

PIEROPAN ★★★ (Veneto) Stunning Soave, in particular La Rocca and Calvarino, both single vineyards. Recioto Le Colombare is divine.

POJER & SANDRI ★ (Trentino) Good quality in reds and whites, and particularly good spumante.

QUINTARELLI ★★ (Veneto) Excellent Valpolicella, especially Amarone and Recioto, though all are equally splendid in my opinion.

REGALEALI ★ (Sicily) Wonderful IGT wines from local varieties: red Rosso del Conte and white Nozze d'Oro. Top Chardonnay. There is a good standard range, too.

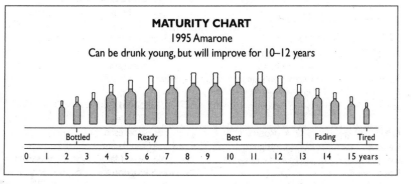

MATURITY CHART
1995 Amarone
Can be drunk young, but will improve for 10–12 years

Bottled	Ready	Best	Fading	Tired

0   1   2   3   4   5   6   7   8   9   10   11   12   13   14   15 years

ITALIAN VINTAGES

2000 Nebbiolo looks terrific, as do most of the reds of Central Italy. Whites in the North seem slightly less good.

1999 Some growers reckon their 1999s are better than their 1998s; others think the opposite. Tuscany seems to have come off well. Overall, a good rather than a great year.

1998 Patchy: go for Piedmontese reds and Tuscan reds, above all. Top Veneto growers will have made decent stuff.

1997 A very good year, but variable: some reds have low acidity and a slightly raisiny character. Central Italy produced excellent whites. Quantity is down, prices up.

1996 Very good for Piedmontese reds, pretty good for Tuscan reds. Variable elsewhere.

1995 Excellent Barolo and Barbaresco, though Dolcetto was below par. Valpolicella was very good, and there'll be wonderful Amarone and Recioto. Also very good for Central Italian reds, though whites had a less good year all over the country.

1994 Central Italy came off best, with good quality across the board. North-eastern whites are also pretty good. In the North-West, Dolcetto, Moscato and Arneis were very good, but now tired. Barbera and Nebbiolo were less good to begin with.

1993 Best in the North-East, where the whites had more richness, perfume, length – well, more of everything – than the 1992s, while the reds are excellent. Central Italy looks fair, and the North-West patchy, though Dolcetto was generally successful.

1992 Light, early-drinking wines were made across most of the country, though Carmignano is nearly as good as in 1990, and the Marche were also fortunate.

1991 A fragmented year. Fair to good overall in the North-West. Tuscany was outstanding, and the Marche, Torgiano, Veneto and Friuli were very good. Trentino-Alto Adige was less so.

1990 A fabulous vintage pretty well everywhere: wines of tremendous colour, richness and perfume, Barolo and Barbaresco for long aging and delicious Barbera. Wonderful Dolcetto again. Tuscan wines are built to last.

1989 Barbera d'Asti is very good, but needs drinking. Other reds are lighter.

1988 Dolcetto and Barbera have concentration and fruit. Nebbiolo is patchier. Tremendous quality in Central Italy and the North-East.

1987 Patchy Barolo and Barbaresco. Central Italian reds are reasonable.

1986 Barbaresco and Barolo are good. Chianti Riserva is very good, and Amarone della Valpolicella is lovely and drinking beautifully now.

1985 Big rich wines in Central Italy. An exciting vintage in the North-West, when more growers decided to emphasize fruit and perfume.

1983 Almost all fading now. Top Amarone is still good.

RICASOLI ★★ (Tuscany) Chianti is currently looking good. Also makes a host of other Tuscan wines at Brolio.

GIUSEPPE RIVETTI ★ (Piedmont) Smallish quantities of magical Moscato d'Asti which sell out in a flash.

RUFFINO ★ (Tuscany) Large Chianti house. Riserva Ducale is its best-known wine. Good IGT wines include lively Cabreo il Borgo (Cabernet) and succulent, oaky Chardonnay, Cabreo la Pietra. Romitorio di Santedame is Prugnolo (alias Sangiovese) and Colorino.

LUCIANO SANDRONE ★★ (Piedmont) A small producer making tiny quantities of perfumed new-style Barolo with lovely raspberry and black cherry flavours. Also excellent Dolcetto.

TENUTA SAN GUIDO ★★★ (Tuscany) Never heard the name? Well, they make Sassicaia, Italy's leading Cabernet. It used to be vino da tavola; now it has the DOC of Bolgheri.

PAOLO SCAVINO ★★ (Piedmont) Hailed as one of the new masters of Barolo: superb wines which combine purity of fruit with depth and structure. Barolo Bric' del Fiasc' is his top wine; Cannubi and straight Barolo are not far behind. Delicious Dolcetto and Barbera.

MARIO SCHIOPETTO ★ (Collio) Lovely whites from Pinot Grigio, Tocai etc, and white blend Rosis.

TERUZZI & PUTHOD ★★ (Tuscany) Commonly acknowledged to be the best producer of Vernaccia di San Gimignano. Its most expensive wine is the oak-aged Terre di Tufo. Whites include Terre di Tufi and Carmen.

VIETTI ★★★ (Piedmont) Classically perfect wines of their type, with a punch of acidity and tannin, plus elegance and class. Barolo (straight plus *crus* Rocche, Villero and Brunate) and Barbaresco (*normale* plus *crus* Masseria, Rabajà) are all intensely complex. Also, very good Dolcetto and Barbera, top Moscato d'Asti and very good Arneis.

ROBERTO VOERZIO ★★★ (Piedmont) Ultra-modern fine wines full of fruit and perfume, made with great skill, giving Roberto (brother Gianni is also on the up) a reputation as a rising star. There is Barolo, Dolcetto d'Alba, Barbera d'Alba, Freisa, and delicious barrique-aged Barbera/Nebbiolo blend Vignaserra. Fine Arneis is also to be had.

CASTELLO DI VOLPAIA ★★ (Tuscany) Leading Chianti estate with elegant wines. Balifico Sangiovese/Cabernet is exotic and oaky-rich; Coltassala is lovely, austere Sangiovese that needs time. Torniello is Sauvignon/Sémillon.

WINE-FINDER: ITALY

In the Price Guides on the next 18 pages, we have divided Italy into the following geographical regions: North-West, North-East, Central and Southern. If you are unsure which part of the country the wine you're looking for comes from, this guide should help. See also the map on page 365.

Asti – *North-West Sparkling*
Barbaresco – *North-West Red*
Barbera – *North-West Red*
Barolo – *North-West Red*
Brunello di Montalcino – *Central Red*
Chianti – *Central Red*
Dolcetto – *North-West Red*
Frascati – *Central White*
Vino Nobile di Montepulciano – *Central Red*
Montepulciano d'Abruzzo – *Central Red*
Orvieto – *Central White*
Soave – *North-East White*
Valpolicella – *North-East Red*
Verdicchio – *Central White*

ITALY PRICES

NORTH-WEST RED

Under £7.00

Barbera d'Alba Punset 1994 £5.99 (WAT)
Barbera d'Asti Ceppi Storici, Araldica
  1998 £5.75 (SOM) £5.99 (VA)
Barbera d'Asti Gemma 1996 £6.65 (CON)
Dolcetto d'Alba Gemma 1998 £6.75 (BALL)

£7.00 → £7.99

Barbera d'Alba Enzo Bogletti 1999 £7.95
  (WS)
Barbera d'Asti Ca' Bianca 1998 £7.95 (BALL)
Bonarda Oltrepò Pavese, Castello di
  Luzzano 1996 £7.95 (RAE)
Dolcetto d'Alba Elio Altare 1996 £7.90
  (JU)
Dolcetto d'Alba, Corino 1996 £7.50 (JU)
Dolcetto d'Alba Enzo Bogletti 1999
  £7.25 (WS)
Dolcetto d'Alba Gemma 1997 £7.25
  (CON)
Dolcetto d'Alba Prunotto 1999 £7.49
  (NEZ)
Dolcetto d'Alba Albino Rocca 1996 £7.90
  (JU)
Dolcetto d'Alba Viberti 2000 £7.59 (BIB)
Dolcetto di Dogliani, Francesco Boschis
  1998 £7.95 (JU)
Monferrato Airone, Chiarlo 1998 £7.99
  (OD)
Nebbiolo delle Langhe Settimo 1997
  £7.95 (WAT)

£8.00 → £9.99

Barbera d'Alba Elio Altare 1998 £9.95 (DI)
Barbera d'Alba Albino Rocca 1995 £8.90
  (JU)
Barbera d'Alba Vigna Vigia, Bricco
  Maiolica 1996 £9.95 (LEA)
Barbera d'Asti, Bertelli 1996 £9.90 (JU)
Barolo Terre del Barolo 1994 £9.17 (FLE)

Bonarda Oltrepò Pavese, Castello di
  Luzzano 1991 £8.95 (RAE)
Dolcetto d'Alba Elio Altare 1998 £8.99
  (DI)
Dolcetto d'Alba, Azelia 1999 £9.50 (JU)
Dolcetto d'Alba Cascina Morassino
  Bianco Mauro 1998 £8.62 (PEN)
Dolcetto d'Alba Clerico 1996 £8.50 (JU)
Dolcetto d'Alba Aldo Conterno 1996
  £8.50 (CRO)
Dolcetto d'Alba Sandrone 1999 £9.30
  (TAN)
Dolcetto d'Alba Sandrone 1996 £9.99
  (RAE)
Dolcetto d'Alba Vajra 1999 £9.99 (VIL)
  £10.49 (LIB)
Dolcetto di Dogliani Sori S. Martino,
  Boschis 1998 £9.99 (DI) £10.29 (YOU)
Dolcetto di Dogliani Sori S. Martino,
  Boschis 1997 £9.95 (JU)
Gutturnio dei Colli Piacentini, Castello di
  Luzzano 1991 £9.95 (RAE)
Monferrato Airone, Chiarlo 1995 £9.99
  (DI)
Monferrato Rosso Il Baciale, Braida di
  Giacomo Bologna 1998 £8.65 (TAN)
  £9.95 (BAL)
Monferrato Rosso Il Baciale, Braida di
  Giacomo Bologna 1996 £9.90 (CRO)
Nebbiolo d'Alba Valmagiore, Bruno
  Giacosa 1997 £9.95 (SOM)
Nebbiolo delle Langhe Cascina Morassino
  1997 £9.99 (PEN)
Spanna Dessilani 1995 £8.50 (RAE)

£10.00 → £12.49

Barbaresco Punset 1995 £11.65 (WAT)
Barbera d'Alba Elio Altare 1999 £10.50
  (JU)
Barbera d'Alba Bric Bertu, Angelo Negro
  & Figli 1998 £10.50 (GW)
Barbera d'Alba Aldo Conterno 1994
  £12.10 (SOM)

RETAILERS SPECIALIZING IN ITALY
see Retailers Directory (page 40) for details

Adnams (AD), Bennetts (BEN), Bibendum (BIB), Butlers Wine Cellar (BU), Anthony Byrne (BY), Cockburns of Leith (COC), Direct Wine Shipments(DI), Lay & Wheeler (LAY), Lea & Sandeman (LEA), Liberty (LIB), James Nicholson (NI), Reid Wines, Roberson, T&W (TW),Valvona & Crolla (VA), Wine Treasury (WT).

Barbera d'Alba Vigna Vigia, Bricco
  Maiolica **1998** £10.50 (LEA)
Barbera d'Alba Vignota, Conterno-
  Fantino **1999** £11.49 (YOU)
Barbera d'Asti Superiore Arbest, Bava
  1996 £12.49 (NEZ)
Barolo Ascheri **1993** £10.72 (FLE)
Barolo Terre del Barolo **1996** £10.99
  (TES) £10.99 (SAF)
Carema Ferrando **1990** £10.90 (BAC)
  £18.99 (RAE)
Dolcetto d'Alba Aldo Conterno **1998**
  £10.95 (LIB) £10.99 (BEN) £10.99 (VIL)
  £13.33 (ARM)
Dolcetto d'Alba Bruno Giacosa **1998**
  £10.00 (ARM)
Dolcetto d'Alba Sandrone **1997** £10.99
  (RAE)
Dolcetto di Dogliani Vigna dei Prey,
  Boschis **1998** £10.90 (JU) £10.99 (YOU)
Dolcetto di Dogliani Vigna Tecc, Luigi
  Einaudi **1998** £10.75 (LEA) £11.95 (BAL)
Inferno Nino Negri **1997** £11.99 (VA)
Nebbiolo d'Alba Valmagiore, Bruno
  Giacosa **1998** £12.08 (ARM) £13.25
  (BU)
Nebbiolo delle Langhe Vajra **1999** £11.99
  (BO) £12.95 (LIB)
Nebbiolo delle Langhe Vajra **1998** £12.44
  (SAV) £12.90 (BAC) £12.95 (POR) £12.99
  (VIL)
Nebbiolo Marengo **1996** £11.50 (JU)
Oltrepo Pavese Vino Cuore, Cabanon
  1998 £10.35 (JER)
Ronco di Mompiano, Pasolini **1985**
  £11.50 (CRO)

£12.50 → £14.99

Barbaresco Campo Quadro, Punset **1995**
  £13.55 (WAT)
Barbera d'Alba Sandrone **1998** £12.85
  (TAN)
Barbera d'Alba Ciabot della Luna, Gianni
  Voerzio **1999** £14.17 (ARM)
Barbera d'Alba Aldo Conterno **1999**
  £13.75 (ARM)
Barbera d'Alba Aldo Conterno **1998**
  £14.58 (ARM) £17.95 (LIB) £17.99 (VIL)
Barolo Cordana, Castiglione Falletto
  1996 £13.95 (SOM)
Barolo Settimo **1995** £13.50 (WAT)
Dolcetto d'Alba Aldo Conterno **1999**
  £12.50 (ARM)
Dolcetto d'Alba Aldo Conterno **1997**
  £13.75 (ARM)

Dolcetto di Dogliani I Filiari, Luigi Einaudi
  1998 £14.50 (BAL)
Inferno Aldo Rainoldi **1995** £14.95 (MAY)
Nebbiolo d'Alba Il Cumot, Bricco
  Maiolica **1998** £12.95 (LEA)

£15.00 → £19.99

Barbaresco Cascina Morassino **1995**
  £16.24 (PEN)
Barbaresco Marchesi di Barolo **1993**
  £15.75 (FRI)
Barbaresco Punset **1996** £18.50 (FORT)
Barbaresco Ronchi Albino Rocca **1994**
  £16.00 (JU)
Barbaresco Serraboella, Cigliuti **1996**
  £19.95 (BAN)
Barbera d'Alba Carati, Paulo Scavino
  1997 £19.00 (JU)
Barbera d'Alba Carati, Paulo Scavino
  1996 £18.95 (DI)
Barbera d'Alba Conca Tre Pile, Aldo
  Conterno **1998** £17.35 (BEN)
Barbera d'Alba Aldo Conterno **1997**
  £16.95 (CON) £21.10 (NI)
Barbera d'Alba Scarrone, Vietti **1998**
  £19.95 (RES)
Barbera d'Alba Paulo Scavino **1998**
  £16.67 (ARM)
Barbera d'Alba Paulo Scavino **1997**
  £16.67 (ARM)
Barbera d'Asti Giarone, Bertelli **1993**
  £16.50 (JU)
Barolo Brunate, Marcarini **1994** £18.70
  (BAC)
Barolo Fontanafredda **1996** £18.50 (STA)
Barolo Marchesi di Barolo **1994** £17.95
  (FRI)
Barolo Monfalletto, Monfalletto-Cordero
  di Montezemolo **1994** £18.25 (STE)
Barolo Sorano, Ascheri **1995** £19.80 (SAV)
Barolo Vigneti Castello Riserva, Terre del
  Barolo **1993** £19.99 (SAF)
Cabernet del Piemonte I Fossaretti,
  Bertelli **1993** £18.00 (JU)
Freisa delle Langhe Vajra **1998** £19.95
  (LIB)
Monferrato Rosso Pin, La Spinetta **1998**
  £18.50 (WS) £28.00 (BAL)
Nebbiolo d'Alba Pio Cesare **1997** £19.95
  (FORT)
Nebbiolo d'Alba San Michele, Vietti **1993**
  £15.13 (PEN)
Sito Moresco, Gaja **1995** £19.95 (BEN)
Sito Moresco, Gaja **1993** £15.95 (DI)
St Marsan, Bertelli **1995** £16.50 (JU)

£20.00 → £29.99

Arte Clerico **1998** £23.00 (JU)
Arte Clerico **1997** £21.00 (JU) £21.99 (YOU)
Barbaresco Sori Paitin, Paitin **1996** £25.99
(WIN)
Barolo Azelia **1995** £21.99 (YOU) £22.00
(JU)
Barolo Brunate, Marcarini **1995** £20.99
(RAE)
Barolo Brunate, Marengo **1996** £28.00
(JU) £31.72 (BODX)
Barolo Bussia, Prunotto **1993** £27.00
(CRO)
Barolo Cannubi, Luigi Einaudi **1996**
£29.95 (LEA) £32.99 (YOU) £38.00 (BAL)
Barolo Chiarlo **1995** £25.50 (DI)
Barolo Ciabot Mentin Ginestra, Clerico
1995 £27.81 (FA)
Barolo Conteisa Cerequio, Gromis **1993**
£22.42 (ARM) £29.75 (LAY) £34.17 (MI)
Barolo Fontanafredda **1971** £25.00 (BU)
Barolo Fontanafredda **1969** £20.00 (BU)
Barolo Paulo Scavino **1996** £26.00 (JU)
Barolo Viberti **1997** £24.97 (BIB)
Barolo Vigna dei Pola, Ascheri **1996**
£22.95 (STA)
Barolo Vigna Giachini, Corino **1996**
£25.00 (JU)
Bricco dell'Uccellone, Braida di Giacomo
Bologna **1998** £28.75 (LAY)
Bricco dell'Uccellone, Braida di Giacomo
Bologna **1997** £23.40 (BODX) £26.00
(BAL)
Bricco dell'Uccellone, Braida di Giacomo
Bologna **1996** £24.75 (TAN)
Bricco dell'Uccellone, Braida di Giacomo
Bologna **1995** £26.00 (CRO)
Monprà Conterno-Fantino **1998** £21.99
(YOU)
Monprà Conterno-Fantino **1997** £21.49
(YOU)
Nebbiolo delle Langhe Il Favot, Aldo
Conterno **1998** £29.99 (VIL)
Sito Moresco, Gaja **1996** £20.49 (YOU)
£21.50 (LAY) £21.67 (ARM) £24.95 (RES)
Sitorey, Gaja **1996** £22.50 (ARM) £23.50
(FORT)
Vignaserra Roberto Voerzio **1996** £20.00
(BU)

A key to name abbreviations
is available on page 7.

£30.00 → £39.99

Barbaresco Gaja **1994** £39.00 (VA) £43.95
(BEN) £44.30 (LAY)
Barbaresco Bruno Giacosa **1996** £38.33
(ARM)
Barolo Arborina, Elio Altare **1996** £33.00
(JU)
Barolo Azelia **1996** £31.00 (JU)
Barolo Bricco Fiasco, Azelia **1996** £34.66
(BODX)
Barolo Bussia Soprana, Aldo Conterno
1997 £38.95 (LIB)
Barolo Bussia Soprana, Aldo Conterno
1996 £30.75 (SOM) £37.25 (CON)
£37.99 (VIL) £38.50 (BEN) £39.00 (POR)
Barolo Bussia Soprana, Aldo Conterno
1994 £34.56 (NO) £34.99 (VA)
Barolo Cannubi Boschis, Sandrone **1991**
£39.50 (RAE)
Barolo Cascina Francia, Giacomo
Conterno **1994** £35.67 (ARM)
Barolo Ciabot Mentin Ginestra, Clerico
1996 £33.50 (JU)
Barolo la Serra di la Morra, Roberto
Voerzio **1996** £30.76 (ARM)
Barolo la Serra di la Morra, Roberto
Voerzio **1995** £35.64 (BODX)
Barolo Riserva Marchesi di Barolo **1990**
£39.95 (FRI)
Barolo Sori Ginestra, Conterno-Fantino
1996 £30.99 (YOU)
Barolo Sperss, Gaja **1994** £35.83 (ARM)
£50.00 (FORT) £53.50 (BEN)
Barolo Vigna Rocche, Corino **1996**
£30.00 (JU)
Barolo Le Vigne, Sandrone **1995** £32.90
(TAN)
Darmagi Gaja **1986** £39.00 (VA) £72.00
(CRO)
Nebbiolo delle Langhe Il Favot, Aldo
Conterno **1997** £31.50 (BEN)

£40.00 → £49.99

Barbaresco Bruno Giacosa **1988** £41.13
(FA)
Barbaresco Il Bricco, Pio Cesare **1995**
£40.00 (FORT)
Barolo Bricco Bussia Colonello, Aldo
Conterno **1996** £48.50 (BEN) £49.99 (VIL)
Barolo Bricco Bussia Colonello, Aldo
Conterno **1993** £48.50 (VA)
Barolo Bussia, Prunotto **1990** £47.00 (FA)
Barolo Cannubi, Prunotto **1989** £47.00
(FA)

Barolo Cannubi Boschis, Sandrone **1998**
£49.84 (BODX)

Barolo la Serra di la Morra, Roberto
Voerzio **1994** £40.00 (VA)

Barolo Pajana, Clerico **1996** £44.45 (FA)

Barolo Sperss, Gaja **1991** £41.13 (FA)
£68.00 (VA)

Barolo Vigna del Gris, Conterno-Fantino
1990 £48.00 (BEN)

Barolo Le Vigne, Sandrone **1998** £45.43
(BODX)

Darmagi Gaja **1994** £43.33 (ARM) £75.00
(MI)

£50.00 → £99.99

Barbaresco Costa Russi, Gaja **1993**
£61.10 (FA) £115.00 (VA)

Barbaresco Costa Russi, Gaja **1988**
£94.00 (FA)

Barbaresco Gaja **1997** £65.00 (ARM)
£66.00 (FA) £67.46 (BODX)

Barbaresco Gaja **1996** £53.33 (ARM)
£59.63 (BODX) £71.67 (MI) £78.00 (RES)

Barbaresco Gaja **1995** £54.25 (FA)

Barbaresco Gaja **1993** £65.00 (VA)

Barbaresco Gaja **1990** £70.50 (FA) £95.00
(CRO) £110.00 (VA)

Barbaresco Gaja **1989** £85.00 (VA)
£141.67 (MI)

Barbaresco Gaja **1988** £55.00 (VA) £58.75
(FA)

Barbaresco Gaja **1983** £85.00 (BU)

Barbaresco Gaja **1978** £89.50 (FA)
£166.55 (TW)

Barbaresco Gaja **1971** £75.00 (VA)

Barbaresco Gallina di Neive, Bruno
Giacosa **1996** £57.17 (ARM)

Barbaresco Gallina di Neive, Bruno
Giacosa **1995** £95.00 (VA)

Barbaresco Sori San Lorenzo, Gaja **1993**
£61.10 (FA) £115.00 (VA)

Barbaresco Sori San Lorenzo, Gaja **1988**
£94.00 (FA)

Barbaresco Sori San Lorenzo, Gaja **1986**
£58.75 (FA)

Barbaresco Sori San Lorenzo, Gaja **1981**
£60.00 (VA)

Barbaresco Sorì Tildìn, Gaja **1993** £61.10
(FA) £115.00 (VA)

Barbaresco Sorì Tildìn, Gaja **1988** £94.00
(FA)

Barolo Bricco Bussia Colonello, Aldo
Conterno **1989** £89.00 (VA)

Barolo Bricco Bussia Colonello, Aldo
Conterno **1988** £69.00 (VA)

Barolo Bricco Rocche Brunate, Ceretto
1990 £60.00 (VA)

Barolo Brunate, Vietti **1996** £60.00 (RES)

Barolo Brunate, Roberto Voerzio **1996**
£60.61 (BODX)

Barolo Bussia, Prunotto **1985** £55.23 (FA)

Barolo Bussia Soprana, Aldo Conterno
1990 £95.00 (VA)

Barolo Cannubi Boschis, Sandrone **1996**
£78.83 (ARM)

Barolo Cascina Francia, Giacomo
Conterno **1996** £64.58 (ARM)

Barolo Cascina Francia, Giacomo
Conterno **1995** £57.17 (ARM)

Barolo la Serra di la Morra, Roberto
Voerzio **1997** £79.21 (BODX)

Barolo Monprivato, Mascarello **1985**
£72.00 (BAL)

Barolo Riserva Borgogno **1985** £55.00
(VA)

Barolo Riserva Borgogno **1978** £57.00
(VA)

Barolo Riserva Borgogno **1971** £65.00
(VA)

Barolo Riserva Borgogno **1947** £65.00
(BU)

Barolo Riserva Marchesi di Barolo **1982**
£66.00 (FRI)

Barolo Rocche, Vietti **1996** £60.00 (RES)

Barolo Sperss, Gaja **1996** £60.00 (VA)
£77.75 (FA) £84.60 (BODX)

Barolo Sperss, Gaja **1995** £59.58 (ARM)
£77.50 (MI)

Barolo Sperss, Gaja **1993** £59.95 (LAY)

Barolo Sperss, Gaja **1990** £97.35 (NO)
£125.00 (VA) £141.67 (MI)

Barolo Sperss, Gaja **1989** £77.75 (FA)
£141.67 (MI)

Barolo Vigna Giachini, Corino **1990**
£55.00 (VA)

Barolo Le Vigne, Sandrone **1997** £82.15
(BODX)

Barolo Le Vigne, Sandrone **1996** £75.83
(ARM) £57.67 (BODX)

£100.00 → £149.99

Barbaresco Costa Russi, Gaja **1996**
£133.56 (BODX) £136.50 (FA) £175.00
(VA)

Barbaresco Costa Russi, Gaja **1995**
£113.98 (FA)

Barbaresco Costa Russi, Gaja **1990**
£142.37 (FA)

Barbaresco Costa Russi, Gaja **1985**
£141.00 (FA)

Barbaresco Sori San Lorenzo, Gaja **1996**
£132.78 (FA) £165.00 (VA)
Barbaresco Sori San Lorenzo, Gaja **1983**
£135.00 (VA)
Barbaresco Sorì Tildìn, Gaja **1996**
£132.78 (FA) £175.00 (VA)
Barolo Bricco Bussia Colonello, Aldo
Conterno **1990** £135.00 (VA)
Barolo Aldo Conterno **1971** £100.00 (VA)
Barolo Granbussia, Aldo Conterno **1990**
£126.90 (FA)
Barolo Monfortino Riserva, Giacomo
Conterno **1993** £110.00 (ARM)

Over £150.00

Barbaresco Costa Russi, Gaja **1982**
£160.00 (VA)
Barbaresco Gaja **1985** £195.00 (VA)
Barbaresco Gaja **1962** £175.00 (VA)
Barbaresco Sori San Lorenzo, Gaja **1995**
£165.00 (VA)
Barbaresco Sori San Lorenzo, Gaja **1985**
£152.75 (FA)
Barbaresco Sori San Lorenzo, Gaja **1982**
£160.00 (VA)
Barbaresco Sorì Tildìn, Gaja **1995**
£165.00 (VA)
Barbaresco Sorì Tildìn, Gaja **1982**
£180.00 (VA)
Barolo Granbussia, Aldo Conterno **1989**
£245.00 (VA)
Barolo Monfortino Riserva, Giacomo
Conterno **1988** £190.00 (VA)

NORTH-WEST WHITE

Under £6.00

Arneis del Roero, Malvirà **1998** £5.49
(OD)
Chardonnay del Piemonte, Alasia **1999**
£4.95 (WS)
Cortese del Piemonte, Araldica **2000**
£4.49 (VA)
Moscato d'Asti, Araldica **Non-vintage**
£3.95 (WS)

- *Wines are listed in A–Z order within each price band.*
- *For each wine, vintages are listed in descending order.*
- *Each vintage of any wine appears only once.*

Moscato d'Asti, Araldica **1999** £4.50 (SOM)
Moscato d'Asti, Araldica **1998** £3.99 (UN)
Moscato d'Asti, Araldica **1994** £5.43 (BY)
Moscato del Piemonte, Gemma **2000**
£3.89 (OD)

£6.00 → £7.99

Gavi Castello di Tassarolo **1999** £7.49 (MAJ)
Gavi La Chiara **2000** £6.49 (OD)
Gavi La Chiara **1998** £7.95 (TAN) £7.95
(BALL) £8.25 (CON)
Gavi La Raia **2000** £6.58 (BIB)

£8.00 → £9.99

Moscato d'Asti la Spinetta, Rivetti **1999**
£9.40 (SAV)
Traminer del Piemonte Plisse, Bertelli
1994 £9.95 (JU)

£10.00 → £19.99

Alteni di Brassica, Gaja **1995** £17.95 (VA)
Arneis del Roero Bruno Giacosa **1999**
£12.50 (ARM)
Chardonnay del Piemonte Giarone,
Bertelli **1995** £16.50 (JU)
Chardonnay Rossj Bass, Gaja **1997**
£19.99 (VA)
Gavi Pio Cesare **1998** £12.25 (FORT)
Langhe Il Fiore, Braida di Giacomo
Bologna **1999** £10.50 (GAU)
Monferrato Bianco Alteserre, Bava **1996**
£14.39 (TW)
St Marsan, Bertelli **1995** £14.90 (JU)

Over £20.00

Alteni di Brassica, Gaja **1997** £25.83
(ARM)
Alteni di Brassica, Gaja **1993** £41.12 (TW)
Chardonnay Gaia & Rey, Gaja **1998**
£43.75 (ARM)
Chardonnay Rossj Bass, Gaja **1999**
£20.00 (ARM) £24.95 (VA)
Rossj-Bass Gaja **1999** £21.90 (LAY)
Rossj-Bass Gaja **1998** £20.49 (YOU)

NORTH-WEST SPARKLING

Under £6.00

Asti Calissano **Non-vintage** £4.95 (BALL)
£5.99 (POR) £5.99 (JON)
Asti Cinzano **Non-vintage** £5.25 (COC)
Asti Martini **Non-vintage** £3.99 (TES)
£4.98 (ASD) £4.99 (UN) £4.99 (SAF) £5.49
(VIC) £5.49 (THR) £5.49 (BOT) £5.49 (WR)

£5.99 (BUD) £5.99 (SO) £5.99 (WAI)
£6.29 (OD) £6.57 (WHI) £6.75 (WRI)
£6.90 (STA) £6.99 (DI) £7.15 (VIN)
Asti Vigna Fiorita, Cantine Gemma Non-vintage £5.79 (CON)

£6.00 → £9.99

Asti Fontanafredda Non-vintage £8.95 (VA)

Over £10.00

Franciacorta Brut, Ca' del Bosco Non-vintage £15.00 (CRO) £17.99 (VA)

NORTH-EAST RED

Under £5.00

Merlot del Veneto, Canaletto 1999 £4.49 (BUD) £4.75 (BAL)
Merlot della Bergamasca, Cantina Sociale Bergamasca 2000 £4.79 (BIB)
Merlot della Bergamasca, Cantina Sociale Bergamasca ½ bottle 2000 £2.69 (BIB)
Merlot della Bergamasca, Cantina Sociale Bergamasca ½ bottle 1999 £2.69 (BIB)
Merlot della Bergamasca, Cantina Sociale Bergamasca ½ bottle 1998 £2.55 (BIB)

Valpolicella Classico Sartori 2000 £4.49 (UN)
Valpolicella Classico Superiore Zenato 1998 £4.99 (VIC) £4.99 (THR) £4.99 (BOT) £4.99 (WR)
Valpolicella Classico Superiore Zenato 1997 £4.99 (BOT) £4.99 (WR) £5.75 (STE)

£5.00 → £5.99

Breganza Rosso, Bartolomeo da Breganze 1996 £5.70 (BAC)
Trentino Cabernet Sauvignon Mezzacorona 1999 £5.99 (NEZ)
Trentino Merlot Mezzacorona 1999 £5.99 (NEZ)
Valpolicella Classico Allegrini 2000 £5.80 (SOM) £6.99 (LIB)
Valpolicella Classico Allegrini 1999 £5.75 (WS) £6.95 (POR) £6.95 (BAC) £7.25 (BEN)
Valpolicella Classico Masi 1999 £5.49 (OD)
Valpolicella Classico Superiore Tommasi 1998 £5.95 (FRI)
Valpolicella Classico Superiore Valverde, Tedeschi 1997 £5.65 (GN)
Valpolicella Classico Superiore Valverde, Tedeschi 1996 £5.99 (COC)

£6.00 → £7.99

Campofiorin Ripasso, Masi 1997 £7.99
(NEZ) £7.99 (OD)
Teroldego Rotaliano Dorigati 1997 £7.85
(CON)
Teroldego Rotaliano Riserva
Mezzacorona 1997 £6.99 (NEZ)
Trentino Rosso Maso Lodron, Letrari
1997 £6.75 (WS)
Valpolicella Classico Allegrini 1997 £7.90
(CRO)
Valpolicella Classico Superiore Allegrini
1998 £7.49 (HED)
Valpolicella Classico Superiore Capitel
San Rocco Vino di Rapasso, Tedeschi
1997 £7.99 (POR)
Valpolicella Classico Superiore Ripassa,
Zenato 1998 £7.99 (WR)
Venegazzù Cabernet Sauvignon
Venegazzù 1997 £6.92 (PEN)

£8.00 → £9.99

Valpolicella Classico la Grola, Allegrini
1997 £9.50 (WS) £10.25 (SOM) £11.90
(BEN) £12.85 (MAY)
Valpolicella Classico Palazzo della Torre,
Allegrini 1995 £9.83 (SUN)
Valpolicella Classico Superiore Palazzo
della Torre, Allegrini 1995 £9.99 (LAI)

£10.00 → £12.99

Amarone della Valpolicella Classico
Tedeschi 1997 £12.99 (MAJ) £14.99 (POR)
Amarone della Valpolicella Classico
Tedeschi 1995 £12.99 (SAF) £16.70
(COC)
Teroldego Rotaliano Foradori 1999
£10.00 (ARM)
Valpolicella Classico Palazzo della Torre,
Allegrini 1998 £12.99 (LIB)
Valpolicella Classico Palazzo della Torre,
Allegrini 1997 £11.90 (BAC) £13.95 (RES)
Valpolicella Classico Superiore La Grola,
Allegrini 1997 £11.95 (POR)
Valpolicella Classico Superiore La Grola,
Allegrini 1996 £12.50 (CON)
Vertigo Livio Felluga 1999 £12.95 (LIB)

- *All prices for each wine are listed
  together in ascending order.*
- *Price bands refer to the lowest price
  for which the wine is available.*

£13.00 → £14.99

Amarone della Valpolicella Classico, Ca'
Fornari 1995 £13.95 (CON)
Amarone della Valpolicella Masi 1997
£14.99 (OD)
Collio Cabernet Franc, Russiz Superiore
1996 £13.99 (NEZ)
Collio Merlot, Russiz Superiore 1997
£13.99 (NEZ)
Recioto della Valpolicella Classico Capitel
Monte Fontana, Tedeschi 1996 £14.99
(SUN) £14.99 (LAI) £15.99 (YOU)
Recioto della Valpolicella Classico Serègo
Alighieri, Masi 1998 £13.69 (OD)
Valpolicella Classico la Grola, Allegrini
1998 £13.75 (LIB)

£15.00 → £19.99

Amarone della Valpolicella Classico,
Zenato 1995 £17.99 (WR) £18.98 (STE)
Amarone della Valpolicella Classico
Allegrini 1996 £19.99 (SOM) £21.99 (VA)
£22.50 (WS) £23.95 (POR) £24.99 (YOU)
£25.00 (BEN) £26.95 (MAY) £27.95 (RES)
£30.74 (FA)
Amarone della Valpolicella Classico
Tedeschi 1996 £17.75 (GN)
Amarone della Valpolicella Tommasi
1995 £15.95 (AD)
Capo di Stato Venegazzù 1996 £19.98 (PEN)
Conte Federico, Bossi Fedrigotti 1990
£18.58 (NO)
Recioto della Valpolicella Classico
Allegrini 1993 £18.00 (CRO)
Teroldego Rotaliano Vigneto Sgarzon,
Foradori 1996 £15.95 (BAL)
Valpolicella Classico Superiore Quintarelli
1994 £17.63 (BIB)
Venegazzù della Casa, Venegazzù 1997
£15.86 (PEN)

£20.00 → £24.99

Amarone della Valpolicella Capitel Monte
Olmi, Tedeschi 1997 £24.99 (POR)
Amarone della Valpolicella Classico,
Tommaso Bussola 1996 £21.00 (BAL)
£24.10 (LAY)
La Poja, Allegrini 1996 £22.60 (SOM)
£27.99 (YOU) £28.50 (BEN) £28.50 (STA)
£29.95 (RES)
Teroldego Rotaliano Granato, Foradori
1998 £21.67 (ARM)
Teroldego Rotaliano Granato, Foradori
1995 £24.00 (BAL)

Over £25.00

Alzero Quintarelli **1994** £165.00 (BEN)
Amarone della Valpolicella Allegrini **1996**
£30.75 (BODX)
Amarone della Valpolicella Classico
Allegrini **1997** £30.95 (LIB)
Amarone della Valpolicella Classico
Allegrini **1995** £25.00 (HED)
Amarone della Valpolicella Quintarelli
1993 £86.16 (BIB) £115.00 (BEN)
Amarone della Valpolicella Riserva,
Quintarelli **1985** £65.00 (BU)
La Poja, Allegrini **1997** £32.95 (LIB)
La Poja, Allegrini **1995** £27.50 (CON)
Recioto della Valpolicella Quintarelli
1993 £76.38 (BIB)
Teroldego Rotaliano Granato, Foradori
1997 £26.83 (FA)

NORTH-EAST WHITE

Under £5.00

Friuli Grave Sauvignon San Simone **2000**
£4.85 (WAI)
Friuli Grave Tocai Friulano San Simone
1999 £4.50 (JU)
Pinot Bianco della Bergamasca, Cantina
Sociale Bergamasca **2000** £4.99 (BIB)
Pinot Grigio Bidoli **2000** £4.99 (UN)
Pinot Grigio Minini **2000** £4.70 (BIB)
Soave Classico Superiore Zenato **2000**
£4.99 (VIC) £4.99 (THR) £4.99 (WR)
Soave Classico Vigneto Colombara,
Zenato **2000** £4.95 (WAI)
Valdadige Pinot Grigio Cantina Sociale
della Valdadige Veronese **2000** £4.95
(LEA)

£5.00 → £5.99

Friuli Grave Pinot Grigio San Simone
2000 £5.45 (JU)
Lugana San Benedetto, Zenato **1999**
£5.95 (STE)
Lugana Villa Flora, Zenato **2000** £5.25
(WAI)
Pinot Grigio Le Due Terre **1999** £5.99
(JON)
Soave Classico Superiore Castelcerino
1999 £5.40 (TAN)
Soave Classico Superiore Castelcerino
1998 £5.49 (CON) £5.69 (JON)
★ Soave Classico Superiore Monte
Fiorentine, Ca' Rugate **2000** £5.99 (UN)

£6.00 → £7.99

Alto Adige Chardonnay Lageder **2000**
£6.96 (BIB)
Alto Adige Pinot Grigio Tiefenbrunner
2000 £6.50 (BAN)
Friuli Grave Pinot Grigio Le Fredis **1999**
£7.49 (CON)
Friuli Grave Pinot Grigio Le Monde **2000**
£6.53 (BIB)
Friuli Grave Sauvignon Le Fredis **1997**
£7.49 (CON)
Lugana Ca' dei Frati **2000** £6.85 (SOM)
Lugana Ca' dei Frati **1999** £7.90 (BAC)
£7.95 (POR) £7.99 (CON) £7.99 (VIL)
£8.95 (MAY)
Soave Classico Pieropan **1999** £7.95 (POR)
Soave Classico Pieropan **1998** £7.99 (HED)
Soave Classico Superiore Gini **1998**
£6.95 (JU)
Soave Classico Superiore Pieropan **1999**
£6.90 (BAC) £7.99 (VIL) £8.35 (STA) £8.99
(VA)
Valdadige Pinot Grigio Vigneti di
Castagnari, Cantina Sociale della
Valdadige Veronese **2000** £6.95 (LEA)

£8.00 → £9.99

Alto Adige Pinot Grigio Lageder **2000**
£8.11 (BIB)
Bianco di Custoza le Vigne di San Pietro
2000 £8.95 (LIB)
Collio Pinot Grigio Puiatti **1999** £9.50
(SOM)
Collio Sauvignon Vigna del Lauro **1998**
£8.45 (JER)
Lugana I Frati, Ca' dei Frati **2000** £8.45
(HAH)
Lugana I Frati, Ca' dei Frati **1999** £8.99
(VA) £9.20 (TAN)
Soave Classico Anselmi **1998** £8.50 (FORT)
Soave Classico Capitel Foscarino, Anselmi
1998 £8.80 (SOM)
Soave Classico la Frosca, Gini **1999** £9.90
(JU)
Soave Classico Monte Carbonare, Suavia
2000 £8.74 (BIB)
Soave Classico San Vincenzo, Anselmi
2000 £8.65 (NI)
Soave Classico Superiore Monte Alto, Ca'
Rugate **1999** £8.99 (VA)
Soave Classico Superiore Pieropan **2000**
£8.49 (LIB)
Soave Classico Superiore Pieropan **1998**
£9.89 (HIC)

Soave Classico Vigneto Calvarino,
   Pieropan 1998 £9.99 (POR)
Soave Classico Vigneto la Rocca, Pieropan
   1998 £9.50 (WS) £11.95 (POR) £12.95
   (BAL) £12.99 (VIL) £14.99 (VA)

£10.00 → £11.99

Lugana Il Brolettino, Ca' dei Frati 1998
   £10.99 (VIL)
Pinot Bianco Jermann 1997 £10.60 (SOM)
Recioto di Soave I Capitelli, Anselmi ½
   bottle 1997 £11.65 (NI)
Soave Classico Capitel Croce, Anselmi
   1999 £10.99 (YOU)
Soave Classico Vigneto Calvarino,
   Pieropan 1999 £11.99 (VIL) £12.99 (VA)
Soave Classico Vigneto la Rocca, Pieropan
   1999 £11.95 (POR)

£12.00 → £14.99

Chardonnay Jermann 1998 £13.99 (VIL)
   £14.99 (VA)
Collio Pinot Bianco Schiopetto 2000
   £12.50 (BAN)
Collio Pinot Grigio, Livio Felluga 2000
   £12.95 (LIB)
Collio Tocai Schiopetto 1998 £12.50
   (BAN)
Lugana Il Brolettino, Ca' dei Frati 1999
   £12.99 (VA)
Pinot Bianco Jermann 1999 £13.99 (VIL)
   £14.99 (VA)
Pinot Grigio Jermann 1999 £13.50 (STA)
   £13.99 (VIL) £14.99 (VA)
★ Recioto di Soave La Perlara, Ca' Rugate
   50cl 1998 £12.99 (VA)
Recioto di Soave Suavia 1999 £13.71 (BIB)
Riesling Renano, Jermann 1998 £13.99
   (VIL)
Soave Classico Capitel Croce, Anselmi
   1998 £12.95 (NI)
★ Torcolato Maculan ½ bottle 1998 £12.99
   (OD)

£15.00 → £19.99

Alto Adige Chardonnay Löwengang,
   Lageder 1998 £16.45 (BIB)
Recioto di Soave le Colombare, Pieropan
   1997 £16.99 (VIL)

Over £20.00

Vintage Tunina Jermann 1999 £23.49 (YOU)
Vintage Tunina Jermann 1998 £24.99 (VIL)
   £26.50 (BAL) £27.99 (VA)
Vintage Tunina Jermann 1995 £23.50 (STA)

NORTH-EAST SPARKLING

Under £8.00

Prosecco di Conegliano Carpenè Malvolti
   Non-vintage £7.95 (LEA)
Prosecco di Valdobbiadene Brut, Bortolin
   Non-vintage £6.99 (OD)
Prosecco Serafino Non-vintage £6.95 (JER)

CENTRAL RED

Under £4.00

Sangiovese di Toscana Cecchi 1999 £3.99
   (SAI) £3.99 (VIC) £3.99 (THR)

£4.00 → £4.99

Chianti Classico Querceto 1996 £4.95 (JU)
Chianti Querceto 1996 £4.95 (JU)
Chianti Rufina Villa di Vetrice 1998 £4.99
   (POR) £5.20 (SOM) £5.99 (VIL)
Col di Sasso Villa Banfi 1998 £4.98 (PEN)
   £4.99 (BO)
Montepulciano d'Abruzzo Minini 2000
   £4.31 (BIB)
Montepulciano d'Abruzzo Roxan 1999
   £4.99 (JON) £4.99 (BAL)
Montepulciano d'Abruzzo Cornacchia
   1999 £4.99 (MAJ) £5.49 (VA)
Montepulciano d'Abruzzo Cornacchia
   1998 £4.98 (PEN)
Montepulciano d'Abruzzo Cornacchia
   1997 £4.99 (BO)
Montepulciano d'Abruzzo Umani Ronchi
   1999 £4.99 (VIL)

£5.00 → £5.99

Chianti Rufina Grati 1997 £5.75 (BALL)
Chianti Rufina Villa di Vetrice 1997 £5.69
   (JON)
Montepulciano d'Abruzzo, Roxan 2000
   £5.80 (LAY)
Montepulciano d'Abruzzo Bianchi 1999
   £5.65 (LLO)
Montepulciano d'Abruzzo Umani Ronchi
   2000 £5.30 (NI)
Santa Cristina, Antinori 1997 £5.99 (NEZ)

£6.00 → £6.99

Carmignano Barco Reale, Capezzana
   1998 £6.50 (WS) £8.00 (FLE)
Centine Rosso Villa Banfi 1998 £6.95 (RES)
Chianti Classico le Capanne, Querceto
   1999 £6.50 (JU)

Chianti Classico Rocca delle Macie **1998**
£6.49 (MAJ)
Chianti Classico Villa Cafaggio **1998**
£6.99 (UN) £7.99 (VIL)
Chianti Rufina Riserva Villa di Vetrice
1996 £6.35 (SOM)
Luce Frescobaldi **2000** £6.39 (COC)
Parrina Rosso, La Parrina **1999** £6.30
(SOM) £6.99 (VA) £7.95 (LIB)
Rosso Conero Brunori **1999** £6.56 (BIB)

£7.00 → £7.99

Carmignano Barco Reale, Capezzana
1999 £7.99 (LIB) £8.40 (HAH) £8.90
(BAC) £8.99 (BAL)
Chianti Classico Aziano, Ruffino **1996**
£7.59 (COC)
Chianti Classico la Lellera, Matta **1998**
£7.27 (WHI)
Chianti Rufina Riserva Villa di Vetrice
1997 £7.99 (VIL)
Chianti Rufina Selvapiana **1998** £7.99 (VA)
£8.95 (RES) £8.99 (VIL) £9.95 (POR) £10.95
(FORT)
Chianti Castello di Volpaia **1998** £7.99 (OD)
Dogajolo Carpineto **1997** £7.05 (TUR)
£8.99 (GN)
Montefalco Rosso, Adanti **1996** £7.95
(BALL)
Morellino di Scansano le Pupille **1999**
£7.50 (WS) £8.90 (BAC) £8.99 (VA) £9.90
(CRO) £9.95 (LIB) £9.99 (VIL)
Morellino di Scansano le Pupille **1997**
£7.30 (SOM)
Parrina Rosso, La Parrina **1998** £7.99 (VIL)
£7.99 (BAL)
Parrina Rosso, La Parrina **1997** £7.95 (POR)
Rosso Conero San Lorenzo, Umani
Ronchi **1998** £7.65 (NI)
Rosso Conero San Lorenzo, Umani
Ronchi **1997** £7.99 (TAN) £7.99 (VIL)
Rosso di Montalcino Campo ai Sassi,
Frescobaldi **1998** £7.99 (OD)
Rosso di Montepulciano Dei **1999** £7.95
(LEA)
Rosso di Montepulciano Sebazio, Antinori
1999 £7.99 (UN)
Rosso Piceno Superiore Il Brecciarolo,
Velenosi **1996** £7.30 (BAC)
Rosso Piceno Vigna Piediprato, Pilastri
1995 £7.49 (BAL)
Val di Cornia Gualdo del Re **1999** £7.95
(LEA)
Vino Nobile di Montepulciano Cerro
1998 £7.99 (OD)

£8.00 → £8.99

Chianti Classico Castello La Leccia **1998**
£8.49 (OD)
Chianti Classico Castello di Fonterutoli
1998 £8.95 (WS) £10.99 (YOU) £11.99
(VIL)
Chianti Classico Melini **1996** £8.99 (JON)
Chianti Classico Montiverdi **1995** £8.25
(CON)
Chianti Classico Riserva Antinori **1997**
£8.99 (WAI) £9.90 (HAH) £14.99 (UN)
Chianti Classico Riserva Antinori **1996**
£8.99 (NEZ)
Chianti Classico Rocca delle Macie **1999**
£8.25 (NI)
Chianti Classico San Jacopo,
Vicchiomaggio **1997** £8.46 (PEN)
Chianti Classico Villa Cafaggio **1999**
£8.95 (WRI) £10.15 (SUN) £10.15 (LAI)
Chianti Classico Castello di Volpaia **1998**
£8.65 (AD)
Montefalco Rosso Caprai **1997** £8.49 (BAL)
Rosso di Montalcino Argiano **1999** £8.75
(SOM) £10.95 (LIB) £11.99 (VA)
Rubesco Rosso di Torgiano Lungarotti
1997 £8.49 (VA) £8.65 (TAN)
Vino Nobile di Montepulciano Baiocchi
1997 £8.99 (VA)
Vino Nobile di Montepulciano Cerro
1997 £8.49 (UN)
Vino Nobile di Montepulciano Fassati
1997 £8.99 (MAJ)

£9.00 → £9.99

Chianti Classico Castellare **1999** £9.99
(DI)
Chianti Classico Castell'in Villa **1992**
£9.69 (CB)
Chianti Classico Fontodi **1998** £9.90
(SOM) £10.99 (VA) £12.95 (POR) £12.99
(VIL)
Chianti Classico Monte Bernardi **1997**
£9.50 (BU) £17.63 (FA) £19.50 (RAE)
Chianti Classico Riserva Villa Antinori,
Antinori **1997** £9.15 (TAN) £9.99 (VA)
Chianti Classico San Jacopo,
Vicchiomaggio **1998** £9.99 (COC)
Chianti Rufina Selvapiana **1999** £9.95 (LIB)
Montefalco Rosso Caprai **1998** £9.00
(ARM) £9.49 (BAL)
Morellino di Scansano Belguardo Castello
di Fonterutoli **1997** £9.25 (GN)
Morellino di Scansano le Pupille **1998**
£9.49 (HED)

Rosso di Montalcino, Lisini **1995** £9.90 (JU)

Rosso di Montalcino Villa Banfi **1998** £9.87 (PEN)

Rosso di Montepulciano Poliziano **1999** £9.99 (VIL)

Vino Nobile di Montepulciano Bindella **1998** £9.99 (BIB)

£10.00 → £11.99

Chianti Classico Castello di Brolio **1999** £11.43 (LLO)

Chianti Classico Casaloste **1997** £10.50 (WS)

Chianti Classico Castellare **1997** £10.50 (BAL)

Chianti Classico Felsina Berardenga **1998** £10.50 (WS) £13.99 (VIL)

Chianti Classico Felsina Berardenga **1997** £10.95 (SOM) £13.50 (BEN) £13.99 (AME)

Chianti Classico Castello di Fonterutoli **1999** £11.75 (NI)

Chianti Classico Fontodi **1996** £11.50 (CRO)

Chianti Classico Isole e Olena **1998** £11.25 (SOM) £13.75 (CON) £13.99 (BEN) £13.99 (VIL) £14.25 (STA) £15.40 (TAN) £15.99 (VA) £16.75 (FORT)

Chianti Classico Isole e Olena **1997** £11.95 (SAV) £13.37 (FLE)

Chianti Classico Nozzole **1998** £10.15 (JER)

Chianti Classico Pèppoli, Antinori **1998** £11.99 (VA)

Chianti Classico Riecine **1997** £11.75 (FORT)

Chianti Classico Riserva Castello di Nipozzano, Frescobaldi **1997** £10.60 (TAN)

Chianti Classico Riserva Fontodi **1998** £10.50 (WS)

Chianti Classico Riserva Querceto **1996** £10.50 (JU)

Chianti Classico Riserva Villa Antinori, Antinori **1998** £10.65 (JER)

Chianti Classico Riserva Castello di Volpaia **1997** £10.99 (OD) £12.75 (AD)

Morellino di Scansano Riserva, le Pupille **1995** £10.65 (SOM)

Parrina Reserva, La Parrina **1997** £10.95 (STA) £10.99 (VIL)

Rosso di Montalcino Argiano **1998** £10.95 (BAL) £12.75 (FORT)

Rosso di Montalcino Col d'Orcia **1999** £10.99 (VA)

Rosso di Montalcino Talenti **1999** £10.28 (BIB)

Vino Nobile di Montepulciano Antinori **1998** £10.99 (NEZ)

Vino Nobile di Montepulciano Avignonesi **1998** £10.95 (WAI)

Vino Nobile di Montepulciano Dei **1997** £11.50 (LEA)

Vino Nobile di Montepulciano Riserva, Baiocchi **1996** £11.99 (VA)

£12.00 → £14.99

Arquata Rosso dell'Umbria, Adanti **1996** £14.95 (CON)

Chianti Classico Castello dei Rampolla **1999** £14.50 (WRI)

Chianti Classico Felsina Berardenga **1999** £14.95 (LIB)

Chianti Classico Fontodi **1999** £12.99 (BEN) £13.95 (LIB)

Chianti Classico Isole e Olena **1999** £13.95 (LIB)

Chianti Classico Monte Bernardi **1994** £13.95 (BAL) £14.99 (RAE)

Chianti Classico Querciabella **1998** £12.49 (YOU) £12.50 (LEA)

Chianti Classico Riserva Fontodi **1996** £13.50 (WS) £16.95 (VA) £16.99 (VIL)

Chianti Classico Riserva Tenute Marchese Antinori **1997** £12.99 (WAI) £16.95 (VA)

Chianti Classico Riserva Tenute Marchese Antinori **1996** £14.99 (SUN) £14.99 (LAI)

Chianti Classico Riserva Castello della Paneretta **1997** £13.51 (PEN) £14.99 (VA)

Chianti Classico Riserva Villa Cafaggio **1997** £12.99 (VIL) £13.99 (SUN) £13.99 (LAI)

Chianti Classico Riserva Villa Cafaggio **1996** £13.50 (BAL)

Chianti Classico San Felice **1998** £13.99 (VA)

Chianti Classico Fattoria Valtellina **1999** £14.30 (SOM)

Chianti Rufina Riserva Selvapiana **1997** £12.99 (VA) £14.75 (LIB) £14.99 (VIL)

Morellino di Scansano Riserva, le Pupille **1997** £14.99 (YOU) £15.99 (HED) £15.99 (VIL) £16.99 (VA)

Parrina Reserva, La Parrina **1998** £13.95 (LIB)

Rosso di Montalcino Costanti **1996** £13.99 (VA)

Tavernelle Villa Banfi **1997** £13.95 (RES)

Vino Nobile di Montepulciano Dei **1996** £14.95 (LEA)

Vino Nobile di Montepulciano Il Macchione **1996** £12.50 (BAN)

Vino Nobile di Montepulciano le Casalte
1996 £12.99 (AME)
Vino Nobile di Montepulciano le Casalte
1990 £14.95 (BAL)
Vino Nobile di Montepulciano Vigneto
Caggiole, Poliziano **1993** £13.65 (SOM)

£15.00 → £19.99

Balifico Castello di Volpaia **1995** £18.95
(DI)
Brancaia, La Brancaia **1998** £16.99 (VA)
Brancaia, La Brancaia **1997** £19.99 (YOU)
£20.99 (VIL) £23.30 (NI)
Brancaia, La Brancaia **1995** £19.95 (LEA)
£19.95 (BAL)
Brunello di Montalcino Castelgiocondo
1994 £19.95 (TAN)
Brunello di Montalcino Col d'Orcia **1994**
£19.95 (VA)
Brunello di Montalcino il Poggione **1993**
£19.99 (SUN) £19.99 (LAI)
Brunello di Montalcino Talenti **1996**
£19.39 (BIB)
Brunello di Montalcino Tenuta Nuova,
Casanova di Neri **1995** £19.50 (WAI)
Brunello di Montalcino Val di Suga **1993**
£17.82 (COC)
Brunello di Montalcino Villa Banfi **1995**
£16.92 (PEN) £24.95 (VA) £24.95 (RES)
Brunello di Montalcino Villa Banfi **1993**
£18.69 (BO)
Ca' del Pazzo Caparzo **1995** £17.95 (DI)
Carmignano Villa di Capezzana **1998**
£15.95 (LIB)
Casalferro Castello di Brolio **1998** £18.99
(YOU)
Cepparello Isole e Olena **1991** £17.63 (FA)
Chianti Classico Castello di Ama **1997**
£17.95 (RES)
Chianti Classico Montagliari **1967** £17.50
(BU)
Chianti Classico Monte Bernardi **1996**
£15.28 (FA) £17.99 (RAE) £18.85 (BIB)
Chianti Classico Monte Bernardi **1995**
£16.95 (BAL)
Chianti Classico Riserva Casaloste **1995**
£17.90 (BAC)
Chianti Classico Riserva Castell'in Villa
1993 £15.79 (CB)
Chianti Classico Riserva Castello dei
Rampolla **1996** £19.95 (BAL)
Chianti Classico Riserva Ducale Oro,
Ruffino **1996** £17.95 (VA)
Chianti Classico Riserva Ducale Oro,
Ruffino **1969** £17.50 (BU)

Chianti Classico Riserva Castello di
Fonterutoli **1996** £19.99 (YOU)
Chianti Classico Riserva Il Picchio,
Querceto **1991** £17.00 (JU)
Chianti Classico Riserva Tenute Marchese
Antinori **1995** £15.99 (DI)
Chianti Classico Riserva Querciabella
1997 £17.50 (LEA)
Chianti Classico Riserva Querciabella
1996 £16.95 (LEA)

Chianti Classico Riserva Torre a Destra,
Castello della Paneretta **1997** £15.16
(PEN)
Chianti Classico Riserva Vigna del Sorbo,
Fontodi **1997** £16.99 (VA) £25.99 (VIL)
Chianti Classico Riserva Vigneto Rancia,
Felsina Berardenga **1997** £17.50 (WS)
£23.79 (YOU)
Chianti Classico Santa Cristina, Antinori
1977 £16.50 (BU)
Chianti Colli Senesi la Torre **1979** £16.50
(BU)
Chianti Rufina Riserva Bucerchiale,
Selvapiana **1998** £17.95 (LIB)
Chianti Rufina Riserva Bucerchiale,
Selvapiana **1996** £17.95 (LIB) £17.99 (VIL)
Chianti Rufina Riserva Bucerchiale,
Selvapiana **1995** £19.95 (VA)
La Corte, Castello di Querceto **1994**
£17.50 (JU)
Elegia Poliziano **1995** £16.95 (SOM)
Federico Primo Gualdo del Re **1997**
£15.95 (LEA)
Flaccianello della Pieve, Fontodi **1995**
£19.99 (VA)
Il Carbonaione, Podere Poggio Scalette
1998 £19.49 (FA)
Lamaione Merlot Frescobaldi **1997**
£18.99 (OD) £38.09 (FA)
Morellino di Scansano Poggio Valente
1998 £19.99 (VIL)
Morellino di Scansano Riserva, le Pupille
1998 £15.95 (LIB)

Palazzo Altesi, Altesino **1995** £17.95 (LEA)

Podere Migliara Manzano **1996** £17.95 (LEA)

Quattro Mori Castel de Paolis **1994** £18.95 (BAL)

Roccato Rocca delle Macie **1996** £15.70 (NI)

Rosso Conero Cúmaro, Umani Ronchi **1997** £15.99 (VIL) £16.99 (VA) £17.99 (UN)

Rubesco Torgiano Riserva Vigna Monticchio Lungarotti **1988** £16.99 (VA)

Sa' etta Monte Bernardi **1994** £18.95 (RAE)

San Giorgio Lungarotti **1990** £19.99 (VA)

Sangioveto di Toscana Badia a Coltibuono **1980** £15.00 (CRO)

Solatio Basilica Villa Cafaggio **1996** £16.50 (BAL)

Tassinaia Tenuta del Terriccio **1998** £18.95 (LEA) £20.69 (YOU)

Tassinaia Tenuta del Terriccio **1995** £16.99 (GN)

Torrione Petrolo **1996** £18.75 (BU)

Vigna il Vallone Villa Sant' Anna **1995** £15.95 (LEA)

Vino Nobile di Montepulciano Poliziano **1997** £15.69 (JON)

£20.00 → £24.99

Brunello di Montalcino Altesino **1988** £23.00 (CRO)

Brunello di Montalcino Argiano **1996** £21.95 (STA) £21.99 (YOU) £22.95 (LIB) £24.99 (POR)

Brunello di Montalcino Argiano **1995** £22.99 (VIL) £24.00 (AME) £27.50 (FORT)

Brunello di Montalcino Casanova di Neri **1994** £22.99 (WR)

Brunello di Montalcino Cantina di Montalcino **1995** £22.50 (UN)

Brunello di Montalcino Riserva, Talenti **1995** £24.48 (BIB)

Brunello di Montalcino Val di Suga **1994** £22.52 (PLAY)

Carmignano Riserva, Villa di Capezzana **1997** £22.95 (RES)

Carmignano Villa di Capezzana **1996** £22.95 (TAN)

Casalferro Castello di Brolio **1996** £20.95 (RES)

Chianti Classico Castello di Brolio **1997** £20.99 (YOU) £24.99 (UN)

Chianti Classico Castello di Fonterutoli **1997** £24.99 (UN)

Chianti Classico I Sodi, Castellare **1993** £21.95 (DI)

Chianti Classico Riserva Castello dei Rampolla **1997** £21.50 (BAL)

★ Chianti Classico Riserva Castello di Fonterutoli **1997** £20.99 (YOU) £22.95 (WAI) £22.99 (VIL) £23.95 (RES)

Chianti Classico Riserva Santa Cristina, Antinori **1983** £21.00 (CRO)

Chianti Classico Riserva Vigna del Sorbo, Fontodi **1995** £21.00 (AME)

Chianti Classico Riserva Vigneto Rancia, Felsina Berardenga **1998** £21.95 (POR) £27.95 (LIB)

Chianti Rufina Riserva Montesodi, Frescobaldi **1996** £20.60 (TAN)

Chianti Rufina Selvapiana **1990** £24.00 (CRO)

Coltassala Castello di Volpaia **1982** £21.00 (CRO)

Concerto Fonterutoli **1994** £24.50 (BAL)

Flaccianello della Pieve, Fontodi **1996** £24.95 (VA)

Fontalloro Felsina Berardenga **1997** £23.40 (BODX) £27.49 (YOU) £28.90 (BEN)

Ghiaie della Furba, Capezzana **1998** £20.49 (YOU)

Il Querciolaia, Querceto **1991** £20.00 (JU)

Percarlo San Giusto a Rentennano **1996** £22.91 (FA) £29.00 (BAL)

Podere Il Bosco Manzano **1998** £22.50 (LEA)

QuerciaGrande, Capaccia **1994** £20.95 (BALL)

Sammarco Castello dei Rampolla **1991** £24.50 (BAL)

I Sodi di San Niccolò, Castellare **1995** £24.50 (BAL)

Le Stanze Poliziano **1998** £22.99 (YOU) £24.95 (VA)

Summus Villa Banfi **1995** £22.56 (PEN)

Syrah Isole e Olena **1996** £24.99 (VIL) £27.95 (RES)

Vino Nobile di Montepulciano Bindella **1986** £20.00 (CRO)

Vino Nobile di Montepulciano Vigna Asinone, Poliziano **1997** £21.99 (YOU)

£25.00 → £29.99

Ardingo Calbello **1999** £29.00 (POR)
Bolgheri Superiore Paleo Rosso, le
  Macchiole **1997** £26.95 (LEA)
Brunello di Montalcino Costanti **1996**
  £29.95 (LIB)
Brunello di Montalcino Fattoria dei Barbi
  1995 £26.25 (FORT)
Brunello di Montalcino Pertimali **1995**
  £25.00 (JU)
Cabernet Sauvignon Isole e Olena **1996**
  £28.99 (VIL) £30.95 (RES)
Camartina Querciabella **1996** £25.95
  (LEA)
Cepparello Isole e Olena **1996** £25.95
  (POR) £27.75 (CON) £27.99 (VIL)
Chianti Classico Felsina Berardenga **1990**
  £28.00 (CRO)
Chianti Classico Giorgio Primo, Fattoria
  La Massa **1997** £26.67 (ARM)
Chianti Classico Riserva Vigna del Sorbo,
  Fontodi **1999** £25.75 (BEN)
Chianti Classico Riserva Vigna del Sorbo,
  Fontodi **1998** £26.95 (LIB)
Chianti Rufina Montesodi, Frescobaldi
  1997 £26.50 (BAL)
Cignale Querceto **1997** £26.50 (JU)
Flaccianello della Pieve, Fontodi **1997**
  £25.95 (BEN) £28.00 (FLE) £28.99 (VIL)
  £30.00 (WS) £35.64 (FA)
Ghiaie della Furba, Capezzana **1997**
  £25.40 (TAN)
Guado al Tasso, Antinori **1993** £26.50
  (VA)
Ornellaia Tenuta dell'Ornellaia **1993**
  £27.99 (YOU)
Sa' etta Monte Bernardi **1997** £26.99 (RAE)
Sa' etta Monte Bernardi **1995** £26.50 (BAL)
Sangioveto di Toscana Badia a Coltibuono
  1990 £29.38 (PEN)
Summus Villa Banfi **1997** £26.95 (RES)
Syrah Isole e Olena **1996** £26.95 (LIB)
Tignanello Antinori **1996** £29.99 (YOU)
  £33.68 (FA) £38.99 (SUN) £38.99 (LAI)
  £50.00 (FORT)

£30.00 → £39.99

Brunello di Montalcino Altesino **1995**
  £35.64 (FA)
Brunello di Montalcino Rennina, Pieve
  Santa Restituta **1995** £33.95 (LAY)
  £41.67 (MI)
Brunello di Montalcino Rennina, Pieve
  Santa Restituta **1993** £34.17 (MI)

Cepparello Isole e Olena **1998** £31.99
  (YOU) £33.50 (LIB)
Cepparello Isole e Olena **1997** £36.95
  (VA) £45.43 (FA)
Chianti Classico Riserva Felsina
  Berardenga **1990** £33.00 (CRO)
Chianti Rufina Riserva Bucerchiale,
  Selvapiana **1990** £31.00 (CRO)
Excelsus Villa Banfi **1997** £35.95 (RES)
Flaccianello della Pieve, Fontodi **1998**
  £30.95 (LIB)
Fontalloro Felsina Berardenga **1998**
  £30.95 (LIB)
Guado al Tasso, Antinori **1997** £34.99
  (NEZ) £38.58 (FA) £41.13 (TUR) £44.00
  (CRO)
Guado al Tasso, Antinori **1996** £35.15
  (BODX) £44.00 (CRO)
Lupicaia Tenuta del Terriccio **1996**
  £38.99 (YOU)
Ornellaia Tenuta dell'Ornellaia **1996**
  £33.19 (BODX) £35.25 (FA) £47.00 (YOU)
Ornellaia Tenuta dell'Ornellaia **1994**
  £32.70 (BODX)
Ornellaia Tenuta dell'Ornellaia **1992**
  £39.99 (VIL) £45.00 (VA)
Rosso Miani, Miani **1994** £39.00 (BAL)
Saffredi le Pupille **1998** £33.98 (SOM)
  £41.00 (YOU) £42.50 (FA) £42.99 (VIL)
  £45.00 (HED)
Sammarco Castello dei Rampolla **1998**
  £39.75 (WRI)
Sammarco Castello dei Rampolla **1995**
  £36.62 (BODX)
San Giorgio Lungarotti **1978** £30.00 (CRO)
Sangioveto di Toscana Badia a Coltibuono
  1997 £38.95 (RES)
Sassicaia Tenuta San Guido **1992** £31.73
  (FA) £85.00 (VA)
Tignanello Antinori **1995** £37.60 (FA)
  £43.50 (BEN)
Tignanello Antinori **1982** £31.82 (TUR)
  £64.63 (FA)
Vino Nobile di Montepulciano Fassati
  1970 £39.00 (CRO)

£40.00 → £49.99

Brunello di Montalcino Riserva, Villa Banfi
  1993 £45.00 (RES)
Brunello di Montalcino Sugarille, Pieve
  Santa Restituta **1993** £47.50 (MI)
Cepparello Isole e Olena **1993** £49.00
  (CRO)
Cepparello Isole e Olena **1990** £47.00
  (FA) £59.00 (CRO)

Flaccianello della Pieve, Fontodi **1990**
£45.00 (VA)

Fontalloro Felsina Berardenga **1990**
£49.00 (VA)

Luce Frescobaldi **1997** £42.99 (YOU)
£44.00 (BAL) £54.25 (FA)

Luce Frescobaldi **1995** £48.18 (FA) £49.84
(BODX)

Ornellaia Tenuta dell'Ornellaia **1995**
£40.54 (BODX) £41.15 (NO) £42.20
(TAN) £45.00 (BAL) £45.00 (FORT)

Saffredi le Pupille **1999** £46.95 (LIB)

Sassicaia Tenuta San Guido **1993** £43.48
(FA) £75.00 (VA) £93.71 (PLAY)

Solaia Antinori **1993** £42.50 (FA)

Tignanello Antinori **1997** £40.00 (UN)
£54.25 (FA) £56.00 (CRO) £58.16 (TUR)

Tignanello Antinori **1983** £48.37 (FA)
£60.00 (YOU)

£50.00 → £69.99

Brunello di Montalcino Rennina, Pieve
Santa Restituta **1990** £50.83 (MI)

Brunello di Montalcino Riserva, Biondi-
Santi **1970** £59.00 (CRO)

Brunello di Montalcino Sugarille, Pieve
Santa Restituta **1995** £50.83 (MI)

Chianti Classico Riserva Badia a
Coltibuono **1968** £50.00 (CRO)

Galatrona Petrolo **1997** £55.00 (BEN)

Lupicaia Tenuta del Terriccio **1998**
£55.00 (LEA)

Masseto Tenuta dell'Ornellaia **1994**
£66.00 (FA) £74.32 (BODX)

Ornellaia Tenuta dell'Ornellaia **1991**
£55.00 (VA)

Rosso Miani, Miani **1997** £53.25 (GAU)

Sammarco Castello dei Rampolla **1990**
£50.33 (FA)

Sammarco Castello dei Rampolla **1988**
£57.67 (BODX)

Sassicaia Tenuta San Guido **1998** £61.00
(LIB) £100.53 (MI)

Sassicaia Tenuta San Guido **1996** £60.00
(VA) £62.08 (FA) £69.91 (TUR) £75.00
(BAL)

Sassicaia Tenuta San Guido **1989** £58.75
(FA) £99.00 (VA)

Solaia Antinori **1996** £57.00 (YOU)

Solaia Antinori **1995** £67.95 (FA) £75.00
(CRO)

Solaia Antinori **1987** £60.12 (FA)

Solengo Argiano **1998** £58.95 (FA) £65.00
(BEN)

Tignanello Antinori **1977** £60.00 (VA)

£70.00 → £99.99

Guado al Tasso, Antinori **1990** £99.29 (FA)

Masseto Tenuta dell'Ornellaia **1996**
£74.81 (BODX) £76.38 (FA)

Masseto Tenuta dell'Ornellaia **1995**
£87.54 (FA)

Ornellaia Tenuta dell'Ornellaia **1997**
£70.00 (VIL) £74.81 (FA)

Ornellaia Tenuta dell'Ornellaia **1990**
£83.62 (FA) £139.00 (VA) £150.00 (FORT)

Ornellaia Tenuta dell'Ornellaia **1986**
£95.00 (BAL)

Saffredi le Pupille **1997** £70.00 (VA)
£74.81 (FA) £76.38 (TUR)

Sassicaia Tenuta San Guido **1997** £79.74
(NO) £97.53 (FA) £117.50 (TUR) £132.20
(MI)

Sassicaia Tenuta San Guido **1994** £77.22
(NO)

Sassicaia Tenuta San Guido **1986** £81.66
(FA) £115.00 (VA)

Sassicaia Tenuta San Guido **1984** £99.00
(VA)

Solaia Antinori **1988** £74.03 (FA)

Solengo Argiano **1997** £87.54 (FA)

Tignanello Antinori **1990** £82.25 (BODX)
£125.00 (VA)

Tignanello Antinori **1987** £99.00 (VA)

Tignanello Antinori **1985** £98.80 (BODX)

Tignanello Antinori **1978** £85.00 (VA)

£100.00 → £149.99

Brunello di Montalcino Biondi-Santi **1988**
£100.00 (VA)

Percarlo San Giusto a Rentennano **1997**
£118.48 (FA)

Sassicaia Tenuta San Guido **1988** £103.40
(FA) £105.00 (CRO)

Sassicaia Tenuta San Guido **1983** £113.00
(FA) £120.00 (VA)

Solaia Antinori **1997** £108.00 (CRO)
£150.00 (VA) £176.25 (BODX) £177.23
(FA) £181.15 (TUR)

Solaia Antinori **1990** £132.78 (FA)
£148.25 (BODX) £195.00 (VA)

Over £150.00

Brunello di Montalcino Riserva, Biondi-
Santi **1990** £160.00 (VA)

Sassicaia Tenuta San Guido **1990** £153.14
(FA) £229.00 (VA)

Sassicaia Tenuta San Guido **1985** £470.00
(FA)

Solaia Antinori **1982** £150.00 (FORT)

CENTRAL WHITE

Under £4.50

Frascati Superiore San Matteo **1999**
£4.39 (CON)
Frascati Superiore Satinata, Colle di
Catone **1999** £3.99 (ASD)
Grechetto dell'Umbria, Il Vignolo **1997**
£4.40 (SOM)
Orvieto Classico Secco Cardeto **1999**
£4.29 (WAI)
Verdicchio dei Castelli di Jesi Classico,
Umani Ronchi **2000** £4.20 (SOM)
Verdicchio dei Castelli di Jesi, Villa Pigna
1998 £4.49 (UN)

£4.50 → £5.49

Frascati Superiore Fontana Candida **2000**
£4.99 (MAJ)
Galestro Antinori **2000** £5.49 (NEZ)
Orvieto Classico Cardetto **2000** £4.99 (UN)
Orvieto Classico Secco Antinori **2000**
£4.99 (VIC) £4.99 (THR) £4.99 (BOT) £5.60
(TAN) £7.15 (JER)
Verdicchio dei Castelli di Jesi Classico,
Brunori **2000** £5.49 (BIB)
Verdicchio dei Castelli di Jesi Classico,
Umani Ronchi **1997** £4.94 (FLE) £6.63
(NO)

£5.50 → £6.99

Bianco Villa Antinori, Antinori **2000**
£6.95 (JER)
Bianco Villa Antinori, Antinori **1999**
£6.20 (TAN) £6.65 (HAH) £6.99 (VA)
Castello della Sala, Antinori **1999** £6.99
(WAI) £8.99 (UN)
Est! Est!! Est!!! di Montefiascone, Bigi
2000 £6.23 (LLO)
Frascati Fontana Candida **2000** £6.20 (NI)
Frascati Fontana Candida **1999** £6.50 (GN)
Frascati Superiore Fontana Candida **1999**
£5.95 (STA) £5.99 (VIL) £7.01 (LLO)
Frascati Superiore Monteporzio **1999**
£6.99 (VA)
Montefalco Bianco, Adanti **1997** £6.89
(JON)
Orvieto Classico Abboccato Antinori
2000 £5.70 (TAN)
Orvieto Classico Abboccato Antinori
1999 £6.49 (VA)
Orvieto Classico Amabile Bigi **1999** £5.99
(VIL) £6.49 (VA)
Orvieto Classico Antinori **1999** £6.58 (CB)

Orvieto Classico Campogrande Castello
della Sala, Antinori **1998** £6.99 (NEZ)
Orvieto Classico Secco Bigi **1999** £5.99
(LLO)
Orvieto Classico Terre Vineate, Il
Palazzone **2000** £6.95 (JU)
Orvieto Classico Terre Vineate, Il
Palazzone **1999** £6.99 (DI) £8.50 (WIN)
Orvieto Classico Vigneto Torricella, Bigi
1999 £5.90 (SOM) £7.25 (STA) £8.25
(FORT)
Orvieto Secco Antinori **2000** £5.99 (VA)
Orvieto Secco Bigi **1999** £6.49 (VA)
Verdicchio dei Castelli di Jesi Classico
Casal di Serra, Umani Ronchi **1998**
£6.20 (SOM) £8.50 (FORT)
Verdicchio dei Castelli di Jesi Classico San
Nicolo, Brunori **2000** £6.56 (BIB)
Verdicchio dei Castelli di Jesi Classico
Villa Bianchi, Ronchi **1999** £5.80 (TAN)
Verdicchio di Matelica, La Monacesca
1998 £5.75 (SOM) £6.95 (BAC)
Verdicchio di Matelica, Filli Bisci **1996**
£6.95 (JU)
Vernaccia di San Gimignano Falchini **1999**
£6.00 (BAC) £6.49 (JON)
Vernaccia di San Gimignano, Fontaleoni
1997 £6.70 (JU)
Vernaccia di San Gimignano Strozzi **1999**
£5.99 (BAL)
Vernaccia di San Gimignano Teruzzi e
Puthod **1999** £6.95 (SOM) £6.99 (VIL)
£7.99 (VA)

£7.00 → £9.99

Frascati Superiore Campovecchio, Castel
de Paolis **1998** £9.95 (BAL)
Orvieto Classico Antinori **1997** £7.80
(CRO)
Orvieto Classico Campo del Guardiano, Il
Palazzone **1995** £7.35 (JU)
Verdicchio dei Castelli di Jesi Classico
Casal di Serra, Umani Ronchi **2000**
£7.65 (NI)
Verdicchio dei Castelli di Jesi Classico
Casal di Serra, Umani Ronchi **1999**
£7.25 (STA) £7.49 (VIL)
Verdicchio dei Castelli di Jesi Classico,
Fazi-Battaglia **1999** £9.49 (VA)
Vernaccia di San Gimignano Fiore,
Montenidoli **2000** £9.96 (BIB)
Vin Santo Antinori **Non-vintage** £9.99
(VA) £10.55 (JER)
Vin Santo Rocca delle Macie **1992** £8.75
(NI)

£10.00 → £12.99

Chardonnay Fontarca, Manzano **1998** £12.69 (YOU)

Chardonnay I Sistri, Felsina Berardenga **1996** £10.95 (SOM)

Frascati Colle Gaio, Colli di Catone **1997** £11.99 (DI)

Frascati Superiore Castel de Paolis **1998** £12.50 (BAL)

Orvieto Classico Campo del Guardiano, Il Palazzone **1998** £11.50 (WIN)

Verdicchio dei Castelli di Jesi Classico Il Coroncino, Coroncino **1999** £10.45 (LAY)

Vernaccia di San Gimignano Terre di Tufi, Teruzzi e Puthod **1999** £11.99 (VIL) £12.99 (VA)

Vernaccia di San Gimignano Terre di Tufi, Teruzzi e Puthod **1998** £11.99 (VIL)

£13.00 → £19.99

Chardonnay I Sistri, Felsina Berardenga **1998** £13.79 (YOU) £13.95 (LIB) £14.00 (STA) £14.99 (VA)

Chardonnay I Sistri, Felsina Berardenga **1997** £13.99 (BEN)

Chardonnay Isole e Olena **1999** £16.99 (YOU) £17.95 (LIB)

Chardonnay Isole e Olena **1998** £17.99 (VIL) £18.99 (VA)

Frascati Superiore Vigna Adriana, Castel de Paolis **1998** £18.95 (LAY)

Pomino Il Benefizio, Frescobaldi **1995** £16.99 (VA)

Saluccio Tenuta del Terriccio **1998** £18.95 (LEA)

Vin Santo di Carmignano, Capezzana **1995** £15.49 (LIB)

Vin Santo Selvapiana 50cl bottle **1995** £19.95 (VIL)

Vin Santo Selvapiana 50cl bottle **1993** £19.99 (VIL)

Over £20.00

Batàr Querciabella **1998** £24.95 (LEA)

Cervaro della Sala, Antinori **1997** £21.99 (NEZ) £25.95 (VA)

Cervaro della Sala, Antinori **1991** £20.95 (DI)

Trebbiano d'Abruzzo Valentini **1993** £32.00 (BAL)

Vin Santo Capelli **1968** £22.00 (CRO)

Vin Santo Isole e Olena **1994** £23.99 (YOU) £24.95 (LIB)

CENTRAL ROSÉ

c. £8.00

Carmignano Vinruspo Rosato, Capezzana **2000** £7.95 (LIB)

SOUTHERN RED

Under £5.00

Cent'Are Rosso Duca di Castelmonte **1997** £4.69 (WAI)

Copertino Eloquenzia, Masseria Monaci **1997** £4.35 (SOM) £5.35 (CON) £5.49 (AME) £5.95 (POR) £5.99 (BAL)

★ Inycon Syrah **2000** £4.99 (SAI)

Negroamaro Promessa **2000** £4.99 (LIB) £4.99 (VA)

Negroamaro Promessa **1999** £4.99 (UN) £4.99 (VIL) £5.29 (JON) £5.35 (STA) £5.49 (POR)

Primitivo del Salento Trulli **1999** £4.49 (TES)

Salice Salentino Riserva Candido **1997** £4.95 (WS) £5.99 (MAJ) £6.49 (VIL) £6.90 (TAN)

Salice Salentino Vallone **1998** £4.99 (BO) £5.75 (BU) £5.79 (AME) £6.55 (LAY)

Salice Salentino Vallone **1997** £4.50 (SOM) £5.65 (LLO) £5.99 (BOT)

£5.00 → £5.99

Barbaglio Santa Barbara **1994** £5.95 (BALL) £6.25 (CON)

Copertino Riserva, Cantina Sociale di Copertino **1997** £5.60 (SOM) £7.49 (VA)

Primitivo A Mano **2000** £5.99 (LIB) £5.99 (AME) £5.99 (VA) £5.99 (BAL) £6.49 (POR)

Primitivo A Mano **1999** £5.99 (BO) £5.99 (BU) £5.99 (VIL) £6.25 (CON) £7.85 (HIC)

Primitivo di Manduria Archidamo, Pervini **1998** £5.80 (SOM) £6.50 (WS) £6.99 (BO) £7.25 (CON) £7.49 (AME)

Rosso Brindisi Santa Barbara **1995** £5.20 (TAN)

Rosso del Salento Notarpanaro Taurino **1996** £5.99 (MAJ)

Salice Salentino Riserva Candido **1996** £5.45 (SOM)

Salice Salentino Vallone **1996** £5.99 (GN)

A key to name abbreviations is available on page 7.

£6.00 → £7.99

Cannonau di Sardegna Costera, Argiolas
1997 £7.50 (BALL)
Cappello di Prete, Candido **1996** £6.30
(SOM)
Carignano del Sulcis Rocca Rubia Riserva,
Santadi **1997** £7.95 (WS)
Carignano del Sulcis, Santadi **1998** £7.99
(VA)
Cirò Classico Librandi **1999** £6.49 (VA)
Copertino Riserva, Cantina Sociale di
Copertino **1994** £6.43 (NO)
Corvo Rosso Duca di Salaparuta **1998**
£6.61 (COC) £6.76 (WHI) £7.99 (VA)
Pier delle Vigne Rosso delle Murge,
Botromagno **1994** £7.49 (BAL)
Primitivo di Manduria Archidamo, Pervini
1997 £7.49 (HED)
Regaleali Rosso, Tasca d'Almerita-
Regaleali **1996** £7.99 (DI)
Salice Salentino Candido **1997** £6.99 (VA)
Simposia Masseria Monaci **1995** £7.99
(AME) £7.99 (BAL)

£8.00 → £9.99

Aglianico del Vulture, Fratelli d'Angelo
1997 £8.95 (TAN)
Pier delle Vigne Rosso delle Murge,
Botromagno **1995** £8.79 (VA)
Rosso del Salento Cappello di Prete **1995**
£8.49 (JON)
Simposia Masseria Monaci **1997** £8.90 (LAY)
Vigna Virzi Rosso, Spadafora **1998** £8.25
(CON) £9.49 (LIB)

£10.00 → £14.99

Aglianico del Vulture, Paternoster **1997**
£11.99 (VA)
Carignano del Sulcis Rocca Rubia Riserva,
Santadi **1996** £10.99 (VIL)
Don Pietro Rosso, Spadafora **1998**
£10.95 (LIB)
Graticciaia Vallone **1994** £13.60 (SOM)
£17.99 (AME) £18.95 (CON) £20.00 (HED)

£15.00 → £19.99

Graticciaia Vallone **1997** £19.99 (WR)
Graticciaia Vallone **1995** £19.99 (POR)
Merlot Planeta **1998** £16.99 (YOU) £17.95
(VA) £18.99 (VIL) £19.95 (RES)
Regaleali Rosso, Tasca d'Almerita-
Regaleali **1997** £18.99 (YOU)
Santa Cecilia Planeta **1998** £16.99 (YOU)
£18.99 (VIL)

Over £20.00

Duca Enrico Duca di Salaparuta **1995**
£35.00 (FORT) ·
Serpico Feudi di San Gregorio **1995**
£25.79 (YOU)
Taurasi Riserva Mastroberardino **1981**
£21.00 (CRO)
Terre Brune, Santadi **1996** £21.99 (VIL)

SOUTHERN WHITE

Under £5.00

Segesta Bianco Kym Milne **1999** £3.99 (UN)
Vermentino di Sardegna, Sella & Mosca
2000 £4.25 (OD)
Zagara Catarratto, Firriato **1999** £3.99
(WAI) ·

£6.00 → £7.99

Corvo Bianco Duca di Salaparuta **1999**
£6.61 (COC) £7.99 (VA)
Corvo Bianco Duca di Salaparuta **1998**
£6.76 (WHI)
Fiano di Avellino Mastroberardino **1999**
£7.95 (VA)
Gravina Bianco, Botromagno **1999** £6.49
(VA)
Greco di Tufo Feudi di San Gregorio
1999 £7.99 (UN) £9.99 (VA)
Regaleali Conte Tasca d'Almerita **1999**
£7.99 (VA)

Over £8.00

Don Pietro Bianco, Spadafora **1998**
£10.49 (LIB)
Lacryma Christi del Vesuvio,
Mastroberardino **1999** £9.99 (VA)

SOUTHERN ROSÉ

c. £6.00

Vigna Flaminio Brindisi Rosato, Vallone
1997 £5.75 (BU)

SOUTHERN FORTIFIED

Under £6.00

Marsala Daniello **Non-vintage** £4.99 (UN)
Marsala Superiore Garibaldi Dolce,
Pellegrino **Non-vintage** £5.99 (DI)
£6.29 (SAF)

NEW ZEALAND

The 2000 vintage produced some stunners here – especially among the Chardonnays

Gosh, New Zealand is making some good Chardonnay these days. Nutty, vegetal, finely balanced and complex – and the oak is nicely judged. You have to pay £10 or a bit over to get the really good ones, but in my book that's good value: perfectly drinkable Chardonnays are ten a penny all over the world, but outstanding ones are like hens' teeth, and expensive with it.

New Zealand Chardonnay has been remarkably good since the mid-1990s. We're now seeing 2000 – and it's a pretty good year for Chardonnay, and also for Sauvignon Blanc. Hawkes Bay Sauvignon is far snappier and more focused than we've seen for a while; Marlborough Sauvignon is back on form with really tangy stuff.

Reds? Pinot Noir has made massive strides in the past few years, and both '99 and 2000 are showing perfume, balance and attractive fruit. They *are* pricey – as are the top Merlots and Cabernets – but it *is* a cool climate, just like Bordeaux and Burgundy – and Kiwi reds aren't nearly as pricey as them.

GRAPES & FLAVOURS

CABERNET SAUVIGNON (red) Even the hotter North Island, where Waiheke, Matakana and Hawkes Bay can make it well in warm years, seldom produces really ripe varietal wines. Blends with Merlot and others are almost always better. Best, including blends: *Babich Patriarch, Delegat's, Esk Valley, Heron's Flight, Matariki Quintology, Matua Valley Ararimu, Morton Estate Black Label, Sacred Hill Basket Press Reserve, Saint Clair, Stonyridge Larose, Te Mata Coleraine, Twin Bays Fenton, Vavasour Reserve, Vidal, Villa Maria Reserve, Waiheke Vineyards Te Motu, Waipara West Ram Paddock Red.*

CHARDONNAY (white) Styles range from the soft peaches-and-cream of Gisborne to the classic nutty warmth of Hawkes Bay and the grapefruity, zesty wines of Marlborough. Auckland, Nelson, Wairarapa and Canterbury all have less defined styles. The best producers are: *Allan Scott, Alpha Domus, Askerne, Babich Patriarch, Chard Farm, Church Road, Cloudy Bay, Collards Rothesay* and *Hawkes Bay, Corbans Marlborough Private Bin* and *Gisborne Cottage Block, Delegat's, Felton Road, Hunter's, Kumeu River, Lawson's Dry Hills, Matua Valley Judd Estate, Montana Ormond Estate, Morton Estate Black Label, Neudorf, Nobilo Dixon* and *Marlborough, Palliser Estate, Sileni Estates, Te Mata, Vidal, Villa Maria, Wither Hills.*

CHENIN BLANC (white) Not widely imported here, and generally sound but not thrilling. Best: *Millton's* barrel-fermented Chenin is a serious heavyweight, whereas *Collards* and *Esk Valley* are lighter, more supple wines.

GEWÜRZTRAMINER (white) Usually pleasant rather than exciting. Try: *Lawson's Dry Hills, Matawhero, Montana 'P'* from *Patutahi Estate, Rippon, Stonecroft. Vidal, Villa Maria,*

MERLOT (red) Increasingly popular in NZ. Blended with Cabernet, it makes some of the country's best reds – and there is an emerging band of top varietals: try (including blends) *Corbans, Delegat's, Esk Valley Reserve, Sileni Estates, Vidal, Villa Maria Reserve.*

MÜLLER-THURGAU (white) The mainstay of bag-in-the-box production. Good ones in bottle include the White Cloud blend from *Nobilo* and *Villa Maria*.

PINOT GRIS (white) Promising, but still not quite making the grade. Try *Dry River, Kim Crawford, Gibbston Valley, Grove Mill, Isabel Estate, St Helena, Seresin*.

PINOT NOIR (red) Not quite at the level of California yet, but making tremendous strides. None is as good as great Burgundy, but then nor is most Burgundy. *Martinborough Vineyard* is closest to the Burgundy benchmark. Try also *Ata Rangi, Chard Farm, Dry River, Felton Road*. Also: *Corbans, Giesen, Neudorf, Palliser Estate, Mark Rattray, Rippon, St Helena, Seresin, Waipara Springs, Waipara West*.

RIESLING (white) There's potential here for very good quality. Try *Corbans, Dry River, Giesen, Hunter's, Neudorf, Palliser Estate* and *Seifried*. For off-dry wines try *Collards, Millton, Montana* and *Stoneleigh*. The best sweet botrytized ones are made by *Collards, Corbans, Seifried* and *Villa Maria*.

SAUVIGNON BLANC (white) New Zealand's best wine. It can be divided into the pungently aromatic, herbaceous and zesty South Island (mainly Marlborough) styles, and the fleshier, riper and softer wines with stone-fruit flavours made on the North Island. There's increasingly a move towards single-vineyard wines, and an emphasis on terroir. Marlborough is becoming divided into Wairau Valley (rich, ripe, powerful) and Awatere (pungent and intense). Best of the South include: *Clifford Bay, Cloudy Bay, Corbans, Kim Crawford, Forrest, Hunter's, Jackson Estate, Montana Brancott Estate, Selaks, Stoneleigh, Vavasour, Villa Maria Wairau Valley* and *Wairau River*. Best North Island: *Matua Valley, Morton Estate, Palliser Estate* and *Vidal*.

SEMILLON (white) Generally ripe and lemony. *Villa Maria* and *Collards* are the best. *Selaks'* Sauvignon-Semillon is clearly the best blend.

WINE REGIONS

AUCKLAND (North Island) A catch-all area that includes such sub-regions as Kumeu/Huapai, Waiheke Island (Bordeaux blends from *Goldwater, Stonyridge* and *Waiheke Vineyards Te Motu*), Henderson and Northland/Matakana. Stars include *Babich, Collards, Corbans, Delegat's, Kumeu River, Matua Valley, Nobilo, Selaks, Villa Maria*.

CANTERBURY (South Island) Dominated by *Giesen*, with a reputation for sweet botrytized Riesling. The Waipara sub-region is home to *Mountford, Pegasus Bay, Mark Rattray, Waipara Springs* and *Waipara West*.

CENTRAL OTAGO (South Island) A fast-growing region in which Pinot Noir is rapidly becoming the most planted vine. *Chard Farm, Felton Road, Gibbston Valley* and *Rippon* are the leading producers.

GISBORNE (North Island) Local growers and winemakers have dubbed this region the Chardonnay capital of NZ. Gisborne is also a spiritual home of Gewürztraminer, and (less promisingly) a centre of bulk production of Müller-Thurgau. There are approximately as many wine styles here as there are wineries. Reds are less exciting than whites, although Pinot Noir is being grown for good Champagne-method fizz.

HAWKES BAY (North Island) Potentially NZ's greatest wine region. Chardonnay, Cabernets Sauvignon and Franc, and Merlot are the leading grapes, though there's also good Sauvignon Blanc, generally softer and riper than that of Marlborough. Best: *Brookfields, Church Road, Esk Valley, Ngatarawa, C J Pask, Sacred Hill, Te Mata, Vidal, Waimarama* and newcomers

Craggy Range and *Unison. Babich, Cooks, Matua Valley, Mills Reef, Morton Estate* and *Villa Maria* also use grapes from here.

MARLBOROUGH (South Island) NZ's biggest region by far specializes in Sauvignon Blanc and makes the archetypal NZ style, all gooseberries and cut grass. Riesling does well here, making wines from dry to sweet; Chardonnay is more difficult, but complex and distinctive when successful. Reds have fared less well although Pinot Noir is in great demand when it can be spared from the buoyant fizz industry. There's good botrytized wine here as well. Best: *Cellier Le Brun* (for fizz), *Cloudy Bay, Corbans, Kim Crawford, Grove Mill, Hunter's, Isabel Estate,* *Jackson Estate, Nautilus, Selaks, Vavasour* and *Wither Hills.*

MARTINBOROUGH (North Island) At the southern end of North Island, this is the source of some of NZ's most exciting Pinot Noirs. *Martinborough Vineyard, Ata Rangi* and *Dry River* are the Pinot stars, all making small quantities from low-yielding vines; *Palliser Estate* makes concentrated Chardonnay and Sauvignon Blanc, and there's promising Riesling and Pinot Gris, too.

NELSON (South Island) *Neudorf,* making subtle, nutty Chardonnay, and *Seifried,* with complex Riesling, are the leading lights in this South Island region.

PRODUCERS WHO'S WHO

ALLAN SCOTT ★ Lively Marlborough Sauvignon Blanc, pungent Riesling and elegant Chardonnay.

ALPHA DOMUS ★★ Lovely Hawkes Bay Sauvignon and Chardonnay.

ASKERNE ★★ Top Hawkes Bay whites such as Chardonnay.

ATA RANGI ★★★ Good subtle Pinot Noir, an intense Cabernet/Merlot/Shiraz blend called Célèbre, and nice Chardonnay.

BABICH ★★ Fresh Fumé Vert (Chardonnay, Semillon, Sauvignon), zesty Marlborough Sauvignon, elegant Irongate Chardonnay and Cabernet/Merlot, smoky The Patriarch Chardonnay.

CELLIER LE BRUN ★★ Excellent, Champenois-run specialist sparkling wine producer.

CLOUDY BAY ★★ Good, complex Sauvignon, fattened with a little Semillon. Top Champagne-method fizz under the Pelorus brand, with the ability to age well, and Chardonnay is also good.

COLLARDS ★★ A top Chardonnay maker. There's buttery Chenin Blanc and luscious botrytized Riesling when the vintage allows.

CORBANS ★ Very good Private Bin Chardonnay and single-vineyard Cottage Block Chardonnay and Pinot Noir.

DELEGAT'S ★ Good Oyster Bay range. Fine Chardonnay and Cabernet with a good botrytized Riesling. Proprietor's Reserve wines are limited-release.

DE REDCLIFFE ★ Consistent Chardonnay and Riesling with occasionally very good oak-aged Sauvignon Blanc. Look out for the Bordeaux-blend reds.

DRY RIVER ★★ The Pinot Noir, Gewürztraminer and Pinot Gris are among the best in the country; Chardonnay and botrytized styles are also up there.

ESK VALLEY ESTATE ★ Reds are based on blends of Bordeaux varieties, but the blend changes according to the year. Decent Chardonnay. Look out for single-vineyard The Terraces.

FROMM ★ Chardonnay is elegant, Cabernet Sauvignon ripe and Pinot Noir very impressive. The winemaking here seems to have a nice sure touch.

GIBBSTON VALLEY ★ Good Pinot Noir and Chardonnay. Sauvignon Blanc is somewhat more variable.

GIESEN ★★ Elegant lime-fruited dry and luscious sweet Riesling are the wines to look for here. There's also big, buttery Chardonnay.

GOLDWATER ★★ Big Waiheke reds, plus good Chardonnay. Sauvignon Blanc is called Dog Point.

GROVE MILL ★★ Weighty Riesling and rich Chardonnay from Marlborough. Top reds in good years.

HUNTER'S ★★ Jane Hunter makes top-of-the-line Sauvignon Blanc and elegant Chardonnay. Fizz is slightly dull.

ISABEL ESTATE ★★ Look out for Marlborough Sauvignon and Pinot Gris.

JACKSON ESTATE ★★ Classic Marlborough Sauvignon Blanc, complex Chardonnay and rather good vintage sparkling wine.

KUMEU RIVER ★★ Excellent single-vineyard Chardonnay from Mate's Vineyard. Good North Island Sauvignon Blanc and a Merlot-Cabernet blend.

LAWSON'S DRY HILLS ★★ Grapefruity Marlborough Sauvignon, and great Chardonnay.

MARTINBOROUGH VINEYARD ★★ NZ's best-known Pinot Noir, big and complex Chardonnay, lovely Riesling.

MATUA VALLEY ★★ Look for top Ararimu Chardonnay and Cabernet; also

---

INSTANT CELLAR:
COOL CHARDONNAYS

• 1999 Kumeu River, £14, New Zealand Wines Direct Lovely toasty wine with terrific texture. The Mate's Vineyard from the same producer is even better: £18, or £13.75 from The Wine Society.

• 1999 Neudorf Moutere, £17.75, The Wine Society Really world-class Chardonnay, very complex and deep.

• 1999 Mount Difficulty, Central Otago, £16.50, Berry Bros Very serious Chardonnay proving that NZ can make complex, top-class examples of the grape. This is minerally and citrus, with a creamy palate and a very long finish.

• 1999 Cloudy Bay, £14.90, Croque-en-Bouche Both crisp and tropical: good, well-made wine. In short supply, like all wines from this estate.

• 1999 Dry River Amaranth, Martinborough, £19, Justerini & Brooks Intensely citrus, peach and mineral wine cropped at very low levels.

Judd Estate Chardonnay. There's luscious Sauvignon and Gewürztraminer, and good Shingle Peak range from Marlborough.

MILLS REEF ★ Big, ripe Hawkes Bay Chardonnay, stylish limy Riesling and rich, ripe, mouthfilling fizz.

MILLTON ★★ New Zealand's first organic winemaker. There's lush, smoky, medium-dry Riesling (look out for Opou Vineyard), big, rich Chenin Blanc and balanced Chardonnay.

MISSION ★ A range of impressive Chardonnays, delicate Riesling and an occasional sweet botrytis-style when the year allows.

MONTANA ★ Top Champagne-method fizz, Lindauer; good Chardonnay and botrytized Riesling. Try Pinot Noir, and single-vineyard wines 'O', 'R' and 'P', after the initial letter of their vineyards' names.

> **ON THE CASE**
> NZ can never be a bargain
> basement: if you want good stuff,
> don't expect rock-bottom prices

MORTON ESTATE ★★ Chardonnay at this estate, especially Black Label, is reliable and attractive. There's also fresh Sauvignon Blanc and Gewürztraminer, and impressive Champagne-method fizz. Reds are pretty good.

NAUTILUS ★ Tight, quality-focused range includes top Marlborough Chardonnay, Sauvignon Blanc and firm, bottle-fermented fizz.

NEUDORF ★★ Remarkably subtle Burgundian-style Chardonnay. There's nice Sauvignon Blanc, too, as well as some Pinot Noir.

NGATARAWA ★ Attractive Chardonnay, Cabernet/Merlot and botrytized Riesling. The Glazebrook label is top of the range.

NOBILO ★ Good Dixon Vineyard Chardonnay. Stylish Sauvignon. Popular White Cloud is a reliable Müller-Thurgau and Sauvignon blend.

PALLISER ★★ Some nice Sauvignon, Pinot Noir and concentrated Chardonnay.

C J PASK ★★ Flavoursome reds from Cabernet, Merlot and Pinot Noir; also makes good Chardonnay from excellent vineyard sites.

PEGASUS BAY ★★ Great Riesling, unconventional Sauvignon Blanc/Semillon and big, chewy Pinot Noir.

MARK RATTRAY VINEYARDS ★★ Very good Waipara-based Pinot Noir producer. Excellent Chardonnay.

RIPPON VINEYARD ★ Organic vineyard with a promising Pinot Noir. There's also some Syrah. The range of whites include decent Chardonnay and Sauvignon Blanc.

ST CLAIR ★ Classic Marlborough Sauvignon Blanc, elegant Chardonnay and pungent medium-dry Riesling.

ST HELENA ★ Good Chardonnay, Pinot Gris and Pinot Blanc.

SEIFRIED ESTATE ★ Very good Riesling, more complex than most. Sauvignon Blanc, too, is distinguished and well-made.

SELAKS ★★ Great Sauvignon and Sauvignon/Semillon. Founder's Selection is the top label.

STONYRIDGE ★★★ NZ's top red producer. Intense, ripe Cabernet blend (Larose) with less intense version as the second label.

TE MATA ★★★ Coleraine and Awatea are sought-after Cabernet/Merlot blends. There's also Burgundian-style Chardonnay under the Elston label, and one of NZ's first Syrahs.

VAVASOUR ★★ Top Chardonnay, promising Pinot Noir and very good Sauvignons.

VIDAL ESTATE ★★ Gewürztraminer and Chardonnay here are very good. Reds have been excellent since 1998.

VILLA MARIA ★★ Top Sauvignon Blanc (look especially for single-vineyard wines) and botrytized Riesling. Also fine Reserve reds.

WAIPARA WEST ★ Good Chardonnay and Sauvignon Blanc. Best is Bordeaux blend Ram Paddock Red.

NEW ZEALAND PRICES

RED

Under £7.00

Cabernet Sauvignon/Merlot Montana
  Timara 2000 £4.99 (THR) £4.99 (WR)
Cabernet Sauvignon/Merlot Montana
  Timara 1998 £5.69 (JON)
Dry Red Waimanu North Island 1998
  £4.49 (UN)

£7.00 → £8.99

Cabernet Franc Kim Crawford Hawkes Bay
  1999 £8.90 (BAC) £8.99 (LIB) £9.99 (VIL)
★ Cabernet Franc Waipara West 1999
  £7.99 (WAT)
Cabernet Sauvignon Delegat's Reserve
  Hawkes Bay 1999 £8.99 (SAF)
Cabernet Sauvignon Delegat's Reserve
  Hawkes Bay 1998 £8.99 (OD)
Cabernet Sauvignon C J Pask 1998 £8.95
  (POR) £9.49 (JON)
Cabernet Sauvignon C J Pask 1997 £8.95
  (BALL)
Cabernet Sauvignon Selaks Hawkes Bay
  1996 £7.95 (STE)
Cabernet Sauvignon Stoneleigh
  Marlborough 1997 £7.99 (VIL)
Cabernet Sauvignon/Merlot Aotea 1998
  £8.25 (LLO)
Cabernet Sauvignon/Merlot Aotea 1997
  £8.77 (PLAY)
Cabernet Sauvignon/Merlot Matua Valley
  Hawkes Bay 1999 £8.95 (STE)
Cabernet Sauvignon/Merlot Montana
  Church Road 1998 £8.95 (COC) £8.99
  (VIC) £8.99 (THR) £8.99 (BOT) £8.99 (WR)
  £8.99 (OD) £9.67 (BY)
Cabernet Sauvignon/Merlot C J Pask
  Hawkes Bay 1999 £8.25 (TAN) £8.95
  (POR) £9.25 (LAY)

Cabernet Sauvignon/Merlot Te Mata
  1998 £8.46 (PEN) £8.49 (VIC) £8.49
  (THR) £8.49 (BOT) £8.79 (AME)
Cabernet Sauvignon/Merlot West Brook
  Blue Ridge 1998 £8.95 (MAY)
Merlot Montana Reserve 1999 £8.77 (COC)
Merlot Montana Reserve 1998 £8.99 (TES)
  £8.99 (VIL)
Merlot Sacred Hill Whitecliff 1998 £7.99
  (UN)
Merlot Saint Clair 2000 £8.49 (COC)
Merlot West Brook 1998 £7.99 (AME)
Pinot Noir Greenstone Point 1999 £8.99
  (POR)
Pinot Noir Jackson Estate 1996 £8.95 (HED)
Ram Paddock Red Waipara West 1996
  £8.59 (WAT) £8.99 (DI)
Syrah Babich Mara Estate 1997 £7.85 (CON)
Syrah Babich Winemaker's Reserve 1999
  £7.49 (TES)
Two Terrace Red Waipara West 1997
  £7.95 (NZW)

£9.00 → £10.99

Cabernet Franc Kim Crawford Wicken
  Hawkes Bay 1999 £9.99 (VA)
Cabernet Sauvignon Redwood Valley 1998
  £9.00 (NZW) £9.39 (DOM) £9.50 (STA)
Cabernet Sauvignon/Merlot Montana
  Church Road 1997 £9.99 (VIL)
Cabernet Sauvignon/Merlot Ngatarawa
  Glazebrook 1999 £10.99 (YOU)
Cabernet Sauvignon/Merlot C J Pask
  Hawkes Bay 1993 £10.90 (CRO)
Cabernet Sauvignon/Merlot Te Mata
  1999 £9.95 (BALL) £10.52 (TW)
Cabernet Sauvignon/Merlot Villa Maria
  Cellar Selection 1998 £9.99 (SAF)
Merlot Kim Crawford Hawkes Bay 1999
  £9.95 (LIB) £9.99 (BAL)
Merlot Kemblefield Estate 1997 £9.95 (STA)

RETAILERS SPECIALIZING IN NEW ZEALAND
see Retailers Directory (page 40) for details

Nobody has very many (except New
Zealand Wines Direct), but for a wider-
than-average choice, try: Adnams (AD),
Averys of Bristol, Ballantynes of
Cowbridge (BAL), Anthony Byrne (BY),

Cockburns of Leith (COC), First Quench
Group (BOT, THR, VIC, WR), New Zealand
Wines Direct (NZW), Lay & Wheeler
(LAY), Tanners (TAN), Wine Society (WS),
Noel Young (YOU).

Merlot Kim Crawford Te Awanga
Hawkes Bay **1999** £9.90 (BAC) £9.99
(VIL) £10.25 (STA)
Merlot Omaka Springs **1999** £9.50 (BALL)
Pinot Noir Giesen Canterbury **1999**
£10.49 (CB)
Pinot Noir Huia Vineyards **2000** £10.48
(BIB)
Pinot Noir Hunter's **1999** £9.99 (DI)
£10.90 (TAN) £10.99 (JON) £10.99 (YOU)
Pinot Noir Jackson Estate **1999** £9.95
(POR) £13.28 (TW)
Pinot Noir Jackson Estate **1998** £9.95
(STA) £10.99 (AME)
Pinot Noir Martinborough **1996** £10.50
(CRO) £13.11 (NO)
Pinot Noir Montana Reserve
Marlborough **1999** £9.99 (TES) £9.99
(WR) £9.99 (WAI) £9.99 (OD) £9.99 (SAF)
Pinot Noir Montana Reserve Marlborough
1998 £9.99 (UN) £9.99 (VIL)
Pinot Noir Mount Riley **1999** £9.99 (VA)
Pinot Noir Palliser Estate **1998** £10.95
(JU) £14.99 (VIL)
Pinot Noir Selaks Drylands Vineyard
1999 £10.75 (STE)
Pinot Noir Te Kairanga **2000** £10.77 (BIB)

£11.00 → £14.99

Cabernet Sauvignon Montana Fairhall
Estate **1998** £11.99 (VIL)
Cabernet Sauvignon Walnut Ridge **1998**
£14.99 (VIL)
Cabernet Sauvignon/Merlot Mills Reef
Elspeth **1997** £12.46 (PEN)
Cabernet Sauvignon/Merlot Montana
Church Road Reserve **1998** £11.99 (WAI)
Cabernet Sauvignon/Merlot Morton
Estate Black Label **1995** £13.99 (NEZ)
Cabernet Sauvignon/Merlot Te Mata
Awatea **1997** £13.99 (WR)
Cabernet Sauvignon/Merlot Te Mata
Awatea **1995** £13.51 (PEN)
Cabernet Sauvignon/Merlot Trinity Hill
Gimblett Road **1998** £14.45 (GN)
Cabernet Sauvignon/Merlot Villa Maria
Reserve **1998** £13.99 (SAF)
Célèbre Ata Rangi **1998** £14.00 (NZW)
£14.95 (WS) £16.75 (STA) £17.75 (FORT)

*Stars (★) indicate wines selected by
Oz Clarke in the Best Buys section which
begins on page 8.*

Merlot/Cabernet Franc Redmetal
Vineyards **1999** £12.00 (NZW)
Merlot/Cabernet Sauvignon Esk Valley
1997 £11.50 (BALL)
Merlot/Cabernet Sauvignon Ngatarawa
Glazebrook **1998** £11.99 (AME)
Merlot/Cabernet Sauvignon Sileni Estates
1998 £11.65 (FA) £12.70 (RIC) £14.75
(MAY) £16.49 (YOU)
Pinot Noir Cloudy Bay **1998** £13.93 (NO)
Pinot Noir Felton Road **1999** £13.25 (SOM)
£14.80 (HAH) £15.99 (RAE) £16.49 (YOU)
Pinot Noir Fromm La Strada **1999** £13.95
(LAY)
Pinot Noir Hunter's **1998** £11.95 (JER)
£12.40 (CRO) £14.50 (BALL)
Pinot Noir Isabel Estate **1999** £13.99
(YOU) £14.50 (MV)
Pinot Noir Isabel Estate **1997** £13.49 (POR)
Pinot Noir Martinborough **1999** £14.50
(AD) £14.99 (VIC) £14.99 (THR)£14.99
(BOT) £14.99 (WR) £15.99 (YOU)
Pinot Noir Martinborough **1998** £13.95
(FORT) £14.25 (CON) £14.99 (VIL)
Pinot Noir Martinborough **1997** £11.50
(SOM)
Pinot Noir Matariki **1999** £12.69 (YOU)
Pinot Noir Muddy Water Waipara **1999**
£13.99 (AME)
Pinot Noir Nautilus **1999** £12.99 (YOU)
Pinot Noir Palliser Estate **1999** £11.49
(VIC) £11.49 (THR) £11.49 (BOT) £11.49
(WR) £12.49 (YOU) £12.65 (BY)
Pinot Noir Rippon Vineyard **1998** £13.99
(UN) £16.75 (STA)
Pinot Noir Seresin Estate **1998** £14.12 (NO)
Pinot Noir Te Kairanga Reserve **2000**
£13.71 (BIB)
Pinot Noir Waipara West **1999** £12.45
(WAT)
Pinot Noir Wither Hills Marlborough
1999 £11.99 (OD) £14.95 (BAL)
Syrah Stonecroft **1998** £12.49 (YOU)
£13.95 (LEA)
Syrah Te Mata Bullnose **1998** £13.51
(PEN) £14.99 (YOU)

£15.00 → £19.99

Cabernet Sauvignon C J Pask Reserve
1995 £19.00 (CRO)
Cabernet Sauvignon Vidal Reserve **1994**
£15.49 (YOU)
Cabernet Sauvignon/Merlot Benfield &
Delamare **1997** £17.99 (VIL) £18.95
(MAY)

Cabernet Sauvignon/Merlot Peninsula
  Estate **1996** £19.99 (VIL) £19.99 (YOU)
Cabernet Sauvignon/Merlot Peninsula
  Estate **1993** £19.00 (FA)
Célèbre Ata Rangi **1997** £16.20 (TAN)
Coleraine Te Mata **1997** £19.70 (TAN)
Coleraine Te Mata **1996** £19.95 (AME)
Coleraine Te Mata **1994** £18.57 (PEN)
Merlot/Cabernet Franc Redmetal Vineyards
  Basket Press **1999** £16.99 (YOU)
Pinot Noir Ata Rangi **1997** £19.00 (FA)
Pinot Noir Cloudy Bay **1999** £15.90 (CRO)
Pinot Noir Felton Road Block 3 **1999**
  £18.99 (VIL)
Pinot Noir Fromm La Strada **1998** £16.49
  (YOU) £21.95 (LAY)
Pinot Noir Gibbston Valley **1998** £15.99
  (YOU) £18.95 (RES)
Pinot Noir Giesen Reserve Canterbury
  1998 £16.10 (CB)
Pinot Noir Mount Difficulty **2000** £19.75
  (NI)
Pinot Noir Mount Difficulty **1999** £16.99
  (YOU) £19.99 (VIL)
Pinot Noir Neudorf Moutere **1999**
  £17.50 (WS)
Pinot Noir Ollsen's of Bannockburn **1999**
  £19.99 (VIL)
Pinot Noir Rippon Vineyard **1999** £15.99
  (YOU)
Pinot Noir Seresin Estate **1999** £15.83
  (ARM)
Pinot Noir Walnut Ridge **1998** £18.49
  (YOU) £19.99 (VIL)
The Terraces Esk Valley **1991** £19.00 (FA)
Unison **1997** £17.67 (NO)
Unison **1996** £15.90 (CRO)
Unison Selection **1999** £15.95 (WAI)

£20.00 → £29.99

Cabernet Sauvignon/Merlot Goldwater
  Estate Waiheke Island **1998** £24.99 (YOU)
Cabernet Sauvignon/Merlot Goldwater
  Estate Waiheke Island **1996** £22.99 (COC)
Cabernet Sauvignon/Merlot Waiheke
  Vineyards Te Motu **1997** £23.00 (NZW)
Cabernet Sauvignon/Merlot Waiheke
  Vineyards Te Motu **1996** £27.25 (FORT)
Cabernet Sauvignon/Merlot Waiheke
  Vineyards Te Motu **1994** £24.87 (FA)
Coleraine Te Mata **1998** £20.95 (FA)
  £21.99 (CRO)
Merlot/Malbec/Cabernet Sauvignon Esk
  Valley Reserve **1996** £22.50 (BALL)
Pinot Noir Ata Rangi **2000** £25.00 (NZW)

Pinot Noir Martinborough Reserve **1998**
  £20.49 (YOU)
Pinot Noir Martinborough Reserve **1997**
  £23.99 (VIL) £25.50 (BEN)
Pinot Noir Mount Difficulty **1998** £20.21
  (NO)
Pinot Noir Mount Edward **2000** £22.50 (NI)
Pinot Noir Mount Edward **1999** £21.99
  (VIL)

Over £30.00

Larose Stonyridge **1999** £32.00 (NZW)
  £39.49 (YOU) £39.95 (TAN) £45.00 (FORT)
Larose Stonyridge **1998** £42.00 (STA)
Larose Stonyridge **1996** £40.95 (PLAY)
Merlot Goldwater Estate Esslin Waiheke
  Island **1999** £33.99 (YOU)
Pinot Noir Martinborough Reserve **1996**
  £36.00 (CRO)

WHITE

Under £4.00

Timara Dry White Montana **2001** £3.99
  (SAF)
Timara Dry White Montana **2000** £3.99
  (VIC) £3.99 (THR) £3.99 (BOT) £3.99 (WR)

£4.00 → £4.99

Chardonnay Coopers Creek Fat Cat
  Hawkes Bay **2000** £4.99 (CO)
Sauvignon Blanc/Semillon Montana Azure
  Bay **2000** £4.99 (VIC) £4.99 (THR)
White Cloud Nobilo **2001** £4.99 (SAF)
White Cloud Nobilo **2000** £4.99 (TES)
White Cloud Nobilo **1999** £4.99 (SO)
  £4.99 (TAN)

£5.00 → £5.99

Chardonnay Corbans Gisborne Estate
  1999 £5.49 (TES)
Chardonnay Corbans Gisborne Estate
  1998 £5.49 (UN)
Chardonnay Grove Mill Sanctuary **1999**
  £5.49 (SAI)
Chardonnay Matua Valley **1999** £5.88
  (PEN) £5.99 (VIL)
Chardonnay Montana Marlborough **2000**
  £5.95 (COC) £5.99 (BUD) £5.99 (VIC)
  £5.99 (THR) £5.99 (BOT) £5.99 (WR)
  £5.99 (OD) £5.99 (SAF) £5.99 (MORR)
Chardonnay Montana Marlborough **1999**
  £5.49 (BO) £5.99 (UN) £5.99 (WAI) £5.99
  (VIL) £6.29 (JON) £6.46 (BY)

Riesling Villa Maria Private Bin **2000** £5.99
(MAJ) £5.99 (VIC) £5.99 (THR) £5.99 (BOT)
£5.99 (WR) £5.99 (WAI)

Sauvignon Blanc Corbans Stoneleigh **2000**
£5.99 (TES)

Sauvignon Blanc Grove Mill Sanctuary
2000 £5.49 (SAI)

Sauvignon Blanc Matua Valley Hawkes Bay
2000 £5.99 (VIL)

Sauvignon Blanc Matua Valley Hawkes Bay
1999 £5.88 (PEN)

Sauvignon Blanc Montana Marlborough
2001 £5.99 (SAF)

Sauvignon Blanc Montana Marlborough
2000 £5.49 (BO) £5.99 (SAI) £5.99 (BUD)
£5.99 (TES) £5.99 (VIC) £5.99 (THR) £5.99
(BOT) £5.99 (WR) £5.99 (VIL) £6.29 (JON)

Sauvignon Blanc Montana Marlborough
1999 £5.95 (COC) £5.99 (UN) £5.99
(OD) £6.46 (BY)

Sauvignon Blanc Nobilo **1999** £5.99 (SO)

Sauvignon Blanc Nobilo Marlborough
2000 £5.95 (BY)

Sauvignon Blanc Seifried Old Coach Road
1999 £5.99 (CON)

Semillon/Chardonnay Babich Gisborne
1999 £5.59 (COC)

Timara Dry White Montana **1999** £5.03
(BY)

£6.00 → £6.99

Chardonnay Babich Gisborne **1999** £6.89
(CON)

Chardonnay Delegat's Oyster Bay **2000**
£6.99 (SAI) £6.99 (MAJ) £6.99 (THR)

Chardonnay Delegat's Oyster Bay **1999**
£6.99 (UN)

Chardonnay Kumeu River Brajkovich
2000 £6.50 (WS)

Chardonnay Mills Reef Moffat Road **1994**
£6.46 (PEN)

Chardonnay C J Pask **1998** £6.99 (TAN)
£7.40 (HAH) £7.50 (BALL) £7.50 (AD)
£7.99 (POR)

Chardonnay Saint Clair Tuatara Bay **1999**
£6.99 (COC)

Chardonnay Selaks **2000** £6.75 (STE)

Please remember that
Oz Clarke's Wine Buying Guide
is a price **guide** *and not a price* **list**. *It is
not meant to replace up-to-date
merchants' lists.*

Chardonnay Villa Maria Private Bin **2000**
£6.99 (OD) £6.99 (SAF)

Chardonnay Villa Maria Private Bin **1999**
£6.99 (UN) £6.99 (SO) £6.99 (BO)

Chardonnay Villa Maria Private Bin **1998**
£6.80 (CRO)

Chardonnay Villa Maria Private Bin East
Coast **1999** £6.99 (WAI)

Chenin Blanc Esk Valley Wood-aged
1998 £6.99 (PLA)

Pinot Gris Babich Marlborough **2000**
£6.99 (WR)

Riesling Jackson Estate **1999** £6.99 (POR)
£6.99 (BO)

Riesling Selaks **1998** £6.95 (STE) £9.82 (HIC)

Sauvignon Blanc Aotea **2000** £6.95 (NZW)
£6.95 (FORT) £7.46 (LLO) £7.50 (LEA)
£7.80 (MV) £7.90 (JER)

Sauvignon Blanc Aotea **1999** £6.95 (STA)

Sauvignon Blanc Babich Hawkes Bay **1999**
£6.59 (COC) £6.89 (CON)

Sauvignon Blanc Babich Marlborough
1999 £6.49 (CON)

Sauvignon Blanc Churton Marlborough
2000 £6.27 (FA) £7.50 (TAN)

Sauvignon Blanc Kim Crawford
Marlborough **2000** £6.75 (SOM) £8.99
(LIB) £8.99 (VIL) £9.16 (FLE)

Sauvignon Blanc Dashwood **2000** £6.99
(VIC) £6.99 (THR) £6.99 (BOT) £6.99 (WR)
£6.99 (OD) £7.88 (LLO) £7.99 (BO)

Sauvignon Blanc De Redcliffe
Marlborough **2000** £6.85 (AS)

Sauvignon Blanc Delegat's Oyster Bay
2001 £6.99 (SAF)

Sauvignon Blanc Delegat's Oyster Bay
2000 £6.99 (UN) £6.99 (MAJ) £6.99
(THR) £6.99 (WAI) £6.99 (CO) £7.35 (BER)

Sauvignon Blanc Mills Reef **1997** £6.46
(PEN)

Sauvignon Blanc C J Pask Hawkes Bay **2000**
£6.25 (TAN) £6.50 (HAH) £6.99 (POR)

Sauvignon Blanc C J Pask Hawkes Bay
1999 £6.25 (BALL) £6.65 (AD) £6.99 (JON)

Sauvignon Blanc Redwood Valley **1999**
£6.75 (WS) £9.00 (NZW) £9.11 (DOM)
£9.40 (STA)

Sauvignon Blanc Saint Clair Tuatara Bay
2000 £6.99 (COC)

Sauvignon Blanc Selaks **2000** £6.75 (STE)
£8.65 (LLO)

Sauvignon Blanc Stoneleigh Marlborough
2000 £6.49 (SAI)

Sauvignon Blanc Stoneleigh Marlborough
1998 £6.99 (VIL)

Sauvignon Blanc Villa Maria Private Bin
   2000 £6.80 (CRO) £6.99 (SAI) £6.99 (TES)
   £6.99 (BO) £6.99 (VIC) £6.99 (THR) £6.99
   (BOT) £6.99 (WR) £6.99 (OD) £6.99 (SAF)
Sauvignon Blanc Villa Maria Private Bin
   1999 £6.75 (POR) £6.99 (UN)
Sauvignon Blanc Wairau River **2000** £6.20
   (SOM) £7.50 (CRO) £8.49 (YOU) £8.75
   (LEA) £9.99 (SUN) £9.99 (LAI)

£7.00 → £7.99

Chardonnay Aotea **1999** £7.20 (NZW)
   £7.95 (STA) £8.39 (LLO)
Chardonnay Babich Hawkes Bay **1998**
   £7.95 (TAN)
Chardonnay Babich Hawkes Bay **1995**
   £7.90 (JU)
Chardonnay Bradshaw Estate Non-
   Wooded **1998** £7.99 (AME)
Chardonnay Cairnbrae **1999** £7.93 (CB)
Chardonnay Kim Crawford Unoaked
   Marlborough **1999** £7.99 (BAL) £8.99
   (UN) £8.99 (VA) £9.16 (FLE)
Chardonnay Kumeu River Brajkovich
   1998 £7.25 (FA)
Chardonnay Lawson's Dry Hills **1999**
   £7.99 (SAF)
Chardonnay Saint Clair **1998** £7.89 (COC)
Chardonnay Stoneleigh **1996** £7.99 (VIL)
Chenin Blanc Esk Valley Wood-aged
   1997 £7.86 (PLAY)
Gewürztraminer Lawson's Dry Hills
   1998 £7.99 (AME)
Gewürztraminer Montana Reserve
   Gisborne **2000** £7.99 (VIC) £7.99 (THR)
   £7.99 (BOT) £7.99 (WR)
Gewürztraminer Seifried **2000** £7.75
   (STA)
Riesling Cairnbrae **2000** £7.93 (CB)
Riesling Clifford Bay Estate **1999** £7.75
   (FRI)
Riesling Grove Mill Marlborough **2000**
   £7.99 (SAF)
Riesling Jackson Estate Dry **1999** £7.49
   (HED) £7.75 (TAN)
Riesling Montana Awatere Reserve **2000**
   £7.99 (OD)
Riesling Palliser Estate **2000** £7.50 (JU)
   £8.17 (BY)
Riesling Saint Clair **1999** £7.89 (COC)
Sauvignon Blanc Babich Mara Estate **1998**
   £7.89 (CON)
Sauvignon Blanc Cairnbrae **2000** £7.93 (CB)
Sauvignon Blanc Chancellor **1999** £7.99
   (GW)

Sauvignon Blanc Clifford Bay Estate **1998**
   £7.95 (FRI)
Sauvignon Blanc Kim Crawford
   Marlborough **1999** £7.99 (BAL) £8.25
   (CON) £8.99 (UN)
Sauvignon Blanc De Gyffarde
   Marlborough **2000** £7.99 (GN)
★ Sauvignon Blanc Forrest Estate **2000**
   £7.95 (AD) £7.99 (BEN) £7.99 (VIL) £8.25
   (NI)
Sauvignon Blanc Forrest Estate **1999**
   £7.10 (FLE)
Sauvignon Blanc Goldwater Estate Dog
   Point Marlborough **2000** £7.99 (MAJ)
Sauvignon Blanc Grove Mill Marlborough
   2000 £7.49 (OD)
Sauvignon Blanc Isabel Estate **2000** £7.94
   (SOM) £9.40 (BAC) £9.45 (BU) £9.50
   (FORT) £9.50 (MV) £9.79 (YOU) £9.95
   (BEN) £9.99 (POR) £10.95 (RES)
Sauvignon Blanc Lawson's Dry Hills **2000**
   £7.95 (LAY) £7.99 (TES) £7.99 (YOU)
Sauvignon Blanc Lawson's Dry Hills **1999**
   £7.99 (AME)
Sauvignon Blanc Lincoln Vineyards
   Heritage Collection **2000** £7.39 (PLA)
Sauvignon Blanc Montana Reserve **2000**
   £7.99 (TES)
Sauvignon Blanc Montana Reserve **1998**
   £7.99 (UN)
Sauvignon Blanc Morton Estate Colefields
   2000 £7.49 (NEZ)
Sauvignon Blanc Saint Clair **2000** £7.89
   (COC)
Sauvignon Blanc Allan Scott **2000** £7.95
   (LAY)
Sauvignon Blanc Allan Scott **1999** £7.95
   (BALL) £8.50 (FORT)
Sauvignon Blanc Trinity Hill **2000** £7.75
   (WS)
Sauvignon Blanc Vidal **1999** £7.34 (DOM)
Sauvignon Blanc West Brook
   Marlborough **2000** £7.49 (AME)
★ Sauvignon Blanc Wither Hills
   Marlborough **2000** £7.99 (GW) £7.99
   (OD) £8.99 (BAL)
Semillon Forrest Estate **1999** £7.75 (FORT)

£8.00 → £8.99

Chardonnay Clifford Bay Estate **1999**
   £8.50 (FRI)
Chardonnay Kim Crawford Unoaked
   Marlborough **2000** £8.90 (BAC) £8.99
   (LIB) £8.99 (VIL)
Chardonnay Dashwood **2000** £8.39 (LLO)

Chardonnay De Redcliffe Mangatawhiri **1997** £8.99 (UN)

★ Chardonnay Delegat's Hawkes Bay Reserve Barrique-Fermented **1998** £8.99 (SAF)

Chardonnay Jackson Estate **1999** £8.95 (TAN) £8.99 (POR) £10.09 (PLA)

Chardonnay Montana Church Road **1998** £8.99 (UN) £8.99 (WR) £9.67 (BY)

Chardonnay C J Pask **1999** £8.99 (JON)

Chardonnay Te Kairanga **2000** £8.72 (BIB)

Chardonnay Trinity Hill **1999** £8.95 (LEA)

Chardonnay Villa Maria Cellar Selection **1999** £8.49 (OD)

Chardonnay Wither Hills Marlborough **1999** £8.95 (WS) £8.99 (OD) £10.99 (BAL)

Gewürztraminer Hunter's **2000** £8.99 (DI)

Gewürztraminer Hunter's **1999** £8.40 (CRO)

Pinot Gris Kim Crawford **2000** £8.95 (STA) £8.99 (LIB) £8.99 (VIL)

Pinot Gris Omaka Springs **2000** £8.95 (RES)

Riesling Kim Crawford Dry Marlborough **2000** £8.90 (BAC) £8.99 (LIB) £8.99 (VIL)

Riesling Kim Crawford Dry Marlborough **1999** £8.25 (CON)

Riesling Forrest Estate **1999** £8.44 (FLE) £9.95 (AD)

Riesling Huia Vineyards **2001** £8.23 (BIB)

Riesling Hunter's Rhine **1998** £8.40 (CRO)

Riesling Kim Crawford Marlborough **2000** £8.95 (STA)

Riesling Kim Crawford Marlborough **1999** £8.25 (CON) £8.99 (VA) £9.16 (FLE)

Riesling Martinborough **1998** £8.95 (AD) £9.50 (BALL)

Riesling Montana Reserve **1999** £8.99 (VIL)

Riesling Neudorf Moutere **2000** £8.95 (WS)

Riesling Omaka Springs **2000** £8.95 (RES)

Riesling Allan Scott **1999** £8.50 (FORT)

★ Riesling Waipara West **1999** £8.29 (WAT)

Sauvignon Blanc Coopers Creek Marlborough **1999** £8.79 (CON)

Sauvignon Blanc Craggy Range Old Renwick Vineyard Marlborough **2000** £8.99 (WAI) £9.79 (AME)

Sauvignon Blanc De Gyffarde Marlborough **1999** £8.99 (PEN)

Sauvignon Blanc Esk Valley **1999** £8.65 (PLAY)

Sauvignon Blanc Goldwater Estate Dog Point Marlborough **1999** £8.99 (COC)

Sauvignon Blanc Hunter's **2000** £8.90 (CRO) £8.99 (DI) £9.99 (SUN) £9.99 (JON) £9.99 (OD) £9.99 (LAI) £9.99 (YOU)

Sauvignon Blanc Jackson Estate **2000** £8.49 (POR) £8.49 (BO) £8.80 (CRO) £8.95 (WRI) £8.99 (HED) £8.99 (TES) £8.99 (AME) £8.99 (WAI) £8.99 (OD) £9.27 (PLA) £9.29 (JON)

Sauvignon Blanc Montana Reserve **1999** £8.99 (VIL)

Sauvignon Blanc Mount Riley **2000** £8.99 (VA)

Sauvignon Blanc Neudorf Marlborough **2000** £8.95 (WS) £10.80 (CRO)

Sauvignon Blanc Neudorf Nelson **2000** £8.71 (FA)

Sauvignon Blanc Ngatarawa Glazebrook **2000** £8.74 (NO)

Sauvignon Blanc Omaka Springs **2000** £8.95 (RES)

Sauvignon Blanc Palliser Estate **2000** £8.16 (BY) £9.49 (YOU) £9.99 (THR) £9.99 (WR)

Sauvignon Blanc Palliser Estate **1998** £8.04 (BY) £9.95 (JU)

Sauvignon Blanc Selaks **1999** £8.32 (HIC)

Sauvignon Blanc Selaks Drylands Vineyard **2000** £8.25 (WS) £9.45 (STE)

Sauvignon Blanc Te Kairanga **2000** £8.27 (BIB)

Sauvignon Blanc Te Mata Castle Hill **2000** £8.79 (AME) £11.22 (TW)

Sauvignon Blanc Te Mata Castle Hill **1997** £8.47 (PEN)

Sauvignon Blanc Villa Maria Cellar Selection **2000** £8.49 (OD)

Sauvignon Blanc Waipara West **1999** £8.29 (WAT) £8.99 (DI)

£9.00 → £10.99

Chardonnay Alpha Domus Hawkes Bay Unwooded **1998** £10.99 (YOU)

Chardonnay Felton Road **1999** £9.95 (HAH)

Chardonnay Forrest Estate **2000** £9.50 (NI)

Chardonnay Forrest Estate **1998** £9.95 (AD)

Chardonnay Goldwater Estate Roseland Marlborough **1998** £9.99 (COC) £9.99 (MAJ) £10.40 (GN)

Chardonnay Huia Vineyards **2000** £9.01 (BIB)

Chardonnay Hunter's **1999** £10.99 (JON)

Chardonnay Jackson Estate **1998** £9.85 (WRI) £9.95 (HED) £9.99 (AME)

Chardonnay Kim Crawford Te Awanga Hawkes Bay **1999** £9.90 (BAC) £9.99 (VIL)

Chardonnay Kumeu River Brajkovich
1999 £9.95 (BEN)
Chardonnay Martinborough **1999** £9.25
(SOM)
Chardonnay Matua Valley Eastern Bays
1999 £10.52 (TW)
Chardonnay Matua Valley Judd Estate
1998 £9.95 (STE)
Chardonnay Montana Church Road **1999**
£9.99 (VIL)
Chardonnay Montana Ormond Estate
Gisborne **1999** £10.99 (VIC) £10.99
(THR) £10.99 (BOT) £10.99 (WR)
Chardonnay Montana Ormond Estate
Gisborne **1998** £10.85 (COC) £10.99
(VIL)
Chardonnay Montana Renwick Estate
1998 £10.99 (VIL)
Chardonnay Montana Renwick Estate
1997 £10.85 (COC)
Chardonnay Ngatarawa Glazebrook
2000 £9.99 (YOU)
Chardonnay Palliser Estate **1999** £10.26
(BY)

Chardonnay Palliser Estate **1997** £10.90
(JU)
Chardonnay Redwood Valley **1999** £9.00
(NZW)
Chardonnay Redwood Valley Barrel-
Fermented **1996** £10.75 (STA)
Chardonnay Selaks Founders **1997** £9.95
(STE)
Chardonnay Seresin Estate **1998** £10.95
(WAI) £11.00 (ARM)
Chardonnay Soljans Hawkes Bay Barrique
1996 £9.50 (FRI)
Chardonnay Te Kairanga Reserve **2000**
£10.28 (BIB)
Chardonnay Trinity Hill **1998** £9.85 (GN)
Chardonnay Vavasour **1999** £10.35 (LLO)
Chardonnay Vavasour **1998** £9.85 (NI)
Chardonnay Waipara West **1996** £9.99
(WAT) £10.99 (DI)
Chenin Blanc Esk Valley **1998** £9.95
(BALL)

Gewürztraminer Montana Patutahi Estate
1999 £10.99 (CON)
Gewürztraminer Montana Patutahi Estate
1998 £10.99 (VIL)
Pinot Gris Brookfields **2000** £10.00 (NZW)
Riesling Hunter's Rhine **1999** £9.99 (DI)
Riesling Isabel Estate **1999** £9.40 (MV)
Riesling Jackson Estate Dry **1997** £9.34
(TW)
Riesling Rippon Vineyard **1999** £10.99
(YOU) £11.27 (BY)
Riesling Selaks Drylands Vineyard Dry
2000 £9.45 (STE)
Riesling Vavasour **1999** £9.85 (NI)
Riesling Waipara West **1998** £10.95 (DI)
Sauvignon Blanc Cloudy Bay **2000** £10.99
(SAF) £12.45 (GN) £12.49 (CON) £12.95
(STE) £13.16 (PLAY) £13.50 (CRO) £14.59
(FA) £14.99 (SUN) £14.99 (LAI)
Sauvignon Blanc Fairhall Downs **2000**
£9.99 (POR)
Sauvignon Blanc Huia Vineyards **2001**
£9.01 (BIB)
Sauvignon Blanc Hunter's **1999** £9.95
(WRI) £9.99 (UN) £10.95 (JER)
Sauvignon Blanc Hunter's **1998** £9.95 (AME)
Sauvignon Blanc Hunter's Wood-aged
1999 £9.99 (DI)
Sauvignon Blanc Hunter's Wood-aged
1998 £10.50 (WRI) £10.50 (TAN)
Sauvignon Blanc Isabel Estate **1999** £9.95
(HED)
Sauvignon Blanc Jackson Estate **1999**
£9.20 (TAN) £10.23 (PLAY)
Sauvignon Blanc Montana Brancott Estate
1999 £10.99 (VIL)
Sauvignon Blanc Montana Brancott Estate
1998 £10.85 (COC)
Sauvignon Blanc Nautilus Marlborough
2000 £10.25 (STE)
Sauvignon Blanc Nautilus Marlborough
1998 £9.91 (SUN)
Sauvignon Blanc Seresin Estate **2000**
£9.83 (ARM) £9.99 (VIL)
Sauvignon Blanc Te Mata Castle Hill **1999**
£9.99 (YOU)
Sauvignon Blanc Torlesse Marlborough
2000 £9.10 (NZW) £9.81 (LLO)
Sauvignon Blanc Torlesse Marlborough
1999 £9.50 (STA)
Sauvignon Blanc Vavasour **2000** £10.35
(LLO)
Sauvignon Blanc Vavasour **1999** £9.49 (BO)
Sauvignon Blanc Villa Maria Reserve
Clifford Bay **2000** £9.99 (OD)

Sauvignon Blanc Villa Maria Reserve
Wairau Valley **2000** £9.99 (VIC) £9.99
(THR) £9.99 (BOT) £9.99 (WR) £9.99 (SAF)
Sauvignon Blanc Villa Maria Reserve
Wairau Valley **1999** £9.99 (UN)
Sauvignon Blanc/Semillon Selaks **1997**
£9.45 (STE)

£11.00 → £12.99

Chardonnay Babich Irongate **1997** £12.50
(TAN)
Chardonnay Babich Irongate **1996** £12.75
(CON)
Chardonnay Corbans Cottage Block
1997 £12.99 (WAI)
Chardonnay Hunter's **1997** £11.49 (DI)
£11.95 (JER)
Chardonnay Hunter's **1996** £11.99 (SUN)
£11.99 (LAI)
Chardonnay Isabel Estate **1999** £11.50 (MV)
Chardonnay Isabel Estate **1997** £11.50
(BALL)
Chardonnay Jackson Estate Reserve **1996**
£11.79 (AME)
Chardonnay Kumeu River **1999** £11.16
(FA) £12.50 (WS) £14.95 (BER) £15.95
(RES) £15.99 (BEN)
Chardonnay Kumeu River **1998** £11.99
(UN) £13.95 (BAL) £15.95 (BEN)
Chardonnay Martinborough **1998** £11.50
(CRO) £11.99 (YOU) £12.50 (AD)
Chardonnay Mills Reef Elspeth **1997**
£12.46 (PEN)
Chardonnay Montana Church Road
Reserve **1998** £11.99 (BOT) £11.99
(WR) £11.99 (VIL)
Chardonnay Redwood Valley **1998**
£11.25 (FORT)
Chardonnay Redwood Valley Barrel-
Fermented **1998** £12.00 (NZW)
Chardonnay Rippon Vineyard **1999**
£11.27 (BY)
Chardonnay Seresin Estate **1999** £11.00
(ARM)
Chardonnay Sileni Estates **1999** £12.95
(MAY)
Chardonnay Sileni Estates **1998** £12.39
(HIC)
Chardonnay Te Mata Elston **1998** £11.16
(FA)
Chardonnay Trinity Hill Gimblett Road
1999 £12.25 (GN)
Pinot Gris Mount Difficulty **1999** £12.99
(YOU) £14.99 (VIL)
Pinot Gris Seresin Estate **2000** £12.67 (ARM)

Riesling Rippon Vineyard **1998** £12.70
(NZW)
Riesling Seresin Estate **2000** £11.33 (ARM)
Sauvignon Blanc Dry River **2000** £11.26
(FA)
Sauvignon Blanc Dry River **1999** £11.95
(RAE)
Sauvignon Blanc Dry River **1998** £11.95
(JU)
Sauvignon Blanc Esk Valley **1998** £11.25
(BALL)
Sauvignon Blanc Kumeu River **1998**
£11.95 (BEN)

£13.00 → £15.99

Chardonnay Cloudy Bay **1999** £14.75
(HAH) £14.95 (STE)
Chardonnay Cloudy Bay **1998** £13.59
(GN) £13.93 (NO) £14.50 (WRI) £14.90
(CRO) £16.55 (BODX) £20.00 (MI)
Chardonnay Coopers Creek Swamp
Reserve Hawkes Bay **1996** £15.25
(CON)
Chardonnay Kim Crawford Tietjen
Gisborne **1998** £14.99 (CON) £15.99 (VIL)
Chardonnay Kim Crawford Tietjen
Gisborne **1996** £14.35 (NO)
Chardonnay Felton Road Barrel-
Fermented **1999** £13.99 (RAE) £16.99
(VIL)
Chardonnay Fromm La Strada Reserve
1999 £15.95 (LAY)
Chardonnay Kumeu River Mate's
Vineyard **1999** £13.75 (WS) £17.45 (BER)
£17.95 (RES) £18.99 (BEN) £19.90 (CRO)
Chardonnay Kumeu River Mate's
Vineyard **1998** £13.61 (FA) £16.95 (BAL)
£18.95 (BEN)
Chardonnay Martinborough **1995** £13.09
(NO)
Chardonnay Mount Difficulty **1999**
£13.99 (YOU) £15.99 (VIL) £16.50 (BER)
Chardonnay Seresin Estate Reserve **1999**
£13.67 (ARM)
Chardonnay Te Mata Elston **1999** £13.99
(BOT) £13.99 (WR) £14.99 (AME) £14.99
(YOU) £17.86 (TW)
Chardonnay Te Mata Elston **1997** £13.50
(PEN) £14.50 (BALL)
Sauvignon Blanc Mount Difficulty **2000**
£15.95 (NI)
Sauvignon Blanc Mount Difficulty **1996**
£14.99 (VIL)
Semillon Kim Crawford Hawkes Bay
1996 £13.95 (FORT)

Over £16.00

Chardonnay Cloudy Bay **1995** £52.88 (WY)

Chardonnay Cloudy Bay **1994** £47.00 (WY)

Chardonnay Cloudy Bay **1991** £58.75 (WY)

Chardonnay Cloudy Bay **1989** £64.63 (WY)

Chardonnay Fromm La Strada Reserve **1998** £17.99 (YOU)

Chardonnay Goldwater Estate Zell Waiheke Island **1999** £16.49 (COC)

Chardonnay Kumeu River **1996** £17.90 (CRO)

Chardonnay Kumeu River Mate's Vineyard **1996** £31.50 (CRO)

Chardonnay Morton Estate Black Label **1996** £18.40 (CRO)

Chardonnay Neudorf Moutere **1999** £17.75 (WS)

Sauvignon Blanc Cloudy Bay **1999** £17.50 (MI) £23.50 (WY)

Sauvignon Blanc Cloudy Bay **1997** £27.03 (WY)

Sauvignon Blanc Cloudy Bay **1994** £29.38 (WY)

SPARKLING

Under £7.50

Lindauer Brut **Non-vintage** £6.45 (GN) £7.49 (BO) £7.49 (BOT) £7.49 (WAI) £7.49 (ASD) £7.99 (UN) £7.99 (BUD) £7.99 (TES) £7.99 (VIC) £7.99 (THR) £7.99 (WR) £7.99 (JON) £7.99 (OD) £7.99 (VIL) £7.99 (SAF)

Lindauer Rosé **Non-vintage** £6.65 (GN) £7.49 (BOT) £7.99 (UN) £7.99 (TES) £7.99 (VIC) £7.99 (THR) £7.99 (WR) £7.99 (VIL)

£7.50 → £9.99

Cellier Le Brun Terrace Road **Non-vintage** £9.95 (HED)

Deutz Marlborough Cuvée Brut **Non-vintage** £9.99 (BO) £10.99 (VIC) £10.99 (THR) £10.99 (BOT) £10.99 (WR) £10.99 (WAI) £10.99 (OD) £11.99 (VIL)

Lindauer Special Reserve **Non-vintage** £8.99 (UN) £8.99 (TES) £8.99 (VIC) £8.99 (THR) £8.99 (BOT) £8.99 (WR) £8.99 (OD) £8.99 (VIL)

★ Morton Estate Premium Brut **Non-vintage** £8.99 (NEZ)

£10.00 → £12.99

Daniel Le Brun Brut **Non-vintage** £12.95 (HED) £12.99 (POR) £13.50 (FORT)

Deutz Marlborough Cuvée Blanc de Blanc Vintage **1996** £12.99 (VIL)

Deutz Marlborough Cuvée Blanc de Blanc Vintage **1994** £11.99 (OD)

Giesen Voyage Traditionelle Brut **Non-vintage** £12.57 (CB)

Hunter's Miru Miru **1998** £10.99 (DI) £11.99 (MAJ)

Hunter's Miru Miru **1997** £10.79 (BO) £10.90 (CRO)

Pelorus **Non-vintage** £10.89 (FLE) £10.99 (POR) £11.50 (RAE) £11.99 (WR) £11.99 (VIL) £13.49 (VA)

Pelorus **1997** £12.99 (WR)

Pelorus Blanc de Blancs **Non-vintage** £11.26 (NO) £11.90 (CRO) £12.49 (JON) £13.75 (NI)

★ Rory Brut Kim Crawford **1996** £10.95 (LIB)

£13.00 → £15.99

Hunter's Miru Miru **Non-vintage** £14.00 (JU)

Jackson Estate Vintage **1994** £14.99 (POR)

Pelorus **1996** £14.95 (HAH) £14.95 (STA) £15.99 (YOU) £16.75 (NI) £17.07 (NO) £17.27 (CB)

Pelorus **1995** £13.50 (BALL) £13.99 (POR) £14.95 (LEA) £14.99 (UN) £14.99 (VIL) £14.99 (RAE) £15.49 (BO) £15.49 (JON) £15.50 (FORT) £15.51 (PLAY) £17.56 (TW)

Pelorus **1994** £13.30 (FLE) £14.10 (PEN) £14.90 (CRO) £14.95 (BAL)

Pelorus **1993** £13.90 (JU)

SWEET

c. £15.00

Riesling Wairau River Botrytised ½ bottle **1998** £14.95 (LEA)

- *Wines are listed in A–Z order within each price band.*
- *For each wine, vintages are listed in descending order.*
- *Each vintage of any wine appears only once.*

PORTUGAL

Some fascinating characters are emerging from Portugal at the moment, many of them at bargain prices. Who cares if you can't pronounce them? Just go out and try them

The hot news in Portugal is still the red table wines – but what to buy? We're seeing an explosion of styles and prices now: whereas it used to be the case that you could shell out £4 or so and be fairly sure of something soft and ripe, now there are spicy, chocolatey reds, young juicy ones and, I regret to say, the sort of over-extracted monsters that plague too many parts of the world, including some pretty smart parts like St-Émilion in Bordeaux.

By 'over-extracted' I mean that the winemaker has flogged the grapes to death, extracting every last molecule of colour and tannin. This doesn't make for wines that are easy to drink – nor, funnily enough, for wines that will age well. Most wine regions grow out of this sort of thing. I'm hoping St-Émilion will, and I'm hoping Portugal will.

Not that this style is ubiquitous. So far it seems to be some of the Douro wines that are falling into the trap, thinking (and no doubt rightly) that they can command higher prices that way. Well, they're not for me. I relish the ripe, spicy fruit of Portugal, but I don't want it encased in too much tannin and oak.

Regional styles are currently all mixed up, too. I can't at the moment tell you precisely what they all taste like. But since the 1999 vintage so many interesting and fruit-driven flavours have been emerging from Alentejo, Ribatejo, Estremadura, Bairrada and Douro that I'm not too worried. There's a joyous riot of experimentation going on, and single-estate wines, especially from consultants like João Portugal Ramos and José Neiva are really worth a try.

WINE REGIONS

ALENTEJO (red, white) This broad region now has a DOC for the better wines, plus eight sub-regional DOCs including Borba, Redondo, Reguengos and Vidigueira. But the Vinhos Regionais can be as good or better. There's not a great deal of regional difference but there are quality differences. Single-estate wines are often very serious, with complex flavours and good concentration. The names to go for include *Caves Aliança, Borba co-op, Quinta do Carmo, Cartuxa, Cortes de Cima, D F J Vinhos, Esporão, José Maria da Fonseca, J P Vinhos, Mouchão, Quinta do Mouro, Pera Manca, João Portugal Ramos, Redondo co-op, Reguengos de Monsaraz co-op* and *Sogrape*.

ALGARVE (red, white) Mostly undistinguished, alcoholic reds. There are four DOCs here, Lagoa, Lagos, Portimão and Tavira, and none of them deserves its status. The *Lagoa co-op* is OK and *José Neiva* has produced a good red, *Cataplana*.

BAIRRADA, DOC (red, white) The reds produced here frequently overshadow the more famous Dão wines. They're apt to be tannic, but with modern winemaking the Baga grape gives rich blackberry and raspberry fruit. The best Bairrada wines age remarkably well. The top red producers are: *Caves Aliança, Quinta das Bágeiras, Quinta do Carvalhinho, Gonçalves Faria, Caves Messias, Luís Pato, Caves Primavera, Quinta da Rigodeira, Casa de Saima, Caves São João, Sidónio de Sousa* and *Sogrape*.

There are also some increasingly good dry whites available. *Casa de Saima, Sogrape, Quinta da Rigodeira* and *Quinta do Valdoeiro* are the best producers to try for these.

BUCELAS, DOC (white) Popular in Wellington's day, this dry white has been enjoying a revival in its fortunes since the 1990s. *Morgado de Santa Catherina* is the best of the modern examples.

CARCAVELOS, DOC (fortified) A tiny historic DOC making a fortified wine rather like an aged Tawny port.

COLARES, DOC (red) Based on the scented Ramisco grape grown in sandy coastal vineyards, the young wine has fabulous cherry perfume but is *numbingly* tannic. The vineyards are shrinking and the grape has yet to catch the imagination of winemakers from outside the region.

DÃO, DOC (red, white) The improvements are beginning here, and not before time: the Alentejo and the North between them have been doing a good job of overshadowing Portugal's most famous table wines. Best buys are from *Caves Aliança, Quinta de Cabriz, José Maria da Fonseca, Quinta das Maias, Quinta dos Roques, Casa de Santar, Caves São João, Sogrape.*

White Dão is now generally light, fresh and fruity. White *Grão Vasco* from *Sogrape* is good and lemony.

DOURO, DOC (red, white) Famous these days for table wine as well as port. The flavour of the red table wines can be delicious – soft and glyceriny, with a rich raspberry-and-peach fruit, and a perfume somewhere between liquorice, smoky bacon and cigar tobacco. But beware of over-extracted monsters. *Casa Ferreirinha* (under the ownership of *Sogrape*) produces a number of goodies, from the rare and expensive *Barca Velha*, through *Casa Ferreirinha Reserva* (formerly known as *Reserva Especial*) to the new *Quinta da Leda* and the young and fruity *Esteva*. Also look for *Altano, Bright Brothers, Quinta do Côtto Grande Escolha, Quinta do Crasto, Duas Quintas, Quinta do Fojo, Quinta da Gaivosa, Niepoort's Passadouro* and *Redoma, Quinta*

do Noval's *Corucho, Quinta do Portal Grande Reserva, Quinta de la Rosa, Quinta do Vale Dona Maria* and *Quinta do Vale da Raposa*.

There are also some good whites, which are best drunk young. *Sogrape's Planalto Douro Reserva, Esteva* from *Casa Ferreirinha* and *Quinta do Valprado* Chardonnay are well worth trying.

ESTREMADURA (red, white) Alias Oeste. It includes the DOCs Alenquer, Arruda, Óbidos and Torres Vedras, plus the IPRs Alcobaça and Encostas d'Aire – and

ON THE CASE

There are some excellent, complex and long-lived Portuguese whites – but not many. Few Portuguese white grapes are that good

the region of Estremadura itself. But don't worry about the DOCs: there are no particular regional differences, and Vinhos Regionais are just as good. Private estates here are making terrific quality. There's that same cherries-and-chocolate fruit in the reds that you get all over the South (the chocolate comes from aging in Portuguese oak, rather than the more international-style American or French oak). Look out for *Quinta de Abrigada, Caves Aliança, Bright Brothers, Casa Santos Lima* own label and brands *Espiga* and *Quinta das Setencostas* and *Palha-Canas. D F J Vinhos* brands *Grand'Arte* and *Manta Preta*, and *Quinta de Pancas. Alta Mesa* and *Portada* are among the best of the cheaper brands. Whites can be nicely aromatic, but need drinking young.

MADEIRA, DOC (fortified) Each Madeira style is supposedly based on the grape from which it takes its name: there are four of them, and they are Malmsey (Malvasia), Bual, Verdelho and Sercial. In practice cheaper Madeiras, those of up to five years old, are almost all made from the inferior Tinta Negra Mole. These call themselves 'Pale Dry', 'Dark Rich', and so on. So anything calling itself Sercial, Verdelho or whatever should be made 85 per cent from that grape.

The Malmsey grape makes the sweetest Madeira, reeking sometimes of Muscovado sugar, dark, rich and brown, but with a smoky bite and surprisingly high acidity that makes it positively refreshing after a long meal. The Bual grape is also rich and strong, less concentrated, sometimes with a faintly rubbery whiff and higher acidity. Verdelho makes pungent, smoky, medium-sweet wine with more obvious, gentle fruit, and the Sercial makes dramatic dry wine, savoury, spirity, tangy, with a steely, piercing acidity. To taste what Madeira is all about you need a 10-year-old; really top Madeira should be two or three times that age.

Blandy, Cossart Gordon, Rutherford & Miles and *Leacock* are all good producers, and all under the same ownership anyway. There is a new emphasis here on a slightly fruitier style, which is worth investigating. *Henriques & Henriques* is the most widely available of the Portuguese-owned houses.

PORT (DOURO, DOC) (fortified) Port falls into two broad categories: that aged in bottle (vintage and single-quinta vintage) and that aged in wood, which is bottled when ready to drink (ruby, tawny, vintage character, late-bottled vintage, crusted and branded ports).

The simplest and cheapest port available in Britain is labelled 'Ruby' or 'Tawny'. Ruby is a tangy, tough, but warmingly sweet wine to knock back uncritically. Cheap Tawny at around the same price as Ruby is a mixture of light Ruby and White ports, and is almost never as good as a straight Ruby.

Calling these inferior concoctions 'Tawnies' is very misleading because there's a genuine 'Tawny', too. Proper Tawnies are

PORTUGUESE CLASSIFICATIONS

Portugal's wines are divided into four tiers of quality. At the top is **Denominação de Origem Controlada** or DOC. **Indicação de Proveniência Regulamentada**, or IPR, is similar to the French VDQS; the wines are referred to as Vinhos de Qualidade Produzidos em Região Determinada (VQPRD). **Vinho Regional**, like the French vin de pays, is more flexible about permitted grape varieties. **Vinho de Mesa** is table wine.

kept in wooden barrels for at least five, but preferably ten or more years, to let a delicate flavour of nuts, brown sugar and raisins develop. These more expensive Tawnies carry an age on the label: 10, 20, 30 or even 40 years old. Those without an age are usually best avoided, though there are some good brands like *Delaforce*'s *His Eminence's Choice* or *Harvey*'s *Director's Bin Very Superior Old Tawny*. For aged Tawnies try *Churchill*, *Cockburn*, *Croft*, *Dow*, *Quinta da Ervamoira* from *Ramos Pinto*, *Ferreira*, *Fonseca*, *Graham*, *Noval*, *Poças*, *Quinta de la Rosa*, *Taylor's*.

Colheitas – single-vintage Tawnies – are increasingly available and can be really delicious. Look for *Barros*, *Kopke*, *Messias*, *Noval*, *Niepoort*, *Poças*, *Warre*.

Vintage ports are the opposite of Tawnies, since the object here is to make a big, concentrated rather than a delicate mouthful. Vintage years are 'declared' by port shippers when the quality seems particularly good – usually about three times a decade. The wines will age for a decade or two in bottle to develop an exciting, complex tangle of flavours; blackcurrant, plums, minty liquorice, pepper and herbs, cough mixture and a lot more.

If you want a peek at what a declared Vintage port can be like, buy single-quinta vintage wine. These are usually from the best vineyards in the less brilliant years; they mature faster and can be extremely good. Look particularly for *Taylor*'s *Quinta da Vargellas*, *Dow*'s *Quinta do Bomfim*, *Warre*'s *Quinta da Cavadinha*, *Fonseca*'s *Quinta do Panascal*, *Niepoort*'s *Quinta do Passadouro*, *Croft*'s *Quinta da Roêda*, *Delaforce*'s *Quinta da Corte*, *Cockburn*'s *Quinta da Eira Velha* and *Quinta dos Canais*, *Churchill*'s *Quinta da Agua Alta* and *Quinta do Vesúvio*, *Quinta de la Rosa* and *Quinta do Crasto*.

Vintage Character is usually short on personality, but traditional Late Bottled can be very good. The best are from *Fonseca*, *Niepoort*, *Smith Woodhouse*, *Ramos Pinto*, *Warre*. Crusted port is also good rich stuff: *Churchill*'s and *Dow*'s are good.

White port, sweet or dry, is seldom exciting. Barros *Very Old Dry White* is special.

RIBATEJO, DOC (red, white) An exciting area for both inexpensive brands and some of Portugal's best *garrafeira* (reserve-style) wines – in particular *Romeira* of *Caves Velhas*. It includes the sub-regional DOCs Almeirim, Cartaxo, Chamusca, Coruche, Santarém and Tomar, but Ribatejo is the name we see most on labels. Don't agonize over the differences between the DOCs: as far as I can see there aren't any, and Vinhos Regionais are just as good. There are lovely chocolaty reds, and fresh whites. Decent brands include *Lezíria*, *Segada*, *Falcoaria*, *Torre Velha* and the wines from the *Almeirim* co-op. Classier wines: *Bright Bros*, *Casa Cadaval*, *Quinta do Casal Branco*, *D F J Vinhos* and *Quinta da Lagoalva*.

SETÚBAL, DOC (fortified) This is good, but it's always a little spirity and never quite

---

INSTANT CELLAR: DOURO REDS

- 1998 Quinta do Côtto Tinto, Champalimaud, £8.95, Laymont & Shaw/£9.99, Villeneuve Wines Tremendously characterful stuff, with soft, leathery, almost animal-perfumed fruit, very long and silky.
- 2000 Redoma Rosé, Quinta de Napoles, £8.99, Bennetts Pink wine from the Douro. Big, serious stuff.
- 1998 Quinta de la Rosa, £7.99, Great Western Wine Utterly modern table wine from a producer that makes port as well. The style is fruit-driven, with lovely spice and weight.
- 1997 Tuella, Cockburn Smithes, £6.42, Hicks & Don Easy-drinking, soft, juicy red with an attractive zestiness.
- 1998 Quinta do Vallado, £6.95, Lea & Sandeman Dense, brambly stuff with a touch of new oak to back up the fruit. Very modern, very dark, very concentrated.
- 1998 Quinta do Crasto, £6.85, Le Fleming Spicy damsons and lots of character.

as perfume-sweet as one would like, perhaps because they don't use the best sort of Muscat. When made from at least 85 per cent Moscatel the wine can be labelled Moscatel de Setúbal; J P Vinhos have a fragrant version. The wines do gain in concentration with age: 20- and 25-year-old versions have a lot more character and less overbearing spiritiness. You can occasionally find older wines from José Maria da Fonseca.

TERRAS DO SADO (red, white) This region includes the Setúbal DOC and also the newly created Palmela DOC, where international grapes have made the most inroads, and local varieties are doing well too. Stars here include *Caves Aliança*, *Bright Brothers*, *José Maria da Fonseca* (fruity rustic red *Periquita*, red and white *Quinta de Camarate* and *Primum*), *J P Vinhos* (oak-aged *Cova da Ursa* Chardonnay) and the

wonderful *Pegos Claros*, made by *João Portugal Ramos*.

VINHO VERDE, DOC (red, white) Roughly half of all Vinho Verde produced is red, wonderfully sharp, harsh even, but hardly ever seen outside Portugal.

But the wine we see is white, and *Verde* means green-youthful, un-aged, not the colour of a croquet lawn. Ideally, the whites are bone dry, positively tart, often aromatic, and brilliantly suited to heavy, oily northern Portuguese food. But we almost always get the wines slightly sweetened and softened, which is a pity, because they're then not nearly so distinctive.

Authentic versions come from *Palácio da Brejoeira*, *Quinta da Aveleda*, *Quinta de Tamariz*, *Quinta da Franqueira*, *Quinta de Azevedo*, *Casa de Sezim*, and *Quinta da Baguinha*. Drink all Vinho Verde young.

PRODUCERS WHO'S WHO

CAVES ALIANÇA ★★ (Bairrada) Up-to-date and quality oriented company who are making good stuff in the Alentejo, Dão and Douro (red Quinta da Terrugem) as well as in Bairrada.

QUINTA DA AVELEDA (Vinho Verde) Largest producer of Vinho Verde, including excellent dry Grinalda and varietal Loureiro. Now Charamba red Douro, too.

BRIGHT BROTHERS ★★ (Several) Aussie Peter Bright gets his fingers into everything. Great Palmela and Cartaxo.

CHURCHILL GRAHAM ★★★ (Port) Intense and concentrated Churchill's Vintage, LBV, 10-Year-Old Tawny and single-quinta Agua Alta.

COCKBURN ★★ (Port) Special Reserve is good Vintage Character, and the 10-Year-Old Tawny is complex and nutty. Look for Quinta dos Canais 1992, and Cockburn 1994.

QUINTA DO CRASTO ★★ (Port/Douro) Estate focusing on vintage port and table wines. Quality is very high, and the wines age well.

CROFT ★★ (Port) Quinta da Roêda is lovely single-quinta vintage, but some wines can be over-delicate.

DELAFORCE ★★★ (Port) Tawny His Eminence's Choice is its best-known wine. Good 1994 Vintage.

D F J VINHOS ★★ (Several) Wines are made by José Neiva, one of Portugal's finest winemakers. At the top end are Grand' Arte reds. There are some well-established brands plus tasty red and white Vale de Rosas and reds Manta Preta and Sendo do Vale.

DOW ★★★ (Port) Deft, complex wines made in a relatively dry style. Its 1994 Vintage is a triumph. Look also for the 10-Year-Old Tawny.

MATURITY CHARTS
VINTAGE PORTS

1983 A vintage for mid-term drinking

| Bottled | | | Ready | Best | Fading | Tired |

0   5   10   15   20   25   30 years

1985 An excellent vintage for laying down

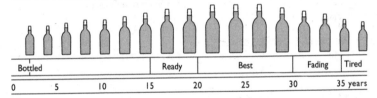

| Bottled | | | Ready | Best | Fading | Tired |

0   5   10   15   20   25   30   35 years

1991 1991 ports are likely to be ready before the 1985s

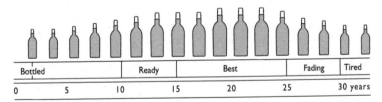

| Bottled | | Ready | Best | Fading | Tired |

0   5   10   15   20   25   30 years

1994 Possibly even better than 1991

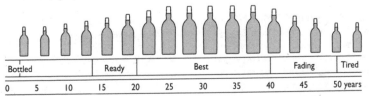

| Bottled | | Ready | Best | Fading | Tired |

0   5   10   15   20   25   30   35   40   45   50 years

ESPORÃO ★ (Alentejo) Australian winemaking plus a combination of local and international grapes. Esporão Reserva and Aragonês are very good reds.

FERREIRA ★★★ (Port/Douro) Elegant, early-maturing Vintages and two superb Tawnies: 10-year-old Quinta do Porto and 20-year-old Duque de Bragança. Also produces some of the top Douro table wines, including the legendary Barca Velha and powerful Quinta da Leda.

FONSECA GUIMARAENS ★★★ (Port) Fonseca's wines are sweeter and less austere than sister company Taylor's. The Vintage ports are often outstanding, as is the 1994, and the quality of its commercial releases is reassuring.

JOSÉ MARIA DA FONSECA ★★ (Countrywide) Delicious range of table wines, particularly Quinta de Camarate red and white, expensive red Primum, oaky d'Avillez and profound José da Sousa Mayor. Not connected to Fonseca port.

GRAHAM ★★ (Port) Usually rich and sweet. Apart from Vintage there is Malvedos, produced in off-vintage years, and fine Tawnies. Very good 1994 Vintage. Six Grapes is attractive Vintage Character.

HENRIQUES & HENRIQUES ★★ (Madeira) Good quality across the board.

J P VINHOS ★★ (Setúbal) Innovative winemaking. Look for João Pires Branco, red Tinto da Ânfora, red Quinta da Bacalhôa and Cova da Ursa Chardonnay.

MADEIRA WINE COMPANY ★★ (Madeira) Blandy, Cossart Gordon, Rutherford & Miles and Leacock are grouped together under this ownership. Rutherford & Miles and Cossart Gordon wines are slightly drier; otherwise there's not much between them. Look for Blandy's new 1994 Colheita Malmsey.

NIEPOORT ★★ (Port) Subtle aged Tawnies, traditional LBVs, Colheitas and long-lasting Vintage (especially 1994), plus single-quinta Quinta do Passadouro.

QUINTA DO NOVAL ★★★ (Port) Huge improvements here: the 10-Year-Old is a stunner, and the Vintage matches it for quality. Noval's Nacional wines, made from ungrafted vines, are legendary and fetch a stratospheric price at auction.

OFFLEY FORRESTER ★★ (Port) Famous for 'Boa Vista' Vintage and LBV ports. Vintage can be insubstantial. Excellent Baron de Forrester Tawnies.

CASA SANTOS LIMA (Estremadura) Good modern winemaking with the emphasis on Portuguese grapes.

RAMOS-PINTO ★★ (Port/Douro) There are delicious Tawnies from two single quintas – Ervamoira and Bom Retiro – both of which are elegant, nutty and delicate. Duas Quintas is good Douro red.

SMITH WOODHOUSE ★★ (Port) Some delicious Vintage and LBVs. Concentrated Vintage wines which tend to mature early, though 1994 is gutsy. Full-flavoured Crusted.

SOGRAPE ★★ (North) Producer of Mateus Rosé, plus excellent Grão Vasco white Dão and many others with emphasis on fruit. Very go-ahead.

TAYLOR, FLADGATE AND YEATMAN ★★★ (Port) Quinta de Vargellas is still one of the best single-quinta wines on the market, and the 10-Year-Old Tawny is superb.

WARRE ★★ (Port) Serious wines: good LBVs and Vintage (especially in 1994) and fine 'Nimrod' Tawny. Quinta da Cavadinha is a single-quinta wine, and the 1986 Colheita is subtle.

PORT VINTAGES

Not every year produces a crop of fine enough quality for vintage-dated wine to be made, and a few houses may not make Vintage port even in a generally good year. Announcing the intention to bottle Vintage port is known as 'declaring'. It all depends on the quality the individual house has produced, although it is extremely rare for a house to declare two consecutive years.

2000   Looks good so far, and could be a vintage year.

1999   Unlikely to be a vintage year: the wines weren't ripe enough.

1998   A small vintage, not good enough for a general declaration. Taylor's declared single-quinta Vintages only.

1997   Varied in quality. Declarations include *Dow, Gould Campbell, Graham's, Fonseca, Quarles Harris, Smith Woodhouse, Taylor* and *Warre*.

1996   Seems an elegant, useful year rather than gutsy.

1995   A vintage with a lot of colour and tannin, but slightly unbalanced. Above average, but missed being top grade.

1994   Excellent year, declared by almost all houses. They're ripe, fleshy and intense, with lovely fruit. They're also much more expensive than the last generally declared year, 1991.

1992   Declared by *Fonseca, Taylor, Niepoort* and *Burmester*. Rich, fruity wines.

1991   Generally declared, but quantities were small. The wines need at least ten years.

1987   *Ferreira, Martinez, Niepoort* and *Offley* declared this small but good vintage. Most shippers opted instead for single-quinta wines for medium-term drinking.

1985   Declared by every important shipper. The quality is exceptionally good, with a juicy ripeness of fruit.

1983   Marvellous wine, strong and aggressive, but with a deep, brooding sweetness which is all ripe, clean fruit. Not one of the most fragrant vintages, but it will be a sturdy classic.

1982   Not as good as it was at first thought. Most need to be drunk.

1980   A good vintage, with a delicious, drier-than-usual style.

1977   Brilliant wine, now mature. The flavour is a marvellous mixture of great fruit sweetness and intense spice and herb fragrance.

1975   These in general don't have the stuffing that a true vintage style demands, but many are still enjoyable, though fading.

1970   Exceptional, balanced port, now good to drink, sweet and ripe with a fascinating citrus freshness – and it'll last.

1966   This has gained body and oomph and can be drunk with pleasure.

1963   The classic year. It's big, deep, and spicy, with remarkable concentration of flavours.

PORTUGAL PRICES

RED

Under £4.00

Bairrada Terra Franca 1997 £3.95 (STE)
Dão Dom Ferraz 1999 £3.99 (MORR)
 £4.95 (BUD) £4.99 (BO) £4.99 (VIC) £4.99
 (THR) £4.99 (BOT)
Dão Duque de Viseu 1996 £3.96 (STE)
Ramada Tinto 1999 £3.30 (BAC) £3.49
 (VIC) £3.49 (THR) £3.79 (BOT) £3.79 (SAF)

£4.00 → £4.99

Alentejano Vinha do Monte, Sogrape
 1999 £4.99 (WAI)
Bairrada Dom Ferraz 1999 £4.75 (MORR)
Bairrada Dom Ferraz 1997 £4.89 (TES)
Bairrada Reserva, Caves Aliança 1997
 £4.99 (PEN) £4.99 (DI)
Beiras Jaen, Bela Fonte 1999 £4.99 (SAF)
Dão Dom Ferraz 1997 £4.99 (TES)
Dão Duque de Viseu 1997 £4.95 (STE)
 £6.67 (MOR)
Dão Grão Vasco 1997 £4.45 (STE)
Dão Reserva, Caves Aliança 1997 £4.99
 (DI)
Dão Reserva, Caves Aliança 1996 £4.99
 (PEN)
Dão Reserva, Dom Ferraz 1998 £4.99
 (UN)
Douro Quinta do Côtto 1997 £4.78 (NO)
 £8.99 (VIL) £9.95 (LA)
Douro Foral Reserva, Caves Aliança
 1997 £4.75 (DI)
Douro Vila Regia 1998 £4.29 (SAF) £4.45
 (STE)
Terras do Sado Pedras do Monte,
 Castelão 1999 £4.85 (BAC) £4.99 (UN)

£5.00 → £5.99

Alenquer Quinta das Setencostas 1999
 £5.99 (OD)
Alentejano Tinto da Ânfora, J P Vinhos
 1998 £5.99 (SAF)
Beiras Jaen, Bela Fonte 1998 £5.50 (BAC)
Dão Garrafeira, Grão Vasco 1996 £5.75
 (STE)
Douro Duas Quintas, Ramos Pinto 1998
 £5.95 (JU) £6.95 (POR) £7.25 (STA)
Douro Quinta de la Rosa 1999 £5.95
 (SOM) £6.99 (BU) £7.40 (TAN) £7.40 (MV)
 £7.95 (BALL)
Terras do Sado Pasmados, J M da Fonseca
 1995 £5.50 (WS)

£6.00 → £6.99

Alentejano Chaminé, Cortes de Cima
 1999 £6.99 (MAJ) £7.95 (NI)
Beira Mar Garrafeira Reserva Particular,
 da Silva 1990 £6.49 (UN) £6.95 (TAN)
 £8.10 (VIN)
Douro Quinta do Crasto 1998 £6.19
 (NO) £6.50 (WS) £7.62 (SAV)
Douro Foral Grande Escolha, Caves
 Aliança 1998 £6.99 (DI)
Douro Quinta de la Rosa 1998 £6.99
 (BO) £7.50 (BEN) £7.95 (BALL)
Palmela Particular, Caves Aliança 1995
 £6.99 (DI)

£7.00 → £9.99

Alentejano Quinta do Carmo 1999 £7.99
 (VIL)
Alentejano Dom Martinho 1996 £7.99 (VIL)
Bairrada Reserva, Casa de Saima 1995
 £9.50 (WRI)

RETAILERS SPECIALIZING IN PORTUGAL
see Retailers Directory (page 40) for details

Nearly all merchants sell some port, but only a few have interesting Portuguese table wines. Adnams (AD), Bibendum (BIB) – especially port, on their fine wine list, D Byrne, Cockburns of Leith (COC) – especially port, Direct Wine (DI) – for port and Madeira, Farr Vintners (FA) – for Vintage port, First Quench Group (BOT, THR, VIC, WR), Justerini & Brooks (JU), Lay & Wheeler (LAY), Laymont & Shaw(LA), Oddbins (OD), Raeburn Fine Wines (RAE) – old colheitas from Niepoort, Reid Wines – particularly for port, T&W Wines (TW) – including ports back to 1944, Tanners (TAN) – particularly port, The Wine Society (WS), Peter Wylie Fine Wines (WY) – old ports and Madeiras.

Dão Fonte do Ouro, Sociedade Agrícola
Boas Quintas 1996 £7.99 (BEN)
Dão Quinta das Maias 1998 £7.95 (POR)
Dão Quinta de Saes 1997 £7.99 (VIL)
£8.25 (LA)
Douro Quinta do Côtto 1998 £8.95 (LA)
£9.99 (VIL)
Douro Quinta do Crasto 1997 £9.34 (TW)
Douro Reserva, Quinta do Crasto 1998
£9.80 (NI) £9.95 (AD)
Douro Reserva, Quinta do Crasto 1996
£7.85 (SOM) £15.83 (MI)
Douro Quinta de la Rosa 2000 £7.75 (NI)
Douro Vale da Raposa 1998 £7.74 (SAV)
Reguengos Reserva, Esporão 1996 £7.99
(OD)
Trás-os-Montes Quinta do Bons Ares,
Ramos Pinto 1992 £9.95 (JU)

£10.00 → £19.99

Alentejano Quinta do Carmo 1996
£10.90 (CRO)
Bairrada Vinha Barrosa, Luis Pato 1998
£16.75 (LA) £19.99 (VIL)
Bairrada Vinha Pan, Luis Pato 1998
£16.75 (LA) £19.99 (VIL)
Dão Reserva, Quinta dos Roques 1997
£12.93 (SAV)
Dão Touriga Nacional, Quinta dos
Carvalhais 1996 £14.25 (STE)
Dão Touriga Nacional, Quinta dos
Roques 1997 £18.95 (GN)
Douro Duas Quintas, Ramos Pinto 1994
£19.50 (FORT)
Douro Duas Quintas Reserva, Ramos
Pinto 1995 £18.99 (VIL)
Douro Redoma, Niepoort 1996 £16.99
(BEN)
Douro Quinta do Vale Dona Maria 1996
£15.83 (MI)
Estremadura Touriz, Quinta da Boavista
1998 £11.99 (YOU)
Evora Cartuxa 1996 £10.95 (BEN) £11.99
(VA)
Evora Cartuxa 1995 £10.95 (WRI)
Terras do Sado Periquita, J M da Fonseca
1987 £10.50 (CRO)

Over £20.00

Dão Garrafeira, Grão Vasco 1975 £20.00
(CRO)
Dão Reserva, Caves São João 1978
£25.00 (CRO)
Douro Barca Velha, Casa Ferreirinha
1991 £41.00 (CRO)

WHITE

Under £4.00

Bairrada Terra Franca 1999 £3.95 (STE)
Bairrada Terra Franca 1997 £3.95 (STE)
Ramada Branco 1999 £3.30 (BAC)
Vinho Verde Cambriz Non-vintage
£3.75 (WS)
Vinho Verde Casal Mendes, Caves Aliança
Non-vintage £3.49 (BO) £4.75 (CON)
£4.99 (GN)
Vinho Verde Gatão Non-vintage £3.99
(SAF)

£4.00 → £4.99

Bairrada Galeria Bical, Caves Aliança
1999 £4.75 (WS)
Dão Grão Vasco 1999 £4.45 (STE)
Dão Grão Vasco 1998 £4.45 (STE)
Terras do Sado J P Branco, J P Vinhos
1996 £4.75 (CON)
Vinho Verde Quinta de Azevedo, Sogrape
1999 £4.95 (STE)
Vinho Verde Gazela, Sogrape Non-
vintage £4.95 (TAN)

Over £5.00

Dão Encruzado, Quinta dos Carvalhais
1998 £10.50 (STE)
Douro Duas Quintas Branco, Ramos
Pinto 1995 £6.95 (JU)
Douro Redoma, Niepoort 1996 £8.99
(RAE)
Douro Reserva, Sogrape 1999 £5.75 (STE)

ROSÉ

Under £4.00

Mateus Rosé Non-vintage £3.89 (TES)
£3.89 (ASD) £3.99 (BUD) £3.99 (SO)
£3.99 (SAF) £4.99 (UN) £5.04 (WHI)

c. £5.00

Nobilis Bairrada, Sogrape 1999 £4.75
(STE)

FORTIFIED

Under £18.00

Moscatel de Setúbal 20-year-old, J M da
Fonseca Non-vintage £17.75 (FORT)
£21.08 (NO)

PORT PRICES

Under £6.00

Churchill's Finest Vintage Character ½ bottle **Non-vintage** £5.50 (LEA)
Cockburn's Special Reserve ½ bottle **Non-vintage** £5.09 (SAF)

£6.00 → £6.99

Cálem Fine White **Non-vintage** £6.99 (UN)
Churchill's Dry White ½ bottle **Non-vintage** £6.07 (VIN)
Fonseca Bin 27 **Non-vintage** £6.92 (LLO) £8.60 (COC) £8.85 (WRI) £8.99 (VIL) £9.90 (GAU) £9.99 (DI) £10.95 (FORT)
Sandeman Fine Old White **Non-vintage** £6.99 (VIC) £6.99 (THR)
Sandeman Tawny **Non-vintage** £6.99 (OD)

£7.00 → £8.99

Cockburn's Fine Ruby **Non-vintage** £7.59 (VIC) £7.59 (THR) £7.59 (BOT) £7.59 (WR) £7.69 (UN) £7.69 (TES) £7.79 (SAF)
Cockburn's Special Reserve **Non-vintage** £8.59 (THR) £8.59 (BOT) £8.59 (WR) £8.69 (UN) £8.69 (WAI) £8.75 (SAF)
Dow's Fine Tawny **Non-vintage** £8.46 (PEN)
Graham Tawny **Non-vintage** £8.79 (BO) £9.26 (PLAY)
Martinez Dry White **Non-vintage** £8.49 (CON)
Martínez Fine Tawny **Non-vintage** £7.29 (CON) £11.20 (VIN)
Niepoort Dry White **Non-vintage** £7.14 (BIB) £7.63 (NO) £7.65 (RAE) £8.99 (BAL)
Niepoort Ruby **Non-vintage** £7.14 (BIB) £7.65 (RAE) £7.89 (BO) £7.99 (GN)
Niepoort Vintage Character **Non-vintage** £8.99 (RAE)
Quinta do Noval Extra Dry White **Non-vintage** £7.04 (PLA)
Quinta do Noval Late-Bottled **Non-vintage** £8.60 (COC) £9.68 (FLE)
Ramos-Pinto Ruby **Non-vintage** £7.98 (LLO)
Royal Oporto **Non-vintage** £8.10 (VIN)
Taylor First Estate **Non-vintage** £7.99 (UN) £7.99 (TES) £7.99 (BO)
Warre's Warrior **Non-vintage** £7.99 (TES) £7.99 (SAF) £8.29 (WAI) £8.49 (UN) £8.49 (VIC) £8.49 (THR) £8.49 (BOT) £8.49 (WR)

£9.00 → £10.99

Cálem Late-Bottled 1994 £9.95 (COC) £9.99 (UN)
Churchill's Late-Bottled 1994 £10.49 (BO) £13.50 (MAY) £27.50 (BAL)
Churchill's Late-Bottled 1992 £9.95 (HED) £9.95 (STA) £11.55 (SAV) £14.35 (VIN)
Churchill's Dry White **Non-vintage** £9.49 (BO) £9.49 (SOM) £9.59 (WAI) £9.95 (HED) £9.95 (AME) £10.50 (STA) £10.75 (AD) £10.90 (TAN) £12.75 (TW)
Churchill's Finest Vintage Character **Non-vintage** £9.00 (PLAY) £9.60 (SAV) £9.95 (HED) £9.95 (LEA) £12.57 (TW)
Dow's Trademark **Non-vintage** £9.99 (CON) £10.65 (HIC)
Dow's Late-Bottled **Non-vintage** £10.53 (PEN)
Dow's Late-Bottled 1995 £9.49 (AME) £9.75 (WAI) £9.99 (OD)
Dow's Late-Bottled 1992 £9.75 (VIC) £9.75 (THR) £9.75 (BOT)
Fonseca 10-year-old Tawny **Non-vintage** £9.99 (VIL) £12.90 (CRO) £13.99 (DI) £15.95 (BALL)
Fonseca Dry White Siroco **Non-vintage** £9.95 (RIC) £9.99 (DI)
Fonseca Late-Bottled **Non-vintage** £9.99 (VIL)
Fonseca Late-Bottled 1996 £10.99 (DI)
Fonseca Late-Bottled 1994 £10.99 (BEN) £12.95 (BALL)
Fonseca Late-Bottled 1990 £9.90 (CRO)
Graham Late-Bottled 1995 £9.95 (SOM) £10.49 (SAF) £10.99 (TAN) £11.75 (CB)
Graham Late-Bottled 1994 £9.99 (WAI) £10.45 (TES) £10.72 (WAT) £10.99 (BO) £11.95 (HAH) £11.99 (GW) £13.25 (FORT)
Graham Late-Bottled 1992 £10.49 (UN) £10.49 (VIC) £10.49 (THR) £10.49 (BOT) £10.49 (WR)
Niepoort ½ bottle 1992 £10.95 (RAE)
Niepoort Late-Bottled 1996 £10.19 (BIB) £11.43 (NO) £12.95 (GN)
Niepoort Late-Bottled 1995 £9.95 (RAE) £11.95 (HAH) £11.99 (BAL) £12.06 (NO)
Niepoort Late-Bottled 1994 £10.75 (BO)
Niepoort Senior Fine Old Tawny **Non-vintage** £10.95 (RAE) £13.35 (GN)
Quinta do Noval Late-Bottled 1994 £9.75 (RIC) £10.99 (TAN) £11.25 (HAH)

Ramos-Pinto Late-Bottled **1994** £10.99 (BO)

Ramos Pinto Quinta da Urtiga **Non-vintage** £9.99 (VIL) £10.89 (JON)

Sandeman Late-Bottled **1994** £9.99 (OD)

Smith Woodhouse Vintage Character **Non-vintage** £9.99 (SUN) £9.99 (LAI)

Taylor Chip Dry White Port **Non-vintage** £10.40 (COC) £10.95 (BALL) £11.15 (STA) £11.75 (STE) £11.80 (BEN) £12.25 (FORT)

Taylor Late-Bottled **Non-vintage** £10.49 (THR) £10.49 (BOT) £10.49 (WR)

Taylor Late-Bottled **1995** £9.99 (UN) £9.99 (MAJ) £10.59 (SAF) £10.99 (TAN) £10.99 (BO) £11.50 (GAU)

Taylor Late-Bottled **1994** £9.99 (STA) £10.99 (WAI) £11.16 (LLO) £11.95 (BALL) £12.25 (FORT) £12.60 (VIN)

Taylor Late-Bottled **1990** £10.25 (COC)

£11.00 → £12.99

★ J W Burmester Late-Bottled **1996** £11.50 (FORT)

Churchill's Traditional Late-Bottled **1992** £11.95 (HED)

Cockburn's Special Reserve 1 litre **Non-vintage** £11.35 (SAF)

Delaforce His Eminence's Choice **Non-vintage** £12.50 (HIG) £14.00 (JU)

Graham Late-Bottled **1991** £11.40 (COC)

Graham Six Grapes Vintage Character **Non-vintage** £11.99 (TES) £11.99 (BOT) £11.99 (WR) £12.49 (JON) £12.49 (WAI) £14.00 (JU) £14.64 (HIC)

Niepoort ½ bottle **1994** £11.99 (FA)

Niepoort ½ bottle **1987** £12.95 (RAE)

Quinta do Noval 10-year-old Tawny **Non-vintage** £12.87 (PLA) £13.95 (WAI) £14.95 (FORT)

Ramos-Pinto Late-Bottled **1996** £12.39 (JON) £13.50 (HAH)

Taylor Late-Bottled **1992** £11.36 (PLAY)

£13.00 → £14.99

Cálem 10-year-old Tawny **Non-vintage** £14.90 (COC) £14.99 (UN)

Churchill's 10-year-old Tawny **Non-vintage** £14.59 (SAV) £14.90 (PLAY) £14.95 (HED) £14.95 (STA)

Croft **1982** £14.20 (FA) £19.59 (YOU)

Croft 10-year-old Tawny **Non-vintage** £14.50 (JU)

Croft Quinta da Roeda **1983** £13.99 (MAJ)

Croft Quinta da Roeda **1980** £14.32 (PLA)

Delaforce Quinta da Corte **1991** £14.99 (OD)

Dow's 10-year-old Tawny **Non-vintage** £14.99 (VIC) £14.99 (THR) £14.99 (WR)

Dow's Crusted Port **Non-vintage** £13.49 (AME)

Fonseca Late-Bottled **1983** £14.55 (WAI)

Hoopers **1985** £13.50 (HIG) £18.50 (BU)

Martinez 10-year-old Tawny **Non-vintage** £14.99 (CON) £18.05 (HIC)

Niepoort 10-year-old Tawny **Non-vintage** £14.95 (RAE) £15.18 (BIB) £17.95 (GN) £18.95 (RES) £18.99 (BAL) £19.20 (HAH) £19.90 (GAU)

Royal Oporto **1982** £13.49 (TES)

Warre's Late-Bottled **1992** £13.85 (HAH)

Warre's Traditional Late-Bottled **1992** £14.95 (WAI) £15.50 (TAN) £15.99 (AME)

Warre's Traditional Late-Bottled **1990** £14.99 (SAF) £15.20 (PEN) £17.10 (HIC) £19.95 (FORT)

£15.00 → £16.99

Churchill's Quinta do Agua Alta **1983** £16.67 (PLA)

Churchill's Traditional Late-Bottled **1990** £16.33 (TW)

Croft Quinta da Roeda **1978** £16.45 (WY)

Fonseca Guimaraens Quinta do Panascal **1987** £15.99 (VIL) £17.50 (BAL) £17.50 (FORT)

Graham 10-year-old Tawny **Non-vintage** £15.99 (OD) £22.68 (TW)

Niepoort Colheita **1987** £15.99 (RAE) £22.64 (NO)

Rebello Valente **1985** £16.65 (FA) £30.00 (JU)

Taylor 10-year-old Tawny **Non-vintage** £15.59 (BO) £15.99 (UN) £16.18 (LLO) £16.20 (VIN) £16.45 (PEN) £16.49 (MAJ) £16.49 (VIC) £16.49 (THR) £16.49 (BOT) £16.49 (WR) £16.49 (SAF) £16.50 (WRI) £16.60 (TAN) £16.75 (STA) £17.20 (BEN) £17.50 (GAU) £17.50 (FORT)

Warre's Late-Bottled **1990** £15.99 (JON)

Warre's Traditional Late-Bottled **1984** £15.95 (CON)

£17.00 → £18.99

Cálem Quinta da Foz **1992** £17.99 (UN)

Croft **1975** £17.63 (FA) £23.50 (WY)

Delaforce **1982** £18.29 (YOU)

Fonseca Guimaraens Quinta do Panascal **1986** £18.00 (VIC) £18.00 (THR) £18.00 (BOT) £18.00 (WR) £24.90 (GAU)

Niepoort Colheita **1985** £18.50 (RAE)
Quinta de la Rosa **1995** £17.95 (BU)
£19.00 (MV) £20.59 (YOU)
Quinta do Noval **1982** £17.00 (COC)
£20.00 (CRO) £22.95 (BALL) £25.85 (PEN)
Warre's ½ bottle **1980** £17.63 (WY)

£19.00 → £20.99

Cálem Colheita **1987** £19.95 (COC)
Churchill's Quinta do Agua Alta **1992**
£20.00 (AS)
Croft **1985** £19.00 (BODX) £21.54 (FA)
£23.50 (WY) £29.50 (UN) £29.95 (LAY)
£70.20 (VIN)
Delaforce **1975** £20.00 (BOT) £20.00 (WR)
Dow **1975** £20.95 (BODX) £25.99 (YOU)
£28.00 (HIG)
Dow's Quinta do Bomfim **1987** £19.99
(OD) £22.86 (HIC)
Dow's Quinta do Bomfim **1986** £19.05
(SOM) £19.99 (TAN) £21.60 (LAY) £22.21
(PEN)
Dow's Quinta do Bomfim **1984** £19.99
(VIC) £19.99 (THR) £19.99 (BOT) £19.99
(WR)
Fonseca **1982** £19.00 (THR)
Fonseca Guimaraens **1984** £19.25 (COC)
£19.99 (VIL) £20.75 (WRI) £21.00 (PEN)
£21.60 (HAH) £21.93 (CB) £22.50 (FORT)
Fonseca Guimaraens **1982** £19.00 (VIC)
£19.00 (BOT) £19.00 (WR)
Gould Campbell **1983** £19.58 (FA)
Graham Malvedos **1998** £19.05 (SOM)
Niepoort **1992** £19.95 (RAE) £32.02 (NO)
Niepoort Colheita **1990** £20.50 (BAL)
£21.16 (NO)
Quinta da Ervamoira 10-year-old Tawny
Non-vintage £20.50 (FORT) £20.99
(JON)
Taylor Quinta de Vargellas **1987** £20.50
(TAN) £21.99 (TES) £21.99 (OD)
Taylor Quinta de Vargellas **1986** £19.25
(COC) £20.00 (THR) £20.00 (BOT) £20.00
(WR) £21.30 (PLAY) £21.50 (FORT) £21.60
(HAH) £21.75 (WRI) £21.99 (UN) £21.99
(JON) £24.90 (GAU) £25.79 (TW)
Warre **1975** £19.00 (BODX)
Warre's Quinta da Cavadinha **1997**
£20.99 (OD)
Warre's Quinta da Cavadinha **1987**
£19.95 (CON) £19.99 (BO) £19.99 (YOU)
£20.50 (WAI) £20.99 (SAF) £21.49 (VIC)
£21.49 (THR) £21.49 (BOT) £21.49 (WR)
£21.95 (STE) £21.97 (PEN) £22.70 (LAY)
£22.99 (POR)

£21.00 → £22.99

Cálem Colheita **1990** £22.99 (UN)
Churchill's **1994** £21.54 (TUR)
Churchill's Quinta do Agua Alta **1995**
£21.50 (TAN) £25.50 (STA)
Cockburn **1994** £21.54 (FA) £22.52 (TUR)
£34.95 (TAN)
Dow **1991** £21.54 (FA) £34.00 (JU) £40.00
(UN)
Graham Malvedos **1988** £21.65 (TAN)
£21.99 (AME) £21.99 (OD) £22.99 (YOU)
Graham Malvedos **1987** £21.99 (POR)
£21.99 (AME) £22.85 (HAH) £24.99 (BO)
£25.00 (FORT)
Graham Malvedos **1986** £21.99 (JON)
£22.47 (PLAY) £22.49 (VIC) £22.49 (THR)
£22.49 (BOT) £22.49 (WR)
Graham Malvedos **1984** £21.00 (VIC)
£21.00 (THR) £21.00 (BOT) £21.00 (WR)
£23.38 (PEN)
Martinez **1994** £21.11 (NO) £23.00 (JU)
£25.90 (LAY)
Niepoort **1991** £22.50 (RAE)
Niepoort Colheita **1979** £21.00 (HIG)
Quarles Harris **1985** £22.00 (HIG) £23.95
(TAN) £25.00 (VIC) £25.00 (THR) £25.00
(BOT) £25.00 (WR)
Ramos-Pinto **1983** £21.99 (GW) £24.99
(SUN) £24.99 (LAI) £28.50 (POR)
Rebello Valente **1983** £21.95 (WAT)
Sandeman **1985** £21.54 (FA) £27.50 (TAN)
£29.50 (UN)
Sandeman **1982** £22.00 (COC) £29.50
(TAN)
Taylor Quinta de Vargellas **1984** £21.95
(BALL)
Warre's Quinta da Cavadinha **1988**
£21.99 (AME)

£23.00 → £24.99

Cockburn **1985** £24.99 (YOU) £29.49
(JON) £30.00 (UN) £32.00 (JU)
Cockburn's Crusted **1968** £23.50 (WY)
Croft **1977** £23.50 (TUR) £34.27 (FA)
£42.50 (BEN) £45.00 (VIC) £45.00 (THR)
£45.00 (BOT) £45.00 (WR)

Dow's 20-year-old Tawny **Non-vintage**
£23.59 (SAF) £24.00 (WAI)
Gould Campbell **1985** £23.88 (PLAY)
£28.29 (JON) £42.00 (JER)
Niepoort **1994** £24.99 (UN) £28.50
(RAE)
Niepoort **1987** £23.99 (RAE) £28.50 (GN)
£29.95 (AME)
Niepoort 20-year-old Tawny **Non-vintage** £23.95 (RAE) £32.45 (GN)
£32.90 (GAU)
Quinta de la Rosa **1994** £23.00 (JU)
£23.20 (TAN)
Ramos-Pinto **1980** £24.99 (SUN) £24.99
(LAI)
Royal Oporto **1987** £23.98 (VIN)
Sandeman 20-year-old Tawny **Non-vintage** £23.50 (LEA)
Sandeman Quinta do Vau **1997** £24.99
(OD)
Smith Woodhouse **1983** £24.00 (VIC)
£24.00 (THR) £24.00 (BOT) £24.00 (WR)
£35.25 (PEN)
Smith Woodhouse **1980** £23.00 (VIC)
£23.00 (THR) £23.00 (BOT) £23.00 (WR)
Warre **1991** £24.50 (STA) £24.50 (CON)
£32.00 (JU) £40.00 (UN)

£25.00 → £29.99

Cálem 20-year-old Tawny **Non-vintage**
£25.99 (UN) £27.50 (COC)
Cálem Quinta da Foz **1987** £25.00 (UN)
Churchill's **1991** £27.00 (JU)
Churchill's **1985** £29.95 (POR) £33.25
(HED) £33.30 (TAN) £34.95 (STA) £39.75
(WRI) £43.47 (TW)
Cockburn **1991** £28.29 (JON) £40.00 (UN)
Delaforce **1994** £28.00 (JU) £28.95 (POR)
Delaforce **1985** £27.00 (VIC) £27.00 (THR)
£27.00 (BOT) £27.00 (WR) £30.00 (JU)
Delaforce Quinta da Corte **1997** £27.32
(BODX) £31.75 (TAN)
Dow **1985** £29.99 (UN) £32.00 (VIC)
£32.00 (THR) £32.00 (BOT) £32.00 (WR)
£39.17 (MI) £43.38 (PLAY)
Dow **1983** £27.50 (CON) £29.99 (SUN)
£29.99 (LAI) £30.00 (VIL) £30.00 (JU)
£35.00 (BALL) £35.20 (TAN) £39.10
(HAH)
Fonseca **1980** £26.93 (FA)
Fonseca 20-year-old Tawny **Non-vintage** £27.95 (DI) £28.99 (VIL) £31.45
(BEN) £31.95 (FORT)
Fonseca Guimaraens **1995** £29.95 (DI)
£35.00 (JU)

Gould Campbell **1997** £29.95 (LEA)
£29.95 (LAY) £32.50 (POR)
Gould Campbell **1994** £25.25 (NI) £26.00
(JU)
Gould Campbell **1991** £25.00 (JU) £35.00
(UN)
Graham **1975** £25.46 (FA) £40.65
(TAN)
Martinez **1985** £25.02 (NO)
Martinez 20-year-old Tawny **Non-vintage** £25.00 (CON)
Niepoort **1985** £27.50 (RAE)
Niepoort **1983** £28.50 (RAE)
Niepoort **1982** £28.50 (RAE)
Niepoort Colheita **1978** £29.50 (RAE)
Offley Boa Vista **1983** £27.60 (TAN)
Quarles Harris **1983** £27.00 (HED)
Quarles Harris **1980** £28.00 (VIC) £28.00
(THR) £28.00 (BOT) £28.00 (WR)
Quinta da Eira Velha **1997** £29.24 (NO)
Quinta da Ervamoira 10-year-old Tawny
1994 £26.99 (VIL)
Quinta de la Rosa **1997** £26.95 (NI)
Quinta do Noval **1991** £26.91 (PEN)
£30.00 (JU) £40.00 (UN)
Quinta do Noval **1985** £25.49 (BO)
£28.00 (CRO) £28.50 (WRI) £28.99 (SUN)
£28.99 (LAI) £43.20 (VIN)
Quinta do Noval 20-year-old Tawny
Non-vintage £28.38 (PLA)
Quinta do Vesuvio **1998** £28.40 (CB)
Quinta do Vesuvio **1996** £28.89 (TUR)
£33.00 (NO) £35.00 (RES)
Quinta do Vesuvio **1992** £26.34 (BODX)
£40.00 (JU)
Rebello Valente **1977** £28.79 (BODX)
£41.99 (JON)
Sandeman Imperial 20-year-old Tawny
Non-vintage £25.99 (OD)
Smith Woodhouse **1994** £27.00 (JU)
Smith Woodhouse **1991** £25.00 (JU)
£35.00 (UN)
Smith Woodhouse **1985** £27.00 (VIC)
£27.00 (THR) £27.00 (BOT) £27.00 (WR)
£28.00 (UN) £30.00 (JU) £32.50 (FORT)
Smith Woodhouse **1970** £29.38 (TUR)
£32.50 (BU)
Smith Woodhouse Fine Crusted **1997**
£29.95 (LEA)
Smith Woodhouse Fine Crusted **1985**
£25.95 (LEA)
Taylor **1980** £27.91 (FA) £38.00 (BAL)
£49.39 (PLAY) £49.94 (TW)
Taylor **1975** £26.93 (FA) £34.95 (TAN)
£37.60 (WY)

Taylor Quinta de Vargellas **1991** £25.00 (UN)

Taylor Quinta de Vargellas **1978** £29.95 (BAL)

Warre **1997** £27.91 (FA) £29.86 (TUR) £35.00 (CON) £36.30 (TAN) £39.50 (POR) £50.00 (BALL)

Warre **1985** £26.00 (BAC) £29.50 (UN) £29.95 (CON) £30.35 (WY) £32.00 (VIC) £32.00 (THR) £32.00 (BOT) £32.00 (WR) £34.95 (STA) £35.00 (MAY) £37.31 (PLAY)

Warre **1983** £28.20 (WY) £29.99 (SUN) £29.99 (LAI) £30.00 (VIL) £30.00 (JU) £32.50 (FORT) £34.25 (TAN) £35.00 (COC) £36.00 (VIC) £36.00 (THR) £36.00 (AME) £36.00 (BOT) £36.00 (WR) £37.50 (JON) £38.35 (HAH) £39.52 (PLAY) £61.20 (VIN)

Warre **1970** £28.49 (SUN) £28.49 (LAI) £47.00 (TUR) £48.96 (FA) £50.00 (FLE) £59.80 (LAY)

£30.00 → £39.99

Cálem **1997** £34.45 (TAN)

Churchill's **1997** £36.07 (CB) £36.25 (TAN)

Churchill's Quinta do Agua Alta **1987** £30.00 (HED)

Cockburn **1997** £38.42 (CB)

Cockburn **1983** £38.75 (WRI)

Cockburn **1970** £38.78 (WY) £45.00 (BAL) £54.90 (PLAY)

Cockburn **1967** £30.26 (BODX)

Cockburn **1960** £31.33 (FA) £49.35 (WY)

Croft **1970** £31.33 (FA) £38.78 (WY)

Croft Quinta da Roeda **1997** £32.25 (CB)

Delaforce **1992** £35.00 (UN)

Delaforce **1977** £35.00 (VIC) £35.00 (THR) £35.00 (BOT) £35.00 (WR)

Dow **1997** £30.35 (TUR) £33.29 (FA) £35.00 (LEA) £35.00 (CON) £36.50 (GAU) £38.45 (SUN) £38.45 (LAI) £50.00 (BALL)

Dow **1994** £38.68 (WY) £40.00 (CON) £60.00 (BALL)

Dow **1980** £34.00 (VIC) £34.00 (THR) £34.00 (BOT) £34.00 (WR) £42.90 (PLAY)

Fonseca **1993** £38.99 (BO)

Fonseca **1983** £31.00 (CRO) £35.00 (COC) £41.13 (WY) £48.00 (VIC) £48.00 (THR) £48.00 (BOT) £48.00 (WR) £50.00 (VIL) £50.89 (JON)

Gould Campbell **1977** £37.50 (TAN) £45.00 (FORT)

Graham **1997** £35.25 (TUR) £35.25 (FA) £37.50 (CON) £38.19 (WY) £39.40 (TAN) £39.90 (GAU) £41.50 (POR) £42.50 (LEA) £43.35 (LAY) £55.00 (BALL)

Graham **1991** £37.00 (TAN) £40.00 (JU) £45.00 (UN) £47.00 (TW)

Graham **1985** £36.00 (VIC) £36.00 (THR) £36.00 (BOT) £36.00 (WR) £38.19 (TUR) £44.70 (LAY) £55.00 (FORT)

Graham **1983** £31.33 (FA) £35.99 (SUN) £35.99 (LAI) £36.00 (LEA) £40.00 (POR) £41.90 (PLAY)

Graham **1980** £34.95 (CON) £36.00 (BAL) £40.00 (VIC) £40.00 (THR) £40.00 (BOT) £40.00 (WR) £41.38 (PLAY)

Graham 20-year-old Tawny **Non-vintage** £37.95 (TW)

Graham Malvedos **1995** £30.80 (LAY) £31.70 (TAN) £32.00 (JU)

Niepoort **1997** £35.00 (BEN) £68.73 (NO)

Niepoort Colheita **1974** £35.00 (RAE)

Offley Boa Vista **1970** £35.00 (BU)

Quarles Harris **1997** £30.45 (TAN) £31.08 (CB)

Quarles Harris **1977** £39.00 (THR) £39.00 (BOT) £39.00 (WR) £70.20 (VIN)

Quinta da Eira Velha **1994** £33.50 (NO)

Quinta do Noval **1995** £30.00 (FORT)

Quinta do Vesuvio **1997** £33.29 (FA) £35.20 (PLAY) £36.00 (YOU) £37.50 (CON) £39.95 (LEA) £41.50 (POR)

Quinta do Vesuvio **1995** £30.00 (FORT) £34.45 (HAH) £35.00 (JU)

Quinta do Vesuvio **1994** £33.99 (UN) £41.66 (SUN) £41.66 (LAI) £42.50 (CON) £70.00 (JU)

Rebello Valente **1970** £30.75 (BODX)

Sandeman **1970** £39.50 (BU) £41.13 (TUR)

Smith Woodhouse **1997** £30.45 (TAN)

> • Wines are listed in A–Z order within each price band.
> • For each wine, vintages are listed in descending order.
> • Each vintage of any wine appears only once.

Taylor **1985** £36.23 (TUR) £38.58 (BODX)
£38.68 (FA) £41.13 (WY) £55.89 (JON)
£56.00 (VIC) £56.00 (THR) £56.00 (BOT)
£56.00 (WR) £64.17 (MI) £80.10 (VIN)
Taylor **1983** £32.00 (CRO) £35.90 (LAY)
£43.50 (WRI) £45.00 (FORT) £45.83 (PEN)
£48.00 (VIC) £48.00 (THR) £48.00 (BOT)
£48.00 (WR) £50.89 (JON) £64.17 (MI)
Taylor 20-year-old Tawny **Non-vintage**
£33.30 (VIN) £33.60 (TAN) £33.68 (PLAY)
£34.00 (VIC) £34.00 (THR) £34.00 (BOT)
£34.90 (GAU) £35.00 (BEN)
Taylor Quinta de Vargellas **1995** £30.95
(LAY) £32.20 (HAH) £35.00 (JU)
Warre **1994** £30.35 (TUR) £35.00 (CON)
£39.50 (LAY) £39.77 (PLAY) £60.00 (BALL)
Warre **1980** £32.95 (CON) £53.95 (VIN)
Warre **1977** £37.50 (BU) £39.17 (TUR)
£41.00 (TAN) £45.00 (VIC) £45.00 (THR)
£45.00 (BOT) £45.00 (WR) £54.50 (BEN)
£55.00 (JON) £56.99 (OD) £59.95 (WAI)

£40.00 → £49.99

Cálem **1994** £42.50 (WRI)
Dow **1977** £43.08 (TUR) £43.47 (BODX)
£45.04 (FA) £48.00 (VIC) £48.00 (THR)
£48.00 (BOT) £48.00 (WR) £50.00 (WAT)
£50.00 (TAN) £51.67 (MI) £75.00 (FORT)
Fonseca **1997** £40.00 (FORT) £47.88
(BODX) £48.47 (WY) £48.47 (FA) £49.95
(CON) £49.95 (DI) £51.70 (TUR) £60.00
(BALL)
Fonseca **1992** £48.37 (BODX) £48.96 (FA)
£49.95 (CON) £50.00 (UN) £53.85 (WY)
£58.75 (WRI) £75.00 (FORT) £88.20 (TAN)
Fonseca **1985** £41.13 (FA) £42.00 (COC)
£49.95 (TAN) £51.50 (STA) £55.00 (FORT)
£56.00 (VIC) £56.00 (THR) £56.00 (BOT)
£56.00 (WR) £57.39 (JON) £60.00 (VIL)
Graham **1994** £41.13 (FA) £42.50 (CON)
£60.00 (JU) £70.00 (BALL)
Graham **1977** £49.35 (TUR) £50.92 (FA)
£52.00 (HIG) £53.50 (WRI) £55.00 (SOM)
£64.60 (TAN) £72.50 (BEN) £75.00 (FORT)
£82.00 (STA) £85.00 (JER)
Niepoort Colheita **1983** £49.00 (RAE)
Offley Boa Vista **1954** £47.00 (FA)
Quinta de la Rosa **1988** £44.10 (VIN)
Quinta do Noval **1970** £45.00 (WRI)
Quinta do Noval **1960** £41.13 (WY)
£60.00 (FORT)
Quinta do Vesuvio **1991** £45.00 (UN)
Quinta do Vesuvio **1990** £47.00 (YOU)
Sandeman **1977** £42.00 (BAL)
Sandeman **1960** £49.35 (WY)

Taylor **1997** £45.00 (WRI) £45.00 (FORT)
£48.47 (FA) £49.95 (CON) £50.43 (WY)
£51.90 (TUR) £60.00 (BALL) £94.00 (BODX)
Taylor ½ bottle **1970** £42.00 (CRO)
Taylor 30-year-old Tawny **Non-vintage**
£49.45 (VIN)
Warre's ½ bottle **1963** £48.00 (CRO)

£50.00 → £74.99

Cálem **1983** £50.00 (UN)
Cálem **1970** £55.00 (COC)
Cálem 40-year-old Tawny **Non-vintage**
£70.50 (UN)
Cockburn **1963** £70.50 (TUR) £75.20 (WY)
£95.00 (RES) £100.00 (HED) £110.00
(BAL) £117.07 (PLAY)
Croft **1963** £70.50 (TUR) £95.00 (RES)
£114.30 (VIN)
Dow **1960** £52.88 (WY) £98.00 (RES)
Dow **1950** £50.00 (CRO)
Fonseca **1994** £65.00 (WRI) £85.00 (CON)
£85.00 (DI) £90.00 (VIL) £105.00 (TAN)
Fonseca 40-year-old Tawny **Non-
vintage** £70.00 (VIL)
Graham **1970** £69.50 (BU) £70.50 (FA)
£115.00 (FRI) £125.00 (FORT)
Graham 40-year-old Tawny **Non-
vintage** £70.00 (JU) £85.54 (TW)
Martinez **1963** £74.90 (TAN)
Niepoort **1963** £72.46 (FA)
Niepoort Colheita **1976** £52.00 (RES)
Niepoort Colheita **1963** £72.00 (RAE)
Offley Boa Vista **1963** £50.00 (BU)
Quinta do Noval **1963** £65.60 (FA) £66.98
(TUR)
Ramos-Pinto Tawny **1937** £55.00 (CRO)
Rebello Valente **1963** £62.50 (BU)
Sandeman **1966** £58.75 (WY)
Sandeman **1963** £65.00 (BEN) £65.60 (FA)
£82.25 (WY) £90.35 (TAN) £110.70 (VIN)
Taylor **1977** £69.52 (FA) £75.00 (CON)
£80.00 (TAN) £89.50 (BEN) £95.00 (FORT)

Taylor **1970** £75.00 (CRO) £75.20 (TUR)
£76.38 (WY) £79.40 (TAN) £95.00 (BU)
£110.00 (RES) £130.50 (VIN)
Taylor **1960** £70.50 (WY) £85.00 (BU)

Taylor 40-year-old Tawny **Non-vintage**
£70.50 (PEN) £74.65 (VIN) £75.95 (STA)
£79.50 (GAU) £80.00 (FORT)
Warre **1966** £58.75 (PLA)
Warre **1927** £52.88 (WY)

£75.00 → £99.99

Dow **1966** £75.40 (FA)
Dow **1963** £85.00 (BEN) £104.77 (FA)
£115.00 (RES)
Fonseca **1977** £94.00 (TAN) £118.50 (NI)
£150.00 (FORT)
Fonseca **1970** £85.19 (FA) £94.00 (WY)
Fonseca **1966** £90.09 (FA)
Fonseca **1960** £76.38 (WY)
Graham **1966** £75.40 (FA) £88.10 (TAN)
£88.13 (WY) £95.00 (VIL)
Martinez **1955** £88.13 (WY)
Niepoort Garrafeira **1952** £93.60 (RAE)
Quinta do Noval **1966** £76.30 (HAH)
Quinta do Noval **1947** £95.00 (CRO)
Quinta do Noval Nacional **1980** £82.75
(TUR) £172.72 (TW)
Quinta do Noval Nacional **1975** £79.80
(TUR)
Rebello Valente **1924** £88.13 (WY)
Smith Woodhouse **1955** £99.88 (WY)
Taylor **1994** £85.00 (CON) £85.19 (FA)
£86.17 (TUR) £87.15 (WY) £120.00
(TAN)
Taylor **1992** £80.29 (FA) £82.25 (WY)
£82.25 (BODX) £88.13 (TUR) £95.00 (JU)
£100.00 (CON) £119.80 (TAN)
Taylor **1966** £80.29 (FA) £110.00 (BAL)
£133.89 (TW)
Warre **1963** £97.53 (WY) £125.00 (FORT)

£100.00 → £149.99

Cockburn **1955** £118.00 (RES) £146.88
(WY)
Cockburn **1927** £105.75 (WY)
Croft **1955** £111.63 (WY) £130.00 (BEN)
Croft **1950** £129.25 (WY)
Ferreira **1945** £129.25 (WY) £146.88
(TUR)
Fonseca **1963** £125.10 (VIN) £160.00
(BEN) £164.50 (WY) £195.00 (CON)
£225.00 (FORT)
Quinta do Noval **1955** £130.00 (BEN)
Quinta do Noval Nacional **1987** £124.80
(NO)
Quinta do Noval Nacional **1978** £146.81
(TW)
Quinta do Noval Nacional **1964** £105.75
(TUR)

Sandeman **1955** £141.00 (WY)
Taylor **1963** £133.56 (BODX) £141.00
(TUR) £147.36 (FA) £200.00 (FORT)
Warre **1955** £141.00 (WY)
Warre **1950** £100.00 (FORT)
Warre **1922** £135.13 (WY)

£150.00 → £199.99

Cockburn **1935** £199.50 (POR) £329.00
(WY)
Dow **1955** £158.63 (WY)
Graham **1963** £155.00 (BEN)
Graham **1955** £150.00 (SOM) £193.88
(WY)
Quinta do Noval Nacional **1967** £183.53
(NO) £200.00 (FORT)
Quinta do Noval Nacional **1960** £178.21
(FA) £450.02 (TW)
Quinta do Noval Tawny **1937** £150.00
(RIC)
Sandeman **1947** £158.63 (WY) £385.00
(FORT)
Taylor **1955** £155.00 (BEN) £186.04 (TUR)
£193.88 (WY) £210.00 (JU)

£200.00 → £299.99

Croft **1927** £205.63 (WY)
Dow **1927** £280.00 (BEN)
Dow **1924** £270.25 (WY)
Fonseca **1955** £264.38 (WY)
Graham **1948** £295.00 (BEN)
Graham **1935** £258.50 (WY)
Niepoort Colheita **1934** £210.00 (RAE)
Quinta do Noval Nacional **1970** £294.03
(NO) £370.12 (TW)
Quinta do Noval Nacional **1966** £271.63
(NO)
Quinta do Noval Nacional **1962** £229.13
(FA)
Smith Woodhouse **1935** £276.13 (WY)

Over £300.00

Croft **1945** £334.88 (WY)
Croft **1920** £329.00 (WY)
Croft **1912** £334.88 (WY)
Dow **1945** £355.50 (VIN)
Quinta do Noval Nacional **1963** £490.00
(JU) £600.00 (NO) £740.25 (TW)
Sandeman **1935** £339.50 (WY)
Sandeman **1927** £317.25 (WY)
Taylor **1948** £446.50 (WY)
Taylor **1935** £428.88 (WY)
Taylor **1920** £381.88 (WY)
Warre **1945** £317.25 (WY)
Warre **1920** £323.13 (WY)

MADEIRA PRICES

Under £9.00

3-year-old Medium Dry Henriques &
Henriques **Non-vintage** £8.95 (STA)
£8.99 (VIL) £11.95 (LEA)

3-year-old Full Rich Henriques &
Henriques **Non-vintage** £8.95 (STA)
£9.95 (FORT) £11.20 (VIN) £11.21 (HIC)

Duke of Clarence Blandy **Non-vintage**
£8.95 (CON) £8.99 (SAF) £9.29 (WAI)
£9.49 (UN) £9.49 (VIC) £9.49 (THR) £9.49
(BOT) £9.49 (WR) £9.99 (GW) £10.39 (VIN)
£10.65 (HAH) £11.00 (JU) £13.28 (TW)

Duke of Sussex Blandy **Non-vintage**
£8.99 (GW) £9.49 (UN) £9.49 (VIC) £9.49
(THR) £9.49 (BOT) £9.49 (WR) £10.52
(VIN) £10.65 (HAH) £11.00 (JU)

Sercial Blandy **Non-vintage** £8.99 (GW)

£9.00 → £9.99

3-year-old Medium Rich Henriques &
Henriques **Non-vintage** £9.95 (FORT)

Duke of Cumberland Blandy **Non-vintage** £9.13 (WAT) £9.49 (UN) £9.49
(VIC) £9.49 (THR) £9.49 (BOT) £9.49 (WR)
£9.99 (GW) £10.52 (VIN)

£10.00 → £14.99

5-year-old Bual Blandy **Non-vintage**
£13.80 (HAH)

5-year-old Bual Cossart Gordon **Non-vintage** £12.95 (CON) £13.50 (DI)
£14.00 (JU) £14.99 (CB)

5-year-old Finest Full Rich Henriques &
Henriques **Non-vintage** £11.00 (COC)
£11.99 (VIL)

5-year-old Finest Medium Dry Henriques
& Henriques **Non-vintage** £10.09 (UN)
£10.99 (AME) £11.95 (LEA) £11.99 (VIL)

5-year-old Finest Medium Rich Henriques
& Henriques **Non-vintage** £11.00
(COC) £11.99 (VIL)

5-year-old Malmsey Cossart Gordon
Non-vintage £12.62 (NO) £12.95 (CON)
£13.50 (DI) £13.95 (FORT) £14.99 (CB)

5-year-old Sercial Blandy **Non-vintage**
£11.80 (WAT)

5-year-old Sercial Cossart Gordon **Non-vintage** £12.95 (CON) £13.50 (DI)
£13.95 (FORT) £14.00 (JU) £14.95 (HAH)
£14.99 (CB)

Malmsey Blandy **1994** £13.95 (STE)

£15.00 → £24.99

10-year-old Bual Cossart Gordon **Non-vintage** £17.49 (JON) £17.95 (DI)

10-year-old Malmsey Blandy **Non-vintage** £15.76 (WAT) £15.95 (WAI)
£15.99 (GW) £16.50 (CON) £16.99 (JON)
£18.80 (HAH) £19.50 (FORT) £22.80 (CB)

10-year-old Malmsey Henriques &
Henriques **Non-vintage** £15.09 (UN)
£15.50 (CRO) £15.99 (VIL) £16.95 (AS)
£16.95 (HED) £17.95 (LEA) £19.21 (HIC)

10-year-old Sercial Henriques &
Henriques **Non-vintage** £15.99 (VIL)
£16.00 (COC) £16.99 (AME) £17.95 (LEA)

10-year-old Verdelho Henriques &
Henriques **Non-vintage** £16.00 (COC)
£16.99 (AME) £17.75 (FORT) £18.79 (HIC)

£25.00 → £49.99

Bual Henriques & Henriques **1964** £37.21
(FA)

Verdelho Henriques & Henriques **1954**
£43.08 (FA)

£50.00 → £99.99

Bual Blandy **1954** £55.00 (BOT) £55.00 (WR)

Bual Henriques & Henriques **1954** £97.00
(JU)

Malmsey Justino Henriques **1933** £82.25
(WY)

Sercial Blandy **1940** £58.75 (FA)

Over £100.00

Bual Blandy **1959** £146.88 (WY)

Bual Vintage Cossart Gordon **1914**
£217.37 (TW)

Bual Vintage Leacocks **1934** £152.75 (TW)

Bual Vintage Leacocks **1914** £193.88 (WY)

Malmsey Henriques & Henriques **1954**
£105.00 (JU) £110.00 (CRO)

Malmsey Powers **1954** £175.00 (JU)

Malmsey Vintage 1880 Blandy **Non-vintage** £158.63 (WY)

Malvazia Reserva Pereira d'Oliveira **1907**
£164.50 (WY)

Malvazia Reserva Pereira d'Oliveira **1900**
£152.95 (GAU)

Sercial Vintage Cossart Gordon **1910**
£117.50 (FA)

Verdelho Vintage Rutherford & Miles
1954 £125.00 (DI)

SOUTH AFRICA

There's a flurry of activity in the Cape's winelands, as growers seek to match vines to their best sites

What, in the future, are going to be the key South African styles? Good question. What's the answer? Sorry, don't ask me – yet.

South Africa is still on a learning curve. There are new wineries and new styles springing up all the time: some of them are genuine stars, and some seem more driven by ego than by genuine quality. But that's par for the course in any newly successful wine region. Some of the stars of ten years ago are still up there, but many have been left by the wayside.

And no wonder. Take Chardonnay. South Africa has only been growing Chardonnay since about 1985, and not surprisingly has yet to discover the best places to plant it. Shiraz is suddenly the grape everyone loves and wants to plant. Well, it wasn't like that a few years ago when only far-sighted pioneers like Fairview were fans. And who'd have thought that warm South Africa would have the potential to make some of the world's best Sauvignon Blanc? So it's a country in flux – but great things are already emerging.

GRAPE VARIETIES

CABERNET SAUVIGNON, CABERNET FRANC AND BORDEAUX BLENDS (red) Good ones have clean, minty aromas and fresh fruit. Bordeaux blends tend to be best, though some producers are now favouring a Bordeaux Right Bank blend of mostly Merlot and Cabernet Franc. Best Cabernets include: *Alto, Backsberg, Bellingham, Beyerskloof, du Plessis, Neil Ellis, Hartenberg, Kanonkop, L'Avenir, Le Bonheur, Nederburg Auction, Plaisir de Merle, Rustenberg Peter Barlow, Saxenburg Private Collection, Springfield, Swartland co-op, Thelema*. Blends: *Backsberg Klein Babylonstoren, Graham Beck Railroad Red, Buitenverwachting Christine, Delheim Grand Reserve, Glen Carlou Grande Classique, Grangehurst, Groot Constantia Gouverneurs Reserve, Kanonkop Paul Sauer, Klein Constantia Marlbrook, Lievland DVB,*

L'Ormarins Optima, Louisvale, Meerlust Rubicon, Meinert, Morgenhof Première Selection, Mulderbosch Faithful Hound, Neetlingshof Lord Neethling Reserve, Overgaauw Tria Corda, Rupert & Rothschild, Rustenberg, Villiera Cru Monro, Vriesenhof Kallista, Warwick Trilogy, Welgemeend, Zonnebloem Lauréat.

CHARDONNAY (white) The best wines have lingering lemon-lime freshness with subtle oak. Inevitably, there's some over-oaking disguising some underpowered winemaking too. Try: *Avontuur, Backsberg, Graham Beck Lone Hill, Bellingham, Bouchard Finlayson, Buitenverwachting, De Leuwen Jagt, De Wetshof, Dieu Donné, Eikendal, Neil Ellis, Glen Carlou, Groot Constantia, Hamilton Russell, Jordan, Klein Constantia, Longridge, Louisvale, Meerlust, Morgenhof, Mulderbosch, Nederburg, Overgaauw, Rustenberg, Saxenburg, Simonsig, Springfield, Thelema, Vergelegen, Weltevrede, Zandvliet.*

CHENIN BLANC (white) Usually simple entry-level stuff, though there's now a Chenin Blanc Association dedicated to improving quality. Bush vine Chenin can be excellent. Best: *Boschendal, Glen Carlou, de Trafford, Ken Forrester, KWV, L'Avenir, Mulderbosch Steen-op-Hout, Spice Route, Villiera, Wildekrans.* Botrytized Chenin Blanc is used for the sweet *Nederburg Edelkeur.*

MERLOT (red) By itself Merlot makes rich, ripe, easy reds – even better aged in new oak. Increasingly popular. Good ones include *Bellingham, Boschendal, Cordoba, de Trafford, Drostdy-Hof, Glen Carlou, Longridge, Meerlust, Meinert, Morgenhof, Overgaauw, Saxenburg, Spice Route, Steenberg, Thelema, Veenwouden, Villiera, Warwick, Yonder Hill.*

MUSCAT (white) Sweet Muscadels are usually the best bet, and include *Klein Constantia Vin de Constance, KWV, Van Loveren Blanc de Noir, Nederburg Eminence.*

PINOTAGE (red) As cleaner, more intense fruit comes to the fore, Pinotage is suddenly very fashionable. Good ones are *Avontuur, Beyerskloof, Clos Malverne, Fairview, Grangehurst, Kaapzicht, Kanonkop, KWV Cathedral Cellar, L'Avenir, Simonsig, Spice Route, Swartland co-op, Thelema, Uiterwyk, Vriesenhof, Warwick* and *Wildekrans.*

PINOT NOIR (red) The coolest parts of the country are producing supple and understated Pinot Noirs of world class. Best are: *Bouchard Finlayson, Glen Carlou, Hamilton Russell, Haute Cabrière, Meerlust.*

SAUVIGNON BLANC (white) Showing vast improvements, there are some lovely pungent, ripe wines from *Bellingham, Buitenverwachting, Neil Ellis, Klein Constantia, Jordan, Morgenhof, Mulderbosch, Saxenburg, Springfield, Steenberg, Stellenryck, Thelema, Vergelegen, Villiera.*

SHIRAZ (red) Better clones of this are promised, which will improve quality – though not immediately. Best: *Graham Beck, Boekenhoutskloof, de Trafford, Fairview, Neil Ellis, Hartenberg, Hunting, Klein Constantia, La Motte, Lievland, Saxenburg, Spice Route, Spier, Stellenzicht Syrah, Thelema, Zandvliet, Zonnebloem.*

SPARKLING WINES 'Methode Cap Classique' is the name for Champagne-method fizz. Best: *Graham Beck, Boschendal, Pierre Jourdan* (from *Cabrière), Pongrácz (J C Le Roux), Simonsig.*

OTHERS Semillon used to be the mainstay of the wine industry, but then went out of fashion. A few people are now looking seriously at it again. Best: *Boekenhoutskloof, Boschendal, Fairview, Steenberg, Vergelegen.* Viognier is also starting to attract attention: look out for *Fairview* and *Spice Route.* Riesling can be interesting too, especially the sweet ones. Try *Danie De Wet Edeloes, Nederburg Noble Late Harvest, Neetlingshof Noble Late Harvest, Stellenzicht Noble Late Harvest.*

WINES & WINE REGIONS

CONSTANTIA There's a new emphasis on cool-climate whites here, especially Sauvignon Blanc. Look for *Buitenverwachting, Klein Constantia* and *Steenberg.*

DURBANVILLE HILLS A small, cool-climate area that is on the up. Look for *Altydgedacht, Bloemendal, Meerendal, Nitida.*

FRANSCHHOEK White grapes rule, yet the new reds are promising. Look for

Cabrière fizz and Pinot Noir, *Bellingham, Boekenhoutskloof, La Motte* and *L'Ormarins.*

OLIFANTS RIVER Irrigated bulk wine area, with some good everyday stuff.

PAARL Good wines from almost every variety, from producers such as *Backsberg, Boschendal, Fairview, Glen Carlou, Plaisir de Merle, Nederburg, Veenwouden, Villiera, Welgemeend.* The *KWV* is based here.

ROBERTSON The country's biggest producer of Chardonnay. There are good value reds, too. *Graham Beck, Bon Courage, De Wetshof, Robertson Winery, Springfield, Van Loveren, Weltevrede, Zandvliet* are names to look for.

STELLENBOSCH The heart of the wine industry. Both reds and whites are successful. Look for: *Avontuur, Beyerskloof, Clos Malverne, Cordoba, Delheim, de Trafford, Eikendal, Neil Ellis, Grangehurst, Hartenberg, Jordan, Kanonkop, L'Avenir, Leef Op Hoop, Lievland, Longridge, Louisvale, Meerlust, Morgenhof, Mulderbosch, Neetlingshof, Overgaauw, Rustenberg, Rust-en-Vrede, Saxenburg, Simonsig, Stellenzicht, Thelema, Vergelegen, Vriesenhof, Warwick.*

> **ON THE CASE**
> Buy Pinotage carefully:
> some are overpriced, overoaked,
> overhyped

SWARTLAND The *Swartland* and *Riebeek co-ops* and *Allesverloren* estate established the potential of this hot, dry area. *Spice Route* is the brightest new star; others are *Darling Cellars* and *Groote Post.*

WALKER BAY Some of the best Pinot Noir comes from here and there's good Chardonnay and Sauvignon Blanc. New producers are now joining the area's top names: *Bouchard Finlayson, Hamilton Russell, WhaleHaven, Wildekrans.*

PRODUCERS WHO'S WHO

BACKSBERG ★★ Luscious Chardonnay and fine reds, including Cabernet, Merlot and Bordeaux blends.

BELLINGHAM ★ Super flinty Sauvignon and an elegant, peachy Chardonnay. Cabernet Franc is impressive.

BOSCHENDAL ★ Intense, peppery Shiraz, juicy, chocolaty Merlot, superb Lanoy red blend, and sparkling white Le Grand Pavillon Blanc de Blancs.

BOUCHARD FINLAYSON ★★ Burgundian-style Chardonnays, flinty fresh Sauvignon Blanc and some of South Africa's best Pinot Noir.

CABRIÈRE ESTATE ★★ Perfumed, raspberry-packed Haute Cabrière Pinot Noir; Pierre Jourdan sparklers.

DE WETSHOF ★★ Danie de Wet makes Chardonnays with great elegance and poise, and spicy Rhine Riesling.

NEIL ELLIS WINES ★★ Top negociant producing excellent Sauvignon, tropical-tasting Chardonnay, intense Cabernet, juicy Pinotage, and brooding Shiraz.

FAIRVIEW ★★ Great Pinotage, Shiraz, Merlot and Zinfandel/Cinsaut. Chardonnay and Semillon are top whites. 'Goats do Roam' is a new Rhône blend. A pioneer of Viognier and Mourvèdre.

GLEN CARLOU ★ Tropically rich, leesy Chardonnay and impressive red Bordeaux blends.

GRANGEHURST ★★★ Look for the excellent mulberry-fruited Nikela blend of Cabernet and Pinotage.

HAMILTON RUSSELL ★★ Elegant Chardonnay and supple, ripe, even silky Pinot Noir that brilliantly straddle Old and New Worlds.

JORDAN ★ International-style reds and whites made with great aplomb.

KANONKOP ★★ Pinotage king of the Cape. There's also rich, mouthfilling Cabernet and Paul Sauer Bordeaux blend.

INSTANT CELLAR: NEW STARS

- **1997 Old Vines Blue White, Irena von Holdt, £6.49, The Nobody Inn** Chenin Blanc of considerable concentration and stylishness, from one of the producers dedicated to taking this variety seriously.
- **1998 Chenin Blanc, Wildekrans, Bot River Valley, £5.75, Bat & Bottle** Cool-climate wine full of concentrated honeyed fruit. Not a bit like most South African Chenin, but then this estate is one of the country's newest stars.
- **1999 Old Vine Semillon, Eikehof Estate, £8.20, Frank Stainton** The vines are 97 years old, apparently, and this Stellenbosch wine has great depth as a result. Good waxy flavours and balancing acidity.
- **1996 Welgemeend Amadé, £6.95, The Wine Society** Grenache, Shiraz and Pinotage go into this soft, lush blend.
- **1998 Sejana Merlot, Jean-Jacques Moueix, £16.70, John Armit Wines** Pricy but good, with smoky, minerally, chocolaty fruit and plenty of tannic backbone.
- **1996 Cordoba Crescendo, Stellenbosch, £15.45, Berry Bros & Rudd** A Cabernet Franc and Merlot blend with considerable depth and finesse.

KLEIN CONSTANTIA ★★ Stunning Sauvignon Blanc, toasty Chardonnay and claret-style Marlbrook red.

LA MOTTE ★ Fine reds: big, spicy Shiraz and ripe, oak-splashed Cabernet.

MEERLUST ★★ Complex Rubicon Cabernet blend and complex Chardonnay.

MULDERBOSCH ★★ Brilliant Sauvignon Blanc, complex Chardonnay and Bordeaux blend Faithful Hound.

PLAISIR DE MERLE ★ Ripe, blackcurranty Cabernet, minty Merlot, lively Sauvignon, and buttery Chardonnay.

RUSTENBERG ★★ Cabernet blends that cellar well and top-quality Chardonnays.

SAXENBERG ★★ Private Collection Shiraz, Cabernet and Merlot are some of the Cape's most sought-after reds. There's equally good Sauvignon Blanc and Chardonnay, too.

SIMONSIG ★★ Concentrated, unwooded Pinotage and brilliant Shiraz; Tiara is the Cabernet/Merlot blend.

SPICE ROUTE ★★ Exciting range includes Pinotage, Shiraz and Merlot, and a promising new red blend called Andrew's Hope.

STEENBERG ★★ Constantia's rising star. Crisp, nettly Sauvignon Blanc and powerful, inky Merlot.

STELLENZICHT ★★ Look out for superb Syrah, good Chardonnay, Semillon, Chenin Blanc.

THELEMA ★★ First-rate Sauvignon Blanc and Chardonnay, gutsy Cabernet Reserve and fruit-driven Cabernet/Merlot.

VEENWOUDEN ★★ Intense, rich reds from warm Paarl: try the Classic.

VERGELEGEN ★★ Top-class Sauvignons and Chardonnays; Mill Race Red is a Cabernet/Merlot blend.

VILLIERA ★★ Tangy Sauvignons and lightly oaked Chenin; Tradition sparklers; Bordeaux-style Cru Monro and consistently excellent Merlot.

VRIESENHOF ★ Very intense Chardonnay; classy Pinotage; super Kallista Bordeaux blend.

WARWICK ★★ Fabulous Pinotage, mouthfilling Cabernet Franc and a complex Bordeaux blend called Trilogy.

WELGEMEEND ★★ Tremendous reds from a variety of grape varieties.

SOUTH AFRICA PRICES

RED

Under £4.50

Cabernet Sauvignon/Shiraz Van Loveren
1999 £4.10 (SOM) £4.99 (VIL)
Cape Red Drostdy-Hof **2001** £4.49 (VIL)
£4.78 (LLO)
Cinsaut/Pinotage Kumala **1999** £4.49 (BOT)

£4.50 → £4.99

Cinsaut/Pinotage Kumala **2000** £4.69
(BUD) £4.79 (SAF)
Goats Do Roam Fairview **2000** £4.99 (TES)
Pinotage Cape Bay **1999** £4.77 (PEN)
Pinotage Culemborg **2000** £4.59 (WAI)
Pinotage Sonop Cape Soleil Organic **2000**
£4.99 (SAF)

£5.00 → £5.99

Cabernet Sauvignon Apostles Falls **1999**
£5.99 (TES)
Cabernet Sauvignon Koopmanskloof
1997 £5.96 (NO)
Cabernet Sauvignon KWV **1999** £5.49 (WR)
Cabernet Sauvignon KWV **1998** £5.16
(COC) £5.49 (CAP)
Cabernet Sauvignon/Merlot Swartland
1996 £5.99 (VIL)
Cabernet Sauvignon Oak Village **1998**
£5.49 (BOT)
Cabernet Sauvignon Robertson Winery
1999 £5.80 (BY)
Cabernet Sauvignon Savanha **1998** £5.99
(UN)
Chateau Libertas **1996** £5.69 (CAP)
Dry Red Stormy Cape Thelema **1999**
£5.75 (FLE)
Le Pavillon Red Boschendal **Non-vintage**
£5.50 (BALL)
Le Pavillon Red Boschendal **1999** £5.25
(STE) £5.39 (PLA)
Merlot Bellingham **1999** £5.99 (SAI)

Merlot De Leuwen Jagt **2000** £5.37 (WIW)
Pinotage Beyerskloof **2000** £5.30 (SOM)
£5.99 (OD) £5.99 (VIL)
Pinotage Clos Malverne **1999** £5.99 (SOM)
£6.95 (POR) £6.99 (WAI) £7.35 (GN)
Pinotage Fairview **1999** £5.99 (SAI)
Pinotage Klippenkop **1999** £5.45 (CON)
Pinotage KWV **1999** £5.49 (VIC) £5.49
(THR) £5.49 (BOT) £5.49 (WR)
Pinotage Robertson Winery **2000** £5.03
(BY)
Pinotage Zonnebloem **1997** £5.95 (BAC)
£6.95 (STE) £7.24 (PLAY) £7.52 (CAP)
Roodeberg KWV **1997** £5.19 (COC)
£5.85 (CAP) £5.99 (UN)
Shiraz KWV **1999** £5.26 (COC) £5.59 (CAP)

£6.00 → £6.99

Cabernet Sauvignon Backsberg **1994**
£6.80 (WHI)
Cabernet Sauvignon Fairview **1999** £6.99
(GW)
Cabernet Sauvignon Hoopenburg **1999**
£6.56 (BY)
Cabernet Sauvignon Nederburg **1997**
£6.21 (COC) £6.50 (CAP)
Cabernet Sauvignon Robertson Winery
Wide River Reserve **1998** £6.37 (BY)
Cabernet Sauvignon/Shiraz Clos Malverne
1997 £6.99 (UN)
Cabernet Sauvignon Villiera **1997** £6.39
(BOT)
Edelrood Nederburg **1997** £6.26 (CAP)
Merlot Fairview **1999** £6.99 (GW) £6.99
(MAJ)
Merlot Fort Simon **1998** £6.75 (STE)
Pinotage Beaumont **1998** £6.95 (BER)
£8.99 (POR)
Pinotage Beyerskloof **1999** £6.49 (UN)
£6.61 (NO)
Pinotage Clos Malverne **1998** £6.99 (UN)
Pinotage Clos Malverne Reserve **1998**
£6.95 (SOM)

RETAILERS SPECIALIZING IN SOUTH AFRICA
see Retailers Directory (page 40) for details

Averys of Bristol, Bibendum (BIB), D Byrne,
Cape Province Wines (CAP), Cockburns of
Leith (COC), Direct Wine Shipments (DI),
First Quench Group (BOT, THR, VIC, WR),

Lay & Wheeler (LAY), Oddbins (OD), Terry
Platt (PLA), Roberson, Sainsbury's (SAI),
Springbok Wines, Tanners (TAN),
Villeneuve Wines (VIL), Waitrose (WAI).

Pinotage Fairview **2000** £6.99 (GW)
Pinotage Fairview Bush Vine **1999** £6.95
(JU)
Pinotage Wildekrans **1998** £6.65 (SOM)
Shiraz Backsberg **1998** £6.57 (WHI)
Zinfandel/Cinsaut Fairview **2000** £6.99 (OD)

£7.00 ➻ £7.99

Auret Clos Malverne **1996** £7.75 (SOM)
£8.99 (GN)
Cabernet Sauvignon Backsberg **1995**
£7.97 (CAP)
Cabernet Sauvignon Groot Constantia
1995 £7.99 (CAP) £8.82 (BY) £8.99 (COC)
Cabernet Sauvignon L'Avenir **1998** £7.75
(SOM)
Cabernet Sauvignon Mooiplaas **1998**
£7.99 (WR)
Cabernet Sauvignon Springfield Estate
1998 £7.44 (BIB) £7.90 (BAC)
Cabernet Sauvignon Vriesenhof **1998**
£7.90 (TAN)
Cabernet Sauvignon Zonnebloem **1997**
£7.55 (CAP)
Cabernet Sauvignon/Merlot Jordan
Chameleon **1997** £7.85 (WRI) £8.95 (BALL)
Cabernet Sauvignon/Merlot Neil Ellis
Stellenbosch **1998** £7.99 (VIL)
Klein Babylonstoren Backsberg **1998**
£7.99 (MORR)
Merlot Cathedral Cellar **1996** £7.99 (MORR)
Pinotage Bellingham **1998** £7.95 (CAP)
Pinotage Neil Ellis Stellenbosch **1998**
£7.64 (PEN)
Pinotage Simonsig **1998** £7.50 (CAP)
Pinotage The Pinotage Co. Trafalgar Bush
Vine **1999** £7.39 (JON)
Pinotage Vriesenhof Paradyskloof **1998**
£7.80 (TAN)
Pinotage Zonnebloem **1998** £7.50 (STA)
Shiraz Graham Beck **1999** £7.01 (BIB)
Shiraz Fairview **1995** £7.45 (JU)
Shiraz Middelvlei **1998** £7.99 (VIL) £9.45
(FORT)
Shiraz Simonsig **1999** £7.95 (CAP)

£8.00 ➻ £8.99

Cabernet Sauvignon Klein Constantia
1996 £8.95 (TAN)
Cabernet Sauvignon Kumala Reserve
1998 £8.99 (TES)
Cabernet Sauvignon Laborie **1995** £8.99
(CAP)
Cabernet Sauvignon Lanzerac **1997** £8.87
(BY)

Cabernet Sauvignon Middelvlei **1996**
£8.99 (VIL)
Cabernet Sauvignon Overgaauw **1998**
£8.69 (GN)
Cabernet Sauvignon Zonnebloem **1998**
£8.46 (TW)
Cabernet Sauvignon/Merlot Jordan
Chameleon **1999** £8.20 (STA)
Kallista Vriesenhof **1998** £8.95 (TAN)
Laureat Zonnebloem **1995** £8.93 (CAP)
Merlot Boschendal **1996** £8.50 (CRO)
Merlot De Leuwen Jagt **1998** £8.29 (HIC)
Merlot Jordan **1999** £8.99 (CON) £9.22
(BY) £9.30 (STA) £10.45 (JER)
Merlot Kaapzicht **1998** £8.99 (JON)
Merlot Lanzerac **1998** £8.87 (BY)
Merlot Villiera **1998** £8.99 (WAI)
Merlot Yonder Hill **1998** £8.99 (OD)
Pinotage Cathedral Cellar **1998** £8.99 (SAF)
Pinotage Clos Malverne Reserve **1997**
£8.75 (CON)
Pinotage Lanzerac **1998** £8.87 (BY)
Pinotage Wildekrans **1999** £8.91 (SAV)
Red Claridge Wellington **1996** £8.90 (BAC)
Shiraz Boschendal **1997** £8.64 (FLE)
Shiraz Groot Constantia **1999** £8.99 (COC)
Shiraz Kaapzicht **1998** £8.99 (JON)
Tinta Barocca Allesverloren **1997** £8.95
(WRI)

£9.00 ➻ £9.99

Cabernet Sauvignon Altydgedacht **1995**
£9.00 (BAC)
Cabernet Sauvignon Bellingham **1996**
£9.45 (CAP)
Cabernet Sauvignon De Trafford **1998**
£9.72 (BIB)
Cabernet Sauvignon Jordan **1998** £9.75
(CON) £9.95 (STA)
Cabernet Sauvignon Steenberg **1997**
£9.58 (ARM)
Cabernet Sauvignon Stellenzicht **1994**
£9.20 (COC)
Cabernet Sauvignon Webersburg **1996**
£9.50 (WS)
Faithful Hound Mulderbosch **1997** £9.99
(VIL) £10.00 (ARM) £10.40 (SOM) £10.95
(BU)
Marlbrook Klein Constantia **1996** £9.45
(WRI)
Merlot Boschendal **1998** £9.95 (GN)
£10.60 (HAH)
Merlot De Trafford **1998** £9.85 (BIB)
Merlot Spice Route Flagship **1999** £9.99
(SOM)

Merlot Steenberg **1999** £9.99 (WAI)
£10.00 (ARM)
Merlot Warwick **1997** £9.50 (WS) £9.50
(BAC) £9.60 (SAV)
Merlot Yonder Hill **1997** £9.99 (VIL)
Pinot Noir Muratie Estate **1999** £9.95 (STA)
Pinot Noir Paul Clüver **1999** £9.95 (LLO)
Pinotage Graham Beck The Old Road
1999 £9.99 (BIB)
Pinotage Kanonkop **1998** £9.40 (SOM)
£10.99 (VIL) £12.68 (NO)
Pinotage L'Avenir **1997** £9.85 (SOM)
Pinotage Longridge **1998** £9.95 (WS)
Pinotage Middelvlei **1997** £9.25 (FORT)
Pinotage Middelvlei **1995** £9.95 (CAP)
Pinotage Spice Route Flagship **1999** £9.99
(SOM)
Pinotage Uiterwyk **1997** £9.95 (LAY)
Pinotage Warwick Old Bush Vine **1998**
£9.50 (BAC)
Shiraz Allesverloren **1998** £9.40 (STA)
Shiraz Allesverloren **1994** £9.35 (CAP)
Shiraz Graham Beck The Ridge **1999**
£9.99 (BIB)
Shiraz Neil Ellis Stellenbosch **1999** £9.99
(VIL)
Shiraz Rust-en-Vrede **1996** £9.80 (RIC)
Syrah Spice Route Flagship **1999** £9.95
(SOM)
Tinta Barocca Allesverloren **1994** £9.00
(CAP)
Trilogy Warwick **1997** £9.95 (RAE)
Trilogy Warwick **1996** £9.80 (BAC)

£10.00 → £12.99

Cabernet Franc Warwick **1997** £10.50
(RAE) £10.95 (STA)
Cabernet Sauvignon Beyerskloof **1996**
£11.99 (OD) £11.99 (VIL) £12.71 (NO)
Cabernet Sauvignon Kanonkop **1996**
£11.99 (VIL)
Cabernet Sauvignon Klein Constantia
1993 £10.42 (CAP)
Cabernet Sauvignon Le Bonheur **1997**
£10.99 (YOU) £11.99 (COC)
Cabernet Sauvignon Plaisir de Merle
1998 £10.99 (SAF)
Cabernet Sauvignon Rust-en-Vrede **1997**
£12.20 (LAY)
Cabernet Sauvignon Stellenryck
Collection **1997** £10.90 (CAP)
Cabernet Sauvignon Stellenryck
Collection **1994** £10.95 (WRI)
Cabernet Sauvignon Vergelegen **1998**
£12.99 (OD)

Catharina Steenberg **1997** £12.50 (ARM)
Dry Red Rustenberg **1996** £11.94 (BY)
Gouverneurs Reserve Groot Constantia
1999 £10.49 (COC)
Grand Classique Glen Carlou **1994**
£10.87 (BY)
Klein Babylonstoren Backsberg **1996**
£10.95 (BALL)
Merlot De Trafford **1999** £10.77 (BIB)
Merlot Môreson Soleil du Matin **1995**
£12.30 (RIC)
Merlot Morgenhof **1998** £10.00 (WRI)
Merlot Veenwouden **1997** £10.90 (SOM)
Merlot Verdun **1997** £10.49 (CON)
£10.52 (DOM)
Pinot Noir Meerlust **1997** £12.50 (FRI)
£15.75 (WRI)
Pinotage Graham Beck The Old Road
1998 £10.22 (NO) £10.99 (YOU)
Pinotage Grangehurst **1997** £12.49 (YOU)
Pinotage Kanonkop **1999** £12.95 (JU)
Pinotage Lanzerac **1999** £10.50 (CRO)
Pinotage L'Avenir **1998** £11.99 (YOU)
Pinotage Môreson Soleil du Matin **1998**
£10.95 (BALL)
Pinotage Saxenburg Private Collection
1998 £10.99 (OD)

Pinotage Spice Route Flagship **1998**
£11.35 (NO) £11.49 (YOU)
Shiraz Graham Beck The Ridge **1998**
£10.99 (YOU)
Shiraz Rust-en-Vrede **1997** £10.95 (LAY)
Shiraz Zandvliet **1993** £11.34 (CAP)
Syrah Boekenhoutskloof **1997** £12.71 (NO)
Syrah Spice Route Flagship **1998** £11.50
(WS)
Tiara Simonsig **1997** £12.95 (CAP) £12.95
(WRI)
Vivat Bacchus Veenwouden **1998** £10.99
(YOU) £11.95 (SAV)

£13.00 → £13.99

Cabernet Sauvignon Neil Ellis **1998**
£13.99 (VIL)
Cabernet Sauvignon Thelema **1997**
£13.99 (FLE) £14.99 (YOU) £15.99 (VIL)
£16.50 (FORT) £16.58 (CAP)
Merlot Meerlust **1997** £13.99 (POR)
Paul Sauer Kanonkop **1996** £13.99 (VIL)
Pinot Noir Hamilton Russell **1997** £13.50
(FLE) £17.10 (PLAY)
Pinot Noir Whalehaven **1997** £13.50
(WRI) £13.95 (LEA)
Pinotage Kanonkop **1997** £13.75 (FORT)
£13.95 (BER)
Pinotage Meerendal **1996** £13.75 (JER)

£14.00 → £15.99

Classic Veenwouden **1998** £14.95 (HED)
£14.99 (YOU)
Estate Wine Rust-en-Vrede **1995** £14.30
(RIC)
Merlot Meerlust **1996** £14.65 (TAN)
£15.47 (CAP) £15.50 (FORT) £15.95 (BALL)
Merlot Thelema **1996** £15.95 (NI)
Merlot Veenwouden **1998** £14.95 (HED)
£14.99 (YOU)
Pinot Noir Bouchard Finlayson Galpin
Peak **1999** £14.55 (BIB)
Pinot Noir Hamilton Russell **1998** £15.25
(GN) £15.99 (POR) £17.99 (VIL) £18.75
(FORT) £18.99 (COC)
Pinot Noir Meerlust **1995** £14.55 (CAP)
Rubicon Meerlust **1996** £15.75 (WRI)
£15.75 (BEN) £15.95 (FRI) £16.30 (HAH)
£20.60 (JER)

---

*Stars (★) indicate wines selected by
Oz Clarke in the Best Buys section which
begins on page 8.*

£16.00 → £19.99

Cabernet Sauvignon Boekenhoutskloof
1998 £17.99 (OD)
Cabernet Sauvignon Thelema **1998**
£16.99 (WR)
Estate Wine Rust-en-Vrede **1997** £16.30
(LAY)
Pinot Noir Meerlust **1996** £17.45 (JER)
Pinotage Kanonkop **1995** £19.00 (CRO)

Over £20.00

Cabernet Sauvignon Warwick **1992**
£20.00 (CRO)
Syrah Stellenzicht **1998** £25.99 (YOU)
Classic Veenwouden **1993** £20.36 (NO)

WHITE

Under £4.00

Blanc de Noir Red Muscadel Van Loveren
2000 £3.99 (VIL)
Chardonnay Van Loveren Spes Bona
2000 £3.99 (SOM) £4.99 (VIL)
Chardonnay/Semillon Robert's Rock
2000 £3.99 (CO)
Chenin Blanc/Chardonnay Kumala **2000**
£3.99 (BUD)
Chenin Blanc KWV **2000** £3.99 (COC)
£4.47 (CAP) £4.49 (VIC) £4.49 (THR)
£4.49 (BOT) £4.49 (WR)
Chenin Blanc Namaqua **2000** £3.99 (VIL)
Chenin Blanc Swartland Reserve **2000**
£3.99 (SAF)
Colombard Namaqua **2000** £3.25 (SOM)
£3.99 (VIL)
Colombard Swartland **2000** £3.49 (MORR)
Pinot Gris Van Loveren **2000** £3.99 (SOM)
Pinot Gris Van Loveren **1999** £3.99 (MORR)
Semillon/Chardonnay Kumala **2000** £3.99
(TES)
Steen Swartland **1999** £3.99 (VIL)

£4.00 → £5.99

Buiten Blanc Buitenverwachting **2000**
£5.99 (NEZ)
Chardonnay Apostles Falls **1999** £5.99 (TES)
Chardonnay Avontuur **1999** £5.95 (WS)
Chardonnay Graham Beck **2000** £5.97 (BIB)
Chardonnay Cape Bay **1999** £4.58 (PEN)
Chardonnay De Leuwen Jagt **2000** £4.98
(WIW)
Chardonnay De Wetshof Lesca **2000**
£5.50 (SOM) £5.99 (MAJ) £6.99 (VIL)

Chardonnay Drostdy-Hof **2001** £5.73 (LLO)
Chardonnay Fairview **1999** £5.99 (UN)
Chardonnay Nederburg **1998** £5.95 (CAP)
Chardonnay Riebeek **2000** £4.99 (MORR)
Chardonnay Sonop Winds of Change
 1999 £4.99 (BO)
Chenin Blanc Cape Bay **1999** £4.11 (PEN)
Chenin Blanc Drostdy-Hof **2000** £4.95 (FRI)
Chenin Blanc Ken Forrester **1999** £5.69
 (OD)
Chenin Blanc Hazendal **1999** £5.80 (RIC)
 £6.50 (WRI)
Chenin Blanc Klippenkop **2000** £4.49
 (CON) £5.95 (JER)
Chenin Blanc KWV **1999** £4.49 (UN)
Chenin Blanc Paarl Heights **1999** £4.15
 (CON)
Chenin Blanc Seidelberg **2000** £5.75 (POR)
Chenin Blanc Thelema Stormy Cape
 2000 £4.50 (WS) £5.35 (FLE) £5.75 (NI)
Chenin Blanc Van Zylshof **1999** £5.25
 (FORT)
Chenin Blanc Villiera **1997** £5.49 (BOT)
Chenin Blanc Wildekrans **1997** £4.75 (SOM)
Chenin Blanc/Chardonnay Arniston Bay
 2000 £4.49 (SO) £4.49 (TES) £4.49 (THR)
 £4.49 (WR) £4.49 (SAF) £4.49 (MORR)
Colombard/Chardonnay Springfield Estate
 2001 £5.09 (BIB)
Colombard/Chardonnay Van Loveren
 2000 £4.99 (VIL)
Gewürztraminer Neethlingshof **2000**
 £5.99 (OD)
Gewürztraminer Special Late-Harvest
 Van Loveren **1999** £4.99 (VIL)
Le Pavillon White Boschendal **1998** £5.25
 (STE)
Roodeberg Blanc KWV **1993** £5.18 (BY)
Sauvignon Blanc De Wetshof **2000** £5.99
 (VIL)
Sauvignon Blanc Douglas Green **2000**
 £4.49 (SAF)
Sauvignon Blanc Kanu **2000** £5.99 (NEZ)
Sauvignon Blanc KWV **2000** £4.71 (COC)
 £4.79 (VIC) £4.79 (THR) £4.79 (BOT)
Sauvignon Blanc Nederburg **1999** £5.95
 (CAP)
Sauvignon Blanc Neil Ellis Elgin **2000** £5.99
 (SOM)
Sauvignon Blanc Spier **2000** £4.49 (ASD)
Sauvignon Blanc Swartland **2000** £4.99 (VIL)
Sauvignon Blanc Wildekrans **2000** £4.95
 (SOM) £6.60 (SAV)
Sauvignon Blanc Zonnebloem **1998** £5.75
 (STE) £7.65 (TW)

Sauvignon Blanc/Chardonnay Fort Simon
 1999 £5.45 (STE)
Sauvignon Blanc/Chenin Blanc Kopland
 1997 £4.95 (JU)
Semillon Fairview **2000** £5.99 (SAF)
Steen Drostdy-Hof **2001** £4.72 (LLO)

£6.00 → £7.99

Chardonnay Agusta Unwooded **1998**
 £7.99 (VA)
Chardonnay Backsberg **1999** £6.87 (WHI)
 £7.39 (JON) £7.89 (CAP)
Chardonnay Boschendal **1999** £6.78
 (CAP) £6.99 (VIL)
Chardonnay Cathedral Cellar **1998** £7.99
 (UN) £8.67 (BY)
Chardonnay De Wetshof **1999** £7.50 (BALL)
Chardonnay De Wetshof Call of the
 African Eagle **2000** £6.99 (SAI)
Chardonnay Delaire **1998** £7.65 (SOM)
 £9.99 (BOT) £9.99 (WR)
Chardonnay Delheim **2000** £7.49 (BOT)
 £7.49 (WR)
Chardonnay Fairview **2000** £6.99 (GW)
Chardonnay Fort Simon **1999** £6.95 (STE)
Chardonnay Groot Constantia **1999**
 £7.33 (CAP)

Chardonnay Laborie **1997** £6.56 (CAP)
Chardonnay Lanzerac **1999** £7.18 (BY)
Chardonnay L'Avenir **1999** £7.95 (WS)
Chardonnay Neil Ellis **1998** £7.99 (GN)
Chardonnay Springfield Estate Wild Yeast **1999** £6.66 (BIB)
Chardonnay Van Loveren **1998** £6.99 (VIL)
Chardonnay Vergelegen **1998** £6.99 (UN)
Chardonnay Vriesenhof **1999** £7.50 (TAN)
Chardonnay Warwick **1999** £6.99 (WAI) £8.50 (STA)
Chardonnay Wildekrans **1999** £6.30 (SOM) £8.62 (SAV)
Chardonnay Zonnebloem **1998** £6.50 (BALL) £7.94 (PLAY) £8.25 (CAP)
Chardonnay/Sauvignon Blanc Jordan Chameleon **2000** £6.75 (CON) £6.95 (STA)
Chenin Blanc Blue White **1997** £6.49 (NO)
Chenin Blanc De Trafford **2000** £7.57 (BIB)
Chenin Blanc L'Avenir **1999** £6.99 (UN)
Chenin Blanc Mulderbosch **1999** £7.67 (ARM) £7.99 (VIL)
Chenin Blanc Verdun **1999** £6.95 (CON)
Gewürztraminer Weltevrede **2000** £6.49 (COC)
Riesling De Wetshof Rhine **2000** £7.99 (VIL)
Sauvignon Blanc Altydgedacht **2000** £7.39 (JON)
Sauvignon Blanc Boschendal **1999** £6.99 (TES) £6.99 (VIL) £7.50 (BALL)
Sauvignon Blanc Buitenverwachting **2000** £7.49 (NEZ) £7.99 (OD)
Sauvignon Blanc Groot Constantia **2000** £7.29 (COC)
Sauvignon Blanc Hazendal **1999** £7.25 (BALL)
Sauvignon Blanc Jordan **2000** £7.30 (FLE)
Sauvignon Blanc Klein Constantia **1999** £7.99 (BO) £8.50 (WRI)
Sauvignon Blanc Neethlingshof **1995** £7.63 (BY)
Sauvignon Blanc Simonsig **2000** £6.35 (DOM)
Sauvignon Blanc Springfield Estate Life from Stone **2000** £6.66 (BIB) £6.90 (BAC) £6.99 (BO) £6.99 (MAR)
Sauvignon Blanc Steenberg **2000** £7.75 (WS) £7.99 (WAI) £8.00 (ARM)
Sauvignon Blanc Uiterwyk **2000** £6.95 (LAY)
Sauvignon Blanc Uitkyk **2000** £6.56 (COC)

£8.00 → £9.99

Chardonnay Bouchard Finlayson Kaaimansgat **1999** £9.08 (BIB)
Chardonnay Bouchard Finlayson Oak Valley **1998** £9.15 (BIB)
Chardonnay Brampton **1997** £8.50 (BEN)

Chardonnay De Wetshof d'Honneur **1999** £8.99 (VIL)
Chardonnay Hamilton Russell **1999** £8.79 (BY) £11.95 (BALL) £11.99 (YOU) £12.90 (CRO) £12.99 (VIL) £13.11 (PLAY) £13.69 (COC)
Chardonnay Jordan **1999** £8.59 (UN) £8.75 (WRI) £8.75 (CON) £8.95 (STA) £8.95 (BY)
Chardonnay Klein Constantia **1997** £9.50 (FORT)
Chardonnay L'Ormarins **1999** £8.49 (COC)
Chardonnay Linton Park **1998** £9.95 (FORT)
Chardonnay Longridge **1999** £8.95 (WS)
Chardonnay Plaisir de Merle **1999** £9.43 (CAP)
Chardonnay Simonsig **1998** £8.17 (DOM)
Chardonnay Stellenryk **1998** £8.30 (CAP)
Chardonnay Verdun **1997** £8.00 (BAC) £8.50 (CON)
Chardonnay Vergelegen Reserve **1998** £9.99 (SAI) £9.99 (OD)
Chardonnay Whalehaven **1998** £8.95 (LEA)
Chenin Blanc De Trafford **1998** £8.90 (BAC)
Sauvignon Blanc Groote Post **1999** £8.56 (HIC)
Sauvignon Blanc Klein Constantia **1998** £8.40 (TAN) £8.75 (FORT) £9.41 (PLAY)
Sauvignon Blanc KWV **1993** £8.79 (BY)
Sauvignon Blanc L'Ormarins **1998** £8.95 (JER)
Sauvignon Blanc Mulderbosch **2000** £9.83 (ARM) £9.99 (VIL) £11.38 (NO)
Sauvignon Blanc Mulderbosch Barrel-Fermented **1997** £9.99 (VIL)
Sauvignon Blanc Plaisir de Merle **1999** £8.96 (CAP)
Sauvignon Blanc Steenberg **1999** £8.00 (ARM)
Sauvignon Blanc Thelema **2000** £9.10 (SOM) £10.79 (YOU) £11.95 (LEA) £11.95 (FORT) £11.99 (VIL)
Semillon Boekenhoutskloof **1998** £9.99 (OD)
Semillon Steenberg Unwooded **1998** £8.63 (NO)

£10.00 → £11.99

Chardonnay Bouchard Finlayson Missionvale **1999** £10.65 (BIB)
Chardonnay Bouchard Finlayson Missionvale **1998** £11.75 (FORT)
Chardonnay De Wetshof Bateleur **2000** £11.99 (VIL)

Chardonnay Glen Carlou **1998** £11.68 (BY)
Chardonnay Glen Carlou Reserve **1999**
£10.99 (OD)
Chardonnay Hamilton Russell **1998**
£11.99 (POR) £11.99 (RAE) £12.99 (VIL)
£12.99 (DI)
Chardonnay Mulderbosch **1997** £10.42
(ARM) £10.95 (BU) £11.25 (FORT) £12.00
(WS)
Chardonnay Thelema **1999** £10.88 (FLE)
£11.99 (YOU) £12.95 (FORT) £12.99 (VIL)
Sauvignon Blanc Klein Constantia **1997**
£11.00 (JER)
Sauvignon Blanc Mulderbosch Barrel-
Fermented **1999** £11.25 (ARM)
Sauvignon Blanc Thelema **1999** £10.05
(NO) £10.50 (FLE)
Semillon Stellenzicht Reserve **1999**
£11.99 (YOU)

£12.00 → £15.99

Chardonnay Agusta Count **1998** £12.25
(FRI)
Chardonnay Hamilton Russell **1997**
£12.85 (WRI)
Chardonnay Neil Ellis **2000** £12.99 (VIL)
Chardonnay Springfield Estate Methode
Ancienne **1999** £12.54 (BIB)
Chardonnay Springfield Estate Wild Yeast
1998 £13.34 (NO)
Chardonnay Thelema **2000** £12.99 (WR)
£13.10 (CAP)
Sauvignon Blanc Thelema **1995** £15.65 (GN)

Over £16.00

Chardonnay Meerlust **1998** £18.99 (POR)
£20.00 (FORT)
Vin de Constance Klein Constancia ½ litre
Non-vintage £26.00 (CRO)

SPARKLING

Under £7.00

Graham Beck Brut **Non-vintage** £6.99
(SAF) £7.98 (BIB) £7.99 (UN) £9.95 (FORT)
KWV Mousseux Blanc Cuvée Brut **Non-
vintage** £6.35 (CAP)
Papillon Van Loveren **Non-vintage** £5.99
(VIL)

£7.00 → £8.49

Laborie Blanc de Noir **1997** £7.96 (CAP)
Nederburg Premiere Cuvée Brut **Non-
vintage** £7.26 (CAP)

Over £8.50

Boschendal Brut Vintage **1993** £11.30 (CAP)
Boschendal Le Grand Pavillon Blanc de
Blancs **Non-vintage** £8.75 (RIC) £9.00
(CRO)
Boschendal Le Grand Pavillon Brut **Non-
vintage** £8.99 (VIL) £9.50 (WRI)
Graham Beck Blanc de Blancs **1996** £9.01
(BIB)
Pongrácz Cap Classique **Non-vintage**
£10.19 (CAP)
Simonsig Kaapse Vonkel **1995** £10.89 (CAP)

FORTIFIED

Under £5.00

Cavendish Cape Extra Dry **Non-vintage**
£4.77 (COC)
Cavendish Cape Medium Dry **Non-
vintage** £4.77 (COC) £5.13 (CAP)

Over £5.00

Cavendish Fine Old Ruby **Non-vintage**
£5.17 (COC)
Cavendish Vintage **1979** £9.62 (CAP)

SPAIN

Good winemaking is now producing new and exciting flavours from a host of recently rediscovered regions all over Spain, which should keep the likes of Rioja on its toes – and that can't be a bad thing

There's such a lot of hype about Spanish wines that sometimes it's difficult to know just what to believe. And sometimes I get a horrible sneaking feeling that the hype has been going on for so long that it has long outpaced the wines themselves. When did you last read anything critical of Spanish wines? And yet do you think everything you've tasted from Spain lately has been fantastic? Quite so.

The truth, it seems to me, is that a great deal of what Spain is making is terrific – but not everything. At the everyday level we're at last seeing imaginative winemaking in the lost hinterlands of places like Calatayud, Jumilla and La Mancha. It's not a country of

great white grapes: Albariño, Godello and Verdejo are really the only ones of interest.

What is genuinely exciting are the new wines coming out of Priorat, Ribera del Duero and, believe it or not, Rioja. The new-style Riojas – many of which ignore classifications like Reserva, and are bottled mercifully young – may be aged in French rather than American oak, and are full of rich, concentrated complexity.

But they're expensive. There's no shortage of cash in Spain. Only the hype comes free. And in all these areas, particularly Rioja, there are producers whose hot-air production outweighs the quality of their wines.

GRAPE VARIETIES

AIRÉN (white) These days Airén is the mainstay of the cheap, fresh whites of La Mancha – even though the reds seem to have taken a bigger hold of the British imagination. Never mind. It's a perfect example of how modern winemaking can turn what was one of the world's dullest grapes into something perfectly drinkable.

ALBARIÑO (white) Lovely, peachy, fresh wines with elegant acid balance from Rías Baixas. From being a rarity it's suddenly everywhere. Why? The growers have realized they can get good money for it – and so they've 'discovered' they have a lot more of it than they thought they had. It's also grown over the border in Portugal for Vinho Verde, but it's called Alvarinho there.

BOBAL (red) Quite good deep-coloured, fruity reds and rosados in Utiel-Requena and Valencia. It has reasonable acidity and relatively low alcohol, which keep the wines comparatively fresh and appetizing.

CABERNET SAUVIGNON (red) Not a native Spanish variety, but making inroads in Penedès and Navarra, where it is generally rich and heavy with oak. Still officially experimental in Rioja, but probably not forever.

CARIÑENA (red) A source of dark and prodigiously tannic wine. It plays only a small part in the DO wine which carries its name, and most Cariñena (it's the same as the Carignan of southern France) is grown in Cataluña, usually as a beefy blender. It is also a minority grape in Rioja under the name Mazuelo. With its high tannin and acidity, and its aroma of ripe plums and cherries, it complements Tempranillo and adds to its aging potential.

CHARDONNAY (white) Usually made in a rich, oaky style, but often blended as well. Found a lot in Navarra and Penedès.

GARNACHA (red) This, known as Grenache in France, grows everywhere in Spain except Andalucia, and makes big, broad, alcoholic, sometimes peppery or spicy wines. The wines are dark, and don't necessarily last well, but they can be delicious young. The greatest examples are to be found in Priorat.

GARNACHA BLANCA (white) This makes wines that are high in alcohol, low in acidity and with a tendency to oxidize, so they are usually blended in with wines of higher acidity, like Viura.

GODELLO (white) Saved from extinction in the 1970s, this interesting and aromatic grape appears in the north-western DOCs of Valdeorras, Ribeiro and Bierzo.

GRACIANO (red) On the verge of extinction, the excellent Graciano grape has been rescued by the DOC upgrade in Rioja, where conscientious winemakers are seeking it out once again for the extra quality it gives to the wine.

MALVASÍA (white) This aromatic, flavourful grape tends, in Spain, to produce wines of low acidity that turn yellow and oxidize rapidly. When well made, it's full-bodied, fairly strongly scented, spicy or musky, often with a hint of apricots, and sometimes slightly nutty as well. Malvasía helps *Marqués de Murrieta* and *CVNE* white Riojas taste the way all white Rioja used to. Malvasía is also widely grown in the Canary Islands, where it makes light, fresh whites, sometimes mixed with Viura/Macabeo.

MENCÍA (red) Mainly used in light, fruity young wines in Ribeiro and Bierzo.

MERSEGUERA (white) Valencia's mainstay white grape, also grown in Alicante and Tarragona, produces light, delicately aromatic and characterful wines.

ON THE CASE
Look for the word 'Joven' on the label if you want something ultra-young and fresh

MONASTRELL (red) Used to add body and guts to many Cataluñan Tempranillo blends. Further south, modern winemaking is paying dividends in Alicante, Almansa, Jumilla, Valencia and Yecla; good wines include *Agapito Rico*'s *Carchelo*, *Castaño*'s *Pozuelo* and *Casa Castillo Pie Franco*.

MOSCATEL (white) Almost all Spanish Moscatel is the second-line Muscat of Alexandria rather than the top-quality Muscat à Petits Grains. But it makes a lot of good wine – rich and brown in Málaga, or fresh and grapy in Valencia. *Torres* makes a good, off-dry, aromatic version mixed with Gewürztraminer in Penedès, as does *de Muller* in Tarragona. Muscat de Chipiona from *Burdon* is rich and peachy. Also used to sweeten cream sherries.

PALOMINO (white) This is the dominant grape of the sherry region, making up all of the dry sherries, and an increasing proportion of the others. Although it produces great fortified wine it is not in itself a great grape. It plays a minor role in Montilla-Moriles. As a table wine grape, it produces dull, fat stuff, even with modern winemaking techniques, but in the sherry bodegas it reacts brilliantly to the *flor* yeast which imparts to *fino* that characteristic bone-dry, stark-sour nose.

PARELLADA (white) Touted as the provider of all the perfume and finesse in Cataluña's whites and in Cava fizz, but Parellada doesn't honestly have much to say for itself, except from the best producers. Blended with Chardonnay, *Torres Gran Viña Sol* is refreshing and lemony.

PEDRO XIMÉNEZ (white) This used to be the chief component of sweet sherries,

and is sometimes made into dessert wine, deeply coloured and thick. It covers most of the nearby Montilla-Moriles vineyards, as well as providing richness in Málaga; otherwise used for rather dull dry whites.

TEMPRANILLO (red) The fine red grape of Rioja and Navarra crops up all over Spain as far south as the province of Cádiz, but with a different name in almost every region. It's known as Cencibel on the plains of La Mancha and Valdepeñas, and as Tinto Fino in Ribera del Duero; elsewhere it may be Tinto de Madrid, Tinto de Toro, Tinto del País, and so on.

The wines have a spicy, herby, tobacco-like character, with plenty of sweet strawberry or black cherry fruit, firm acidity and some tannin. Tempranillo makes vibrantly fruity wines ideal for gulping down young, as well as more robust wines suitable for aging – and it mixes brilliantly with oak. It's often blended, especially with Garnacha.

VERDEJO (white) One of Spain's more interesting white grapes. In Rueda it makes soft, creamy and slightly nutty white, sometimes a touch honeyed, sometimes herby, with good, green acidity.

VIURA (white) The main white grape of Rioja, made nowadays apple-fresh and clean and, at best, rather neutral; at worst it is sharp and grapefruity. It achieves similarly mixed results, under the name Macabeo, in Cataluña. Made in this light, modern style, it's a wine for gulping down young, in its first year. But if you take the trouble to blend it with Malvasía, top it up with a slug of acidity and leave it to age for a while in oak barrels, Viura can make wonderful, rich, almost Burgundy-like white Rioja.

XAREL-LO (white) One of the three main white grapes of Cataluña, this is heavier, more alcoholic and even less aromatic than the barely aromatic Parellada and Macabeo, with which it is blended.

WINE REGIONS

ALELLA, DO (white) Catalan region whose best-known wine is the off-dry, very fruity *Marqués de Alella*. Also look for the light, pineapple-fresh Chardonnay and appley *Marqués de Alella Seco*, as well as the sparkling, greengagy *Parxet*, which beats most famous Cavas hands down.

ALICANTE, DO (red) Heavy, earthy reds made in south-east Spain from Monastrell and mostly useful for blending.

ALMANSA, DO (red) Strong spicy reds from Monastrell and Garnacha, and even better reds from Tempranillo. *Bodegas Piqueras* makes very good wines under the *Castillo de Almansa* and *Marius* labels.

AMPURDÁN-COSTA BRAVA, DO (red, white, rosado) Suddenly there are some good juicy reds being exported from here. The best are very good indeed. Start by looking for *Cellars Santamaría*.

BIERZO, DO (red) Emergent zone for the promising Mencía grape. Older wines are blends from before it became a DO. The *Vinos del Bierzo co-op* is good.

BINISSALEM, DO (red, white, rosado) Young and *crianza* reds and light young whites and rosados from Mallorca. The main producer is *Bodegas Franja Roja*.

BULLAS, DO (red) In the province of Murcia, making great big heady Monastrell reds, mostly from co-operatives.

CALATAYUD, DO (red) Hot, dry area adjoining Cariñena, making mainly Garnacha reds, plus some Tempranillo, usually for drinking young.

CAMPO DE BORJA, DO (red) Hefty alcoholic reds made from Cariñena and Garnacha, now making way for lighter reds and good rosados. *Bodegas Bordejé* and the *Borja* and *Santo Cristo* co-ops look promising.

CANARY ISLANDS There are eight DOs in the islands: Abona, El Hierro, Lanzarote, La Palma, Tacoronte-Acentejo, Valle de Güímar, Valle de la Orotava and Ycoden-Daute-Isora. Most of the wines are white (Tacoronte-Acentejo is the only serious producer of red) and mainly

SPANISH CLASSIFICATIONS

Denominación de Origen Calificada (DOC) is a new super-category (equivalent to the Italian DOCG) for wines which have a long tradition of high quality and are prepared to submit themselves to more rigorous quality scrutiny. So far there's only one DOC, and that's Rioja.

Denominación de Origen (DO) is roughly equivalent to the French AC: the basic quality wine designation. There are 51 of them.

Country wines fall into two groups: there are **Vinos Comarcales**: perhaps 'county wines' is the nearest translation into English. These have some local significance but few pretensions to promotion. The second and more important group comprises 22 **Vinos de la Tierra**, which translates as 'country wines', like French vins de pays. These are smaller areas, more tightly controlled and, in many cases, with ambitions to apply for DO status at some time in the future.

Vino de Mesa, basic table wine, doesn't usually carry any kind of regional name, nor a vintage date. A few maverick winemakers such as the Marqués de Griñón in Toledo and the Yllera family in Rueda use a legal nicety to put a general regional name on the label.

pleasant enough for the beach. There is still some sweet, fortified Malvasía, but it's not seen outside the islands.

CARIÑENA, DO (red, rosado, white) The best here are the pleasant, full, soft reds, mostly made from the fat, jammy Garnacha. The reds of the Bodegas San Valero co-op are sold here as *Don Mendo* and *Monte Ducay*.

CAVA, DO (white, rosado) The Spanish name for Champagne-method fizz, nearly all of which is from Cataluña. When Cava was promoted to DO status, several regions lost the right to use the name, and their wines (some, admittedly excellent) must now be called *Método Tradicional*. However, the two biggest outsiders, *Bodegas Inviosa* in Extremadura and *Torre Oria* in Valencia, have permission to continue using the name.

Most Cava is fresh and clean, and though it doesn't improve with bottle age, it is almost always a decent, good-humoured mouthful of fizz at a fair price. Most appetizing are *Albet i Noya, Cavas Hill, Codorníu, Jané Ventura, Juvé y Camps, Marqués de Monistrol, Mont Marçal Cava Nature* (and *Chardonnay*), *Parxet, Raïmat, Raventos i Blanc, Rovellats* and *Segura Viudas*.

CHACOLÍ, DO (red, white) There are two of these, in neighbouring Basque provinces: Chacolí de Getaria (the local spelling is Getariako Txakolina) and Chacolí

de Bizcaia/Vizcaya (Bizkaiko Txakolina). The wines are sharp, fresh and uncomplicated, suited to the local seafood.

CIGALES, DO (red, rosado) Near Ribera del Duero, famed for rosados but with some serious reds as well, made from Tempranillo/Garnacha mixes.

CONCA DE BARBERÁ, DO (red, white) Useful source of grapes just inland from Tarragona. Good reds and whites, including international varieties like Merlot. *Torres Grans Muralles* is an elegant red blend of Spanish grapes.

CONDADO DE HUELVA, DO (white, fortified) Wines not unlike Montilla are made and mostly drunk locally.

COSTERS DEL SEGRE, DO (red, white) Formerly a virtual one-producer DO, in the form of *Raïmat*, whose initial 'New World' approach made the wines a hit here. Reds and whites are now far leaner, and consequently we drink less of them. *Castell del Remei*, producing Cabernet, Merlot, Chardonnay, Macabeo and Tempranillo, is now also in Britain.

JUMILLA, DO (red) Much fruitier wines than of yore. This is one of Spain's most promising new regions. Look for the *Condestable* brands, *Casa Castillo, Casa de la Ermita* and the *San Isidro co-op*.

MATURITY CHART
1998 Ribera del Duero Crianza
The best growers have produced wines of good concentration

Bottled		Ready		Best				Fading			Tired		
0	1	2	3	4	5	6	7	8	9	10	11	12	13	14 years

MÁLAGA, DO (fortified) Rarer than ever, now that *Scholtz Hermanos* has closed, leaving only one producer, *Bodega López Hermanos*, of any size. Málaga is (was?) usually full, brown and sweet in a raisiny, but not a gooey way, and is slightly smoky too. Star roving winemaker *Telmo Rodriguez* looks set to raise the stakes with his new *Molino Real Mountain Wine* – but it fails to meet one of the DO requirements, so is currently Vino de Mesa.

LA MANCHA, DO (red, white) Spain's enormous central plateau has learnt how to make good fresh flavours in spite of searing summer heat. Irrigation is now permitted, and vineyards are being planted with Cencibel (Tempranillo), Cabernet, Syrah and Merlot; whites are mostly Airén, with some Viura and Chardonnay. Reds have soft tannins and whites are fresh, but need drinking young. *Arboles de Castillejo* from *Bodegas Torres Filoso, Rodríguez y Berger, Casa Gualda, Casa la Teja, Castillo de Alhambra, Castillo de Manzanares, Lazarillo, Señorío de Guadianeja, Tierra Seca, Viña Santa Elena, Vinicola de Castilla, Yuntero* and *Zagarrón* are all producing the goods.

MANCHUELA, DO (red, white) New DO on the western edge of Utiel-Requena. Some high-altitude vineyards are potentially exciting.

MÉNTRIDA, DO (red) Strong, sturdy reds produced bang in the middle of Spain and seldom travelling much further.

MONTERREI, DO (white) Another of Galicia's new 'superwhite' DOs. Good value whites from Godello, Doña Blanca and even Palomino.

MONTILLA-MORILES, DO (fortified) Montilla wines are usually thought of as lower-priced – and lower-strength – sherry lookalikes but there is a great deal of reasonably good wine here, even if it lacks the bite of really good sherry.

NAVARRA, DO (red, white, rosado) Suffering from lack of direction: should it be making top-class wines, or everyday cheapies? There's a huge gap between the top producers and the rest. The best are *Chivite, Guelbenzu, Monjardin, Monte Ore, Ochoa* and *Nekeas*.

PENEDÈS, DO (red, white, rosado) Cataluña's leading region, though no longer as exciting as it used to be. *Torres* wines run from the rich, rather sweetly oaky basic reds, right up to the periodically exciting Cabernet Sauvignon-based *Mas La Plana* and the 100 per cent Pinot Noir *Mas Borras*. Torres also extracts a lean, lemony, sharply refreshing flavour from Parellada. *Jean León* makes a rich, oaky, pineappley Chardonnay and a rich Cabernet. Also look out for *René Barbier, Can Ràfols dels Caus, Cavas Hill, Masía Bach, Mont Marçal, Jaume Serra, Vallformosa*.

PRIORAT, DO (red) Wonderful big, rich Garnacha-based reds, blended with Syrah, Cabernet and a bit of everything else. *Clos Erasmus, Clos Martinet, Clos Mogador, Clos de l'Obac, Clos & Terrasses, Costers del Siurana, Finca Dofi, Mas d'en Gil, Rottlan Torra* and, for lottery winners, *L'Ermita* are the stars. Also look for *Capafons-Ossó, Cims de Porrera, de Muller, Masía Barril, Onix, Pasanau* and *Scala Dei*.

RÍAS BAIXAS, DO (red, white) Fresh and fragrant white Albariño wines are the stars of Galicia's best DO: *Agro de Bazán, Martín Codax, Granxa Fillaboa, Lusco do Miño, Pazo de Señorans, Quinta de Couselo, Santiago Ruiz* and *Terras Gauda* are all good.

RIBEIRA SACRA, DO (white) Galician DO making excellent and good value whites from Godello, Albariño and others.

RIBEIRO, DO (red, white) There is fresh white wine made from Treixadura and Torrontés here: try *Casal da Barca* from *Bodega Alanis*.

RIBERA DEL DUERO, DO (red) The big name in this region has traditionally been *Vega Sicilia*; its wines are among the best in Spain. Modern-day Ribera del Duero now has a whole clutch of very expensive superstars, often of excellent quality – like *Pesquera* from Alejandro Fernández and *Pingus* – and a gaggle of hangers-on, occasionally of good quality. However, the area's outstanding potential and real quality is at the moment clouded by puffery and silly prices. Good producers include *Alión, Ismael Arroyo, Arzuaga, Balbás, Briego, Hermanos Cuadrado García, Moro, Señorío de Nava, Pago de Carraovejas, Viña Pedrosa, Protos, Teófilo Reyes, Hermanos Sastre, Valtravieso*.

RIBERA DEL GUADIANA, DO (red, white) DO created in 1997, producing wines for drinking young: whites from Viura, Chardonnay and local speciality Alarije; reds from Garnacha, Tempranillo and others.

RIOJA, DOC (red, white) Another area that suffers from believing its own promotional material. Prices recently have gone far too high, and much quality has lagged far behind. This is a pity, because Rioja can be one of the classic reds, tasting of oak and vanilla toffee, plus rather light, sometimes peppery fruit with a strawberry jam sweetness. New-wave Riojas are bottled younger, aged in French wood and are more modern, gutsy propositions. *Finca Allende, Remirez de la Gamuza, Roda* and *San Vicente* are among the leaders here, and many traditional bodegas are making wines in the same style, often from single estates: look for *Remelluri, Palacio, Marqués de Murrieta, Muga, Baron de Oña* from La Rioja Alta, *Finca Valpiedra* from *Martínez Bujanda, Bodegas Amezola de la Mora*.

The red blend is Tempranillo (for character), Garnacha (for fatness), and perhaps some Graciano and Mazuelo, but it's not unusual for producers to add some Cabernet to the blend. Traditional wines come from *Artadi, Barón de Ley, Bodegas Bretón, Campillo, Campo Viejo, CVNE, El Coto, Faustino, Viña Ijalba, López de Heredia, Marqués de Cáceres, Marqués de Murrieta, Marqués de Riscal, Martínez Bujanda, Montecillo, Muga, Olarra, Palacio, La Rioja Alta* and *Bodegas Riojanas*.

White Rioja *can* be buttery and rich, slightly Burgundian. *Marqués de Murrieta*

RIOJA CLASSIFICATIONS

Rioja is divided into three geographical sub-regions: Rioja Alta, Rioja Alavesa and Rioja Baja: most wines will be a blend from all three. The wine's age, indicated on the label, falls into one of four categories.

Sin crianza Without aging, or with less than a year in wood; wine sold in its first or second year. (The words *sin crianza* are not seen on the label.)

Crianza With a minimum of 12 months in wood and some further months in bottle; cannot be sold before its third year. Whites will have had a minimum of six months in cask before bottling.

Reserva Selected wine from a good harvest with a minimum of 36 months' aging, in cask and bottle, of which 12 months minimum in cask. It cannot leave the bodega until the fifth year after the vintage. Whites have at least six months in cask, and 24 months' aging in total.

Gran Reserva Wine from an excellent vintage (supposedly) that will stand up to aging: 24 months minimum in cask and 36 months in bottle, or vice-versa. It cannot leave the bodega until the sixth year after the vintage. White wines have six months in cask and 48 months' aging in total.

makes a good example of this style, and so does *CVNE* with its *Viña Real*, and *Bodegas Riojanas* with its *Monte Real*. *López de Heredia* makes an old-fashioned style, while *Navajas, Viña Soledad* from *Franco Españolas* and *Siglo Gold* from *AGE* are all oak aged.

RUEDA, DO (white) A brilliant source of light table wines, picked early and fresh and fermented cool. The local grape, the Verdejo, makes soft, full, nutty wines, sometimes padded out with the dull Palomino, or sharpened up with the more acid Viura and Sauvignon Blanc. Most are best young, but there are oaked ones. Look for *Alvarez y Díez, Belondrade y Lurton, Bodegas Castilla La Vieja, Hermanos Lurton, Marqués de Griñon, Marqués de Riscal*.

SHERRY (JEREZ-XÉRÈS-SHERRY, DO) (fortified) There are two basic sherry styles, *fino* and *oloroso*, each with sub-divisions. *Fino*, from Jerez or Puerto de Santa Maria, should be pale and dry, with an unnerving dry austerity. The tang comes from a layer of natural yeast, called *flor*, that forms on the surface of the wine in the barrels. The lightest wines are selected for *fino*, which is drunk cool and fresh, often as an apéritif.

Manzanilla is a form of *fino* matured by the sea at Sanlúcar de Barrameda. It can be almost savoury-dry, and you might imagine a whiff of sea salt – if you catch it fresh enough. Best: *Barbadillo, Caballero, Diez-Merito, Don Zoilo, Garvey, La Gitana, Hidalgo, La Ina, Inocente, Lustau, La Riva, Sanchez Romate, Tío Pepe*. Good Puerto *fino* comes from *Burdon* and *Osborne*.

In Britain there can be a problem with freshness: *fino* and *manzanilla* won't usually keep longer than six months in bottle.

Real *amontillado* begins life as *fino*, aged in cask until the flor dies and the wine deepens and darkens to a tantalizing, nutty dryness. In the natural state, as drunk in Spain, it is *completely* dry, and a proper *amontillado* will usually say *seco* ('dry'), on the label. But we've adulterated the word in

English to mean a bland, downmarket drink of no interest. Look out for *almacenista* sherries, wines from small stockholders, which can be wonderful.

Look out also for *Solear* from *Barbadillo*, *La Goya Manzanilla Pasada* and *Amontillado Fino Zuleta (Delgado Zuleta), Amontillado del Duque (González Byass), Hidalgo Manzanilla Pasada, Valdespino's Amontillado Coliseo* and *Don Tomás. (Manzanilla Pasada* has extra barrel age, and should be wonderful.)

Real *olorosos*, made from richer, fatter wines without any flor, are deep and dark, packed with violent burnt flavours – and usually dry, though you may find *oloroso dulce* (sweet). In Britain most are sweetened with Pedro Ximénez or Moscatel. They usually come as 'Milk', 'Cream' or 'Brown'. Pale Creams are sweetened (inferior) *fino*, and are some of the dullest drinks around. For the real, dry thing, once again, look for *almacenista olorosos* from *Lustau* and *seco* examples from top companies like *Barbadillo, González Byass* and *Valdespino*. There are a few good, concentrated sweetened *olorosos* around, like *Apostoles* and *Matusalem*, both from *González Byass*, *Solera 1842 (Valdespino)*. Dry: *Barbadillo, Don Zoilo, Sandeman, Valdespino Don Gonzalo, Williams & Humbert Dos Cortados*. These intense old wines are one of today's great bargains.

SOMONTANO, DO (red, white, rosado) The most exciting of Spain's newer regions, with a long tradition of both Spanish and international grape varieties. *Enate* and *Viños del Vero* are the star producers, making substantial, ageworthy reds and good whites from Chardonnay and Gewürztraminer. Look also for *Covisa, Bodegas Pirineos* and the *Co-operativa de Sobrarbe* under the *Camporocal* label.

TARRAGONA, DO (red, white, rosado) Now benefiting from its proximity to Priorat, and making new-wave wines in a similar style. They are all spice, figs and richness. Look out for *Capafons-Ossó, Finca*

**INSTANT CELLAR:
BEEFY REDS**

• 1995 Priorat Clos Mogador, £25,
Moreno Wines Cult wine that is as beefy as
they come – but can be drunk early.
• 1998 Priorat Coma Vella, Mas d'en Gil,
£18, Bibendum A Priorat new to Britain,
from low-yielding vines. The wines are
dense and concentrated.
• 1996 Rioja Allende, Finca Allende,
£12.49, Moreno Wines Sexy, cult modern
Rioja with masses of fruit and lots of
complexity.
• 1996 Rioja Reserva, Roda II, £17.50, John
Armit Wines I'm sorry about these prices,
but Spain is awash with money at the
moment and Spaniards will pay anything for
top wines. And this really is good, from one
of the best new-wave names in Rioja. It's
intense, tarry and leathery.
• 1997 Rioja Crianza, Domaine Ostatu,
£9.70, H&H Bancroft Concentrated
Tempranillo, Graciano and Mazuelo from
old vines, made with great care.
• 1998 Syrah Dominio de Valdepusa,
Marqués de Griñon, £10.99, Waitrose
Wonderfully exotic stuff, all spices and
leather and lovely concentration.
• 1997 Ribera del Duero Teófilo Reyes,
£17.50, Laymont & Shaw All tar, mulberries
and damsons, very long and concentrated
and ripe. First-class wine.

---

d'Argata, de Muller, and the co-ops at
Capçanes and Falset.

TERRA ALTA, DO (red) Decent
Tempranillo. Good producers include the
Gandesa co-op, Ferrer Escod.

**TIERRA DE BARROS, Vino de la
Tierra** (red) One major bodega (Inviosa)
has blazed a trail with its excellent Lar de
Barros from Cencibel and Cabernet
Sauvignon. Viniberia heads the followers.

TORO, DO (red) Beefy fruity reds from
the Tinto de Toro – alias Tempranillo.
Bodegas Fariña' Gran Colegiata is not quite
what it was, and prices have risen too fast.

Too many of the wines are rustic and not
that well made. Interest from neighbouring
Ribera del Duero – in particular from Vega
Sicilia – may pep things up.

UTIEL-REQUENA, DO (red, rosado)
The reds, from the Bobal grape, are robust,
rather hot and southern. The rosados can
be better – delicate and fragrant.

VALDEORRAS, DO (red, white) The
reds are best young. The ordinary whites,
fresh and fruity at their best, are made from
Palomino and Doña Blanca, but there is
work being done with Godello.

VALDEPEÑAS, DO (red, white) The
best reds here are from Cencibel
(Tempranillo) and turn out deep and herby
with good strawberry fruit – and excellent
value at very low prices, even for gran
reservas with a decade's aging, which is
what the region is famous for. Look for the
soft wines, aged in new oak, of Señorío de
Los Llanos (including Pata Negra Gran
Reserva), Viña Albali from Bodegas Felix
Solís, Bodegas Luís Megía (including Duque
de Estrada and Marqués de Gastañaga) and
Casa de la Viña.

VALENCIA, DO (red, white, rosado)
Large quantities of wines fine for the beach.
Some low-priced reds from Schenk and
Gandía Pla can be good, and sweet
Moscatels can be tasty and good value.
Gandía's Castillo de Liria is an attractive red.

YECLA, DO (red, white) Fairly full-
bodied reds and more dubious whites.
Some decent wines from Bodegas Castaño,
from the cheap and cheerful Dominio de
Espinal to the better Pozuelo Reserva.

OTHER REGIONS There is a whole
new generation of high-priced, high-quality
table wines: look for Mauro, from the
Duero, and Abadia Retuerta, from Pascal
Delbeck. He's the winemaker at Château
Belair in St-Émilion.

PRODUCERS WHO'S WHO

ANTONIO BARBADILLO ★★
(Sanlúcar de Barrameda) Top *manzanilla* bodega producing consistently fresh wines. Older *amontillados* are superb, too. Buy the *manzanilla* in half bottles.

RENÉ BARBIER ★★ (Priorat) The Clos Mogador is one of the top wines of Priorat.

JULIÁN CHIVITE ★ (Navarra) Clean white from Viura, attractive rosado from Garnacha, and a good Tempranillo-based red, all under the Gran Feudo label.

CODORNÍU ★ (Penedès) Giant Cava company making likeably reliable fizz. Good soft and honeyed Anna de Codorníu, and a very good, creamy Chardonnay Cava.

CONTINO ★ (Rioja) Single-vineyard Viña del Olivo is big, plummy and spicily complex.

CVNE ★★ (Rioja) Excellent *crianza* and *reserva* whites (Monopole and CVNE Reserva). Best reds are Imperial and Viña Real, *reservas* upwards. Younger reds are currently looking a bit uninspired.

FINCA ALLENDE ★★ (Rioja) Small winery producing top-quality new-wave stuff, all lush fruit and French oak.

FREIXENET ★ (Penedès) Disappointing Cordon Negro; vintage-dated Brut Nature and Reserva are much better, as is non-vintage Reserva Real Gran Reserva.

GONZÁLEZ BYASS ★★★ (Jerez) Producer of the best-selling (and very good) fino Tío Pepe. Gonzalez Byass makes an impressive top range of wines, and a Rioja, Bodegas Beronia.

CAVAS HILL (Penedès) Table wines as well as fresh, clean Cava Reserva Oro Brut Natur. Look out for Blanc Cru and Oro Penedès Blanco Suave whites, and Rioja-style reds, Gran Civet and Gran Toc.

COSTERS DEL SIURANA ★★
(Priorat) A Priorat pioneer, with fabulously lush wines. Look for Clos de l'Obac.

JEAN LEÓN ★ (Penedès) Some of Spain's most 'Californian' wines: super-oaky, pineapple-and-honey Chardonnay, and soft, blackcurranty Cabernet Sauvignon.

LOS LLANOS ★ (Valdepeñas) Reliable bodega producing wonderfully soft, oaky reds and uncomplicated whites.

LÓPEZ DE HEREDIA ★ (Rioja) Rich, complex whites, Viña Tondonia and Viña Gravonia, and delicate, ethereal reds, Viña Cubillo and Viña Tondonia. The most traditional of all Riojan bodegas.

LUSTAU ★★ (Jerez) 'Reviving Traditional Sherry Values', to use its own phrase, with its range of *almacenista* wines.

MARQUÉS DE CÁCERES ★ (Rioja) Whites are cool-fermented and fresh, and reds have less wood-aging than usual, but still keep an attractive style.

MARQUÉS DE GRIÑÓN ★★
(Toledo) Very good Cabernet, Syrah and Petit Verdot from his family estate, Dominio de Valdepusa. Also a joint venture with Berberana in Rioja which is so far disappointing.

MARQUÉS DE MURRIETA ★★
(Rioja) An ultra-traditional winery with wines oak-aged far longer than in any other Rioja bodega, that is nevertheless reinventing itself with modern, fruity, early-bottled wines to sit alongside the traditional range. Castillo Ygay wines (from top years) may sit in barrel for 40 years. But Viña Albina is deep, modern and lush.

MAS MARTINET ★★★ (Priorat) Look for Martinet Bru and Clos Martinet from this Priorat leader.

MARTÍNEZ BUJANDA ★★ (Rioja) Super-fresh and lively Valdemar white and strongly oaky Reserva and Gran Reserva Conde de Valdemar. New-style Rioja at its best.

MONTECILLO ★ (Rioja) Aromatic white Viña Cumbrero, a raspberry and oak Viña Cumbrero red *crianza*, and a Gran Reserva, Viña Monty.

MUGA ★★ (Rioja) Newly revived, and far more modern than it was. Prado Enea Reserva or Gran Reserva is complex, but still subtle and elegant. It's not cheap, though. Also good white.

ALVARO PALACIOS ★★ (Priorat) One of the pioneers of new-style Priorat. The wines are called L'Ermita, Finca Dofi and Les Terrasses.

PESQUERA/ALEJANDRO FERNÁNDEZ ★★★ (Ribera del Duero) Pesquera wines, richly coloured, firm, fragrant and plummy-tobaccoey are among Spain's best reds. Made from Tempranillo, they are sold as *crianzas*, with Reservas and Gran Reservas in the best years.

PRÍNCIPE DE VIANA (Navarra) Innovative bodega which used to be a co-op, and became known as Bodegas Cenalsa. Agramont is its best-known UK brand. Look out for Bodegas Guelbenzu, Cabernet/Tempranillo blends.

RAÏMAT ★ (Costers del Segre) A trailblazer in Spain's new wave, now looking tired. The wines are perfectly pleasant, but have lost the New World swagger that made everyone sit up and take notice.

REMELLURI ★★ (Rioja) Single-estate wine, not that common in Rioja; the bodega

makes a fine, meaty Reserva and subtle Gran Reserva. Into biodynamic viticulture, which involves incredible degrees of care of the organically grown vines.

LA RIOJA ALTA ★★ (Rioja) A traditional bodega making two styles of Reserva, the elegant Viña Arana and the rich Viña Ardanza. Viña Alberdi is aged for longer than most *crianzas*. Also exceptional Gran Reservas, Reserva 904 and Reserva 890.

RIOJANAS ★ (Rioja) The best reds here are the Reservas: the plummy Viña Albina and the richer, more concentrated Monte Reál. White Monte Reál *crianza* is soft and peachy, with just enough oak to fatten it.

RODA ★★ (Rioja) A leader of the new generation, making three red wines: Roda I, Roda II and Cirsion.

MIGUEL TORRES ★ (Penedès) One of the leaders of modern Spanish wine, now rather overtaken by other winemakers, other regions. The superstar white is Milmanda Chardonnay; Mas la Plana Cabernet Sauvignon is the top red. Grans Muralles is a blend of red Spanish grapes made very much in the current mode: highly extracted, highly concentrated.

VALDESPINO ★★★ (Jerez) No longer family owned; the fear is quality may slip. We pray not, because Valdespino is sherry's jewel. Inocente is masterful *fino*, and *amontillados* and *olorosos* are about as good as you can get.

VEGA SICILIA ★★★ (Ribera del Duero) Makers of Spain's most famous and expensive red wine – Vega Sicilia Unico, sometimes kept in barrel for ten years. The second wine, Valbuena, offers a cheaper glimpse of Vega Sicilia's glories. Cheaper, you understand. Not cheap. Newest is more modern Alión, from a separate winery.

SPAIN PRICES

RIOJA RED

Under £5.00

Artadi Orobio Tempranillo 1999 £4.99
(TES)
Berberana Tempranillo 1999 £4.99 (BUD)
£4.99 (VIC) £4.99 (THR)
Campo Viejo Albor 1999 £4.45 (STE)
Faustino Rivero Orla Dorado Crianza
1997 £4.99 (UN)
Bodegas Olarra Añares Crianza 1997
£4.95 (SOM)

£5.00 → £5.99

Artadi Orobio Tempranillo 2000 £5.99
(COC) £6.35 (COC)
Campo Viejo Crianza 1999 £5.99 (SAF)
Campo Viejo Crianza 1996 £5.99 (TES)
£6.95 (STE)
CVNE ½ bottle 1998 £5.17 (BIB)
CVNE Viña Real ½ bottle 1998 £5.92 (BIB)
Marqués de Griñon 1998 £5.99 (UN)
£5.99 (TES) £5.99 (MAJ)
Bodegas Muerza Vega 1999 £5.75 (COC)
Olarra 1998 £5.99 (GN)

£6.00 → £6.99

Berberana Carta de Oro 1996 £6.49 (UN)
Berberana Carta de Oro 1995 £6.90 (CRO)
El Coto Crianza 1997 £6.39 (JON)
CVNE Crianza 1997 £6.69 (BO) £7.94
(JON) £9.62 (VIN)
CVNE Viña Real Crianza 1994 £6.49 (BOT)
Marqués de Cáceres Crianza 1997 £6.99
(POR) £7.15 (HAH) £7.60 (LAY)
Marqués de Cáceres Crianza 1996 £6.36
(TUR) £6.45 (WHI) £6.95 (TAN) £6.96
(COC) £7.04 (PLA) £7.99 (DI)
Marqués de Cáceres Crianza 1995 £6.95
(BALL) £7.95 (STE)
Marqués de Cáceres Crianza 1994 £6.80
(CRO)

Martinez Bujanda Conde de Valdemar
Crianza 1998 £6.49 (VIC) £6.49 (THR)
£6.49 (BOT) £6.99 (OD) £8.49 (SUN)
Bodegas Olarra Añares Crianza 1998
£6.49 (CON)
Bodegas Palacio Cosme Palacio y
Hermanos 1998 £6.99 (WAI) £6.99 (OD)
Bodegas Palacio Cosme Palacio y
Hermanos 1997 £6.99 (UN) £6.99 (SAF)
Bodegas Palacio Glorioso Crianza 1998
£6.99 (OD)

£7.00 → £7.99

Alavesas Solar de Samaniego Crianza
1998 £7.76 (CB)
Amezola de la Mora Amezola Crianza
1997 £7.49 (BO) £8.32 (BIB)
Amezola de la Mora Amezola Crianza
1996 £7.50 (RAE) £7.95 (JU) £8.19 (JON)
Artadi Viñas de Gain 1997 £7.99 (BO)
£7.99 (MAJ) £8.55 (TAN) £8.85 (GAU)
£8.99 (GW) £9.49 (CON) £9.65 (RAE)
£9.66 (SUN) £9.99 (BAL) £10.65 (GN)
£12.40 (TW)
Barón de Ley 1996 £7.10 (SOM) £7.99 (WR)
Berberana Reserva 1996 £7.99 (MAJ)
Campo Viejo Reserva 1995 £7.95 (POR)
£8.75 (STE)
CVNE Crianza 1996 £7.00 (HIG)
CVNE Crianza 1994 £7.49 (BOT)
Domecq Marqués de Arienzo 1997 £7.57
(FLE)
Faustino V Reserva 1994 £7.49 (VIC)
£7.49 (THR) £8.49 (MOR) £9.89 (CON)
Viña Ijalba Múrice Crianza 1998 £7.04
(WHI)
Bodegas Lan Crianza 1997 £7.36 (BY)
Bodegas Olarra Cerro Anon Reserva
1996 £7.10 (SOM)
Bodegas Riojanas Puerta Vieja 1997 £7.75
(WRI) £8.50 (RIC)
Viña Salceda Crianza 1997 £7.95 (TAN)
£7.99 (DI) £8.09 (JON) £9.50 (LEA)

RETAILERS SPECIALIZING IN SPAIN

see Retailers Directory (page 40) for details

Adnams (AD), Ballantynes (BAL), Bibendum
(BIB), D Byrne, Direct Wine (DI), Cockburns
of Leith (COC), Lay & Wheeler (LAY),
Laymont & Shaw (LA), Lea & Sandeman
(LEA), Moreno Wines (MOR) – a mostly
Spanish list, Playford Ros (PLAY), Reid Wines
(REI) – good sherries, Roberson, Tanners
(TAN), Villeneuve (VIL), Wine Society (WS).

£8.00 → £8.99

Artadi **2000** £8.20 (TAN)
Artadi **1999** £8.45 (CON) £8.99 (BAL)
Artadi Viñas de Gain **1996** £8.50 (WS)
   £11.75 (BODX)
Barón de Ley Reserva **1995** £8.50 (CRO)
Briego Tinto Roble, Ribera del Duero
   1999 £8.99 (RAE)
CVNE Viña Real Crianza **1998** £8.21 (PLA)
   £9.89 (BIB)
Faustino V Reserva **1997** £8.99 (SAF)
Martinez Bujanda Conde de Valdemar
   Crianza **1996** £8.95 (GN)
Martinez Bujanda Conde de Valdemar
   Reserva **1996** £8.99 (VIC) £8.99 (THR)
   £8.99 (BOT) £8.99 (WR) £9.45 (NI) £9.49
   (OD) £10.99 (SUN) £11.75 (LA)
Muga Reserva **1996** £8.21 (WHI) £8.75
   (WRI) £8.95 (CON) £8.95 (LA) £9.87 (PEN)
   £9.99 (BAL) £10.79 (JON)
Muga Reserva **1995** £8.21 (WHI) £9.85 (GN)
Bodegas Olarra Cerro Anon Reserva
   1994 £8.50 (CON)
La Rioja Alta Vina Alberdi **1996** £8.20
   (SOM) £10.49 (AME)
La Rioja Alta Viña Alberdi Reserva **1995**
   £8.50 (WS) £9.25 (RIC) £10.70 (HIC)
Viña Salceda Crianza **1998** £8.95 (LEA)
   £8.95 (BER)

£9.00 → £9.99

Faustino V Reserva **1995** £9.62 (WHI)
Marqués de Cáceres Reserva **1994** £9.99
   (POR) £11.45 (HAH) £11.95 (BER) £11.99
   (DI)
Marqués de Murrieta Reserva **1997** £9.99
   (SAF) £10.49 (POR) £11.17 (PLA)
Marqués de Murrieta Reserva **1996** £9.95
   (FRI) £9.99 (SAI) £9.99 (MAJ) £9.99 (PEN)
   £9.99 (OD) £10.65 (WRI) £10.95 (CON)
   £10.99 (VIL) £11.95 (PLAY) £11.95 (NI)
   £12.00 (JU)
Marqués de Riscal Reserva **1996** £9.99
   (MAJ) £10.75 (GW) £11.10 (PLA) £11.25
   (LA) £11.45 (VA)

• *Wines are listed in A–Z order within
   each price band.*
• *For each wine, vintages are listed in
   descending order.*
• *Each vintage of any wine appears
   only once.*

Marqués de Riscal Reserva **1995** £9.99
   (UN)
Martinez Bujanda Conde de Valdemar
   Reserva **1995** £9.75 (TAN)
Remelluri **1995** £9.70 (SOM) £17.00 (CRO)
La Rioja Alta Vina Alberdi **1995** £9.95
   (POR)
La Rioja Alta Viña Alberdi Reserva **1996**
   £9.25 (LA) £9.95 (BER) £9.99 (VIL) £10.69
   (JON)

£10.00 → £11.99

Baron de Oña Torre de Oña Reserva
   1996 £10.95 (JER)
Baron de Oña Torre de Oña Reserva
   1995 £10.75 (LA) £10.99 (VIL) £11.50
   (STA) £12.49 (AME)
Campillo Reserva **1998** £11.95 (POR)
Campillo Reserva **1995** £10.99 (TES)
Campo Viejo Gran Reserva **1993** £10.95
   (POR) £11.99 (WR)
Campo Viejo Gran Reserva **1991** £11.95
   (STE)
CVNE Reserva **1995** £10.99 (GW) £11.89
   (WAT)
CVNE Viña Real Reserva **1989** £11.99
   (MOR) £12.49 (BOT)
Domecq Marqués de Arienzo Reserva
   1995 £10.37 (FLE)
Faustino I Gran Reserva **1990** £10.99 (BOT)
Viña Ijalba Reserva **1997** £10.16 (WHI)
Lagunilla Gran Reserva **1994** £10.28 (WHI)
Lagunilla Gran Reserva **1990** £10.99 (PLA)
López de Heredia Viña Bosconia **1993**
   £11.55 (SAV)
Marqués de Cáceres Gran Reserva **1991**
   £10.15 (MOR)
Marqués de Cáceres Reserva **1992**
   £10.99 (JON)
Marqués de Griñon **1996** £11.50 (CRO)
Marqués de Murrieta **1996** £11.35 (BEN)
Marqués de Murrieta Reserva **1993**
   £11.49 (UN)
Marqués de Riscal Reserva **1991** £10.95
   (GN)
Martinez Bujanda Conde de Valdemar
   Reserva **1994** £11.40 (PEN)
Remelluri **1998** £11.78 (FLE)
Bodegas Riojanas Monte Real Reserva
   1996 £10.75 (BU)
Bodegas Riojanas Viña Albina Reserva
   1995 £10.75 (RIC)
Viña Salceda Reserva **1996** £10.99 (DI)
Urbina Gran Reserva **1991** £11.95 (POR)
   £12.69 (JON) £12.95 (RES)

£12.00 → £13.99

Alavesas Solar de Samaniego Gran
   Reserva 1991 £13.40 (CB)
Amezola de la Mora Gran Reserva 1990
   £12.99 (RAE)
Artadi Viñas de Gain 1998 £13.95 (LIB)
Bretón Dominio de Conte Reserva 1995
   £13.25 (FORT)
Faustino I Gran Reserva 1994 £12.04
   (WHI) £12.69 (CON) £12.69 (OD) £12.99
   (SAF)
Marqués de Cáceres Gran Reserva 1990
   £13.95 (HAH)
Marqués de Murrieta Reserva 1984
   £13.00 (CRO)
Marqués de Murrieta Reserva Especial
   1995 £12.99 (MOR) £15.75 (FORT)
   £15.79 (JON) £15.80 (BEN) £15.95 (FRI)
Marqués de Murrieta Reserva Especial
   1991 £13.50 (BOT)
Marqués de Vargas Reserva 1997 £12.90
   (TAN) £16.50 (LEA) £16.50 (LEA) £16.99
   (JON) £17.99 (POR)
Marqués de Vargas Reserva 1996 £13.99
   (DI)
Remelluri 1997 £12.83 (SAV) £13.29 (YOU)
   £15.00 (CRO)
Remelluri 1996 £13.20 (TAN) £16.00 (CRO)
La Rioja Alta Viña Arana Reserva 1994
   £12.50 (WS) £12.50 (LA) £12.99 (VIL)
La Rioja Alta Viña Ardanza Reserva 1994
   £12.25 (SOM) £12.99 (SAI) £12.99 (YOU)
   £13.25 (LA) £13.75 (JER) £13.99 (VIL)
   £14.00 (JU) £14.95 (POR) £15.25 (STA)
   £15.80 (BEN) £16.25 (FORT)
La Rioja Alta Viña Ardanza Reserva 1989
   £13.90 (CRO)
Viña Salceda Reserva 1995 £12.95 (LEA)

£14.00 → £15.99

Campillo Gran Reserva 1992 £14.99 (UN)
   £14.99 (TES)
Campo Viejo Dominio de Montalvo Gran
   Reserva 1994 £14.99 (AME)
CVNE Imperial Gran Reserva 1989
   £15.75 (MOR) £21.00 (HIG)
CVNE Imperial Gran Reserva 1988
   £15.86 (PEN) £19.99 (BOT)
CVNE Viña Real Reserva 1994 £15.25
   (LA) £17.00 (WS)
López de Heredia Viña Tondonia Reserva
   1993 £14.00 (HIG)
Marqués de Cáceres Gran Reserva 1989
   £14.99 (DI)

Marqués de Murrieta Castillo Ygay Gran
   Reserva Especial 1994 £14.50 (BALL)
Marqués de Murrieta Prado Lagar Reserva
   1995 £14.99 (VIL)
Martinez Bujanda Conde de Valdemar
   Gran Reserva 1994 £14.50 (NI)
Martinez Bujanda Garnacha 1982 £14.69
   (PEN)
Martinez Bujanda Gran Reserva 1993
   £15.99 (UN) £19.98 (PEN)
Muga Prado Enea Gran Reserva 1994
   £14.95 (RES)
Muga Prado Enea Gran Reserva 1991
   £14.99 (BAL) £15.10 (SOM) £18.75 (LA)
   £19.00 (WS) £19.99 (MAJ) £19.99 (MOR)
   £20.99 (JON)
Muga Reserva Selección Especial 1995
   £14.99 (JON)
Muga Reserva Selección Especial 1994
   £15.00 (WRI) £15.95 (BAL)
La Rioja Alta Viña Ardanza Reserva 1995
   £14.59 (JON)
La Rioja Alta Viña Ardanza Reserva 1993
   £14.70 (RIC) £14.99 (AME)

£16.00 → £19.99

Contino Reserva 1996 £19.50 (LAY)
   £22.25 (WAT)
CVNE Imperial Gran Reserva 1994
   £18.95 (STE) £21.95 (STA)
CVNE Imperial Gran Reserva 1991
   £19.35 (JON) £19.75 (GW) £19.95 (LA)
   £20.25 (VIN) £20.50 (TAN) £22.13 (BIB)
CVNE Imperial Reserva 1995 £18.58
   (GW) £18.99 (WAT)
CVNE Imperial Reserva 1994 £16.25 (LA)
   £17.95 (STA)
CVNE Viña Real Gran Reserva 1994
   £17.95 (LAY)
CVNE Viña Real Gran Reserva 1991
   £16.85 (GW) £17.03 (PLA) £17.50 (STA)
   £17.50 (LA)
CVNE Viña Real Gran Reserva 1988
   £16.95 (BALL) £18.49 (BOT)
CVNE Viña Real Reserva 1995 £16.95
   (TAN) £17.89 (JON)
CVNE Viña Real Reserva 1991 £16.95
   (STA)

> • All prices for each wine are listed
>   together in ascending order.
> • Price bands refer to the lowest price
>   for which the wine is available.

Bodegas Lan Viña Lanciano Reserva **1995**
£16.99 (WAI) £17.13 (BY) £19.50 (CRO)
Bodegas Lan Viña Lanciano Reserva **1975**
£17.98 (BY)
López de Heredia Viña Tondonia Reserva
1991 £17.45 (LA) £17.63 (SAV)
Marqués de Griñon **1990** £17.90 (CRO)
Marqués de Murrieta Castillo Ygay Gran
Reserva **1996** £19.95 (POR)
Marqués de Murrieta Castillo Ygay Gran
Reserva **1991** £19.99 (SAF)
Marqués de Murrieta Castillo Ygay Gran
Reserva **1989** £18.75 (LAY) £18.99 (RAE)
Marqués de Murrieta Castillo Ygay Gran
Reserva Especial **1989** £19.50 (HAH)
£19.50 (BOT)
Marqués de Murrieta Castillo Ygay Gran
Reserva **1989** £19.92 (PLA)
Marqués de Murrieta Castillo Ygay Gran
Reserva Especial **1989** £19.99 (VIL)
Marqués de Murrieta Castillo Ygay Gran
Reserva **1989** £19.99 (MOR) £20.00
(FORT) £20.75 (NI) £21.95 (FRI) £29.00
(CRO)
Marqués de Murrieta Castillo Ygay Gran
Reserva Especial **1987** £18.49 (BOT)
Marqués de Riscal Gran Reserva **1994**
£17.99 (SAF) £23.00 (LA)
Martinez Bujanda Conde de Valdemar
Gran Reserva **1997** £19.95 (GN)
Muga Prado Enea Gran Reserva **1985**
£19.98 (PEN)
Remelluri Reserva **1995** £17.63 (NO)
La Rioja Alta Gran Reserva 904 **1990**
£19.65 (SOM) £19.95 (LA) £20.99 (YOU)
£22.00 (JU) £22.99 (VIL) £24.69 (JON)
£24.99 (BEN) £25.90 (JER) £25.95 (BER)
La Rioja Alta Viña Arana Reserva **1987**
£18.00 (LA)
La Rioja Alta Viña Ardanza Reserva **1990**
£17.00 (LA)
Bodegas Riojanas Viña Albina Gran
Reserva **1973** £18.95 (BU)
Roda II Reserva **1996** £17.50 (ARM)

£20.00 → £29.99

Artadi Pagos Viejos Reserva **1997** £25.85
(FA) £29.95 (GN) £31.20 (TW) £31.50
(CON)
Artadi Viñas El Pison Reserva **1995**
£25.99 (CON)
Bretón Alba de Bretón Reserva **1996**
£24.45 (FORT)
CVNE Imperial Gran Reserva **1990**
£23.00 (FORT)

López de Heredia Viña Bosconia Gran
Reserva **1976** £27.22 (SAV)
López de Heredia Viña Tondonia Reserva
1981 £27.22 (SAV)
Marqués de Murrieta Gran Reserva **1983**
£26.00 (CRO)
Marqués de Murrieta Reserva **1985**
£20.00 (CRO)
Marqués de Riscal Gran Reserva **1988**
£21.00 (LA)
Martinez Bujanda Conde de Valdemar
Gran Reserva **1981** £23.00 (CRO)
Miguel Merino Reserva **1994** £20.00 (BU)
Muga Torre Reserva Especial **1996**
£29.95 (RES)
Paternina Banda Azul **1982** £25.00 (BU)
La Rioja Alta Gran Reserva 890 **1989**
£22.00 (WAI)
La Rioja Alta Gran Reserva 904 **1989**
£21.00 (RIC) £21.90 (CRO) £22.00 (WS)
£22.95 (POR) £22.95 (GN) £26.50 (FORT)
La Rioja Alta Viña Arana Reserva **1984**
£20.00 (LA)
La Rioja Alta Viña Arana Reserva **1981**
£25.00 (LA)
La Rioja Alta Viña Arana Reserva **1976**
£28.00 (LA)
La Rioja Alta Viña Ardanza Reserva **1987**
£25.00 (LA)
La Rioja Alta Viña Ardanza Reserva **1983**
£25.00 (LA)
La Rioja Alta Viña Ardanza Reserva **1978**
£27.00 (LA)
Roda I Reserva **1995** £24.38 (BODX)
£27.50 (ARM)
Roda I Reserva **1986** £22.00 (WS)

£30.00 → £49.99

Artadi Pagos Viejos Reserva **1998** £39.56
(FA) £43.48 (TUR)
Artadi Pagos Viejos Reserva **1996** £31.99
(RAE) £40.07 (TW) £60.00 (GAU)
Artadi Pagos Viejos Reserva **1995** £42.50
(FA) £49.84 (BODX)
Artadi Viñas El Pison Reserva **1994**
£45.00 (BU)
Berberana Gran Reserva **1970** £39.00
(CRO)
Bilbainas Viña Pomal **1970** £45.00 (BU)
López de Heredia Viña Bosconia Gran
Reserva **1973** £43.50 (BAL)
López de Heredia Viña Tondonia Gran
Reserva **1978** £35.25 (SAV)
López de Heredia Viña Tondonia Gran
Reserva **1968** £49.50 (BAL)

Marqués de Murrieta Castillo Ygay Gran
   Reserva **1978** £34.95 (BOT) £59.00
   (CRO)
Marqués de Murrieta Dalmau Reserva
   1995 £48.99 (RAE) £55.00 (FRI) £55.99
   (MOR)
La Rioja Alta Gran Reserva 890 **1985**
   £45.50 (LA) £51.85 (JER) £52.99 (VIL)
La Rioja Alta Gran Reserva 904 **1968**
   £47.50 (BU) £95.00 (LA)
La Rioja Alta Viña Arana Reserva **1988**
   £30.00 (LA)
La Rioja Alta Viña Arana Reserva **1982**
   £45.00 (LA)

£50.00 → £69.99

Artadi Viñas El Pison Reserva **1998**
   £54.50 (TW) £75.00 (GAU) £82.25 (TUR)
CVNE Imperial Gran Reserva **1976**
   £59.99 (BOT)
CVNE Imperial Gran Reserva **1975**
   £50.00 (LA)
CVNE Viña Real Gran Reserva **1975**
   £50.00 (LA) £59.99 (BOT)
López de Heredia Viña Tondonia Gran
   Reserva **1964** £53.00 (BAL) £59.22 (SAV)
   £64.00 (RIC)
Marqués de Murrieta Gran Reserva **1964**
   £50.00 (CRO)
Marqués de Riscal Reserva **1960** £60.00
   (BU)
La Rioja Alta Gran Reserva 890 **1982**
   £53.00 (POR)
La Rioja Alta Gran Reserva 890 **1981**
   £50.00 (LA)
La Rioja Alta Gran Reserva 904 **1985**
   £65.00 (LA)
La Rioja Alta Gran Reserva 904 **1970**
   £60.00 (BU)
La Rioja Alta Viña Ardanza Reserva **1985**
   £50.00 (LA)

Over £70.00

Artadi Viñas El Pison Reserva **1996**
   £84.60 (FA) £85.78 (TUR)
Marqués de Murrieta Castillo Ygay Gran
   Reserva **1970** £93.00 (RAE) £100.00
   (FRI) £115.00 (RES)
Marqués de Murrieta Castillo Ygay Gran
   Reserva **1968** £110.00 (CRO)
Marqués de Murrieta Castillo Ygay Gran
   Reserva **1959** £87.54 (FA)
Marqués de Murrieta Castillo Ygay Gran
   Reserva Especial **1970** £105.00 (VIL)
   £106.90 (NO)

La Rioja Alta Gran Reserva 904 **1981**
   £85.00 (LA)
La Rioja Alta Gran Reserva 904 **1978**
   £75.00 (LA)
La Rioja Alta Gran Reserva 904 **1975**
   £85.00 (LA)

RIOJA WHITE

Under £5.00

Viña Ijalba Genoli **1999** £4.69 (WHI)
Marqués de Cáceres **2000** £4.49 (POR)
   £4.71 (COC) £4.99 (BO) £5.15 (HAH)
   £5.20 (TAN)
Marqués de Cáceres **1999** £4.41 (TUR)
   £4.64 (WHI) £4.90 (CRO) £5.49 (DI)
   £5.95 (STE)
Marqués de Cáceres **1998** £4.50 (BALL)

£5.00 → £5.99

CVNE Monopole **1998** £5.99 (WAI) £7.85
   (TAN)
Faustino V **1997** £5.99 (SAF)
Marqués de Cáceres Satinela Semi-Dulce
   1999 £5.99 (DI)

£6.00 → £7.99

Artadi Blanco **1998** £6.75 (CON)
CVNE Monopole Barrel-Fermented **1998**
   £7.99 (GW) £8.97 (BIB)
CVNE Viura **2000** £7.25 (MOR)
Bodegas Lan **1999** £6.90 (CRO)
Marqués de Cáceres Antea **1998** £6.99 (DI)
Marqués de Cáceres Antea **1997** £6.99
   (JON)
Marqués de Cáceres sin Crianza **1999**
   £6.29 (VIN)
Marqués de Murrieta **1997** £7.99 (BO)
Marqués de Murrieta Misela de Murrieta
   1993 £6.57 (NO)
Muga **1999** £6.49 (CON) £6.69 (JON) £6.80
   (GN)
Muga **1998** £6.66 (PEN)
Muga **1997** £6.15 (MOR)
Navajas **1995** £7.99 (POR)
Navajas **1994** £6.49 (MOR) £7.50 (BAC)

Please remember that
Oz Clarke's Wine Buying Guide
*is a price **guide** and not a price **list**. It is
not meant to replace up-to-date
merchants' lists.*

£8.00 → £11.99

CVNE Monopole **1997** £8.95 (BALL)
Marqués de Murrieta **1995** £11.00 (JU)
Marqués de Murrieta Capellania Reserva
  1996 £8.99 (SAF)
Marqués de Murrieta Capellania Reserva
  1995 £8.75 (WS) £8.99 (POR) £8.99 (VIL)
  £9.10 (PLA) £9.70 (LAY)
Marqués de Murrieta Reserva **1995** £8.46
  (PEN) £8.49 (MAJ)
Marqués de Murrieta Reserva **1994**
  £10.90 (CRO)
Marqués de Murrieta Reserva **1993** £8.99
  (BOT)
Marqués de Murrieta Reserva Especial
  1996 £9.50 (RAE)
Marqués de Murrieta Reserva Especial
  1995 £8.50 (FRI) £8.65 (WRJ) £8.95 (LA)
  £9.50 (FORT)
Marqués de Murrieta Reserva Especial
  1994 £8.99 (MOR)
Martinez Bujanda Conde de Valdemar
  1999 £8.20 (NI)
Martinez Bujanda Conde de Valdemar
  1997 £8.75 (CON) £9.95 (WR) £9.95 (LA)
Martinez Bujanda Conde de Valdemar
  1994 £10.43 (VIN)

£12.00 → £19.99

López de Heredia Tondonia **1985** £16.45
  (LA)
López de Heredia Tondonia Reserva
  1993 £15.50 (SAV)
Marqués de Murrieta Castillo Ygay Gran
  Reserva **1986** £19.99 (RAE) £21.95
  (BOT) £23.00 (JU)

Over £20.00

López de Heredia Tondonia Gran
  Reserva **1976** £31.00 (HIG)
Marqués de Murrieta Castillo Ygay Gran
  Reserva **1962** £60.00 (CRO)

RIOJA ROSÉ

Under £5.50

Marqués de Cáceres Rosado **2000** £5.49
  (OD)
Marqués de Cáceres Rosado **1999** £4.80
  (COC) £4.99 (POR) £6.45 (STE)

c. £7.00

Artadi Rosado **1998** £6.75 (CON)

NAVARRA RED

Under £5.00

Baso **2000** £4.50 (CRO)
Baso **1999** £4.39 (FLE) £4.80 (BEN)
Baso **1998** £4.25 (SOM)
Orvalaiz Tempranillo **1999** £4.89 (JON)
Bodegas Principe de Viana Agramont
  Tinto **1998** £4.99 (OD)

£5.00 → £6.99

Chivite Gran Feudo Crianza **1997** £5.49
  (OD) £5.56 (COC) £5.99 (DI) £7.33 (PLAY)
Chivite Gran Feudo Crianza **1996** £6.99
  (DI)
Chivite Gran Feudo Crianza **1995** £6.99
  (DI)
Chivite Gran Feudo Reserva **1996** £6.29
  (OD)
Chivite Gran Feudo Reserva **1995** £6.29
  (VIC) £6.29 (THR) £6.29 (BOT)
Guelbenzu **1998** £6.99 (BO) £6.99 (BU)
Guelbenzu Crianza **1999** £6.99 (GW)
Guelbenzu Jardin **1998** £5.74 (NO)
Castillo de Monjardin Merlot **1996** £6.05
  (SOM) £6.75 (WRI) £6.95 (LA) £6.99 (VIL)
  £7.95 (POR)
Ochoa Tempranillo Crianza **1997** £6.89
  (BO) £6.99 (UN) £6.99 (MAJ) £7.49 (POR)
  £7.50 (GW) £7.50 (BALL) £7.90 (TAN)
  £7.99 (JON) £8.75 (FORT)
Palacio de la Vega Cabernet/Tempranillo
  Crianza **1998** £5.49 (BUD)
Bodegas Principe de Viana Agramont
  Tinto **1997** £5.95 (LA)

£7.00 → £9.99

Guelbenzu Crianza **1998** £8.35 (TAN)
Ochoa Merlot Crianza **1997** £8.75 (BALL)
Ochoa Tempranillo Crianza **1998** £7.74
  (PLA) £9.75 (LAY)
Ochoa Tempranillo Crianza **1996** £8.05
  (WAT) £8.40 (GN)

Over £10.00

Chivite Colección 125 Reserva **1995**
  £13.99 (DI)
Chivite Colección 125 Reserva **1994**
  £14.95 (BER)
Guelbenzu Evo **1998** £18.50 (TAN)
Guelbenzu Lautus **1996** £24.00 (WS)
  £24.75 (NO) £29.00 (POR)
Ochoa Gran Reserva **1994** £12.95 (GN)
Ochoa Reserva **1995** £10.45 (WAT)

NAVARRA WHITE

Under £6.00

Nekeas Vega Sindoa Chardonnay **1998** £5.29 (UN) £7.25 (FORT)
Bodegas Principe de Viana Agramont Blanco **1999** £5.95 (LA)

c. £10.00

Ochoa Vino Dulce de Moscatel 50cl **1999** £9.91 (STA)
Ochoa Vino Dulce de Moscatel 50cl **1998** £10.50 (LA)

OTHER SPANISH RED

Under £4.00

Elegido, Vino de Mesa **1998** £3.20 (SOM)
Vicente Gandia Castillo de Liria, Valencia **Non-vintage** £3.39 (UN) £3.49 (BOT)
Bodegas Inviosa, Lar de Barros Tempranillo **1999** £3.99 (SOM) £4.75 (SAV) £4.80 (TAN)
Los Llanos Señorio de los Llanos Reserva, Valdepeñas **1996** £3.99 (TES) £4.99 (VIL) £5.45 (LA) £5.73 (HIC)
Vitorianas Don Darias, Vino de Mesa **Non-vintage** £3.49 (TES) £3.49 (ASD) £3.79 (SAF) £3.89 (UN)

£4.00 → £4.99

Frutos Villar Conde Ansurez, Cigales **1998** £4.99 (VIL)
Los Llanos Señorio de los Llanos Gran Reserva, Valdepeñas **1995** £4.95 (JU)
Los Llanos Señorio de los Llanos Reserva, Valdepeñas **1995** £4.99 (POR)
Los Llanos Señorio de los Llanos, Valdepeñas **1997** £4.49 (VIL) £4.95 (LA)
Los Llanos Señorio de los Llanos, Valdepeñas **1996** £4.99 (JON)
Viña Montana, Yecla **1999** £4.99 (TES)
Bodegas Piqueras Marius Tinto Reserva, Almansa **1995** £4.49 (POR) £4.49 (BO) £4.99 (JON) £5.20 (TAN)
Felix Solis Viña Albali Gran Reserva, Valdepeñas **1993** £4.95 (MORR) £5.69 (BO) £5.84 (ASD) £5.99 (BUD)
Felix Solis Viña Albali Reserva, Valdepeñas **1995** £4.49 (BUD) £4.49 (VIC) £4.49 (THR) £4.49 (WR) £4.99 (UN)
★ Viñedos del Jalon Poema Garnacha Viñas Viejas, Calatayud **1999** £4.99 (MOR)

£5.00 → £5.99

Abadia Retuerta Primicia, Vina de Mesa **1999** £5.69 (JON) £5.99 (BAL) £6.95 (RES)
Abadia Retuerta Primicia, Vina de Mesa **1998** £5.99 (DI)
Frutos Villar Conde Ansurez, Cigales **1999** £5.75 (LA)
Los Llanos Pata Negra Gran Reserva, Valdepeñas **1991** £5.50 (SOM) £6.45 (JU) £6.49 (VIL) £6.50 (CRO) £6.50 (LA) £6.99 (POR) £7.45 (BEN) £7.65 (WRI)
Los Llanos Señorio de los Llanos Gran Reserva, Valdepeñas **1994** £5.49 (MAJ) £5.99 (VIL) £6.25 (LA)
Marques de Velilla, Ribera del Duero **1999** £5.99 (MOR)
Palacio de León, Vino de Mesa **1998** £5.20 (LAY)
San Valero Monte Ducay, Cariñena **1995** £5.99 (JON)
Torres Coronas, Penedès **1998** £5.99 (TES) £5.99 (DI) £6.60 (LA) £6.66 (BY) £6.95 (BALL)
Torres Coronas, Penedès **1996** £5.99 (SAF)
Torres Sangre de Toro, Penedès **1999** £5.29 (MORR) £5.49 (ASD) £5.69 (DI) £6.30 (BY)
Torres Sangre de Toro, Penedès **1998** £5.49 (TES) £5.82 (WHI) £6.25 (LA) £6.95 (BALL)
Torres Sangre de Toro, Penedès **1997** £5.86 (PEN)
Viñas del Vero Cabernet Sauvignon, Somontano **1998** £5.99 (UN) £7.95 (BALL)

£6.00 → £7.99

Abadia Retuerta Rivola, Vina de Mesa **1998** £7.99 (DI) £7.99 (BAL) £8.95 (RES)
Abadia Retuerta Rivola, Vina de Mesa **1997** £7.49 (BOT)
Enate Crianza, Somontano **1996** £7.20 (CRO)
Fariña Gran Colegiata Reserva, Toro **1994** £7.99 (DI)
Frutos Villar Miralmonte Crianza, Toro **1997** £7.95 (LA) £7.99 (VIL)
Los Llanos Pata Negra Gran Reserva, Valdepeñas **1992** £6.45 (JU) £7.99 (CB)
Masía Barril Típico, Priorat **1991** £7.49 (MOR) £10.95 (TAN)
Mont Marçal Cabernet Sauvignon, Penedès **1995** £6.25 (CON)
Raïmat Abadia, Costers del Segre **1998** £6.99 (OD)

Cellers Santamaria Gran Recosind, Ampurdan Costa Brava **1993** £7.25 (LA) £7.50 (RAE)

Cellers Scala Dei Crianza, Priorat **1993** £6.99 (MOR)

★ Bodegas Toresanas Deheso Gago, Toro **1999** £6.50 (AD)

Torres Atrium, Penedès **1999** £6.99 (OD) £6.99 (DI)

Torres Atrium, Penedès **1998** £7.25 (LA)

Torres Gran Coronas Reserva, Penedès **1997** £7.99 (DI) £8.99 (WR)

Torres Gran Sangre de Toro, Penedès **1998** £6.99 (VIC) £6.99 (THR) £6.99 (BOT) £6.99 (WR) £6.99 (DI)

Torres Gran Sangre de Toro, Penedès **1997** £6.99 (UN) £6.99 (DI) £7.41 (COC)

Torres Gran Sangre de Toro, Penedès **1995** £7.58 (PEN)

£8.00 → £9.99

Callejo, Ribera del Duero **1996** £9.59 (JON)

Celler de Capçanes Costers de Gravet, Tarragona **1998** £9.95 (BAL) £10.40 (GAU) £11.90 (CRO)

Condado de Haza, Ribera del Duero **1998** £9.85 (TAN) £10.95 (GAU) £11.50 (ARM) £11.95 (BAL) £12.30 (NI)

Bodegas Inviosa, Lar de Lares Gran Reserva, Ribera del Guadiana **1994** £8.85 (TAN)

Jean León Cabernet Sauvignon Reserva, Penedès **1991** £9.78 (PEN) £11.95 (DI)

Marqués de Griñon Dominio de Valdepusa Cabernet Sauvignon, Vino de Mesa **1996** £9.99 (UN)

Protos, Ribera del Duero **1998** £8.99 (COC)

Torres Gran Coronas Reserva, Penedès **1996** £9.75 (PEN) £9.95 (STA) £9.95 (LA) £10.30 (BY) £10.59 (JON)

£10.00 → £19.99

Alión Reserva, Ribera del Duero **1996** £17.95 (DI)

Alión, Ribera del Duero **1997** £19.79 (YOU)

Alión, Ribera del Duero **1996** £19.50 (BEN) £20.95 (FA) £21.50 (JER)

Ismael Arroyo Val Sotillo Crianza, Ribera del Duero **1997** £16.50 (JU)

Ismael Arroyo Val Sotillo Crianza, Ribera del Duero **1996** £15.57 (BODX) £17.49 (YOU)

Celler de Capçanes Costers de Gravet, Tarragona **1999** £10.50 (NI)

Cillar de Silos Crianza, Ribero del Duero **1995** £14.80 (CRO)

Cillar de Silos Reserva, Ribero del Duero **1995** £19.40 (CRO)

Condado de Haza, Ribera del Duero **1997** £10.99 (NI) £12.99 (MOR)

Condado de Haza, Ribera del Duero **1996** £10.95 (VA) £11.90 (CRO)

Costers del Siurana Miserere, Priorat **1997** £19.99 (DI) £21.99 (VIL) £22.50 (LA)

Gutiérrez de la Vega Rojo y Negro, Alicante **1996** £11.95 (DI)

Gutiérrez de la Vega Viña Ulises, Alicante **1997** £12.95 (DI)

Hacienda Monasterio Crianza, Ribera del Duero **1997** £19.04 (CB)

Marqués de Griñon Dominio de Valdepusa Petit Verdot, Vino de Mesa **1998** £15.90 (CRO)

Marqués de Griñon Dominio de Valdepusa Petit Verdot, Vino de Mesa **1997** £12.49 (YOU)

Marqués de Griñon Dominio de Valdepusa Syrah, Vino de Mesa **1998** £10.99 (WR) £14.90 (CRO)

Marqués de Griñon Dominio de Valdepusa Syrah, Vino de Mesa **1997** £11.99 (YOU)

Marques de Velilla Monte Villalobon, Ribera del Duero **1996** £19.99 (MOR)

Masía Barril Típico, Priorat **1993** £10.75 (LA)

Matarromera Crianza, Ribera del Duero **1996** £14.50 (CRO)

Mauro Crianza, Ribera del Duero **1998** £16.00 (ARM)

Mauro Crianza, Ribera del Duero **1995** £11.95 (LEA)

Mauro, Vino de Mesa **1996** £13.95 (GAU)

Pago de Carraovejas Crianza, Ribera del Duero **1998** £15.99 (POR)

Pago de Carraovejas Crianza, Ribera del Duero **1997** £13.99 (MOR) £14.50 (GW) £14.95 (BAL)

Alvaro Palacios Les Terrasses, Priorat **1998** £11.99 (CB) £19.99 (WR)

Alvaro Palacios Les Terrasses, Priorat **1997** £10.38 (FA) £12.95 (BU) £14.50 (CRO)

Stars (★) indicate wines selected by Oz Clarke in the Best Buys section which begins on page 8.

Pesquera Crianza, Ribera del Duero **1998**
£11.50 (TAN) £12.63 (FA) £13.95 (NI)
£14.79 (YOU) £14.99 (OD)

Pesquera Crianza, Ribera del Duero **1997**
£11.20 (TAN) £12.63 (FA) £13.95 (BAL)
£14.08 (ARM) £16.99 (MOR) £17.95 (VA)

Protos Crianza, Ribera del Duero **1996**
£15.99 (COC)

Cellers Santamaria Gran Recosind Gran
Reserva, Ampurdan Costa Brava **1988**
£10.99 (RAE)

Cellers Scala Dei Negre, Priorat **1991**
£19.95 (POR)

Señorio de Nava Crianza, Ribera del
Duero **1996** £10.45 (LAY)

Torres Gran Coronas Reserva, Penedès
1995 £11.33 (VIN) £12.99 (GN)

Torres Mas Borras Pinot Noir, Penedès
1998 £13.69 (MOR)

Torres Mas la Plana, Penedès **1995**
£18.60 (TAN) £18.99 (DI) £19.75 (LA)
£19.99 (POR) £20.59 (JON) £20.95 (GN)
£21.33 (BY)

Torres Mas la Plana, Penedès **1994**
£19.62 (PEN) £19.99 (MOR) £21.50 (STA)
£27.39 (PLAY)

Bodegas Valduero Crianza, Ribera del
Duero **1997** £10.00 (JER)

Bodegas Valduero Reserva, Ribera del
Duero **1991** £13.95 (JU)

£20.00 → £29.99

Abadia Retuerta Cuvée Campanario, Vina
de Mesa **1996** £24.50 (BAL) £25.95 (DI)

Abadia Retuerta Cuvée Palomar, Vina de
Mesa **1996** £23.95 (DI)

Alión, Ribera del Duero **1995** £20.95 (FA)

Clos Mogador, Priorat **1997** £20.00 (WS)

Clos Mogador, Priorat **1995** £25.00 (MOR)

Costers del Siurana Clos de l'Obac,
Priorat **1997** £23.95 (DI) £25.99 (VIL)
£26.50 (LA) £28.99 (MOR) £29.95 (TAN)

Costers del Siurana Clos de l'Obac,
Priorat **1996** £25.75 (LA) £27.99 (YOU)
£37.00 (JU)

Costers del Siurana Miserere, Priorat
1996 £22.50 (LA) £28.00 (JU)

Costers del Siurana Miserere, Priorat
1995 £23.99 (YOU) £24.50 (LA) £25.50
(FORT) £28.50 (CRO)

Costers del Siurana Miserere, Priorat
1994 £24.06 (NO)

Joset Maria Fuentes Gran Clos, Priorat
1997 £22.00 (FORT) £27.50 (BAL) £28.00
(NI)

Joset Maria Fuentes Gran Clos, Priorat
1996 £25.50 (BAL)

Hacienda Monasterio Crianza, Ribera del
Duero **1996** £25.00 (CRO)

Mauro Vendimia Seleccionada, Vino de
Mesa **1995** £29.17 (ARM)

Alvaro Palacios Finca Dofi, Priorat **1996**
£28.30 (FA) £39.60 (MOR) £42.00 (DI)
£46.95 (TAN) £59.95 (WR)

Pesquera Reserva, Ribera del Duero
1997 £24.50 (NI)

Pesquera Reserva, Ribera del Duero
1995 £22.91 (FA) £25.00 (ARM) £26.00
(CRO) £35.00 (MOR)

Protos Reserva, Ribera del Duero **1996**
£21.99 (COC)

Rotllan Torra Amadis, Priorat **1996**
£23.95 (POR)

Rotllan Torra Amadis, Priorat **1995**
£21.50 (MOR)

Torres Mas la Plana, Penedès **1993**
£22.00 (WRI)

Torres Mas la Plana, Penedès **1990**
£25.00 (LA)

£30.00 → £49.99

Condado de Haza Alenza, Ribera del
Duero **1997** £46.25 (NI)

Condado de Haza Alenza, Ribera del
Duero **1996** £44.06 (TUR) £45.83 (ARM)
£49.50 (BAL)

Costers del Siurana Dolç de l'Obac,
Priorat **1997** £36.95 (DI) £39.00 (LA)

Costers del Siurana Dolç de l'Obac,
Priorat **1996** £36.50 (LA) £43.99 (YOU)

Mauro Vendimia Selecciónada, Vino de
Mesa **1996** £38.33 (ARM)

Alvaro Palacios Finca Dofi, Priorat **1998**
£39.36 (CB)

Alvaro Palacios Finca Dofi, Priorat **1997**
£35.00 (FORT) £59.95 (WR)

Alvaro Palacios Finca Dofi, Priorat **1994**
£41.74 (NO) £59.00 (CRO) £59.95 (BOT)

Pesquera Crianza, Ribera del Duero **1995**
£39.22 (BY)

Pesquera Gran Reserva, Ribera del Duero
  1992 £38.58 (FA)
Pesquera Gran Reserva, Ribera del Duero
  1990 £45.43 (FA)
Pesquera Reserva, Ribera del Duero
  1986 £49.00 (CRO)
Rotllan Torra Tirant, Priorat **1997** £35.00
  (MOR)
Torres Gran Muralles, Penedès **1997**
  £35.95 (DI) £38.50 (POR) £41.00 (YOU)
Torres Gran Muralles, Penedès **1996**
  £35.95 (DI) £38.50 (POR) £39.50 (LA)
  £39.95 (PEN) £45.00 (MOR)
Torres Mas la Plana, Penedès **1983**
  £32.00 (CRO) £45.00 (LA)
Vega Sicilia Valbuena 5th year, Ribera del
  Duero **1995** £42.00 (DI) £42.50 (FA)
Vega Sicilia Valbuena 5th year, Ribera del
  Duero **1994** £31.00 (GN) £40.00 (MOR)
Vega Sicilia Valbuena, Ribera del Duero
  Non-vintage £35.00 (RIC)
Vega Sicilia Valbuena, Ribera del Duero
  1996 £43.00 (MV) £45.00 (YOU)
Vega Sicilia Valbuena, Ribera del Duero
  1995 £42.50 (BU) £44.00 (FORT) £49.50
  (LEA)
Vega Sicilia Valbuena, Ribera del Duero
  1994 £43.00 (LA)

£50.00 → £99.99

Condado de Haza Alenza, Ribera del
  Duero **1995** £52.88 (TUR) £54.17 (ARM)
  £85.00 (DI)
Costers del Siurana Dolç de l'Obac,
  Priorat **1994** £53.89 (NO)
Pesquera Gran Reserva, Ribera del Duero
  1997 £54.80 (NI)
Pesquera Gran Reserva, Ribera del Duero
  1995 £59.00 (YOU)
Pesquera Janus, Ribero del Duero **1994**
  £84.99 (NO)
Pesquera Janus, Ribero del Duero **1991**
  £64.63 (FA)
Pesquera Reserva, Ribera del Duero
  1985 £75.00 (BU)
Vega Sicilia Unico, Ribera del Duero **1990**
  £92.00 (LA) £92.50 (POR) £99.00 (YOU)
  £100.00 (MV) £117.50 (TUR) £118.87
  (FA)
Vega Sicilia Unico, Ribera del Duero **1981**
  £96.00 (LA) £102.50 (TAN) £120.00 (VA)
  £120.00 (GN) £122.75 (STA) £135.13
  (TUR) £140.00 (MOR)
Vega Sicilia Valbuena 5th year, Ribera del
  Duero **1984** £57.50 (BU)

£100.00 → £124.99

Vega Sicilia Reserva Especial, Ribera del
  Duero **Non-vintage** £110.00 (YOU)
  £114.00 (FA)
Vega Sicilia Unico, Ribera del Duero **1982**
  £117.50 (FA) £165.00 (BU)

Over £125.00

Dominio de Pingus, Ribera del Duero
  1999 £200.00 (FORT) £260.85 (BODX)
Dominio de Pingus, Ribera del Duero
  1998 £216.79 (BODX)
Dominio de Pingus, Ribera del Duero
  1996 £280.43 (FA) £365.00 (CRO)
Alvaro Palacios l'Ermita, Priorat **1998**
  £151.81 (CB)
Alvaro Palacios l'Ermita, Priorat **1996**
  £145.00 (DI) £147.99 (MOR)
Alvaro Palacios l'Ermita, Priorat **1994**
  £154.47 (NO)
Alvaro Palacios l'Ermita, Priorat **1993**
  £136.50 (FA)
Vega Sicilia Unico, Ribera del Duero **1970**
  £236.37 (FA)
Vega Sicilia Unico, Ribera del Duero **1968**
  £211.50 (FA) £246.75 (TUR)
Vega Sicilia Unico, Ribera del Duero **1962**
  £150.00 (LA) £205.63 (TUR) £205.63 (FA)

OTHER SPANISH WHITE

Under £4.00

★ Bodessa Moscatel de Valencia, **1999**
  £3.99 (MAR)
Vicente Gandia Castillo de Liria Moscatel,
  Valencia **Non-vintage** £3.99 (UN)
  £4.25 (TAN)
Vicente Gandia Castillo de Liria, Valencia
  Non-vintage £3.39 (UN)
Pazo Ribeiro, Ribeiro **2000** £3.70 (SOM)
Tierra Seca, Penedès **1999** £3.95 (WS)

£4.00 → £4.99

Basa, Rueda **2000** £4.50 (CRO)
Basa, Rueda **1999** £4.25 (SOM) £4.39 (FLE)
  £4.80 (BEN)
Basa, Rueda **1998** £4.39 (FLE)
Castilla la Vieja Palacio de Bornos, Rueda
  2000 £4.40 (SOM) £4.79 (BO) £6.29 (MOR)
Marqués de Alella Clasico, Alella **1999**
  £4.95 (WS) £5.83 (NO) £5.90 (BAC)
  £5.99 (DI) £5.99 (MOR) £6.49 (POR)
  £7.85 (LA)

Pazo Ribeiro, Ribeiro **1999** £4.99 (MOR)

Torres San Valentin, Penedès **1999** £4.99 (DI)

Torres San Valentin, Penedès **1998** £4.95 (LA)

Torres Viña Esmeralda, Penedès **1998** £4.99 (DI) £5.43 (NO) £5.64 (PEN)

Torres Viña Sol, Penedès **2000** £4.34 (WHI) £4.49 (BO) £4.49 (BOT) £4.49 (WAI) £4.49 (MORR) £4.59 (VIC) £4.59 (THR) £4.59 (WR) £4.99 (DI)

Torres Viña Sol, Penedès **1999** £4.49 (TES) £4.58 (COC) £4.95 (LA) £4.99 (UN) £4.99 (DI) £5.06 (BY) £5.45 (STE) £5.85 (VIN) £5.99 (MOR)

Viñas del Vero Chardonnay, Somontano **1998** £4.99 (UN) £7.99 (GN)

£5.00 → £5.99

Alvarez y Diez Mantel Blanco, Rueda **1999** £5.99 (BO) £6.25 (STE) £6.25 (BALL)

Alvarez y Diez Mantel Blanco, Rueda **1998** £5.99 (DI)

Castilla la Vieja Palacio de Bornos, Rueda **1999** £5.59 (JON)

Bodegas Inviosa Lar de Barros Blanco **1999** £5.60 (CRO)

Marqués de Riscal, Rueda **2000** £5.49 (MAJ)

Marqués de Riscal, Rueda **1999** £5.49 (WR) £6.57 (PLA) £6.95 (LA)

Marqués de Riscal Sauvignon, Rueda **1999** £5.99 (UN)

Masía Bach Extrísimo Seco, Penedès **2000** £5.66 (MOR)

Cellers Scala Dei Blanc, Priorat **1996** £5.49 (MOR)

Torres Viña Esmeralda, Penedès **1999** £5.28 (WHI) £5.29 (UN) £5.49 (BO) £5.49 (VIC) £5.49 (THR) £5.49 (BOT) £5.49 (WR) £5.49 (DI) £5.75 (TAN) £5.89 (JON) £5.95 (STA) £5.95 (LA) £5.95 (AME) £6.03 (BY) £6.45 (STE) £6.95 (BALL) £6.99 (MOR)

Bodegas Valduero Azumbre Blanco, Ribera del Duero **1996** £5.45 (JU)

£6.00 → £9.99

Castilla la Vieja Palacio de Bornos, Rueda **1997** £6.35 (GN)

Martin Códax Albariño, Rias Baixas **2000** £8.50 (WRI) £8.79 (JON)

Lagar de Fornelos Lagar de Cervera, Rías Baixas **2000** £9.40 (TAN)

Lagar de Fornelos Lagar de Cervera, Rías Baixas **1999** £7.65 (SOM) £8.95 (LA) £8.99 (VIL) £9.30 (STA) £10.50 (WRI)

Marqués de Alella Clasico, Alella **Non-vintage** £7.60 (RIC)

Marqués de Alella Clasico, Alella **1998** £7.90 (CRO)

Marqués de Riscal Sauvignon, Rueda **1998** £7.95 (LA)

Marqués de Riscal Superior, Rueda **1999** £6.55 (GN)

Mont Marçal Chardonnay, Penedès **1997** £6.25 (CON)

Pazo de Señorans Albariño, Rias Baixas **1999** £8.99 (BO)

Pazo de Señorans Albariño, Rias Baixas **1998** £9.85 (NI)

Torres Fransola, Penedès **1999** £9.99 (DI) £10.49 (POR) £10.95 (STA)

Torres Gran Viña Sol, Penedès **2000** £6.05 (WHI)

Torres Gran Viña Sol, Penedès **1999** £6.05 (WHI) £6.29 (VIC) £6.29 (THR) £6.29 (BOT) £6.29 (WR) £6.49 (DI) £6.79 (JON) £6.82 (BY) £6.95 (HAH) £7.25 (BALL) £8.46 (TW)

Torres Gran Viña Sol, Penedès **1998** £6.65 (LA) £6.75 (WRI) £6.75 (GN)

Torres Moscatel Malvasia de Oro, Penedès **Non-vintage** £7.22 (NO)

Txomin Etxaniz, Getariako Txakolina **1998** £9.94 (NO) £11.25 (MOR)

Viñas del Vero Barrel-Fermented Chardonnay, Somontano **1998** £6.99 (OD)

Viñas del Vero Chardonnay, Somontano **1999** £6.95 (BALL)

Viñas del Vero Gewürztraminer, Somontano **1999** £9.35 (PLA)

£10.00 → £14.99

Belondrade y Lurton, Rueda **1998** £12.99 (YOU)

Belondrade y Lurton, Rueda **1997** £11.70 (BAC)

Belondrade y Lurton, Rueda **1996** £10.50 (BALL)

Martin Códax Organistrum, Rias Baixas **1998** £10.95 (DI)

Jean León Chardonnay, Penedès **1998** £10.99 (MOR)

Jean León Chardonnay, Penedès **1997** £10.18 (PEN)

A key to name abbreviations is available on page 7.

Hermanos Lurton Rueda, Rueda **1999**
£14.49 (BIB)

Pazo de Barrantes Albariño, Rias Baixas
1999 £10.99 (RAE) £11.71 (NO)

Pazo de Barrantes Albariño, Rias Baixas
1998 £12.50 (FORT)

Pazo de Señorans Albariño, Rias Baixas
2000 £10.40 (TAN)

Cellers Puig & Roca, Augustus Chardonnay,
Penedès **1998** £11.99 (DI)

Cellers Puig & Roca, Augustus Chardonnay,
Penedès **1997** £10.95 (WS)

Cellers Puig & Roca, Augustus Chardonnay,
Penedès **1996** £13.25 (MOR)

Torres Fransola, Penedès **1998** £10.50
(LA) £10.99 (MOR)

Over £15.00

Pazo de Señorans Selección de Anada,
Rias Baixas **1996** £21.90 (GAU)

Scholtz Solera 1885, Málaga **Non-
vintage** £24.00 (CRO)

Torres Milmanda Chardonnay, Penedès
1998 £17.50 (LA) £17.99 (DI) £17.99
(MOR) £17.99 (YOU)

OTHER SPANISH ROSÉ

Under £5.00

Chivite Gran Feudo, Navarra **2000** £4.49
(OD)

Chivite Gran Feudo, Navarra **1999** £4.99
(DI)

Torres de Casta, Penedès **1999** £4.99 (DI)

£5.00 → £5.99

Ochoa Rosado, Navarra **1999** £5.99 (UN)
£6.50 (BALL) £7.25 (FORT)

Torres de Casta, Penedès **1998** £5.75 (LA)

Over £6.00

Masía Bach Rosado, Penedès **2000** £6.70
(MOR)

Ochoa Rosado, Navarra **1998** £6.99 (GN)

SPANISH SPARKLING

Under £6.00

Condé de Caralt Brut, Cava **Non-
vintage** £5.99 (SAF) £6.54 (GW) £6.69
(WAI)

Marqués de Monistrol Brut, Cava **Non-
vintage** £5.39 (WHI)

Palau Brut, Cava **Non-vintage** £4.99 (BO)
£5.49 (CON)

Palau Rosé **Non-vintage** £5.49 (CON)

Sumarroca Extra Brut, Cava **1995** £5.95
(WS)

£6.00 → £6.99

Castellblanch Brut Zero, Cava **Non-
vintage** £6.79 (JON)

Castellblanch Cristal Seco, Cava **Non-
vintage** £6.45 (GN) £6.56 (BIB)

Castellblanch Rosado **Non-vintage**
£6.66 (BIB)

Freixenet Brut Rosé, Cava **Non-vintage**
£6.99 (SAF) £7.70 (WHI)

Freixenet Carta Nevada, Cava **Non-
vintage** £6.49 (BO)

Freixenet Cordon Negro Brut, Cava
Non-vintage £6.99 (UN) £6.99 (WAI)
£6.99 (SAF) £7.23 (PLA) £7.39 (BO) £7.49
(MAJ) £7.49 (VIC) £7.49 (THR) £7.49 (BOT)
£7.49 (WR) £7.49 (ASD) £7.70 (WHI)

Bodegas Inviosa Bonaval Brut, Cava **Non-
vintage** £6.50 (FLE)

Raventos I Blanc Cava l'Hereau **Non-
vintage** £6.65 (WAT)

Segura Viudas Brut Reserva, Cava **Non-
vintage** £6.49 (OD) £6.75 (DI)

Torre del Gall Brut, Cava **1994** £6.90 (SOM)

£7.00 → £7.99

Condé de Caralt Blanc de Blancs, Cava
Non-vintage £7.95 (BALL)

Juvé y Camps Brut, Cava **1998** £7.45
(STA) £8.50 (LA) £10.15 (JER)

Juvé y Camps Brut, Cava **1997** £7.99 (VIL)
£8.50 (LA)

Parxet Extra Brut Nature, Cava **Non-
vintage** £7.95 (FORT)

Segura Viudas Brut, Cava **1996** £7.99 (OD)

£8.00 → £9.99

Freixenet Brut Nature, Cava **1997** £8.99
(MAJ)

Juvé y Camps Reserva de la Familia, Cava
1996 £9.99 (VIL) £10.95 (LA) £13.95
(FORT)

Raventos I Blanc Cava Brut Reserva **1998**
£8.25 (WAT)

Over £10.00

Juvé y Camps Reserva de la Familia, Cava
1997 £10.95 (LA)

Raventos I Blanc Cava Gran Reserva
Personal MRN **1992** £14.55 (WAT)

SHERRY PRICES

DRY

Under £4.00

Manzanilla La Gitana, Hidalgo ½ bottle
£3.15 (SOM) £3.25 (TAN) £3.35 (BALL)
£3.49 (VIL) £3.75 (LA) £3.80 (JER)

£4.00 → £4.99

Amontillado Hidalgo £4.99 (MAJ) £5.95 (NI)
Fino Barbadillo £4.99 (CON) £5.59 (PLAY)
£5.80 (HIG) £5.97 (LLO)
Fino Hidalgo £4.92 (PLA) £4.99 (MAJ) £5.35
(HAH) £6.99 (VIL)
Fino Puerto, Lustau £4.50 (SOM) £7.99
(GW) £8.95 (DI) £8.99 (BEN) £8.99 (AME)
£8.99 (CON) £9.20 (MV) £9.25 (FORT)
★ Fino The Society's £4.25 (WS)
Fino Valdespino £4.95 (LEA) £5.00 (WAT)
Oloroso Seco, Barbadillo £4.99 (CON)
£5.46 (COC) £5.65 (GN) £6.41 (HIC)

£5.00 → £6.99

Amontillado Conquinero, Osborne £6.99
(OD)
Amontillado de Sanlúcar, Barbadillo £6.09
(CB) £6.41 (HIC) £7.30 (JER)
Amontillado Napoleon, Hidalgo £6.70 (SOM)
£7.44 (SAV) £7.99 (MAJ) £7.99 (VIL) £8.95
(LA) £9.20 (NI) £9.50 (BEN) £9.99 (TW)
Croft Delicado £6.49 (WAI) £6.55 (SAF)
Elegante, González Byass £5.89 (COC)
£5.89 (TES) £5.89 (THR) £5.89 (WAI) £5.99
(UN) £5.99 (OD) £5.99 (VIL) £6.19 (SAF)
Fino de Sanlúcar, Barbadillo £5.49 (AME)
£5.65 (GN) £7.30 (JER)
Harvey's Dune £5.99 (BOT) £5.99 (WR)
La Ina, Domecq £6.91 (COC) £7.21 (WAT)
£7.49 (VIL) £7.95 (WRI) £8.25 (FORT)
£8.30 (HAH) £9.90 (JU)
Manzanilla Deliciosa, Valdespino £6.95 (LEA)
Manzanilla La Gitana, Hidalgo £5.99 (MAJ)
£5.99 (WAI) £6.35 (HAH) £6.46 (SAV)
£7.60 (NI) £7.75 (TW)
Manzanilla Pasada Solear, Barbadillo £6.25
(CON) £7.23 (COC) £8.96 (HIC)
Manzanilla de Sanlúcar, Barbadillo £5.49
(AME) £5.49 (OD) £5.49 (MOR) £5.65
(GN) £5.80 (HIG) £5.97 (LLO) £6.41 (HIC)
Palo Cortado de Jerez Vides, Lustau ½
bottle £5.95 (GN) £8.95 (FORT) £8.99
(AME)

£7.00 → £8.99

Amontillado Los Arcos, Lustau £7.99
(GW) £8.95 (DI) £9.50 (FORT) £9.60 (WRI)
£9.75 (MOR)
Fino Don Zoilo £7.35 (COC)
Fino Inocente, Valdespino £7.43 (WAT)
£7.95 (LEA)
Fino San Patricio, Garvey £7.45 (COC)
Manzanilla La Guita, Hidalgo £7.50 (STA)
Manzanilla Papirusa, Lustau £8.95 (DI)
£9.95 (FORT)
Manzanilla Pasada, Hidalgo £8.99 (VIL)
£9.39 (JON) £9.75 (LA) £10.51 (TW)
Manzanilla La Pastrana, Hidalgo £7.85
(SOM) £7.95 (TAN) £8.99 (VIL) £9.25 (LA)
Manzanilla Solear, Barbadillo £7.00 (HIG)
£7.29 (MOR)
Oloroso Anada 1918 Solera, Lustau ½
bottle £8.95 (MAY) £8.99 (BEN) £8.99
(CON)
Oloroso Don Zoilo Old Dry £7.85 (COC)
Oloroso Dry, Lustau £8.99 (STA)
Oloroso Seco, Hidalgo £8.50 (TAN)
Palo Cortado de Jerez, Hidalgo £7.99 (VIL)
£9.60 (SAV) £10.59 (JON) £10.95 (TAN)
£13.86 (TW)
Palo Cortado del Carrascal, Valdespino
£8.49 (OD) £11.28 (WAT)
Tio Pepe González Byass £7.65 (VIN) £7.79
(TES) £7.79 (WAI) £7.89 (COC) £7.95
(PLAY) £7.99 (VIL) £8.29 (OD) £8.50 (WRI)
£8.50 (STA) £8.95 (HAH) £8.95 (FORT)
Tio Pepe Lustau £7.89 (UN)

£9.00 → £9.99

Amontillado Tio Diego, Valdespino £9.28
(WAT) £9.95 (LEA)
Fino Quinta, Osborne £9.50 (FORT)
Oloroso Dos Cortados Old Dry, Williams
& Humbert £9.91 (COC) £9.99 (UN)
Oloroso Seco Napoleon, Hidalgo £9.50
(LAY)

£10.00 → £19.99

Amontillado de Jerez Fino, Alberto
Lorente Piaget £11.70 (JU)
Fino Superior, Hidalgo £10.40 (LAY)
Oloroso Especial, Hidalgo £10.51 (TW)
Palo Cortado Cardenal, Valdespino £14.81
(WAT)
Palo Cortado Peninsula, Lustau £12.93 (CB)

Over £20.00

Amontillado del Duque, González Byass
£20.99 (COC) £21.99 (VIL) £22.00 (MOR)
£22.75 (FORT) £24.00 (LA)

Amontillado Viejo, Hidalgo £21.95 (BALL)
£23.50 (SAV) £25.00 (JU) £28.20 (TAN)
£28.75 (HAH) £36.42 (TW)

MEDIUM

Under £7.00

Amontillado Caballero, González Byass
£5.89 (TES) £5.99 (VIL)
Amontillado La Concha, González Byass
£5.89 (COC) £5.89 (VIC) £5.89 (WR) £5.89
(WAI) £5.99 (UN) £5.99 (VIL) £6.19 (SAF)
Amontillado Principe, Barbadillo £5.97 (LLO)
Amontillado Valdespino £4.79 (OD) £4.95
(LEA) £5.00 (WAT)
Croft Particular £6.49 (THR) £6.49 (BOT)
£6.49 (WAI) £6.55 (UN) £6.55 (SAF)
Dry Sack Williams & Humbert £5.49 (TES)
£6.52 (COC) £8.25 (FORT)
Harvey's Club Amontillado £5.59 (VIC)
£5.59 (THR) £5.59 (BOT) £5.59 (WR)
£5.69 (SAF) £5.84 (COC)

£7.00 → £10.99

**Amontillado del Puerto, José Luis
Gonzalez Obregon** ½ bottle £8.00 (MV)
Amontillado Lustau £7.49 (OD)
**Oloroso de Jerez Almacenista Viuda de
Antonio Borrego, Lustau** ½ bottle £8.95
(FORT)
Oloroso Solera 1842, Valdespino £9.28
(WAT) £9.49 (OD) £9.95 (LEA)

Over £13.00

Oloroso Apostoles, González Byass
£20.99 (COC) £21.38 (VIN) £24.00 (LA)
Oloroso Royal Corregidor, Sandeman
£13.75 (FORT) £17.00 (CRO)

SWEET

Under £7.00

Cream Hidalgo £5.95 (NI)
Croft Original Pale Cream £6.20 (COC)
£6.29 (VIN) £6.49 (VIC) £6.49 (THR) £6.49
(BOT) £6.49 (WR) £6.49 (WAI) £6.52 (TES)
£6.55 (UN) £6.55 (OD) £6.55 (SAF) £6.95
(JU) £6.99 (VIL) £7.10 (WRI) £7.35 (HAH)
Dark Cream, Valdespino £4.95 (LEA)
Harvey's Bristol Cream £6.25 (VIN) £6.48
(TES) £6.49 (VIC) £6.49 (THR) £6.49 (BOT)
£6.49 (WR) £6.49 (WAI) £6.55 (SAF)
£6.59 (UN) £6.59 (BO) £6.69 (OD) £6.94
(COC) £6.99 (VIL) £8.07 (PLAY) £8.35
(WRI) £8.95 (HAH) £8.95 (FORT)
Sanlúcar Cream, Barbadillo £6.41 (HIC)

£7.00 → £9.99

Croft Original Pale Cream 1 litre £8.29 (UN)
Harvey's Bristol Cream 1 litre £7.99 (VIC)
£7.99 (THR) £7.99 (BOT) £7.99 (WR)
£8.29 (UN) £8.29 (WAI) £8.35 (SAF)
Old East India, Lustau £9.99 (UN) £9.99
(GW) £9.99 (DI) £10.99 (BEN) £10.99
(BO) £10.99 (BU) £10.99 (CON) £11.00
(MV) £11.50 (FORT) £11.55 (MOR)
Oloroso Old Jerez Cream, Valdespino
£7.60 (LEA)
Pedro Ximénez, Barbadillo £7.49 (MOR)
£8.95 (CON) £9.50 (HIG)
**Pedro Ximénez Solera Superior,
Valdespino** £8.23 (WAT) £8.49 (OD)
£8.95 (LEA)
Pedro Ximénez Viejo, Hidalgo £8.50
(TAN) £8.99 (MAJ) £11.28 (TW)
Pedro Ximénez Viejo Napoleon, Hidalgo
£8.99 (VIL) £9.75 (LA)

£10.00 → £11.99

Moscatel Emilin, Lustau £10.99 (DI) £11.80
(MV) £12.99 (CON)
Oloroso Matusalem, González Byass
£10.25 (WAI) £20.99 (COC) £21.37 (VIN)
£21.99 (VIL) £22.00 (MOR) £22.95 (FORT)
£24.00 (LA)
Pedro Ximénez San Emilio, Lustau £10.99
(DI) £11.80 (MV) £11.99 (BEN) £11.99
(BO) £11.99 (CON)

Over £20.00

Pedro Ximénez Noé, González Byass
£21.99 (VIL) £22.00 (MOR) £22.75 (FORT)
Solera India, Osborne £30.00 (FORT)

UNITED STATES

**America's national grape is enjoying a boom. Can we afford to miss it?
Can we afford it, period?**

You want to know which Californian wines inspire the most passion in California? Not top Cabernets like Martha's Vineyard; not even new cult wines like Screaming Eagle. No, it's Zinfandel. The US Senate has touchingly declared it a national treasure and, less touchingly, Italian producers of Primitivo (the same grape, dammit) are forbidden to export their wines to the US under the name of Zin.

Zinfandel fans have a lot in common with trainspotters or birdwatchers. They want rare Zins, and they'll go anywhere, pay anything, to get them. One company, Rosenblum, produces no fewer than 26 different Zins, all from different vineyards or different parcels of vines. Its winemaker, Jeff Cohn, also releases wines under his own label, JC Cellars: he may make only 75 cases of some wines. That's how Zin watchers like it.

And they buy to drink, not to collect. (Just as well, since Zin does not usually improve much in bottle.) Do they drink them with food? It's hard to imagine, since the fashion is for monstrous alcohol levels of 16 or 17%. That sort of thing is no fun with food. But there's something terrifically macho about it – mine's bigger than yours.

And the prices? Equally monstrous. A top cult Zin can set you back around $70 a bottle. Most good Zins here in Britain cost around £20-plus – and these are not the rarest wines, which never see a shop shelf. Are they worth it? If you're a Zin freak, yes. But if you're going to compare them with what's on offer from the rest of the world – well, that's another matter.

GRAPE VARIETIES

BARBERA (red) The most successful Italian variety in California. It's been there for donkey's years as a workhorse grape, and is now beginning a revival as a quality number. Look for *Bonny Doon, La Famiglia di Robert Mondavi, Il Podere dell' Olivos, Preston Vineyards, Redwood* and *Sebastiani*.

CABERNET SAUVIGNON (red) Still the top grape for premium California reds. Napa Cabernet is the classic: rich, tannic yet seductive at a young age. For the top wines, complexity and finesse are the new watchwords, especially for wines from hillside vineyards (as opposed to the flat floor of the Napa). Washington State Cab continues to improve as the vines age, yielding more concentration. For cellaring (never as long as for the equivalent quality Bordeaux), try: *Arrowood, Beaulieu Vineyards Georges de Latour Private Reserve, Beringer Reserve, Bernardus, Buena Vista, Burgess, Cain, Carmenet Moon Mountain, Caymus Special Selection, Chimney Rock, Clos du Val, Conn Creek, Cuvaison, Dalla Valle, Diamond Creek, Dominus, Dunn, Flora Springs Hillside Reserve, Franciscan, Grgich Hills, Groth, Heitz Bella Oaks, Hess Collection, Kenwood Artist Series, La Jota, Laurel Glen, Louis M Martini, Robert Mondavi Reserve* and *Opus One, Chateau Montelena, Newton, Niebaum-Coppola, Raymond Private Reserve, Ridge Monte Bello, Sequoia Grove, Shafer Hillside Select, Silver Oak, Spottswoode, Stag's Leap Cask 23, Sterling Vineyards Diamond Mountain Ranch, Stonestreet* (California); *Andrew Will, Chateau Ste Michelle, Columbia, Hogue Cellars, Quilceda Creek* (Washington). For light Cabernet, try: *Beringer, Chateau Souverain, Clos du Bois, Cosentino, Fetzer, Estancia, Foppiano, Kendall-Jackson* (California); *Columbia Crest* (Washington).

CHARDONNAY (white) Top wines are becoming more subtle and Burgundian. Many of the more popular brands – such as *Kendall-Jackson* and *Gallo* – have a slightly sweet finish to make them more commercial. The best can age, but seldom need to, since they often don't gain any extra dimension. For balance and poise look for: *Acacia, Arrowood, Au Bon Climat, Beringer, Buena Vista, Byron Reserve, Chalone, Chateau St Jean, Cuvaison, Dehlinger, Far Niente, Flora Springs, Flowers, Franciscan, Kistler, Kunde, Lambert Bridge, Landmark, Matanzas Creek, Mondavi Reserve, Newton, Ramey, Rabbit Ridge, Ridge, Shafer Red Shoulder Ranch, Simi* and *Sonoma-Cutrer* (California); *Gristina* (NY). For simpler wines, try *Clos du Bois, Estancia, Matanzas Creek, Kendall-Jackson, Morgan, Mirassou, Phelps, Wente* (California); *Chateau Ste Michelle, Columbia Crest, Woodward Canyon* (Washington).

GEWÜRZTRAMINER (white) Often made with a touch of residual sugar, which suits it. Look for *Adler Fels, Babcock, Nalle, Fetzer, Firestone,* (California); *Columbia, Chateau Ste Michelle* (Washington).

MERLOT (red) When it's good it's very, very good, full of lovely black cherry fruit with a pleasing brambly edge. But it's frighteningly fashionable, and too many are overcropped and insipid. Some producers do the opposite, and treat it like Cabernet, with huge extraction and as much tannin as possible. Best are *Arrowood, Clos du Val, Cuvaison, Duckhorn, Geyser Peak, Gundlach-Bundschu, Monticello Cellars, Murphy-Goode, Newton, St Francis, Pine Ridge, Ridge Santa Cruz, Silverado, Sinskey, St Clement, Sterling, Swanson, Vichon,* (California); *Bedell Cellars, Hargrave, Peconic Bay* (New York); *Chateau Ste Michelle, Columbia, Columbia Crest, Hogue Cellars, Leonetti Cellar, Staton Hills, Paul Thomas* (Washington).

PETITE SIRAH (red) This is emphatically not the same as the great Syrah grape of the Rhône Valley or the Shiraz of Australia.

It produces big, stark, almost tarry wines – impressive, but needing a good winemaker. *Ridge* is superb. Also look for *Foppiano, Ravenswood, Stag's Leap* and *Turley*.

PINOT GRIS (white) Oregon's other speciality, after Pinot Noir. Most are light and spicy, but less vinous than Alsace versions. Try *Elk Cove, Erath, Eyrie, Ponzi*.

PINOT NOIR (red) At its best, from a leading producer in California and Oregon, US Pinot is almost as good as very good Burgundy. Most, though, settles for charm rather than excitement, and lesser wines can be dilute. Try *Acacia, Au Bon Climat, Byron, Calera, Carneros Creek, Chalone, Dehlinger, Fetzer, De Loach, Gary Farrell, Iron Horse, Kendall-Jackson, Kistler, Lazy Creek, Robert Mondavi, Rochioli, Lane Tanner, Saintsbury, Sanford, Sinskey, Rodney Strong, Wild Horse, Zaca Mesa, ZD* (California); *Hargrave* (NY); *Adelsheim, Amity, Archery Summit, Bethel Heights, Broadley, Drouhin, Erath, Eyrie, Scott Henry, King Estate, Panther Creek, Rex Hill, Sokol Blosser, Ken Wright* (Oregon).

RIESLING (white) Seldom that successful in California. Good ones are *Alexander Valley Vineyards, Konocti, Navarro* (California); *Lamoreaux Landing, Wagner Vineyards* (New York); *Amity* (Oregon); *Hogue Cellars, Columbia Cellars, Chateau Ste Michelle, Kiona* (Washington).

SANGIOVESE (red) California's latest love affair, and not always entirely successful. Best: *Atlas Peak, Dalle Valle, Iron Horse, Renwood, Seghesio, Silverado, Vina Noceto*. There's also some Nebbiolo, but that's proving even trickier.

SAUVIGNON BLANC/FUMÉ BLANC (white) Generally riper and broader than the New Zealand or Loire prototypes, and often oaked, usually to excess. Try *Babcock, Caymus, Chalk Hill, Chateau Potelle, Chateau St Jean, Dry Creek Vineyards, Ferrari-Carano, Geyser Peak,*

Kenwood, Kunde, Matanzas Creek, Robert Mondavi, Murphy-Goode, Navarro, Quivira, Rochioli, Sanford, Simi, Stag's Leap (California); Hargrave (NY); Columbia, L'Ecole No 41 (Washington).

SEMILLON (white) Usually added to Sauvignon Blanc for complexity (try Carmenet, Clos du Val, St Supéry and Vichon in California).

SYRAH/RHÔNE VARIETIES (red) There has been an explosion of interest in these. Most eyes are on Syrah, but there is also Mourvèdre, Cinsaut, Grenache and Carignan. Whites include Viognier and Marsanne. The best are from California: Bonny Doon, Cline, Dehlinger, Duxoup, Fetzer, Kendall-Jackson, Jade Mountain, Jensen, La Jota, McDowell Valley, Joseph Phelps Mistral

series, RH Phillips, Preston Vineyards, Qupé, Rabbit Ridge, Santino, Thackrey, Zaca Mesa. In Washington: Columbia, Columbia Crest.

ZINFANDEL (red) Americans are passionate about this. Styles range from the dreaded 'blush' to light, berryish wines to big, rich, brambly old vine wines of terrific density and sometimes terrific alcohol. Very few (a handful, no more) benefit from ageing. Big Zins include: Chateau Potelle, Cline Cellars, Deer Park, Peter Franus, Grgich Hills, Kendall-Jackson, Kunde, La Jota, Martinelli, Murrieta's Well, Preston Vineyards, A Rafanelli, Ravenswood, Ridge Lytton Springs, Rosenblum, Shenandoah, Storybook Mountain, Joseph Swan. Lighter ones: Buehler, Buena Vista, Burgess, Clos du Val, Fetzer, Haywood, Howell Mountain, Kendall-Jackson Kenwood, Louis M Martini, Nalle, Quivira.

WINE REGIONS

CARNEROS (California; red, white) One of California's top spots for Pinot Noir and Chardonnay – for both still and sparkling wine. It straddles the southern end of Napa and Sonoma. Look for Acacia, Carneros Creek, Domaine Carneros, David Ramey, Rasmussen, Saintsbury.

CENTRAL VALLEY (California; red, white) Huge and hot. This is where much of California's everyday jug wine comes from, and it's usually drinkable. Chardonnay, especially, is much improved.

IDAHO (red, white) The potato state produces wines of intensity and elegance, the best of which age well. Most of the vineyards are along the Snake River Valley, and most are planted with Riesling and Chardonnay. New plantings are mostly of red varieties. Best: Ste Chapelle, Vickers.

LAKE COUNTY (California; red, white) Good Cabernet Sauvignon and Sauvignon Blanc territory. Guenoc, Konocti, Louis M Martini and Steele have vines here.

LIVERMORE VALLEY (California; red, white) Currently reviving. Stars include Bonny Doon, Concannon, Wente.

MENDOCINO COUNTY (California; red, white) Good Zin, Italian and Rhône varietals. The cool Anderson Valley makes good fizz, led by Roederer Estate and Handley Cellars. Elegant Riesling, Gewürztraminer, Pinot Noir and Chardonnay comes from here, too. Some Cabernet Sauvignon is good.

MONTEREY COUNTY (California; red, white) The North is top Pinot Noir country (Calera, Chalone) and Carmel Valley is giving nice Cabernets. Jekel makes excellent Chardonnay and Riesling in Arroyo Seco.

NAPA COUNTY (California; red, white) This is California's classic wine country. Napa's strong suit is red – Cabernet Sauvignon and Merlot – with Pinot Noir in Carneros. Star producers are too many to list, but include Beaulieu, Beringer, Dalla Valle, Diamond Creek, Dominus, Mondavi,

Newton, Opus One, Phelps, Spottswoode, Stag's Leap, Turley.

NEW MEXICO (red, white) Good producers here are *Anderson Valley*, especially for Chardonnay, and *Gruet* for fizz.

NEW YORK STATE (red, white) Long Island Chardonnays are very different from those of California, with more austere flavours, a bit like ripe Chablis. There's also good Chardonnay and Riesling coming from the Finger Lakes and Hudson River Valley areas. Try *Bedell Cellars, Fox Run, Hargrave, Lamoreaux Landing, Lenz, Millbrook, Wagner.*

OREGON (red, white) Most famous for Pinot Noir, which is patchy but excellent at its best. Next comes Pinot Gris, which can be delicious and refreshing. Riesling can also be quite good, but Chardonnay has never really taken off. Indeed Oregon as a whole is still struggling to find out what it does best. The main regions are the Willamette Valley, Umpqua Valley and Rogue Valley. For Pinot Gris, go for *Adelsheim, Archery Summit, Eyrie, King Estate, Ponzi, Rex Hill.* Oak Knoll has the best Riesling. For Pinot Noir, try *Adelsheim, Amity, Archery Summit, Beaux Frères, Bethel Heights, Drouhin, Eyrie, King Estate, Panther Creek, Sokol Blosser, Ken Wright.*

SAN LUIS OBISPO COUNTY (California; red, white) Has some good sites for Pinot Noir and Chardonnay, and there are a few surprising old Zinfandel vineyards. Edna Valley is the chief sub-region with a deserved reputation for Chardonnay.

SANTA BARBARA COUNTY (California; red, white) Some outstanding Pinot Noirs from the Santa Maria and Santa Ynez valleys, plus some good Sauvignon and Merlot. Best names: *Au Bon Climat, Firestone, Qupé, Sanford, Zaca Mesa.*

SANTA CRUZ MOUNTAINS (California; red, white) Pinot Noir here is promising, but still patchy. *David Bruce* and *Santa Cruz Mountain Winery* have had various degrees of success. *Mount Eden* and *Ridge Vineyards* are good for Cabernet.

SIERRA FOOTHILLS (California; red, white) California's gold country was one of its busiest wine zones until Prohibition, but only a few Zinfandel vineyards survived. These are the basis of the area's reputation, plus good Sauvignon Blanc and Barbera. Best: *Amador Foothill Winery, Boeger, Monteviña, Santino* and *Shenandoah Vineyards.*

SONOMA COUNTY (California; red, white) Sonoma Valley is the main sub-region, but there are many others, in particular Alexander Valley, Chalk Hill, Dry Creek, Knight's Valley, and the Russian River Valley (including its sub-region Green Valley). Cabernet Sauvignon is the star grape, and it and Chardonnay are usually a

MATURITY CHART
1997 Napa Cabernet Sauvignon (premium)
An outstanding vintage for Napa Cabernet
The top wines will age well

Bottled	Ready	Best	Fading	Tired

| 0 | 2 | 4 | 6 | 8 | 10 | 12 | 14 | 16 | 18 | 20 | 22 | 24 years |

little fruitier and softer than they are in Napa. There's also some first-rate Pinot Noir emerging from the lower Russian River Valley, and exciting Zinfandel and Merlot. Look for *Carmenet, Chateau St Jean, Dehlinger, De Loach, Iron Horse, Jordan, Kistler, Simi, Sonoma-Cutrer, Williams-Selyem.*

TEXAS (red, white) Cabernet Sauvignons from Texas have a drink-me-now rich fruitiness and the Chardonnays and Sauvignon Blancs are looking better every year. The best producers currently are: *Fall Creek, Llano Estacado, Messina Hof, Oberhellmann* and *Pheasant Ridge.*

VIRGINIA (red, white) Growing good wine grapes in Virginia's hot, humid climate is a man-over-nature drama. Nevertheless, there are some good Rieslings and Chardonnays. Top producers are *Horton, Ingleside Plantation* and *Prince Michel.*

> **ON THE CASE**
> *Washington State has, from the 2000 vintage, a Washington Wine Quality Alliance: look for the logo on bottles. It is voluntary and self-regulating*

WASHINGTON STATE (red, white) Intense, clear fruit is the hallmark here for Cabernet, Merlot, Syrah, Sauvignon Blanc, Semillon, Riesling and Chardonnay. Appellations include Columbia Valley, Yakima Valley, Walla Walla Valley and Puget Sound. Good names include *Andrew Will, Apex, Canoe Ridge, Chateau Ste Michelle, Chinook, Columbia, Columbia Crest, Covey Run, Durham Cellars, Hedges Wine Cellars, Hogue Cellars, Kiona, L'Ecole No 41, Leonetti Cellar, Matthews, McCrea Cellars, Quilceda Creek, Paul Thomas* and *Woodward Canyon.*

PRODUCERS WHO'S WHO

ACACIA ★★ (Carneros/Napa) Very attractive Pinot Noir and Chardonnay.

ADLER FELS ★ (Sonoma) A quirky winery, taking chances that sometimes miss. Top Gewürztraminer and an unusual Riesling sparkler.

ANDREW WILL ★★ (Washington) Ripe, spicy Merlot and intense Cabernet Sauvignon, and superb red blend, Sorella.

ARROWOOD ★★ (Sonoma) Beautifully balanced Cabernet Sauvignon, Merlot and Chardonnay, plus peachy Viognier.

AU BON CLIMAT ★★ (Santa Barbara) Fine Pinot Noir with intense black cherry fruit. Chardonnay can also be impressive. The Podere dell' Olivos label is for quirky, characterful Italian varietals.

BEAULIEU VINEYARDS ★ (Napa) Top-of-the-line George de Latour Private

Reserve Cabernet Sauvignon is still marvellous. Also lean, supple Carneros Chardonnay, and red blend, Tapestry.

BEDELL CELLARS (New York) Long Island pioneer of Bordeaux-styled Merlot, Cabernet and red blend Cupola.

BERINGER (Napa) Reserve Cabernets are top of the line. Reserve Chardonnay is rich and loaded with buttery oak. The second label, Napa Ridge, is good value.

BETHEL HEIGHTS ★★ (Oregon) Impressive, intense Pinot Noirs. The Reserves can be among Oregon's finest and most concentrated.

BONNY DOON ★★ (Santa Cruz) One of California's most innovative winemakers, Grenache (Le Cigare Volant) and Mourvèdre (Old Telegram) and a line of Italian styles called Ca' Del Solo. New ideas and new wines appear every year.

BUENA VISTA (Sonoma/Carneros) Balanced, understated Merlot, Pinot Noir and Cabernet Sauvignon. Reserve wines have great intensity and depth. Very good Lake County Sauvignon Blanc.

CAIN CELLARS ★ (Napa) Superb Cain Five Bordeaux blend red, and excellent across the board.

CALERA ★★ (San Benito) Possibly the best Pinot Noir in California. Rich and intense; Jensen Vineyard is tops. Also fine Viognier and Chardonnay.

CAYMUS ★ (Napa) Benchmark California Cabernet which shows no sign of faltering. Special Selection is the top wine. Liberty School is the second label.

CHALONE ★ (Monterey) Individualistic, ageworthy Pinot Noir and harmonious Chardonnay. Also some nice Pinot Blanc and Chenin Blanc.

CHATEAU MONTELENA ★★ (Napa) Chardonnay and Cabernet that both need time and repay the wait.

CHATEAU POTELLE ★★ (Napa) Very good Sauvignon Blanc and Cabernet, outstanding Zinfandel.

CHATEAU ST JEAN ★★ (Sonoma) Rich Chardonnay, outstanding Cabernet and Merlot, and justly famous botrytized Rieslings.

CHATEAU STE MICHELLE ★★ (Washington) Consistently good with Cabernet Sauvignon and Merlot being the real strengths; Riesling, both dry and sweet, is also worth trying. Col Solare is a ludicrously pricey Cab-Merlot.

CHIMNEY ROCK ★ (Napa) Powerful yet elegant Cabernet Sauvignon and Bordeaux blend called Elevage with deep, rich and complex fruit.

CLOS DU BOIS ★★ (Sonoma) Consistently good Merlots, Chardonnays and a Bordeaux-style blend called Marlstone.

CLOS DU VAL ★ (Napa) Elegant, ageworthy, well-balanced reds. Best are Cabernet and Zinfandel. Ariadne is a beautifully made Semillon/Sauvignon/Viognier blend.

COLUMBIA ★ (Washington) Reds are excellent: Syrah, soft, peppery Pinot Noir, seductive Merlot (Red Willow vineyard), and ripe Cabernet (Otis vineyard). Very good whites include Semillon and Gewürztraminer.

COLUMBIA CREST (Washington) Highly drinkable wines, not expensive: Cabernet, Merlot, Chardonnay.

CUVAISON ★★ (Napa) Delicious Merlot, Pinot Noir and Cabernet: elegant, understated, with unexpected complexity.

DEHLINGER ★★ (Sonoma) One of the best Pinots in North America; also good Cabernets, Chardonnay and Syrah.

DOMAINE CARNEROS ★★ (Napa) This Taittinger-owned sparkling wine house makes remarkable vintage Brut and silky, powerful Blanc de Blancs.

DOMAINE CHANDON ★★ (Napa) Owned by Champagne house Moët & Chandon, and making consistently good non-vintage bubblies, plus rich and creamy Reserve and Carneros Blanc de Blancs.

DROUHIN ★★ (Oregon) Top wine Cuvée Laurène is often Oregon's best Pinot Noir. The regular release is delicious in warm years. Very good Chardonnay, too.

DUCKHORN ★★ (Napa) Intensely flavoured, deep and rich Three Palms Vineyard Merlot, and a weighty Cabernet.

ELK COVE VINEYARDS ★ (Oregon) One of Oregon's best Pinot Noirs, and very good Pinot Gris.

EYRIE ★ (Oregon) David Lett is Oregon's Pinot pioneer, and he continues to make wine in his own idiosyncratic style, even if the results are sometimes unfashionably lean. Good Pinot Gris.

FETZER ★ (Mendocino) A good range of tasty reds and whites. Also a leader in organic wines under the Bonterra label.

FLORA SPRINGS ★★ (Napa) Excellent Chardonnay and a fair Bordeaux blend called Trilogy. Soliloquy is a creamy, rich, floral white that belies its Sauvignon Blanc base.

FRANCISCAN ★★ (Napa) The estate-bottled Chardonnays, especially the Cuvée Sauvage, are outstanding. Sleek Magnificat Bordeaux blend.

GRGICH HILLS ★ (Sonoma) Ageworthy Cabernet and rich Zinfandel.

HANDLEY CELLARS ★ (Mendocino) Excellent fizz, especially Brut and rosé. Very good Chardonnay and Sauvignon, promising Pinot Noir.

HEITZ ★ (Napa) Martha's Vineyard Cabernet is a California blue chip, dark, uncompromising and expensive.

HESS COLLECTION ★★ (Napa) Chardonnay and Cabernet with balance and finesse.

JORDAN ★★ (Sonoma) The rich, ripe Cabernet Sauvignon ages well, and there's a classic, biscuity fizz called 'J'.

KENDALL-JACKSON ★ (Sonoma) Makes massive amounts of smooth, rich, off-dry Chardonnay. Also owns estates, which are much more interesting.

INSTANT CELLAR:
COOL-CLIMATE

• **1999 Sleepy Hollow Chardonnay, Testarossa, £27.95, Liberty Wines** Complex, nutty wine from a new small-scale producer. The vineyard is in cool Monterey County – in the Santa Lucia Highlands, to be precise.
• **1997 Unfiltered Chardonnay, Carneros, Saintsbury, £13.99, Villeneuve Wines** Good, complex, tight-grained Chardonnay; rich but subtle.
• **1996 Meritage Reserve, Paragon Vineyard, Edna Valley, Carmenet, £12.50, The Wine Society** A white Graves-style blend from California. It's two-thirds Sauvignon and one-third Semillon, barrel-fermented and with lots of rich, dry depth.
• **1997 Pinot Noir Single Vineyard, Carneros, Clos du Val, £17.50, Mayfair Cellars** Quite Burgundian in style, with pure fruit and a touch of smoke.
• **1997 Zinfandel The Adventures of Commander Zinskey, Robert Sinskey, £13.99, The Winery** Daft name, but rather good wine. It's Zin from Carneros, which is unusual – most Zin comes from hotter climates. This is all damsons and cherries, with good length.

KENWOOD ★★ (Sonoma) Consistent quality, including one of California's best Sauvignon Blancs. Jack London and Artist Series Cabernets are outstanding, as is the Zinfandel.

KUNDE ESTATE (Sonoma) First-rate Chardonnays (especially Reserve and single-vineyard Kinneybrook and Wildwood), fine Syrah and Viognier, rich old vine Zinfandel, and classy Sauvignon Blanc.

LAMOREAUX LANDING ★ (New York) Chardonnay is rather good; the Pinot Noir improves with each vintage.

LAUREL GLEN ★ (Sonoma) Intense, black cherry Cabernet Sauvignon is the only wine here, very good at its best.

LENZ ★ (New York) Elegant and quite powerful Merlot; tasty dry Gewürztraminer.

LOUIS M MARTINI (Napa) Quality is somewhat patchy these days. Highlights are Monte Rosso Cabernet, and Zinfandel, Chardonnay and Carneros Pinot Noir.

MAYACAMAS ★★ (Napa) Firm Cabernet and rich Chardonnay are the stars here; there's some Pinot Noir as well.

ROBERT MONDAVI ★★ (Napa) Mondavi's prices seem to have risen so much it isn't easy to judge the wines. Woodbridge and regular releases are OK, sometimes good; Reserves can be superb. Opus One is very good, but rarely memorable. New is a line of Italian varietals under the La Famiglia label.

MUMM NAPA ★★ (Napa) Good fizz, better than that made by the parent company in Champagne. Look for the Brut and impressive Blanc de Noirs.

NEWTON ★★ (Napa) Excellent, unfiltered Chardonnay; cedary, cinnamon-spiced Cabernet and succulent Merlot.

PHELPS ★ (Napa) Best here is the Insignia Bordeaux blend. Mistral label is for interesting Rhône varieties.

QUPÉ ★★ (Santa Maria) Specialist in Rhône-style wines – superb Syrah – and very fine Chardonnay.

RAVENSWOOD ★★ (Sonoma) Superlative Zinfandel. Fans have the winery logo tattooed on their backs.

RIDGE ★★★ (Santa Clara) Benchmark Zinfandel, probably California's best. The Monte Bello Cabernets are also remarkable, with great balance and long-lasting, perfumed fruit. Petite Sirah from York Creek is brilliant, and there's also a top-class red blend, Geyserville.

ROEDERER ESTATE ★★ (Mendocino County) Excellent sparklers from a company owned by Roederer Champagne. Very good Brut and rosé. Top of the range l'Ermitage is rich and concentrated.

SAINTSBURY ★★ (Napa) Stylish, supple, elegant Pinot Noir and Chardonnay. Lovely Garnet, from young Pinot Noir vines.

SANFORD WINERY ★ (Santa Barbara) At its best, Sanford Pinot Noir can be a real treat, with spicy, lush, intense fruit. Good Sauvignon and Chardonnay.

SCHRAMSBERG ★★ (Napa) Big, lush fizz. Reserve Brut is best, often world class. Blanc de Noirs is big and bold.

SCREAMING EAGLE ★★★ (Napa) Cult Cabernet, made in tiny quantities.

SHAFER ★★ (Napa) Very good, very long-lived Cabernet Sauvignon and Merlot, and classic cool-climate Chardonnay.

SIMI ★★ (Sonoma) Rich, sometimes voluptuous, always reliable Chardonnay, concentrated Cabernets. Reserves are excellent, as is Sauvignon Blanc.

SONOMA-CUTRER ★★ (Sonoma) Chardonnay specialist: rich, complex Les Pierres and Cutrer are made to age. Russian River Ranches is more forward.

STAG'S LEAP WINE CELLARS ★★ (Napa) Splendid, ageworthy and elegant Cask 23, SLV and Fay Vineyard Cabs. Good Chardonnay, too.

STEELE WINES ★ (Lake County) Expensive, vivid Chardonnays. Good Zinfandel and Pinot Noir. Shooting Star is a budget label.

RODNEY STRONG ★★ (Sonoma) Fine single-vineyard Cabernet Sauvignon, Pinot Noir, Chardonnay.

UNITED STATES PRICES

CALIFORNIA RED

Under £5.00

Cabernet Sauvignon E&J Gallo **1999**
£4.69 (ASD) £4.99 (BUD) £4.99 (SAF)
£4.99 (MORR)

Cabernet Sauvignon Sutter Home **1998**
£4.99 (MORR)

Cabernet Sauvignon Sutter Home **1997**
£4.99 (VIL) £5.35 (CON)

Cabernet Sauvignon/Merlot E&J Gallo
Garnet Point **1998** £4.99 (BUD)

Californian Red Paul Masson **Non-
vintage** £3.99 (ASD)

Dry Reserve E&J Gallo **Non-vintage**
£4.69 (BUD)

Pinot Noir Thornhill **1996** £4.99 (UN)

Zinfandel E&J Gallo **Non-vintage** £4.69
(SAF)

Zinfandel E&J Gallo **1999** £4.69 (BUD)

Zinfandel E&J Gallo **1996** £4.69 (UN)

Zinfandel Sutter Home **1998** £4.69 (VIL)
£4.99 (CON) £4.99 (MORR) £5.72 (LLO)

Zinfandel/Barbera E&J Gallo Garnet Point
1999 £3.49 (MORR) £3.99 (BUD)

£5.00 → £5.99

Cabernet Sauvignon Glen Ellen **1999**
£5.49 (BUD)

Cabernet Sauvignon Glen Ellen **1997**
£5.49 (SAF)

Cabernet Sauvignon Sutter Home **1996**
£5.99 (UN)

Pinot Noir Redwood Trail **1998** £5.99
(WAI) £6.49 (VIC) £6.49 (THR) £6.49
(BOT) £6.49 (WR) £6.49 (OD) £6.90
(CRO)

Starboard Batch 88 Quady ½ bottle **Non-
vintage** £5.05 (PEN)

Zinfandel Sutter Home **1997** £5.25 (STE)
£5.39 (JON) £5.49 (UN)

£6.00 → £7.99

Barbera Monteviña **1997** £7.99 (VIL) £8.75
(STE)

Barbera Monteviña **1994** £7.50 (CRO)

Big House Red Bonny Doon Ca' del Solo
1998 £6.99 (SOM) £7.99 (POR) £8.40
(BEN) £8.40 (MV) £8.50 (TAN) £8.65
(CON) £8.70 (GW) £8.99 (VIL) £9.50 (NI)

Black Muscat Quady Elysium ½ bottle
Non-vintage £6.95 (NI) £7.73 (COC)
£7.95 (FORT)

Black Muscat Quady Elysium ½ bottle
1999 £7.25 (STA)

Black Muscat Quady Elysium ½ bottle
1998 £6.46 (PEN) £6.99 (MAJ) £6.99
(JON) £9.50 (JER)

Black Muscat Quady Elysium ½ bottle
1995 £6.95 (CON) £7.95 (LEA) £11.00
(CRO)

Black Muscat Quady Elysium ½ bottle
1994 £7.91 (NO)

Cabernet Franc Pepperwood Grove
1997 £6.35 (BAC)

Cabernet Sauvignon Fetzer Valley Oaks
1998 £6.99 (SAI) £6.99 (WR)

Cabernet Sauvignon Fetzer Valley Oaks
1997 £6.99 (JON) £6.99 (WAI)

Cabernet Sauvignon E&J Gallo Turning
Leaf **1998** £6.45 (TES) £6.49 (MORR)

Cabernet Sauvignon E&J Gallo Turning
Leaf **1997** £6.49 (UN)

Cabernet Sauvignon Jekel **1998** £7.99
(WR)

Cabernet Sauvignon Robert Mondavi
Woodbridge **1998** £7.49 (POR)

Cabernet Sauvignon Wente **1997** £7.85
(COC)

Cabernet Sauvignon Wente **1996** £7.99
(UN)

Côtes d'Oakley Cline Cellars **1997** £6.99
(VIL) £7.00 (GW)

RETAILERS SPECIALIZING IN UNITED STATES
see Retailers Directory (page 40) for details

see Retailers Directory (page 40) for details

Adnams (AD), Averys, Bennetts (BEN),
Berrys (BER), Bibendum (BIB), D Byrne, Cave
Cru Classé, Croque-en-Bouche (CRO), Lay
& Wheeler (LAY), Majestic (MAJ), Morris &
Verdin (MV), Oddbins (OD), J Nicholson (NI),
The Nobody Inn (NO), Penistone Ct (PEN),
Reid Wines, Savage Selection (SAV), T&W
(TW), Villeneuve (VIL), Wine Treasury (WT),

Framboise Bonny Doon ½ bottle **Non-vintage** £7.35 (NI)
Petite Syrah Parducci **1995** £7.99 (DI)
Starboard Batch 88 Quady **Non-vintage** £6.70 (RIC) £9.75 (STA)
Valdiguie Beringer California **1998** £6.49 (NEZ)
Zinfandel Beringer California **1999** £6.99 (NEZ)
Zinfandel Fetzer **1997** £6.99 (OD)
Zinfandel Fetzer **1996** £7.65 (JU)
Zinfandel Fetzer Valley Oaks **1998** £6.99 (SO)
Zinfandel E&J Gallo Turning Leaf **1998** £6.49 (UN)
Zinfandel E&J Gallo Turning Leaf **1997** £6.49 (TES) £6.49 (MORR)
Zinfandel Robert Mondavi Woodbridge **1998** £7.49 (POR) £8.75 (STE)
Zinfandel Monteviña **1997** £7.81 (LLO)
Zinfandel Monteviña **1996** £6.90 (CRO) £6.99 (VIL)
Zinfandel Wente **1998** £7.35 (COC)

£8.00 → £9.99

Allure Rabbit Ridge **1996** £8.99 (WIN)
Barbera Bonny Doon Ca' del Solo **1996** £8.50 (CRO) £13.09 (NO)
Barbera Monteviña **1998** £8.49 (WR)
Barbera Monteviña **1996** £8.95 (VA) £9.00 (WRI) £9.04 (PLA)
Big House Red Bonny Doon Ca' del Solo **1996** £8.40 (CRO)
Cabernet Sauvignon Beringer California **1997** £8.99 (NEZ)
Cabernet Sauvignon Bonterra **1999** £8.99 (BOT) £8.99 (WR)
Cabernet Sauvignon Bonterra **1998** £8.99 (SAI) £8.99 (MORR)
Cabernet Sauvignon Bonterra **1997** £8.99 (WAI)
Cabernet Sauvignon Hawk Crest **1998** £8.21 (DOM) £8.99 (GW)
Cabernet Sauvignon Seven Peaks **1996** £8.99 (UN)
Carignane Bonny Doon **1999** £9.95 (FRI) £10.99 (VIL)
Merlot Seven Peaks **1998** £9.99 (BAN)
Petite Syrah Parducci **1998** £8.69 (GN)

*Stars (★) indicate wines selected by
Oz Clarke in the Best Buys section which
begins on page 8.*

Pinot Noir Saintsbury Garnet **1998** £9.75 (SOM) £11.75 (CON) £11.90 (JU)
Pinot Noir Saintsbury Garnet **1995** £9.50 (CRO)
Starboard Batch 88 Quady **1988** £8.12 (NO)
Zinfandel Beringer California **1996** £8.99 (MAJ)
Zinfandel Bonterra **1997** £9.59 (JON)
Zinfandel Cline Cellars California **1997** £8.50 (GW) £8.99 (VIL)
Zinfandel Fetzer Barrel Select **1997** £8.99 (TES)
Zinfandel Madrona **1998** £9.99 (BAL)
Zinfandel Pedroncelli Mother Clone **1997** £9.90 (RIC)
Zinfandel Ravenswood Vintners Blend **1998** £8.75 (ARM)
Zinfandel Ravenswood Vintners Blend **1997** £8.25 (WS) £8.99 (OD)
Zinfandel Sebastiani Sonoma Old Vines **1998** £9.99 (CO)
Zinfandel Seghesio Sonoma County **1997** £9.50 (WS)
Zinfandel Villa Mt Eden Coastal **1996** £8.29 (CON)

£10.00 → £11.99

Cabernet Sauvignon Kendall-Jackson Vintner's Reserve **1997** £11.99 (DI)
Cabernet Sauvignon St Supéry **1997** £10.95 (LIB)
Cabernet Sauvignon Wente Charles Wetmore Reserve **1995** £10.99 (UN)
Il Fiasco Bonny Doon Ca' del Solo **1998** £11.85 (NI)
Il Fiasco Bonny Doon Ca' del Solo **1997** £11.99 (VIL)
Merlot Wente Crane Ridge Reserve **1998** £10.99 (UN)
Pinot Noir Kendall-Jackson Vintner's Reserve **1997** £10.99 (DI)
Pinot Noir Robert Mondavi Coastal **1999** £11.95 (POR)
Pinot Noir Kent Rasmussen Ramsay **1999** £10.49 (OD)
Pinot Noir Kent Rasmussen Ramsay **1998** £10.95 (STE)
Pinot Noir Schug Cellars **1996** £11.99 (UN)
Pinot Noir Wente Reliz Creek Reserve **1996** £10.50 (COC) £10.99 (UN)
Sangiovese Noceto **1997** £11.79 (YOU)
Syrah Qupé Central Coast **1997** £11.50 (FRI)
Zinfandel Burgess Cellars **1995** £11.50 (RIC)

£12.00 → £13.99

Cabernet Sauvignon Beringer California
1996 £12.99 (MAJ)
Cabernet Sauvignon Carmenet Dynamite
1998 £12.43 (BIB)
Cabernet Sauvignon Clos du Val Stags
Leap 1985 £13.50 (CRO)
Cabernet Sauvignon Rutherford Hill 1994
£12.10 (PEN)
Charbono Duxoup 1998 £12.73 (BIB)
Cotes du Soleil Jade Mountain 1997
£12.50 (BEN) £12.50 (BAC) £13.00 (MV)
Counterpoint Laurel Glen 1994 £13.90
(NO)
Los Olivos Cuvée Qupé 1996 £13.71 (NO)
Merlot Clos du Bois Sonoma 1997
£13.99 (BOT) £13.99 (WR)
Montepiano Rabbit Ridge 1996 £13.95
(WIN)
Mourvèdre Cline Cellars Ancient Vines
1997 £12.99 (VIL)
Nebbiolo Il Podere dell'Olivos 1995
£12.99 (YOU)
Nero Misto Elyse 1998 £13.22 (BIB)
Petite Sirah Ridge York Creek 1997
£12.85 (SOM) £15.50 (FRI) £15.65 (CON)
Pinot Noir Beringer North Coast 1997
£12.90 (CRO)
Pinot Noir La Crema 1998 £12.99 (DI)
Pinot Noir Saintsbury Carneros 1997
£12.75 (SOM) £12.90 (CRO) £14.50 (JU)
£14.99 (WR)
Pinot Noir Saintsbury Garnet 1999
£13.50 (AD) £13.75 (NI)
Pinot Noir Seven Peaks 1997 £12.99 (BAN)
Sangiovese Noceto 1995 £12.99 (VA)
Zinfandel Cline Cellars Ancient Vines
1998 £12.99 (VIL)
Zinfandel Clos du Val 1998 £13.95 (STA)
Zinfandel Clos du Val 1997 £13.50 (MAY)
Zinfandel Frog's Leap 1996 £13.89 (FLE)
Zinfandel Heitz 1996 £12.50 (JU)
Zinfandel Kenwood 1997 £13.50 (BU)
Zinfandel Renwood Old Vine 1998
£13.99 (OD)
Zinfandel Seghesio Sonoma County 1999
£13.95 (LIB) £13.99 (YOU)

£14.00 → £15.99

Cabernet Sauvignon Carmenet Dynamite
1999 £14.19 (BIB)
Cabernet Sauvignon Clos La Chance
Santa Cruz Mountains 1997 £14.99
(OD)

La Provençale Jade Mountain 1999
£15.50 (MV)
La Provençale Jade Mountain 1997
£14.95 (FORT) £15.50 (BEN)
La Provençale Jade Mountain 1996
£14.95 (VA)
Mataro Ridge Bridgehead 1997 £15.75
(FORT) £16.25 (NI) £16.95 (VA)
Merlot Frog's Leap 1995 £15.32 (FLE)
Mondouse/Pinot Noir Au Bon Climat
1999 £15.50 (MV)
Mourvèdre Jade Mountain 1990 £15.50
(CRO)
Pinot Noir Au Bon Climat 1999 £14.99
(GW)
Pinot Noir Byron 1995 £14.10 (PEN)
Pinot Noir Clos du Val Carneros 1994
£15.95 (STA)
Pinot Noir Morgan 1999 £15.66 (BIB)
★ Pinot Noir Saintsbury Carneros 1998
£14.09 (FLE) £14.99 (SUN) £14.99 (LAI)
£15.50 (HAH) £15.60 (TAN) £15.75
(CON) £16.50 (FORT) £16.95 (TES) £16.99
(VIL) £18.65 (NI) £18.95 (AD)
Pleiades Thackrey Non-vintage £15.99
(OD)
Syrah Duxoup 1998 £15.66 (BIB)
Syrah Duxoup 1997 £14.49 (YOU)
Zinfandel Cline Cellars Ancient Vines
1996 £14.50 (FORT)
Zinfandel Cline Cellars Big Break 1997
£15.99 (VIL)
Zinfandel Cline Cellars Bridgehead 1997
£15.99 (VIL)
Zinfandel Frog's Leap 1999 £15.49 (YOU)
Zinfandel Frog's Leap 1998 £14.50 (BAC)
£15.50 (FORT) £15.95 (LAY) £17.95 (RES)
Zinfandel Frog's Leap 1997 £14.99 (CON)
£15.10 (NO) £15.10 (RIC)
Zinfandel Niebaum-Coppola Edizione
Pennino 1994 £15.99 (YOU)
Zinfandel Rocking Horse 1998 £15.99 (OD)
Zinfandel St Francis Old Vines 1997
£14.95 (VA)

£16.00 → £17.99

Cabernet Sauvignon Heitz 1993 £16.95 (JU)
Cabernet Sauvignon Rancho Sisquoc
1997 £17.50 (JER)
Cabernet Sauvignon Simi 1985 £16.00
(CRO)
Le Cigare Volant Bonny Doon 1997
£16.95 (FRI)
Le Cigare Volant Bonny Doon 1996
£16.95 (NI)

Merlot Havens 1998 £16.39 (DOM)
Merlot Silverado 1996 £16.50 (WIN)
Pinot Noir Acacia Carneros 1999 £17.63
(BIB)
Pinot Noir Au Bon Climat 1998 £16.30
(BEN) £16.95 (FORT) £17.95 (RES)
Pinot Noir Calera Central Coast 1999
£16.65 (BIB)
Pinot Noir Calera Central Coast 1998
£16.99 (DI)
Pinot Noir Calera Central Coast 1997
£16.49 (WAI)
Pinot Noir Clos du Val Carneros 1997
£17.50 (MAY)
Pinot Noir Sanford 1997 £17.99 (VIL)
Pinot Noir Marimar Torres Estate Don
Miguel Vineyard 1995 £17.50 (CRO)
Syrah Havens 1998 £17.63 (DOM)
Syrah Qupé Bien Nacido Reserve 1998
£17.99 (GW) £17.99 (YOU) £19.00 (MV)
Syrah Qupé Bien Nacido Reserve 1997
£17.04 (FA) £17.99 (YOU)
Zinfandel Elyse Morisoli 1998 £17.63 (BIB)
Zinfandel Fife Old Vine 1998 £16.75 (WRI)
Zinfandel Fife Old Vine 1996 £16.00
(BAC)
Zinfandel Fritz Old Vine 1997 £17.99 (VIL)
Zinfandel Nalle 1998 £17.63 (DOM)
Zinfandel Ridge Lytton Springs 1998
£16.25 (SOM) £19.65 (CON) £19.95 (FRI)
£19.99 (VIL) £20.30 (BEN) £21.95 (RES)
Zinfandel Ridge Lytton Springs 1997
£17.70 (FLE) £18.99 (LAI) £19.95 (BEN)
£19.99 (VA) £22.00 (WS)
Zinfandel Joseph Swan Frati Ranch 1996
£17.99 (RAE)

£18.00 → £19.99

Alluvium Red Beringer Private Reserve
1996 £18.99 (SUN) £18.99 (LAI)
Cabernet Sauvignon Clos du Val Stags
Leap 1996 £18.95 (MAY)
Cabernet Sauvignon Clos du Val Stags
Leap 1994 £19.50 (STA)
Cabernet Sauvignon Mayacamas 1982
£19.00 (CRO)

* Wines are listed in A–Z order within
  each price band.
* For each wine, vintages are listed in
  descending order.
* Each vintage of any wine appears
  only once.

Cabernet Sauvignon Monticello Jefferson
Cuvée 1997 £19.85 (LAY)
Cabernet Sauvignon Ridge Santa Cruz
Mountains 1997 £19.65 (CON) £19.95
(FRI) £19.99 (SUN) £19.99 (LAI) £20.25
(BEN) £21.50 (FORT) £21.95 (RES) £22.95
(VA)
Cabernet Sauvignon Ridge Santa Cruz
Mountains 1996 £18.20 (TAN) £19.58
(FLE)
Cabernet Sauvignon Stag's Leap Wine
Cellars Napa 1998 £19.99 (GW) £27.95
(RES) £30.00 (JER)
Cabernet Sauvignon Stag's Leap Wine
Cellars Napa 1985 £19.00 (CRO)
Geyserville Ridge 1997 £19.00 (FLE)
£20.00 (VA) £20.95 (STA)
Geyserville Ridge 1996 £19.65 (CON)
Le Mistral Joseph Phelps 1997 £18.99
(YOU) £19.99 (VIL)
Mataro Ridge Bridgehead 1995 £18.50
(FRI)
Merlot Frog's Leap 1997 £18.99 (RIC)
£20.95 (CON) £21.50 (FORT) £21.71
(NO)
Merlot Ravenswood Sangiacomo 1995
£18.33 (ARM)
Merlot Robert Sinskey Carneros 1997
£19.99 (WIN)
Merlot Stag's Leap Wine Cellars Napa
1996 £19.99 (VIL)
Mourvèdre Jade Mountain 1996 £18.00
(GW) £18.00 (MV) £18.20 (BEN)
Petite Sirah Ridge York Creek 1998
£19.49 (YOU) £19.95 (NI)
Petite Syrah Stag's Leap Wine Cellars
Napa 1996 £19.99 (VIL)
Pinot Noir Robert Mondavi 1996 £18.95
(STE) £22.20 (TAN) £22.49 (JON)
Pinot Noir Kent Rasmussen 1997 £18.99
(SUN) £18.99 (LAI)
Pinot Noir Robert Sinskey Carneros
1997 £19.99 (WIN)
Pinot Noir Marimar Torres Estate Don
Miguel Vineyard 1998 £18.75 (PEN)
£19.99 (POR)
Pinot Noir Marimar Torres Estate Don
Miguel Vineyard 1997 £18.95 (BALL)
Syrah Jade Mountain 1996 £19.30 (BEN)
Syrah Jade Mountain 1995 £19.00 (MV)
£19.50 (FORT) £34.95 (RES) £36.89 (NO)
Syrah Ojai 1998 £19.79 (YOU)
Syrah Joseph Phelps 1994 £19.99 (VIL)
Zinfandel Green & Red Chiles Mill
Vineyard 1998 £19.99 (WIN)

£20.00 → £29.99

Bourriquot Havens **1997** £23.50 (DOM)

Cabernet Sauvignon Chalk Hill **1995**
£20.00 (JU)

Cabernet Sauvignon Cuvaison **1984**
£22.00 (CRO)

Cabernet Sauvignon Elyse Morisoli **1996**
£25.46 (BIB)

Cabernet Sauvignon Far Niente **1986**
£21.00 (CRO)

Cabernet Sauvignon Firestone **1975**
£20.00 (CRO)

Cabernet Sauvignon Freemark Abbey
1983 £23.00 (CRO)

Cabernet Sauvignon Frog's Leap **1998**
£23.50 (LAY)

Cabernet Sauvignon Frog's Leap **1997**
£21.50 (CON) £23.95 (RES)

Cabernet Sauvignon Frog's Leap **1987**
£26.00 (CRO)

Cabernet Sauvignon Jordan **1992** £25.00
(BU)

Cabernet Sauvignon Robert Mondavi
1995 £20.50 (WRI)

Cabernet Sauvignon Robert Mondavi
Oakville **1993** £21.00 (CRO)

Cabernet Sauvignon Robert Mondavi
Oakville **1992** £23.50 (PEN)

Cabernet Sauvignon Joseph Phelps **1996**
£21.99 (YOU) £22.99 (VIL)

Cabernet Sauvignon Ridge Santa Cruz
Mountains **1998** £20.99 (YOU) £21.00
(MV) £22.40 (NI)

Cabernet Sauvignon Shafer **1996** £27.99
(VIL)

Cabernet Sauvignon Shafer Stag's Leap
District **1998** £27.95 (RES)

Cabernet Sauvignon Simi Reserve **1994**
£28.00 (PEN)

Cabernet Sauvignon Simi Reserve **1982**
£27.00 (CRO)

Cabernet Sauvignon Stag's Leap Wine
Cellars Napa **1997** £22.99 (VIL)

Cain Five Cain Cellars **1995** £29.00 (JU)

Chardonney Robert Sinskey Carneros
1998 £21.99 (WIN)

Firebreak Shafer **1997** £23.95 (RES)

Firebreak Shafer **1996** £22.99 (VIL)

Geyserville Ridge **1999** £22.40 (NI)

Geyserville Ridge **1998** £20.49 (YOU)
£20.50 (TAN) £20.95 (FRI) £20.95 (SUN)
£20.95 (LAI) £21.50 (FORT) £21.54 (SAV)
£21.95 (AD) £21.99 (VIL) £22.50 (JER)
£22.50 (BAL)

Le Cigare Volant Bonny Doon **1998**
£21.69 (GW) £21.79 (YOU) £22.00 (MV)
£22.50 (WRI) £22.99 (VIL)

Max Cuvée Fife **1997** £24.95 (BAL)

Merlot Cuvaison **1996** £20.95 (TAN)

Merlot Cuvaison **1994** £26.93 (NO)

Merlot Duckhorn **1997** £29.65 (LAY)

Merlot Frog's Leap **1998** £22.00 (MV)
£24.95 (RES)

Merlot Havens Reserve **1997** £22.91
(DOM)

Merlot Havens Reserve **1996** £20.56
(DOM)

Merlot Ravenswood Sangiacomo **1996**
£20.83 (ARM)

Merlot Ravenswood Sangiacomo **1994**
£23.35 (NO)

Merlot Ridge Santa Cruz Mountains **1997**
£22.25 (SOM) £28.95 (AD) £29.95 (RES)
£31.25 (NI) £31.95 (VA)

Merlot Ridge Santa Cruz Mountains **1996**
£27.75 (FORT) £28.50 (BEN) £29.95 (FRI)

Merlot Ridge Santa Cruz Mountains **1995**
£27.18 (NO)

Merlot Shafer Napa **1997** £25.99 (VIL)
£27.95 (RES)

Merlot Shafer Napa **1996** £20.95 (AD)

Moon Mountain Reserve Carmenet **1996**
£23.70 (BIB)

Moon Mountain Reserve Carmenet **1995**
£26.00 (WS)

Mourvèdre Jade Mountain **1995** £21.26
(NO)

Old Telegram Bonny Doon **1998** £27.99
(YOU) £32.00 (NI)

Old Telegram Bonny Doon **1993** £22.00
(NO)

Pinot Noir Chalone **1999** £22.52 (BIB)

Pinot Noir Chalone **1998** £20.99 (YOU)

Pinot Noir Cristom Reserve **1997** £25.99
(VIL)

Pinot Noir Etude Carneros **1998** £26.44
(DOM)

Pinot Noir Monticello Corley Family
Vineyards **1998** £21.35 (LAY)

Pinot Noir Saintsbury Carneros **1999**
£25.35 (NI)

Please remember that
Oz Clarke's Wine Buying Guide
*is a price **guide** and not a price list. It is
not meant to replace up-to-date
merchants' lists.*

Pinot Noir Saintsbury Reserve 1997
£26.00 (WS)
Pinot Noir Saintsbury Reserve 1996
£22.00 (CRO) £22.50 (JU)
Pinot Noir Sanford Barrel Select 1997
£29.99 (VIL)
Pinot Noir Sanford Barrel Select 1996
£26.00 (WS)
Syrah Jade Mountain 1990 £28.00 (CRO)
Syrah Qupé Bien Nacido Hillside Select
1997 £25.85 (FA) £27.99 (YOU)
Syrah Qupé Bien Nacido Reserve 1994
£20.35 (NO)

Viader 1995 £25.95 (DI)
Viader 1994 £24.75 (NO)
Zinfandel Cline Cellars Jacuzzi Family
Reserve 1994 £29.99 (VIL)
Zinfandel Grgich Hills 1996 £20.95 (RES)
Zinfandel Ravenswood 1995 £23.35 (NO)
Zinfandel Ridge Lytton Springs 1999
£20.99 (YOU) £21.00 (MV) £22.40 (NI)
Zinfandel Seghesio Cortina 1999 £21.99
(YOU) £23.50 (LIB)
Zinfandel Seghesio Old Vines 1999
£21.99 (YOU) £23.50 (LIB)
Zinfandel Joseph Swan Frati Ranch 1995
£24.30 (GAU)

£30.00 → £39.99

Cabernet Sauvignon Beaulieu Vineyard
Georges de Latour Private Reserve
1996 £39.50 (FORT)
Cabernet Sauvignon Caymus Vineyards
1996 £34.66 (FA) £39.95 (DI)
Cabernet Sauvignon Corison 1997
£32.31 (DOM)
Cabernet Sauvignon Duckhorn 1995
£39.99 (VIL)
Cabernet Sauvignon Fife 1997 £32.50
(BAL)
Cabernet Sauvignon Heitz 1978 £35.25
(WY)
Cabernet Sauvignon Heitz 1973 £39.00
(CRO)

Cabernet Sauvignon Heitz Trailside 1994
£37.00 (JU)
Cabernet Sauvignon Jekel Private Reserve
1978 £30.00 (CRO)
Cabernet Sauvignon Jordan 1980 £30.00
(CRO)
Cabernet Sauvignon Lewis Reserve 1997
£38.99 (WIN)
Cabernet Sauvignon Livingston Moffet
Vineyard 1995 £35.99 (WIN)
Cabernet Sauvignon Newton 1998
£34.17 (ARM)
Cabernet Sauvignon Paradigm 1997
£32.31 (DOM)
Cabernet Sauvignon Plumpjack 1997
£38.00 (BAL)
Cabernet Sauvignon Shafer Stag's Leap
District 1996 £30.00 (FORT)
Cabernet Sauvignon Spottswoode 1997
£38.19 (DOM)
Merlot Duckhorn 1996 £31.75 (FORT)
Merlot Duckhorn 1995 £39.99 (VIL)
Merlot Matanzas Creek 1997 £34.95
(BEN)
Merlot Stag's Leap Wine Cellars Napa
1998 £30.00 (JER)
Moon Mountain Reserve Carmenet 1998
£31.82 (BIB)
Paraduxx Duckhorn 1997 £30.65 (LAY)
Petite Sirah Ridge York Creek 1990
£35.25 (TUR)
Pinot Noir Calera Jensen 1995 £31.62
(NO)
Pinot Noir Gary Farrell Russian River
1998 £31.00 (BAL)
Pinot Noir Patz & Hall Sonoma County
1999 £33.95 (RES)
Pinot Noir Saintsbury Reserve 1994
£35.00 (CRO)
Pinot Noir Robert Sinskey Reserve
Carneros 1997 £32.99 (WIN)
Pinot Noir Testarossa Gary's 1999
£32.99 (YOU) £34.95 (LIB)
Rubicon Niebaum-Coppola 1993 £38.99
(YOU) £59.95 (RES)
Zinfandel Cline Cellars Jacuzzi Family
Reserve 1996 £32.95 (RES)

£40.00 → £49.99

Bacio Divino 1995 £41.00 (DI) £59.99 (WIN)
Cabernet Sauvignon Beaulieu Vineyard
Georges de Latour Private Reserve
1982 £49.50 (BU)
Cabernet Sauvignon Beringer Private
Reserve 1993 £41.00 (CRO)

Cabernet Sauvignon Etude **1997** £41.13 (DOM)

Cabernet Sauvignon Robert Mondavi Reserve **1994** £48.00 (CRO)

Cabernet Sauvignon Robert Mondavi Reserve **1982** £48.37 (FA)

Monte Bello Ridge **1995** £45.25 (NI)

Howell Mountain Duckhorn **1994** £44.99 (VIL)

Merlot Duckhorn Three Palms **1997** £46.30 (LAY)

Opus One Mondavi/Rothschild **1996** £44.03 (NO) £89.50 (CON) £89.99 (UN) £129.25 (BODX) £132.58 (FA) £141.00 (TUR) £146.88 (WY) £150.00 (VIL)

Pinot Noir Calera Jensen **1997** £42.10 (BIB)

Pinot Noir Calera Jensen **1996** £45.00 (DI)

Viader **1998** £41.13 (DOM)

£50.00 → £59.99

Cabernet Sauvignon Beringer Private Reserve **1994** £50.33 (FA)

Cabernet Sauvignon Chateau Montelena **1996** £59.50 (BAL)

Cabernet Sauvignon Dalla Valle Estate **1994** £50.52 (NO)

Cabernet Sauvignon Dunn Howell Mountain **1995** £53.27 (FA)

Cabernet Sauvignon Far Niente **1993** £58.75 (PEN)

Cabernet Sauvignon Robert Mondavi Reserve **1997** £58.16 (FA)

Cabernet Sauvignon Robert Mondavi Reserve **1995** £57.20 (HAH)

Cabernet Sauvignon Robert Mondavi Reserve **1985** £58.75 (FA)

Monte Bello Ridge **1997** £53.85 (SAV) £56.93 (NO) £75.00 (BEN)

Cabernet Sauvignon Stag's Leap Wine Cellars Fay Estate **1996** £59.99 (VIL)

Cabernet Sauvignon Stag's Leap Wine Cellars SLV **1996** £59.99 (VIL)

Dominus Christian Moueix **1995** £59.00 (CB) £75.00 (YOU) £77.75 (TUR)

Pinot Noir Gary Farrell Rochioli Vineyard **1997** £55.00 (BAL)

£60.00 → £69.99

Bacio Divino **1996** £61.95 (DI)

Cabernet Sauvignon Dalla Valle Estate **1995** £60.05 (NO)

Cabernet Sauvignon Heitz Fay Vineyard **1975** £66.00 (CRO)

Cabernet Sauvignon Heitz Martha's Vineyard **1982** £61.00 (CRO)

Monte Bello Ridge **1996** £62.69 (NO) £66.85 (SOM) £67.95 (FA) £70.00 (FORT) £79.50 (YOU) £80.00 (MV) £85.00 (VIL) £89.00 (FRI) £89.50 (BAL)

Monte Bello Ridge **1994** £65.00 (CON) £80.00 (FORT) £85.00 (VIL)

Dominus Christian Moueix **1996** £63.00 (CB) £79.21 (FA) £120.00 (JER)

Opus One Mondavi/Rothschild **1994** £63.00 (CRO) £112.80 (FA)

Petite Syrah Turley Cellars Aida Vineyard **1997** £61.99 (YOU)

£70.00 → £99.99

Cabernet Sauvignon Caymus Vineyards Special Selection **1994** £75.00 (DI)

Cabernet Sauvignon Chateau Montelena **1997** £84.00 (BAL)

Cabernet Sauvignon Heitz Martha's Vineyard **1996** £85.00 (JU)

Cabernet Sauvignon Joseph Phelps Backus Vineyard **1996** £85.00 (VIL)

Cabernet Sauvignon Shafer Hillside Select **1993** £94.00 (TUR)

Cabernet Sauvignon Philip Togni **1994** £85.00 (YOU)

Dominus Christian Moueix **1997** £83.62 (FA)

Dominus Christian Moueix **1989** £83.62 (FA)

Dominus Christian Moueix **1988** £77.75 (FA)

Dominus Christian Moueix **1985** £88.13 (FA)

Dominus Christian Moueix **1984** £89.50 (FA)

Dominus Christian Moueix **1983** £79.70 (FA)

Gravelly Meadow Diamond Creek **1997** £89.50 (LAY)

Insignia Joseph Phelps **1996** £85.00 (VIL)

Insignia Joseph Phelps **1986** £88.13 (BODX)

Opus One Mondavi/Rothschild **1995** £72.00 (UN) £113.98 (FA) £115.02 (NO) £141.00 (TUR)

Opus One Mondavi/Rothschild **1982** £89.50 (FA) £152.75 (TUR)

• All prices for each wine are listed together in ascending order.
• Price bands refer to the lowest price for which the wine is available.

Over £100.00

Cabernet Sauvignon Caymus Vineyards
Special Selection **1995** £103.20 (FA)
Cabernet Sauvignon Caymus Vineyards
Special Selection **1989** £118.87 (FA)
Cabernet Sauvignon Caymus Vineyards
Special Selection **1988** £129.25 (FA)
Cabernet Sauvignon Dalla Valle Maya
1996 £423.00 (TUR)
Monte Bello Ridge **1987** £145.00 (FORT)
Dominus Christian Moueix **1994** £105.00
(YOU) £117.50 (FA)
Dominus Christian Moueix **1991** £118.87
(FA)
Dominus Christian Moueix **1990** £107.12
(FA)
Opus One Mondavi/Rothschild **1997**
£105.00 (YOU) £110.00 (FORT) £113.98
(FA) £118.87 (BODX) £141.00 (TUR)
£150.00 (VIL)
Opus One Mondavi/Rothschild **1993**
£156.66 (TUR) £164.50 (WY)
Opus One Mondavi/Rothschild **1990**
£105.75 (FA)
Opus One Mondavi/Rothschild **1988**
£164.50 (TUR)
Opus One Mondavi/Rothschild **1981**
£217.38 (WY)

CALIFORNIA WHITE

Under £4.00

Blossom Hill White **Non-vintage** £3.99
(UN)
Chardonnay/Chenin Blanc E&J Gallo
Garnet Point **1999** £3.49 (MORR) £3.99
(BUD)
Chenin Blanc E&J Gallo **Non-vintage**
£3.99 (UN)
Chenin Blanc E&J Gallo **1999** £3.99 (BUD)
Colombard E&J Gallo **Non-vintage**
£3.99 (UN) £3.99 (SO) £3.99 (SAF)
Colombard E&J Gallo **2000** £3.99 (BUD)
£3.99 (ASD) £3.99 (MORR)
Colombard E&J Gallo **1999** £3.99 (VIC)
£3.99 (THR)

£4.00 → £5.99

Chardonnay E&J Gallo **1999** £4.69 (ASD)
£4.99 (BUD) £4.99 (WR) £4.99 (SAF)
£4.99 (MORR)
Chardonnay E&J Gallo **1998** £4.99 (VIC)
£4.99 (THR)

Chardonnay E&J Gallo Turning Leaf **1999**
£5.99 (MORR)
Chardonnay E&J Gallo Turning Leaf **1998**
£5.99 (TES)
Chardonnay E&J Gallo Turning Leaf **1997**
£5.99 (UN)
Chardonnay Glen Ellen **1999** £5.49 (BUD)
Chardonnay Redwood Trail **1998** £5.99
(UN) £5.99 (WAI)
Chardonnay Sutter Home **1999** £4.99 (SAF)
£4.99 (MORR) £5.25 (STE) £5.72 (LLO)
Chardonnay Sutter Home **1998** £4.69
(VIL) £4.99 (CON) £5.49 (UN)
Chardonnay Sutter Home **1997** £5.39
(JON)
Sauvignon Blanc E&J Gallo **1999** £4.69
(BUD) £4.69 (BO) £4.69 (SAF)
Sauvignon Blanc E&J Gallo **1997** £4.69 (UN)
Sauvignon Blanc Sutter Home **1998** £4.69
(VIL) £4.99 (CON)

£6.00 → £7.99

Chardonnay Bonterra **1998** £7.99 (BO)
£7.99 (JON) £8.49 (UN) £8.49 (WR) £8.49
(SAF)
Chardonnay Edna Valley ½ bottle **2000**
£6.62 (BIB)
Chardonnay Fetzer Barrel Select **1998**
£7.99 (TES)
Chardonnay Fetzer Sundial **1999** £6.49
(SO) £6.49 (VIC) £6.49 (THR) £6.49 (BOT)
£6.49 (WR)
Chardonnay Fetzer Sundial **1998** £6.49
(UN) £6.49 (WR)
Chardonnay Jekel **1998** £7.49 (VIC) £7.49
(THR) £7.49 (BOT) £7.49 (WR)
Chardonnay Wente **1997** £7.35 (COC)
£7.49 (UN)
Cotes d'Oakley Cline Cellars **1997** £6.48
(GW) £6.99 (VIL)
Fumé Blanc Beringer **1999** £7.99 (MAJ)
Fumé Blanc Beringer **1998** £7.99 (OD)
Fumé Blanc Monteviña **2000** £7.81 (LLO)
Fumé Blanc Monteviña **1999** £6.99 (VIL)
£7.39 (JON) £7.50 (PLA)
Fumé Blanc Monteviña **1998** £7.79 (PLAY)
Fumé Blanc Monteviña **1997** £7.25 (STE)
£7.80 (RIC)
Malvasia Bianca Bonny Doon Ca' del Solo
1999 £7.99 (BO) £8.20 (TAN) £8.40
(CRO) £8.70 (GW)
Malvasia Bianca Bonny Doon Ca' del Solo
1998 £7.99 (POR) £7.99 (AME) £7.99
(CON) £8.40 (BEN) £8.40 (BAC) £8.99
(VIL)

Orange Muscat Quady Essensia ½ bottle
Non-vintage £6.95 (NI) £7.73 (COC)
Orange Muscat Quady Essensia ½ bottle
1999 £7.95 (LEA)
Orange Muscat Quady Essensia ½ bottle
1998 £6.46 (PEN) £6.95 (STA) £6.99
(MAJ) £7.15 (WRI)
Orange Muscat Quady Essensia ½ bottle
1997 £7.43 (NO) £8.95 (JER)
Orange Muscat Quady Essensia ½ bottle
1996 £6.95 (CON)
Sauvignon Blanc Robert Mondavi
Woodbridge **1998** £6.99 (POR)
Sauvignon Blanc Robert Mondavi
Woodbridge **1997** £7.75 (STE)
Sauvignon Blanc Wente **1998** £6.80 (COC)
Viognier Fetzer **1999** £6.99 (TES) £7.99
(VIC) £7.99 (THR) £7.99 (BOT) £7.99 (WAI)
Viognier Fetzer **1998** £6.99 (OD)

£8.00 → £9.99

Chardonnay Beringer California **1998**
£8.99 (MAJ) £8.99 (NEZ)
Chardonnay Bonterra **1999** £8.49 (SAI)
£8.49 (WR) £8.49 (WAI) £8.49 (MORR)
Chardonnay Cartlidge & Browne **1999**
£8.95 (BER)
Chardonnay Hawk Crest **1999** £8.21 (DOM)
Chardonnay Hawk Crest **1998** £8.99 (GW)
Chardonnay Robert Mondavi **1997** £9.99
(UN) £15.99 (POR)
Chardonnay Robert Mondavi Coastal
1998 £9.09 (JON)
Chardonnay Murphy-Goode **1998** £9.95
(AD)
Chardonnay Pedroncelli **1998** £8.95 (LAY)
Chardonnay St Francis **1997** £9.99 (VA)
Chardonnay Sebastiani Sonoma **1998**
£9.99 (CO)
Chardonnay Seven Peaks **1998** £9.99 (BAN)
Chardonnay Seven Peaks **1997** £8.99 (UN)
Chardonnay Villa Mt Eden Coastal **1996**
£8.29 (CON)
Chardonnay Wente Riva Ranch **1997**
£8.99 (WR)
Chardonnay Wente Riva Ranch **1996**
£9.99 (UN)
Fumé Blanc Murphy-Goode **1998** £8.95
(AD)
Malvasia Bianca Bonny Doon Ca' del Solo
1997 £8.60 (WRI)
Riesling Bonny Doon Pacific Rim **1998**
£8.40 (MV) £8.99 (VIL) £9.50 (NI)
Viognier Bonterra **1999** £9.99 (BOT)
Viognier Bonterra **1998** £9.99 (UN)

£10.00 → £11.99

Chardonnay Kendall-Jackson Vintner's
Reserve **1998** £10.99 (DI)
Chardonnay Rochioli **1994** £10.99 (RAE)
Chardonnay Saintsbury Carneros **1999**
£11.75 (SOM) £13.95 (FLE)
Il Pescatore Bonny Doon Ca' del Solo
1996 £10.95 (FRI)
Malvasia Bianca Bonny Doon Ca' del Solo
2000 £11.60 (NI)
Riesling Joseph Phelps Johannisberg
Selected Late-Harvest ½ bottle **1986**
£11.00 (CRO)
Riesling Mark West Johannisberg Late-
Harvest ½ bottle **1983** £10.00 (CRO)
Roussanne Bonny Doon **1998** £11.99
(VIL) £11.99 (YOU) £13.95 (FRI)
Sauvignon Blanc Rochioli **1999** £11.90
(CRO)
Sauvignon Blanc St Supéry **1999** £11.95
(RES)

£12.00 → £14.99

Chardonnay Au Bon Climat **1998** £14.99
(GW) £15.00 (MV) £15.50 (BEN) £15.95
(LEA) £16.95 (RES)
Chardonnay Clos La Chance Santa Cruz
Mountains **1997** £13.99 (OD)
Chardonnay Cuvaison **1998** £13.99 (YOU)
£15.50 (TAN) £16.49 (AME)
Chardonnay De Loach **1997** £13.50 (DI)
Chardonnay Edna Valley **2000** £12.24 (BIB)
Chardonnay Landmark Overlook **1998**
£14.99 (OD)
Chardonnay Saintsbury Carneros **1998**
£13.90 (HAH) £14.95 (AD)
Chardonnay Saintsbury Carneros **1997**
£13.00 (JU) £13.50 (WS) £13.95 (FORT)
Chardonnay Saintsbury Carneros **1996**
£12.90 (CRO) £13.79 (NO)
Chardonnay Simi **1993** £13.04 (PEN)
Chardonnay Sonoma-Cutrer Russian
River **1997** £13.51 (PEN)
Fumé Blanc Robert Mondavi **1998** £13.25
(STE) £15.95 (POR)
Gewürztraminer Joseph Phelps **1998**
£14.99 (VIL)
Il Pescatore Bonny Doon Ca' del Solo
1997 £12.00 (GW)
Moscato d'Oro Robert Mondavi **1979**
£14.50 (BU)
Pinot Blanc Chalone **1996** £13.50 (WS)
Riesling Freemark Abbey Edelwein Gold
Johannisberg ½ bottle **1986** £14.00 (CRO)

Riesling Joseph Phelps Johannisberg
Selected Late-Harvest ½ bottle **1985**
£12.97 (NO)
Riesling Stag's Leap Wine Cellars Napa
1998 £13.99 (VIL)
Roussanne Cline Cellars Los Carneros
1997 £12.99 (VIL)
Pinot Grigio Seghesio **2000** £14.95 (LIB)
Sauvignon Blanc Chalk Hill **1996** £13.00
(JU)
Sauvignon Blanc Frog's Leap **2000** £13.50
(MV)
Sauvignon Blanc Frog's Leap **1999** £13.45
(LAY)
Sauvignon Blanc Frog's Leap **1997** £12.32
(NO)
Sauvignon Blanc Rochioli **2000** £13.75 (NI)
Sauvignon Blanc St Supéry **2000** £14.49
(LIB)
Sauvignon Blanc Sanford **1998** £12.99 (VIL)
Sauvignon Blanc Stag's Leap Wine Cellars
Napa **1997** £12.99 (VIL) £22.99 (POR)
Viognier Cline Cellars Los Carneros
1998 £12.99 (VIL)
Viognier/Chardonnay Qupé Bien Nacido
Cuvée **1998** £14.50 (WRI) £14.50 (FRI)
£14.80 (BAC)

£15.00 → £19.99

Chardonnay Au Bon Climat **1997** £15.95
(FORT) £18.80 (TAN)
Chardonnay Au Bon Climat Le Bouge d'à
Côté **1996** £18.54 (NO)
Chardonnay Au Bon Climat Talley
Vineyard **1998** £19.99 (YOU)
Chardonnay Chalk Hill **1996** £17.00 (JU)
Chardonnay Chalk Hill **1993** £19.80 (CRO)
Chardonnay Clos du Val Carneros **1999**
£15.50 (MAY)
Chardonnay Clos du Val Carneros **1996**
£15.95 (STA)
Chardonnay Cuvaison Carneros **1997**
£15.50 (STA)
Chardonnay De Loach **1998** £16.95 (GN)
Chardonnay Fritz Dutton Ranch **1996**
£18.99 (VIL)
Chardonnay Frog's Leap **1999** £19.75
(LAY)
Chardonnay Frog's Leap **1998** £17.75
(CON)

A key to name abbreviations
is available on page 7.

Chardonnay Mer Soleil **1996** £19.95 (DI)
Chardonnay Robert Mondavi **1998**
£16.30 (TAN)
Chardonnay Joseph Phelps Los Carneros
1997 £17.99 (VIL)
Chardonnay Rancho Sisquoc **1998** £16.50
(JER)
Chardonnay Kent Rasmussen Napa Valley
1998 £15.99 (OD)
Chardonnay Ridge Santa Cruz Mountains
1998 £17.10 (SOM) £20.95 (FRI)
Chardonnay Ridge Santa Cruz Mountains
1996 £16.00 (CRO) £19.95 (AD)
Chardonnay Ridge Santa Cruz Mountains
1995 £16.62 (NO)
Chardonnay Rutherford Hill Jaeger **1991**
£17.63 (PEN)
Chardonnay St Supéry **1999** £17.95 (LIB)
Chardonnay Saintsbury Carneros **2000**
£17.50 (NI)
Chardonnay Sanford **1996** £15.99 (VIL)
Chardonnay Shafer **1995** £18.49 (NO)
Chardonnay Sonoma-Cutrer Russian
River **1999** £16.95 (RES) £18.50 (LEA)
Chardonnay Stag's Leap Wine Cellars
Napa **1997** £17.50 (GW) £17.99 (VIL)
£19.39 (DOM)
Chardonnay Swanson **1988** £17.51 (PEN)
Chardonnay Marimar Torres Estate Don
Miguel Vineyard **1998** £16.03 (PEN)
Chardonnay Marimar Torres Estate Don
Miguel Vineyard **1997** £17.99 (POR)
Chardonnay Marimar Torres Estate Don
Miguel Vineyard **1996** £16.95 (BALL)
Chardonnay Marimar Torres Estate Don
Miguel Vineyard **1995** £16.99 (DI)
£21.00 (CRO)
Fumé Blanc Robert Mondavi **1997** £16.30
(TAN)
Pinot Blanc Chalone **1999** £17.13 (BIB)
£18.90 (BAC)
Pinot Blanc Chalone **1998** £16.99 (YOU)
Roussanne Bonny Doon **1997** £16.68 (NO)
Sauvignon Blanc Duckhorn **1998** £16.95
(LAY) £18.50 (FORT)

£20.00 → £29.99

Chardonnay Au Bon Climat Alban
Vineyard **1997** £25.99 (YOU)
Chardonnay Au Bon Climat Le Bouge d'à
Côté **1998** £20.00 (MV)
Chardonnay Au Bon Climat Le Bouge d'à
Côté **1995** £28.20 (CRO)
Chardonnay Au Bon Climat Talley
Vineyard **1995** £24.00 (YOU)

Chardonnay Beringer Private Reserve
1996 £27.00 (CRO)
Chardonnay Chalone **1999** £22.52 (BIB)
Chardonnay Chalone **1997** £21.50 (FORT)
Chardonnay Chateau Montelena **1998**
£21.50 (BAL)
Chardonnay Fritz Poplar Ranch **1996**
£21.99 (VIL)
Chardonnay Grgich Hills **1997** £29.95
(RES) £32.00 (JER)
Chardonnay Lewis Reserve **1998** £29.99
(WIN)
Chardonnay Matanzas Creek **1997**
£24.50 (BEN)
Chardonnay Matanzas Creek **1995**
£22.50 (BAL) £23.95 (RES)
Chardonnay Mer Soleil **1997** £23.95 (DI)
Chardonnay Monticello Corley Family
Vineyards **1995** £20.50 (FORT)
Chardonnay Monticello Corley Select
Reserve **1997** £22.90 (LAY)
Chardonnay Newton Red Label **1999**
£20.83 (ARM)
Chardonnay Joseph Phelps Ovation **1997**
£25.99 (YOU) £28.99 (VIL)
Chardonnay Ridge Santa Cruz Mountains
1997 £21.35 (BEN)
Chardonnay Rochioli **1999** £20.75 (NI)
Chardonnay Saintsbury Reserve **1998**
£23.95 (CON) £24.99 (VIL)
Chardonnay Saintsbury Reserve **1997**
£24.00 (WS)
Chardonnay Saintsbury Reserve **1996**
£21.00 (CRO) £21.00 (JU) £24.00 (WS)
£25.75 (AD)
Chardonnay Sanford Estate **1996** £21.99
(VIL)
Chardonnay Sanford Barrel Select **1995**
£23.99 (VIL)
Chardonnay Shafer Red Shoulder Ranch
1998 £25.99 (VIL)
Chardonnay Sonoma-Cutrer les Pierres
1998 £23.95 (RES)
Chardonnay Sonoma-Cutrer les Pierres
1996 £21.74 (PEN) £24.95 (LEA)
Chardonnay Stag's Leap Wine Cellars
Napa **1999** £24.50 (JER)
Chardonnay Stag's Leap Wine Cellars
Beckstoffer Ranch **1997** £23.99 (VIL)
Chardonnay Stags' Leap Winery **1999**
£21.95 (RES)
Chardonnay Testarossa Sleepy Hollow
1999 £26.49 (YOU) £27.95 (LIB)
Chardonnay Villa Mt Eden Coastal **1997**
£29.00 (WS)

Riesling Firestone Selected Harvest
Johannisberg ½ bottle **1985** £22.00 (CRO)
Riesling Joseph Phelps Johannisberg
Selected Late-Harvest ½ bottle **1997**
£27.99 (VIL)
Sauvignon Blanc Frog's Leap **1994** £25.00
(BU)
Viognier Calera **1997** £24.95 (RES)
Viognier Joseph Phelps **1997** £22.99 (VIL)
£24.95 (RES)
Viognier Phelps Vin du Mistral **1995**
£28.25 (NO)
Viognier Sanford & Benedict Cold Heaven
1998 £22.00 (MV)

Over £30.00

Chardonnay Far Niente **1994** £34.07 (PEN)
Chardonnay Ramey Hyde Vineyard **1998**
£33.99 (YOU)
Viognier Calera **1996** £31.62 (NO)

CALIFORNIA ROSÉ

Under £4.50

White Grenache E&J Gallo **Non-vintage**
£4.38 (ASD)

£4.50 → £6.49

White Grenache E&J Gallo **1999** £4.69
(UN) £4.69 (BUD) £4.69 (VIC) £4.69 (THR)
£4.69 (BOT) £4.69 (SAF)
White Zinfandel Sutter Home **1999**
£4.69 (SAF) £4.99 (BUD)
White Zinfandel Sutter Home **1998**
£4.69 (VIL) £4.99 (JON)
White Zinfandel Wente **1998** £6.49 (UN)

Over £6.50

Vin Gris de Cigare, Bonny Doon **2000**
£8.00 (MV) £9.50 (NI)
Vin Gris de Cigare, Bonny Doon **1999**
£8.99 (VIL)

CALIFORNIA SPARKLING

Under £10.00

Gallo Brut **Non-vintage** £6.05 (BY)
Mumm Cuvée Napa Brut **Non-vintage**
£9.99 (WR) £9.99 (WAI) £9.99 (ASD)
£10.99 (UN) £10.99 (BUD) £10.99 (MAJ)
£10.99 (VIC) £10.99 (THR) £10.99 (BOT)
£10.99 (OD) £10.99 (VIL) £10.99 (SAF)
£11.95 (JER) £12.89 (BY)

Mumm Cuvée Napa Rosé **Non-vintage**
£9.95 (JER) £10.99 (MAJ) £10.99 (VIC)
£10.99 (THR) £10.99 (BOT) £10.99 (WR)
£10.99 (VIL)

£10.00 → £15.99

Mumm Cuvée Napa Brut Blanc de Blancs
Non-vintage £11.99 (OD) £12.49 (VIL)
Mumm Cuvée Napa Rosé **1991** £12.99
(OD) £12.99 (VIL)
Roederer Estate Quartet **Non-vintage**
£14.21 (NO) £14.90 (CRO) £14.95 (BALL)
£15.00 (JU) £15.40 (HIC) £15.99 (BEN)
£15.99 (POR) £16.45 (PEN) £16.95 (FORT)
£17.49 (MAJ) £17.99 (JON)

c. £17.00

Schramsberg Blanc de Blancs **1995**
£16.95 (LEA)

OREGON/WASHINGTON RED

Under £10.00

Pinot Noir Firesteed **1997** £7.95 (SOM)
£9.75 (WRI) £9.85 (CON)
Pinot Noir Rex Hill Kings Ridge **1997**
£9.99 (MOR)

£10.00 → £14.99

Cabernet Sauvignon Chateau Ste Michelle
1993 £10.50 (WRI)
Cabernet Sauvignon Chateau Ste Michelle
1988 £14.00 (CRO)
Cabernet Sauvignon Columbia Crest
1997 £11.50 (FORT)
Cabernet Sauvignon Columbia Crest
1993 £11.00 (CRO)
Cabernet Sauvignon Staton Hills **1994**
£13.45 (CB)
Cabernet Sauvignon Staton Hills **1993**
£13.45 (CB) £15.50 (CRO)
Merlot Canoe Ridge **1997** £13.98 (BIB)
£16.99 (YOU)
Merlot Chateau Ste Michelle **1998** £14.65
(GN)
Merlot Columbia Crest **1990** £12.50 (CRO)
Pinot Meunier Eyrie Vineyard **1997**
£12.53 (SAV)
Pinot Noir Eyrie Vineyard **1997** £14.10
(SAV)
Pinot Noir Firesteed **1999** £10.95 (LIB)
Pinot Noir Firesteed **1998** £10.75 (NI)
Pinot Noir Rex Hill Kings Ridge **1995**
£11.06 (LLO)

£15.00 → £19.99

Cabernet Sauvignon Chateau Ste Michelle
1985 £16.00 (CRO)
Cabernet Sauvignon Columbia Otis
Vineyard **1985** £19.98 (PEN)
Merlot Canoe Ridge **1998** £16.65 (BIB)
Pinot Noir Amity **1995** £16.70 (JER)
Pinot Noir Eyrie Vineyard **1999** £16.25
(SAV)

Over £20.00

Merlot L'École No. 41 **1996** £24.85 (JER)
Pinot Noir Amity Winemakers Reserve
1993 £34.40 (JER)
Pinot Noir Domaine Drouhin **1997**
£23.95 (BEN) £25.00 (FORT)
Pinot Noir Domaine Drouhin **1996**
£22.21 (PEN) £23.95 (STA)
Pinot Noir Domaine Drouhin Laurène
1996 £28.90 (BEN)
Pinot Noir Domaine Drouhin Laurène
1995 £31.25 (NI)

OREGON/WASH. WHITE

Under £7.00

Chardonnay Columbia Crest **1998** £5.99
(MORR)
Sauvignon Blanc Columbia Crest **1996**
£6.99 (VA)

£7.00 → £9.99

Chardonnay Columbia Crest **1997** £9.50
(FORT)
Chardonnay Salishan **1997** £8.79 (SAV)
Gewürztraminer Columbia **1999** £8.20
(GN)
Riesling Amity **1996** £7.95 (WS)
Sémillon Chateau Ste Michelle **1998**
£7.80 (GN)

Over £10.00

Chardonnay Canoe Ridge **1997** £17.50
(CON)
Chardonnay Eyrie Vineyard **1997** £11.95
(SAV)

OTHER USA WHITE

c. £12.50

★ Chardonnay Vicker's Vineyard, Idaho
1993 £12.53 (SAV)

OTHER REGIONS

The countries to which we give whole chapters are not the only story. Austria is producing world-class wines now, and Greece is showing that it can make more than retsina. Canada and Uruguay are up-and-coming, and other countries can field a few stars

AUSTRIA

Austrian wines have been busy finding their feet in the last few years. And where are they now that they've found them? Firmly in their native soil, that's for sure. They've evolved a style that is elegant and structured (I'm talking about white wines here, if you were wondering), with good acidity but not the over-high acidity that some of them went in for a while ago. There's often a minerally flavour to them, and they're not designed for immensely long aging. Even the Rieslings of the Wachau region don't live as long as, say, German examples – and Riesling is a grape generally given to age. They're also much drier, and have higher alcohol content than German wines, but it's actually best not to compare them at all, since that particular comparison is only misleading.

Gruner Veltliner, which used to be thought of as something best glugged back by the half litre and forgotten about, turns out to be potentially a rather serious grape. It's got a lovely subtle pepper and bay leaf flavour, which may not sound much, but you don't want massive flavours all the time.

New oak? Inevitably there's some. It's not necessarily to the advantage of the wines, particularly since it's often still a new toy, and they don't know when to stop. But on the reds it can be a useful extra.

I'm not sure that Austria has any red grapes that are as good as its whites. Blaufränkisch can be good, all cherries and redcurrants, but if the yields are too high the natural acidity takes over and it just goes thin and weedy. It generally needs a bit of help from something else, and that

something else is usually Cabernet. Blauburgunder is Pinot Noir, and seldom that amazing. Zweigelt is attractive, with celery and blueberry fruit flavours. It's mostly treated as everyday stuff, but it can be concentrated and lush, too. St Laurent makes attractive Beaujolais-lookalikes. There are lots of red blends, often with French grapes, and Merlot usually ripens better than Cabernet.

One of Austria's greatest contributions to the multi-faceted world of wine is the revival of Ruster Ausbruch, a sweet wine from the town of Rust, on the shore of Lake Neusiedl. It doesn't seem to matter much which grapes are used – some producers grow Gelber Muskateller (one of the better Muscats), others use Pinot Blanc, Sauvignon Blanc or Hungary's Furmint – as long as they are overripe and affected by noble rot. The result is closer to Sauternes than to Germany's sweet styles, with less fruit flavour but more complexity.

Austria's best producers include *Bründlmayer, Feiler-Artinger, Freie Weingärtner Wachau, Gesellmann, Heinrich, Franz Hirtzberger, Josef Jamek, Juris (Georg Stiegelmar), Kollwentz, Emmerich Knoll, Alois Kracher, Krutzler, Lenz Moser, Malat, Nigl, Nikolaihof, H & A Nittnaus, Willi Opitz, F-X Pichler, Prager, Prieler, Fritz Salomon, Heidi Schröck, Ernst Triebaumer, Umathum, Velich, Robert Wenzel* and *Fritz Wieninger.*

CANADA

Cool-climate wines that are mostly sound rather than exciting, though the icewines (sweet wines made from grapes frozen on the vine in winter) are some of the world's most original sweet wines. Grape varieties include Chardonnay (of course), Pinot Blanc, Pinot Gris, Riesling, Gewürztraminer and sometimes Merlot. The good news is that as of 2001 icewine will be allowed into the EU: the reason you've never seen it in the shops is because it wasn't allowed in. These wines are intensely sweet and very concentrated; the grapes most used are Riesling and Vidal – and the latter is a hybrid, which is an additional irritation for the Eurocrats. Best names include *Blue Mountain, Calona, Cave Spring, Cedar Creek, Chateau des Charmes, Gehringer Brothers, Gray Monk, Hainle Vineyards, Henry of Pelham, Hillebrand, Inniskillin, Mission Hill, Quail's Gate, Sumac Ridge, Summerhill* and *Thirty Bench.*

CYPRUS

At last, Cyprus is modernizing its wine industry: with government support, wineries are being built in or near the vineyards; the leading producers, *Etko, Keo, Loel* and *Sodap,* are making efforts to match grape varieties to vineyard sites. Experiments with international varieties such as Cabernet, Shiraz, Chardonnay and Sémillon alongside indigenous grapes are already paying off. Commandaria is the island's raisiny, treacly-sweet – but slightly dull – fortified.

GREECE

Expect changes in the appellation system here, as winemakers plant increasing amounts of non-authorized varieties. In fact there's something of a 'Super-Tuscan' situation developing, as these new high-quality wines are denied appellation status and have to settle for calling themselves vins de pays; producers are making up their own names for their wines. Well, that situation didn't do Italy any harm, and perhaps Greece will battle its way to fame and fortune by the same route.

There are about 250 indigenous grape varieties in Greece, so if I don't list them all you'll probably forgive me. Only(!) about 30 varieties are commonly grown, anyway,

among whites – and there are some terrific new-style whites in Greece. Robola is lemony and flinty; Moschophilero is aromatic, a bit like a cross between Muscat and Gewürztraminer; Savatiano is more neutral and much used for retsina. Malagousia has fat, ripe, peachy flavours, and often gets blended with Assyrtiko, which is altogether steelier. Assyrtiko is a good bet generally: it's minerally and well balanced, rather polished.

The main red grapes are rather more familiar: there's Agiorgitiko and Mavrodaphne, Xynomavro and Limnio: expect earthy, minerally flavours and good fruit. Agiorgitiko can be a bit low in acidity, but has good plum and cherry fruit; Mavrodaphne is aromatic and often made sweet and fortified. Xynomavro is of potentially very high quality, and ages well; Limnio is every bit as good, full bodied and with good acidity.

Some of the best reds are the powerful, concentrated wines that blend native Greek and international varieties, such as *Megas Oenos* from *Skouras, Antonopoulos Collection* and *Chateau Carras* from *Domaine Carras.*

My only quarrel with Greek wines these days is that when they start playing with new oak, they tend to overdo it. It's a common problem, and they'll get over it. Well, I have one other quarrel: a lot of their wines are exported with labels in Greek. And the Greeks don't use the same alphabet as the rest of us.

Best producers include *Achaia-Clauss, Antonopoulos, Boutari, Domaine Carras, Gaia, Gentilini, Gerovassiliou, Chateau Harlaftis, Domaine Kokotos (formerly Semeli), Dom. Constantin Lazaridi, Domaine Mercouri, Kourtakis, Skouras, Spiropoulos, Strofilia* and *Tsantalis.*

Greece's other treasures are the rich, sweet Muscat wines produced by the co-ops on the island of Samos: honeyed Samos Nectar is made from sun-dried grapes; Samos Anthemis is fortified and cask-aged for up to five years.

INDIA

Bordeaux oenologist Michel Rolland is the consultant winemaker for *Grover*, which is turning out respectable whites and reds, and *Chateau Indage* is making considerable efforts with both red and white from high-altitude vineyards near Pune. *Chateau Indage's* greatest success so far has been with *Omar Khayyam* – a surprisingly good Champagne-method fizz. There are a handful of other producers, but India isn't very suited to wine grapes and the vast majority of her vines produce grapes for the table.

ISRAEL

The *Golan Heights* winery is the best producer. *Carmel* is bigger, and has recently improved its act, but the emphasis on producing Kosher wine means that the supervision of a rabbi can take precedence over the ideas of the winemaker. The idea that Kosher wine might also be nice to drink is of fairly recent date.

LEBANON

Chateau Musar is still the star here, making gutsy, spicy reds that will live 30 years. Serge Hochar, whose baby Musar is, reckons it's at its peak at 15 years, which means you have to stash it away for quite a while after buying it. It's worth the wait, though it's temptingly good young, as well. *Chateau Ksara* is another producer whose wines impressed me when I tasted them recently.

LUXEMBOURG

Difficult to find outside the Grand Duchy itself, and frankly not that exciting when you do find them. I mean, don't make a journey specially. Most are light and made from Müller-Thurgau, alias Rivaner. The vineyards are on the banks of the Mosel (or Moselle if you prefer), but don't start expecting the thrills of German Mosel – because you won't get them.

MEXICO

If you happen to have some of the folding stuff about you, you might want to try Mexico's current star wine: it's called *Monte Xanic,* and it aspires to be the Mondavi of Mexico. And it is good, actually: full and rich. It's probably the best thing to have come out of Mexico in the last ten or 15 years. But it is expensive.

Otherwise, *LA Cetto* is still there, making good Zinfandel, Petite Sirah and Cabernet Sauvignon, and *Santo Tomas* has a joint venture with Wente of California, which uses grapes from both wineries. *Casa Madero* is making a fair stab at things near Monterey, and actually produces rather good white wine, while the rest of Mexico clearly seems better suited to red.

NORTH AFRICA

This had a ready market for its wines in colonial days, but until now it's been steadily downhill ever since. Now a mixture of European and Antipodean investment and knowhow is at last beginning to make its mark in both Tunisia and Morocco, and if first releases of wines like Syrah, Cabernet Sauvignon and Carignan are anything to go by, North Africa could be back with a bang. But it'll be tough, because under the influence of Islam, these countries tend not to look kindly on their indigenous wine industries.

Meknes is traditionally one of the better areas in Morocco; giant French producer Castel Frères now have vineyards and a large modern winery there. Look for oak-aged Cabernet/Merlot blends *Baraka* and *L'Excellence de Bonassia*, and Moroccan Syrah and Cabernet Sauvignon under *Sainsbury's* own label.

Tunisia's most exciting wines are made by a producer not that far across the Mediterranean, in Sicily: look for the names *Accademia del Sole* and *Selian*. Tunisian Muscat can be reasonable.

SWITZERLAND

I like Swiss wines – I certainly drink them whenever I'm in Switzerland – but very few are exported. The real stars of Swiss wine are the oddities – the Petite Arvine, rich, aromatic and often made sweet, from late-picked grapes; the Amigne, also headily aromatic; the Humagne Blanche, rich, with good acidity. These are curiously a world apart from the usual Swiss white, which is made from the Chasselas grape, also called Fendant, Perlan or Dorin. It's a fairly neutral grape variety, but these are perfectly nice wines, and they do reflect their site quite strongly. The Swiss do have an interesting way with Pinot Gris: when I was there in January I drank a spicy, honeyed *mi-fletris* Malvoisie (a local name for a late-harvested Pinot Gris) with a hunk of Argentinian steak – and it was fab.

There's some surprisingly good Syrah from the Valais; perhaps not that surprising when you consider that the Rhône Valley starts here, and even in the depths of winter, skiers in Verbier can see the snow melting away fom this Alpine suntrap. The French-speaking cantons also produce Pinot Noir and Gamay; the Pinot Noir/Gamay blend, Dole, is typically light, fruity and must be drunk young. The Italian-speaking canton of Ticino concentrates on Merlot, which ranges, as befits Italian individuality, from pale rosés to intensely fruity oak-aged reds.

Can you get Swiss wines over here? Yes, sometimes. Names to look for include *Charles Bonvin, Louis Bovard, Germanier Bon Père, Caves Imesch* and *Provins.* If want to find out more, you could try contacting Swiss Wine UK, tel 020-7851 1731.

TURKEY

Not a serious wine-producing country: only a tiny proportion of the grape harvest, some two or three per cent, is turned into wine. Turkish restaurants (the better kind, at least) in Britain seem to be able to find perfectly decent house wines from Turkey, though.

UNITED KINGDOM

Even with vineyards concentrated in the south of England and Wales, ripeness is a problem, and early-ripening Germanic crosses like Bacchus, Müller-Thurgau and Huxelrebe are the usual solution. Some of the best wines come from Seyval Blanc, a hybrid disliked by the EU; there's also some Chardonnay, Riesling, Gewürztraminer and Pinot Blanc. Flavours seem to fall into two broad groups: there's the pungent elderflower kind, which usually has some highly perfumed grapes in it, and there's the nuttier, leafier, more neutral kind, rather like a sub-Soave. Both kinds sometimes have some residual sugar. There are also some properly sweet wines, made with botrytized grapes. There are reds, too, from Dornfelder and Dunkelfelder, and sometimes from Cabernet and Merlot, those these usually have to be grown under plastic. Pinot Noir is grown, though mostly for rosés and sparkling wines.

Sparkling wines may indeed be the future for England and Wales. So far the sparklers do not lack elegance and refinement, though a bit more character would not come amiss.

Best producers include *Biddenden, Beenleigh Manor, Breaky Bottom, Bruisyard, Carr Taylor, Chapel Down, Chiltern Valley, Denbies, Hidden Spring, Lamberhurst, Nyetimber, Penshurst, Ridgeview, Sharpham, Three Choirs, Valley Vineyards, Wyken.*

Some of the supermarkets are beginning to stock English wines from the larger producers such as *Chapel Down* and *Three Choirs,* and branches in wine-producing areas sometimes stock locally made wines. Many more are sold direct from the vineyard. If you're interested in tasting them, look on the English Wine Producers website (www.englishwineproducers.com) or telephone (01536) 772264 for further information.

URUGUAY

Tannat is the great discovery here: an obscure grape from South-West France is suddenly blossoming into lovely spicy reds. The whites, when they're made in a modern style, are perfectly nice.

OTHER REGIONS PRICES

AUSTRIA

Under £10.00

Blauer Zweigelt Heinrich 1999 £8.70
(BAC)

Blauer Zweigelt Weinbau Krutzler 1995
£8.95 (JU)

Blaufränkisch Paul Achs 1998 £8.90
(BAC)

Chardonnay Paul Achs 1999 £7.90
(BAC)

Grüner Veltliner Weissenkirchner
Achleiten Smaragd, Freie Weingärtner
Wachau 1998 £9.89 (HIC)

Zierfandler Ried Badnerweg Trocken,
Schellmann 1998 £7.90 (BAC)

£10.00 → £14.99

Bouvier/Neuburger
Trockenbeerenauslese, Lenz Moser ½
bottle 1995 £13.20 (NO)

Cuvée Eiswein Alois Kracher ½ bottle
1998 £12.99 (YOU)

Grüner Veltliner Schütt Smaragd,
Emmerich Knoll 1999 £14.29 (PAU)

Grüner Veltliner Smaragd Achleiten,
Prager 1999 £13.33 (PAU) £17.49
(YOU)

Grüner Veltliner Weissenkirchner
Achleiten Smaragd, Freie Weingärtner
Wachau 1999 £14.25 (MAY)

Pannobile Heinrich 1998 £12.90 (BAC)

Riesling Loibenberg Smaragd, Emmerich
Knoll 1999 £14.29 (PAU)

Riesling Loibenberg Smaragd, Emmerich
Knoll 1998 £14.29 (PAU) £21.95
(RAE)

Riesling Viesslinger Federspiel, Freie
Weingärtner Wachau 1999 £14.25
(MAY)

Riesling vom Stein Federspiel, Nikolaihof
1998 £13.50 (RAE) £14.01 (BIB)

Riesling vom Stein Federspiel, Nikolaihof
1997 £13.50 (RAE)

Riesling vom Stein Federspiel, Nikolaihof
1996 £13.50 (BAL) £13.71 (BIB)

Ruster Ausbruch Gelber Muskateller,
Heidi Schröck 50cl 1998 £12.52 (SAV)

Seewinkel Beerenauslese, Velich 1998
£10.26 (NO)

£15.00 → £24.99

Gabarinza Heinrich 1998 £15.90 (BAC)

Grüner Veltliner Ried Grub, Schloss
Gobelsburg 1998 £16.50 (FORT)

Grüner Veltliner Ried Lamm, Schloss
Gobelsburg 1998 £17.25 (FORT)

Grüner Veltliner Smaragd Honivogl, Franz
Hirtzberger 1999 £22.95 (GAU)

Grüner Veltliner von den Terrassen
Smaragd, F-X Pichler 1999 £16.99
(YOU)

Grüner Veltliner von den Terrassen
Smaragd, F-X Pichler 1998 £19.99
(RAE)

Riesling Loibenberg Smaragd, Emmerich
Knoll 1997 £20.95 (RAE)

Riesling Smaragd Achleiten, Prager 1999
£17.46 (PAU) £20.99 (YOU)

Riesling Smaragd Achleiten, Prager 1998
£16.83 (PAU)

Riesling Smaragd Klaus, Prager 1999
£18.73 (PAU) £20.99 (YOU)

Riesling Smaragd Klaus, Prager 1998
£18.73 (PAU)

RETAILERS SPECIALIZING IN THESE COUNTRIES
see Retailers Directory (page 40) for details

Good retailers often stock a scattering of wines from these countries. The following have a slightly better choice: **Austria** Adnams (AD), Bacchus (BAC), D Byrne, Justerini & Brooks (JU), Lay & Wheeler (LAY), Christopher Piper Wines (PIP), T & W Wines (TW), Noel Young (YOU); **Canada** Averys of Bristol, Corney & Barrow (CB), Terry Platt (PLA), Stevens Garnier (STE); **Greece** Direct Wine Shipments (DI), Oddbins (OD), Tanners (TAN); **Israel** no actual specialists but Averys of Bristol, Corney & Barrow (CB), and Safeway (SAF) have some; **Lebanon** Chateau Musar is widely available. For older vintages try Roberson.

METOXI

TSANTALI

intense
and generous
with a velvety texture,
from the pristine

"Mount Athos
Vineyard"

TSANTALI

Riesling Steiner Hund Spatlese, Nikolaihof
1997 £22.95 (RAE)
Riesling Steinertal Smaragd, F-X Pichler
1999 £18.73 (PAU) £25.49 (YOU)
Riesling vom Stein Smaragd, Nikolaihof
1998 £21.95 (RAE)
Riesling vom Stein Smaragd, Nikolaihof
1997 £20.00 (WS) £21.95 (RAE) £24.24
(BIB)
Riesling vom Stein Smaragd, Nikolaihof
1995 £22.50 (RAE)
Trockenbeerenauslese Erwin Tinhof ½
bottle **1995** £15.50 (SAV)
Viognier V, Graf Hardegg **1999** £19.59
(YOU)

Over £25.00

Grüner Veltliner von den Terrassen
Smaragd, F-X Pichler **1992** £26.98
(PAU)
Muskat Schilfmandl Weisser, Willi Opitz
1990 £53.96 (NO)
St Laurent Reserve, Joseph Umathum
1995 £25.00 (FORT)
Welschriesling Trockenbeerenauslese No
1, Alois Kracher **1995** £26.00 (JU)

CANADA

Under £10.00

Chardonnay Inniskillin **1996** £6.99
(VIL)
Riesling Chateau des Charmes
Late-Harvest ½ bottle **1997** £8.45
(STE)

c. £13.00

Pinot Noir Inniskillin Reserve **1995**
£12.99 (VIL)

CYPRUS

Under £5.00

Aphrodite Keo White **Non-vintage**
£4.99 (DI)
Commandaria St John **Non-vintage**
£4.99 (UN) £8.99 (VA)
St Panteleimon Keo White **Non-vintage**
£4.99 (UN)

GREECE RED

Under £4.00

VdP de Crète Kourtakis **1999** £3.45
(MORR)
VdP de Crète Kourtakis **1998** £3.45
(WAI) £3.49 (BUD)

£4.00 → £5.99

Mavrodaphne Patras, Cambas **Non-
vintage** £5.19 (JON)
Mavrodaphne Patras, Kourtakis **Non-
vintage** £4.29 (WAI) £4.29 (SAF)
Mavrodaphne Patras, Tsantalis **Non-
vintage** £5.40 (TAN)
Nemea Boutari **1999** £4.99 (OD)
Notios Gaia **2000** £5.99 (OD)
Syrah Tsantalis **1997** £5.99 (OD)

Over £6.00

Amethystos Domaine Lazaridi **1998**
£8.99 (OD)
Domaine Gerovassiliou **1997** £6.99
(OD)
Mavrodaphne Patras, Tsantalis **1944**
£8.82 (NO)
Metoxi Tsantalis **1997** £7.49 (OD)
Strofilia **1997** £6.49 (OD)
Syrah Ktima Kyr-Yianni **1998** £8.99 (OD)

GREECE WHITE

Under £3.50

Retsina Kourtakis **Non-vintage** £3.29
(BUD) £3.29 (SAF) £3.35 (WAI) £3.59 (VIC)
£3.59 (THR) £3.59 (BOT) £3.59 (WR)
£3.59 (OD) £3.79 (UN)

£3.50 → £4.99

Mantinia Cambas **Non-vintage** £4.99
(JON)
Notios Gaia **2000** £4.99 (OD)
Retsina Tsantalis **Non-vintage** £4.15
(TAN)
Santorini Boutari **2000** £4.99 (OD)
Strofilia **1999** £4.99 (OD)

Over £5.00

Amethystos Domaine Lazaridi **2000**
£6.99 (OD)
Chardonnay Antonopoulos **1998** £9.99
(OD)
Chromitsa Tsantalis **2000** £6.99 (OD)
Classico White, Gentilini **2000** £6.49 (OD)
Domaine Gerovassiliou **2000** £6.49 (OD)
Nafsika Strofilia **1999** £5.99 (OD)
Samos Nectar, Vinicoles de Samos **Non-vintage** £9.40 (TAN)

INDIA

c. £10.00

Omar Khayyam **1990** £9.84 (NO)

ISRAEL

Under £6.00

Palwin No. 4 **Non-vintage** £5.69 (SAF)
Palwin No. 10 **Non-vintage** £4.99 (SAF)

c. £6.50

Carmel Cabernet Sauvignon **1995** £6.49
(SAF)

LEBANON RED

Under £10.00

Chateau Musar **1994** £9.69 (BODX) £9.69
(FA) £9.99 (BO) £10.28 (TUR) £10.49
(POR) £10.50 (BAC) £10.93 (PEN) £10.95
(WS) £10.99 (MAJ) £10.99 (VIL) £11.00

(HIG) £11.25 (VIN) £11.25 (CON) £11.29
(UN) £11.30 (TAN) £11.32 (PLAY) £11.40
(GN) £11.75 (BEN) £11.75 (FORT) £11.95
(STE) £11.95 (LEA) £11.95 (RES) £11.95
(AD) £12.49 (YOU) £12.50 (BALL) £12.69
(JON) £12.75 (WRI) £13.90 (CRO) £14.85
(NI)
Chateau Musar **1993** £9.69 (BODX) £9.69
(FA) £10.48 (TUR) £11.90 (GAU) £11.99
(VIL) £12.95 (BALL) £12.99 (YOU) £13.75
(WRI)

£10.00 → £19.99

Chateau Musar **1995** £11.95 (SAV) £11.99
(YOU) £12.56 (PLA) £12.69 (JON) £13.20
(JER)
Chateau Musar **1991** £10.18 (BODX)
£10.18 (FA) £11.26 (TUR) £12.99 (VIL)
Chateau Musar **1989** £19.00 (FA)

£20.00 → £29.99

Chateau Musar **1988** £21.65 (WRI) £33.44
(PLAY)
Chateau Musar **1986** £27.50 (WRI) £30.26
(FA)
Chateau Musar **1981** £27.03 (FA)
Chateau Musar **1980** £28.30 (FA)

Over £30.00

Chateau Musar **1979** £30.75 (FA)
Chateau Musar **1977** £34.50 (BEN)
Chateau Musar **1972** £55.23 (FA)
Chateau Musar **1966** £71.87 (FA)

LEBANON WHITE

Under £8.00

Chateau Musar Blanc **1996** £6.76 (FA)
£7.49 (POR) £7.65 (CON) £7.99 (VIL)
Chateau Musar Blanc **1995** £7.05 (FA)
£7.49 (BO) £7.70 (WRI) £7.80 (HIG) £8.79
(GN)
Chateau Musar Blanc **1993** £7.05 (FA)
£8.95 (VIN)
Chateau Musar Blanc **1992** £7.25 (FA)
Chateau Musar Blanc **1991** £7.74 (FA)
Chateau Musar Blanc **1990** £7.74 (FA)
Chateau Musar Blanc **1989** £7.74 (FA)

Over £9.50

Chateau Musar Blanc **1986** £17.53 (FA)
Chateau Musar Blanc **1969** £39.56 (FA)
Chateau Musar Blanc **1967** £43.48 (FA)
Chateau Musar Blanc **1966** £52.78 (FA)

MEXICO

Under £6.00

L A Cetto Cabernet Sauvignon **1997** £4.99 (UN)
L A Cetto Petite Sirah **1998** £5.40 (TAN) £5.75 (PLA)
L A Cetto Petite Sirah **1997** £4.99 (UN) £4.99 (WAI) £5.95 (CRO)

c. £10.00

L A Cetto Nebbiolo **1996** £9.95 (TAN)

UNITED KINGDOM WHITE

Under £5.00

Chapel Down, Epoch V **1999** £4.99 (SAF)
★ Dry English Table Wine **1999** £4.95 (NO)
Three Choirs **1999** £4.99 (NO)
Three Choirs **1996** £3.99 (CON)
Three Choirs Medium Dry **1999** £4.99 (JON) £5.20 (TAN)
Tudor Rose Cream **Non-vintage** £2.49 (UN)

Over £5.00

Astley Severn Vale **1997** £5.90 (TAN)
Chiddingstone Seyval/Kerner **1998** £6.95 (FORT)
Monnow Valley Huxelrebe/Seyval **1996** £6.45 (PLA)
Wroxeter Roman Vineyard Madeleine Angevine, Medium Dry **1998** £7.95 (TAN)

UNITED KINGDOM RED

c. £6.00

Chapel Down Epoch I **1998** £5.99 (BO) £7.95 (FORT)

c. £27.00

Beenleigh Red **1998** £26.66 (NO)

UNITED KINGDOM SPARKLING

Under £18.00

Carr Taylor **Non-vintage** £10.50 (CRO)
Nyetimber Blanc de Blancs Vintage Brut **1993** £17.75 (FORT)

INDEX

References to the Price Guides
are in **bold** and indicate the first
entry of the wine in each of the
sections in which it appears.

A

Abadia Retuerta **459**
Abbazia dell'Annunziata 374
Acacia 471, **478**
Accabailles de Barréjats **217**
Achs, Paul **491**
Aconcagua Valley 125
Adams, Tim 94, **104**, **116**
Adelaide Hills 90
Adler Fels 471
Aglianico del Vulture 368, **397**
Aglianico (grape) 364
Agramont 452, **459**
Aguirre, Francisco de 126, **128**, **134**
Agusta **439**
Ahr 352
Aiguilhe, Ch. d' **175**
Airén 443
Alamosa, Viña **130**, **133**
Alavesas **453**
Albana di Romagna 368
Alban Vineyards **484**
Albariño 443
Aldridge Estate **99**, **113**, **121**
Alella 445
Alentejo 412
Algarve 412
Aliança, Caves 416, **420**, **421**
Alicante 445
Aligoté 221 see also
   Bourgogne Aligoté
Alkoomi **105**, **116**
Allandale 94, **117**
Allan Scott 400, **407**
Allegrini 374, **385**
Allesverloren **436**
Almansa 445
Aloxe-Corton 222, **249**
Alpha Domus 400, **408**
Alsace: classifications 144–145;
   grapes & producers
   143–144; specialist
   merchants 146; vintages 145;
   wines **146–152**
Alta Agrelo **83**
Altare **380**

Altare, Elio 374
Alta Vista 82, **84**
Altesino 374, **392**
Alto Adige 368, **387**
Altydgedacht **440**
Alvarez y Diez **463**
Ama, Castello di 374
Amalia, Viña **85**, **86**
Amarone della Valpolicella **386**
Amberley Estate **118**
Amézola de la Mora **453**
Amiral-de-Beychevelle **175**
Amity **486**
Ampurdán-Costa Brava 445
Andrew Will 471
Andron-Blanquet, Ch. **175**
Angas Brut 121
l'Angélus, Ch. 162, **175**
Angludet, Ch. d' 162, **175**
Angove's **99**
Anjou 302, **308**, **312**, **313**
Annereaux, Ch. des **175**
Anselmi 374, **387**
Anthonic, Ch. **175**
Antinori, Ludovico 375, **388**, **389**, **395**
Antonins, Ch. **215**
Antu Mapu **132**
Anubis 82, **84**, **85**
Aotea **403**, **406**
Arbois 300
Arche, Ch. d' (Sauternes) 162, **217**
Ardanza, Viña **455**
d'Ardèche, V de P **321**
Ardennes, Ch. d' **175**
Arena Negra **128**
Aresti Montemar **129**, **133**
Argentina 80–82, **83–86**;
   specialist merchants 83
Armailhac, Ch. d' 162, **175**
Arnauld, Ch. **176**
Arneis 368, **384**
Arniston Bay **439**
Arquata Rosso dell'Umbria **390**
Arricaud, Ch. d' **176**
l'Arrosée, Ch. **176**
Arroucats, Ch. des **216**
Arrowood 471
Artadi **453**, **457**, **458**
Artina **83**, **86**
Ashton Hills **106**, **119**

Askerne 400
Asti 368, **384**
Ata Rangi 400, **404**
Atuel **83**
Au Bon Climat 471, **477**, **483**
Auckland 399
Ausone, Ch. 162, **176**
Australia: grapes 87–90;
   producers 94–98; specialist
   merchants 99; wine regions
   90–93; wines **99–123**
Austria 487, **491**; specialist
   merchants 491
Auxerrois 143
Auxey-Duresses 222, **248**, **271**
Aveleda, Quinta da 416
Avignonesi 375, **390**
Avontuur **438**
Ayala **291**

B

Babich 400, **403**, **406**
Bacio Divino **480**
Backsberg 433, **435**, **439**
Baden 352
Badia a Coltibuono 375, **392**
Bahans-Haut-Brion **176**
Baileys of Glenrowan 94, **105**
Bairrada 412, **420**, **421**
Balbi **83**
Balestard-la-Tonnelle, Ch. **176**
Balgownie **105**
Bandol 335, **343**, **347**, **348**
Banfi 375, **388**
Bannockburn (Australia) 94, **120**
Bannockburn (NZ) **405**
Banrock Station **121**
Banyuls 335, **348**
Barbadillo **465**
Barbadillo, Antonio 451
Barbaresco 368, **380**
Barbera: d' Alba **380**; d' Asti **380**; Oltrepò Pavese **380**
Barbera DOC 368
Barbera (grape) 80, 364, 467
Barbi, Fattoria dei 375, **393**
Barbier, René 451
Barca Velha **421**
Bardolino 369
Baret, Ch. **176**, **215**
Barolo 369, **380**
Barón de Ley **453**

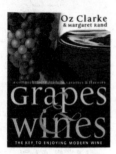